**NZC**

# 2022
# NEW ZEALAND
## CRICKET ALMANACK

EDITED BY
FRANCIS PAYNE
IAN SMITH

mower

**The editors welcome contributions from readers for inclusion in the *2023 Almanack***

*Please correspond directly with the editors:*

Francis Payne,
97 Bond Crescent,
Forrest Hill,
AUCKLAND.
Email: francisp@xtra.co.nz

Ian Smith,
98C Taita Drive,
Lower Hutt,
WELLINGTON.
Email: ianelizabeth2@outlook.com

**Front cover:** Ajaz Patel on his way to all ten wickets in a test innings          Photosport

ISBN 978-1-990003-49-3

A Mower Book
© 2022 F. Payne & I. Smith
Published in 2022 by Upstart Press Ltd
Level 6, BDO Tower, 19-21 Como Street, Takapuna, Auckland, New Zealand
Printed by Everbest Printing, China.

# CONTENTS

New Zealand First-class Records
New Zealand Test Records
New Zealand Limited-over Records
New Zealand One-day International Records
New Zealand Twenty20 International Records

# Office Bearers
*2021/22*

**Patron**
Her Excellency The Right Honourable Dame Cindy Kiro GNZM, QSO, DSTJ
Governor-General of New Zealand

**President**
D.A. Hockley CNZM, MNZM

**Vice President**
L.J. Murdoch ONZM, MBE

**Board**
M.C. Snedden CNZM *(chair)*, W.N. Birnie CNZM, A.W. Campbell, J.M. Lloyd
K.M. Malloy, D.M. Puketapu, R.J. Rolls, R.G. Twose

**Chief Executive Officer**
D.J. White

**Auditors**
PWC

**Bankers**
ANZ Bank

**Life Members**
S.L. Boock ONZM, J.G. Bracewell, M.J. Brito, J.V. Coney MBE
J.J. Crowe, D.S. Currie QSO, E.C. Drumm MNZM, S.P. Fleming ONZM
Sir Richard Hadlee MBE, D.A. Hockley CNZM, MNZM
G.P. Howarth OBE, A.R. Isaac CNZM, B.B. McCullum ONZM, J.D. McCarthy
P.F. McKelvey CNZM, MBE, L.J. Murdoch ONZM, MBE, D.O. Neely MNZM, MBE *(deceased)*
Hon. Justice B.J. Paterson CNZM, OBE, QC, I.D.S. Smith MBE, Y.G. Taylor, G.M. Turner
D.L. Vettori ONZM, Sir Allan Wright KBE, J.G. Wright MBE

**Honorary Members**
J.C. Alabaster, B.L. Aldridge QSM *(deceased)*, A.M. Astle, E.A. Badham, S.E. Bond
B.F. Bowden, B.A. Brentnall, M.G. Burgess, B.L. Cairns, F.J. Cameron MBE
P.F. Carrick, E.J. Chatfield MBE, R.O. Collinge, K. Cross, A.E. Dick
G.T. Dowling OBE, J.W. Guy, D.R. Hadlee, B.F. Hastings, J. Lord, A. McKenna
D.J. Nash, M.H. Peters, V. Pollard, S.J. Rattray, E.F. Rouse QSM
J.M. Saulbury, B.W. Sinclair MNZM *(deceased)*, J.T. Sparling

**National Code of Conduct Commissioner**
M. Heron QC

**Statistician**
F. Payne

# FROM THE EDITORS

The 75th edition of the *New Zealand Cricket Almanack* (and the 40th under the current editors) covers another full and eventful year of cricket. This edition begins with the White Ferns in England in August and the Black Caps in Bangladesh in September and ends with New Zealand's tour of England in June.

Despite problems caused by the Covid pandemic, a near complete season of domestic cricket took place, the Black Caps hosted Bangladesh, South Africa and the Netherlands while the Women's World Cup went ahead as planned. Credit is due to everyone who overcame the logistical challenges which confronted them.

### The Black Caps
The World Test Championship win of the previous year was always going to be a hard act to follow and so it proved. There were just two wins in nine tests with six defeats. The loss at home to Bangladesh, who had previously lost every international game they had played against New Zealand in New Zealand, must go down as one of the most unexpected results in the long history of test cricket.

The Black Caps' season started with a low-scoring Twenty20 series in Bangladesh which the hosts won 3-2. This should have been followed by one-day games and Twenty20s in Pakistan but the tour was called off at the last minute due to security concerns.

Following this, New Zealand reached the final of the Twenty20 World Cup played in the United Arab Emirates. They lost their first game to Pakistan but then won their next four group games and defeated England in the semi-final before going down to Australia in the final.

The Black Caps then went to India to play three Twenty20s (all won by the home side) and two test matches. New Zealand drew the first game, in a tense finish being nine wickets down when play was called off, while India won the second test. This game saw the individual highlight of the season when Ajaz Patel became just the third bowler in test history to take all ten wickets in an innings.

The Black Caps' home season consisted of two tests each against Bangladesh and South Africa and one-day games against the Netherlands. Proposed games against Australia (home and away) did not go ahead due to lack of managed isolation availability. New Zealand bounced back after their unexpected loss to Bangladesh with an emphatic victory in the second test and another in the first test against South Africa. The visitors regrouped, however, and comfortably won the second test, leaving both series drawn 1-1.

The Netherlands played three one-day internationals at the end of the season (after a scheduled Twenty20 was rained off). New Zealand won all three games, the last of which was Ross Taylor's 450th and final appearance for New Zealand.

New Zealand then went to England for a three-test series. Despite the first innings differences in the three games being minimal, England were able to win all three matches chasing sizeable targets with eventual ease on each occasion. New Zealand were in a dominant position several times during the series but were never able to translate this into victory.

Key players in the test side such as Devon Conway, Kane Williamson and Trent Boult were not always available during the year while Kyle Jamieson and Colin de Grandhomme returned home early after suffering injuries in England.

While Patel's all-ten was New Zealand's bowling highlight of the year, Daryl Mitchell provided the batting equivalent during the series in England. He scored a century in three successive tests and became the first New Zealand player to reach fifty in five successive test innings. Mitchell and Tom Blundell had as many as four century stands during the series. Trent Boult had earlier reached 300 test wickets in the second game against Bangladesh.

### The White Ferns
The White Ferns lost both the Twenty20 and one-day series in England in September but hopes were high for the World Cup in New Zealand in March. The New Zealand players had been playing regular domestic cricket and there were no injury concerns when the World Cup squad was announced. A subsequent 4-1 series win over India prior to the tournament was another confidence booster.

However, a narrow loss to West Indies in the first game of the World Cup immediately put New Zealand on the back foot. They never recovered and failed to make the semi-finals. Australia, who defeated England in the final and won every game, were deserved winners.

Amelia Kerr was the standout player with both bat and ball and is now one of the top all-rounders in the game. The New Zealand selectors made changes for the Commonwealth Games side, introducing several newcomers.

This edition of the *Almanack* contains an expanded women's cricket records section. One notable feature is the full list of all New Zealand women's internationals. There had previously been many gaps in White Ferns records but all the missing player details have now been found and the complete list is published here for the first time.

## The Domestic Scene

The domestic competitions started in October and finished in April. A Covid outbreak just before the start of the season, and subsequent travel restrictions, meant last-minute changes to the schedule. Northern Districts and Auckland thus had delayed starts to their seasons although this seemed to make little difference as Auckland won the Plunket Shield (with a game still to play) and Ford Trophy while Northern won the Super Smash.

In the event that competitions could not be completed, provision was made for positions to be calculated on a points per game basis. As it turned out, this was hardly needed and played no significant part in the final outcome. What was disappointing was the number of games which were completely washed out. A total of eight Ford Trophy games and eleven Hallyburton Johnstone Shield matches were abandoned without any play at all.

Otago won the Hallyburton Johnstone Shield for the first time since 2013/14, defeating previously unbeaten Wellington in the final at Queenstown. Wellington had earlier won the Super Smash title for the fourth time in five seasons. The Super Smash again featured men's and women's double-headers.

Only two Hawke Cup challenges took place because of Covid-related problems with Hawke's Bay retaining the trophy.

## Changes

During the year former New Zealand players Viv Stephens (nee Sexton) and Barry Sinclair, former international umpires Fred Goodall, Brian Aldridge, Tony MacKintosh and Chris King and former national selector and New Zealand Cricket president, New Zealand Cricket life member and noted historian Don Neely passed away.

Neil Broom, Anaru Kitchen, Hamish Bennett, Anna Petersen and Katey Martin announced their retirements from all cricket while Ross Taylor and Amy Satterthwaite stepped down from international duties. Heinrich Malan left Auckland to coach Ireland and was replaced by Doug Watson. Glenn Pocknall resigned as Wellington coach with Bruce Edgar and BJ Watling taking over. Bob Carter finished his term as White Ferns coach and was replaced by Ben Sawyer, who was previously bowling coach of the Australian women's team.

## Coming Up

The cricket never stops. As we write, the Black Caps are due to play white-ball games in Ireland, Scotland, Netherlands and West Indies while the White Ferns will take part in the Commonwealth Games in England and also tour West Indies. The men's Twenty20 World Cup takes place in Australia in October and November while the women's tournament is set down for February 2023 in South Africa. The 2022/23 home season will see the Black Caps face Bangladesh, Pakistan, India, England and Sri Lanka while the White Ferns will host Bangladesh.

## Acknowledgments

We again wish to thank the associations, scorers and officials throughout the country who supplied information to us. In particular, we would like to acknowledge the help of Catherine Campbell and the rest of the staff at New Zealand Cricket.

We are also grateful to Evan Watkin, Lindsay Knight, Euan West and Brian Adams for their help with obituaries and other information.

*Francis Payne & Ian Smith*
*July 2022*

# DIARY OF THE SEASON

## July

26  Alan Whimp passes away in Auckland aged 87. He was a Northern Districts life member, Bert Sutcliffe Medal Winner and ICC Centenary Medal recipient for a lifetime of service to the game.

28  Central Districts captain Anlo van Deventer announces she will not be available for the 2021/22 season after accepting a full-time position as physiotherapist for the Brisbane Heat and Queensland women's teams.

## August

24  Eight of New Zealand's most promising women's players sign development contracts for 2021/22. They are: Kate Anderson, Bella Armstrong, Sarah Asmussen, Claudia Green, Fran Jonas, Nensi Patel, Molly Penfold, Gabby Sullivan. Armstrong and Jonas had also received contracts for the previous year.

## September

7  Queen's Park in Invercargill is removed from New Zealand's list of first-class grounds for the 2021/22 season. Drainage problems have to be addressed before it can regain its first-class status while a new electronic scoreboard is also required.

9  Northern Districts announce that men's coach Graeme Aldridge has his contract extended for a further two seasons.

29  Roz McNeil announces her retirement after ten seasons with Auckland. She played 66 one-day games, taking 62 wickets at 25, and 38 Twenty20s.

## October

1  Millie Cowan announces her retirement after ten seasons with Otago. The Otago hockey and cricket representative had been juggling her sporting commitments with her teaching role at Gore High School and felt it was the right time to let some young players have their time. She played 64 one-day and 52 Twenty20 games for the province.

5  Anna Peterson announces her retirement from international cricket but plans to continue in domestic cricket. Peterson played 32 one-day internationals for New Zealand and also 33 Twenty20s, taking a hat-trick against Australia at Geelong in 2016/17.

15  Grant Bradburn steps down as the head of coaching at Pakistan's high-performance centre 18 months before his contract was due to end to pursue further coaching opportunities.

18  Former international umpire Fred Goodall passes away in Wellington aged 83. Goodall stood in 102 first-class matches, including 24 tests, and 15 one-day internationals. He was appointed as an Officer of the New Zealand Order of Merit in the 1999 New Year Honours list for services to sport.

19  Sara McGlashan, who made 212 appearances for New Zealand, is named as an MCC honorary life member in the club's 2021 list of new members.

28  Auckland and Otago announce the Ross Dykes Memorial Trophy will be contested for in games between the two provinces in the future. The first Ford Trophy fixture between Otago and Auckland will see the winner retain the trophy for the summer.

## November

10  Lesley Murdoch is appointed vice-president at New Zealand Cricket's 127th annual general meeting. Her appointment is for one year after which she will be eligible for nomination for NZC president. The AGM also featured the re-election of Martin Snedden as board chair, the formal election of Roger Twose, who was co-opted to the board in January, the retirement of board member Geoff Allott, and the addition of Bill Birnie to the board. NZC reported a $160,000 surplus after budgeting for a $3.5 million dollar loss, partly due to the increased cost ($2.4 million) in hosting tours due to MIQ and other Covid-19 enforced measures. It put the positive result down to being "heavily influenced by the successful delivery of a full season of professional cricket and prudent cost-cutting".

17 Australia and New Zealand are named as joint hosts of the 2028 ICC Men's Twenty20 World Cup.

18 New Zealand Cricket confirm they will not send a team to the 2022 men's Under 19 World Cup in West Indies, owing to "extensive mandatory quarantine restrictions for minors on their return home". Scotland, who initially missed qualification in the Europe qualifiers, became the 16th team to participate in New Zealand's absence.

## December

9 Former international umpire Brian Aldridge passes away in Christchurch aged 81. He stood in 84 first-class games (including 26 test matches) and 45 one-day internationals (including the 1992 World Cup final). He was New Zealand Cricket's national umpiring manager for eleven years following his retirement and was awarded the Queen's Service Medal in the 2012 New Year Honours list for services to cricket administration.

10 Will Young signs for Northamptonshire for the 2022 season. He is expected to be available for the majority of the County Championship and Royal London Cup.

20 New Zealand Cricket announce the Black Caps will tour Pakistan twice in 2022/23. They will play two tests and three one-day internationals in December 2022 and January 2023 before returning in April for five one-day games and five Twenty20s.

30 Ross Taylor announces he will retire from test cricket after the Bangladesh series and from all international cricket at the end of the season. He subsequently says he intends to continue to be available for Central Districts.

## January

3 Former test umpire Tony MacKintosh passes away at Rosebud, Victoria aged 90. He stood in 32 first-class games, including eight test matches.

4 Auckland coach Heinrich Malan is named to succeed Graham Ford as coach of the Ireland men's side. Malan will take up the role in March 2022 on a three-year contract. Malan had been coach of Auckland since 2019/20.

19 New Zealand's tour of Australia, with three one-day internationals and a Twenty 20 scheduled for 30 January and 2, 5, 8 February at Perth, Hobart, Sydney and Canberra is postponed due to uncertainty over when the squad would be able to return to New Zealand. Despite a proposal from New Zealand Cricket and Cricket Australia to extend the length of the tour so the team could return home at a time more manageable for the mandatory isolation process, the Government confirmed it had no capacity to meet the request.

23 Former New Zealand umpire Chris King passes away in Portsmouth, England aged 77. He stood in 54 first-class games, including three test matches, and 25 one-day internationals. Born in London, King came to New Zealand in 1978 and returned to England in 1999. He continued umpiring at club level and stood in several games with another former New Zealand test umpire, Steve Dunne, in the early 2000s.

25 Northamptonshire announce the signing of James Neesham for their T20 Blast campaign and also for county championship games in June.

27 New Zealand Cricket streamlines its remaining home international schedule in order to mitigate the risk of an Omicron outbreak compromising the fixtures. The second test against South Africa is moved from Wellington to Christchurch, the first and second Twenty20s against Australia are moved from Wellington to Napier and the first one-day game against the Netherlands is moved from Dunedin to Mount Maunganui. The White Ferns' Twenty20 and first one-day game, scheduled for Napier, and the second and third games, set down for Nelson, are all moved to Queenstown.

## February

9 The three Twenty20s between New Zealand and Australia, set down for Napier in March, are cancelled because no quarantine accommodation is available for the Australians. The Twenty20 against Netherlands on 25 March, previously scheduled for Tauranga, will now be played in Napier.

Neil Broom announces that he will retire after the Ford Trophy. He played two tests, 39 one-day internationals and 11 Twenty20 internationals and is Otago's leading scorer in fifty-over and Twenty20 cricket and behind only Craig Cumming in first-class cricket.

16 Luke Ronchi is named as interim coach of Auckland from 2 March through to the end of the domestic season. Heinrich Malan will continue until the end of the Ford Trophy, before departing to take the reins as the Ireland men's coach.

22 Anaru Kitchen announces his retirement, hours before scoring a century against Auckland in his final game. He played for Auckland and Otago over a 14-season career and appeared in five Twenty20 internationals in 2017/18.

**March**

1 Anna Peterson announces her retirement. She played for Northern Districts and Auckland over 15 seasons and appeared in 32 one-day internationals and 33 Twenty20 internationals. She is the only New Zealand women's player with a hat-trick in Twenty20 internationals.

9 Black Caps' manager Mike Sandle announces he will step down at the end of the summer to take on the role of CEO of Taranaki Rugby. Sandle had been in his role since 2011.

**April**

4 Yorkshire announce the signing of Finn Allen for the 2022 Vitality Blast. He will be available from the sixth match of the competition until the end of the group stage.

11 Doug Watson is named as coach of Auckland for the next three years. Watson, who was previously Auckland assistant coach, had spent a season as Wellington batting coach. He also had coaching spells in South Africa, Namibia and India.

12 The New Zealand Cricket awards are held online.

New Zealand umpire of the year: Chris Gaffaney
Men's domestic player of the year: Tom Bruce and Robbie O'Donnell
Women's domestic player of the year: Nensi Patel
Ruth Martin Cup *(women's domestic batting)*: Suzie Bates
Phyl Blackler Cup *(women's domestic bowling)*: Eden Carson
Dream11 Super Smash men's player of the year: Michael Bracewell
Dream11 Super Smash women's player of the year: Amelia Kerr
Redpath Cup *(first-class batting)*: Devon Conway
Winsor Cup *(first-class bowling)*: Tim Southee
ANZ women's one-day international player of the year: Amelia Kerr
ANZ women's Twenty20 international player of the year: Sophie Devine
ANZ test player of the year: Devon Conway
ANZ men's one-day international player of the year: Will Young
ANZ men's Twenty20 international player of the year: Trent Boult
Sir Richard Hadlee medal for player of the year: Tim Southee
Bert Sutcliffe medal for outstanding service: Penny Kinsella

Hamish Bennett announces his retirement. He played one test match, 19 one-day internationals and 11 Twenty20 internationals. He made his debut for Canterbury in the 2005/06 season and played for Wellington from 2016/17. He took 261 wickets in first-class cricket and 160 in List A matches.

13 Wellington's Luke Georgeson signs a two-year central contract with Cricket Ireland. Georgeson is an Irish passport-holder and spent 2021 playing inter-provincial cricket in that country.

26 Colin de Grandhomme signs for Surrey for three county championship matches in April and May.

30 Luke Georgeson and Cricket Ireland announce the termination of Georgeson's central contract by mutual consent. Georgeson cited his ambition to play for New Zealand as the reason for his change of plans.

## May

11 Brendon McCullum is named as England's test coach, on a four-year contract.

Sussex announce the signing Tim Seifert for the Twenty20 Blast. Seifert subsequently also appeared for Sussex in the county championship.

12 The 20 players offered New Zealand Cricket men's contracts for 2022/23 are Tom Blundell, Trent Boult, Michael Bracewell, Devon Conway, Colin de Grandhomme, Lockie Ferguson, Martin Guptill, Matt Henry, Kyle Jamieson, Tom Latham, Daryl Mitchell, Henry Nicholls, Ajaz Patel, Glenn Phillips, Mitchell Santner, Ish Sodhi, Tim Southee, Neil Wagner, Kane Williamson and Will Young. Patel returns to the list while Bracewell features for the first time. Ross Taylor and James Neesham drop out.

18 Katey Martin announces her retirement. She played 199 games for New Zealand across three formats and 272 games for Otago.

Glenn Pocknall steps down as coach of Wellington to lead Cricket Wellington's new Talent Acceleration Programme.

19 Simon Insley is named as the Black Caps' Performance Manager, replacing Mike Sandle who stepped down at the end of the season.

22 Ish Sodhi signs for Canterbury for the 2022/23 season. Sodhi had been living in Christchurch for the past five years.

23 Hamish Rutherford signs for Leicestershire for the Twenty20 Blast and is released from the New Zealand squad in England.

25 Amy Satterthwaite retires from international cricket after being advised she would not be offered a New Zealand Cricket contract for the 2022/23 season. Satterthwaite played a New Zealand record 145 one-day internationals and also 111 Twenty20 internationals.

26 Lance Hamilton is named as Central Districts' new chief executive, following Peter de Wet's departure to lead Triathlon New Zealand.

27 The 17 players offered New Zealand Cricket women's contracts for 2022/23 are Suzie Bates, Eden Carson, Sophie Devine, Lauren Down, Maddy Green, Izzy Gaze, Brooke Halliday, Hayley Jensen, Fran Jonas, Amelia Kerr, Jess Kerr, Jess McFadyen, Rosemary Mair, Nensi Patel, Molly Penfold, Georgia Plimmer, Hannah Rowe. Jonas, Penfold, Gaze, Patel, Plimmer and Carson are offered contracts for the first time while Katey Martin (retired), Amy Satterthwaite, Lea Tahuhu, Frances Mackay, Leigh Kasperek and Thamsyn Newton drop off the list.

31 Glenn Phillips announces he is moving from Auckland to Otago.

Rob Nicol is named as coach of the Auckland women's team.

## June

6 Ross Taylor is appointed a Companion of the New Zealand Order of Merit (CNZM) in the Queen's Birthday Honours, for services to cricket and Pacific communities. Former New Zealand test cricketer Paul McEwan is appointed a Member of the New Zealand Order of Merit (MNZM) for services to neonatal care.

Ben Sawyer, bowling coach of the Australian women's team, is named as White Ferns coach, taking over from Bob Carter whose contract ended after the World Cup.

7 Bruce Edgar is appointed Cricket Wellington director of cricket and Plunket Shield coach for the 2022/23 season.

Kent sign Jacob Duffy for two county championship games.

8 The White Ferns squad to take part in the Commonwealth Games in Birmingham in July and August is named. It is: Sophie Devine *(captain)*, Suzie Bates, Eden Carson, Lauren Down, Izzy Gaze, Maddy Green, Brooke Halliday, Hayley Jensen, Fran Jonas, Amelia Kerr, Jess Kerr, Rosemary Mair, Jess McFadyen, Georgia Plimmer, Hannah Rowe.

9 BJ Watling is named as white-ball coach of the Wellington men's team. He will join Bruce Edgar as support coach in the Plunket Shield and will offer specialist wicketkeeping coaching across the men's, women's and Cricket Wellington pathway teams.

11  Lancashire sign Will Williams on a short-term county championship contract.

Rachin Ravindra, having been released from New Zealand's test squad, joins Durham for one county championship game as cover for Keegan Petersen.

14  James Neesham opts not to take up a domestic contract with Wellington after four seasons with the province.

Ollie Pringle announces his retirement from professional cricket.

17  Alicia Rout announces her retirement after ten seasons with Northen Districts.

18  Mitch Renwick makes himself unavailable for an Otago contract in 2022/23 as he explores future career options.

20  New Zealand white-ball squads are named. The one-day squad for Ireland is Tom Latham *(captain)*, Finn Allen, Michael Bracewell, Dane Cleaver, Jacob Duffy, Lockie Ferguson, Martin Guptill, Matt Henry, Adam Milne, Henry Nicholls, Glenn Phillips, Mitchell Santner, Ish Sodhi, Blair Tickner, Will Young. The squad for Twenty20s in Ireland and matches in Scotland and the Netherlands is Mitchell Santner *(captain)*, Finn Allen, Michael Bracewell, Mark Chapman, Dane Cleaver, Lockie Ferguson, Martin Guptill, Adam Milne, Daryl Mitchell, James Neesham, Glenn Phillips, Michael Rippon, Ben Sears, Ish Sodhi, Blair Tickner.

## July

5  Lauren Down withdraws from the Commonwealth Games squad, citing a need to take time away from the game. Jess Kerr is also ruled out due to a foot injury suffered in the World Cup match against Pakistan. They are replaced by Lea Tahuhu and Claudia Green.

6  Will Williams signs a three-year deal with Lancashire, thereby ruling him out of the Canterbury contract list for 2022/23.

8  The six Major Associations announce their 16 contracted players for 2022/23. Notable changes are Glenn Phillips *(Auckland)* and Andrew Hazeldine *(Canterbury)* to Otago, Nick Kelly *(Otago)* and Adam Milne *(Central Districts)* to Wellington, Angus McKenzie *(Otago)* to Canterbury and Brett Randell *(Northern Districts)* to Central Districts. Quinn Sunde *(Auckland)*, Matt Boyle *(Canterbury)* and Tim Pringle *(Northern Districts)* are the only players who have not appeared at provincial level.

15  Adam Milne is ruled out of the remainder of New Zealand's tour of Ireland, Scotland and Netherlands because of injury. He is replaced by Jacob Duffy who had previously been selected only for the one-day games in Ireland.

21  Glamorgan sign Ajaz Patel for their final four matches of the 2022 county championship.

# PLAYERS OF THE YEAR

**Daryl Mitchell** began this past season with a reputation as someone who could come into the national side and do a good job whenever and wherever he was required. However, he was by no means always guaranteed a spot. The season before, even a maiden test hundred had not been enough to see him in the eleven when New Zealand had played their next test.

Mitchell, well known as an effective finisher in white-ball cricket, was thrust into a new role in the Twenty20 World Cup in October. Promoted to open for the first time, he made 49 off 35 balls against India, to help New Zealand to their first victory of the tournament, and 72 not out off 47 balls in the semi-final win against England. His final tally was 208 runs at a strike rate of 140, the best scoring rate of any of the New Zealand top order.

Mitchell was not required for the first test in India but replaced the injured Kane Williamson, batted at number three for the first time, and top scored with 60 in New Zealand's second innings.

The return of Devon Conway for the home series saw Mitchell drop out again but he was recalled for the final three tests, with a best score of 60 against South Africa.

With Williamson available for the first test in England, Mitchell looked unlikely to play. Henry Nicholl's absence, however, earned Mitchell a reprieve and he responded with 108 in New Zealand's second innings.

Scores of 190, 62 not out, 109 and 56 followed in the next two games to dispel any doubts as to Mitchell's quality as a test match player. He became the first New Zealander to hit centuries in successive test innings in England for almost 50 years, the first to reach fifty in five successive test innings and only the second (after Ross Taylor) to hit a century in each test of a three-match series.

Mitchell ended as New Zealand's highest scorer in tests over the year with 709 runs at 64.45. He also formed a formidable combination with wicketkeeper Tom Blundell with the pair combining for as many as four century partnerships during the series.

In what was a difficult year for the New Zealand test team, **Tim Southee** was the only bowler (and one of only four players overall) to appear in every match. He sent down well over 100 overs more than any other New Zealand bowler and was the most successful with 33 wickets. He also had to carry the attack in the absence of Trent Boult for four tests. Southee's total of 39 wickets in first-class cricket for the year was also the highest by any player.

Southee was one of New Zealand's key performers in their successful run in the Twenty World Cup. In the six matches leading up to the final he never once conceded more than 26 runs off his four overs and finished the tournament with the commendable economy rate of just 6.50 runs per over.

Southee's performance in the first test against India at Kanpur might well rank as one of the finest displays by a New Zealand pace bowler in the subcontinent. He took 5-69 off 27.4 overs in the first innings and captured three more wickets in the second. Although he went wicketless in the next test, he was still able to contain the strong Indian batting lineup as figures of 22-6-43-0 in the first innings testify.

Southee took seven wickets in two tests against Bangladesh, with best figures of 3-28 in New Zealand's win at Christchurch. He followed this up with 5-35 against South Africa who were bowled out for 111 and lost by an innings.

The series in England started well enough for Southee. After New Zealand had been bowled out for just 132 and England had reached 59-0 in reply, Southee (4-55) played a major role in a fightback which saw the home side dismissed for 141.

Southee found the going more difficult for the remainder of the series, with the often depleted New Zealand attack under pressure from the rampant England batting lineup but he finished the year just three short of 350 test wickets. He also reached the 500 wicket milestone in first-class cricket.

Southee also made his mark in domestic cricket when his international commitments allowed. He took 3-20 for Northern Districts when they won the final of the Super Smash tournament and 5-65 against Auckland in his only Plunket Shield appearance of the summer.

# PROMISING PLAYERS

**Troy Johnson** started the season for Wellington with scores of 78 and 28 against Otago in October but then suffered concussion which forced him to miss the next three Plunket Shield games. He returned to action in December, scoring 73 against Otago in the Ford Trophy and followed this with 54 against Central Districts in the Super Smash. He finished with 140 runs in the Twenty20 tournament.

Johnson made 88 and 84 in his next two Ford Trophy outings. In total he scored 281 runs at 40, heading the Wellington aggregates. He scored a career best 194 not out in the Plunket Shield against Otago in March, narrowly missing a double century after dominating a last wicket stand of 50 with Michael Snedden (who scored 2).

Johnson finished the first-class season with 389 runs at 55 and after 12 first-class games has a career average of over 50. He is part of the leadership group for Wellington and is highly regarded in the capital. Still only 24, he has many years in front of him and could be in contention for national honours.

**Simon Keene** made his debut for Auckland in their second Plunket Shield game against Otago and made an immediate impact getting 2-14 and 5-24. He then took 4-47 against the same team in his one-day debut.

In Auckland's next Plunket Shield game Keene took 2-32 and 6-44 against Canterbury and later in the month he had another six wicket haul against Wellington. He went wicketless in the next game against Central Districts but showed his prowess with the bat, scoring 65 after coming in with Auckland in trouble at 84-6.

Keene ended the season with 25 wickets at 14 in just five games and was Auckland's leading wicket-taker. He has had a tremendous start to his first-class career and the 21-year-old will be keenly watched next season to see if he can continue this great start.

**Ben Sears** started the season as part of the New Zealand Twenty20 squad touring Bangladesh and Pakistan. He played in two Twenty20 internationals against Bangladesh before the Pakistan leg was called off.

In his three Plunket Shield games before the break he took 14 wickets for Wellington, including 5-88 against Central Districts. He was Wellington's leading wicket-taker in the Super Smash with 13 at 20, including 3-22 against Auckland. He finished with 18 wickets at 23 in the Plunket Shield.

Sears was selected in the New Zealand squad for the Twenty20 game against the Netherlands but the game was abandoned due to bad weather. He also played for a New Zealand XI against the tourists. Sears (24) is acknowledged as one of the fastest bowlers in the country and his progress will be watched closely.

# HAPPENINGS

As far as can be ascertained there are just ten surviving New Zealand first-class cricketers who were born in 1930 or earlier. Any additions or amendments to the following list are very welcome:

|  |  | Born |  |  |
|---|---|---|---|---|
| W.C. Crump | *Auckland* | 3 | February | 1928 |
| D.J. Reid | *Canterbury* | 17 | October | 1928 |
| J.D. Alderson | *Canterbury* | 3 | February | 1929 |
| G.E. Royfee | *Canterbury* | 20 | February | 1929 |
| T.G. McMahon | *Wellington* | 8 | November | 1929 |
| D.V. Spence | *Central Districts* | 8 | January | 1930 |
| I.B. Leggat | *Central Districts* | 7 | June | 1930 |
| J.C. Alabaster | *Otago* | 11 | July | 1930 |
| J.A. Harliwich | *Canterbury* | 14 | July | 1930 |
| I.N. Brennan | *Wellington* | 17 | July | 1930 |

Missing from the previous year's list of oldest players are Peter Arnold (who was the oldest), John Kiddey, Malcom McCaw and Noel Dellow.

Bruce Pairaudeau, born 14 April 1931, is the oldest Northern Districts player and Trevor McMahon, Ian Leggat and Jack Alabaster are New Zealand's oldest living test cricketers.

* * *

Peter Arnold, who died at Northampton on 6 September 2021 at the age of 94, tried his luck in professional cricket in England after the war and ended up playing ten seasons for Northamptonshire from 1951 to 1960, scoring 7420 runs at 26 in 167 games. He played one season for Canterbury in 1953/54, making 412 runs at 68. He served as Northamptonshire president from 1997-2000 and founded a successful engineering business. He was also Northamptonshire's oldest living player.

* * *

Noel Dellow, who died at Timaru on 1 September 2021 aged 92, was a medium-pace bowler who played five games for Canterbury in the 1950s. In the history of South Canterbury cricket, written by Rex Bowden, Dellow recalled that in his first Plunket Shield match he came to the crease as the number eleven batsman. "The slip cordon was strengthened and the fast bowler, eager to wrap up the innings, thundered in."

Halfway through the long run up Dellow turned to the men behind the stumps and muttered "Sorry about this, I'm a left-hand batsman." Dellow explained that "As I came out of the pavilion, Sam Guillen, already dismissed, gave me so much advice that I became so confused that when I took guard it was as a right-hand batsman. The bowler was Bob Blair and he hit me in the ribs and I am still looking for the ball. We had no one that fast in Timaru."

Dellow served as executive director of the South Canterbury Cricket Association from 1996 to 1998 and was awarded life membership of the association in 1998.

* * *

Former Canterbury left-arm pace bowler John Kiddey, who died at Christchurch on 13 November at the age of 92, took 141 wickets at 20.17 in 44 games for Canterbury from 1956/57 to 1964/65. He was renowned for his accuracy (conceding just 1.69 runs per over during his first-class career) and ability to bowl long spells. He also took 864 wickets in Christchurch senior club cricket.

He believed much of his accuracy could be attributed to coaching during his schooldays from former New Zealand captain Ian Cromb. Kiddey was a Canterbury selector for four seasons from 1979/80 and also represented New Zealand at hockey in 1955 and 1958.

Malcolm McCaw, who died in Wellington on 28 July at the age of 91, played three first-class games for Wellington opening the batting in 1952/53, scoring 51 against Auckland on debut. He was prominent in business and was chairman of the New Zealand Society of Chartered Accountants. He was a Trustee of the Wellington Cricket Trust and was president of the Wellington association from 1984 to 1987. He was made a life member of Cricket Wellington in 2004.

• • •

Bill Crump became New Zealand's oldest living first-class player following Peter Arnold's death on 7 September 2021, courtesy of one game as wicketkeeper for Auckland against Fiji in April 1948.

In an unusual twist of fate, Crump would never have been a first-class cricketer at all, let alone New Zealand's oldest, had it not been for P.A. Snow's efforts to get Fiji's games against the New Zealand major associations in 1947/48 recognised as first-class. The New Zealand Cricket Council had ruled at the time, and on several subsequent occasions, that the games were not to be regarded as first-class.

Snow, a colonial administrator and captain of the Fiji team, was an honorary life member of the MCC and also the permanent representative for Fiji on the ICC panel. He launched a concerted campaign at Lord's to have the five three-day games that Fiji played against the New Zealand major associations to be recognised as first-class.

It took Snow 40 years of diligent persistence to achieve his goal and when the ICC ruled the games were to be considered first-class, Snow found himself ranked as a first-class cricketer at the age of 74. Crump was quite amused when told he had just become a first-class cricketer aged almost 60.

• • •

Tom Larkin, who died at Wellington on 17 August aged 103, had been the last survivor from the game between Taranaki and MCC played at Pukekura Park in January 1936.

The MCC side was captained by Charles Lyttelton (later Lord Cobham) who was Governor-General of New Zealand from 1957 to 1962. The Taranaki side included three eighteen-year-olds in Larkin, future test batsman Martin Donnelly and Tom Pritchard, who took 818 wickets in 200 first-class games, most of those in a long career in county cricket.

In 1936 Donnelly and Larkin shared a partnership of 234 for New Plymouth Boys' High School, a record which stood until 1965.

Larkin had made his debut for Taranaki in the 1932/33 season, aged just 15, and appeared once for Wellington in a two-day game in 1946/47. He later had a distinguished public service career, including a spell as the New Zealand ambassador to Japan. He was appointed as an Officer of the New Zealand Order of Merit in the 2008 Queen's Birthday Honours list for services to New Zealand-Japan relations.

• • •

There was the unusual sight of a player scoring seven runs off one ball in the second test between New Zealand and Bangladesh at Christchurch. Will Young edged a delivery from Ebadot Hossain to Liton Das at first slip but he spilled the ball which raced toward fine leg. Young and Tom Latham ran three and when the throw came in wicketkeeper Nurul Hasan threw the ball back to the bowler, who wasn't backing up, and then ended chasing it all the way to the boundary himself but in vain.

As if that wasn't enough frustration for the bowler, in Ebadot's next over Young scored five runs off one delivery after a quick single resulted in a further four overthrows.

It was not the first time that a seven and a five had been recorded in the same test innings but it was the first time that the same batsman and same bowler were involved.

Andy Sandham scored seven off Frank Martin and five off Herman Griffith for England against West Indies at Kingston in 1929/30 and Alan Knott took a seven off Vanburn Holder and Tony Greig a five off Collis King for England against West Indies at Leeds in 1976.

Cole McConchie captained Canterbury in all 26 matches of the three domestic competitions in 2021/22 while Robbie O'Donnell led Auckland in 26 out of 27 games. Central Districts, Northern Districts and Wellington appointed separate captains for different formats.

| | *Official captain* | *Replacement/Alternate* |
|---|---|---|
| Auckland | Robbie O'Donnell | Ben Horne |
| Canterbury | Cole McConchie | – |
| Central Districts | Greg Hay | Tom Bruce, Dane Cleaver |
| Northern Districts | Joe Carter | Jeet Raval, Ish Sodhi |
| Otago | Hamish Rutherford | Nick Kelly |
| Wellington | Michael Bracewell | Hamish Bennett, Tom Blundell |

•   •   •

New Zealand played nine test matches during the past twelve months, winning two, losing six and drawing one. Daryl Mitchell (709) was the leading run scorer while Tim Southee took the most wickets (33).

Mitchell (three), Devon Conway (two) and Colin de Grandhomme, Tom Blundell, Tom Latham and Henry Nicholls scored centuries. Southee and Trent Boult (twice) and Matt Henry and Ajaz Patel took five wickets in an innings and Patel took ten in a match. Latham, Southee, Blundell and Will Young were the only players to appear in every game.

•   •   •

New Zealand took part in just three one-day internationals in the same period, winning them all. Will Young was the leading scorer with 224 runs, including two centuries. Tom Latham and Martin Guptill also scored hundreds. Kyle Jamieson took the most wickets (six) while Colin de Grandhomme (3.33 runs per over) was the most economical bowler.

•   •   •

New Zealand played 15 Twenty20 internationals over the year, winning seven and losing eight. Martin Guptill was the leading scorer with 360 runs while Trent Boult (16) was the leading wicket taker.

Guptill (93 v Scotland in the Twenty20 World Cup) made the highest score and Ajaz Patel, who played in five games in Bangladesh, had the best economy rate of 3.65 runs per over.

•   •   •

The highest run scorer in New Zealand first-class cricket over the past twelve months was Tom Bruce who totalled 858, followed by Tom Latham (829). The most first-class wickets were taken by Tim Southee (39) while Matt Henry took 37.

•   •   •

A number of New Zealand players have a high ratio of catches per match over their first-class careers. Ross Taylor has 250 in 192 games while Jeet Raval (141 in 132), Martin Guptill (138 in 118), Daryl Mitchell (101 in 88), Tom Bruce (88 in 59), Robbie O'Donnell (75 in 61) and James Neesham (67 in 67) also average at least one catch per game. Included in Taylor's record are 163 catches in 112 test matches.

•   •   •

By the end of his international career, Ross Taylor had taken 351 catches as a fielder for New Zealand in international cricket – 163 in tests, 142 in one-day internationals and 46 in Twenty20 internationals. Stephen Fleming (305), Martin Guptill (211), Kane Williamson (168), Nathan Astle (156), Tim Southee (155) and Daniel Vettori (153) are the only other fielders to have taken 150 catches or more for New Zealand in international cricket.

Taylor was also the longest-serving player to appear in New Zealand first-class cricket in 2021/22. He made his debut for Central Districts against Canterbury at Timaru on 9 January 2003, batting at number seven and scoring 12 in his only innings (bowled by Craig McMillan, who opened the bowling with Chris Martin).

He was followed by Will Somerville who made his debut in the 2004/05 season. Neil Broom also made his first-class debut in 2002/03 but appeared only in Ford Trophy and Super Smash games in 2021/22 (and subsequently announced his retirement from all forms).

Due to Covid travel restrictions, Taylor twice missed playing Plunket Shield games for Central Districts so did not add to his first-class record for the association. Taylor and Mike Shrimpton thus remain tied as Central's longest serving first-class cricketers with careers spanning 19 seasons.

•   •   •

Neil Broom ended his career with 101 first-class appearances for Otago, meaning Warren Lees' long-standing Otago record of 108 games remained intact. Hamish Rutherford (71 games) is now the closest to the record amongst current players.

Robbie O'Donnell (61 appearances) is the closest to Tim McIntosh's Auckland record of 102 games while Peter Fulton's Canterbury record of 121 games is safe for the time being with Cameron Fletcher (64 games) being his nearest challenger.

James Marshall's Northern Districts record of 127 matches is also safe for some time with Scott Kuggeleijn (63 games) being the next closest and Luke Woodcock's Wellington record of 143 games (also the record for any New Zealand province) will not be threatened for some seasons. Tom Blundell (62 matches) has the most first-class games for Wellington amongst current players. Greg Hay (92 matches) is the nearest challenger to Mathew Sinclair's Central Districts record of 119 games.

•   •   •

The finals of the Gillette Cup for secondary school boys and the Gillette Venus Cup for girls did not take place in 2021/22 due to a COVID-19 outbreak and subsequent travel restrictions. The teams that had qualified were: **Gillette Cup** – Hamilton Boys' High School, Palmerston North Boys' High School, Wellington College and Otago Boys' High School. **Gillette Venus Cup** – Epsom Girls' Grammar School, Gisborne Girls' High School, St Matthew's Collegiate, Tawa College, Christchurch Girls' High School and St Hilda's Collegiate.

•   •   •

Former Canterbury and Central Districts left-arm spinner Marty Kain, who had last played in New Zealand in 2016/17, played two Twenty20 internationals for the United States against Ireland at Lauderhill in Florida in December 2021. He scored 39 not out in the first game, which the United States won. Former West Indies test player Xavier Marshall was also a member of the United States team.

•   •   •

Auckland won the Plunket Shield for the 2021/22 season, the first time they had won the competition since 2015/16. The overall list of winners of the New Zealand first-class competition (Plunket Shield, Shell Trophy, State Championship) is Auckland 24, Wellington 21, Canterbury 20, Otago 13, Central Districts 11, Northern Districts 8.

This does not include matches from the seasons 1907/08 to 1920/21 when the Plunket Shield was first played on a challenge basis. Otago, whose last success was in 1987/88 (Shell Trophy) have gone by far the longest without winning the title.

Otago also won the one-day competition (Shell Cup) that season when they fielded the same eleven in all five games. Five of those players, Bruce Blair, Stephen Boock, Kevin Burns, Richard Hoskin and Derek Walker also played in all eight Shell Trophy fixtures.

A uckland also won the New Zealand domestic one-day competition which was introduced in the 1971/72 season. It was the first time that Auckland had won both titles in the same season since 1980/81 when the one-day competition was played as a round-robin programme for the first time.

The winners have been: Canterbury (15), Auckland (13), Wellington (8), Northern Districts (7), Central Districts (6), Otago (2).

Canterbury (in 1975/76-1977/78 and 1991/92-1993/94) are the only side to win the competition three times in a row (winning seven times in nine seasons during the 1990s).

Winners of both the first-class and one-day titles in the same season are: Canterbury (5 times), Wellington (2), Northern Districts (2), Auckland (2), Otago (1).

• • •

N orthern Districts won the domestic Twenty20 title for the first time since 2017/18, defeating Canterbury in the final. It was Northern's third success in five final appearances.

A summary of winners is: **Auckland** — eight finals, four wins, **Canterbury** — five finals, one win, **Central Districts** — six finals, three wins, **Northern Districts** — five finals, three wins, **Otago** — five finals, two wins, **Wellington** — five finals, four wins.

Ten finals have been won by the team batting first, six by the team batting second while one was abandoned with the higher placed team (Otago) being declared winners.

• • •

I n the sixteen years that three titles have been available, no team has won all three in the same season. Canterbury (2005/06) and Auckland (2006/07 and 2010/11) won the one-day and Twenty20 competitions in the same season while Northern Districts (2009/10), Canterbury (2020/21) and Auckland, this past season, won the Plunket Shield and one-day titles in the same season.

Auckland (in 2015/16), Central Districts (2018/19) and Wellington (2019/20) are the only teams to win the first-class and Twenty20 titles in the same season. Over the 2012/13 and 2013/14 seasons all six teams won a trophy each.

• • •

W ith home umpires again officiating in international games due to the Covid situation, New Zealand umpire Chris Gaffaney, who was on the ICC's elite panel, officiated in three of the four tests played in New Zealand during the season. Chris Brown also stood in three and Wayne Knights in two. Gaffaney also stood in the three one-day internationals between New Zealand and Netherlands with Brown, Knights and Shaun Haig his partners. Gaffaney (seven games) and Brown (five) were also involved in the Twenty20 World Cup in United Arab Emirates. Gaffaney also officiated in one test in West Indies in June 2002.

Kim Cotton stood in six games of the women's World Cup (including a semi-final and the final). Former New Zealand captain Jeff Crowe was the ICC Match Referee throughout the season for the Black Caps' games.

• • •

D evon Conway was 99 not out at the end of the first day of the test against Bangladesh at Christchurch and went on to complete his hundred the following morning. The only other New Zealand player to be 99 not out at stumps in a test match is Glenn Turner.

He was one short of his maiden test hundred at the end of the opening day against Pakistan at Dacca in 1969/70 and was also 99 not out at the end of the second day against Australia at Christchurch in 1973/74.

Turner reached his century on both occasions and both matches provided notable milestones for New Zealand. The match at Dacca was drawn, giving New Zealand their first test series win and the game at Christchurch was New Zealand's first test win against Australia. Turner scored a century in each innings of that game.

Don McKechnie, who died in Balcutha on 10 August aged 77, took 37 wickets as a left-arm spinner for Otago in 17 games from 1975/76 to 1980/81. He also umpired eight first-class games, the last of which was between Canterbury and Wellington at Lancaster Park in 1989/90. McKechnie was at the bowler's end in this game when Robert Vance sent down a 22-ball over which cost 77 runs.

It was Wellington's last game of the season and they needed to win to ensure that they secured the Shell Trophy title for that season. Canterbury had been set 291 and had slumped to 108-8 but Lee Germon and Roger Ford looked set to hold out for a draw.

In an effort to entice Canterbury to chase their target, and with just two overs remaining, Wellington's captain, Erv McSweeney, instructed part-timer Vance to bowl deliberate no-balls and full-tosses. Confusion ensued with the scorers when McKechnie soon stopped signalling the no-balls and it was several hours after the game finished before the final score was confirmed.

Canterbury's official tally was found to be 290-8, which was just one short of a victory which would have eventually given them the title over Wellington for that season.

With the players unaware of the score, Ford had blocked the last ball of the game (from Evan Gray) with the scores level and it was later discovered that Vance had sent down only five legal deliveries before McKechnie had finally called "over".

• • •

Wellington wicketkeeper Callum McLachlan had a unique debut in New Zealand first-class cricket when he made nine dismissals and was dismissed for a king pair (out first ball in each innings) against Canterbury at the Basin Reserve in November. McLachlan became the sixth player to record five dismissals in an innings on debut and the first to make nine in a match (the previous record was seven).

### Most dismissals in an innings on first-class debut

| | | | |
|---|---|---|---|
| 5 – O.R.D. Whitford (4c, 1s) | Canterbury v Otago | Dunedin | 1947/48 |
| 5 – A.S. Mills (1c, 4s) | Otago v Fiji | Dunedin | 1947/48 |
| 5 – L.W. Downes (5c) | Central Districts v Wellington | Masterton | 1975/76 |
| 5 – A.C. Parore (5c) | Auckland v Otago | Dunedin | 1988/89 |
| 5 – O.G. Ivins (5c) | Northern Districts v Otago | Queenstown | 2010/11 |
| 5 – C.R. McLachlan (5c) | Wellington v Canterbury | Wellington | 2021/22 |

This was Dick Mills' only first-class game. He was in his mid-60s when the match was eventually given first-class status.

### Most dismissals in a match on first-class debut

| | | | |
|---|---|---|---|
| 9 – C.R. McLachlan (8c, 1s) | Wellington v Canterbury | Wellington | 2021/22 |
| 7 – W.R. Garrard (5c, 2s) | Auckland v Canterbury | Christchurch | 1918/19 |
| 7 – C.J. Nevin (7c) | Wellington v Northern Districts | Wellington | 1995/96 |
| 7 – M.J. Sale (6c, 1s) | Otago v Central Districts | Dunedin | 1997/98 |
| 7 – F.G. Anderson (7c) | Canterbury v Central Districts | Christchurch | 2014/15 |

Robin Schofield took seven catches in an innings and nine in the match for Central Districts against Wellington at Wellington in 1964/65. This was Schofield's first match as wicketkeeper but he had previously made three appearances for Central in 1959/60 as a bowler.

• • •

Ma'ara Ave created history during the season by appearing for two different teams in the Plunket Shield. He made his first-class debut for Central Districts and was later used by Otago as a loan player when their regular keeper, Max Chu, was unavailable.

Three players, Bert Sutcliffe (Otago and Auckland in 1946/47), Alan Clark (Otago and Auckland in 1959/60) and Bryan Andrews (Canterbury and Central Districts in 1966/67) had previously played for two different first-class teams in one season but the second game was not part of the domestic competition.

By the end of the season, Robbie O'Donnell had played 61 first-class games, all of which are for Auckland. Shanan Stewart (96 games for Canterbury) holds the overall New Zealand record for most first-class games in a career all for one team. The most first-class games for each New Zealand province without playing for any other first-class side is:

| | |
|---|---|
| Auckland | 68 – Michael Bates |
| Canterbury | 96 – Shanan Stewart |
| Central Districts | 67 – Ben Smith |
| Northern Districts | 90 – Cliff Dickeson |
| Otago | 75 – Stu McCullum |
| Wellington | 52 – Brian Cederwall |

•　　•　　•

Henry Cooper became the fourth player to be dismissed for exactly 200 in New Zealand first-class cricket during the Plunket Shield match between Northern Districts and Otago at Alexandra in November.

The other players to record this score are Robbie Lawson (Otago v Central Districts in 1995/96), Ross Taylor (New Zealand v Bangladesh in 2018/19) and Devon Conway (New Zealand v England in 2021). Archie MacLaren (MCC), Warren Bardsley (New South Wales), Graham Thorpe (England) and Kane Williamson (New Zealand) all had a score of 200 not out.

McLaren was aged 51 when he made his double century against New Zealand at the Basin Reserve on New Year's Day in 1923. The oldest New Zealand player to record a double century is Bert Kortlang who was 45 when he made 214 not out for Wellington against Auckland at the Basin Reserve in 1925/26.

•　　•　　•

The first official test match between Australia and New Zealand was played at the Basin Reserve in 1946. The tour was arranged at short notice to help New Zealand for morale boosting purposes. Australia sent a strong side which ran up scores of 579 against Auckland, 415-8 declared against Canterbury, 420 against Otago and 415 against Wellington, winning three of the games by an innings and one by eight wickets.

In the test match, which only went ahead for the sake of the big crowd in poor conditions after wet weather, New Zealand made 42 and 54 while Australia's 199-8 declared was enough for another innings victory. The match was only given official status in 1948 and some of the Australians were reported to be somewhat surprised to find that they had not made their test debuts against England in 1946/47 as they had originally believed.

The circumstances behind giving the match official test status do not appear to be widely known. However, an opportunity to check the MCC committee minutes of 8 March 1948 reveals that the agreement of all bodies concerned had been received to the request made by the Australian Board of Control that their tour to New Zealand in 1946 should be regarded as official. The MCC recommended to the boards of South Africa, India and West Indies that the tour should be regarded as official, subject to the concurrence of the New Zealand Cricket Council. The Imperial Cricket Conference (ICC) subsequently endorsed the decision.

Australia were due to return to New Zealand for official tests in 1951/52. However, when they subsequently learned that West Indies would visit Australia that season, the New Zealand Cricket Council asked for permission for West Indies to come to New Zealand afterwards instead, thus postponing Australia's visit.

Planned test series in Australia in 1953/54 and 1961/62 also did not go ahead while Australia's scheduled tour to New Zealand in 1939/40 was cancelled because of the war. A strong Australian team, expected to be led by Don Bradman, had been due to play fourteen matches, including three tests.

The two sides did not meet again in official tests until 1973/74, when three-match series were played in Australia and New Zealand. *(Thanks to Lynn McConnell for his assistance with this article).*

Maurie Langdon, who died at Tauranga on 27 March 2022 aged 87, was a very useful all-rounder for Northern Districts, appearing in 25 games from 1957/58 to 1964/65. He is best remembered for a sensational bowling performance against Auckland on Eden Park in 1963/64 when he took 8-21 from 19.3 overs to help dismiss Auckland for a meagre 69 runs.

This still stands as the second best bowling figures for Northern Districts, bettered only by Alex Tait's 9-48 against Auckland in 1996/97. Langdon finished that season with 19 wickets at 19 and overall captured 60 wickets at 24 with his right-arm medium pacers.

Auckland had to follow on after Langdon's heroics but eventually won a thrilling contest by eight runs and went on to win the Plunket Shield that season by one point from Wellington.

Langdon did have the misfortune to record four consecutive ducks in his first three first-class games but hit an unbeaten 70 in the next match against Wellington, one of five half-centuries he made for Northern. He played his early district association cricket for Bay of Plenty and later represented Waikato.

•　•　•

Tom Bruce became the first player in first-class cricket in New Zealand to record double centuries in consecutive innings when he made 208 not out for Central Districts against Northern Districts and 204 not out against Auckland.

However, he is not the first New Zealand player to achieve the feat. Glenn Turner did so twice in West Indies in 1972, including famously making 259 twice within a week at Bourda in Georgetown, batting for almost 23 hours in total. Turner had earlier made 202 against the President's XI and followed with 223 not out in the first test in his next innings.

No one has scored double centuries in three consecutive first-class innings but these players did so in two consecutive innings more than once: Don Bradman (four times), Walter Hammond, Everton Weekes (three), K.S. Ranjitsinhji, Patsy Hendren, Bill Ponsford, Vijay Merchant, Bob Simpson and Glenn Turner (twice).

•　•　•

Bruce did become the first New Zealand player to amass 500 runs in first-class cricket without being dismissed. He ended the season with unbeaten innings of 90, 208 and 204. The overall record in first-class cricket is 709 by K.C. Ibrahim in India in 1947/48 when he had not out scores of 218, 36, 234, 77 and was finally dismissed for 144.

•　•　•

After a Covid outbreak had caused their penultimate Plunket Shield game to be called off, Northern Districts were forced to field an entirely new squad for their last game against Wellington.

With nineteen players unavailable in total, the eventual playing eleven included seven players making their first-class debut, two with one game each and one with two games, a total of four games between ten players. The eleventh player was Ish Sodhi, who captained a side for the first time at any level.

The seven players on debut equalled the number in Northern Districts' first Plunket Shield match which began on Christmas Day 1956. Len Wyatt, Doug Gray, Peter Smith, Tom Puna, Ken Hough, Des Ferrow, Dave Hoskin all made their debuts while Eric Petrie, Allen Lissette, Jim Everest, Bernie Graham had all previously played for Auckland. Petrie and Lissette had also already played for New Zealand.

•　•　•

A triple century partnership was recorded in Auckland women's club cricket at Huapai Domain in February 2022. Kumeu premier reserve grade openers Jessica Smith (153 not out) and Hayley Courtney (104 not out) batted through the entire 35 overs, during which (and boosted by 66 extras) they posted 323 without loss. Their opponents, Waitakere, responded with 144-7.

Ross Taylor had an interesting end to both his test and one-day international careers. In the test against Bangladesh at Christchurch, the visitors were nine wickets down and facing an innings defeat near the end of the third day.

The umpires had informed Tom Latham that the light was not good enough for faster bowlers to operate so, with encouragement from the crowd, he gave the ball to Ross Taylor to try his off-spin. Ebadot Hossain went for a big hit from Taylor's third ball, Latham got under it and duly took his fourth catch of the innings and sixth of the match.

It was the first time that Taylor had bowled since New Zealand's game against the Cricket Australia XI at Sydney in October 2015. This was the bizarre game where the local side had an opening stand of 503, declared and the match was then called off with the wicket's deteriorating surface having been deemed unfit for first-class cricket.

Taylor's 450th and final game for New Zealand was the one-day international against the Netherlands at Hamilton on 4 April. Taylor again had the final say when he caught Aryan Dutt at mid-wicket off Matt Henry's bowling to end the game and bring his international career to a close.

•   •   •

The Bracewell cousins, Doug and Michael, played together for New Zealand for the first time in the one-day series against the Netherlands. In the third game, at Hamilton, they were at the crease together but for just two balls before Michael was dismissed.

The only previous time that two Bracewells had batted together for New Zealand was in November 1980 in the test against Australia at Brisbane. John and his brother Brendon (father of Doug) batted together for eight minutes, which thus remains the Bracewell record in all games for New Zealand. John Bracewell was part of the radio commentary team for the Netherlands series.

•   •   •

Kristian Clarke had an extraordinary and unique introduction to first-class cricket for Northern Districts against Wellington at Whangarei in March. He top scored with 63 not out, batting at number ten, and then captured the wicket of Jamie Gibson (inevitably caught by namesake Katene Clarke) with his first ball in first-class cricket. New Zealand players with a wicket with their first ball in first-class cricket are:

| Bowler | Batsman | | | |
|---|---|---|---|---|
| R.B. Strange | T.H. Dent | Canterbury v Hawke's Bay | Christchurch | 1901/02 |
| S.J. Hotter | K.R. Rutherford | Wellington v Otago | Dunedin | 1988/89 |
| A.C. Barnes | M.E.L. Lane | Auckland v CD | Palmerston North | 1993/94 |
| R.A. Jones | G.E. Bradburn | Wellington v ND | Wellington | 2000/01 |
| L.J. Woodcock | C.D. Cumming | Wellington v Otago | Wellington | 2001/02 |
| B. Cachopa | Craig Cachopa | Auckland v Wellington | Auckland | 2011/12 |
| O.R. Newton | M.L. Guptill-Bunce | Wellington v Auckland | Wellington | 2017/18 |
| F.H. Allen | H.D. Rutherford | Wellington v Otago | Wellington | 2020/21 |
| K.D.C. Clarke | J.D. Gibson | ND v Wellington | Whangarei | 2021/22 |

Clarke is the only player in New Zealand first-class cricket to make a fifty and take a wicket with his first ball on debut.

•   •   •

In March 2006 Will Somerville played for Otago alongside Craig Cumming at Dunedin's University Oval. Sixteen years later in February 2022, at the same ground, Somerville played for Auckland against Otago whose team included Craig's son Jacob, who was making his debut in first-class cricket.

Matt Henry had figures of 7-23 against South Africa on the first day of the first test at Christchurch. This was the equal third best for New Zealand after Ajaz Patel's 10-119 in India, Richard Hadlee's 9-52 against Australia at Brisbane in 1985/86 and equalled Hadlee's 7-23 against India at Wellington in 1975/76. Hadlee and Henry both took their 7-23 on 17 February.

The only other bowler to finish an innings with figures of exactly 7-23 on the first day of a test was 48-year-old Bert Ironmonger against West Indies at Melbourne in 1930/31.

Henry also achieved the very rare feat of taking five wickets in an innings and also making a fifty (58 not out) batting at number eleven in the same test. The only other player to do so was Wes Hall (50 not out and 5-20) against India at Port-of-Spain in 1961/62.

• • •

South Africa were bowled out for 95 in the first test at Christchurch, only the sixth time in their history that they had been dismissed for under 100 in the first innings of a test and the first time since 1932. This list is:

| | | |
|---|---|---|
| 84 v England | Port Elizabeth | 1888/89 |
| 97 v England | Cape Town | 1891/92 |
| 58 v England | Lord's | 1912 |
| 95 v England | The Oval | 1912 |
| 36 v Australia | Melbourne | 1931/32 |
| 95 v New Zealand | Christchurch | 2021/22 |

• • •

Glenn Phillips reached fifty of just 21 balls for Auckland against Otago at Dunedin in February, with seven fours and three sixes. This was just short of the fastest known fifty in New Zealand first-class cricket (by balls faced) which was scored by former Auckland player Andre Adams.

On his first-class debut (and facing a pair) Adams reached fifty off 20 balls against Otago in 1997/98 and scored fifty off 21 balls against Canterbury in 2006/07, both games on the outer oval at Eden Park. Another ex-Auckland player, Rob Nicol, took 19 balls to get to fifty for Gloucestershire against Yorkshire in 2012 but this was in highly contrived circumstances.

• • •

Although New Zealand named a squad of twenty for their tour of England, only twelve players were available for the first warm-up game against Sussex. Blair Tickner and Henry Nicholls (and bowling coach Shane Jurgensen) were isolating due to Covid, Devon Conway, Trent Boult, Tim Southee and Daryl Mitchell were involved with the IPL and Kane Williamson and Neil Wagner were in New Zealand awaiting the birth of their children. All twelve available players took part in the four-day game (which was not first-class). No play was possible on the first and last days.

• • •

Tom Latham's 252 against Bangladesh at Christchurch was the first time that score had been recorded in all test cricket and in all New Zealand first-class cricket. Kane Williamson scored 251 against West Indies the previous season while Chris Harris made 251 not out for Canterbury in 1996/97. The lowest individual score not yet made in test cricket is 229 with 265 now the next lowest.

It was Latham's fifth double century in first-class cricket putting him level with Mathew Sinclair and Kane Williamson. Only Bert Sutcliffe, with eight double centuries (including two triples), has scored more in New Zealand first-class cricket. Glenn Turner scored ten double centuries but six (including a triple) were for Worcestershire.

Latham was 186 not out at the close of the first day of the test against Bangladesh at Chistchurch. This was just short of Brendon McCullum's New Zealand record of most runs on the first day of a test. McCullum made 195 against Sri Lanka in 2014/15 at the same ground, coming in at number five and being dismissed well before the end of the day.

Ian Smith made 169 not out on the first day against India at Auckland in 1989/90, batting at number nine, while Bryan Young batted through the first day for 154 not out against Sri Lanka at Dunedin in 1996/97.

The most runs by a New Zealand player on any day of a test are 222 by Nathan Astle against England at Christchutch in 2001/02 (day four) and 209 by Ross Taylor against Australia at Perth in 2015/16 (day three).

• • •

Covid restrictions meant that Ross Taylor was twice unable to join the Central Districts team for Plunket Shield games during the season and he eventually did not play for them at all in that format this past summer. He was therefore unable to extend his first-class career span of 19 seasons for Central, leaving him tied with Mike Shrimpton for the longest first-class career for the association. The longest career spans (seasons) for each New Zealand province are:

| Auckland | 25 – Raoul Garrard | 1917/18-1941/42 |
|---|---|---|
| Canterbury | 34 – Reg Read | 1904/05-1937/38 |
| Central Districts | 19 – Mike Shrimpton | 1961/62-1979/80 |
| | 19 – Ross Taylor | 2002/03-2020/21 |
| Northern Districts | 19 – Michael Parlane | 1992/93-2010/11 |
| Otago | 27 – Alex Downes | 1887/88-1913/14 |
| Wellington | 29 – Martin Luckie | 1891/92-1918/19 |

Parlane had a spell at Wellington and Shrimpton played one season for Northern Districts. Luckie, who was twice deputy mayor of Wellington, made just two appearances for Wellington. Stewie Dempster (27 seasons) has the next longest career for Wellington.

• • •

The first game of New Zealand's Twenty20 series in Bangladesh in September produced some interesting results. New Zealand were bowled out for 60 in 16.5 overs. The previous time the two sides had met, in Auckland in April, Bangladesh had been dismissed for 76 in 9.3 overs. Twenty wickets had therefore fallen in 26.2 overs in successive innings.

Cole McConchie took a wicket with his first ball on debut. The only other New Zealand player to take a wicket with his first ball on Twenty20 international debut was Lockie Ferguson, also against Bangladesh, at Napier in 2016/17. Ferguson also got a wicket with his second ball.

Rachin Ravindra and McConchie were both dismissed without scoring. Mathew Sinclair and Kyle Mills, against Australia at Auckland in 2004/05, provide the only other instance of two New Zealand players making ducks on their Twenty20 international debut in the same game. This was the very first men's international Twenty20.

Ravindra became just the second New Zealand opener to be dismissed first ball on debut (all formats) after Finn Allen, also against Bangladesh, at Hamilton in 2020/21.

• • •

New Zealand drew the first test against India at Kanpur with nine wickets down, after Ajaz Patel and Rachin Ravindra survived for 8.4 overs before play was halted. The only other time that New Zealand had drawn a test match with one wicket remaining was against Australia at Hobart in 1997/98 when Simon Doull and Shayne O'Connor saw out the last 38 minutes. New Zealand ended on 223-9 after being set 288 to win.

In the test between India and New Zealand at Kanpur, substitute K.S. Bharat kept wicket in place of Wriddhiman Saha who was unable to keep due to injury. Bharat caught Will Young and Ross Taylor and stumped Tom Latham. It was just the third instance of a subsitute (i.e. someone not in the playing eleven) making a stumping in a test match. Neville Tufnell (England v South Africa at Durban in 1909/10) and Bevan Congdon (New Zealand v Pakistan at Lahore in 1964/65) provide the only other cases.

Congdon was later on the receiving end of such a dismissal when he was stumped by substitute Peter Burge while playing for Central Districts against the Australians at Palmerston North in 1966/67.

• • •

New Zealand were set a target of 540 by India in the test at Mumbai but were bowled out for 167, losing by 372 runs. This was India's biggest winning margin by runs and New Zealand's biggest loss. The only higher totals New Zealand has been set for victory are 617 by India at Wellington in 2008/09 (scored 281-8), 553 by England at Napier in 2007/08 (all out 431) and 550 by England at Christchurch in 2001/02 (all out 451).

• • •

Ajaz Patel became just the third bowler in test history to take all ten wickets in an innings when he returned figures of 47.5-12-119-10 against India at Mumbai in December. Jim Laker (10-53 for England against Australia at Manchester in 1956) and Anil Kumble (10-74 against Pakistan at Delhi in 1998/99) are the others.

He was the only one of the trio who still had to bat, on the same day as it turned out, having just 27.5 overs to reflect on his bowling effort before returning to the field of play. Although Patel became the first bowler to take all ten wickets in an away test, he was actually born in Mumbai (or Bombay as it then was).

Patel finished with match figures of 14-225, the most wickets in a test against India (Ian Botham took 13 wickets at Bombay in 1979/80) or by a visiting bowler in a test in India. Only Narendra Hirwani (16 wickets on debut) and Harbhajan Singh (15) have taken more wickets in a test in India.

There had been just one previous instance of a bowler taking all ten wickets in an innings in New Zealand first-class cricket. Albert Moss took 10-28 for Canterbury against Wellington in Christchurch in 1889/90 (on his first-class debut).

• • •

The feat of taking all ten wickets in an innings in first-class cricket in India had happened just six times previously as this list shows:

| 10-90 | F.A. Tarrant | Cooch-Behar's XI v Willingdon's XI | Poona | 1918/19 |
| 10-78 | S.P. Gupte | Bombay v Combined XI | Bombay | 1954/55 |
| 10-20 | P.M. Chatterjee | Bengal v Assam | Jorhat | 1956/57 |
| 10-78 | P. Sunderam | Rajasthan v Vidarbha | Jodhpur | 1985/86 |
| 10-74 | A. Kumble | India v Pakistan | Delhi | 1998/99 |
| 10-46 | D.S. Mohanty | East Zone v South Zone | Agartala | 2000/01 |
| 10-119 | A.Y. Patel | New Zealand v India | Mumbai | 2021/22 |

• • •

Prior to Ajaz Patel's all-ten at Mumbai, the most number of consecutive wickets taken by a New Zealand bowler from the start of a test innings was eight, by Richard Hadlee against Australia at Brisbane in 1985/86. Simon Doull took the first seven against India at Wellington in 1998/99 while Lance Cairns took the first six and seven out of the first eight (the other was run out) against England at Wellington in 1983/84.

There was an interesting game at Gordon Spratt Reserve in Papamoa, in the Bay of Plenty B Grade competition in March 2022.

Te Puke B Grade Green won the toss and decided to bat but were quickly reduced to 18-4. Karan Bains 216 (98 balls, 28 fours, 11 sixes) and Sukhpreet Singh 119 not out (103 balls, 16 fours, one six) then put on 337 for the fifth wicket in 29 overs, enabling the team to reach 387-8 in its 40 overs. The next highest score was 6 and the rest of the team scored 13 runs between them. Te Puke then dismissed Greerton for 79 to win by 308 runs.

The previous highest fifth wicket partnership on record in minor cricket in New Zealand was 335 between future test cricketer Trevor Barber (254) & Ken Parkin (120 not out) for Wellington College Old Boys against Karori in 1951/52.

•   •   •

Former Auckland off-spinner Teja Nidamanuru made his one-day international debut when he appeared for Netherlands against West Indies at Amstelveen in May. He scored 58 not out off 51 balls but was not required at the bowling crease. Nidamanuru played five Super Smash games in 2017/18 and made one Ford Trophy appearance the following season.

•   •   •

Auckland opening bowler Arlene Kelly made her international debut when she played for Ireland against South Africa at Dublin in June. She appeared in all six games of the series (three Twenty20 games and three one-day internationals).

•   •   •

Will Young was dismissed for 1 in each innings of the first test against England at Lord's. It was just the sixth time that an opener had been dismissed for a single run in each innings of a test with New Zealand players accounting for four of those cases.

| Gordon Leggat | New Zealand v Pakistan | Dacca | 1955/56 |
| Bruce Murray | New Zealand v England | Christchurch | 1970/71 |
| Wasim Jaffer | India v West Indies | Kingston | 2006 |
| Moeen Ali | England v Pakistan | Dubai | 2015/16 |
| Jeet Raval | New Zealand v Australia | Perth | 2019/20 |
| Will Young | New Zealand v England | Lord's | 2022 |

•   •   •

Tom Blundell became the first New Zealand wicketkeeper to score a test century in England when he reached three figures in the second test at Trent Bridge. He had come close in the previous test, making 96 at Lord's (the second time in three tests that he had been dismissed for that score). The highest individual scores by New Zealand keepers in England are:

| 106 | Tom Blundell | Nottingham | 2022 |
| 97 | Brendon McCullum | Lord's | 2008 |
| 96 | Brendon McCullum | Lord's | 2004 |
| 96 | Tom Blundell | Lord's | 2022 |

BJ Watling scored 120 at Leeds in 2015 but did not keep wicket due to injury. Luke Ronchi replaced Watling behind the stumps and made 88 on debut. The highest score by a New Zealand keeper in an overseas test is 152 by Warren Lees at Karachi in 1976/77 and in all tests 205 by BJ Watling against England at Mount Maunganui in 2019/20.

Alan Knott (135 for England against Australia in 1977) and Matt Prior (102 not out for England against Pakistan in 2010) are the only other wicketkeepers to score a test century at Trent Bridge.

Daryl Mitchell and Tom Blundell shared a stand of 236 in the second test against England at Trent Bridge, the highest fifth wicket partnership for New Zealand in all tests. The previous record was 222 by Nathan Astle and Craig McMillan against Zimbabwe at Wellington in December 2000. Just over a year later 222 and Nathan Astle took on a completely new meaning when he played his famous innings against England at Christchurch.

• • •

Mitchell and Blundell had shared a partnership of 195 in the first test and had partnerships of 120 and 113 in the third. They became just the fifth pair to record as many as four century partnerships in the same series after David Boon and Mark Waugh (5) for Australia against England in 1993 (six tests), Jack Hobbs and Herbert Sutcliffe (4) for England against Australia in 1924/25 (five tests), Vijay Hazare and Rusi Modi (4) for India against West Indies in 1948/49 (five tests) and Mohammad Yousuf and Younis Khan (4) for Pakistan against India in 2005/06 (three tests).

• • •

Daryl Mitchell's 190 against England at Trent Bridge followed his 108 in the second innings of the first test at Lord's. The only other instances of a New Zealand player scoring centuries in successive test innings in England happened during the 1973 series. Bevan Congdon made 176 at Trent Bridge and 175 at Lord's while Vic Pollard, in the same two innings, made 116 and 105 not out.

Pollard had waited eight years and 55 innings for a test century then got two in a row. He then made 62 in his next test innings at Leeds but that turned out to be the final test of his career. He played in the two one-day internationals at the end of the tour and one against Australia in 1973/74 and for Canterbury until 1974/75. However, the increase in Sunday play saw Pollard's career come to an end before he turned 30.

• • •

Mitchell scored another century in the third test making him the fifth New Zealand player to register hundreds in three successive test matches.

Mark Burgess was the first to do so (all in different countries) while Ross Taylor was the first to score a hundred for New Zealand in each match of a three test series. Tom Latham and Kane Williamson have also scored centuries in three successive tests (but not the same series). Andrew Jones remains the only New Zealand player to make centuries in three successive innings (against Sri Lanka in 1990/91).

Mitchell became the first New Zealand player to reach fifty in five successive test innings. *(Full details in New Zealand Test Records).*

• • •

Michael Bracewell became New Zealand test cricketer number 283 when he made his debut against England in the second test at Nottingham. The provinces from which New Zealand players made their tests debuts are: Auckland (64), Canterbury (61), Wellington (57), Otago (35), Central Districts (34), Northern Districts (32). The last three debutants are all from Wellington (Devon Conway, Rachin Ravindra and Bracewell) while Canterbury have gone the longest without a new test match player. Henry Nicholls, who made his debut against Australia in 2015/16, was their last one.

• • •

Ross Taylor ended his international career with 450 appearances for New Zealand across the three formats. Players with the most appearances for New Zealand are: Ross Taylor 450, Daniel Vettori 437, Brendon McCullum 432, Stephen Fleming 395, Martin Guptill 348, Tim Southee 323, Kane Williamson 313, Nathan Astle 308.

Tim Southee, Trent Boult and Neil Wagner have appeared in 40 test matches together. In those games Southee has taken 182 wickets at 25, Boult 182 at 25 and Wagner 171 at 25. All other bowlers used took 166 wickets between them. Kyle Jamieson (36 wickets at 15) is next on the list. New Zealand won 24, drew eight and lost eight of the 40 games where Southee, Boult and Wagner all played.

• • •

Tim Southee and Trent Boult have taken the most wickets for New Zealand in test match victories. Southee tops the list with 185 wickets at 21.57 in 38 games while Boult has 182 at 22.17, also in 38 wins. Richard Hadlee (173 wickets at 13.06 in 22 victories) is next.

Kane Williamson (4094 runs at 78.73) has scored the most runs for New Zealand in test match wins. Ross Taylor is next with 3272 runs at 55.45.

Taylor was on the winning side in test matches on 44 occasions, a New Zealand record. In all formats he was on the winning side 216 times, ahead of Brendon McCullum (198 times) and Daniel Vettori (193). Taylor scored 24 centuries in those 216 games.

• • •

Rachin Ravindra played one county championship match for Durham in 2022, signing as a replacement for Keegan Petersen who had returned to South Africa for personal reasons. Ravindra scored 217 and 46 not out and thus joined Devon Conway (200 against England at Lord's in 2021) as the only New Zealand players to score a double century on first-class debut in a particular overseas country.

• • •

The second test between England and New Zealand at Trent Bridge became the first test match to include 1000 or more runs in boundaries. The two sides hit 225 fours and 24 sixes, a total of 1044 runs in boundaries. New Zealand hit 116 fours and six sixes (500 runs) while the England players struck 109 fours and 18 sixes (544 runs).

The previous most runs from boundaries in a test was 976 in the Sydney test between Australia and India in 2003/04. The most in a test in New Zealand is 862 when New Zealand (366 and 464-8d) met India (416 and 249-2) at Hamilton in 1998/99.

• • •

Bay of Plenty left-arm spinner Tim Pringle made his List A and one-day international debuts for the Netherlands against England at Amstelveen in June 2022. Pringle (19), the son of former New Zealand pace bowler Chris Pringle, was born in The Hague. He was a member of the New Zealand XI which played Bangladesh in a two-day game in December.

• • •

Rodney Reid, who died at Blenheim on 12 May aged 82, is believed to be the first player of Samoan ancestry to play first-class cricket in New Zealand. Born in Apia, he came to New Zealand as a child.

He represented Wellington in 13 matches as a right-arm pace bowler from 1958/59 to 1960/61. He took a hat-trick against Otago in his first season, with Bert Sutcliffe being the second victim (lbw first ball). At age 19, Reid was the youngest to perform the feat in New Zealand at that time (Gary Bartlett, aged 18, did so the following season). Reid took 33 wickets at 29.72 with best figures of 6-57 against Auckland at Eden Park in January 1960.

Reid played football for New Zealand (two games in 1958 and two in 1961) and in 1965 represented Australia, where he lived for many years. He was prominent as a player and coach in Perth during the 1960s.

# OBITUARIES

## Donald Owen NEELY

*Born: Wellington, 21 December, 1935*

*Died: Wellington, 16 June, 2022*

*Right-hand bat, right-arm medium-pace bowler*

Don Neely played 34 first-class games, representing Wellington and Auckland, but is best remembered for his work as a cricket historian and writer. He also enjoyed a lengthy spell as a New Zealand selector.

Neely played for Wellington age-group sides and in minor association cricket but was 29-years-old before he made his first-class debut against Canterbury at Lancaster Park in December 1964, scoring 76 and 27.

He was appointed Wellington captain the following sesason, following Bob Blair's retirement, and led Wellington to the Plunket Shield title. Neely's best season for Wellington was in 1967/68 when he scored 317 runs at 39.62. This included his only century, an unbeaten 132 against Otago at the Basin Reserve. Neely then had three seasons with Auckland, scoring 276 runs at 55.20 in 1969/70. He finished with 1301 runs at 28.91 in his 34 first-class games.

Neely was a national selector from 1979 and was convener until 1993. He was awarded life membership of New Zealand Cricket in 1995. He was President of New Zealand Cricket from 2006 to 2009, a role which he also held at Cricket Wellington. He was also a trustee and chair of the New Zealand Cricket Museum and a member of the Basin Reserve Trust.

He was appointed as a Member of the Order of the British Empire (MBE) for services to cricket in the 1995 New Year Honours list and in the 2011 New Year Honours list he became a Member of the New Zealand Order of Merit (MNZM) for services to cricket.

In 2008, the Basin Reserve unveiled a new electronic scoreboard which was officially named the Don Neely Scoreboard.

Neely was involved with the following publications: *100 Summers: The History of Wellington Cricket* (1975), *Men in White: The History of New Zealand International Cricket, 1894–1985* (1986), *The Summer Game – The Illustrated History of New Zealand Cricket* (1994), *The Basin: An Illustrated History of the Basin Reserve* (2003), *Men in White: The History of New Zealand International Test Cricket* (2008), *The First 50 Tests* (2010) and he also edited the New Zealand *Cricket Annual* for 19 seasons from 1973.

## Vivian Sherill STEPHENS

*Born: Lower Hutt, 8 November, 1953*

*Died: Taradale, 5 September, 2021*

*Right-hand bat, right-arm medium-pace bowler*

Viv Stephens (nee Sexton) represented New Zealand in the 1977/78 World Cup in India, playing in all three games of the four-team tournament, scoring twelve runs in her two innings. She was also a member of the New Zealand side which toured India in 1975/76 and played one game in Australia en route to the World Cup two years later.

Stephens was a life member of Central Districts Cricket Association and one of the driving forces behind establishing the Central Districts women's side in 1979. She was the team's first captain and she also scored the first century for them with a fine knock of 135 against Auckland at Palmerston North in December 1980.

Like a number of talented female players who hailed from what is now Central's catchment area, Stephens had to carve out her cricketing reputation elsewhere (for Wellington). Amalgamation between the New Zealand men's and women's cricket councils, leading to integration at domestic level, was still in the future during her playing days.

During her teacher training days in Palmerston North, playing cricket meant playing for men's club sides. A lecturer suggested Stephens travel to Wellington to play in its dedicated women's club competition at weekends and that was how she came to join the capital's Varsity-Tech Old Girls' club where her promise was soon apparent.

When she was 21, Stephens made her one-day debut for Wellington against Australia at Anderson Park in March 1975, a match in which she shared the opening bowling duties. As her career progressed, she would shift towards the batting end of the all-rounder spectrum.

In 22 first-class games Stephens scored 705 runs at 24.31 and took 16 wickets at 23.43. In her 15 one-day games she made 250 runs at 25 and took nine wickets at 19.22. In her last first-class game, in 1980/81, she made 82 (with 17 boundaries) against Otago and played her last one-day games for Central the following season.

Stephens remained closely involved with the game and was a long-serving Central Districts board member. She was based in Napier with her husband, broadcaster and bowls identity Philip Stephens, and was digital technology and physical education teacher at Taradale High School.

*Barry Sinclair passed away at Auckland on 10 July, 2022. His obituary will appear in the 2023 Almanack.*

# NEW ZEALAND
# IN BANGLADESH & PAKISTAN

New Zealand visited Bangladesh and Pakistan in September. The side, which did not include any players who were to play in the Twenty20 World Cup, lost the Twenty20 series in Bangladesh 3-2 and were due to play the first one-day game against Pakistan when the tour was called off for security reasons on the morning of the match. The team which was due to play Pakistan in Twenty20 games included five members of the Twenty20 world cup squad.

In a low-scoring series in Bangladesh, Latham was the only batsman from either side to reach fifty, doing so twice. New Zealand's score of 60 in the first game equalled their lowest in a Twenty20 international. Patel (ten wickets) was the top wicket-taker from either side while fellow slow bowlers McConchie and Ravindra (both playing for New Zealand for the first time) also enjoyed success.

New Zealand had new coaches to lighten the load on the established staff with Glenn Pocknall in charge and Graeme Aldridge and Tilan Samaraweera assisting. The squads were:

Bangladesh Twenty20s and Pakistan one-day internationals: T.W.M. Latham *(captain, Canterbury)*, F.H. Allen *(Wellington)*, H.K. Bennett *(Wellington)*, T.A. Blundell *(Wellington)*, D.A.J. Bracewell *(Central Districts)*, C. de Grandhomme *(Northern Districts)*, J.A. Duffy *(Otago)*, S.C. Kuggeleijn *(Northern Districts)*, C.E. McConchie *(Canterbury)*, H.M. Nicholls *(Canterbury)*, A.Y. Patel *(Central Districts)*, R. Ravindra *(Wellington)*, B.V. Sears *(Wellington)*, B.M. Tickner *(Central Districts)*, W.A. Young *(Central Districts)*.

Pakistan Twenty20s: T.W.M. Latham *(captain, Canterbury)*, F.H. Allen *(Wellington)*, T.D. Astle *(Canterbury)*, H.K. Bennett *(Wellington)*, T.A. Blundell *(Wellington)*, M.S. Chapman *(Auckland)*, C. de Grandhomme *(Northern Districts)*, M.J. Guptill *(Auckland)*, M.J. Henry *(Canterbury)*, D.J. Mitchell *(Canterbury)*, A.Y. Patel *(Central Districts)*, I.S. Sodhi *(Northern Districts)*, B.V. Sears *(Wellington)*, B.M. Tickner *(Central Districts)*, W.A. Young *(Central Districts)*.

Coach, G.D. Pocknall; Batting coach, T.T. Samaraweera; Bowling coach, G.W. Aldridge; Manager, M. Sandle; Trainer, C. Miles; Physiotherapist, S. Nishil.

Sears was selected for Twenty20s only. When Allen tested positive for Covid prior to the Bangladesh series, Henry (originally Pakistan leg only) joined the squad. Blundell was ruled out of the Pakistan one-day games through injury (but stayed with the team) and Mitchell, who was originally set to join the team for the Twenty20 leg of the Pakistan tour, was brought in early and was due to be available for selection from the second one-day international once he had completed his mandatory isolation.

When the tour was called off, as many as 21 players were in Pakistan, with Guptill, Chapman, Mitchell, Astle and Sodhi still in isolation and not set to be released until the following day.

The Pakistan itinerary included one-day internationals on 17, 19, 21 September at Rawalpindi and Twenty20s on 25, 26, 29 September and 1, 3 October at Lahore.

# BANGLADESH v NEW ZEALAND First Twenty20 International

*at Sher-e-Bangla National Stadium, Mirpur on 1 September, 2021 (d/n)*
*Toss : New Zealand. Umpires : Gazi Sohel & Sharfuddoula*
**Bangladesh won by 7 wickets**

McConchie and Ravindra made their debuts for New Zealand who won the toss and decided to bat first. They lost a wicket in the first over and were soon 9-4 before Latham and Nicholls added 34 from 41 balls. Wickets fell regularly and the visitors were dismissed for 60, equalling their lowest Twenty20 international score. Mustafizur took three wickets while Nasum, Shakib and Saifuddin all took two wickets.

Bangladesh also started badly and were 7-2 in the third over but then two stands enabled them to reach their target with five overs to spare. McConchie took a wicket with his first ball in international cricket.

## NEW ZEALAND

| | Runs | Mins | Balls | 6s | 4s |
|---|---|---|---|---|---|
| T.A.Blundell b Nasum | 2 | 19 | 6 | - | - |
| R.Ravindra c & b Mehedi | 0 | 4 | 1 | - | - |
| W.A.Young b Shakib | 5 | 7 | 11 | - | 1 |
| C.de Grandhomme c Naim b Nasum | 1 | 4 | 4 | - | - |
| T.W.M.Latham*† c Nasum b Saifuddin | 18 | 31 | 25 | - | 1 |
| H.M.Nicholls c Mushfiqur b Saifuddin | 18 | 39 | 24 | - | 1 |
| C.E.McConchie c Mushfiqur b Shakib | 0 | 5 | 3 | - | - |
| D.A.J.Bracewell c Mehedi b Mustafizur | 5 | 16 | 7 | - | - |
| A.Y.Patel b Mustafizur | 3 | 6 | 6 | - | - |
| B.M.Tickner not out | 3 | 13 | 9 | - | - |
| J.A.Duffy c Saifuddin b Mustafizur | 3 | 10 | 5 | - | - |
| Extras (b 2) | 2 | | | | |
| **TOTAL** (16.5 overs) | **60** | 72 | | | |

## BANGLADESH

| | Runs | Mins | Balls | 6s | 4s |
|---|---|---|---|---|---|
| Mohammad Naim c Nicholls b McConchie | 1 | 5 | 6 | - | - |
| Liton Das c Latham b Patel | 1 | 12 | 3 | - | - |
| Shakib Al Hasan c Latham b Ravindra | 25 | 32 | 33 | - | 2 |
| Mushfiqur Rahim not out | 16 | 47 | 26 | - | 1 |
| Mahmudullah* not out | 14 | 21 | 22 | - | 2 |
| Nurul Hasan† | | | | | |
| Afif Hossain | | | | | |
| Mehedi Hasan | | | | | |
| Nasum Ahmed | | | | | |
| Mohammad Saifuddin | | | | | |
| Mustafizur Rahman | | | | | |
| Extras (w 5) | 5 | | | | |
| **TOTAL** (15 overs) (3 wkts) | **62** | 58 | | | |

| Bowling | O | M | R | W |
|---|---|---|---|---|
| **BANGLADESH** | | | | |
| Mehedi | 4 | 0 | 15 | 1 |
| Nasum | 2 | 0 | 5 | 2 |
| Shakib | 4 | 0 | 10 | 2 |
| Mustafizur | 2.5 | 0 | 13 | 3 |
| Mahmudullah | 2 | 0 | 8 | 0 |
| Saifuddin | 2 | 0 | 7 | 2 |
| **NEW ZEALAND** | | | | |
| Patel | 4 | 0 | 7 | 1 |
| McConchie | 4 | 0 | 19 | 1 |
| Ravindra | 4 | 0 | 21 | 1 |
| Duffy | 1 | 0 | 3 | 0 |
| Bracewell | 1 | 0 | 3 | 0 |
| Tickner | 1 | 0 | 9 | 0 |

| Fall of Wickets | NZ | B |
|---|---|---|
| 1st | 1 | 1 |
| 2nd | 7 | 7 |
| 3rd | 8 | 37 |
| 4th | 9 | - |
| 5th | 43 | - |
| 6th | 45 | - |
| 7th | 49 | - |
| 8th | 52 | - |
| 9th | 55 | - |
| 10th | 60 | - |

# BANGLADESH v NEW ZEALAND Second Twenty20 International

*at Sher-e-Bangla National Stadium, Mirpur on 3 September, 2021 (d/n)*
*Toss : Bangladesh.  Umpires : Masudur Rahman & Tanvir Ahmed*
**Bangladesh won by 4 runs**

Sears made his debut for New Zealand. Bangladesh won the toss and decided to bat on a different pitch to the one used for the low scoring first game, and they got off to a good start with a 59 run opening stand off 57 balls. Mahmudullah then held the innings together with an unbeaten 37 while Ravindra took three wickets as Bangladesh made 141-6.

New Zealand were soon 18-2 but Latham made an unbeaten 65 with fifty coming from 38 balls. He and McConchie had an unbroken stand of 45 from 27 balls but New Zealand just fell short and lost by four rus after Latham had needed a six off the last ball to win the game.

## BANGLADESH

| | Runs | Mins | Balls | 6s | 4s |
|---|---|---|---|---|---|
| Mohammad Naim c Blundell | | | | | |
| b Ravindra | 39 | 70 | 39 | - | 3 |
| Liton Das b Ravindra | 33 | 39 | 29 | 1 | 3 |
| Mushfiqur Rahim st Latham | | | | | |
| b Ravindra | 0 | 1 | 1 | - | - |
| Shakib Al Hasan c Sears | | | | | |
| b McConchie | 12 | 6 | 7 | - | 2 |
| Mahmudullah* not out | 37 | 43 | 32 | - | 5 |
| Afif Hossain c de Grandhomme | | | | | |
| b Patel | 3 | 3 | 3 | - | - |
| Nurul Hasan† c Young b Bennett | 13 | 19 | 9 | - | 1 |
| Mehedi Hasan | | | | | |
| Nasum Ahmed | | | | | |
| Mohammad Saifuddin | | | | | |
| Mustafizur Rahman | | | | | |
| Extras (lb 2, w 2) | 4 | | | | |
| **TOTAL** (20 overs) (6 wkts) . | **141** | 93 | | | |

## NEW ZEALAND

| | Runs | Mins | Balls | 6s | 4s |
|---|---|---|---|---|---|
| T.A.Blundell st Nurul b Mehedi | 6 | 12 | 8 | - | 1 |
| R.Ravindra b Shakib | 10 | 8 | 9 | 1 | - |
| T.W.M.Latham*† not out | 65 | 95 | 49 | 1 | 6 |
| W.A.Young c Saifuddin b Shakib | 22 | 30 | 28 | - | 3 |
| C.de Grandhomme c Mushfiqur | | | | | |
| b Nasum | 8 | 19 | 10 | - | - |
| H.M.Nicholls c Mushfiqur | | | | | |
| b Mehedi | 6 | 5 | 5 | - | 1 |
| C.E.McConchie not out | 15 | 32 | 12 | - | - |
| A.Y.Patel | | | | | |
| D.A.J.Bracewell | | | | | |
| H.K.Bennett | | | | | |
| B.V.Sears | | | | | |
| Extras (lb 2, w 2, nb 1) | 5 | | | | |
| **TOTAL** (20 overs) (5 wkts) . | **137** | 104 | | | |

| Bowling | O | M | R | W |
|---|---|---|---|---|
| **NEW ZEALAND** | | | | |
| Patel | 4 | 0 | 20 | 1 |
| McConchie | 4 | 0 | 24 | 1 |
| Bennett | 4 | 0 | 32 | 1 |
| Bracewell | 3 | 0 | 30 | 0 |
| Ravindra | 4 | 0 | 22 | 3 |
| Sears | 1 | 0 | 11 | 0 |
| **BANGLADESH** | | | | |
| Mehedi | 4 | 0 | 12 | 2 |
| Nasum | 3 | 0 | 17 | 1 |
| Shakib | 4 | 0 | 29 | 2 |
| Mustafizur | 4 | 0 | 34 | 0 |
| Mahmudullah | 1 | 0 | 7 | 0 |
| Saifuddin | 4 | 0 | 36 | 0 |

| Fall of Wickets | B | NZ |
|---|---|---|
| 1st | 59 | 16 |
| 2nd | 59 | 18 |
| 3rd | 72 | 61 |
| 4th | 106 | 85 |
| 5th | 109 | 92 |
| 6th | 141 | - |
| 7th | - | - |
| 8th | - | - |
| 9th | - | - |
| 10th | - | - |

**NZC**

# BANGLADESH v NEW ZEALAND Third Twenty20 International

*at Sher-e-Bangla National Stadium, Mirpur on 5 September, 2021 (d/n)*
*Toss : New Zealand. Umpires : Masudur Rahman & Sharfuddoula*
**New Zealand won by 52 runs**

New Zealand won the toss and batted. Allen rejoined the side after he had tested positive for Covid on arrival in Bangladesh. New Zealand were 62-5 after 10.5 overs before Nicholls and Blundell added an unbroken 66 from 55 balls to get the total to 128-5. Saifuddin took two wickets.

Bangladesh went from 23-0 to 25-3 and then lost wickets regularly being dismissed for 76 from 19.4 overs. Patel took four wickets and McConchie three as New Zealand kept the series alive.

| NEW ZEALAND | Runs | Mins | Balls | 6s | 4s |
|---|---|---|---|---|---|
| F.H.Allen c Mahmudullah | | | | | |
| b Mustafizur | 15 | 8 | 10 | - | 3 |
| R.Ravindra b Mahmudullah | 20 | 41 | 20 | - | 2 |
| W.A.Young lbw b Saifuddin | 20 | 19 | 20 | - | 3 |
| C.de Grandhomme | | | | | |
| lbw b Saifuddin | 0 | 2 | 2 | - | - |
| T.W.M.Latham*† c & b Mehedi | 5 | 14 | 9 | - | - |
| H.M.Nicholls not out | 36 | 53 | 29 | - | 3 |
| T.A.Blundell not out | 30 | 48 | 30 | - | 3 |
| C.E.McConchie | | | | | |
| A.Y.Patel | | | | | |
| J.A.Duffy | | | | | |
| S.C.Kuggeleijn | | | | | |
| Extras (w 2) | 2 | | | | |
| **TOTAL** (20 overs) (5 wkts) | **128** | 95 | | | |

| BANGLADESH | Runs | Mins | Balls | 6s | 4s |
|---|---|---|---|---|---|
| Mohammad Naim b Ravindra | 13 | 30 | 19 | - | 2 |
| Liton Das lbw b McConchie | 15 | 10 | 11 | - | 3 |
| Mehedi Hasan c Nicholls b Patel | 1 | 4 | 4 | - | - |
| Shakib Al Hasan c Blundell | | | | | |
| b Patel | 0 | 2 | 2 | - | - |
| Mushfiqur Rahim not out | 20 | 74 | 37 | - | - |
| Mahmudullah* c Nicholls b Patel | 3 | 11 | 7 | - | - |
| Afif Hossain b Patel | 0 | 1 | 1 | - | - |
| Nurul Hasan† c Blundell | | | | | |
| b McConchie | 8 | 18 | 11 | - | - |
| Mohammad Saifuddin | | | | | |
| lbw b McConchie | 8 | 11 | 11 | - | 1 |
| Nasum Ahmed b Kuggeleijn | 1 | 6 | 5 | - | - |
| Mustafizur Rahman c sub (D.A.J.Bracewell) | | | | | |
| b de Grandhomme | 4 | 10 | 10 | - | - |
| Extras (w 3) | 3 | | | | |
| **TOTAL** (19.4 overs) | **76** | 93 | | | |

| Bowling | O | M | R | W |
|---|---|---|---|---|
| **BANGLADESH** | | | | |
| Mehedi | 4 | 0 | 27 | 1 |
| Nasum | 2 | 0 | 10 | 0 |
| Mustafizur | 4 | 1 | 29 | 1 |
| Shakib | 4 | 0 | 24 | 0 |
| Saifuddin | 4 | 0 | 28 | 2 |
| Mahmudullah | 2 | 0 | 10 | 1 |
| **NEW ZEALAND** | | | | |
| Duffy | 4 | 0 | 15 | 0 |
| Patel | 4 | 0 | 16 | 4 |
| McConchie | 4 | 0 | 15 | 3 |
| Ravindra | 4 | 0 | 13 | 1 |
| Kuggeleijn | 3 | 0 | 14 | 1 |
| de Grandhomme | 0.4 | 0 | 3 | 1 |

| Fall of Wickets | NZ | B |
|---|---|---|
| 1st | 16 | 23 |
| 2nd | 46 | 24 |
| 3rd | 46 | 25 |
| 4th | 58 | 32 |
| 5th | 62 | 43 |
| 6th | - | 43 |
| 7th | - | 57 |
| 8th | - | 66 |
| 9th | - | 70 |
| 10th | - | 76 |

# BANGLADESH v NEW ZEALAND Fourth Twenty20 International

*at Sher-e-Bangla National Stadium, Mirpur on 8 September, 2021 (d/n)*
*Toss : New Zealand. Umpires : Gazi Sohel & Tanvir Ahmed*
**Bangladesh won by 6 wickets**

New Zealand again batted first after winning the toss but struggled as only three players reached double figures. Young made 46 out of a total of 93 from 19.3 overs while Nasum (4-10) and Mustafizur (4-12) were the most successful bowlers.

Bangladesh were soon 32-3 in reply but then had two good stands to get to 96-4 with five balls remaining. Mahmudullah scored 43 not out and Patel took two wickets as Bangladesh secured a series win.

## NEW ZEALAND

| | Runs | Mins | Balls | 6s | 4s |
|---|---|---|---|---|---|
| R.Ravindra c Saifuddin b Nasum | 0 | 3 | 5 | - | - |
| F.H.Allen c Saifuddin b Nasum | 12 | 11 | 8 | 1 | - |
| T.W.M.Latham*† st Nurul b Mehedi | 21 | 42 | 26 | - | 1 |
| W.A.Young c Mahmudullah b Mustafizur | 46 | 83 | 48 | 1 | 5 |
| H.M.Nicholls b Nasum | 1 | 4 | 5 | - | - |
| C.de Grandhomme c Nurul b Nasum | 0 | 1 | 1 | - | - |
| T.A.Blundell c Naim b Mustafizur | 4 | 20 | 10 | - | - |
| C.E.McConchie c & b Mustafizur | 0 | 3 | 3 | - | - |
| A.Y.Patel b Saifuddin | 4 | 12 | 8 | - | - |
| B.M.Tickner c Mehedi b Mustafizur | 2 | 6 | 3 | - | - |
| H.K.Bennett not out | 0 | 1 | 0 | - | - |
| Extras (lb 2, w 1) | 3 | | | | |
| **TOTAL** (19.3 overs) | **93** | 98 | | | |

## BANGLADESH

| | Runs | Mins | Balls | 6s | 4s |
|---|---|---|---|---|---|
| Mohammad Naim run out | 29 | 59 | 35 | 1 | 1 |
| Liton Das c Allen b McConchie | 6 | 8 | 11 | - | 1 |
| Shakib Al Hasan st Latham b Patel | 8 | 14 | 8 | - | 1 |
| Mushfiqur Rahim b Patel | 0 | 2 | 3 | - | - |
| Mahmudullah* not out | 43 | 60 | 48 | 2 | 1 |
| Afif Hossain not out | 6 | 25 | 10 | - | - |
| Mehedi Hasan | | | | | |
| Nurul Hasan† | | | | | |
| Mohammad Saifuddin | | | | | |
| Nasum Ahmed | | | | | |
| Mustafizur Rahman | | | | | |
| Extras (lb 2, w 2) | 4 | | | | |
| **TOTAL** (19.1 overs) (4 wkts) | **96** | 87 | | | |

| Bowling | O | M | R | W |
|---|---|---|---|---|
| **BANGLADESH** | | | | |
| Nasum | 4 | 2 | 10 | 4 |
| Shakib | 4 | 0 | 25 | 0 |
| Mehedi | 4 | 0 | 21 | 1 |
| Mustafizur | 3.3 | 0 | 12 | 4 |
| Saifuddin | 3 | 0 | 16 | 1 |
| Mahmudullah | 1 | 0 | 7 | 0 |
| **NEW ZEALAND** | | | | |
| Bennett | 3 | 0 | 17 | 0 |
| Patel | 4 | 0 | 9 | 2 |
| McConchie | 3.1 | 0 | 34 | 1 |
| Ravindra | 4 | 0 | 8 | 0 |
| de Grandhomme | 3 | 0 | 13 | 0 |
| Tickner | 2 | 0 | 13 | 0 |

| Fall of Wickets | NZ | B |
|---|---|---|
| 1st | 0 | 8 |
| 2nd | 16 | 32 |
| 3rd | 51 | 32 |
| 4th | 52 | 67 |
| 5th | 52 | - |
| 6th | 72 | - |
| 7th | 74 | - |
| 8th | 91 | - |
| 9th | 93 | - |
| 10th | 93 | - |

NZC

# BANGLADESH v NEW ZEALAND  Fifth Twenty20 International

*at Sher-e-Bangla National Stadium, Mirpur on 10/09/2021 (d/n)*
*Toss : New Zealand.  Umpires : Sharfoudulla & Tanvir Ahmed*
**New Zealand won by 27 runs**

New Zealand won the toss and batted first for the fourth time in the series, reaching 161-5, which was the highest total in the five-match series. Allen made 41 from 24 balls and Latham got his second fifty of the series from 37 deliveries.

Bangladesh struggled after a promising start. Afif (49 not out) put on 63 from 43 balls for the fifth wicket with Mahmudullah but the home side could reach just 134-8. Patel and Kuggeleijn each took two wickets as Bangladesh won the series 3-2.

| NEW ZEALAND | Runs | Mins | Balls | 6s | 4s |
|---|---|---|---|---|---|
| F.H.Allen b Shoriful | 41 | 34 | 24 | 3 | 4 |
| R.Ravindra c Mushfiqur b Shoriful | 17 | 30 | 12 | - | 3 |
| T.W.M.Latham*† not out | 50 | 71 | 37 | 2 | 2 |
| W.A.Young c Nurul b Afif | 6 | 13 | 8 | - | 1 |
| C.de Grandhomme c Shamim b Nasum | 9 | 10 | 8 | 1 | - |
| H.M.Nicholls c Nurul b Taskin | 20 | 23 | 21 | - | 2 |
| C.E.McConchie not out | 17 | 23 | 10 | - | 3 |
| A.Y.Patel | | | | | |
| J.A.Duffy | | | | | |
| B.V.Sears | | | | | |
| S.C.Kuggeleijn | | | | | |
| Extras (lb 1) | 1 | | | | |
| **TOTAL** (20 overs) (5 wkts) | **161** | 99 | | | |

| BANGLADESH | Runs | Mins | Balls | 6s | 4s |
|---|---|---|---|---|---|
| Mohammad Naim c Latham b Sears | 23 | 33 | 21 | - | 3 |
| Liton Das c Kuggeleijn b Patel | 10 | 19 | 12 | - | 1 |
| Soumya Sarkar c Ravindra b McConchie | 4 | 10 | 9 | - | - |
| Mushfiqur Rahim c de Grandhomme b Ravindra | 3 | 12 | 8 | - | - |
| Afif Hossain not out | 49 | 58 | 33 | 3 | 2 |
| Mahmudullah* c Allen b Kuggeleijn | 23 | 33 | 21 | 1 | 1 |
| Nurul Hasan† lbw b Patel | 4 | 4 | 4 | - | 1 |
| Shamim Hossain b Duffy | 2 | 6 | 5 | - | - |
| Taskin Ahmed b Kuggeleijn | 9 | 5 | 4 | - | 2 |
| Nasum Ahmed not out | 3 | 2 | 3 | - | - |
| Shoriful Islam | | | | | |
| Extras (w 4) | 4 | | | | |
| **TOTAL** (20 overs) (8 wkts) | **134** | 92 | | | |

| Bowling | O | M | R | W |
|---|---|---|---|---|
| **BANGLADESH** | | | | |
| Taskin | 4 | 0 | 34 | 1 |
| Nasum | 3 | 0 | 25 | 1 |
| Shoriful | 4 | 0 | 48 | 2 |
| Mahmudullah | 3 | 0 | 17 | 0 |
| Sarkar | 2 | 0 | 14 | 0 |
| Afif | 3 | 0 | 18 | 1 |
| Shamim | 1 | 0 | 4 | 0 |
| **NEW ZEALAND** | | | | |
| Duffy | 4 | 0 | 25 | 1 |
| Patel | 4 | 0 | 21 | 2 |
| Kuggeleijn | 3 | 0 | 23 | 2 |
| McConchie | 3 | 0 | 25 | 1 |
| Sears | 3 | 0 | 21 | 1 |
| Ravindra | 3 | 0 | 19 | 1 |

| Fall of Wickets | NZ | B |
|---|---|---|
| 1st | 58 | 26 |
| 2nd | 58 | 38 |
| 3rd | 71 | 39 |
| 4th | 83 | 46 |
| 5th | 118 | 109 |
| 6th | - | 113 |
| 7th | - | 116 |
| 8th | - | 127 |
| 9th | - | - |
| 10th | - | - |

# ICC TWENTY20 WORLD CUP

The ICC Twenty20 World Cup was held in Oman and United Arab Emirates in October and November 2021. The top eight sides in the world rankings automatically qualified for the main stage while Sri Lanka, Namibia, Bangladesh and Scotland joined them after a first round qualifying tournament.

Australia claimed the Twenty20 title for the first time, defeating New Zealand by eight wickets in the final. New Zealand lost their first game to group winners Pakistan before bouncing back with victories over India, Scotland, Namibia and Afghanistan to reach the semi-final where they defeated England. In the final New Zealand made 172-4 but Australia won with seven balls to spare.

Williamson was New Zealand's leading run-scorer with 216 followed by Guptill and Mitchell with 208. Boult was the leading wicket-taker with 13 followed by Sodhi with nine.

The New Zealand squad was: K.S. Williamson *(captain, Northern Districts)*, T.D. Astle *(Canterbury)*, T.A. Boult *(Northern Districts)*, M.S. Chapman *(Auckland)*, D.P. Conway *(Wellington)*, L.H. Ferguson *(Auckland)*, M.J. Guptill *(Auckland)*, K.A. Jamieson *(Auckland)*, A.F. Milne *(Central Districts)*, D.J. Mitchell *(Canterbury)*, J.D.S. Neesham *(Wellington)*, G.D. Phillips *(Auckland)*, M.J. Santner *(Northern Districts)*, T.L. Seifert *(Northern Districts)*, I.S. Sodhi *(Northern Districts)*, T.G. Southee *(Northern Districts)*.

Milne was selected as the sixteenth man and replaced Ferguson who was injured before the tournament began. Coach, G.R. Stead; Assistant coach, S.J. Jurgensen; Fielding coach, L. Ronchi; Bowling coach, S.E. Bond; Manager, R. Muller; Physiotherapist, T. Simsek; Trainer, C.L. Donaldson; Video analyst, P. Warren.

## New Zealand Averages

| BATTING | M | I | NO | HS | Agg | Ave | 100s | 50s | Ct | St | SR |
|---|---|---|---|---|---|---|---|---|---|---|---|
| K.S. Williamson | 7 | 7 | 2 | 85 | 216 | 43.20 | - | 1 | 2 | - | 115 |
| J.D. S.Neesham | 7 | 5 | 3 | 35* | 86 | 43.00 | - | - | 1 | - | 175 |
| D.J. Mitchell | 7 | 7 | 1 | 72* | 208 | 34.66 | - | 1 | 3 | - | 140 |
| D.P. Conway | 6 | 6 | 2 | 46 | 129 | 32.25 | - | - | 5 | - | 108 |
| M.J. Guptill | 7 | 7 | 0 | 93 | 208 | 29.71 | - | 1 | 4 | - | 120 |
| G.D. Phillips | 7 | 5 | 1 | 39* | 105 | 26.25 | - | - | 1 | - | 111 |
| T.L. Seifert | 2 | 2 | 1 | 8* | 16 | 16.00 | - | - | - | - | 114 |
| M.J. Santner | 7 | 3 | 2 | 6 | 9 | 9.00 | - | - | 2 | - | 100 |
| I.S. Sodhi | 7 | 1 | 1 | 2* | 2 | - | - | - | 1 | - | 100 |
| T.G. Southee | 7 | - | - | - | - | - | - | - | 3 | - | - |
| T.A. Boult | 7 | - | - | - | - | - | - | - | 2 | - | - |
| A.F. Milne | 6 | - | - | - | - | - | - | - | - | - | - |

| BOWLING | O | M | R | W | Ave | Best | R/O |
|---|---|---|---|---|---|---|---|
| T.A. Boult | 27.4 | 0 | 173 | 13 | 13.30 | 3-17 | 6.25 |
| I.S. Sodhi | 24 | 0 | 194 | 9 | 21.55 | 2-17 | 8.08 |
| T.G. Southee | 27.5 | 0 | 181 | 8 | 22.62 | 2-15 | 6.50 |
| J.D.S. Neesham | 11 | 0 | 81 | 3 | 27.00 | 1-6 | 7.36 |
| A.F. Milne | 24 | 1 | 169 | 3 | 56.33 | 1-17 | 7.04 |
| M.J. Santner | 22 | 0 | 149 | 2 | 74.50 | 1-20 | 6.77 |
| G.D. Phillips | 1 | 0 | 11 | 0 | - | - | 11.00 |

## FIRST ROUND GROUP A

*18 October at Abu Dhabi*
**Netherlands** 106 lost to **Ireland** 107-3 by 7 wickets

*18 October at Abu Dhabi*
**Namibia** 96 lost to **Sri Lanka** 100-3 by 7 wickets

*20 October at Abu Dhabi*
**Netherlands** 164-4 lost to **Namibia** 166-4 by 6 wickets

*20 October at Abu Dhabi*
**Sri Lanka** 171-7 defeated **Ireland** 101 by 70 runs

*22 October at Abu Dhabi*
**Ireland** 125-8 lost to **Namibia** 126-2 by 8 wickets

*22 October at Abu Dhabi*
**Netherlands** 44 lost to **Sri Lanka** 45-2 by 8 wickets

**Points:** Sri Lanka 6, Namibia 4, Ireland 2, Netherlands 0.

## FIRST ROUND GROUP B

*17 October at Al Amerat*
**Papua New Guinea** 129-9 lost to **Oman** 131-0 by 10 wickets

*17 October at Al Amerat*
**Scotland** 140-9 defeated **Bangladesh** 134-7 by 6 runs

*19 October at Al Amerat*
**Scotland** 165-9 defeated **Papua New Guinea** 148 by 17 runs

*19 October at Al Amerat*
**Bangladesh** 153 defeated **Oman** 127-9 by 26 runs

*21 October at Al Amerat*
**Bangladesh** 181-7 defeated **Papua New Guinea** 97 by 84 runs

*21 October at Al Amerat*
**Oman** 122 lost to **Scotland** 123-2 by 8 wickets

**Points:** Scotland 6, Bangladesh 4, Oman 2, Papua New Guinea 0.

## GROUP 1

*23 October at Sharjah*
**South Africa** 118-9 lost to **Australia** 121-5 by 5 wickets

*23 October at Dubai*
**West Indies** 55 lost to **England** 56-4 by 6 wickets

*24 October at Sharjah*
**Bangladesh** 171-4 lost to **Sri Lanka** 172-5 by 5 wickets

*26 October at Dubai*
**West Indies** 143-8 lost to **South Africa** 144-2 by 8 wickets

*27 October at Abu Dhabi*
**Bangladesh** 124-9 lost to **England** 126-2 by 8 wickets

*28 October at Dubai*
**Sri Lanka** 154-6 lost to **Australia** 155-3 by 7 wickets

*29 October at Sharjah*
**West Indies** 142-7 defeated **Bangladesh** 139-5 by 3 runs

*30 October at Sharjah*
**Sri Lanka** 142 lost to **South Africa** 146-6 by 4 wickets

*30 October at Dubai*
**Australia** 125 lost to **England** 126-2 by 8 wickets

*1 November at Sharjah*
**England** 163-4 defeated **Sri Lanka** 137 by 26 runs

*2 November at Abu Dhabi*
**Bangladesh** 84 lost to **South Africa** 86-4 by 6 wickets

*4 November at Dubai*
**Bangladesh** 73 lost to **Australia** 78-2 by 8 wickets

*4 November at Abu Dhabi*
**Sri Lanka** 189-3 defeated **West Indies** 169-8 by 20 runs

*6 November at Abu Dhabi*
**West Indies** 157-7 lost to **Australia** 161-2 by 8 wickets

*6 November at Sharjah*
**South Africa** 189-2 defeated **England** 179-8 by 10 runs

**Points:** England 8, Australia 8, South Africa 8, Sri Lanka 4, West Indies 2, Bangladesh 0.

## GROUP 2

*24 October at Dubai*
**India** 151-7 lost to **Pakistan** 152-0 by 10 wickets

*25 October at Sharjah*
**Afghanistan** 190-4 defeated **Scotland** 60 by 130 runs

*27 October at Abu Dhabi*
**Scotland** 109-8 lost to **Namibia** 115-6 by 4 wickets

*29 October at Dubai*
**Afghanistan** 147-6 lost to **Pakistan** 148-5 by 5 wickets

*31 October at Abu Dhabi*
**Afghanistan** 160-5 defeated **Namibia** 98-9 by 62 runs

*2 November at Abu Dhabi*
**Pakistan** 189-2 defeated **Namibia** 144-5 by 45 runs

*3 November at Abu Dhabi*
**India** 210-2 defeated **Afghanistan** 144-7 by 66 runs

*5 November at Abu Dhabi*
**Scotland** 85 lost to **India** 89-2 by 8 wickets

*7 November at Sharjah*
**Pakistan** 189-4 defeated **Scotland** 117-6 by 72 runs

*8 November at Dubai*
**Pakistan** 201-5 defeated **Bangladesh** 146-6 by 55 runs

**Points:** Pakistan 10, New Zealand 8, India 6, Afghanistan 4, Namibia 2, Scotland 0.

### NEW ZEALAND v NETHERLANDS
*At ICC Cricket Academy Ground, Dubai    16 October, 2021*
**New Zealand** 154-8 (D.J. Mitchell 40, J.D.S. Neesham 33, M.J. Guptill 32) **defeated Netherlands** 138-8 (B.F.W. de Leede 35) by 16 runs

### NEW ZEALAND v AUSTRALIA
*At Sheikh Zayed Stadium Nursery 2, Abu Dhabi    18 October, 2021*
**New Zealand** 158-7 (K.S. Williamson 37, D.J. Mitchell 33*, M.J. Guptill 30, K.W. Richardson 3-24) **lost to Australia** 159-7 (S.P.D. Smith 35, M.J. Santner 3-22) by 3 wickets

### NEW ZEALAND v ENGLAND
*At Sheikh Zayed Stadium Nursery 2, Abu Dhabi    20 October, 2021*
**England** 163-6 (J.C. Buttler 73, J.M. Bairstow 30, I.S. Sodhi 3-26) **defeated New Zealand** 150 (M.J. Guptill 41, M.A. Wood 4-23, A.J. Rashid 3-15) by 13 runs

# NEW ZEALAND v PAKISTAN                    Group 2

*at Sharjah C.A. Stadium on 26 October, 2021 (d/n)*
*Toss : Pakistan. Umpires : M.A. Gough & R.A. Kettleborough*
**Pakistan won by 5 wickets**

Pakistan won the toss and decided to bowl first. Guptill became New Zealand's most capped Twenty20 international player with his 103rd game. Astle, Chapman, Jamieson and Ferguson (who was injured) were omitted from the New Zealand squad. Milne, who had replaced Ferguson in the squad, was deemed not eligible to play in this game.

Mitchell opened the innings for the first time in an international and equal top scored with Conway, both making 27. Rauf took 4-22 as Pakistan limited New Zealand to 134-8. Rizwan top scored with 33 as Pakistan reached the target with eight balls to spare. Southee took his 100th Twenty20 international wicket when he dismissed the Pakistan captain Babar Azam and Sodhi took 2-28.

### NEW ZEALAND

| | Runs | Mins | Balls | 6s | 4s |
|---|---|---|---|---|---|
| M.J.Guptill b Rauf | 17 | 25 | 20 | - | 3 |
| D.J.Mitchell c Fakhar b Imad | 27 | 38 | 20 | 2 | 1 |
| K.S.Williamson* run out | 25 | 38 | 26 | 1 | 2 |
| J.D.S.Neesham c Fakhar b Hafeez | 1 | 5 | 2 | - | - |
| D.P.Conway c Babar b Rauf | 27 | 40 | 24 | - | 3 |
| G.D.Phillips c Hasan b Rauf | 13 | 25 | 15 | - | 1 |
| T.L.Seifert† c Hafeez b Afridi | 8 | 12 | 8 | - | 1 |
| M.J.Santner b Rauf | 6 | 12 | 5 | - | 1 |
| I.S.Sodhi not out | 2 | 3 | 2 | - | - |
| T.G.Southee | | | | | |
| T.A.Boult | | | | | |
| Extras (b 1, lb 5, nb 2) | 8 | | | | |
| **TOTAL** (20 overs) (8 wkts) | **134** | 100 | | | |

### PAKISTAN

| | Runs | Mins | Balls | 6s | 4s |
|---|---|---|---|---|---|
| Mohammad Rizwan† lbw b Sodhi | 33 | 57 | 34 | - | 5 |
| Babar Azam* b Southee | 9 | 23 | 11 | - | 1 |
| Fakhar Zaman lbw b Sodhi | 11 | 18 | 17 | 1 | - |
| Mohammad Hafeez c Conway b Santner | 11 | 12 | 6 | 1 | - |
| Shoaib Malik not out | 26 | 43 | 20 | 1 | 2 |
| Imad Wasim lbw b Boult | 11 | 17 | 12 | - | 1 |
| Asif Ali not out | 27 | 23 | 12 | 3 | 1 |
| Shadab Khan | | | | | |
| Hasan Ali | | | | | |
| Shaheen Afridi | | | | | |
| Haris Rauf | | | | | |
| Extras (lb 2, w 5) | 7 | | | | |
| **TOTAL** (18.4 overs) (5 wkts) | **135** | 95 | | | |

| Bowling | O | M | R | W |
|---|---|---|---|---|
| **PAKISTAN** | | | | |
| Afridi | 4 | 1 | 21 | 1 |
| Imad | 4 | 0 | 24 | 1 |
| Hasan | 3 | 0 | 26 | 0 |
| Rauf | 4 | 0 | 22 | 4 |
| Shadab | 3 | 0 | 19 | 0 |
| Hafeez | 2 | 0 | 16 | 1 |
| **NEW ZEALAND** | | | | |
| Santner | 4 | 0 | 33 | 1 |
| Southee | 4 | 0 | 25 | 1 |
| Boult | 3.4 | 0 | 29 | 1 |
| Neesham | 3 | 0 | 18 | 0 |
| Sodhi | 4 | 0 | 28 | 2 |

| Fall of Wickets | | |
|---|---|---|
| | NZ | P |
| 1st | 36 | 28 |
| 2nd | 54 | 47 |
| 3rd | 56 | 63 |
| 4th | 90 | 69 |
| 5th | 116 | 87 |
| 6th | 116 | - |
| 7th | 125 | - |
| 8th | 134 | - |
| 9th | - | - |
| 10th | - | - |

**NZC**

# NEW ZEALAND v INDIA                              Group 2

*at Dubai Sports City Stadium on 31 October, 2021 (d/n)*
*Toss : New Zealand.  Umpires : M. Erasmus & R.A. Kettleborough*
**New Zealand won by 8 wickets**

New Zealand made one change with Milne, who had replaced the injured Ferguson in the New Zealand squad, coming in for Seifert while Conway kept wicket. New Zealand decided to bowl first on winning the toss and restricted India to 110-7. India went from 35-1 to 48-4 and never recovered. Boult took 3-20 and Thakur became his 50th Twenty20 international wicket.

New Zealand had a second wicket stand of 72 from 54 balls between Mitchell and Williamson to help them win the game with 33 deliveries remaining. Mitchell's 49 was his highest score.

| INDIA | Runs | Mins | Balls | 6s | 4s |
|---|---|---|---|---|---|
| K.L.Rahul c Mitchell b Southee | 18 | 29 | 16 | - | 3 |
| I.P.Kishan c Mitchell b Boult | 4 | 14 | 8 | - | 1 |
| R.G.Sharma c Guptill b Sodhi | 14 | 23 | 14 | 1 | 1 |
| V.Kohli* c Boult b Sodhi | 9 | 20 | 17 | - | - |
| R.R.Pant† b Milne | 12 | 33 | 19 | - | - |
| H.H.Pandya c Guptill b Boult | 23 | 39 | 24 | - | 1 |
| R.A.Jadeja not out | 26 | 27 | 19 | 1 | 2 |
| S.N.Thakur c Guptill b Boult | 0 | 3 | 3 | - | - |
| Mohammad Shami not out | 0 | 6 | 0 | - | - |
| V.V.Chakravarthy | | | | | |
| J.J.Bumrah | | | | | |
| Extras (lb 2, w 2) | 4 | | | | |
| **TOTAL** (20 overs) (7 wkts) . | **110** | 96 | | | |

| NEW ZEALAND | Runs | Mins | Balls | 6s | 4s |
|---|---|---|---|---|---|
| M.J.Guptill c Thakur b Bumrah . | 20 | 15 | 17 | - | 3 |
| D.J.Mitchell c Rahul b Bumrah . | 49 | 57 | 35 | 3 | 4 |
| K.S.Williamson* not out | 33 | 53 | 31 | - | 3 |
| D.P.Conway† not out | 2 | 19 | 4 | - | - |
| G.D.Phillips | | | | | |
| J.D.S.Neesham | | | | | |
| M.J.Santner | | | | | |
| T.G.Southee | | | | | |
| A.F.Milne | | | | | |
| I.S.Sodhi | | | | | |
| T.A.Boult | | | | | |
| Extras (lb 1, w 6) | 7 | | | | |
| **TOTAL** (14.3 overs) (2 wkts) | **111** | 67 | | | |

| Bowling NEW ZEALAND | O | M | R | W |
|---|---|---|---|---|
| Boult | 4 | 0 | 20 | 3 |
| Southee | 4 | 0 | 26 | 1 |
| Santner | 4 | 0 | 15 | 0 |
| Milne | 4 | 0 | 30 | 1 |
| Sodhi | 4 | 0 | 17 | 2 |
| INDIA | | | | |
| Chakravarthy | 4 | 0 | 23 | 0 |
| Bumrah | 4 | 0 | 19 | 2 |
| Jadeja | 2 | 0 | 23 | 0 |
| Shami | 1 | 0 | 11 | 0 |
| Thakur | 1.3 | 0 | 17 | 0 |
| Pandya | 2 | 0 | 17 | 0 |

| Fall of Wickets | I | NZ |
|---|---|---|
| 1st | 11 | 24 |
| 2nd | 35 | 96 |
| 3rd | 40 | - |
| 4th | 48 | - |
| 5th | 70 | - |
| 6th | 94 | - |
| 7th | 94 | - |
| 8th | - | - |
| 9th | - | - |
| 10th | - | - |

# NEW ZEALAND v SCOTLAND                    Group 2

*at Dubai Sports City Stadium on 3 November, 2021*
*Toss : Scotland.  Umpires : Ahsan Raza & M. Erasmus*
**New Zealand won by 16 runs**

Scotland won the toss and bowled first. After a 35 run opening stand New Zealand fell to 52-3 before Guptill and Phillips added 105 from 73 balls. Guptill became the second batsman to reach 3000 international Twenty20 runs and reached his fifty from 35 balls. New Zealand reached 172-5.

The Scottish top order all contributed with the top six reaching double figures. Leask finished unbeaten on 42 from just 20 balls as Scotland finished on 156-5. Boult and Sodhi both took two wickets.

| NEW ZEALAND | Runs | Mins | Balls | 6s | 4s |
|---|---|---|---|---|---|
| M.J.Guptill c MacLeod b Wheal | 93 | 92 | 56 | 7 | 6 |
| D.J.Mitchell lbw b Sharif | 13 | 21 | 11 | - | 1 |
| K.S.Williamson* c Cross b Sharif | 0 | 4 | 4 | - | - |
| D.P.Conway† c Cross b Watt | 1 | 11 | 3 | - | - |
| G.D.Phillips c Greaves b Wheal | 33 | 55 | 37 | 1 | - |
| J.D.S.Neesham not out | 10 | 11 | 6 | - | 1 |
| M.J.Santner not out | 2 | 9 | 3 | - | - |
| I.S.Sodhi | | | | | |
| A.F.Milne | | | | | |
| T.G.Southee | | | | | |
| T.A.Boult | | | | | |
| Extras (lb 5, w 15) | 20 | | | | |
| **TOTAL** (20 overs) (5 wkts) | **172** | 101 | | | |

| SCOTLAND | Runs | Mins | Balls | 6s | 4s |
|---|---|---|---|---|---|
| H.G.Munsey c Southee b Sodhi | 22 | 39 | 18 | 2 | 1 |
| K.J.Coetzer* c Southee b Boult | 17 | 16 | 11 | - | 4 |
| M.H.Cross† b Southee | 27 | 39 | 29 | - | 5 |
| R.D.Berrington c Conway b Sodhi | 20 | 37 | 17 | 1 | 1 |
| C.S.MacLeod b Boult | 12 | 16 | 15 | - | - |
| M.A.Leask not out | 42 | 26 | 20 | 3 | 3 |
| C.N.Greaves not out | 8 | 19 | 10 | - | - |
| M.R.J.Watt | | | | | |
| S.M.Sharif | | | | | |
| A.C.Evans | | | | | |
| B.T.J.Wheal | | | | | |
| Extras (lb 2, w 6) | 8 | | | | |
| **TOTAL** (20 overs) (5 wkts) | **156** | 95 | | | |

| Bowling | O | M | R | W |
|---|---|---|---|---|
| **SCOTLAND** | | | | |
| Wheal | 4 | 0 | 40 | 2 |
| Sharif | 4 | 0 | 28 | 2 |
| Evans | 4 | 0 | 48 | 0 |
| Watt | 4 | 0 | 13 | 1 |
| Greaves | 3 | 0 | 26 | 0 |
| Leask | 1 | 0 | 12 | 0 |
| **NEW ZEALAND** | | | | |
| Boult | 4 | 0 | 29 | 2 |
| Southee | 4 | 0 | 24 | 1 |
| Milne | 4 | 1 | 36 | 0 |
| Santner | 4 | 0 | 23 | 0 |
| Sodhi | 4 | 0 | 42 | 2 |

| Fall of Wickets | NZ | S |
|---|---|---|
| 1st | 35 | 21 |
| 2nd | 35 | 66 |
| 3rd | 52 | 76 |
| 4th | 157 | 102 |
| 5th | 157 | 106 |
| 6th | - | - |
| 7th | - | - |
| 8th | - | - |
| 9th | - | - |
| 10th | - | - |

NZC

# NEW ZEALAND v NAMIBIA    Group 2

*at Sharjah C.A. Stadium on 5 November, 2021*
*Toss : Namibia.  Umpires : P.R. Reiffel & P. Wilson*
**New Zealand won by 52 runs**

Namibia continued the trend of bowling first after winning the toss. All the New Zealand batsmen reached double figures and an unbeaten stand of 76 from 36 balls for the fifth wicket by Phillips and Neesham took the final score to 163-4.

Namibia had a promising opening stand of 47 from 44 balls but lost three quick wickets and never recovered and finished on 111-7. Boult and Southee took two wickets each.

### NEW ZEALAND

| | Runs | Mins | Balls | 6s | 4s |
|---|---|---|---|---|---|
| M.J.Guptil c Trumpelmann b Wiese | 18 | 20 | 18 | 1 | 1 |
| D.J.Mitchell c van Lingen b Scholtz | 19 | 29 | 15 | - | 2 |
| K.S.Williamson* b Erasmus | 28 | 38 | 25 | 1 | 2 |
| D.P.Conway† run out | 17 | 36 | 18 | - | 1 |
| G.D.Phillips not out | 39 | 41 | 21 | 3 | 1 |
| J.D.S.Neesham not out | 35 | 33 | 23 | 2 | 1 |
| M.J.Santner | | | | | |
| I.S.Sodhi | | | | | |
| A.F.Milne | | | | | |
| T.G.Southee | | | | | |
| T.A.Boult | | | | | |
| Extras (lb 1, w 6) | 7 | | | | |
| **TOTAL** (20 overs) (4 wkts) . **163** | | 95 | | | |

### NAMIBIA

| | Runs | Mins | Balls | 6s | 4s |
|---|---|---|---|---|---|
| S.J.Baard b Santner | 21 | 37 | 27 | - | 2 |
| M.van Lingen b Neesham | 25 | 32 | 25 | 1 | 2 |
| M.G.Erasmus* c Conway b Sodhi | 3 | 11 | 4 | - | - |
| Z.E.Green† c Boult b Southee | 23 | 44 | 27 | 1 | 1 |
| D.Wiese lbw b Southee | 16 | 22 | 17 | 1 | 1 |
| J.J.Smit not out | 9 | 27 | 17 | - | 1 |
| J.N.Loftie-Eaton c Guptill b Boult | 0 | 4 | 2 | - | - |
| C.G.Williams c Phillips b Boult | 0 | 3 | 2 | - | - |
| R.C.Trumpelmann not out | 6 | 6 | 4 | - | 1 |
| K.J.Birkenstock | | | | | |
| B.M.Scholtz | | | | | |
| Extras (lb 3, w 5) | 8 | | | | |
| **TOTAL** (20 overs) (7 wkts) . **111** | | 93 | | | |

| Bowling | O | M | R | W |
|---|---|---|---|---|
| **NAMIBIA** | | | | |
| Scholtz | 3 | 0 | 15 | 1 |
| Trumpelmann | 3 | 0 | 25 | 0 |
| Wiese | 4 | 0 | 40 | 1 |
| Smit | 2 | 0 | 27 | 0 |
| Loftie-Eaton | 2 | 0 | 24 | 0 |
| Erasmus | 4 | 0 | 22 | 1 |
| Birkenstock | 2 | 0 | 9 | 0 |
| **NEW ZEALAND** | | | | |
| Southee | 4 | 0 | 15 | 2 |
| Boult | 4 | 0 | 20 | 2 |
| Milne | 4 | 0 | 25 | 0 |
| Santner | 4 | 0 | 20 | 1 |
| Neesham | 1 | 0 | 6 | 1 |
| Sodhi | 3 | 0 | 22 | 1 |

| Fall of Wickets | NZ | N |
|---|---|---|
| 1st | 30 | 47 |
| 2nd | 43 | 51 |
| 3rd | 81 | 55 |
| 4th | 87 | 86 |
| 5th | - | 102 |
| 6th | - | 103 |
| 7th | - | 105 |
| 8th | - | - |
| 9th | - | - |
| 10th | - | - |

# NEW ZEALAND v AFGHANISTAN                    Group 2

*at Sheikh Zayed Stadium, Abu Dhabi on 7 November, 2021*
*Toss : Afghanistan.  Umpires : H.D.P.K. Dharmasena & L. Rusere*
**New Zealand won by 8 wickets**

This game would decide second place in the group and Afghanistan bucked the trend by batting first. They were soon 19-3 and then 56-4 but Najibullah scored 73 off 48 deliveries, with his fifty coming from 33 balls. Afghanistan finished with 124-8 while Boult took three wickets and Southee two.

New Zealand were steady in their reply with Williamson and Conway sharing an unbroken stand of 68 from 56 balls to see New Zealand home and into the semi-finals with eleven balls left.

| AFGHANISTAN | Runs | Mins | Balls | 6s | 4s |
|---|---|---|---|---|---|
| Hazratullah Zazai c Santner | | | | | |
|   b Boult | 2 | 16 | 4 | - | - |
| Mohammad Shahzad† c Conway | | | | | |
|   b Milne | 4 | 12 | 11 | - | 1 |
| Rahmanullah Gurbaz | | | | | |
|   lbw b Southee | 6 | 15 | 9 | - | 1 |
| Gulbadeen Naib b Sodhi | 15 | 31 | 18 | - | 1 |
| Najibullah Zadaran c Neesham | | | | | |
|   b Boult | 73 | 61 | 48 | 3 | 6 |
| Mohammad Nabi* | | | | | |
|   c & b Southee | 14 | 35 | 20 | - | - |
| Karim Janat c Sodhi b Boult | 2 | 5 | 2 | - | - |
| Rashid Khan c Williamson | | | | | |
|   b Neesham | 3 | 10 | 7 | - | - |
| Mujeeb Zadran not out | 0 | 8 | 1 | - | - |
| Naveen-ul-Haq | | | | | |
| Hamid Hassan | | | | | |
| Extras (b 1, lb 1, w 3) | 5 | | | | |
| **TOTAL** (20 overs) (8 wkts) | **124** | 94 | | | |

| NEW ZEALAND | Runs | Mins | Balls | 6s | 4s |
|---|---|---|---|---|---|
| M.J.Guptill b Rashid | 28 | 34 | 23 | - | 4 |
| D.J.Mitchell c Shahzad b Zadran | 17 | 13 | 12 | - | 3 |
| K.S.Williamson* not out | 40 | 63 | 42 | - | 3 |
| D.P.Conway† not out | 36 | 42 | 32 | - | 4 |
| G.D.Phillips | | | | | |
| J.D.S.Neesham | | | | | |
| M.J.Santner | | | | | |
| A.F.Milne | | | | | |
| T.G.Southee | | | | | |
| I.S.Sodhi | | | | | |
| T.A.Boult | | | | | |
| Extras (lb 2, w 2) | 4 | | | | |
| **TOTAL** (18.1 overs) (2 wkts) | **125** | 75 | | | |

| Bowling NEW ZEALAND | O | M | R | W |
|---|---|---|---|---|
| Southee | 4 | 0 | 24 | 2 |
| Boult | 4 | 0 | 17 | 3 |
| Milne | 4 | 0 | 17 | 1 |
| Neesham | 4 | 0 | 24 | 1 |
| Santner | 2 | 0 | 27 | 0 |
| Sodhi | 2 | 0 | 13 | 1 |
| **AFGHANISTAN** | | | | |
| Nabi | 4 | 0 | 26 | 0 |
| Zadran | 4 | 0 | 31 | 1 |
| Naveen | 2 | 0 | 16 | 0 |
| Hassan | 3 | 0 | 14 | 0 |
| Rashid | 4 | 0 | 27 | 1 |
| Naib | 1.1 | 0 | 9 | 0 |

| Fall of Wickets | A | NZ |
|---|---|---|
| 1st | 8 | 26 |
| 2nd | 12 | 57 |
| 3rd | 19 | - |
| 4th | 56 | - |
| 5th | 115 | - |
| 6th | 119 | - |
| 7th | 121 | - |
| 8th | 124 | - |
| 9th | - | - |
| 10th | - | - |

# NEW ZEALAND v ENGLAND                        Semi-final

*at Sheikh Zayed Stadium, Abu Dhabi on 10 November, 2021 (d/n)*
*Toss : New Zealand.  Umpires : H.D.P.K. Dharmasena & M. Erasmus*
**New Zealand won by 5 wickets**

New Zealand won the toss and bowled first in the first semi-final. Malan and Moeen (50 from 36 balls) added 63 from 43 balls to enable England to reach 166-4.

New Zealand were soon 13-2 before Mitchell and Conway added 82 from 72 balls. Mitchell reached his first fifty from 41 balls. Phillips was out to the first ball of the sixteenth over to leave New Zealand struggling at 107-4. However, some lusty hitting from Mitchell, assisted by Neesham, saw his team home and into the final with an over to spare.

## ENGLAND

| | Runs | Mins | Balls | 6s | 4s |
|---|---|---|---|---|---|
| J.C.Buttler† lbw b Sodhi | 29 | 41 | 24 | - | 4 |
| J.M.Bairstow c Williamson b Milne | 13 | 27 | 17 | - | 2 |
| D.J.Malan c Conway b Southee | 41 | 48 | 30 | 1 | 4 |
| M.M.Ali not out | 51 | 59 | 37 | 2 | 3 |
| L.S.Livingstone c Santner b Neesham | 17 | 20 | 10 | 1 | 1 |
| E.J.G.Morgan* not out | 4 | 5 | 2 | - | - |
| S.W.Billings | | | | | |
| A.U.Rashid | | | | | |
| C.J.Jordan | | | | | |
| C.R.Woakes | | | | | |
| M.A.Wood | | | | | |
| Extras (lb 2, w 9) | 11 | | | | |
| **TOTAL** (20 overs) (4 wkts) . | **166** | 99 | | | |

## NEW ZEALAND

| | Runs | Mins | Balls | 6s | 4s |
|---|---|---|---|---|---|
| M.J.Guptill c Ali b Woakes | 4 | 3 | 3 | - | 1 |
| D.J.Mitchell not out | 72 | 102 | 47 | 4 | 4 |
| K.S.Williamson* c Ali b Woakes | 5 | 12 | 11 | - | - |
| D.P.Conway† st Buttler b Livingstone | 46 | 53 | 38 | 1 | 5 |
| G.D.Phillips c Billings b Livingstone | 2 | 11 | 4 | - | - |
| J.D.S.Neesham c Morgan b Rashid | 27 | 18 | 11 | 3 | 1 |
| M.J.Santner not out | 1 | 7 | 1 | - | - |
| I.S.Sodhi | | | | | |
| A.F.Milne | | | | | |
| T.G.Southee | | | | | |
| T.A.Boult | | | | | |
| Extras (b 1, lb 4, w 4, nb 1) | 10 | | | | |
| **TOTAL** (19 overs) (5 wkts) . | **167** | 101 | | | |

| Bowling | O | M | R | W |
|---|---|---|---|---|
| **NEW ZEALAND** | | | | |
| Southee | 4 | 0 | 24 | 1 |
| Boult | 4 | 0 | 40 | 0 |
| Milne | 4 | 0 | 31 | 1 |
| Sodhi | 4 | 0 | 32 | 1 |
| Santner | 1 | 0 | 8 | 0 |
| Neesham | 2 | 0 | 18 | 1 |
| Phillips | 1 | 0 | 11 | 0 |
| **ENGLAND** | | | | |
| Woakes | 4 | 1 | 36 | 2 |
| Jordan | 3 | 0 | 31 | 0 |
| Rashid | 4 | 0 | 39 | 1 |
| Wood | 4 | 0 | 34 | 0 |
| Livingstone | 4 | 0 | 22 | 2 |

| Fall of Wickets | E | NZ |
|---|---|---|
| 1st | 37 | 4 |
| 2nd | 53 | 13 |
| 3rd | 116 | 95 |
| 4th | 156 | 107 |
| 5th | - | 147 |
| 6th | - | - |
| 7th | - | - |
| 8th | - | - |
| 9th | - | - |
| 10th | - | - |

**AUSTRALIA v PAKISTAN** *(Semi-final)*
*At Dubai International Cricket Stadium  11 November, 2021*
**Pakistan** 176-4 **lost to Australia** 177-5 by 5 wickets

# NEW ZEALAND v AUSTRALIA                    Final

*at Dubai Sports City Stadium on 14 November, 2021 (d/n)*
*Toss : Australia.  Umpires : M. Erasmus & R.A. Kettleborough*
**Australia won by 8 wickets**

Australia won the toss and bowled first. New Zealand were forced to make a change with Seifert replacing Conway, who had broken his hand. Williamson reached 2000 runs in his innings of 85, with his fifty coming from 32 balls. New Zealand finished with 172-4 while Hazlewood took 3-16.

Australia lost Finch early  but then Warner and Marsh added 92 from 59 balls for the second wicket. Warner got fifty from 34 balls, three more than Marsh, who made his highest score. Marsh finished on 77 not out as Australia got to their target with seven balls to spare to claim their first Twenty20 World Cup.

## NEW ZEALAND

| | Runs | Mins | Balls | 6s | 4s |
|---|---|---|---|---|---|
| M.J.Guptill c Stoinis b Zampa ... | 28 | 53 | 35 | - | 3 |
| D.J.Mitchell c Wade b Hazlewood .......................... | 11 | 18 | 8 | 1 | - |
| K.S.Williamson* c Smith b Hazlewood ........................... | 85 | 69 | 48 | 3 | 10 |
| G.D.Phillips c Maxwell b Hazlewood .......................... | 18 | 32 | 17 | 1 | 1 |
| J.D.S.Neesham not out ............. | 13 | 17 | 7 | 1 | - |
| T.L.Seifert† not out ...................... | 8 | 15 | 6 | - | 1 |
| M.J.Santner | | | | | |
| I.S.Sodhi | | | | | |
| A.F.Milne | | | | | |
| T.G.Southee | | | | | |
| T.A.Boult | | | | | |
| Extras (b 1, lb 3, w 4, nb 1) ...... | 9 | | | | |
| **TOTAL** (20 overs) (4 wkts) . | **172** | 100 | | | |

## AUSTRALIA

| | Runs | Mins | Balls | 6s | 4s |
|---|---|---|---|---|---|
| D.A.Warner b Boult ................... | 53 | 57 | 38 | 3 | 4 |
| A.J.Finch* c Mitchell b Boult ....... | 5 | 12 | 7 | - | 1 |
| M.R.Marsh not out ................... | 77 | 80 | 50 | 4 | 6 |
| G.J.Maxwell not out .................. | 28 | 33 | 18 | 1 | 4 |
| S.P.D.Smith | | | | | |
| M.P.Stoinis | | | | | |
| M.S.Wade† | | | | | |
| A.Zampa | | | | | |
| P.J.Cummins | | | | | |
| M.A.Starc | | | | | |
| J.R.Hazlewood | | | | | |
| Extras (lb 4, w 6) .................... | 10 | | | | |
| **TOTAL** (18.5 overs) (2 wkts) | **173** | 91 | | | |

| Bowling | O | M | R | W |
|---|---|---|---|---|
| **AUSTRALIA** | | | | |
| Starc | 4 | 0 | 60 | 0 |
| Hazlewood | 4 | 0 | 16 | 3 |
| Maxwell | 3 | 0 | 28 | 0 |
| Cummins | 4 | 0 | 27 | 0 |
| Zampa | 4 | 0 | 26 | 1 |
| Marsh | 1 | 0 | 11 | 0 |
| **NEW ZEALAND** | | | | |
| Boult | 4 | 0 | 18 | 2 |
| Southee | 3.5 | 0 | 43 | 0 |
| Milne | 4 | 0 | 30 | 0 |
| Sodhi | 3 | 0 | 40 | 0 |
| Santner | 3 | 0 | 23 | 0 |
| Neesham | 1 | 0 | 15 | 0 |

| Fall of Wickets | | |
|---|---|---|
| | NZ | A |
| 1st | 28 | 15 |
| 2nd | 76 | 107 |
| 3rd | 144 | - |
| 4th | 148 | - |
| 5th | - | - |
| 6th | - | - |
| 7th | - | - |
| 8th | - | - |
| 9th | - | - |
| 10th | - | - |

# NEW ZEALAND
# IN INDIA

New Zealand made a five-match tour of India immediately after the Twenty20 World Cup in November and December. The tour was made up of of three Twenty20 internationals and two test matches.

India won the three Twenty20 games and the test series 1-0 with the first match drawn with New Zealand nine wickets down. The highlight of the whole tour came in the second test when Ajaz Patel became only the third bowler and first left-arm bowler to take ten wickets in a test innings. His finished with 10-119 and his four second innings wickets gave him the most wickets by any player in a test against India.

New Zealand had no luck with the toss, losing all five, but in general the batting struggled in the Indian conditions. In the Twenty20 games Guptill (twice) and Chapman scored fifties while in the tests Latham (twice), Young and Mitchell reached half-centuries. Patel took 17 wickets in the two tests followed by Southee who took eight and Jamieson six.

The New Zealand squads were:

Twenty20: K.S. Williamson *(captain, Northern Districts)*, T.D. Astle *(Canterbury)*, T.A. Boult *(Northern Districts)*, M.S. Chapman *(Auckland)*, L.H. Ferguson *(Auckland)*, M.J. Guptill *(Auckland)*, K.A. Jamieson *(Auckland)*, A.F. Milne *(Central Districts)*, D.J. Mitchell *(Canterbury)*, J.D.S. Neesham *(Wellington)*, G.D. Phillips *(Auckland)*, M.J. Santner *(Northern Districts)*, T.L. Seifert *(Northern Districts)*, I.S. Sodhi *(Northern Districts)*, T.G. Southee *(Northern Districts)*.

Test: K.S. Williamson *(captain, Northern Districts)*, T.A. Blundell *(Wellington)*, K.A. Jamieson *(Auckland)*, T.W.M. Latham *(Canterbury)*, D.J. Mitchell *(Canterbury)*, H.M. Nicholls *(Canterbury)*, A.Y. Patel *(Central Districts)*, G.D. Phillips *(Auckland)*, R. Ravindra *(Wellington)*, M.J. Santner *(Northern Districts)*, W.E.R. Somerville *(Auckland)*, T.G. Southee *(Northern Districts)*, L.R.P.L. Taylor *(Central Districts)*, W.A. Young *(Central Districts)*, N. Wagner *(Northern Districts)*.

Boult (tests) and C. de Grandhomme were not available for selection. D.P. Conway, who was in both squads, was injured during the Twenty20 World Cup and replaced in the test squad by Mitchell. No replacement was named in the Twenty20 squad. Williamson and Jamieson subsequently withdrew from the Twenty20 squad after arriving in India. Ravindra was added to the Twenty20 squad after Neesham was unwell prior to the first game.

Coach, G.R. Stead; Assistant coaches, L. Ronchi and J.I. Pamment; Bowling coaches, S.E. Bond and S.J. Jurgensen; Manager, M. Sandle; Physiotherapist, V. Villabh; Trainer, C.L. Donaldson; Video analyst, P. Warren.

# New Zealand Test Averages

| BATTING | M | I | NO | HS | Agg | Ave | 100s | 50s | Ct | St |
|---|---|---|---|---|---|---|---|---|---|---|
| T.W.M. Latham | 2 | 4 | 0 | 95 | 163 | 40.75 | - | 2 | 2 | - |
| D.J. Mitchell | 1 | 2 | 0 | 60 | 68 | 34.00 | - | 1 | - | - |
| W.A. Young | 2 | 4 | 0 | 89 | 115 | 28.75 | - | 1 | 2 | - |
| K.S. Williamson | 1 | 2 | 0 | 24 | 42 | 21.00 | - | - | - | - |
| R. Ravindra | 2 | 4 | 1 | 18* | 53 | 17.66 | - | - | 2 | - |
| H.M. Nicholls | 2 | 4 | 0 | 44 | 54 | 13.50 | - | - | - | - |
| K.A. Jamieson | 2 | 4 | 0 | 23 | 45 | 11.25 | - | - | 1 | - |
| W.E.R. Somerville | 2 | 4 | 0 | 36 | 43 | 10.75 | - | - | - | - |
| T.A. Blundell | 2 | 4 | 0 | 13 | 23 | 5.75 | - | - | 8 | 1 |
| L.R.P.L. Taylor | 2 | 4 | 0 | 11 | 20 | 5.00 | - | - | 2 | - |
| T.G. Southee | 2 | 4 | 0 | 5 | 9 | 2.25 | - | - | - | - |
| A.Y. Patel | 2 | 4 | 4 | 5* | 7 | - | - | - | 1 | - |

| BOWLING | O | M | R | W | Ave | Best | 5w | 10w |
|---|---|---|---|---|---|---|---|---|
| A.Y. Patel | 120 | 25 | 375 | 17 | 22.05 | 10-119 | 1 | 1 |
| T.G. Southee | 84.4 | 15 | 218 | 8 | 27.25 | 5-69 | 1 | - |
| K.A. Jamieson | 60.2 | 17 | 182 | 6 | 30.33 | 3-40 | - | - |
| R. Ravindra | 33 | 6 | 121 | 3 | 40.33 | 3-56 | - | - |
| D.J. Mitchell | 5 | 3 | 9 | 0 | - | - | - | - |
| W.E.R. Somerville | 69 | 4 | 237 | 0 | - | - | - | - |

# India Test Averages

| BATTING | M | I | NO | HS | Agg | Ave | 100s | 50s | Ct | St |
|---|---|---|---|---|---|---|---|---|---|---|
| A.R. Patel | 2 | 4 | 2 | 52 | 124 | 62.00 | - | 1 | 1 | - |
| M.A. Agarwal | 2 | 4 | 0 | 150 | 242 | 60.50 | 1 | 1 | 1 | - |
| S.S. Iyer | 2 | 4 | 0 | 105 | 202 | 50.50 | 1 | 1 | 2 | - |
| S. Gill | 2 | 4 | 0 | 52 | 144 | 36.00 | - | 1 | 1 | - |
| W.P. Saha | 2 | 4 | 1 | 61* | 102 | 34.00 | - | 1 | - | 1 |
| R.A. Jadeja | 1 | 2 | 0 | 50 | 50 | 25.00 | - | 1 | - | - |
| C.A. Pujara | 2 | 4 | 0 | 47 | 95 | 23.75 | - | - | 3 | - |
| R. Ashwin | 2 | 3 | 0 | 38 | 70 | 23.33 | - | - | - | - |
| A.M. Rahane | 1 | 2 | 0 | 35 | 39 | 19.50 | - | - | - | - |
| V. Kohli | 1 | 2 | 0 | 36 | 36 | 18.00 | - | - | 2 | - |
| J. Yadav | 1 | 2 | 0 | 12 | 18 | 9.00 | - | - | 1 | - |
| M. Siraj | 1 | 1 | 0 | 4 | 4 | 4.00 | - | - | 1 | - |
| I. Sharma | 1 | 1 | 0 | 0 | 0 | 0.00 | - | - | - | - |
| U.T. Yadav | 2 | 2 | 2 | 10* | 10 | - | - | - | - | - |

| BOWLING | O | M | R | W | Ave | Best | 5w | 10w |
|---|---|---|---|---|---|---|---|---|
| M. Siraj | 9 | 2 | 32 | 3 | 10.66 | 3-19 | - | - |
| R. Ashwin | 103 | 33 | 159 | 14 | 11.35 | 4-8 | - | - |
| J. Yadav | 16 | 4 | 62 | 5 | 12.40 | 4-49 | - | - |
| A.R. Patel | 74.1 | 23 | 141 | 9 | 15.66 | 5-62 | 1 | - |
| R.A. Jadeja | 61 | 20 | 97 | 5 | 19.40 | 4-40 | - | - |
| U.T. Yadav | 40 | 8 | 110 | 2 | 55.00 | 1-34 | - | - |
| I. Sharma | 22 | 6 | 55 | 0 | - | - | - | - |

**NZC**

# INDIA v NEW ZEALAND　　First Twenty20 International

*at Sawai Mansingh Stadium, Jaipur on 17 November, 2021 (d/n)*
*Toss : India. Umpires : K.N. Ananthapadmanabhan & V.K. Sharma*
**India won by 5 wickets**

India won the toss and decided to bowl first. They had immediate success getting Mitchell in the first over. Guptill and Chapman then added 109 from 77 balls for the second wicket with Guptill reaching fifty from 31 balls, 14 faster than Chapman. New Zealand finished on 164-6 after 20 overs.

India had a strong start with 50 coming from five overs. Yadav got fifty from 34 deliveries as India lost five wickets getting to its target with two balls to spare.

## NEW ZEALAND

| | Runs | Mins | Balls | 6s | 4s |
|---|---|---|---|---|---|
| M.J.Guptill c Iyer S.S. b Chahar | 70 | 87 | 42 | 4 | 3 |
| D.J.Mitchell b Kumar | 0 | 5 | 1 | - | - |
| M.S.Chapman b Ashwin | 63 | 61 | 50 | 2 | 6 |
| G.D.Phillips lbw b Ashwin | 0 | 4 | 3 | - | - |
| T.L.Seifert† c Yadav b Kumar | 12 | 27 | 11 | - | 2 |
| R.Ravindra b Siraj | 7 | 19 | 8 | - | 1 |
| M.J.Santner not out | 4 | 13 | 4 | - | - |
| T.G.Southee* not out | 0 | 2 | 1 | - | - |
| T.D.Astle | | | | | |
| L.H.Ferguson | | | | | |
| T.A.Boult | | | | | |

Extras (b 2, lb 3, w 3) .............. 8
**TOTAL** (20 overs) (6 wkts) . **164**　107

## INDIA

| | Runs | Mins | Balls | 6s | 4s |
|---|---|---|---|---|---|
| K.L.Rahul c Chapman b Santner | 15 | 27 | 14 | 1 | 1 |
| R.G.Sharma* c Ravindra | | | | | |
| 　b Boult | 48 | 63 | 36 | 2 | 5 |
| S.A.Yadav b Boult | 62 | 56 | 40 | 3 | 6 |
| R.R.Pant† not out | 17 | 38 | 17 | - | 2 |
| S.S.Iyer c Boult b Southee | 5 | 14 | 8 | - | - |
| V.R.Iyer c Ravindra b Mitchell | 4 | 5 | 2 | - | 1 |
| A.R.Patel not out | 1 | 4 | 1 | - | - |
| R.Ashwin | | | | | |
| B.Kumar | | | | | |
| D.L.Chahar | | | | | |
| Mohammad Siraj | | | | | |

Extras (lb 7, w 7) .................... 14
**TOTAL** (19.4 overs) (5 wkts) **166**　101

| Bowling | O | M | R | W |
|---|---|---|---|---|
| **INDIA** | | | | |
| Kumar | 4 | 0 | 24 | 2 |
| Chahar | 4 | 0 | 42 | 1 |
| Siraj | 4 | 0 | 39 | 1 |
| Ashwin | 4 | 0 | 23 | 2 |
| Patel | 4 | 0 | 31 | 0 |
| **NEW ZEALAND** | | | | |
| Southee | 4 | 0 | 40 | 1 |
| Boult | 4 | 0 | 31 | 2 |
| Ferguson | 4 | 0 | 24 | 0 |
| Santner | 4 | 0 | 19 | 1 |
| Astle | 3 | 0 | 34 | 0 |
| Mitchell | 0.4 | 0 | 11 | 1 |

**Fall of Wickets**

| | NZ | I |
|---|---|---|
| 1st | 1 | 50 |
| 2nd | 110 | 109 |
| 3rd | 110 | 144 |
| 4th | 150 | 155 |
| 5th | 153 | 160 |
| 6th | 162 | - |
| 7th | - | - |
| 8th | - | - |
| 9th | - | - |
| 10th | - | - |

## INDIA v NEW ZEALAND      Second Twenty20 International

*at Jharkhand State C.A. Oval Ground, Ranchi on 19 November, 2021 (d/n)*
*Toss : India. Umpires : A.K. Chaudhary & J. Madanagopal*
**India won by 7 wickets**

New Zealand again batted first and made 153-6. During his innings, Guptill became the leading run scorer in Twenty20 Internationals, passing Virat Kohli. Three players reached 30 but no one was able to reach a half century.

India had a 117 run opening stand from 80 balls. Sharma got fifty from 35 balls, five faster than Rahul. Southee took three wickets but India sealed the series winning by seven wickets with 16 balls to spare.

### NEW ZEALAND

| | Runs | Mins | Balls | 6s | 4s |
|---|---|---|---|---|---|
| M.J.Guptill c Pant b Chahar | 31 | 25 | 15 | 2 | 3 |
| D.J.Mitchell c Yadav | | | | | |
|   b Patel H.V. | 31 | 63 | 28 | - | 3 |
| M.S.Chapman c Rahul | | | | | |
|   b Patel A.R. | 21 | 22 | 17 | - | 3 |
| G.D.Phillips c sub (R.D.Gaikwad) | | | | | |
|   b Patel H.V. | 34 | 47 | 21 | 3 | 1 |
| T.L.Seifert† c Kumar b Ashwin | 13 | 22 | 15 | - | 1 |
| J.D.S.Neesham c Pant b Kumar | 3 | 20 | 12 | - | - |
| M.J.Santner not out | 8 | 22 | 9 | - | - |
| A.F.Milne not out | 6 | 13 | 4 | - | - |
| I.S.Sodhi | | | | | |
| T.G.Southee* | | | | | |
| T.A.Boult | | | | | |
| Extras (lb 1, w 4, nb 1) | 6 | | | | |
| **TOTAL** (20 overs) (6 wkts) | **153** | 116 | | | |

### INDIA

| | Runs | Mins | Balls | 6s | 4s |
|---|---|---|---|---|---|
| K.L.Rahul c Phillips b Southee | 65 | 80 | 49 | 2 | 6 |
| R.G.Sharma* c Guptill | | | | | |
|   b Southee | 55 | 90 | 36 | 5 | 1 |
| V.R.Iyer not out | 12 | 22 | 11 | - | 2 |
| S.A.Yadav b Southee | 1 | 3 | 2 | - | - |
| R.R.Pant† not out | 12 | 8 | 6 | 2 | - |
| S.S.Iyer | | | | | |
| A.R.Patel | | | | | |
| R.Ashwin | | | | | |
| B.Kumar | | | | | |
| D.L.Chahar | | | | | |
| H.V.Patel | | | | | |
| Extras (lb 6, w 4) | 10 | | | | |
| **TOTAL** (17.2 overs) (3 wkts) | **155** | 100 | | | |

| Bowling | O | M | R | W |
|---|---|---|---|---|
| **INDIA** | | | | |
| Kumar | 4 | 0 | 39 | 1 |
| Chahar | 4 | 0 | 43 | 1 |
| Patel A.R. | 4 | 0 | 26 | 1 |
| Ashwin | 4 | 0 | 19 | 1 |
| Patel H.V. | 4 | 0 | 25 | 2 |
| **NEW ZEALAND** | | | | |
| Southee | 4 | 0 | 16 | 3 |
| Boult | 4 | 0 | 36 | 0 |
| Santner | 4 | 0 | 33 | 0 |
| Milne | 3 | 0 | 39 | 0 |
| Sodhi | 2 | 0 | 13 | 0 |
| Neesham | 0.2 | 0 | 12 | 0 |

| Fall of Wickets | | |
|---|---|---|
| | NZ | I |
| 1st | 48 | 117 |
| 2nd | 79 | 135 |
| 3rd | 90 | 137 |
| 4th | 125 | - |
| 5th | 137 | - |
| 6th | 140 | - |
| 7th | - | - |
| 8th | - | - |
| 9th | - | - |
| 10th | - | - |

# INDIA v NEW ZEALAND     Third Twenty20 International

*aat Eden Gardens, Kolkata on 21 November, 2021 (d/n)*
*Toss : India. Umpires : K.N. Ananthapadmanabhan & V.K. Sharma*
**India won by 73 runs**

Santner captained New Zealand as Southee was rested for the test series. India batted first and had an opening stand of 69 from 38 balls with Sharma getting a 28-ball fifty. Santner took three wickets as India made 184-7.

The New Zealand reply was disappointing with only Guptill (fifty from 33 balls) able to reach 20. Patel took 3-9 as New Zealand were bowled out for 111 thus giving India a clean sweep of the series.

## INDIA

| | Runs | Mins | Balls | 6s | 4s |
|---|---|---|---|---|---|
| R.G.Sharma* c & b Sodhi | 56 | 60 | 31 | 3 | 5 |
| I.P.Kishan c Seifert b Santner | 29 | 35 | 21 | - | 6 |
| S.A.Yadav c Guptill b Santner | 0 | 5 | 4 | - | - |
| R.R.Pant† c Neesham b Santner | 4 | 9 | 6 | - | - |
| S.S.Iyer c Mitchell b Milne | 25 | 38 | 20 | - | 2 |
| V.R.Iyer c Chapman b Boult | 20 | 24 | 15 | 1 | 1 |
| A.R.Patel not out | 2 | 26 | 4 | - | - |
| H.V.Patel hit wicket b Ferguson | 18 | 15 | 11 | 1 | 2 |
| D.L.Chahar not out | 21 | 8 | 8 | 1 | 2 |
| Y.S.Chahal | | | | | |
| B.Kumar | | | | | |

Extras (b 2, lb 1, w 6) ............... 9
**TOTAL** (20 overs) (7 wkts) . **184**   107

## NEW ZEALAND

| | Runs | Mins | Balls | 6s | 4s |
|---|---|---|---|---|---|
| M.J.Guptill c Yadav b Chahal | 51 | 52 | 36 | 4 | 4 |
| D.J.Mitchell c Patel H.V. b Patel A.R. | 5 | 13 | 6 | - | 1 |
| M.S.Chapman st Pant b Patel A.R. | 0 | 5 | 2 | - | - |
| G.D.Phillips b Patel A.R. | 0 | 7 | 4 | - | - |
| T.L.Seifert† run out | 17 | 35 | 18 | - | 1 |
| J.D.S.Neesham c Pant b Patel H.V. | 3 | 14 | 7 | - | - |
| M.J.Santner* run out | 2 | 12 | 4 | - | - |
| A.F.Milne c Sharma b Iyer V.R. | 7 | 15 | 6 | 1 | - |
| I.S.Sodhi c Yadav b Patel H.V. | 9 | 13 | 11 | - | 2 |
| L.H.Ferguson c & b Chahar | 14 | 11 | 8 | 2 | - |
| T.A.Boult not out | 2 | 7 | 2 | - | - |

Extras (w 1) ............................. 1
**TOTAL** (17.2 overs) ............ **111**   88

| Bowling | O | M | R | W |
|---|---|---|---|---|
| **NEW ZEALAND** | | | | |
| Boult | 4 | 0 | 31 | 1 |
| Milne | 4 | 0 | 47 | 1 |
| Ferguson | 4 | 0 | 45 | 1 |
| Santner | 4 | 0 | 27 | 3 |
| Sodhi | 4 | 0 | 31 | 1 |
| **INDIA** | | | | |
| Kumar | 2 | 0 | 12 | 0 |
| Chahar | 2.2 | 0 | 26 | 1 |
| Patel A.R. | 3 | 0 | 9 | 3 |
| Chahal | 4 | 0 | 26 | 1 |
| Iyer V.R. | 3 | 0 | 12 | 1 |
| Patel H.V. | 3 | 0 | 26 | 2 |

| Fall of Wickets | I | NZ |
|---|---|---|
| 1st | 69 | 21 |
| 2nd | 71 | 22 |
| 3rd | 83 | 30 |
| 4th | 103 | 69 |
| 5th | 139 | 76 |
| 6th | 140 | 76 |
| 7th | 162 | 84 |
| 8th | - | 93 |
| 9th | - | 95 |
| 10th | - | 111 |

# INDIA v NEW ZEALAND                    First Test

*at Modi Stadium, Kanpur on 25, 26, 27, 28, 29 November, 2021*
*Toss : India. Umpires : N.N. Menon & V.K. Sharma*
*Close of play: 1st day: India 258-4, Iyer 75, Jadeja 50; 2nd day: NZ 129-0, Latham 50, Young 75*
*3rd day: India 14-1, Agarwal 4, Pujara 9; 4th day: NZ 4-1, Latham 2, Somerville 0*

**Match drawn**

Both sides had debutants in Iyer (India) and Ravindra (New Zealand). India decided to bat after winning the toss and were indebted to a 121 run fifth wicket stand between Iyer and Jadeja. Iyer got fifty off 94 balls and became the 16th Indian batsman to score a century on debut after he had faced 157 deliveries. Jadeja needed 99 balls for his fifty. Southee was the leading bowler with 5-69 being his 13th five wicket haul. Jamieson took three wickets and India were bowled out for 345.

New Zealand had a 151 run opening stand. Latham reached fifty from 157 balls while Young needed 88. It was his highest score. However Patel and Ashwin then took eight wickets between them as New Zealand were dismissed for 296. India had a 49 run lead and were 103-6 before Iyer and Saha both scored fifties. Iyer needed 109 balls for his fifty, six fewer than Saha, as India declared at 234-7. Southee and Jamieson both took three wickets.

Needing 284 to win New Zealand struggled with Young going early. Latham and Somerville (who was the nightwatchman) batted through the first session on day five but Somerville's dismissal to the first ball after lunch triggered a collapse. Bad light brought an end to the game a few minutes early after Ravindra and Patel had survived 50 balls to save the game with New Zealand finishing on 165-9.

## INDIA

| FIRST INNINGS | Runs | Mins | Balls | 6s | 4s | SECOND INNINGS | Runs | Mins | Balls | 6s | 4s |
|---|---|---|---|---|---|---|---|---|---|---|---|
| M.A.Agarwal c Blundell b Jamieson | 13 | 35 | 28 | - | 2 | c Latham b Southee | 17 | 96 | 53 | - | 3 |
| S.Gill b Jamieson | 52 | 122 | 93 | 1 | 5 | b Jamieson | 1 | 6 | 3 | - | - |
| C.A.Pujara c Blundell b Southee | 26 | 121 | 88 | - | 2 | c Blundell b Jamieson | 22 | 50 | 33 | - | 3 |
| A.M.Rahane* b Jamieson | 35 | 89 | 63 | - | 6 | lbw b Patel | 4 | 19 | 15 | - | 1 |
| S.S.Iyer c Young b Southee | 105 | 267 | 171 | 2 | 13 | c Blundell b Southee | 65 | 194 | 125 | 1 | 8 |
| R.A.Jadeja b Southee | 50 | 162 | 112 | - | 6 | lbw b Southee | 0 | 4 | 2 | - | - |
| W.P.Saha† c Blundell b Southee | 1 | 27 | 12 | - | - | (8) not out | 61 | 187 | 126 | 1 | 4 |
| R.Ashwin b Patel | 38 | 81 | 56 | - | 5 | (7) b Jamieson | 32 | 78 | 62 | - | 5 |
| A.R.Patel c Blundell b Southee | 3 | 14 | 9 | - | - | not out | 28 | 95 | 67 | 1 | 2 |
| U.T.Yadav not out | 10 | 53 | 43 | 1 | - | | | | | | |
| I.Sharma lbw b Patel | 0 | 10 | 5 | - | - | | | | | | |
| Extras (b 5, lb 2, w 1, nb 4) | 12 | | | | | (b 3, lb 1) | 4 | | | | |
| **TOTAL (111.1 overs)** | **345** | 494 | | | | (81 overs) (7 wkts dec) | **234** | 365 | | | |

## NEW ZEALAND

| | Runs | Mins | Balls | 6s | 4s | | Runs | Mins | Balls | 6s | 4s |
|---|---|---|---|---|---|---|---|---|---|---|---|
| T.W.M.Latham st sub (K.S.Bharat) b Patel | 95 | 401 | 282 | - | 10 | b Ashwin | 52 | 218 | 146 | - | 3 |
| W.A.Young c sub (K.S.Bharat) b Ashwin | 89 | 255 | 214 | - | 15 | lbw b Ashwin | 2 | 12 | 6 | - | - |
| K.S.Williamson* lbw b Yadav | 18 | 78 | 64 | - | 2 | (4) lbw b Jadeja | 24 | 139 | 112 | - | 3 |
| L.R.P.L.Taylor c sub (K.S.Bharat) b Patel | 11 | 38 | 28 | - | 1 | (5) b Jadeja | 2 | 36 | 24 | - | - |
| H.M.Nicholls lbw b Patel | 2 | 11 | 9 | - | - | (6) lbw b Patel | 1 | 6 | 4 | - | - |
| T.A.Blundell† b Patel | 13 | 97 | 94 | - | - | (7) b Ashwin | 2 | 44 | 38 | - | - |
| R.Ravindra b Jadeja | 13 | 26 | 23 | - | 2 | (8) not out | 18 | 91 | 91 | - | 2 |
| K.A.Jamieson c Patel b Ashwin | 23 | 94 | 75 | - | 1 | (9) lbw b Jadeja | 5 | 27 | 30 | - | - |
| T.G.Southee b Patel | 5 | 12 | 13 | - | 1 | (10) lbw b Jadeja | 4 | 10 | 8 | - | 1 |
| W.E.R.Somerville b Ashwin | 6 | 49 | 52 | - | - | (3) c Gill b Yadav | 36 | 125 | 110 | - | 5 |
| A.Y.Patel not out | 5 | 16 | 6 | - | 1 | not out | 2 | 29 | 23 | - | - |
| Extras (b 6, lb 4, w 1, nb 5) | 16 | | | | | (b 12, lb 10, nb 4) | 17 | | | | |
| **TOTAL (142.3 overs)** | **296** | 542 | | | | (98 overs) (9 wkts) | **165** | 438 | | | |

| Bowling | O | M | R | W | O | M | R | W |
|---|---|---|---|---|---|---|---|---|
| **NEW ZEALAND** | | | | | | | | |
| Southee | 27.4 | 6 | 69 | 5 | 22 | 2 | 75 | 3 |
| Jamieson | 23.2 | 6 | 91 | 3 | 17 | 6 | 40 | 3 |
| Patel | 29.1 | 7 | 90 | 2 | 17 | 3 | 60 | 1 |
| Somerville | 24 | 2 | 60 | 0 | 16 | 2 | 38 | 0 |
| Ravindra | 7 | 1 | 28 | 0 | 9 | 3 | 17 | 0 |
| **INDIA** | | | | | | | | |
| Sharma | 15 | 5 | 35 | 0 | 7 | 1 | 20 | 0 |
| Yadav | 18 | 3 | 50 | 1 | 12 | 2 | 34 | 1 |
| Ashwin | 42.3 | 10 | 82 | 3 | 30 | 12 | 35 | 3 |
| Jadeja | 33 | 10 | 57 | 1 | 28 | 10 | 40 | 4 |
| Patel | 34 | 6 | 62 | 5 | 21 | 12 | 23 | 1 |

| Fall of Wickets | I | NZ | I | NZ |
|---|---|---|---|---|
| | 1st | 1st | 2nd | 2nd |
| 1st | 21 | 151 | 2 | 3 |
| 2nd | 82 | 197 | 32 | 79 |
| 3rd | 106 | 214 | 41 | 118 |
| 4th | 145 | 218 | 51 | 125 |
| 5th | 266 | 227 | 51 | 126 |
| 6th | 288 | 241 | 103 | 128 |
| 7th | 305 | 258 | 167 | 138 |
| 8th | 313 | 270 | - | 147 |
| 9th | 339 | 284 | - | 155 |
| 10th | 345 | 296 | - | - |

*Bharat kept wicket in New Zealand's first innings from the start of day three and in the second innings from the third over on day four.*

**NZC**

# INDIA v NEW ZEALAND Second Test

*at Wankhede Stadium, Mumbai on 3, 4, 5, 6 December, 2021*
*Toss : India. Umpires : A.K. Chaudhary & N.N. Menon*
*Close of play: 1st day: India 221-4, Agarwal 120, Saha 25; 2nd day: India 69-0, Agarwal 38, Pujara 29*
*3rd day: NZ 140-5, Nicholls 36, Ravindra 2*
**India won by 372 runs**

Both sides made changes through injury. Kohli, Jayant Yadav and Siraj replaced Rahane, Jadeja and Ishant in the Indian side while Mitchell replaced Williamson for New Zealand. India had an 80 run opening stand but then lost three wickets in 15 balls.

Agarwal got a century from 196 balls but the hero of the innings and match was Ajaz Patel. He became the third bowler (and first left-arm bowler) to take all ten wickets in an innings of a test match. He finished with 10-119 as India made 325. New Zealand were then bowled out for just 62, their lowest total against India. Only two players reached double figures while Ashwin took 4-8 and Siraj 3-19.

India decided not to enforce the follow on and got 276-7 before declaring. Agarwal scored fifty and four other batsmen made over 30. Patel took another four wickets and his 14 wickets in a match were the most against India. Ravindra got his first test wickets.

New Zealand were set 540 to win but Latham went early. Mitchell attacked the bowling and scored 60 with his fifty coming from 76 balls. Ashwin and Yadav both took four wickets as New Zealand were bowled out for 167. The 372 run margin represented India's biggest win and New Zealand's heaviest defeat.

## INDIA

| FIRST INNINGS | Runs | Mins | Balls | 6s | 4s | SECOND INNINGS | Runs | Mins | Balls | 6s | 4s |
|---|---|---|---|---|---|---|---|---|---|---|---|
| M.A.Agarwal c Blundell b Patel | 150 | 432 | 311 | 4 | 17 | c Young b Patel | 62 | 140 | 108 | 1 | 9 |
| S.Gill c Taylor b Patel | 44 | 112 | 71 | 1 | 7 | (3) c Latham b Ravindra | 47 | 118 | 75 | 1 | 4 |
| C.A.Pujara b Patel | 0 | 11 | 5 | - | - | (2) c Taylor b Patel | 47 | 167 | 97 | 1 | 6 |
| V.Kohli* lbw b Patel | 0 | 8 | 4 | - | - | b Ravindra | 36 | 111 | 84 | 1 | 1 |
| S.S.Iyer c Blundell b Patel | 18 | 73 | 41 | - | 3 | st Blundell b Patel | 14 | 10 | 8 | 2 | - |
| W.P.Saha† lbw b Patel | 27 | 106 | 62 | 1 | 3 | c Jamieson b Ravindra | 13 | 20 | 12 | - | 2 |
| R.Ashwin b Patel | 0 | 2 | 1 | - | - | | | | | | |
| A.R.Patel lbw b Patel | 52 | 149 | 128 | 1 | 5 | (7) not out | 41 | 32 | 26 | 4 | 3 |
| J.Yadav c Ravindra b Patel | 12 | 39 | 31 | - | 2 | (8) c & b Patel | 6 | 17 | 11 | 1 | - |
| U.T.Yadav not out | 0 | 12 | 2 | - | - | | | | | | |
| M.Siraj c Ravindra b Patel | 4 | 5 | 3 | - | 1 | | | | | | |
| Extras (b 13, lb 5) | 18 | | | | | (b 6, lb 3, nb 1) | 10 | | | | |
| **TOTAL** (109.5 overs) | **325** | 478 | | | | (70 overs) (7 wkts dec) | **276** | 311 | | | |

## NEW ZEALAND

| | Runs | Mins | Balls | 6s | 4s | | Runs | Mins | Balls | 6s | 4s |
|---|---|---|---|---|---|---|---|---|---|---|---|
| T.W.M.Latham* c Iyer b Siraj | 10 | 22 | 14 | - | 2 | lbw b Ashwin | 6 | 16 | 15 | - | 1 |
| W.A.Young c Kohli b Siraj | 4 | 17 | 9 | - | 1 | c sub (S.A.Yadav) b Ashwin | 20 | 59 | 41 | - | 4 |
| D.J.Mitchell lbw b Patel | 8 | 33 | 11 | - | - | c Yadav J. b Patel | 60 | 129 | 92 | 2 | 7 |
| L.R.P.L.Taylor b Siraj | 1 | 10 | 2 | - | - | c Pujara b Ashwin | 6 | 9 | 8 | - | 1 |
| H.M.Nicholls b Ashwin | 7 | 41 | 31 | - | 1 | st Saha b Ashwin | 44 | 158 | 111 | - | 8 |
| T.A.Blundell† c Pujara b Ashwin | 8 | 48 | 24 | - | 1 | run out | 0 | 8 | 6 | - | - |
| R.Ravindra c Kohli b Yadav J. | 4 | 13 | 15 | - | - | c Pujara b Yadav J. | 18 | 48 | 50 | - | 4 |
| K.A.Jamieson c Iyer b Patel | 17 | 44 | 36 | - | 2 | lbw b Yadav J. | 0 | 9 | 4 | - | - |
| T.G.Southee c sub (S.A.Yadav) b Ashwin | 0 | 2 | 2 | - | - | b Yadav J. | 0 | 3 | 2 | - | - |
| W.E.R.Somerville c Siraj b Ashwin | 0 | 24 | 26 | - | - | c Agarwal b Yadav J. | 1 | 9 | 7 | - | - |
| A.Y.Patel not out | 0 | 4 | 1 | - | - | not out | 0 | 5 | 5 | - | - |
| Extras (lb 1, nb 2) | 3 | | | | | (b 9, lb 1, nb 2) | 12 | | | | |
| **TOTAL** (28.1 overs) | **62** | 128 | | | | (56.3 overs) | **167** | 221 | | | |

| Bowling | O | M | R | W | O | M | R | W |
|---|---|---|---|---|---|---|---|---|
| **NEW ZEALAND** | | | | | | | | |
| Southee | 22 | 6 | 43 | 0 | 13 | 2 | 31 | 0 |
| Jamieson | 12 | 3 | 36 | 0 | 8 | 2 | 15 | 0 |
| Patel | 47.5 | 12 | 119 | 10 | 26 | 3 | 106 | 4 |
| Somerville | 19 | 0 | 80 | 0 | 10 | 0 | 59 | 0 |
| Ravindra | 4 | 0 | 20 | 0 | 13 | 2 | 56 | 3 |
| Mitchell | 5 | 3 | 9 | 0 | | | | |
| **INDIA** | | | | | | | | |
| Yadav U.T. | 5 | 2 | 7 | 0 | 5 | 1 | 19 | 0 |
| Siraj | 4 | 0 | 19 | 3 | 5 | 2 | 13 | 0 |
| Ashwin | 8 | 2 | 8 | 4 | 22.3 | 9 | 34 | 4 |
| Yadav J. | 2 | 0 | 13 | 1 | 14 | 4 | 49 | 4 |
| Patel | 9.1 | 3 | 14 | 2 | 10 | 2 | 42 | 1 |

| Fall of Wickets | I | NZ | I | NZ |
|---|---|---|---|---|
| | 1st | 1st | 2nd | 2nd |
| 1st | 80 | 10 | 107 | 13 |
| 2nd | 80 | 15 | 115 | 45 |
| 3rd | 80 | 17 | 197 | 55 |
| 4th | 160 | 27 | 211 | 128 |
| 5th | 224 | 31 | 217 | 129 |
| 6th | 224 | 38 | 238 | 162 |
| 7th | 291 | 53 | 276 | 165 |
| 8th | 316 | 53 | - | 165 |
| 9th | 321 | 62 | - | 167 |
| 10th | 325 | 62 | - | 167 |

*Latham kept wicket for over 93 on the second day*

# BANGLADESH
# IN NEW ZEALAND

Bangladesh played a two-test match series in New Zealand in January in which they recorded their first test match win over New Zealand in the first game with an emphatic eight wicket victory. This was New Zealand's first home defeat since 2017.

However the tables were turned in the second game where New Zealand won by an innings. Bangladesh were without two of their main players in Shakib al Hasan and Tamim Iqbal but the young side performed well. Liton Das scored the only century while five players reached fifties. Ebadot Hossain had career best figures with 6-46 at Mount Maunganui.

The Bangladesh squad was: Mominul Haque *(captain)*, Abu Jayed, Ebadot Hossain, Fazle Mahmud, Khaled Ahmed, Liton Das, Mahmudul Hasan, Mehidy Hasan, Mohammad Naim, Mushfiqur Rahim, Nazmul Hossain, Nurul Hasan, Shadman Islam, Shohidul Islam, Shoriful Islam, Taijul Islam, Taskin Ahmed, Yasir Ali. Coach, R.C. Domingo; Managers, Khaled Mahmud and Nafees Iqbal.

## New Zealand Test Averages

| BATTING | M | I | NO | HS | Agg | Ave | 100s | 50s | Ct | St |
|---|---|---|---|---|---|---|---|---|---|---|
| T.W.M. Latham | 2 | 3 | 0 | 252 | 267 | 89.00 | 1 | - | 6 | - |
| D.P. Conway | 2 | 3 | 0 | 122 | 244 | 81.33 | 2 | - | - | - |
| W.A. Young | 2 | 3 | 0 | 69 | 175 | 58.33 | - | 3 | 2 | - |
| T.A. Blundell | 2 | 3 | 1 | 57* | 68 | 34.00 | - | 1 | 6 | - |
| L.R.P.L. Taylor | 2 | 3 | 0 | 40 | 99 | 33.00 | - | - | 2 | - |
| H.M. Nicholls | 2 | 3 | 0 | 75 | 75 | 25.00 | - | 1 | 1 | - |
| T.A. Boult | 2 | 2 | 1 | 9* | 17 | 17.00 | - | - | 1 | - |
| R. Ravindra | 1 | 2 | 0 | 16 | 20 | 10.00 | - | - | - | - |
| K.A. Jamieson | 2 | 3 | 1 | 6 | 10 | 5.00 | - | - | - | - |
| T.G. Southee | 2 | 2 | 0 | 6 | 6 | 3.00 | - | - | 1 | - |
| D.J. Mitchell | 1 | 1 | 0 | 3 | 3 | 3.00 | - | - | 1 | - |
| N. Wagner | 2 | 2 | 1 | 0* | 0 | 0.00 | - | - | 2 | - |

| BOWLING | O | M | R | W | Ave | Best | 5w | 10w |
|---|---|---|---|---|---|---|---|---|
| L.R.P.L. Taylor | 0.3 | 0 | 0 | 1 | 0.00 | 1-0 | - | - |
| D.J. Mitchell | 6 | 1 | 18 | 1 | 18.00 | 1-18 | - | - |
| T.A. Boult | 69.4 | 23 | 174 | 9 | 19.33 | 5-43 | 1 | - |
| K.A. Jamieson | 65.5 | 19 | 204 | 8 | 25.50 | 4-82 | - | - |
| T.G. Southee | 72 | 16 | 217 | 7 | 31.00 | 3-28 | - | - |
| N. Wagner | 72 | 18 | 205 | 6 | 34.16 | 3-77 | - | - |
| R. Ravindra | 28 | 5 | 67 | 0 | - | - | - | - |

# Bangladesh Test Averages

| BATTING | M | I | NO | HS | Agg | Ave | 100s | 50s | Ct | St |
|---|---|---|---|---|---|---|---|---|---|---|
| Mahmudul Hasan | 1 | 1 | 0 | 78 | 78 | 78.00 | - | 1 | - | - |
| Liton Das | 2 | 3 | 0 | 102 | 196 | 65.33 | 1 | 1 | 4 | - |
| Mominul Haque | 2 | 4 | 1 | 88 | 138 | 46.00 | - | 1 | 1 | - |
| Nurul Hasan | 1 | 2 | 0 | 41 | 77 | 38.50 | - | - | 2 | - |
| Nazmul Hossain | 2 | 4 | 0 | 64 | 114 | 28.50 | - | 1 | - | - |
| Yasir Ali | 2 | 3 | 0 | 55 | 83 | 27.66 | - | 1 | 1 | - |
| Mehidy Hasan | 2 | 3 | 0 | 47 | 55 | 18.33 | - | - | - | - |
| Mushfiqur Rahim | 1 | 2 | 1 | 12 | 17 | 17.00 | - | - | - | - |
| Shadman Islam | 2 | 4 | 0 | 22 | 53 | 13.25 | - | - | 5 | - |
| Mohammad Naim | 1 | 2 | 0 | 24 | 24 | 12.00 | - | - | 1 | - |
| Taskin Ahmed | 2 | 3 | 1 | 9* | 16 | 8.00 | - | - | - | - |
| Ebadot Hossain | 2 | 3 | 2 | 4 | 4 | 4.00 | - | - | - | - |
| Shoriful Islam | 2 | 3 | 0 | 7 | 9 | 3.00 | - | - | 2 | - |

| BOWLING | O | M | R | W | Ave | Best | 5w | 10w |
|---|---|---|---|---|---|---|---|---|
| Mominul Haque | 11.1 | 0 | 47 | 3 | 15.66 | 2-6 | - | - |
| Ebadot Hossain | 69 | 12 | 264 | 9 | 29.33 | 6-46 | 1 | - |
| Shoriful Islam | 66 | 18 | 178 | 5 | 35.60 | 3-69 | - | - |
| Mehidy Hasan | 85.4 | 16 | 254 | 4 | 63.50 | 3-86 | - | - |
| Taskin Ahmed | 72.5 | 15 | 230 | 3 | 76.66 | 3-36 | - | - |
| Nazmul Hossain | 6 | 0 | 25 | 0 | - | - | - | - |

**NEW ZEALAND XI v BANGLADESH**
*At Bay Oval No.2, Mt Maunganui    28, 29 December, 2021*

**New Zealand XI** 146-7d (J.J.N.P. Bhula 57, M.T.M.M.J. Ave 33, Abu Jayed 3-36) **drew with Bangladesh** 269-8 (Mahmudul Hasan 66, Mushfiqur Rahim 66, Liton Das 41)

# NEW ZEALAND v BANGLADESH                First Test

*at Bay Oval, Mt Maunganui on 1, 2, 3, 4, 5 January, 2022*
*Toss : Bangladesh. Umpires : C.M. Brown & C.B. Gaffaney*
*Close of play: 1st day: NZ 258-5, Nicholls 32; 2nd day: Bangladesh 175-2, Mominul 8*
*3rd day: Bangladesh 401-6, Yasir 11, Mehidy 20; 4th day: NZ 147-5, Taylor 37, Ravindra 6*
**Bangladesh won by 8 wickets**

Bangladesh won the toss and decided to bowl first. Young and Conway added 138 for the second wicket after Latham went early. Young got fifty from 131 balls while Conway needed 101 for his half-century and went to his second test century after 186 balls. His dismissal signalled a collapse from 227-3 to 328 all out with Nicholls (75) the only player to make any real contribution thereafter. Shoriful and Mehidy both took three wickets.

Four of the Bangladesh batsmen made fifties. Mahmudul scored his maiden fifty and Nazmul, Mominul and Liton all made telling contributions. This included a record partnership for the second wicket for Bangladesh against New Zealand and a 158 run stand for the fifth wicket. Bangladesh were finally dismissed for 458. Boult took four wickets and Wagner three.

With a deficit of 130 New Zealand reached 136-2. Young got his second fifty of the game but then New Zealand lost eight wickets for 33 runs, being dismissed for 169. Ebadot had career best figures with 6-46 and Taskin gave good support with 3-36. Bangladesh lost two wickets before getting a deserved first test win over New Zealand at their 16th attempt.

## NEW ZEALAND

| FIRST INNINGS | Runs | Mins | Balls | 6s | 4s | SECOND INNINGS | Runs | Mins | Balls | 6s | 4s |
|---|---|---|---|---|---|---|---|---|---|---|---|
| T.W.M.Latham* c Liton b Shoriful | 1 | 15 | 14 | - | - | b Taskin | 14 | 41 | 30 | - | 2 |
| W.A.Young run out | 52 | 214 | 135 | - | 6 | b Ebadot | 69 | 239 | 172 | - | 7 |
| D.P.Conway c Liton b Mominul | 122 | 328 | 227 | 1 | 16 | c Shadman b Ebadot | 13 | 70 | 40 | - | 1 |
| L.R.P.L.Taylor c Shadman b Shoriful | 31 | 80 | 64 | - | 5 | b Ebadot | 40 | 179 | 104 | - | 2 |
| H.M.Nicholls c Shadman b Mominul | 75 | 192 | 127 | - | 12 | b Ebadot | 0 | 3 | 2 | - | - |
| T.A.Blundell† b Ebadot | 11 | 43 | 25 | - | 2 | lbw b Ebadot | 0 | 9 | 4 | - | - |
| R.Ravindra c Shadman b Shoriful | 4 | 25 | 18 | - | 1 | c Liton b Taskin | 16 | 59 | 49 | - | 3 |
| K.A.Jamieson c Shadman b Mehidy | 6 | 43 | 20 | - | 1 | c Shoriful b Ebadot | 0 | 14 | 8 | - | - |
| T.G.Southee c Mominul b Mehidy | 6 | 19 | 16 | - | 1 | b Taskin | 0 | 13 | 4 | - | - |
| N.Wagner c Liton b Mehidy | 0 | 3 | 1 | - | - | not out | 0 | 29 | 17 | - | - |
| T.A.Boult not out | 9 | 8 | 5 | - | 2 | c sub (Taijul Islam) b Mehidy | 8 | 21 | 13 | - | 2 |
| Extras (b 1, lb 4, w 3, nb 3) | 11 | | | | | (b 2, lb 5, w 1, nb 1) | 9 | | | | |
| **TOTAL** (108.1 overs) | **328** | 487 | | | | (73.4 overs) | **169** | 340 | | | |

## BANGLADESH

| | Runs | Mins | Balls | 6s | 4s | | Runs | Mins | Balls | 6s | 4s |
|---|---|---|---|---|---|---|---|---|---|---|---|
| Shadman Islam c & b Wagner | 22 | 76 | 55 | - | 1 | c Blundell b Southee | 3 | 6 | 10 | - | - |
| Mahmudul Hasan c Nicholls b Wagner | 78 | 292 | 228 | - | 7 | | | | | | |
| Nazmul Hossain c Young b Wagner | 64 | 160 | 109 | 1 | 7 | (2) c Taylor b Jamieson | 17 | 59 | 41 | - | 3 |
| Mominul Haque* lbw b Boult | 88 | 370 | 244 | - | 12 | (3) not out | 13 | 65 | 44 | - | 3 |
| Mushfiqur Rahim b Boult | 12 | 85 | 53 | - | 1 | (4) not out | 5 | 12 | 7 | - | 1 |
| Liton Das† c Blundell b Boult | 86 | 247 | 177 | - | 10 | | | | | | |
| Yasir Ali c Blundell b Jamieson | 26 | 153 | 85 | - | 1 | | | | | | |
| Mehidy Hasan c Blundell b Southee | 47 | 121 | 88 | - | 8 | | | | | | |
| Taskin Ahmed lbw b Southee | 5 | 24 | 12 | - | 1 | | | | | | |
| Shoriful Islam b Boult | 7 | 11 | 10 | - | 1 | | | | | | |
| Ebadot Hossain not out | 0 | 2 | 0 | - | - | | | | | | |
| Extras (lb 8, w 7, nb 3, pen 5) | 23 | | | | | (lb 1, w 2, nb 1) | 4 | | | | |
| **TOTAL** (176.2 overs) | **458** | 772 | | | | (16.5 overs) (2 wkts) | **42** | 72 | | | |

| Bowling | O | M | R | W | O | M | R | W |
|---|---|---|---|---|---|---|---|---|
| **BANGLADESH** | | | | | | | | |
| Taskin | 26 | 7 | 77 | 0 | 14 | 3 | 36 | 3 |
| Shoriful | 26 | 7 | 69 | 3 | 12 | 2 | 30 | 0 |
| Ebadot | 18 | 3 | 75 | 1 | 21 | 6 | 46 | 6 |
| Mehidy | 32 | 9 | 86 | 3 | 22.4 | 5 | 43 | 1 |
| Nazmul | 2 | 0 | 10 | 0 | | | | |
| Mominul | 4.1 | 0 | 6 | 2 | 4 | 0 | 7 | 0 |
| **NEW ZEALAND** | | | | | | | | |
| Southee | 38 | 4 | 114 | 2 | 5 | 2 | 21 | 1 |
| Boult | 35.2 | 11 | 85 | 4 | 5 | 3 | 4 | 0 |
| Jamieson | 35 | 11 | 78 | 1 | 3.5 | 1 | 12 | 1 |
| Wagner | 40 | 9 | 101 | 3 | 3 | 1 | 4 | 0 |
| Ravindra | 28 | 5 | 67 | 0 | | | | |

| Fall of Wickets | NZ | B | NZ | B |
|---|---|---|---|---|
| | 1st | 1st | 2nd | 2nd |
| 1st | 1 | 43 | 29 | 3 |
| 2nd | 139 | 147 | 63 | 34 |
| 3rd | 189 | 184 | 136 | - |
| 4th | 227 | 203 | 136 | - |
| 5th | 258 | 361 | 136 | - |
| 6th | 265 | 370 | 154 | - |
| 7th | 297 | 445 | 160 | - |
| 8th | 316 | 450 | 160 | - |
| 9th | 316 | 458 | 161 | - |
| 10th | 328 | 458 | 169 | - |

# NEW ZEALAND v BANGLADESH                Second Test

*at Hagley Oval, Christchurch on 9, 10, 11 January, 2022*
*Toss : Bangladesh. Umpires : C.B. Gaffaney & W.R. Knights*
*Close of play: 1st day: NZ 349-1, Latham 186, Conway 99; 2nd day: Bangladesh 126 all out*
**New Zealand won by an innings and 117 runs**

Both sides made changes. Mitchell replaced Ravindra in the home side while Naim made his debut for the visitors replacing the injured Mahmudul. Taylor was making his last test appearance, equalling Daniel Vettori's New Zealand record of 112 matches.

Bangladesh again won the toss and decided to bowl. New Zealand had an opening stand of 148 with Young scoring his third successive fifty from 98 balls. Latham and Conway then added 215 for the second wicket. Latham went to his 12th Test century off 133 balls while Conway needed 149 for his third hundred. Latham was dismissed for 252, the highest score in a test at the venue. New Zealand declared at 521-6.

Bangladesh had a disastrous start losing wickets in the second and third overs and were 27-5 after 12 overs. Yasir hit his maiden fifty from 85 balls as he and Nurul added 60 for the sixth wicket. Mehidy became Boult's 300th test wicket and Boult's 5-43 his ninth five wicket bag. Southee took three wickets and Jamieson two as Bangladesh were dismissed for 126.

New Zealand enforced the follow-on and the tourists showed improved form in the second innings with the top four players all reaching twenty but Bangladesh then went from 105-2 to 128-5 before Liton and Nurul added 101 for the sixth wicket. Liton scored his second test century after 106 balls but there was then another collapse from 229-5 to 278 all out. Jamieson took four wickets and Wagner three as New Zealand had an innings and 117 run win.

## NEW ZEALAND

| FIRST INNINGS | Runs | Mins | Balls | 6s | 4s | SECOND INNINGS | Runs | Mins | Balls | 6s | 4s |
|---|---|---|---|---|---|---|---|---|---|---|---|
| T.W.M.Latham* c Yasir b Mominul ... | 252 | 552 | 373 | 2 | 34 | | | | | | |
| W.A.Young c Naim b Shoriful ............ | 54 | 176 | 114 | - | 5 | | | | | | |
| D.P.Conway run out ........................ | 109 | 227 | 166 | 1 | 12 | | | | | | |
| L.R.P.L.Taylor c Shoriful b Ebadot ..... | 28 | 56 | 39 | - | 4 | | | | | | |
| H.M.Nicholls c Nurul b Ebadot ............ | 0 | 20 | 4 | - | - | | | | | | |
| D.J.Mitchell c Nurul b Shoriful ............ | 3 | 18 | 11 | - | - | | | | | | |
| T.A.Blundell† not out ........................ | 57 | 66 | 60 | - | 8 | | | | | | |
| K.A.Jamieson not out ........................ | 4 | 14 | 7 | - | - | | | | | | |
| T.G.Southee | | | | | | | | | | | |
| N.Wagner | | | | | | | | | | | |
| T.A.Boult | | | | | | | | | | | |
| Extras (lb 8, w 5, nb 1) ........................ | 14 | | | | | | | | | | |
| **TOTAL** (128.5 overs) (6 wkts dec) ... | **521** | 566 | | | | | | | | | |

## BANGLADESH

| | | | | | | | | | | | |
|---|---|---|---|---|---|---|---|---|---|---|---|
| Shadman Islam c Latham b Boult .......... | 7 | 5 | 8 | - | - | c Blundell b Jamieson ......... | 21 | 55 | 48 | - | 3 |
| Mohammad Naim b Southee ................. | 0 | 14 | 5 | - | - | c Latham b Southee ............ | 24 | 160 | 98 | - | 1 |
| Nazmul Hossain c Latham b Boult ........ | 4 | 19 | 12 | - | - | c Boult b Wagner ................. | 29 | 58 | 36 | 1 | 5 |
| Mominul Haque* b Southee ................. | 0 | 15 | 8 | - | - | c Taylor b Wagner ............... | 37 | 90 | 63 | - | 4 |
| Liton Das c Blundell b Boult................. | 8 | 26 | 18 | - | 1 | lbw b Jamieson ................... | 102 | 189 | 114 | 1 | 14 |
| Yasir Ali c Mitchell b Jamieson ........... | 55 | 160 | 95 | - | 7 | c Latham b Wagner ................ | 2 | 11 | 9 | - | - |
| Nurul Hasan† lbw b Southee ............... | 41 | 80 | 62 | - | 6 | c Wagner b Mitchell ............. | 36 | 76 | 54 | - | 7 |
| Mehidy Hasan b Boult ............................ | 5 | 39 | 33 | - | - | c Latham b Jamieson ............ | 3 | 33 | 30 | - | - |
| Taskin Ahmed c Young b Jamieson ....... | 2 | 6 | 3 | - | - | not out ................................... | 9 | 43 | 17 | - | 2 |
| Shoriful Islam b Boult ............................ | 2 | 16 | 3 | - | - | c Southee b Jamieson ........... | 0 | 9 | 6 | - | - |
| Ebadot Hossain not out ........................ | 0 | 4 | 2 | - | - | c Latham b Taylor ................... | 4 | 9 | 6 | - | 1 |
| Extras (w 1, nb 1) ................................ | 2 | | | | | (b 4, lb 1, w 2, nb 4) ........... | 11 | | | | |
| **TOTAL** (41.2 overs) ........................ | **126** | 194 | | | | (79.3 overs) ...................... | **278** | 369 | | | |

| Bowling | O | M | R | W | O | M | R | W | | Fall of Wickets | | | |
|---|---|---|---|---|---|---|---|---|---|---|---|---|---|
| **BANGLADESH** | | | | | | | | | | | NZ | B | B |
| Taskin | 32.5 | 5 | 117 | 0 | | | | | | | 1st | 1st | 2nd |
| Shoriful | 28 | 9 | 79 | 2 | | | | | | 1st | 148 | 7 | 27 |
| Ebadot | 30 | 3 | 143 | 2 | | | | | | 2nd | 363 | 11 | 71 |
| Mehidy | 31 | 2 | 125 | 0 | | | | | | 3rd | 411 | 11 | 105 |
| Nazmul | 4 | 0 | 15 | 0 | | | | | | 4th | 414 | 11 | 123 |
| Mominul | 3 | 0 | 34 | 1 | | | | | | 5th | 423 | 27 | 128 |
| **NEW ZEALAND** | | | | | | | | | | 6th | 499 | 87 | 229 |
| Southee | 12 | 4 | 28 | 3 | 17 | 6 | 54 | 1 | | 7th | - | 109 | 244 |
| Boult | 13.2 | 3 | 43 | 5 | 16 | 6 | 42 | 0 | | 8th | - | 118 | 269 |
| Jamieson | 9 | 3 | 32 | 2 | 18 | 4 | 82 | 4 | | 9th | - | 126 | 269 |
| Wagner | 7 | 1 | 23 | 0 | 22 | 7 | 77 | 3 | | 10th | - | 126 | 278 |
| Mitchell | | | | | 6 | 1 | 18 | 1 | | | | | |
| Taylor | | | | | 0.3 | 0 | 0 | 1 | | | | | |

# SOUTH AFRICA IN NEW ZEALAND

South Africa made a two-test tour to New Zealand with games counting for the new world test championship cycle. The visitors had a disastrous first test and were soundly beaten but fortunes changed in the second game where they gained a dominant win.

Erwee and Verreynne both recorded maiden test centuries in the second test to lead the run scorers while Rabada was the leading bowler and achieved his eleventh five wicket haul in test cricket.

The South African squad was: D. Elgar *(captain)*, T. Bavuma, S.J. Erwee, M.Z. Hamza, S.R. Harmer, M. Jansen, K.A. Maharaj, A.K. Markram, P.W.A. Mulder, L. Ngidi, D. Olivier, K. Rabada, R.D. Rickelton, L. Sipamla, G.A. Stuurman, H.E. van der Dussen, K. Verreynne. Coach, M.V. Boucher; Manager, K. Masubelele.

## New Zealand Test Averages

| BATTING | M | I | NO | HS | Agg | Ave | 100s | 50s | Ct | St |
|---|---|---|---|---|---|---|---|---|---|---|
| C. de Grandhomme | 2 | 3 | 1 | 120* | 183 | 91.50 | 1 | - | 3 | - |
| H.M. Nicholls | 2 | 3 | 0 | 105 | 151 | 50.33 | 1 | - | 1 | - |
| T.A. Blundell | 2 | 3 | 0 | 96 | 146 | 48.66 | - | 1 | 10 | - |
| D.P. Conway | 2 | 3 | 0 | 92 | 144 | 48.00 | - | 1 | 1 | - |
| N. Wagner | 2 | 3 | 1 | 49 | 80 | 40.00 | - | - | 1 | - |
| D.J. Mitchell | 2 | 3 | 0 | 60 | 100 | 33.33 | - | 1 | 6 | - |
| M.J. Henry | 2 | 3 | 1 | 58* | 58 | 29.00 | - | 1 | - | - |
| K.A. Jamieson | 2 | 3 | 0 | 15 | 40 | 13.33 | - | - | 1 | - |
| T.G. Southee | 2 | 3 | 0 | 17 | 26 | 8.66 | - | - | 4 | - |
| T.W.M. Latham | 2 | 3 | 0 | 15 | 16 | 5.33 | - | - | 2 | - |
| W.A. Young | 2 | 3 | 0 | 8 | 11 | 3.66 | - | - | 1 | - |

| BOWLING | O | M | R | W | Ave | Best | 5w | 10w |
|---|---|---|---|---|---|---|---|---|
| M.J. Henry | 85 | 26 | 226 | 14 | 16.14 | 7-23 | 1 | - |
| N. Wagner | 70.2 | 17 | 213 | 9 | 23.66 | 4-102 | - | - |
| T.G. Southee | 87.4 | 24 | 233 | 9 | 25.88 | 5-35 | 1 | - |
| C. de Grandhomme | 16 | 6 | 33 | 1 | 33.00 | 1-16 | - | - |
| K.A. Jamieson | 65 | 16 | 198 | 6 | 33.00 | 2-74 | - | - |

## South Africa Test Averages

| BATTING | M | I | NO | HS | Agg | Ave | 100s | 50s | Ct | St |
|---|---|---|---|---|---|---|---|---|---|---|
| K. Verreynne | 2 | 4 | 1 | 136* | 188 | 62.66 | 1 | - | 5 | - |
| S.J. Erwee | 2 | 4 | 0 | 108 | 126 | 31.50 | 1 | - | 2 | - |
| M. Jansen | 2 | 4 | 2 | 37* | 58 | 29.00 | - | - | 2 | - |
| T. Bavuma | 2 | 4 | 0 | 41 | 100 | 25.00 | - | - | 3 | - |
| P.W.A. Mulder | 1 | 2 | 0 | 35 | 49 | 24.50 | - | - | 2 | - |
| H.E. van der Dussen | 2 | 4 | 0 | 45 | 97 | 24.25 | - | - | 3 | - |
| K.A. Maharaj | 1 | 2 | 0 | 36 | 40 | 20.00 | - | - | - | - |
| A.K. Markram | 2 | 4 | 0 | 42 | 73 | 18.25 | - | - | 1 | - |
| M.Z. Hamza | 1 | 2 | 0 | 25 | 31 | 15.50 | - | - | - | - |
| D. Elgar | 2 | 4 | 0 | 41 | 55 | 13.75 | - | - | 1 | - |
| K. Rabada | 2 | 4 | 0 | 47 | 53 | 13.25 | - | - | 2 | - |
| L.L. Sipamla | 1 | 2 | 1 | 10* | 10 | 10.00 | - | - | 1 | - |
| G.A. Stuurman | 1 | 2 | 0 | 11 | 11 | 5.50 | - | - | - | - |
| D. Olivier | 1 | 2 | 1 | 1 | 1 | 1.00 | - | - | - | - |

| BOWLING | O | M | R | W | Ave | Best | 5w | 10w |
|---|---|---|---|---|---|---|---|---|
| A.K. Markram | 8 | 0 | 27 | 2 | 13.50 | 2-27 | - | - |
| K. Rabada | 68 | 14 | 219 | 10 | 21.90 | 5-60 | 1 | - |
| M. Jansen | 74.5 | 11 | 257 | 9 | 28.55 | 4-98 | - | - |
| K.A. Maharaj | 47.5 | 11 | 121 | 4 | 30.25 | 3-75 | - | - |
| D. Olivier | 21 | 1 | 100 | 3 | 33.33 | 3-100 | - | - |
| L.L. Sipamla | 30 | 9 | 78 | 1 | 78.00 | 1-29 | - | - |
| G.A. Stuurman | 29 | 5 | 124 | 1 | 124.00 | 1-124 | - | - |
| P.W.A. Mulder | 13 | 3 | 47 | 0 | - | - | - | - |

# NEW ZEALAND v SOUTH AFRICA    First Test

*at Hagley Oval, Christchurch on 17, 18, 19 February, 2022*
*Toss : New Zealand. Umpires : C.M. Brown & C.B. Gaffaney*
*Close of play: 1st day: NZ 116-3, Nicholls 37, Wagner 2; 2nd day: South Africa 34-3, van der Dussen 9, Bavuma 22*
**New Zealand won by an innings and 276 runs**

South Africa had two debutants in Erwee and Stuurman. New Zealand won the toss and decided to bowl. South Africa lost Elgar in the second over and never recovered, being dismissed for 95. It was their lowest score against New Zealand. Henry took 7-23, his first five wicket bag, and equalled the best bowling figures by a New Zealand bowler at home.

New Zealand had a cautious start being 36-2 but then positive batting saw them reach 482. Nicholls scored his eighth century from 156 balls and Blundell was last out for 96. Henry (half-century from 54 balls) became the third New Zealander to score a fifty from number eleven. The last wicket stand of 94 was a record for New Zealand against South Africa.

South Africa again struggled losing three wickets in nine overs on the second evening. They managed to get to 111 before being dismissed just before the lunch interval, which had been delayed with the visitors eight wickets down. Southee recorded his 14th five wicket haul.

## SOUTH AFRICA

| FIRST INNINGS | Runs | Mins | Balls | 6s | 4s | SECOND INNINGS | Runs | Mins | Balls | 6s | 4s |
|---|---|---|---|---|---|---|---|---|---|---|---|
| D.Elgar* c Southee b Henry | 1 | 8 | 9 | - | - | (2) c Blundell b Henry | 0 | 14 | 9 | - | - |
| S.J.Erwee c Mitchell b Jamieson | 10 | 41 | 30 | - | 1 | (1) lbw b Southee | 0 | 1 | 2 | - | - |
| A.K.Markram c Blundell b Henry | 15 | 75 | 43 | - | 2 | c Mitchell b Southee | 2 | 17 | 11 | - | - |
| H.E.van der Dussen c Southee b Henry | 8 | 46 | 29 | - | 1 | b Henry | 9 | 26 | 14 | - | - |
| T.Bavuma c Conway b Southee | 7 | 42 | 31 | - | - | lbw b Wagner | 41 | 112 | 73 | - | 6 |
| M.Z.Hamza c Blundell b Henry | 25 | 93 | 74 | - | 3 | c Mitchell b Jamieson | 6 | 39 | 32 | - | 1 |
| K.Verreynne† lbw b Henry | 18 | 74 | 52 | - | 2 | c de Grandhomme b Southee | 30 | 57 | 38 | - | 3 |
| M.Jansen not out | 2 | 34 | 17 | - | - | c Blundell b Wagner | 10 | 45 | 24 | - | 1 |
| K.Rabada c Blundell b Henry | 0 | 3 | 4 | - | - | c Jamieson b Southee | 0 | 15 | 8 | - | - |
| G.A.Stuurman c Blundell b Henry | 0 | 2 | 1 | - | - | lbw b Southee | 11 | 38 | 30 | - | 2 |
| D.Olivier c Latham b Wagner | 1 | 10 | 6 | - | - | not out | 0 | 16 | 10 | - | - |
| Extras (b 4, lb 4) | 8 | | | | | (lb 1, nb 1) | 2 | | | | |
| **TOTAL** (49.2 overs) | **95** | 217 | | | | (41.4 overs) | **111** | 192 | | | |

## NEW ZEALAND

| | Runs | Mins | Balls | 6s | 4s |
|---|---|---|---|---|---|
| T.W.M.Latham* b Olivier | 15 | 78 | 61 | - | 2 |
| W.A.Young c Verreynne b Jansen | 8 | 47 | 32 | - | 2 |
| D.P.Conway b Olivier | 36 | 112 | 76 | - | 3 |
| H.M.Nicholls c Markram b Olivier | 105 | 267 | 163 | - | 11 |
| N.Wagner c van der Dussen b Rabada | 49 | 83 | 56 | 2 | 7 |
| D.J.Mitchell c Elgar b Stuurman | 16 | 59 | 46 | - | 2 |
| T.A.Blundell† c Verreynne b Jansen | 96 | 215 | 138 | - | 12 |
| C.de Grandhomme c Jansen b Markram | 45 | 59 | 42 | 1 | 5 |
| K.A.Jamieson c Rabada b Markram | 15 | 20 | 19 | - | 2 |
| T.G.Southee c Erwee b Rabada | 4 | 18 | 13 | - | 1 |
| M.J.Henry not out | 58 | 73 | 68 | - | 8 |
| Extras (b 9, lb 13, w 6, nb 7) | 35 | | | | |
| **TOTAL** (117.5 overs) | **482** | 517 | | | |

| Bowling | O | M | R | W | O | M | R | W | | Fall of Wickets | | | |
|---|---|---|---|---|---|---|---|---|---|---|---|---|---|
| **NEW ZEALAND** | | | | | | | | | | | SA | NZ | SA |
| Southee | 12 | 2 | 33 | 1 | 17.4 | 6 | 35 | 5 | | | 1st | 1st | 2nd |
| Henry | 15 | 7 | 23 | 7 | 11 | 4 | 32 | 2 | | 1st | 1 | 18 | 0 |
| Jamieson | 11 | 4 | 19 | 1 | 6 | 0 | 24 | 1 | | 2nd | 20 | 36 | 2 |
| Wagner | 9.2 | 2 | 11 | 1 | 7 | 2 | 19 | 2 | | 3rd | 36 | 111 | 4 |
| de Grandhomme | 2 | 1 | 1 | 0 | | | | | | 4th | 37 | 191 | 34 |
| **SOUTH AFRICA** | | | | | | | | | | 5th | 52 | 239 | 46 |
| Rabada | 30 | 6 | 113 | 2 | | | | | | 6th | 85 | 273 | 87 |
| Stuurman | 29 | 5 | 124 | 1 | | | | | | 7th | 88 | 349 | 91 |
| Jansen | 29.5 | 3 | 96 | 2 | | | | | | 8th | 88 | 368 | 97 |
| Olivier | 21 | 1 | 100 | 3 | | | | | | 9th | 88 | 388 | 105 |
| Markram | 8 | 0 | 27 | 2 | | | | | | 10th | 95 | 482 | 111 |

NZC

# NEW ZEALAND v SOUTH AFRICA                     Second Test

*at Hagley Oval, Christchurch on 25, 26, 27, 28 February, 1 March, 2022*
*Toss : South Africa. Umpires : C.M. Brown & W.R. Knights*
*Close of play: 1st day: South Africa 238-3, van der Dussen 13, Bavuma 22;*
*2nd day: NZ 157-5, Mitchell 29, de Grandhomme 54; 3rd day: South Africa 140-5, Verreynne 22, Mulder 10;*
*4th day: NZ 94-4, Conway 60, Blundell 1*
**South Africa won by 198 runs**

South Africa made three changes with Mulder, Maharaj and Sipamla replacing Hamza (injured), Olivier and Stuurman. New Zealand were unchanged.

South Africa won the toss and decided to bat first and they made a great start with a century opening stand. Elgar then became Southee's 500th first class wicket while Erwee made fifty from 92 balls and went to a maiden century after a further 96. Jansen and Maharaj set a ninth wicket record for South Africa against New Zealand with their 62 run stand as South Africa made 364. Wagner took 4-102 and Henry 3-90.

New Zealand made a bad start being 9-2 in the fifth over and struggled throughout apart from a 133 run stand for the sixth wicket. Mitchell got fifty from 106 balls while de Grandhomme needed 36 balls for fifty and went to his second test century after 138 deliveries. His unbeaten 120 was his highest test score. Rabada had his 11th five wicket bag and Jansen took 4-98.

With a 71 run lead the visitors were soon in trouble at 38-3 and then 114-5 but Verreynne held the innings together getting his maiden century from 158 balls. The lower order helped South Africa declare at 354-9, a lead of 425. New Zealand were soon in trouble at 25-3 but Conway stood firm. He got fifty from 106 balls and reached 8000 first-class runs. When he was dismissed the innings fell away and New Zealand were dismissed for 227. Rabada, Jansen and Marahaj each took three wickets. The 198 run win enabled South Africa to level the series.

## SOUTH AFRICA

| FIRST INNINGS | Runs | Mins | Balls | 6s | 4s | SECOND INNINGS | Runs | Mins | Balls | 6s | 4s |
|---|---|---|---|---|---|---|---|---|---|---|---|
| D.Elgar* b Southee | 41 | 153 | 101 | - | 3 | (2) c Blundell b Southee | 13 | 43 | 28 | - | 2 |
| S.J.Erwee c Blundell b Henry | 108 | 293 | 221 | - | 14 | (1) lbw b Southee | 8 | 10 | 9 | - | 1 |
| A.K.Markram c Mitchell b Wagner | 42 | 137 | 103 | - | 8 | b Henry | 14 | 61 | 44 | - | 3 |
| H.E.van der Dussen c Mitchell b Wagner | 35 | 173 | 124 | - | 1 | c & b Wagner | 45 | 103 | 85 | - | 5 |
| T.Bavuma b Henry | 29 | 107 | 81 | - | 5 | c Southee b Wagner | 23 | 104 | 51 | - | 2 |
| K.Verreynne† c Latham b Henry | 4 | 15 | 10 | - | - | not out | 136 | 299 | 187 | 1 | 16 |
| P.W.A.Mulder c Blundell b Wagner | 14 | 68 | 42 | - | 2 | c Blundell b Jamieson | 35 | 111 | 91 | - | 4 |
| M.Jansen not out | 37 | 96 | 51 | - | 6 | c Young b de Grandhomme | 9 | 51 | 41 | - | 1 |
| K.Rabada c Mitchell b Wagner | 6 | 17 | 14 | - | 1 | c de Grandhomme b Henry . | 47 | 44 | 34 | 4 | 4 |
| K.A.Maharaj c Nicholls b Jamieson | 36 | 51 | 50 | - | 6 | c de Grandhomme b Jamieson | 4 | 15 | 4 | - | 1 |
| L.L.Sipamla c Southee b Jamieson | 0 | 6 | 5 | - | - | not out | 10 | 46 | 28 | - | 1 |
| Extras (lb 7, w 1, nb 4) | 12 | | | | | (lb 5, w 3, nb 2) | 10 | | | | |
| **TOTAL** (133 overs) | **364** | 559 | | | | (100 overs) (9 wkts dec) ... | **354** | 447 | | | |

## NEW ZEALAND

| | Runs | Mins | Balls | 6s | 4s | | Runs | Mins | Balls | 6s | 4s |
|---|---|---|---|---|---|---|---|---|---|---|---|
| T.W.M.Latham* c Verreynne b Rabada | 0 | 2 | 4 | - | - | c van der Dussen b Rabada | 1 | 11 | 2 | - | - |
| W.A.Young c Verreynne b Rabada | 3 | 17 | 8 | - | - | c Bavuma b Rabada | 0 | 2 | 2 | - | - |
| D.P.Conway c Verreynne b Jansen | 16 | 75 | 52 | - | 3 | lbw b Sipamla | 92 | 269 | 188 | - | 13 |
| H.M.Nicholls c Erwee b Jansen | 39 | 89 | 63 | - | 8 | b Maharaj | 7 | 38 | 32 | - | - |
| D.J.Mitchell lbw b Maharaj | 60 | 196 | 134 | - | 8 | b Maharaj | 24 | 98 | 72 | 2 | 2 |
| T.A.Blundell† b Rabada | 6 | 10 | 6 | - | 1 | c Bavuma b Jansen | 44 | 158 | 109 | - | 7 |
| C.de Grandhomme not out | 120 | 228 | 158 | 3 | 12 | c Mulder b Jansen | 18 | 42 | .34 | - | 2 |
| K.A.Jamieson c Mulder b Jansen | 13 | 38 | 30 | - | - | c Rabada b Jansen | 12 | 31 | 23 | - | 2 |
| T.G.Southee c Bavuma b Jansen | 5 | 7 | 8 | - | - | c Sipamla b Rabada | 17 | 47 | 41 | - | 2 |
| N.Wagner c Jansen b Rabada | 21 | 24 | 18 | 1 | 3 | not out | 10 | 59 | 38 | - | 1 |
| M.J.Henry c van der Dussen b Rabada | 0 | 2 | 1 | - | - | lbw b Maharaj | 0 | 34 | 23 | - | - |
| Extras (lb 6, w 2, nb 2) | 10 | | | | | (lb 1, nb 1) | 2 | | | | |
| **TOTAL** (80 overs) | **293** | 346 | | | | (93.5 overs) | **227** | 397 | | | |

| Bowling | O | M | R | W | O | M | R | W | | Fall of Wickets | | | |
|---|---|---|---|---|---|---|---|---|---|---|---|---|---|
| **NEW ZEALAND** | | | | | | | | | | SA | NZ | SA | NZ |
| Southee | 32 | 11 | 75 | 1 | 26 | 5 | 90 | 2 | | 1st | 1st | 2nd | 2nd |
| Henry | 35 | 10 | 90 | 3 | 24 | 5 | 81 | 2 | 1st | 111 | 4 | 12 | 1 |
| Jamieson | 27 | 10 | 74 | 2 | 21 | 2 | 81 | 2 | 2nd | 199 | 9 | 23 | 6 |
| de Grandhomme | 8 | 3 | 16 | 0 | 6 | 2 | 16 | 1 | 3rd | 199 | 51 | 38 | 25 |
| Wagner | 31 | 10 | 102 | 4 | 23 | 3 | 81 | 2 | 4th | 257 | 83 | 103 | 81 |
| **SOUTH AFRICA** | | | | | | | | | 5th | 261 | 91 | 114 | 166 |
| Rabada | 19 | 3 | 60 | 5 | 19 | 5 | 46 | 3 | 6th | 277 | 224 | 192 | 187 |
| Jansen | 22 | 2 | 98 | 4 | 23 | 6 | 63 | 3 | 7th | 296 | 249 | 219 | 188 |
| Sipamla | 16 | 4 | 49 | 0 | 14 | 5 | 29 | 1 | 8th | 302 | 255 | 297 | 201 |
| Mulder | 7 | 2 | 34 | 0 | 6 | 1 | 13 | 0 | 9th | 364 | 293 | 322 | 220 |
| Maharaj | 16 | 2 | 46 | 1 | 31.5 | 9 | 75 | 3 | 10th | 364 | 293 | - | 227 |

# NETHERLANDS
# IN NEW ZEALAND

The Netherlands made a tour of New Zealand in March and April. They were to play one Twenty20 international (but this was abandoned due to rain) and three one-day internationals. Three warm-up games were added (one of which was also called off).

New Zealand won all three one-day internationals. In the first one-day game the Netherlands recovered from a perilous position to reach 202 and in the second game had New Zealand at 32-5, only for the home side to end up with 264-9. In the third game, chasing New Zealand's 333-8, they had a flying start but collapsed.

Two players, Rippon and van Beek, had been playing in New Zealand domestic competitions while Myburgh, O'Dowd, Klaasen and Floyd had New Zealand connections. Rippon and Myburgh both scored fifties, while van Beek was the leading wicket-taker.

The squad was: P.M. Seelaar *(captain)*, P.R.P. Boissevain, B.F.W. de Leede, A. Dutt, S.A. Edwards, C. Floyd, B.D. Glover, B.H.G. Gorlee, F.J. Klaassen, R. Klein, S.J. Myburgh, M.P. O'Dowd, M.J.G. Rippon, Shariz Ahmad, L.V. van Beek, Vikramjit Singh.

Coach, R.J. Campbell; Manager, R.P. Lefebvre

## New Zealand  One-day International Averages

| BATTING | M | I | NO | HS | Agg | Ave | 100s | 50s | Ct | St | SR |
|---|---|---|---|---|---|---|---|---|---|---|---|
| T.W.M. Latham | 3 | 3 | 2 | 140* | 171 | 171.00 | 1 | - | 3 | 1 | 113 |
| W.A. Young | 3 | 3 | 1 | 120 | 224 | 112.00 | 2 | - | 1 | - | 96 |
| M.J. Guptill | 3 | 3 | 0 | 106 | 114 | 38.00 | 1 | - | 4 | - | 81 |
| D.A.J. Bracewell | 2 | 2 | 0 | 41 | 63 | 31.50 | - | - | 2 | - | 105 |
| I.S. Sodhi | 3 | 2 | 1 | 18 | 31 | 31.00 | - | - | 2 | - | 103 |
| H.M. Nicholls | 3 | 3 | 0 | 57 | 78 | 26.00 | - | 1 | 1 | - | 65 |
| C. de Grandhomme | 3 | 2 | 0 | 16 | 20 | 10.00 | - | - | 3 | - | 44 |
| K.A. Jamieson | 3 | 2 | 1 | 6* | 9 | 9.00 | - | - | - | - | 128 |
| L.R.P.L. Taylor | 3 | 3 | 0 | 14 | 26 | 8.66 | - | - | 3 | - | 60 |
| M.G. Bracewell | 3 | 2 | 0 | 3 | 4 | 2.00 | - | - | 3 | - | 57 |
| B.M. Tickner | 2 | 1 | 1 | 1* | 1 | - | - | - | - | - | 33 |
| M.J. Henry | 2 | - | - | - | - | - | - | - | - | - | - |

| BOWLING | O | M | R | W | Ave | Best | R/O |
|---|---|---|---|---|---|---|---|
| M.J. Henry | 15.3 | 2 | 67 | 5 | 13.40 | 4-36 | 4.32 |
| D.A.J. Bracewell | 14 | 3 | 47 | 3 | 15.66 | 2-23 | 3.36 |
| C. de Grandhomme | 15 | 1 | 50 | 3 | 16.66 | 1-10 | 3.33 |
| B.M. Tickner | 15 | 0 | 88 | 5 | 17.60 | 4-50 | 5.87 |
| K.A. Jamieson | 22.4 | 2 | 110 | 6 | 18.33 | 3-45 | 4.85 |
| M.G. Bracewell | 19 | 1 | 96 | 5 | 19.20 | 3-21 | 5.05 |
| I.S. Sodhi | 25.1 | 1 | 96 | 3 | 32.00 | 2-17 | 3.81 |

# Netherlands One-day International Averages

| BATTING | M | I | NO | HS | Agg | Ave | 100s | 50s | Ct | St | SR |
|---|---|---|---|---|---|---|---|---|---|---|---|
| M.J.G. Rippon | 3 | 3 | 0 | 67 | 109 | 36.33 | - | 1 | - | - | 76 |
| S.J. Myburgh | 3 | 3 | 0 | 64 | 79 | 26.33 | - | 1 | - | - | 123 |
| Vikramjit Singh | 3 | 3 | 0 | 31 | 75 | 25.00 | - | - | 2 | - | 63 |
| B.F.W. de Leede | 3 | 3 | 0 | 37 | 65 | 21.66 | - | - | 2 | - | 57 |
| L.V. van Beek | 3 | 3 | 0 | 32 | 53 | 17.66 | - | - | 2 | - | 81 |
| P.M. Seelaar | 3 | 3 | 0 | 43 | 52 | 17.33 | - | - | - | - | 58 |
| P.R.P. Boissevain | 1 | 1 | 0 | 15 | 15 | 15.00 | - | - | - | - | 55 |
| F.J. Klaasen | 3 | 3 | 2 | 8* | 12 | 12.00 | - | - | 1 | - | 57 |
| A. Dutt | 2 | 2 | 0 | 9 | 17 | 8.50 | - | - | - | - | 43 |
| B.D. Glover | 2 | 2 | 1 | 6* | 8 | 8.00 | - | - | 1 | - | 72 |
| M.P. O'Dowd | 3 | 3 | 0 | 16 | 20 | 6.66 | - | - | - | - | 46 |
| S.A. Edwards | 3 | 3 | 0 | 9 | 16 | 5.33 | - | - | 6 | 1 | 66 |
| C. Floyd | 1 | 1 | 0 | 2 | 2 | 2.00 | - | - | - | - | 40 |

| BOWLING | O | M | R | W | Ave | Best | R/O |
|---|---|---|---|---|---|---|---|
| C. Floyd | 7 | 0 | 41 | 2 | 20.50 | 2-41 | 5.86 |
| L.V. van Beek | 25 | 2 | 148 | 7 | 21.14 | 4-56 | 5.92 |
| F.J. Klaasen | 26 | 1 | 121 | 5 | 24.20 | 3-36 | 4.65 |
| A. Dutt | 9 | 0 | 65 | 2 | 32.50 | 2-49 | 7.22 |
| M.J.G. Rippon | 25 | 0 | 132 | 3 | 44.00 | 2-32 | 5.28 |
| P.M. Seelaar | 24 | 0 | 105 | 1 | 105.00 | 1-48 | 4.38 |
| P.R.P. Boissevain | 3.3 | 0 | 35 | 0 | - | - | 10.00 |
| B.F.W. de Leede | 8 | 0 | 54 | 0 | - | - | 6.75 |
| B.D. Glover | 11 | 0 | 84 | 0 | - | - | 7.64 |

**NEW ZEALAND XI v NETHERLANDS**
*At McLean Park, Napier   17 March, 2022*

**New Zealand XI** 280-8 (M.G. Bracewell 127*, F.J. Klaasen 3-54) **defeated Netherlands**
117-4 (B.F.W. de Leede 47*, Vikramjit Singh 45) by 42 runs *(D/L)*

**NEW ZEALAND XI v NETHERLANDS**
*At McLean Park, Napier   19 March, 2022*

**Netherlands** 214-9 (B.F.W. de Leede 74, L.V. van Beek 37, M.P. O'Dowd 30, A.W. McKenzie
4-33) **lost to New Zealand XI** 215-6 (M.G. Bracewell 81, M.W.T. Boyle 41) by 4 wickets

**NEW ZEALAND XI v NETHERLANDS**
*At McLean Park, Napier   21 March, 2022*

**Abandoned without a ball being bowled**

## NEW ZEALAND v NETHERLANDS — Twenty20 International

*at McLean Park, Napier on 25 March, 2022 (d/n)*
**Abandoned without a ball being bowled**

## NEW ZEALAND v NETHERLANDS — First One-day International

*at Bay Oval, Mt Maunganui on 29 March, 2022 (d/n)*
*Toss : Netherlands. Umpires : C.B. Gaffaney & W.R. Knights*
**New Zealand won by 7 wickets**

Vikramjit Singh made his debut for the Netherlands while Michael Bracewell and Tickner made their one-day international debuts. The Netherlands won the toss and decided to bat first. However they lost two wickets in the first six overs and were soon 45-5 before Rippon and Seelaar added 80 for the sixth wicket. Both players recorded their highest scores with Rippon getting fifty from 81 balls. The Netherlands finished on 202 after 49.4 overs.

New Zealand lost Guptill early and then Nicholls and Young added 162 for the second wicket. Nicholls got fifty from 65 balls while Young needed 54 for his half-century and then reached his maiden century after 114 deliveries. New Zealand scored the required runs in 38.3 overs.

### NETHERLANDS

| | Runs | Mins | Balls | 6s | 4s |
|---|---|---|---|---|---|
| S.J.Myburgh c Guptill b Henry | 11 | 22 | 16 | - | 2 |
| M.P.O'Dowd c Latham b Jamieson | 4 | 11 | 9 | - | - |
| Vikramjit Singh c Sodhi b Tickner | 19 | 32 | 21 | - | 4 |
| B.F.W.de Leede c de Grandhomme b Tickner | 7 | 35 | 21 | - | 1 |
| S.A.Edwards† c & b de Grandhomme | 1 | 4 | 7 | - | - |
| M.J.G.Rippon c Guptill b Jamieson | 67 | 160 | 97 | 1 | 4 |
| P.M.Seelaar* c Latham b Tickner | 43 | 81 | 75 | - | 3 |
| L.V.van Beek c Young b Tickner | 14 | 18 | 14 | 1 | 1 |
| P.R.P.Boissevain c & b Bracewell | 15 | 28 | 27 | - | 1 |
| F.J.Klaasen c de Grandhomme b Jamieson | 3 | 11 | 8 | - | - |
| B.D.Glover not out | 6 | 11 | 5 | - | 1 |
| Extras (lb 4, w 6, nb 2) | 12 | | | | |
| **TOTAL (49.4 overs)** | **202** | 209 | | | |

### NEW ZEALAND

| | Runs | Mins | Balls | 6s | 4s |
|---|---|---|---|---|---|
| M.J.Guptill c Edwards b van Beek | 2 | 13 | 10 | - | - |
| H.M.Nicholls b Rippon | 57 | 130 | 79 | 1 | 3 |
| W.A.Young not out | 103 | 150 | 114 | 3 | 8 |
| L.R.P.L.Taylor b Rippon | 11 | 19 | 17 | - | 1 |
| T.W.M.Latham*† not out | 8 | 13 | 11 | - | - |
| M.G.Bracewell | | | | | |
| C.de Grandhomme | | | | | |
| I.S.Sodhi | | | | | |
| K.A.Jamieson | | | | | |
| M.J.Henry | | | | | |
| B.M.Tickner | | | | | |
| Extras (b 5, lb 4, w 14) | 23 | | | | |
| **TOTAL (38.3 overs) (3 wkts)** | **204** | 163 | | | |

| Bowling | O | M | R | W |
|---|---|---|---|---|
| **NEW ZEALAND** | | | | |
| Jamieson | 9.4 | 1 | 45 | 3 |
| Henry | 8 | 1 | 31 | 1 |
| Tickner | 10 | 0 | 50 | 4 |
| de Grandhomme | 5 | 0 | 10 | 1 |
| Bracewell | 8 | 1 | 22 | 1 |
| Sodhi | 9 | 0 | 40 | 0 |
| **NETHERLANDS** | | | | |
| Klaasen | 6 | 1 | 23 | 0 |
| van Beek | 6 | 0 | 34 | 1 |
| de Leede | 2 | 0 | 17 | 0 |
| Glover | 3 | 0 | 24 | 0 |
| Seelaar | 10 | 0 | 30 | 0 |
| Rippon | 8 | 0 | 32 | 2 |
| Boissevain | 3.3 | 0 | 35 | 0 |

**Fall of Wickets**

| | N | NZ |
|---|---|---|
| 1st | 9 | 12 |
| 2nd | 17 | 174 |
| 3rd | 41 | 186 |
| 4th | 42 | - |
| 5th | 45 | - |
| 6th | 125 | - |
| 7th | 147 | - |
| 8th | 175 | - |
| 9th | 183 | - |
| 10th | 202 | - |

# NEW ZEALAND v NETHERLANDS Second One-day International

*at Seddon Park, Hamilton on 2 April, 2022 (d/n)*
*Toss : Netherlands. Umpires : C.M. Brown & C.B. Gaffaney*
**New Zealand won by 118 runs**

Netherlands decided to bowl first and soon had New Zealand in serious trouble at 32-5. However, the sixth wicket added 57 and the seventh put on 90 to enable the home side to reach 264-9. Latham made his sixth century off 101 balls while van Beek had career best bowling figures with 4-56 and Klaasen took 3-36.

Netherlands were 4-2 after seven balls and never recovered. They did have a 77 run stand for the third wicket off 89 balls but then collapsed to be dismissed for 146 after 34.1 overs. Michael Bracewell took three wickets and Jamieson and Sodhi two each.

## NEW ZEALAND

| | Runs | Mins | Balls | 6s | 4s |
|---|---|---|---|---|---|
| M.J.Guptill c de Leede b Klaasen | 6 | 19 | 7 | - | 1 |
| H.M.Nicholls c Vikramjit b van Beek | 19 | 36 | 29 | - | 4 |
| W.A.Young b van Beek | 1 | 5 | 5 | - | - |
| L.R.P.L.Taylor c van Beek b Klaasen | 1 | 12 | 10 | - | - |
| T.W.M.Latham*† not out | 140 | 187 | 123 | 5 | 10 |
| M.G.Bracewell c Klaasen b van Beek | 1 | 2 | 5 | - | - |
| C.de Grandhomme c Edwards b Seelaar | 16 | 56 | 40 | - | 1 |
| D.A.J.Bracewell c Glover b Rippon | 41 | 66 | 51 | 2 | 2 |
| I.S.Sodhi c Vikramjit b Klaasen | 18 | 30 | 25 | 1 | - |
| K.A.Jamieson lbw b van Beek | 3 | 9 | 4 | - | - |
| B.M.Tickner not out | 1 | 11 | 3 | - | - |
| Extras (lb 3, w 12, nb 2) | 17 | | | | |
| **TOTAL** (50 overs) (9 wkts) . | **264** | 225 | | | |

## NETHERLANDS

| | Runs | Mins | Balls | 6s | 4s |
|---|---|---|---|---|---|
| S.J.Myburgh c & b Bracewell D.A.J. | 4 | 3 | 5 | - | 1 |
| M.P.O'Dowd c Guptill b Jamieson | 0 | 6 | 1 | - | - |
| Vikramjit Singh c Sodhi b de Grandhomme | 31 | 66 | 51 | - | 7 |
| B.F.W.de Leede c Bracewell M.G. b Sodhi | 37 | 89 | 58 | - | 5 |
| S.A.Edwards† c Nicholls b Tickner | 6 | 12 | 8 | - | - |
| M.J.G.Rippon st Latham b Bracewell M.G. | 18 | 34 | 22 | 1 | 2 |
| P.M.Seelaar* b Bracewell M.G. | 9 | 13 | 13 | 1 | - |
| L.V.van Beek c Taylor b Bracewell M.G. | 7 | 16 | 15 | - | 1 |
| A.Dutt b Jamieson | 8 | 19 | 17 | - | 1 |
| F.J.Klaasen not out | 8 | 19 | 9 | - | 1 |
| B.D.Glover c Taylor b Sodhi | 2 | 6 | 6 | - | - |
| Extras (lb 4, w 12) | 16 | | | | |
| **TOTAL** (34.1 overs) | **146** | 150 | | | |

| Bowling | O | M | R | W |
|---|---|---|---|---|
| **NETHERLANDS** | | | | |
| Klaasen | 10 | 0 | 36 | 3 |
| van Beek | 10 | 2 | 56 | 4 |
| Glover | 8 | 0 | 60 | 0 |
| Rippon | 10 | 0 | 45 | 1 |
| Seelaar | 9 | 0 | 48 | 1 |
| Dutt | 3 | 0 | 16 | 0 |
| **NEW ZEALAND** | | | | |
| Bracewell D.A.J. | 7 | 2 | 24 | 1 |
| Jamieson | 7 | 0 | 22 | 2 |
| Tickner | 5 | 0 | 38 | 1 |
| de Grandhomme | 4 | 0 | 20 | 1 |
| Sodhi | 6.1 | 0 | 17 | 2 |
| Bracewell M.G. | 5 | 0 | 21 | 3 |

| Fall of Wickets | NZ | N |
|---|---|---|
| 1st | 22 | 4 |
| 2nd | 25 | 4 |
| 3rd | 30 | 81 |
| 4th | 31 | 89 |
| 5th | 32 | 103 |
| 6th | 89 | 119 |
| 7th | 179 | 122 |
| 8th | 221 | 129 |
| 9th | 235 | 138 |
| 10th | - | 146 |

# NEW ZEALAND v NETHERLANDS Third One-day International

*at Seddon Park, Hamilton on 4 April, 2022 (d/n)*
*Toss : New Zealand. Umpires : C.B. Gaffaney & S.B. Haig*
**New Zealand won by 115 runs**

Taylor was making his final appearance for New Zealand before retiring from international play. It was also a farewell game for long-time manager Mike Sandle. New Zealand won the toss and batted first.

Nicholls went early and then Guptill and Young added 203, a record second wicket stand for New Zealand against all comers. Guptill went to his 17th century after 119 balls and also reached 7000 runs in one-day internationals during the innings. Young went to his second hundred after 102 deliveries.

The Netherlands openers got off to a flying start putting on 81 before being parted in the twelfth over. Myburgh, who was also playing his last game, made a 33-ball fifty but his dismissal started another slump as the Netherlands were dismissed for 218 after 42.3 overs. Van Beek made his highest score and Henry took his 100th wicket in one-day internationals when he dismissed Vikramjit Singh. Henry finished with 4-36 as New Zealand won the series 3-0.

### NEW ZEALAND

| | Runs | Mins | Balls | 6s | 4s |
|---|---|---|---|---|---|
| M.J.Guptill c Edwards | | | | | |
| b Klaasen | 106 | 159 | 123 | 2 | 11 |
| H.M.Nicholls c Edwards | | | | | |
| b Klaasen | 2 | 17 | 12 | - | - |
| W.A.Young lbw b Dutt | 120 | 168 | 112 | 4 | 6 |
| L.R.P.L.Taylor c & b van Beek | 14 | 21 | 16 | 1 | - |
| M.G.Bracewell st Edwards | | | | | |
| b Floyd | 3 | 14 | 2 | - | - |
| C.de Grandhomme c Edwards | | | | | |
| b Floyd | 4 | 4 | 5 | - | - |
| D.A.J.Bracewell c de Leede | | | | | |
| b Dutt | 22 | 20 | 9 | 2 | 1 |
| T.W.M.Latham*† c Edwards | | | | | |
| b van Beek | 23 | 24 | 17 | - | 3 |
| I.S.Sodhi not out | 13 | 11 | 51 | 1 | 1 |
| K.A.Jamieson not out | 6 | 3 | 3 | - | 1 |
| M.J.Henry | | | | | |
| Extras (lb 4, w 12, nb 4) | 20 | | | | |
| **TOTAL** (50 overs) (8 wkts) . | **333** | 228 | | | |

### NETHERLANDS

| | Runs | Mins | Balls | 6s | 4s |
|---|---|---|---|---|---|
| S.J.Myburgh c Bracewell D.A.J. | | | | | |
| b de Grandhomme | 64 | 45 | 43 | 1 | 13 |
| M.P.O'Dowd | | | | | |
| lbw b Bracewell D.A.J. | 16 | 52 | 33 | - | 2 |
| Vikramjit Singh lbw b Henry | 25 | 53 | 47 | 1 | 1 |
| B.F.W.de Leede b Henry | 21 | 62 | 34 | - | 2 |
| S.A.Edwards† c Latham | | | | | |
| b Jamieson | 9 | 9 | 9 | - | 1 |
| M.J.G.Rippon c Bracewell M.G. | | | | | |
| b Sodhi | 24 | 39 | 23 | 1 | 3 |
| P.M.Seelaar* c Guptill b Henry | 0 | 1 | 1 | - | - |
| L.V.van Beek | | | | | |
| lbw b Bracewell M.G. | 32 | 52 | 36 | 3 | 1 |
| A.Dutt c Taylor b Henry | 9 | 32 | 22 | - | 1 |
| C.Floyd b Bracewell D.A.J. | 2 | 7 | 5 | - | - |
| F.J.Klaasen not out | 1 | 4 | 4 | - | - |
| Extras (lb 4, w 9, nb 2) | 15 | | | | |
| **TOTAL** (42.3 overs) | **218** | 183 | | | |

| Bowling | O | M | R | W |
|---|---|---|---|---|
| **NETHERLANDS** | | | | |
| Klaasen | 10 | 0 | 62 | 2 |
| van Beek | 9 | 0 | 58 | 2 |
| Floyd | 7 | 0 | 41 | 2 |
| de Leede | 6 | 0 | 37 | 0 |
| Seelaar | 5 | 0 | 27 | 0 |
| Rippon | 7 | 0 | 55 | 0 |
| Dutt | 6 | 0 | 49 | 2 |
| **NEW ZEALAND** | | | | |
| Henry | 7.3 | 1 | 36 | 4 |
| Jamieson | 6 | 1 | 43 | 1 |
| Bracewell D.A.J. | 7 | 1 | 23 | 2 |
| Bracewell M.G. | 6 | 0 | 53 | 1 |
| de Grandhomme | 6 | 1 | 20 | 1 |
| Sodhi | 10 | 1 | 39 | 1 |

| Fall of Wickets | NZ | N |
|---|---|---|
| 1st | 12 | 81 |
| 2nd | 215 | 82 |
| 3rd | 253 | 128 |
| 4th | 260 | 144 |
| 5th | 265 | 144 |
| 6th | 267 | 144 |
| 7th | 306 | 177 |
| 8th | 325 | 211 |
| 9th | - | 215 |
| 10th | - | 218 |

# NEW ZEALAND IN ENGLAND

New Zealand toured England in May and June, playing three test matches. The tour party was disrupted with de Grandhomme and Jamieson departing with injury while five players tested positive for Covid. New Zealand struggled for consistency with the bat, with collapses in the first two games, while dropped chances also cost the side any chance of victory.

The highlight of the tour was the emergence of Daryl Mitchell who scored a century in each test as well as two other fifties. He scored 538 runs in the three games. He was ably assisted by Tom Blundell and the pair had a century partnership in every test. Trent Boult was the outstanding bowler taking 16 wickets, including the only five wicket haul at Nottingham. In general the New Zealand bowlers struggled to contain the England scoring rate.

The touring squad was: K.S. Williamson, *(captain, Northern Districts)*, T.A. Blundell *(Wellington)*, T.A. Boult *(Northern Districts)*, M.G. Bracewell *(Wellington)*, D.P. Conway *(Wellington)*, C. de Grandhomme *(Northern Districts)*, J.A. Duffy *(Otago)*, C.D. Fletcher *(Canterbury)*, M.J. Henry *(Canterbury)*, K.A. Jamieson *(Auckland)*, T.W.M. Latham *(Canterbury)*, D.J. Mitchell *(Canterbury)*, H.M. Nicholls *(Canterbury)*, A.Y. Patel *(Central Districts)*, R. Ravindra *(Wellington)*, H.D. Rutherford *(Otago)*, T.G. Southee *(Northern Districts)*, B.M. Tickner *(Central Districts)*, N. Wagner *(Northern Districts)*, W.A. Young *(Central Districts)*.

Coach, G.R. Stead; Assistant coach, D.D. Ebrahim; Batting coach, L. Ronchi; Bowling coach, S.E. Jurgensen; Manager, R. Muller; Trainer, C. Donaldson; Physiotherapist, V. Vallabh; Doctor, J. Cameron.

Rutherford was released to play for Leicestershire after the first warm-up game and the squad was reduced to fifteen before the first test. Duffy, Ravindra and Tickner were omitted while Bracewell was kept on as injury cover for Nicholls for the first test and retained after de Grandhomme was injured during the game. Rutherford was recalled when Williamson tested positive for Covid before the second test and Tickner and D. Cleaver *(Central Districts)* added to the squad when Jamieson and Fletcher were injured during the second test. Rutherford was released after Williamson recovered.

## New Zealand Test Averages

| BATTING | M | I | NO | HS | Agg | Ave | 100s | 50s | Ct | St |
|---|---|---|---|---|---|---|---|---|---|---|
| D.J. Mitchell | 3 | 6 | 1 | 190 | 538 | 107.60 | 3 | 2 | 6 | - |
| T.A. Blundell | 3 | 6 | 1 | 106 | 383 | 76.60 | 1 | 3 | 10 | 1 |
| C. de Grandhomme | 1 | 2 | 1 | 42* | 42 | 42.00 | - | - | - | - |
| D.P. Conway | 3 | 6 | 0 | 52 | 151 | 25.16 | - | 1 | - | - |
| K.S. Williamson | 2 | 4 | 0 | 48 | 96 | 24.00 | - | - | 2 | - |
| M.G. Bracewell | 2 | 4 | 0 | 49 | 96 | 24.00 | - | - | - | - |
| W.A. Young | 3 | 6 | 0 | 56 | 133 | 22.16 | - | 1 | - | - |
| T.W.M. Latham | 3 | 6 | 0 | 76 | 121 | 20.16 | - | 1 | - | - |
| T.A. Boult | 3 | 6 | 3 | 17 | 55 | 18.33 | - | - | 3 | - |
| H.M. Nicholls | 2 | 4 | 0 | 30 | 59 | 14.75 | - | - | - | - |
| T.G. Southee | 3 | 6 | 0 | 33 | 86 | 14.33 | - | - | 4 | - |
| M.J. Henry | 1 | 2 | 0 | 18 | 18 | 9.00 | - | - | 1 | - |
| A.Y. Patel | 1 | 2 | 0 | 7 | 11 | 5.50 | - | - | - | - |
| K.A. Jamieson | 2 | 4 | 0 | 14 | 21 | 5.25 | - | - | - | - |
| N. Wagner | 1 | 2 | 0 | 4 | 4 | 2.00 | - | - | - | - |

**BOWLING**

| | O | M | R | W | Ave | Best | 5w | 10w |
|---|---|---|---|---|---|---|---|---|
| C. de Grandhomme | 11.5 | 3 | 27 | 1 | 27.00 | 1-24 | - | - |
| K.A. Jamieson | 48.3 | 10 | 165 | 6 | 27.50 | 4-79 | - | - |
| T.A. Boult | 121.2 | 22 | 463 | 16 | 28.93 | 5-106 | 1 | - |
| N. Wagner | 20 | 3 | 108 | 2 | 54.00 | 2-75 | - | - |
| M.G. Bracewell | 47.4 | 2 | 285 | 5 | 57.00 | 3-62 | - | - |
| T.G. Southee | 122.5 | 16 | 531 | 9 | 59.00 | 4-55 | - | - |
| M.J. Henry | 42 | 8 | 195 | 2 | 97.50 | 1-67 | - | - |
| A.Y. Patel | 2 | 0 | 22 | 0 | - | - | - | - |
| D.J. Mitchell | 5.1 | 0 | 24 | 0 | - | - | - | - |

# England Test Averages

**BATTING**

| | M | I | NO | HS | Agg | Ave | 100s | 50s | Ct | St |
|---|---|---|---|---|---|---|---|---|---|---|
| J.E. Root | 3 | 6 | 2 | 176 | 396 | 99.00 | 2 | 1 | 4 | - |
| J. Overton | 1 | 1 | 0 | 97 | 97 | 97.00 | - | 1 | - | - |
| J.M. Bairstow | 3 | 6 | 1 | 162 | 394 | 78.80 | 2 | 1 | 8 | - |
| B.A. Stokes | 3 | 5 | 1 | 75* | 194 | 48.50 | - | 2 | 5 | - |
| O.J.D. Pope | 3 | 6 | 0 | 145 | 267 | 44.50 | 1 | 1 | 3 | - |
| B.T. Foakes | 3 | 5 | 2 | 56 | 107 | 35.66 | - | 1 | 12 | - |
| A.Z. Lees | 3 | 6 | 0 | 67 | 169 | 28.16 | - | 1 | 2 | - |
| S.C.J. Broad | 3 | 3 | 0 | 42 | 60 | 20.00 | - | - | 1 | - |
| J.M. Anderson | 2 | 2 | 1 | 9 | 16 | 16.00 | - | - | - | - |
| Z. Crawley | 3 | 6 | 0 | 43 | 87 | 14.50 | - | - | 4 | - |
| M.J. Leach | 2 | 2 | 1 | 8 | 8 | 8.00 | - | - | 1 | - |
| M.W. Parkinson | 1 | 1 | 0 | 8 | 8 | 8.00 | - | - | - | - |
| M.J. Potts | 3 | 3 | 1 | 3 | 4 | 2.00 | - | - | 3 | - |
| S.W. Billings | 1 | - | - | - | - | - | - | - | 1 | - |

**BOWLING**

| | O | M | R | W | Ave | Best | 5w | 10w |
|---|---|---|---|---|---|---|---|---|
| J.M. Anderson | 72.4 | 23 | 205 | 11 | 18.63 | 4-66 | - | - |
| M.J. Potts | 125.5 | 35 | 326 | 14 | 23.28 | 4-13 | - | - |
| M.J. Leach | 129.5 | 31 | 392 | 13 | 30.15 | 5-66 | 2 | 1 |
| S.C.J. Broad | 132 | 30 | 423 | 12 | 35.25 | 3-62 | - | - |
| M.W. Parkinson | 15.3 | 0 | 47 | 1 | 47.00 | 1-47 | - | - |
| J. Overton | 37 | 4 | 146 | 2 | 73.00 | 1-61 | - | - |
| B.A. Stokes | 53.4 | 6 | 225 | 3 | 75.00 | 2-85 | - | - |
| J.E. Root | 18 | 0 | 77 | 1 | 77.00 | 1-29 | - | - |

## SUSSEX v NEW ZEALAND
*At County Ground, Hove   20, 21, 22, 23 May, 2022*

**New Zealand** 342-7d (T.W.M.Latham 65, W.A. Young 55, M.G.Bracewell 51, T.A. Blundell 51, H.D. Rutherford 31) and 40-0 **drew with Sussex** 247 (A.G.H. Orr 59, T.J. Haines 41, O.E. Robinson 36, F.J. Hudson-Prentice 34, O.J. Carter 31)

## FIRST-CLASS COUNTIES SELECT XI v NEW ZEALAND
*At County Ground, Chelmsford   26, 27, 28, 29 May, 2022*

**New Zealand** 362-9d (M.J. Henry 65, D.J. Mitchell 58, C.D. Fletcher 50, W.A. Young 46, C. de Grandhomme 39, A.Y Patel 36*, L.A. Patterson-White 3-60) and 148 (N. Wagner 36, K.A. Jamieson 36, T.G. Southee 34, J.A. Porter 5-31, B.J. Gibbon 3-36) **lost to First-Class Counties Select XI** 247 (L.W. James 52, T.J. Haines 42, B.G. Compton 39, J.A. Porter 31, A.Y. Patel 3-32) and 264-3 (B.G. Compton 119, N.R.T. Gubbins 67*, D.P, Sibley 34) by 7 wickets

# ENGLAND v NEW ZEALAND First Test

*at Lord's on 2, 3, 4, 5 June, 2022*
*Toss : New Zealand. Umpires : M.A. Gough & R.J. Tucker*
*Close of play: 1st day: England 116-7, Foakes 6, Broad 4; 2nd day: NZ 236-4, Mitchell 97, Blundell 90*
*3rd day: England 216-5, Root 77, Foakes 9*
**England won by 5 wickets**

Potts made his England debut as did Parkinson, who replaced Leach as a concussion substitute after the 23rd over of the match. New Zealand won the toss and batted but were soon in trouble and never recovered. They were 12-4 and 45-7 but finally reached 132, with de Grandhomme making an unbeaten 42. Potts took 4-13 and Anderson 4-66.

England had an opening stand of 59 but went from 92-2 to 100-7 before eventually reaching 141 and securing a nine run lead. Southee took 4-55 and Boult 3-21. New Zealand were again in trouble when they batted but Mitchell and Blundell added 195, a record for New Zealand's fifth wicket against England. Mitchell reached his second test hundred after 189 balls. Mitchell, de Grandhomme and Jamieson went in successive balls. Blundell was dismissed for 96 and New Zealand went from 251-4 to 285 all out. Broad and Potts both took three wickets.

Set 277 to win, England were soon 69-4 but then had stands of 90 for the fifth wicket and an unbeaten 120 for the sixth wicket to secure a five wicket win. Root scored his 26th test hundred and reached 10,000 test runs at the same time. Jamieson was the best of the bowlers with 4-79.

## NEW ZEALAND

| FIRST INNINGS | Runs | Mins | Balls | 6s | 4s | SECOND INNINGS | Runs | Mins | Balls | 6s | 4s |
|---|---|---|---|---|---|---|---|---|---|---|---|
| T.W.M.Latham c Bairstow b Anderson | 1 | 23 | 17 | - | - | c Foakes b Potts | 14 | 66 | 33 | - | 2 |
| W.A.Young c Bairstow b Anderson | 1 | 11 | 2 | - | - | c Foakes b Anderson | 1 | 11 | 6 | - | - |
| K.S.Williamson* c Foakes b Potts | 2 | 43 | 22 | - | - | c Bairstow b Potts | 15 | 43 | 34 | - | 2 |
| D.P.Conway c Bairstow b Broad | 3 | 17 | 7 | - | - | c Foakes b Broad | 13 | 59 | 34 | - | 1 |
| D.J.Mitchell b Potts | 13 | 53 | 35 | - | 3 | c Foakes b Broad | 108 | 307 | 203 | - | 12 |
| T.A.Blundell† b Potts | 14 | 59 | 39 | - | 2 | lbw b Anderson | 96 | 281 | 198 | - | 12 |
| C.de Grandhomme not out | 42 | 115 | 50 | - | 4 | run out | 0 | 3 | 1 | - | - |
| K.A.Jamieson c Potts b Anderson | 6 | 17 | 11 | - | 1 | b Broad | 0 | 2 | 1 | - | - |
| T.G.Southee c Potts b Anderson | 26 | 27 | 23 | - | 4 | c Root b Parkinson | 21 | 46 | 26 | - | 4 |
| A.Y.Patel lbw b Potts | 7 | 28 | 18 | - | 1 | lbw b Potts | 4 | 23 | 13 | - | - |
| T.A.Boult c Pope b Stokes | 14 | 25 | 16 | - | 1 | not out | 4 | 8 | 3 | - | 1 |
| Extras (lb 3) | 3 | | | | | (b 1, lb 4, w 1, nb 3) | 9 | | | | |
| **TOTAL** (40 overs) | **132** | 218 | | | | (91.3 overs) | **285** | 434 | | | |

## ENGLAND

| FIRST INNINGS | Runs | Mins | Balls | 6s | 4s | SECOND INNINGS | Runs | Mins | Balls | 6s | 4s |
|---|---|---|---|---|---|---|---|---|---|---|---|
| A.Z.Lees lbw b Southee | 25 | 139 | 77 | - | 2 | b Jamieson | 20 | 35 | 32 | - | 4 |
| Z.Crawley c Blundell b Jamieson | 43 | 61 | 56 | - | 7 | c Southee b Jamieson | 9 | 54 | 29 | - | 1 |
| O.J.D.Pope c Blundell b Jamieson | 7 | 50 | 27 | - | 1 | b Boult | 10 | 40 | 27 | - | - |
| J.E.Root c Southee b de Grandhomme | 11 | 21 | 15 | - | 2 | not out | 115 | 327 | 170 | - | 12 |
| J.M.Bairstow b Boult | 1 | 24 | 9 | - | - | b Jamieson | 16 | 21 | 15 | - | 3 |
| B.A.Stokes* c Blundell b Southee | 1 | 9 | 9 | - | - | c Blundell b Jamieson | 54 | 142 | 110 | 3 | 5 |
| B.T.Foakes† c Mitchell b Southee | 7 | 45 | 22 | - | - | not out | 32 | 140 | 92 | - | 3 |
| M.J.Potts c Mitchell b Boult | 0 | 3 | 2 | - | - | | | | | | |
| S.C.J.Broad b Southee | 9 | 25 | 14 | - | 1 | | | | | | |
| J.M.Anderson not out | 7 | 25 | 19 | - | - | | | | | | |
| M.W.Parkinson c Mitchell b Boult | 8 | 15 | 8 | - | 1 | | | | | | |
| M.J.Leach | | | | | | | | | | | |
| Extras (b 14, lb 7, nb 1) | 22 | | | | | (b 6, lb 9, w 6, nb 2) | 23 | | | | |
| **TOTAL** (42.5 overs) | **141** | 218 | | | | (78.5 overs) (5 wkts) | **279** | 385 | | | |

| Bowling | O | M | R | W | O | M | R | W |
|---|---|---|---|---|---|---|---|---|
| **ENGLAND** | | | | | | | | |
| Anderson | 16 | 6 | 66 | 4 | 21 | 7 | 57 | 2 |
| Broad | 13 | 0 | 45 | 1 | 26 | 7 | 76 | 3 |
| Potts | 9.2 | 4 | 13 | 4 | 20 | 3 | 55 | 3 |
| Stokes | 1.4 | 0 | 5 | 1 | 8 | 1 | 43 | 0 |
| Parkinson | | | | | 15.3 | 0 | 47 | 1 |
| Root | | | | | 1 | 0 | 2 | 0 |
| **NEW ZEALAND** | | | | | | | | |
| Southee | 14 | 3 | 55 | 4 | 23.5 | 5 | 87 | 0 |
| Boult | 13.5 | 4 | 21 | 3 | 24 | 3 | 73 | 1 |
| de Grandhomme | 8 | 2 | 24 | 1 | 3.5 | 1 | 3 | 0 |
| Jamieson | 7 | 3 | 20 | 2 | 25 | 4 | 79 | 4 |
| Mitchell | | | | | 0.1 | 0 | 0 | 0 |
| Patel | | | | | 2 | 0 | 22 | 0 |

| Fall of Wickets | | | | |
|---|---|---|---|---|
| | NZ | E | NZ | E |
| | 1st | 1st | 2nd | 2nd |
| 1st | 1 | 59 | 5 | 31 |
| 2nd | 2 | 75 | 30 | 32 |
| 3rd | 7 | 92 | 35 | 46 |
| 4th | 12 | 96 | 56 | 69 |
| 5th | 27 | 96 | 251 | 159 |
| 6th | 36 | 100 | 251 | - |
| 7th | 45 | 100 | 251 | - |
| 8th | 86 | 125 | 265 | - |
| 9th | 102 | 130 | 281 | - |
| 10th | 132 | 141 | 285 | - |

*Parkinson was a concussion substitute for Leach*

# ENGLAND v NEW ZEALAND — Second Test

*at Trent Bridge, Nottingham on 10, 11, 12, 13, 14 June, 2022*
*Toss : England. Umpires : M.A. Gough & P.R. Reiffel*
*Close of play: 1st day: NZ 349-1, Latham 186, Conway 99; 2nd day: Bangladesh 126 all out*
**England won by 5 wickets**

England were unchanged from their original side at Lord's while New Zealand made three changes. Williamson (Covid), Patel and the injured de Grandhomme were replaced by Nicholls, Henry and the debutant Bracewell.

England won the toss and decided to bowl. New Zealand had an 84 run opening stand but then lost both openers in successive balls. Mitchell and Blundell had another record fifth wicket stand. This time they added 236, the best against all comers for New Zealand's fifth wicket. Both scored their third test century, Mitchell from 184 balls, seven fewer than Blundell. The total of 553 was New Zealand's best in England. Anderson took three wickets.

England lost Crawley in the second over but then had a stand of 141 for the second wicket. Lees got his maiden fifty while Pope went on to his second hundred off 160 balls. Pope and Root added 187 for the third wicket. Root scored his 27th century from 116 balls. England were dismissed for 539 giving New Zealand a slender 14 run lead. Boult got his tenth five wicket haul and Bracewell took three wickets.

Latham then went in the first over to give Anderson his 650th test wicket before Young and Conway added 100 for the second wicket. Both got fifties from 98 and 108 balls respectively. Mitchell continued his good run getting an unbeaten 62 as New Zealand were bowled out for 284. Broad got three wickets.

Set 299 to win off 72 overs, England again lost Crawley in the second over and were soon 93-4 but Bairstow and Stokes added 179 for the fifth wicket off 121 balls. Bairstow reached his ninth hundred from 77 balls while Stokes hit an unbeaten 75 as England won by five wickets, with 20 overs to spare, and clinched the series. Boult took another three wickets.

## NEW ZEALAND

| FIRST INNINGS | Runs | Mins | Balls | 6s | 4s | SECOND INNINGS | Runs | Mins | Balls | 6s | 4s |
|---|---|---|---|---|---|---|---|---|---|---|---|
| T.W.M.Latham* c Potts b Anderson | 26 | 103 | 60 | - | 6 | b Anderson | 4 | 6 | 5 | - | 1 |
| W.A.Young c Crawley b Stokes | 47 | 99 | 70 | - | 9 | run out | 56 | 185 | 113 | - | 8 |
| D.P.Conway c Foakes b Anderson | 46 | 103 | 62 | - | 7 | c Bairstow b Leach | 52 | 139 | 109 | - | 8 |
| H.M.Nicholls c Foakes b Stokes | 30 | 82 | 52 | - | 4 | c Lees b Potts | 3 | 22 | 18 | - | - |
| D.J.Mitchell c Foakes b Potts | 190 | 477 | 318 | 4 | 23 | not out | 62 | 223 | 131 | 1 | 4 |
| T.A.Blundell† c Stokes b Leach | 106 | 297 | 198 | - | 14 | c Stokes b Broad | 24 | 82 | 53 | - | 4 |
| M.G.Bracewell c Root b Anderson | 49 | 111 | 87 | - | 9 | c Broad b Potts | 25 | 23 | 17 | 1 | 4 |
| K.A.Jamieson c Foakes b Broad | 14 | 15 | 12 | - | 3 | (10) c Foakes b Broad | 1 | 10 | 6 | - | - |
| T.G.Southee c Root b Broad | 4 | 4 | 3 | - | 1 | (8) run out | 0 | 9 | 1 | - | - |
| M.J.Henry c Crawley b Leach | 0 | 4 | 1 | - | - | (9) c Foakes b Broad | 18 | 53 | 46 | - | 4 |
| T.A.Boult not out | 16 | 33 | 18 | - | 4 | c Stokes b Anderson | 17 | 31 | 15 | - | 3 |
| Extras (b 1, lb 16, nb 8) | 25 | | | | | (b 9, lb 5, w 2, nb 6) | 22 | | | | |
| **TOTAL (145.3 overs)** | **553** | 674 | | | | **(84.4 overs)** | **284** | 401 | | | |

## ENGLAND

| | Runs | Mins | Balls | 6s | 4s | | Runs | Mins | Balls | 6s | 4s |
|---|---|---|---|---|---|---|---|---|---|---|---|
| A.Z.Lees c Mitchell b Henry | 67 | 180 | 125 | - | 11 | c Blundell b Southee | 44 | 116 | 81 | 1 | 7 |
| Z.Crawley c Blundell b Boult | 4 | 9 | 6 | - | 1 | c Southee b Boult | 0 | 8 | 4 | - | - |
| O.J.D.Pope c Henry b Boult | 145 | 353 | 239 | 3 | 13 | c Blundell b Henry | 18 | 56 | 34 | - | 3 |
| J.E.Root c Southee b Boult | 176 | 353 | 211 | 1 | 26 | c & b Boult | 3 | 5 | 4 | - | - |
| J.M.Bairstow c Blundell b Boult | 8 | 14 | 11 | - | 2 | c Blundell b Boult | 136 | 150 | 92 | 7 | 14 |
| B.A.Stokes* c Boult b Bracewell | 46 | 45 | 33 | 2 | 6 | not out | 75 | 125 | 70 | 4 | 10 |
| B.T.Foakes† run out | 56 | 135 | 104 | - | 10 | not out | 12 | 23 | 15 | - | 2 |
| S.C.J.Broad c Mitchell b Bracewell | 9 | 15 | 13 | - | 2 | | | | | | |
| M.J.Potts b Boult | 3 | 14 | 8 | - | - | | | | | | |
| M.J.Leach not out | 0 | 22 | 9 | - | - | | | | | | |
| J.M.Anderson st Blundell b Bracewell | 9 | 17 | 11 | - | 2 | | | | | | |
| Extras (b 12, lb 3, w 1) | 16 | | | | | (b 5, lb 6) | 11 | | | | |
| **TOTAL (128.2 overs)** | **539** | 588 | | | | **(50 overs) (5 wkts)** | **299** | 240 | | | |

| Bowling | O | M | R | W | O | M | R | W | | Fall of Wickets | | | |
|---|---|---|---|---|---|---|---|---|---|---|---|---|---|
| **ENGLAND** | | | | | | | | | | | NZ | E | NZ | E |
| Anderson | 27 | 9 | 62 | 3 | 8.4 | 1 | 20 | 2 | | | 1st | 1st | 2nd | 2nd |
| Broad | 26 | 4 | 107 | 2 | 20 | 4 | 70 | 3 | 1st | 84 | 6 | 4 | 12 |
| Potts | 30.3 | 6 | 126 | 1 | 15 | 6 | 32 | 2 | 2nd | 84 | 147 | 104 | 53 |
| Stokes | 23 | 2 | 85 | 2 | 17 | 3 | 62 | 0 | 3rd | 161 | 334 | 115 | 56 |
| Leach | 35 | 6 | 140 | 2 | 24 | 5 | 86 | 1 | 4th | 169 | 344 | 131 | 93 |
| Root | 4 | 0 | 16 | 0 | | | | | 5th | 405 | 405 | 176 | 272 |
| **NEW ZEALAND** | | | | | | | | | 6th | 496 | 516 | 204 | - |
| Southee | 32 | 1 | 154 | 0 | 11 | 0 | 67 | 1 | 7th | 513 | 527 | 213 | - |
| Boult | 33.3 | 8 | 106 | 5 | 16 | 1 | 94 | 3 | 8th | 517 | 522 | 245 | - |
| Henry | 27 | 5 | 128 | 1 | 15 | 3 | 67 | 1 | 9th | 520 | 530 | 249 | - |
| Jamieson | 16.3 | 3 | 66 | 0 | | | | | 10th | 553 | 539 | 284 | - |
| Bracewell | 17.2 | 2 | 62 | 3 | 8 | 0 | 60 | 0 | | | | | |
| Mitchell | 2 | 0 | 8 | 0 | | | | | | | | | |

NZC

# ENGLAND v NEW ZEALAND                                          Third Test

*at Headingley, Leeds on 23, 24, 25, 26, 27 June, 2022*
*Toss : New Zealand. Umpires : M. Erasmus & R.A. Kettleborough*
*Close of play: 1st day: NZ 225-5, Mitchell 78, Blundell 45; 2nd day: England 264-6, Bairstow 130, Overton 89*
*3rd day: NZ 168-5, Mitchell 4, Blundell 5; 4th day: England 183-2, Pope 81, Root 55*
**England won by 7 wickets**

Both sides made changes with England bringing in Overton for his debut for the injured Anderson. New Zealand brought in Williamson and Wagner for Henry and the injured Jamieson. New Zealand won the toss and decided to bat but lost Latham in the first over. Mitchell and Blundell again rescued the side with another century stand, adding 120 for the sixth wicket. Mitchell got fifty off 100 deliveries, 11 fewer than Blundell, and reached his fourth test hundred from 213 balls. Leach took 5-100, his third five wicket bag, as New Zealand made 329.

England had a poor start losing Lees in the first over and being 55-6 before Bairstow and Overton broke the England seventh wicket record against all comers with 241 off 274 balls. Bairstow got his tenth century off just 95 balls while Overton got fifty from 68 balls. Boult got four wickets as England were dismissed for 360.

New Zealand had a stand of 97 for the second wicket when they batted again but slumped to 161-5 before Mitchell and Blundell had another century stand. Blundell reached fifty off 105 balls, 40 fewer than Mitchell, and New Zealand reached 326. Leach took another five wickets for his first ten wicket haul.

England were set 296 to win and Pope and Root added 134 for the third wicket. Bairstow joined Root on the last morning to add an unbroken stand of 111 to give England a seven wicket win and a 3-0 series win. Bairstow reached fifty off 30 balls.

## NEW ZEALAND

| FIRST INNINGS | Runs | Mins | Balls | 6s | 4s | SECOND INNINGS | Runs | Mins | Balls | 6s | 4s |
|---|---|---|---|---|---|---|---|---|---|---|---|
| T.W.M.Latham c Root b Broad | 0 | 5 | 6 | - | - | c Bairstow b Overton | 76 | 141 | 100 | - | 12 |
| W.A.Young lbw b Leach | 20 | 57 | 42 | - | 2 | c Pope b Potts | 8 | 35 | 19 | - | 2 |
| K.S.Williamson* c Foakes b Broad | 31 | 97 | 64 | - | 5 | c Bairstow b Potts | 48 | 168 | 115 | - | 8 |
| D.P.Conway b Overton | 26 | 100 | 62 | - | 5 | c Pope b Root | 11 | 50 | 23 | - | 2 |
| H.M.Nicholls c Lees b Leach | 19 | 137 | 99 | - | 1 | c & b Leach | 7 | 36 | 26 | - | 1 |
| D.J.Mitchell c Stokes b Leach | 109 | 342 | 228 | 3 | 9 | lbw b Potts | 56 | 207 | 152 | - | 9 |
| T.A.Blundell† lbw b Potts | 55 | 162 | 122 | - | 7 | not out | 88 | 247 | 161 | - | 15 |
| M.G.Bracewell c Crawley b Broad | 13 | 58 | 46 | - | 2 | c Crawley b Leach | 9 | 19 | 13 | 1 | - |
| T.G.Southee c Stokes b Leach | 33 | 45 | 29 | 1 | 5 | b Leach | 2 | 22 | 12 | - | - |
| N.Wagner c Bairstow b Leach | 4 | 10 | 8 | - | 1 | c Billings b Leach | 0 | 5 | 5 | - | - |
| T.A.Boult not out | 0 | 3 | 0 | - | - | b Leach | 4 | 17 | 8 | - | 1 |
| Extras (b 4, lb 14, nb 1) | 19 | | | | | (b 9, lb 2, w 4, nb 2) | 17 | | | | |
| **TOTAL** (117.3 overs) | **329** | 517 | | | | (105.2 overs) | **326** | 466 | | | |

## ENGLAND

| | Runs | Mins | Balls | 6s | 4s | | Runs | Mins | Balls | 6s | 4s |
|---|---|---|---|---|---|---|---|---|---|---|---|
| A.Z.Lees b Boult | 4 | 5 | 5 | - | 1 | run out | 9 | 21 | 18 | - | 2 |
| Z.Crawley b Boult | 6 | 33 | 24 | - | 1 | c Williamson b Bracewell | 25 | 56 | 33 | - | 6 |
| O.J.D.Pope b Boult | 5 | 17 | 8 | - | 1 | b Southee | 82 | 158 | 108 | - | 12 |
| J.E.Root c Blundell b Southee | 5 | 16 | 9 | - | 1 | not out | 86 | 186 | 125 | 1 | 11 |
| J.M.Bairstow c Boult b Bracewell | 162 | 304 | 157 | - | 24 | not out | 71 | 62 | 44 | 3 | 8 |
| B.A.Stokes* c Williamson b Wagner | 18 | 23 | 13 | 1 | 2 | | | | | | |
| B.T.Foakes† lbw b Wagner | 0 | 4 | 3 | - | - | | | | | | |
| J.Overton c Mitchell b Boult | 97 | 231 | 136 | 2 | 13 | | | | | | |
| S.C.J.Broad b Southee | 42 | 38 | 36 | 2 | 6 | | | | | | |
| M.J.Potts not out | 1 | 12 | 4 | - | - | | | | | | |
| M.J.Leach lbw b Southee | 8 | 10 | 7 | - | 2 | | | | | | |
| S.W.Billings | | | | | | | | | | | |
| Extras (lb 11, w 1) | 12 | | | | | (b 9, lb 12, nb 2) | 23 | | | | |
| **TOTAL** (67 overs) | **360** | 356 | | | | (54.2 overs) (3 wkts) | **296** | 245 | | | |

| Bowling | O | M | R | W | O | M | R | W |
|---|---|---|---|---|---|---|---|---|
| **ENGLAND** | | | | | | | | |
| Broad | 23 | 8 | 62 | 3 | 24 | 7 | 63 | 0 |
| Potts | 26 | 11 | 34 | 1 | 25 | 5 | 66 | 3 |
| Overton | 23 | 2 | 85 | 1 | 14 | 2 | 61 | 1 |
| Leach | 38.3 | 8 | 100 | 5 | 32.2 | 12 | 66 | 5 |
| Root | 7 | 0 | 30 | 0 | 6 | 0 | 29 | 1 |
| Stokes | | | | | 4 | 0 | 30 | 0 |
| **NEW ZEALAND** | | | | | | | | |
| Boult | 22 | 4 | 104 | 4 | 12 | 2 | 65 | 0 |
| Southee | 23 | 2 | 100 | 3 | 19 | 5 | 68 | 1 |
| Wagner | 12 | 1 | 75 | 2 | 8 | 2 | 33 | 0 |
| Bracewell | 7 | 0 | 54 | 1 | 15.2 | 0 | 109 | 1 |
| Mitchell | 3 | 0 | 16 | 0 | | | | |

| Fall of Wickets | NZ | E | NZ | E |
|---|---|---|---|---|
| | 1st | 1st | 2nd | 2nd |
| 1st | 0 | 4 | 28 | 17 |
| 2nd | 35 | 14 | 125 | 51 |
| 3rd | 62 | 17 | 152 | 185 |
| 4th | 83 | 21 | 153 | - |
| 5th | 123 | 55 | 161 | - |
| 6th | 243 | 55 | 274 | - |
| 7th | 265 | 296 | 291 | - |
| 8th | 325 | 351 | 305 | - |
| 9th | 329 | 351 | 305 | - |
| 10th | 329 | 360 | 326 | - |

*In New Zealand's second innings Bairstow kept wicket on day 3 (Foakes injured) and Billings kept wicket on day 4 (Covid replacement for Foakes)*

# INTERNATIONAL SUMMARY

## 2021/22

## Test Matches

| | Played | Won | Lost | Drawn |
|---|---|---|---|---|
| India | 2 | – | 1 | 1 |
| Bangladesh | 2 | 1 | 1 | – |
| South Africa | 2 | 1 | 1 | – |
| England | 3 | – | 3 | – |
| **TOTAL** | **9** | **2** | **6** | **1** |

## New Zealand Test Averages

| BATTING | M | I | NO | HS | Agg | Ave | 100s | 50s | Ct | St |
|---|---|---|---|---|---|---|---|---|---|---|
| C. de Grandhomme | 3 | 5 | 2 | 120* | 225 | 75.00 | 1 | - | 3 | - |
| D.J. Mitchell | 7 | 12 | 1 | 190 | 709 | 64.45 | 3 | 4 | 13 | - |
| D.P. Conway | 7 | 12 | 0 | 122 | 539 | 44.91 | 2 | 2 | 1 | - |
| T.A. Blundell | 9 | 16 | 2 | 106 | 620 | 44.28 | 1 | 5 | 34 | 2 |
| T.W.M. Latham | 9 | 16 | 0 | 252 | 567 | 35.43 | 1 | 3 | 10 | - |
| W.A. Young | 9 | 16 | 0 | 89 | 434 | 27.12 | - | 5 | 5 | - |
| H.M. Nicholls | 8 | 14 | 0 | 105 | 339 | 24.21 | 1 | 1 | 2 | - |
| M.G. Bracewell | 2 | 4 | 0 | 49 | 96 | 24.00 | - | - | - | - |
| K.S. Williamson | 3 | 6 | 0 | 48 | 138 | 23.00 | - | - | 2 | - |
| M.J. Henry | 3 | 5 | 1 | 58* | 76 | 19.00 | - | 1 | 1 | - |
| T.A. Boult | 5 | 8 | 4 | 17 | 72 | 18.00 | - | - | 4 | - |
| L.R.P.L. Taylor | 4 | 7 | 0 | 40 | 119 | 17.00 | - | - | 4 | - |
| N. Wagner | 5 | 7 | 2 | 49 | 84 | 16.80 | - | - | 3 | - |
| R. Ravindra | 3 | 6 | 1 | 18* | 73 | 14.60 | - | - | 2 | - |
| W.E.R. Somerville | 2 | 4 | 0 | 36 | 43 | 10.75 | - | - | - | - |
| A.Y. Patel | 3 | 6 | 4 | 7 | 18 | 9.00 | - | - | 1 | - |
| K.A. Jamieson | 8 | 14 | 1 | 23 | 116 | 8.92 | - | - | 2 | - |
| T.G. Southee | 9 | 15 | 0 | 33 | 127 | 8.46 | - | - | 9 | - |

| BOWLING | O | M | R | W | Ave | Best | 5 | 10w |
|---|---|---|---|---|---|---|---|---|
| L.R.P.L. Taylor | 0.3 | 0 | 0 | 1 | 0.00 | 1-0 | - | - |
| A.Y. Patel | 122 | 25 | 397 | 17 | 23.35 | 10-119 | 1 | 1 |
| T.A. Boult | 191 | 45 | 637 | 25 | 25.48 | 5-43 | 2 | - |
| M.J. Henry | 127 | 34 | 421 | 16 | 26.31 | 7-23 | 1 | - |
| K.A. Jamieson | 239.4 | 62 | 749 | 26 | 28.80 | 4-79 | - | - |
| C. de Grandhomme | 27.5 | 9 | 60 | 2 | 30.00 | 1-16 | - | - |
| N. Wagner | 162.2 | 38 | 526 | 17 | 30.94 | 4-102 | - | - |
| T.G. Southee | 367.1 | 72 | 1199 | 33 | 36.33 | 5-35 | 2 | - |
| D.J. Mitchell | 16.1 | 4 | 51 | 1 | 51.00 | 1-18 | - | - |
| M.G. Bracewell | 47.4 | 2 | 285 | 5 | 57.00 | 3-62 | - | - |
| R. Ravindra | 61 | 11 | 188 | 3 | 62.66 | 3-56 | - | - |
| W.E.R. Somerville | 69 | 4 | 237 | 0 | - | - | - | - |

## One-day Internationals

|             | *Played* | *Won* | *Lost* | *Tied* | *NR* |
|-------------|----------|-------|--------|--------|------|
| Netherlands | 3        | 3     | –      | –      | –    |
| **TOTAL**   | **3**    | **3** | **–**  | **–**  | **–** |

# New Zealand One-day International Averages

| BATTING | M | I | NO | HS | Agg | Ave | 100s | 50s | Ct | St | SR |
|---------|---|---|----|----|-----|-----|------|-----|----|----|----|
| T.W.M. Latham | 3 | 3 | 2 | 140* | 171 | 171.00 | 1 | - | 3 | 1 | 113 |
| W.A. Young | 3 | 3 | 1 | 120 | 224 | 112.00 | 2 | - | 1 | - | 96 |
| M.J. Guptill | 3 | 3 | 0 | 106 | 114 | 38.00 | 1 | - | 4 | - | 81 |
| D.A.J. Bracewell | 2 | 2 | 0 | 41 | 63 | 31.50 | - | - | 2 | - | 105 |
| I.S. Sodhi | 3 | 2 | 1 | 18 | 31 | 31.00 | - | - | 2 | - | 103 |
| H.M. Nicholls | 3 | 3 | 0 | 57 | 78 | 26.00 | - | 1 | 1 | - | 65 |
| C. de Grandhomme | 3 | 2 | 0 | 16 | 20 | 10.00 | - | - | 3 | - | 44 |
| K.A. Jamieson | 3 | 2 | 1 | 6* | 9 | 9.00 | - | - | - | - | 128 |
| L.R.P.L. Taylor | 3 | 3 | 0 | 14 | 26 | 8.66 | - | - | 3 | - | 60 |
| M.G. Bracewell | 3 | 2 | 0 | 3 | 4 | 2.00 | - | - | 3 | - | 57 |
| B.M. Tickner | 2 | 1 | 1 | 1* | 1 | - | - | - | - | - | 33 |
| M.J. Henry | 2 | - | - | - | - | - | - | - | - | - | - |

| BOWLING | O | M | R | W | Ave | Best | R/O |
|---------|---|---|---|---|-----|------|-----|
| M.J. Henry | 15.3 | 2 | 67 | 5 | 13.40 | 4-36 | 4.32 |
| D.A.J. Bracewell | 14 | 3 | 47 | 3 | 15.66 | 2-23 | 3.36 |
| C. de Grandhomme | 15 | 1 | 50 | 3 | 16.66 | 1-10 | 3.33 |
| B.M. Tickner | 15 | 0 | 88 | 5 | 17.60 | 4-50 | 5.87 |
| K.A. Jamieson | 22.4 | 2 | 110 | 6 | 18.33 | 3-45 | 4.85 |
| M.G. Bracewell | 19 | 1 | 96 | 5 | 19.20 | 3-21 | 5.05 |
| I.S. Sodhi | 25.1 | 1 | 96 | 3 | 32.00 | 2-17 | 3.81 |

## Twenty20 Internationals

|             | *Played* | *Won* | *Lost* | *Tied* | *NR* |
|-------------|----------|-------|--------|--------|------|
| Bangladesh  | 5  | 2 | 3 | – | – |
| India       | 4  | 1 | 3 | – | – |
| Australia   | 1  | – | 1 | – | – |
| Pakistan    | 1  | – | 1 | – | – |
| Scotland    | 1  | 1 | – | – | – |
| Namibia     | 1  | 1 | – | – | – |
| Afghanistan | 1  | 1 | – | – | – |
| England     | 1  | 1 | – | – | – |
| **TOTAL**   | **15** | **7** | **8** | **–** | **–** |

## New Zealand Twenty20 International Averages

| BATTING | M | I | NO | HS | Agg | Ave | 100s | 50s | Ct | St | SR |
|---|---|---|---|---|---|---|---|---|---|---|---|
| T.W.M. Latham | 5 | 5 | 2 | 65* | 159 | 53.00 | - | 2 | 3 | 2 | 108 |
| K.S. Williamson | 7 | 7 | 2 | 85 | 216 | 43.20 | - | 1 | 2 | - | 115 |
| M.J. Guptill | 10 | 10 | 0 | 93 | 360 | 36.00 | - | 3 | 6 | - | 135 |
| D.P. Conway | 6 | 6 | 2 | 46 | 129 | 32.25 | - | - | 5 | - | 108 |
| M.S. Chapman | 3 | 3 | 0 | 63 | 84 | 28.00 | - | 1 | 2 | - | 121 |
| D.J. Mitchell | 10 | 10 | 1 | 72* | 244 | 27.11 | - | 1 | 4 | - | 133 |
| J.D.S. Neesham | 9 | 7 | 3 | 35* | 92 | 23.00 | - | - | 2 | - | 135 |
| F.H. Allen | 3 | 3 | 0 | 41 | 68 | 22.66 | - | - | 2 | - | 161 |
| H.M. Nicholls | 5 | 5 | 1 | 36* | 81 | 20.25 | - | - | 3 | - | 96 |
| G.D. Phillips | 10 | 8 | 1 | 39* | 139 | 19.85 | - | - | 2 | - | 113 |
| W.A. Young | 5 | 5 | 0 | 46 | 99 | 19.80 | - | - | 1 | - | 86 |
| C.E. McConchie | 5 | 4 | 2 | 17* | 32 | 16.00 | - | - | - | - | 114 |
| T.L. Seifert | 5 | 5 | 1 | 17 | 58 | 14.50 | - | - | 1 | - | 100 |
| L.H. Ferguson | 2 | 1 | 0 | 14 | 14 | 14.00 | - | - | - | - | 175 |
| T.A. Blundell | 4 | 4 | 1 | 30* | 42 | 14.00 | - | - | 3 | - | 77 |
| A.F. Milne | 8 | 2 | 1 | 7 | 13 | 13.00 | - | - | - | - | 120 |
| M.J. Santner | 10 | 6 | 4 | 8* | 23 | 11.50 | - | - | 2 | - | 88 |
| I.S. Sodhi | 9 | 2 | 1 | 9 | 11 | 11.00 | - | - | 2 | - | 84 |
| R. Ravindra | 6 | 6 | 0 | 20 | 54 | 9.00 | - | - | 3 | - | 98 |
| D.A.J. Bracewell | 2 | 1 | 0 | 5 | 5 | 5.00 | - | - | - | - | 71 |
| B.M. Tickner | 2 | 2 | 1 | 3* | 5 | 5.00 | - | - | - | - | 41 |
| C. de Grandhomme | 5 | 5 | 0 | 9 | 18 | 3.60 | - | - | 2 | - | 72 |
| A.Y. Patel | 5 | 2 | 0 | 4 | 7 | 3.50 | - | - | - | - | 50 |
| J.A. Duffy | 3 | 1 | 0 | 3 | 3 | 3.00 | - | - | - | - | 60 |
| T.A. Boult | 10 | 1 | 1 | 2* | 2 | - | - | - | 3 | - | 100 |
| T.D. Astle | 1 | 0 | 0 | 0 | 0 | - | - | - | - | - | 0 |
| H.K. Bennett | 2 | 1 | 1 | 0* | 0 | - | - | - | - | - | 0 |
| T.G. Southee | 9 | 1 | 1 | 0* | 0 | - | - | - | 3 | - | 0 |
| S.C. Kuggeleijn | 2 | - | - | - | - | - | - | - | 1 | - | - |
| B.V. Sears | 2 | - | - | - | - | - | - | - | 1 | - | - |

| BOWLING | O | M | R | W | Ave | Best | R/O |
|---|---|---|---|---|---|---|---|
| A.Y. Patel | 20 | 0 | 73 | 10 | 7.30 | 4-16 | 3.65 |
| D.J. Mitchell | 0.4 | 0 | 11 | 1 | 11.00 | 1-11 | 16.50 |
| S.C. Kuggeleijn | 6 | 0 | 37 | 3 | 12.33 | 2-23 | 6.16 |
| R. Ravindra | 19 | 0 | 83 | 6 | 13.83 | 3-22 | 4.36 |
| C. de Grandhomme | 3.4 | 0 | 16 | 1 | 16.00 | 1-3 | 4.36 |
| C.E. McConchie | 18.1 | 0 | 117 | 7 | 16.71 | 3-15 | 6.44 |
| T.A. Boult | 39.4 | 0 | 271 | 16 | 16.93 | 3-17 | 6.83 |
| T.G. Southee | 35.5 | 0 | 237 | 12 | 19.75 | 3-16 | 6.61 |
| I.S. Sodhi | 30 | 0 | 238 | 10 | 23.80 | 2-17 | 7.93 |
| J.D.S. Neesham | 11.2 | 0 | 93 | 3 | 31.00 | 1-6 | 8.20 |
| B.V. Sears | 4 | 0 | 32 | 1 | 32.00 | 1-21 | 8.00 |
| M.J. Santner | 34 | 0 | 228 | 6 | 38.00 | 3-27 | 6.70 |
| J.A. Duffy | 9 | 0 | 43 | 1 | 43.00 | 1-25 | 4.66 |
| H.K. Bennett | 7 | 0 | 49 | 1 | 49.00 | 1-32 | 7.00 |
| A.F. Milne | 31 | 1 | 255 | 4 | 63.75 | 1-17 | 8.22 |
| L.H. Ferguson | 8 | 0 | 69 | 1 | 69.00 | 1-45 | 8.62 |
| G.D. Phillips | 1 | 0 | 11 | 0 | - | - | 11.00 |
| B.M. Tickner | 3 | 0 | 22 | 0 | - | - | 7.33 |
| D.A.J. Bracewell | 4 | 0 | 33 | 0 | - | - | 8.25 |
| T.D. Astle | 3 | 0 | 34 | 0 | - | - | 11.33 |

# PROVINCIAL SUMMARIES

## AUCKLAND CRICKET ASSOCIATION

*Formed 1883, affiliated 1894/95.*

**Selectors:** H. Malan, I. West, Azhar Abbas, J.R.M. Bassett-Graham and D. Archer

Auckland had a late start to the season due to Covid restrictions but they overcame this to win the Ford Trophy, after coming second in the round-robin series, and the Plunket Shield. They finished fifth in the Super Smash.

Robbie O'Donnell scored 539 runs in the Plunket Shield with brother Will getting 335. Martin Guptill scored 358 and Sean Solia got 344. Debutant Simon Keene was the leading wicket-taker with 25 while Will Somerville took 22. George Worker (672 runs with four centuries) was the overall leading scorer in the Ford Trophy. Mark Chapman (465), Glenn Phillips (378) and Guptill (367) all topped the 300-run mark. Lockie Ferguson was the competition's equal leading wicket-taker with 14 victims. Robbie O'Donnell was Auckland's leading Super Smash scorer with 227 runs while Ferguson took 17 wickets. Ben Horne was the wicketkeeper getting 24 catches and three stumpings in the first-class programme.

Robbie O'Donnell captained the side in all formats. Heinrich Malan coached the side until the end of the Ford Trophy when he took up a position with Ireland. Luke Ronchi took over as coach and a selector after Malan's departure.

Contracted players were: Adithya Ashok, Cole Briggs, Mark Chapman, Louis Delport, Danru Ferns, Matthew Gibson, Ryan Harrison, Ben Horne, Ben Lister, Robbie O'Donnell, Will O'Donnell, Ollie Pringle, Sean Solia, Will Somerville, Ross ter Braak, George Worker.

## CANTERBURY CRICKET ASSOCIATION

*Formed 1877, affiliated 1894/95.*

**Selectors:** B.P. Donkers and P.G. Fulton

Canterbury finished second in the Plunket Shield and Super Smash and fifth in the Ford Trophy. Chad Bowes was their top run scorer in the Plunket Shield getting 570 runs. He was followed by Cole McConchie (445), Cam Fletcher (364) and Ken McClure (320). Will Williams took 25 wickets and Matt Henry 21. Leo Carter scored 267 runs in the Ford Trophy.

Bowes scored 333 runs in the Super Smash with Fletcher getting 305. Henry Shipley was the competition's leading wicket-taker with 18. Ed Nuttall took 15 wickets and Henry 14. Fletcher was the wicketkeeper in all formats. McConchie captained the side in every game while Peter Fulton again coached the side.

Contracted players were: Todd Astle, Chad Bowes, Jack Boyle, Leo Carter, Harry Chamberlain, Sean Davey, Cam Fletcher, Andrew Hazeldine, Ken McClure, Cole McConchie, Ed Nuttall, Will O'Rourke, Fraser Sheat, Henry Shipley, Theo van Woerkom, Will Williams.

## CENTRAL DISTRICTS CRICKET ASSOCIATION

*Formed 1950, affiliated 1954/55.*

**Selectors:** R. Walter and D.T. Meiring

Central Districts finished fifth in the Plunket Shield, runner-up in the Ford Trophy final, after being top qualifier, and fourth in the Super Smash.

Tom Bruce was the Plunket Shield's top run scorer with 858, including consecutive double centuries. Brad Schmulian scored 541, Greg Hay 403, Dane Cleaver 393 and Bayley Wiggins 353. Blair Tickner and Ray Toole both took 23 wickets. Ross Taylor scored 279 runs in the Ford Trophy, including the fastest-ever hundred, and Seth Rance took 12 wickets. Cleaver got 369 runs in the Super Smash, including a century, while Bruce (267) and Hay (234) followed. Rance took 15 wickets and Doug Bracewell took 14.

Hay led the Plunket Shield side while Bruce was captain in white-ball games. Cleaver was the first choice wicketkeeper with Wiggins deputising. Rob Walter coached the side.

Contracted players were: Doug Bracewell, Tom Bruce, Josh Clarkson, Dane Cleaver, Joey Field, Greg Hay, Jayden Lennox, Adam Milne, Ajaz Patel, Seth Rance, Brad Schmulian, Ben Smith, Blair Tickner, Ray Toole, Ben Wheeler, Bayley Wiggins.

# NORTHERN DISTRICTS CRICKET ASSOCIATION
*Formed 1953, granted Plunket Shield status 1956/57*
**Selectors:** P.J. Malcon, G.W. Aldridge and S. Krishnamurthy

Northern Districts won the Super Smash final, finished third in the Plunket Shield and fourth in the Ford Trophy. As happened with Auckland, they were affected by Covid restrictions and had early games postponed.

Jeet Raval scored 491 runs in the Plunket Shield with Henry Cooper getting 314. Brett Randell was the joint leading wicket-taker in the competition with 31 victims. Raval was Northern's leading scorer in the Ford Trophy with 226 runs while Joe Carter got 205. Colin de Grandhomme led the way in the Super Smash with 240 runs, Tim Seifert got 239 and Katene Clarke 228. Joe Walker took 16 wickets and Anurag Verma 14. Carter captained the side in the Plunket Shield while Raval skippered the white-ball teams.

Wicketkeeping duties were shared by Seifert and Peter Bocock and Graeme Aldridge again coached the side.

Contracted players were: Peter Bocock, Joe Carter, Katene Clarke, Kristian Clarke, Henry Cooper, Matthew Fisher, Zak Gibson, Brett Hampton, Scott Kuggeleijn, Bharat Popli, Brett Randell, Jeet Raval, Tim Seifert, Anurag Verma, Freddy Walker, Joe Walker.

# OTAGO CRICKET ASSOCIATION
*Formed 1876, affiliated 1894/95.*
**Selectors:** D.D. Ebrahim, S. Martin, W.C. McSkimming and H.D. Rutherford

Otago finished fourth in the Plunket Shield, fifth in the Ford Trophy and sixth in the Super Smash competition.

Nick Kelly scored 675 runs in the Plunket Shield followed by Hamish Rutherford (593), Dale Phillips (587), Mitch Renwick (467) and Max Chu (307). Michael Rippon took 22 wickets. Anaru Kitchen scored 205 runs in the Ford Trophy while Matt Bacon took 14 wickets (equal most in the competition) and Kitchen and Rippon both took 11. Rutherford scored 229 runs in the Super Smash and Kitchen took 11 wickets.

Chu was the wicketkeeper in all formats. The side was coached by Dion Ebrahim and captained by Rutherford. During the season Kitchen and Neil Broom announced their retirements.

Contracted players were: Matt Bacon, Neil Broom, Max Chu, Jacob Duffy, Josh Finnie, Jake Gibson, Nick Kelly, Anaru Kitchen, Angus McKenzie, Jarrod McKay, Travis Muller, Dale Phillips, Michael Rae, Michael Rippon, Mitch Renwick, Hamish Rutherford.

# WELLINGTON CRICKET ASSOCIATION
*Formed 1875, affiliated 1894/95.*
**Selectors:** G.D. Pocknall and D.J. Watson

Wellington finished third in both the Ford Trophy and Super Smash and sixth in the Plunket Shield.

Troy Johnson top scored in the Plunket Shield with 389 runs followed by Rachin Ravindra with 343. Nathan Smith was the joint leading wicket-taker in the competition with 31 wickets. Johnson got 281 runs in the Ford Trophy followed by Finn Allen (244) and Smith (200). Logan van Beek was the leading bowler with 11 wickets. Michael Bracewell was the Super Smash top scorer with 478 runs, including a New Zealand domestic record score of 141 not out, and Allen got 280. Ben Sears took 13 wickets.

Tom Blundell and Callum McLachlan kept wicket in the Plunket Shield while Allen kept in the white-ball games. Glenn Pocknall again coached the side. Hamish Bennett announced his retirement at the end of the season.

Contracted players were: Finn Allen, Hamish Bennett, Jakob Bhula, Michael Bracewell, Luke Georgeson, Jamie Gibson, Troy Johnson, Callum McLachlan, Iain McPeake, Ollie Newton, Rachin Ravindra, Ben Sears, Nathan Smith, Michael Snedden, Logan van Beek, Peter Younghusband.

# PLUNKET SHIELD REVIEW 2021/22

The Plunket Shield was again scheduled to be played over eight rounds with four rounds due to be played from 23 October before the Dream11 Super Smash started. However, Covid restrictions forced fixtures to be rearranged and when the Super Smash began only nine games had taken place. Northern Districts did not play their first game until 15 November while Auckland had to wait until the second half of the season to begin their campaign.

At the scheduled half-way break the points were: Canterbury 56 (four games), Central Districts 39 (four games), Otago 31 (four games), Wellington 28 (four games), Northern Districts 22 (two games).

As it was uncertain as to whether the domestic competitions would be played in full, it was decided that placings would be decided on average points per game.

The Super Smash began on 26 November and the Ford Trophy four days later. The Plunket Shield resumed on 4 February and finished on 15 April. Auckland made up for their late start by winning five games in a row (while one was abandoned without any play). With two games remaining, Auckland were all but assured of the title which they confirmed when they took their first batting point in their game against Central Districts.

Auckland had finished fourth the previous season, while previous winners Canterbury ended in second place. Northern Districts dropped from second to third, Central Districts went from fifth to fourth while Otago went from third to fifth. Wellington, who had won the competition in 2019/20, finished last for the second season in a row.

No team went through the competition unbeaten and every team won at least one game. Auckland (twice) and Central Districts gained the maximum twenty points from a game.

Bonus points for batting and bowling were again available for the first 110 overs of the first innings. No points were awarded for a first innings lead. Playing time was six hours per day, although this was extended if the number of overs to be bowled in the day had not been completed. Teams were required to bowl 96 overs a day with no reduction for change of innings. Penalties for slow over rates were calculated round by round instead of over the whole season.

Points were awarded as follows:

    a)   twelve points for an outright win
    b)   six points for a tie
    c)   batting points at 200, 250, 300 and 350 runs
          *(available in first innings up to 110 overs)*
    d)   bowling points at 3, 5, 7 and 9 wickets
          *(available in first innings up to 110 overs)*

Final points and placings were:

| | P | OW | OL | Draw | Bat | Bowl | TOTAL | AVE |
|---|---|---|---|---|---|---|---|---|
| Auckland* | 8 | 5 | 1 | 1 | 17 | 23 | 104 | 13.000 |
| Canterbury | 8 | 4 | 1 | 3 | 16 | 28 | 92 | 11.500 |
| Northern Districts*† | 8 | 3 | 3 | 1 | 5 | 23 | 68 | 9.714 |
| Central Districts† | 8 | 1 | 2 | 5 | 20 | 24 | 56 | 8.000 |
| Otago | 8 | 2 | 4 | 2 | 12 | 25 | 61 | 7.625 |
| Wellington | 8 | 2 | 6 | – | 7 | 27 | 58 | 7.250 |

*Northern Districts and Auckland were each awarded four points for their abandoned match*

†*No points were awarded for the match between Northern Districts and Central Districts at Whangarei and it was not included in the points per game calculation*

# CANTERBURY v CENTRAL DISTRICTS                    Plunket Shield

*at Hagley Oval, Christchurch on 23, 24, 25, 26 October, 2021*
*Toss : Central Districts. Umpires : J.A.K. Bromley & D.J. Walker*
*Close of play: 1st day: CD 355-9, Tickner 26, Toole 3; 2nd day: CD 16-1, Hay 3, Lennox 1*
*        3rd day: Canterbury 61-0, Latham 30, Nicholls 28*
**Match drawn.** *Points: Central Districts 8 (4 bat, 4 bowl), Canterbury 5 (1 bat, 4 bowl)*

Central batted through the first day with Wiggins scoring a hundred on first-class debut. He came in with his team in trouble at 101-5 and reached his century off 101 balls. He shared a seventh wicket stand of 183 with Wheeler.

    Five wickets from Tickner saw Central gain a lead of 128 on the first innings which they extended to 449 before declaring late on the third day. Hay reached his century off 224 balls. Latham responded with a hundred from 210 balls on the last day before play was called off.

## CENTRAL DISTRICTS

| FIRST INNINGS | Runs | Mins | Balls | 6s | 4s |
|---|---|---|---|---|---|
| G.R.Hay* b Henry | 0 | 11 | 11 | - | - |
| B.S.Smith c Fletcher b Nuttall | 0 | 15 | 8 | - | - |
| B.D.Schmulian c Fletcher b Henry | 20 | 42 | 31 | - | 3 |
| D.Cleaver† c Fletcher b Williams | 44 | 162 | 110 | - | 7 |
| T.C.Bruce lbw b Henry | 33 | 72 | 50 | - | 3 |
| D.A.J.Bracewell c Nicholls b Williams | 2 | 20 | 13 | - | - |
| B.L.Wiggins c Fletcher b Henry | 133 | 219 | 138 | 3 | 16 |
| B.M.Wheeler b Williams | 74 | 168 | 138 | - | 10 |
| B.M.Tickner not out | 37 | 77 | 61 | - | 4 |
| J.R.Lennox c Bowes b Nuttall | 8 | 32 | 27 | - | - |
| R.L.Toole b Sheat | 5 | 23 | 13 | - | - |
| Extras (lb 5, w 4, nb 4) | 13 | | | | |
| **TOTAL** (99.2 overs) | **369** | 423 | | | |

| SECOND INNINGS | Runs | Mins | Balls | 6s | 4s |
|---|---|---|---|---|---|
| st Fletcher b van Woerkom | 101 | 320 | 228 | - | 9 |
| c Nuttall b Henry | 11 | 20 | 13 | - | 2 |
| (4) b Nuttall | 35 | 85 | 55 | - | 3 |
| (5) c Fletcher b Sheat | 48 | 59 | 56 | 1 | 4 |
| (6) not out | 55 | 65 | 48 | 2 | 4 |
| (7) b McConchie | 15 | 11 | 11 | 1 | - |
| (8) not out | 9 | 13 | 11 | - | 1 |
| | | | | | |
| (3) b Williams | 43 | | | | |
| | | | | | |
| (w 2, nb 2) | 4 | | | | |
| (83 overs) (6 wkts dec) | **321** | 344 | | | |

## CANTERBURY

| | Runs | Mins | Balls | 6s | 4s |
|---|---|---|---|---|---|
| T.W.M.Latham c Wheeler b Tickner | 11 | 62 | 37 | - | 1 |
| C.J.Bowes c Lennox b Tickner | 42 | 101 | 63 | 1 | 6 |
| H.M.Nicholls b Toole | 6 | 53 | 40 | - | 3 |
| C.E.McConchie* c Cleaver b Tickner | 29 | 103 | 63 | - | 3 |
| L.J.Carter c & b Wheeler | 1 | 23 | 13 | - | - |
| C.D.Fletcher† c Wiggins b Lennox | 50 | 131 | 100 | - | 9 |
| T.F.van Woerkom c Toole b Lennox | 36 | 134 | 86 | 2 | 1 |
| M.J.Henry c Lennox b Tickner | 29 | 45 | 46 | - | 4 |
| W.S.A.Williams c Schmulian b Lennox | 2 | 15 | 14 | - | - |
| F.W.Sheat not out | 6 | 12 | 9 | - | - |
| E.J.Nuttall c Cleaver b Tickner | 0 | 4 | 2 | - | - |
| Extras (b 1, lb 6, w 2, nb 9) | 18 | | | | |
| **TOTAL** (77.2 overs) | **241** | 343 | | | |

| | Runs | Mins | Balls | 6s | 4s |
|---|---|---|---|---|---|
| c Bruce b Lennox | 104 | 333 | 227 | 1 | 9 |
| (3) lbw b Wheeler | 6 | 56 | 33 | - | - |
| (2) b Toole | 44 | 149 | 95 | - | 3 |
| c Cleaver b Toole | 24 | 100 | 90 | - | 1 |
| c Wiggins b Lennox | 4 | 6 | 7 | - | 1 |
| not out | 27 | 95 | 70 | - | 4 |
| not out | 27 | 74 | 64 | - | 2 |
| | | | | | |
| (b 1, lb 2, nb 10) | 13 | | | | |
| (96 overs) (5 wkts) | **249** | 407 | | | |

| Bowling | O | M | R | W | O | M | R | W |
|---|---|---|---|---|---|---|---|---|
| **CANTERBURY** | | | | | | | | |
| Henry | 27 | 7 | 82 | 4 | 9 | 2 | 20 | 1 |
| Nuttall | 18 | 3 | 105 | 2 | 11 | 0 | 46 | 1 |
| Williams | 23 | 8 | 66 | 3 | 15 | 5 | 43 | 1 |
| Sheat | 16.2 | 1 | 46 | 1 | 15 | 2 | 53 | 1 |
| van Woerkom | 8 | 0 | 35 | 0 | 25 | 1 | 121 | 1 |
| McConchie | 7 | 0 | 30 | 0 | 8 | 0 | 38 | 1 |
| **CENTRAL DISTRICTS** | | | | | | | | |
| Bracewell | 17 | 3 | 59 | 0 | 18 | 2 | 48 | 0 |
| Wheeler | 14 | 3 | 35 | 1 | 15 | 0 | 70 | 1 |
| Tickner | 17.2 | 2 | 64 | 5 | 18 | 0 | 44 | 0 |
| Toole | 13 | 5 | 35 | 1 | 20 | 4 | 39 | 2 |
| Lennox | 15 | 4 | 38 | 3 | 22 | 12 | 36 | 2 |
| Schmulian | 1 | 0 | 3 | 0 | 3 | 0 | 9 | 0 |

| Fall of Wickets | CD | C | CD | C |
|---|---|---|---|---|
| | 1st | 1st | 2nd | 2nd |
| 1st | 0 | 51 | 13 | 90 |
| 2nd | 0 | 77 | 88 | 113 |
| 3rd | 25 | 81 | 142 | 185 |
| 4th | 84 | 89 | 216 | 190 |
| 5th | 101 | 129 | 269 | 195 |
| 6th | 128 | 180 | 296 | - |
| 7th | 311 | 228 | - | - |
| 8th | 325 | 234 | - | - |
| 9th | 346 | 241 | - | - |
| 10th | 369 | 241 | - | - |

**NZC**

# WELLINGTON v OTAGO                    **Plunket Shield**

*at Cello Basin Reserve, Wellington on 23, 24, 25, 26 October, 2021*
*Toss : Wellington.  Umpires : S.B. Haig & T.J. Parlane*
*Close of play: 1st day: Wellington 91-2, Johnson 52, Bracewell 22; 2nd day: Otago 143-7, Muller 0, Gibson 0*
*3rd day: Wellington 95-0, Georgeson 50, Johnson 23*
**Wellington won by 6 wickets.** *Points: Wellington 16 (4 bowl), Otago 5 (1 bat, 4 bowl)*

Jacob Gibson made his first-class debut while Smith made his first appearance for Wellington. A low scoring game saw Otago dismissed for 207 on the first day with Muller top-scoring with 30 while five players were dismissed in the twenties.Wellington reached 99-2 but collapsed to be all out for 195. Muller returned career best figures of 6-52.

Otago again struggled with the bat in their second innings and only Rutherford (who was seventh out at 143 for 77) reached twenty. Smith had his best bowling figures in first-class cricket at the expense of his former team. Wellington needed 193 to win and reached their target on the final day with six wickets in hand. Georgeson made his highest score in the process.

## OTAGO

| FIRST INNINGS | Runs | Mins | Balls | 6s | 4s |
|---|---|---|---|---|---|
| H.D.Rutherford* lbw b Smith | 2 | 7 | 7 | - | - |
| M.Renwick lbw b Snedden | 20 | 103 | 63 | - | 3 |
| D.N.Phillips lbw b Newton | 0 | 6 | 5 | - | - |
| N.F.Kelly lbw b McPeake | 16 | 58 | 38 | - | 4 |
| A.K.Kitchen c Gibson b Smith | 23 | 46 | 32 | - | 4 |
| M.J.G.Rippon c Johnson b Smith | 9 | 26 | 17 | - | 2 |
| M.W.Chu† c Gibson b Snedden | 23 | 61 | 38 | - | 3 |
| T.Muller c Bracewell b McPeake | 30 | 95 | 63 | - | 5 |
| J.M.Gibson c Georgeson b Snedden | 23 | 66 | 51 | - | 3 |
| J.A.Duffy lbw b Ravindra | 24 | 60 | 35 | - | 4 |
| M.D.Rae not out | 9 | 39 | 28 | - | 1 |
| Extras (b 12, lb 6, w 6, nb 4) | 28 | | | | |
| **TOTAL (62.1 overs)** | **207** | 286 | | | |

| SECOND INNINGS | Runs | Mins | Balls | 6s | 4s |
|---|---|---|---|---|---|
| c Georgeson b McPeake | 77 | 214 | 143 | - | 12 |
| c Blundell b Snedden | 15 | 63 | 42 | - | 1 |
| c Blundell b Smith | 19 | 56 | 44 | - | 4 |
| b Newton | 5 | 21 | 16 | - | 1 |
| c Gibson b Newton | 4 | 3 | 2 | - | 1 |
| b Smith | 0 | 5 | 3 | - | - |
| c Johnson b Smith | 10 | 41 | 26 | - | 2 |
| not out | 14 | 94 | 61 | - | 3 |
| c Snedden b Smith | 19 | 60 | 40 | - | 3 |
| c Ravindra b Smith | 0 | 8 | 4 | - | - |
| lbw b Smith | 0 | 1 | 1 | - | - |
| (b 5, lb 6, nb 6) | 17 | | | | |
| **(62.4 overs)** | **180** | 285 | | | |

## WELLINGTON

| FIRST INNINGS | Runs | Mins | Balls | 6s | 4s |
|---|---|---|---|---|---|
| L.I.Georgeson c Chu b Duffy | 0 | 2 | 4 | - | - |
| R.Ravindra c Chu b Gibson | 11 | 34 | 22 | - | 2 |
| T.M.Johnson c Rutherford b Gibson | 78 | 211 | 166 | - | 14 |
| M.G.Bracewell* c Renwick b Muller | 30 | 110 | 77 | - | 6 |
| T.A.Blundell† lbw b Muller | 0 | 1 | 1 | - | - |
| F.H.Allen c Kelly b Duffy | 18 | 45 | 28 | - | 4 |
| J.D.Gibson c Kitchen b Muller | 14 | 64 | 45 | - | 2 |
| N.G.Smith c Chu b Muller | 10 | 23 | 18 | - | 2 |
| O.R.Newton b Muller | 10 | 39 | 29 | - | 2 |
| I.G.McPeake not out | 15 | 26 | 16 | - | 3 |
| M.W.Snedden c Kitchen b Muller | 0 | 7 | 3 | - | - |
| Extras (lb 3, w 1, nb 5) | 9 | | | | |
| **TOTAL (67.2 overs)** | **195** | 284 | | | |

| SECOND INNINGS | Runs | Mins | Balls | 6s | 4s |
|---|---|---|---|---|---|
| c sub (J.L.Finnie) b Rippon | 74 | 264 | 196 | - | 11 |
| retired hurt | 18 | 42 | 33 | - | 3 |
| c Kitchen b Muller | 28 | 115 | 84 | - | 5 |
| run out | 24 | 77 | 56 | - | 4 |
| not out | 22 | 61 | 46 | - | 3 |
| run out | 4 | 4 | 4 | - | 1 |
| not out | 8 | 26 | 22 | - | - |
| (b 4, lb 8, nb 3) | 15 | | | | |
| **(73 overs) (4 wkts)** | **193** | 296 | | | |

| Bowling | O | M | R | W | O | M | R | W |
|---|---|---|---|---|---|---|---|---|
| **WELLINGTON** | | | | | | | | |
| Newton | 13 | 3 | 47 | 1 | 14 | 0 | 45 | 2 |
| Smith | 19 | 5 | 60 | 3 | 24.4 | 9 | 54 | 6 |
| McPeake | 10 | 5 | 18 | 2 | 12 | 4 | 26 | 1 |
| Snedden | 16 | 6 | 48 | 3 | 8 | 1 | 22 | 1 |
| Gibson | 4 | 0 | 16 | 0 | | | | |
| Ravindra | 0.1 | 0 | 0 | 1 | | | | |
| Bracewell | | | | | 4 | 0 | 22 | 0 |
| **OTAGO** | | | | | | | | |
| Duffy | 20 | 9 | 33 | 2 | 19 | 5 | 58 | 0 |
| Gibson | 15 | 3 | 59 | 2 | 9 | 2 | 34 | 0 |
| Muller | 17.2 | 5 | 52 | 6 | 17 | 6 | 43 | 1 |
| Rae | 4 | 2 | 17 | 0 | | | | |
| Rippon | 11 | 4 | 31 | 0 | 28 | 12 | 46 | 1 |

| Fall of Wickets | O | W | O | W |
|---|---|---|---|---|
| | 1st | 1st | 2nd | 2nd |
| 1st | 3 | 0 | 40 | 102 |
| 2nd | 4 | 23 | 94 | 148 |
| 3rd | 39 | 99 | 108 | 168 |
| 4th | 49 | 99 | 112 | 172 |
| 5th | 65 | 133 | 113 | - |
| 6th | 74 | 145 | 130 | - |
| 7th | 123 | 167 | 143 | - |
| 8th | 155 | 174 | 176 | - |
| 9th | 175 | 191 | 180 | - |
| 10th | 207 | 195 | 180 | - |

*Ravindra retired hurt at 34-0*

# OTAGO v CENTRAL DISTRICTS                    Plunket Shield

*at University of Otago Oval, Dunedin on 31, October, 1, 2, 3 November, 2021*
*Toss : Central Districts. Umpires : J.A.K. Bromley & S.B. Haig*
*Close of play: 1st day: CD 321-6, Hay 127, Wheeler 29; 2nd day: Otago 223-0, Rutherford 118, Renwick 100*
*3rd day: Otago 542-5, Kelly 169, Chu 73*
**Match drawn.** *Points: Otago 6 (3 bat, 3 bowl), Central Districts 5 (4 bat, 1 bowl)*

Hay decided to bat first and reached his second century in successive innings before the close, from 228 balls. Otago began batting on the second day and had lost just six wickets when they declared on the fourth.

Rutherford and Renwick began with an opening stand of 251, reaching their hundreds from 173 and 227 balls. Kelly and Chu, both making their highest scores, added 256 for the sixth wicket, an Otago record against all teams. Kelly made his hundred off 149 balls and his double century came just 86 balls later. Otago's total was their highest against Central and just nine runs short of their highest against anyone.

With conditions very much in favour of batting, Central had no trouble is seeing out the game safely. Schmulian and Cleaver reached their hundreds from 143 and 170 deliveries. This was the 100th first-class game between the two sides.

## CENTRAL DISTRICTS

| FIRST INNINGS | Runs | Mins | Balls | 6s | 4s | SECOND INNINGS | Runs | Mins | Balls | 6s | 4s |
|---|---|---|---|---|---|---|---|---|---|---|---|
| G.R.Hay* c Muller b Gibson | 152 | 486 | 331 | 1 | 18 | retired ill | 13 | 87 | 53 | - | 1 |
| B.L.Wiggins c Chu b Gibson | 0 | 7 | 3 | - | - | c Phillips b Gibson | 15 | 33 | 21 | - | 3 |
| B.D.Schmulian c Chu b Duffy | 1 | 15 | 10 | - | - | b Muller | 117 | 245 | 167 | - | 15 |
| D.Cleaver† b Gibson | 30 | 81 | 66 | - | 5 | not out | 108 | 234 | 171 | 3 | 16 |
| T.C.Bruce c Phillips b Duffy | 74 | 142 | 96 | - | 10 | not out | 13 | 42 | 30 | - | 1 |
| D.A.J.Bracewell c Phillips b Duffy | 15 | 33 | 24 | - | 2 | | | | | | |
| J.A.Clarkson c Kelly b Rippon | 31 | 46 | 43 | 1 | 4 | | | | | | |
| B.M.Wheeler b McKenzie | 31 | 90 | 71 | - | 4 | | | | | | |
| B.M.Tickner c Chu b Duffy | 7 | 16 | 19 | - | - | | | | | | |
| J.R.Lennox not out | 26 | 63 | 42 | - | 3 | | | | | | |
| R.L.Toole c Kitchen b Gibson | 8 | 11 | 9 | - | 2 | | | | | | |
| Extras (b 1, lb 11, w 1, nb 6) | 19 | | | | | (lb 4, nb 4) | 8 | | | | |
| **TOTAL** (118 overs) | **394** | 498 | | | | (73 overs) (2 wkts) | **274** | 321 | | | |

## OTAGO

| | Runs | Mins | Balls | 6s | 4s |
|---|---|---|---|---|---|
| H.D.Rutherford* b Wheeler | 144 | 375 | 250 | - | 18 |
| M.Renwick lbw b Bracewell | 107 | 339 | 265 | 2 | 10 |
| D.N.Phillips b Toole | 14 | 69 | 35 | - | 2 |
| N.F.Kelly not out | 234 | 370 | 245 | 9 | 25 |
| A.K.Kitchen lbw b Tickner | 3 | 39 | 21 | - | - |
| M.J.G.Rippon c Lennox b Wheeler | 21 | 78 | 76 | - | - |
| M.W.Chu† c Lennox b Clarkson | 94 | 191 | 171 | 1 | 11 |
| A.W.McKenzie not out | 13 | 19 | 12 | 1 | - |
| J.M.Gibson | | | | | |
| J.A.Duffy | | | | | |
| T.Muller | | | | | |
| Extras (b 3, lb 7, w 1, nb 1) | 12 | | | | |
| **TOTAL** (179 overs) (6 wkts dec) | **642** | 745 | | | |

| Bowling | O | M | R | W | O | M | R | W | | Fall of Wickets | | | |
|---|---|---|---|---|---|---|---|---|---|---|---|---|---|
| **OTAGO** | | | | | | | | | | | CD | O | CD |
| | | | | | | | | | | | 1st | 1st | 2nd |
| Duffy | 34 | 8 | 106 | 4 | 18 | 5 | 56 | 0 | | 1st | 0 | 251 | 22 |
| Gibson | 21 | 4 | 84 | 4 | 7 | 1 | 31 | 1 | | 2nd | 11 | 265 | 214 |
| Muller | 23 | 3 | 74 | 0 | 11 | 2 | 38 | 1 | | 3rd | 66 | 292 | - |
| McKenzie | 26 | 6 | 59 | 1 | 8 | 2 | 34 | 0 | | 4th | 191 | 305 | - |
| Rippon | 14 | 0 | 59 | 1 | 22 | 2 | 84 | 0 | | 5th | 214 | 337 | - |
| Kelly | | | | | 3 | 0 | 22 | 0 | | 6th | 259 | 593 | - |
| Kitchen | | | | | 4 | 1 | 5 | 0 | | 7th | 326 | - | - |
| **CENTRAL DISTRICTS** | | | | | | | | | | 8th | 335 | - | - |
| Bracewell | 28 | 4 | 98 | 1 | | | | | | 9th | 379 | - | - |
| Wheeler | 29 | 8 | 52 | 2 | | | | | | 10th | 394 | - | - |
| Tickner | 32 | 7 | 98 | 1 | | | | | | | | | |
| Toole | 27 | 8 | 74 | 1 | | | | | | | | | |
| Lennox | 41 | 1 | 172 | 0 | | | | | | *Hay retired ill at 55-1* | | | |
| Schmulian | 10 | 0 | 66 | 0 | | | | | | | | | |
| Clarkson | 12 | 0 | 72 | 1 | | | | | | | | | |

**NZC**

# WELLINGTON v CANTERBURY          Plunket Shield

*at Cello Basin Reserve, Wellington on 31 October, 1, 2, 3 November, 2021*
*Toss : Wellington. Umpires : K.D. Cotton & D.J. Walker*
*Close of play: 1st day: Canterbury 246-6, Fletcher 87, Shipley 15; 2nd day: Wellington 135-7, Gibson 10, Sears 5*
*3rd day: Wellington 30-4, Ravindra 16*
**Canterbury won by 294 runs.** *Points: Canterbury 19 (3 bat, 4 bowl), Wellington 3 (3 bowl)*

Canterbury were 56-5 after being sent but were rescued by Nicholls and Fletcher (hundred from 245 balls). Shipley and Henry assisted and Canterbury were able to declare at 379-9.

Wellington reached 46 without loss but were all out for 161, with Sheat taking five wickets. McConchie did not enforce the follow on and Latham (hundred off 156 balls) and Bowes took the chance to register a double century opening stand.

Wellington needed 449 to win but lost Georgeson in the third over and were 30-4 at the close. Canterbury duly completed an emphatic victory on the final day. Greenwood made his first-class debut in this game.

## CANTERBURY

| FIRST INNINGS | Runs | Mins | Balls | 6s | 4s | SECOND INNINGS | Runs | Mins | Balls | 6s | 4s |
|---|---|---|---|---|---|---|---|---|---|---|---|
| T.W.M.Latham c Blundell b Sears | 20 | 92 | 65 | - | 2 | not out | 127 | 220 | 184 | 1 | 14 |
| C.J.Bowes c Blundell b Smith | 1 | 19 | 11 | - | - | c Greenwood b Ravindra | 95 | 213 | 137 | 1 | 7 |
| K.J.McClure c Blundell b Gibson | 8 | 34 | 26 | - | 1 | not out | 2 | 7 | 5 | - | - |
| H.M.Nicholls b Smith | 97 | 287 | 189 | - | 10 | | | | | | |
| C.E.McConchie* c Allen b Smith | 4 | 21 | 8 | - | - | | | | | | |
| L.J.Carter c Georgeson b Gibson | 2 | 19 | 17 | - | - | | | | | | |
| C.D.Fletcher† c Bracewell b Smith | 110 | 304 | 258 | 1 | 14 | | | | | | |
| H.B.Shipley c Gibson b Smith | 59 | 140 | 87 | - | 10 | | | | | | |
| M.J.Henry c Sears b Ravindra | 43 | 79 | 48 | 1 | 6 | | | | | | |
| W.S.A.Williams not out | 14 | 36 | 36 | - | 2 | | | | | | |
| F.W.Sheat | | | | | | | | | | | |
| Extras (lb 8, w 3, nb 10) | 21 | | | | | (lb 2, w 2, nb 2) | 6 | | | | |
| **TOTAL** (122.3 overs) (9 wkts dec) | **379** | 518 | | | | (54 overs) (1 wkt dec) | **230** | 220 | | | |

## WELLINGTON

| | Runs | Mins | Balls | 6s | 4s | | Runs | Mins | Balls | 6s | 4s |
|---|---|---|---|---|---|---|---|---|---|---|---|
| L.I.Georgeson c Fletcher b Shipley | 15 | 82 | 60 | - | 3 | c Nicholls b Henry | 1 | 9 | 6 | - | - |
| R.Ravindra c Nicholls b Sheat | 26 | 76 | 60 | - | 4 | c & b Henry | 70 | 355 | 247 | - | 10 |
| N.A.Greenwood c Fletcher b Shipley | 14 | 83 | 50 | - | 2 | c Latham b Shipley | 13 | 68 | 50 | - | 2 |
| M.G.Bracewell* lbw b Williams | 14 | 46 | 36 | - | 1 | c Nicholls b Shipley | 0 | 10 | 6 | - | - |
| T.A.Blundell† b Sheat | 13 | 104 | 81 | - | 2 | (6) lbw b Henry | 17 | 90 | 57 | - | 3 |
| F.H.Allen c Fletcher b Sheat | 21 | 44 | 30 | - | 4 | (7) b McConchie | 44 | 101 | 81 | - | 7 |
| J.D.Gibson c & b Sheat | 18 | 110 | 80 | - | 2 | (8) c Fletcher b Williams | 6 | 47 | 35 | - | 1 |
| N.G.Smith lbw b Williams | 8 | 35 | 22 | - | 1 | (9) lbw b Williams | 0 | 11 | 7 | - | - |
| B.V.Sears c Fletcher b Sheat | 15 | 64 | 55 | - | 3 | (5) lbw b Shipley | 0 | 19 | 15 | - | - |
| I.G.McPeake b Shipley | 5 | 22 | 9 | - | - | not out | 0 | 8 | 0 | - | - |
| M.W.Snedden not out | 0 | 4 | 1 | - | - | c Latham b Henry | 1 | 3 | 3 | - | - |
| Extras (lb 3, w 1, nb 8) | 12 | | | | | (w 1, nb 1) | 2 | | | | |
| **TOTAL** (79.2 overs) | **161** | 338 | | | | (84.2 overs) | **154** | 363 | | | |

| Bowling | | | | | | | | | | Fall of Wickets | | | | |
|---|---|---|---|---|---|---|---|---|---|---|---|---|---|---|
| **WELLINGTON** | O | M | R | W | O | M | R | W | | | C | W | C | W |
| Smith | 23 | 8 | 51 | 5 | 4 | 0 | 8 | 0 | | | 1st | 1st | 2nd | 2nd |
| McPeake | 22 | 1 | 66 | 0 | 8 | 0 | 39 | 0 | | 1st | 7 | 46 | 223 | 4 |
| Gibson | 24 | 7 | 76 | 2 | 6 | 1 | 24 | 0 | | 2nd | 23 | 46 | - | 30 |
| Snedden | 18 | 4 | 57 | 0 | 9 | 0 | 23 | 0 | | 3rd | 37 | 70 | - | 30 |
| Sears | 15 | 2 | 57 | 1 | 2 | 0 | 15 | 0 | | 4th | 50 | 76 | - | 30 |
| Bracewell | 17 | 4 | 52 | 0 | 10 | 0 | 41 | 0 | | 5th | 56 | 103 | - | 71 |
| Ravindra | 3.3 | 0 | 12 | 1 | 15 | 0 | 78 | 1 | | 6th | 207 | 114 | - | 140 |
| **CANTERBURY** | | | | | | | | | | 7th | 296 | 126 | - | 153 |
| Henry | 20 | 8 | 43 | 0 | 21.2 | 6 | 43 | 4 | | 8th | 343 | 149 | - | 153 |
| Williams | 19 | 10 | 32 | 2 | 18 | 10 | 26 | 2 | | 9th | 379 | 161 | - | 153 |
| Shipley | 17.2 | 3 | 46 | 3 | 16 | 7 | 23 | 3 | | 10th | - | 161 | - | 154 |
| Sheat | 20 | 9 | 30 | 5 | 14 | 3 | 39 | 0 | | | | | | |
| McConchie | 3 | 1 | 7 | 0 | 15 | 7 | 23 | 1 | | | | | | |

# CENTRAL DISTRICTS v OTAGO Plunket Shield

*at Saxton Oval, Nelson on 7, 8, 9, 10 November, 2021*
*Toss : Central Districts. Umpires : J.A.K. Bromley & T.J. Parlane*
*Close of play: 1st day: CD 21-0, Hay 12, Wiggins 8; 2nd day: Otago 45-0, Rutherford 27, Renwick 18*
*3rd day: Otago 374-6, Rippon 7*
**Otago won by 161 runs.** *Points: Otago 17 (1 bat, 4 bowl), Central Districts 6 (2 bat, 4 bowl)*

Otago were sent in and owed much to Phillips (hundred off 190 balls) who scored almost half the runs off the bat. In response, most of the Central players got starts but only Schmulian reached fifty and the home side had to be content with a lead of just 21.

Otago were much improved in their second innings with Rutherford (120 balls) and Renwick (217 balls) both making hundreds for the second game in a row.

Central were left to score an unlikely 402 on the last day but at 108-1 seemed safe. Wickets began to fall and no one was able to stay with Bruce, who ended unbeaten on 77. Last man Toole resisted for 28 minutes without scoring until bowled by Kitchen who finished with 2-2.

## OTAGO

| FIRST INNINGS | Runs | Mins | Balls | 6s | 4s | SECOND INNINGS | Runs | Mins | Balls | 6s | 4s |
|---|---|---|---|---|---|---|---|---|---|---|---|
| H.D.Rutherford* c Wiggins b Bracewell | 6 | 38 | 33 | - | 1 | c Bracewell b Field | 101 | 204 | 121 | 1 | 14 |
| M.Renwick c Cleaver b Bracewell | 6 | 27 | 17 | - | - | c Cleaver b Tickner | 134 | 358 | 268 | - | 18 |
| D.N.Phillips lbw b Bracewell | 113 | 308 | 209 | - | 14 | lbw b Lennox | 18 | 102 | 85 | - | 1 |
| N.F.Kelly c Cleaver b Tickner | 12 | 33 | 27 | - | 1 | c Field b Lennox | 66 | 147 | 82 | 1 | 7 |
| A.K.Kitchen c Wiggins b Toole | 1 | 15 | 14 | - | - | b Bracewell | 20 | 45 | 37 | - | 4 |
| M.J.G.Rippon c Schmulian b Field | 19 | 45 | 31 | - | 3 | not out | 35 | 84 | 69 | - | 3 |
| M.W.Chu† c Wheeler b Toole | 31 | 102 | 74 | - | 5 | c Bruce b Schmulian | 12 | 5 | 4 | - | 3 |
| A.W.McKenzie b Tickner | 0 | 4 | 3 | - | - | b Lennox | 9 | 13 | 8 | 1 | - |
| T.Muller not out | 41 | 120 | 90 | 1 | 6 | not out | 7 | 16 | 9 | - | 1 |
| M.B.Bacon c Wiggins b Bracewell | 3 | 12 | 9 | - | - | | | | | | |
| J.D.McKay b Wheeler | 2 | 12 | 8 | - | - | | | | | | |
| Extras (lb 8, w 2) | 10 | | | | | (b 6, lb 8, w 4, nb 2) | 20 | | | | |
| **TOTAL** (85.5 overs) | **244** | 361 | | | | (113.3 overs) (7 wkts dec) | **422** | 489 | | | |

## CENTRAL DISTRICTS

| | Runs | Mins | Balls | 6s | 4s | | Runs | Mins | Balls | 6s | 4s |
|---|---|---|---|---|---|---|---|---|---|---|---|
| G.R.Hay* c Chu b Muller | 13 | 52 | 46 | - | 2 | run out | 18 | 27 | 19 | - | 3 |
| B.L.Wiggins lbw b McKenzie | 30 | 99 | 53 | - | 5 | b Bacon | 41 | 116 | 72 | - | 7 |
| B.D.Schmulian b Bacon | 60 | 194 | 134 | - | 5 | b Rippon | 44 | 78 | 56 | - | 8 |
| D.Cleaver† run out | 48 | 119 | 77 | - | 7 | b Rippon | 4 | 17 | 10 | - | 1 |
| T.C.Bruce c Chu b Bacon | 35 | 57 | 51 | - | 7 | not out | 77 | 218 | 150 | - | 14 |
| D.A.J.Bracewell b Rippon | 26 | 78 | 55 | - | 4 | b Muller | 1 | 19 | 13 | - | - |
| B.M.Wheeler b McKenzie | 18 | 51 | 39 | - | 3 | lbw b McKay | 17 | 26 | 28 | 1 | 1 |
| J.F.A.Field b Rippon | 20 | 63 | 40 | - | 3 | lbw b Rippon | 17 | 115 | 88 | - | 1 |
| B.M.Tickner b Rippon | 1 | 32 | 29 | - | - | b McKenzie | 3 | 14 | 8 | - | - |
| J.R.Lennox b Muller | 1 | 8 | 10 | - | - | b Kitchen | 0 | 8 | 6 | - | - |
| R.L.Toole not out | 0 | 19 | 12 | - | - | b Kitchen | 0 | 28 | 21 | - | - |
| Extras (lb 5, w 5, nb 3) | 13 | | | | | (b 6, lb 6, w 2, nb 4) | 18 | | | | |
| **TOTAL** (90.3 overs) | **265** | 388 | | | | (77.5 overs) | **240** | 335 | | | |

| Bowling | O | M | R | W | O | M | R | W |
|---|---|---|---|---|---|---|---|---|
| **CENTRAL DISTRICTS** | | | | | | | | |
| Bracewell | 19 | 6 | 53 | 4 | 21 | 5 | 55 | 1 |
| Wheeler | 11.5 | 1 | 36 | 1 | 13 | 1 | 53 | 0 |
| Toole | 18 | 2 | 49 | 2 | 13 | 2 | 39 | 0 |
| Tickner | 17 | 5 | 33 | 2 | 25 | 3 | 86 | 1 |
| Field | 8 | 2 | 28 | 1 | 9 | 0 | 45 | 1 |
| Lennox | 11 | 2 | 32 | 0 | 29.3 | 5 | 112 | 3 |
| Schmulian | 1 | 0 | 5 | 0 | 3 | 0 | 18 | 1 |
| **OTAGO** | | | | | | | | |
| Bacon | 19 | 4 | 59 | 2 | 11 | 1 | 35 | 1 |
| Muller | 19 | 5 | 48 | 2 | 14 | 2 | 40 | 1 |
| McKenzie | 15 | 6 | 32 | 2 | 13 | 6 | 25 | 1 |
| McKay | 11 | 2 | 42 | 0 | 11 | 2 | 41 | 1 |
| Kitchen | 3 | 0 | 12 | 0 | 4.5 | 3 | 2 | 2 |
| Rippon | 23.3 | 9 | 67 | 3 | 24 | 7 | 85 | 3 |

| Fall of Wickets | O | CD | O | CD |
|---|---|---|---|---|
| | 1st | 1st | 2nd | 2nd |
| 1st | 11 | 28 | 173 | 39 |
| 2nd | 16 | 55 | 234 | 108 |
| 3rd | 46 | 153 | 284 | 114 |
| 4th | 49 | 181 | 322 | 118 |
| 5th | 91 | 208 | 362 | 120 |
| 6th | 152 | 239 | 374 | 147 |
| 7th | 153 | 239 | 393 | 221 |
| 8th | 234 | 242 | - | 232 |
| 9th | 239 | 243 | - | 232 |
| 10th | 244 | 265 | - | 240 |

NZC

# WELLINGTON v CANTERBURY                    Plunket Shield

*at Cello Basin Reserve, Wellington on 7, 8, 9 November, 2021*
*Toss : Wellington.  Umpires : C.A. Black & D.J. Walker*
*Close of play: 1st day: Wellington 102-8, Sears 11, Newton 11; 2nd day: Canterbury 247-4, Carter 46, Fletcher 22*
**Canterbury won by 314 runs.** *Points: Canterbury 16 (4 bowl), Wellington 4 (4 bowl)*

Eighteen wickets fell on the first day after Canterbury had been 86-0 after being sent in. Wellington were all out early on the second day and the visitors fared better in their second innings. McClure reached a century from 174 balls and Carter and Fletcher made fifties.

Wellington thus needed 430 to win but were bowled out within fifty overs, giving Canterbury a win by 314 runs with a day to spare. McLachlan made nine dismissals in his first-class debut and also bagged a king pair.

## CANTERBURY

| FIRST INNINGS | Runs | Mins | Balls | | 4s | SECOND INNINGS | Runs | Mins | Balls | 6s | 4s |
|---|---|---|---|---|---|---|---|---|---|---|---|
| C.J.Bowes run out | 59 | 107 | 72 | 1 | 9 | (2) lbw b Gibson | 21 | 67 | 49 | - | 4 |
| K.J.McClure c McLachlan b Smith | 34 | 131 | 83 | - | 7 | (1) b Sears | 130 | 258 | 193 | 3 | 20 |
| H.J.Chamberlain c McLachlan b Smith | 0 | 5 | 3 | - | - | b Gibson | 0 | 1 | 1 | - | - |
| C.E.McConchie* lbw b Snedden | 0 | 6 | 5 | - | - | lbw b Bracewell | 15 | 80 | 64 | - | 1 |
| L.J.Carter c Snedden b Sears | 22 | 68 | 42 | 1 | 2 | c McLachlan b Smith | 56 | 199 | 144 | - | 11 |
| C.D.Fletcher† c McLachlan b Snedden | 23 | 93 | 64 | - | 3 | not out | 78 | 246 | 164 | 1 | 11 |
| H.B.Shipley c McLachlan b Newton | 2 | 21 | 19 | - | - | c McLachlan b Sears | 25 | 51 | 36 | 2 | 3 |
| M.J.Henry c Allen b Sears | 5 | 11 | 3 | - | 1 | c McLachlan b Sears | 20 | 11 | 10 | 3 | - |
| W.S.A.Williams c McLachlan b Sears | 0 | 10 | 5 | - | - | lbw b Smith | 9 | 40 | 28 | - | 1 |
| F.W.Sheat c & b Snedden | 0 | 11 | 7 | - | - | st McLachlan b Bracewell | 30 | 48 | 34 | 1 | 4 |
| E.J.Nuttall not out | 4 | 6 | 5 | - | 1 | b Bracewell | 4 | 3 | 4 | - | 1 |
| Extras (lb 6, w 1) | 7 | | | | | (b 1, lb 4, w 6, nb 8) | 19 | | | | |
| **TOTAL** (51.2 overs) | **156** | 237 | | | | (119.5 overs) | **407** | 504 | | | |

## WELLINGTON

| | Runs | Mins | Balls | | 4s | | Runs | Mins | Balls | 6s | 4s |
|---|---|---|---|---|---|---|---|---|---|---|---|
| L.I.Georgeson c Fletcher b Henry | 4 | 24 | 13 | - | - | c Fletcher b Williams | 1 | 33 | 22 | - | - |
| J.J.N.P.Bhula b Shipley | 29 | 109 | 90 | - | 4 | b Henry | 2 | 19 | 15 | - | - |
| N.A.Greenwood b Nuttall | 9 | 46 | 37 | - | 1 | c Shipley b Nuttall | 21 | 61 | 46 | - | 3 |
| M.G.Bracewell* c McClure b Nuttall | 2 | 11 | 9 | - | - | b Nuttall | 8 | 64 | 41 | - | 1 |
| F.H.Allen b Henry | 17 | 39 | 22 | - | 4 | lbw b Williams | 38 | 112 | 75 | - | 8 |
| J.D.Gibson c Nuttall b Shipley | 6 | 18 | 12 | - | 1 | c Carter b Henry | 25 | 124 | 76 | - | 4 |
| N.G.Smith c Fletcher b Henry | 5 | 13 | 6 | - | 1 | b Henry | 1 | 11 | 5 | - | - |
| C.R.McLachlan† b Shipley | 0 | 1 | 1 | - | - | c Fletcher b Henry | 0 | 2 | 1 | - | - |
| B.V.Sears not out | 24 | 113 | 86 | - | 4 | not out | 2 | 22 | 15 | - | - |
| O.R.Newton retired hurt | 11 | 42 | 22 | - | 2 | absent hurt | | | | | |
| M.W.Snedden lbw b Nuttall | 16 | 65 | 52 | - | 2 | (10) lbw b Williams | 0 | 8 | 7 | - | - |
| Extras (lb 8, nb 3) | 11 | | | | | (b 4, lb 7, w 2, nb 4) | 17 | | | | |
| **TOTAL** (57.5 overs) | **134** | 243 | | | | (49.5 overs) | **115** | 230 | | | |

| Bowling | O | M | R | W | O | M | R | W | | | Fall of Wickets | | | | |
|---|---|---|---|---|---|---|---|---|---|---|---|---|---|---|---|
| **WELLINGTON** | | | | | | | | | | | | C | W | C | W |
| | | | | | | | | | | | | 1st | 1st | 2nd | 2nd |
| Newton | 15 | 4 | 47 | 1 | | | | | | | 1st | 86 | 9 | 58 | 4 |
| Smith | 14 | 8 | 22 | 2 | 25 | 8 | 61 | 2 | | | 2nd | 90 | 27 | 58 | 16 |
| Gibson | 2 | 0 | 13 | 0 | 18 | 4 | 83 | 2 | | | 3rd | 91 | 33 | 116 | 39 |
| Sears | 10 | 1 | 40 | 3 | 23 | 1 | 102 | 3 | | | 4th | 97 | 60 | 212 | 44 |
| Snedden | 10.2 | 3 | 28 | 3 | 28 | 5 | 81 | 0 | | | 5th | 131 | 72 | 263 | 95 |
| Bracewell | | | | | 25.5 | 8 | 75 | 3 | | | 6th | 137 | 78 | 306 | 102 |
| **CANTERBURY** | | | | | | | | | | | 7th | 152 | 78 | 326 | 102 |
| Henry | 19 | 5 | 53 | 3 | 17 | 7 | 37 | 4 | | | 8th | 152 | 84 | 349 | 110 |
| Williams | 10 | 5 | 7 | 0 | 12.5 | 5 | 21 | 3 | | | 9th | 152 | 134 | 403 | 115 |
| Sheat | 9 | 2 | 26 | 0 | 7 | 1 | 22 | 0 | | | 10th | 156 | - | 407 | - |
| Nuttall | 9.5 | 2 | 21 | 3 | 8 | 3 | 14 | 2 | | | | | | | |
| Shipley | 10 | 4 | 19 | 3 | 5 | 2 | 10 | 0 | | | | | | | |

# NORTHERN DISTRICTS v CANTERBURY          Plunket Shield

*at Bay Oval, Mt Maunganui on 15, 16, 17 November, 2021*
*Toss : Northern Districts. Umpires : C.A. Black & D.J. Walker*
*Close of play: 1st day: Canterbury 82-9, Carter 17; 2nd day: Canterbury 170-8, Fletcher 32, Williams 7*
**Canterbury won by 2 wickets.** *Points: Canterbury 16 (4 bowl), Northern Districts 4 (4 bowl)*

Northern Districts made their belated entry into the competition and decided to bat. However, apart from Carter, who made an unbeaten 74, their was little else of note in their batting. Number eleven Gibson made the next best score of 22.

Canterbury fared even worse and were 82-9 at stumps and dismissed without addition the next morning for the lowest total in a first-class game at Bay Oval. Northern were unable to take advantage of their unexpected 105 run lead and were bowled out for 123, with no player reaching thirty.

Canterbury needed 229 to win but at 156-8 were in trouble. In a tense finish Williams helped Fletcher to take their side to victory with an unbeaten stand of 73 for the ninth wicket.

## NORTHERN DISTRICTS

| FIRST INNINGS | Runs | Mins | Balls | 6s | 4s | SECOND INNINGS ........ | Runs | Mins | Balls | 6s | 4s |
|---|---|---|---|---|---|---|---|---|---|---|---|
| J.A.Raval c Carter b Nuttall ................ | 21 | 55 | 48 | - | 3 | (2) b Henry ........................... | 25 | 69 | 45 | - | 4 |
| H.R.Cooper c Carter b Shipley .............. | 6 | 58 | 36 | - | 6 | (1) c Carter b Henry .............. | 0 | 1 | 1 | - | - |
| B.Popli b Shipley ...................................... | 1 | 15 | 10 | - | - | b Williams ............................. | 2 | 22 | 13 | - | - |
| J.F.Carter* not out ................................ | 74 | 223 | 136 | 2 | 7 | c Bowes b Williams ................ | 3 | 11 | 11 | - | - |
| C.de Grandhomme c Fletcher b Williams | 15 | 55 | 40 | - | 2 | c Shipley b Williams .............. | 5 | 8 | 8 | - | - |
| S.C.Kuggeleijn c Bowes b Shipley ........ | 4 | 23 | 17 | - | - | c Carter b Henry .................. | 10 | 44 | 30 | - | - |
| P.D.Bocock† c Fletcher b Nuttall ........ | 21 | 39 | 23 | - | 2 | run out ................................. | 28 | 86 | 55 | - | 2 |
| B.R.Hampton c Fletcher b Williams ......5 | 25 | 22 | - | - | c Fletcher b Nuttall .............. | 21 | 32 | 21 | - | 4 |
| J.G.Walker lbw b Henry ........................ | 2 | 15 | 12 | - | - | c McClure b Henry ................ | 2 | 49 | 35 | - | - |
| B.G.Randell lbw b Williams .................. | 0 | 12 | 6 | - | - | not out ................................. | 13 | 40 | 30 | - | 1 |
| Z.N.Gibson c McConchie b Shipley .... | 22 | 40 | 38 | - | 4 | c Fletcher b Nuttall .............. | 6 | 28 | 17 | - | - |
| Extras (b 8, lb 7, nb 1) .................. | 16 | | | | | (b 4, lb 3, nb 1) .................. | 8 | | | | |
| **TOTAL** (64.3 overs) ...................... | **187** | 282 | | | | (44.1 overs) ...................... | **123** | 196 | | | |

## CANTERBURY

| | | | | | | | | | | | |
|---|---|---|---|---|---|---|---|---|---|---|---|
| C.J.Bowes c Cooper b Hampton ........ | 25 | 68 | 46 | - | 4 | (2) c Popli b Randell .............. | 0 | 6 | 4 | - | - |
| K.J.McClure c Cooper b Randell .......... | 5 | 44 | 35 | - | 1 | (1) lbw b Kuggeleijn ............ | 19 | 67 | 46 | - | 3 |
| H.J.Chamberlain c Bocock b Randell ....4 | 7 | 4 | - | 1 | c Bocock b Randell ................ | 2 | 6 | 3 | - | - |
| C.E.McConchie* lbw b de Grandhomme | 3 | 23 | 14 | - | - | b Gibson ............................... | 34 | 63 | 48 | 1 | 6 |
| L.J.Carter not out ............................... | 17 | 75 | 56 | - | 2 | c Carter b Gibson ................ | 17 | 27 | 24 | - | 3 |
| C.D.Fletcher† lbw b de Grandhomme ...0 | 8 | 6 | - | - | not out ................................. | 56 | 230 | 154 | - | 6 |
| H.B.Shipley c Popli b Randell ............. | 1 | 22 | 15 | - | - | c Bocock b Randell .............. | 10 | 30 | 15 | - | 2 |
| T.F.van Woerkom lbw b Gibson ........... | 0 | 14 | 12 | - | - | lbw b de Grandhomme .......... | 7 | 37 | 25 | - | 1 |
| M.J.Henry b Randell ............................ | 4 | 17 | 6 | - | - | c Kuggeleijn b Gibson ........ | 19 | 28 | 24 | - | 3 |
| W.S.A.Williams lbw b Gibson .............. | 0 | 4 | 4 | - | - | not out ................................. | 27 | 114 | 81 | - | 4 |
| E.J.Nuttall b Gibson ............................ | 0 | 1 | 3 | - | - | | | | | | |
| Extras (b 4, lb 4, nb 15) .................. | 23 | | | | | (b 12, lb 1, w 8, nb 17) ....... | 38 | | | | |
| **TOTAL** (31 overs) ............................ | **82** | 143 | | | | (67.5 overs) (8 wkts) ........ | **229** | 308 | | | |

| Bowling | O | M | R | W | O | M | R | W | | Fall of Wickets | | | |
|---|---|---|---|---|---|---|---|---|---|---|---|---|---|
| **CANTERBURY** | | | | | | | | | | | ND | C | ND | C |
| Henry | 20 | 6 | 49 | 1 | 17 | 6 | 46 | 4 | | | 1st | 1st | 2nd | 2nd |
| Williams | 20 | 7 | 51 | 3 | 10 | 2 | 24 | 3 | | 1st | 33 | 29 | 0 | 4 |
| Nuttall | 12 | 1 | 46 | 2 | 6.1 | 0 | 24 | 2 | | 2nd | 33 | 39 | 7 | 10 |
| Shipley | 12.3 | 7 | 26 | 4 | 11 | 1 | 22 | 0 | | 3rd | 34 | 46 | 11 | 49 |
| **NORTHERN DISTRICTS** | | | | | | | | | | 4th | 69 | 49 | 17 | 67 |
| Kuggeleijn | 5 | 1 | 11 | 0 | 10 | 0 | 40 | 1 | | 5th | 74 | 49 | 44 | 83 |
| Randell | 11 | 3 | 32 | 4 | 16 | 5 | 41 | 3 | | 6th | 101 | 58 | 51 | 106 |
| de Grandhomme | 6 | 4 | 8 | 2 | 23 | 6 | 54 | 1 | | 7th | 113 | 63 | 86 | 129 |
| Hampton | 4 | 1 | 9 | 1 | 3 | 0 | 14 | 0 | | 8th | 130 | 80 | 104 | 156 |
| Gibson | 5 | 1 | 14 | 3 | 15.5 | 1 | 67 | 3 | | 9th | 145 | 82 | 106 | - |
| | | | | | | | | | | 10th | 187 | 82 | 123 | - |

# WELLINGTON v CENTRAL DISTRICTS          Plunket Shield

*at Cello Basin Reserve, Wellington on 15, 16, 17, 18 November, 2021*
*Toss : Central Districts. Umpires : J.A.K. Bromley & T.J. Parlane*
*Close of play: 1st day: Wellington 233-9, Smith 55, Hartshorn 13; 2nd day: CD 285-6, Bracewell 53, Wheeler 23*
*          3rd day: Wellington 225-6, Smith 60, McLachlan 25*
**Central Districts won by 7 wickets.** *Points: Central Districts 20 (4 bat, 4 bowl), Wellington 5 (1 bat, 4 bowl)*

Fifties from Bracewell and Smith enabled Wellington to reach 238 by the time they were bowled out early on the second day. Central had secured a lead by the close and ended with a 120 run advantage by the time their innings ended.

Smith hit his second fifty of the game when Wellington batted again but their score of 250 left Central with a straightforward target which they achieved with seven wickets in hand. Ave and Hartshorn (son of former Canterbury and Central Districts player David) made their first-class debuts in this game.

## WELLINGTON

| FIRST INNINGS | Runs | Mins | Balls | 6s | 4s | SECOND INNINGS | Runs | Mins | Balls | 6s | 4s |
|---|---|---|---|---|---|---|---|---|---|---|---|
| L.I.Georgeson c Wheeler b Rance | 1 | 16 | 12 | - | - | c Field b Tickner | 28 | 103 | 73 | - | 5 |
| J.J.N.P.Bhula b Tickner | 27 | 95 | 59 | - | 4 | b Rance | 0 | 5 | 1 | - | - |
| N.A.Greenwood c Bruce b Bracewell | 23 | 111 | 75 | - | 2 | run out | 26 | 91 | 63 | - | 4 |
| M.G.Bracewell* c Wheeler b Field | 51 | 147 | 120 | - | 3 | c Schmulian b Bracewell | 46 | 172 | 97 | - | 5 |
| F.H.Allen c Cleaver b Tickner | 33 | 81 | 42 | - | 5 | c Cleaver b Bracewell | 8 | 17 | 10 | - | 1 |
| J.D.Gibson lbw b Tickner | 1 | 37 | 24 | - | - | c Hay b Wheeler | 23 | 81 | 66 | - | 4 |
| N.G.Smith c Wiggins b Rance | 56 | 182 | 115 | - | 9 | not out | 72 | 184 | 126 | 1 | 9 |
| C.R.McLachlan† c Cleaver b Tickner | 0 | 9 | 7 | - | - | c Cleaver b Wheeler | 25 | 69 | 56 | - | 5 |
| B.V.Sears c Bruce b Rance | 7 | 89 | 65 | - | - | lbw b Wheeler | 2 | 19 | 8 | - | - |
| M.W.Snedden c & b Rance | 7 | 35 | 33 | - | - | lbw b Wheeler | 2 | 9 | 7 | - | - |
| J.W.Hartshorn not out | 17 | 42 | 34 | - | 3 | c & b Rance | 4 | 19 | 15 | - | - |
| Extras (lb 9, w 4, nb 2) | 15 | | | | | (b 1, lb 12, w 1) | 14 | | | | |
| **TOTAL** (97.2 overs) | **238** | 425 | | | | (87 overs) | **250** | 386 | | | |

## CENTRAL DISTRICTS

| | Runs | Mins | Balls | 6s | 4s | | Runs | Mins | Balls | 6s | 4s |
|---|---|---|---|---|---|---|---|---|---|---|---|
| G.R.Hay* c McLachlan b Sears | 18 | 94 | 60 | - | 1 | c Smith b Hartshorn | 22 | 133 | 84 | - | 1 |
| B.L.Wiggins c Bracewell b Smith | 16 | 29 | 23 | - | 4 | c Gibson b Sears | 29 | 40 | 36 | - | 6 |
| B.D.Schmulian c Allen b Sears | 88 | 144 | 93 | 1 | 13 | c Allen b Sears | 4 | 10 | 6 | - | 1 |
| D.Cleaver† c Gibson b Sears | 39 | 129 | 85 | - | 5 | not out | 54 | 134 | 100 | - | 7 |
| T.C.Bruce c & b Sears | 17 | 28 | 18 | - | 3 | not out | 23 | 52 | 39 | - | 3 |
| D.A.J.Bracewell c Georgeson | | | | | | | | | | | |
| b Snedden | 68 | 162 | 96 | - | 12 | | | | | | |
| M.T.M.M.J.Ave c Allen b Sears | 24 | 83 | 55 | - | 4 | | | | | | |
| B.M.Wheeler c Bracewell b Smith | 59 | 116 | 94 | - | 6 | | | | | | |
| J.F.A.Field b Smith | 15 | 43 | 31 | - | 2 | | | | | | |
| B.M.Tickner not out | 1 | 21 | 12 | - | - | | | | | | |
| S.H.A.Rance b Hartshorn | 3 | 6 | 6 | - | - | | | | | | |
| Extras (lb 9, w 1) | 10 | | | | | (lb 2) | 2 | | | | |
| **TOTAL** (95.3 overs) | **358** | 430 | | | | (44.1 overs) (3 wkts) | **134** | 185 | | | |

| Bowling | O | M | R | W | O | M | R | W | | Fall of Wickets | | | | |
|---|---|---|---|---|---|---|---|---|---|---|---|---|---|---|
| **CENTRAL DISTRICTS** | | | | | | | | | | | W | CD | W | CD |
| Bracewell | 23 | 5 | 51 | 1 | 16 | 3 | 52 | 2 | | | 1st | 1st | 2nd | 2nd |
| Rance | 20.2 | 6 | 52 | 4 | 21 | 6 | 53 | 2 | | 1st | 3 | 25 | 4 | 30 |
| Wheeler | 21 | 5 | 41 | 0 | 24 | 5 | 54 | 4 | | 2nd | 46 | 84 | 56 | 34 |
| Tickner | 23 | 7 | 56 | 4 | 13 | 4 | 45 | 1 | | 3rd | 55 | 159 | 58 | 83 |
| Field | 9 | 3 | 27 | 1 | 11 | 3 | 30 | 0 | | 4th | 125 | 181 | 70 | - |
| Schmulian | 1 | 0 | 2 | 0 | 2 | 0 | 3 | 0 | | 5th | 140 | 188 | 109 | - |
| **WELLINGTON** | | | | | | | | | | 6th | 140 | 258 | 177 | - |
| Smith | 24 | 4 | 69 | 3 | 12 | 5 | 17 | 0 | | 7th | 140 | 312 | 227 | - |
| Hartshorn | 13.3 | 3 | 46 | 1 | 9 | 3 | 26 | 1 | | 8th | 192 | 344 | 233 | - |
| Sears | 20 | 4 | 88 | 5 | 9 | 1 | 40 | 2 | | 9th | 204 | 355 | 239 | - |
| Georgeson | 2 | 0 | 15 | 0 | | | | | | 10th | 238 | 358 | 250 | - |
| Gibson | 6 | 0 | 26 | 0 | | | | | | | | | | |
| Snedden | 21 | 8 | 64 | 1 | 8.1 | 3 | 27 | 0 | | | | | | |
| Bracewell | 9 | 1 | 41 | 0 | 6 | 0 | 22 | 0 | | | | | | |

# OTAGO v NORTHERN DISTRICTS

**Plunket Shield**

at Molyneux Park, Alexandra on 22, 23, 24, 25 November, 2021
Toss : Northern Districts. Umpires : E.D. Sanders & D.J. Walker
*Close of play: 1st day: Otago 185-7, Chu 30, McKenzie 2; 2nd day: ND 162-1, Cooper 63, Randell 0*
*3rd day: ND 547-7, Bocock 23, Walker 10*
**Northern Districts won by an innings and 74 runs.** Points: Northern Districts 18 (3 bat, 3 bowl), Otago 3 (3 bat)

Northern decided to bowl and took the wicket of Renwick in the first over. Otago were still in trouble at 125-6 but a maiden hundred from Chu (245 balls) and a first fifty from Gibson saw the home team to 342. Randell took five wickets in an innings for the first time.

Northern's reply was based around Cooper's maiden double century, reached from 378 balls. His hundred had come from 239 deliveries. Fifties from Raval, nightwatchman Randell and Popli saw Northern end on 553, the highest total at Molyneux Park.

Facing a deficit of 211, Otago were unable to see the day out and were dismissed for 137. Phillips, coming in at number three, was left unbeaten on 68.

## OTAGO

| FIRST INNINGS | Runs | Mins | Balls | 6s | 4s | SECOND INNINGS | Runs | Mins | Balls | 6s | 4s |
|---|---|---|---|---|---|---|---|---|---|---|---|
| H.D.Rutherford* c Popli b de Grandhomme | 37 | 107 | 59 | - | 6 | lbw b Randell | 4 | 4 | 6 | - | 1 |
| M.Renwick lbw b Randell | 0 | 2 | 2 | - | - | b Walker | 11 | 60 | 43 | - | 1 |
| D.N.Phillips b Randell | 7 | 44 | 32 | - | - | not out | 68 | 277 | 179 | - | 7 |
| N.F.Kelly c Cooper b Kuggeleijn | 57 | 113 | 78 | 1 | 8 | run out | 0 | 4 | 0 | - | - |
| A.K.Kitchen b Randell | 8 | 24 | 25 | - | 1 | lbw b Randell | 16 | 41 | 37 | - | 2 |
| M.J.G.Rippon c Bocock b Gibson | 7 | 41 | 27 | - | 1 | b Walker | 4 | 22 | 16 | - | 1 |
| M.W.Chu† not out | 103 | 352 | 246 | - | 14 | c Bocock b Gibson | 10 | 53 | 37 | - | 1 |
| T.Muller c Randell b Walker | 30 | 136 | 103 | - | 5 | b Walker | 11 | 46 | 39 | - | - |
| A.W.McKenzie c sub (F.L.Walker) b Randell | 10 | 36 | 28 | - | - | c Bocock b Gibson | 4 | 32 | 27 | - | - |
| J.M.Gibson c Bocock b Randell | 50 | 130 | 95 | - | 6 | c Cooper b Gibson | 0 | 2 | 2 | - | - |
| J.A.Duffy c Hampton b Gibson | 12 | 36 | 22 | - | 3 | c Raval b Walker | 0 | 18 | 11 | - | - |
| Extras (b 4, lb 4, w 4, nb 9) | 21 | | | | | (lb 5, w 2, nb 2) | 9 | | | | |
| **TOTAL** (117.5 overs) | **342** | 512 | | | | (66 overs) | **137** | 282 | | | |

## NORTHERN DISTRICTS

| | Runs | Mins | Balls | 6s | 4s |
|---|---|---|---|---|---|
| J.A.Raval lbw b Rippon | 89 | 206 | 158 | - | 13 |
| H.R.Cooper lbw b Rippon | 200 | 550 | 379 | 4 | 23 |
| B.G.Randell c Chu b Muller | 50 | 185 | 155 | 1 | 5 |
| B.Popli c Rutherford b Duffy | 86 | 172 | 119 | 1 | 10 |
| C.de Grandhomme c Chu b Rippon | 21 | 9 | 18 | - | 1 |
| J.F.Carter* c Phillips b Muller | 20 | 29 | 23 | - | 2 |
| P.D.Bocock† lbw b Rippon | 28 | 49 | 26 | 1 | - |
| S.C.Kuggeleijn c Chu b Rippon | 11 | 13 | 9 | 1 | - |
| J.G.Walker run out | 11 | 21 | 11 | - | 2 |
| Z.N.Gibson not out | 0 | 1 | 0 | - | - |
| B.R.Hampton absent hurt | | | | | |
| Extras (b 3, lb 10, w 15, nb 9) | 37 | | | | |
| **TOTAL** (148.1 overs) | **553** | 629 | | | |

| Bowling | O | M | R | W | O | M | R | W |
|---|---|---|---|---|---|---|---|---|
| **NORTHERN DISTRICTS** | | | | | | | | |
| Randell | 26 | 7 | 56 | 5 | 17 | 3 | 39 | 2 |
| Gibson | 28.5 | 5 | 104 | 2 | 17 | 6 | 30 | 3 |
| Kuggeleijn | 14.3 | 3 | 44 | 1 | | | | |
| de Grandhomme | 18 | 4 | 53 | 1 | 4 | 0 | 12 | 0 |
| Hampton | 11.3 | 0 | 37 | 0 | | | | |
| Walker | 19 | 7 | 40 | 1 | 27 | 9 | 47 | 4 |
| Raval | | | | | 1 | 0 | 4 | 0 |
| **OTAGO** | | | | | | | | |
| Duffy | 30 | 5 | 93 | 1 | | | | |
| Muller | 28 | 1 | 126 | 2 | | | | |
| McKenzie | 23 | 6 | 44 | 0 | | | | |
| Gibson | 19 | 2 | 83 | 0 | | | | |
| Rippon | 37.1 | 7 | 142 | 5 | | | | |
| Kitchen | 11 | 2 | 52 | 0 | | | | |

| Fall of Wickets | O | ND | O |
|---|---|---|---|
| | 1st | 1st | 2nd |
| 1st | 1 | 161 | 4 |
| 2nd | 30 | 268 | 29 |
| 3rd | 79 | 447 | 33 |
| 4th | 92 | 474 | 61 |
| 5th | 115 | 491 | 72 |
| 6th | 125 | 508 | 99 |
| 7th | 181 | 532 | 115 |
| 8th | 203 | 550 | 126 |
| 9th | 307 | 550 | 126 |
| 10th | 342 | - | 137 |

**NZC**

# AUCKLAND v NORTHERN DISTRICTS    Plunket Shield

*at Kennards Hire Community Oval, Auckland on 4, 5, 6, 7 February, 2022*
*Toss : Auckland. Umpires : C.M. Brown & W.R. Knights*
*Close of play: 1st day: Auckland 32-0, Guptill 23, Worker 8; 2nd day: ND 68-3, Wagner 1, Carter 0*
*3rd day: ND 155-7, Santner 13, Southee 4*
**Auckland won by 4 wickets.** *Points: Auckland 17 (1 bat, 4 bowl), Northern Districts 5 (1 bat, 4 bowl)*

Auckland finally got their first-class season underway and decided to bowl first. They soon accounted for Northern's openers and the visitors fell to 127-7. Fifties to Santner and Randell steadied things but the innings ended at 230 and Auckland were 32-0 by the close of play.

Test bowlers Southee, Wagner and de Grandhomme struck the next morning and Auckland were suddenly 55-5 and then 100-6. Despite Solia's 72, Northern gained an unexpected lead of 22 but lost the advantage when they were seven down by the close.

Auckland soon finished off the innings on the last day but had to work hard to reach their target of 196 after a promising start. Chapman was unbeaten on 53 when the winning runs came. Worker made his Auckland debut in this match.

## NORTHERN DISTRICTS

| FIRST INNINGS | Runs | Mins | Balls | 6s | 4s |
|---|---|---|---|---|---|
| J.A.Raval b Jamieson | 3 | 37 | 15 | - | - |
| H.R.Cooper lbw b ter Braak | 8 | 62 | 59 | - | 1 |
| K.D.Clarke c O'Donnell b ter Braak | 29 | 55 | 35 | - | 6 |
| J.F.Carter* b ter Braak | 22 | 105 | 70 | - | 4 |
| T.L.Seifert† b Somerville | 18 | 83 | 56 | - | 1 |
| C.de Grandhomme c Phillips b Somerville | 13 | 31 | 14 | - | 2 |
| M.J.Santner c Horne b Somerville | 59 | 141 | 97 | 2 | 5 |
| T.G.Southee c Worker b Lister | 8 | 12 | 12 | 1 | - |
| B.G.Randell c Horne b Phillips | 51 | 126 | 96 | - | 11 |
| N.Wagner c Jamieson b Phillips | 1 | 13 | 12 | - | - |
| J.G.Walker not out | 4 | 6 | 6 | - | 1 |
| Extras (b 3, lb 7, w 2, nb 2) | 14 | | | | |
| **TOTAL (78.2 overs)** | **230** | 337 | | | |

| SECOND INNINGS | Runs | Mins | Balls | 6s | 4s |
|---|---|---|---|---|---|
| (2) c Jamieson b ter Braak | 32 | 84 | 48 | - | 5 |
| (1) lbw b Solia | 24 | 114 | 89 | - | 2 |
| b Solia | 9 | 19 | 11 | - | 2 |
| (5) b Jamieson | 0 | 17 | 10 | - | - |
| (6) b Somerville | 9 | 91 | 49 | - | - |
| (7) c Guptill b Phillips | 17 | 53 | 38 | - | - |
| (8) b Somerville | 19 | 80 | 62 | - | 2 |
| (9) c Horne b Lister | 8 | 15 | 9 | - | 2 |
| (10) run out | 8 | 29 | 17 | - | 2 |
| (4) st Horne b Somerville | 36 | 94 | 74 | 1 | 5 |
| not out | 0 | 7 | 6 | - | - |
| (b 5, lb 3, w 2, nb 1) | 11 | | | | |
| **(68.4 overs)** | **173** | 304 | | | |

## AUCKLAND

| | Runs | Mins | Balls | 6s | 4s |
|---|---|---|---|---|---|
| M.J.Guptill c Randell b Southee | 63 | 186 | 141 | 1 | 9 |
| G.H.Worker c Raval b Southee | 12 | 74 | 46 | - | 2 |
| G.D.Phillips lbw b Southee | 0 | 9 | 6 | - | - |
| M.S.Chapman c Southee b Wagner | 7 | 16 | 14 | - | 1 |
| R.R.O'Donnell* lbw b Southee | 0 | 5 | 3 | - | - |
| B.J.Horne† c Raval b de Grandhomme | 3 | 16 | 10 | - | - |
| S.M.Solia c Walker b Randell | 72 | 218 | 160 | 2 | 7 |
| K.A.Jamieson c Clarke b Wagner | 28 | 102 | 66 | 1 | 1 |
| W.E.R.Somerville b Walker | 14 | 29 | 36 | - | 1 |
| R.M.ter Braak lbw b Southee | 0 | 15 | 12 | - | - |
| B.G.Lister not out | 0 | 2 | 2 | - | - |
| Extras (lb 1, w 2, nb 6) | 9 | | | | |
| **TOTAL (81.4 overs)** | **208** | 339 | | | |

| | Runs | Mins | Balls | 6s | 4s |
|---|---|---|---|---|---|
| b Southee | 31 | 92 | 55 | - | 6 |
| lbw b Randell | 29 | 68 | 57 | - | 4 |
| c Santner b Wagner | 41 | 67 | 42 | 1 | 6 |
| not out | 53 | 125 | 72 | 1 | 6 |
| b Walker | 4 | 20 | 13 | - | 1 |
| c Seifert b Randell | 5 | 14 | 9 | - | 1 |
| b Wagner | 26 | 48 | 37 | - | 4 |
| not out | 1 | 1 | 2 | - | - |
| (w 6) | 6 | | | | |
| **(47.5 overs) (6 wkts)** | **196** | 218 | | | |

| Bowling | O | M | R | W | O | M | R | W |
|---|---|---|---|---|---|---|---|---|
| **AUCKLAND** | | | | | | | | |
| Jamieson | 14 | 3 | 29 | 1 | 17 | 7 | 34 | 1 |
| Lister | 12 | 5 | 23 | 1 | 12 | 1 | 33 | 1 |
| Solia | 11 | 3 | 25 | 0 | 8 | 3 | 21 | 2 |
| ter Braak | 13 | 3 | 59 | 3 | 10 | 1 | 28 | 1 |
| Somerville | 22 | 5 | 68 | 3 | 19.4 | 8 | 41 | 3 |
| Worker | 4 | 1 | 12 | 0 | | | | |
| Phillips | 2.2 | 2 | 4 | 2 | 2 | 0 | 8 | 1 |
| **NORTHERN DISTRICTS** | | | | | | | | |
| Southee | 17 | 6 | 35 | 5 | 13 | 2 | 54 | 1 |
| Wagner | 22 | 4 | 39 | 2 | 7.5 | 0 | 53 | 2 |
| Randell | 13.4 | 3 | 39 | 1 | 11 | 2 | 40 | 2 |
| Walker | 13 | 1 | 39 | 1 | 5 | 0 | 14 | 1 |
| de Grandhomme | 11 | 5 | 31 | 1 | 4 | 1 | 11 | 0 |
| Santner | 5 | 1 | 24 | 0 | 7 | 1 | 24 | 0 |

| Fall of Wickets | ND | A | ND | A |
|---|---|---|---|---|
| | 1st | 1st | 2nd | 2nd |
| 1st | 13 | 38 | 54 | 59 |
| 2nd | 28 | 38 | 67 | 83 |
| 3rd | 49 | 49 | 68 | 116 |
| 4th | 90 | 50 | 69 | 137 |
| 5th | 92 | 55 | 112 | 148 |
| 6th | 115 | 100 | 131 | 195 |
| 7th | 127 | 175 | 151 | - |
| 8th | 221 | 198 | 160 | - |
| 9th | 222 | 206 | 173 | - |
| 10th | 230 | 208 | 173 | - |

# OTAGO v AUCKLAND                                    Plunket Shield

*at University of Otago Oval, Dunedin on 11, 12, 13, 14 February, 2022*
*Toss : Otago. Umpires : B.F. Bowden & T.J. Parlane*
*Close of play: 1st day: Otago 8-1, Renwick 1, Muller 1; 2nd day: Otago 86-4, Renwick 38, Parkes 4*
*3rd day: no pplay*
**Auckland won by 213 runs.** *Points: Auckland 16 (3 bat, 1 bowl), Otago 4 (4 bowl)*

Keene, Cumming (son of Craig) and Parkes all made their first-class debuts while Kelly was captain in a first-class game for the first time.

Auckland were sent in to bat and fifties from Phillips, Chapman and Somerville (highest score) saw them reach 325 and take the wicket of Cumming before stumps. Just 35.1 overs were bowled over the next two days and Otago declared before play resumed on the last day.

Auckland scored 84 off nine overs (Phillips fifty off 21 balls) and also declared, leaving Otago 324 runs to win. Renwick went in the first over and wickets continued to fall. Keene marked his debut by taking 5-24 from 8.1 overs as Auckland won by 213 runs.

## AUCKLAND

| FIRST INNINGS | Runs | Mins | Balls | 6s | 4s | SECOND INNINGS | Runs | Mins | Balls | 6s | 4s |
|---|---|---|---|---|---|---|---|---|---|---|---|
| G.H.Worker c Chu b McKenzie | 9 | 89 | 66 | - | 1 | run out | 14 | 40 | 20 | - | 1 |
| W.T.O'Donnell c Renwick b Muller | 0 | 16 | 12 | - | - | b Muller | 0 | 6 | 4 | - | - |
| G.D.Phillips c Chu b McKenzie | 61 | 85 | 48 | 2 | 9 | not out | 53 | 43 | 24 | 3 | 7 |
| M.S.Chapman c Kelly b McKay | 97 | 237 | 160 | 1 | 17 | not out | 8 | 10 | 6 | 1 | - |
| R.R.O'Donnell* c Chu b Duffy | 5 | 29 | 20 | - | 1 | | | | | | |
| B.J.Horne† b Rippon | 45 | 132 | 99 | 1 | 7 | | | | | | |
| S.M.Solia b Rippon | 16 | 74 | 46 | - | 2 | | | | | | |
| W.E.R.Somerville not out | 60 | 68 | 48 | 2 | 9 | | | | | | |
| S.B.Keene c Chu b McKay | 6 | 9 | 5 | - | 1 | | | | | | |
| R.M.ter Braak c Cumming b Rippon | 0 | 3 | 2 | - | - | | | | | | |
| B.G.Lister not out | 8 | 43 | 29 | - | - | | | | | | |
| Extras (b 2, lb 10, w 5, nb 1) | 18 | | | | | (lb 4, w 5) | 9 | | | | |
| **TOTAL** (89 overs) (9 wkts dec) | **325** | 395 | | | | (9 overs) (2 wkts dec) | **84** | 50 | | | |

## OTAGO

| | | | | | | | | | | | |
|---|---|---|---|---|---|---|---|---|---|---|---|
| M.Renwick not out | 38 | 161 | 125 | - | 6 | c Phillips b Lister | 0 | 2 | 4 | - | - |
| J.M.Cumming c Horne b Solia | 0 | 6 | 5 | - | - | c Horne b ter Braak | 8 | 57 | 38 | - | 1 |
| T.Muller c Horne b Solia | 7 | 42 | 27 | - | 1 | (8) lbw b Keene | 6 | 52 | 49 | - | 1 |
| D.N.Phillips c Phillips b Keene | 24 | 59 | 44 | 1 | 2 | (3) c & b Solia | 18 | 30 | 19 | 1 | 3 |
| N.F.Kelly* c O'Donnell R.R. b Keene | 4 | 23 | 14 | - | 1 | (4) c O'Donnell W.T. b Keene | 48 | 159 | 109 | 2 | 6 |
| T.K.Parkes not out | 4 | 28 | 26 | - | - | (5) c O'Donnell R.R. b Keene | 1 | 6 | 4 | - | - |
| M.W.Chu† | | | | | | c Phillips b Somerville | 2 | 22 | 15 | - | - |
| M.J.G.Rippon | | | | | | (6) c O'Donnell R.R. b Lister | 19 | 67 | 44 | - | 2 |
| A.W.McKenzie | | | | | | c Horne b Keene | 0 | 3 | 3 | - | - |
| J.A.Duffy | | | | | | c Phillips b Keene | 4 | 16 | 8 | - | - |
| J.D.McKay | | | | | | not out | 0 | 5 | 2 | - | - |
| Extras (lb 6, w 3) | 9 | | | | | (lb 1, w 3) | 4 | | | | |
| **TOTAL** (40.1 overs) (4 wkts dec) | **86** | 161 | | | | (49.1 overs) | **110** | 211 | | | |

| Bowling | O | M | R | W | O | M | R | W | | Fall of Wickets | | | | |
|---|---|---|---|---|---|---|---|---|---|---|---|---|---|---|
| **OTAGO** | | | | | | | | | | | A | O | A | O |
| Duffy | 23 | 11 | 67 | 1 | 5 | 0 | 41 | 0 | | | 1st | 1st | 2nd | 2nd |
| Muller | 18 | 6 | 47 | 1 | 4 | 0 | 39 | 1 | | 1st | 4 | 0 | 2 | 0 |
| McKenzie | 20 | 7 | 59 | 2 | | | | | | 2nd | 71 | 20 | 71 | 26 |
| McKay | 12 | 2 | 75 | 2 | | | | | | 3rd | 76 | 66 | - | 29 |
| Rippon | 16 | 2 | 65 | 3 | | | | | | 4th | 87 | 74 | - | 30 |
| **AUCKLAND** | | | | | | | | | | 5th | 200 | - | - | 84 |
| Lister | 6 | 3 | 9 | 0 | 11 | 4 | 19 | 2 | | 6th | 248 | - | - | 95 |
| Solia | 8 | 2 | 25 | 2 | 8 | 2 | 24 | 1 | | 7th | 251 | - | - | 106 |
| ter Braak | 5 | 0 | 16 | 0 | 7 | 0 | 29 | 1 | | 8th | 265 | - | - | 106 |
| Keene | 8 | 2 | 14 | 2 | 8.1 | 4 | 24 | 5 | | 9th | 266 | - | - | 107 |
| Somerville | 10 | 5 | 11 | 0 | 10 | 4 | 6 | 1 | | 10th | - | - | - | 110 |
| Phillips | 3.1 | 1 | 5 | 0 | 5 | 2 | 7 | 0 | | | | | | |

# AUCKLAND v CANTERBURY          **Plunket Shield**

*at Kennards Hire Community Oval, Auckland on 3, 4, 5, 6 March, 2022*
*Toss : Auckland. Umpires : C.M. Brown & J.M. Dempsey*
*Close of play: 1st day: Auckland 403-4, R.R.O'Donnell 160, Horne 14; 2nd day: Canterbury 135-7, Shipley 35, Williams 12*
        *3rd day: Canterbury 81-2, Foulkes 35, Boyle 7*
**Auckland won by 224 runs.** *Points: Auckland 20 (4 bat, 4 bowl), Canterbury 3 (1 bat, 2 bowl)*

Auckland decided to bat and made full use of this decision by reaching 403-4 by stumps, after they had been 87-3. Guptill and O'Donnell put on 278, an Auckland fourth wicket record against Canterbury. O'Donnell had reached his hundred from 205 balls and next day went to his first double century from 338 deliveries.

Canterbury made a disastrous reply and were soon 39-5. A fifty to Shipley saw a recovery but the vistors ended 347 runs behind. Auckland batted again, with Phillips scoring fifty from 29 balls, and set Canterbury a target of 479 runs to win.

Shipley scored his second fifty of the match but it was not enough to stop Auckland winning by 224 runs. Keene took another five wicket haul with new best figures of 6-44. Foulkes made his first-class debut in this match.

## AUCKLAND

| FIRST INNINGS | Runs | Mins | Balls | 6s | 4s | SECOND INNINGS | Runs | Mins | Balls | 6s | 4s |
|---|---|---|---|---|---|---|---|---|---|---|---|
| M.J.Guptill c McClure b Sheat | 195 | 364 | 212 | 5 | 24 | c Carter b Foulkes | 36 | 45 | 29 | 2 | 3 |
| G.H.Worker b Shipley | 9 | 66 | 38 | - | 1 | run out | 16 | 30 | 19 | 1 | 1 |
| G.D.Phillips c Fletcher b Shipley | 1 | 8 | 3 | - | - | not out | 57 | 49 | 31 | 4 | 5 |
| M.S.Chapman c Fletcher b Shipley | 11 | 27 | 17 | - | 2 | not out | 10 | 34 | 12 | - | 1 |
| R.R.O'Donnell* c McConchie b van Woerkom | 223 | 450 | 354 | 9 | 20 | | | | | | |
| B.J.Horne† lbw b Sheat | 14 | 57 | 45 | - | 1 | | | | | | |
| S.M.Solia c McClure b Boyle | 33 | 109 | 80 | 1 | 2 | | | | | | |
| S.B.Keene c Carter b Boyle | 0 | 2 | 4 | - | - | | | | | | |
| O.M.R.Pringle c Sheat b Boyle | 28 | 29 | 29 | 2 | 2 | | | | | | |
| L.J.Delport not out | 12 | 11 | 11 | 1 | - | | | | | | |
| B.G.Lister | | | | | | | | | | | |
| W.T.O'Donnell | | | | | | | | | | | |
| Extras (b 8, lb 3, w 8, nb 2) | 21 | | | | | (lb 9, w 2, nb 1) | 12 | | | | |
| **TOTAL** (131.5 overs) (9 wkts dec) | **547** | 566 | | | | (15 overs) (2 wkts dec) | **131** | 79 | | | |

## CANTERBURY

| | Runs | Mins | Balls | 6s | 4s | | Runs | Mins | Balls | 6s | 4s |
|---|---|---|---|---|---|---|---|---|---|---|---|
| K.J.McClure c & b Lister | 0 | 11 | 13 | - | - | c Horne b Keene | 14 | 53 | 39 | - | 1 |
| Z.G.Foulkes c Horne b Keene | 3 | 46 | 26 | - | - | c Horne b Keene | 35 | 179 | 136 | - | 3 |
| C.E.McConchie* lbw b Solia | 22 | 64 | 46 | - | 4 | c Chapman b Keene | 23 | 83 | 69 | - | 4 |
| J.C.T.Boyle b Lister | 5 | 42 | 29 | - | - | c Horne b Lister | 7 | 43 | 42 | - | 1 |
| L.J.Carter c Guptill b Solia | 38 | 76 | 60 | 1 | 6 | c & b Keene | 5 | 36 | 18 | - | 1 |
| C.D.Fletcher† b Solia | 2 | 15 | 11 | - | - | c Horne b Keene | 10 | 42 | 30 | - | 1 |
| H.B.Shipley c Guptill b Lister | 61 | 240 | 168 | 2 | 3 | lbw b Phillips | 70 | 171 | 126 | 1 | 10 |
| T.F.van Woerkom c Horne b Phillips | 12 | 43 | 43 | 1 | 1 | c Guptill b Delport | 7 | 48 | 43 | - | - |
| W.S.A.Williams c Worker b Phillips | 14 | 100 | 85 | - | 2 | not out | 37 | 199 | 160 | 1 | 3 |
| A.T.E.Hazeldine c Chapman b Keene | 27 | 77 | 75 | - | 4 | c O'Donnell R.R. b Keene | 24 | 38 | 23 | - | 5 |
| F.W.Sheat not out | 3 | 28 | 20 | - | - | lbw b Lister | 11 | 47 | 37 | - | 2 |
| Extras (b 4, lb 1, w 2, nb 6) | 13 | | | | | (b 4, lb 3, w 1, nb 3) | 11 | | | | |
| **TOTAL** (95 overs) | **200** | 376 | | | | (120 overs) | **254** | 472 | | | |

| Bowling | O | M | R | W | O | M | R | W |
|---|---|---|---|---|---|---|---|---|
| **CANTERBURY** | | | | | | | | |
| Williams | 28 | 8 | 70 | 0 | 4 | 1 | 35 | 0 |
| Sheat | 24 | 7 | 90 | 2 | 4 | 0 | 26 | 0 |
| Foulkes | 18.2 | 2 | 52 | 0 | 4 | 0 | 27 | 1 |
| Shipley | 13.4 | 1 | 59 | 3 | | | | |
| Hazeldine | 17 | 1 | 65 | 0 | 3 | 0 | 34 | 0 |
| van Woerkom | 14 | 0 | 106 | 1 | | | | |
| McConchie | 12 | 0 | 73 | 0 | | | | |
| Boyle | 4.5 | 1 | 21 | 3 | | | | |
| **AUCKLAND** | | | | | | | | |
| Lister | 14 | 3 | 31 | 3 | 21 | 7 | 42 | 2 |
| Keene | 13 | 5 | 32 | 2 | 27 | 12 | 44 | 6 |
| Pringle | 16 | 7 | 35 | 0 | 21 | 7 | 48 | 0 |
| Solia | 11 | 5 | 17 | 3 | | | | |
| Delport | 23 | 5 | 58 | 0 | 29 | 8 | 61 | 1 |
| Phillips | 17 | 7 | 18 | 2 | 14 | 3 | 42 | 1 |
| O'Donnell | 1 | 0 | 4 | 0 | 6 | 3 | 8 | 0 |
| Worker | | | | | 2 | 0 | 2 | 0 |

| Fall of Wickets | A | C | A | C |
|---|---|---|---|---|
| | 1st | 1st | 2nd | 2nd |
| 1st | 61 | 2 | 44 | 22 |
| 2nd | 64 | 17 | 70 | 69 |
| 3rd | 87 | 33 | - | 81 |
| 4th | 365 | 35 | - | 81 |
| 5th | 405 | 39 | - | 97 |
| 6th | 501 | 91 | - | 98 |
| 7th | 501 | 118 | - | 120 |
| 8th | 521 | 152 | - | 193 |
| 9th | 547 | 184 | - | 231 |
| 10th | - | 200 | - | 254 |

*W.T.O'Donnell was a Covid substitute for Solia from the third day*

# NORTHERN DISTRICTS v WELLINGTON                 Plunket Shield

*at Cobham Oval, Whangarei on 3, 4, 5, 6 March, 2022*
*Toss : Northern Districts.  Umpires : C.A. Black & B.F. Bowden*
*Close of play: 1st day: ND 188-8, Randall 10, K.D.C.Clarke 36; 2nd day: ND 68-0, Cooper 34, Raval 29*
*3rd day: Wellington 55-5, Gibson 1, Smith 0*
**Northern Districts won by 213 runs.** *Points: Northern Districts 17 (1 bat, 4 bowl), Wellington 4 (4 bowl),*

Northern Districts decided to bat first but managed just 188-8 on a shortened first day. They eventually reached 243 thanks to Kristian Clarke's 63 not out on debut. This turned out to be more than enough to gain a sizeable lead as Wellington were dismissed for just 119, after being 43-8 at one stage. Kristian Clarke dismissed Gibson with his first ball in first-class cricket, caught by Katene Clarke who equalled the Northern record of four catches in an innings.

Carter and Santner hit seventies in Northern's second innings and the home side declared leaving Wellington needing 439 to win. By the close, Wellington were 55-5 and on the last day were bowled out for 225. Smith's 70 and McLachlan's maiden fifty were the only highlight for the visitors.

## NORTHERN DISTRICTS

| FIRST INNINGS | Runs | Mins | Balls | 6s | 4s | SECOND INNINGS | Runs | Mins | Balls | 6s | 4s |
|---|---|---|---|---|---|---|---|---|---|---|---|
| J.A.Raval c Ravindra b Neesham | 25 | 125 | 88 | - | 1 | (2) c Sears b van Beek | 38 | 159 | 132 | - | 4 |
| H.R.Cooper c McLachlan b Neesham | 14 | 28 | 19 | - | 1 | (1) lbw b Ravindra | 45 | 164 | 117 | - | 5 |
| K.D.Clarke b Neesham | 15 | 73 | 41 | - | 3 | c van Beek b Bracewell | 10 | 23 | 16 | - | 1 |
| J.F.Carter* c Neesham b Bracewell | 3 | 29 | 19 | - | - | c Gibson b Bracewell | 76 | 152 | 121 | - | 11 |
| T.L.Seifert† c McLachlan b Ravindra | 24 | 111 | 78 | - | 2 | b Bracewell | 3 | 13 | 11 | - | - |
| M.J.Santner c Younghusband b Sears | 40 | 76 | 67 | 1 | 4 | c Younghusband b Sears | 74 | 146 | 140 | 1 | 8 |
| S.C.Kuggeleijn b Sears | 0 | 1 | 2 | - | - | not out | 25 | 64 | 33 | 1 | 2 |
| I.S.Sodhi c Georgeson b Ravindra | 10 | 26 | 19 | - | 2 | c Younghusband b Sears | 6 | 15 | 15 | - | - |
| B.G.Randell lbw b Ravindra | 18 | 89 | 68 | - | 1 | c McLachlan b Younghusband | 14 | 9 | 7 | 2 | - |
| K.D.C.Clarke not out | 63 | 128 | 94 | - | 4 | not out | 11 | 12 | 11 | - | 1 |
| J.G.Walker c Bracewell b van Beek | 9 | 41 | 35 | - | 2 | | | | | | |
| Extras (b 7, lb 5, w 7, nb 3) | 22 | | | | | (b 4, lb 3, w 2, nb 3) | 12 | | | | |
| **TOTAL** (87.4 overs) | **243** | 365 | | | | (100 overs) (8 wkts dec) | **314** | 381 | | | |

## WELLINGTON

| | Runs | Mins | Balls | 6s | 4s | | Runs | Mins | Balls | 6s | 4s |
|---|---|---|---|---|---|---|---|---|---|---|---|
| L.I.Georgeson c Clarke K.D. b Randell | 4 | 19 | 17 | - | - | c Seifert b Clarke K.D.C. | 17 | 54 | 31 | - | 3 |
| R.Ravindra c Raval b Walker | 10 | 111 | 55 | - | - | c Raval b Randell | 3 | 19 | 12 | - | - |
| T.M.Johnson lbw b Neesham | 0 | 9 | 8 | - | - | c Seifert b Sodhi | 13 | 88 | 70 | - | 1 |
| M.G.Bracewell* c Clarke K.D. b Kuggeleijn | 13 | 42 | 32 | - | 1 | c Carter b Clarke K.D.C. | 2 | 3 | 2 | - | - |
| J.J.N.P.Bhula lbw b Kuggeleijn | 0 | 3 | 3 | - | - | b Walker | 16 | 61 | 49 | - | 2 |
| J.D.S.Neesham b Randell | 0 | 3 | 1 | - | - | | | | | | |
| J.D.Gibson c Clarke K.D. b Clarke K.D.C. | 9 | 25 | 17 | - | - | (6) lbw b Walker | 14 | 80 | 58 | - | 1 |
| P.F.Younghusband c Seifert b Walker | 1 | 13 | 11 | - | - | c Raval b Sodhi | 6 | 33 | 22 | - | - |
| L.V.van Beek c Clarke K.D. b Santner | 35 | 87 | 51 | 1 | 2 | c Clarke K.D.C. b Sodhi | 21 | 57 | 41 | - | 2 |
| C.R.McLachlan† not out | 40 | 87 | 70 | - | 4 | st Seifert b Walker | 56 | 130 | 105 | 1 | 5 |
| B.V.Sears c Seifert b Santner | 1 | 7 | 7 | - | - | not out | 1 | 56 | 48 | - | - |
| N.G.Smith | | | | | | (7) st Seifert b Walker | 70 | 233 | 189 | 1 | 6 |
| Extras (b 2, w 2, nb 1) | 5 | | | | | (b 4, w 2) | 6 | | | | |
| **TOTAL** (45.1 overs) | **119** | 206 | | | | (104.3 overs) | **225** | 410 | | | |

| Bowling | O | M | R | W | O | M | R | W |
|---|---|---|---|---|---|---|---|---|
| **WELLINGTON** | | | | | | | | |
| Neesham | 18 | 4 | 46 | 3 | 6 | 3 | 11 | 0 |
| van Beek | 19.4 | 4 | 48 | 1 | 19 | 5 | 54 | 1 |
| Sears | 15 | 2 | 34 | 2 | 10 | 1 | 43 | 2 |
| Georgeson | 2 | 0 | 8 | 0 | | | | |
| Bracewell | 15 | 3 | 42 | 1 | 33 | 3 | 107 | 3 |
| Ravindra | 10 | 2 | 38 | 3 | 22 | 8 | 55 | 1 |
| Gibson | 4 | 1 | 6 | 0 | | | | |
| Younghusband | 4 | 1 | 9 | 0 | 10 | 1 | 37 | 1 |
| **NORTHERN DISTRICTS** | | | | | | | | |
| Randell | 13 | 3 | 36 | 3 | 12 | 5 | 27 | 1 |
| Kuggeleijn | 13 | 4 | 28 | 2 | 10 | 1 | 33 | 0 |
| Walker | 9 | 1 | 29 | 2 | 27.3 | 10 | 50 | 4 |
| Clarke K.D.C. | 6 | 1 | 23 | 1 | 12 | 4 | 41 | 2 |
| Santner | 4.1 | 3 | 1 | 2 | 21 | 5 | 31 | 0 |
| Sodhi | | | | | 22 | 7 | 39 | 3 |

| Fall of Wickets | | | | |
|---|---|---|---|---|
| | ND | W | ND | W |
| | 1st | 1st | 2nd | 2nd |
| 1st | 18 | 4 | 89 | 7 |
| 2nd | 55 | 6 | 93 | 31 |
| 3rd | 63 | 23 | 105 | 33 |
| 4th | 63 | 23 | 113 | 46 |
| 5th | 120 | 26 | 245 | 52 |
| 6th | 120 | 38 | 263 | 89 |
| 7th | 140 | 38 | 276 | 106 |
| 8th | 140 | 43 | 295 | 143 |
| 9th | 208 | 115 | - | 188 |
| 10th | 243 | 119 | - | 225 |

*Smith was a Covid substitute for Neesham from the third day*

**NZC**

# CENTRAL DISTRICTS v NORTHERN DISTRICTS Plunket Shield

*at McLean Park, Napier on 11, 12, 13, 14 March, 2022*
*Toss : Central Districts. Umpires : J.M. Dempsey & W.R. Knights*
*Close of play: 1st day: CD 114-4, Field 8, Bruce 13; 2nd day: ND 91-5, de Grandhomme 12, Clarke 14*
*3rd day: CD 28-0, Young 14, Smith 14*
**Northern Districts won by 141 runs.** *Points: Northern Districts 16 (4 bowl), Central Districts 5 (1 bat, 4 bowl)*

Fourteen wickets fell on the first day with no player able to reach fifty. Central gained a lead of 77 on the second day and looked set for victory when they reduced Northern to 119-6 in the second innings.

De Grandhomme had other ideas and reached his hundred from 148 balls. He had good support from Sodhi and then Johnston (making his first-class debut) who batted for 76 minutes in a 60 run last wicket partnership. Toole recorded his first five wicket haul.

Central found themselves needing 224 to win but from 32-0 collapsed to be all out for 82. Randell had career best figures as Northern won by 141 runs. Cleaver was captain in a first-class game for the first time.

## NORTHERN DISTRICTS

| FIRST INNINGS | Runs | Mins | Balls | 6s | 4s |
|---|---|---|---|---|---|
| J.A.Raval c Bruce b Bracewell | 16 | 63 | 43 | - | 2 |
| H.R.Cooper b Tickner | 11 | 30 | 24 | - | 1 |
| B.Popli c Cleaver b Tickner | 17 | 74 | 53 | - | 3 |
| J.F.Carter* c Cleaver b Field | 16 | 49 | 36 | - | 4 |
| T.L.Seifert† c Bruce b Toole | 10 | 25 | 11 | - | 1 |
| C.de Grandhomme c Young b Field | 37 | 97 | 59 | - | 4 |
| K.D.C.Clarke b Bracewell | 10 | 20 | 16 | - | 1 |
| I.S.Sodhi lbw b Bracewell | 6 | 28 | 25 | - | - |
| B.G.Randell lbw b Toole | 0 | 4 | 4 | - | - |
| J.G.Walker not out | 25 | 77 | 64 | 1 | 2 |
| S.S.Johnston c Cleaver b Toole | 10 | 51 | 40 | 1 | 1 |
| Extras (lb 12, w 1, nb 1) | 14 | | | | |
| **TOTAL (62.2 overs)** | **172** | 262 | | | |

| SECOND INNINGS | Runs | Mins | Balls | 6s | 4s |
|---|---|---|---|---|---|
| (2) lbw b Toole | 30 | 126 | 89 | - | 3 |
| (1) c Cleaver b Bracewell | 6 | 36 | 24 | - | 1 |
| run out | 0 | 4 | 1 | - | - |
| c Cleaver b Toole | 25 | 47 | 38 | - | 4 |
| c Wiggins b Toole | 0 | 9 | 6 | - | - |
| not out | 164 | 349 | 233 | 7 | 11 |
| c Tickner b Bracewell | 16 | 65 | 45 | - | 3 |
| c Patel b Toole | 34 | 126 | 107 | - | 5 |
| c Schmulian b Toole | 0 | 10 | 12 | - | - |
| lbw b Tickner | 3 | 42 | 33 | - | - |
| lbw b Toole | 7 | 76 | 42 | - | 1 |
| (b 3, lb 8, w 2, nb 2) | 15 | | | | |
| **(104.4 overs)** | **300** | 447 | | | |

## CENTRAL DISTRICTS

| FIRST INNINGS | Runs | Mins | Balls | 6s | 4s |
|---|---|---|---|---|---|
| W.A.Young st Seifert b Walker | 42 | 96 | 79 | - | 8 |
| B.S.Smith lbw b Clarke | 12 | 51 | 31 | - | 1 |
| B.D.Schmulian c Seifert b Walker | 28 | 54 | 34 | - | 5 |
| D.Cleaver*† b Randell | 1 | 16 | 14 | - | - |
| J.F.A.Field c Walker b Sodhi | 38 | 154 | 114 | - | 4 |
| T.C.Bruce lbw b Randell | 25 | 41 | 32 | - | 5 |
| D.A.J.Bracewell c Seifert b Clarke | 25 | 87 | 62 | - | - |
| B.L.Wiggins b de Grandhomme | 35 | 106 | 82 | - | 5 |
| A.Y.Patel b de Grandhomme | 27 | 102 | 88 | - | 4 |
| B.M.Tickner not out | 0 | 27 | 18 | - | - |
| R.L.Toole c Raval b Clarke | 1 | 13 | 13 | - | - |
| Extras (b 1, lb 8, w 4, nb 2) | 15 | | | | |
| **TOTAL (94.5 overs)** | **249** | 376 | | | |

| SECOND INNINGS | Runs | Mins | Balls | 6s | 4s |
|---|---|---|---|---|---|
| c Seifert b Randell | 20 | 68 | 48 | - | 3 |
| lbw b de Grandhomme | 14 | 47 | 38 | - | 2 |
| lbw b Randell | 7 | 27 | 18 | - | 1 |
| c Seifert b de Grandhomme | 0 | 15 | 8 | - | - |
| (9) lbw b Raval | 12 | 104 | 91 | - | 2 |
| (5) b Randell | 4 | 4 | 4 | - | 1 |
| (6) lbw b Randell | 0 | 2 | 1 | - | - |
| (7) b de Grandhomme | 1 | 21 | 12 | - | - |
| (8) c & b Randell | 7 | 22 | 14 | - | 1 |
| c & b Randell | 13 | 34 | 26 | - | 2 |
| not out | 1 | 66 | 51 | - | - |
| (b 1, lb 1, w 1) | 3 | | | | |
| **(51.5 overs)** | **82** | 207 | | | |

| Bowling | O | M | R | W | O | M | R | W |
|---|---|---|---|---|---|---|---|---|
| **CENTRAL DISTRICTS** | | | | | | | | |
| Bracewell | 15 | 5 | 35 | 3 | 24 | 10 | 46 | 2 |
| Tickner | 16 | 4 | 39 | 2 | 23 | 4 | 72 | 1 |
| Toole | 14.2 | 3 | 33 | 3 | 22.4 | 5 | 54 | 6 |
| Field | 12 | 3 | 33 | 2 | 12 | 1 | 59 | 0 |
| Patel | 5 | 0 | 20 | 0 | 19 | 4 | 45 | 0 |
| Schmulian | | | | | 4 | 0 | 13 | 0 |
| **NORTHERN DISTRICTS** | | | | | | | | |
| Randell | 21 | 3 | 63 | 2 | 19 | 6 | 45 | 6 |
| Clarke | 17.5 | 3 | 47 | 3 | 4 | 1 | 14 | 0 |
| de Grandhomme | 20 | 8 | 49 | 2 | 12 | 6 | 13 | 3 |
| Johnston | 9 | 2 | 29 | 0 | | | | |
| Walker | 15 | 5 | 28 | 2 | 6 | 5 | 1 | 0 |
| Sodhi | 12 | 3 | 24 | 1 | 10 | 7 | 7 | 0 |
| Raval | | | | | 0.5 | 0 | 0 | 1 |

| Fall of Wickets | ND | CD | ND | CD |
|---|---|---|---|---|
| | 1st | 1st | 2nd | 2nd |
| 1st | 18 | 38 | 12 | 32 |
| 2nd | 35 | 90 | 12 | 40 |
| 3rd | 62 | 91 | 50 | 42 |
| 4th | 68 | 92 | 50 | 46 |
| 5th | 89 | 129 | 71 | 46 |
| 6th | 102 | 172 | 119 | 46 |
| 7th | 115 | 184 | 202 | 55 |
| 8th | 116 | 239 | 204 | 55 |
| 9th | 134 | 248 | 240 | 74 |
| 10th | 172 | 249 | 300 | 82 |

# OTAGO v AUCKLAND                    Plunket Shield

*at Molyneux Park, Alexandria on 11, 12, 13, 14 March, 2022*
*Toss : Auckland. Umpires : B.F. Bowden & J.A.K. Bromley*
*Close of play: 1st day: Auckland 299-5, R.R.O'Donnell 73, Jamieson 29; 2nd day: Otago 167-3, Kelly 51, Cumming 33*
*3rd day: Auckland 216-4, R.R.O'Donnell 26*
**Auckland won by 158 runs.** *Points: Auckland 19 (4 bat, 3 bowl), Otago 5 (2 bat, 3 bowl)*

Auckland decided to bat and the first nine players all reached double figures with Worker, Robbie O'Donnell and Somerville scoring fifties. Kelly made 75 for Otago while Muller registered his maiden fifty. Auckland had a lead of 55 which they extended to 314 when they batted again with Phillips and both O'Donnells this time making half-centuries.

Otago struggled in their chase and wickets fell regularly until they were all out for 156. Auckland's spinners, Somerville and Delport, picked up seven wickets between them. Ave, who had earlier played for Central Districts, appeared for Otago as a loan player.

## AUCKLAND

| FIRST INNINGS | Runs | Mins | Balls | 6s | 4s | SECOND INNINGS | Runs | Mins | Balls | 6s | 4s |
|---|---|---|---|---|---|---|---|---|---|---|---|
| G.H.Worker c Ave b McKay | 80 | 202 | 133 | 1 | 11 | c Rippon b Duffy | 18 | 41 | 41 | - | 3 |
| W.T.O'Donnell c Ave b Muller | 41 | 151 | 109 | - | 3 | c Renwick b Duffy | 70 | 152 | 104 | - | 7 |
| G.D.Phillips c Kelly b Muller | 10 | 9 | 13 | - | 2 | c Muller b Rippon | 73 | 102 | 59 | 4 | 7 |
| M.S.Chapman c Rippon b McKay | 25 | 75 | 61 | - | 4 | lbw b Rippon | 14 | 31 | 20 | - | 1 |
| R.R.O'Donnell* lbw b Duffy | 84 | 212 | 140 | - | 9 | not out | 56 | 38 | 33 | 3 | 6 |
| B.J.Horne† c Ave b Rippon | 24 | 59 | 48 | - | 3 | not out | 8 | 16 | 8 | - | - |
| K.A.Jamieson c & b Duffy | 32 | 84 | 69 | - | 5 | | | | | | |
| W.E.R.Somerville lbw b McKay | 54 | 92 | 71 | - | 8 | | | | | | |
| O.M.R.Pringle c Renwick b McKay | 16 | 66 | 49 | 1 | 1 | | | | | | |
| L.J.Delport c Renwick b Rippon | 4 | 13 | 7 | - | 1 | | | | | | |
| B.G.Lister not out | 0 | 6 | 5 | - | - | | | | | | |
| Extras (b 6, lb 3, w 5, nb 5) | 19 | | | | | (b 2, lb 9, w 8, nb 1) | 20 | | | | |
| **TOTAL** (116.4 overs) | **389** | 487 | | | | (44 overs) (4 wkts dec) | **259** | 191 | | | |

## OTAGO

| | Runs | Mins | Balls | 6s | 4s | | Runs | Mins | Balls | 6s | 4s |
|---|---|---|---|---|---|---|---|---|---|---|---|
| H.D.Rutherford* c Lister b Delport | 38 | 165 | 114 | - | 5 | c Worker b Lister | 13 | 17 | 16 | - | 2 |
| M.Renwick c & b Jamieson | 27 | 90 | 63 | - | 4 | b Somerville | 45 | 136 | 90 | - | 5 |
| D.N.Phillips c Phillips b Delport | 6 | 40 | 30 | - | - | c Chapman b Somerville | 14 | 74 | 48 | - | 2 |
| N.F.Kelly b Lister | 75 | 235 | 128 | 1 | 9 | b Delport | 2 | 13 | 11 | - | - |
| J.M.Cumming c & b Somerville | 37 | 140 | 126 | - | 5 | c O'Donnell R.R. b Delport | 16 | 42 | 33 | - | 2 |
| M.J.G.Rippon c Lister b Somerville | 9 | 29 | 23 | - | 1 | lbw b Phillips | 22 | 99 | 83 | - | 2 |
| M.T.M.M.J.Ave† c Phillips b Lister | 34 | 91 | 82 | - | 5 | c Pringle b Delport | 9 | 50 | 49 | - | 2 |
| T.Muller not out | 65 | 131 | 87 | 2 | 7 | st Horne b Somerville | 14 | 60 | 47 | 1 | - |
| J.A.Duffy c Chapman b Phillips | 13 | 33 | 27 | - | 2 | b Delport | 6 | 43 | 41 | - | 1 |
| B.N.J.Lockrose c Chapman b Somerville | 9 | 36 | 32 | - | 1 | b Jamieson | 6 | 46 | 45 | - | 1 |
| J.D.McKay b Somerville | 0 | 1 | 1 | - | - | b Jamieson | 0 | 25 | 27 | - | - |
| Extras (b 5, lb 6, w 3, nb 7) | 21 | | | | | (b 6, lb 1, w 1, nb 1) | 9 | | | | |
| **TOTAL** (117.4 overs) | **334** | 497 | | | | (81.3 overs) | **156** | 305 | | | |

| Bowling | O | M | R | W | O | M | R | W |
|---|---|---|---|---|---|---|---|---|
| **OTAGO** | | | | | | | | |
| Duffy | 28 | 5 | 56 | 2 | 13 | 0 | 38 | 2 |
| Muller | 22 | 5 | 85 | 2 | 5 | 0 | 41 | 0 |
| McKay | 25 | 4 | 85 | 4 | 5 | 0 | 26 | 0 |
| Lockrose | 25 | 4 | 98 | 0 | 8 | 0 | 44 | 0 |
| Rippon | 16.4 | 0 | 56 | 2 | 13 | 0 | 99 | 2 |
| **AUCKLAND** | | | | | | | | |
| Jamieson | 18 | 7 | 37 | 1 | 10.3 | 3 | 18 | 1 |
| Lister | 20 | 3 | 60 | 2 | 7 | 1 | 21 | 1 |
| Pringle | 16 | 3 | 31 | 0 | 4 | 2 | 14 | 0 |
| Somerville | 28.4 | 7 | 66 | 4 | 24 | 12 | 22 | 3 |
| Phillips | 10 | 1 | 45 | 1 | 6 | 3 | 15 | 1 |
| Delport | 25 | 5 | 84 | 2 | 30 | 12 | 59 | 4 |

**Fall of Wickets**

| | A | O | A | O |
|---|---|---|---|---|
| | 1st | 1st | 2nd | 2nd |
| 1st | 106 | 50 | 36 | 13 |
| 2nd | 116 | 66 | 172 | 68 |
| 3rd | 151 | 99 | 176 | 73 |
| 4th | 174 | 183 | 216 | 99 |
| 5th | 236 | 201 | - | 99 |
| 6th | 305 | 211 | - | 119 |
| 7th | 336 | 251 | - | 135 |
| 8th | 378 | 283 | - | 140 |
| 9th | 385 | 334 | - | 148 |
| 10th | 389 | 334 | - | 156 |

NZC

# NORTHERN DISTRICTS v AUCKLAND    Plunket Shield

*at Cobham Oval, Whangarei on 20, 21, 22, 23 March, 2022*
**Abandoned without a ball being bowled**

# OTAGO v WELLINGTON    Plunket Shield

*at University of Otago Oval, Dunedin on 20, 21, 22, 23 March, 2022*
*Toss : Otago. Umpires : T.J. Parlane & D.J. Walker*
*Close of play: 1st day: Wellington 319-7, Johnson 116, Newton 16; 2nd day: Otago 164-5, Cumming 22, Chu 2*
       *3rd day: no play*
**Otago won by 7 wickets.** *Points: Otago 15 (3 bowl), Wellington 6 (4 bat, 2 bowl)*

Otago decided to bowl but saw Wellington's openers, Ravindra and Vishvaka (on debut), respond with a century opening stand. Robinson also made a fifty on debut while Johnson and Newton made their highest scores. Johnson reached his hundred from 180 balls but was left six runs short of a double century. Snedden (who made 2) had helped add 50 for the last wicket.

In response to Wellington's 469, Otago were 164-5 by the end of the second day. No play was possible on the third day and Wellington forfeited their innings on the last morning after Otago declared. Otago reached their target for the loss of just three wickets with Phillips reaching his century from 147 balls and sharing a 178 run partnership with Kelly.

## WELLINGTON

| FIRST INNINGS | Runs | Mins | Balls | 6s | 4s | SECOND INNINGS | Runs | Mins | Balls | 6s | 4s |
|---|---|---|---|---|---|---|---|---|---|---|---|
| R.Ravindra c Chu b Rae | 56 | 124 | 90 | - | 9 | | | | | | |
| K.L.D.Vishvaka c Kelly b Duffy | 56 | 129 | 82 | 1 | 9 | | | | | | |
| T.M.Johnson not out | 194 | 411 | 299 | 3 | 27 | | | | | | |
| J.J.N.P.Bhula lbw b McKay | 6 | 16 | 12 | - | 1 | | | | | | |
| T.B.Robinson b Rae | 54 | 169 | 114 | - | 8 | | | | | | |
| T.A.Blundell*† c Phillips b Rae | 0 | 6 | 4 | - | - | | | | | | |
| J.D.Gibson c Chu b Rippon | 0 | 6 | 5 | - | - | | | | | | |
| N.G.Smith lbw b Muller | 8 | 31 | 21 | - | 1 | | | | | | |
| O.R.Newton c Muller b McKay | 70 | 100 | 87 | 2 | 11 | | | | | | |
| I.G.McPeake b McKay | 9 | 29 | 22 | - | - | | | | | | |
| M.W.Snedden b Rippon | 2 | 44 | 19 | - | - | | | | | | |
| Extras (lb 5, w 4, nb 5) | 14 | | | | | | | | | | |
| **TOTAL** (125 overs) | **469** | 536 | | | | Innings forfeited | | | | | |

## OTAGO

| | Runs | Mins | Balls | 6s | 4s | | Runs | Mins | Balls | 6s | 4s |
|---|---|---|---|---|---|---|---|---|---|---|---|
| H.D.Rutherford* c Johnson b Smith | 44 | 132 | 81 | - | 8 | c Blundell b McPeake | 36 | 62 | 44 | - | 7 |
| M.Renwick c Ravindra b McPeake | 20 | 90 | 69 | - | 3 | c Robinson b McPeake | 27 | 73 | 45 | - | 5 |
| D.N.Phillips run out | 12 | 87 | 63 | 1 | - | c Vishvaka b Newton | 114 | 178 | 158 | - | 21 |
| N.F.Kelly c Robinson b Smith | 48 | 117 | 84 | 1 | 5 | not out | 85 | 224 | 133 | - | 13 |
| J.M.Cumming not out | 22 | 98 | 72 | - | 2 | not out | 28 | 57 | 46 | - | 4 |
| M.J.G.Rippon c Smith b Ravindra | 0 | 10 | 3 | - | - | | | | | | |
| M.W.Chu† not out | 2 | 15 | 11 | - | - | | | | | | |
| T.Muller | | | | | | | | | | | |
| J.A.Duffy | | | | | | | | | | | |
| M.D.Rae | | | | | | | | | | | |
| J.D.McKay | | | | | | | | | | | |
| Extras (lb 9, w 2, nb 5) | 16 | | | | | (b 6, lb 2, w 1, nb 10) | 19 | | | | |
| **TOTAL** (63 overs) (5 wkts dec) | **164** | 276 | | | | (69.2 overs) (3 wkts) | **309** | 298 | | | |

| Bowling | O | M | R | W | O | M | R | W |
|---|---|---|---|---|---|---|---|---|
| **OTAGO** | | | | | | | | |
| Duffy | 28 | 9 | 79 | 1 | | | | |
| Muller | 17 | 5 | 58 | 1 | | | | |
| Rae | 27 | 6 | 135 | 3 | | | | |
| McKay | 22 | 3 | 99 | 3 | | | | |
| Rippon | 31 | 4 | 93 | 2 | | | | |
| **WELLINGTON** | | | | | | | | |
| Smith | 16 | 5 | 34 | 2 | 12 | 1 | 63 | 0 |
| Newton | 15 | 5 | 37 | 0 | 15 | 2 | 64 | 1 |
| McPeake | 11 | 4 | 20 | 1 | 8 | 1 | 36 | 2 |
| Snedden | 11 | 2 | 30 | 0 | 17 | 1 | 63 | 0 |
| Gibson | 1 | 0 | 5 | 0 | 4 | 0 | 24 | 0 |
| Ravindra | 9 | 1 | 29 | 1 | 13.2 | 1 | 51 | 0 |

| Fall of Wickets | | | | |
|---|---|---|---|---|
| | W | O | W | O |
| | 1st | 1st | 2nd | 2nd |
| 1st | 113 | 54 | - | 64 |
| 2nd | 113 | 80 | - | 71 |
| 3rd | 119 | 104 | - | 249 |
| 4th | 263 | 158 | - | - |
| 5th | 265 | 161 | - | - |
| 6th | 266 | - | - | - |
| 7th | 291 | - | - | - |
| 8th | 393 | - | - | - |
| 9th | 419 | - | - | - |
| 10th | 469 | - | - | - |

## CENTRAL DISTRICTS v CANTERBURY — Plunket Shield

*at Fitzherbert Park, Palmerston North on 20, 21, 22, 23 March, 2022*
*Toss : Canterbury. Umpires : C.A. Black, J.M. Dempsey & G.M. Walklin*
*Close of play: 1st day: Canterbury 341-8, McConchie 136, Sheat 15;*
*2nd day: Canterbury 438-8, McConchie 187, Sheat 60; 3rd day: Canterbury 81-3, Nicholls 20*
**Match drawn.** *Points: Canterbury 6 (4 bat, 2 bowl), Central Districts 4 (1 bat, 3 bowl)*

Canterbury decided to bat and were 341-8 at the close of play. McConchie's hundred had come from 168 balls. Just 16 overs were possible on the second day with Canterbury scoring 97 runs, McConchie reaching his highest score and Sheat making his first fifty. Their unbeaten partnership of 138 was a Canterbury ninth wicket record against Central.

McConchie declared before the third day began and saw Central reach 203-5 before they also declared and Canterbury were batting again before stumps. Only 32 overs were possible on the last day, with Central reaching 99-0.

Clark and O'Rourke (son of former Wellington player Paddy) made their first-class debuts in this game and Dudding made his first appearance since 2016/17.

### CANTERBURY

| FIRST INNINGS | Runs | Mins | Balls | 6s | 4s |
|---|---|---|---|---|---|
| C.J.Bowes c Dudding b Field | 50 | 95 | 70 | - | 6 |
| K.J.McClure c Bruce b Toole | 13 | 29 | 20 | - | 3 |
| H.M.Nicholls c Bruce b Clark | 2 | 33 | 24 | - | - |
| C.E.McConchie* not out | 187 | 405 | 246 | 2 | 20 |
| L.J.Carter c Field b Toole | 24 | 42 | 30 | 1 | 3 |
| C.D.Fletcher† c Leopard b Toole | 4 | 14 | 10 | - | 1 |
| Z.G.Foulkes c Wiggins b Dudding | 49 | 88 | 79 | 1 | 4 |
| T.F.van Woerkom c Patel b Clark | 32 | 106 | 97 | - | 5 |
| W.S.A.Williams c & b Toole | 1 | 13 | 15 | - | - |
| F.W.Sheat not out | 60 | 106 | 81 | 1 | 10 |
| W.P.O'Rourke | | | | | |
| Extras (b 3, lb 12, w 1) | 16 | | | | |
| **TOTAL** (112 overs) (8 wkts dec) | **438** | 468 | | | |

| SECOND INNINGS | Runs | Mins | Balls | 6s | 4s |
|---|---|---|---|---|---|
| (2) b Toole | 22 | 26 | 18 | - | 5 |
| (1) lbw b Patel | 36 | 43 | 35 | - | 3 |
| not out | 20 | 22 | 9 | 1 | 2 |
| c Schmulian b Toole | 0 | 5 | 1 | - | - |
| (lb 2, w 1) | 3 | | | | |
| (10.3 overs) (3 wkts dec) | 81 | 49 | | | |

### CENTRAL DISTRICTS

| | Runs | Mins | Balls | 6s | 4s |
|---|---|---|---|---|---|
| G.R.Hay* b Foulkes | 18 | 59 | 42 | - | 3 |
| B.S.Smith c Nicholls b Foulkes | 21 | 124 | 90 | - | 3 |
| B.D.Schmulian c McConchie b O'Rourke | 1 | 25 | 15 | - | - |
| T.C.Bruce not out | 90 | 222 | 152 | 1 | 9 |
| C.K.Leopard c McClure b Foulkes | 0 | 2 | 2 | - | - |
| B.L.Wiggins† c & b van Woerkom | 23 | 53 | 35 | - | 5 |
| J.F.A.Field not out | 34 | 127 | 111 | - | 3 |
| W.J.Clark | | | | | |
| A.Y.Patel | | | | | |
| R.L.Toole | | | | | |
| L.R.Dudding | | | | | |
| Extras (b 4, lb 5, w 4, nb 3) | 16 | | | | |
| **TOTAL** (74 overs) (5 wkts dec) | **203** | 307 | | | |

| | Runs | Mins | Balls | 6s | 4s |
|---|---|---|---|---|---|
| not out | 41 | 143 | 80 | - | 7 |
| not out | 40 | 143 | 112 | - | 6 |
| (b 1, lb 13, w 4) | 18 | | | | |
| (32 overs) (0 wkts) | 99 | 143 | | | |

| Bowling | O | M | R | W | O | M | R | W |
|---|---|---|---|---|---|---|---|---|
| **CENTRAL DISTRICTS** | | | | | | | | |
| Toole | 30 | 5 | 119 | 4 | 5.3 | 0 | 36 | 2 |
| Dudding | 17 | 2 | 63 | 1 | 4 | 0 | 39 | 0 |
| Field | 20 | 3 | 78 | 1 | | | | |
| Clark | 22 | 3 | 78 | 2 | | | | |
| Patel | 19 | 2 | 74 | 0 | 1 | 0 | 4 | 1 |
| Schmulian | 3 | 1 | 10 | 0 | | | | |
| Bruce | 1 | 0 | 1 | 0 | | | | |
| **CANTERBURY** | | | | | | | | |
| Williams | 14 | 6 | 25 | 0 | 10 | 5 | 22 | 0 |
| Sheat | 14 | 4 | 32 | 0 | 11 | 5 | 21 | 0 |
| Foulkes | 12 | 2 | 32 | 3 | 4 | 0 | 20 | 0 |
| O'Rourke | 11 | 5 | 27 | 1 | 7 | 1 | 22 | 0 |
| van Woerkom | 17 | 4 | 60 | 1 | | | | |
| Nicholls | 1 | 0 | 1 | 0 | | | | |
| McConchie | 5 | 0 | 17 | 0 | | | | |

| Fall of Wickets | C | CD | C | CD |
|---|---|---|---|---|
| | 1st | 1st | 2nd | 2nd |
| 1st | 25 | 36 | 41 | - |
| 2nd | 55 | 41 | 79 | - |
| 3rd | 75 | 44 | 81 | - |
| 4th | 115 | 44 | - | - |
| 5th | 125 | 92 | - | - |
| 6th | 211 | - | - | - |
| 7th | 297 | - | - | - |
| 8th | 300 | - | - | - |
| 9th | - | - | - | - |
| 10th | - | - | - | - |

*Walklin replaced Black as umpire after the second day*

**NZC**

# AUCKLAND v WELLINGTON                    Plunket Shield

*at Kennards Hire Community Oval, Auckland on 28, 29, 30 March, 2022*
*Toss : Auckland.  Umpires : C.A. Black & B.F. Bowden*
*Close of play: 1st day: Auckland 349-3, R.R.O'Donnell 118, Delport 16;*
*          2nd day: Wellington 36-1, Ravindra 14, Johnson 3*
**Auckland won by 10 wickets.** *Points: Auckland 20 (4 bat, 4 bowl), Wellington 2 (2 bowl)*

Auckland reached 349-3 by the end of the first day, after deciding to bat. Solia made his maiden hundred from 249 balls and Robbie O'Donnell scored his century from 132 deliveries. Their partnership of 213 was an Auckland third wicket record against Wellington.

Auckland finally declared at 469-8 and then took a wicket in the first over when they bowled. Robinson (maiden hundred from 112 balls) was the only Wellington player to offer any significant resistance. He was on 88 when the ninth wicket fell and hit 6-1-6 over the next seven deliveries to reach his hundred.

Wellington followed on and were all out for 281 on the third day with all six of the Auckland bowlers being successful. The home side needed just nine balls to record a ten wicket win with a day to spare.

## AUCKLAND

| FIRST INNINGS | Runs | Mins | Balls | 6s | 4s | SECOND INNINGS | Runs | Mins | Balls | 6s | 4s |
|---|---|---|---|---|---|---|---|---|---|---|---|
| W.T.O'Donnell c Bhula b McPeake ..... | 36 | 92 | 61 | 1 | 6 | not out ................................... 5 | | 7 | 8 | - | 1 |
| S.M.Solia c Bhula b Snedden ........... | 135 | 360 | 301 | 2 | 19 | not out ................................... 4 | | 7 | 1 | - | 1 |
| C.J.Briggs run out ............................. | 20 | 62 | 36 | - | 3 | | | | | | |
| R.R.O'Donnell* c Blundell b Snedden | 130 | 246 | 173 | 4 | 17 | | | | | | |
| L.J.Delport b Smith .......................... | 16 | 58 | 34 | - | 4 | | | | | | |
| R.D.Harrison run out ......................... | 46 | 79 | 51 | 2 | 7 | | | | | | |
| B.J.Horne† c Ravindra b Younghusband | 38 | 72 | 47 | - | 5 | | | | | | |
| W.E.R.Somerville c Blundell | | | | | | | | | | | |
| b Younghusband ............................. | 15 | 12 | 10 | 1 | 1 | | | | | | |
| S.B.Keene not out ............................ | 1 | 2 | 1 | - | - | | | | | | |
| O.M.R.Pringle | | | | | | | | | | | |
| B.G.Lister | | | | | | | | | | | |
| Extras (b 4, lb 8, w 13, nb 7) ............ 32 | | | | | | ................................................ 0 | | | | | |
| **TOTAL** (118 overs) (8 wkts dec) ... **469** | 495 | | | | | (1.3 overs) (0 wkts) ............... **9** | | 7 | | | |

## WELLINGTON

| | Runs | Mins | Balls | 6s | 4s | | Runs | Mins | Balls | 6s | 4s |
|---|---|---|---|---|---|---|---|---|---|---|---|
| K.L.D.Vishvaka c O'Donnell R.R. b Lister | 0 | 3 | 6 | - | - | c Somerville b Lister ............ | 14 | 20 | 18 | - | 3 |
| R.Ravindra c Horne b Keene .............. | 23 | 66 | 37 | - | 4 | c Horne b Solia ................... | 58 | 244 | 161 | - | 9 |
| T.M.Johnson c Horne b Keene ........... | 19 | 40 | 32 | - | 2 | b Keene .............................. | 12 | 68 | 48 | - | 1 |
| J.J.N.P.Bhula c O'Donnell W.T. b Keene | 0 | 2 | 3 | - | - | c O'Donnell W.T. b Somerville | 1 | 6 | 7 | - | - |
| T.B.Robinson not out ........................ | 103 | 188 | 116 | 3 | 14 | lbw b Delport ...................... | 28 | 71 | 55 | - | 6 |
| T.A.Blundell*† c O'Donnell W.T. b Keene | 20 | 64 | 41 | - | 2 | c Horne b Solia ................... | 33 | 101 | 75 | - | 6 |
| N.G.Smith lbw b Keene .................... | 6 | 17 | 13 | - | 1 | c O'Donnell W.T. b Delport .... | 1 | 32 | 13 | - | - |
| P.F.Younghusband c Horne b Keene .... | 1 | 9 | 6 | - | - | not out ............................... | 36 | 134 | 95 | 1 | 4 |
| O.R.Newton run out ........................... | 6 | 12 | 9 | - | 1 | c Harrison b Pringle ............. | 40 | 65 | 51 | 3 | 3 |
| I.G.McPeake c O'Donnell W.T. | | | | | | c O'Donnell R.R. b Keene ..... | 6 | 26 | 19 | - | 1 |
| b Somerville ................................... | 15 | 48 | 39 | - | 1 | | | | | | |
| M.W.Snedden c Briggs b Somerville .... | 1 | 15 | 9 | - | - | c Harrison b Delport ........... | 19 | 34 | 31 | - | 3 |
| Extras (nb 1) ................................... | 1 | | | | | (b 19, lb 6, nb 8) ................. | 33 | | | | |
| **TOTAL** (51.4 overs) ..................... **195** | 236 | | | | | (94.1 overs) ...................... **281** | 405 | | | | |

| Bowling | O | M | R | W | O | M | R | W |
|---|---|---|---|---|---|---|---|---|
| **WELLINGTON** | | | | | | | | |
| Smith | 22 | 6 | 67 | 1 | 1 | 0 | 5 | 0 |
| Newton | 21 | 4 | 75 | 0 | | | | |
| Snedden | 20 | 6 | 57 | 2 | 0.3 | 0 | 4 | 0 |
| McPeake | 17 | 2 | 71 | 1 | | | | |
| Ravindra | 23 | 3 | 97 | 0 | | | | |
| Younghusband | 13 | 0 | 79 | 2 | | | | |
| Bhula | 2 | 0 | 11 | 0 | | | | |
| **AUCKLAND** | | | | | | | | |
| Lister | 8 | 1 | 30 | 1 | 18 | 3 | 63 | 1 |
| Pringle | 6 | 1 | 16 | 0 | 9 | 1 | 38 | 1 |
| Keene | 13 | 5 | 51 | 6 | 20 | 7 | 38 | 2 |
| Solia | 7 | 1 | 33 | 0 | 14 | 4 | 43 | 2 |
| Somerville | 12.4 | 0 | 48 | 2 | 14 | 6 | 30 | 1 |
| Delport | 5 | 0 | 17 | 0 | 19.1 | 7 | 44 | 3 |

| Fall of Wickets | A | W | W | A |
|---|---|---|---|---|
| | 1st | 1st | 2nd | 2nd |
| 1st | 70 | 0 | 18 | - |
| 2nd | 110 | 42 | 53 | - |
| 3rd | 323 | 42 | 54 | - |
| 4th | 362 | 43 | 107 | - |
| 5th | 371 | 89 | 151 | - |
| 6th | 448 | 113 | 163 | - |
| 7th | 461 | 121 | 163 | - |
| 8th | 469 | 133 | 234 | - |
| 9th | - | 179 | 247 | - |
| 10th | - | 195 | 281 | - |

# NORTHERN DISTRICTS v CENTRAL DISTRICTS Plunket Shield

*at Cobham Oval, Whangarei on 29, 30, 31 March, 1 April, 2022*
*Toss : Northern Districts. Umpires : J.M. Dempsey & D.J. Walker*
*Close of play: 1st day: ND 303-0, Raval 163, Popli 133; 2nd day: CD 131-2, Schmulian 39, Bruce 50*
*3rd day: ND 25-1, Popli 9, Clarke 11*
**Match drawn.** *Points: not awarded*

Northern Districts batted first and recorded the highest partnership in their first-class history. It was also the highest first wicket partenship by any team against Central. Raval reached his hundred from 218 balls and his two hundred 147 balls later. Popli's hundred came from 209 balls. Raval's score was the highest in a first-class game at the ground.

Central also found batting conditions to their liking. Bruce reached his hundred from 169 balls and his first double century from 305 deliveries. There was no play on the last day after the match was called off because of a Covid outbreak amongst the players. Freddy Walker made his first-class debut in this game.

## NORTHERN DISTRICTS

| FIRST INNINGS | Runs | Mins | Balls | 6s | 4s | SECOND INNINGS | Runs | Mins | Balls | 6s | 4s |
|---|---|---|---|---|---|---|---|---|---|---|---|
| J.A.Raval c Lennox b Patel | 209 | 497 | 373 | 4 | 18 | c Field b Clark | 3 | 6 | 7 | - | - |
| B.Popli c Hay b Toole | 150 | 422 | 295 | 1 | 13 | not out | 9 | 52 | 29 | - | 1 |
| K.D.Clarke b Patel | 8 | 14 | 9 | 1 | - | not out | 11 | 45 | 36 | - | 1 |
| J.F.Carter* c Bruce b Toole | 43 | 106 | 85 | 1 | 3 | | | | | | |
| B.R.Hampton c Lennox b Patel | 47 | 60 | 41 | 3 | 1 | | | | | | |
| P.D.Bocock† c Hay b Patel | 15 | 17 | 14 | - | 2 | | | | | | |
| S.C.Kuggeleijn not out | 12 | 9 | 6 | - | 2 | | | | | | |
| B.G.Randell not out | 1 | 6 | 3 | - | - | | | | | | |
| N.Wagner | | | | | | | | | | | |
| J.G.Walker | | | | | | | | | | | |
| F.L.Walker | | | | | | | | | | | |
| Extras (lb 2, w 5, nb 4) | 11 | | | | | (lb 2) | 2 | | | | |
| **TOTAL** (137 overs) (6 wkts dec) | **496** | 567 | | | | (12 overs) (1 wkt) | **25** | 52 | | | |

## CENTRAL DISTRICTS

| | Runs | Mins | Balls | 6s | 4s |
|---|---|---|---|---|---|
| G.R.Hay* c Kuggeleijn b Hampton | 7 | 53 | 30 | - | - |
| W.J.Clark c Carter b Walker J.G. | 14 | 87 | 68 | - | 1 |
| B.D.Schmulian b Randell | 98 | 320 | 234 | - | 7 |
| T.C.Bruce not out | 208 | 498 | 308 | 2 | 19 |
| J.A.Clarkson c Bocock b Randell | 0 | 15 | 4 | - | - |
| J.F.A.Field st Bocock b Walker J.G. | 16 | 65 | 56 | - | 3 |
| A.Y.Patel c Randell b Walker J.G. | 14 | 57 | 55 | - | 1 |
| D.Cleaver† c Carter b Hampton | 17 | 61 | 55 | - | 1 |
| J.R.Lennox not out | 4 | 11 | 4 | - | - |
| B.S.Smith | | | | | |
| R.L.Toole | | | | | |
| Extras (b 8, lb 7, w 11, nb 4) | 30 | | | | |
| **TOTAL** (135 overs) (7 wkts dec) | **408** | 586 | | | |

| Bowling | O | M | R | W | | | | | | | | Fall of Wickets | | | |
|---|---|---|---|---|---|---|---|---|---|---|---|---|---|---|---|
| **CENTRAL DISTRICTS** | | | | | | | | | | | | | ND | CD | ND |
| Toole | 29 | 7 | 104 | 2 | 5 | 1 | 15 | 0 | | | | | 1st | 1st | 2nd |
| Clark | 14 | 3 | 60 | 0 | 3 | 1 | 5 | 1 | | | | 1st | 334 | 28 | 3 |
| Field | 18 | 2 | 55 | 0 | | | | | | | | 2nd | 350 | 36 | - |
| Clarkson | 5 | 2 | 15 | 0 | | | | | | | | 3rd | 399 | 254 | - |
| Patel | 46 | 8 | 133 | 4 | 3 | 3 | 0 | 0 | | | | 4th | 462 | 256 | - |
| Lennox | 15 | 1 | 76 | 0 | 1 | 0 | 3 | 0 | | | | 5th | 479 | 294 | - |
| Bruce | 7 | 0 | 25 | 0 | | | | | | | | 6th | 484 | 330 | - |
| Schmulian | 3 | 0 | 26 | 0 | | | | | | | | 7th | - | 394 | - |
| **NORTHERN DISTRICTS** | | | | | | | | | | | | 8th | - | - | - |
| Wagner | 28 | 6 | 64 | 0 | | | | | | | | 9th | - | - | - |
| Randell | 22 | 8 | 42 | 2 | | | | | | | | 10th | - | - | - |
| Kuggeleijn | 15 | 2 | 46 | 0 | | | | | | | | | | | |
| Hampton | 10 | 1 | 29 | 2 | | | | | | | | | | | |
| Walker J.G. | 35 | 3 | 99 | 3 | | | | | | | | | | | |
| Walker F.L. | 17 | 4 | 63 | 0 | | | | | | | | | | | |
| Raval | 8 | 0 | 50 | 0 | | | | | | | | | | | |

*Smith and B.L.Wiggins (sub) replaced Cleaver as wicketkeeper during Northern Districts' first innings. Wiggins kept in the second innings*

# CANTERBURY v OTAGO

**Plunket Shield**

*at MainPower Oval, Rangiora on 29, 30, 31 March, 1 April, 2022*
*Toss : Canterbury. Umpires : J.A.K. Bromley & T.J. Parlane*
*Close of play: 1st day: Otago 196-4, Cumming 15, Chu 14; 2nd day: Canterbury 153-2, Bowes 79, Boyle 32*
*3rd day: Otago 107-3, Phillips 65, Lockrose 0*
**Match drawn.** *Points: Canterbury 8 (4 bat, 4 bowl), Otago 6 (2 bat, 4 bowl)*

Fifties to Rutherford and Phillips were the highlight of Otago's first innings. In Canterbury's innings Bowes was run out the ball after reaching his century while Hay (on debut) and Davey both registered maiden fifties.

Otago had almost erased their deficit of 112 by the end of the third day. Just 29.4 overs were possible on the last day with Phillips being on 97 when the game was called off.

## OTAGO

| FIRST INNINGS | Runs | Mins | Balls | 6s | 4s |
|---|---|---|---|---|---|
| H.D.Rutherford* b O'Rourke | 70 | 245 | 164 | - | 7 |
| M.Renwick c McClure b Davey | 17 | 65 | 46 | - | 3 |
| D.N.Phillips c Davey b McConchie | 63 | 165 | 126 | - | 7 |
| N.F.Kelly c Hay b Sheat | 3 | 26 | 16 | - | - |
| J.M.Cumming c Bowes b Sheat | 37 | 155 | 107 | - | 5 |
| M.W.Chu† c McClure b Williams | 20 | 105 | 82 | - | 3 |
| J.M.Gibson c Hay b Williams | 0 | 15 | 11 | - | - |
| J.A.Duffy c Foulkes b O'Rourke | 24 | 47 | 31 | - | 3 |
| B.N.J.Lockrose b Sheat | 0 | 9 | 2 | - | - |
| M.D.Rae b O'Rourke | 8 | 16 | 12 | - | - |
| J.D.McKay not out | 0 | 1 | 0 | - | - |
| T.Muller | | | | | |
| Extras (b 4, lb 2, w 5, nb 4) | 15 | | | | |
| **TOTAL** (98.5 overs) | **257** | 427 | | | |

| SECOND INNINGS | Runs | Mins | Balls | 6s | 4s |
|---|---|---|---|---|---|
| lbw b Davey | 21 | 86 | 56 | - | 2 |
| lbw b Sheat | 0 | 5 | 2 | - | - |
| not out | 97 | 295 | 175 | - | 10 |
| b Williams | 20 | 75 | 45 | - | 3 |
| (6) c Williams b O'Rourke | 13 | 65 | 50 | - | 1 |
| (7) b O'Rourke | 0 | 9 | 7 | - | - |
| | | | | | |
| | | | | | |
| (5) c Hay b Williams | 1 | 18 | 16 | - | - |
| | | | | | |
| | | | | | |
| (8) not out | 5 | 45 | 36 | - | - |
| (b 8, lb 1, w 2, nb 1) | 12 | | | | |
| (64.2 overs) (6 wkts) | **169** | 300 | | | |

## CANTERBURY

| | Runs | Mins | Balls | 6s | 4s |
|---|---|---|---|---|---|
| C.J.Bowes run out | 100 | 258 | 168 | - | 12 |
| K.J.McClure c Chu b McKay | 21 | 83 | 66 | - | 1 |
| C.E.McConchie* lbw b Gibson | 14 | 23 | 19 | - | 3 |
| J.C.T.Boyle c Gibson b McKay | 43 | 123 | 103 | - | 3 |
| L.J.Carter lbw b Gibson | 3 | 18 | 10 | - | - |
| Z.G.Foulkes c Chu b McKay | 11 | 71 | 50 | - | - |
| M.J.Hay† c Kelly b Gibson | 62 | 137 | 92 | - | 6 |
| S.B.Davey c Chu b Rae | 55 | 100 | 72 | - | 9 |
| W.S.A.Williams c McKay b Lockrose | 21 | 38 | 30 | - | 2 |
| F.W.Sheat c Chu b Lockrose | 18 | 23 | 12 | - | 3 |
| W.P.O'Rourke not out | 6 | 8 | 5 | - | 1 |
| Extras (lb 6, w 8, nb 1) | 15 | | | | |
| **TOTAL** (104.2 overs) | **369** | 445 | | | |

| Bowling | O | M | R | W | O | M | R | W |
|---|---|---|---|---|---|---|---|---|
| **CANTERBURY** | | | | | | | | |
| Williams | 23 | 8 | 41 | 2 | 13 | 2 | 28 | 2 |
| Sheat | 21 | 6 | 55 | 3 | 20 | 6 | 38 | 1 |
| Davey | 21 | 4 | 60 | 1 | 12 | 3 | 29 | 1 |
| O'Rourke | 17.5 | 4 | 56 | 3 | 15.2 | 2 | 51 | 2 |
| Foulkes | 12 | 2 | 37 | 0 | 4 | 0 | 14 | 0 |
| McConchie | 4 | 3 | 2 | 1 | | | | |
| **OTAGO** | | | | | | | | |
| Duffy | 27 | 6 | 86 | 0 | | | | |
| Rae | 29 | 5 | 118 | 1 | | | | |
| McKay | 19 | 5 | 59 | 3 | | | | |
| Gibson | 21 | 4 | 70 | 3 | | | | |
| Lockrose | 8.2 | 0 | 30 | 2 | | | | |

**Fall of Wickets**

| | O | C | O |
|---|---|---|---|
| | 1st | 1st | 2nd |
| 1st | 39 | 56 | 2 |
| 2nd | 158 | 79 | 53 |
| 3rd | 161 | 177 | 107 |
| 4th | 163 | 189 | 109 |
| 5th | 213 | 192 | 150 |
| 6th | 217 | 227 | 153 |
| 7th | 231 | 314 | - |
| 8th | 237 | 339 | - |
| 9th | 257 | 355 | - |
| 10th | 257 | 369 | - |

*Muller was a Covid substitute for Gibson on the fourth day*

# CENTRAL DISTRICTS v AUCKLAND

**Plunket Shield**

*at McLean Park, Napier on 5, 6, 7, 8 April, 2022*
*Toss : Central Districts. Umpires : B.F. Bowden & J.M. Dempsey*
*Close of play: 1st day: Auckland 84-5, McGregor-Sumpter 14, Somerville 0; 2nd day: CD 131-4. Bruce 62, Wiggins 21*
*3rd day: Auckland 9-1, O'Donnell 1, Briggs 1*
**Match drawn.** *Points: Central Districts 8 (4 bat, 4 bowl), Auckland 4 (1 bat, 3 bowl)*

McGregor-Sumpter and Sussex made their first-class debuts while Horne was captain for the first time in a first-class game. Auckland required one point to ensure they won the Plunket Shield for 2021/22 and they duly obtained this with a batting point when their score reached 200. Keene made his maiden fifty.

Central were struggling at 131-5 before Clarkson joined Bruce. Clarkson hit his first fifty while Bruce reached his hundred from 148 balls and, after facing 293 deliveries, became the first player in first-class cricket in New Zealand to register double centuries in successive innings. It was the highest score by a Central Districts player against Auckland.

With no chance of a victory, Auckland played out the last day with O'Donnell scoring 46 in 256 minutes and Harrison 23 in 255 minutes.

## AUCKLAND

| FIRST INNINGS | Runs | Mins | Balls | 6s | 4s | SECOND INNINGS | Runs | Mins | Balls | 6s | 4s |
|---|---|---|---|---|---|---|---|---|---|---|---|
| W.T.O'Donnell lbw b Tickner | 9 | 20 | 17 | - | 1 | c Wiggins b Schmulian | 46 | 256 | 179 | - | 5 |
| S.M.Solia c Wiggins b Tickner | 12 | 82 | 48 | - | 1 | b Clarkson | 6 | 14 | 11 | - | - |
| C.J.Briggs b Tickner | 22 | 46 | 40 | - | 4 | c & b Field | 15 | 25 | 22 | - | 3 |
| F.McGregor-Sumpter c Cleaver b Patel | 56 | 260 | 165 | - | 5 | c Bruce b Tickner | 0 | 11 | 7 | - | - |
| R.D.Harrison c Cleaver b Clarkson | 0 | 10 | 7 | - | - | lbw b Patel | 23 | 255 | 197 | - | 1 |
| B.J.Horne*† c Cleaver b Tickner | 23 | 51 | 49 | 1 | 3 | not out | 89 | 123 | 92 | 1 | 12 |
| W.E.R.Somerville c Clarkson b Tickner | 0 | 8 | 3 | - | - | | | | | | |
| S.B.Keene c Cleaver b Field | 65 | 142 | 108 | 1 | 7 | (7) lbw b Patel | 17 | 57 | 47 | - | 2 |
| O.M.R.Pringle c Wiggins b Field | 19 | 26 | 22 | 1 | 1 | | | | | | |
| L.J.Delport not out | 7 | 11 | 7 | - | 1 | | | | | | |
| J.D.Sussex c Wiggins b Field | 0 | 5 | 1 | - | - | | | | | | |
| R.M.ter Braak | | | | | | (8) not out | 0 | 14 | 14 | - | - |
| Extras (b 1, lb 1, w 1, nb 5) | 8 | | | | | (b 8, lb 6, w 3, nb 5) | 22 | | | | |
| **TOTAL** (77 overs) | **221** | 333 | | | | (94 overs) (6 wkts) | **218** | 379 | | | |

## CENTRAL DISTRICTS

| | Runs | Mins | Balls | 6s | 4s |
|---|---|---|---|---|---|
| G.R.Hay* b Sussex | 0 | 1 | 4 | - | - |
| B.S.Smith c Horne b Solia | 3 | 41 | 23 | - | - |
| B.D.Schmulian c McGregor-Sumpter b ter Braak | 38 | 131 | 86 | - | 6 |
| D.Cleaver† c Horne b Solia | 0 | 3 | 2 | - | - |
| T.C.Bruce not out | 204 | 455 | 302 | 2 | 23 |
| B.L.Wiggins b Sussex | 21 | 53 | 45 | - | 4 |
| J.A.Clarkson c Horne b Pringle | 83 | 198 | 144 | 3 | 9 |
| J.F.A.Field c Horne b Pringle | 5 | 25 | 19 | - | 1 |
| A.Y.Patel c Harrison b Solia | 5 | 19 | 11 | - | 1 |
| W.J.Clark c Sussex b ter Braak | 41 | 66 | 62 | 2 | 5 |
| B.M.Tickner c Delport b Sussex | 0 | 4 | 2 | - | - |
| Extras (lb 7, w 2, nb 6) | 15 | | | | |
| **TOTAL** (115.4 overs) | **415** | 500 | | | |

| Bowling | O | M | R | W | O | M | R | W |
|---|---|---|---|---|---|---|---|---|
| **CENTRAL DISTRICTS** | | | | | | | | |
| Tickner | 23 | 6 | 69 | 5 | 20 | 8 | 48 | 1 |
| Field | 19 | 4 | 50 | 3 | 14 | 3 | 39 | 1 |
| Clark | 13 | 4 | 33 | 0 | 5 | 1 | 15 | 0 |
| Clarkson | 9 | 0 | 30 | 1 | 7 | 1 | 28 | 1 |
| Patel | 13 | 0 | 37 | 1 | 34 | 23 | 37 | 2 |
| Schmulian | | | | | 9 | 2 | 28 | 1 |
| Bruce | | | | | 5 | 3 | 9 | 0 |
| **AUCKLAND** | | | | | | | | |
| Sussex | 16.4 | 5 | 36 | 3 | | | | |
| ter Braak | 17 | 1 | 56 | 2 | | | | |
| Keene | 20 | 3 | 84 | 0 | | | | |
| Solia | 22 | 1 | 76 | 3 | | | | |
| Pringle | 17 | 4 | 60 | 2 | | | | |
| Delport | 23 | 5 | 96 | 0 | | | | |

| Fall of Wickets | | A | CD | A |
|---|---|---|---|---|
| | | 1st | 1st | 2nd |
| 1st | | 11 | 0 | 7 |
| 2nd | | 37 | 11 | 24 |
| 3rd | | 50 | 11 | 25 |
| 4th | | 52 | 93 | 103 |
| 5th | | 84 | 131 | 132 |
| 6th | | 84 | 322 | 209 |
| 7th | | 191 | 336 | - |
| 8th | | 212 | 344 | - |
| 9th | | 214 | 414 | - |
| 10th | | 221 | 415 | - |

*In Auckland's first innings, Wiggins caught Pringle and Sussex while keeping wicket and Cleaver caught Keene and McGregor-Sumpter in the field. Ter Braak was a Covid substitute for Somerville on the second day.*

**NZC**

# NORTHERN DISTRICTS v WELLINGTON          Plunket Shield

*at Cobham Oval, Whangarei on 6, 7, 8 April, 2022*
*Toss : Northern Districts. Umpires : C.M. Brown & D.J. Walker*
*Close of play: 1st day: ND 183-9, Johnston 20, Fisher 28; 2nd day: Wellington 264-6, Blundell 42, Younghusband 25*
**Wellington won by 9 wickets.** *Points: Wellington 18 (2 bat, 4 bowl) Northern Districts 4 (4 bowl)*

After the Covid outbreak in their previous game, Northern were required to select an entirely new squad for this game. Lellman, Varcoe, Patel, Swanson, Drysdale, Pomare and Brown made their first-class debuts while Sodhi was captain at first-class level for the first time. McComb was also making his debut.

The inexperienced Northern batting lineup made 188 from 92.3 overs, with the last wicket contributing 57 runs. Wellington were 160-1 before Vishvaka fell for his highest score and Northern did well to restrict the visitors to 296.

Northern's second innings began badly and they were 8-3 after seven overs. Drysdale made 62 but the innings ended at 161. Wellington hit off the required runs in 12.4 overs to win with a day to spare.

## NORTHERN DISTRICTS

| FIRST INNINGS | | Runs | Mins | Balls | 6s | 4s | SECOND INNINGS | | Runs | Mins | Balls | 6s | 4s |
|---|---|---|---|---|---|---|---|---|---|---|---|---|---|
| F.F.Lellman | c & b Ravindra | 20 | 88 | 65 | - | 3 | b Smith | | 6 | 29 | 20 | - | 1 |
| S.S.Varcoe | c Johns b Hartshorn | 16 | 106 | 83 | - | - | b Smith | | 0 | 17 | 15 | - | - |
| S.K.Patel | lbw b Smith | 15 | 63 | 40 | - | 1 | lbw b Smith | | 0 | 1 | 1 | - | - |
| C.J.Swanson | c Blundell b McPeake | 45 | 128 | 120 | - | 6 | lbw b Smith | | 11 | 36 | 24 | - | 1 |
| R.P.O.Drysdale | lbw b Smith | 5 | 36 | 31 | - | - | lbw b Younghusband | | 62 | 129 | 89 | 1 | 5 |
| B.J.Pomare† | lbw b Younghusband | 0 | 12 | 10 | - | - | b Smith | | 23 | 39 | 32 | - | 1 |
| K.D.C.Clarke | c Smith b McPeake | 9 | 54 | 30 | - | - | lbw b McComb | | 26 | 88 | 77 | 1 | 1 |
| I.S.Sodhi* | c Smith b McPeake | 6 | 8 | 11 | - | 1 | c Hartshorn b Younghusband | 3 | 20 | 20 | - | - |
| J.H.Brown | c Blundell b McPeake | 8 | 20 | 14 | - | - | c Johnson b Younghusband | .. 1 | 7 | 5 | - | - |
| S.S.Johnston | c Johnson b McPeake | .. 25 | 87 | 72 | - | 2 | c Ravindra b McComb | | 3 | 35 | 33 | - | - |
| M.J.Fisher | not out | 28 | 79 | 84 | - | 3 | not out | | 5 | 31 | 31 | - | 1 |
| | Extras (b 5, lb 1, nb 5) | 11 | | | | | (b 16, lb 4, w 1) | | 21 | | | | |
| | **TOTAL** (92.3 overs) | **188** | 345 | | | | (57.5 overs) | | **161** | | | | |

## WELLINGTON

| | | Runs | Mins | Balls | 6s | 4s | | | Runs | Mins | Balls | 6s | 4s |
|---|---|---|---|---|---|---|---|---|---|---|---|---|---|
| K.L.D.Vishvaka | st Pomare b Sodhi | 80 | 194 | 137 | - | 9 | lbw b Drysdale | | 16 | 31 | 24 | - | 2 |
| R.Ravindra | c Pomare b Brown | 39 | 99 | 63 | - | 4 | not out | | 29 | 50 | 40 | - | 3 |
| T.M.Johnson | c Patel b Sodhi | 35 | 102 | 72 | - | 4 | not out | | 9 | 19 | 12 | - | 1 |
| T.B.Robinson | lbw b Fisher | 0 | 11 | 7 | - | - | | | | | | | |
| L.R.Johns | c Brown b Johnston | 21 | 33 | 27 | - | 3 | | | | | | | |
| T.A.Blundell*† | not out | 55 | 213 | 151 | - | 3 | | | | | | | |
| N.G.Smith | st Pomare b Sodhi | 2 | 25 | 20 | - | - | | | | | | | |
| P.F.Younghusband | lbw b Fisher | 36 | 126 | 112 | - | 4 | | | | | | | |
| I.G.McPeake | lbw b Fisher | 0 | 2 | 1 | - | - | | | | | | | |
| J.W.Hartshorn | c Pomare b Brown | 0 | 6 | 7 | - | - | | | | | | | |
| K.J.McComb | b Sodhi | 0 | 17 | 12 | - | - | | | | | | | |
| | Extras (b 15, lb 4, w 6, nb 3) | 28 | | | | | | | 0 | | | | |
| | **TOTAL** (101 overs) | **296** | 420 | | | | (12.4 overs) (1 wkt) | | **54** | 50 | | | |

| Bowling | O | M | R | W | O | M | R | W |
|---|---|---|---|---|---|---|---|---|
| **WELLINGTON** | | | | | | | | |
| Smith | 20 | 11 | 25 | 2 | 15 | 7 | 35 | 5 |
| McPeake | 18.3 | 5 | 36 | 5 | 6 | 1 | 22 | 0 |
| Hartshorn | 11 | 2 | 35 | 1 | 8 | 1 | 20 | 0 |
| Ravindra | 10 | 4 | 41 | 1 | 1 | 0 | 10 | 0 |
| McComb | 18 | 7 | 23 | 0 | 7.5 | 2 | 11 | 2 |
| Younghusband | 15 | 5 | 22 | 1 | 20 | 7 | 43 | 3 |
| **NORTHERN DISTRICTS** | | | | | | | | |
| Clarke | 15 | 1 | 60 | 0 | | | | |
| Fisher | 19 | 5 | 67 | 2 | 4 | 0 | 21 | 0 |
| Johnston | 11 | 3 | 31 | 1 | | | | |
| Brown | 16 | 2 | 31 | 2 | | | | |
| Sodhi | 32 | 6 | 65 | 5 | 3.4 | 0 | 22 | 0 |
| Drysdale | 8 | 1 | 23 | 0 | 5 | 1 | 11 | 1 |

| Fall of Wickets | | | | |
|---|---|---|---|---|
| | ND | W | ND | W |
| | *1st* | *1st* | *2nd* | *2nd* |
| 1st | 35 | 94 | 5 | 37 |
| 2nd | 39 | 160 | 5 | - |
| 3rd | 64 | 161 | 8 | - |
| 4th | 83 | 162 | 32 | - |
| 5th | 84 | 194 | 82 | - |
| 6th | 113 | 199 | 126 | - |
| 7th | 119 | 283 | 144 | - |
| 8th | 127 | 283 | 146 | - |
| 9th | 131 | 285 | 146 | - |
| 10th | 188 | 296 | 161 | - |

# CANTERBURY v AUCKLAND · Plunket Shield

*at Bert Sutcliffe Oval, Lincoln on 12, 13, 14, 15 April, 2022*
*Toss : Canterbury. Umpires : J.M. Dempsey & W.R. Knights*
*Close of play: 1st day: Canterbury 154-1, Bowes 90, Nicholls 33; 2nd day: Auckland 88-6, Solia 6, Somerville 2*
*3rd day: Auckland 6-0, Guptill 6, Worker 0*
**Canterbury won by 98 runs.** *Points: Canterbury 19 (3 bat, 4 bowl), Auckland 4 (4 bowl)*

Auckland, who had already won the Plunket Shield, bowled on a shortened first day. Canterbury reached 154-1 at stumps and went on to total 325 the following day. Bowes took 129 balls for his hundred. Delport returned his best figures and the best in a first-class game at the ground.

Auckland were 88-6 at the end of the second day and it was left to Somerville (37) to make the highest score the next day while van Woerkom had his first five wicket bag. Canterbury extended their lead of 153 and left Auckland to score 372 for victory.

Will O'Donnell was Auckland's main contributor in their second innings and was unbeaten on 119 when the innings ended. He took 233 balls to reach his hundred as Auckland suffered their only loss of the competition.

## CANTERBURY

| FIRST INNINGS | Runs | Mins | Balls | 6s | 4s | SECOND INNINGS | Runs | Mins | Balls | 6s | 4s |
|---|---|---|---|---|---|---|---|---|---|---|---|
| C.J.Bowes c Horne b Delport | 127 | 249 | 166 | 1 | 19 | (2) c Keene b Somerville | 22 | 54 | 54 | - | 2 |
| K.J.McClure c Horne b Solia | 22 | 49 | 40 | - | 4 | (1) c Guptill b Somerville | 16 | 45 | 36 | - | 2 |
| H.M.Nicholls c Chapman b Keene | 45 | 111 | 73 | 1 | 7 | lbw b Keene | 72 | 103 | 74 | 2 | 8 |
| C.E.McConchie* c O'Donnell W.T. b Delport | 56 | 105 | 91 | - | 12 | c Chapman b Solia | 34 | 60 | 39 | 1 | 5 |
| L.J.Carter not out | 39 | 121 | 102 | - | 6 | not out | 36 | 77 | 49 | - | 4 |
| C.D.Fletcher† c Worker b Delport | 0 | 10 | 9 | - | - | c Worker b Somerville | 4 | 12 | 11 | - | - |
| Z.G.Foulkes c Somerville b Delport | 0 | 9 | 10 | - | - | c Guptill b Somerville | 11 | 20 | 19 | 1 | - |
| S.B.Davey st Horne b Delport | 0 | 16 | 13 | - | - | not out | 13 | 11 | 6 | 1 | 1 |
| T.F.van Woerkom lbw b Delport | 9 | 31 | 27 | - | 1 | | | | | | |
| W.S.A.Williams lbw b Somerville | 0 | 10 | 10 | - | - | | | | | | |
| W.P.O'Rourke c Guptill b Delport | 4 | 25 | 20 | - | 1 | | | | | | |
| Extras (b 9, lb 6, w 1, nb 7) | 23 | | | | | (b 4, lb 4, w 2) | 10 | | | | |
| **TOTAL** (92.2 overs) | **325** | 371 | | | | (48 overs) (6 wkts dec) | **218** | 192 | | | |

## AUCKLAND

| | Runs | Mins | Balls | 6s | 4s | | Runs | Mins | Balls | 6s | 4s |
|---|---|---|---|---|---|---|---|---|---|---|---|
| M.J.Guptill c Fletcher b Williams | 0 | 1 | 1 | - | - | lbw b McConchie | 33 | 54 | 40 | 1 | 5 |
| G.H.Worker c Carter b van Woerkom | 29 | 74 | 65 | 1 | 3 | lbw b Williams | 7 | 11 | 8 | 1 | - |
| W.T.O'Donnell c Carter b McConchie | 9 | 29 | 18 | - | 2 | not out | 119 | 323 | 241 | 1 | 16 |
| M.S.Chapman c Nicholls b McConchie | 14 | 32 | 28 | - | 2 | b McConchie | 17 | 26 | 26 | - | 2 |
| R.R.O'Donnell* c Nicholls b van Woerkom | 6 | 17 | 15 | - | 1 | c McClure b Williams | 31 | 68 | 53 | - | 4 |
| B.J.Horne† lbw b McConchie | 16 | 23 | 20 | - | 3 | b Davey | 35 | 91 | 73 | - | 4 |
| S.M.Solia c & b van Woerkom | 29 | 136 | 125 | - | 4 | c Fletcher b O'Rourke | 11 | 40 | 36 | - | 2 |
| W.E.R.Somerville c sub (F.W.Sheat) b van Woerkom | 37 | 100 | 92 | - | 4 | c Fletcher b O'Rourke | 2 | 9 | 8 | - | - |
| S.B.Keene c Carter b McConchie | 5 | 42 | 26 | - | - | b O'Rourke | 0 | 7 | 5 | - | - |
| L.J.Delport st Fletcher b van Woerkom | 12 | 20 | 16 | 1 | - | b van Woerkom | 4 | 7 | 5 | - | 1 |
| B.G.Lister not out | 0 | 4 | 3 | - | - | c McClure b Williams | 5 | 28 | 19 | - | 1 |
| Extras (b 11, lb 4) | 15 | | | | | (b 9) | 9 | | | | |
| **TOTAL** (68.1 overs) | **172** | 240 | | | | (85.4 overs) | **273** | 334 | | | |

| Bowling | O | M | R | W | O | M | R | W |
|---|---|---|---|---|---|---|---|---|
| **AUCKLAND** | | | | | | | | |
| Lister | 12 | 0 | 60 | 0 | | | | |
| Keene | 14 | 3 | 44 | 1 | 4 | 0 | 26 | 1 |
| Solia | 12 | 4 | 46 | 1 | 3 | 0 | 18 | 1 |
| Somerville | 31 | 7 | 82 | 1 | 20 | 4 | 75 | 4 |
| Delport | 23.2 | 8 | 78 | 7 | 21 | 2 | 91 | 0 |
| **CANTERBURY** | | | | | | | | |
| Williams | 3 | 0 | 10 | 1 | 10.4 | 4 | 37 | 3 |
| O'Rourke | 12 | 6 | 26 | 0 | 14 | 2 | 56 | 3 |
| McConchie | 26.1 | 6 | 73 | 4 | 24 | 9 | 63 | 2 |
| van Woerkom | 25 | 13 | 42 | 5 | 30 | 6 | 97 | 1 |
| Davey | 2 | 0 | 6 | 0 | 6 | 2 | 10 | 1 |
| Nicholls | | | | | 1 | 0 | 1 | 0 |

| Fall of Wickets | C | A | C | A |
|---|---|---|---|---|
| | 1st | 1st | 2nd | 2nd |
| 1st | 50 | 0 | 39 | 13 |
| 2nd | 170 | 18 | 46 | 50 |
| 3rd | 261 | 48 | 112 | 72 |
| 4th | 274 | 60 | 171 | 119 |
| 5th | 274 | 65 | 176 | 194 |
| 6th | 275 | 85 | 194 | 215 |
| 7th | 279 | 141 | - | 221 |
| 8th | 299 | 151 | - | 223 |
| 9th | 304 | 168 | - | 228 |
| 10th | 325 | 172 | - | 273 |

# 2021/22 FIRST-CLASS STATISTICS

## REGISTER OF PLAYERS

The following players appeared in first-class cricket for New Zealand teams during the 2021/22 season.

| Name | | Born | At | Type | | | First-class debut | |
|---|---|---|---|---|---|---|---|---|
| **Allen** Finnley Hugh | W | 22. 4.99 | Auckland | RHB | | WK | A v CD | 17/18 |
| **Ave** Mea Tangi Me Ma'ara Joseph | CD, O | 6. 7.98 | Wellington | RHB | | WK | CD v W | 21/22 |
| **Bacon** Matthew Boyce | O | 13. 4.93 | Auckland | RHB | RM | | W v O | 15/16 |
| **Bhula** Jakob Jarrod Naran Patel | W | 12.12.98 | Wellington | RHB | ROB | | W v ND | 18/19 |
| **Blundell** Thomas Ackland | W, NZ | 1. 9.90 | Wellington | RHB | ROB | WK | W v A | 12/13 |
| **Bocock** Peter David | ND | 12. 4.91 | Te Awamutu | RHB | | WK | ND v O | 17/18 |
| **Boult** Trent Alexander | NZ | 22. 7.89 | Rotorua | RHB | LFM | | NZ A v India A | 08/09 |
| **Bowes** Chad Jayson | C | 19.10.92 | Benoni, S. Africa | RHB | RFM | | KZN v FS | 10/11 |
| **Boyle** John Christopher Thwaites | C | 24. 3.96 | Christchurch | RHB | ROB | | C v A | 16/17 |
| **Bracewell** Douglas Andrew John | CD | 28. 9.90 | Tauranga | RHB | RM | | CD v A | 08/09 |
| **Bracewell** Michael Gordon | W, NZ | 14. 2.91 | Masterton | LHB | | WK | O v CD | 10/11 |
| **Briggs** Cole Jeffery | A | 20. 8.97 | Pretoria, S.Africa | RHB | | WK | A v O | 20/21 |
| **Brown** Joshua Harvey | ND | 9. 8.00 | Johannesburg, S.Africa | RHB | RM | | ND v W | 21/22 |
| **Bruce** Thomas Charles | CD | 2. 8.91 | Te Kuiti | RHB | ROB | | CD v O | 14/15 |
| **Carter** Joseph Franklyn | ND | 17.12.92 | Hemel Hempstead, Eng | RHB | ROB | | ND v A | 13/14 |
| **Carter** Leo James | C | 10.12.94 | Wellington | LHB | RLB | | C v ND | 14/15 |
| **Chamberlain** Harry John | C | 16.11.95 | Christchurch | RHB | RM | | C v A | 20/21 |
| **Chapman** Mark Sinclair | A | 27. 6.94 | Hong Kong, China | LHB | SLA | | A v ND | 15/16 |
| **Chu** Max Wilkie | O | 21. 3.00 | Dunedin | LHB | | WK | O v CD | 18/19 |
| **Clark** William James | CD | 5. 9.01 | Hastings | RHB | RM | | CD v C | 21/22 |
| **Clarke** Katene Dalton | ND | 21. 9.99 | Pukekohe | RHB | RSM | | ND v CD | 19/20 |
| **Clarke** Kristian David Charles | ND | 6. 3.01 | Te Awamutu | RHB | RM | | ND v W | 21/22 |
| **Clarkson** Joshua Andrew | CD | 21. 1.97 | Christchurch | RHB | RM | | CD v O | 15/16 |
| **Cleaver** Dane | CD | 1. 1.92 | Auckland | RHB | | WK | CD v ND | 10/11 |
| **Conway** Devon Philip | NZ | 8. 7.91 | Johannesburg, S.Africa | LHB | RM | WK | Gaut v East | 08/09 |
| **Cooper** Henry Ross | ND | 20. 5.93 | Whangarei | RHB | ROB | | ND v CD | 16/17 |
| **Cumming** Jacob Mark | O | 14.12.03 | Dunedin | LHB | RM | | O v A | 21/22 |
| **Davey** Sean Benjamin | C | 8. 4.93 | Tauranga | RHB | RM | | C v ND | 20/21 |
| **de Grandhomme** Colin | ND, NZ | 22. 7.86 | Harare, Zimbabwe | RHB | RM | | Zim A v Kenya | 05/06 |
| **Delport** Louis Johannes | A | 12. 2.88 | Nelspruit, S.Africa | LHB | SLA | | WP v Boland | 14/15 |
| **Drysdale** Rupert Peter Owens | ND | 7. 1.89 | Forest Row, England | LHB | ROB | | ND v W | 21/22 |
| **Dudding** Liam Raymond | CD | 13. 6.94 | Hamilton | RHB | RM | | CD v ND | 15/16 |
| **Duffy** Jacob Andrew | O | 2. 8.94 | Lumsden | RHB | RFM | | O v W | 11/12 |
| **Field** Joseph Francis Alexander | CD | 19.12.00 | Hamilton | RHB | RM | | CD v A | 20/21 |
| **Fisher** Matthew John | ND | 10.11.99 | Auckland | RHB | RFM | | ND v W | 20/21 |
| **Fletcher** Cameron Dean | C | 1. 3.93 | Auckland | RHB | | WK | ND v CD | 12/13 |
| **Foulkes** Zakary Glen | C | 5. 6.02 | Christchurch | RHB | RM | | C v A | 21/22 |
| **Georgeson** Luke Ian | W | 14. 4.99 | Wellington | LHB | RM | | W v CD | 20/21 |
| **Gibson** James David | W | 29. 4.93 | Greytown | RHB | RM | | W v C | 19/20 |
| **Gibson** Jacob Michael | O | 7. 8.97 | Hamilton | RHB | RM | | O v W | 21/22 |
| **Gibson** Zakary Neil | ND | 19. 3.97 | Hamilton | RHB | RM | | ND v CD | 15/16 |
| **Greenwood** Nicholas Anthony | W | 21.10.99 | Jersey | RHB | | | W v C | 21/22 |
| **Guptill** Martin John | A | 30. 9.86 | Auckland | RHB | ROB | | A v W | 05/06 |
| **Hampton** Brett Raymond | ND | 30. 9.96 | Tauranga | RHB | RM | | ND v A | 15/16 |
| **Harrison** Ryan David | A | 10.10.99 | Auckland | RHB | RM | | A v C | 20/21 |
| **Hartshorn** James William | W | 28. 9.97 | Palmerston North | RHB | RM | | W v CD | 21/22 |
| **Hay** Gregory Robert | CD | 14. 7.84 | Rotorua | RHB | ROB | | CD v W | 06/07 |
| **Hay** Mitchell James | C | 20. 8.00 | Christchurch | RHB | | WK | C v O | 21/22 |
| **Hazeldine** Andrew Thomas Edward | C | 13. 7.94 | Portsmouth, England | LHB | LFM | | C v W | 17/18 |
| **Henry** Matthew James | C, NZ | 14.12.91 | Christchurch | RHB | RFM | | C v W | 10/11 |
| **Horne** Benjamin James | A | 4. 3.93 | Auckland | RHB | SLA | WK | A v CD | 16/17 |
| **Jamieson** Kyle Alex | A, NZ | 30.12.94 | Auckland | RHB | RFM | | C v W | 14/15 |
| **Johns** Lauchlan Ritchie | W | 1. 7.96 | Wellington | RHB | | WK | W v CD | 17/18 |
| **Johnson** Troy Manning | W | 1.10.97 | Lower Hutt | RHB | ROB | | W v C | 19/20 |
| **Johnston** Scott Sangster | ND | 6. 2.97 | Auckland | RHB | RM | | ND v CD | 21/22 |
| **Keene** Simon Brian | A | 21.10.00 | Auckland | RHB | RM | | A v O | 21/22 |
| **Kelly** Nicholas Fred | O | 25. 7.93 | Melbourne, Australia | LHB | SLA | | ND v A | 15/16 |
| **Kitchen** Anaru Kyle | O | 21. 2.84 | Auckland | RHB | SLA | | A v ND | 08/09 |
| **Kuggeleijn** Scott Christopher | ND | 3. 1.92 | Hamilton | RHB | RFM | | W v CD | 11/12 |
| **Latham** Thomas William Maxwell | C, NZ | 2. 4.92 | Christchurch | LHB | RM | WK | C v ND | 10/11 |
| **Lellman** Fergus Fraser | ND | 16. 7.01 | Tauranga | RHB | RM | | ND v W | 21/22 |

103

**NZC**

| | | Born | At | Type | | | First-class debut | |
|---|---|---|---|---|---|---|---|---|
| **Lennox** Jayden Richard | CD | 14.12.94 | Napier | LHB | SLA | | CD v C | 20/21 |
| **Leopard** Christian Kevin | CD | 17. 9.97 | Hastings | RHB | RM | | CD v O | 16/17 |
| **Lister** Benjamin George | A | 1. 1.96 | Auckland | RHB | LFM | | A v O | 17/18 |
| **Lockrose** Benjamin Nicholas John | O | 24. 3.00 | Portsmouth, England | RHB | SLA | | O v CD | 18/19 |
| **McClure** Kenneth James | C | 25.10.94 | Christchurch | RHB | RLB | | C v A | 15/16 |
| **McComb** Kieran Jordan | W | 28.12.94 | Leeds, England | LHB | SLA | | W v ND | 21/22 |
| **McConchie** Cole Edward | C | 12. 1.92 | Christchurch | RHB | ROB | | C v O | 12/13 |
| **McGregor-Sumpter** Flynn | A | 11. 7.98 | Auckland | LHB | | | A v CD | 21/22 |
| **McKay** Jarrod Douglas | O | 8. 6.00 | Nelson | RHB | RM | | CD v ND | 19/20 |
| **McLachlan** Callum Ross | W | 17. 5.99 | Lower Hutt | RHB | | WK | W v C | 21/22 |
| **McPeake** Iain Geoffrey | W | 24. 5.91 | Lower Hutt | RHB | RM | | W v ND | 15/16 |
| **McKenzie** Angus William | O | 17. 7.98 | Wellington | LHB | RM | | O v A | 20/21 |
| **Mitchell** Daryl Joseph | NZ | 20. 5.91 | Hamilton | RHB | RM | | ND v A | 11/12 |
| **Muller** Travis | O | 4. 3.93 | Cape Town, S.Africa | RHB | RFM | | WP v Namibia | 11/12 |
| **Neesham** James Douglas Sheehan | W | 17. 9.90 | Auckland | LHB | RFM | | A v C | 09/10 |
| **Newton** Oliver Robert | W | 22. 8.88 | Dunedin | LHB | RM | | W v A | 17/18 |
| **Nicholls** Henry Michael | C, NZ | 15.11.91 | Christchurch | LHB | ROB | | C v O | 11/12 |
| **Nuttall** Edward James | C | 15. 7.93 | Christchurch | LHB | LFM | | C v O | 11/12 |
| **O'Donnell** Robert Roux | A | 12. 9.94 | Kimberley, S.Africa | RHB | ROB | | A v CD | 14/15 |
| **O'Donnell** William Taylor | A | 29. 9.97 | Randburg, S.Africa | RHB | ROB | | A v O | 18/19 |
| **O'Rourke** William Peter | C | 6. 8.01 | Kingston upon Thames | RHB | RM | | C v CD | 21/22 |
| **Parkes** Thorn Kiwa | O | 10. 8.00 | Gisborne | LHB | RLBG | | O v A | 21/22 |
| **Patel** Ajaz Yunus | CD, NZ | 21.10.88 | Bombay, India | LHB | SLA | | CD v W | 12/13 |
| **Patel** Sandeep Kumar | ND | 30.10.98 | Auckland | RHB | RM | | ND v W | 21/22 |
| **Phillips** Dale Nathan | O | 15.10.98 | Johannesburg, S.Africa | RHB | RM | | O v W | 19/20 |
| **Phillips** Glenn Dominic | A | 6.12.96 | East London, S.Africa | RHB | ROB | WK | A v C | 16/17 |
| **Pomare** Benjamin James | ND | 15. .9.00 | Tauranga | RHB | ROB | WK | ND v W | 21/22 |
| **Popli** Bharat | ND | 30. 5.90 | New Delhi, India | RHB | RLB | | ND v A | 13/14 |
| **Pringle** Oliver Morgan Reynolds | A | 27. 5.92 | Auckland | LHB | RM | | A v O | 20/21 |
| **Rae** Michael David | O | 13. 6.95 | Dunedin | RHB | RFM | | O v ND | 14/15 |
| **Rance** Seth Hayden Arnold | CD | 23. 8.87 | Wellington | RHB | RM | | CD v W | 08/09 |
| **Randell** Brett Graham | ND | 20. 5.95 | Auckland | RHB | RM | | ND v W | 16/17 |
| **Raval** Jeet Ashok | ND | 22. 5.88 | Ahmedabad, India | LHB | RLB | | A v WI | 05/06 |
| **Ravindra** Rachin | W, NZ | 18.11.99 | Wellington | LHB | SLA | | NZ A v Pak A | 18/19 |
| **Renwick** Mitchell | O | 23. 2.93 | Palmerston North | RHB | RLB | | CD v W | 15/16 |
| **Rippon** Michael James Gratton | O | 14. 9.91 | Cape Town, S.Africa | RHB | SLC | | WP v KZN | 11/12 |
| **Robinson** Timothy Blake | W | 28. 4.02 | Wellington | RHB | RM | | W v O | 21/22 |
| **Rutherford** Hamish Duncan | O | 27. 4.89 | Dunedin | LHB | SLA | | O v ND | 08/09 |
| **Santner** Mitchell Josef | ND | 5. 2.92 | Hamilton | LHB | SLA | | ND v O | 11/12 |
| **Schmulian** Bradley Dean | CD | 3. 8.90 | Cape Town, S.Africa | RHB | RLB | | CD v ND | 17/18 |
| **Sears** Benjamin Vincent | W | 11. 2.98 | Lower Hutt | RHB | RFM | | W v ND | 18/19 |
| **Seifert** Tim Louis | ND | 14.12.94 | Wanganui | RHB | | WK | ND v O | 14/15 |
| **Sheat** Fraser William | C | 29. 4.98 | Christchurch | RHB | RM | | C v O | 17/18 |
| **Shipley** Henry Burton | C | 10. 5.96 | Darfield | RHB | RM | | C v ND | 16/17 |
| **Smith** Benjamin Seth | CD | 7. 1.91 | Hamilton | RHB | ROB | | CD v W | 10/11 |
| **Smith** Nathan Gregory | W | 15. 7.98 | Dunedin | RHB | RFM | | O v ND | 15/16 |
| **Snedden** Michael Warwick | W | 20. 9.92 | Auckland | RHB | RM | | W v C | 19/20 |
| **Sodhi** Inderbir Singh | ND | 31.10.92 | Ludhiana, India | RHB | RLB | | ND v O | 12/13 |
| **Solia** Sean Mikaele | A | 15.12.92 | Auckland | LHB | RM | | A v C | 16/17 |
| **Somerville** William Edgar Richard | A, NZ | 9. 8.84 | Wellington | RHB | ROB | | O v W | 04/05 |
| **Southee** Timothy Grant | ND, NZ | 11.12.88 | Whangarei | RHB | RFM | | ND v O | 06/07 |
| **Sussex** Jordan David | A | 3. 3.94 | Auckland | RHB | RFM | | A v CD | 21/22 |
| **Swanson** Christopher John | ND | 14. 7.97 | Johannesburg, S.Africa | RHB | RM | | ND v W | 21/22 |
| **Taylor** Luteru Ross Poutoa Lote | NZ | 8. 3.84 | Lower Hutt | RHB | ROB | | CD v C | 02/03 |
| **ter Braak** Ross Matthew | A | 5. 6.97 | Auckland | RHB | LM | | A v ND | 20/21 |
| **Tickner** Blair Marshall | CD | 13.10.93 | Napier | RHB | RFM | | CD v A | 14/15 |
| **Toole** Raymond Lawrence | CD | 30.10.97 | Johannesburg, S.Africa | LHB | LM | | CD v ND | 19/20 |
| **van Beek** Logan Verjus | W | 7. 9.90 | Christchurch | RHB | RFM | | C v CD | 09/10 |
| **van Woerkom** Theo Francis | C | 26. 7.93 | Christchurch | RHB | SLA | | C v A | 15/16 |
| **Varcoe** Samuel Scott | ND | 11. 4.93 | Wellington | LHB | SLA | | ND v W | 21/22 |
| **Vishvaka** Kalupahana Liyanage Devan | W | 17.10.00 | Lower Hutt | RHB | RLBG | | W v O | 21/22 |
| **Wagner** Neil | ND, NZ | 13. 3.86 | Pretoria, S.Africa | LHB | LFM | | NW v Nthns | 05/06 |
| **Walker** Frederick Leonard | ND | 26. 7.94 | Hamilton | LHB | SLA | | ND v CD | 21/22 |
| **Walker** Josef Grant | ND | 6. 9.92 | Hamilton | RHB | ROB | | ND v C | 10/11 |
| **Wheeler** Ben Matthew | CD | 10.11.91 | Blenheim | RHB | LM | | CD v A | 09/10 |
| **Wiggins** Bayley Luke | CD | 3. 9.98 | Hastings | RHB | | WK | CD v C | 21/22 |
| **Williams** William Salter Austen | C | 6.10.92 | Christchurch | RHB | RM | | C v O | 12/13 |
| **Williamson** Kane Stuart | NZ | 8. 8.90 | Tauranga | RHB | ROB | | ND v A | 07/08 |
| **Worker** George Herrick | A | 23. 8.89 | Palmerston North | LHB | SLA | | CD v W | 07/08 |
| **Young** William Alexander | CD, NZ | 22.11.92 | New Plymouth | RHB | ROB | | CD v A | 11/12 |
| **Younghusband** Peter Francis | W | 17. 2.90 | Harare, Zimbabwe | RHB | RLBG | | W v C | 16/17 |

# FIRST-CLASS UMPIRES

*2021/22*

Sixteen umpires officiated in international, first-class and limited-overs games. With test matches being umpired by local officials due to Covid, Chris Gaffaney, Chris Brown and Wayne Knights stood in the four home tests. Gaffaney was again on the ICC elite panel while Brown, Knights and Shaun Haig were again on the ICC International Panel. Kim Cotton was again on the ICC Associate Panel and umpired the finals of the ICC Women's T20 and one-day World Cups.

**Black**, Cory Alan *(Wellington)*. Age 41. Made his debut in 2019/20 and has now umpired six first-class matches as well as seven one-day and five Twenty20 games.

**Bowden**, Brent Fraser *(Auckland)*. Age 59. Debut in 1992/93 and has now umpired 192 first-class matches including 84 tests. Has stood in 341 one-day matches, including 200 one-day internationals. Also officiated in 157 Twenty20 games of which 24 are internationals

**Bromley**, John Arthur Kinneir *(South Canterbury)*. Age 54. Debut in 2013/14 and has now umpired 29 first-class games, 34 one-day matches and 29 Twenty20 fixtures.

**Brown**, Christopher Mark, *(Auckland)*. Age 49. Former first-class player with Auckland from 1993 to 1999. Made his umpiring debut in 2012/13 and has now stood in 46 first-class matches of which five are tests . Also umpired 49 one-day games, 19 of which are internationals, and 81 Twenty20 games, including 40 internationals.

**Cotton**, Kim Diane *(Canterbury)*. Age 44. Made her debut in 2019/20 and has now umpired two first-class matches, four one-day and seven Twenty20 matches. She has also umpired 14 women's one-day internationals and 30 women's Twenty20 internationals. Stood in the finals of one-day and Twenty20 World Cups.

**Dempsey**, John Michael *(Counties-Manukau)*. Age 56. Debut in 2015/16 and has now umpired 28 first-class, 27 one-day and 24 Twenty20 matches.

**Gaffaney**, Christopher Blair *(Otago)*. Age 46. Former Otago player who made his umpiring debut in 2007/08. Member of ICC Elite Panel and has umpired 72 first-class matches including 41 tests. Has stood in 102 one-day games, including 74 one-day internationals, and 153 Twenty20 games, which include 35 internationals.

**Haig**, Shaun Barry *(Otago)*. Age 40. Former Otago player who made his umpiring debut in 2015/16. Has now officiated in 22 first-class fixtures, 29 one-day games, including seven internationals, and 67 Twenty20 matches, including 25 internationals.

**Jagannathan**, Kannan Sudarsanam *(Otago)*. Age 35. Made his debut in 2019/20 and has now umpired six one-day and four Twenty20 matches.

**Knights**, Wayne Roger *(Auckland)*. Age 51. Made his debut in 2001/02 and has now umpired 77 first-class matches, including four tests. Also officiated in 78 one-day games, 18 of which are internationals, and 89 Twenty20 games, including 24 internationals.

**Morrow**, Damian Ross *(Hamilton)*. Age 41. Debut in 2015/16 and has now  umpired one first-class match as a substitute, 16 one-day games and six Twenty20 fixtures.

**Parlane**, Timothy James *(Canterbury)*. Age 64. Made his debut in 2001/02 and has now stood in 117 first-class matches, 123 one-day games and 92 Twenty20 games.

**Pasco**, Peter John *(Southland)*. Age 51. Debut in 2020/21 and has now umpired three one-day and three Twenty20 games.

**Sanders**, Eugene Dalaine *(Canterbury)*. Age 49. Made his debut in 2016/17 and has now umpired five first-class matches, 14 one-day games and seven Twenty20 matches.

**Walker**, Derek John *(North Otago)*. Age 62. Former Otago player who made his umpiring debut in 2004/05. Has now umpired 115 first-class games, 111 one-day matches, which include nine internationals, and 115 Twenty20 games, including eight internationals.

**Walklin**, Glen Michael *(Hawke's Bay)*. Age 48. Made his debut in 2018/19 and has now umpired one first-class game as a substitute and four one-day and four Twenty20 matches.

# COMPLETE AVERAGES

*Averages for Bangladesh and South Africa are on pages 57 and 60*

| | M | In | NO | HS | Runs | Ave | 100 | 50 | Ct | St | O | M | R | W | Ave | 5WI | 10WM | Best |
|---|---|---|---|---|---|---|---|---|---|---|---|---|---|---|---|---|---|---|
| F.H.Allen | 4 | 8 | 0 | 44 | 183 | 22.87 | - | - | 5 | - | | | | | | | | |
| M.T.M.M.J.Ave | 2 | 3 | 0 | 34 | 67 | 22.33 | - | - | 3 | - | | | | | | | | |
| M.B.Bacon | 1 | 1 | 0 | 3 | 3 | 3.00 | - | - | - | - | 30 | 5 | 94 | 3 | 31.33 | - | - | 2-59 |
| J.J.N.P.Bhula | 5 | 9 | 0 | 29 | 81 | 9.00 | - | - | 2 | - | 2 | 0 | 11 | 0 | | - | - | - |
| T.A.Blundell | 9 | 14 | 3 | 96 | 374 | 34.00 | - | 3 | 26 | - | | | | | | | | |
| P.D.Bocock | 3 | 4 | 0 | 28 | 92 | 23.00 | - | - | 8 | 1 | | | | | | | | |
| T.A.Boult | 2 | 2 | 1 | 9* | 17 | 17.00 | - | - | 1 | - | 69.4 | 23 | 174 | 9 | 19.33 | 1 | - | 5-43 |
| C.J.Bowes | 7 | 13 | 0 | 127 | 570 | 43.84 | 2 | 3 | 4 | - | | | | | | | | |
| J.C.T.Boyle | 2 | 3 | 0 | 43 | 55 | 18.33 | - | - | - | - | 4.5 | 1 | 21 | 3 | 7.00 | - | - | 3-21 |
| D.A.J.Bracewell | 5 | 8 | 0 | 68 | 152 | 19.00 | - | 1 | 1 | - | 181 | 43 | 497 | 14 | 35.50 | - | - | 4-53 |
| M.G.Bracewell | 5 | 10 | 0 | 51 | 190 | 19.00 | - | 1 | 5 | - | 119.5 | 19 | 402 | 7 | 57.42 | - | - | 3-75 |
| C.J.Briggs | 2 | 3 | 0 | 22 | 57 | 19.00 | - | - | 1 | - | | | | | | | | |
| J.H.Brown | 1 | 2 | 0 | 8 | 9 | 4.50 | - | - | 1 | - | 16 | 2 | 31 | 2 | 15.50 | - | - | 2-31 |
| T.C.Bruce | 8 | 13 | 7 | 208* | 858 | 143.00 | 2 | 4 | 10 | - | 13 | 3 | 35 | 0 | | - | - | - |
| J.F.Carter | 6 | 10 | 1 | 76 | 282 | 31.33 | - | 2 | 4 | - | | | | | | | | |
| L.J.Carter | 8 | 13 | 3 | 56 | 264 | 26.40 | - | 1 | 10 | - | | | | | | | | |
| H.J.Chamberlain | 2 | 4 | 0 | 4 | 6 | 1.50 | - | - | - | - | | | | | | | | |
| M.S.Chapman | 5 | 10 | 3 | 97 | 256 | 36.57 | - | 2 | 7 | - | | | | | | | | |
| M.W.Chu | 7 | 11 | 2 | 103* | 307 | 34.11 | 1 | 1 | 21 | - | | | | | | | | |
| W.J.Clark | 3 | 2 | 0 | 41 | 55 | 27.50 | - | - | - | - | 57 | 12 | 191 | 3 | 63.66 | - | - | 2-78 |
| K.D.Clarke | 3 | 6 | 1 | 29 | 82 | 16.40 | - | - | 5 | - | | | | | | | | |
| K.D.C.Clarke | 3 | 6 | 2 | 63* | 135 | 33.75 | - | 1 | 1 | - | 54.5 | 10 | 185 | 6 | 30.83 | - | - | 3-47 |
| J.A.Clarkson | 3 | 3 | 0 | 83 | 114 | 38.00 | - | 1 | 1 | - | 33 | 3 | 145 | 3 | 48.33 | - | - | 1-28 |
| D.Cleaver | 7 | 12 | 2 | 108* | 393 | 39.30 | 1 | 1 | 19 | - | | | | | | | | |
| D.P.Conway | 4 | 6 | 0 | 122 | 388 | 64.66 | 2 | 1 | 1 | - | | | | | | | | |
| H.R.Cooper | 5 | 9 | 0 | 200 | 314 | 34.88 | 1 | - | 4 | - | | | | | | | | |
| J.M.Cumming | 4 | 8 | 2 | 37 | 161 | 26.83 | - | - | - | - | | | | | | | | |
| S.B.Davey | 2 | 3 | 1 | 55 | 68 | 34.00 | - | 1 | 1 | - | 41 | 9 | 105 | 3 | 35.00 | - | - | 1-10 |
| C.de Grandhomme | 6 | 10 | 2 | 164* | 455 | 56.87 | 2 | - | 3 | - | 114 | 40 | 264 | 11 | 24.00 | - | - | 3-13 |
| L.J.Delport | 5 | 6 | 2 | 16 | 55 | 13.75 | - | - | 1 | - | 198.3 | 52 | 588 | 17 | 34.58 | 1 | - | 7-78 |
| R.P.O.Drysdale | 1 | 2 | 0 | 62 | 67 | 33.50 | - | 1 | - | - | 13 | 2 | 34 | 1 | 34.00 | - | - | 1-11 |
| L.R.Dudding | 1 | - | - | - | - | - | - | - | 1 | - | 21 | 2 | 102 | 1 | 102.00 | - | - | 1-63 |
| J.A.Duffy | 7 | 8 | 0 | 24 | 83 | 10.37 | - | - | 1 | - | 245 | 63 | 713 | 13 | 54.84 | - | - | 4-106 |
| J.F.A.Field | 6 | 8 | 1 | 38 | 157 | 22.42 | - | - | 5 | - | 132 | 24 | 444 | 10 | 44.40 | - | - | 3-50 |
| M.J.Fisher | 1 | 2 | 2 | 28* | 33 | | - | - | - | - | 23 | 5 | 88 | 2 | 44.00 | - | - | 2-67 |
| C.D.Fletcher | 7 | 12 | 3 | 110 | 364 | 40.44 | 1 | 3 | 24 | 2 | | | | | | | | |
| Z.G.Foulkes | 4 | 6 | 0 | 49 | 109 | 18.16 | - | - | 1 | - | 54.2 | 6 | 182 | 4 | 45.50 | - | - | 3-32 |
| L.I.Georgeson | 5 | 10 | 0 | 74 | 145 | 14.50 | - | 1 | 5 | - | 4 | 0 | 23 | 0 | | - | - | - |
| J.D.Gibson | 6 | 11 | 1 | 25 | 124 | 12.40 | - | - | 7 | - | 69 | 13 | 273 | 4 | 68.25 | - | - | 2-76 |
| J.M.Gibson | 4 | 5 | 0 | 50 | 92 | 18.40 | - | 1 | 1 | - | 92 | 16 | 361 | 10 | 36.10 | - | - | 4-84 |
| Z.N.Gibson | 2 | 3 | 1 | 22 | 28 | 14.00 | - | - | - | - | 66.4 | 13 | 215 | 11 | 19.54 | - | - | 3-14 |
| N.A.Greenwood | 3 | 6 | 0 | 26 | 106 | 17.66 | - | - | 1 | - | | | | | | | | |
| M.J.Guptill | 3 | 6 | 0 | 195 | 358 | 59.66 | 1 | 1 | 7 | - | | | | | | | | |
| B.R.Hampton | 3 | 3 | 0 | 47 | 73 | 24.33 | - | - | 1 | - | 28.3 | 2 | 89 | 3 | 29.66 | - | - | 2-29 |
| R.D.Harrison | 2 | 3 | 0 | 46 | 69 | 23.00 | - | - | 3 | - | | | | | | | | |
| J.W.Hartshorn | 2 | 3 | 1 | 17* | 21 | 10.50 | - | - | 1 | - | 41.3 | 9 | 127 | 3 | 42.33 | - | - | 1-26 |
| G.R.Hay | 7 | 12 | 2 | 152 | 403 | 40.30 | 2 | - | 3 | - | | | | | | | | |
| M.J.Hay | 1 | 1 | 0 | 62 | 62 | 62.00 | - | 1 | 3 | - | | | | | | | | |
| A.T.E.Hazeldine | 1 | 2 | 0 | 27 | 51 | 25.50 | - | - | - | - | 20 | 1 | 99 | 0 | | - | - | - |
| M.J.Henry | 6 | 9 | 1 | 58* | 178 | 22.25 | - | 1 | 1 | - | 235.2 | 73 | 599 | 35 | 17.11 | 1 | - | 7-23 |
| B.J.Horne | 7 | 11 | 2 | 89* | 300 | 33.33 | - | 1 | 24 | 3 | | | | | | | | |
| K.A.Jamieson | 6 | 9 | 2 | 32 | 111 | 15.85 | - | - | 4 | - | 190.2 | 55 | 520 | 18 | 28.88 | - | - | 4-82 |
| L.R.Johns | 1 | 1 | 0 | 21 | 21 | 21.00 | - | - | 1 | - | | | | | | | | |
| T.M.Johnson | 5 | 9 | 2 | 194* | 389 | 55.57 | 1 | 1 | 5 | - | | | | | | | | |
| S.S.Johnston | 2 | 4 | 0 | 25 | 45 | 11.25 | - | - | - | - | 20 | 5 | 60 | 1 | 60.00 | - | - | 1-31 |
| S.B.Keene | 5 | 7 | 1 | 65 | 94 | 15.66 | - | 1 | 2 | - | 127.1 | 41 | 357 | 25 | 14.28 | 3 | - | 6-44 |
| N.F.Kelly | 8 | 15 | 2 | 234* | 675 | 51.92 | 1 | 4 | 6 | - | 3 | 0 | 22 | 0 | | - | - | - |
| A.K.Kitchen | 4 | 7 | 0 | 23 | 75 | 10.71 | - | - | 4 | - | 22.5 | 6 | 71 | 2 | 35.50 | - | - | 2-2 |
| S.C.Kuggeleijn | 4 | 6 | 2 | 25* | 62 | 15.50 | - | - | 2 | - | 67.3 | 11 | 202 | 4 | 50.50 | - | - | 2-28 |
| T.W.M.Latham | 6 | 10 | 1 | 252 | 545 | 60.55 | 3 | - | 10 | - | | | | | | | | |
| F.F.Lellman | 1 | 2 | 0 | 20 | 26 | 13.00 | - | - | - | - | | | | | | | | |
| J.R.Lennox | 4 | 6 | 2 | 43 | 82 | 20.50 | - | - | 6 | - | 134.3 | 25 | 469 | 8 | 58.62 | - | - | 3-38 |
| C.K.Leopard | 1 | 1 | 0 | 0 | 0 | 0.00 | - | - | 1 | - | | | | | | | | |
| B.G.Lister | 6 | 5 | 4 | 8* | 13 | 13.00 | - | - | 3 | - | 141 | 31 | 391 | 14 | 27.92 | - | - | 3-31 |

| | M | In | NO | HS | Runs | Ave | 100 | 50 | Ct | St | O | M | R | W | Ave | 5WI | 10WM | Best |
|---|---|---|---|---|---|---|---|---|---|---|---|---|---|---|---|---|---|---|
| B.N.J.Lockrose | 2 | 4 | 1 | 9 | 16 | 5.33 | - | - | - | - | 41.2 | 4 | 172 | 2 | 86.00 | - | - | 2-30 |
| K.J.McClure | 7 | 13 | 1 | 130 | 320 | 26.66 | 1 | - | 9 | - | | | | | | | | |
| K.J.McComb | 1 | 1 | 0 | 0 | 0 | 0.00 | - | - | - | - | 25.5 | 9 | 34 | 2 | 17.00 | - | - | 2-11 |
| C.E.McConchie | 8 | 14 | 1 | 187* | 445 | 34.23 | 1 | 1 | 3 | - | 104.1 | 26 | 326 | 9 | 36.22 | - | - | 4-73 |
| F.McGregor-Sumpter | 1 | 2 | 0 | 56 | 56 | 28.00 | - | 1 | 1 | - | | | | | | | | |
| J.D.McKay | 5 | 5 | 2 | 2 | 2 | 0.66 | - | - | 1 | - | 105 | 18 | 427 | 13 | 32.84 | - | - | 4-85 |
| A.W.McKenzie | 4 | 6 | 1 | 13* | 36 | 7.20 | - | - | - | - | 105 | 33 | 253 | 6 | 42.16 | - | - | 2-32 |
| C.R.McLachlan | 3 | 6 | 1 | 56 | 121 | 24.20 | - | 1 | 12 | 1 | | | | | | | | |
| I.G.McPeake | 5 | 7 | 2 | 15* | 50 | 10.00 | - | - | - | - | 112.3 | 23 | 334 | 12 | 27.83 | 1 | - | 5-36 |
| D.J.Mitchell | 3 | 4 | 0 | 60 | 103 | 25.75 | - | 1 | 7 | - | 6 | 1 | 18 | 1 | 18.00 | - | - | 1-18 |
| T.Muller | 8 | 11 | 5 | 65* | 230 | 38.33 | - | 1 | 3 | - | 195.2 | 40 | 691 | 18 | 38.38 | 1 | - | 6-52 |
| J.D.S.Neesham | 1 | 1 | 0 | 0 | 0 | 0.00 | - | 0 | 1 | - | 24 | 7 | 57 | 3 | 19.00 | - | - | 3-46 |
| O.R.Newton | 4 | 5 | 1 | 70 | 137 | 34.25 | - | 1 | - | - | 93 | 18 | 315 | 5 | 63.00 | - | - | 2-45 |
| H.M.Nicholls | 8 | 13 | 1 | 105 | 523 | 43.58 | 1 | 3 | 9 | - | 2 | 0 | 2 | 0 | | - | - | - |
| E.J.Nuttall | 3 | 4 | 1 | 4* | 8 | 2.66 | - | - | 2 | - | 65 | 9 | 256 | 12 | 21.33 | - | - | 3-21 |
| R.R.O'Donnell | 6 | 9 | 1 | 223 | 539 | 67.37 | 2 | 2 | 8 | - | 7 | 3 | 12 | 0 | | - | - | - |
| W.T.O'Donnell | 6 | 10 | 2 | 119* | 335 | 41.87 | 1 | 1 | 7 | - | | | | | | | | |
| W.P.O'Rourke | 3 | 2 | 1 | 6* | 10 | 10.00 | - | - | - | - | 77.1 | 20 | 238 | 9 | 26.44 | - | - | 3-56 |
| T.K.Parkes | 1 | 2 | 1 | 4* | 5 | 5.00 | - | - | - | - | | | | | | | | |
| A.Y.Patel | 4 | 4 | 0 | 27 | 53 | 13.25 | - | - | 2 | - | 140 | 40 | 350 | 8 | 43.75 | - | - | 4-133 |
| S.K.Patel | 1 | 2 | 0 | 15 | 15 | 7.50 | - | - | 1 | - | | | | | | | | |
| D.N.Phillips | 8 | 15 | 2 | 114 | 587 | 45.15 | 2 | 3 | 5 | - | | | | | | | | |
| G.D.Phillips | 4 | 8 | 2 | 73 | 296 | 49.33 | - | 4 | 7 | - | 59.3 | 19 | 144 | 8 | 18.00 | - | - | 2-4 |
| B.J.Pomare | 1 | 2 | 0 | 23 | 23 | 11.50 | - | - | 2 | 2 | | | | | | | | |
| B.Popli | 4 | 7 | 1 | 150 | 265 | 44.16 | 1 | 1 | 3 | - | | | | | | | | |
| O.M.R.Pringle | 4 | 3 | 0 | 28 | 63 | 21.00 | - | - | 1 | - | 89 | 25 | 242 | 3 | 80.66 | - | - | 2-60 |
| M.D.Rae | 3 | 3 | 1 | 9* | 17 | 8.50 | - | - | - | - | 60 | 13 | 270 | 4 | 67.50 | - | - | 3-135 |
| S.H.A.Rance | 1 | 1 | 0 | 3 | 3 | 3.00 | - | - | 2 | - | 41.2 | 12 | 105 | 6 | 17.50 | - | - | 4-52 |
| B.G.Randell | 6 | 10 | 2 | 51 | 155 | 19.37 | - | 2 | 5 | - | 181.4 | 48 | 460 | 31 | 14.83 | 2 | - | 6-45 |
| J.A.Raval | 6 | 11 | 0 | 209 | 491 | 44.63 | 1 | 1 | 7 | - | 9.5 | 0 | 54 | 1 | 54.00 | - | - | 1-0 |
| R.Ravindra | 7 | 13 | 2 | 70 | 363 | 33.00 | - | 3 | 6 | - | 135 | 24 | 478 | 9 | 53.11 | - | - | 3-38 |
| M.Renwick | 8 | 15 | 1 | 134 | 467 | 33.35 | 2 | - | 6 | - | | | | | | | | |
| M.J.G.Rippon | 7 | 11 | 1 | 35* | 145 | 14.50 | - | - | 2 | - | 236.2 | 47 | 827 | 22 | 37.59 | 1 | - | 5-142 |
| T.B.Robinson | 3 | 4 | 1 | 103* | 185 | 61.66 | 1 | 1 | 2 | - | | | | | | | | |
| H.D.Rutherford | 7 | 13 | 0 | 144 | 593 | 45.61 | 2 | 2 | 2 | - | | | | | | | | |
| M.J.Santner | 2 | 4 | 0 | 74 | 192 | 48.00 | - | 2 | 1 | - | 37.1 | 10 | 80 | 2 | 40.00 | - | - | 2-1 |
| B.D.Schmulian | 8 | 13 | 0 | 117 | 541 | 41.61 | 1 | 3 | 5 | - | 40 | 3 | 183 | 2 | 91.50 | - | - | 1-18 |
| B.V.Sears | 4 | 8 | 3 | 24* | 52 | 10.40 | - | - | 3 | - | 104 | 12 | 419 | 18 | 23.27 | 1 | - | 5-88 |
| T.L.Seifert | 3 | 6 | 0 | 24 | 64 | 10.66 | - | - | 9 | 3 | | | | | | | | |
| F.W.Sheat | 6 | 7 | 3 | 60* | 128 | 32.00 | - | 1 | 2 | - | 175.2 | 46 | 478 | 13 | 36.76 | 1 | - | 5-30 |
| H.B.Shipley | 4 | 7 | 0 | 70 | 228 | 32.57 | - | 3 | 2 | - | 85.3 | 25 | 205 | 16 | 12.81 | - | - | 4-26 |
| B.S.Smith | 5 | 7 | 1 | 40* | 101 | 16.83 | - | - | - | - | | | | | | | | |
| N.G.Smith | 8 | 12 | 1 | 72* | 239 | 21.72 | - | 3 | 4 | - | 231.4 | 77 | 571 | 31 | 18.41 | 3 | - | 6-54 |
| M.W.Snedden | 6 | 10 | 1 | 19 | 48 | 5.33 | - | - | 3 | - | 167 | 39 | 504 | 10 | 50.40 | - | - | 3-28 |
| I.S.Sodhi | 3 | 6 | 0 | 34 | 65 | 10.83 | - | - | - | - | 79.4 | 23 | 157 | 9 | 17.44 | 1 | - | 5-65 |
| S.M.Solia | 6 | 10 | 1 | 135 | 344 | 38.22 | 1 | 1 | 1 | - | 104 | 25 | 328 | 15 | 21.86 | - | - | 3-17 |
| W.E.R.Somerville | 6 | 7 | 1 | 60* | 182 | 30.33 | - | 2 | 3 | - | 192 | 58 | 449 | 22 | 20.40 | - | - | 4-66 |
| T.G.Southee | 5 | 7 | 1 | 17 | 48 | 6.85 | - | - | 6 | - | 189.4 | 48 | 539 | 22 | 24.50 | 2 | - | 5-35 |
| J.D.Sussex | 1 | 1 | 0 | 0 | 0 | 0.00 | - | - | 1 | - | 16.4 | 5 | 36 | 3 | 12.00 | - | - | 3-36 |
| C.J.Swanson | 1 | 2 | 0 | 45 | 56 | 28.00 | - | - | - | - | | | | | | | | |
| L.R.P.L.Taylor | 2 | 3 | 0 | 40 | 99 | 33.00 | - | - | 2 | - | 0.3 | 0 | 0 | 1 | 0.00 | - | - | 1-0 |
| R.M.ter Braak | 3 | 3 | 1 | 0* | 0 | 0.00 | - | - | - | - | 52 | 5 | 188 | 7 | 26.85 | - | - | 3-59 |
| B.M.Tickner | 6 | 8 | 3 | 37* | 62 | 12.40 | - | - | 1 | - | 227.2 | 50 | 654 | 23 | 28.43 | 2 | - | 5-64 |
| R.L.Toole | 6 | 6 | 2 | 8 | 15 | 3.75 | - | - | 2 | - | 197.3 | 42 | 597 | 23 | 25.95 | 1 | - | 6-54 |
| L.V.van Beek | 1 | 2 | 0 | 35 | 56 | 28.00 | - | - | 1 | - | 38.4 | 9 | 102 | 2 | 51.00 | - | - | 1-48 |
| T.F.van Woerkom | 5 | 8 | 1 | 36 | 130 | 18.57 | - | - | 2 | - | 119 | 24 | 461 | 9 | 51.22 | 1 | - | 5-42 |
| S.S.Varcoe | 1 | 2 | 0 | 16 | 16 | 8.00 | - | - | - | - | | | | | | | | |
| K.L.D.Vishvaka | 3 | 5 | 0 | 80 | 166 | 33.20 | - | 2 | 1 | - | | | | | | | | |
| N.Wagner | 6 | 7 | 2 | 49 | 117 | 23.40 | - | - | 3 | - | 200.1 | 45 | 574 | 19 | 30.21 | - | - | 4-102 |
| F.L.Walker | 1 | - | - | - | - | - | - | - | - | - | 17 | 4 | 63 | 0 | | - | - | - |
| J.G.Walker | 6 | 8 | 3 | 25* | 56 | 11.20 | - | - | 2 | - | 156.3 | 41 | 347 | 18 | 19.27 | - | - | 4-47 |
| B.M.Wheeler | 4 | 5 | 0 | 74 | 199 | 39.80 | - | 2 | 5 | - | 127.5 | 23 | 341 | 9 | 37.88 | - | - | 4-54 |
| B.L.Wiggins | 7 | 12 | 1 | 133 | 353 | 32.09 | 1 | - | 12 | - | | | | | | | | |
| W.S.A.Williams | 8 | 11 | 3 | 37* | 125 | 15.62 | - | - | 1 | - | 233.3 | 86 | 538 | 25 | 21.52 | - | - | 3-21 |
| G.H.Worker | 5 | 10 | 0 | 80 | 223 | 22.30 | - | 1 | 5 | - | 6 | 1 | 14 | 0 | | - | - | - |
| W.A.Young | 5 | 8 | 0 | 69 | 248 | 31.00 | - | 3 | 4 | - | | | | | | | | |
| P.F.Younghusband | 3 | 5 | 1 | 36* | 80 | 20.00 | - | - | 3 | - | 62 | 14 | 190 | 7 | 27.14 | - | - | 3-43 |

# LEADING AVERAGES

***BATTING*** *(top 20, qualification six innings)*

| | M | I | NO | HS | Runs | Ave | 100s | 50s |
|---|---|---|---|---|---|---|---|---|
| T.C. Bruce | 8 | 13 | 7 | 208* | 858 | 143.00 | 2 | 4 |
| R.R. O'Donnell | 6 | 9 | 1 | 223 | 539 | 67.37 | 2 | 2 |
| D.P. Conway | 4 | 6 | 0 | 122 | 388 | 64.66 | 2 | 1 |
| T.W.M. Latham | 6 | 10 | 1 | 252 | 545 | 60.55 | 3 | - |
| M.J. Guptill | 3 | 6 | 0 | 195 | 358 | 59.66 | 1 | 1 |
| C. de Grandhomme | 6 | 10 | 2 | 164* | 455 | 56.87 | 2 | - |
| T.M. Johnson | 5 | 9 | 2 | 194* | 389 | 55.57 | 1 | 1 |
| N.F. Kelly | 8 | 15 | 2 | 234* | 675 | 51.92 | 1 | 4 |
| G.D. Phillips | 4 | 8 | 2 | 73 | 296 | 49.33 | - | 4 |
| H.D. Rutherford | 7 | 13 | 0 | 144 | 593 | 45.61 | 2 | 2 |
| D.N. Phillips | 8 | 15 | 2 | 114 | 587 | 45.15 | 2 | 3 |
| J.A. Raval | 6 | 11 | 0 | 209 | 491 | 44.63 | 1 | 1 |
| B. Popli | 4 | 7 | 1 | 150 | 265 | 44.16 | 1 | 1 |
| C.J. Bowes | 7 | 13 | 0 | 127 | 570 | 43.84 | 2 | 3 |
| H.M. Nicholls | 8 | 13 | 1 | 105 | 523 | 43.58 | 1 | 3 |
| W.T. O'Donnell | 6 | 10 | 2 | 119* | 335 | 41.87 | 1 | 1 |
| B.D. Schmulian | 8 | 13 | 0 | 117 | 541 | 41.61 | 1 | 3 |
| C.D. Fletcher | 7 | 12 | 3 | 110 | 364 | 40.44 | 1 | 3 |
| G.R. Hay | 7 | 12 | 2 | 152 | 403 | 40.30 | 2 | - |
| D. Cleaver | 7 | 12 | 2 | 108* | 393 | 39.30 | 1 | 1 |

***BOWLING*** *(top 20, qualification 10 wickets)*

| | Overs | Mdns | Runs | Wkts | Ave | 5WI | 10WM | Best |
|---|---|---|---|---|---|---|---|---|
| H.B. Shipley | 85.2 | 25 | 205 | 16 | 12.81 | - | - | 4-26 |
| S.B. Keene | 127.1 | 41 | 357 | 25 | 14.28 | 3 | - | 6-44 |
| B.G. Randell | 181.4 | 48 | 460 | 31 | 14.83 | 2 | - | 6-45 |
| M.J. Henry | 235.2 | 73 | 599 | 35 | 17.11 | 1 | - | 7-23 |
| N.G. Smith | 231.4 | 77 | 571 | 31 | 18.41 | 3 | - | 6-54 |
| J.G. Walker | 156.3 | 41 | 347 | 18 | 19.27 | - | - | 4-47 |
| Z.N. Gibson | 66.4 | 13 | 215 | 11 | 19.54 | - | - | 3-14 |
| W.E.R. Somerville | 192 | 58 | 449 | 22 | 20.40 | - | - | 4-66 |
| E.J. Nuttall | 65 | 9 | 256 | 12 | 21.33 | - | - | 3-21 |
| W.S.A. Williams | 233.3 | 86 | 538 | 25 | 21.52 | - | - | 3-21 |
| S.M. Solia | 104 | 25 | 328 | 15 | 21.86 | - | - | 3-17 |
| K. Rabada | 68 | 14 | 219 | 10 | 21.90 | 1 | - | 5-60 |
| B.V. Sears | 104 | 12 | 419 | 18 | 23.27 | 1 | - | 5-88 |
| C. de Grandhomme | 114 | 40 | 264 | 11 | 24.00 | - | - | 3-13 |
| T.G. Southee | 189.4 | 48 | 539 | 22 | 24.50 | 2 | - | 5-35 |
| R.L. Toole | 197.3 | 42 | 597 | 23 | 25.95 | 1 | - | 6-54 |
| I.G. McPeake | 112.3 | 23 | 334 | 12 | 27.83 | 1 | - | 5-36 |
| B.G. Lister | 141 | 31 | 391 | 14 | 27.92 | - | - | 3-31 |
| B.M. Tickner | 227.2 | 50 | 654 | 23 | 28.43 | 2 | - | 5-64 |
| K.A. Jamieson | 190.2 | 55 | 520 | 18 | 28.88 | - | - | 4-82 |

# CENTURIES

There were 41 centuries scored in first-class cricket in 2021/22 compared to 53 the previous season and the record of 84 in 2008/09. Thirty players scored hundreds during the season with T.W.M.Latham scoring three and C.J. Bowes, T.C. Bruce, D.P. Conway, C. de Grandhomme, G.R. Hay, R.R. O'Donnell, D.N. Phillips, M. Renwick and H.D. Rutherford getting two each.

The fastest century of the season was scored by B.L.Wiggins off 101 balls for Central Districts against Canterbury.

| | | | |
|---|---|---|---|
| 252 | T.W.M. Latham | New Zealand v Bangladesh *(Second Test)* | Christchurch |
| 234* | N.F. Kelly | Otago v Central Districts | Dunedin |
| 223 | R.R. O'Donnell | Auckland v Canterbury | Auckland |
| 209 | J.A. Raval | Northern Districts v Central Districts | Whangarei |
| 208* | T.C. Bruce | Central Districts v Northern Districts | Whangarei |
| 204* | T.C. Bruce | Central Districts v Auckland | Napier |
| 200 | H.R. Cooper | Northern Districts v Otago | Alexandra |
| 195 | M.J. Guptill | Auckland v Canterbury | Auckland |
| 194* | T.M. Johnson | Wellington v Otago | Dunedin |
| 187* | C.E. McConchie | Canterbury v Central Districts | Palmerston North |
| 164* | C. de Grandhomme | Northern Districts v Central Districts | Napier |
| 152 | G.R. Hay | Central Districts v Otago | Dunedin |
| 150 | B. Popli | Northern Districts v Central Districts | Whangarei |
| 144 | H.D. Rutherford | Otago v Central Districts | Dunedin |
| 136* | K. Verreynne | South Africa v New Zealand *(Second Test)* | Christchurch |
| †135 | S.M. Solia | Auckland v Wellington | Auckland |
| 134 | M. Renwick | Otago v Central Districts | Nelson |
| †133 | B.L. Wiggins | Central Districts v Canterbury | Christchurch |
| 130 | K.J. McClure | Canterbury v Wellington | Wellington |
| 130 | R.R. O'Donnell | Auckland v Wellington | Auckland |
| 127* | T.W.M. Latham | Canterbury v Wellington | Wellington |
| 127 | C.J. Bowes | Canterbury v Auckland | Lincoln |
| 122 | D.P. Conway | New Zealand v Bangladesh *(First Test)* | Mt Maunganui |
| 120* | C. de Grandhomme | New Zealand v South Africa *(Second Test)* | Christchurch |
| 119* | W.T. O'Donnell | Auckland v Canterbury | Lincoln |
| 117 | B.D. Schmulian | Central Districts v Otago | Dunedin |
| 114 | D.N. Phillips | Otago v Wellington | Dunedin |
| 113 | D.N. Phillips | Otago v Central Districts | Nelson |
| 110 | C.D. Fletcher | Canterbury v Wellington | Wellington |
| 109 | D.P. Conway | New Zealand v Bangladesh *(Second Test)* | Christchurch |
| 108* | D. Cleaver | Central Districts v Otago | Dunedin |
| 108 | S.J. Erwee | South Africa v New Zealand *(Second Test)* | Christchurch |
| 107 | M. Renwick | Otago v Central Districts | Dunedin |
| 105 | H.M. Nicholls | New Zealand v South Africa *(First Test)* | Christchurch |
| 104 | T.W.M. Latham | Canterbury v Central Districts | Christchurch |
| †103* | M.W. Chu | Otago v Northern Districts | Alexandra |
| †103* | T.B. Robinson | Wellington v Auckland | Auckland |
| 102 | Liton Das | Bangladesh v New Zealand *(Second Test)* | Christchurch |
| 101 | G.R. Hay | Central Districts v Canterbury | Christchurch |
| 101 | H.D. Rutherford | Otago v Central Districts | Nelson |
| 100 | C.J. Bowes | Canterbury v Otago | Rangiora |

† *maiden first-class century*

# CENTURY PARTNERSHIPS

There were 38 century partnerships in 2021/22 compared to 57 the previous season and the record of 92 in 2009/10.

**FIRST WICKET**
| | | | |
|---|---|---|---|
| 334 | J.A.Raval & B.Popli | Northern Districts v Central Districts | Whangarei |
| 251 | H.D.Rutherford & M.Renwick | Otago v Central Districts | Dunedin |
| 223 | T.W.M.Latham & C.J.Bowes | Canterbury v Wellington | Wellington |
| 173 | H.D.Rutherford & M.Renwick | Otago v Central Districts | Nelson |
| 161 | J.A.Raval & H.R.Cooper | Northern Districts v Otago | Alexandra |
| 148 | T.W.M.Latham & W.A.Young | New Zealand v Bangladesh *(Second Test)* | Christchurch |
| 113 | R.Ravindra & K.L.D.Vishvaka | Wellington v Otago | Dunedin |
| 111 | D.Elgar & S.J.Erwee | South Africa v New Zealand *(Second Test)* | Christchurch |
| 106 | G.H.Worker & W.T.O'Donnell | Auckland v Otago | Alexandra |

**SECOND WICKET**
| | | | |
|---|---|---|---|
| 215 | T.W.M.Latham & D.P.Conway | New Zealand v Bangladesh *(Second Test)* | Christchurch |
| 159 | B.D.Schmulian & D Cleaver | Central Districts v Otago | Dunedin |
| 138 | W.A.Young & D.P.Conway | New Zealand v Bangladesh *(First Test)* | Mt Maunganui |
| 136 | W.T.O'Donnell & G.D.Phillips | Auckland v Otago | Alexandra |
| 120 | C.J.Bowes & H.M.Nicholls | Canterbury v Auckland | Lincoln |
| 119 | H.D.Rutherford & D.N.Phillips | Otago v Canterbury | Rangiora |
| 107 | H.R.Cooper & B.G.Randell | Northern Districts v Otago | Alexandra |
| 104 | Nazmul Hossain & Mahmudul Hasan | Bangladesh v New Zealand *(First Test)* | Mt Maunganui |

**THIRD WICKET**
| | | | |
|---|---|---|---|
| 218 | B.D.Schmulian & T.C.Bruce | Central Districts v Northern Districts | Whangarei |
| 213 | S.M.Solia & R.R.O'Donnell | Auckland v Wellington | Auckland |
| 179 | H.R.Cooper & B.Popli | Northern Districts v Otago | Alexandra |
| 178 | D.N.Phillips & N.F.Kelly | Otago v Wellington | Dunedin |

**FOURTH WICKET**
| | | | |
|---|---|---|---|
| 278 | M.J.Guptill & R.R.O'Donnell | Auckland v Canterbury | Auckland |
| 144 | T.M.Johnson & T.B.Robinson | Wellington v Otago | Dunedin |
| 125 | G.R.Hay & T.C.Bruce | Central Districts v Otago | Dunedin |

**FIFTH WICKET**
| | | | |
|---|---|---|---|
| 158 | Mominul Haq & Liton Das | Bangladesh v New Zealand *(First Test)* | Mt Maunganui |
| 132 | J.F.Carter & M.J.Santner | Northern Districts v Wellington | Whangarei |
| 113 | M.S.Chapman & B.J.Horne | Auckland v Otago | Dunedin |

**SIXTH WICKET**
| | | | |
|---|---|---|---|
| 256 | N.F.Kelly & M.W.Chu | Otago v Central Districts | Dunedin |
| 191 | T.C.Bruce & J.A.Clarkson | Central Districts v Auckland | Napier |
| 151 | H.M.Nicholls & C.D.Fletcher | Canterbury v Wellington | Wellington |
| 133 | D.J.Mitchell & C.de Grandhomme | New Zealand v South Africa *(Second Test)* | Christchurch |
| 111* | T.C.Bruce & J.F.A.Field | Central Districts v Canterbury | Palmerston North |
| 101 | Nazmul Hossain & Liton Das | Bangladesh v New Zealand *(Second Test)* | Christchurch |

**SEVENTH WICKET**
| | | | |
|---|---|---|---|
| 183 | B.L.Wiggins & B.M.Wheeler | Central Districts v Canterbury | Christchurch |
| 107 | F.H.McGregor-Sumpter& S.B.Keene | Auckland v Central Districts | Napier |

**EIGHTH WICKET**
| | | | |
|---|---|---|---|
| 102 | T.M.Johnson & O.R.Newton | Wellington v Otago | Dunedin |

**NINTH WICKET**
| | | | |
|---|---|---|---|
| 138* | C.E.McConchie & F.W.Sheat | Canterbury v Central Districts | Palmerston North |
| 104 | M.W.Chu & J.M.Gibson | Otago v Northern Districts | Alexandra |

# BOWLING PERFORMANCES

There were 25 instances of bowlers taking five wickets or more in an innings in 2021/22 compared with 27 in 2020/21. Eighteen players achieved the feat with S.B. Keene and N.G. Smith doing so on three occasions while T.G. Southee, B.G. Randell and B.M. Tickner each did so twice. No player took ten wickets in a match or performed the hat-trick.

### FIVE WICKETS IN AN INNINGS

| | | | |
|---|---|---|---|
| 7-23 | M.J. Henry | New Zealand v South Africa *(First Test)* | Christchurch |
| 7-78 | L.J. Delport | Auckland v Canterbury | Lincoln |
| 6-44 | S.B. Keene | Auckland v Canterbury | Auckland |
| 6-45 | B.G. Randell | Northern Districts v Central Districts | Napier |
| 6-46 | Ebadot Hossain | Bangladesh v New Zealand *(First Test)* | Mt Maunganui |
| 6-51 | S.B. Keene | Auckland v Wellington | Auckland |
| 6-52 | T. Muller | Otago v Wellington | Wellington |
| 6-54 | N.G. Smith | Wellington v Otago | Wellington |
| 6-54 | R.L. Toole | Central Districts v Northern Districts | Napier |
| 5-24 | S.B. Keene | Auckland v Otago | Dunedin |
| 5-30 | F.W. Sheat | Canterbury v Wellington | Wellington |
| 5-35 | T.G. Southee | Northern Districts v Auckland | Auckland |
| 5-35 | T.G. Southee | New Zealand v South Africa *(First Test)* | Christchurch |
| 5-35 | N.G. Smith | Wellington v Northern Districts | Whangarei |
| 5-36 | I.G. McPeake | Wellington v Northern Districts | Whangarei |
| 5-42 | T.F. van Woerkom | Canterbury v Auckland | Lincoln |
| 5-43 | T.A. Boult | New Zealand v Bangladesh *(Second Test)* | Christchurch |
| 5-51 | N.G. Smith | Wellington v Canterbury | Wellington |
| 5-56 | B.G. Randell | Northern Districts v Otago | Alexandra |
| 5-60 | K. Rabada | South Africa v New Zealand *(Second Test)* | Christchurch |
| 5-64 | B.M. Tickner | Central Districts v Canterbury | Christchurch |
| 5-65 | I.S. Sodhi | Northern Districts v Wellington | Whangarei |
| 5-69 | B.M. Tickner | Central Districts v Auckland | Napier |
| 5-88 | B.V. Sears | Wellington v Central Districts | Wellington |
| 5-142 | M.J.G. Rippon | Otago v Northern Districts | Alexandra |

# WICKETKEEPING DISMISSALS

The following New Zealand players who appeared in 2021/22 have made at least one dismissal in first-class cricket while keeping wicket.

| | ct | st | total | | ct | st | total |
|---|---|---|---|---|---|---|---|
| C.D.Fletcher * | 233 | 13 | 246 | D.P.Conway | 19 | – | 19 |
| T.A.Blundell | 187 | 8 | 195 | B.S.Smith | 15 | 2 | 17 |
| D.Cleaver | 179 | 11 | 190 | C.R.McLachlan * | 12 | 1 | 13 |
| B.J. Horne * | 139 | 6 | 145 | B.J.Pomare * | 2 | 2 | 4 |
| T.L.Seifert | 124 | 12 | 136 | M.G.Bracewell | 3 | – | 3 |
| M.W.Chu * | 49 | 1 | 50 | M.J.Hay * | 3 | – | 3 |
| T.W.M.Latham | 38 | 1 | 39 | M.T.M.M.J.Ave * | 3 | – | 3 |
| L.R.Johns | 33 | 2 | 35 | B.L.Wiggins | 3 | – | 3 |
| P.D.Bocock * | 33 | 2 | 35 | J.F.Carter | 1 | – | 1 |
| M.Renwick | 27 | 1 | 28 | G.D.Phillips | 1 | – | 1 |

*\* no further catches taken as fielder*

# NEW ZEALANDERS
# IN OVERSEAS CRICKET

Devon Conway *(Somerset)*, Colin de Grandhomme *(Hampshire)*, Kyle Jamieson *(Surrey)*, Daryl Mitchell *(Middlesex)*, James Neesham *(Essex)*, Glenn Phillips *(Gloucestershire)*, Matt Quinn *(Kent)* Hamish Rutherford *(Glamorgan)*, Ish Sodhi *(Worcestershire)* and Will Young *(Durham)* appeared in county cricket in 2021. The details are:

| | M | I | NO | HS | Runs | Ave | 100 | 50 | ct/st |
|---|---|---|---|---|---|---|---|---|---|
| D.P. Conway | 2 | 3 | 0 | 88 | 121 | 40.33 | - | 1 | 3 |
| C. de Grandhomme | 2 | 3 | 2 | 174* | 186 | 186.00 | 1 | - | 2 |
| K.A. Jamieson | 1 | 1 | 1 | 0* | 0 | | - | - | - |
| D.J. Mitchell | 2 | 4 | 0 | 73 | 134 | 33.50 | - | 1 | - |
| J.D.S. Neesham | 1 | 1 | 1 | 10* | 10 | | - | - | - |
| G.D. Phillips | 3 | 6 | 0 | 49 | 147 | 18.16 | - | - | 5 |
| M.R. Quinn | 6 | 5 | 3 | 13* | 32 | 16.00 | - | - | - |
| H.D. Rutherford | 4 | 7 | 0 | 71 | 260 | 37.14 | - | 2 | - |
| I.S. Sodhi | 1 | 1 | 0 | 13 | 13 | 13.00 | - | - | - |
| W.A. Young | 4 | 7 | 0 | 124 | 278 | 39.71 | 2 | - | 1 |

| | O | M | R | W | Ave | 5WI | 10WM | Best |
|---|---|---|---|---|---|---|---|---|
| C. de Grandhomme | 37 | 20 | 68 | 6 | 11.33 | - | - | 4-31 |
| K.A. Jamieson | 6 | 3 | 10 | 0 | | - | - | - |
| D.J. Mitchell | 44 | 8 | 142 | 9 | 15.77 | - | - | 4-42 |
| J.D.S. Neesham | 4.1 | 0 | 15 | 2 | 7.50 | - | - | 2-15 |
| G.D. Phillips | 40 | 3 | 159 | 4 | 39.75 | - | - | 2-67 |
| M.R. Quinn | 149.3 | 34 | 413 | 18 | 22.94 | - | - | 4-54 |
| H.D. Rutherford | 8 | 1 | 26 | 1 | 26.00 | - | - | 1-26 |
| I.S. Sodhi | 49.2 | 3 | 148 | 6 | 24.66 | 1 | - | 6-89 |

**NZC**

# CAREER AVERAGES

*as at 1 July, 2022 for players active during the 2021/22 season*

| | M | In | NO | HS | Runs | Ave | 100 | 50 | Ct | St | Wkts | Runs | Ave | 5WI | 10WM | Best |
|---|---|---|---|---|---|---|---|---|---|---|---|---|---|---|---|---|
| F.H.Allen | 16 | 28 | 2 | 66 | 526 | 20.23 | - | 3 | 17 | - | 1 | 15 | 15.00 | - | - | 1-15 |
| M.T.M.M.J.Ave | 2 | 3 | 0 | 34 | 67 | 22.33 | - | - | 3 | - | | | | | | |
| M.B.Bacon | 20 | 28 | 7 | 43 | 205 | 9.76 | - | - | 9 | - | 56 | 1757 | 31.37 | 1 | 1 | 6-73 |
| J.J.N.P.Bhula | 10 | 17 | 0 | 55 | 203 | 11.94 | - | 1 | 7 | - | 0 | 11 | - | - | - | - |
| T.A.Blundell | 86 | 145 | 19 | 153 | 4636 | 36.79 | 11 | 22 | 199 | 8 | 1 | 65 | 65.00 | - | - | 1-15 |
| P.D.Bocock | 12 | 18 | 1 | 56 | 358 | 21.05 | - | 1 | 33 | 2 | | | | | | |
| T.A.Boult | 113 | 136 | 56 | 61 | 1212 | 15.15 | - | 2 | 59 | - | 433 | 11,634 | 26.86 | 18 | 1 | 6-30 |
| C.J.Bowes | 79 | 130 | 8 | 155 | 3532 | 28.95 | 6 | 14 | 49 | - | 1 | 129 | 129.00 | - | - | 1-22 |
| J.C.T.Boyle | 21 | 36 | 1 | 108 | 658 | 18.80 | 1 | 1 | 15 | - | 4 | 25 | 6.25 | - | - | 3-21 |
| D.A.J.Bracewell | 114 | 171 | 23 | 105 | 3930 | 26.55 | 3 | 20 | 52 | - | 348 | 11,301 | 32.47 | 10 | - | 7-35 |
| M.G.Bracewell | 98 | 175 | 13 | 190 | 5358 | 32.55 | 11 | 22 | 94 | - | 32 | 1568 | 49.00 | 1 | - | 5-43 |
| C.J.Briggs | 5 | 8 | 1 | 30 | 148 | 21.14 | - | - | 7 | - | | | | | | |
| J.H.Brown | 1 | 2 | 0 | 8 | 9 | 4.50 | - | - | 1 | - | 2 | 31 | 15.50 | - | - | 2-31 |
| T.C.Bruce | 59 | 104 | 20 | 208* | 3959 | 47.13 | 6 | 26 | 88 | - | 21 | 727 | 34.61 | - | - | 2-17 |
| J.F.Carter | 58 | 102 | 4 | 169 | 3206 | 32.71 | 6 | 16 | 42 | - | | | | | | |
| L.J.Carter | 43 | 72 | 6 | 226* | 2198 | 33.30 | 3 | 12 | 41 | - | 0 | 4 | - | - | - | - |
| H.J.Chamberlain | 4 | 7 | 0 | 132 | 169 | 24.14 | 1 | - | 1 | - | | | | | | |
| M.S.Chapman | 35 | 60 | 5 | 146 | 2287 | 41.58 | 4 | 14 | 31 | - | 1 | 222 | 222.00 | - | - | 1-60 |
| M.W.Chu | 17 | 28 | 5 | 103* | 654 | 28.43 | 1 | 2 | 49 | 1 | | | | | | |
| W.J.Clark | 3 | 2 | 0 | 41 | 55 | 27.50 | - | - | - | - | 3 | 191 | 63.66 | - | - | 2-78 |
| K.D.Clarke | 10 | 19 | 2 | 41 | 324 | 19.05 | - | - | 10 | - | | | | | | |
| K.D.C.Clarke | 3 | 6 | 2 | 63* | 135 | 33.75 | - | 1 | 1 | - | 6 | 185 | 30.83 | - | - | 3-47 |
| J.A.Clarkson | 10 | 14 | 1 | 83 | 268 | 20.61 | - | 1 | 6 | - | 15 | 587 | 39.13 | - | - | 2-28 |
| D.Cleaver | 66 | 109 | 12 | 201 | 3991 | 41.14 | 7 | 26 | 182 | 11 | | | | | | |
| D.P.Conway | 120 | 195 | 23 | 327* | 8169 | 47.49 | 21 | 37 | 100 | - | 9 | 467 | 51.88 | - | - | 3-36 |
| H.R.Cooper | 40 | 70 | 2 | 200 | 2422 | 35.61 | 6 | 12 | 21 | - | 2 | 56 | 28.00 | - | - | 1-8 |
| J.M.Cumming | 4 | 8 | 2 | 37 | 161 | 26.83 | - | - | - | - | | | | | | |
| S.B.Davey | 6 | 7 | 2 | 55 | 85 | 17.00 | - | 1 | 2 | - | 18 | 384 | 21.33 | 1 | - | 5-19 |
| C.de Grandhomme | 126 | 202 | 29 | 174* | 6592 | 38.10 | 15 | 36 | 113 | - | 205 | 6070 | 29.60 | 2 | - | 6-24 |
| L.J.Delport | 17 | 18 | 7 | 53* | 191 | 17.36 | - | 1 | 6 | - | 58 | 1747 | 30.12 | 3 | - | 7-78 |
| R.P.O.Drysdale | 1 | 2 | 0 | 62 | 67 | 33.50 | - | 1 | - | - | 1 | 34 | 34.00 | - | - | 1-11 |
| J.A.Duffy | 78 | 104 | 30 | 71 | 914 | 12.35 | - | 1 | 34 | - | 218 | 7328 | 33.61 | 9 | - | 7-89 |
| L.R.Dudding | 5 | 5 | 0 | 16 | 33 | 6.60 | - | - | 2 | - | 12 | 514 | 42.83 | - | - | 3-85 |
| J.F.A.Field | 7 | 10 | 1 | 38 | 194 | 21.55 | - | - | 5 | - | 12 | 506 | 42.16 | - | - | 3-50 |
| M.J.Fisher | 2 | 2 | 2 | 28* | 33 | - | - | - | - | - | 2 | 176 | 88.00 | - | - | 2-67 |
| C.D.Fletcher | 72 | 113 | 23 | 157 | 3179 | 35.32 | 6 | 16 | 233 | 13 | | | | | | |
| Z.G.Foulkes | 4 | 6 | 0 | 49 | 109 | 18.16 | - | - | 1 | - | 4 | 182 | 45.50 | - | - | 3-32 |
| L.I.Georgeson | 9 | 17 | 0 | 74 | 388 | 19.88 | - | 3 | 6 | - | 5 | 106 | 21.20 | - | - | 3-39 |
| J.D.Gibson | 20 | 33 | 4 | 116* | 704 | 24.27 | 1 | 2 | 21 | - | 22 | 899 | 40.86 | - | - | 3-36 |
| J.M.Gibson | 4 | 5 | 0 | 50 | 92 | 18.40 | - | 1 | 1 | - | 10 | 361 | 36.10 | - | - | 4-84 |
| Z.N.Gibson | 17 | 18 | 9 | 31* | 123 | 13.66 | - | - | 5 | - | 30 | 1402 | 46.73 | - | - | 4-62 |
| N.A.Greenwood | 3 | 6 | 0 | 26 | 106 | 17.66 | - | - | 1 | - | | | | | | |
| M.J.Guptill | 118 | 214 | 13 | 227 | 7747 | 38.54 | 17 | 40 | 138 | - | 11 | 674 | 61.27 | - | - | 3-11 |
| B.R.Hampton | 17 | 26 | 6 | 63* | 527 | 26.35 | - | 4 | 8 | - | 24 | 849 | 35.37 | - | - | 4-78 |
| R.D.Harrison | 4 | 6 | 0 | 46 | 84 | 14.00 | - | - | 7 | - | 2 | 120 | 60.00 | - | - | 1-29 |
| J.W.Hartshorn | 2 | 3 | 1 | 17* | 21 | 10.50 | - | - | 1 | - | 3 | 127 | 42.33 | - | - | 1-26 |
| G.R.Hay | 94 | 165 | 13 | 226 | 6367 | 41.88 | 15 | 31 | 49 | - | 2 | 201 | 100.50 | - | - | 1-8 |
| M.J.Hay | 1 | 1 | 0 | 62 | 62 | 62.00 | - | 1 | 3 | - | | | | | | |
| A.T.E.Hazeldine | 16 | 23 | 2 | 41 | 331 | 15.76 | - | - | 5 | - | 35 | 1383 | 39.51 | 1 | - | 5-33 |
| M.J.Henry | 81 | 106 | 17 | 81 | 1758 | 19.75 | - | 6 | 34 | - | 351 | 8700 | 24.78 | 16 | 3 | 7-23 |
| B.J.Horne | 42 | 67 | 12 | 162 | 1772 | 32.21 | 2 | 9 | 139 | 6 | | | | | | |
| K.A.Jamieson | 47 | 64 | 11 | 67 | 980 | 18.49 | - | 5 | 12 | - | 168 | 3758 | 22.36 | 11 | 2 | 8-74 |
| L.R.Johns | 12 | 17 | 1 | 40 | 222 | 13.87 | - | - | 34 | 2 | | | | | | |
| T.M.Johnson | 12 | 20 | 5 | 194* | 751 | 50.06 | 2 | 2 | 12 | - | | | | | | |
| S.S.Johnston | 2 | 4 | 0 | 25 | 45 | 11.25 | - | - | - | - | 1 | 60 | 60.00 | - | - | 1-31 |
| S.B.Keene | 5 | 7 | 1 | 65 | 94 | 15.6 | - | 1 | 2 | - | 25 | 357 | 14.28 | 3 | - | 6-44 |
| N.F.Kelly | 35 | 62 | 6 | 234* | 1980 | 35.35 | 2 | 11 | 27 | - | 0 | 77 | - | - | - | - |
| A.K.Kitchen | 92 | 167 | 13 | 207 | 5194 | 33.72 | 10 | 26 | 75 | - | 36 | 1797 | 49.91 | - | - | 3-19 |
| S.C.Kuggeleijn | 87 | 134 | 23 | 142* | 3105 | 27.97 | 3 | 16 | 33 | - | 270 | 8676 | 32.13 | 9 | - | 7-45 |
| T.W.M.Latham | 137 | 236 | 15 | 264* | 9497 | 42.97 | 23 | 51 | 175 | 1 | 1 | 18 | 18.00 | - | - | 1-7 |
| F.F.Lellman | 1 | 2 | 0 | 20 | 26 | 13.00 | - | - | - | - | | | | | | |
| J.R.Lennox | 6 | 10 | 2 | 43 | 96 | 12.00 | - | - | 8 | - | 10 | 617 | 61.70 | - | - | 3-38 |
| C.K.Leopard | 5 | 8 | 2 | 52 | 203 | 33.83 | - | 1 | 2 | - | 2 | 124 | 62.00 | - | - | 1-21 |

| | M | In | NO | HS | Runs | Ave | 100 | 50 | Ct | St | | Wkts | Runs | Ave | 5WI | 10WM | Best |
|---|---|---|---|---|---|---|---|---|---|---|---|---|---|---|---|---|---|
| B.G.Lister | 25 | 28 | 12 | 19* | 137 | 8.56 | - | - | 13 | - | | 61 | 1596 | 26.16 | 1 | - | 5-29 |
| B.N.J.Lockrose | 3 | 6 | 2 | 9 | 17 | 4.25 | - | - | - | - | | 3 | 295 | 98.33 | - | - | 2-30 |
| K.J.McClure | 48 | 81 | 8 | 210 | 2605 | 35.68 | 6 | 8 | 37 | - | | 0 | 2 | - | - | - | - |
| K.J.McComb | 1 | 1 | 0 | 0 | 0 | 0.00 | - | - | - | - | | 2 | 34 | 17.00 | - | - | 2-11 |
| C.E.McConchie | 51 | 81 | 7 | 187* | 2523 | 34.09 | 6 | 10 | 20 | - | | 44 | 1623 | 36.88 | - | - | 4-46 |
| F.McGregor-Sumpter | 1 | 2 | 0 | 56 | 56 | 28.00 | - | 1 | 1 | - | | | | | | | |
| J.D.McKay | 7 | 8 | 3 | 2 | 2 | 0.40 | - | - | 4 | - | | 15 | 612 | 40.80 | - | - | 4-85 |
| A.W.McKenzie | 7 | 10 | 2 | 34* | 106 | 13.25 | - | - | 1 | - | | 12 | 463 | 38.58 | - | - | 3-77 |
| C.R.McLachlan | 3 | 6 | 1 | 56 | 121 | 24.20 | - | 1 | 12 | 1 | | | | | | | |
| I.G.McPeake | 48 | 65 | 15 | 48 | 578 | 11.56 | - | - | 10 | - | | 132 | 3929 | 29.76 | 4 | 1 | 5-21 |
| D.J.Mitchell | 88 | 141 | 18 | 190 | 4987 | 40.54 | 13 | 27 | 101 | - | | 90 | 2715 | 30.16 | 1 | - | 5-44 |
| T.Muller | 59 | 70 | 26 | 65* | 891 | 20.25 | - | 1 | 21 | - | | 153 | 4235 | 27.67 | 7 | - | 6-52 |
| J.D.S.Neesham | 67 | 112 | 10 | 147 | 3249 | 31.85 | 5 | 17 | 67 | - | | 123 | 4012 | 32.61 | 2 | - | 5-65 |
| O.R.Newton | 24 | 33 | 4 | 70 | 464 | 16.00 | - | 2 | 1 | - | | 55 | 1821 | 33.10 | - | - | 4-26 |
| H.M.Nicholls | 103 | 168 | 12 | 174 | 6072 | 38.92 | 13 | 33 | 81 | - | | 0 | 26 | - | - | - | - |
| E.J.Nuttall | 38 | 35 | 22 | 24* | 136 | 10.46 | - | - | 11 | - | | 117 | 3650 | 31.19 | 4 | - | 6-35 |
| R.R.O'Donnell | 61 | 105 | 7 | 223 | 3588 | 36.61 | 7 | 19 | 75 | - | | 8 | 420 | 52.50 | - | - | 3-74 |
| W.T.O'Donnell | 12 | 21 | 4 | 137* | 756 | 44.47 | 3 | 3 | 12 | - | | 1 | 47 | 47.00 | - | - | 1-39 |
| W.P.O'Rourke | 3 | 2 | 1 | 6* | 10 | 10.00 | - | - | - | - | | 9 | 238 | 26.44 | - | - | 3-56 |
| T.K.Parkes | 1 | 2 | 1 | 4* | 5 | 5.00 | - | - | - | - | | | | | | | |
| A.Y.Patel | 74 | 106 | 29 | 52 | 1043 | 13.54 | - | 1 | 50 | - | | 273 | 8759 | 32.08 | 19 | 4 | 10-119 |
| S.K.Patel | 1 | 2 | 0 | 15 | 15 | 7.50 | - | - | 1 | - | | | | | | | |
| D.N.Phillips | 17 | 31 | 3 | 149 | 1047 | 37.39 | 3 | 6 | 24 | - | | 0 | 40 | - | - | - | - |
| G.D.Phillips | 46 | 80 | 6 | 138* | 2948 | 39.83 | 7 | 19 | 43 | - | | 35 | 1352 | 38.62 | - | - | 4-70 |
| B.J.Pomare | 1 | 2 | 0 | 23 | 23 | 11.50 | - | - | 2 | 2 | | | | | | | |
| B.Popli | 53 | 90 | 5 | 172 | 3154 | 37.10 | 4 | 21 | 50 | - | | 0 | 16 | - | - | - | - |
| O.M.R.Pringle | 10 | 10 | 4 | 28 | 112 | 18.66 | - | - | 4 | - | | 10 | 509 | 50.90 | - | - | 2-29 |
| M.D.Rae | 43 | 56 | 15 | 36 | 332 | 8.09 | - | - | 10 | - | | 118 | 4146 | 35.13 | 2 | - | 5-18 |
| S.H.A.Rance | 49 | 67 | 15 | 71 | 910 | 17.50 | - | 4 | 17 | - | | 152 | 4188 | 27.55 | 7 | - | 6-26 |
| B.G.Randell | 18 | 31 | 6 | 56 | 329 | 13.16 | - | 3 | 8 | - | | 52 | 1296 | 39.80 | 2 | - | 6-45 |
| J.A.Raval | 132 | 232 | 11 | 256 | 8323 | 37.66 | 18 | 38 | 141 | - | | 24 | 1138 | 47.41 | - | - | 2-10 |
| R.Ravindra | 36 | 61 | 8 | 217 | 2149 | 40.54 | 4 | 12 | 21 | - | | 34 | 1910 | 56.17 | 1 | - | 6-89 |
| M.Renwick | 41 | 76 | 3 | 134 | 1832 | 25.23 | 3 | 5 | 44 | 1 | | | | | | | |
| M.J.G.Rippon | 43 | 74 | 7 | 106 | 1876 | 28.00 | 1 | 8 | 16 | - | | 108 | 3730 | 34.53 | 4 | - | 6-66 |
| T.B.Robinson | 3 | 4 | 1 | 103* | 185 | 61.66 | 1 | 1 | 2 | - | | | | | | | |
| H.D.Rutherford | 122 | 212 | 3 | 239 | 7683 | 36.76 | 17 | 39 | 75 | - | | 1 | 107 | 107.00 | - | - | 1-26 |
| M.J.Santner | 56 | 85 | 5 | 126 | 2344 | 29.30 | 3 | 14 | 46 | - | | 86 | 4061 | 47.22 | - | - | 4-111 |
| B.D.Schmulian | 30 | 50 | 2 | 203 | 1893 | 39.43 | 3 | 12 | 17 | - | | 23 | 817 | 35.52 | - | - | 4-34 |
| B.V.Sears | 14 | 19 | 7 | 41 | 129 | 10.75 | - | - | 10 | - | | 46 | 1183 | 25.71 | 2 | - | 6-43 |
| T.L.Seifert | 55 | 94 | 6 | 167* | 2986 | 33.93 | 6 | 14 | 137 | 12 | | | | | | | |
| F.W.Sheat | 23 | 29 | 14 | 60* | 295 | 19.66 | - | 1 | 11 | - | | 76 | 1907 | 25.09 | 3 | - | 5-25 |
| H.B.Shipley | 17 | 27 | 2 | 76 | 560 | 22.40 | - | 5 | 9 | - | | 40 | 1111 | 27.77 | 1 | - | 5-37 |
| B.S.Smith | 67 | 114 | 8 | 244 | 3414 | 32.20 | 6 | 17 | 39 | 2 | | 1 | 59 | 59.00 | - | - | 1-17 |
| N.G.Smith | 37 | 59 | 9 | 114 | 1349 | 26.98 | 1 | 7 | 18 | - | | 81 | 2463 | 30.40 | 4 | - | 6-54 |
| M.W.Snedden | 12 | 15 | 4 | 19 | 59 | 5.36 | - | - | 8 | - | | 22 | 880 | 40.00 | - | - | 3-28 |
| I.S.Sodhi | 88 | 130 | 18 | 82* | 2337 | 20.86 | - | 11 | 38 | - | | 279 | 8410 | 33.72 | 16 | 2 | 7-30 |
| S.M.Solia | 40 | 65 | 6 | 135 | 1671 | 28.32 | 1 | 12 | 15 | - | | 68 | 1830 | 26.91 | - | - | 5-8 |
| W.E.R.Somerville | 45 | 58 | 9 | 60* | 918 | 18.73 | - | 3 | 17 | - | | 135 | 4026 | 29.82 | 4 | - | 8-136 |
| T.G.Southee | 129 | 176 | 16 | 156 | 2682 | 16.76 | 1 | 7 | 82 | - | | 511 | 13,680 | 26.77 | 25 | 1 | 8-27 |
| J.D.Sussex | 1 | 1 | 0 | 0 | 0 | 0.00 | - | - | 1 | - | | 3 | 36 | 12.00 | - | - | 3-36 |
| C.J.Swanson | 1 | 2 | 0 | 45 | 56 | 28.00 | - | - | - | - | | | | | | | |
| L.R.P.L.Taylor | 192 | 323 | 27 | 290 | 12,369 | 41.78 | 27 | 65 | 250 | - | | 7 | 378 | 54.00 | - | - | 2-4 |
| R.M.ter Braak | 7 | 8 | 1 | 58 | 92 | 18.40 | - | 1 | 1 | - | | 13 | 415 | 31.92 | - | - | 4-67 |
| B.M.Tickner | 58 | 63 | 24 | 37* | 416 | 10.66 | - | - | 24 | - | | 171 | 6011 | 35.15 | 5 | - | 5-23 |
| R.L.Toole | 17 | 23 | 13 | 17* | 59 | 5.90 | - | - | 5 | - | | 53 | 1454 | 27.43 | 1 | - | 6-54 |
| L.V.van Beek | 62 | 85 | 19 | 111* | 1535 | 22.91 | 1 | 7 | 43 | - | | 157 | 5106 | 32.52 | 6 | 1 | 6-46 |
| T.F.van Woerkom | 29 | 35 | 8 | 63* | 527 | 19.51 | - | 3 | 10 | - | | 45 | 1765 | 39.22 | 1 | - | 5-42 |
| S.S.Varcoe | 1 | 2 | 0 | 16 | 16 | 8.00 | - | - | - | - | | | | | | | |
| K.L.D.Vishvaka | 3 | 5 | 0 | 80 | 166 | 32.20 | - | 2 | 1 | - | | | | | | | |
| N.Wagner | 191 | 250 | 55 | 70 | 3260 | 16.71 | - | 9 | 58 | - | | 783 | 20,996 | 26.81 | 36 | 2 | 7-39 |
| F.L.Walker | 1 | - | - | - | - | - | - | - | - | - | | 0 | 63 | - | - | - | - |
| J.G.Walker | 41 | 53 | 17 | 87 | 664 | 18.44 | - | 1 | 19 | - | | 80 | 2997 | 37.46 | 3 | - | 5-25 |
| B.M.Wheeler | 42 | 51 | 7 | 81* | 854 | 19.40 | - | 6 | 22 | - | | 121 | 3472 | 28.69 | 3 | - | 6-60 |
| B.L.Wiggins | 7 | 12 | 1 | 133 | 353 | 32.09 | 1 | - | 12 | - | | | | | | | |
| W.S.A.Williams | 43 | 59 | 15 | 38 | 578 | 13.13 | - | - | 18 | - | | 123 | 2848 | 23.15 | 2 | - | 5-26 |
| K.S.Williamson | 156 | 267 | 21 | 284* | 12,179 | 49.50 | 34 | 60 | 138 | - | | 86 | 3721 | 43.26 | 1 | - | 5-75 |
| G.H.Worker | 110 | 199 | 7 | 210 | 5451 | 28.39 | 9 | 27 | 104 | - | | 58 | 3892 | 67.10 | - | - | 4-58 |
| W.A.Young | 100 | 166 | 13 | 162 | 6333 | 41.39 | 13 | 37 | 56 | - | | 0 | 8 | - | - | - | - |
| P.F.Younghusband | 15 | 23 | 6 | 97 | 562 | 33.05 | - | 2 | 13 | - | | 17 | 768 | 45.17 | 1 | - | 5-89 |

# FORD TROPHY

*2021/22*

Auckland won the Ford Trophy for the third time in five seasons defeating Central Districts in the final at Queenstown. The competition got off to a slow start with Auckland and Northern Districts starting late due to Covid restrictions and when the competition got into full swing, eight games were abandoned without any play, due to rain, and others were shortened. Auckland and Otago played only nine matches so final places were determined by average points per game (which made no difference to the placings at it turned out).

Auckland's George Worker became the first player to score four centuries in a season and finished with 672 runs. The next four leading run scorers were Mark Chapman (465), Glenn Phillips (378), Martin Guptill (367) and Robbie O'Donnell (283) who were also from Auckland. Wellington's Troy Johnson was next with 281.

Lockie Ferguson *(Auckland)* and Matt Bacon *(Otago)* were the leading wicket takers with 14 while Seth Rance *(Central Districts)* took 12.

Final points were:

|  | P | W | L | T | NR | Bonus | Points |
|---|---|---|---|---|---|---|---|
| Central Districts | 10 | 5 | 1 | – | 4 | 4 | 32 |
| Auckland | 9 | 6 | 3 | – | – | 3 | 27 |
| Wellington | 10 | 4 | 3 | – | 3 | 1 | 23 |
| Northern Districts | 10 | 2 | 4 | – | 4 | 2 | 18 |
| Otago | 9 | 3 | 5 | – | 1 | 1 | 15 |
| Canterbury | 10 | 1 | 5 | – | 4 | – | 12 |

# Games 1-3

Gibson made his Otago debut and Smith made his Wellington debut.

The Northern versus Canterbury match was reduced to 32 overs-per-side. Northern Districts lost wickets in each of the first two overs before a 119 run stand from 90 balls for the third wicket between Raval (fifty from 45 balls and reached 2000 career runs) and Carter (fifty from 41 balls). Cooper then got fifty from 35 balls to enable Northern to reach 239-8. McClure and McConchie added 71 off 51 balls for Canterbury's third wicket and McConchie and Carter finished the game with an unbeaten century stand. Carter got his fifty from just 20 balls as Canterbury got to their target with 28 balls to spare.

Allen became Duffy's 100th victim when Wellington batted first. Johnson scored a 72-ball fifty and Smith hit an unbeaten 44 as Wellington made 255-7. Rippon took 4-41. Rutherford reached 2000 runs during his innings but Broom was the Otago backbone with fifty from 67 balls. Otago were in a promising position at 202-4 with 61 balls left but they collapsed to be all out for 242 with an over remaining. Younghusband took three wickets.

The Canterbury versus Northern Districts game was abandoned without a ball being bowled.

## NORTHERN DISTRICTS v CANTERBURY      Ford Trophy

*at Seddon Park, Hamilton on 30 November, 2021*
*Toss : Canterbury. Umpires : C.M. Brown & T.J. Parlane*
**Canterbury won by 7 wickets.** *Points: Canterbury 4, Northern Districts 0*

### NORTHERN DISTRICTS

| | Runs | Mins | Balls | 6s | 4s |
|---|---|---|---|---|---|
| K.D.Clarke c Shipley b Nuttall .... | 1 | 3 | 2 | - | - |
| J.A.Raval c McClure b Nuttall ... | 74 | 75 | 57 | 3 | 6 |
| B.Popli c Carter b Henry ............. | 2 | 6 | 4 | - | - |
| J.F.Carter* c McConchie b Henry | 52 | 83 | 46 | 2 | 4 |
| H.R.Cooper c Shipley b Williams | 52 | 43 | 40 | 3 | 4 |
| C.de Grandhomme c McClure | | | | | |
| b van Woerkom ...................... | 7 | 17 | 10 | - | 1 |
| P.D.Bocock† run out ................ | 20 | 26 | 17 | - | 2 |
| A.Verma run out ......................... | 9 | 12 | 6 | 1 | - |
| B.G.Randell not out .................... | 9 | 13 | 6 | 1 | - |
| Z.N.Gibson not out .................... | 4 | 5 | 4 | - | - |
| J.G.Walker | | | | | |
| Extras (lb 2, w 7) ...................... | 9 | | | | |
| **TOTAL** (32 overs) (8 wkts) . | **239** | 144 | | | |

### CANTERBURY

| | Runs | Mins | Balls | 6s | 4s |
|---|---|---|---|---|---|
| C.J.Bowes c Bocock b Randell . | 12 | 14 | 14 | 1 | 1 |
| J.C.T.Boyle st Bocock b Walker | 16 | 47 | 27 | - | 1 |
| K.J.McClure c Clarke | | | | | |
| b de Grandhomme ................ | 87 | 68 | 55 | 5 | 9 |
| C.E.McConchie* not out ........... | 57 | 71 | 46 | 3 | 3 |
| L.J.Carter not out ...................... | 54 | 35 | 23 | 6 | 2 |
| C.D.Fletcher† | | | | | |
| H.B.Shipley | | | | | |
| T.F.van Woerkom | | | | | |
| M.J.Henry | | | | | |
| W.S.A.Williams | | | | | |
| E.J.Nuttall | | | | | |
| Extras (b 1, w 12, nb 1) .......... | 14 | | | | |
| **TOTAL** (27.2 overs) (3 wkts) | **240** | 118 | | | |

| Bowling | O | M | R | W |
|---|---|---|---|---|
| **CANTERBURY** | | | | |
| Nuttall | 7 | 0 | 58 | 2 |
| Henry | 7 | 0 | 42 | 2 |
| Shipley | 4 | 0 | 33 | 0 |
| Williams | 6 | 0 | 51 | 1 |
| McConchie | 2 | 0 | 21 | 0 |
| van Woerkom | 6 | 0 | 32 | 1 |
| **NORTHERN DISTRICTS** | | | | |
| Gibson | 5 | 1 | 25 | 0 |
| Randell | 6.2 | 0 | 69 | 1 |
| de Grandhomme | 5 | 0 | 63 | 1 |
| Verma | 6 | 0 | 48 | 0 |
| Walker | 5 | 0 | 34 | 1 |

| Fall of Wickets | ND | C |
|---|---|---|
| 1st | 4 | 18 |
| 2nd | 8 | 68 |
| 3rd | 127 | 139 |
| 4th | 155 | - |
| 5th | 194 | - |
| 6th | 197 | - |
| 7th | 215 | - |
| 8th | 233 | - |
| 9th | - | - |
| 10th | - | - |

# WELLINGTON v OTAGO  **Ford Trophy**

*at Cello Basin Reserve, Wellington on 1 December, 2021*
*Toss : Otago.  Umpires : C.A. Black & S.B. Haig*
**Wellington won by 13 runs.** *Points: Wellington 4, Otago 0*

## WELLINGTON

| | Runs | Mins | Balls | 6s | 4s |
|---|---|---|---|---|---|
| F.H.Allen† c Phillips b Duffy | 23 | 35 | 25 | 1 | 3 |
| L.I.Georgeson c Chu b Rippon | 44 | 81 | 70 | - | 6 |
| J.J.N.P.Bhula c & b Rippon | 21 | 60 | 32 | - | 1 |
| T.M.Johnson c & b Duffy | 73 | 103 | 87 | 1 | 9 |
| M.G.Bracewell b Rippon | 4 | 14 | 13 | - | - |
| J.D.Gibson c Duffy b Rippon | 21 | 42 | 35 | 1 | - |
| N.G.Smith not out | 44 | 48 | 29 | 3 | 2 |
| L.V.van Beek c Kelly b Gibson | 13 | 14 | 9 | 1 | - |
| P.F.Younghusband not out | 0 | 2 | 0 | - | - |
| B.V.Sears | | | | | |
| H.K.Bennett* | | | | | |
| Extras (lb 7, w 5) | 12 | | | | |
| **TOTAL** (50 overs) (7 wkts) | **255** | 201 | | | |

## OTAGO

| | Runs | Mins | Balls | 6s | 4s |
|---|---|---|---|---|---|
| H.D.Rutherford* c Allen | | | | | |
|   b van Beek | 23 | 33 | 27 | - | 3 |
| D.N.Phillips lbw b Younghusband | 33 | 69 | 38 | - | 5 |
| N.T.Broom c Georgeson b Sears | 72 | 145 | 94 | - | 6 |
| N.F.Kelly c van Beek | | | | | |
|   b Younghusband | 0 | 3 | 2 | - | - |
| J.L.Finnie c Smith | | | | | |
|   b Younghusband | 28 | 29 | 26 | - | 5 |
| A.K.Kitchen run out | 41 | 93 | 59 | - | 3 |
| M.J.G.Rippon c Smith b Bennett | 18 | 51 | 27 | - | 1 |
| M.W.Chu† c sub (M.W.Snedden) | | | | | |
|   b Bhula | 0 | 4 | 1 | - | - |
| J.M.Gibson c Georgeson b Gibson | 2 | 7 | 7 | - | - |
| J.A.Duffy c Johnson b Bennett | 11 | 23 | 13 | - | 1 |
| M.B.Bacon not out | 0 | 1 | 0 | - | - |
| Extras (b 4, lb 1, w 9) | 14 | | | | |
| **TOTAL** (49 overs) | **242** | 231 | | | |

| Bowling | O | M | R | W |
|---|---|---|---|---|
| **OTAGO** | | | | |
| Duffy | 10 | 0 | 58 | 2 |
| Bacon | 6 | 0 | 41 | 0 |
| Kitchen | 10 | 0 | 26 | 0 |
| Gibson | 6 | 0 | 45 | 1 |
| Rippon | 10 | 2 | 41 | 4 |
| Finnie | 8 | 0 | 37 | 0 |
| **WELLINGTON** | | | | |
| Smith | 6 | 0 | 38 | 0 |
| Bennett | 7 | 0 | 30 | 2 |
| van Beek | 6 | 1 | 26 | 1 |
| Sears | 8 | 0 | 36 | 1 |
| Younghusband | 10 | 1 | 56 | 3 |
| Bhula | 5 | 0 | 19 | 1 |
| Gibson | 7 | 0 | 32 | 1 |

### Fall of Wickets

| | W | O |
|---|---|---|
| 1st | 44 | 41 |
| 2nd | 92 | 65 |
| 3rd | 107 | 65 |
| 4th | 121 | 113 |
| 5th | 157 | 202 |
| 6th | 209 | 214 |
| 7th | 249 | 216 |
| 8th | - | 219 |
| 9th | - | 242 |
| 10th | - | 242 |

# CANTERBURY v NORTHERN DISTRICTS  **Ford Trophy**

*at MainPower Oval, Rangiora on 6 December, 2021*
**Abandoned without a ball being bowled.** *Points: Canterbury 2, Northern Districts 2*

## Games 4-6

Johnson *(Otago)* made his debut against Wellington.

Canterbury batted first against Otago and made 222, thanks largely to highest scores by Shipley (55) and van Woerkom (41) who added 96 for the seventh wicket. Bacon had career best figures of 4-45 and Kitchen took three wickets. Finnie and Broom both scored fifties as they added 95 off 59 balls to give Otago a win by five wickets with 43 balls to spare.

The game between Northern Districts and Central Districts was abandoned.

Wellington batted first against Otago and made an imposing 333-9. After Wellington lost Allen early, Ravindra and Blundell added 98 from 102 balls. Blundell got fifty from 80 balls. Johnson scored a fifty from 51 deliveries and made 88 to top score. Duffy took 3-70. Otago lost two wickets in the first five overs and were then 54-4. Kelly and Rippon both scored fifties but Otago were dismissed for 238 from 43.4 overs. Bracewell took three wickets.

## OTAGO v CANTERBURY                                    Ford Trophy

*at University of Otago Oval, Dunedin on 14 December, 2021*
*Toss : Otago.  Umpires : J.A.K. Bromley & D.J. Walker*
**Otago won by 5 wickets.** *Points: Otago 4, Canterbury 0*

### CANTERBURY

| | Runs | Mins | Balls | 6s | 4s |
|---|---|---|---|---|---|
| J.C.T.Boyle c Chu b Bacon | 6 | 20 | 15 | - | 1 |
| C.J.Bowes c Chu b Muller | 23 | 43 | 31 | - | 4 |
| K.J.McClure c Chu b Duffy | 14 | 14 | 13 | - | 3 |
| C.E.McConchie* b Kitchen | 2 | 12 | 9 | - | - |
| L.J.Carter c Rippon b Kitchen | 25 | 46 | 35 | 3 | 1 |
| C.D.Fletcher† c Broom b Kitchen | 12 | 35 | 21 | - | 3 |
| H.B.Shipley c Kelly b Duffy | 55 | 97 | 67 | 3 | 2 |
| T.F.van Woerkom c Duffy b Bacon | 41 | 76 | 78 | 2 | 3 |
| M.J.Henry c Duffy b Bacon | 15 | 17 | 12 | - | 2 |
| W.S.A.Williams not out | 4 | 13 | 7 | - | - |
| E.J.Nuttall c Duffy b Bacon | 8 | 9 | 8 | - | 1 |
| Extras (lb 2, w 15) | 17 | | | | |
| **TOTAL** (49.2 overs) | **222** | 194 | | | |

### OTAGO

| | Runs | Mins | Balls | 6s | 4s |
|---|---|---|---|---|---|
| H.D.Rutherford* c Fletcher b Williams | 24 | 31 | 16 | - | 5 |
| D.N.Phillips lbw b Shipley | 43 | 67 | 62 | - | 7 |
| N.T.Broom c & b Williams | 50 | 100 | 64 | - | 5 |
| N.F.Kelly b van Woerkom | 1 | 6 | 5 | - | - |
| J.L.Finnie not out | 72 | 98 | 74 | - | 9 |
| A.K.Kitchen b van Woerkom | 1 | 7 | 9 | - | - |
| M.J.G.Rippon not out | 26 | 32 | 27 | - | 4 |
| M.W.Chu† | | | | | |
| T.Muller | | | | | |
| J.A.Duffy | | | | | |
| M.B.Bacon | | | | | |
| Extras (lb 1, w 5) | 6 | | | | |
| **TOTAL** (42.5 overs) (5 wkts) | **223** | 172 | | | |

| Bowling | O | M | R | W |
|---|---|---|---|---|
| **OTAGO** | | | | |
| Duffy | 10 | 3 | 28 | 2 |
| Bacon | 7.2 | 1 | 45 | 4 |
| Kitchen | 10 | 1 | 36 | 3 |
| Muller | 8 | 0 | 41 | 1 |
| Rippon | 10 | 1 | 42 | 0 |
| Finnie | 4 | 0 | 28 | 0 |
| **CANTERBURY** | | | | |
| Henry | 8 | 2 | 44 | 0 |
| Nuttall | 6 | 0 | 49 | 0 |
| Williams | 10 | 0 | 28 | 2 |
| McConchie | 4 | 0 | 27 | 0 |
| van Woerkom | 9.5 | 1 | 49 | 2 |
| Shipley | 5 | 0 | 25 | 1 |

| Fall of Wickets | C | O |
|---|---|---|
| 1st | 20 | 48 |
| 2nd | 43 | 84 |
| 3rd | 50 | 87 |
| 4th | 52 | 182 |
| 5th | 89 | 185 |
| 6th | 90 | - |
| 7th | 186 | - |
| 8th | 208 | - |
| 9th | 211 | - |
| 10th | 222 | - |

# NORTHERN DISTRICTS v CENTRAL DISTRICTS    Ford Trophy

*at Seddon Park, Hamilton on 15 December, 2021*
**Abandoned without a ball being bowled.** *Points: Northern Districts 2, Central Districts 2*


# WELLINGTON v OTAGO                                    Ford Trophy

*at Cello Basin Reserve, Wellington on 21 December, 2021*
*Toss : Otago. Umpires : S.B. Haig & E.D. Sanders*
**Wellington won by 95 runs.** *Points: Wellington 5, Otago 0*

## WELLINGTON

|  | Runs | Mins | Balls | 6s | 4s |
|---|---|---|---|---|---|
| F.H.Allen c Johnson b Duffy | 8 | 8 | 11 | - | 2 |
| R.Ravindra c Muller b Duffy | 46 | 88 | 41 | - | 7 |
| T.A.Blundell† b Kitchen | 53 | 107 | 84 | - | 5 |
| T.M.Johnson c Duffy b Bacon | 88 | 111 | 78 | 4 | 7 |
| M.G.Bracewell b Kitchen | 39 | 53 | 38 | 2 | 2 |
| J.D.Gibson c Muller b Duffy | 2 | 13 | 7 | - | - |
| N.G.Smith not out | 28 | 46 | 20 | - | 4 |
| L.V.van Beek c Chu b McKenzie | 2 | 5 | 5 | - | - |
| B.V.Sears c Johnson b Bacon | 15 | 12 | 9 | - | 2 |
| O.R.Newton c Duffy b McKenzie | 25 | 11 | 10 | 2 | 1 |
| H.K.Bennett* | | | | | |

Extras (b 2, lb 7, w 15, nb 3) .. 27
**TOTAL** (50 overs) (9 wkts) . **333** 228

## OTAGO

|  | Runs | Mins | Balls | 6s | 4s |
|---|---|---|---|---|---|
| H.D.Rutherford* c Blundell | | | | | |
| b Newton | 8 | 22 | 14 | - | 1 |
| D.N.Phillips c Allen b Newton | 0 | 4 | 2 | - | - |
| N.F.Kelly b Bracewell | 67 | 103 | 71 | 4 | 5 |
| A.K.Kitchen b van Beek | 17 | 33 | 15 | - | 3 |
| L.C.Johnson c Allen b Smith | 0 | 6 | 6 | - | - |
| M.W.Chu† c van Beek | | | | | |
| b Bracewell | 32 | 67 | 42 | - | 5 |
| M.J.G.Rippon not out | 68 | 93 | 65 | 2 | 6 |
| A.W.McKenzie c Newton | | | | | |
| b Bracewell | 6 | 22 | 14 | - | - |
| T.Muller c van Beek b Bennett | 18 | 33 | 23 | - | 1 |
| J.A.Duffy c Gibson b Bennett | 17 | 13 | 10 | 1 | 1 |
| M.B.Bacon run out | 0 | 1 | 0 | - | - |
| Extras (lb 1, w 4) | 5 | | | | |
| **TOTAL** (43.4 overs) | **238** | 201 | | | |

| Bowling | O | M | R | W |
|---|---|---|---|---|
| **NORTHERN DISTRICTS** | | | | |
| Bacon | 10 | 2 | 66 | 2 |
| Duffy | 7 | 0 | 70 | 3 |
| McKenzie | 9 | 1 | 59 | 2 |
| Muller | 5 | 0 | 34 | 0 |
| Rippon | 10 | 0 | 44 | 0 |
| Kitchen | 9 | 0 | 51 | 2 |
| **WELLINGTON** | | | | |
| Newton | 8 | 0 | 44 | 2 |
| Bennett | 7.4 | 0 | 38 | 2 |
| van Beek | 6 | 0 | 43 | 1 |
| Smith | 3 | 0 | 13 | 1 |
| Sears | 4 | 0 | 28 | 0 |
| Bracewell | 8 | 0 | 36 | 3 |
| Ravindra | 7 | 0 | 35 | 0 |

| Fall of Wickets | W | O |
|---|---|---|
| 1st | 9 | 1 |
| 2nd | 107 | 13 |
| 3rd | 144 | 53 |
| 4th | 218 | 54 |
| 5th | 238 | 119 |
| 6th | 274 | 143 |
| 7th | 277 | 167 |
| 8th | 301 | 218 |
| 9th | 333 | 238 |
| 10th | - | 238 |

# Games 7-9

Ashok *(Auckland)* and O'Rourke *(Canterbury)* made their debuts. Worker made his Auckland debut.

Wellington batted first against Auckland and made 307-9 with fifties to Allen, Georgeson and Johnson. Georgeson made his highest score after sharing an opening stand of 125 from 85 balls. Ferns took 3-68. Worker and Chapman broke the Auckland second wicket record with a 237 run stand from 229 balls. Both players scored centuries. Worker's 13th domestic century took 107 balls while Chapman's fourth came from 108 balls. Auckland won by six wickets and with two balls to spare.

Otago had an opening stand of 105 against Canterbury. Renwick scored 55 and Chu reached his highest score as Otago totalled 258-7. Canterbury started badly being 15-3 and then 77-5 before fifties to Carter and Shipley got them to 205. Shipley made his highest score of 78. Bacon took 4-51 and Lockrose had career best figures with his three wickets. Otago won by 53 runs.

Wellington captain Bracewell was playing his 100th domestic one-day game. Auckland batted first and made 207. Guptill had to retire hurt and Auckland were 103-5 at one stage. Solia and Somerville added 74 with Somerville getting a fifty. Newton and van Beek both took three wickets. Allen was dismissed first ball in Wellington's reply but then came a 69 run stand for the second wicket. Georgeson got fifty from 49 balls. After being 110-4 Wellington had two stands of fifty to register a five wicket win with 43 balls to spare.

# WELLINGTON v AUCKLAND      Ford Trophy

*at Cello Basin Reserve, Wellington on 1 January, 2022*
*Toss : Wellington.  Umpires : K.D. Cotton & D.J. Walker*
**Auckland won by 6 wickets.** *Points: Auckland 4, Welllington 0*

| WELLINGTON | Runs | Mins | Balls | 6s | 4s |
|---|---|---|---|---|---|
| F.H.Allen† c Horne b Solia | 86 | 81 | 55 | 5 | 11 |
| L.I.Georgeson b Phillips | 56 | 158 | 74 | 1 | 4 |
| J.J.N.P.Bhula c Solia b Ashok | 9 | 22 | 26 | - | 1 |
| T.M.Johnson run out | 84 | 125 | 87 | 3 | 4 |
| M.G.Bracewell c Worker b Delport | 10 | 19 | 19 | - | - |
| N.G.Smith c b Delport | 14 | 13 | 12 | - | 2 |
| L.V.van Beek b Ferns | 19 | 22 | 17 | - | 3 |
| O.R.Newton lbw b Ferns | 8 | 10 | 7 | - | 1 |
| P.F.Younghusband not out | 1 | 7 | 3 | - | - |
| B.V.Sears c Chapman b Ferns | 0 | 1 | 1 | - | - |
| H.K.Bennett* not out | 0 | 3 | 0 | - | - |

Extras (b 1, lb 3, w 15, nb 1) .. 20
**TOTAL (50 overs) (9 wkts) .** **307** 232

| AUCKLAND | Runs | Mins | Balls | 6s | 4s |
|---|---|---|---|---|---|
| M.J.Guptill c Allen b Newton | 10 | 13 | 11 | 1 | 1 |
| G.H.Worker c Johnson b Bracewell | 132 | 176 | 128 | 7 | 9 |
| M.S.Chapman c Bracewell b Younghusband | 105 | 168 | 113 | 4 | 6 |
| G.D.Phillips run out | 30 | 43 | 21 | 1 | 3 |
| R.R.O'Donnell* not out | 16 | 40 | 24 | - | - |
| S.M.Solia not out | 4 | 2 | 1 | - | 1 |
| B.J.Horne† | | | | | |
| D.K.Ferns | | | | | |
| A.Ashok | | | | | |
| L.J.Delport | | | | | |
| B.G.Lister | | | | | |

Extras (b 4, w 9) .. 13
**TOTAL (49.4 overs) (4 wkts)** **310** 223

| Bowling | O | M | R | W |
|---|---|---|---|---|
| **AUCKLAND** | | | | |
| Lister | 9 | 0 | 70 | 0 |
| Ferns | 10 | 1 | 68 | 3 |
| Ashok | 10 | 0 | 70 | 1 |
| Solia | 5 | 1 | 23 | 1 |
| Delport | 10 | 0 | 43 | 2 |
| Chapman | 2 | 0 | 13 | 0 |
| Phillips | 4 | 0 | 16 | 1 |
| **WELLINGTON** | | | | |
| Newton | 10 | 1 | 57 | 1 |
| Bennett | 6 | 0 | 32 | 0 |
| van Beek | 6 | 0 | 53 | 0 |
| Bhula | 2 | 0 | 15 | 0 |
| Sears | 7.4 | 0 | 41 | 0 |
| Bracewell | 10 | 0 | 61 | 1 |
| Younghusband | 8 | 0 | 47 | 1 |

| Fall of Wickets | W | A |
|---|---|---|
| 1st | 125 | 15 |
| 2nd | 140 | 252 |
| 3rd | 207 | 261 |
| 4th | 230 | 305 |
| 5th | 250 | - |
| 6th | 288 | - |
| 7th | 304 | - |
| 8th | 306 | - |
| 9th | 306 | - |
| 10th | - | - |

# CANTERBURY v OTAGO                     Ford Trophy

*at Dudley Park, Rangiora on 3 January, 2022*
*Toss : Canterbury.  Umpires : J.M. Dempsey & T.J. Parlane*
**Otago won by 53 runs.** Points: Otago 5, Canterbury 0

## OTAGO

| | Runs | Mins | Balls | 6s | 4s |
|---|---|---|---|---|---|
| H.D.Rutherford* st Fletcher b McConchie | 45 | 104 | 66 | - | 4 |
| M.Renwick c Fletcher b Nuttall | 55 | 123 | 85 | - | 4 |
| N.T.Broom c Shipley b O'Rourke | 41 | 70 | 43 | - | 3 |
| N.F.Kelly c Fletcher b Nuttall | 1 | 9 | 8 | - | - |
| L.C.Johnson b O'Rourke | 26 | 45 | 30 | - | 3 |
| A.K.Kitchen b Shipley | 1 | 10 | 3 | - | - |
| M.W.Chu† not out | 44 | 54 | 41 | - | 6 |
| J.A.Duffy run out | 6 | 23 | 7 | - | - |
| B.N.J.Lockrose not out | 18 | 22 | 17 | 1 | 1 |
| M.D.Rae | | | | | |
| M.B.Bacon | | | | | |
| Extras (b 1, lb 4, w 16) | 21 | | | | |
| **TOTAL** (50 overs) (7 wkts) | **258** | 232 | | | |

| Bowling | O | M | R | W |
|---|---|---|---|---|
| **CANTERBURY** | | | | |
| Williams | 10 | 1 | 40 | 0 |
| Nuttall | 10 | 0 | 64 | 2 |
| Shipley | 9 | 0 | 50 | 1 |
| O'Rourke | 10 | 1 | 31 | 2 |
| van Woerkom | 6 | 0 | 43 | 0 |
| McConchie | 5 | 0 | 25 | 1 |

## CANTERBURY

| | Runs | Mins | Balls | 6s | 4s |
|---|---|---|---|---|---|
| C.J.Bowes lbw b Bacon | 11 | 5 | 6 | - | 2 |
| J.C.T.Boyle c Renwick b Duffy | 4 | 18 | 10 | - | - |
| K.J.McClure lbw b Bacon | 0 | 3 | 3 | - | - |
| L.J.Carter st Chu b Lockrose | 63 | 107 | 81 | - | 8 |
| C.E.McConchie* b Kitchen | 14 | 38 | 28 | - | 1 |
| C.D.Fletcher† b Kitchen | 2 | 19 | 11 | - | - |
| H.B.Shipley c Renwick b Bacon | 78 | 106 | 64 | 3 | 8 |
| T.F.van Woerkom c Kelly b Lockrose | 9 | 18 | 16 | - | 1 |
| W.S.A.Williams b Lockrose | 0 | 11 | 7 | - | - |
| W.P.O'Rourke c sub (A.W.McKenzie) b Bacon | 11 | 23 | 19 | - | 2 |
| E.J.Nuttall not out | 3 | 17 | 12 | - | - |
| Extras (lb 4, w 6) | 10 | | | | |
| **TOTAL** (43.3 overs) | **205** | 183 | | | |

| Bowling | O | M | R | W |
|---|---|---|---|---|
| **OTAGO** | | | | |
| Duffy | 6 | 0 | 27 | 1 |
| Bacon | 9.3 | 1 | 51 | 4 |
| Rae | 9 | 0 | 43 | 0 |
| Kitchen | 7 | 0 | 32 | 2 |
| Lockrose | 10 | 2 | 36 | 3 |
| Rutherford | 2 | 0 | 12 | 0 |

### Fall of Wickets

| | O | C |
|---|---|---|
| 1st | 105 | 11 |
| 2nd | 132 | 11 |
| 3rd | 140 | 15 |
| 4th | 186 | 63 |
| 5th | 186 | 77 |
| 6th | 188 | 141 |
| 7th | 217 | 161 |
| 8th | - | 166 |
| 9th | - | 185 |
| 10th | - | 205 |

# WELLINGTON v AUCKLAND                     Ford Trophy

*at Cello Basin Reserve, Wellington on 3 January, 2022*
*Toss : Auckland.  Umpires : K.D. Cotton & D.J. Walker*
**Wellington won by 5 wickets.** Points: Wellington 4, Auckland 0

## AUCKLAND

| | Runs | Mins | Balls | 6s | 4s |
|---|---|---|---|---|---|
| M.J.Guptill retired hurt | 32 | 56 | 35 | - | 4 |
| G.H.Worker c Younghusband b Newton | 6 | 27 | 14 | - | 1 |
| M.S.Chapman b Smith | 12 | 14 | 10 | - | 2 |
| G.D.Phillips c Allen b van Beek | 27 | 77 | 36 | 1 | 3 |
| R.R.O'Donnell* c & b van Beek | 20 | 48 | 41 | - | 3 |
| B.J.Horne† c Allen b van Beek | 0 | 3 | 4 | - | - |
| S.M.Solia c Gibson b Bracewell | 39 | 76 | 62 | 1 | 3 |
| W.E.R.Somerville b Bracewell | 59 | 83 | 77 | 1 | 4 |
| L.H.Ferguson c Georgeson b Newton | 4 | 19 | 9 | - | - |
| D.K.Ferns c Gibson b Newton | 2 | 6 | 3 | - | - |
| L.J.Delport not out | 0 | 3 | 0 | - | - |
| Extras (lb 2, w 4) | 6 | | | | |
| **TOTAL** (48.3 overs) | **207** | 208 | | | |

| Bowling | O | M | R | W |
|---|---|---|---|---|
| **WELLINGTON** | | | | |
| Smith | 7 | 0 | 23 | 1 |
| Newton | 6.3 | 0 | 43 | 3 |
| Sears | 6 | 0 | 30 | 0 |
| van Beek | 10 | 2 | 29 | 3 |
| Younghusband | 10 | 2 | 34 | 0 |
| Bracewell | 9 | 0 | 46 | 2 |
| **AUCKLAND** | | | | |
| Ferguson | 8 | 0 | 37 | 1 |
| Ferns | 4.5 | 0 | 42 | 0 |
| Solia | 3 | 1 | 9 | 0 |
| Somerville | 10 | 2 | 28 | 2 |
| Delport | 10 | 0 | 45 | 2 |
| Phillips | 3 | 0 | 19 | 0 |
| Chapman | 2 | 0 | 17 | 0 |
| Worker | 2 | 0 | 11 | 0 |

## WELLINGTON

| | Runs | Mins | Balls | 6s | 4s |
|---|---|---|---|---|---|
| F.H.Allen† lbw b Ferguson | 0 | 1 | 1 | - | - |
| L.I.Georgeson c Horne b Delport | 51 | 97 | 52 | 1 | 9 |
| J.J.N.P.Bhula lbw b Somerville | 38 | 59 | 50 | 2 | 3 |
| T.M.Johnson b Delport | 8 | 33 | 27 | - | 1 |
| M.G.Bracewell* lbw b Somerville | 30 | 54 | 40 | - | 3 |
| N.G.Smith not out | 47 | 87 | 56 | 1 | 5 |
| J.D.Gibson not out | 22 | 35 | 31 | - | 3 |
| L.V.van Beek | | | | | |
| O.R.Newton | | | | | |
| P.F.Younghusband | | | | | |
| B.V.Sears | | | | | |
| Extras (lb 2, w 12) | 14 | | | | |
| **TOTAL** (42.5 overs) (5 wkts) | **210** | 185 | | | |

### Fall of Wickets

| | A | W |
|---|---|---|
| 1st | 33 | 0 |
| 2nd | 50 | 69 |
| 3rd | 100 | 109 |
| 4th | 100 | 110 |
| 5th | 103 | 160 |
| 6th | 177 | - |
| 7th | 204 | - |
| 8th | 204 | - |
| 9th | 207 | - |
| 10th | - | - |

*Guptill retired hurt at 57-2*

# Games 10-12

Northern were dismissed for just 143 from 35.4 overs with Carter top scoring with 38. Rance had career best figures of 4-25. Central cruised to a bonus point win achieving their target while losing four wickets in 30.4 overs. Clarkson hit a 34-ball fifty.

Auckland made 221 against Northern with Horne top scoring with 45. Verma took 3-29. Northern lost Seifert early and then Raval and Carter added 177 from 180 balls for the second wicket, a record for Northern against Auckland. Raval got fifty from 51 balls while Carter needed 67 for fifty and reached his second century and highest score off 95. Northern won by eight wickets with 11.5 overs to spare.

In the return fixture Auckland batted first and made 303-7. The fourth wicket stand of 185 was an Auckland record. O'Donnell got fifty from 62 balls, ten faster than Worker who went to his 13th domestic hundred from 124 balls. Gibson took 4-61. Northern lost its first four wickets for 37 and only a fifth wicket stand of 145 gave them respectability. Santner got fifty from 45 balls and de Grandhomme got his fifty from 27 balls and his second domestic century from 76 balls. Ferguson did the damage getting his second six wicket bag with 6-34. Northern were dismissed for 256 after 39.5 overs.

## CENTRAL DISTRICTS v NORTHERN DISTRICTS   Ford Trophy

*at Pukekura Park, New Plymouth on 6 January, 2022*
*Toss : Central Districts. Umpires : C.A. Black & B.F. Bowden*
**Central Districts won by 6 wickets.** *Points: Central Districts 5,  Northern Districts 0*

### NORTHERN DISTRICTS

| | Runs | Mins | Balls | 6s | 4s |
|---|---|---|---|---|---|
| J.A.Raval c Patel b Field | 26 | 68 | 44 | 1 | 3 |
| T.L.Seifert† c Wiggins b Bracewell | 1 | 4 | 3 | - | - |
| J.F.Carter* c Wiggins b Tickner | 38 | 82 | 54 | - | 7 |
| H.R.Cooper c Wiggins b Rance | 29 | 80 | 52 | - | 3 |
| C.de Grandhomme c Bruce b Tickner | 7 | 16 | 8 | - | 1 |
| M.J.Santner c Wiggins b Patel | 5 | 15 | 11 | - | - |
| B.R.Hampton not out | 21 | 51 | 26 | - | 3 |
| S.C.Kuggeleijn c Wiggins b Rance | 1 | 7 | 6 | - | - |
| A.Verma c Patel b Rance | 0 | 5 | 5 | - | - |
| J.G.Walker c Smith b Patel | 0 | 2 | 2 | - | - |
| Z.N.Gibson b Rance | 0 | 5 | 4 | - | - |
| Extras (b 5, lb 5, w 4, nb 1) | 15 | | | | |
| **TOTAL** (35.4 overs) | **143** | 170 | | | |

### CENTRAL DISTRICTS

| | Runs | Mins | Balls | 6s | 4s |
|---|---|---|---|---|---|
| M.T.M.M.J.Ave lbw b Kuggeleijn | 26 | 54 | 46 | - | 4 |
| B.L.Wiggins† b Verma | 0 | 1 | 2 | - | - |
| B.S.Smith c Seifert b Verma | 34 | 77 | 47 | - | 5 |
| B.D.Schmulian not out | 20 | 76 | 47 | - | 1 |
| T.C.Bruce* run out | 2 | 14 | 8 | - | - |
| J.A.Clarkson not out | 50 | 37 | 34 | 4 | 4 |
| D.A.J.Bracewell | | | | | |
| J.F.A.Field | | | | | |
| A.Y.Patel | | | | | |
| S.H.A.Rance | | | | | |
| B.M.Tickner | | | | | |
| Extras (lb 1, w 12) | 13 | | | | |
| **TOTAL** (30.4 overs) (4 wkts) | **145** | 131 | | | |

| Bowling | O | M | R | W |
|---|---|---|---|---|
| **CENTRAL DISTRICTS** | | | | |
| Bracewell | 8 | 0 | 37 | 1 |
| Rance | 7.4 | 1 | 25 | 4 |
| Field | 6 | 0 | 27 | 1 |
| Tickner | 6 | 1 | 18 | 2 |
| Patel | 8 | 0 | 26 | 2 |
| **NORTHERN DISTRICTS** | | | | |
| Verma | 8.4 | 0 | 49 | 2 |
| Gibson | 7 | 2 | 20 | 0 |
| de Grandhomme | 4 | 0 | 16 | 0 |
| Kuggeleijn | 7 | 1 | 39 | 1 |
| Hampton | 1 | 0 | 2 | 0 |
| Santner | 3 | 0 | 18 | 0 |

| Fall of Wickets | ND | CD |
|---|---|---|
| 1st | 3 | 1 |
| 2nd | 67 | 54 |
| 3rd | 82 | 79 |
| 4th | 93 | 84 |
| 5th | 104 | - |
| 6th | 129 | - |
| 7th | 135 | - |
| 8th | 137 | - |
| 9th | 138 | - |
| 10th | 143 | - |

# AUCKLAND v NORTHERN DISTRICTS — Ford Trophy

*at Kennards Hire Community Oval, Auckland on 10 January, 2022*
*Toss : Northern Districts. Umpires : B.F. Bowden & J.A.K. Bromley*
**Northern Districts won by 8 wickets.** *Points: Northern Districts 5, Auckland 0*

## AUCKLAND

| | Runs | Mins | Balls | 6s | 4s |
|---|---|---|---|---|---|
| G.H.Worker run out | 15 | 33 | 30 | - | 2 |
| C.J.Briggs c Raval b Verma | 2 | 11 | 7 | - | - |
| M.S.Chapman c Verma | | | | | |
| b de Grandhomme | 13 | 40 | 24 | - | 2 |
| G.D.Phillips c Kuggeleijn b Sodhi | 33 | 74 | 44 | 1 | 2 |
| R.R.O'Donnell* c Raval b Santner | 31 | 82 | 51 | - | 4 |
| B.J.Horne† c Gibson b Walker | 45 | 72 | 57 | - | 4 |
| S.M.Solia c Kuggeleijn b Santner | 6 | 18 | 17 | - | - |
| W.E.R.Somerville st Seifert b Sodhi | 27 | 40 | 33 | 1 | 1 |
| R.M.ter Braak c Carter b Verma | 15 | 29 | 15 | 1 | - |
| D.K.Ferns c Carter b Verma | 4 | 7 | 8 | - | - |
| L.J.Delport not out | 7 | 8 | 10 | - | - |
| Extras (b 4, w 19) | 23 | | | | |
| **TOTAL** (49.2 overs) | **221** | 210 | | | |

## NORTHERN DISTRICTS

| | Runs | Mins | Balls | 6s | 4s |
|---|---|---|---|---|---|
| J.A.Raval c Horne b Somerville | 97 | 146 | 107 | - | 12 |
| T.L.Seifert† lbw b ter Braak | 1 | 20 | 13 | - | - |
| J.F.Carter* not out | 105 | 143 | 95 | 4 | 7 |
| H.R.Cooper not out | 9 | 17 | 15 | - | 1 |
| C.de Grandhomme | | | | | |
| M.J.Santner | | | | | |
| S.C.Kuggeleijn | | | | | |
| A.Verma | | | | | |
| I.S.Sodhi | | | | | |
| J.G.Walker | | | | | |
| Z.N.Gibson | | | | | |
| Extras (lb 5, w 5) | 10 | | | | |
| **TOTAL** (38.1 overs) (2 wkts) | **222** | 164 | | | |

| Bowling | O | M | R | W |
|---|---|---|---|---|
| **NORTHERN DISTRICTS** | | | | |
| Verma | 6.2 | 1 | 29 | 3 |
| Gibson | 5 | 0 | 11 | 0 |
| Kuggeleijn | 6 | 0 | 24 | 0 |
| de Grandhomme | 4 | 0 | 14 | 1 |
| Santner | 10 | 0 | 47 | 2 |
| Sodhi | 8 | 0 | 54 | 2 |
| Walker | 10 | 0 | 38 | 1 |
| **AUCKLAND** | | | | |
| ter Braak | 7 | 0 | 32 | 1 |
| Ferns | 5 | 0 | 24 | 0 |
| Delport | 10 | 0 | 47 | 0 |
| Solia | 5 | 0 | 34 | 0 |
| Somerville | 9.1 | 0 | 71 | 1 |
| Phillips | 2 | 0 | 9 | 0 |

| Fall of Wickets | A | ND |
|---|---|---|
| 1st | 5 | 18 |
| 2nd | 27 | 195 |
| 3rd | 41 | - |
| 4th | 89 | - |
| 5th | 121 | - |
| 6th | 139 | - |
| 7th | 183 | - |
| 8th | 199 | - |
| 9th | 212 | - |
| 10th | 221 | - |

---

# AUCKLAND v NORTHERN DISTRICTS — Ford Trophy

*at Kennards Hire Community Oval, Auckland on 12 January, 2022*
*Toss : Northern Districts. Umpires : B.F. Bowden & T.J. Parlane*
**Auckland won by 47 runs.** *Points: Auckland 4, Northern Districts 0*

## AUCKLAND

| | Runs | Mins | Balls | 6s | 4s |
|---|---|---|---|---|---|
| G.H.Worker c Hampton b Gibson | 132 | 295 | 142 | 6 | 7 |
| C.J.Briggs lbw b Gibson | 0 | 5 | 2 | - | - |
| M.S.Chapman lbw b Santner | 37 | 74 | 47 | 1 | 4 |
| G.D.Phillips b Santner | 0 | 2 | 2 | - | - |
| R.R.O'Donnell* c Santner | | | | | |
| b Hampton | 95 | 115 | 90 | 4 | 7 |
| B.J.Horne† c Seifert b Gibson | 2 | 7 | 2 | - | - |
| S.M.Solia not out | 15 | 13 | 9 | - | 1 |
| W.E.R.Somerville c Kuggeleijn | | | | | |
| b Gibson | 5 | 9 | 7 | - | - |
| L.H.Ferguson not out | 0 | 1 | 0 | - | - |
| D.K.Ferns | | | | | |
| A.Ashok | | | | | |
| Extras (b 2, lb 6, w 8, nb 1) | 17 | | | | |
| **TOTAL** (50 overs) (7 wkts) | **303** | 218 | | | |

## NORTHERN DISTRICTS

| | Runs | Mins | Balls | 6s | 4s |
|---|---|---|---|---|---|
| J.A.Raval b Ferguson | 0 | 1 | 1 | - | - |
| T.L.Seifert† c Briggs b Ferguson | 9 | 31 | 18 | - | 1 |
| J.F.Carter* c Horne b Ferguson | 2 | 1 | 2 | - | - |
| H.R.Cooper c Horne b Ferguson | 4 | 9 | 5 | - | 1 |
| C.de Grandhomme c Solia | | | | | |
| b Ferguson | 126 | 155 | 104 | 6 | 8 |
| M.J.Santner c Horne b Solia | 74 | 72 | 57 | 5 | 4 |
| B.R.Hampton c Horne b Ferguson | 0 | 6 | 2 | - | - |
| S.C.Kuggeleijn c & b Somerville | 15 | 40 | 28 | - | - |
| I.S.Sodhi c Worker b Ferns | 13 | 23 | 14 | 1 | 1 |
| J.G.Walker not out | 0 | 10 | 5 | - | - |
| Z.N.Gibson c Solia b Ferns | 0 | 4 | 3 | - | - |
| Extras (lb 2, w 10, nb 1) | 13 | | | | |
| **TOTAL** (39.5 overs) | **256** | 179 | | | |

| Bowling | O | M | R | W |
|---|---|---|---|---|
| **NORTHERN DISTRICTS** | | | | |
| Kuggeleijn | 9 | 2 | 43 | 0 |
| Gibson | 10 | 0 | 61 | 4 |
| Walker | 7 | 0 | 48 | 0 |
| de Grandhomme | 5 | 0 | 20 | 0 |
| Hampton | 5 | 1 | 39 | 1 |
| Santner | 10 | 1 | 47 | 2 |
| Sodhi | 4 | 0 | 37 | 0 |
| **AUCKLAND** | | | | |
| Ferguson | 8 | 2 | 34 | 6 |
| Ferns | 6.5 | 0 | 73 | 2 |
| Ashok | 10 | 0 | 64 | 0 |
| Somerville | 10 | 0 | 53 | 1 |
| Solia | 5 | 0 | 30 | 1 |

| Fall of Wickets | A | ND |
|---|---|---|
| 1st | 1 | 0 |
| 2nd | 85 | 2 |
| 3rd | 85 | 11 |
| 4th | 270 | 37 |
| 5th | 282 | 182 |
| 6th | 282 | 188 |
| 7th | 301 | 231 |
| 8th | - | 256 |
| 9th | - | 256 |
| 10th | - | 256 |

## Games 13-15

Central Districts made 296-7 with the batting honours going to Young who scored his fourth century from 103 balls. Bruce scored fifty from 38 balls. Ashok had career best figures of 3-53. Only Guptill was able to reach fifty in Auckland's reply, getting his fifty from 77 balls. Auckland could only manage 183 from 39.3 overs. Tickner had career best figures with 4-37 and Bracewell took three wickets.

Canterbury batted first against Wellington and their innings was centred around Bowes. He got fifty from 59 balls and was dismissed for 99 as Canterbury reached 218-8. Van Beek and Neesham both took two wickets. Wellington had a good start with an opening stand of 90 thanks to a 46-ball fifty from Allen but they then went to 140-6. Wellington reached their target after 42.2 overs thanks to an unbroken 56 run stand for the eighth wicket between Smith and van Beek.

The game between Otago and Central Districts was abandoned.

## CENTRAL DISTRICTS v AUCKLAND                Ford Trophy

*at Fitzherbert Park, Palmerston North on 1 February, 2022*
*Toss : Auckland.  Umpires : J.A.K. Bromley & S.B. Haig*
**Central Districts won by 113 runs.** *Points: Central Districts 5, Auckland 0*

### CENTRAL DISTRICTS

| | Runs | Mins | Balls | 6s | 4s |
|---|---|---|---|---|---|
| D.Cleavert c Somerville b Lister | 7 | 35 | 22 | - | 1 |
| B.S.Smith b Somerville | 32 | 75 | 59 | 1 | 2 |
| W.A.Young c Phillips b Solia | 107 | 181 | 110 | 1 | 9 |
| L.R.P.L.Taylor c Horne b Ashok | 9 | 21 | 16 | - | 1 |
| T.C.Bruce* c Chapman b Ashok | 50 | 46 | 39 | - | 7 |
| J.A.Clarkson c sub (R.M.ter Braak) b Ashok | 8 | 30 | 19 | - | - |
| D.A.J.Bracewell lbw b Lister | 42 | 38 | 29 | 2 | 2 |
| A.F.Milne not out | 16 | 9 | 7 | 1 | 1 |
| S.H.A.Rance not out | 0 | 4 | 0 | - | - |
| B.M.Tickner | | | | | |
| J.R.Lennox | | | | | |

Extras (lb 4, w 20, nb 1) ......... 25
**TOTAL** (50 overs) (7 wkts) . **296** 221

### AUCKLAND

| | Runs | Mins | Balls | 6s | 4s |
|---|---|---|---|---|---|
| M.J.Guptill c Cleaver b Bracewell | 54 | 136 | 83 | - | 7 |
| G.H.Worker b Rance | 1 | 12 | 5 | - | - |
| M.S.Chapman c Bruce b Lennox | 22 | 47 | 34 | - | 3 |
| G.D.Phillips c Rance b Tickner | 25 | 54 | 43 | 1 | 1 |
| R.R.O'Donnell* c Bruce b Bracewell | 5 | 20 | 13 | - | - |
| B.J.Hornet c sub (J.F.A.Field) b Tickner | 30 | 49 | 21 | 2 | 2 |
| S.M.Solia c Rance b Milne | 21 | 27 | 17 | - | 3 |
| W.E.R.Somerville c Smith b Bracewell | 1 | 7 | 5 | - | - |
| A.Ashok c Taylor b Tickner | 14 | 22 | 14 | - | 2 |
| B.G.Lister not out | 1 | 12 | 2 | - | - |
| L.H.Ferguson c Taylor b Tickner | 0 | 2 | 1 | - | - |

Extras (lb 2, w 6, nb 1) ............ 9
**TOTAL** (39.3 overs) ............ **183** 195

| Bowling | O | M | R | W |
|---|---|---|---|---|
| **CENTRAL DISTRICTS** | | | | |
| Lister | 10 | 1 | 48 | 2 |
| Ferguson | 4 | 0 | 24 | 0 |
| Solia | 10 | 0 | 73 | 1 |
| Somerville | 10 | 0 | 48 | 1 |
| Ashok | 10 | 0 | 53 | 3 |
| Phillips | 4 | 0 | 26 | 0 |
| Chapman | 2 | 0 | 20 | 0 |
| **CENTRAL DISTRICTS** | | | | |
| Rance | 8 | 0 | 30 | 1 |
| Milne | 8 | 0 | 42 | 1 |
| Bracewell | 8 | 2 | 42 | 3 |
| Lennox | 8 | 0 | 30 | 1 |
| Tickner | 7.3 | 0 | 37 | 4 |

| Fall of Wickets | CD | A |
|---|---|---|
| 1st | 35 | 5 |
| 2nd | 63 | 51 |
| 3rd | 88 | 98 |
| 4th | 161 | 114 |
| 5th | 199 | 114 |
| 6th | 277 | 145 |
| 7th | 279 | 148 |
| 8th | - | 169 |
| 9th | - | 182 |
| 10th | - | 183 |

*Smith caught Somerville while keeping wicket*

# WELLINGTON v CANTERBURY — Ford Trophy

*at Cello Basin Reserve, Wellington on 4 February, 2022*
*Toss : Wellington.  Umpires : B.F. Bowden & J.M. Dempsey*
**Wellington won by 3 wickets.** *Points: Wellington 4, Canterbury 0*

## CANTERBURY

| | Runs | Mins | Balls | 6s | 4s |
|---|---|---|---|---|---|
| C.J.Bowes c van Beek b Bracewell | 99 | 174 | 116 | - | 12 |
| K.J.McClure c & b Newton | 4 | 9 | 6 | - | 1 |
| D.J.Mitchell c & b van Beek | 12 | 30 | 20 | - | 2 |
| T.W.M.Latham† c Sears b Neesham | 4 | 7 | 6 | - | 1 |
| L.J.Carter c Allen b Ravindra | 31 | 72 | 48 | - | 5 |
| C.E.McConchie* c Smith b Neesham | 18 | 37 | 38 | - | 2 |
| H.B.Shipley c Neesham b Sears | 14 | 35 | 26 | - | 1 |
| T.F.van Woerkom not out | 12 | 42 | 24 | - | - |
| M.J.Henry c Blundell b van Beek | 3 | 12 | 8 | - | - |
| W.S.A.Williams not out | 11 | 11 | 8 | 1 | - |
| E.J.Nuttall | | | | | |
| Extras (b 4, lb 1, w 5) | 10 | | | | |
| **TOTAL (50 overs) (8 wkts)** | **218** | 216 | | | |

## WELLINGTON

| | Runs | Mins | Balls | 6s | 4s |
|---|---|---|---|---|---|
| F.H.Allen c Williams b van Woerkom | 68 | 92 | 65 | 2 | 9 |
| R.Ravindra st Latham b Williams | 34 | 64 | 39 | 2 | 2 |
| D.P.Conway c Latham b Henry | 0 | 5 | 3 | - | - |
| T.A.Blundell† c Latham b Shipley | 12 | 37 | 22 | - | - |
| M.G.Bracewell* b Nuttall | 17 | 39 | 23 | 1 | - |
| J.D.S.Neesham run out | 4 | 14 | 13 | - | - |
| T.M.Johnson b Henry | 8 | 39 | 35 | - | - |
| N.G.Smith not out | 43 | 60 | 33 | 2 | 4 |
| L.V.van Beek not out | 24 | 31 | 21 | - | 4 |
| O.R.Newton | | | | | |
| B.V.Sears | | | | | |
| Extras (lb 2, w 7) | 9 | | | | |
| **TOTAL (42.2 overs) (7 wkts)** | **219** | 193 | | | |

| Bowling | O | M | R | W |
|---|---|---|---|---|
| **WELLINGTON** | | | | |
| Smith | 4 | 1 | 15 | 0 |
| Newton | 5 | 0 | 35 | 1 |
| van Beek | 5 | 0 | 28 | 2 |
| Neesham | 8 | 0 | 31 | 2 |
| Sears | 8 | 0 | 33 | 1 |
| Bracewell | 10 | 0 | 35 | 1 |
| Ravindra | 10 | 0 | 36 | 1 |
| **CANTERBURY** | | | | |
| Henry | 9 | 1 | 47 | 2 |
| Shipley | 9 | 0 | 62 | 1 |
| Nuttall | 5 | 0 | 31 | 1 |
| Williams | 7 | 1 | 26 | 1 |
| van Woerkom | 7 | 0 | 26 | 1 |
| McConchie | 5 | 0 | 24 | 0 |
| Mitchell | 0.2 | 0 | 1 | 0 |

| Fall of Wickets | C | W |
|---|---|---|
| 1st | 5 | 90 |
| 2nd | 40 | 91 |
| 3rd | 45 | 111 |
| 4th | 127 | 125 |
| 5th | 163 | 134 |
| 6th | 183 | 140 |
| 7th | 195 | 163 |
| 8th | 204 | - |
| 9th | - | - |
| 10th | - | - |

# OTAGO v CENTRAL DISTRICTS — Ford Trophy

*at University of Otago Oval, Dunedin on 4 February, 2022*
**Abandoned without a ball being bowled.** *Points: Otago 2, Central Districts 2*

# Games 16-18

Central Districts made 314-7 in a 37-over game. Wiggins scored fifty off 45 balls at the top of the innings and added 111 off 69 balls with Young for the second wicket. Bracewell and Milne added 76 off 31 balls with Milne scoring the second-fastest fifty in New Zealand one-day games off 18 balls. Otago lost five wickets in the first eight overs and never threatened. Rance took three wickets while Milne, Bracewell and Lennox all took two as Otago were dismissed for 114 after 23.5 overs.

The games between Wellington and Canterbury and Canterbury and Central Districts were abandoned without any play.

## OTAGO v CENTRAL DISTRICTS                              Ford Trophy

*at University of Otago Oval, Dunedin on 6 February, 2022*
*Toss : Otago. Umpires : C.B. Gaffaney & S.B. Haig*
**Central Districts won by 200 runs.** Points: Central Districts 5, Otago 0

### CENTRAL DISTRICTS

| | Runs | Mins | Balls | 6s | 4s |
|---|---|---|---|---|---|
| B.S.Smith c Kitchen b Bacon .... | 10 | 21 | 17 | - | 2 |
| B.L.Wiggins† c McKay b Rippon | 80 | 81 | 64 | 1 | 14 |
| W.A.Young b Bacon .................. | 40 | 52 | 26 | 2 | 3 |
| L.R.P.L.Taylor st Chu b Kitchen | 45 | 66 | 36 | 2 | 2 |
| T.C.Bruce* c Chu b Duffy ........... | 2 | 6 | 4 | - | - |
| J.A.Clarkson c Kelly b Kitchen . | 27 | 44 | 34 | - | 4 |
| D.A.J.Bracewell not out ............. | 29 | 38 | 17 | 3 | - |
| A.F.Milne c Chu b McKay ......... | 50 | 25 | 21 | 5 | 2 |
| J.R.Lennox not out ................... | 11 | 4 | 3 | 1 | 1 |
| S.H.A.Rance | | | | | |
| B.M.Tickner | | | | | |
| Extras (b 1, w 19) ................... | 20 | | | | |
| **TOTAL** (37 overs) (7 wkts) . | **314** | 170 | | | |

### OTAGO

| | Runs | Mins | Balls | 6s | 4s |
|---|---|---|---|---|---|
| D.N.Phillips c Wiggins b Milne .... | 6 | 10 | 9 | - | 1 |
| M.Renwick c Taylor b Rance ...... | 3 | 16 | 8 | - | - |
| N.T.Broom b Milne ...................... | 2 | 9 | 7 | - | - |
| N.F.Kelly* c Wiggins b Rance .... | 1 | 20 | 6 | - | - |
| M.J.G.Rippon c Wiggins b Rance | 6 | 8 | 7 | - | 1 |
| M.W.Chu† c Milne b Bracewell | 31 | 58 | 38 | 1 | 3 |
| A.K.Kitchen c Wiggins | | | | | |
| b Bracewell ............................ | 18 | 50 | 25 | 1 | 1 |
| J.A.Duffy not out ........................ | 23 | 32 | 21 | 1 | 3 |
| M.B.Bacon c Milne b Lennox ...... | 1 | 14 | 5 | - | - |
| J.D.McKay c Smith b Lennox .... | 14 | 17 | 17 | 1 | 1 |
| M.D.Rae absent hurt | | | | | |
| Extras (lb 1, w 8) ...................... | 9 | | | | |
| **TOTAL** (23.5 overs) ............. | **114** | 119 | | | |

| Bowling | O | M | R | W |
|---|---|---|---|---|
| **OTAGO** | | | | |
| Duffy | 7 | 1 | 35 | 1 |
| Bacon | 6 | 0 | 59 | 2 |
| McKay | 6 | 0 | 81 | 1 |
| Rae | 2 | 0 | 23 | 0 |
| Kitchen | 8 | 0 | 69 | 2 |
| Rippon | 8 | 0 | 46 | 1 |
| **CENTRAL DISTRICTS** | | | | |
| Milne | 4 | 0 | 15 | 2 |
| Rance | 5 | 0 | 19 | 3 |
| Bracewell | 5 | 0 | 24 | 2 |
| Tickner | 5 | 0 | 34 | 0 |
| Lennox | 4.5 | 0 | 21 | 2 |

| Fall of Wickets | | |
|---|---|---|
| | CD | O |
| 1st | 19 | 9 |
| 2nd | 130 | 13 |
| 3rd | 140 | 13 |
| 4th | 143 | 20 |
| 5th | 214 | 24 |
| 6th | 220 | 72 |
| 7th | 296 | 72 |
| 8th | - | 83 |
| 9th | - | 114 |
| 10th | - | - |

## WELLINGTON v CANTERBURY                              Ford Trophy

*at Cello Basin Reserve, Wellington on 6 February, 2022*
**Abandoned without a ball being bowled.** Points: Wellington 2, Canterbury 2

## CANTERBURY v CENTRAL DISTRICTS                       Ford Trophy

*at MainPower Oval, Rangiora on 11 February, 2022*
**Abandoned without a ball being bowled.** Points: Canterbury 2, Central Districts 2

## Games 19-21

Two games between Northern Districts and Wellington and the match between Canterbury and Central Districts were all abandoned without a ball being bowled.

### NORTHERN DISTRICTS v WELLINGTON      Ford Trophy

*at Seddon Park, Hamilton on 11 February, 2022*
**Abandoned without a ball being bowled.** *Points: Northern Districts 2, Wellington 2*

### CANTERBURY v CENTRAL DISTRICTS      Ford Trophy

*at MainPower Oval, Rangiora on 13 February, 2022*
**Abandoned without a ball being bowled.** *Points: Canterbury 2, Central Districts 2*

### NORTHERN DISTRICTS v WELLINGTON      Ford Trophy

*at Seddon Park, Hamilton on 13 February, 2022*
**Abandoned without a ball being bowled.** *Points: Northern Districts 2, Wellington 2*

# Games 22-24

Swanson *(Northern Districts)* made his debut.

Auckland scored 365-5 against Canterbury. Guptill scored 90 (fifty from 43 balls) eight fewer than Chapman who got 64. O'Donnell scored his first century from the last ball of the innings. The fourth wicket stand of 149 between Chapman and O'Donnell was an Auckland record against Canterbury. Canterbury struggled with no player being able to reach 40. Ashok had career best figures of 4-25 while ter Braak got three wickets as Canterbury made 146 in 32.2 overs. The 219 run win was Auckland's biggest by runs.

Otago made 139 against Northern Districts. Kelly made 59 (fifty from 72 deliveries) and was the only player to reach 20. Fisher took three wickets while Kuggeleijn and Walker took two. Northern were never troubled with Seifert getting fifty from 43 balls. Rippon took three wickets as Northern won by six wickets with 27.2 overs to spare.

Central Districts and Wellington had a 29 over game. Central batted first and amassed 310-5 with Taylor scoring a 49-ball century, the fastest in New Zealand one-day cricket. His fifty came from 25 balls. Taylor and Clarkson added 115 for the fourth wicket off 9.2 overs. Clarkson got fifty from 32 balls and Smith took three wickets. Wellington lost early wickets but Bracewell scored a 31-ball fifty in making 93 before bad light ended the game with Wellington 184-6 after 20 overs. This gave Central a 43 run win by the DLS system and ensured them of being the top qualifier for the final.

## AUCKLAND v CANTERBURY                     Ford Trophy

*at Kennards Hire Community Oval, Auckland on 18 February, 2022*
*Toss : Canterbury. Umpires : B.F. Bowden & P.J. Pasco*
**Auckland won by 219 runs.** Points: Auckland 5, Canterbury 0

### AUCKLAND

| | Runs | Mins | Balls | 6s | 4s |
|---|---|---|---|---|---|
| M.J.Guptill c Shipley b O'Rourke | 90 | 113 | 83 | 6 | 7 |
| G.H.Worker b Shipley | 24 | 55 | 31 | 1 | 4 |
| G.D.Phillips c Boyle | | | | | |
| b McConchie | 45 | 52 | 31 | 3 | 4 |
| M.S.Chapman c McConchie | | | | | |
| b van Woerkom | 64 | 93 | 59 | 3 | 3 |
| R.R.O'Donnell* not out | 100 | 116 | 79 | 5 | 6 |
| S.M.Solia c Bowes b Shipley | 0 | 7 | 2 | - | - |
| B.J.Horne† not out | 24 | 19 | 15 | 1 | 1 |
| W.E.R.Somerville | | | | | |
| A.Ashok | | | | | |
| R.M.ter Braak | | | | | |
| B.G.Lister | | | | | |
| Extras (lb 6, w 12) | 18 | | | | |
| **TOTAL** (50 overs) (5 wkts) | **365** | 230 | | | |

### CANTERBURY

| | Runs | Mins | Balls | 6s | 4s |
|---|---|---|---|---|---|
| C.J.Bowes b ter Braak | 22 | 44 | 28 | - | 3 |
| J.C.T.Boyle c Chapman | | | | | |
| b ter Braak | 15 | 32 | 26 | - | 2 |
| K.J.McClure c Horne b ter Braak | 0 | 3 | 1 | - | - |
| L.J.Carter run out | 36 | 49 | 38 | 2 | 3 |
| C.E.McConchie* c Lister | | | | | |
| b Phillips | 35 | 76 | 51 | - | 2 |
| M.J.Hay† c O'Donnell b Ashok | 8 | 16 | 16 | - | 1 |
| H.B.Shipley lbw b Ashok | 9 | 22 | 15 | - | - |
| T.F.van Woerkom not out | 5 | 16 | 7 | - | - |
| W.S.A.Williams c Guptill b Ashok | 0 | 1 | 3 | - | - |
| W.P.O'Rourke c Guptill b Ashok | 0 | 2 | 2 | - | - |
| E.J.Nuttall c Lister b Somerville | 1 | 7 | 8 | - | - |
| Extras (b 1, lb 6, w 7, nb 1) | 15 | | | | |
| **TOTAL** (32.2 overs) | **146** | 138 | | | |

| Bowling | O | M | R | W |
|---|---|---|---|---|
| **CANTERBURY** | | | | |
| Nuttall | 10 | 0 | 74 | 0 |
| O'Rourke | 10 | 2 | 71 | 1 |
| Williams | 10 | 0 | 77 | 0 |
| Shipley | 10 | 0 | 65 | 2 |
| van Woerkom | 6 | 0 | 51 | 1 |
| McConchie | 4 | 0 | 21 | 1 |
| **AUCKLAND** | | | | |
| Lister | 5 | 0 | 22 | 0 |
| ter Braak | 5 | 0 | 20 | 3 |
| Somerville | 7.2 | 0 | 17 | 1 |
| Solia | 4 | 0 | 35 | 0 |
| Ashok | 7 | 1 | 25 | 4 |
| Phillips | 4 | 0 | 20 | 1 |

| Fall of Wickets | | |
|---|---|---|
| | A | C |
| 1st | 80 | 33 |
| 2nd | 165 | 34 |
| 3rd | 166 | 43 |
| 4th | 315 | 97 |
| 5th | 327 | 115 |
| 6th | - | 139 |
| 7th | - | 141 |
| 8th | - | 141 |
| 9th | - | 141 |
| 10th | - | 146 |

# NORTHERN DISTRICTS v OTAGO — Ford Trophy

*at Cobham Oval, Whangarei on 18 February, 2022*
*Toss : Northern Districts. Umpires : D.R. Morrow & T.J. Parlane*
**Northern Districts won by 6 wickets.** *Points: Northern Districts 5, Otago 0*

## OTAGO

| | Runs | Mins | Balls | 6s | 4s |
|---|---|---|---|---|---|
| D.N.Phillips c Seifert b Kuggeleijn | 16 | 26 | 25 | - | 1 |
| M.Renwick b Kuggeleijn | 4 | 31 | 14 | - | - |
| N.T.Broom run out | 13 | 62 | 37 | - | 1 |
| N.F.Kelly* b Walker | 59 | 132 | 82 | - | 4 |
| M.J.G.Rippon st Seifert b Santner | 8 | 25 | 20 | - | - |
| A.K.Kitchen c Clarke b Walker | 18 | 39 | 33 | 1 | - |
| M.W.Chu† b Fisher | 2 | 7 | 6 | - | - |
| T.Muller not out | 3 | 20 | 9 | - | - |
| J.A.Duffy c Santner b Fisher | 0 | 6 | 7 | - | - |
| B.N.J.Lockrose run out | 0 | 6 | 2 | - | - |
| M.B.Bacon c Seifert b Fisher | 1 | 5 | 4 | - | - |
| Extras (b 6, lb 3, w 6) | 15 | | | | |
| **TOTAL** (39.5 overs) | **139** | 181 | | | |

## NORTHERN DISTRICTS

| | Runs | Mins | Balls | 6s | 4s |
|---|---|---|---|---|---|
| J.A.Raval* c Kelly b Rippon | 11 | 41 | 23 | - | 2 |
| K.D.Clarke b Muller | 28 | 14 | 12 | - | 6 |
| T.L.Seifert† lbw b Rippon | 51 | 81 | 46 | 2 | 3 |
| C.J.Swanson c Renwick b Rippon | 41 | 46 | 52 | - | 6 |
| M.J.Santner not out | 0 | 10 | 2 | - | - |
| P.D.Bocock not out | 3 | 1 | 2 | - | - |
| B.R.Hampton | | | | | |
| S.C.Kuggeleijn | | | | | |
| A.Verma | | | | | |
| J.G.Walker | | | | | |
| M.J.Fisher | | | | | |
| Extras (lb 1, w 4, nb 1) | 6 | | | | |
| **TOTAL** (22.4 overs) (4 wkts) | **140** | 98 | | | |

| Bowling | O | M | R | W |
|---|---|---|---|---|
| **NORTHERN DISTRICTS** | | | | |
| Kuggeleijn | 7 | 0 | 26 | 2 |
| Verma | 7 | 0 | 20 | 0 |
| Fisher | 8.5 | 1 | 24 | 3 |
| Walker | 10 | 1 | 35 | 2 |
| Santner | 7 | 0 | 25 | 1 |
| **OTAGO** | | | | |
| Duffy | 4 | 0 | 46 | 0 |
| Muller | 4 | 0 | 17 | 1 |
| Rippon | 8.4 | 1 | 50 | 3 |
| Kitchen | 4 | 2 | 9 | 0 |
| Lockrose | 2 | 0 | 17 | 0 |

| Fall of Wickets | O | ND |
|---|---|---|
| 1st | 20 | 32 |
| 2nd | 21 | 63 |
| 3rd | 57 | 128 |
| 4th | 84 | 137 |
| 5th | 125 | - |
| 6th | 129 | - |
| 7th | 129 | - |
| 8th | 130 | - |
| 9th | 133 | - |
| 10th | 139 | - |

# CENTRAL DISTRICTS v WELLINGTON — Ford Trophy

*at Pukekura Park, New Plymouth on 18 February, 2022*
*Toss : Wellington. Umpires : S.J. Kannan & E.D. Sanders*
**Central Districts won by 43 runs (D/L).** *Points: Central Districts 4, Wellington 0*

## CENTRAL DISTRICTS

| | Runs | Mins | Balls | 6s | 4s |
|---|---|---|---|---|---|
| B.L.Wiggins† b van Beek | 46 | 65 | 39 | 1 | 8 |
| B.S.Smith c Johns b Smith | 37 | 48 | 30 | - | 9 |
| L.R.P.L.Taylor not out | 111 | 106 | 51 | 5 | 14 |
| T.C.Bruce* c Bhula b Smith | 25 | 27 | 17 | 1 | 3 |
| J.A.Clarkson b van Beek | 58 | 53 | 35 | 4 | 6 |
| D.A.J.Bracewell c Allen b Smith | 15 | 5 | 5 | 1 | 2 |
| A.F.Milne not out | 0 | 4 | 0 | - | - |
| B.D.Schmulian | | | | | |
| S.H.A.Rance | | | | | |
| J.F.A.Field | | | | | |
| J.R.Lennox | | | | | |
| Extras (lb 4, w 11, nb 3) | 18 | | | | |
| **TOTAL** (29 overs) (5 wkts) | **310** | 155 | | | |

## WELLINGTON

| | Runs | Mins | Balls | 6s | 4s |
|---|---|---|---|---|---|
| F.H.Allen lbw b Lennox | 49 | 65 | 29 | 3 | 6 |
| L.I.Georgeson c Field b Rance | 5 | 21 | 13 | - | 1 |
| J.J.N.P.Bhula c Bracewell b Rance | 2 | 16 | 12 | - | - |
| T.M.Johnson c Milne b Lennox | 2 | 11 | 11 | - | - |
| M.G.Bracewell c Bruce b Lennox | 93 | 40 | 42 | 8 | 6 |
| N.G.Smith st Wiggins b Schmulian | 12 | 13 | 8 | 1 | - |
| L.V.van Beek not out | 5 | 12 | 5 | - | - |
| L.R.Johns† not out | 0 | 1 | 0 | - | - |
| O.R.Newton | | | | | |
| B.V.Sears | | | | | |
| H.K.Bennett* | | | | | |
| Extras (lb 4, w 12) | 16 | | | | |
| **TOTAL** (20 overs) (6 wkts) | **184** | 90 | | | |

| Bowling | O | M | R | W |
|---|---|---|---|---|
| **WELLINGTON** | | | | |
| Newton | 6 | 0 | 77 | 0 |
| Bennett | 6 | 1 | 51 | 0 |
| Smith | 6 | 1 | 51 | 3 |
| van Beek | 6 | 0 | 54 | 2 |
| Sears | 2 | 0 | 33 | 0 |
| Georgeson | 3 | 0 | 40 | 0 |
| **CENTRAL DISTRICTS** | | | | |
| Milne | 3 | 0 | 21 | 0 |
| Bracewell | 4 | 0 | 28 | 0 |
| Rance | 3 | 0 | 15 | 2 |
| Lennox | 6 | 1 | 57 | 3 |
| Bruce | 2 | 0 | 31 | 0 |
| Schmulian | 2 | 0 | 28 | 1 |

| Fall of Wickets | CD | W |
|---|---|---|
| 1st | 71 | 36 |
| 2nd | 107 | 41 |
| 3rd | 162 | 56 |
| 4th | 277 | 100 |
| 5th | 292 | 134 |
| 6th | - | 184 |
| 7th | - | - |
| 8th | - | - |
| 9th | - | - |
| 10th | - | - |

# Games 25-27

Foulkes *(Canterbury)* made his debut.

Canterbury lost two early wickets to be 23-2 but Carter (fifty from 63 balls) steadied the innings to enable them to reach 226-9. Ferguson, Somerville and Ashok each took two wickets. Auckland had a second wicket stand of 122 from 108 balls to set them on their way. Phillips reached his fourth domestic century from 79 deliveries and Horne reached 1000 runs. Auckland reached their target with 79 balls to spare.

Wellington made 191-8 against Central in a game reduced to 32 overs. Bhula top scored with 50. Central won with 43 balls to spare but lost eight wickets. Taylor top scored, also with exactly 50.

Otago were dismissed for 132 against Northern, losing their last four wickets for 14 runs. Fisher had career best figures of 4-34. There was rain during the interval and the match was reduced to 40 overs with a target of 120. Northern seemed to be well on track at 96-3 but then lost seven wickets for 22 to finish on 118 all out after 26.3 overs. Lockrose (career best) and Rippon both took three wickets as Otago won by 1 run.

# AUCKLAND v CANTERBURY                    Ford Trophy

*at Kennards Hire Community Oval, Auckland on 20 February, 2022*
*Toss : Canterbury.  Umpires : B.F. Bowden & P.J. Pasco*
**Auckland won by 6 wickets.** *Points: Auckland 5, Canterbury  0*

## CANTERBURY

| | Runs | Mins | Balls | 6s | 4s |
|---|---|---|---|---|---|
| J.C.T.Boyle c Phillips | | | | | |
| b Somerville | 29 | 69 | 57 | - | 4 |
| C.J.Bowes b Ferguson | 0 | 6 | 3 | - | - |
| K.J.McClure b Ferguson | 9 | 24 | 18 | - | 2 |
| L.J.Carter c Phillips b Ashok | 58 | 124 | 73 | 2 | 2 |
| C.E.McConchie* c Chapman | | | | | |
| b Phillips | 33 | 64 | 61 | - | 3 |
| Z.G.Foulkes c Solia b Ashok | 19 | 40 | 25 | - | 2 |
| M.J.Hay† lbw b Solia | 24 | 38 | 28 | 1 | 1 |
| H.B.Shipley c Guptill b Somerville | 0 | 4 | 1 | - | - |
| T.F.van Woerkom b Lister | 16 | 21 | 16 | - | 1 |
| W.S.A.Williams not out | 15 | 16 | 12 | - | 1 |
| W.P.O'Rourke not out | 7 | 9 | 8 | - | - |
| Extras (lb 9, w 5, nb 2) | 16 | | | | |
| **TOTAL** (50 overs) (9 wkts) | **226** | 212 | | | |

## AUCKLAND

| | Runs | Mins | Balls | 6s | 4s |
|---|---|---|---|---|---|
| M.J.Guptill c Carter b Shipley | 21 | 11 | 14 | 1 | 3 |
| G.H.Worker run out | 36 | 85 | 53 | 1 | 4 |
| G.D.Phillips not out | 122 | 139 | 102 | 8 | 13 |
| M.S.Chapman c Boyle | | | | | |
| b O'Rourke | 30 | 41 | 36 | - | 4 |
| R.R.O'Donnell* c O'Rourke | | | | | |
| b van Woerkom | 2 | 8 | 4 | - | - |
| B.J.Horne† not out | 14 | 14 | 12 | - | 2 |
| S.M.Solia | | | | | |
| W.E.R.Somerville | | | | | |
| L.H.Ferguson | | | | | |
| A.Ashok | | | | | |
| B.G.Lister | | | | | |
| Extras (w 2) | 2 | | | | |
| **TOTAL** (36.5 overs) (4 wkts) | **227** | 151 | | | |

| **Bowling** | O | M | R | W |
|---|---|---|---|---|
| **AUCKLAND** | | | | |
| Lister | 9 | 1 | 29 | 1 |
| Ferguson | 7 | 1 | 25 | 2 |
| Solia | 6 | 0 | 37 | 1 |
| Somerville | 10 | 0 | 40 | 2 |
| Ashok | 10 | 0 | 53 | 2 |
| Phillips | 8 | 0 | 33 | 1 |
| **CANTERBURY** | | | | |
| Shipley | 7 | 0 | 53 | 1 |
| O'Rourke | 7 | 1 | 40 | 1 |
| Williams | 2.5 | 0 | 24 | 0 |
| Foulkes | 3 | 0 | 20 | 0 |
| McConchie | 7 | 1 | 34 | 0 |
| van Woerkom | 10 | 0 | 56 | 1 |

| **Fall of Wickets** | | |
|---|---|---|
| | **C** | **A** |
| 1st | 1 | 22 |
| 2nd | 23 | 144 |
| 3rd | 67 | 197 |
| 4th | 128 | 205 |
| 5th | 153 | - |
| 6th | 169 | - |
| 7th | 177 | - |
| 8th | 201 | - |
| 9th | 208 | - |
| 10th | - | - |

# CENTRAL DISTRICTS v WELLINGTON     Ford Trophy

*at Pukekura Park, New Plymouth on 20 February, 2022*
*Toss : Wellington. Umpires : S.J. Kannan & E.D. Sanders*
**Central Districts won by 2 wickets.** Points: Central Districts 5, Wellington 0

| WELLINGTON | Runs | Mins | Balls | 6s | 4s |
|---|---|---|---|---|---|
| F.H.Allen† c Taylor b Milne | 10 | 13 | 11 | 1 | 1 |
| L.I.Georgeson c Milne b Bracewell | 23 | 62 | 31 | - | 4 |
| J.J.N.P.Bhula c Bruce b Schmulian | 50 | 69 | 56 | - | 7 |
| T.M.Johnson c Schmulian b Milne | 18 | 24 | 16 | - | 3 |
| M.G.Bracewell c Bruce b Lennox | 4 | 20 | 9 | - | - |
| N.G.Smith b Milne | 12 | 23 | 21 | - | 1 |
| L.V.van Beek c Lennox b Field | 18 | 22 | 14 | 1 | 1 |
| P.F.Younghusband not out | 14 | 36 | 20 | - | 1 |
| O.R.Newton lbw b Rance | 0 | 4 | 3 | - | - |
| B.V.Sears not out | 19 | 16 | 11 | - | 3 |
| H.K.Bennett* | | | | | |
| Extras (lb 3, w 20) | 23 | | | | |
| **TOTAL** (32 overs) (8 wkts) | **191** | 146 | | | |

| CENTRAL DISTRICTS | Runs | Mins | Balls | 6s | 4s |
|---|---|---|---|---|---|
| B.L.Wiggins† c Bhula b Newton | 5 | 5 | 5 | - | 1 |
| B.S.Smith c Allen b Newton | 12 | 19 | 10 | - | 3 |
| B.D.Schmulian c Allen b van Beek | 48 | 57 | 37 | 2 | 5 |
| L.R.P.L.Taylor b Sears | 50 | 49 | 31 | 2 | 6 |
| T.C.Bruce* not out | 47 | 56 | 33 | 1 | 6 |
| J.A.Clarkson b van Beek | 6 | 13 | 8 | - | 1 |
| D.A.J.Bracewell c van Beek b Smith | 16 | 17 | 15 | - | 3 |
| A.F.Milne hit wicket b Bracewell | 3 | 15 | 8 | - | - |
| J.F.A.Field run out | 0 | 2 | 2 | - | - |
| J.R.Lennox not out | 0 | 1 | 0 | - | - |
| S.H.A.Rance | | | | | |
| Extras (b 1, lb 2, w 4) | 7 | | | | |
| **TOTAL** (24.5 overs) (8 wkts) | **194** | 119 | | | |

| Bowling | O | M | R | W |
|---|---|---|---|---|
| **CENTRAL DISTRICTS** | | | | |
| Milne | 7 | 1 | 35 | 3 |
| Rance | 6 | 0 | 29 | 1 |
| Bracewell | 6 | 0 | 49 | 1 |
| Field | 4 | 0 | 32 | 1 |
| Lennox | 7 | 0 | 36 | 1 |
| Schmulian | 2 | 0 | 7 | 1 |
| **WELLINGTON** | | | | |
| Bennett | 2 | 0 | 20 | 0 |
| Newton | 5 | 0 | 46 | 2 |
| Smith | 3 | 0 | 23 | 1 |
| Younghusband | 4 | 0 | 24 | 0 |
| Sears | 5 | 0 | 39 | 1 |
| van Beek | 4 | 0 | 34 | 2 |
| Bracewell | 1.5 | 0 | 5 | 1 |

| Fall of Wickets | W | CD |
|---|---|---|
| 1st | 20 | 10 |
| 2nd | 87 | 35 |
| 3rd | 118 | 114 |
| 4th | 118 | 124 |
| 5th | 138 | 151 |
| 6th | 138 | 175 |
| 7th | 162 | 190 |
| 8th | 163 | 190 |
| 9th | - | - |
| 10th | - | - |

# NORTHERN DISTRICTS v OTAGO     Ford Trophy

*at Cobham Oval, Whangarei on 20 February, 2022*
*Toss : Otago. Umpires : D.R. Morrow & T.J. Parlane*
**Otago won by 1 run (D/L).** Points: Otago 4, Northern Districts 0

| OTAGO | Runs | Mins | Balls | 6s | 4s |
|---|---|---|---|---|---|
| D.N.Phillips c Raval b Santner | 36 | 96 | 54 | - | 3 |
| M.Renwick c Raval b Kuggeleijn | 4 | 27 | 17 | - | - |
| N.T.Broom c Verma b Fisher | 9 | 34 | 24 | - | 1 |
| N.F.Kelly* c Raval b Fisher | 11 | 23 | 19 | - | 1 |
| M.J.G.Rippon lbw b Raval | 31 | 93 | 61 | - | 1 |
| A.K.Kitchen lbw b Santner | 3 | 9 | 9 | - | - |
| M.W.Chu† c Seifert b Fisher | 6 | 28 | 25 | - | - |
| T.Muller c Raval b Walker | 9 | 3 | 28 | - | 1 |
| J.A.Duffy not out | 10 | 20 | 13 | - | 1 |
| B.N.J.Lockrose b Raval | 0 | 3 | 3 | - | - |
| M.B.Bacon c Clarke b Fisher | 0 | 4 | 3 | - | - |
| Extras (b 3, lb 4, w 6) | 13 | | | | |
| **TOTAL** (42.4 overs) | **132** | 187 | | | |

| NORTHERN DISTRICTS | Runs | Mins | Balls | 6s | 4s |
|---|---|---|---|---|---|
| K.D.Clarke b Muller | 11 | 16 | 18 | - | - |
| J.A.Raval c Bacon b Lockrose | 18 | 49 | 21 | - | 3 |
| T.L.Seifert † run out | 45 | 62 | 44 | 2 | 3 |
| B.R.Hampton b Rippon | 10 | 12 | 9 | - | 1 |
| J.F.Carter* c Duffy b Rippon | 8 | 9 | 6 | 1 | - |
| M.J.Santner c Chu b Rippon | 0 | 2 | 1 | - | - |
| H.R.Cooper b Kitchen | 8 | 15 | 12 | - | 1 |
| S.C.Kuggeleijn not out | 10 | 44 | 22 | - | 1 |
| A.Verma lbw b Kitchen | 4 | 18 | 14 | - | - |
| J.G.Walker b Lockrose | 0 | 6 | 3 | - | - |
| M.J.Fisher b Lockrose | 0 | 9 | 9 | - | - |
| Extras (lb 2, w 2) | 4 | | | | |
| **TOTAL** (26.3 overs) | **118** | 122 | | | |

| Bowling | O | M | R | W |
|---|---|---|---|---|
| **NORTHERN DISTRICTS** | | | | |
| Kuggeleijn | 8 | 1 | 21 | 1 |
| Verma | 4 | 0 | 17 | 0 |
| Fisher | 8.4 | 0 | 34 | 4 |
| Santner | 10 | 1 | 25 | 2 |
| Walker | 10 | 2 | 22 | 1 |
| Raval | 2 | 1 | 6 | 2 |
| **OTAGO** | | | | |
| Duffy | 4 | 0 | 19 | 0 |
| Muller | 3 | 0 | 14 | 1 |
| Bacon | 2 | 0 | 12 | 0 |
| Rippon | 8 | 1 | 41 | 3 |
| Lockrose | 3.3 | 0 | 17 | 3 |
| Kitchen | 6 | 2 | 13 | 2 |

| Fall of Wickets | O | ND |
|---|---|---|
| 1st | 20 | 13 |
| 2nd | 43 | 54 |
| 3rd | 63 | 80 |
| 4th | 71 | 96 |
| 5th | 77 | 96 |
| 6th | 98 | 97 |
| 7th | 118 | 109 |
| 8th | 131 | 115 |
| 9th | 131 | 116 |
| 10th | 132 | 118 |

# Games 28-29 and Final

Keene *(Auckland)* made his debut.

Auckland's openers set a record for the Auckland's first wicket, putting on 260. Guptill got his ninth domestic hundred from 83 balls while Worker needed 95 for his 15th century. Auckland finished on 380-6. Otago never threatened the large total but an unbroken Otago seventh wicket record stand of 122 from 130 balls got the reply to 284-6. Kitchen, in his last innings before retirement, scored his fifth century off 89 balls while Muller reached his maiden fifty off 72 deliveries.

Central made 301 off 49.2 overs in the final round-robin match. Schmulian made his highest score with 75 (fifty from 65 balls) and Taylor hit a 47-ball fifty. Pringle had best figures of 4-51. Auckland had a third wicket stand of 182 from 178 balls after being 19-2. Worker went to his 16th century and became the first player to score four hundreds in a season. Chapman got 88 and Auckland won by three wickets with three balls left.

Central made 213 off 49.5 overs batting first in the final. Bruce got fifty from 56 balls and top scored with 63. Ferguson took four wickets. Auckland were 60-2 before Worker and Chapman had an unbroken third wicket stand of 157 off 149 balls. Chapman got fifty from 55 balls , thirty faster than Worker, as Auckland won the Ford Trophy for the third time in five seasons with 13.5 overs to spare.

## AUCKLAND v OTAGO                              Ford Trophy

*at Kennards Hire Community Oval, Auckland on 22 February, 2022*
*Toss : Auckland.  Umpires : B.F. Bowden & T.J. Parlane*
**Auckland won by 96 runs.** *Points: Auckland 5, Otago 0*

| AUCKLAND | Runs | Mins | Balls | 6s | 4s |
|---|---|---|---|---|---|
| M.J.Guptill c Phillips b McKenzie | 137 | 160 | 106 | 7 | 10 |
| G.H.Worker b McKenzie | 122 | 169 | 114 | 2 | 14 |
| G.D.Phillips b Bacon | 68 | 64 | 41 | 4 | 6 |
| M.S.Chapman c Kelly b McKenzie | 2 | 9 | 4 | - | - |
| R.R.O'Donnell* c Muller b Bacon | 7 | 14 | 11 | - | 1 |
| B.J.Horne† b Duffy | 14 | 27 | 16 | - | 1 |
| S.M.Solia not out | 10 | 10 | 5 | - | 1 |
| W.E.R.Somerville not out | 7 | 5 | 4 | - | 1 |
| A.Ashok | | | | | |
| B.G.Lister | | | | | |
| S.B.Keene | | | | | |
| Extras (lb 4, w 8, nb 1) | 13 | | | | |
| **TOTAL** (50 overs) (6 wkts) | **380** | 230 | | | |

| OTAGO | Runs | Mins | Balls | 6s | 4s |
|---|---|---|---|---|---|
| D.N.Phillips c Ashok b Keene | 47 | 64 | 47 | - | 7 |
| M.Renwick c O'Donnell b Keene | 28 | 40 | 27 | - | 6 |
| N.T.Broom c Chapman b Keene | 2 | 8 | 6 | - | - |
| N.F.Kelly* c Chapman b Somerville | 23 | 46 | 35 | - | 2 |
| M.J.G.Rippon c Somerville b Keene | 0 | 5 | 3 | - | - |
| A.K.Kitchen not out | 106 | 136 | 95 | 7 | 2 |
| M.W.Chu† c Ashok b Phillips | 5 | 27 | 11 | - | - |
| T.Muller not out | 54 | 82 | 76 | 1 | 5 |
| M.B.Bacon | | | | | |
| J.A.Duffy | | | | | |
| A.W.McKenzie | | | | | |
| Extras (lb 9, w 10) | 19 | | | | |
| **TOTAL** (50 overs) (6 wkts) | **284** | 206 | | | |

| Bowling OTAGO | O | M | R | W |
|---|---|---|---|---|
| Duffy | 10 | 0 | 76 | 1 |
| Muller | 7 | 0 | 67 | 0 |
| Kitchen | 10 | 0 | 59 | 0 |
| McKenzie | 10 | 0 | 66 | 3 |
| Bacon | 8 | 0 | 55 | 2 |
| Rippon | 5 | 0 | 53 | 0 |
| **AUCKLAND** | | | | |
| Lister | 5 | 0 | 31 | 0 |
| Solia | 9 | 0 | 58 | 0 |
| Keene | 10 | 0 | 47 | 4 |
| Somerville | 10 | 1 | 38 | 1 |
| Ashok | 10 | 0 | 67 | 0 |
| Phillips | 6 | 0 | 34 | 1 |

| Fall of Wickets | A | O |
|---|---|---|
| 1st | 260 | 71 |
| 2nd | 273 | 81 |
| 3rd | 283 | 91 |
| 4th | 305 | 94 |
| 5th | 362 | 125 |
| 6th | 366 | 162 |
| 7th | - | - |
| 8th | - | - |
| 9th | - | - |
| 10th | - | - |

# AUCKLAND v CENTRAL DISTRICTS                    Ford Trophy

*at Kennards Hire Community Oval, Auckland on 24 February, 2022*
*Toss : Central Districts.  Umpires : B.F. Bowden & T.J. Parlane*
**Auckland won by 3 wickets.** Points: Auckland 4, Central Districts 0

## CENTRAL DISTRICTS

| | Runs | Mins | Balls | 6s | 4s |
|---|---|---|---|---|---|
| B.L.Wiggins† c Keene b Ferguson | 41 | 25 | 25 | - | 9 |
| B.S.Smith c O'Donnell b Phillips | 32 | 90 | 56 | - | 2 |
| B.D.Schmulian c Guptill b Somerville | 75 | 135 | 98 | - | 6 |
| L.R.P.L.Taylor c Guptill b Phillips | 59 | 91 | 54 | 4 | 1 |
| T.C.Bruce* c Worker b Somerville | 4 | 3 | 3 | - | 1 |
| J.A.Clarkson b Pringle | 31 | 32 | 23 | 1 | 4 |
| D.A.J.Bracewell b Pringle | 8 | 11 | 8 | - | 1 |
| A.F.Milne run out | 25 | 25 | 14 | - | 3 |
| J.F.A.Field lbw b Pringle | 0 | 1 | 1 | - | - |
| J.R.Lennox c Chapman b Pringle | 8 | 17 | 12 | - | - |
| S.H.A.Rance not out | 0 | 4 | 2 | - | - |
| Extras (b 1, lb 4, w 13) | 18 | | | | |
| **TOTAL** (49.2 overs) | **301** | 219 | | | |

## AUCKLAND

| | Runs | Mins | Balls | 6s | 4s |
|---|---|---|---|---|---|
| M.J.Guptill c Taylor b Milne | 0 | 3 | 5 | - | - |
| G.H.Worker not out | 139 | 225 | 144 | 3 | 11 |
| G.D.Phillips b Bracewell | 5 | 21 | 9 | - | 1 |
| M.S.Chapman c Wiggins b Milne | 88 | 126 | 92 | 2 | 6 |
| R.R.O'Donnell* b Lennox | 7 | 13 | 9 | - | 1 |
| B.J.Horne† c Rance b Bracewell | 35 | 37 | 26 | 1 | 3 |
| W.E.R.Somerville run out | 13 | 9 | 7 | - | 3 |
| L.H.Ferguson c Smith b Field | 0 | 2 | 1 | - | - |
| S.B.Keene not out | 4 | 10 | 4 | - | - |
| A.Ashok | | | | | |
| O.M.R.Pringle | | | | | |
| Extras (b 1, lb 6, w 7) | 14 | | | | |
| **TOTAL** (49.3 overs) (7 wkts) | **305** | 225 | | | |

| Bowling | O | M | R | W |
|---|---|---|---|---|
| **AUCKLAND** | | | | |
| Ferguson | 7.2 | 0 | 53 | 1 |
| Keene | 7 | 0 | 41 | 0 |
| Pringle | 9 | 0 | 51 | 4 |
| Somerville | 10 | 0 | 44 | 2 |
| Ashok | 10 | 0 | 65 | 0 |
| Phillips | 6 | 0 | 42 | 2 |
| **CENTRAL DISTRICTS** | | | | |
| Milne | 6 | 2 | 18 | 2 |
| Bracewell | 8 | 1 | 51 | 2 |
| Rance | 6 | 0 | 38 | 0 |
| Field | 10 | 0 | 64 | 1 |
| Bruce | 6 | 0 | 41 | 0 |
| Lennox | 10 | 0 | 50 | 1 |
| Schmulian | 3.3 | 0 | 36 | 0 |

| Fall of Wickets | CD | A |
|---|---|---|
| 1st | 48 | 4 |
| 2nd | 117 | 19 |
| 3rd | 208 | 201 |
| 4th | 212 | 212 |
| 5th | 246 | 270 |
| 6th | 267 | 286 |
| 7th | 268 | 287 |
| 8th | 268 | - |
| 9th | 295 | - |
| 10th | 301 | - |

---

# CENTRAL DISTRICTS v AUCKLAND                    Final

*at John Davies Oval, Queenstown on 26 February, 2022*
*Toss : Auckland.  Umpires : J.A.K. Bromley & D.J. Walker*
**Auckland won by 8 wickets**

## CENTRAL DISTRICTS

| | Runs | Mins | Balls | 6s | 4s |
|---|---|---|---|---|---|
| B.L.Wiggins† c O'Donnell b Ferguson | 14 | 24 | 13 | - | 3 |
| B.S.Smith run out | 9 | 43 | 28 | - | - |
| B.D.Schmulian b Ferguson | 44 | 96 | 66 | - | 2 |
| L.R.P.L.Taylor c Horne b Solia | 5 | 21 | 15 | - | 1 |
| T.C.Bruce* c O'Donnell b Phillips | 63 | 105 | 66 | 1 | 5 |
| J.A.Clarkson c Horne b Ashok | 15 | 18 | 21 | - | 2 |
| D.A.J.Bracewell c Solia b Ferguson | 21 | 42 | 36 | - | 1 |
| A.F.Milne c Horne b Solia | 21 | 45 | 28 | - | 1 |
| B.M.Tickner c Horne b Ferguson | 2 | 13 | 8 | - | - |
| J.R.Lennox run out | 9 | 19 | 18 | - | 1 |
| S.H.A.Rance not out | 0 | | | | |
| Extras (lb 2, w 8) | 10 | | | | |
| **TOTAL** (49.5 overs) | **213** | 215 | | | |

## AUCKLAND

| | Runs | Mins | Balls | 6s | 4s |
|---|---|---|---|---|---|
| M.J.Guptill c Lennox b Milne | 23 | 33 | 21 | - | 4 |
| G.H.Worker not out | 65 | 172 | 109 | - | 4 |
| G.D.Phillips c Bracewell b Rance | 23 | 23 | 13 | - | 4 |
| M.S.Chapman not out | 92 | 115 | 75 | 1 | 12 |
| R.R.O'Donnell* | | | | | |
| B.J.Horne† | | | | | |
| S.M.Solia | | | | | |
| W.E.R.Somerville | | | | | |
| L.H.Ferguson | | | | | |
| A.Ashok | | | | | |
| B.G.Lister | | | | | |
| Extras (w 13, nb 1) | 14 | | | | |
| **TOTAL** (36.1 overs) (2 wkts) | **217** | 172 | | | |

| Bowling | O | M | R | W |
|---|---|---|---|---|
| **AUCKLAND** | | | | |
| Lister | 10 | 1 | 36 | 0 |
| Ferguson | 10 | 0 | 32 | 4 |
| Solia | 6.5 | 0 | 36 | 2 |
| Somerville | 10 | 1 | 44 | 0 |
| Ashok | 6 | 0 | 29 | 1 |
| Phillips | 7 | 0 | 34 | 1 |
| **CENTRAL DISTRICTS** | | | | |
| Milne | 8 | 1 | 43 | 1 |
| Rance | 6 | 0 | 25 | 1 |
| Bracewell | 7 | 1 | 36 | 0 |
| Tickner | 7 | 0 | 52 | 0 |
| Lennox | 6 | 0 | 33 | 0 |
| Schmulian | 1.1 | 0 | 12 | 0 |
| Bruce | 1 | 0 | 16 | 0 |

| Fall of Wickets | CD | A |
|---|---|---|
| 1st | 20 | 28 |
| 2nd | 32 | 60 |
| 3rd | 44 | - |
| 4th | 110 | - |
| 5th | 130 | - |
| 6th | 170 | - |
| 7th | 183 | - |
| 8th | 191 | - |
| 9th | 207 | - |
| 10th | 213 | - |

# 2021/22 FORD TROPHY AVERAGES

| | M | In | NO | HS | Runs | Ave | 100s | 50s | Ct | St | O | M | R | W | Ave | R/O | Best |
|---|---|---|---|---|---|---|---|---|---|---|---|---|---|---|---|---|---|
| F.H.Allen | 7 | 7 | 0 | 86 | 244 | 34.85 | - | 2 | 10 | - | | | | | | | |
| A.Ashok | 8 | 1 | 0 | 14 | 14 | 14.00 | - | - | 2 | - | 73 | 1 | 426 | 11 | 38.72 | 5.84 | 4-25 |
| M.T.M.M.J.Ave | 1 | 1 | 0 | 26 | 26 | 26.00 | - | - | - | - | | | | | | | |
| M.B.Bacon | 8 | 5 | 1 | 1 | 2 | 0.50 | - | - | 1 | - | 48.5 | 4 | 329 | 14 | 23.50 | 6.74 | 4-45 |
| H.K.Bennett | 5 | 1 | 1 | 0* | 0 | - | - | - | - | - | 28.4 | 1 | 171 | 4 | 42.75 | 5.97 | 2-30 |
| J.J.N.P.Bhula | 5 | 5 | 0 | 50 | 120 | 24.00 | - | 1 | 2 | - | 7 | 0 | 34 | 1 | 34.00 | 4.86 | 1-19 |
| T.A.Blundell | 2 | 2 | 0 | 53 | 65 | 32.50 | - | 1 | 2 | - | | | | | | | |
| P.D.Bocock | 2 | 2 | 1 | 20 | 23 | 23.00 | - | - | 1 | 1 | | | | | | | |
| C.J.Bowes | 6 | 6 | 0 | 99 | 167 | 27.83 | - | 1 | 1 | - | | | | | | | |
| J.C.T.Boyle | 5 | 5 | 0 | 29 | 70 | 14.00 | - | - | 2 | - | | | | | | | |
| D.A.J.Bracewell | 7 | 6 | 1 | 42 | 131 | 26.20 | - | - | 2 | - | 46 | 4 | 267 | 9 | 29.66 | 5.80 | 3-42 |
| M.G.Bracewell | 7 | 7 | 0 | 93 | 197 | 28.14 | - | 1 | 1 | - | 38.5 | 0 | 183 | 8 | 22.87 | 4.71 | 3-36 |
| C.J.Briggs | 2 | 2 | 0 | 2 | 2 | 1.00 | - | - | 1 | - | | | | | | | |
| N.T.Broom | 7 | 7 | 0 | 72 | 189 | 27.00 | - | 2 | 1 | - | | | | | | | |
| T.C.Bruce | 7 | 7 | 1 | 63 | 193 | 32.16 | - | 2 | 6 | - | 9 | 0 | 88 | 0 | - | 9.78 | - |
| J.F.Carter | 5 | 5 | 1 | 105* | 205 | 51.25 | 1 | 1 | 2 | - | | | | | | | |
| L.J.Carter | 6 | 6 | 1 | 63 | 267 | 53.40 | - | 3 | 2 | - | | | | | | | |
| M.S.Chapman | 10 | 10 | 1 | 105 | 465 | 51.66 | 1 | 3 | 7 | - | 6 | 0 | 50 | 0 | - | 8.33 | - |
| M.W.Chu | 8 | 7 | 1 | 44* | 120 | 20.00 | - | - | 8 | 2 | | | | | | | |
| K.D.Clarke | 3 | 3 | 0 | 28 | 40 | 13.33 | - | - | 3 | - | | | | | | | |
| J.A.Clarkson | 7 | 7 | 1 | 58 | 195 | 32.50 | - | 2 | - | - | | | | | | | |
| D.Cleaver | 1 | 1 | 0 | 7 | 7 | 7.00 | - | - | 1 | - | | | | | | | |
| D.P.Conway | 1 | 1 | 0 | 0 | 0 | 0.00 | - | - | - | - | | | | | | | |
| H.R.Cooper | 5 | 5 | 1 | 52 | 102 | 25.50 | - | 1 | - | - | | | | | | | |
| C.de Grandhomme | 4 | 3 | 0 | 126 | 140 | 46.66 | 1 | - | - | - | 18 | 0 | 113 | 2 | 56.50 | 6.28 | 1-14 |
| L.J.Delport | 3 | 2 | 2 | 7* | 7 | - | - | - | 1 | - | 30 | 0 | 135 | 4 | 33.75 | 4.50 | 2-43 |
| J.A.Duffy | 8 | 6 | 2 | 23* | 67 | 16.75 | - | - | 8 | - | 58 | 4 | 359 | 10 | 35.90 | 6.19 | 3-70 |
| L.H.Ferguson | 6 | 4 | 1 | 4 | 4 | 1.33 | - | - | - | - | 44.2 | 3 | 205 | 14 | 14.64 | 4.62 | 6-34 |
| D.K.Ferns | 4 | 2 | 0 | 4 | 6 | 3.00 | - | - | 1 | - | 26.4 | 1 | 207 | 5 | 41.40 | 7.76 | 3-68 |
| J.F.A.Field | 4 | 2 | 0 | 0 | 0 | 0.00 | - | - | 1 | - | 20 | 0 | 123 | 3 | 41.00 | 6.15 | 1-27 |
| J.L.Finnie | 2 | 2 | 1 | 72* | 100 | 100.00 | - | 1 | - | - | 12 | 0 | 65 | 0 | - | 5.42 | - |
| M.J.Fisher | 2 | 1 | 0 | 0 | 0 | 0.00 | - | - | - | - | 17.3 | 1 | 58 | 7 | 8.28 | 3.31 | 4-34 |
| C.D.Fletcher | 3 | 2 | 0 | 12 | 14 | 7.00 | - | - | 3 | 1 | | | | | | | |
| Z.G.Foulkes | 1 | 1 | 0 | 19 | 19 | 19.00 | - | - | - | - | 3 | 0 | 20 | 0 | - | 6.67 | - |
| L.I.Georgeson | 5 | 5 | 0 | 56 | 179 | 35.80 | - | 2 | 3 | - | 3 | 0 | 40 | 0 | - | 13.33 | - |
| J.D.Gibson | 3 | 3 | 1 | 22* | 45 | 22.50 | - | - | 3 | - | 7 | 0 | 32 | 1 | 32.00 | 4.57 | 1-32 |
| J.M.Gibson | 1 | 1 | 0 | 2 | 2 | 2.00 | - | - | - | - | 6 | 0 | 45 | 1 | 45.00 | 7.50 | 1-45 |
| Z.N.Gibson | 4 | 3 | 1 | 4* | 4 | 2.00 | - | - | 1 | - | 27 | 3 | 117 | 4 | 29.25 | 4.33 | 4-61 |
| M.J.Guptill | 8 | 8 | 1 | 137 | 367 | 52.42 | 1 | 2 | 5 | - | | | | | | | |
| B.R.Hampton | 4 | 3 | 1 | 21* | 31 | 15.50 | - | - | 1 | - | 6 | 1 | 41 | 1 | 41.00 | 6.83 | 1-39 |
| M.J.Hay | 2 | 2 | 0 | 24 | 32 | 16.00 | - | - | - | - | | | | | | | |
| M.J.Henry | 3 | 2 | 0 | 15 | 18 | 9.00 | - | - | - | - | 24 | 3 | 133 | 4 | 33.25 | 5.54 | 2-42 |
| B.J.Horne | 10 | 8 | 2 | 45 | 164 | 27.33 | - | - | 13 | - | | | | | | | |
| L.R.Johns | 1 | 1 | 1 | 0* | 0 | - | - | - | 1 | - | | | | | | | |
| L.C.Johnson | 2 | 2 | 0 | 26 | 26 | 13.00 | - | - | 2 | - | | | | | | | |
| T.M.Johnson | 7 | 7 | 0 | 88 | 281 | 40.14 | - | 3 | 2 | - | | | | | | | |
| S.B.Keene | 2 | 1 | 1 | 4* | 4 | - | - | - | 1 | - | 17 | 0 | 88 | 4 | 22.00 | 5.18 | 4-47 |
| N.F.Kelly | 8 | 8 | 0 | 67 | 163 | 20.37 | - | 2 | 6 | - | | | | | | | |
| A.K.Kitchen | 8 | 8 | 1 | 106* | 205 | 29.28 | 1 | - | 1 | - | 64 | 5 | 295 | 11 | 26.81 | 4.61 | 3-36 |
| S.C.Kuggeleijn | 5 | 3 | 1 | 15 | 26 | 13.00 | - | - | 3 | - | 37 | 4 | 153 | 4 | 38.25 | 4.14 | 2-26 |
| T.W.M.Latham | 1 | 1 | 0 | 4 | 4 | 4.00 | - | - | 2 | 1 | | | | | | | |
| J.R.Lennox | 6 | 4 | 2 | 11* | 28 | 14.00 | - | - | 2 | - | 41.5 | 1 | 227 | 8 | 28.37 | 5.43 | 3-57 |
| B.G.Lister | 6 | 1 | 1 | 1* | 1 | - | - | - | 2 | - | 48 | 3 | 236 | 3 | 78.66 | 4.92 | 2-48 |
| B.N.J.Lockrose | 3 | 3 | 1 | 18* | 18 | 9.00 | - | - | - | - | 15.3 | 2 | 70 | 6 | 11.66 | 4.52 | 3-17 |
| K.J.McClure | 6 | 6 | 0 | 87 | 114 | 19.00 | - | 1 | 2 | - | | | | | | | |
| C.E.McConchie | 6 | 6 | 1 | 57* | 159 | 31.80 | - | 1 | 2 | - | 27 | 1 | 152 | 2 | 76.00 | 5.63 | 1-21 |
| J.D.McKay | 1 | 1 | 0 | 14 | 14 | 14.00 | - | 1 | - | - | 6 | 0 | 81 | 1 | 81.00 | 13.50 | 1-81 |
| A.W.McKenzie | 2 | 1 | 0 | 6 | 6 | 6.00 | - | - | - | - | 19 | 1 | 125 | 5 | 25.00 | 6.58 | 3-66 |
| A.F.Milne | 6 | 6 | 2 | 50 | 115 | 28.75 | - | 1 | 4 | - | 36 | 4 | 174 | 9 | 19.33 | 4.83 | 3-35 |
| D.J.Mitchell | 1 | 1 | 0 | 12 | 12 | 12.00 | - | - | - | - | 0.2 | 0 | 1 | 0 | - | - | - |
| T.Muller | 5 | 4 | 2 | 54* | 84 | 42.00 | - | 1 | 3 | - | 27 | 0 | 173 | 3 | 57.66 | 6.41 | 1-14 |
| J.D.S.Neesham | 1 | 1 | 0 | 4 | 4 | 4.00 | - | - | 1 | - | 8 | 0 | 31 | 2 | 15.50 | 3.88 | 2-31 |
| O.R.Newton | 6 | 3 | 0 | 25 | 33 | 11.00 | - | - | 2 | - | 40.3 | 1 | 302 | 9 | 33.55 | 7.46 | 3-43 |
| E.J.Nuttall | 5 | 3 | 1 | 8 | 12 | 6.00 | - | - | 1 | - | 38 | 0 | 276 | 5 | 55.20 | 7.26 | 2-58 |
| R.R.O'Donnell | 10 | 9 | 2 | 100* | 283 | 40.42 | 1 | 1 | 5 | - | | | | | | | |

| | M | In | NO | HS | Runs | Ave | 100s | 50s | Ct | St | O | M | R | W | Ave | R/O | Best |
|---|---|---|---|---|---|---|---|---|---|---|---|---|---|---|---|---|---|
| W.P.O'Rourke | 3 | 3 | 1 | 11 | 18 | 9.00 | - | - | 1 | - | 27 | 4 | 142 | 4 | 35.50 | 5.26 | 2-31 |
| A.Y.Patel | 1 | - | - | - | - | - | - | - | 2 | - | 8 | 0 | 26 | 2 | 13.00 | 3.25 | 2-26 |
| D.N.Phillips | 7 | 7 | 0 | 47 | 181 | 25.85 | - | - | 2 | - | | | | | | | |
| G.D.Phillips | 10 | 10 | 1 | 122* | 378 | 42.00 | 1 | 1 | 3 | - | 44 | 0 | 233 | 7 | 33.28 | 5.30 | 2-42 |
| B.Popli | 1 | 1 | 0 | 2 | 2 | 2.00 | - | - | - | - | | | | | | | |
| O.M.R.Pringle | 1 | - | - | - | - | - | - | - | - | - | 9 | 0 | 51 | 4 | 12.75 | 5.67 | 4-51 |
| M.D.Rae | 2 | - | - | - | - | - | - | - | - | - | 11 | 0 | 66 | 0 | - | 6.00 | - |
| S.H.A.Rance | 7 | 3 | 3 | 0* | 0 | - | - | - | 3 | - | 41.4 | 1 | 181 | 12 | 15.08 | 4.34 | 4-25 |
| B.G.Randell | 1 | 1 | 1 | 9* | 9 | - | - | - | - | - | 6.2 | 0 | 69 | 1 | 69.00 | 10.90 | 1-69 |
| J.A.Raval | 6 | 6 | 0 | 97 | 226 | 37.66 | - | 2 | 6 | - | 2 | 1 | 6 | 2 | 3.00 | 3.00 | 2-6 |
| R.Ravindra | 2 | 2 | 0 | 46 | 80 | 40.00 | - | - | - | - | 17 | 0 | 71 | 1 | 71.00 | 4.18 | 1-36 |
| M.Renwick | 5 | 5 | 0 | 55 | 94 | 18.80 | - | 1 | 3 | - | | | | | | | |
| M.J.G.Rippon | 7 | 7 | 2 | 68* | 157 | 31.40 | - | 1 | 2 | - | 59.4 | 5 | 317 | 11 | 28.81 | 5.31 | 4-41 |
| H.D.Rutherford | 4 | 4 | 0 | 45 | 100 | 25.00 | - | - | - | - | 2 | 0 | 12 | 0 | - | 6.00 | - |
| M.J.Santner | 5 | 4 | 1 | 74 | 79 | 26.33 | - | 1 | 2 | - | 40 | 2 | 162 | 7 | 23.14 | 4.05 | 2-25 |
| B.D.Schmulian | 5 | 4 | 1 | 75 | 187 | 62.33 | - | 1 | 1 | - | 8.4 | 0 | 83 | 2 | 41.50 | 9.58 | 1-7 |
| B.V.Sears | 7 | 3 | 1 | 19* | 34 | 17.00 | - | - | 1 | - | 40.4 | 0 | 240 | 3 | 80.00 | 5.90 | 1-33 |
| T.L.Seifert | 5 | 5 | 0 | 51 | 107 | 21.40 | - | 1 | 5 | 2 | | | | | | | |
| H.B.Shipley | 6 | 5 | 0 | 78 | 156 | 31.20 | - | 2 | 4 | - | 44 | 0 | 288 | 6 | 48.00 | 6.55 | 2-65 |
| B.S.Smith | 7 | 7 | 0 | 37 | 166 | 23.71 | - | - | 4 | - | | | | | | | |
| N.G.Smith | 7 | 7 | 4 | 47* | 200 | 66.66 | - | - | 3 | - | 29 | 2 | 163 | 6 | 27.16 | 5.62 | 3-51 |
| I.S.Sodhi | 2 | 1 | 0 | 13 | 13 | 13.00 | - | - | - | - | 12 | 0 | 91 | 2 | 45.50 | 7.58 | 2-54 |
| S.M.Solia | 9 | 7 | 3 | 39 | 95 | 23.75 | - | - | 5 | - | 53.5 | 2 | 335 | 6 | 55.83 | 6.22 | 2-36 |
| W.E.R.Somerville | 9 | 6 | 1 | 59 | 112 | 22.40 | - | 1 | 3 | - | 86.3 | 4 | 383 | 11 | 34.81 | 4.43 | 2-28 |
| C.J.Swanson | 1 | 1 | 0 | 41 | 41 | 41.00 | - | - | - | - | | | | | | | |
| L.R.P.L.Taylor | 6 | 6 | 1 | 111* | 279 | 55.80 | 1 | 2 | 5 | - | | | | | | | |
| R.M.ter Braak | 2 | 1 | 0 | 15 | 15 | 15.00 | - | - | - | - | 12 | 0 | 52 | 4 | 13.00 | 4.33 | 3-20 |
| B.M.Tickner | 4 | 1 | 0 | 2 | 2 | 2.00 | - | - | - | - | 25.3 | 1 | 141 | 6 | 23.50 | 5.53 | 4-37 |
| L.V.van Beek | 7 | 6 | 2 | 24* | 81 | 20.25 | - | - | 7 | - | 43 | 3 | 267 | 11 | 24.27 | 6.21 | 3-29 |
| T.F.van Woerkom | 6 | 5 | 2 | 41 | 83 | 27.66 | - | - | - | - | 44.5 | 1 | 257 | 6 | 42.83 | 5.73 | 2-49 |
| A.Verma | 5 | 3 | 0 | 9 | 13 | 4.33 | - | - | - | - | 32 | 1 | 163 | 5 | 32.60 | 5.09 | 3-29 |
| J.G.Walker | 6 | 3 | 1 | 0* | 0 | 0.00 | - | - | - | - | 42 | 3 | 177 | 5 | 35.40 | 4.21 | 2-35 |
| B.L.Wiggins | 6 | 6 | 0 | 80 | 186 | 31.00 | - | 1 | 10 | 1 | | | | | | | |
| W.S.A.Williams | 6 | 5 | 3 | 15* | 30 | 15.00 | - | - | 2 | - | 45.5 | 2 | 246 | 4 | 61.50 | 5.37 | 2-28 |
| G.H.Worker | 10 | 10 | 2 | 139* | 672 | 84.00 | 4 | 1 | 3 | - | 2 | 0 | 11 | 0 | - | 5.50 | - |
| W.A.Young | 2 | 2 | 0 | 107 | 147 | 73.50 | 1 | - | - | - | | | | | | | |
| P.F.Younghusband | 4 | 3 | 3 | 14* | 15 | - | - | - | 1 | - | 32 | 3 | 161 | 4 | 40.25 | 5.03 | 3-56 |

## HIGHEST STRIKE RATES (qualification 150 runs)

| | | Runs | Balls | S/R | | | | Runs | Balls | S/R |
|---|---|---|---|---|---|---|---|---|---|---|
| L.R.P.L.Taylor | CD | 279 | 203 | 137 | | N.G.Smith | W | 200 | 179 | 111 |
| B.L.Wiggins | CD | 186 | 148 | 125 | | G.D.Phillips | A | 378 | 342 | 110 |
| F.H.Allen | W | 244 | 197 | 123 | | B.J.Horne | A | 164 | 153 | 107 |
| T.C.Bruce | CD | 193 | 170 | 113 | | M.G.Bracewell | W | 197 | 184 | 107 |
| J.A.Clarkson | CD | 195 | 174 | 112 | | M.J.Guptill | A | 367 | 358 | 102 |

## MOST ECONOMICAL BOWLING (qualification 30 overs)

| | | O | M | R | W | Ave | R/O |
|---|---|---|---|---|---|---|---|
| M.J.Santner | ND | 40 | 2 | 162 | 7 | 23.14 | 4.05 |
| S.C.Kuggeleijn | ND | 37 | 4 | 153 | 4 | 38.25 | 4.14 |
| J.G.Walker | ND | 42 | 3 | 177 | 5 | 35.40 | 4.21 |
| S.H.A.Rance | CD | 41.4 | 1 | 181 | 12 | 15.08 | 4.34 |
| W.E.R.Somerville | A | 86.3 | 4 | 383 | 11 | 34.81 | 4.43 |
| L.J.Delport | A | 30 | 0 | 135 | 4 | 33.75 | 4.50 |
| A.K.Kitchen | O | 64 | 5 | 295 | 11 | 26.81 | 4.61 |
| L.H.Ferguson | A | 44.2 | 3 | 205 | 14 | 14.64 | 4.62 |
| M.G.Bracewell | W | 38.5 | 0 | 183 | 8 | 22.87 | 4.71 |
| A.F.Milne | CD | 36 | 4 | 174 | 9 | 19.33 | 4.83 |

# CAREER RECORDS

| | M | In | NO | HS | Runs | Ave | 100s | 50s | Ct | St | O | M | R | W | Ave | R/O | Best |
|---|---|---|---|---|---|---|---|---|---|---|---|---|---|---|---|---|---|
| F.H.Allen | 25 | 25 | 0 | 128 | 644 | 25.76 | 1 | 2 | 18 | - | | | | | | | |
| A.Ashok | 8 | 1 | 0 | 14 | 14 | 14.00 | - | - | 2 | - | 73 | 1 | 426 | 11 | 38.72 | 5.84 | 4-25 |
| M.T.M.M.J.Ave | 9 | 9 | 2 | 26 | 77 | 11.00 | - | - | 8 | 4 | | | | | | | |
| M.B.Bacon | 34 | 19 | 6 | 21* | 99 | 7.61 | - | - | 10 | - | 231.4 | 8 | 1456 | 43 | 33.86 | 6.28 | 4-45 |
| H.K.Bennett | 82 | 27 | 16 | 20* | 73 | 6.63 | - | - | 11 | - | 586.1 | 34 | 3025 | 112 | 27.00 | 5.16 | 6-45 |
| J.J.N.P.Bhula | 29 | 28 | 1 | 99 | 605 | 22.40 | - | 4 | 15 | - | 44.2 | 0 | 216 | 11 | 19.63 | 4.87 | 3-13 |
| T.A.Blundell | 42 | 36 | 1 | 151 | 1113 | 31.80 | 1 | 6 | 33 | 4 | | | | | | | |
| P.D.Bocock | 22 | 20 | 3 | 57* | 394 | 23.17 | - | 3 | 28 | 2 | | | | | | | |
| C.J.Bowes | 53 | 53 | 4 | 114* | 1737 | 35.44 | 4 | 7 | 25 | - | | | | | | | |
| J.C.T.Boyle | 33 | 33 | 1 | 126 | 1182 | 36.93 | 3 | 5 | 13 | - | | | | | | | |
| D.A.J.Bracewell | 48 | 41 | 5 | 80 | 980 | 27.22 | - | 4 | 16 | - | 347.3 | 22 | 1860 | 55 | 33.81 | 5.35 | 4-43 |
| M.G.Bracewell | 103 | 98 | 5 | 120 | 2977 | 32.01 | 1 | 24 | 52 | - | 149.5 | 3 | 769 | 23 | 33.43 | 5.13 | 3-30 |
| C.J.Briggs | 6 | 6 | 0 | 101 | 254 | 42.33 | 1 | 1 | 2 | - | | | | | | | |
| N.T.Broom | 137 | 127 | 13 | 164 | 4644 | 40.73 | 9 | 30 | 46 | - | 51.2 | 1 | 306 | 4 | 76.50 | 5.96 | 1-10 |
| T.C.Bruce | 52 | 52 | 6 | 100 | 1614 | 35.08 | 1 | 15 | 26 | - | 27 | 0 | 218 | 2 | 109.00 | 8.07 | 1-13 |
| J.F.Carter | 42 | 40 | 5 | 105* | 1266 | 36.17 | 2 | 8 | 21 | - | | | | | | | |
| L.J.Carter | 33 | 28 | 5 | 63* | 634 | 27.56 | - | 5 | 9 | - | | | | | | | |
| M.S.Chapman | 34 | 33 | 5 | 157 | 1509 | 53.89 | 4 | 8 | 20 | - | 79.5 | 1 | 536 | 12 | 44.66 | 6.71 | 3-41 |
| M.W.Chu | 12 | 10 | 1 | 44* | 152 | 16.88 | - | - | 12 | 2 | | | | | | | |
| K.D.Clarke | 24 | 24 | 0 | 82 | 713 | 29.70 | - | 6 | 14 | - | | | | | | | |
| J.A.Clarkson | 51 | 48 | 8 | 111 | 1452 | 36.30 | 2 | 8 | 11 | - | 81.2 | 2 | 454 | 14 | 32.42 | 5.58 | 3-30 |
| D.Cleaver | 57 | 49 | 4 | 124* | 1358 | 30.17 | 2 | 8 | 61 | 9 | | | | | | | |
| D.P.Conway | 30 | 30 | 3 | 138 | 1227 | 45.44 | 2 | 10 | 10 | - | | | | | | | |
| H.R.Cooper | 32 | 32 | 3 | 146* | 994 | 34.27 | 1 | 8 | 8 | - | 25.3 | 1 | 157 | 5 | 31.40 | 6.16 | 2-9 |
| C.de Grandhomme | 85 | 79 | 9 | 126 | 1865 | 26.64 | 2 | 6 | 43 | - | 361 | 8 | 1979 | 47 | 42.10 | 5.48 | 4-37 |
| L.J.Delport | 19 | 11 | 7 | 16* | 58 | 14.50 | - | - | 5 | - | 183 | 8 | 809 | 27 | 29.96 | 4.42 | 3-41 |
| J.A.Duffy | 60 | 36 | 16 | 39 | 250 | 12.50 | - | - | 22 | - | 482.4 | 25 | 2667 | 109 | 24.46 | 5.53 | 6-35 |
| L.H.Ferguson | 31 | 20 | 7 | 24 | 80 | 6.15 | - | - | 6 | - | 263.5 | 18 | 1352 | 57 | 23.71 | 5.12 | 6-27 |
| D.K.Ferns | 21 | 15 | 6 | 35* | 135 | 15.00 | - | - | 8 | - | 150 | 11 | 906 | 27 | 33.55 | 6.04 | 4-35 |
| J.F.A.Field | 12 | 7 | 1 | 31 | 52 | 8.66 | - | - | 3 | - | 67 | 0 | 466 | 10 | 46.60 | 6.96 | 4-42 |
| J.L.Finnie | 40 | 37 | 6 | 73* | 867 | 27.96 | - | 6 | 10 | - | 58 | 0 | 378 | 4 | 94.50 | 6.52 | 1-14 |
| M.J.Fisher | 8 | 3 | 1 | 2 | 2 | 1.00 | - | - | 2 | - | 70.3 | 3 | 338 | 18 | 18.77 | 4.79 | 4-34 |
| C.D.Fletcher | 65 | 50 | 14 | 73 | 1062 | 29.50 | - | 3 | 70 | 10 | | | | | | | |
| Z.G.Foulkes | 1 | 1 | 0 | 19 | 19 | 19.00 | - | - | - | - | 3 | 0 | 20 | 0 | - | 6.67 | - |
| L.I.Georgeson | 6 | 6 | 0 | 56 | 197 | 32.83 | - | 2 | 4 | - | 3 | 0 | 40 | 0 | - | 13.33 | - |
| J.D.Gibson | 25 | 24 | 6 | 64* | 455 | 25.27 | - | 2 | 16 | - | 83 | 1 | 537 | 6 | 89.50 | 6.47 | 2-31 |
| J.M.Gibson | 6 | 6 | 1 | 7 | 20 | 4.00 | - | - | - | - | 40.5 | 2 | 223 | 13 | 17.15 | 5.46 | 5-31 |
| Z.N.Gibson | 27 | 15 | 7 | 18 | 57 | 7.12 | - | - | 10 | - | 195.1 | 11 | 1045 | 24 | 43.54 | 5.35 | 4-31 |
| M.J.Guptill | 53 | 52 | 3 | 156 | 2213 | 45.16 | 9 | 8 | 30 | - | | | | | | | |
| B.R.Hampton | 62 | 53 | 13 | 95 | 1114 | 27.85 | - | 4 | 20 | - | 352.4 | 10 | 1891 | 52 | 36.36 | 5.36 | 4-30 |
| M.J.Hay | 3 | 3 | 0 | 24 | 35 | 11.66 | - | - | - | - | | | | | | | |
| M.J.Henry | 50 | 34 | 8 | 37* | 355 | 13.65 | - | - | 21 | - | 407.5 | 35 | 2051 | 82 | 25.01 | 5.03 | 6-45 |
| B.J.Horne | 49 | 44 | 7 | 101 | 1050 | 28.37 | 1 | 5 | 56 | 7 | | | | | | | |
| L.R.Johns | 23 | 19 | 4 | 25* | 219 | 14.60 | - | - | 33 | 4 | | | | | | | |
| L.C.Johnson | 2 | 2 | 0 | 26 | 26 | 13.00 | - | - | 2 | - | | | | | | | |
| T.M.Johnson | 17 | 17 | 1 | 113 | 651 | 40.68 | 1 | 6 | 8 | - | | | | | | | |
| S.B.Keene | 2 | 1 | 1 | 4* | 4 | - | - | - | 1 | - | 17 | 0 | 88 | 4 | 22.00 | 5.18 | 4-47 |
| N.F.Kelly | 56 | 54 | 2 | 120 | 1659 | 31.90 | 3 | 13 | 32 | - | 8 | 0 | 60 | 2 | 30.00 | 7.50 | 2-55 |
| A.K.Kitchen | 115 | 111 | 11 | 143* | 3193 | 31.93 | 5 | 15 | 48 | - | 408.2 | 13 | 2163 | 57 | 37.94 | 5.30 | 4-23 |
| S.C.Kuggeleijn | 71 | 57 | 12 | 85* | 914 | 20.31 | - | 3 | 27 | - | 589.5 | 36 | 3285 | 106 | 30.99 | 5.57 | 5-24 |
| T.W.M.Latham | 49 | 46 | 6 | 130 | 1734 | 43.35 | 3 | 9 | 54 | 6 | | | | | | | |
| J.R.Lennox | 19 | 10 | 4 | 11* | 45 | 7.50 | - | - | 4 | - | 138.5 | 2 | 720 | 21 | 34.28 | 5.19 | 3-30 |
| B.G.Lister | 35 | 15 | 9 | 30 | 78 | 13.00 | - | - | 15 | - | 274.2 | 16 | 1550 | 43 | 36.04 | 5.65 | 6-51 |
| B.N.J.Lockrose | 4 | 3 | 1 | 18* | 18 | 9.00 | - | - | 1 | - | 21.3 | 2 | 104 | 7 | 14.85 | 4.84 | 3-17 |
| K.J.McClure | 27 | 23 | 3 | 107 | 751 | 37.55 | 2 | 4 | 6 | - | | | | | | | |
| C.E.McConchie | 57 | 45 | 3 | 90 | 1063 | 25.30 | - | 6 | 15 | - | 251 | 5 | 1426 | 31 | 46.00 | 5.68 | 3-28 |
| J.D.McKay | 3 | 2 | 1 | 14 | 18 | 18.00 | - | - | 2 | - | 18 | 0 | 174 | 2 | 87.00 | 9.67 | 1-52 |
| A.W.McKenzie | 7 | 4 | 1 | 22 | 39 | 13.00 | - | - | 2 | - | 47 | 1 | 264 | 8 | 33.00 | 5.62 | 3-66 |
| A.F.Milne | 30 | 19 | 7 | 50 | 264 | 22.00 | - | 1 | 8 | - | 241.2 | 22 | 1268 | 48 | 26.41 | 5.25 | 4-48 |
| D.J.Mitchell | 70 | 66 | 8 | 126* | 2273 | 39.18 | 3 | 17 | 35 | - | 235 | 4 | 1462 | 44 | 33.22 | 6.22 | 3-34 |
| T.Muller | 11 | 8 | 2 | 54* | 137 | 22.83 | - | 1 | 5 | - | 68 | 0 | 431 | 11 | 39.18 | 6.34 | 5-34 |
| J.D.S.Neesham | 57 | 51 | 9 | 120* | 1625 | 38.69 | 2 | 11 | 27 | - | 312.5 | 15 | 1759 | 71 | 24.77 | 5.62 | 5-29 |
| O.R.Newton | 28 | 19 | 7 | 35* | 183 | 15.25 | - | - | 4 | - | 219.1 | 10 | 1137 | 49 | 23.20 | 5.19 | 5-46 |
| E.J.Nuttall | 38 | 15 | 8 | 8 | 17 | 2.42 | - | - | 9 | - | 285.2 | 17 | 1639 | 57 | 28.75 | 5.74 | 4-50 |
| R.R.O'Donnell | 61 | 59 | 6 | 100* | 1670 | 31.50 | 1 | 10 | 32 | - | 51 | 0 | 281 | 8 | 35.12 | 5.51 | 2-19 |

| | M | In | NO | HS | Runs | Ave | 100s | 50s | Ct | St | O | M | R | W | Ave | R/O | Best |
|---|---|---|---|---|---|---|---|---|---|---|---|---|---|---|---|---|---|
| W.P.O'Rourke | 3 | 3 | 1 | 11 | 18 | 9.00 | - | - | 1 | - | 27 | 4 | 142 | 4 | 35.50 | 5.26 | 2-31 |
| A.Y.Patel | 29 | 17 | 7 | 45 | 179 | 17.90 | - | - | 14 | - | 240.1 | 6 | 1281 | 29 | 44.17 | 5.33 | 3-43 |
| D.N.Phillips | 23 | 21 | 2 | 62 | 484 | 25.47 | - | 1 | 12 | - | 4.1 | 0 | 41 | 0 | - | 9.84 | - |
| G.D.Phillips | 37 | 37 | 1 | 156 | 1384 | 38.44 | 4 | 3 | 24 | 2 | 63 | 0 | 330 | 11 | 30.00 | 5.24 | 3-40 |
| B.Popli | 16 | 15 | 1 | 69 | 396 | 28.28 | - | 3 | 5 | - | | | | | | | |
| O.M.R.Pringle | 5 | 3 | 1 | 13 | 14 | 7.00 | - | - | - | - | 29 | 0 | 198 | 8 | 24.75 | 6.83 | 4-51 |
| M.D.Rae | 15 | 9 | 4 | 33 | 76 | 15.20 | - | - | 2 | - | 112.2 | 6 | 693 | 22 | 31.50 | 6.17 | 7-35 |
| S.H.A.Rance | 59 | 36 | 14 | 41* | 216 | 9.81 | - | - | 11 | - | 444.1 | 34 | 2208 | 95 | 23.24 | 4.97 | 4-25 |
| B.G.Randell | 26 | 14 | 7 | 25 | 81 | 11.57 | - | - | 10 | - | 210.2 | 11 | 1146 | 47 | 24.38 | 5.45 | 5-22 |
| J.A.Raval | 71 | 71 | 0 | 149 | 2181 | 30.71 | 4 | 10 | 44 | - | 25 | 1 | 139 | 5 | 27.80 | 5.56 | 2-6 |
| R.Ravindra | 6 | 6 | 0 | 130 | 280 | 46.66 | 1 | 1 | 1 | - | 50 | 1 | 225 | 5 | 45.00 | 4.50 | 2-53 |
| M.Renwick | 33 | 33 | 1 | 75 | 837 | 26.15 | - | 4 | 32 | 5 | | | | | | | |
| M.J.G.Rippon | 47 | 44 | 9 | 84 | 1295 | 37.00 | - | 8 | 19 | - | 390.4 | 19 | 2071 | 60 | 34.51 | 5.30 | 5-21 |
| H.D.Rutherford | 62 | 60 | 3 | 155 | 2090 | 36.66 | 7 | 5 | 20 | - | 9 | 0 | 45 | 1 | 45.00 | 5.00 | 1-4 |
| M.J.Santner | 24 | 23 | 1 | 86 | 600 | 27.27 | - | 4 | 14 | - | 189.4 | 11 | 815 | 28 | 29.10 | 4.30 | 3-70 |
| B.D.Schmulian | 15 | 12 | 4 | 75 | 388 | 48.50 | - | 2 | 3 | - | 51 | 1 | 376 | 3 | 125.33 | 7.37 | 1-7 |
| B.V.Sears | 22 | 9 | 4 | 19* | 52 | 10.40 | - | - | 10 | - | 164.4 | 7 | 919 | 28 | 32.82 | 5.58 | 3-40 |
| T.L.Seifert | 34 | 34 | 3 | 104 | 737 | 23.77 | 1 | 4 | 42 | 6 | | | | | | | |
| H.B.Shipley | 31 | 21 | 3 | 78 | 398 | 22.11 | - | 3 | 12 | - | 215.4 | 7 | 1311 | 24 | 54.62 | 6.08 | 4-60 |
| B.S.Smith | 19 | 19 | 3 | 83 | 429 | 26.81 | - | 3 | 8 | - | | | | | | | |
| N.G.Smith | 36 | 33 | 9 | 81 | 702 | 29.25 | - | 3 | 19 | - | 253.4 | 10 | 1411 | 44 | 32.06 | 5.56 | 3-21 |
| I.S.Sodhi | 39 | 26 | 4 | 44* | 263 | 11.95 | - | - | 9 | - | 357.5 | 15 | 1686 | 58 | 29.06 | 4.71 | 4-85 |
| S.M.Solia | 48 | 46 | 7 | 152 | 1586 | 40.66 | 3 | 8 | 14 | - | 202 | 4 | 1236 | 36 | 34.33 | 6.12 | 4-38 |
| W.E.R.Somerville | 28 | 22 | 5 | 59 | 319 | 18.76 | - | 2 | 10 | - | 265 | 6 | 1264 | 35 | 36.11 | 4.77 | 4-48 |
| C.J.Swanson | 1 | 1 | 0 | 41 | 41 | 41.00 | - | - | - | - | | | | | | | |
| L.R.P.L.Taylor | 47 | 47 | 6 | 132* | 1990 | 48.53 | 5 | 15 | 31 | - | 31 | 0 | 140 | 2 | 70.00 | 4.52 | 1-13 |
| R.M.ter Braak | 11 | 8 | 1 | 42* | 155 | 22.14 | - | - | 4 | - | 73.4 | 3 | 461 | 17 | 27.11 | 6.26 | 4-27 |
| B.M.Tickner | 31 | 10 | 8 | 24* | 58 | 29.00 | - | - | 9 | - | 243.3 | 5 | 1368 | 39 | 35.07 | 5.62 | 4-37 |
| L.V.van Beek | 66 | 42 | 8 | 53 | 457 | 13.44 | - | 1 | 37 | - | 426.5 | 18 | 2433 | 72 | 33.79 | 5.70 | 4-23 |
| T.F.van Woerkom | 20 | 12 | 3 | 41 | 140 | 15.55 | - | - | 2 | - | 163 | 2 | 858 | 18 | 47.66 | 5.26 | 2-31 |
| A.Verma | 59 | 39 | 13 | 58 | 574 | 22.07 | - | 2 | 30 | - | 437.4 | 20 | 2494 | 81 | 30.79 | 5.70 | 5-44 |
| J.G.Walker | 35 | 22 | 8 | 31* | 170 | 12.14 | - | - | 4 | - | 261.1 | 7 | 1275 | 29 | 43.96 | 4.88 | 3-35 |
| B.L.Wiggins | 15 | 14 | 0 | 103 | 569 | 40.64 | 1 | 3 | 14 | 1 | | | | | | | |
| W.S.A.Williams | 41 | 24 | 10 | 19* | 145 | 10.35 | - | - | 18 | - | 311.4 | 20 | 1603 | 51 | 31.43 | 5.14 | 4-34 |
| G.H.Worker | 117 | 116 | 9 | 194 | 5069 | 47.37 | 16 | 27 | 40 | - | 358.4 | 6 | 1985 | 54 | 36.75 | 5.53 | 4-22 |
| W.A.Young | 55 | 55 | 4 | 107 | 1796 | 35.21 | 4 | 11 | 22 | - | | | | | | | |
| P.F.Younghusband | 38 | 29 | 10 | 52* | 315 | 16.57 | - | 1 | 22 | - | 297.4 | 5 | 1597 | 38 | 42.02 | 5.37 | 3-42 |

# DREAM11
# SUPER SMASH
### *2021/22*

Northern Districts won their first Twenty20 title since 2017/18 when they defeated Canterbury in the final at Hamilton. After a no result and a loss in their first two games, Northern had eight successive wins to top the table and go through to the final. Canterbury finished in second place and defeated the 2020/21 winners, Wellington, in the elimination final.

Wellington's Michael Bracewell was the leading scorer with 478 runs, which included the highest individual score (141 not out v Central Districts) in New Zealand domestic Twenty20 history. He was followed by Dane Cleaver (369 runs), Chad Bowes (333) and Cam Fletcher (305). Cleaver also scored a century (114 not out for Central Districts v Otago). The fastest century was scored by Bracewell off 46 balls, while the fastest fifty came from Katene Clarke off 19 balls in the final.

Henry Shipley was the leading wicket-taker with 18 wickets followed by Lockie Ferguson (17) and Joe Walker (16). Seth Rance took the only five wicket bag with 5-19 for Central Districts v Otago. All games were televised live on Spark Sport with some shown on free to air television.

Final points were:

|                     | P  | W | L | NR | Points |
|---------------------|----|---|---|----|--------|
| Northern Districts  | 10 | 8 | 1 | 1  | 34     |
| Canterbury          | 10 | 7 | 3 | –  | 28     |
| Wellington          | 10 | 5 | 5 | –  | 20     |
| Central Districts   | 10 | 4 | 6 | –  | 16     |
| Auckland            | 10 | 4 | 6 | –  | 16     |
| Otago               | 10 | 1 | 8 | 1  | 6      |

## CANTERBURY v WELLINGTON                    Super Smash

*at Hagley Oval, Christchurch on 26 November, 2021 (d/n)*
*Toss : Canterbury. Umpires : K.D. Cotton & T.J. Parlane*
**Wellington won by 27 runs.** *Points: Wellington 4, Canterbury 0*

### WELLINGTON

|                                          | Runs | Mins | Balls | 6s | 4s |
|------------------------------------------|------|------|-------|----|----|
| F.H.Allen† c Shipley b Nuttall           | 57   | 39   | 30    | 4  | 4  |
| L.I.Georgeson c Coburn b Nuttall         | 30   | 37   | 22    | 1  | 3  |
| N.A.Greenwood c Williams b Shipley       | 14   | 17   | 12    | 1  | 1  |
| M.G.Bracewell* c Henry b McConchie       | 27   | 20   | 17    | 1  | 3  |
| T.B.Robinson c Bowes b Nuttall           | 2    | 7    | 4     | -  | -  |
| J.D.Gibson not out                       | 22   | 27   | 19    | 1  | -  |
| N.G.Smith c Williams b Henry             | 4    | 8    | 5     | -  | -  |
| L.V.van Beek run out                     | 17   | 14   | 11    | 1  | 1  |
| P.F.Younghusband not out                 | 0    | 2    | 0     | -  | -  |
| B.V.Sears                                |      |      |       |    |    |
| H.K.Bennett                              |      |      |       |    |    |
| Extras (lb 2, w 2)                       | 4    |      |       |    |    |
| **TOTAL** (20 overs) (7 wkts)            | **177** | 88 |       |    |    |

### CANTERBURY

|                                          | Runs | Mins | Balls | 6s | 4s |
|------------------------------------------|------|------|-------|----|----|
| C.J.Bowes c Bracewell b van Beek         | 9    | 15   | 10    | -  | 1  |
| K.J.McClure c Smith b Bennett            | 0    | 3    | 2     | -  | -  |
| J.C.T.Boyle c Georgeson b Younghusband   | 31   | 37   | 25    | 1  | 2  |
| C.E.McConchie* b Bracewell               | 12   | 21   | 12    | -  | 1  |
| C.D.Fletcher† c Georgeson b Bracewell    | 7    | 7    | 6     | -  | -  |
| H.B.Shipley c Younghusband b Smith       | 25   | 24   | 21    | 1  | 2  |
| M.W.Hay c Gibson b Bracewell             | 11   | 13   | 10    | -  | 2  |
| M.J.Henry c Bracewell b Bennett          | 4    | 6    | 6     | -  | -  |
| W.S.A.Williams not out                   | 29   | 24   | 17    | 1  | 3  |
| B.P.Coburn b Smith                       | 7    | 21   | 10    | -  | -  |
| E.J.Nuttall not out                      | 1    | 1    | 1     | -  | -  |
| Extras (lb 4, w 10)                      | 14   |      |       |    |    |
| **TOTAL** (20 overs) (9 wkts)            | **150** | 88 |       |    |    |

| Bowling | | | | |
|---------|---|---|---|---|
| **CANTERBURY** | O | M | R | W |
| Nuttall    | 4 | 0 | 31 | 3 |
| Henry      | 4 | 0 | 32 | 1 |
| Shipley    | 3 | 0 | 37 | 1 |
| McConchie  | 3 | 0 | 29 | 1 |
| Williams   | 2 | 0 | 17 | 0 |
| Coburn     | 4 | 0 | 29 | 0 |
| **WELLINGTON** | | | | |
| Bennett    | 4 | 0 | 30 | 2 |
| Smith      | 4 | 0 | 40 | 2 |
| van Beek   | 4 | 0 | 23 | 1 |
| Sears      | 2 | 0 | 23 | 0 |
| Bracewell  | 4 | 0 | 22 | 3 |
| Younghusband | 2 | 0 | 8 | 1 |

| Fall of Wickets | | |
|------|-----|-----|
|      | W   | C   |
| 1st  | 89  | 1   |
| 2nd  | 89  | 15  |
| 3rd  | 122 | 55  |
| 4th  | 133 | 61  |
| 5th  | 133 | 63  |
| 6th  | 144 | 94  |
| 7th  | 171 | 101 |
| 8th  | -   | 105 |
| 9th  | -   | 148 |
| 10th | -   | -   |

# OTAGO v CENTRAL DISTRICTS

**Super Smash**

*at University of Otago Oval, Dunedin on 28 November, 2021*
*Toss : Otago. Umpires : S.B. Haig & S.J. Kannan*
**Central Districts won by 5 wickets.** *Points: Central Districts  4, Otago 0*

| OTAGO | Runs | Mins | Balls | 6s | 4s |
|---|---|---|---|---|---|
| H.D.Rutherford* c Tickner b Rance | 82 | 77 | 47 | 7 | 4 |
| J.L.Finnie c Rance b Bracewell | 12 | 14 | 10 | - | 3 |
| N.T.Broom c Bruce b Lennox | 30 | 46 | 26 | - | 3 |
| N.F.Kelly not out | 24 | 38 | 20 | - | 2 |
| A.K.Kitchen c Cleaver b Wheeler | 25 | 12 | 14 | 2 | 2 |
| D.N.Phillips not out | 8 | 9 | 4 | - | 1 |
| M.J.G.Rippon | | | | | |
| M.W.Chu† | | | | | |
| J.A.Duffy | | | | | |
| J.M.Gibson | | | | | |
| M.B.Bacon | | | | | |
| Extras (lb 1, w 1, nb 1) | 3 | | | | |
| **TOTAL** (20 overs) (4 wkts) . | **184** | 99 | | | |

| CENTRAL DISTRICTS | Runs | Mins | Balls | 6s | 4s |
|---|---|---|---|---|---|
| B.L.Wiggins c Kelly b Kitchen | 6 | 6 | 5 | - | 1 |
| G.R.Hay run out | 56 | 64 | 46 | - | 6 |
| D.Cleaver† not out | 114 | 70 | 54 | 4 | 14 |
| T.C.Bruce* c Gibson b Duffy | 0 | 1 | 1 | - | - |
| C.K.Leopard c Broom b Bacon | 5 | 5 | 4 | - | 1 |
| D.A.J.Bracewell c Gibson b Bacon | 0 | 1 | 1 | - | - |
| B.M.Wheeler not out | 0 | 2 | 3 | - | - |
| B.S.Smith | | | | | |
| J.R.Lennox | | | | | |
| B.M.Tickner | | | | | |
| S.H.A.Rance | | | | | |
| Extras (lb 2, w 2) | 4 | | | | |
| **TOTAL** (19 overs) (5 wkts) . | **185** | 76 | | | |

| Bowling | O | M | R | W |
|---|---|---|---|---|
| **CENTRAL DISTRICTS** | | | | |
| Rance | 4 | 0 | 33 | 1 |
| Wheeler | 4 | 0 | 40 | 1 |
| Bracewell | 4 | 0 | 29 | 1 |
| Tickner | 4 | 0 | 47 | 0 |
| Lennox | 3 | 0 | 23 | 1 |
| Bruce | 1 | 0 | 11 | 0 |
| **OTAGO** | | | | |
| Duffy | 4 | 0 | 32 | 1 |
| Kitchen | 4 | 0 | 33 | 1 |
| Gibson | 2 | 0 | 22 | 0 |
| Bacon | 4 | 0 | 27 | 2 |
| Rippon | 3 | 0 | 50 | 0 |
| Finnie | 2 | 0 | 19 | 0 |

| Fall of Wickets | O | CD |
|---|---|---|
| 1st | 27 | 9 |
| 2nd | 111 | 165 |
| 3rd | 145 | 166 |
| 4th | 171 | 183 |
| 5th | - | 183 |
| 6th | - | - |
| 7th | - | - |
| 8th | - | - |
| 9th | - | - |
| 10th | - | - |

# NORTHERN DISTRICTS v OTAGO

**Super Smash**

*at Seddon Park, Hamilton on 3 December, 2021 (d/n)*
*Toss : Otago. Umpires : C.M. Brown & D.R. Morrow*
**No result.** *Points: Northern Districts 2, Otago 2*

| NORTHERN DISTRICTS | Runs | Mins | Balls | 6s | 4s |
|---|---|---|---|---|---|
| J.A.Raval* st Chu b Rippon | 33 | 28 | 18 | 2 | 4 |
| K.D.Clarke c Phillips b Bacon | 2 | 8 | 4 | - | - |
| J.F.Carter c Johnson b Kitchen | 20 | 34 | 18 | - | 3 |
| H.R.Cooper lbw b Rippon | 19 | 17 | 14 | 1 | 1 |
| C.de Grandhomme c Finnie b Rippon | 6 | 12 | 7 | - | 1 |
| P.D.Bocock† not out | 13 | 17 | 11 | 1 | - |
| S.C.Kuggeleijn c Johnson b Gibson | 8 | 6 | 5 | 1 | - |
| A.Verma not out | 0 | 2 | 1 | - | - |
| J.G.Walker | | | | | |
| Z.N.Gibson | | | | | |
| M.J.Fisher | | | | | |
| Extras (lb 4, w 1) | 5 | | | | |
| **TOTAL** (13 overs) (6 wkts) . | **106** | 78 | | | |

| OTAGO |
|---|
| H.D.Rutherford* |
| L.C.Johnson |
| N.T.Broom |
| D.N.Phillips |
| A.K.Kitchen |
| M.J.G.Rippon |
| J.L.Finnie |
| M.W.Chu† |
| J.M.Gibson |
| J.A.Duffy |
| M.B.Bacon |

| Bowling | O | M | R | W |
|---|---|---|---|---|
| **OTAGO** | | | | |
| Duffy | 2 | 0 | 13 | 0 |
| Kitchen | 3 | 0 | 15 | 1 |
| Bacon | 2 | 0 | 22 | 1 |
| Rippon | 4 | 0 | 32 | 3 |
| Gibson | 2 | 0 | 20 | 1 |

| Fall of Wickets | ND | O |
|---|---|---|
| 1st | 17 | - |
| 2nd | 55 | - |
| 3rd | 77 | - |
| 4th | 80 | - |
| 5th | 89 | - |
| 6th | 105 | - |
| 7th | - | - |
| 8th | - | - |
| 9th | - | - |
| 10th | - | - |

# WELLINGTON v CENTRAL DISTRICTS — Super Smash

at Cello Basin Reserve, Wellington on 5 December, 2021
Toss : Wellington.  Umpires : C.A. Black & S.B. Haig
**Central Districts won by 14 runs.** Points: Central Districts 4, Wellington 0

## CENTRAL DISTRICTS

| | Runs | Mins | Balls | 6s | 4s |
|---|---|---|---|---|---|
| B.L.Wiggins c Allen b Smith ....... | 9 | 8 | 8 | - | 2 |
| G.R.Hay c Robinson b Bennett .. | 1 | 14 | 4 | - | - |
| D.Cleavert b van Beek ............ | 16 | 14 | 9 | 1 | 2 |
| C.K.Leopard c van Beek b Sears | 19 | 33 | 19 | - | 2 |
| T.C.Bruce* not out ................... | 69 | 70 | 48 | 2 | 8 |
| J.A.Clarkson not out ................ | 71 | 45 | 32 | 6 | 3 |
| D.A.J.Bracewell | | | | | |
| B.M.Wheeler | | | | | |
| J.R.Lennox | | | | | |
| B.M.Tickner | | | | | |
| S.H.A.Rance | | | | | |
| Extras (b 1, lb 3, w 1) ............. | 5 | | | | |
| **TOTAL** (20 overs) (4 wkts) . | **190** | 93 | | | |

## WELLINGTON

| | Runs | Mins | Balls | 6s | 4s |
|---|---|---|---|---|---|
| F.H.Allent c Rance b Bracewell . | 0 | 3 | 1 | - | - |
| L.I.Georgeson c Wheeler b Bracewell | 0 | 6 | 1 | - | - |
| N.A.Greenwood b Rance ............ | 9 | 16 | 11 | - | 1 |
| T.M.Johnson lbw b Rance ........ | 54 | 79 | 46 | - | 7 |
| N.G.Smith c Bracewell b Wheeler | 25 | 20 | 16 | 1 | 3 |
| J.D.Gibson c Clarkson b Wheeler | 0 | 4 | 1 | - | - |
| T.B.Robinson c Bruce b Lennox . | 5 | 11 | 6 | - | - |
| L.V.van Beek not out ................ | 61 | 41 | 33 | 2 | 7 |
| P.F.Younghusband not out ........ | 8 | 12 | 5 | - | 1 |
| B.V.Sears | | | | | |
| H.K.Bennett* | | | | | |
| Extras (b 1, lb 2, w 11) .......... | 14 | | | | |
| **TOTAL** (20 overs) (7 wkts) . | **176** | 97 | | | |

| Bowling WELLINGTON | O | M | R | W |
|---|---|---|---|---|
| Bennett | 4 | 0 | 36 | 1 |
| Smith | 4 | 0 | 44 | 1 |
| van Beek | 4 | 0 | 36 | 1 |
| Gibson | 1 | 0 | 10 | 0 |
| Sears | 3 | 0 | 27 | 1 |
| Younghusband | 4 | 0 | 33 | 0 |
| **CENTRAL DISTRICTS** | | | | |
| Bracewell | 4 | 0 | 31 | 2 |
| Rance | 4 | 0 | 23 | 2 |
| Tickner | 4 | 0 | 48 | 0 |
| Wheeler | 4 | 0 | 42 | 2 |
| Lennox | 4 | 0 | 29 | 1 |

| Fall of Wickets | CD | W |
|---|---|---|
| 1st | 9 | 0 |
| 2nd | 11 | 2 |
| 3rd | 30 | 19 |
| 4th | 81 | 55 |
| 5th | - | 55 |
| 6th | - | 72 |
| 7th | - | 138 |
| 8th | - | - |
| 9th | - | - |
| 10th | - | - |

# CANTERBURY v CENTRAL DISTRICTS — Super Smash

at Hagley Oval, Christchurch on 10 December, 2021 (d/n)
Toss : Canterbury.  Umpires : C.M. Brown & P.J. Pasco
**Canterbury won by 47 runs.** Points: Canterbury 4, Central Districts 0

## CANTERBURY

| | Runs | Mins | Balls | 6s | 4s |
|---|---|---|---|---|---|
| K.J.McClure c Bruce b Tickner . | 24 | 18 | 19 | - | 5 |
| C.J.Bowes c Clarkson b Tickner | 5 | 12 | 6 | - | 1 |
| L.J.Carter b Wheeler ............... | 1 | 11 | 2 | - | - |
| C.E.McConchie* c Clarkson | | | | | |
| b Lennox ................. | 84 | 72 | 54 | 3 | 6 |
| C.D.Fletchert c Cleaver | | | | | |
| b Bracewell ............. | 18 | 21 | 17 | 2 | - |
| M.J.Hay c Bruce b Bracewell .... | 29 | 26 | 16 | 2 | 3 |
| M.W.Hay run out ..................... | 2 | 17 | 4 | - | - |
| M.J.Henry b Lennox .................. | 0 | 2 | 1 | - | - |
| T.D.Astle not out ..................... | 0 | 2 | 0 | - | - |
| W.S.A.Williams not out .............. | 1 | 1 | 1 | - | - |
| E.J.Nuttall | | | | | |
| Extras (b 2, lb 3, w 3) ............. | 8 | | | | |
| **TOTAL** (20 overs) (8 wkts) . | **172** | 93 | | | |

## CENTRAL DISTRICTS

| | Runs | Mins | Balls | 6s | 4s |
|---|---|---|---|---|---|
| B.L.Wiggins c Nuttall b Henry ... | 13 | 8 | 9 | - | 2 |
| G.R.Hay c Nuttall b Henry ........ | 12 | 21 | 15 | - | - |
| D.Cleavert c Carter b Nuttall .... | 0 | 3 | 2 | - | - |
| C.K.Leopard st Fletcher b Astle | 25 | 34 | 23 | 1 | 1 |
| T.C.Bruce* run out ..................... | 6 | 23 | 12 | - | - |
| J.A.Clarkson run out ................. | 25 | 14 | 11 | 2 | 1 |
| D.A.J.Bracewell c Bowes | | | | | |
| b Henry ................... | 14 | 22 | 16 | - | 1 |
| B.M.Wheeler lbw b Astle ............ | 2 | 6 | 5 | - | - |
| B.M.Tickner c Astle b Williams ... | 1 | 9 | 5 | - | - |
| S.H.A.Rance run out .................. | 8 | 20 | 9 | - | 1 |
| J.R.Lennox not out .................. | 17 | 15 | 13 | - | 3 |
| Extras (w 2) ............................. | 2 | | | | |
| **TOTAL** (20 overs) ............... | **125** | 90 | | | |

| Bowling CENTRAL DISTRICTS | O | M | R | W |
|---|---|---|---|---|
| Bracewell | 4 | 0 | 24 | 2 |
| Rance | 4 | 0 | 37 | 0 |
| Tickner | 4 | 0 | 33 | 2 |
| Wheeler | 4 | 0 | 22 | 1 |
| Lennox | 4 | 0 | 51 | 2 |
| **CANTERBURY** | | | | |
| Nuttall | 4 | 0 | 32 | 1 |
| Henry | 4 | 0 | 11 | 3 |
| McConchie | 4 | 0 | 27 | 0 |
| Astle | 4 | 0 | 13 | 2 |
| Williams | 4 | 0 | 42 | 1 |

| Fall of Wickets | C | CD |
|---|---|---|
| 1st | 22 | 15 |
| 2nd | 31 | 18 |
| 3rd | 38 | 28 |
| 4th | 73 | 58 |
| 5th | 140 | 59 |
| 6th | 169 | 88 |
| 7th | 171 | 98 |
| 8th | 171 | 100 |
| 9th | - | 105 |
| 10th | - | 125 |

# OTAGO v NORTHERN DISTRICTS

**Super Smash**

*at University of Otago Oval, Dunedin on 12 December, 2021*
*Toss : Otago. Umpires : C.A. Black & D.J. Walker*
**Otago won by 3 wickets.** *Points: Otago 4, Northern Districts 0*

### NORTHERN DISTRICTS

| | Runs | Mins | Balls | 6s | 4s |
|---|---|---|---|---|---|
| K.D.Clarke c Phillips b Finnie ... | 49 | 46 | 37 | 1 | 6 |
| T.L.Seifert† c Phillips b Muller .. | 14 | 16 | 7 | 1 | 2 |
| J.A.Raval* st Chu b Kitchen ....... | 3 | 8 | 3 | - | - |
| H.R.Cooper st Chu b Finnie ...... | 24 | 23 | 24 | 1 | 1 |
| C.de Grandhomme c Phillips | | | | | |
| b Rippon ................................. | 4 | 8 | 5 | - | - |
| P.D.Bocock lbw b Rippon .......... | 5 | 8 | 7 | - | - |
| S.C.Kuggeleijn not out ............. | 14 | 27 | 13 | - | 1 |
| A.Verma run out ....................... | 22 | 23 | 23 | - | 2 |
| F.L.Walker run out .................... | 1 | 2 | 1 | - | - |
| J.G.Walker | | | | | |
| M.J.Fisher | | | | | |
| Extras (lb 4, w 6) .................... | 10 | | | | |
| **TOTAL** (20 overs) (8 wkts) . | **146** | 82 | | | |

| Bowling | O | M | R | W |
|---|---|---|---|---|
| **OTAGO** | | | | |
| McKenzie | 3 | 0 | 18 | 0 |
| Kitchen | 4 | 0 | 19 | 1 |
| Duffy | 4 | 0 | 38 | 0 |
| Muller | 1 | 0 | 18 | 1 |
| Finnie | 4 | 0 | 22 | 2 |
| Rippon | 4 | 0 | 27 | 2 |
| **NORTHERN DISTRICTS** | | | | |
| Kuggeleijn | 3.4 | 0 | 51 | 1 |
| Verma | 4 | 0 | 22 | 2 |
| Fisher | 4 | 0 | 21 | 2 |
| Walker F.L. | 4 | 0 | 23 | 2 |
| Walker J.G. | 4 | 0 | 33 | 0 |

### OTAGO

| | Runs | Mins | Balls | 6s | 4s |
|---|---|---|---|---|---|
| H.D.Rutherford* c Cooper | | | | | |
| b Kuggeleijn ............................. | 8 | 4 | 5 | - | 2 |
| J.L.Finnie c Seifert b Fisher ...... | 10 | 17 | 10 | - | 2 |
| N.T.Broom c Bocock b Verma .. | 62 | 80 | 53 | - | 6 |
| A.K.Kitchen c sub (J.M.Gibson) | | | | | |
| b Walker F.L. ............................ | 16 | 26 | 16 | 1 | - |
| D.N.Phillips b Walker F.L. .......... | 6 | 9 | 9 | - | - |
| L.C.Johnson c de Grandhomme | | | | | |
| b Fisher .................................... | 25 | 20 | 13 | 1 | 3 |
| M.J.G.Rippon c Fisher b Verma . | 3 | 7 | 5 | - | - |
| M.W.Chu† not out ..................... | 10 | 10 | 5 | 1 | - |
| A.W.McKenzie not out ............... | 7 | 7 | 2 | 1 | - |
| T.Muller | | | | | |
| J.A.Duffy | | | | | |
| Extras (b 1, w 3) ...................... | 4 | | | | |
| **TOTAL** (19.4 overs) (7 wkts) | **151** | 92 | | | |

**Fall of Wickets**

| | ND | O |
|---|---|---|
| 1st | 39 | 8 |
| 2nd | 53 | 26 |
| 3rd | 95 | 71 |
| 4th | 95 | 83 |
| 5th | 104 | 129 |
| 6th | 104 | 134 |
| 7th | 145 | 135 |
| 8th | 146 | - |
| 9th | - | - |
| 10th | - | - |

---

# NORTHERN DISTRICTS v AUCKLAND

**Super Smash**

*at Seddon Park, Hamilton on 17 December, 2021 (d/n)*
*Toss : Northern Districts. Umpires : J.M. Dempsey & T.J. Parlane*
**Northern Districts won by 4 wickets.** *Points: Northern Districts 4, Auckland 0*

### AUCKLAND

| | Runs | Mins | Balls | 6s | 4s |
|---|---|---|---|---|---|
| M.J.Guptill c Cooper b Kuggeleijn . | 47 | 50 | 31 | 2 | 4 |
| G.H.Worker b Walker ................ | 36 | 35 | 24 | 2 | 2 |
| M.S.Chapman c Sodhi | | | | | |
| b Kuggeleijn .......................... | 22 | 19 | 16 | - | 3 |
| R.R.O'Donnell* b Walker .......... | 22 | 19 | 14 | 2 | 1 |
| B.J.Horne† lbw b Walker .......... | 4 | 11 | 5 | - | - |
| S.M.Solia run out ..................... | 1 | 6 | 3 | - | - |
| C.J.Briggs c Carter b Kuggeleijn | 6 | 22 | 8 | - | - |
| L.J.Delport c de Grandhomme | | | | | |
| b Walker ................................. | 6 | 6 | 7 | 1 | - |
| L.H.Ferguson c Raval b Kuggeleijn | 7 | 8 | 6 | 1 | - |
| A.Ashok not out ....................... | 2 | 7 | 2 | - | - |
| B.G.Lister c Carter b Verma ...... | 5 | 4 | 4 | - | 1 |
| Extras (lb 2, w 4, nb 1) ............. | 7 | | | | |
| **TOTAL** (19.5 overs) ............. | **165** | 95 | | | |

| Bowling | O | M | R | W |
|---|---|---|---|---|
| **NORTHERN DISTRICTS** | | | | |
| Boult | 4 | 0 | 19 | 0 |
| Verma | 2.5 | 0 | 25 | 1 |
| Kuggeleijn | 4 | 0 | 34 | 4 |
| de Grandhomme | 1 | 0 | 17 | 0 |
| Sodhi | 4 | 0 | 37 | 0 |
| Walker | 4 | 0 | 31 | 4 |
| **AUCKLAND** | | | | |
| Lister | 3 | 0 | 24 | 1 |
| Delport | 4 | 0 | 37 | 2 |
| Ferguson | 3 | 0 | 25 | 2 |
| Ashok | 4 | 0 | 36 | 0 |
| Solia | 1 | 0 | 16 | 0 |
| Chapman | 2.5 | 0 | 27 | 1 |

### NORTHERN DISTRICTS

| | Runs | Mins | Balls | 6s | 4s |
|---|---|---|---|---|---|
| K.D.Clarke st Horne b Delport .. | 11 | 8 | 5 | 1 | 1 |
| T.L.Seifert† c Lister b Ferguson | 14 | 11 | 10 | 1 | 1 |
| J.A.Raval* c Guptill b Ferguson . | 0 | 6 | 1 | - | - |
| J.F.Carter not out ...................... | 75 | 66 | 53 | 2 | 8 |
| C.de Grandhomme c Guptill | | | | | |
| b Delport ................................. | 53 | 40 | 29 | 4 | 4 |
| H.R.Cooper c Lister b Chapman | 3 | 11 | 7 | - | - |
| S.C.Kuggeleijn c Horne b Lister . | 1 | 4 | 2 | - | - |
| A.Verma not out ......................... | 2 | 6 | 2 | - | - |
| I.S.Sodhi | | | | | |
| J.G.Walker | | | | | |
| T.A.Boult | | | | | |
| Extras (lb 2, w 4, nb 2) ............. | 8 | | | | |
| **TOTAL** (17.5 overs) (6 wkts) | **167** | 78 | | | |

**Fall of Wickets**

| | A | ND |
|---|---|---|
| 1st | 81 | 25 |
| 2nd | 108 | 25 |
| 3rd | 110 | 26 |
| 4th | 129 | 126 |
| 5th | 136 | 142 |
| 6th | 136 | 146 |
| 7th | 145 | - |
| 8th | 156 | - |
| 9th | 158 | - |
| 10th | 165 | - |

# CENTRAL DISTRICTS v OTAGO　　　Super Smash

*at McLean Park, Napier on 18 December, 2021*
*Toss : Otago. Umpires : B.F. Bowden & W.R. Knights*
**Central Districts won by 53 runs.** *Points: Central Districts 4, Otago 0*

| CENTRAL DISTRICTS | Runs | Mins | Balls | 6s | 4s |
|---|---|---|---|---|---|
| B.L.Wiggins c & b Gibson | 22 | 12 | 15 | - | 4 |
| G.R.Hay b Duffy | 76 | 83 | 55 | 1 | 10 |
| D.Cleaver† c Johnson b Kitchen | 45 | 44 | 32 | 1 | 5 |
| J.A.Clarkson c Johnson b Rutherford | 3 | 2 | 3 | - | - |
| T.C.Bruce* not out | 26 | 23 | 15 | 1 | 2 |
| C.K.Leopard | | | | | |
| D.A.J.Bracewell | | | | | |
| A.F.Milne | | | | | |
| B.M.Tickner | | | | | |
| S.H.A.Rance | | | | | |
| J.R.Lennox | | | | | |
| Extras (lb 4, w 4) | 8 | | | | |
| **TOTAL** (20 overs) (4 wkts) . | **180** | 83 | | | |

| OTAGO | Runs | Mins | Balls | 6s | 4s |
|---|---|---|---|---|---|
| H.D.Rutherford* b Rance | 7 | 15 | 9 | - | 1 |
| D.N.Phillips c Clarkson b Rance | 7 | 14 | 7 | - | 1 |
| N.T.Broom c Clarkson b Lennox | 7 | 21 | 12 | - | 1 |
| N.F.Kelly c Clarkson b Rance | 4 | 11 | 8 | - | - |
| A.K.Kitchen b Rance | 12 | 23 | 11 | - | 2 |
| L.C.Johnson b Bracewell | 38 | 25 | 23 | 2 | 2 |
| M.J.G.Rippon b Bruce | 7 | 15 | 7 | - | - |
| M.W.Chu† c Hay b Bruce | 12 | 16 | 12 | - | 2 |
| J.M.Gibson b Bruce | 0 | 1 | 1 | - | - |
| J.A.Duffy b Rance | 16 | 13 | 8 | 1 | 1 |
| M.B.Bacon not out | 2 | 4 | 3 | - | - |
| Extras (b 1, lb 10, w 4) | 15 | | | | |
| **TOTAL** (16.5 overs) | **127** | 82 | | | |

| Bowling | O | M | R | W |
|---|---|---|---|---|
| **OTAGO** | | | | |
| Duffy | 4 | 0 | 38 | 1 |
| Kitchen | 4 | 0 | 29 | 1 |
| Bacon | 4 | 0 | 38 | 0 |
| Gibson | 3 | 0 | 30 | 1 |
| Rippon | 4 | 0 | 35 | 0 |
| Rutherford | 1 | 0 | 6 | 1 |
| **CENTRAL DISTRICTS** | | | | |
| Milne | 2 | 0 | 11 | 0 |
| Bracewell | 4 | 0 | 37 | 1 |
| Rance | 3.5 | 0 | 19 | 5 |
| Lennox | 2 | 0 | 14 | 1 |
| Tickner | 3 | 0 | 26 | 0 |
| Bruce | 2 | 0 | 9 | 3 |

| Fall of Wickets | CD | O |
|---|---|---|
| 1st | 27 | 25 |
| 2nd | 116 | 25 |
| 3rd | 120 | 35 |
| 4th | 180 | 44 |
| 5th | - | 73 |
| 6th | - | 92 |
| 7th | - | 98 |
| 8th | - | 98 |
| 9th | - | 119 |
| 10th | - | 127 |

# WELLINGTON v CANTERBURY　　　Super Smash

*at Cello Basin Reserve, Wellington on 19 December, 2021*
*Toss : Wellington. Umpires : S.B. Haig & E.D. Sanders*
**Canterbury won by 6 wickets.** *Points: Canterbury 4, Wellington 0*

| WELLINGTON | Runs | Mins | Balls | 6s | 4s |
|---|---|---|---|---|---|
| F.H.Allen† b Henry | 20 | 13 | 9 | 2 | 1 |
| L.I.Georgeson c Fletcher b Nuttall | 1 | 5 | 3 | - | - |
| T.M.Johnson c Fletcher b Nuttall | 10 | 16 | 7 | - | 2 |
| M.G.Bracewell* c Henry b Coburn | 20 | 35 | 22 | - | 3 |
| N.G.Smith c & b Shipley | 6 | 11 | 9 | - | 1 |
| J.D.Gibson b Astle | 10 | 19 | 12 | - | - |
| T.B.Robinson c Carter b Nuttall | 32 | 37 | 26 | - | 2 |
| L.V.van Beek c Bowes b Henry | 22 | 16 | 14 | - | 4 |
| P.F.Younghusband c Shipley b Henry | 21 | 18 | 15 | - | 3 |
| B.V.Sears not out | 3 | 5 | 2 | - | - |
| H.K.Bennett not out | 1 | 2 | 1 | - | - |
| Extras (w 5) | 5 | | | | |
| **TOTAL** (20 overs) (9 wkts) . | **151** | 91 | | | |

| CANTERBURY | Runs | Mins | Balls | 6s | 4s |
|---|---|---|---|---|---|
| C.J.Bowes b van Beek | 62 | 66 | 41 | 1 | 7 |
| K.J.McClure c Georgeson b van Beek | 13 | 18 | 10 | - | 2 |
| L.J.Carter c Allen b Sears | 9 | 10 | 7 | - | 1 |
| C.E.McConchie* c Allen b Sears | 6 | 10 | 10 | - | - |
| C.D.Fletcher† not out | 52 | 31 | 28 | 4 | 5 |
| M.J.Hay not out | 8 | 5 | 3 | 1 | - |
| H.B.Shipley | | | | | |
| M.J.Henry | | | | | |
| T.D.Astle | | | | | |
| B.P.Coburn | | | | | |
| E.J.Nuttall | | | | | |
| Extras (lb 4, w 3) | 7 | | | | |
| **TOTAL** (16.3 overs) (4 wkts) | **157** | 71 | | | |

| Bowling | O | M | R | W |
|---|---|---|---|---|
| **CANTERBURY** | | | | |
| Henry | 4 | 0 | 48 | 3 |
| Nuttall | 4 | 0 | 28 | 3 |
| McConchie | 2 | 0 | 21 | 0 |
| Astle | 4 | 0 | 19 | 1 |
| Shipley | 2 | 0 | 9 | 1 |
| Coburn | 4 | 0 | 26 | 1 |
| **WELLINGTON** | | | | |
| Bennett | 2 | 0 | 22 | 0 |
| Smith | 2 | 0 | 23 | 0 |
| van Beek | 3 | 0 | 20 | 2 |
| Sears | 3.3 | 0 | 38 | 2 |
| Bracewell | 4 | 0 | 27 | 0 |
| Younghusband | 2 | 0 | 23 | 0 |

| Fall of Wickets | W | C |
|---|---|---|
| 1st | 4 | 37 |
| 2nd | 26 | 62 |
| 3rd | 44 | 75 |
| 4th | 50 | 144 |
| 5th | 68 | - |
| 6th | 76 | - |
| 7th | 110 | - |
| 8th | 141 | - |
| 9th | 147 | - |
| 10th | - | - |

# AUCKLAND v NORTHERN DISTRICTS          Super Smash

*at Kennards Hire Community Oval, Auckland on 20 December, 2021*
*Toss : Northern Districts. Umpires : B.F. Bowden & W.R. Knights*
**Northern Districts won by 6 wickets.** *Points: Northern Districts 4, Auckland 0*

### AUCKLAND

| | Runs | Mins | Balls | 6s | 4s |
|---|---|---|---|---|---|
| M.J.Guptill b Verma | 4 | 19 | 13 | - | - |
| G.H.Worker c Raval b Verma | 5 | 6 | 4 | - | 1 |
| M.S.Chapman run out | 8 | 10 | 6 | - | 1 |
| C.J.Briggs c Sodhi b Fisher | 1 | 10 | 3 | - | - |
| R.R.O'Donnell* c Gibson b Walker | 7 | 21 | 16 | - | 1 |
| B.J.Horne† c Fisher b Walker | 8 | 14 | 9 | - | - |
| S.M.Solia lbw b Sodhi | 5 | 16 | 9 | - | - |
| L.H.Ferguson c Raval b Walker | 26 | 38 | 24 | - | 4 |
| L.J.Delport c Clarke b Verma | 3 | 5 | 3 | - | - |
| A.Ashok b Sodhi | 0 | 2 | 4 | - | - |
| B.G.Lister not out | 17 | 15 | 13 | 2 | - |
| Extras(lb 5, w 3) | 8 | | | | |
| **TOTAL** (17.2 overs) | **92** | 81 | | | |

### NORTHERN DISTRICTS

| | Runs | Mins | Balls | 6s | 4s |
|---|---|---|---|---|---|
| K.D.Clarke b Solia | 28 | 44 | 32 | 1 | 2 |
| T.L.Seifert† not out | 38 | 74 | 42 | 1 | 3 |
| J.A.Raval* c Ashok b Delport | 1 | 6 | 3 | - | - |
| J.F.Carter c Briggs b Solia | 2 | 7 | 6 | - | - |
| C.de Grandhomme c Ferguson b Ashok | 11 | 13 | 8 | - | 2 |
| H.R.Cooper not out | 1 | 1 | 1 | - | - |
| A.Verma | | | | | |
| I.S.Sodhi | | | | | |
| Z.N.Gibson | | | | | |
| F.L.Walker | | | | | |
| M.J.Fisher | | | | | |
| Extras (w 11, nb 1) | 12 | | | | |
| **TOTAL** (15.1 overs) (4 wkts) | **93** | 74 | | | |

| Bowling | O | M | R | W |
|---|---|---|---|---|
| **NORTHERN DISTRICTS** | | | | |
| Gibson | 4 | 0 | 31 | 0 |
| Verma | 3 | 0 | 14 | 3 |
| Fisher | 4 | 1 | 27 | 1 |
| Walker | 2.2 | 0 | 10 | 3 |
| Sodhi | 4 | 0 | 5 | 2 |
| **AUCKLAND** | | | | |
| Lister | 3 | 0 | 20 | 0 |
| Ferguson | 3 | 0 | 15 | 0 |
| Ashok | 3 | 0 | 22 | 1 |
| Delport | 3.1 | 0 | 20 | 1 |
| Solia | 3 | 0 | 16 | 2 |

| Fall of Wickets | | |
|---|---|---|
| | A | ND |
| 1st | 6 | 65 |
| 2nd | 23 | 69 |
| 3rd | 23 | 73 |
| 4th | 28 | 92 |
| 5th | 39 | - |
| 6th | 40 | - |
| 7th | 55 | - |
| 8th | 61 | - |
| 9th | 61 | - |
| 10th | 92 | - |

# NORTHERN DISTRICTS v CANTERBURY          Super Smash

*at Bay Oval, Mt Maunganui on 23 December, 2021 (d/n)*
*Toss : Northern Districts. Umpires : W.R. Knights & D.R. Morrow*
**Northern Districts won by 1 wicket.** *Points: Central Districts 4, Otago 0*

### CANTERBURY

| | Runs | Mins | Balls | 6s | 4s |
|---|---|---|---|---|---|
| K.J.McClure c Kuggeleijn b Boult | 8 | 3 | 6 | 1 | - |
| C.J.Bowes c Seifert b Boult | 3 | 14 | 6 | - | - |
| H.M.Nicholls c Raval b Sodhi | 35 | 31 | 21 | 2 | 3 |
| L.J.Carter c Cooper b Hampton | 4 | 9 | 4 | - | - |
| C.E.McConchie* c Verma b Walker | 8 | 26 | 12 | - | - |
| C.D.Fletcher† lbw b Walker | 15 | 17 | 15 | 1 | - |
| H.B.Shipley c Raval b Verma | 11 | 29 | 19 | - | - |
| T.D.Astle c Seifert b Walker | 5 | 10 | 8 | - | - |
| M.J.Henry c Carter b Sodhi | 1 | 3 | 3 | - | - |
| B.P.Coburn not out | 11 | 15 | 10 | - | 2 |
| E.J.Nuttall c Seifert b Verma | 0 | 2 | 1 | - | - |
| Extras (lb 1, w 4, nb 1) | 6 | | | | |
| **TOTAL** (17.2 overs) | **107** | 82 | | | |

### NORTHERN DISTRICTS

| | Runs | Mins | Balls | 6s | 4s |
|---|---|---|---|---|---|
| K.D.Clarke not out | 32 | 18 | 12 | 4 | 1 |
| T.L.Seifert† run out | 15 | 32 | 17 | 1 | 1 |
| J.A.Raval* c Astle b Henry | 0 | 9 | 5 | - | - |
| J.F.Carter st Fletcher b Coburn | 13 | 38 | 30 | - | 1 |
| B.R.Hampton lbw b Coburn | 11 | 21 | 17 | - | - |
| H.R.Cooper b Astle | 7 | 14 | 10 | - | 1 |
| S.C.Kuggeleijn c Coburn b McConchie | 6 | 18 | 7 | - | 6 |
| A.Verma c Henry b Nuttall | 8 | 18 | 17 | - | 1 |
| I.S.Sodhi c Bowes b Nuttall | 2 | 5 | 2 | - | - |
| T.A.Boult not out | 7 | 6 | 2 | 1 | - |
| J.G.Walker c Bowes b Nuttall | 0 | 2 | 1 | - | - |
| Extras (lb 2, w 5) | 7 | | | | |
| **TOTAL** (20 overs) (9 wkts) | **108** | 93 | | | |

| Bowling | O | M | R | W |
|---|---|---|---|---|
| **NORTHERN DISTRICTS** | | | | |
| Boult | 3 | 0 | 21 | 2 |
| Verma | 3.2 | 0 | 26 | 2 |
| Kuggeleijn | 1 | 0 | 15 | 0 |
| Hampton | 2 | 0 | 9 | 1 |
| Sodhi | 4 | 0 | 22 | 2 |
| Walker | 4 | 0 | 13 | 3 |
| **CANTERBURY** | | | | |
| Henry | 4 | 1 | 8 | 1 |
| Nuttall | 4 | 0 | 43 | 3 |
| Shipley | 1 | 0 | 14 | 0 |
| Astle | 4 | 0 | 8 | 1 |
| McConchie | 3 | 0 | 17 | 1 |
| Coburn | 4 | 0 | 16 | 2 |

| Fall of Wickets | | |
|---|---|---|
| | C | ND |
| 1st | 8 | 46 |
| 2nd | 17 | 48 |
| 3rd | 35 | 72 |
| 4th | 55 | 81 |
| 5th | 75 | 83 |
| 6th | 75 | 98 |
| 7th | 85 | 100 |
| 8th | 88 | 100 |
| 9th | 105 | 101 |
| 10th | 107 | - |

*Clarke retired hurt on 31 at*
*33-0 and returned at 101-9*

# WELLINGTON v AUCKLAND    **Super Smash**

*at Cello Basin Reserve, Wellington on 24 December, 2021*
*Toss : Auckland. Umpires : J.M. Dempsey & S.J. Kannan*
**Auckland won by 13 runs.** *Points: Auckland 4, Wellington 0*

## AUCKLAND

| | Runs | Mins | Balls | 6s | 4s |
|---|---|---|---|---|---|
| M.J.Guptill c Allen b Bennett | 4 | 2 | 3 | - | 1 |
| G.H.Worker c Johnson b Sears | 23 | 35 | 25 | 1 | 1 |
| M.S.Chapman c Younghusband b van Beek | 55 | 72 | 48 | 1 | 3 |
| C.J.Briggs run out | 0 | 3 | 0 | - | - |
| R.R.O'Donnell* c Bracewell b Sears | 0 | 6 | 3 | - | - |
| B.J.Horne† c Bracewell b Sears | 10 | 14 | 12 | 1 | - |
| S.M.Solia b Newton | 19 | 29 | 19 | - | 2 |
| L.H.Ferguson run out | 0 | 3 | 0 | - | - |
| L.J.Delport c Robinson b Younghusband | 0 | 2 | 2 | - | - |
| A.Ashok not out | 6 | 11 | 6 | - | - |
| B.G.Lister not out | 1 | 2 | 2 | - | - |
| Extras (lb 9, w 7) | 16 | | | | |
| **TOTAL** (20 overs) (9 wkts) . **134** | | 92 | | | |

## WELLINGTON

| | Runs | Mins | Balls | 6s | 4s |
|---|---|---|---|---|---|
| F.H.Allen† c Horne b Lister | 0 | 1 | 2 | - | - |
| T.B.Robinson b Lister | 9 | 11 | 7 | - | 2 |
| L.V.van Beek c Briggs b Lister | 0 | 3 | 4 | - | - |
| T.M.Johnson b Ashok | 24 | 32 | 2 | 1 | 3 |
| M.G.Bracewell* not out | 58 | 73 | 46 | 2 | 3 |
| N.G.Smith lbw b Ashok | 0 | 2 | 3 | - | - |
| J.D.Gibson c Guptill b Delport | 5 | 12 | 14 | - | - |
| P.F.Younghusband st Horne b Ashok | 2 | 8 | 10 | - | - |
| O.R.Newton c Solia b Delport | 9 | 11 | 10 | - | 1 |
| B.V.Sears not out | 5 | 12 | 3 | - | 1 |
| H.K.Bennett | | | | | |
| Extras (b 1, lb 6, w 1, nb 1) | 9 | | | | |
| **TOTAL** (20 overs) (8 wkts) . **121** | | 84 | | | |

| Bowling | O | M | R | W |
|---|---|---|---|---|
| **WELLINGTON** | | | | |
| Bennett | 3 | 0 | 18 | 1 |
| Newton | 3 | 0 | 26 | 1 |
| van Beek | 3 | 0 | 19 | 1 |
| Bracewell | 4 | 0 | 22 | 0 |
| Sears | 4 | 0 | 22 | 3 |
| Younghusband | 3 | 0 | 18 | 1 |
| **AUCKLAND** | | | | |
| Lister | 4 | 0 | 27 | 3 |
| Ferguson | 4 | 0 | 28 | 0 |
| Solia | 2 | 0 | 13 | 0 |
| Delport | 4 | 0 | 20 | 2 |
| Ashok | 4 | 1 | 8 | 3 |
| Chapman | 2 | 0 | 18 | 0 |

| Fall of Wickets | A | W |
|---|---|---|
| 1st | 4 | 0 |
| 2nd | 61 | 1 |
| 3rd | 63 | 10 |
| 4th | 68 | 53 |
| 5th | 91 | 53 |
| 6th | 115 | 65 |
| 7th | 116 | 73 |
| 8th | 116 | 92 |
| 9th | 132 | - |
| 10th | - | - |

---

# CANTERBURY v OTAGO    **Super Smash**

*at Hagley Oval, Christchurch on 26 December, 2021*
*Toss : Canterbury. Umpires : K.D. Cotton & T.J. Parlane*
**Canterbury won by 36 runs.** *Points: Canterbury 4, Otago 0*

## CANTERBURY

| | Runs | Mins | Balls | 6s | 4s |
|---|---|---|---|---|---|
| C.J.Bowes c Bacon b McKenzie | 50 | 54 | 32 | 1 | 7 |
| K.J.McClure c Rutherford b Rippon | 34 | 33 | 27 | 2 | 3 |
| H.M.Nicholls not out | 49 | 58 | 37 | 1 | 4 |
| C.E.McConchie* st Chu b Kitchen | 1 | 7 | 4 | - | - |
| C.D.Fletcher† c Broom b Duffy | 2 | 6 | 4 | - | - |
| L.J.Carter c Duffy b Bacon | 2 | 4 | 3 | - | - |
| H.B.Shipley c Chu b McKenzie | 2 | 6 | 4 | - | - |
| M.J.Henry not out | 23 | 12 | 9 | 2 | 1 |
| T.D.Astle | | | | | |
| B.P.Coburn | | | | | |
| E.J.Nuttall | | | | | |
| Extras (b 1, lb 5, w 4) | 10 | | | | |
| **TOTAL** (20 overs) (6 wkts) . **173** | | 91 | | | |

## OTAGO

| | Runs | Mins | Balls | 6s | 4s |
|---|---|---|---|---|---|
| H.D.Rutherford* run out | 62 | 73 | 48 | 1 | 7 |
| J.J.Tasman-Jones c Carter b Shipley | 2 | 14 | 5 | - | - |
| N.T.Broom c & b Shipley | 2 | 8 | 6 | - | - |
| N.F.Kelly st Fletcher b Astle | 22 | 14 | 16 | 2 | 2 |
| A.K.Kitchen c Fletcher b Nuttall | 2 | 9 | 4 | - | - |
| L.C.Johnson b Astle | 4 | 7 | 5 | - | - |
| M.J.G.Rippon c Shipley b Henry | 16 | 33 | 21 | - | - |
| M.W.Chu† c Fletcher b Henry | 11 | 7 | 7 | - | 2 |
| A.W.McKenzie not out | 5 | 10 | 4 | - | 1 |
| J.A.Duffy not out | 4 | 2 | 4 | - | 1 |
| M.B.Bacon | | | | | |
| Extras (lb 5, w 2) | 7 | | | | |
| **TOTAL** (20 overs) (8 wkts) . **137** | | 91 | | | |

| Bowling | O | M | R | W |
|---|---|---|---|---|
| **OTAGO** | | | | |
| Duffy | 4 | 0 | 43 | 1 |
| Kitchen | 4 | 0 | 33 | 1 |
| Bacon | 4 | 0 | 35 | 1 |
| McKenzie | 4 | 0 | 28 | 2 |
| Rippon | 4 | 0 | 28 | 1 |
| **CANTERBURY** | | | | |
| Henry | 4 | 0 | 19 | 2 |
| Nuttall | 4 | 0 | 35 | 1 |
| Shipley | 3 | 0 | 17 | 2 |
| Astle | 4 | 0 | 25 | 2 |
| McConchie | 4 | 0 | 20 | 0 |
| Coburn | 1 | 0 | 16 | 0 |

| Fall of Wickets | C | O |
|---|---|---|
| 1st | 75 | 21 |
| 2nd | 112 | 34 |
| 3rd | 118 | 67 |
| 4th | 126 | 83 |
| 5th | 129 | 91 |
| 6th | 139 | 107 |
| 7th | - | 120 |
| 8th | - | 132 |
| 9th | - | - |
| 10th | - | - |

# CENTRAL DISTRICTS v AUCKLAND

**Super Smash**

*at Fitzherbert Park, Palmerston North on 27 December, 2021*
*Toss : Central Districts. Umpires : B.F. Bowden & C.M. Brown*
**Auckland won by 4 wickets.** *Points: Auckland 4, Central Districts 0*

## CENTRAL DISTRICTS

| | Runs | Mins | Balls | 6s | 4s |
|---|---|---|---|---|---|
| B.L.Wiggins c O'Donnell b Ferguson | 37 | 32 | 25 | 2 | 2 |
| G.R.Hay b Delport | 57 | 63 | 45 | 2 | 4 |
| D.Cleavert c & b Ferguson | 42 | 48 | 27 | - | 4 |
| T.C.Bruce* c Lister b Ashok | 4 | 4 | 4 | - | - |
| J.A.Clarkson b Delport | 1 | 6 | 2 | - | - |
| C.K.Leopard not out | 8 | 16 | 11 | - | - |
| B.S.Smith not out | 6 | 10 | 7 | - | 1 |
| B.M.Tickner | | | | | |
| S.H.A.Rance | | | | | |
| J.F.A.Field | | | | | |
| A.Y.Patel | | | | | |
| Extras (lb 1, w 11, nb 1) | 13 | | | | |
| **TOTAL** (20 overs) (5 wkts) . | **168** | 91 | | | |

## AUCKLAND

| | Runs | Mins | Balls | 6s | 4s |
|---|---|---|---|---|---|
| M.J.Guptill not out | 79 | 96 | 58 | 3 | 7 |
| G.H.Worker b Tickner | 1 | 5 | 2 | - | - |
| M.S.Chapman c Bruce b Tickner | 14 | 15 | 12 | - | 2 |
| C.J.Briggs c Patel b Leopard | 3 | 11 | 8 | - | - |
| R.R.O'Donnell* b Rance | 34 | 37 | 26 | 1 | 4 |
| S.M.Solia c Cleaver b Tickner | 0 | 8 | 2 | - | - |
| B.J.Horne c & b Rance | 27 | 10 | 9 | 2 | 3 |
| L.H.Fergusont not out | 7 | 6 | 3 | 1 | - |
| L.J.Delport | | | | | |
| A.Ashok | | | | | |
| B.G.Lister | | | | | |
| Extras (b 1, lb 1, w 2, nb 1) | 5 | | | | |
| **TOTAL** (19.5 overs) (6 wkts) | **170** | 96 | | | |

| Bowling | O | M | R | W |
|---|---|---|---|---|
| **AUCKLAND** | | | | |
| Lister | 4 | 0 | 20 | 0 |
| Solia | 3 | 0 | 39 | 0 |
| Delport | 4 | 0 | 51 | 2 |
| Ferguson | 4 | 0 | 24 | 2 |
| Ashok | 4 | 0 | 24 | 1 |
| Chapman | 1 | 0 | 9 | 0 |
| **CENTRAL DISTRICTS** | | | | |
| Rance | 4 | 0 | 43 | 2 |
| Tickner | 4 | 0 | 40 | 3 |
| Field | 3.5 | 0 | 30 | 0 |
| Leopard | 2 | 0 | 18 | 1 |
| Bruce | 2 | 0 | 12 | 0 |
| Patel | 4 | 0 | 25 | 0 |

| Fall of Wickets | CD | A |
|---|---|---|
| 1st | 59 | 6 |
| 2nd | 127 | 28 |
| 3rd | 132 | 34 |
| 4th | 145 | 104 |
| 5th | 155 | 130 |
| 6th | - | 160 |
| 7th | - | - |
| 8th | - | - |
| 9th | - | - |
| 10th | - | - |

# OTAGO v WELLINGTON

**Super Smash**

*at John Davies Oval, Queenstown on 28 December, 2021*
*Toss : Otago. Umpires : S.B. Haig & D.J. Walker*
**Wellington won by 5 wickets.** *Points: Wellington 4, Otago 0*

## OTAGO

| | Runs | Mins | Balls | 6s | 4s |
|---|---|---|---|---|---|
| H.D.Rutherford* c Bennett | | | | | |
| b van Beek | 12 | 14 | 10 | - | 2 |
| J.J.Tasman-Jones b Neesham . | 35 | 28 | 26 | 3 | 3 |
| N.T.Broom lbw b Younghusband | 6 | 18 | 9 | - | - |
| N.F.Kelly c Bennett b Sears | 8 | 15 | 7 | - | 1 |
| L.C.Johnson c Allen b Neesham | 0 | 2 | 1 | - | - |
| A.K.Kitchen c Younghusband | | | | | |
| b Smith | 54 | 45 | 34 | 3 | 5 |
| M.J.G.Rippon not out | 28 | 48 | 25 | - | 3 |
| M.W.Chut c Bracewell b Bennett | 9 | 10 | 8 | - | 1 |
| A.W.McKenzie | | | | | |
| J.A.Duffy | | | | | |
| M.B.Bacon | | | | | |
| Extras (lb 6, w 8) | 14 | | | | |
| **TOTAL** (20 overs) (7 wkts) . | **166** | 92 | | | |

## WELLINGTON

| | Runs | Mins | Balls | 6s | 4s |
|---|---|---|---|---|---|
| F.H.Allent c Kitchen b Bacon .. | 32 | 20 | 13 | 3 | 3 |
| T.B.Robinson b Kitchen | 65 | 81 | 49 | 1 | 8 |
| T.M.Johnson c Kelly | | | | | |
| b Rutherford | 18 | 25 | 21 | - | 3 |
| M.G.Bracewell* c Chu b Rippon . | 1 | 5 | 5 | - | - |
| J.D.S.Neesham c McKenzie | | | | | |
| b Rippon | 4 | 7 | 7 | - | - |
| N.G.Smith not out | 38 | 32 | 18 | - | 4 |
| J.D.Gibson not out | 2 | 9 | 4 | - | - |
| L.V.van Beek | | | | | |
| P.F.Younghusband | | | | | |
| B.V.Sears | | | | | |
| H.K.Bennett | | | | | |
| Extras (b 1, lb 2, w 6, nb 1) .... | 10 | | | | |
| **TOTAL** (19.2 overs) (5 wkts) | **170** | 91 | | | |

| Bowling | O | M | R | W |
|---|---|---|---|---|
| **WELLINGTON** | | | | |
| Bennett | 4 | 0 | 32 | 1 |
| Smith | 2 | 0 | 21 | 1 |
| van Beek | 4 | 0 | 39 | 1 |
| Sears | 3 | 0 | 26 | 1 |
| Neesham | 3 | 0 | 17 | 2 |
| Younghusband | 3 | 0 | 17 | 1 |
| Bracewell | 1 | 0 | 8 | 0 |
| **OTAGO** | | | | |
| Duffy | 3.2 | 0 | 50 | 0 |
| Rippon | 4 | 1 | 24 | 2 |
| Bacon | 4 | 0 | 40 | 1 |
| Kitchen | 4 | 0 | 26 | 1 |
| McKenzie | 1 | 0 | 9 | 0 |
| Rutherford | 3 | 0 | 18 | 1 |

| Fall of Wickets | O | W |
|---|---|---|
| 1st | 41 | 40 |
| 2nd | 57 | 90 |
| 3rd | 62 | 92 |
| 4th | 63 | 100 |
| 5th | 77 | 145 |
| 6th | 152 | - |
| 7th | 166 | - |
| 8th | - | - |
| 9th | - | - |
| 10th | - | - |

# OTAGO v AUCKLAND

**Super Smash**

*at John Davies Oval, Queenstown on 29 December, 2021*
*Toss : Otago.  Umpires : S.B. Haig & P.J. Pasco*
**Auckland won by 8 wickets.** *Points: Auckland 4, Otago 0*

### OTAGO

| | Runs | Mins | Balls | 6s | 4s |
|---|---|---|---|---|---|
| H.D.Rutherford* c O'Donnell b Ferguson | 11 | 15 | 15 | - | 1 |
| J.J.Tasman-Jones c Worker b Ferguson | 24 | 52 | 23 | - | 3 |
| N.T.Broom c Horne b Ferguson . | 0 | 2 | 2 | - | - |
| N.F.Kelly c Lister b Somerville . | 58 | 53 | 39 | 3 | 5 |
| L.C.Johnson st Horne b Ashok ... | 3 | 11 | 5 | - | - |
| A.K.Kitchen lbw b Lister | 16 | 21 | 13 | - | 2 |
| M.W.Chu† b Solia | 6 | 9 | 5 | - | 1 |
| B.R.Wheeler-Greenall not out ... | 5 | 16 | 12 | - | - |
| A.W.McKenzie lbw b Lister | 0 | 2 | 3 | - | - |
| J.A.Duffy c Solia b Ferguson | 0 | 2 | 1 | - | - |
| M.B.Bacon not out | 3 | 5 | 2 | - | - |
| Extras (b 1, w 2) | 3 | | | | |
| **TOTAL** (20 overs) (9 wkts) . | **129** | 96 | | | |

### AUCKLAND

| | Runs | Mins | Balls | 6s | 4s |
|---|---|---|---|---|---|
| M.J.Guptill c Rutherford b Bacon | 1 | 3 | 3 | - | - |
| G.H.Worker not out | 53 | 64 | 45 | 1 | 5 |
| M.S.Chapman c & b Wheeler-Greenall | 55 | 47 | 42 | 2 | 4 |
| G.D.Phillips not out | 14 | 13 | 13 | - | 3 |
| R.R.O'Donnell* | | | | | |
| B.J.Horne† | | | | | |
| S.M.Solia | | | | | |
| W.E.R.Somerville | | | | | |
| L.H.Ferguson | | | | | |
| A.Ashok | | | | | |
| B.G.Lister | | | | | |
| Extras (lb 2, w 5) | 7 | | | | |
| **TOTAL** (17.1 overs) (2 wkts) | **130** | | | | |

| Bowling | O | M | R | W |
|---|---|---|---|---|
| **AUCKLAND** | | | | |
| Lister | 4 | 0 | 14 | 2 |
| Solia | 3 | 0 | 25 | 1 |
| Ferguson | 4 | 0 | 19 | 4 |
| Somerville | 4 | 0 | 27 | 1 |
| Ashok | 4 | 0 | 31 | 1 |
| Chapman | 1 | 0 | 12 | 0 |
| **OTAGO** | | | | |
| Bacon | 3 | 0 | 25 | 1 |
| Kitchen | 4 | 0 | 19 | 0 |
| McKenzie | 2.1 | 0 | 16 | 0 |
| Duffy | 3 | 0 | 24 | 0 |
| Rutherford | 3 | 0 | 29 | 0 |
| Wheeler-Greenall | 2 | 0 | 15 | 1 |

| Fall of Wickets | | |
|---|---|---|
| | O | A |
| 1st | 17 | 4 |
| 2nd | 17 | 110 |
| 3rd | 70 | - |
| 4th | 86 | - |
| 5th | 100 | - |
| 6th | 116 | - |
| 7th | 122 | - |
| 8th | 122 | - |
| 9th | 123 | - |
| 10th | - | - |

# CENTRAL DISTRICTS v NORTHERN DISTRICTS  Super Smash

*at Pukekura Park, New Plymouth on 30 December, 2021*
*Toss : Northern Districts.  Umpires : B.F. Bowden & G.M. Walklin*
**Northern Districts won by 6 wickets.** *Points: Northern Districts 4, Central Districts 0*

### CENTRAL DISTRICTS

| | Runs | Mins | Balls | 6s | 4s |
|---|---|---|---|---|---|
| B.L.Wiggins c Fisher b Kuggeleijn | 0 | 2 | 3 | - | - |
| G.R.Hay run out | 6 | 16 | 8 | - | 1 |
| D.Cleaver† b Fisher | 65 | 71 | 42 | 2 | 9 |
| C.K.Leopard c Carter b Verma ... | 1 | 10 | 6 | - | - |
| T.C.Bruce* c Walker J.G. b Kuggeleijn | 17 | 20 | 17 | - | 2 |
| J.A.Clarkson c Hampton b Kuggeleijn | 0 | 3 | 2 | - | - |
| D.A.J.Bracewell not out | 36 | 48 | 28 | 1 | 3 |
| J.F.A.Field c Verma b Hampton . | 9 | 16 | 11 | - | 1 |
| A.Y.Patel run out | 4 | 9 | 4 | - | - |
| S.H.A.Rance | | | | | |
| B.M.Tickner | | | | | |
| Extras (lb 1, w 5, nb 1) | 7 | | | | |
| **TOTAL** (20 overs) (8 wkts) . | **145** | 99 | | | |

### NORTHERN DISTRICTS

| | Runs | Mins | Balls | 6s | 4s |
|---|---|---|---|---|---|
| J.A.Raval* not out | 66 | 88 | 46 | 3 | 6 |
| T.L.Seifert† c Bruce b Bracewell | 8 | 12 | 10 | - | 1 |
| B.R.Hampton b Field | 11 | 11 | 9 | - | 2 |
| J.F.Carter lbw b Field | 32 | 41 | 27 | 1 | 3 |
| C.de Grandhomme b Tickner | 4 | 5 | 3 | - | 1 |
| H.R.Cooper not out | 25 | 17 | 12 | 1 | 4 |
| S.C.Kuggeleijn | | | | | |
| A.Verma | | | | | |
| J.G.Walker | | | | | |
| F.L.Walker | | | | | |
| M.J.Fisher | | | | | |
| Extras (w 1) | 1 | | | | |
| **TOTAL** (17.5 overs) (4 wkts) | **147** | 88 | | | |

| Bowling | O | M | R | W |
|---|---|---|---|---|
| **NORTHERN DISTRICTS** | | | | |
| Kuggeleijn | 3 | 0 | 22 | 3 |
| Verma | 4 | 0 | 27 | 1 |
| Fisher | 4 | 0 | 20 | 1 |
| Walker F.L. | 4 | 0 | 25 | 0 |
| Walker J.G. | 2 | 0 | 24 | 0 |
| Hampton | 3 | 0 | 26 | 1 |
| **CENTRAL DISTRICTS** | | | | |
| Bracewell | 3.5 | 0 | 28 | 1 |
| Rance | 3 | 0 | 31 | 0 |
| Tickner | 4 | 0 | 23 | 1 |
| Field | 4 | 0 | 28 | 2 |
| Patel | 3 | 0 | 37 | 0 |

| Fall of Wickets | | |
|---|---|---|
| | CD | ND |
| 1st | 0 | 15 |
| 2nd | 22 | 27 |
| 3rd | 33 | 101 |
| 4th | 71 | 106 |
| 5th | 72 | - |
| 6th | 107 | - |
| 7th | 131 | - |
| 8th | 145 | - |
| 9th | - | - |
| 10th | - | - |

# CENTRAL DISTRICTS v CANTERBURY — Super Smash

*at Pukekura Park, New Plymouth on 31 December, 2021*
*Toss : Central Districts. Umpires : J.A.K. Bromley & E.D. Sanders*
**Canterbury won by 5 wickets.** *Points: Canterbury 4, Central Districts 0*

### CENTRAL DISTRICTS

| | Runs | Mins | Balls | 6s | 4s |
|---|---|---|---|---|---|
| G.R.Hay c Coburn b Williams ... | 26 | 27 | 20 | - | 4 |
| B.S.Smith c Hay b Astle ........... | 22 | 34 | 19 | - | 3 |
| D.Cleavert c Hay b Williams .... | 61 | 51 | 32 | 5 | 3 |
| M.T.M.M.J.Ave b Shipley ........... | 6 | 8 | 10 | - | - |
| T.C.Bruce* not out .................... | 93 | 52 | 36 | 8 | 8 |
| J.A.Clarkson not out .................. | 1 | 17 | 3 | - | - |
| D.A.J.Bracewell | | | | | |
| J.F.A.Field | | | | | |
| A.Y.Patel | | | | | |
| S.H.A.Rance | | | | | |
| B.M.Tickner | | | | | |
| Extras (lb 4, w 4) ...................... | 8 | | | | |
| **TOTAL** (20 overs) (4 wkts) . | **217** | 95 | | | |

### CANTERBURY

| | Runs | Mins | Balls | 6s | 4s |
|---|---|---|---|---|---|
| C.J.Bowes c Bracewell b Field . | 28 | 33 | 13 | 2 | 3 |
| K.J.McClure lbw b Rance ......... | 13 | 8 | 7 | 1 | 1 |
| L.J.Carter c Tickner b Field ...... | 56 | 46 | 35 | 3 | 4 |
| C.E.McConchie* b Bracewell .... | 19 | 29 | 15 | 1 | 2 |
| C.D.Fletchert not out ............... | 48 | 36 | 21 | 6 | 1 |
| M.J.Hay c Field b Patel ............. | 8 | 5 | 4 | 1 | - |
| H.B.Shipley not out .................. | 39 | 22 | 11 | 5 | 1 |
| T.D.Astle | | | | | |
| W.S.A.Williams | | | | | |
| B.P.Coburn | | | | | |
| E.J.Nuttall | | | | | |
| Extras (b 1, lb 2, w 5, nb 2) .... | 10 | | | | |
| **TOTAL** (17.2 overs) (5 wkts) | **221** | 91 | | | |

| Bowling | O | M | R | W |
|---|---|---|---|---|
| **CANTERBURY** | | | | |
| McConchie | 3 | 0 | 29 | 0 |
| Nuttall | 4 | 0 | 54 | 0 |
| Shipley | 4 | 0 | 35 | 1 |
| Astle | 4 | 0 | 41 | 1 |
| Williams | 3 | 0 | 28 | 2 |
| Coburn | 2 | 0 | 26 | 0 |
| **CENTRAL DISTRICTS** | | | | |
| Bracewell | 4 | 0 | 40 | 1 |
| Rance | 2.2 | 0 | 36 | 1 |
| Tickner | 3 | 0 | 47 | 0 |
| Field | 2.2 | 0 | 37 | 2 |
| Patel | 2 | 0 | 31 | 1 |
| Bruce | 3.4 | 0 | 27 | 0 |

| Fall of Wickets | | |
|---|---|---|
| | CD | C |
| 1st | 48 | 15 |
| 2nd | 64 | 73 |
| 3rd | 73 | 117 |
| 4th | 157 | 125 |
| 5th | - | 134 |
| 6th | - | - |
| 7th | - | - |
| 8th | - | - |
| 9th | - | - |
| 10th | - | - |

# WELLINGTON v OTAGO — Super Smash

*at Cello Basin Reserve, Wellington on 6 January, 2022*
*Toss : Otago. Umpires : D.J. Walker & G.M. Walklin*
**Wellington won by 8 wickets (D/L).** *Points: Wellington 4, Otago 0*

### OTAGO

| | Runs | Mins | Balls | 6s | 4s |
|---|---|---|---|---|---|
| H.D.Rutherford* c Younghusband | | | | | |
| b van Beek ............................. | 16 | 28 | 14 | - | 2 |
| J.J.Tasman-Jones b Bracewell . | 35 | 37 | 24 | 1 | 4 |
| N.T.Broom c Neesham | | | | | |
| b Younghusband | 25 | 44 | 32 | - | 2 |
| N.F.Kelly b Younghusband ....... | 35 | 37 | 31 | 2 | 3 |
| L.C.Johnson c Neesham | | | | | |
| b Bracewell ............................. | 8 | 6 | 4 | - | 1 |
| A.K.Kitchen not out .................. | 20 | 15 | 12 | 1 | 1 |
| B.R.Wheeler-Greenall not out .... | 7 | 11 | 4 | - | 1 |
| M.W.Chut | | | | | |
| A.W.McKenzie | | | | | |
| J.A.Duffy | | | | | |
| M.B.Bacon | | | | | |
| Extras (b 2, lb 2, w 6, nb 1) .... | 11 | | | | |
| **TOTAL** (20 overs) (5 wkts) . | **157** | 90 | | | |

### WELLINGTON

| | Runs | Mins | Balls | 6s | 4s |
|---|---|---|---|---|---|
| F.H.Allent c McKenzie | | | | | |
| b Kitchen ................................. | 68 | 37 | 32 | 5 | 4 |
| T.B.Robinson c McKenzie | | | | | |
| b Wheeler-Greenall ............... | 18 | 41 | 19 | - | 2 |
| M.G.Bracewell* not out ............ | 18 | 22 | 13 | - | 1 |
| T.M.Johnson not out ................. | 12 | 18 | 15 | 1 | - |
| J.D.S.Neesham | | | | | |
| N.G.Smith | | | | | |
| J.J.N.P.Bhula | | | | | |
| J.D.Gibson | | | | | |
| L.V.van Beek | | | | | |
| P.F.Younghusband | | | | | |
| H.K.Bennett | | | | | |
| Extras (lb 1, w 2) ...................... | 3 | | | | |
| **TOTAL** (13.1 overs) (2 wkts) | **119** | 59 | | | |

| Bowling | O | M | R | W |
|---|---|---|---|---|
| **WELLINGTON** | | | | |
| Bennett | 4 | 0 | 39 | 0 |
| Smith | 1 | 0 | 14 | 0 |
| Younghusband | 4 | 0 | 19 | 2 |
| van Beek | 4 | 0 | 31 | 1 |
| Bracewell | 4 | 0 | 25 | 2 |
| Bhula | 2 | 0 | 17 | 0 |
| Neesham | 1 | 0 | 8 | 0 |
| **OTAGO** | | | | |
| Bacon | 2 | 0 | 24 | 0 |
| Kitchen | 2 | 0 | 22 | 1 |
| Duffy | 3 | 0 | 21 | 0 |
| McKenzie | 1.1 | 0 | 11 | 0 |
| Wheeler-Greenall | 3 | 0 | 26 | 1 |
| Rutherford | 2 | 0 | 14 | 0 |

| Fall of Wickets | | |
|---|---|---|
| | O | W |
| 1st | 48 | 82 |
| 2nd | 61 | 88 |
| 3rd | 121 | - |
| 4th | 121 | - |
| 5th | 131 | - |
| 6th | - | - |
| 7th | - | - |
| 8th | - | - |
| 9th | - | - |
| 10th | - | - |

# AUCKLAND v CANTERBURY Super Smash

*at Kennards Hire Community Oval, Auckland on 7 January, 2022*
*Toss : Canterbury.  Umpires : J.M. Dempsey & P.J. Pasco*
**Canterbury won by 5 wickets.** *Points: Canterbury 4, Auckland 0*

## AUCKLAND

| | Runs | Mins | Balls | 6s | 4s |
|---|---|---|---|---|---|
| G.H.Worker c Hay b Nuttall | 26 | 52 | 27 | - | 2 |
| G.D.Phillips c Shipley b Astle | 53 | 26 | 27 | 5 | 3 |
| S.M.Solia lbw b McConchie | 0 | 1 | 1 | - | - |
| G.K.Beghin b Astle | 23 | 20 | 23 | - | 1 |
| R.R.O'Donnell* c McClure | | | | | |
| b Nuttall | 22 | 17 | 12 | 1 | 2 |
| B.J.Hornet c Nuttall b Williams | 18 | 19 | 13 | 2 | - |
| C.J.Briggs c Hay b Shipley | 3 | 11 | 6 | - | - |
| L.H.Ferguson c Hay b Shipley | 0 | 6 | 2 | - | - |
| W.E.R.Somerville not out | 12 | 8 | 6 | - | 2 |
| A.Ashok not out | 4 | 6 | 3 | - | - |
| B.G.Lister | | | | | |
| Extras (b 1, lb 2, w 3) | 6 | | | | |
| **TOTAL** (20 overs) (8 wkts) | 167 | 88 | | | |

## CANTERBURY

| | Runs | Mins | Balls | 6s | 4s |
|---|---|---|---|---|---|
| C.J.Bowes lbw b Lister | 26 | 17 | 13 | 1 | 4 |
| K.J.McClure c Ashok b Ferguson | 5 | 5 | 3 | - | 1 |
| L.J.Carter c Worker | | | | | |
| b Somerville | 33 | 37 | 22 | 3 | 1 |
| C.E.McConchie* b Ferguson | 5 | 9 | 5 | - | 1 |
| C.D.Fletchert not out | 57 | 54 | 39 | 4 | 2 |
| M.J.Hay c O'Donnell b Phillips | 2 | 6 | 4 | - | - |
| H.B.Shipley not out | 37 | 30 | 22 | 2 | 3 |
| T.D.Astle | | | | | |
| W.S.A.Williams | | | | | |
| W.P.O'Rourke | | | | | |
| E.J.Nuttall | | | | | |
| Extras (lb 1, w 5, nb 1) | 7 | | | | |
| **TOTAL** (17.5 overs) (5 wkts) | 172 | 81 | | | |

| Bowling CANTERBURY | O | M | R | W |
|---|---|---|---|---|
| Shipley | 3 | 0 | 26 | 2 |
| Nuttall | 4 | 0 | 27 | 2 |
| O'Rourke | 3 | 0 | 21 | 0 |
| Astle | 4 | 0 | 45 | 2 |
| McConchie | 4 | 0 | 26 | 1 |
| Williams | 2 | 0 | 19 | 1 |
| **AUCKLAND** | | | | |
| Lister | 3 | 0 | 35 | 1 |
| Ferguson | 3.5 | 0 | 39 | 2 |
| Solia | 2 | 0 | 20 | 0 |
| Somerville | 3 | 0 | 31 | 1 |
| Ashok | 3 | 0 | 23 | 0 |
| Phillips | 3 | 0 | 23 | 1 |

| Fall of Wickets | A | C |
|---|---|---|
| 1st | 62 | 19 |
| 2nd | 62 | 43 |
| 3rd | 97 | 57 |
| 4th | 108 | 89 |
| 5th | 133 | 96 |
| 6th | 147 | - |
| 7th | 151 | - |
| 8th | 152 | - |
| 9th | - | - |
| 10th | - | - |

# CENTRAL DISTRICTS v WELLINGTON Super Smash

*at Pukekura Park, New Plymouth on 8 January, 2022*
*Toss : Wellington.  Umpires : B.F. Bowden & K.D. Cotton*
**Wellington won by 2 wickets.** *Points: Wellington 4, Central Districts 0*

## CENTRAL DISTRICTS

| | Runs | Mins | Balls | 6s | 4s |
|---|---|---|---|---|---|
| M.G.Hughes c Neesham | | | | | |
| b Bennett | 12 | 17 | 6 | 1 | 1 |
| B.S.Smith c Allen b Sears | 29 | 40 | 26 | 1 | 3 |
| B.L.Wigginst c Bracewell | | | | | |
| b Sears | 45 | 43 | 30 | 2 | 4 |
| J.A.Clarkson not out | 76 | 63 | 38 | 4 | 7 |
| T.C.Bruce* c van Beek | | | | | |
| b Neesham | 36 | 37 | 17 | 4 | 1 |
| D.A.J.Bracewell not out | 3 | 5 | 3 | - | - |
| M.T.M.M.J.Ave | | | | | |
| J.F.A.Field | | | | | |
| A.Y.Patel | | | | | |
| S.H.A.Rance | | | | | |
| B.M.Tickner | | | | | |
| Extras (b 4, lb 6, w 16) | 26 | | | | |
| **TOTAL** (20 overs) (4 wkts) | 227 | 103 | | | |

## WELLINGTON

| | Runs | Mins | Balls | 6s | 4s |
|---|---|---|---|---|---|
| F.H.Allent c Wiggins b Bracewell | 4 | 2 | 3 | - | 1 |
| T.B.Robinson b Bracewell | 0 | 5 | 1 | - | - |
| M.G.Bracewell* not out | 141 | 98 | 65 | 11 | 11 |
| T.M.Johnson c Wiggins b Rance | 4 | 5 | 3 | - | 1 |
| J.D.S.Neesham b Rance | 5 | 7 | 6 | - | 1 |
| N.G.Smith lbw b Field | 2 | 7 | 4 | - | - |
| J.D.Gibson run out | 21 | 31 | 14 | 1 | 2 |
| L.V.van Beek b Bracewell | 37 | 27 | 18 | 4 | 1 |
| O.R.Newton run out | 3 | 13 | 4 | - | - |
| B.V.Sears not out | 1 | 2 | 1 | - | - |
| H.K.Bennett | | | | | |
| Extras (lb 1, w 9) | 10 | | | | |
| **TOTAL** (19.5 overs) (8 wkts) | 228 | 101 | | | |

| Bowling WELLINGTON | O | M | R | W |
|---|---|---|---|---|
| Bennett | 4 | 0 | 46 | 1 |
| Newton | 3 | 0 | 32 | 0 |
| van Beek | 4 | 0 | 44 | 0 |
| Sears | 4 | 0 | 35 | 2 |
| Neesham | 3 | 0 | 35 | 1 |
| Bracewell | 2 | 0 | 25 | 0 |
| **CENTRAL DISTRICTS** | | | | |
| Bracewell | 4 | 0 | 33 | 3 |
| Rance | 3 | 0 | 53 | 2 |
| Field | 2 | 0 | 32 | 1 |
| Tickner | 4 | 0 | 34 | 0 |
| Patel | 3 | 0 | 32 | 0 |
| Bruce | 3.5 | 0 | 43 | 0 |

| Fall of Wickets | CD | W |
|---|---|---|
| 1st | 33 | 4 |
| 2nd | 62 | 5 |
| 3rd | 109 | 18 |
| 4th | 213 | 24 |
| 5th | - | 43 |
| 6th | - | 120 |
| 7th | - | 199 |
| 8th | - | 217 |
| 9th | - | - |
| 10th | - | - |

# NORTHERN DISTRICTS v CENTRAL DISTRICTS    Super Smash

*at Bay Oval, Mt Maunganui on 14 January, 2022*
*Toss : Central Districts. Umpires : T.J. Parlane & D.J. Walker*
**Northern Districts won by 19 runs.** Points: Northern Districts 4, Central Districts 0

## NORTHERN DISTRICTS

| | Runs | Mins | Balls | 6s | 4s |
|---|---|---|---|---|---|
| J.A.Raval* c Cleaver b Tickner . | 11 | 11 | 10 | - | 1 |
| T.L.Seifert† b Tickner | 10 | 23 | 14 | - | 1 |
| J.F.Carter c Bracewell b Lennox | 32 | 62 | 28 | - | 2 |
| C.de Grandhomme c Bracewell | | | | | |
| b Tickner | 86 | 59 | 45 | 5 | 4 |
| M.J.Santner c Cleaver b Lennox | 0 | 2 | 1 | - | - |
| H.R.Cooper lbw b Patel | 3 | 7 | 5 | - | - |
| S.C.Kuggeleijn c Cleaver b Bracewell | 3 | 7 | 3 | - | - |
| A.Verma not out | 11 | 14 | 9 | - | 1 |
| I.S.Sodhi not out | 8 | 8 | 5 | - | 1 |
| J.G.Walker | | | | | |
| M.J.Fisher | | | | | |
| Extras (b 1, lb 7, w 4) | 12 | | | | |
| **TOTAL** (20 overs) (7 wkts) . | **176** | 99 | | | |

## CENTRAL DISTRICTS

| | Runs | Mins | Balls | 6s | 4s |
|---|---|---|---|---|---|
| M.G.Hughes c Carter b Verma ... | 5 | 8 | 7 | - | 1 |
| B.S.Smith c Kuggeleijn b Walker | 68 | 86 | 53 | 2 | 5 |
| D.Cleavert run out | 6 | 8 | 6 | - | 1 |
| M.T.M.M.J.Ave c de Grandhomme | | | | | |
| b Santner | 12 | 18 | 11 | - | 2 |
| T.C.Bruce* lbw b Sodhi | 8 | 11 | 7 | - | 1 |
| J.A.Clarkson c Carter b Fisher . | 20 | 20 | 12 | 2 | - |
| D.A.J.Bracewell c Raval b Verma | 1 | 9 | 3 | - | - |
| A.Y.Patel c Raval b Santner | 11 | 7 | 6 | - | 2 |
| J.R.Lennox not out | 6 | 14 | 9 | - | 1 |
| S.H.A.Rance not out | 10 | 12 | 8 | 1 | - |
| B.M.Tickner | | | | | |
| Extras (b 1, lb 3, w 4, nb 2) .... | 10 | | | | |
| **TOTAL** (20 overs) (8 wkts) . | **157** | 98 | | | |

| Bowling | O | M | R | W |
|---|---|---|---|---|
| **CENTRAL DISTRICTS** | | | | |
| Bracewell | 4 | 0 | 33 | 1 |
| Rance | 4 | 0 | 44 | 0 |
| Tickner | 4 | 0 | 20 | 3 |
| Patel | 2 | 0 | 23 | 1 |
| Lennox | 4 | 0 | 23 | 2 |
| Clarkson | 1 | 0 | 15 | 0 |
| Bruce | 1 | 0 | 10 | 0 |
| **NORTHERN DISTRICTS** | | | | |
| Kuggeleijn | 4 | 0 | 27 | 0 |
| Verma | 4 | 0 | 36 | 2 |
| Fisher | 3 | 0 | 34 | 1 |
| Santner | 4 | 0 | 25 | 2 |
| Sodhi | 4 | 0 | 29 | 1 |
| Walker | 1 | 0 | 2 | 1 |

| Fall of Wickets | | |
|---|---|---|
| | ND | CD |
| 1st | 19 | 7 |
| 2nd | 33 | 16 |
| 3rd | 145 | 53 |
| 4th | 146 | 70 |
| 5th | 150 | 109 |
| 6th | 151 | 122 |
| 7th | 157 | 137 |
| 8th | - | 137 |
| 9th | - | - |
| 10th | - | - |

# AUCKLAND v OTAGO    Super Smash

*at Kennards Hire Community Oval, Auckland on 15 January, 2022*
*Toss : Otago. Umpires : J.A.K. Bromley & J.M. Dempsey*
**Auckland won by 1 wicket.** Points: Wellington 4, Canterbury 0

## OTAGO

| | Runs | Mins | Balls | 6s | 4s |
|---|---|---|---|---|---|
| H.D.Rutherford* c Chapman | | | | | |
| b Somerville | 25 | 35 | 20 | - | 5 |
| N.T.Broom c O'Donnell b Ferguson | 32 | 27 | 17 | 1 | 4 |
| N.F.Kelly b Ashok | 7 | 16 | 12 | - | 1 |
| D.N.Phillips b Phillips | 7 | 15 | 12 | - | - |
| L.C.Johnson c Beghin b Phillips | 14 | 24 | 17 | - | 1 |
| A.K.Kitchen lbw b Somerville | 7 | 8 | 6 | - | 1 |
| M.J.G.Rippon c Phillips b Ashok | 7 | 15 | 10 | - | - |
| M.W.Chu† c Lister b Ferguson ... | 9 | 18 | 10 | - | - |
| A.W.McKenzie c Horne b Lister | 11 | 17 | 11 | - | 1 |
| J.M.Gibson lbw b Lister | 2 | 6 | 3 | - | - |
| J.A.Duffy not out | 1 | 2 | 1 | - | - |
| Extras (lb 4, w 3, nb 1) | 8 | | | | |
| **TOTAL** (19.4 overs) | **130** | 93 | | | |

## AUCKLAND

| | Runs | Mins | Balls | 6s | 4s |
|---|---|---|---|---|---|
| G.H.Worker c Phillips b Kitchen . | 9 | 5 | 8 | - | 2 |
| G.D.Phillips b Duffy | 0 | 12 | 1 | - | - |
| M.S.Chapman b Kitchen | 0 | 1 | 2 | - | - |
| G.K.Beghin b Kitchen | 0 | 2 | 1 | - | - |
| R.R.O'Donnell* b Rippon | 8 | 22 | 12 | - | 1 |
| B.J.Horne† lbw b Duffy | 0 | 1 | 2 | - | - |
| S.M.Solia not out | 67 | 78 | 54 | 3 | 4 |
| W.E.R.Somerville b Kitchen | 25 | 41 | 27 | 1 | - |
| L.H.Ferguson lbw b Duffy | 14 | 8 | 5 | 2 | - |
| A.Ashok c Gibson b McKenzie ... | 5 | 9 | 5 | - | 1 |
| B.G.Lister not out | 4 | 2 | 1 | - | 1 |
| Extras (w 1) | 1 | | | | |
| **TOTAL** (19.4 overs) (9 wkts) | **133** | 93 | | | |

| Bowling | O | M | R | W |
|---|---|---|---|---|
| **AUCKLAND** | | | | |
| Lister | 3.4 | 0 | 21 | 2 |
| Solia | 2 | 0 | 24 | 0 |
| Ferguson | 4 | 0 | 35 | 2 |
| Somerville | 4 | 0 | 18 | 2 |
| Ashok | 4 | 0 | 17 | 2 |
| Phillips | 2 | 0 | 11 | 2 |
| **OTAGO** | | | | |
| Duffy | 4 | 0 | 30 | 3 |
| Kitchen | 4 | 0 | 11 | 4 |
| McKenzie | 2.4 | 0 | 16 | 1 |
| Gibson | 4 | 0 | 31 | 0 |
| Rippon | 4 | 0 | 39 | 1 |
| Rutherford | 1 | 0 | 6 | 0 |

| Fall of Wickets | | |
|---|---|---|
| | O | A |
| 1st | 58 | 9 |
| 2nd | 66 | 9 |
| 3rd | 71 | 9 |
| 4th | 77 | 13 |
| 5th | 89 | 13 |
| 6th | 100 | 26 |
| 7th | 106 | 103 |
| 8th | 128 | 120 |
| 9th | 129 | 128 |
| 10th | 130 | - |

# NORTHERN DISTRICTS v WELLINGTON — Super Smash

*at Cobham Oval, Whangarei on 16 January, 2022*
*Toss : Wellington.  Umpires : B.F. Bowden & G.M. Walklin*
**Northern Districts won by 6 wickets.** Points: Northern Districts 4, Wellington 0

## WELLINGTON

| | Runs | Mins | Balls | 6s | 4s |
|---|---|---|---|---|---|
| F.H.Allen† b Verma | 7 | 7 | 6 | - | 1 |
| T.B.Robinson c Walker b Kuggeleijn | 12 | 15 | 10 | - | 2 |
| M.G.Bracewell* b Sodhi | 15 | 37 | 17 | - | 1 |
| T.M.Johnson c Raval b Walker | 18 | 24 | 19 | - | 2 |
| R.Ravindra b Walker | 14 | 23 | 21 | - | - |
| J.D.S.Neesham c Kuggeleijn b Verma | 20 | 30 | 21 | - | - |
| N.G.Smith b Santner | 1 | 3 | 2 | - | - |
| L.V.van Beek c Walker b Santner | 5 | 11 | 5 | - | - |
| P.F.Younghusband lbw b Verma | 5 | 11 | 6 | - | - |
| B.V.Sears run out | 0 | 3 | 1 | - | - |
| H.K.Bennett not out | 4 | 4 | 3 | - | - |
| Extras (lb 2, w 1) | 3 | | | | |
| **TOTAL** (18.3 overs) | **104** | 89 | | | |

### Bowling

| NORTHERN DISTRICTS | O | M | R | W |
|---|---|---|---|---|
| Kuggeleijn | 2 | 0 | 13 | 1 |
| Verma | 3.3 | 0 | 25 | 3 |
| Santner | 3 | 0 | 15 | 2 |
| Fisher | 2 | 0 | 13 | 0 |
| Sodhi | 4 | 0 | 22 | 1 |
| Walker | 4 | 0 | 14 | 2 |

## NORTHERN DISTRICTS

| | Runs | Mins | Balls | 6s | 4s |
|---|---|---|---|---|---|
| J.A.Raval* c Sears b Bracewell | 15 | 45 | 28 | - | - |
| T.L.Seifert† c Younghusband b Ravindra | 15 | 16 | 12 | 1 | 1 |
| J.F.Carter b Younghusband | 0 | 3 | 1 | - | - |
| C.de Grandhomme not out | 41 | 61 | 46 | 3 | - |
| M.J.Santner c & b Ravindra | 7 | 13 | 8 | - | 1 |
| H.R.Cooper not out | 17 | 21 | 19 | 1 | - |
| S.C.Kuggeleijn | | | | | |
| A.Verma | | | | | |
| I.S.Sodhi | | | | | |
| J.G.Walker | | | | | |
| M.J.Fisher | | | | | |
| Extras (b 1, lb 3, w 6) | 10 | | | | |
| **TOTAL** (19 overs) (4 wkts) | **105** | 81 | | | |

### Bowling

| WELLINGTON | O | M | R | W |
|---|---|---|---|---|
| Bennett | 3 | 0 | 22 | 0 |
| van Beek | 2 | 0 | 13 | 0 |
| Ravindra | 4 | 0 | 16 | 2 |
| Younghusband | 4 | 1 | 22 | 1 |
| Neesham | 1 | 0 | 3 | 0 |
| Bracewell | 4 | 0 | 22 | 1 |
| Sears | 1 | 0 | 3 | 0 |

### Fall of Wickets

| | W | ND |
|---|---|---|
| 1st | 9 | 21 |
| 2nd | 23 | 21 |
| 3rd | 53 | 57 |
| 4th | 55 | 70 |
| 5th | 83 | - |
| 6th | 84 | - |
| 7th | 94 | - |
| 8th | 98 | - |
| 9th | 99 | - |
| 10th | 104 | - |

# CANTERBURY v AUCKLAND — Super Smash

*at Hagley Oval, Christchurch on 18 January, 2022 (d/n)*
*Toss : Auckland.  Umpires : W.R. Knights & T.J. Parlane*
**Canterbury won by 18 runs.** Points: Canterbury 4, Otago 0

## CANTERBURY

| | Runs | Mins | Balls | 6s | 4s |
|---|---|---|---|---|---|
| C.J.Bowes c Somerville b Lister | 2 | 2 | 4 | - | - |
| T.W.M.Latham lbw b Ferguson | 34 | 27 | 19 | 2 | 4 |
| D.J.Mitchell c Chapman b Ashok | 30 | 47 | 22 | 1 | 3 |
| C.E.McConchie* c & b Ashok | 10 | 11 | 9 | - | 2 |
| C.D.Fletcher† c Ferguson b Somerville | 22 | 29 | 20 | 1 | 1 |
| M.J.Hay run out | 6 | 9 | 5 | - | - |
| H.B.Shipley c Horne b Ferguson | 21 | 30 | 20 | 1 | 2 |
| T.D.Astle run out | 1 | 4 | 1 | - | - |
| M.J.Henry c Lister b Ashok | 13 | 8 | 8 | 1 | - |
| W.P.O'Rourke c Chapman b Lister | 10 | 13 | 8 | - | 1 |
| E.J.Nuttall not out | 1 | 5 | 3 | - | - |
| Extras (w 4) | 4 | | | | |
| **TOTAL** (19.5 overs) | **154** | 95 | | | |

### Bowling

| AUCKLAND | O | M | R | W |
|---|---|---|---|---|
| Lister | 3.5 | 0 | 22 | 2 |
| ter Braak | 1 | 0 | 18 | 0 |
| Ferguson | 4 | 0 | 22 | 2 |
| Somerville | 4 | 0 | 37 | 1 |
| Ashok | 4 | 0 | 33 | 3 |
| Solia | 3 | 0 | 22 | 0 |

| CANTERBURY | O | M | R | W |
|---|---|---|---|---|
| Shipley | 4 | 0 | 14 | 3 |
| Henry | 4 | 0 | 34 | 1 |
| O'Rourke | 3 | 0 | 23 | 0 |
| McConchie | 2 | 0 | 13 | 0 |
| Astle | 4 | 0 | 21 | 1 |
| Nuttall | 2 | 0 | 23 | 2 |
| Mitchell | 1 | 0 | 6 | 0 |

## AUCKLAND

| | Runs | Mins | Balls | 6s | 4s |
|---|---|---|---|---|---|
| G.H.Worker c Henry b Shipley | 2 | 9 | 4 | - | - |
| S.M.Solia c Fletcher b Shipley | 8 | 22 | 19 | - | - |
| M.S.Chapman c Shipley b Nuttall | 18 | 40 | 19 | - | - |
| G.D.Phillips c Nuttall b Shipley | 0 | 2 | 2 | - | - |
| R.R.O'Donnell* c Hay b Nuttall | 56 | 42 | 37 | - | 8 |
| B.J.Horne† st Fletcher b Astle | 3 | 12 | 6 | - | - |
| W.E.R.Somerville not out | 12 | 29 | 13 | - | - |
| L.H.Ferguson b Henry | 30 | 23 | 19 | 2 | 1 |
| R.M.ter Braak not out | 2 | 1 | 1 | - | - |
| A.Ashok | | | | | |
| B.G.Lister | | | | | |
| Extras (lb 2, w 3) | 5 | | | | |
| **TOTAL** (20 overs) (7 wkts) | **136** | 92 | | | |

### Fall of Wickets

| | C | A |
|---|---|---|
| 1st | 3 | 8 |
| 2nd | 52 | 16 |
| 3rd | 69 | 16 |
| 4th | 92 | 56 |
| 5th | 103 | 78 |
| 6th | 116 | 90 |
| 7th | 118 | 134 |
| 8th | 132 | - |
| 9th | 146 | - |
| 10th | 154 | - |

# AUCKLAND v WELLINGTON

**Super Smash**

*at Kennards Hire Community Oval, Auckland on 20 January, 2022*
*Toss : Auckland. Umpires : C.A. Black & J.A.K. Bromley*
**Wellington won by 8 wickets.** *Points: Wellington 4, Auckland 0*

## AUCKLAND

| | Runs | Mins | Balls | 6s | 4s |
|---|---|---|---|---|---|
| G.H.Worker c Ravindra b van Beek | 13 | 27 | 17 | - | 2 |
| W.T.O'Donnell c Conway b Smith | 6 | 7 | 8 | - | - |
| M.S.Chapman c Bracewell b Sears | 7 | 12 | 8 | - | - |
| G.D.Phillips b Bennett | 39 | 52 | 31 | 2 | 2 |
| R.R.O'Donnell* c Ravindra b Sears | 10 | 13 | 11 | - | 1 |
| B.J.Horne† c Younghusband | | | | | |
| b Bennett | 27 | 46 | 29 | 1 | 2 |
| S.M.Solia c Smith b Bennett | 0 | 2 | 3 | - | - |
| W.E.R.Somerville c & b van Beek | 0 | 6 | 2 | - | - |
| L.H.Ferguson c Younghusband | | | | | |
| b Neesham | 9 | 9 | 8 | 1 | - |
| A.Ashok not out | 1 | 6 | 2 | - | - |
| B.G.Lister not out | 1 | 1 | 1 | - | - |
| Extras (b 1, lb 2, w 5) | 8 | | | | |
| **TOTAL** (20 overs) (9 wkts) . | **121** | 95 | | | |

## WELLINGTON

| | Runs | Mins | Balls | 6s | 4s |
|---|---|---|---|---|---|
| F.H.Allen lbw b Somerville | 16 | 27 | 12 | - | 3 |
| D.P.Conway b Ferguson | 7 | 6 | 5 | - | 1 |
| M.G.Bracewell* not out | 54 | 59 | 44 | 1 | 5 |
| T.A.Blundell† not out | 41 | 39 | 25 | 3 | 1 |
| J.D.S.Neesham | | | | | |
| R.Ravindra | | | | | |
| N.G.Smith | | | | | |
| L.V.van Beek | | | | | |
| P.F.Younghusband | | | | | |
| B.V.Sears | | | | | |
| H.K.Bennett | | | | | |
| Extras (lb 1, w 2, nb 1) | 4 | | | | |
| **TOTAL** (14.1 overs) (2 wkts) | **122** | 66 | | | |

| Bowling | O | M | R | W |
|---|---|---|---|---|
| **WELLINGTON** | | | | |
| Bennett | 4 | 0 | 15 | 3 |
| Smith | 1 | 0 | 4 | 1 |
| van Beek | 4 | 0 | 26 | 2 |
| Sears | 4 | 0 | 15 | 2 |
| Younghusband | 1 | 0 | 10 | 0 |
| Ravindra | 4 | 0 | 29 | 0 |
| Neesham | 2 | 0 | 19 | 1 |
| **AUCKLAND** | | | | |
| Lister | 3 | 0 | 31 | 0 |
| Ferguson | 4 | 0 | 35 | 1 |
| Solia | 1 | 0 | 17 | 0 |
| Somerville | 3.1 | 0 | 20 | 1 |
| Ashok | 3 | 0 | 18 | 0 |

| Fall of Wickets | A | W |
|---|---|---|
| 1st | 8 | 12 |
| 2nd | 21 | 52 |
| 3rd | 28 | - |
| 4th | 43 | - |
| 5th | 102 | - |
| 6th | 102 | - |
| 7th | 105 | - |
| 8th | 111 | - |
| 9th | 118 | - |
| 10th | - | - |

# CANTERBURY v NORTHERN DISTRICTS

**Super Smash**

*at Hagley Oval, Christchurch on 21 January, 2022 (d/n)*
*Toss : Northern Districts. Umpires : S.B. Haig & T.J. Parlane*
**Northern Districts won by 8 wickets.** *Points: Northern Districts 4, Canterbury 0*

## CANTERBURY

| | Runs | Mins | Balls | 6s | 4s |
|---|---|---|---|---|---|
| C.J.Bowes c Southee b Santner | 58 | 63 | 40 | 2 | 5 |
| T.W.M.Latham c Boult b Santner | 34 | 33 | 22 | 2 | 2 |
| D.J.Mitchell c Sodhi b Walker | 23 | 19 | 11 | 4 | - |
| L.J.Carter c Seifert b Boult | 6 | 23 | 7 | - | - |
| C.D.Fletcher† c Boult b Kuggeleijn | 12 | 11 | 9 | 1 | - |
| C.E.McConchie* not out | 25 | 18 | 20 | - | 1 |
| H.B.Shipley c sub (M.J. Fisher) | | | | | |
| b Boult | 5 | 10 | 3 | - | 1 |
| M.J.Henry not out | 0 | 3 | 0 | - | - |
| T.D.Astle | | | | | |
| W.P.O'Rourke | | | | | |
| E.J.Nuttall | | | | | |
| Extras (b 1, w 1) | 2 | | | | |
| **TOTAL** (20 overs) (6 wkts) . | **173** | 93 | | | |

## NORTHERN DISTRICTS

| | Runs | Mins | Balls | 6s | 4s |
|---|---|---|---|---|---|
| K.D.Clarke c Henry b Shipley | 31 | 35 | 23 | 1 | 4 |
| T.L.Seifert† not out | 88 | 88 | 62 | 1 | 7 |
| J.A.Raval* c Mitchell | | | | | |
| b McConchie | 36 | 37 | 23 | 1 | 4 |
| C.de Grandhomme not out | 10 | 16 | 7 | 1 | - |
| M.J.Santner | | | | | |
| H.R.Cooper | | | | | |
| S.C.Kuggeleijn | | | | | |
| T.G.Southee | | | | | |
| I.S.Sodhi | | | | | |
| J.G.Walker | | | | | |
| T.A.Boult | | | | | |
| Extras (b 1, lb 5, w 3) | 9 | | | | |
| **TOTAL** (19.1 overs) (2 wkts) | **174** | 88 | | | |

| Bowling | O | M | R | W |
|---|---|---|---|---|
| **NORTHERN DISTRICTS** | | | | |
| Boult | 4 | 0 | 37 | 2 |
| Southee | 3 | 0 | 32 | 0 |
| Santner | 4 | 0 | 34 | 2 |
| Kuggeleijn | 3 | 0 | 22 | 1 |
| Sodhi | 2 | 0 | 18 | 0 |
| Walker | 4 | 0 | 29 | 1 |
| **CANTERBURY** | | | | |
| Shipley | 3 | 0 | 28 | 1 |
| Henry | 4 | 0 | 37 | 0 |
| O'Rourke | 1 | 0 | 8 | 0 |
| Astle | 4 | 0 | 29 | 0 |
| Nuttall | 2 | 0 | 21 | 0 |
| McConchie | 4 | 0 | 29 | 1 |
| Mitchell | 1.1 | 0 | 16 | 0 |

| Fall of Wickets | C | ND |
|---|---|---|
| 1st | 66 | 81 |
| 2nd | 110 | 153 |
| 3rd | 126 | - |
| 4th | 143 | - |
| 5th | 147 | - |
| 6th | 166 | - |
| 7th | - | - |
| 8th | - | - |
| 9th | - | - |
| 10th | - | - |

# AUCKLAND v CENTRAL DISTRICTS

**Super Smash**

*at Eden Park, Auckland on 22 January, 2022*
*Toss : Auckland. Umpires : J.M. Dempsey & W.R. Knights*
**Central Districts won by 10 runs.** *Points: Central Districts 4, Auckland 0*

## CENTRAL DISTRICTS

| | Runs | Mins | Balls | 6s | 4s |
|---|---|---|---|---|---|
| W.A.Young st Phillips b Ashok . | 23 | 28 | 15 | 1 | 3 |
| B.S.Smith c O'Donnell W.T. | | | | | |
| b Somerville | 80 | 77 | 49 | 2 | 10 |
| D.Cleaver† c O'Donnell W.T. | | | | | |
| b Ashok | 20 | 28 | 18 | - | 2 |
| T.C.Bruce* c Chapman b Somerville | 8 | 6 | 6 | 1 | - |
| J.A.Clarkson c & b Ashok | 4 | 7 | 4 | - | - |
| D.A.J.Bracewell c Phillips | | | | | |
| b Ferguson | 18 | 18 | 13 | - | 2 |
| A.F.Milne c Chapman b Ferguson | 8 | 10 | 8 | - | 1 |
| A.Y.Patel not out | 4 | 6 | 4 | - | - |
| S.H.A.Rance not out | 2 | 5 | 3 | - | - |
| B.M.Tickner | | | | | |
| J.R.Lennox | | | | | |
| Extras (b 1, lb 3, w 5) | 9 | | | | |
| **TOTAL (20 overs) (7 wkts)** . | **176** | 94 | | | |

## AUCKLAND

| | Runs | Mins | Balls | 6s | 4s |
|---|---|---|---|---|---|
| M.J.Guptill c Milne b Bracewell | 16 | 31 | 21 | 1 | 1 |
| G.H.Worker c Cleaver b Rance .. | 4 | 3 | 3 | - | 1 |
| M.S.Chapman c Tickner b Rance | 5 | 10 | 6 | - | 1 |
| G.D.Phillips† c sub (J.F.A.Field) | | | | | |
| b Bracewell | 52 | 59 | 34 | 3 | 5 |
| R.R.O'Donnell* c Milne | | | | | |
| b Tickner | 68 | 61 | 37 | 2 | 8 |
| W.T.O'Donnell c & b Lennox | 2 | 8 | 3 | - | - |
| S.M.Solia not out | 5 | 24 | 8 | - | - |
| W.E.R.Somerville b Milne | 1 | 3 | 2 | - | - |
| L.H.Ferguson not out | 9 | 9 | 6 | - | 1 |
| B.G.Lister | | | | | |
| A.Ashok | | | | | |
| Extras (lb 2, w 2) | 4 | | | | |
| **TOTAL (20 overs) (7 wkts)** . | **166** | 106 | | | |

| Bowling | O | M | R | W |
|---|---|---|---|---|
| **AUCKLAND** | | | | |
| Lister | 4 | 0 | 28 | 0 |
| Ferguson | 4 | 0 | 32 | 2 |
| Solia | 2 | 0 | 25 | 0 |
| Somerville | 4 | 0 | 41 | 2 |
| Ashok | 4 | 0 | 28 | 3 |
| Chapman | 2 | 0 | 18 | 0 |
| **CENTRAL DISTRICTS** | | | | |
| Rance | 4 | 0 | 15 | 2 |
| Milne | 4 | 0 | 22 | 1 |
| Bracewell | 4 | 0 | 53 | 2 |
| Tickner | 4 | 0 | 36 | 1 |
| Lennox | 3 | 0 | 28 | 1 |
| Patel | 1 | 0 | 10 | 0 |

| Fall of Wickets | | |
|---|---|---|
| | CD | A |
| 1st | 58 | 5 |
| 2nd | 118 | 14 |
| 3rd | 128 | 29 |
| 4th | 138 | 115 |
| 5th | 148 | 127 |
| 6th | 169 | 150 |
| 7th | 169 | 152 |
| 8th | - | - |
| 9th | - | - |
| 10th | - | - |

# OTAGO v CANTERBURY

**Super Smash**

*at University of Otago Oval, Dunedin on 23 January, 2022*
*Toss : Otago. Umpires : K.D. Cotton & S.B. Haig*
**Canterbury won by 8 wickets.** *Points: Canterbury 4, Otago 0*

## OTAGO

| | Runs | Mins | Balls | 6s | 4s |
|---|---|---|---|---|---|
| H.D.Rutherford* c Latham b Shipley | 6 | 9 | 6 | - | 1 |
| N.T.Broom c Mitchell b McConchie | 34 | 31 | 23 | 3 | 2 |
| N.F.Kelly c Mitchell b Shipley | 0 | 2 | 1 | - | - |
| D.N.Phillips c Nuttall b Shipley . | 65 | 40 | 34 | 5 | 4 |
| A.W.McKenzie run out | 1 | 5 | 2 | - | - |
| A.K.Kitchen c Bowes b Mitchell | 28 | 39 | 24 | 1 | 1 |
| M.W.Chu† b Henry | 6 | 10 | 8 | - | - |
| M.J.G.Rippon not out | 38 | 36 | 19 | 2 | 4 |
| J.A.Duffy c & b Shipley | 0 | 5 | 1 | - | - |
| M.D.Rae not out | 6 | 17 | 3 | - | 1 |
| M.B.Bacon | | | | | |
| Extras (nb 1) | 1 | | | | |
| **TOTAL (20 overs) (8 wkts)** . | **185** | 99 | | | |

## CANTERBURY

| | Runs | Mins | Balls | 6s | 4s |
|---|---|---|---|---|---|
| C.J.Bowes c Bacon b Rae | 20 | 20 | 15 | - | 4 |
| T.W.M.Latham st Chu b Rippon | 66 | 53 | 35 | 5 | 4 |
| D.J.Mitchell not out | 68 | 62 | 39 | 4 | 5 |
| L.J.Carter not out | 26 | 20 | 15 | 1 | 1 |
| C.E.McConchie | | | | | |
| C.D.Fletcher† | | | | | |
| H.B.Shipley | | | | | |
| M.J.Henry | | | | | |
| T.D.Astle | | | | | |
| B.P.Coburn | | | | | |
| E.J.Nuttall | | | | | |
| Extras (w 5, nb 1) | 6 | | | | |
| **TOTAL (17.1 overs) (2 wkts)** | **186** | 83 | | | |

| Bowling | O | M | R | W |
|---|---|---|---|---|
| **CANTERBURY** | | | | |
| Shipley | 4 | 0 | 23 | 4 |
| Henry | 4 | 0 | 57 | 1 |
| Nuttall | 2 | 0 | 17 | 0 |
| Mitchell | 2 | 0 | 17 | 1 |
| Astle | 4 | 0 | 29 | 0 |
| McConchie | 3 | 0 | 27 | 1 |
| Coburn | 1 | 0 | 15 | 0 |
| **OTAGO** | | | | |
| Duffy | 3 | 0 | 29 | 0 |
| Rae | 4 | 0 | 38 | 1 |
| Bacon | 2 | 0 | 30 | 0 |
| Kitchen | 3 | 0 | 35 | 0 |
| Rippon | 4 | 0 | 41 | 1 |
| McKenzie | 1.1 | 0 | 13 | 0 |

| Fall of Wickets | | |
|---|---|---|
| | O | C |
| 1st | 24 | 58 |
| 2nd | 24 | 121 |
| 3rd | 67 | - |
| 4th | 76 | - |
| 5th | 121 | - |
| 6th | 132 | - |
| 7th | 148 | - |
| 8th | 159 | - |
| 9th | - | - |
| 10th | - | - |

# WELLINGTON v NORTHERN DISTRICTS — Super Smash

*at Cello Basin Reserve, Wellington on 24 January, 2022*
*Toss : Northern Districts.  Umpires : C.A. Black & T.J. Parlane*
**Northern Districts won by 2 wickets.** Points: Northern Districts 4, Wellington 0

## WELLINGTON

| | Runs | Mins | Balls | 6s | 4s |
|---|---|---|---|---|---|
| F.H.Allen c Clarke b Walker ..... | 64 | 43 | 28 | 3 | 10 |
| D.P.Conway c Seifert b Southee | 0 | 8 | 3 | - | - |
| M.G.Bracewell* c Raval b Walker ................................. | 63 | 56 | 38 | 2 | 7 |
| T.A.Blundell† c Verma b Southee | 2 | 13 | 6 | - | - |
| J.D.S.Neesham c Raval b Sodhi | 2 | 10 | 6 | - | - |
| R.Ravindra c Cooper b Santner . | 7 | 19 | 11 | - | - |
| N.G.Smith b Walker ..................... | 1 | 4 | 2 | - | - |
| L.V.van Beek lbw b Southee ..... | 18 | 24 | 17 | 1 | - |
| P.F.Younghusband c Seifert b Boult.......................................... | 1 | 5 | 2 | - | - |
| O.R.Newton c Raval b Boult ....... | 0 | 1 | 1 | - | - |
| B.V.Sears not out ...................... | 4 | 6 | 4 | - | - |
| Extras (lb 2, w 3) ...................... | 5 | | | | |
| **TOTAL** (19.4 overs) ............. | **167** | 97 | | | |

## NORTHERN DISTRICTS

| | Runs | Mins | Balls | 6s | 4s |
|---|---|---|---|---|---|
| K.D.Clarke c Blundell b Smith .... | 4 | 2 | 2 | - | 1 |
| T.L.Seifert† c Smith b Neesham | 32 | 27 | 15 | 2 | 4 |
| J.A.Raval* c Smith b van Beek . | 10 | 19 | 12 | - | 1 |
| C.de Grandhomme c van Beek b Sears .................................. | 16 | 18 | 10 | 1 | 1 |
| M.J.Santner c Ravindra b Younghusband .................. | 59 | 42 | 35 | 4 | 6 |
| H.R.Cooper run out .................. | 21 | 19 | 10 | 2 | 1 |
| A.Verma c Conway b Neesham | 11 | 26 | 15 | - | 1 |
| T.G.Southee c Bracewell b Sears | 10 | 22 | 14 | - | 1 |
| I.S.Sodhi not out ......................... | 2 | 7 | 4 | - | - |
| J.G.Walker not out ...................... | 0 | 1 | 0 | - | - |
| T.A.Boult | | | | | |
| Extras (lb 1, w 2) ...................... | 3 | | | | |
| **TOTAL** (19.3 overs) (8 wkts) | **168** | 93 | | | |

### Bowling
#### NORTHERN DISTRICTS

| | O | M | R | W |
|---|---|---|---|---|
| Boult | 3 | 0 | 40 | 2 |
| Southee | 3.4 | 0 | 20 | 3 |
| Verma | 2 | 0 | 23 | 0 |
| Sodhi | 3 | 0 | 23 | 1 |
| Santner | 4 | 0 | 23 | 1 |
| Walker | 4 | 0 | 36 | 3 |

#### WELLINGTON

| | O | M | R | W |
|---|---|---|---|---|
| Smith | 2 | 0 | 12 | 1 |
| Newton | 1 | 0 | 9 | 0 |
| Sears | 3.3 | 0 | 47 | 2 |
| van Beek | 4 | 0 | 26 | 1 |
| Neesham | 3 | 0 | 18 | 2 |
| Ravindra | 2 | 0 | 24 | 0 |
| Bracewell | 2 | 0 | 20 | 0 |
| Younghusband | 2 | 0 | 11 | 1 |

### Fall of Wickets

| | W | ND |
|---|---|---|
| 1st | 16 | 4 |
| 2nd | 100 | 42 |
| 3rd | 125 | 50 |
| 4th | 134 | 69 |
| 5th | 134 | 125 |
| 6th | 137 | 148 |
| 7th | 151 | 164 |
| 8th | 156 | 167 |
| 9th | 156 | - |
| 10th | 167 | - |

# CANTERBURY v WELLINGTON — Elimination Final

*at University of Otago Oval, Dunedin on 27 January, 2022*
*Toss : Canterbury.  Umpires : B.F. Bowden & S.B. Haig*
**Canterbury won by 6 wickets**

## WELLINGTON

| | Runs | Mins | Balls | 6s | 4s |
|---|---|---|---|---|---|
| F.H.Allen c Astle b Henry .......... | 12 | 3 | 4 | 2 | - |
| D.P.Conway not out .................. | 74 | 88 | 52 | 2 | 5 |
| T.A.Blundell† lbw b Henry .......... | 0 | 1 | 1 | - | - |
| M.G.Bracewell* c McConchie b Shipley ................................. | 81 | 68 | 54 | 4 | 6 |
| J.D.S.Neesham not out ............. | 16 | 14 | 10 | - | 2 |
| R.Ravindra | | | | | |
| N.G.Smith | | | | | |
| L.V.van Beek | | | | | |
| P.F.Younghusband | | | | | |
| B.V.Sears | | | | | |
| H.K.Bennett | | | | | |
| Extras (w 6, nb 1) ..................... | 7 | | | | |
| **TOTAL** (20 overs) (3 wkts) . | **190** | 88 | | | |

## CANTERBURY

| | Runs | Mins | Balls | 6s | 4s |
|---|---|---|---|---|---|
| C.J.Bowes c van Beek b Younghusband .................. | 51 | 58 | 41 | 1 | 6 |
| T.W.M.Latham b van Beek ....... | 16 | 13 | 5 | 2 | 1 |
| D.J.Mitchell c Conway b Ravindra | 11 | 24 | 14 | - | 1 |
| L.J.Carter not out ...................... | 44 | 57 | 30 | 2 | 3 |
| C.E.McConchie* c Sears b Younghusband .................. | 0 | 1 | 2 | - | - |
| C.D.Fletcher† not out ............... | 63 | 34 | 25 | 3 | 6 |
| H.B.Shipley | | | | | |
| M.J.Henry | | | | | |
| T.D.Astle | | | | | |
| M.J.Hay | | | | | |
| E.J.Nuttall | | | | | |
| Extras (lb 1, w 5) ...................... | 6 | | | | |
| **TOTAL** (19.3 overs) (4 wkts) | **191** | 94 | | | |

### Bowling
#### CANTERBURY

| | O | M | R | W |
|---|---|---|---|---|
| Henry | 4 | 0 | 47 | 2 |
| Shipley | 4 | 0 | 21 | 1 |
| Nuttall | 3 | 0 | 37 | 0 |
| Mitchell | 3 | 0 | 41 | 0 |
| McConchie | 4 | 0 | 24 | 0 |
| Astle | 2 | 0 | 20 | 0 |

#### WELLINGTON

| | O | M | R | W |
|---|---|---|---|---|
| Bennett | 2 | 0 | 11 | 0 |
| Smith | 1 | 0 | 21 | 0 |
| van Beek | 4 | 0 | 49 | 1 |
| Neesham | 3 | 0 | 38 | 0 |
| Sears | 3 | 0 | 27 | 0 |
| Ravindra | 3 | 0 | 24 | 1 |
| Younghusband | 3.3 | 0 | 20 | 2 |

### Fall of Wickets

| | W | C |
|---|---|---|
| 1st | 12 | 37 |
| 2nd | 12 | 65 |
| 3rd | 155 | 93 |
| 4th | - | 93 |
| 5th | - | - |
| 6th | - | - |
| 7th | - | - |
| 8th | - | - |
| 9th | - | - |
| 10th | - | - |

# NORTHERN DISTRICTS v CANTERBURY                    Final

*at Seddon Park, Hamilton on 29 January, 2022*
*Toss : Canterbury.  Umpires : C.M. Brown & W.R. Knights*
**Northern Districts won by 56 runs**

## NORTHERN DISTRICTS

| | Runs | Mins | Balls | 6s | 4s |
|---|---|---|---|---|---|
| K.D.Clarke c McConchie | | | | | |
| b Mitchell | 71 | 42 | 34 | 4 | 8 |
| T.L.Seifert† c Bowes b Shipley | 5 | 5 | 5 | - | 1 |
| J.A.Raval* c Fletcher b Shipley | 9 | 18 | 15 | - | 1 |
| C.de Grandhomme c Bowes | | | | | |
| b McConchie | 9 | 13 | 8 | 1 | - |
| M.J.Santner not out | 92 | 62 | 40 | 9 | 4 |
| H.R.Cooper run out | 16 | 29 | 14 | 1 | - |
| S.C.Kuggeleijn not out | 6 | 8 | 4 | - | - |
| A.Verma | | | | | |
| T.G.Southee | | | | | |
| I.S.Sodhi | | | | | |
| J.G.Walker | | | | | |
| Extras (w 9) | 9 | | | | |
| **TOTAL** (20 overs) (5 wkts) | **217** | 100 | | | |

## CANTERBURY

| | Runs | Mins | Balls | 6s | 4s |
|---|---|---|---|---|---|
| C.J.Bowes c Raval b Kuggeleijn | 19 | 22 | 13 | - | 3 |
| T.W.M.Latham b Southee | 11 | 12 | 9 | - | 2 |
| D.J.Mitchell c Santner b Sodhi | 8 | 20 | 12 | 1 | - |
| L.J.Carter st Seifert b Walker | 11 | 18 | 8 | 1 | - |
| C.E.McConchie* c Clarke | | | | | |
| b Sodhi | 23 | 16 | 10 | 2 | 1 |
| C.D.Fletcher† c Raval b Santner | 9 | 12 | 6 | 1 | - |
| M.J.Hay b Walker | 2 | 9 | 5 | - | - |
| H.B.Shipley c Verma b Sodhi | 4 | 11 | 8 | - | - |
| M.J.Henry b Southee | 44 | 24 | 22 | 3 | 4 |
| T.D.Astle not out | 13 | 27 | 12 | - | 1 |
| E.J.Nuttall c Clarke b Southee | 11 | 10 | 8 | 1 | 1 |
| Extras (lb 1, w 5) | 6 | | | | |
| **TOTAL** (18.5 overs) | **161** | 93 | | | |

| Bowling | O | M | R | W |
|---|---|---|---|---|
| **CANTERBURY** | | | | |
| Henry | 4 | 0 | 36 | 0 |
| Shipley | 4 | 0 | 30 | 2 |
| Nuttall | 4 | 0 | 42 | 0 |
| Astle | 3 | 0 | 40 | 0 |
| McConchie | 3 | 0 | 36 | 1 |
| Mitchell | 2 | 0 | 33 | 1 |
| **NORTHERN DISTRICTS** | | | | |
| Southee | 3.5 | 0 | 39 | 3 |
| Verma | 3 | 0 | 19 | 0 |
| Santner | 3 | 0 | 23 | 1 |
| Kuggeleijn | 1 | 0 | 6 | 1 |
| Sodhi | 4 | 0 | 48 | 3 |
| Walker | 4 | 0 | 25 | 2 |

| Fall of Wickets | | |
|---|---|---|
| | ND | C |
| 1st | 10 | 21 |
| 2nd | 41 | 36 |
| 3rd | 77 | 40 |
| 4th | 127 | 57 |
| 5th | 200 | 76 |
| 6th | - | 86 |
| 7th | - | 90 |
| 8th | - | 104 |
| 9th | - | 147 |
| 10th | - | 161 |

**NZC**

# 2021/22 DREAM11 SUPER SMASH AVERAGES

| | M | In | NO | HS | Runs | Ave | 100s | 50s | Ct | St | O | M | R | W | Ave | R/O | Best |
|---|---|---|---|---|---|---|---|---|---|---|---|---|---|---|---|---|---|
| F.H.Allen | 11 | 11 | 0 | 68 | 280 | 25.45 | - | 3 | 6 | 1 | | | | | | | |
| A.Ashok | 10 | 6 | 4 | 6* | 18 | 9.00 | - | - | 4 | - | 37 | 1 | 240 | 14 | 17.14 | 6.49 | 3-8 |
| T.D.Astle | 11 | 4 | 2 | 13* | 19 | 9.50 | - | - | 3 | - | 41 | 0 | 290 | 10 | 29.00 | 7.07 | 2-13 |
| M.T.M.M.J.Ave | 3 | 2 | 0 | 12 | 18 | 9.00 | - | - | - | - | | | | | | | |
| M.B.Bacon | 8 | 2 | 2 | 3* | 5 | - | - | - | 2 | - | 25 | 0 | 241 | 6 | 40.16 | 9.64 | 2-27 |
| G.K.Beghin | 2 | 2 | 0 | 23 | 23 | 11.50 | - | - | 1 | - | | | | | | | |
| H.K.Bennett | 10 | 2 | 2 | 4* | 5 | - | - | - | 2 | - | 34 | 0 | 271 | 9 | 30.11 | 7.97 | 3-15 |
| J.J.N.P.Bhula | 1 | - | - | - | - | - | - | - | - | - | 2 | 0 | 17 | 0 | - | 8.50 | - |
| T.A.Blundell | 3 | 3 | 1 | 41* | 43 | 21.50 | - | - | 1 | - | | | | | | | |
| P.D.Bocock | 2 | 2 | 1 | 13* | 18 | 18.00 | - | - | 1 | - | | | | | | | |
| T.A.Boult | 4 | 1 | 1 | 7* | 7 | - | - | - | 2 | - | 14 | 0 | 117 | 6 | 19.50 | 8.36 | 2-21 |
| C.J.Bowes | 12 | 12 | 0 | 62 | 333 | 27.75 | - | 4 | 8 | - | | | | | | | |
| J.C.T.Boyle | 1 | 1 | 0 | 31 | 31 | 31.00 | - | - | - | - | | | | | | | |
| D.A.J.Bracewell | 9 | 6 | 2 | 36* | 72 | 18.00 | - | - | 4 | - | 35.5 | 0 | 308 | 14 | 22.00 | 8.60 | 3-33 |
| M.G.Bracewell | 10 | 10 | 4 | 141* | 478 | 79.66 | 1 | 4 | 8 | - | 25 | 0 | 171 | 6 | 28.50 | 6.84 | 3-22 |
| C.J.Briggs | 5 | 5 | 0 | 6 | 13 | 2.60 | - | - | 2 | - | | | | | | | |
| N.T.Broom | 10 | 9 | 0 | 62 | 198 | 22.00 | - | 1 | 2 | - | | | | | | | |
| T.C.Bruce | 10 | 10 | 3 | 93* | 267 | 38.14 | - | 2 | 6 | - | 13.3 | 0 | 112 | 3 | 37.33 | 8.30 | 3-9 |
| J.F.Carter | 7 | 7 | 1 | 75* | 174 | 29.00 | - | 1 | 6 | - | | | | | | | |
| L.J.Carter | 10 | 10 | 2 | 56 | 192 | 24.00 | - | 1 | 3 | - | | | | | | | |
| M.S.Chapman | 9 | 9 | 0 | 55 | 184 | 20.44 | - | 2 | 5 | - | 8.5 | 0 | 84 | 1 | 84.00 | 9.51 | 1-27 |
| M.W.Chu | 10 | 7 | 1 | 12 | 63 | 10.50 | - | - | 2 | 5 | | | | | | | |
| K.D.Clarke | 8 | 8 | 1 | 71 | 228 | 32.57 | - | 1 | 4 | - | | | | | | | |
| J.A.Clarkson | 9 | 9 | 3 | 76* | 201 | 33.50 | - | 2 | 6 | - | 1 | 0 | 15 | 0 | - | 15.00 | - |
| D.Cleaver | 9 | 9 | 1 | 114* | 369 | 46.12 | 1 | 2 | 7 | - | | | | | | | |
| B.P.Coburn | 6 | 2 | 1 | 11* | 18 | 18.00 | - | - | 3 | - | 16 | 0 | 128 | 3 | 42.66 | 8.00 | 2-16 |
| D.P.Conway | 3 | 3 | 1 | 74* | 81 | 40.50 | - | 1 | 3 | - | | | | | | | |
| H.R.Cooper | 11 | 10 | 3 | 25* | 136 | 19.42 | - | - | 4 | - | | | | | | | |
| C.de Grandhomme | 10 | 10 | 2 | 86 | 240 | 30.00 | - | 2 | 3 | - | 1 | 0 | 17 | 0 | - | 17.00 | - |
| L.J.Delport | 4 | 3 | 0 | 6 | 9 | 3.00 | - | - | - | - | 15.1 | 0 | 128 | 7 | 18.28 | 8.44 | 2-20 |
| J.A.Duffy | 10 | 5 | 2 | 16 | 21 | 7.00 | - | - | 1 | - | 34.2 | 0 | 318 | 6 | 53.00 | 9.26 | 3-30 |
| L.H.Ferguson | 10 | 9 | 2 | 30 | 102 | 14.57 | - | - | 3 | - | 37.5 | 0 | 274 | 17 | 16.11 | 7.24 | 4-19 |
| J.F.A.Field | 4 | 1 | 0 | 9 | 9 | 9.00 | - | - | 1 | - | 12.1 | 0 | 127 | 5 | 25.40 | 10.44 | 2-28 |
| J.L.Finnie | 3 | 2 | 0 | 12 | 22 | 11.00 | - | - | 1 | - | 6 | 0 | 41 | 2 | 20.50 | 6.83 | 2-22 |
| M.J.Fisher | 6 | 0 | 0 | 0 | 0 | - | - | - | 3 | - | 17 | 1 | 115 | 5 | 23.00 | 6.76 | 2-21 |
| C.D.Fletcher | 12 | 11 | 4 | 63* | 305 | 43.57 | - | 3 | 6 | 4 | | | | | | | |
| L.I.Georgeson | 3 | 3 | 0 | 30 | 31 | 10.33 | - | - | 3 | - | | | | | | | |
| J.D.Gibson | 7 | 6 | 2 | 22* | 60 | 15.00 | - | - | 1 | - | 1 | 0 | 10 | 0 | - | 10.00 | - |
| J.M.Gibson | 4 | 2 | 0 | 2 | 2 | 1.00 | - | - | 4 | - | 11 | 0 | 103 | 2 | 51.50 | 9.36 | 1-20 |
| Z.N.Gibson | 2 | - | - | - | - | - | - | - | 1 | - | 4 | 0 | 31 | 0 | - | 7.75 | - |
| N.A.Greenwood | 2 | 2 | 0 | 14 | 23 | 11.50 | - | - | - | - | | | | | | | |
| M.J.Guptill | 6 | 6 | 1 | 79* | 151 | 30.20 | - | 1 | 3 | - | | | | | | | |
| B.R.Hampton | 2 | 2 | 0 | 11 | 22 | 11.00 | - | - | 1 | - | 5 | 0 | 35 | 2 | 17.50 | 7.00 | 1-9 |
| G.R.Hay | 7 | 7 | 0 | 76 | 234 | 33.42 | - | 3 | 1 | - | | | | | | | |
| M.J.Hay | 7 | 6 | 1 | 29 | 55 | 11.00 | - | - | 6 | - | | | | | | | |
| M.W.Hay | 2 | 2 | 0 | 11 | 13 | 6.50 | - | - | - | - | | | | | | | |
| M.J.Henry | 10 | 7 | 2 | 44 | 85 | 17.00 | - | - | 5 | - | 40 | 1 | 329 | 14 | 23.50 | 8.23 | 3-11 |
| B.J.Horne | 9 | 8 | 0 | 27 | 97 | 12.12 | - | - | 5 | 3 | | | | | | | |
| M.G.Hughes | 2 | 2 | 0 | 12 | 17 | 8.50 | - | - | - | - | | | | | | | |
| L.C.Johnson | 8 | 7 | 0 | 38 | 92 | 13.14 | - | - | 4 | - | | | | | | | |
| T.M.Johnson | 7 | 7 | 1 | 54 | 140 | 23.33 | - | 1 | 1 | - | | | | | | | |
| N.F.Kelly | 8 | 8 | 1 | 58 | 158 | 22.57 | - | 1 | 2 | - | | | | | | | |
| A.K.Kitchen | 10 | 9 | 1 | 54 | 180 | 22.50 | - | 1 | 1 | - | 36 | 0 | 242 | 11 | 22.00 | 6.72 | 4-11 |
| S.C.Kuggeleijn | 9 | 6 | 2 | 14* | 38 | 9.50 | - | - | 3 | - | 21.4 | 0 | 190 | 11 | 17.27 | 8.77 | 4-34 |
| T.W.M.Latham | 5 | 5 | 0 | 66 | 161 | 32.20 | - | 1 | 1 | - | | | | | | | |
| J.R.Lennox | 6 | 2 | 2 | 17* | 23 | - | - | - | 1 | - | 20 | 0 | 168 | 8 | 21.00 | 8.40 | 2-23 |
| C.K.Leopard | 6 | 5 | 1 | 25 | 58 | 14.50 | - | - | - | - | 2 | 0 | 18 | 1 | 18.00 | 9.00 | 1-18 |
| B.G.Lister | 10 | 5 | 4 | 17* | 28 | 28.00 | - | - | 6 | - | 35.3 | 0 | 242 | 11 | 22.00 | 6.82 | 3-27 |
| K.J.McClure | 7 | 7 | 0 | 34 | 97 | 13.85 | - | - | 1 | - | | | | | | | |
| C.E.McConchie | 12 | 11 | 1 | 84 | 193 | 19.30 | - | 1 | 2 | - | 39 | 0 | 298 | 6 | 49.66 | 7.64 | 1-17 |
| A.W.McKenzie | 7 | 5 | 2 | 11 | 24 | 8.00 | - | - | 3 | - | 15.1 | 0 | 111 | 3 | 37.00 | 7.32 | 2-28 |
| A.F.Milne | 2 | 1 | 0 | 8 | 8 | 8.00 | - | - | 2 | - | 6 | 0 | 33 | 1 | 33.00 | 5.50 | 1-22 |
| D.J.Mitchell | 5 | 5 | 1 | 68* | 148 | 37.00 | - | 1 | 3 | - | 9.1 | 0 | 113 | 2 | 56.50 | 12.33 | 1-17 |
| T.Muller | 1 | - | - | - | - | - | - | - | - | - | 1 | 0 | 18 | 1 | 18.00 | 18.00 | 1-18 |
| J.D.S.Neesham | 7 | 5 | 1 | 20 | 47 | 11.75 | - | - | 3 | - | 16 | 0 | 138 | 6 | 23.00 | 8.63 | 2-17 |
| O.R.Newton | 3 | 3 | 0 | 9 | 12 | 4.00 | - | - | - | - | 7 | 0 | 67 | 1 | 67.00 | 9.57 | 1-26 |
| H.M.Nicholls | 2 | 2 | 1 | 49* | 84 | 84.00 | - | - | - | - | | | | | | | |

| | M | In | NO | HS | Runs | Ave | 100s | 50s | Ct | St | O | M | R | W | Ave | R/O | Best |
|---|---|---|---|---|---|---|---|---|---|---|---|---|---|---|---|---|---|
| E.J.Nuttall | 12 | 4 | 2 | 11 | 13 | 6.50 | - | - | 5 | - | 41 | 0 | 390 | 15 | 26.00 | 9.51 | 3-28 |
| R.R.O'Donnell | 10 | 9 | 0 | 68 | 227 | 25.22 | - | 2 | 4 | - | | | | | | | |
| W.T.O'Donnell | 2 | 2 | 0 | 6 | 8 | 4.00 | - | - | 2 | - | | | | | | | |
| W.P.O'Rourke | 3 | 1 | 0 | 10 | 10 | 10.00 | - | - | - | - | 7 | 0 | 52 | 0 | - | 7.43 | - |
| A.Y.Patel | 6 | 3 | 1 | 11 | 19 | 9.50 | - | - | 1 | - | 15 | 0 | 158 | 2 | 79.00 | 10.53 | 1-23 |
| D.N.Phillips | 6 | 5 | 1 | 65 | 93 | 23.25 | - | 1 | 5 | - | | | | | | | |
| G.D.Phillips | 6 | 6 | 1 | 53 | 158 | 31.60 | - | 2 | 2 | 1 | 5 | 0 | 34 | 3 | 11.33 | 6.80 | 2-11 |
| M.D.Rae | 1 | 1 | 1 | 6* | 6 | - | - | - | - | - | 4 | 0 | 38 | 1 | 38.00 | 9.50 | 1-38 |
| S.H.A.Rance | 10 | 3 | 2 | 10* | 20 | 20.00 | - | - | 3 | - | 36.1 | 0 | 334 | 15 | 22.26 | 9.24 | 5-19 |
| J.A.Raval | 11 | 11 | 1 | 66* | 184 | 18.40 | - | 1 | 13 | - | | | | | | | |
| R.Ravindra | 4 | 2 | 0 | 14 | 21 | 10.50 | - | - | 4 | - | 13 | 0 | 93 | 3 | 31.00 | 7.15 | 2-16 |
| M.J.G.Rippon | 8 | 6 | 2 | 38* | 99 | 24.75 | - | - | - | - | 31 | 1 | 276 | 10 | 27.60 | 8.90 | 3-32 |
| T.B.Robinson | 8 | 8 | 0 | 65 | 143 | 17.87 | - | 1 | 2 | - | | | | | | | |
| H.D.Rutherford | 10 | 9 | 0 | 82 | 229 | 25.44 | - | 2 | 2 | - | 10 | 0 | 73 | 2 | 36.50 | 7.30 | 1-6 |
| M.J.Santner | 5 | 4 | 1 | 92* | 158 | 52.66 | - | 2 | 1 | - | 18 | 0 | 120 | 8 | 15.00 | 6.67 | 2-15 |
| B.V.Sears | 10 | 5 | 4 | 5* | 13 | 13.00 | - | - | 2 | - | 31 | 0 | 263 | 13 | 20.23 | 8.48 | 3-22 |
| T.L.Seifert | 10 | 10 | 2 | 88* | 239 | 29.87 | - | 1 | 7 | 1 | | | | | | | |
| H.B.Shipley | 11 | 8 | 2 | 39* | 144 | 24.00 | - | - | 8 | - | 35 | 0 | 254 | 18 | 14.11 | 7.26 | 4-23 |
| B.S.Smith | 6 | 5 | 1 | 80 | 205 | 51.25 | - | 2 | - | - | | | | | | | |
| N.G.Smith | 11 | 8 | 1 | 38* | 77 | 11.00 | - | - | 4 | - | 17 | 0 | 179 | 6 | 29.83 | 10.53 | 2-40 |
| I.S.Sodhi | 8 | 3 | 2 | 8* | 12 | 12.00 | - | - | 3 | - | 29 | 0 | 204 | 10 | 20.40 | 7.03 | 3-48 |
| S.M.Solia | 10 | 9 | 2 | 67* | 105 | 15.00 | - | 1 | 2 | - | 22 | 0 | 217 | 3 | 72.33 | 9.86 | 2-16 |
| W.E.R.Somerville | 6 | 5 | 2 | 25 | 50 | 16.66 | - | - | 1 | - | 22.1 | 0 | 174 | 8 | 21.75 | 7.85 | 2-18 |
| T.G.Southee | 3 | 1 | 0 | 10 | 10 | 10.00 | - | - | 1 | - | 10.3 | 0 | 91 | 6 | 15.16 | 8.67 | 3-20 |
| J.J.Tasman-Jones | 4 | 4 | 0 | 35 | 96 | 24.00 | | | | | | | | | | | |
| R.M.ter Braak | 1 | 1 | 1 | 2* | 2 | - | - | - | - | - | 1 | 0 | 18 | 0 | - | 18.00 | - |
| B.M.Tickner | 10 | 1 | 0 | 1 | 1 | 1.00 | - | - | 3 | - | 38 | 0 | 354 | 10 | 35.40 | 9.32 | 3-20 |
| L.V.van Beek | 11 | 7 | 1 | 61* | 160 | 26.66 | - | 1 | 5 | - | 40 | 0 | 326 | 11 | 29.63 | 8.15 | 2-20 |
| A.Verma | 10 | 6 | 3 | 22 | 54 | 18.00 | - | - | 4 | - | 29.4 | 0 | 217 | 14 | 15.50 | 7.31 | 3-14 |
| F.L.Walker | 3 | 1 | 0 | 1 | 1 | 1.00 | - | - | - | - | 10.2 | 0 | 58 | 5 | 11.60 | 5.61 | 3-10 |
| J.G.Walker | 10 | 2 | 1 | 0* | 0 | 0.00 | - | - | 3 | - | 31 | 0 | 207 | 16 | 12.93 | 6.68 | 4-31 |
| B.M.Wheeler | 3 | 2 | 1 | 2 | 2 | 2.00 | - | - | 1 | - | 12 | 0 | 104 | 4 | 26.00 | 8.67 | 2-42 |
| B.R.Wheeler-Greenall | 2 | 2 | 2 | 7* | 12 | - | - | - | 1 | - | 5 | 0 | 41 | 2 | 20.50 | 8.20 | 1-15 |
| B.L.Wiggins | 7 | 7 | 0 | 45 | 132 | 18.85 | - | - | 2 | - | | | | | | | |
| W.S.A.Williams | 4 | 2 | 2 | 29* | 30 | - | - | - | 2 | - | 11 | 0 | 106 | 4 | 26.50 | 9.64 | 2-28 |
| G.H.Worker | 10 | 10 | 1 | 53* | 172 | 19.11 | - | 1 | 2 | - | | | | | | | |
| W.A.Young | 1 | 1 | 0 | 23 | 23 | 23.00 | - | - | - | - | | | | | | | |
| P.F.Younghusband | 10 | 6 | 2 | 21 | 37 | 9.25 | - | - | 7 | - | 28.3 | 1 | 181 | 9 | 20.11 | 6.35 | 2-19 |

## HIGHEST STRIKE RATES *(qualification 100 runs)*

| | | Runs | Balls | S/R | | | | Runs | Balls | S/R |
|---|---|---|---|---|---|---|---|---|---|---|
| F.H.Allen | W | 280 | 140 | 200 | | T.C.Bruce | CD | 267 | 163 | 163 |
| M.J.Santner | ND | 158 | 84 | 188 | | C.D.Fletcher | C | 305 | 190 | 160 |
| J.A.Clarkson | CD | 201 | 107 | 187 | | L.V.van Beek | W | 160 | 102 | 156 |
| T.W.M.Latham | C | 161 | 90 | 178 | | K.D.Clarke | ND | 228 | 149 | 153 |
| D.Cleaver | CD | 369 | 222 | 166 | | M.G.Bracewell | W | 478 | 321 | 148 |

## MOST ECONOMICAL BOWLING *(qualification 20 overs)*

| | | O | M | R | W | Ave | R/O |
|---|---|---|---|---|---|---|---|
| P.F.Younghusband | W | 28.3 | 1 | 181 | 9 | 20.11 | 6.35 |
| A.Ashok | A | 37 | 1 | 240 | 14 | 17.14 | 6.49 |
| J.G.Walker | ND | 31 | 0 | 207 | 16 | 12.93 | 6.68 |
| A.K.Kitchen | O | 36 | 0 | 242 | 11 | 22.00 | 6.72 |
| B.G.Lister | A | 35.3 | 0 | 242 | 11 | 22.00 | 6.82 |
| M.G.Bracewell | W | 25 | 0 | 171 | 6 | 28.50 | 6.84 |
| I.S.Sodhi | ND | 29 | 0 | 204 | 10 | 20.40 | 7.03 |
| T.D.Astle | C | 41 | 0 | 290 | 10 | 29.00 | 7.07 |
| L.H.Ferguson | A | 37.5 | 0 | 274 | 17 | 16.11 | 7.24 |
| H.B.Shipley | C | 35 | 0 | 254 | 18 | 14.11 | 7.26 |

# CAREER RECORDS

| | M | In | NO | HS | Runs | Ave | 100s | 50s | Ct | St | O | M | R | W | Ave | R/O | Best |
|---|---|---|---|---|---|---|---|---|---|---|---|---|---|---|---|---|---|
| F.H.Allen | 23 | 23 | 2 | 92* | 797 | 37.95 | - | 9 | 9 | 1 | 1 | 0 | 8 | 0 | - | 8.00 | - |
| A.Ashok | 10 | 6 | 4 | 6* | 18 | 9.00 | - | - | 4 | - | 37 | 1 | 240 | 14 | 17.14 | 6.49 | 3-8 |
| T.D.Astle | 78 | 40 | 20 | 37* | 364 | 18.20 | - | - | 30 | - | 239 | 1 | 1678 | 56 | 29.96 | 7.02 | 3-18 |
| M.T.M.M.J.Ave | 3 | 2 | 0 | 12 | 18 | 9.00 | - | - | - | - | | | | | | | |
| M.B.Bacon | 20 | 5 | 3 | 3* | 6 | 3.00 | - | - | 5 | - | 67.5 | 1 | 609 | 26 | 23.42 | 8.98 | 4-31 |
| G.K.Beghin | 8 | 6 | 0 | 32 | 69 | 11.50 | - | - | 3 | - | | | | | | | |
| H.K.Bennett | 73 | 14 | 10 | 12* | 30 | 7.50 | - | - | 15 | - | 240.4 | 1 | 1850 | 68 | 27.20 | 7.69 | 3-15 |
| J.J.N.P.Bhula | 1 | - | - | - | - | - | - | - | - | - | 2 | 0 | 17 | 0 | - | 8.50 | - |
| T.A.Blundell | 50 | 45 | 4 | 79 | 1013 | 24.70 | - | 8 | 33 | 2 | 0.1 | 0 | 4 | 0 | - | - | - |
| P.D.Bocock | 20 | 16 | 6 | 29* | 159 | 15.90 | - | - | 12 | 1 | | | | | | | |
| T.A.Boult | 36 | 9 | 7 | 7* | 23 | 11.50 | - | - | 15 | - | 120.2 | 2 | 958 | 32 | 29.93 | 7.96 | 3-35 |
| C.J.Bowes | 61 | 61 | 2 | 95 | 1642 | 27.83 | - | 13 | 31 | - | | | | | | | |
| J.C.T.Boyle | 20 | 20 | 1 | 69* | 417 | 21.94 | - | 1 | 8 | - | | | | | | | |
| D.A.J.Bracewell | 53 | 42 | 16 | 55* | 760 | 29.23 | - | 2 | 24 | - | 172.4 | 2 | 1439 | 58 | 24.81 | 8.33 | 3-21 |
| M.G.Bracewell | 99 | 89 | 21 | 141* | 2171 | 31.92 | 1 | 12 | 63 | 1 | 51 | 0 | 380 | 20 | 19.00 | 7.45 | 4-28 |
| C.J.Briggs | 5 | 5 | 0 | 6 | 13 | 2.60 | - | - | 2 | - | | | | | | | |
| N.T.Broom | 124 | 121 | 11 | 96* | 3037 | 27.60 | - | 19 | 51 | - | 25 | 0 | 241 | 8 | 30.12 | 9.64 | 2-19 |
| T.C.Bruce | 66 | 65 | 9 | 93* | 1768 | 31.57 | - | 12 | 43 | 1 | 22.4 | 0 | 195 | 6 | 32.50 | 8.60 | 3-9 |
| J.F.Carter | 25 | 23 | 3 | 75* | 348 | 17.40 | - | 2 | 12 | - | | | | | | | |
| L.J.Carter | 52 | 47 | 11 | 70* | 663 | 18.41 | - | 2 | 16 | - | | | | | | | |
| M.S.Chapman | 56 | 50 | 6 | 101 | 1337 | 30.38 | 1 | 11 | 22 | - | 52.5 | 0 | 416 | 15 | 27.73 | 7.87 | 3-22 |
| M.W.Chu | 23 | 11 | 4 | 21* | 94 | 13.42 | - | - | 4 | 6 | | | | | | | |
| K.D.Clarke | 16 | 16 | 1 | 71 | 336 | 22.40 | - | 1 | 6 | - | | | | | | | |
| J.A.Clarkson | 69 | 64 | 18 | 78 | 1288 | 28.00 | - | 6 | 27 | - | 26 | 0 | 238 | 8 | 29.75 | 9.15 | 2-21 |
| D.Cleaver | 74 | 70 | 7 | 114* | 1458 | 23.14 | 1 | 5 | 57 | 5 | | | | | | | |
| B.P.Coburn | 14 | 4 | 1 | 11* | 32 | 10.66 | - | - | 4 | - | 41 | 0 | 351 | 10 | 35.10 | 8.56 | 4-17 |
| D.P.Conway | 40 | 39 | 10 | 105* | 1607 | 55.41 | 2 | 12 | 19 | 1 | 2 | 0 | 14 | 2 | 7.00 | 7.00 | 2-14 |
| H.R.Cooper | 15 | 14 | 3 | 25* | 176 | 16.00 | - | - | 4 | - | 111.4 | 0 | 1037 | 38 | 27.28 | 9.29 | 3-22 |
| C.de Grandhomme | 98 | 91 | 21 | 86 | 1886 | 26.94 | - | 8 | 40 | - | 111.4 | 0 | 1037 | 38 | 27.28 | 9.29 | 3-22 |
| L.J.Delport | 12 | 4 | 1 | 6 | 12 | 4.00 | - | - | - | - | 37.1 | 0 | 318 | 11 | 28.90 | 8.56 | 2-20 |
| J.A.Duffy | 85 | 33 | 19 | 16 | 124 | 8.85 | - | - | 17 | - | 285.5 | 3 | 2508 | 89 | 28.17 | 8.77 | 5-18 |
| L.H.Ferguson | 30 | 14 | 5 | 30 | 118 | 13.11 | - | - | 6 | - | 97.5 | 1 | 761 | 28 | 27.17 | 7.78 | 4-19 |
| J.F.A.Field | 15 | 7 | 4 | 9 | 27 | 9.00 | - | - | 13 | - | 45.1 | 0 | 434 | 15 | 28.93 | 9.61 | 2-26 |
| J.L.Finnie | 53 | 41 | 7 | 71* | 596 | 17.52 | - | 1 | 21 | - | 37 | 0 | 329 | 8 | 41.12 | 8.89 | 4-11 |
| M.J.Fisher | 12 | 4 | 4 | 1* | 2 | - | - | - | 4 | - | 35 | 1 | 311 | 9 | 34.55 | 8.89 | 2-21 |
| C.D.Fletcher | 81 | 70 | 26 | 74* | 1573 | 35.75 | - | 8 | 46 | 17 | | | | | | | |
| L.I.Georgeson | 3 | 3 | 0 | 30 | 31 | 10.33 | - | - | 3 | - | | | | | | | |
| J.D.Gibson | 29 | 19 | 4 | 28 | 228 | 15.20 | - | - | 12 | - | 6 | 0 | 49 | 2 | 24.50 | 8.17 | 1-19 |
| J.M.Gibson | 4 | 2 | 0 | 2 | 2 | 1.00 | - | - | 4 | - | 11 | 0 | 103 | 2 | 51.50 | 9.36 | 1-20 |
| Z.N.Gibson | 13 | 7 | 3 | 9 | 30 | 7.50 | - | - | 8 | - | 32 | 0 | 281 | 8 | 35.12 | 8.78 | 3-17 |
| N.A.Greenwood | 2 | 2 | 0 | 14 | 23 | 11.50 | - | - | - | - | | | | | | | |
| M.J.Guptill | 68 | 64 | 11 | 120* | 2115 | 39.90 | 1 | 14 | 47 | - | 1 | 0 | 8 | 0 | - | 8.00 | - |
| B.R.Hampton | 45 | 39 | 3 | 64 | 556 | 15.44 | - | 3 | 26 | - | 28.4 | 0 | 244 | 9 | 27.11 | 8.51 | 3-21 |
| G.R.Hay | 23 | 20 | 5 | 76 | 467 | 31.13 | - | 4 | 6 | - | 0.3 | 0 | 12 | 0 | - | - | - |
| M.J.Hay | 7 | 6 | 1 | 29 | 55 | 11.00 | - | - | 6 | - | | | | | | | |
| M.W.Hay | 4 | 2 | 0 | 11 | 13 | 6.50 | - | - | - | - | | | | | | | |
| M.J.Henry | 60 | 38 | 19 | 44 | 263 | 13.84 | - | - | 23 | - | 205.3 | 3 | 1664 | 65 | 25.60 | 8.10 | 4-43 |
| B.J.Horne | 37 | 34 | 7 | 63 | 466 | 17.25 | - | 1 | 23 | 7 | 6 | 0 | 66 | 3 | 22.00 | 11.00 | 2-46 |
| M.G.Hughes | 2 | 2 | 0 | 12 | 17 | 8.50 | - | - | - | - | | | | | | | |
| L.C.Johnson | 17 | 16 | 0 | 72 | 228 | 14.25 | - | 1 | 8 | - | | | | | | | |
| T.M.Johnson | 21 | 18 | 5 | 54 | 281 | 21.61 | - | 2 | 10 | - | 4 | 0 | 38 | 1 | 38.00 | 9.50 | 1-22 |
| N.F.Kelly | 57 | 49 | 6 | 85 | 1085 | 25.23 | - | 7 | 26 | - | 199 | 0 | 1540 | 36 | 42.77 | 7.74 | 4-11 |
| A.K.Kitchen | 127 | 115 | 10 | 66 | 2214 | 21.08 | - | 7 | 56 | - | 295.4 | 3 | 2582 | 91 | 28.37 | 8.73 | 4-18 |
| S.C.Kuggeleijn | 90 | 62 | 26 | 41 | 628 | 17.44 | - | - | 35 | - | | | | | | | |
| T.W.M.Latham | 37 | 32 | 1 | 110 | 878 | 28.32 | 1 | 5 | 14 | 2 | 35 | 0 | 250 | 14 | 17.85 | 7.14 | 3-20 |
| J.R.Lennox | 10 | 2 | 2 | 17* | 23 | - | - | - | - | - | 3 | 0 | 22 | 3 | 7.33 | 7.33 | 2-4 |
| C.K.Leopard | 26 | 24 | 5 | 52 | 339 | 17.84 | - | 1 | 7 | - | 116.3 | 0 | 947 | 34 | 27.85 | 8.13 | 3-21 |
| B.G.Lister | 34 | 11 | 7 | 17* | 37 | 9.25 | - | - | 15 | - | | | | | | | |
| K.J.McClure | 22 | 22 | 1 | 40 | 313 | 14.90 | - | - | 2 | - | | | | | | | |
| C.E.McConchie | 75 | 60 | 9 | 84 | 1092 | 21.41 | - | 5 | 24 | - | 197 | 0 | 1482 | 47 | 31.53 | 7.52 | 3-18 |
| A.W.McKenzie | 7 | 5 | 2 | 11 | 24 | 8.00 | - | - | 3 | - | 15.1 | 0 | 111 | 3 | 37.00 | 7.32 | 2-28 |
| A.F.Milne | 40 | 16 | 9 | 18* | 118 | 16.85 | - | - | 8 | - | 138.3 | 5 | 1069 | 44 | 24.29 | 7.72 | 3-12 |
| D.J.Mitchell | 91 | 80 | 22 | 88* | 2067 | 35.63 | - | 9 | 46 | - | 127.4 | 0 | 1172 | 45 | 26.04 | 9.18 | 4-32 |
| T.Muller | 3 | 1 | 0 | 3 | 3 | 3.00 | - | - | 1 | - | 9 | 0 | 89 | 4 | 22.25 | 9.89 | 2-29 |
| J.D.S.Neesham | 57 | 47 | 12 | 59* | 911 | 26.02 | - | 1 | 20 | - | 143.5 | 1 | 1242 | 61 | 20.36 | 8.63 | 4-24 |
| O.R.Newton | 30 | 14 | 5 | 17 | 66 | 7.33 | - | - | 5 | - | 100.2 | 0 | 851 | 35 | 24.31 | 8.48 | 5-45 |

| | M | In | NO | HS | Runs | Ave | 100s | 50s | Ct | St | O | M | R | W | Ave | R/O | Best |
|---|---|---|---|---|---|---|---|---|---|---|---|---|---|---|---|---|---|
| H.M.Nicholls | 35 | 34 | 7 | 67* | 959 | 35.51 | - | 8 | 16 | - | | | | | | | |
| E.J.Nuttall | 68 | 17 | 13 | 13* | 42 | 10.50 | - | - | 20 | - | 225.1 | 2 | 1895 | 64 | 29.60 | 8.42 | 3-13 |
| R.R.O'Donnell | 52 | 43 | 16 | 68 | 1009 | 37.37 | - | 6 | 24 | - | 5 | 0 | 45 | 1 | 45.00 | 9.00 | 1-30 |
| W.T.O'Donnell | 10 | 9 | 1 | 50* | 220 | 27.50 | - | 1 | 8 | - | | | | | | | |
| W.P.O'Rourke | 3 | 1 | 0 | 10 | 10 | 10.00 | - | - | - | - | 7 | 0 | 52 | 0 | - | 7.43 | - |
| A.Y.Patel | 58 | 22 | 11 | 12* | 111 | 10.09 | - | - | 12 | - | 195.1 | 1 | 1604 | 60 | 26.73 | 8.22 | 3-20 |
| D.N.Phillips | 14 | 12 | 5 | 65 | 181 | 25.85 | - | 1 | 9 | - | 1 | 0 | 20 | 0 | - | 20.00 | - |
| G.D.Phillips | 53 | 51 | 5 | 116* | 1233 | 26.80 | 2 | 8 | 28 | 5 | 16 | 0 | 131 | 6 | 21.83 | 8.19 | 2-11 |
| M.D.Rae | 21 | 6 | 3 | 16 | 39 | 13.00 | - | - | 5 | - | 65 | 0 | 585 | 22 | 26.59 | 9.00 | 3-14 |
| S.H.A.Rance | 73 | 20 | 10 | 42 | 129 | 12.90 | - | - | 21 | - | 247.3 | 0 | 1977 | 91 | 21.72 | 7.99 | 5-19 |
| J.A.Raval | 47 | 46 | 2 | 70 | 954 | 21.68 | - | 5 | 24 | - | | | | | | | |
| R.Ravindra | 26 | 20 | 1 | 40* | 312 | 16.42 | - | - | 10 | - | 84 | 0 | 659 | 22 | 29.95 | 7.85 | 3-32 |
| M.J.G.Rippon | 40 | 32 | 12 | 38* | 381 | 19.05 | - | - | 9 | - | 145.4 | 1 | 1174 | 33 | 35.57 | 8.06 | 3-32 |
| T.B.Robinson | 8 | 8 | 0 | 65 | 143 | 17.87 | - | 1 | 2 | - | | | | | | | |
| H.D.Rutherford | 100 | 97 | 3 | 106 | 2338 | 24.87 | 1 | 11 | 33 | - | 11 | 0 | 84 | 2 | 42.00 | 7.64 | 1-6 |
| M.J.Santner | 28 | 25 | 8 | 92* | 530 | 31.17 | - | 2 | 7 | - | 100 | 0 | 724 | 25 | 28.96 | 7.24 | 2-15 |
| B.V.Sears | 21 | 7 | 5 | 12 | 27 | 13.50 | - | - | 7 | - | 66 | 2 | 510 | 27 | 18.88 | 7.73 | 4-16 |
| T.L.Seifert | 76 | 69 | 8 | 107 | 1660 | 27.21 | 1 | 8 | 63 | 11 | | | | | | | |
| H.B.Shipley | 29 | 18 | 3 | 39* | 291 | 19.40 | - | 1 | 13 | - | 68 | 1 | 549 | 23 | 23.86 | 8.07 | 4-23 |
| B.S.Smith | 32 | 28 | 3 | 80 | 550 | 22.00 | - | 3 | 13 | - | | | | | | | |
| N.G.Smith | 33 | 18 | 3 | 38* | 146 | 9.73 | - | - | 9 | - | 89.2 | 1 | 836 | 34 | 24.58 | 9.36 | 5-14 |
| I.S.Sodhi | 65 | 20 | 10 | 51 | 120 | 12.00 | - | 1 | 14 | - | 227.5 | 1 | 1679 | 59 | 28.45 | 7.37 | 3-12 |
| S.M.Solia | 45 | 40 | 9 | 75 | 687 | 22.16 | - | 3 | 13 | - | 59.3 | 0 | 578 | 13 | 44.46 | 9.71 | 2-16 |
| W.E.R.Somerville | 34 | 16 | 9 | 37* | 190 | 27.14 | - | - | 4 | - | 108.5 | 0 | 911 | 34 | 26.79 | 8.37 | 3-18 |
| T.G.Southee | 46 | 24 | 4 | 35* | 191 | 9.55 | - | - | 18 | - | 163.4 | 2 | 1337 | 58 | 23.05 | 8.17 | 3-15 |
| J.J.Tasman-Jones | 8 | 8 | 0 | 35 | 104 | 13.00 | - | - | 2 | - | 8 | 0 | 76 | 1 | 76.00 | 9.50 | 1-24 |
| R.M.ter Braak | 11 | 4 | 3 | 2* | 3 | 3.00 | - | - | 2 | - | 31.5 | 0 | 280 | 13 | 21.53 | 8.80 | 3-26 |
| B.M.Tickner | 58 | 10 | 7 | 3* | 8 | 2.66 | - | - | 14 | - | 211 | 2 | 1825 | 89 | 20.50 | 8.65 | 5-19 |
| L.V.van Beek | 87 | 49 | 16 | 61* | 453 | 13.72 | - | 1 | 45 | - | 266.3 | 2 | 2286 | 84 | 27.21 | 8.58 | 3-15 |
| A.Verma | 52 | 24 | 8 | 22 | 136 | 8.50 | - | - | 17 | - | 163.4 | 1 | 1410 | 62 | 22.74 | 8.62 | 4-27 |
| F.L.Walker | 7 | 2 | 1 | 3* | 4 | 4.00 | - | - | 3 | - | 24.1 | 0 | 142 | 10 | 14.20 | 5.88 | 3-10 |
| J.G.Walker | 22 | 5 | 1 | 16 | 22 | 5.50 | - | - | 6 | - | 63.2 | 0 | 437 | 27 | 16.18 | 6.90 | 4-31 |
| B.M.Wheeler | 52 | 35 | 17 | 47 | 335 | 18.61 | - | - | 14 | - | 184.3 | 2 | 1579 | 49 | 32.22 | 8.56 | 4-8 |
| B.R.Wheeler-Greenall | 2 | 2 | 2 | 7* | 12 | | - | - | 1 | - | 5 | 0 | 41 | 2 | 20.50 | 8.20 | 1-15 |
| B.L.Wiggins | 12 | 12 | 1 | 45 | 174 | 15.81 | - | - | 4 | - | | | | | | | |
| W.S.A.Williams | 37 | 13 | 10 | 29* | 76 | 25.33 | - | - | 27 | - | 82.1 | 0 | 787 | 30 | 26.23 | 9.58 | 5-12 |
| G.H.Worker | 122 | 117 | 9 | 106 | 2970 | 27.50 | 1 | 15 | 41 | - | 109.4 | 1 | 922 | 35 | 26.34 | 8.41 | 5-10 |
| W.A.Young | 72 | 68 | 4 | 101 | 1726 | 26.96 | 1 | 9 | 33 | - | | | | | | | |
| P.F.Younghusband | 27 | 11 | 5 | 21 | 50 | 8.33 | - | - | 15 | - | 76.3 | 1 | 550 | 20 | 27.50 | 7.19 | 2-16 |

# NEW ZEALAND DEVELOPMENT XI

A New Zealand Development XI played nine games against Provincial A teams in January and February. The squad was: M.W.T. Boyle *(Canterbury)*, J.M. Cumming *(Otago)*, S. Devereaux *(Auckland)*, E.M.I. Falanitule *(Auckland)*, Z.G. Foulkes *(Canterbury)*, D.B. Hancock *(Wellington)*, M.J. Hay *(Canterbury)*, C.G. Heaphy *(Central Districts)*, H.W.W. McIntyre *(Wellington)*, J.J. McKenzie *(Auckland)*, Mohammed Abbas *(Auckland)*, J.M. Parker *(Northern Districts)*, N.S. Perera *(Auckland)*, B.J. Pomare *(Northern Districts)*, T.J.G. Pringle *(Northern Districts)*, F.P. Raxworthy *(Central Districts)*, T.B. Robinson *(Wellington)*, Samrath Singh *(Auckland)*, A.H. Sidey *(Canterbury)*, P.C. Spencer *(Northern Districts)*, J.M. Tashkoff *(Wellington)*, J.T. Todd *(Auckland)*, K.L.D. Vishvaka *(Wellington)*, K.S. Weerasundara *(Wellington)*, O.J. White *(Northern Districts)*, Y.B. Zeb *(Auckland)*.

## WELLINGTON A v NEW ZEALAND DEVELOPMENT XI
*Kelburn Park, Wellington   6 January, 2022*

**New Zealand Development XI** 191-8 (T.J.G. Pringle 56*, M.W. Snedden 3-26) **v Wellington A** 72-1 (K.L.D. Vishvaka 40*) no result

## WELLINGTON A v NEW ZEALAND DEVELOPMENT XI
*Cello Basin Reserve, Wellington   7 January, 2022*

**Wellington A** 257-8 (N.A. Greenwood 77, J.J.N.P. Bhula 42, G.R. Severin 39, P.C. Spencer 4-53) **defeated New Zealand Development XI** 160 (O.J. White 29, J.W. Hartshorn 3-18, B.M. Johnson 3-24) by 97 runs

## CENTRAL DISTRICTS A v NEW ZEALAND DEVELOPMENT XI
*Nelson Park, Napier   10, 11, 12 January, 2022*

**Central Districts A** 330-5d (B.L. Wiggins 93, B.D. Schmulian 78, A.R. Schaw 56*. M.T.M.M.J. Ave 47*, N.C. Clark 38) and 180-9d (W.J. Clark 54, F.P. Raxworthy 46, M.G. Hughes 36, T.J.G. Pringle 6-50) **lost to New Zealand Development XI** 240-8d (J.M. Tashkoff 65, J.M. Cumming 59, M.W.T. Boyle 40, B.P. Stoyanoff 4-38) and 274-3 (J.M. Cumming 133*, M.W.T Boyle 88, J.M. Tashkoff 32*) by 7 wickets

## CANTERBURY A v NEW ZEALAND DEVELOPMENT XI
*Lincoln No.3   24 January, 2022*

**New Zealand Development XI** 294-5 (J.M. Cumming 131*, C.G. Heaphy 81) **lost to Canterbury A** 297-6 (O.C. Wilson 89, S.B. Davey 64*, R.A. Mariu 44, Samrath Singh 3-36) **by 4 wickets**

## OTAGO A v NEW ZEALAND DEVELOPMENT XI
*Lincoln No.3   25 January, 2022*

**Otago A** 334 (L.C. Johnson 186, J.M. Gibson 55, T.K. Parkes 42, Samrath Singh 5-34, Z.G. Foulkes 3-55) **defeated New Zealand Development XI** 315-8 (C.G. Heaphy 79*, T.J.G. Pringle 46, Z.G. Foulkes 44, M.W.T. Boyle 43) by 19 runs

## AUCKLAND A v NEW ZEALAND DEVELOPMENT XI
*Colin Maiden Park, Auckland   14 February, 2022*

**New Zealand Development XI** 264-7 (J.T. Todd 95, J.M. Tashkoff 65*, T.B. Robinson 46) **defeated Auckland A** 220 (L.M.J. Dasent 51, R. Mudford 42, C.J. Briggs 36, J.M. Tashkoff 4-34) by 44 runs

## AUCKLAND A v NEW ZEALAND DEVELOPMENT XI
*Colin Maiden Park, Auckland    15 February, 2022*

**Auckland A** 247 (R.W. Schierhout 51, M.P. O'Dowd 37, D. Kharel 30, H.W.W. McIntyre 3-39, J.M. Tashkoff 3-58) **defeated New Zealand Development XI** 218 (J.T. Todd 47, J.M. Tashkoff 43, T.B. Robinson 41, L.J. Delport 5-30) by 29 runs

## NORTHERN DISTRICTS A v NEW ZEALAND DEVELOPMENT XI
*St Paul's Collegiate, Hamilton    17 February, 2022*

**Northern Districts A** 341-7 (R.P.O. Drysdale 84, F.F. Lellman 82, K.R.S. Price 65, S.K. Patel 34) **lost to New Zealand Development XI** 343-3 (C.G. Heaphy 96, K.L.D. Vishvaka 84, J.J. McKenzie 70*, T.B. Robinson 51, O.J. White 34) by 7 wickets

## NORTHERN DISTRICTS A v NEW ZEALAND DEVELOPMENT XI
*St Paul's Collegiate, Hamilton    18 February, 2022*

**New Zealand Development XI** 352-8 (J.J. McKenzie 119, J.M. Tashkoff 74, K.L.D. Vishvaka 42) **defeated Northern Districts A** 260 Z.N. Gibson 42* S.K. Patel 36, E.W. Schreuder 36, B.J. Pomare 34, J.H. Brown 32, J.T. Todd  5-71) by 92 runs

*Photosport*

**NEW ZEALAND v NETHERLANDS** *(Third one-day international)* — **2021/22**
**Back row:** M.J. Henry, M.G Bracewell, G.H. Worker, D.A.J. Bracewell, I.S. Sodhi, K.A. Jamieson, H.M. Nicholls.
**Front row:** C. de Grandhomme, M.J. Guptill, L.R.P.L. Taylor, T.W.M. Latham *(captain)*, W.A. Young.

*Photosport*

**NEW ZEALAND WOMEN v INDIA** — **2021/22**
**Back row:** R.A. Mair, M.L. Green, H.M. Rowe, L.M.M. Tahuhu, J.M. Kerr, H.N.K. Jensen.
**Front row:** L.R. Down, K.J. Martin, A.C. Kerr, S.W. Bates, S.F.M. Devine *(captain)*,
A.E. Satterthwaite, F.L. Mackay, F.C. Jonas.

**AUCKLAND — 2021/22**

**Back row:** W.E.R. Somerville, G.H. Worker, K.A. Jamieson, S.M. Solia, B.G. Lister, J.D. Sussex, L.J. Delport.
**Front row:** S.B. Keene, W.T. O'Donnell, M.S. Chapman, R.R. O'Donnell *(captain)*, B.J. Horne, M.J. Guptill.

**CENTRAL DISTRICTS — 2021/22**

**Back row:** R. Walter *(coach)*, N. Arnold *(physiotherapist)*, J.R. Lennox, J.F.A. Field, B.M. Tickner, R.L. Toole, B.D. Schmulian, M.T.M.M.J. Ave, K. Malcolm *(strength and conditioning)*.
**Front row:** B.M. Wheeler, D.A.J. Bracewell, D. Cleaver, G.R. Hay *(captain)*, T.C. Bruce, B.L.Wiggins.

*Margot Butcher*

The scoreboard records Eden Carson's five-wicket haul for Otago against Wellington in the Hallyburton Johnstone Shield final at Queenstown.

*Photosport*

**CENTRAL DISTRICTS WOMEN — 2021/22**

**Back row:** J. Stewart *(strength and conditioning*, A.M. Gaging, G.K. Atkinson, K.J. Gaging, G. Sims, H.M. Rowe, M.J. Hansen, K.A. Tomlinson, G.L. Hermansson *(mental skills coach)*.

**Second row:** J.A. Watkins *(coach)*, M.J. Greig, C.S. Pedersen, C.L. Green, J.M. Watkin *(captain)*, M.S. Rees, A. Kumar.

### NORTHERN DISTRICTS — 2021/22

**Back row:** C. de Grandhomme, B.R. Hampton, S.C. Kuggeleijn, M.J. Santner, I.S. Sodhi.
**Front row:** H.R. Cooper, T.L. Seifert, J.G. Walker, J.A. Raval *(captain)*, M.J. Fisher, A. Verma, J.F. Carter.

### NORTHERN DISTRICTS WOMEN — 2021/22

**Back row:** S.R.H. Curtis, K.A. Knight, C.A. Gurrey, E.L. Baker, L.F. Boucher, L.H. Heaps, S.R. Naidu.
**Front row:** M.B. Templeton, K.G. Anderson, C.L. Agafili, E.A.J. Richardson *(captain)*, C.R. Sarsfield, A.M. Ewart, N.H. Patel.

Photosport

### OTAGO — 2021/22

**Back row:** S. Wilson *(physiotherapist)*, D.N. Phillips, J.L. Finnie, T. Muller, A.W. McKenzie,
M.W. Chu, M. Renwick, J.M. Gibson, D.D. Ebrahim *(coach)*, B.E.W. McCord *(assistant coach)*.
**Front row:** M.J.G. Rippon, M.D. Rae, J.A. Duffy, H.D. Rutherford *(captain)*, N.F. Kelly,
A.K. Kitchen.

Photosport

### OTAGO WOMEN — 2021/22

**Back row:** E.M. Campbell *(manager)*, H. Littleworth *(physiotherapist)*, P.R. Loggenberg,
S.A. Oldershaw, H.O. Cuttance, S.R. Wilson, C.G. Blakely, C.D. Cumming *(coach)*.
**Front row:** K.E. Ebrahim *(captain)*, P.M. Inglis, I.R. James, M.B.A. Lamplough, E.J. Carson,
E.J. Black, C.M. Deerness.

Photosport

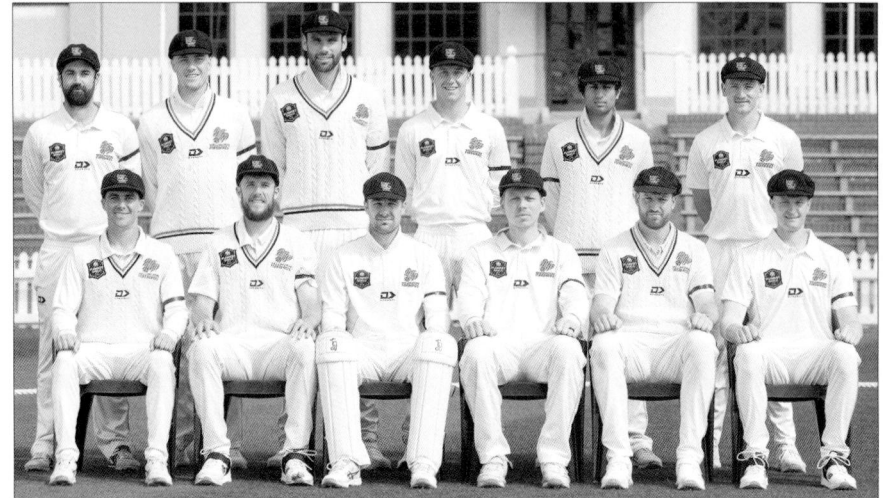

**WELLINGTON — 2021/22**

**Back row:** T.M. Johnson, F.H. Allen, M.W. Snedden, L.I. Georgeson, R. Ravindra, N.G. Smith.
**Front row:** P.F. Younghusband, J.D. Gibson, T.A. Blundell, M.G. Bracewell *(captain)*, I.G. McPeake, O.R. Newton.

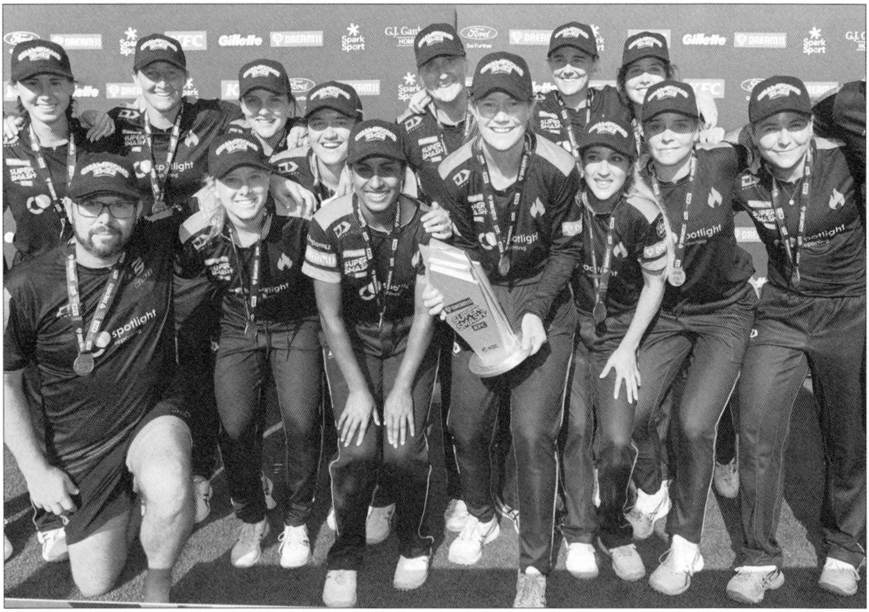

Photosport

**WELLINGTON WOMEN — 2021/22**

**Back row:** N.E. Codyre, S.F.M. Devine, A.C. Kerr, T.M.M. Newton, R.M. Burns, J.T. McFadyen, G.E. Plimmer.
**Front row:** L.R. Dry *(coach)*, L.M. Kasperek, M.P. Singh, M.L. Green *(captain)*, X.A.R. Jetly, J.M. Kerr, C.R. King.

Tom Bruce reaches two hundred in consecutive innings, for Central Districts against Auckland at McLean Park.

Ross Taylor on his way to the fastest century (49 balls) in New Zealand domestic one-day cricket, for Central Districts against Wellington at Pukekura Park.

# NATIONAL UNDER 19 TOURNAMENT

The National Under 19 tournament was held at Christchurch and Lincoln from 15 to 21 January 2022. The tournament consisted of five rounds of fifty-over matches and one round of Twenty20 games. Final positions were: Central Districts, Wellington, Canterbury, Northern Districts, Auckland, Otago.

FIRST ROUND

**AUCKLAND v WELLINGTON** *Wellington won by 14 runs*

**Wellington** 270-8 L.J.Bailey 67, O.T.Jackson 58, K.S.Weerasundara 31*, H.W.W.McIntyre 31, Mohammad Abbas 3-17)

**Auckland** 256 (J.T. Todd 97, K. Prakash 66, K.S. Weerasundara 3-58)


**CENTRAL DISTRICTS v NORTHERN DISTRICTS** *Central Districts won by 3 wkts*

**Northern Districts** 211 (N.J. Dovey 70, K.R.S. Price 45, L.J. Marconi 31, R.J. Restieaux 3-38)

**Central Districts** 212-7 (C.G. Heaphy 83*, B.L. Latter 46, J.L. Raxworthy 36)


**CANTERBURY v OTAGO** *Canterbury won by 31 runs*

**Canterbury** 292-9 (M.W.T. Boyle 116, M.C. McMillan 52, K.D. McKay 3-45)

**Otago** 261 (X.J. Chisholm 47, T. O'Connor 41, J.M. Cumming 36, K.D. McKay 35, O.D. Curtis 3-40, M.W.T Boyle 3-40)

SECOND ROUND

**AUCKLAND v OTAGO** *Auckland won by 4 wickets*

**Otago** 255-4 (J.M. Cumming 106*, J.T. Ingram 64, S.F. Kyle 44, Samrath Singh 3-49)

**Auckland** 256-6 (K. Prakash 58, H.S. Lowe 54, S.A. Prasad 34, Mohammad Abbas 31)


**CANTERBURY v NORTHERN DISTRICTS** *Canterbury won by 2 wickets*

**Northern Districts** 229 (K.R.S. Price 48, B. Vyver 32, M.W.T Boyle 3-53)

**Canterbury** 230-8 (O.D. Curtis 50, M.C. McMillan 38, K.M. Challu 35)


**CENTRAL DISTRICTS v WELLINGTON** *Central Districts won by 5 runs*

**Central Districts** 236 (B.L. Latter 75, F.P. Raxworthy 51, J.L. Raxworthy 43, K.S. Weerasundara 3-32, Y.S. Kalsi 3-52)

**Wellington** 231 (S.J. French 81, O.T. Jackson 79, T.M. Annand 3-19)


THIRD ROUND

**CANTERBURY v AUCKLAND** *Canterbury won by 5 wickets*

**Auckland** 285-9 (B.P. Harrison 81, H.S. Lowe 71, S.A. Prasad 37, S.J.G. Janett 3-34)

**Canterbury** 286-5 (M.W.T. Boyle 107, K.M. Challu 96)

**OTAGO v CENTRAL DISTRICTS**　　　　　*Central Districts won by 2 wickets*
**Otago** 221 (B.J. Culhane 48, J.M. Cumming 45, J.T. Ingram 33)
**Central Districts** 222-8 (J.M. Fleck 72*, T.A. Findlay 57, C.G. Heaphy 41, B. McCall 3-36)


**NORTHERN DISTRICTS v WELLINGTON**　　*Northern Districts won by 5 wickets*
**Wellington** 220-8 (F.S. Harding 62, O.T. Jackson 38, L.J. Bailey 33)
**Northern Districts** 222-5 (R. Patel 66, J.M. Parker 52, K.R.S. Price 41*, P.C. Spencer 33*)


FOURTH ROUND

**AUCKLAND v NORTHERN DISTRICTS**　　　*Auckland won by 7 runs (D/L)*
**Northern Districts** 275-7 (N.J. Dovey 116, R. Patel 79, L.J. Marconi 41, Y.B. Zeb 4-65)
**Auckland** 159-2 (B.P. Harrison 46*, H.S. Lowe 40, K. Prakash 39)


**CANTERBURY *v* CENTRAL DISTRICTS**　　　*Central Districts won by 2 wickets*
**Canterbury** 295-7 (M.W.T. Boyle 91, O.D. Curtis 47, S.T. Ashwin 45, K.M. Challu 32, J.M. Fleck 4-50)
**Central Districts** 296-8 (C.G. Heaphy 98, J.W. Rawnsley 64, J.L. Fairbrother 51, F.P. Raxworthy 49)


**OTAGO v WELLINGTON**　　　　　　　*Wellington won by 2 runs (D/L)*
**Otago** 303-7 (B.J. Culhane 85, T.G. Mockford 77, X.J. Chisholm 54, T. O'Connor 46)
**Wellington** 193-4 (S.J. French 79*, W.J. Stevenson 43, O.T. Jackson 30*)


FIFTH ROUND

**AUCKLAND v CENTRAL DISTRICTS**　　　*Central Districts won by 8 wickets*
**Auckland** 109 (S.A. Prasad 30, L.T. Carr 3-21)
**Central Districts** 113-2 (F.P. Raxworthy 59*)


**CANTERBURY v WELLINGTON**　　　　　*Wellington won by 40 runs*
**Wellington** 201 (O.T. Jackson 47, L.J. Bailey 31, M.R. Hamilton 3-31)
**Canterbury** 161 (M.W.T. Boyle 38, K.S. Weerasundara 5-23)


**NORTHERN DISTRICTS v OTAGO**　　　　　*Otago won by 7 wickets*
**Northern Districts** 195 (R. Patel 44, L. Direen 4-34)
**Otago** 199-3 (J.M. Cumming 81, T.G. Mockford 62*, J.T. Ingram 31*)

SIXTH ROUND

**OTAGO v WELLINGTON**　　　　　　　*Wellington won by 105 runs*
**Wellington** 184-6 (L.J. Bailey 44*, O.T. Jackson 43, P. Bonar 36, W.J. Stevenson 32)
**Otago** 79 (Z.A.J. Cumming 22, Y.S. Kalsi 4-13)

**CENTRAL DISTRICTS v CANTERBURY**          *Canterbury won by 25 runs*

**Canterbury** 144-6 (K.M. Challu 75)

**Central Districts** 119-8 (J.L. Raxworthy 21, S.J.G. Janett 3-20)


**AUCKLAND v NORTHERN DISTRICTS**          *Northern Districts won by 58 runs*

**Northern Districts** 171-8 (A.J. Wilton 44, R. Patel 36*, D.C. Laban-Jeffries 4-39, Samrath Singh 3-41)

**Auckland** 113 (J.T. Todd 35, L.W. Collett 3-18)

# HAWKE CUP

The major competition for the District (formerly Minor) Associations reverted to the Hawke Cup from 1999/00. The Fuji Xerox Cup since 1995/96, it was renamed the National District Championship in 1998/99. The competition was for the U-Bix Cup from 1985/86 to 1994/95.

Apart from tournaments in 1910/11, 1912/13 and 2000/01, the competition has always been on a challenge basis. To reduce the number of challenges received by the holders it was decided to pair off all the Minor Associations. This scheme commenced in the 1924/25 season, when the first three elimination matches were played. Since then numerous elimination matches have been staged to determine the right to challenge the holders of the cup.

At the end of 1999/00 it was decided to exclude the teams from the four major centres who had taken part in the tournament from 1995/96. As Dunedin Metropolitan held the trophy at the time, a national zonal tournament was held to find a new holder in 2000/01 and the challenge format resumed in 2001/02.

## Holders

Southland, 1910/11; won the tournament of six matches.
Southland, March 14, 1911, to March 25, 1913; resisted one challenge.
South Auckland, 1912/13; won the tournament of four matches.

*Challenges resisted*

Wanganui, December 26, 1913, to March 28, 1919 ............................ 5
Poverty Bay, March 28, 1919, to February 15, 1921 ......................... 4
Wairarapa, February 15, 1921, to December 26, 1921 ...................... 1
Rangitikei, December 26, 1921, to January 3, 1922 ......................... —
Nelson, January 3, 1922, to April 1, 1922 ......................................... 2
Wanganui, April 1, 1922, to January 22, 1924 ................................... 7
Nelson, January 22, 1924, to February 2, 1926 ................................. 7
Wanganui, February 2, 1926, to December 6, 1926 .......................... 2
Taranaki, December 6, 1926, to December 20, 1927 ......................... 3
Wanganui, December 20, 1927, to February 23, 1928 ...................... 2
Manawatu, February 23, 1928, to March 29, 1930 ............................. 9
Rangitikei, March 29, 1930, to December 15, 1930 ......................... —
Waikato, December 15, 1930, to January 2, 1933 ............................. 11
Nelson, January 2, 1933, to December 27, 1933 ............................... 2
Taranaki, December 27, 1933, to December 27, 1934 ....................... 3
Manawatu, December 27, 1934, to February 14, 1938 ..................... 15
Waikato, February 14, 1938, to January 30, 1940 ............................. 7
Manawatu, January 30, 1940, to April 7, 1947 .................................. 9
Hawke's Bay, April 7, 1947, to February 14, 1948 ........................... 1
Wanganui, February 14, 1948, to December 13, 1948 ...................... 1
Hutt Valley, December 13, 1948, to April 11, 1950 .......................... 7
Hawke's Bay, April 11, 1950, to January 3, 1951 .............................. 2
Wairarapa, January 3, 1951, to March 12, 1951 ................................ 1
Waikato, March 12, 1951, to December 10, 1951 ............................. —
Nelson, December 10, 1951, to December 30, 1952 .......................... 6
Wanganui, December 30, 1952, to December 28, 1955 .................... 13
Hutt Valley, December 28, 1955, to January 2, 1956 ....................... —
Northland, January 2, 1956, to December 8, 1956 ............................ 2
Waikato, December 8, 1956, to December 8, 1958 ............................ 9
Nelson, December 8, 1958, to February 1, 1965 .............................. 28
Manawatu, February 1, 1965, to January 24, 1967 ............................ 9
North Canterbury, January 24, 1967, to February 27, 1967 ............. —
Nelson, February 27, 1967, to December 17, 1967 ........................... —
Hutt Valley, December 17, 1967, to January 7, 1968 ........................ 1
Marlborough, January 7, 1968, to March 3, 1968 .............................. 1
Hawke's Bay, March 3, 1968, to February 23, 1969 ......................... 4

*Challenges resisted*

Waikato, February 23, 1969, to February 7, 1970 .............................. 3
Southland, February 7, 1970, to December 29, 1970 ......................... 1
Taranaki, December 29, 1970, to March 12, 1973 ........................... 12
Southland, March 12, 1973, to February 27, 1977 ........................... 14
Wairarapa, February 27, 1977, to February 5, 1979 .......................... 6
Nelson, February 5, 1979, to February 21, 1983 .............................. 14
Northland, February 21, 1983, to March 14, 1983 ........................... 2
Hawke's Bay, March 14, 1983, to February 20, 1984 ........................ 2
Northland, February 20, 1984, to February 27, 1984 ...................... —
Nelson, February 27, 1984, to February 24, 1986 .............................. 8
Hawke's Bay, February 24, 1986, to March 18, 1986 ....................... 1
Bay of Plenty, March 18, 1986, to February 23, 1987 ....................... 2
Hawke's Bay, February 23, 1987, to March 16, 1987 ...................... —
Bay of Plenty, March 16, 1987, to March 23, 1987 .......................... —
Southland, March 23, 1987, to March 15, 1988 ................................ 4
North Canterbury, March 15, 1988, to March 22, 1988 ................... —
Taranaki, March 22, 1988, to February 13, 1989 ............................. —
Northland, February 13, 1989, to February 27, 1989 ...................... —
Southland, February 27, 1989, to February 24, 1992 ....................... 15
Northland, February 24, 1992, to March 23, 1992 ............................. 1
Nelson, March 23, 1992, to March 15, 1993 ..................................... 3
Canterbury Country, March 15, 1993, to March 29, 1993 ................ —
Manawatu, March 29, 1993, to February 28, 1994 ............................. 2
Marlborough, February 28, 1994 to March 14, 1994 ...................... —
Taranaki, March 14, 1994 to January 29, 1996 .................................. 7
Central Otago, January 29, 1996 to February 12, 1996 .................... —
Nelson, February 12, 1996 to February 26, 1996 .............................. —
Hutt Valley, February 26, 1996 to January 20, 1997 ......................... 2
Nelson, January 20, 1997 to February 17, 1997 ................................ 1
Auckland-Manukau, February 17, 1997 to March 3, 1997 .............. —
Bay of Plenty, March 3, 1997 to January 26, 1998 ............................ 1
Wellington City, January 26, 1998 to February 9, 1998 ................... —
Manawatu, February 9, 1998 to February 23, 1998 ......................... —
Auckland-Waitakere, February 23, 1998 to March 9, 1998 ............. —
Northland, March 9, 1998 to February 8, 1999 ................................ 2
Wellington City, February 8, 1999 to February 22, 1999 ................ —
Canterbury Country, February 22, 1999 to January 24, 2000 ............ 2
South Canterbury, January 24, 2000 to February 7, 2000 ................ —
Dunedin Metropolitan, February 7, 2000 to March 26, 2001 ............ 3
Hamilton, March 26, 2001 to March 25, 2002 ................................. 4
Manawatu, March 25, 2002 to February 17, 2003 ........................... —
Hawke's Bay, February 17, 2003 to 3 March, 2003 ......................... —
Northland, 3 March, 2003 to 16 February, 2004 ............................... 2
Mid-Canterbury, 16 February, 2004 to 7 February, 2005 ................... 1
Canterbury Country, 7 February, 2005 to 7 March, 2005 ................... 1
Hamilton, 7 March, 2005 to 12 March, 2007 ................................... 5
Taranaki, 12 March, 2007 to 18 February, 2008 ............................... —
Canterbury Country, 18 February 2008 to 17 March, 2008 ............... 1
Hamilton, 17 March, 2008 to 16 February, 2009 ............................. —
Hawke's Bay, 16 February, 2009 to 8 February, 2010 ....................... 2
Manawatu, 8 February, 2010 to 15 March, 2010 ............................... 2
North Otago, 15 March, 2010 to 30 January, 2011 .......................... —
Otago Country, 30 January, 2011 to 13 February, 2011 ................... —
Marlborough, 13 February, 2011 to 13 March, 2011 ......................... 1
Hamilton, 13 March, 2011 to 27 January, 2013 ................................ 4
Bay of Plenty, 27 January, 2013 to 9 February, 2014 ........................ 4

*Challenges resisted*

Manawatu, 9 February, 2014 to 1 March, 2015 .................................... 4
Canterbury Country, 1 March, 2015 to 31 January, 2016 .................. 1
Buller, 31 January, 2016 to 14 February, 2016 ................................. —
North Otago, 14 February, 2016 to 27 February, 2016 ..................... —
Hawke's Bay, 27 February, 2016 to 13 March, 2016 ........................ —
Bay of Plenty, 13 March, 2016 to 29 January, 2018 .......................... 4
Counties-Manukau, 29 January, 2018 to 11 March, 2018 .................. 2
Southland, 11 March 2018 to 17 February, 2019 ............................... 1
Nelson, 17 February, 2019 to 3 March, 2019 .................................... —
Hawke's Bay, 3 March, 2019 to 17 March, 2019 .............................. —
Hamilton, 17 March, 2019 to 1 March, 2020 ..................................... 2
Canterbury Country, 1 March 2020 to 31 January 2021 .................... 1
Nelson, 31 January 2021 to 14 February 2021 .................................. —
North Otago, 14 February 2021 to 27 February 2021 ....................... —
Hawke's Bay, 27 February 2021 ......................................................... 3

# Career Aggregates

| BATTING | M | I | NO | HS | Runs | Ave |
|---|---|---|---|---|---|---|
| Leggat I.B. *(Nelson)*, 1948-68 ............................................. | 38 | 56 | 1 | 130 | 1968 | 35.78 |
| Reade L.B. *(Nelson)*, 1958-73 ............................................ | 35 | 57 | 2 | 117 | 1951 | 35.47 |
| Lowans G.E. *(Nelson)*, 1958-73 ........................................ | 30 | 48 | 1 | 148 | 1811 | 38.53 |
| Anderson R.W. *(Northland and Southland)*, 1970-77 ...... | 16 | 31 | 6 | 255 | 1773 | 70.92 |
| McVicar C.C. *(Manawatu)*, 1935-54 ................................ | 28 | 44 | 1 | 180 | 1754 | 40.79 |
| Spence D.V. *(Hawkes Bay and Nelson)*, 1949-67 .......... | 34 | 51 | 8 | 151 | 1574 | 36.60 |
| Hoskin R.N.*(Southland and Central Otago)*, 1978-96 .... | 31 | 35 | 4 | 162 | 1429 | 46.09 |
| Pierce R.A. *(Nelson)*, 1969-89 ......................................... | 24 | 31 | 2 | 150 | 1426 | 49.17 |
| Congdon B.E. *(Nelson)*, 1959-65 ..................................... | 19 | 28 | 2 | 133 | 1413 | 54.34 |
| Gallichan N. *(Manawatu)*, 1925-47 .................................. | 29 | 48 | 5 | 142 | 1409 | 32.76 |
| Hampton B.L. *(Nelson)*, 1960-75 ..................................... | 21 | 32 | 3 | 236 | 1391 | 49.26 |
| Hodgson W.G. *(Nelson)*, 1978-86 .................................... | 24 | 29 | 2 | 265 | 1348 | 49.92 |
| Norris W.E. *(Manawatu)*, 1926-47 ................................... | 42 | 61 | 6 | 84 | 1242 | 22.58 |
| Orton R.W. *(Rangitikei and Wanganui)*, 1911-26 .......... | 20 | 33 | 1 | 204 | 1222 | 38.18 |
| Hayward R.E. *(Nelson)*, 1979-89 ..................................... | 23 | 26 | 2 | 113 | 1115 | 46.45 |
| Holland C.A. *(Wanganui)*, 1912-28 .................................. | 24 | 38 | 4 | 111 | 1060 | 31.17 |
| Robinson G.G. *(Hamilton)*, 2000-09 ............................... | 11 | 16 | 1 | 268 | 1039 | 69.26 |
| Edwards G.N. *(Nelson)*, 1972-86 ..................................... | 24 | 30 | 2 | 236 | 1038 | 37.07 |
| Toynbee M.H. *(Nelson)*, 1974-81 ..................................... | 13 | 17 | 3 | 200* | 1031 | 73.64 |

| BOWLING | M | Runs | Wkts | Ave |
|---|---|---|---|---|
| Holland C.A. *(Wanganui)*, 1912-28 ................................................... | 24 | 2202 | 189 | 11.65 |
| Gallichan N. *(Manawatu)*, 1925-47 ................................................... | 29 | 2053 | 177 | 11.59 |
| Leggat I.B. *(Nelson)*, 1948-68 ........................................................... | 38 | 2149 | 134 | 16.03 |
| Spence D.V. *(Hawkes Bay and Nelson)*, 1949-67 ........................... | 34 | 1697 | 110 | 15.42 |
| Alabaster G.D. *(Thames Valley and Southland)*, 1961-79 ............... | 20 | 1508 | 102 | 14.78 |
| Newman J. *(Nelson)*, 1922-46 ............................................................ | 20 | 1348 | 97 | 13.89 |
| Alabaster J.C. *(Southland)*, 1955-74 ................................................. | 14 | 1223 | 92 | 13.29 |
| Bernau E.H.L. *(Wanganui and Hawkes Bay)*, 1912-28 ................... | 14 | 1009 | 90 | 11.21 |

## Highest Individual Innings

| | | | | |
|---|---|---|---|---|
| 272* | Kinzett C.A. | Nelson v Marlborough | Nelson | 1933/34 |
| 268 | Robinson G.G. | Hamilton v Northland | Hamilton | 2005/06 |
| 265 | Hodgson W.G. | Nelson v Taranaki | Nelson | 1983/84 |
| 264 | Everest J.K. | Waikato v Manawatu | Hamilton | 1956/57 |
| 255 | Anderson R.W. | Southland v Ashburton County | Invercargill | 1976/77 |
| 242 | Edmondson M.J. | Hawke's Bay v Nelson | Nelson | 2018/19 |
| 236 | Hampton B.L. | Nelson v Waikato | Nelson | 1963/64 |
| 236 | Edwards G.N. | Nelson v North Canterbury | Nelson | 1984/85 |
| 229 | Douglas M.W. | Nelson v Southland | Nelson | 1992/93 |

## Best Bowling in an Innings

| | | | | |
|---|---|---|---|---|
| 10-35 | Holland C.A. | Wanganui v South Taranaki | Wanganui | 1922/23 |
| 9-38 | Williams W.S.A. | Canterbury Country v Buller | Rangiora | 2015/16 |
| 9-103 | Jordan A.B. | Taranaki v Hutt Valley | New Plymouth | 1971/72 |
| 8-9 | Clough R. | Waikato v Bay of Plenty | Hamilton | 1938/39 |
| 8-20 | Andrews S.L. | Hamilton v Northland | Hamilton | 2001/02 |
| 8-25 | Smith J.D. | Waikato v Horowhenua | Hamilton | 1969/70 |
| 8-25 | Jordan A.B. | Taranaki v Franklin | New Plymouth | 1971/72 |
| 8-26 | Haycock R.S. | Nelson v Marlborough | Nelson | 1924/25 |

## Best Bowling in a Match

| | | | | |
|---|---|---|---|---|
| 14-79 | Holland C.A. | Wanganui v South Taranaki | Wanganui | 1922/23 |
| 14-89 | Jordan A.B. | Taranaki v Franklin | New Plymouth | 1971/72 |
| 14-133 | Upston I.A. | Hutt Valley v Wanganui | Wanganui | 1955/56 |
| 14-149 | Sulzberger G.P. | Taranaki v Manawatu | New Plymouth | 1994/95 |

# HAWKE'S BAY v MANAWATU

## Hawke Cup

*at Nelson Park, Napier on 28, 29, 30 January, 2022*
*Toss : Hawke's Bay.  Umpires : D.R. Morrow & G.M. Walklin*
*Close of play: 1st day: Manawatu 184-6, Cleaver 19, Richards 0; 2nd day: Hawke's Bay 61-0, Whitley 29, Clark 27*
**Match drawn**

## MANAWATU

| FIRST INNINGS | Runs | Mins | Balls | 6s | 4s |
|---|---|---|---|---|---|
| M.G.Hughes c Wiggins b Schaw | 54 | 144 | 142 | - | 3 |
| B.J.Small c Weeks b Clark | 30 | 61 | 38 | 1 | 2 |
| M.T.M.M.J.Ave† b Watson | 4 | 25 | 17 | - | - |
| A.W.Noema-Barnett b Schaw | 9 | 93 | 68 | - | - |
| C.G.Heaphy c Wiggins b Clark | 37 | 195 | 140 | - | 1 |
| T.A.McGrath c Leopard b Schmulian | 20 | 109 | 109 | - | 2 |
| B.S.Cleaver c Dudding b Stoyanoff | 60 | 242 | 174 | - | 5 |
| T.J.Richards* lbw b Schaw | 11 | 64 | 52 | - | 2 |
| R.L.Toole c & b Schaw | 34 | 166 | 149 | - | 3 |
| J.T.Harris lbw b Schaw | 11 | 66 | 36 | - | - |
| R.B.J.Fulton not out | 0 | 16 | 12 | - | - |
| Extras (b 3, lb 16, w 1) | 20 | | | | |
| **TOTAL** (156.1 overs) | **290** | 623 | | | |

## HAWKE'S BAY

| | Runs | Mins | Balls | 6s | 4s |
|---|---|---|---|---|---|
| J.D.Whitley c Noema-Barnett b Harris | 68 | 312 | 244 | - | 3 |
| W.J.Clark c Ave b Fulton | 34 | 195 | 154 | - | 3 |
| B.D.Schmulian c Ave b Toole | 64 | 166 | 124 | - | 6 |
| B.L.Wiggins not out | 72 | 131 | 98 | 1 | 9 |
| C.K.Leopard not out | 46 | 82 | 72 | - | 7 |
| A.R.Schaw* | | | | | |
| D.R.Thompson | | | | | |
| T.J.Watson | | | | | |
| K.A.Weeks† | | | | | |
| L.R.Dudding | | | | | |
| B.P.Stoyanoff | | | | | |
| Extras (b 1, lb 2, nb 5) | 8 | | | | |
| **TOTAL** (114.3 overs) (3 wkts) | **292** | 444 | | | |

| Bowling | O | M | R | W |
|---|---|---|---|---|
| **HAWKE'S BAY** | | | | |
| Dudding | 27 | 5 | 79 | 0 |
| Stoyanoff | 30 | 9 | 62 | 1 |
| Watson | 16 | 4 | 27 | 1 |
| Clark | 24 | 13 | 30 | 2 |
| Schaw | 43.1 | 22 | 47 | 5 |
| Schmulian | 16 | 4 | 26 | 1 |
| **MANAWATU** | | | | |
| Toole | 28.3 | 14 | 62 | 1 |
| Harris | 25 | 5 | 64 | 1 |
| Fulton | 12 | 3 | 39 | 1 |
| McGrath | 12 | 6 | 23 | 0 |
| Richards | 18 | 8 | 46 | 0 |
| Noema-Barnett | 18 | 7 | 49 | 0 |
| Cleaver | 1 | 0 | 6 | 0 |

**Fall of Wickets**

| | M | HB |
|---|---|---|
| | 1st | 1st |
| 1st | 50 | 78 |
| 2nd | 59 | 159 |
| 3rd | 99 | 187 |
| 4th | 108 | - |
| 5th | 148 | - |
| 6th | 179 | - |
| 7th | 204 | - |
| 8th | 255 | - |
| 9th | 281 | - |
| 10th | 290 | - |

# HAWKE'S BAY v BAY OF PLENTY

**Hawke Cup**

*at Nelson Park, Napier on 11, 12, 13 February, 2022*
*Toss : Bay of Plenty. Umpires : S.R. Oliver & T.S. Shirriffs*
*Close of play: 1st day: Bay of Plenty 155-5, White 69, Drysdale 34; 2nd day: no play*
**Match drawn**

## BAY OF PLENTY

| FIRST INNINGS | Runs | Mins | Balls | 6s | 4s |
|---|---|---|---|---|---|
| N.J.Dovey c Thompson b Dudding | 0 | 2 | 2 | - | - |
| T.J.Bettleheim c Leopard b Stoyanoff | 10 | 24 | 14 | - | 1 |
| B.J.McKenzie c Weeks b Dudding | 10 | 48 | 29 | - | 1 |
| F.F.Lellman lbw b Clark | 13 | 52 | 24 | - | 1 |
| O.J.White not out | 69 | 178 | 134 | - | 3 |
| T.J.G.Pringle b Schaw | 18 | 38 | 21 | - | - |
| R.P.O.Drysdale not out | 34 | 113 | 94 | - | 2 |
| B.J.Pomare*† | | | | | |
| D.P.Crombie | | | | | |
| D.B.Hancock | | | | | |
| L.W.Collett | | | | | |
| Extras (w 1) | 1 | | | | |
| **TOTAL** (53 overs) (5 wkts) | **155** | 229 | | | |

## HAWKE'S BAY

J.D.Whitley
W.J.Clark
C.K.Leopard
B.Z.Meehan
A.R.Schaw*
D.R.Thompson
T.J.Watson
K.A.Weeks†
T.A.Findlay
L.R.Dudding
B.P.Stoyanoff

| Bowling | O | M | R | W |
|---|---|---|---|---|
| **HAWKE'S BAY** | | | | |
| Dudding | 16 | 5 | 28 | 2 |
| Stoyanoff | 10 | 1 | 28 | 1 |
| Clark | 6 | 0 | 23 | 1 |
| Watson | 5 | 0 | 20 | 0 |
| Schaw | 14 | 1 | 49 | 1 |
| Findlay | 2 | 0 | 7 | 0 |

| Fall of Wickets | |
|---|---|
| | BOP |
| | 1st |
| 1st | 0 |
| 2nd | 16 |
| 3rd | 30 |
| 4th | 46 |
| 5th | 86 |
| 6th | - |
| 7th | - |
| 8th | - |
| 9th | - |
| 10th | - |

# WOMEN'S CRICKET

*Compiled by Catherine Campbell*

With Covid restrictions present in New Zealand, the 2021/22 domestic and international programmes were still able to be completed in their entirety, albeit with a delayed start for both Auckland and Northern Districts in the Hallyburton Johnstone Shield.

New Zealand's World Cup preparation started in September with a tour to England, where they lost the Twenty20 series 2-1 and the one-day series 4-1, followed by a series against India, where New Zealand won the only Twenty20 and the one-day series 4-1.

The ICC Women's Cricket World Cup was the highlight of the summer with Australia defeating England in a high-scoring final at Hagley Oval, Christchurch. The White Ferns beat Bangladesh, India and Pakistan in round-robin play but were unable to qualify for the semi-finals and finished the tournament in sixth place. Molly Penfold, the right-arm pace bowler from Auckland, made her White Ferns debut during the year.

Otago won the Hallyburton Johnstone Shield beating Wellington in the final at Queenstown, with captain Kate Ebrahim top scoring with 92 off 138 balls and Eden Carson taking 5-17 with her right-arm off-spin. Ebrahim was the leading run scorer in the competition with 451 runs and Nensi Patel from Northern Districts took the most wickets with 18.

In the Super Smash competition grand final, Wellington beat Otago by 75 runs at Hamilton. The highlight of the match was Sophie Devine's rollicking 92 off 62 balls. Suzie Bates was the leading run scorer in the competition with 504 runs while Leigh Kasperek *(Wellington)* took the most wickets with 20.

Central Districts won the national Under 19 tournament played at Lincoln University but due to Covid the Gillette Venus Cup and the Primary School Cup were not played.

Contracted players were: Auckland: Skye Bowden, Izzy Gaze, Holly Huddleston, Arlene Kelly, Tariel Lamb, Regina Lili'i, Katie Perkins, Anna Peterson, Jesse Prasad.

Canterbury: Melissa Banks, Natalie Cox, Abigale Gerken, Laura Hughes, Emma Kench, Kirsty Nation, Jacinta Savage, Jessica Simmons, Kate Sims.

Central Districts: Georgia Atkinson, Emily Cunningham, Natalie Dodd, Kate Gaging, Mikaela Greig, Melissa Hansen, Monique Rees, Kerry Tomlinson, Jess Watkin.

Northern Districts: Sam Curtis, Lucy Boucher, Caitlin Gurrey, Georgina Harris, Lauren Heaps, Kayley Knight, Eimear Richardson, Charlotte Sarsfield, Makayla Templeton.

Otago: Emma Black, Caitlin Blakely, Eden Carson, Kate Ebrahim, Polly Inglis, Bella James, Felicity Leydon-Davis, Molly Loe, Sophie Oldershaw.

Wellington: Rebecca Burns, Natasha Codyre, Deanna Doughty, Rose Fenton, Xara Jetly, Caitlin King, Beth Molony, Georgia Plimmer, Maneka Singh.

## PLAYER OF THE YEAR

**Amelia Kerr** *(Wellington)* is the Player of the Year. She was unavailable for the tour to England but her performances in the home series against India and at the World Cup resulted in her being named the ANZ one-day player of the year. In 12 one-day games she scored 554 runs at 61, with a highest score of 119 not out, and took 16 wickets at an economy rate of 4.98.

Kerr scored 178 runs at 59.33 in the Hallyburton Johnstone Shield and took 14 wickets at 11.14 with an economy rate of 3.90. In the Super Smash she scored 346 runs at 34.60 and a strike rate of 115 with a highest score of 71. She also took 17 wickets at 11.29 with an economy rate of 4.57. She was the leading player across both domestic competitions and the White Ferns' home international programme.

## PROMISING PLAYER

**Nensi Patel** *(Northern Districts)* is the Promising Player of the Year. The right-arm off-spinner was the leading wicket taker in the Hallyburton Johnstone Shield with 18 wickets at 17.83, best bowling figures of 6-25 and an economy rate of 4.92. In the Super Smash Twenty 20 competition she took 11 wickets at 21.36, with best bowling figures of 3-13 and an economy rate of 6.53. Patel was also in form with the bat, making 236 runs at 78.67 in the Hallyburton Johnstone Shield, with a highest score of 71 not out.

# NEW ZEALAND IN ENGLAND

The White Ferns undertook a three-match Twenty20 and five-match one-day international tour of England in September. To allow for any possible Covid issues, sixteen players were selected. Rosemary Mair withdrew due to injury ahead of departure and was replaced by Auckland's Molly Penfold, who made her debut in the third one-day game at Leicester. Amelia Kerr was unavailable for the tour.

England won the Twenty20 Series with the White Ferns fighting back to lock up the series 1-1 before England won the decider at Taunton. England also won the one-day series 4-1. They led 2-nil before the White Ferns won the third game at Leicester. However, New Zealand lost the fourth game and then suffered their biggest defeat, losing by 203 runs in the fifth and final match at Canterbury.

Amy Satterthwaite was the leading run scorer in the one-day games with 173 runs at an average of 43.25 and Hannah Rowe was the leading wicket taker with ten wickets, including 4-47 in the fourth game at Derby.

The New Zealand squad was: Sophie Devine *(captain)*, Maddy Green, Leigh Kasperek, Jess Kerr, Jessie McFadyen, Thamsyn Newton *(Wellington)*, Lauren Down, Molly Penfold *(Auckland)*, Brooke Halliday *(Northern Districts)*, Claudia Green, Hannah Rowe *(Central Districts)*, Amy Satterthwaite, Lea Tahuhu *(Canterbury)*, Suzie Bates, Hayley Jensen, Katey Martin *(Otago)*.

Coach, Bob Carter; Batting coach, Rob Nicol; Bowling coach, Jacob Oram; Manager, Belinda Muller; Physiotherapist, Zoe Russell; Trainer, Scott Wrenn.

## New Zealand One-day International Averages

| BATTING | M | I | NO | HS | Agg | Ave | 100s | 50s | Ct | St | SR |
|---|---|---|---|---|---|---|---|---|---|---|---|
| A.E. Satterthwaite | 5 | 5 | 1 | 79* | 173 | 43.25 | - | 2 | 2 | - | 67 |
| M.L. Green | 5 | 5 | 1 | 70* | 120 | 30.00 | - | 1 | 2 | - | 63 |
| S.F.M. Devine | 5 | 5 | 0 | 41 | 109 | 21.80 | - | - | - | - | 64 |
| B.M. Halliday | 5 | 5 | 0 | 29 | 109 | 21.80 | - | - | 3 | - | 72 |
| K.J. Martin | 5 | 5 | 1 | 65* | 87 | 21.75 | - | 1 | 7 | - | 75 |
| L.M.M. Tahuhu | 4 | 4 | 1 | 25 | 49 | 16.33 | - | - | 1 | - | 128 |
| L.R. Down | 5 | 5 | 0 | 27 | 72 | 14.40 | - | - | 2 | - | 53 |
| L.M. Kasperek | 4 | 2 | 0 | 15 | 25 | 12.50 | - | - | 1 | - | 55 |
| J.M. Kerr | 3 | 3 | 2 | 6* | 12 | 12.00 | - | - | 1 | - | 109 |
| S.W. Bates | 5 | 5 | 0 | 28 | 57 | 11.40 | - | - | 1 | - | 54 |
| H.M. Rowe | 4 | 4 | 0 | 20 | 43 | 10.75 | - | - | - | - | 70 |
| H.N.K. Jensen | 3 | 3 | 0 | 19 | 21 | 7.00 | - | - | - | - | 77 |
| M.M. Penfold | 2 | 1 | 1 | 0* | 0 | - | - | - | - | - | 0 |

| BOWLING | O | M | R | W | Ave | Best | R/O |
|---|---|---|---|---|---|---|---|
| L.M.M. Tahuhu | 39 | 1 | 180 | 9 | 20.00 | 5-37 | 4.62 |
| H.M. Rowe | 38 | 2 | 200 | 10 | 20.00 | 4-47 | 5.26 |
| L.M. Kasperek | 31 | 1 | 137 | 5 | 27.40 | 3-31 | 4.42 |
| S.F.M. Devine | 44 | 2 | 241 | 7 | 34.42 | 2-29 | 5.48 |
| J.M. Kerr | 28.3 | 2 | 120 | 3 | 40.00 | 3-42 | 4.21 |
| M.M. Penfold | 17 | 1 | 85 | 2 | 42.50 | 2-42 | 5.00 |
| H.N.K. Jensen | 29.3 | 3 | 134 | 2 | 67.00 | 1-40 | 4.54 |
| A.E. Satterthwaite | 14 | 0 | 89 | 1 | 89.00 | 1-34 | 6.36 |

# England One-day International Averages

| BATTING | M | I | NO | HS | Agg | Ave | 100s | 50s | Ct | St | SR |
|---|---|---|---|---|---|---|---|---|---|---|---|
| K.H. Brunt | 2 | 2 | 1 | 49* | 92 | 92.00 | - | - | - | - | 61 |
| D.N. Wyatt | 4 | 4 | 2 | 63* | 143 | 71.50 | - | 1 | 1 | - | 102 |
| H.C. Knight | 5 | 5 | 0 | 101 | 214 | 42.80 | 1 | 1 | 3 | - | 88 |
| T.T. Beaumont | 5 | 5 | 0 | 102 | 175 | 35.00 | 1 | - | 3 | - | 74 |
| L. Winfield-Hill | 5 | 5 | 0 | 43 | 140 | 28.00 | - | - | 2 | - | 67 |
| A.E. Jones | 5 | 5 | 0 | 60 | 124 | 24.80 | - | 1 | 2 | 1 | 79 |
| N.E. Farrant | 2 | 2 | 0 | 22 | 34 | 17.00 | - | - | - | - | 69 |
| S.I.R. Dunkley | 5 | 5 | 1 | 33* | 55 | 13.75 | - | - | - | - | 67 |
| N.R. Sciver | 4 | 4 | 0 | 39 | 53 | 13.25 | - | - | 2 | - | 75 |
| K.L. Cross | 4 | 3 | 0 | 29 | 35 | 11.66 | - | - | - | - | 72 |
| C.E. Dean | 5 | 3 | 0 | 10 | 19 | 6.33 | - | - | 1 | - | 50 |
| S. Ecclestone | 5 | 4 | 1 | 8 | 17 | 5.66 | - | - | 2 | - | 56 |
| A. Shrubsole | 2 | 1 | 1 | 6* | 6 | - | - | - | 1 | - | 120 |
| F.R. Davies | 2 | 1 | 1 | 0* | 0 | - | - | - | 2 | - | 0 |

| BOWLING | O | M | R | W | Ave | Best | R/O |
|---|---|---|---|---|---|---|---|
| K.H. Brunt | 18 | 6 | 44 | 5 | 8.80 | 4-22 | 2.44 |
| H.C. Knight | 9 | 0 | 42 | 3 | 14.00 | 3-24 | 4.67 |
| C.E. Dean | 41.2 | 1 | 192 | 10 | 19.20 | 4-36 | 4.65 |
| K.L. Cross | 32.3 | 1 | 156 | 8 | 19.50 | 3-43 | 4.80 |
| A. Shrubsole | 13 | 0 | 63 | 3 | 21.00 | 2-43 | 4.85 |
| F.R. Davies | 15 | 0 | 86 | 3 | 28.66 | 2-46 | 5.73 |
| S. Ecclestone | 47 | 3 | 184 | 6 | 30.66 | 2-31 | 3.91 |
| N.R. Sciver | 26 | 1 | 95 | 3 | 31.66 | 2-10 | 3.65 |
| N.E. Farrant | 14.5 | 1 | 68 | 2 | 34.00 | 1-23 | 4.58 |

**ENGLAND A v NEW ZEALAND**
*At County Ground, Derby     23 August, 2021*

**New Zealand** 223 (S.W. Bates 70, K.J. Martin 52) **lost to England A** 226-6 (B.F. Smith 53, A.N. Davidson-Richards 43*, G.E. Scrivens 39) by 4 wickets

NZC

# ENGLAND v NEW ZEALAND  First Twenty20 International

*at County Ground, Chelmsford on 1 September, 2021*
*Toss : New Zealand. Umpires : G.D. Lloyd & S. Redfern*
**England won by 46 runs**

New Zealand won the toss in their first game of the season and decided to field but saw Beaumont and Wyatt get away to a brisk start. Wyatt fell in the third over but Beaumont got good support from Sciver, Jones and Dunkley in partnerships of 43, 53 and 53. Beaumont reached fifty off 41 balls and was dismissed off the penultimate delivery of the innings for 97.

New Zealand had lost both openers by the third over and found it difficult to recover. Satterthwaite made 43 off 31 balls before she was sixth out at 82. No other player reached twenty as England won comfortably by 46 runs.

## ENGLAND

| | Runs | Mins | Balls | 6s | 4s |
|---|---|---|---|---|---|
| T.T.Beaumont c Halliday | | | | | |
| b Jensen | 97 | 79 | 65 | 1 | 13 |
| D.N.Wyatt st Martin b Kasperek | 14 | 14 | 8 | - | 3 |
| N.R.Sciver* b Jensen | 14 | 28 | 16 | 1 | - |
| A.E.Jones† st Martin | | | | | |
| b Satterthwaite | 31 | 16 | 15 | - | 6 |
| S.I.R.Dunkley not out | 23 | 23 | 17 | - | 2 |
| E.L.Lamb not out | 0 | 1 | 0 | - | - |
| K.H.Brunt | | | | | |
| S.Ecclestone | | | | | |
| S.Glenn | | | | | |
| M.K.Villiers | | | | | |
| N.E.Farrant | | | | | |
| Extras (w 4, nb 1) | 5 | | | | |
| **TOTAL** (20 overs) (4 wkts) | **184** | 79 | | | |

## NEW ZEALAND

| | Runs | Mins | Balls | 6s | 4s |
|---|---|---|---|---|---|
| S.F.M.Devine* lbw b Farrant | 2 | 9 | 7 | - | - |
| S.W.Bates b Brunt | 1 | 13 | 5 | - | - |
| A.E.Satterthwaite c Villiers | | | | | |
| b Brunt | 43 | 46 | 31 | - | 8 |
| M.L.Green c Farrant | | | | | |
| b Ecclestone | 19 | 22 | 18 | 1 | 2 |
| K.J.Martin† b Glenn | 7 | 11 | 7 | - | 1 |
| B.M.Halliday b Villiers | 2 | 6 | 4 | - | - |
| H.N.K.Jensen b Glenn | 16 | 14 | 11 | - | 3 |
| T.M.M.Newton run out | 14 | 23 | 12 | - | 1 |
| H.M.Rowe c Jones b Sciver | 11 | 9 | 8 | - | 2 |
| J.M.Kerr not out | 12 | 10 | 8 | 1 | 1 |
| L.M.Kasperek st Jones | | | | | |
| b Ecclestone | 0 | 3 | 2 | - | - |
| Extras (b 8, lb 1, w 2) | 11 | | | | |
| **TOTAL** (18.5 overs) | **138** | 81 | | | |

| Bowling | O | M | R | W |
|---|---|---|---|---|
| **NEW ZEALAND** | | | | |
| Kerr | 2 | 0 | 20 | 0 |
| Devine | 4 | 0 | 24 | 0 |
| Kasperek | 4 | 0 | 54 | 1 |
| Rowe | 3 | 0 | 29 | 0 |
| Jensen | 4 | 0 | 26 | 2 |
| Satterthwaite | 3 | 0 | 31 | 1 |
| **ENGLAND** | | | | |
| Brunt | 3 | 0 | 9 | 2 |
| Farrant | 4 | 1 | 24 | 1 |
| Ecclestone | 3.5 | 0 | 24 | 2 |
| Sciver | 3 | 0 | 31 | 1 |
| Glenn | 3 | 0 | 24 | 2 |
| Villiers | 2 | 0 | 17 | 1 |

| Fall of Wickets | E | NZ |
|---|---|---|
| 1st | 31 | 4 |
| 2nd | 74 | 4 |
| 3rd | 127 | 52 |
| 4th | 180 | 67 |
| 5th | - | 70 |
| 6th | - | 82 |
| 7th | - | 98 |
| 8th | - | 116 |
| 9th | - | 133 |
| 10th | - | 138 |

# ENGLAND v NEW ZEALAND      Second Twenty20 International

*at County Ground, Hove on 4 September, 2021*
*Toss : New Zealand.  Umpires : N.J. Llong & M.J. Saggers*
**New Zealand won by 4 wickets**

New Zealand again won the toss and fielded. Wyatt scored 35 off 29 balls but the other top-order batsmen went cheaply. Dunkley and Bouchier provided some support but the New Zealand bowlers were able to restrict England to 127-7.

Devine, with 50 off 41 balls, dominated New Zealand's reply, being third out at 100 in the fifteenth over. New Zealand lost three more wickets before the target was reached but two lots of two wides off Farrant settled the issue. The series was now level at 1-1.

## ENGLAND

| | Runs | Mins | Balls | 6s | 4s |
|---|---|---|---|---|---|
| D.N.Wyatt c Kerr b Rowe | 35 | 67 | 29 | - | 4 |
| T.T.Beaumont b Kerr | 13 | 13 | 15 | - | 2 |
| N.R.Sciver* c Rowe b Devine | 4 | 7 | 7 | - | 1 |
| A.E.Jones† c Newton b Devine | 0 | 1 | 1 | - | - |
| S.I.R.Dunkley c & b Kasperek | 21 | 20 | 20 | - | 4 |
| M.E.Bouchier c Martin b Rowe | 25 | 25 | 24 | - | 3 |
| S.Ecclestone c Bates b Kasperek | 5 | 10 | 7 | - | - |
| S.Glenn not out | 8 | 16 | 13 | - | - |
| M.K.Villiers not out | 9 | 9 | 6 | - | 1 |
| N.E.Farrant | | | | | |
| F.R.Davies | | | | | |
| Extras (lb 2, w 3, nb 2) | 7 | | | | |
| **TOTAL** (20 overs) (7 wkts) | **127** | 86 | | | |

## NEW ZEALAND

| | Runs | Mins | Balls | 6s | 4s |
|---|---|---|---|---|---|
| S.W.Bates run out | 8 | 21 | 16 | - | 1 |
| S.F.M.Devine* c Villiers b Farrant | 50 | 61 | 41 | 4 | 2 |
| A.E.Satterthwaite b Davies | 11 | 21 | 15 | - | 1 |
| M.L.Green c & b Villiers | 21 | 23 | 19 | - | 3 |
| B.M.Halliday c Villiers b Glenn | 3 | 11 | 5 | - | - |
| K.J.Martin† not out | 7 | 14 | 8 | - | 1 |
| H.N.K.Jensen c Jones b Farrant | 7 | 5 | 6 | - | 1 |
| T.M.M.Newton not out | 0 | 3 | 0 | - | - |
| H.M.Rowe | | | | | |
| J.M.Kerr | | | | | |
| L.M.Kasperek | | | | | |
| Extras (lb 2, w 19) | 21 | | | | |
| **TOTAL** (18.2 overs) (6 wkts) | **128** | 81 | | | |

| Bowling | O | M | R | W |
|---|---|---|---|---|
| **NEW ZEALAND** | | | | |
| Kasperek | 4 | 0 | 20 | 2 |
| Kerr | 4 | 0 | 23 | 1 |
| Devine | 4 | 0 | 28 | 2 |
| Satterthwaite | 2 | 0 | 11 | 0 |
| Jensen | 4 | 0 | 31 | 0 |
| Rowe | 2 | 0 | 12 | 2 |
| **ENGLAND** | | | | |
| Sciver | 3 | 0 | 17 | 0 |
| Farrant | 3.2 | 0 | 32 | 2 |
| Davies | 3 | 0 | 25 | 1 |
| Ecclestone | 4 | 0 | 20 | 0 |
| Glenn | 4 | 0 | 24 | 1 |
| Villiers | 1 | 0 | 8 | 1 |

| Fall of Wickets | E | NZ |
|---|---|---|
| 1st | 20 | 31 |
| 2nd | 25 | 68 |
| 3rd | 25 | 100 |
| 4th | 61 | 107 |
| 5th | 105 | 115 |
| 6th | 106 | 124 |
| 7th | 113 | - |
| 8th | - | - |
| 9th | - | - |
| 10th | - | - |

**NZC**

# ENGLAND v NEW ZEALAND     Third Twenty20 International

*at County Ground, Taunton on 9 September, 2021*
*Toss : England. Umpires : N.J. Llong & S. Redfern*
**England won by 4 wickets**

New Zealand batted first for the first time in the series after England won the toss. The New Zealand openers put on 45 before Bates went in the seventh over. The innings threatened to lose momentum but Halliday and Martin put on 36 from the last 14 balls to take New Zealand to 144-4.

Beaumont and Sciver went cheaply in England's reply but Wyatt, Knight and Jones all passed thirty and Dunkley, with 22 off 21 balls, was able to see England home with one ball remaining, hitting a Satterthwaite full toss to the boundary. England thus won the series 2-1.

## NEW ZEALAND

| | Runs | Mins | Balls | 6s | 4s |
|---|---|---|---|---|---|
| S.W.Bates b Farrant | 34 | 27 | 30 | - | 6 |
| S.F.M.Devine* b Ecclestone | 35 | 57 | 33 | - | 3 |
| A.E.Satterthwaite c Brunt | | | | | |
|   b Glenn | 13 | 24 | 21 | - | - |
| M.L.Green c Jones b Sciver | 16 | 17 | 14 | - | 2 |
| B.M.Halliday not out | 25 | 23 | 16 | - | 3 |
| K.J.Martin† not out | 13 | 13 | 6 | - | 3 |
| H.N.K.Jensen | | | | | |
| T.M.M.Newton | | | | | |
| H.M.Rowe | | | | | |
| J.M.Kerr | | | | | |
| L.M.Kasperek | | | | | |
| Extras (b 5, lb 1, w 2) | 8 | | | | |
| **TOTAL** (20 overs) (4 wkts) | **144** | 80 | | | |

## ENGLAND

| | Runs | Mins | Balls | 6s | 4s |
|---|---|---|---|---|---|
| D.N.Wyatt c Newton b Kasperek | 35 | 29 | 23 | 1 | 6 |
| T.T.Beaumont c Devine b Kerr | 3 | 13 | 11 | - | - |
| N.R.Sciver c Jensen b Kasperek | 2 | 15 | 5 | - | - |
| H.C.Knight* c Bates b Devine | 42 | 52 | 36 | - | 5 |
| A.E.Jones† b Kasperek | 32 | 29 | 19 | - | 5 |
| S.I.R.Dunkley not out | 22 | 27 | 21 | - | 1 |
| M.E.Bouchier b Satterthwaite | 1 | 4 | 2 | - | - |
| K.H.Brunt not out | 1 | 3 | 2 | - | - |
| S.Ecclestone | | | | | |
| S.Glenn | | | | | |
| N.E.Farrant | | | | | |
| Extras (lb 1, w 6) | 7 | | | | |
| **TOTAL** (19.5 overs) (6 wkts) | **145** | 85 | | | |

| Bowling | O | M | R | W |
|---|---|---|---|---|
| **ENGLAND** | | | | |
| Brunt | 4 | 0 | 25 | 0 |
| Farrant | 4 | 0 | 34 | 1 |
| Sciver | 4 | 0 | 29 | 1 |
| Ecclestone | 4 | 0 | 30 | 1 |
| Glenn | 4 | 0 | 20 | 1 |
| **NEW ZEALAND** | | | | |
| Kasperek | 4 | 0 | 25 | 3 |
| Kerr | 4 | 0 | 27 | 1 |
| Devine | 4 | 0 | 29 | 1 |
| Jensen | 2 | 0 | 21 | 0 |
| Rowe | 2 | 0 | 14 | 0 |
| Satterthwaite | 3.5 | 0 | 28 | 1 |

| Fall of Wickets | NZ | E |
|---|---|---|
| 1st | 45 | 16 |
| 2nd | 84 | 42 |
| 3rd | 90 | 42 |
| 4th | 108 | 97 |
| 5th | - | 137 |
| 6th | - | 138 |
| 7th | - | - |
| 8th | - | - |
| 9th | - | - |
| 10th | - | - |

## ENGLAND v NEW ZEALAND                    First One-day International

*at County Ground, Bristol on 16 September, 2021*
*Toss : New Zealand. Umpires : P.R. Pollard & S. Redfern*
**England won by 30 runs**

New Zealand won the toss and fielded in the opening one-day international. Winfield-Hill and Beaumont gave England a bright start and Knight (fifty from 64 balls) and Brunt put on 88 for the sixth wicket. The innings then fell away with five wickets falling for 13 runs as England were dismissed in the final over.

New Zealand made a very slow start and after ten overs were 17-2. Satterthwaite and Devine put on 78 for the fourth wicket but five wickets fell quickly to leave New Zealand 143-8. Satterthwaite (fifty from 58 balls) got support from Tahuhu and Kasperek, adding 68 for last two wickets, before she finally ran out of partners. England won by 30 runs. Dean made her one-day international debut in this game.

### ENGLAND

| | Runs | Mins | Balls | 6s | 4s |
|---|---|---|---|---|---|
| L.Winfield-Hill c Martin b Rowe | 21 | 33 | 24 | - | 3 |
| T.T.Beaumont lbw b Devine | 44 | 91 | 75 | - | 6 |
| H.C.Knight* c & b Kasperek | 89 | 155 | 107 | - | 8 |
| N.R.Sciver b Tahuhu | 2 | 10 | 10 | - | - |
| A.E.Jones† b Tahuhu | 2 | 14 | 7 | - | - |
| S.I.R.Dunkley c Martin b Kerr | 5 | 14 | 9 | - | 1 |
| K.H.Brunt b Kerr | 43 | 63 | 51 | - | 5 |
| S.Ecclestone run out | 5 | 18 | 6 | - | - |
| K.L.Cross c Halliday b Devine | 5 | 8 | 5 | - | 1 |
| C.E.Dean lbw b Kerr | 1 | 5 | 2 | - | - |
| F.R.Davies not out | 0 | 3 | 2 | - | - |

Extras (b 1, lb 7, w 15, nb 1) .. 24
**TOTAL** (49.3 overs) ............ **241** 205

### NEW ZEALAND

| | Runs | Mins | Balls | 6s | 4s |
|---|---|---|---|---|---|
| L.R.Down c Jones b Sciver | 5 | 37 | 26 | - | - |
| S.W.Bates c Knight b Sciver | 1 | 13 | 13 | - | - |
| M.L.Green c Knight b Cross | 19 | 35 | 32 | - | 2 |
| A.E.Satterthwaite not out | 79 | 148 | 87 | - | 10 |
| S.F.M.Devine* c Winfield-Hill | | | | | |
| b Cross | 34 | 63 | 59 | - | 3 |
| K.J.Martin† c Davies | | | | | |
| b Ecclestone | 9 | 12 | 11 | - | 1 |
| B.M.Halliday b Ecclestone | 0 | 4 | 1 | - | - |
| H.M.Rowe lbw b Brunt | 1 | 14 | 11 | - | - |
| J.M.Kerr b Dean | 5 | 10 | 5 | - | 1 |
| L.M.M.Tahuhu b Davies | 25 | 15 | 14 | - | 5 |
| L.M.Kasperek run out | 15 | 24 | 21 | - | 3 |

Extras (lb 10, w 7, nb 1) ........ 18
**TOTAL** (46.3 overs) ............ **211** 186

| **Bowling** | O | M | R | W |
|---|---|---|---|---|
| **NEW ZEALAND** | | | | |
| Devine | 10 | 0 | 57 | 2 |
| Kerr | 9.3 | 1 | 42 | 3 |
| Tahuhu | 10 | 0 | 32 | 2 |
| Rowe | 9 | 0 | 47 | 1 |
| Kasperek | 10 | 0 | 48 | 1 |
| Satterthwaite | 1 | 0 | 7 | 0 |
| **ENGLAND** | | | | |
| Brunt | 8 | 4 | 22 | 1 |
| Sciver | 5 | 0 | 10 | 2 |
| Cross | 8.3 | 0 | 37 | 2 |
| Davies | 7 | 0 | 40 | 1 |
| Dean | 8 | 0 | 53 | 1 |
| Ecclestone | 10 | 1 | 39 | 2 |

| **Fall of Wickets** | E | NZ |
|---|---|---|
| 1st | 44 | 2 |
| 2nd | 109 | 17 |
| 3rd | 113 | 31 |
| 4th | 132 | 109 |
| 5th | 140 | 124 |
| 6th | 228 | 124 |
| 7th | 232 | 132 |
| 8th | 240 | 143 |
| 9th | 241 | 177 |
| 10th | 241 | 211 |

# ENGLAND v NEW ZEALAND — Second One-day International

*at County Ground, Worcester on 19 September, 2021*
*Toss : New Zealand. Umpires : A.Y. Harris & D.J. Millns*
**England won by 13 runs (D/L)**

Devine again won the toss and decided to bowl first. Beaumont hit three fours in her first five balls but was bowled by the sixth. The England batting struggled to gather momentum and Winfield-Hill was run out for 39 to make the score 118-6. The ninth wicket fell at 146 but Wyatt (fifty off 63 balls) and Farrant then added an invaluable 51 for the last wicket. Rowe and Kasperek each took three wickets.

The New Zealand opening pair were more positive on this occasion and had reached 40 before Bates fell in the ninth over. Rain interrupted play with New Zealand 111-4 and the revised target was 183 off 42 overs. Devine went almost immediately, Martin and Rowe soon followed and New Zealand were eventually bowled out for 169 in 39 overs. England thus took a 2-0 series lead.

## ENGLAND

| | Runs | Mins | Balls | 6s | 4s |
|---|---|---|---|---|---|
| L.Winfield-Hill run out | 39 | 120 | 66 | - | 4 |
| T.T.Beaumont b Devine | 12 | 8 | 6 | - | 3 |
| H.C.Knight* c Martin b Rowe | 18 | 36 | 22 | - | 3 |
| N.R.Sciver† c Green b Rowe | 1 | 10 | 8 | - | - |
| A.E.Jones† c Halliday b Devine | 1 | 6 | 7 | - | - |
| S.I.R.Dunkley c sub (H.N.K.Jensen) b Tahuhu | 11 | 26 | 27 | - | 1 |
| D.N.Wyatt not out | 63 | 97 | 72 | 2 | 4 |
| C.E.Dean c Martin b Kasperek | 8 | 13 | 11 | - | 1 |
| S.Ecclestone c Satterthwaite b Rowe | 4 | 13 | 8 | - | - |
| K.L.Cross c Down b Kasperek | 1 | 3 | 3 | - | - |
| N.E.Farrant c Green b Kasperek | 22 | 34 | 31 | - | 3 |
| Extras (lb 1, w 16) | 17 | | | | |
| **TOTAL** (43.3 overs) | **197** | 185 | | | |

## NEW ZEALAND

| | Runs | Mins | Balls | 6s | 4s |
|---|---|---|---|---|---|
| S.W.Bates c Wyatt b Cross | 28 | 33 | 34 | - | 5 |
| L.R.Down lbw b Cross | 22 | 55 | 33 | - | 3 |
| M.L.Green c Dean b Ecclestone | 9 | 20 | 18 | - | 2 |
| A.E.Satterthwaite c Jones b Cross | 1 | 24 | 15 | - | - |
| S.F.M.Devine* b Sciver | 28 | 44 | 41 | - | 4 |
| B.M.Halliday st Jones b Dean | 29 | 59 | 42 | - | 4 |
| K.J.Martin† b Dean | 6 | 6 | 7 | - | 1 |
| H.M.Rowe lbw b Dean | 7 | 17 | 9 | - | 1 |
| L.M.Kasperek lbw b Dean | 10 | 23 | 24 | - | - |
| L.M.M.Tahuhu c Knight b Farrant | 4 | 14 | 6 | - | - |
| J.M.Kerr not out | 6 | 7 | 5 | - | 1 |
| Extras (lb 4, w 15) | 19 | | | | |
| **TOTAL** (39 overs) | **169** | 217 | | | |

### Bowling

| NEW ZEALAND | O | M | R | W |
|---|---|---|---|---|
| Kerr | 9 | 1 | 31 | 0 |
| Devine | 5 | 0 | 29 | 2 |
| Tahuhu | 10 | 0 | 48 | 1 |
| Rowe | 9 | 1 | 41 | 3 |
| Kasperek | 7.3 | 0 | 31 | 3 |
| Satterthwaite | 3 | 0 | 16 | 0 |
| **ENGLAND** | | | | |
| Sciver | 7 | 0 | 33 | 1 |
| Farrant | 7 | 0 | 23 | 1 |
| Cross | 8 | 0 | 43 | 3 |
| Ecclestone | 9 | 1 | 30 | 1 |
| Dean | 8 | 0 | 36 | 4 |

### Fall of Wickets

| | E | NZ |
|---|---|---|
| 1st | 14 | 40 |
| 2nd | 59 | 63 |
| 3rd | 67 | 64 |
| 4th | 68 | 85 |
| 5th | 85 | 114 |
| 6th | 118 | 121 |
| 7th | 134 | 135 |
| 8th | 145 | 151 |
| 9th | 146 | 161 |
| 10th | 197 | 169 |

# ENGLAND v NEW ZEALAND          Third One-day International

*at County Ground, Leicester on 21 September, 2021*
*Toss : New Zealand.  Umpires : P.R. Pollard & S. Redfern*
**New Zealand won by 3 wickets**

New Zealand won the toss and fielded for the third game in a row with Penfold playing her first game for New Zealand. England were in early trouble with their top three dismissed by the time the score reached 20. The eighth wicket fell at 101 but Brunt, who finished one short of a half-century, was supported by Cross and Farrant in adding 77 runs for the last two wickets. Tahuhu had her first five wicket haul.

New Zealand also made a poor start and were 13-2 before Green came to the rescue. She added 72 for the third wicket with Satterthwaite and 52 for the fifth wicket with Halliday. Green (fifty from 80 balls) was unbeaten on 70 when the winning runs came with Tahuhu hitting Farrant for six.

## ENGLAND

| | Runs | Mins | Balls | 6s | 4s |
|---|---|---|---|---|---|
| L.Winfield-Hill lbw b Tahuhu | 4 | 19 | 13 | - | 1 |
| T.T.Beaumont lbw b Tahuhu | 1 | 11 | 10 | - | - |
| H.C.Knight* c Martin b Tahuhu | 6 | 16 | 5 | - | 1 |
| A.E.Jones† b Penfold | 21 | 37 | 33 | - | 4 |
| S.I.R.Dunkley b Tahuhu | 6 | 7 | 16 | - | 1 |
| D.N.Wyatt c Down b Penfold | 10 | 36 | 20 | - | 2 |
| C.E.Dean b Tahuhu | 10 | 34 | 25 | - | 2 |
| K.H.Brunt not out | 49 | 122 | 98 | - | 4 |
| S.Ecclestone lbw b Kasperek | 8 | 33 | 16 | - | 1 |
| K.L.Cross run out | 29 | 47 | 40 | - | 4 |
| N.E.Farrant lbw b Jensen | 12 | 26 | 18 | - | 2 |
| Extras (lb 5, w 14, nb 3) | 22 | | | | |
| **TOTAL** (48.3 overs) | **178** | 200 | | | |

## NEW ZEALAND

| | Runs | Mins | Balls | 6s | 4s |
|---|---|---|---|---|---|
| S.W.Bates b Brunt | 5 | 19 | 19 | - | 1 |
| L.R.Down c Beaumont b Brunt | 7 | 28 | 13 | - | 1 |
| M.L.Green not out | 70 | 155 | 106 | - | 6 |
| A.E.Satterthwaite c Ecclestone b Dean | 33 | 60 | 54 | - | 5 |
| S.F.M.Devine* b Brunt | 3 | 13 | 12 | - | - |
| B.M.Halliday b Farrant | 25 | 41 | 38 | - | 3 |
| K.J.Martin† b Ecclestone | 2 | 6 | 5 | - | - |
| H.N.K.Jensen lbw b Brunt | 2 | 17 | 13 | - | - |
| L.M.M.Tahuhu not out | 19 | 13 | 15 | 1 | 3 |
| L.M.Kasperek | | | | | |
| M.M.Penfold | | | | | |
| Extras (lb 3, w 12) | 15 | | | | |
| **TOTAL** (45.5 overs) (7 wkts) | **181** | 176 | | | |

| Bowling | O | M | R | W |
|---|---|---|---|---|
| **NEW ZEALAND** | | | | |
| Tahuhu | 10 | 1 | 37 | 5 |
| Devine | 9 | 1 | 26 | 0 |
| Penfold | 10 | 1 | 42 | 2 |
| Jensen | 9.3 | 1 | 40 | 1 |
| Kasperek | 10 | 1 | 28 | 1 |
| **ENGLAND** | | | | |
| Brunt | 10 | 2 | 22 | 4 |
| Farrant | 7.5 | 1 | 45 | 1 |
| Cross | 8 | 1 | 32 | 0 |
| Ecclestone | 10 | 0 | 41 | 1 |
| Dean | 10 | 0 | 38 | 1 |

| Fall of Wickets | E | NZ |
|---|---|---|
| 1st | 6 | 12 |
| 2nd | 11 | 13 |
| 3rd | 20 | 85 |
| 4th | 27 | 94 |
| 5th | 48 | 146 |
| 6th | 59 | 149 |
| 7th | 78 | 158 |
| 8th | 101 | - |
| 9th | 154 | - |
| 10th | 178 | - |

NZC

# ENGLAND v NEW ZEALAND          Fourth One-day International

*at County Ground, Derby on 23 September, 2021*
*Toss : England. Umpires : A.Y. Harris & D.J. Millns*
**England won by 3 wickets**

England won the toss for the first time in the series and bowled first, with New Zealand needing to win the game to keep the series alive. New Zealand recovered from 33-3 thanks to fifties from Satterthwaite (82 balls) and Martin (65 balls) and 41 from Devine and reached 244-8 in their fifty overs.

Winfield-Hill and Beaumont put on 52 for the first wicket in England's response and Knight and Jones added 100 for the fourth wicket. The England captain reached fifty from 58 balls and her century from 103. She was sixth out with eight runs still needed from ten balls and Wyatt went four balls later, leaving England to score six runs off the last over. Shrubsole hit a four and took a single and the game finished in unusual fashion when Ecclestone was stumped off a wide from Kasperek. England thus secured a series win with one game remaining.

## NEW ZEALAND

| | Runs | Mins | Balls | 6s | 4s |
|---|---|---|---|---|---|
| S.W.Bates run out .................... | 17 | 24 | 24 | - | 3 |
| L.R.Down b Shrubsole ............. | 11 | 37 | 19 | - | 2 |
| M.L.Green c Davies b Shrubsole | 0 | 7 | 5 | - | - |
| A.E.Satterthwaite b Dean ......... | 54 | 116 | 86 | - | 4 |
| S.F.M.Devine* lbw b Dean ........ | 41 | 57 | 48 | 1 | 5 |
| K.J.Martin† not out .................. | 65 | 97 | 83 | - | 7 |
| B.M.Halliday c Sciver b Dean ... | 28 | 19 | 19 | 1 | 4 |
| H.N.K.Jensen b Davies ............. | 0 | 6 | 1 | - | - |
| H.M.Rowe b Davies .................. | 15 | 15 | 14 | - | 1 |
| J.M.Kerr not out ...................... | 1 | 6 | 1 | - | - |
| L.M.Kasperek | | | | | |
| Extras (w 12) .......................... | 12 | | | | |
| **TOTAL** (50 overs) (8 wkts) . | **244** | 192 | | | |

## ENGLAND

| | Runs | Mins | Balls | 6s | 4s |
|---|---|---|---|---|---|
| L.Winfield-Hill b Rowe .............. | 33 | 46 | 46 | - | 5 |
| T.T.Beaumont c Martin b Rowe | 16 | 54 | 31 | - | 2 |
| H.C.Knight* c Halliday | | | | | |
|    b Devine ............................. | 101 | 140 | 107 | - | 10 |
| N.R.Sciver lbw b Rowe ............. | 11 | 12 | 14 | - | 2 |
| A.E.Jones† c Kerr b Rowe ........ | 40 | 77 | 63 | - | 2 |
| S.I.R.Dunkley lbw b Satterthwaite | 0 | 10 | 5 | - | - |
| D.N.Wyatt lbw b Devine ........... | 27 | 39 | 27 | 1 | 1 |
| A.Shrubsole not out .................. | 6 | 10 | 5 | - | 1 |
| S.Ecclestone not out ................ | 0 | 6 | 0 | - | - |
| C.E.Dean | | | | | |
| F.R.Davies | | | | | |
| Extras (w 10, nb 1) ................ | 11 | | | | |
| **TOTAL** (49.3 overs) (7 wkts) | **245** | 198 | | | |

| Bowling | O | M | R | W |
|---|---|---|---|---|
| **ENGLAND** | | | | |
| Sciver | 10 | 1 | 42 | 0 |
| Shrubsole | 8 | 0 | 43 | 2 |
| Davies | 8 | 0 | 46 | 2 |
| Ecclestone | 10 | 0 | 43 | 0 |
| Dean | 10 | 1 | 52 | 3 |
| Knight | 4 | 0 | 18 | 0 |
| **NEW ZEALAND** | | | | |
| Kerr | 10 | 0 | 47 | 0 |
| Devine | 10 | 0 | 55 | 2 |
| Rowe | 10 | 0 | 47 | 4 |
| Jensen | 10 | 2 | 32 | 0 |
| Kasperek | 3.3 | 0 | 30 | 0 |
| Satterthwaite | 6 | 0 | 34 | 1 |

| Fall of Wickets | NZ | E |
|---|---|---|
| 1st | 24 | 52 |
| 2nd | 24 | 59 |
| 3rd | 33 | 71 |
| 4th | 89 | 171 |
| 5th | 173 | 185 |
| 6th | 209 | 237 |
| 7th | 216 | 239 |
| 8th | 236 | - |
| 9th | - | - |
| 10th | - | - |

## ENGLAND v NEW ZEALAND          Fifth One-day International

*at St Lawrence Ground, Canterbury on 26 September, 2021*
*Toss : New Zealand. Umpires : P.R. Pollard & S. Redfern*
**England won by 203 runs**

New Zealand won the toss and bowled for the fourth time in the series but had to wait until the 17th over before they captured a wicket. Knight then fell without scoring but Beaumont had partnerships of 69 with Sciver and 97 with Jones (fifty off 36 balls) before she was fifth out at 268. Beaumont's fifty took 55 balls and her century came from 111.
Dunkley and Wyatt then proceeded to flay the attack and scored 79 from just 6.2 overs. England's final total of 347 was the highest conceded by New Zealand in a one-day international.
New Zealand made a poor start and were 38-2 after 11.2 overs. No player was able to reach 30 and the innings folded in the 36th over. Cross and Knight took three wickets each as England won the match by 203 runs and the series 4-1.

### AUSTRALIA

| | Runs | Mins | Balls | 6s | 4s |
|---|---|---|---|---|---|
| L.Winfield-Hill c Satterthwaite b Jensen | 43 | 71 | 57 | 1 | 4 |
| T.T.Beaumont c Bates b Rowe | 102 | 179 | 114 | - | 11 |
| H.C.Knight* c Martin b Tahuhu | 0 | 5 | 2 | - | - |
| N.R.Sciver lbw b Rowe | 39 | 41 | 38 | - | 7 |
| A.E.Jones† c Tahuhu b Devine | 60 | 58 | 46 | 1 | 9 |
| S.I.R.Dunkley not out | 33 | 25 | 25 | - | 5 |
| D.N.Wyatt not out | 43 | 29 | 20 | 4 | 3 |
| C.E.Dean | | | | | |
| S.Ecclestone | | | | | |
| K.L.Cross | | | | | |
| A.Shrubsole | | | | | |
| Extras (lb 8, w 17, nb 2) | 27 | | | | |
| **TOTAL** (50 overs) (5 wkts) | **347** | 210 | | | |

### NEW ZEALAND

| | Runs | Mins | Balls | 6s | 4s |
|---|---|---|---|---|---|
| S.W.Bates c Beaumont b Shrubsole | 6 | 25 | 15 | - | - |
| L.R.Down b Ecclestone | 27 | 41 | 43 | - | 3 |
| M.L.Green c & b Ecclestone | 22 | 33 | 28 | - | 4 |
| A.E.Satterthwaite c Sciver b Cross | 6 | 22 | 15 | - | 1 |
| S.F.M.Devine* lbw b Cross | 3 | 12 | 8 | - | - |
| B.M.Halliday c Beaumont b Knight | 27 | 61 | 51 | - | 3 |
| K.J.Martin† b Cross | 5 | 15 | 9 | - | 1 |
| H.N.K.Jensen c Shrubsole b Knight | 19 | 14 | 13 | - | 4 |
| H.M.Rowe lbw b Knight | 20 | 30 | 27 | - | 2 |
| L.M.M.Tahuhu c Winfield-Hill b Dean | 1 | 4 | 3 | - | - |
| M.M.Penfold not out | 0 | 2 | 0 | - | - |
| Extras (lb 2, w 6) | 8 | | | | |
| **TOTAL** (35.2 overs) | **144** | 128 | | | |

| Bowling | O | M | R | W |
|---|---|---|---|---|
| **NEW ZEALAND** | | | | |
| Tahuhu | 9 | 0 | 63 | 1 |
| Devine | 10 | 1 | 74 | 1 |
| Penfold | 7 | 0 | 43 | 0 |
| Rowe | 10 | 1 | 65 | 2 |
| Jensen | 10 | 0 | 62 | 1 |
| Satterthwaite | 4 | 0 | 32 | 0 |
| **ENGLAND** | | | | |
| Shrubsole | 5 | 0 | 20 | 1 |
| Sciver | 4 | 0 | 10 | 0 |
| Ecclestone | 8 | 1 | 31 | 2 |
| Cross | 8 | 0 | 44 | 3 |
| Dean | 5.2 | 0 | 13 | 1 |
| Knight | 5 | 0 | 24 | 3 |

**Fall of Wickets**

| | E | NZ |
|---|---|---|
| 1st | 95 | 25 |
| 2nd | 96 | 38 |
| 3rd | 165 | 59 |
| 4th | 262 | 63 |
| 5th | 268 | 66 |
| 6th | - | 90 |
| 7th | - | 113 |
| 8th | - | 142 |
| 9th | - | 144 |
| 10th | - | 144 |

# INDIA IN
# NEW ZEALAND

India arrived in New Zealand ahead of the ICC Women's Cricket World Cup and played one Twenty20 and five one-day internationals at John Davies Oval, Queenstown.

The White Ferns' World Cup squad assembled for the Indian series. They convincingly won the only Twenty20 and in the one-day games, Suzie Bates began the series with 106 off 111 balls, leading the team to 275 in 48.1 overs and subsequent victory. This win was followed by three more before India won the last game, leaving New Zealand a 4-1 series winner.

The highlight of the series, after Bates century in the first match, was Amelia Kerr's 353 runs in the series at 117.66, including an unbeaten 119 in the second one-day game. She also captured seven wickets. During the series, Lauren Down sustained an injury that forced her withdrawal from the World Cup.

The New Zealand squad was: Sophie Devine *(captain)*, Maddy Green, Amelia Kerr, Jess Kerr *(Wellington)*, Lauren Down, Fran Jonas *(Auckland)*, Brooke Halliday *(Northern Districts)*, Rosemary Mair, Hannah Rowe *(Central Districts)*, Frances Mackay, Amy Satterthwaite, Lea Tahuhu *(Canterbury)*, Suzie Bates, Hayley Jensen, Katey Martin *(Otago)*.

Coach, Bob Carter; Batting coach, Rob Nicol; Bowling coach, Jacob Oram; Manager, Belinda Muller; Physiotherapist, Tim Dovbysh; Trainer, Scott Wrenn.

## New Zealand One-day International Averages

| BATTING | M | I | NO | HS | Agg | Ave | 100s | 50s | Ct | St | SR |
|---|---|---|---|---|---|---|---|---|---|---|---|
| A.C. Kerr | 5 | 5 | 2 | 119* | 353 | 117.66 | 1 | 3 | 9 | - | 97 |
| L.R. Down | 3 | 3 | 1 | 64* | 99 | 49.50 | - | 1 | 1 | - | 106 |
| S.W. Bates | 5 | 5 | 0 | 106 | 185 | 37.00 | 1 | - | 7 | - | 101 |
| A.E. Satterthwaite | 5 | 5 | 0 | 63 | 166 | 33.20 | - | 2 | 3 | - | 91 |
| M.L. Green | 3 | 3 | 0 | 52 | 93 | 31.00 | - | 1 | 3 | - | 80 |
| S.F.M. Devine | 5 | 5 | 0 | 34 | 112 | 22.40 | - | - | - | - | 100 |
| F.L. Mackay | 3 | 3 | 1 | 17* | 39 | 19.50 | - | - | - | - | 63 |
| K.J. Martin | 5 | 4 | 0 | 35 | 76 | 19.00 | - | - | 3 | 1 | 91 |
| H.M. Rowe | 4 | 2 | 1 | 13 | 18 | 18.00 | - | - | 1 | - | 112 |
| H.N.K. Jensen | 4 | 3 | 0 | 30 | 40 | 13.33 | - | - | - | - | 90 |
| J.M. Kerr | 3 | 3 | 2 | 6* | 11 | 11.00 | - | - | - | - | 137 |
| B.M. Halliday | 2 | 2 | 0 | 13 | 19 | 9.50 | - | - | 1 | - | 79 |
| L.M.M. Tahuhu | 2 | 2 | 0 | 8 | 9 | 4.50 | - | - | 1 | - | 90 |
| R.A. Mair | 4 | 1 | 1 | 7* | 7 | - | - | - | - | 2 | - | 116 |
| F.C. Jonas | 2 | - | - | - | - | - | - | - | - | - | - |

| BOWLING | O | M | R | W | Ave | Best | R/O |
|---|---|---|---|---|---|---|---|
| J.M. Kerr | 20.4 | 2 | 92 | 7 | 13.14 | 4-35 | 4.45 |
| A.E. Satterthwaite | 3 | 0 | 19 | 1 | 19.00 | 1-19 | 6.33 |
| H.N.K. Jensen | 26 | 0 | 141 | 6 | 23.50 | 3-32 | 5.42 |
| S.F.M. Devine | 22 | 0 | 118 | 4 | 29.50 | 2-42 | 5.36 |
| H.M. Rowe | 22 | 0 | 118 | 4 | 29.50 | 2-52 | 5.36 |
| F.L. Mackay | 22.3 | 0 | 101 | 3 | 33.66 | 2-22 | 4.49 |
| A.C. Kerr | 41.5 | 0 | 242 | 7 | 34.57 | 3-30 | 5.78 |
| R.A. Mair | 21 | 0 | 121 | 3 | 40.33 | 2-43 | 5.76 |
| F.C. Jonas | 18 | 0 | 100 | 2 | 50.00 | 1-40 | 5.56 |
| L.M.M. Tahuhu | 16 | 1 | 72 | 1 | 72.00 | 1-36 | 4.50 |

# India One-day International Averages

| BATTING | M | I | NO | HS | Agg | Ave | 100s | 50s | Ct | St | SR |
|---|---|---|---|---|---|---|---|---|---|---|---|
| M. Raj | 5 | 5 | 2 | 66* | 232 | 77.33 | - | 3 | 3 | - | 82 |
| R.M. Ghosh | 4 | 4 | 1 | 65 | 146 | 48.66 | - | 2 | 4 | 1 | 114 |
| S.S. Mandhana | 2 | 2 | 0 | 71 | 84 | 42.00 | - | 1 | 1 | - | 84 |
| D.B. Sharma | 5 | 5 | 2 | 69* | 116 | 38.66 | - | 1 | 1 | - | 80 |
| S. Meghana | 3 | 3 | 0 | 61 | 114 | 38.00 | - | 1 | 1 | - | 108 |
| H. Kaur | 4 | 4 | 0 | 63 | 96 | 24.00 | - | 1 | 2 | - | 75 |
| Y.H. Bhatia | 4 | 4 | 0 | 41 | 91 | 22.75 | - | - | 3 | - | 71 |
| J.N. Goswami | 3 | 2 | 1 | 13* | 21 | 21.00 | - | - | 1 | - | 63 |
| S. Verma | 5 | 5 | 0 | 51 | 96 | 19.20 | - | 1 | 2 | - | 77 |
| P. Vastrakar | 3 | 3 | 0 | 23 | 38 | 12.66 | - | - | - | - | 84 |
| S. Rana | 3 | 2 | 0 | 11 | 20 | 10.00 | - | - | 1 | - | 74 |
| T. Bhatia | 1 | 1 | 0 | 8 | 8 | 8.00 | - | - | 1 | - | 44 |
| E.K. Bisht | 1 | 1 | 0 | 3 | 3 | 3.00 | - | - | - | - | 60 |
| P. Yadav | 3 | 1 | 0 | 3 | 3 | 3.00 | - | - | - | - | 37 |
| R.S. Gayakwad | 4 | 2 | 0 | 4 | 4 | 2.00 | - | - | 1 | - | 100 |
| Renuka Singh | 2 | 2 | 0 | 0 | 0 | 0.00 | - | - | 1 | - | 0 |
| Meghna Singh | 2 | 1 | 1 | 0* | 0 | - | - | - | - | - | 0 |

| BOWLING | | O | M | R | W | Ave | Best | R/O |
|---|---|---|---|---|---|---|---|---|
| D.B. Sharma | | 41.1 | 1 | 247 | 10 | 24.70 | 4-52 | 6.00 |
| R.S. Gayakwad | | 31.1 | 0 | 168 | 6 | 28.00 | 2-28 | 5.39 |
| J.N. Goswami | | 27 | 3 | 145 | 5 | 29.00 | 3-47 | 5.37 |
| Renuka Singh | | 14 | 0 | 92 | 3 | 30.66 | 2-33 | 6.57 |
| Meghna Singh | | 9 | 0 | 67 | 2 | 33.50 | 1-22 | 7.44 |
| S. Rana | | 22 | 0 | 118 | 3 | 39.33 | 2-40 | 5.36 |
| P. Yadav | | 29 | 2 | 133 | 3 | 44.33 | 1-41 | 4.59 |
| P. Vastrakar | | 17 | 0 | 112 | 2 | 56.00 | 2-55 | 6.59 |
| E.K. Bisht | | 10 | 0 | 62 | 1 | 62.00 | 1-62 | 6.20 |
| H. Kaur | | 13 | 0 | 93 | 1 | 93.00 | 1-63 | 7.15 |
| S.D. Bahadur | | 3 | 0 | 18 | 0 | - | - | 6.00 |

# NEW ZEALAND v INDIA

## Twenty20 International

*at John Davies Oval, Queenstown on 9 February, 2022*
*Toss : India. Umpires : C.A. Black & J.M. Dempsey*
**New Zealand won by 17 runs**

India won the toss in the only Twenty20 of the tour and decided to bowl. Bates and Devine had fifty up in 38 balls before Devine fell in the eighth over. Green hit 26 off 20 balls and Tahuhu, promoted in the order, made 27 off just 14 balls. Halliday and Martin took 14 off the last over as New Zealand finished on 155-5.

India reached 41 before losing Bhatia in the seventh over and Verma followed two balls later. Meghana made 37 off 30 balls but there were no other contributions of note and India finished 18 runs short.

| NEW ZEALAND | Runs | Mins | Balls | 6s | 4s |
|---|---|---|---|---|---|
| S.W.Bates b Gayakwad | 36 | 47 | 34 | - | 2 |
| S.F.M.Devine* c Rana b Sharma | 31 | 31 | 23 | 2 | 2 |
| A.C.Kerr c Verma b Vestrakar .. | 17 | 30 | 20 | - | 1 |
| M.L.Green c Yadav b Sharma .. | 26 | 25 | 20 | - | 3 |
| L.M.M.Tahuhu c Verma | | | | | |
| b Vestrakar | 27 | 17 | 14 | 1 | 4 |
| B.M.Halliday not out | 7 | 12 | 6 | - | - |
| K.J.Martin† not out | 9 | 6 | 3 | - | 2 |
| L.R.Down | | | | | |
| H.N.K.Jensen | | | | | |
| J.M.Kerr | | | | | |
| H.M.Rowe | | | | | |
| Extras (lb 2) | 2 | | | | |
| **TOTAL** (20 overs) (5 wkts) . | **155** | 85 | | | |

| INDIA | Runs | Mins | Balls | 6s | 4s |
|---|---|---|---|---|---|
| Y.H.Bhatia b Kerr A.C. | 26 | 25 | 26 | 1 | 2 |
| S.Verma c Green b Kerr A.C. ... | 13 | 28 | 14 | - | 2 |
| H.Kaur* b Kerr J.M. | 12 | 18 | 13 | - | - |
| S.Meghana c Bates b Tahuhu .. | 37 | 32 | 30 | - | 6 |
| R.M.Ghosh† b Devine | 12 | 20 | 9 | - | 2 |
| P.Vestrakar c Bates b Jensen .. | 10 | 16 | 9 | - | 1 |
| S.Rana c Martin b Jensen | 6 | 9 | 9 | - | - |
| D.B.Sharma not out | 3 | 8 | 3 | - | - |
| S.D.Bahadur b Kerr J.M. | 10 | 6 | 6 | - | 2 |
| P.Yadav not out | 1 | 1 | 1 | - | - |
| R.S.Gayakwad | | | | | |
| Extras (lb 1, w 6) | 7 | | | | |
| **TOTAL** (20 overs) (8 wkts) . | **137** | 83 | | | |

| Bowling | O | M | R | W |
|---|---|---|---|---|
| **INDIA** | | | | |
| Vestrakar | 4 | 1 | 16 | 2 |
| Bahadur | 2 | 0 | 26 | 0 |
| Gayakwad | 4 | 0 | 39 | 1 |
| Yadav | 4 | 0 | 34 | 0 |
| Sharma | 4 | 0 | 26 | 2 |
| Rana | 2 | 0 | 12 | 0 |
| **NEW ZEALAND** | | | | |
| Kerr J.M. | 4 | 0 | 20 | 2 |
| Rowe | 2 | 0 | 18 | 0 |
| Tahuhu | 4 | 0 | 27 | 1 |
| Kerr A.C. | 4 | 0 | 25 | 2 |
| Devine | 3 | 0 | 21 | 1 |
| Jensen | 3 | 0 | 25 | 2 |

| Fall of Wickets | | |
|---|---|---|
| | NZ | I |
| 1st | 60 | 41 |
| 2nd | 80 | 42 |
| 3rd | 102 | 67 |
| 4th | 123 | 101 |
| 5th | 140 | 107 |
| 6th | - | 120 |
| 7th | - | 122 |
| 8th | - | 136 |
| 9th | - | - |
| 10th | - | - |

# NEW ZEALAND v INDIA          **First One-day International**

*at John Davies Oval, Queenstown on 12 February, 2022*
*Toss : India. Umpires : J.A.K. Bromley & D.J. Walker*
**New Zealand won by 62 runs**

India decided to field in the opening game of the one-day series and Bates and Green responded with an opening stand of 54. Bates reached fifty off 66 balls and her eleventh one-day hundred from 107 deliveries. She shared a 98 run stand with Satterthwaite who took 51 balls for her fifty. From 204-2, New Zealand were bowled out for 275 in the 49th over with four Indian bowlers taking two wickets each.

In India's reply Meghana (on debut) went early and Verma soon followed. Bhatia and Raj (fifty from 63 balls) put on 88 for the third wicket but India were always struggling and were dismissed for 213. Jess Kerr returned her best one-day figures for New Zealand.

| NEW ZEALAND | Runs | Mins | Balls | 6s | 4s |
|---|---|---|---|---|---|
| S.W.Bates c Verma b Sharma | 106 | 148 | 111 | - | 10 |
| M.L.Green c Bhatia b Sharma .. | 17 | 51 | 28 | - | - |
| A.C.Kerr b Yadav | 33 | 36 | 39 | - | 5 |
| A.E.Satterthwaite c Ghosh | | | | | |
| b Goswami | 63 | 96 | 67 | - | 4 |
| S.F.M.Devine* c Raj b Vastrakar | 13 | 11 | 15 | - | - |
| L.M.M.Tahuhu c Kaur b Vastrakar | 8 | 8 | 7 | - | 1 |
| K.J.Martin† run out | 6 | 10 | 4 | - | 1 |
| B.M.Halliday c Ghosh b Goswami | 6 | 13 | 7 | - | - |
| H.N.K.Jensen c Raj b Gayakwad | 6 | 4 | 3 | - | 1 |
| J.M.Kerr c Meghana b Gayakwad | 4 | 9 | 4 | - | - |
| H.M.Rowe not out | 5 | 5 | 4 | - | 1 |
| Extras (b 3, lb 3, w 2) | 8 | | | | |
| **TOTAL** (48.1 overs) | **275** | 199 | | | |

| INDIA | Runs | Mins | Balls | 6s | 4s |
|---|---|---|---|---|---|
| S.Meghana c Green b Tahuhu ... | 4 | 17 | 14 | - | 1 |
| S.Verma lbw b Devine | 12 | 21 | 16 | - | 2 |
| Y.H.Bhatia c Green b Jensen ... | 41 | 78 | 63 | - | 4 |
| M.Raj* c Kerr A.C. b Kerr J.M. | 59 | 95 | 73 | - | 6 |
| H.Kaur c Halliday b Kerr J.M. ... | 10 | 32 | 22 | - | - |
| R.M.Ghosh† st Martin b Rowe . | 22 | 32 | 27 | 1 | - |
| D.B.Sharma c Green b Kerr A.C. | 16 | 45 | 24 | - | - |
| P.Vastrakar c Bates b Jensen .. | 23 | 33 | 29 | - | 3 |
| J.N.Goswami not out | 13 | 21 | 21 | - | - |
| P.Yadav c Martin b Kerr J.M. ...... | 3 | 11 | 8 | - | - |
| R.S.Gayakwad b Kerr J.M. ......... | 0 | 1 | 1 | - | - |
| Extras (b 1, lb 3, w 6) | 10 | | | | |
| **TOTAL** (49.4 overs) | **213** | 195 | | | |

| Bowling | O | M | R | W |
|---|---|---|---|---|
| **INDIA** | | | | |
| Goswami | 10 | 0 | 58 | 2 |
| Vastrakar | 9 | 0 | 55 | 2 |
| Gayakwad | 7.1 | 0 | 28 | 2 |
| Sharma | 8 | 0 | 47 | 2 |
| Yadav | 10 | 1 | 51 | 1 |
| Kaur | 4 | 0 | 30 | 0 |
| **NEW ZEALAND** | | | | |
| Tahuhu | 9 | 1 | 36 | 1 |
| Kerr J.M. | 9.4 | 2 | 35 | 4 |
| Devine | 7 | 0 | 23 | 1 |
| Jensen | 8 | 0 | 36 | 2 |
| Rowe | 6 | 0 | 25 | 1 |
| Kerr A.C. | 10 | 0 | 54 | 1 |

| Fall of Wickets | | |
|---|---|---|
| | NZ | I |
| 1st | 54 | 13 |
| 2nd | 106 | 17 |
| 3rd | 204 | 105 |
| 4th | 222 | 130 |
| 5th | 236 | 139 |
| 6th | 250 | 164 |
| 7th | 258 | 190 |
| 8th | 265 | 201 |
| 9th | 269 | 213 |
| 10th | 275 | 213 |

# NEW ZEALAND v INDIA          Second One-day International

*at John Davies Oval, Queenstown on 15 February, 2022*
*Toss : India. Umpires : J.M. Dempsey & D.J. Walker*
**New Zealand won by 3 wickets**

India again won the toss but decided to bat first. Meghana and Verma began with an opening stand of 61 and fifties from Raj (67 balls) and Ghosh (49 balls) saw India reach 270-6 in their fifty overs. Raj and Ghosh put on 108 for the fifth wicket.

Devine and Bates began briskly before the first wicket fell in the fifth over. When Satterthwaite went for a duck, New Zealand were 55-3 and in some trouble. Green joined Amelia Kerr and the pair added 128 to put New Zealand back on course. Kerr took 69 balls for her fifty and a further 56 to reach her hundred. Green's fifty came from 57 balls.

Kerr got further support from Halliday and Martin and Jess Kerr hit the boundary which gave New Zealand the win with an over to spare. Bahadur made her one-day international debut in this game.

## INDIA

| | Runs | Mins | Balls | 6s | 4s |
|---|---|---|---|---|---|
| S.Meghana c & b Kerr A.C. ...... | 49 | 85 | 50 | - | 7 |
| S.Verma c Satterthwaite b Mair | 24 | 46 | 38 | 1 | 1 |
| Y.H.Bhatia c Bates b Devine .... | 31 | 35 | 38 | - | 4 |
| M.Raj *not out ........................... | 66 | 120 | 81 | - | 3 |
| H.Kaur c Kerr A.C. b Jonas ...... | 10 | 27 | 18 | - | - |
| R.M.Ghosh† c Kerr A.C. | | | | | |
| b Devine ................................. | 65 | 70 | 64 | 1 | 6 |
| P.Vastrakar c Kerr A.C. | | | | | |
| b Kerr J.M. ............................. | 11 | 18 | 11 | - | 1 |
| D.B.Sharma not out ................... | 1 | 1 | 1 | - | - |
| S.D.Bahadur | | | | | |
| R.S.Gayakwad | | | | | |
| P.Yadav | | | | | |
| Extras (lb 2, w 10, nb 1) ......... 13 | | | | | |
| **TOTAL** (50 overs) (6 wkts) . **270** | 202 | | | | |

## NEW ZEALAND

| | Runs | Mins | Balls | 6s | 4s |
|---|---|---|---|---|---|
| S.F.M.Devine c Bhatia | | | | | |
| b Gayakwad .......................... | 33 | 27 | 30 | - | 5 |
| S.W.Bates st sub (T.Bhatia) | | | | | |
| b Sharma .............................. | 16 | 16 | 14 | - | 4 |
| A.C.Kerr not out ...................... | 119 | 164 | 135 | - | 7 |
| A.E.Satterthwaite* c Kaur | | | | | |
| b Sharma .............................. | 0 | 2 | 1 | - | - |
| M.L.Green c Bhatia b Yadav ..... | 52 | 88 | 61 | - | 5 |
| B.M.Halliday c Sharma b Kaur . | 13 | 15 | 17 | - | 1 |
| K.J.Martin† b Sharma .............. | 20 | 27 | 25 | - | - |
| H.N.K.Jensen b Sharma ............ | 4 | 9 | 8 | - | - |
| J.M.Kerr not out ....................... | 6 | 8 | 3 | - | 1 |
| R.A.Mair | | | | | |
| F.C.Jonas | | | | | |
| Extras (lb 1, w 9) ................... 10 | | | | | |
| **TOTAL** (49 overs) (7 wkts) . **273** | 181 | | | | |

| Bowling | O | M | R | W |
|---|---|---|---|---|
| **NEW ZEALAND** | | | | |
| Jensen | 10 | 0 | 44 | 0 |
| Kerr J.M. | 8 | 0 | 46 | 1 |
| Mair | 6 | 0 | 33 | 1 |
| Jonas | 10 | 0 | 60 | 1 |
| Kerr A.C. | 8 | 0 | 43 | 1 |
| Devine | 8 | 0 | 42 | 2 |
| **INDIA** | | | | |
| Vastrakar | 7 | 0 | 45 | 0 |
| Gayakwad | 10 | 0 | 53 | 1 |
| Sharma | 10 | 1 | 52 | 4 |
| Yadav | 10 | 0 | 41 | 1 |
| Bahadur | 3 | 0 | 18 | 0 |
| Kaur | 9 | 0 | 63 | 1 |

### Fall of Wickets

| | I | NZ |
|---|---|---|
| 1st | 61 | 35 |
| 2nd | 110 | 52 |
| 3rd | 111 | 55 |
| 4th | 135 | 183 |
| 5th | 243 | 200 |
| 6th | 268 | 239 |
| 7th | - | 253 |
| 8th | - | - |
| 9th | - | - |
| 10th | - | - |

*Substitute T.Bhatia kept wicket in the New Zealand innings after Ghosh was injured while batting*

# NEW ZEALAND v INDIA          Third One-day International

*at John Davies Oval, Queenstown on 18 February, 2022*
*Toss : New Zealand. Umpires : C.A. Black & J.M. Dempsey*
**New Zealand won by 3 wickets**

New Zealand decided to bowl only to see Meghana (fifty from 33 balls) and Verma (fifty from 54 balls) amass a century opening stand inside 13 overs. Sharma also hit a quick fifty (55 balls) and India reached 279, being bowled out in the final over.

New Zealand lost both openers in the first three overs but Kerr and Satterthwaite (fifties from 59 and 55 balls) shared a century stand to put the game in the balance. At 171-6 in the 35th over, India had fought back but Down (fifty from 45 balls) and Martin added 76 to again give New Zealand some hope.

Mackay joined Down and kept the runs coming until six were needed from the final over. Down made sure there were no further problems by hitting Sharma's first ball for six and securing a series win. Renuka Singh made her one-day international debut in this game.

## INDIA

| | Runs | Mins | Balls | 6s | 4s |
|---|---|---|---|---|---|
| S.Meghana c Martin b Mair | 61 | 56 | 41 | 2 | 9 |
| S.Verma c Bates b Kerr | 51 | 78 | 57 | - | 7 |
| Y.H.Bhatia c Tahuhu b Mair | 19 | 34 | 25 | - | 1 |
| M.Raj* c Martin b Rowe | 23 | 55 | 33 | - | 1 |
| H.Kaur run out | 13 | 23 | 22 | - | 1 |
| D.B.Sharma not out | 69 | 90 | 69 | 1 | 7 |
| S.Rana c Rowe b Devine | 11 | 18 | 13 | - | 2 |
| T.Bhatia† run out | 8 | 25 | 18 | - | - |
| J.N.Goswami c Kerr b Rowe | 8 | 14 | 12 | - | - |
| E.K.Bisht c Kerr b Satterthwaite | 3 | 7 | 5 | - | - |
| Renuka Singh c Bates b Mackay | 0 | 3 | 2 | - | - |
| Extras (lb 1, w 12) | 13 | | | | |
| **TOTAL** (49.3 overs) | **279** | 203 | | | |

## NEW ZEALAND

| | Runs | Mins | Balls | 6s | 4s |
|---|---|---|---|---|---|
| S.F.M.Devine* lbw b Goswami | 0 | 2 | 2 | - | - |
| S.W.Bates b Goswami | 5 | 14 | 7 | - | 1 |
| A.C.Kerr c Renuka b Rana | 67 | 117 | 80 | - | 8 |
| A.E.Satterthwaite c Raj b Goswami | 59 | 79 | 76 | - | 6 |
| M.L.Green b Renuka | 24 | 41 | 27 | - | 2 |
| L.R.Down not out | 64 | 80 | 52 | 2 | 6 |
| L.M.M.Tahuhu c Verma b Bisht | 1 | 5 | 3 | - | - |
| K.J.Martin† c Bhatia T. b Sharma | 35 | 44 | 37 | - | 1 |
| F.L.Mackay not out | 17 | 16 | 12 | - | 2 |
| H.M.Rowe | | | | | |
| R.A.Mair | | | | | |
| Extras (lb 2, w 5, nb 1) | 8 | | | | |
| **TOTAL** (49.1 overs) (7 wkts) | **280** | 201 | | | |

| Bowling | O | M | R | W |
|---|---|---|---|---|
| **NEW ZEALAND** | | | | |
| Tahuhu | 7 | 0 | 36 | 0 |
| Rowe | 7 | 0 | 52 | 2 |
| Devine | 3 | 0 | 36 | 1 |
| Mair | 10 | 0 | 43 | 2 |
| Kerr | 10 | 0 | 60 | 1 |
| Mackay | 9.3 | 0 | 32 | 1 |
| Satterthwaite | 3 | 0 | 19 | 1 |
| **INDIA** | | | | |
| Goswami | 10 | 2 | 47 | 3 |
| Renuka | 10 | 0 | 59 | 1 |
| Bisht | 10 | 0 | 62 | 1 |
| Sharma | 9.1 | 0 | 57 | 1 |
| Rana | 10 | 0 | 53 | 1 |

| Fall of Wickets | I | NZ |
|---|---|---|
| 1st | 100 | 2 |
| 2nd | 131 | 14 |
| 3rd | 147 | 117 |
| 4th | 166 | 152 |
| 5th | 187 | 166 |
| 6th | 211 | 171 |
| 7th | 245 | 247 |
| 8th | 264 | - |
| 9th | 277 | - |
| 10th | 279 | - |

# NEW ZEALAND v INDIA          Fourth One-day International

*at John Davies Oval, Queenstown on 22 February, 2022*
*Toss : India. Umpires : J.A.K. Bromley & D.J. Walker*
**New Zealand won by 63 runs**

India chose to bowl in a game reduced to 20 overs per side. Devine and Bates had the fifty up in the sixth over before the New Zealand captain went. Amelia Kerr hit a 28-ball fifty while Satterthwaite made 32 off just 16 balls to help the home team to 191-5.

India made a disastrous reply and were 19-4 inside five overs. Ghosh reached fifty off just 26 balls and Raj made 30 but it was never going to be enough as India were dismissed for 128 in the 18th over. Kerr and Jensen took three wickets each.

### NEW ZEALAND

| | Runs | Mins | Balls | 6s | 4s |
|---|---|---|---|---|---|
| S.F.M.Devine* c Mandhana b Renuka | 32 | 27 | 24 | - | 6 |
| S.W.Bates st Ghosh b Gayakwad | 41 | 41 | 26 | - | 7 |
| A.C.Kerr not out | 68 | 62 | 33 | 1 | 11 |
| A.E.Satterthwaite b Meghna | 32 | 17 | 16 | 2 | 3 |
| F.L.Mackay b Renuka | 7 | 21 | 16 | - | - |
| L.R.Down b Sharma | 5 | 4 | 4 | - | 1 |
| J.M.Kerr not out | 1 | 3 | 1 | - | - |
| K.J.Martin† | | | | | |
| H.N.K.Jensen | | | | | |
| H.M.Rowe | | | | | |
| R.A.Mair | | | | | |
| Extras (lb 1, w 4) | 5 | | | | |
| **TOTAL** (20 overs) (5 wkts) | **191** | 89 | | | |

### INDIA

| | Runs | Mins | Balls | 6s | 4s |
|---|---|---|---|---|---|
| S.S.Mandhana c Kerr A.C. b Jensen | 13 | 20 | 15 | - | 2 |
| S.Verma c Bates b Mackay | 0 | 4 | 2 | - | - |
| Y.H.Bhatia c Bates b Kerr J.M. | 0 | 3 | 1 | - | - |
| P.Vastrakar c Satterthwaite b Jensen | 4 | 4 | 5 | - | 1 |
| M.Raj* b Kerr J.M. | 30 | 50 | 28 | 1 | 2 |
| R.M.Ghosh† c Kerr A.C. b Jensen | 52 | 37 | 29 | 4 | 4 |
| D.B.Sharma b Kerr A.C. | 9 | 20 | 9 | - | - |
| S.Rana c Mair b Mackay | 9 | 14 | 14 | - | - |
| Meghna Singh not out | 0 | 4 | 0 | - | - |
| Renuka Singh b Kerr A.C. | 0 | 1 | 1 | - | - |
| R.S.Gayakwad b Kerr A.C. | 4 | 2 | 3 | - | 1 |
| Extras (lb 4, w 3) | 7 | | | | |
| **TOTAL** (17.5 overs) | **128** | 81 | | | |

| Bowling | O | M | R | W |
|---|---|---|---|---|
| **INDIA** | | | | |
| Meghna | 4 | 0 | 45 | 1 |
| Renuka | 4 | 0 | 33 | 2 |
| Vastrakar | 1 | 0 | 12 | 0 |
| Gayakwad | 4 | 0 | 26 | 1 |
| Sharma | 4 | 0 | 49 | 1 |
| Rana | 3 | 0 | 25 | 0 |
| **NEW ZEALAND** | | | | |
| Mackay | 3 | 0 | 22 | 2 |
| Kerr J.M. | 3 | 0 | 11 | 2 |
| Jensen | 4 | 0 | 32 | 3 |
| Mair | 3 | 0 | 27 | 0 |
| Kerr A.C. | 3.5 | 0 | 30 | 3 |
| Devine | 1 | 0 | 2 | 0 |

| Fall of Wickets | | |
|---|---|---|
| | NZ | I |
| 1st | 53 | 7 |
| 2nd | 84 | 8 |
| 3rd | 132 | 12 |
| 4th | 164 | 19 |
| 5th | 176 | 96 |
| 6th | - | 105 |
| 7th | - | 124 |
| 8th | - | 124 |
| 9th | - | 124 |
| 10th | - | 128 |

# NEW ZEALAND v INDIA

## Fifth One-day International

*at John Davies Oval, Queenstown on 24 February, 2022*
*Toss : New Zealand. Umpires : J.M. Dempsey & D.J. Walker*
**India won by 6 wickets**

New Zealand batted after winning the toss. Kerr top scored with 66, her fourth successive score of fifty or more, with the half-century coming off 60 balls. Devine, Down and Jensen all made thirties.

India lost Verma at 29 but fifties from Mandhana (63 balls), Kaur (58 balls) and Raj (63 balls) saw India reach their target with four overs to spare. New Zealand thus won the series 4-1.

### NEW ZEALAND

| | Runs | Mins | Balls | 6s | 4s |
|---|---|---|---|---|---|
| S.W.Bates lbw b Meghna | 17 | 26 | 25 | - | 3 |
| S.F.M.Devine* c Gayakwad b Rana | 34 | 80 | 41 | 1 | 2 |
| A.C.Kerr c Ghosh b Sharma | 66 | 91 | 75 | - | 6 |
| A.E.Satterthwaite c Rana b Sharma | 12 | 23 | 21 | - | 1 |
| L.R.Down lbw b Rana | 30 | 48 | 37 | 2 | 1 |
| K.J.Martin† c Ghosh b Yadav | 15 | 27 | 17 | - | 1 |
| H.N.K.Jensen c Goswami b Gayakwad | 30 | 37 | 33 | - | 4 |
| F.L.Mackay b Gayakwad | 15 | 37 | 33 | - | 1 |
| H.M.Rowe run out | 13 | 16 | 12 | 1 | - |
| R.A.Mair not out | 7 | 8 | 6 | - | 1 |
| F.C.Jonas | | | | | |
| Extras (lb 5, w 7) | 12 | | | | |
| **TOTAL** (50 overs) (9 wkts) | **251** | 198 | | | |

### INDIA

| | Runs | Mins | Balls | 6s | 4s |
|---|---|---|---|---|---|
| S.Verma c Down b Jensen | 9 | 18 | 11 | - | 1 |
| S.S.Mandhana c Bates b Kerr | 71 | 108 | 84 | - | 9 |
| D.B.Sharma c Mair b Jonas | 21 | 54 | 41 | - | 1 |
| H.Kaur c Satterthwaite b Rowe | 63 | 86 | 66 | 1 | 6 |
| M.Raj* not out | 54 | 65 | 66 | - | 5 |
| R.M.Ghosh† not out | 7 | 15 | 8 | - | 1 |
| S.Rana | | | | | |
| J.N.Goswami | | | | | |
| Meghna Singh | | | | | |
| R.S.Gayakwad | | | | | |
| P.Yadav | | | | | |
| Extras (lb 7, w 20) | 27 | | | | |
| **TOTAL** (46 overs) (4 wkts) | **252** | 174 | | | |

| Bowling | O | M | R | W |
|---|---|---|---|---|
| **INDIA** | | | | |
| Goswami | 7 | 1 | 40 | 0 |
| Meghna | 5 | 0 | 22 | 1 |
| Gayakwad | 10 | 0 | 61 | 2 |
| Sharma | 10 | 0 | 42 | 2 |
| Rana | 9 | 0 | 40 | 2 |
| Yadav | 9 | 1 | 41 | 1 |
| **NEW ZEALAND** | | | | |
| Jensen | 4 | 0 | 29 | 1 |
| Rowe | 9 | 0 | 41 | 1 |
| Mackay | 10 | 0 | 47 | 0 |
| Mair | 2 | 0 | 18 | 0 |
| Jonas | 8 | 0 | 40 | 1 |
| Kerr | 10 | 0 | 55 | 1 |
| Devine | 3 | 0 | 15 | 0 |

| Fall of Wickets | NZ | I |
|---|---|---|
| 1st | 27 | 29 |
| 2nd | 95 | 89 |
| 3rd | 123 | 153 |
| 4th | 139 | 225 |
| 5th | 177 | - |
| 6th | 187 | - |
| 7th | 225 | - |
| 8th | 234 | - |
| 9th | 251 | - |
| 10th | - | - |

# ICC WOMEN'S WORLD CUP

After a convincing series win against India the White Ferns arrived at the tournament with confidence. In the two warm-up matches played at Lincoln University the team lost to Pakistan and defeated Australia with Sophie Devine scoring 161 not out and Amelia Kerr unbeaten on 92 chasing 321 in 43.1 overs.

In tournament round-robin play New Zealand lost their opening match against West Indies in the last over but then beat Bangladesh in Dunedin, with Suzie Bates unbeaten on 79 at her home ground. The White Ferns then beat India by 62 runs in Hamilton, to continue their dominance over them during the summer, but then lost to Australia, South Africa and England which effectively ruined any chances of the team making the semi-finals. New Zealand won their last match against Pakistan at Hagley Oval, Christchurch but to no avail. Sophie Devine and Suzie Bates scored centuries during the tournament while Lea Tahuhu and Frances Mackay each took ten wickets.

The New Zealand squad was: Sophie Devine *(captain)*, Maddy Green, Amelia Kerr, Jess Kerr *(Wellington)*, Lauren Down, Fran Jonas *(Auckland)*, Brooke Halliday *(Northern Districts)*, Rosemary Mair, Hannah Rowe *(Central Districts)*, Frances Mackay, Amy Satterthwaite, Lea Tahuhu *(Canterbury)*, Suzie Bates, Hayley Jensen, Katey Martin *(Otago)*. Down was injured during the series against India and was replaced by Georgia Plimmer *(Wellington)*. Molly Penfold *(Auckland)* joined the squad as a non-playing 16th member in case a Covid replacement player was required.

Coach, Bob Carter; Bowling coach, Jacob Oram; Coaching support, Freddie Anderson; Manager, Belinda Muller; Physiotherapist, Tim Dovbysh; Trainer, Scott Wrenn.

## New Zealand Averages

| BATTING | M | I | NO | HS | Agg | Ave | 100s | 50s | Ct | St | SR |
|---|---|---|---|---|---|---|---|---|---|---|---|
| S.F.M. Devine | 7 | 7 | 0 | 108 | 309 | 44.14 | 1 | 1 | 4 | - | 91 |
| S.W. Bates | 7 | 7 | 1 | 126 | 255 | 42.50 | 1 | 1 | 3 | - | 87 |
| A.C. Kerr | 7 | 7 | 1 | 50 | 201 | 33.50 | - | 1 | 2 | - | 80 |
| K.J. Martin | 7 | 6 | 1 | 44 | 149 | 29.80 | - | - | 10 | 2 | 85 |
| A.E. Satterthwaite | 7 | 6 | 0 | 75 | 175 | 29.16 | - | 1 | 2 | - | 69 |
| M.L. Green | 7 | 6 | 1 | 52* | 144 | 28.80 | - | 1 | 3 | - | 60 |
| F.L. Mackay | 6 | 5 | 3 | 13* | 31 | 15.50 | - | - | 2 | - | 88 |
| B.M. Halliday | 4 | 4 | 0 | 29 | 58 | 14.50 | - | - | 1 | - | 69 |
| J.M. Kerr | 7 | 6 | 1 | 25 | 57 | 11.40 | - | - | 1 | - | 114 |
| L.M.M. Tahuhu | 6 | 5 | 0 | 23 | 30 | 6.00 | - | - | 1 | - | 75 |
| H.M. Rowe | 7 | 6 | 2 | 6 | 15 | 3.75 | - | - | 3 | - | 55 |
| H.N.K. Jensen | 3 | 2 | 0 | 1 | 1 | 0.50 | - | - | - | - | 12 |
| F.C. Jonas | 1 | 1 | 0 | 0 | 0 | 0.00 | - | - | 1 | - | 0 |
| R.A. Mair | 1 | - | - | - | - | - | - | - | 1 | - | - |

| BOWLING | O | M | R | W | Ave | Best | R/O |
|---|---|---|---|---|---|---|---|
| A.E. Satterthwaite | 10 | 0 | 48 | 3 | 16.00 | 3-25 | 4.80 |
| B.M. Halliday | 3.4 | 1 | 18 | 1 | 18.00 | 1-18 | 4.91 |
| F.L. Mackay | 48.3 | 2 | 195 | 10 | 19.50 | 4-34 | 4.02 |
| L.M.M. Tahuhu | 43.4 | 3 | 208 | 10 | 20.80 | 3-17 | 4.76 |
| H.N.K. Jensen | 17.4 | 0 | 103 | 4 | 25.75 | 2-30 | 5.83 |
| R.A. Mair | 8 | 1 | 29 | 1 | 29.00 | 1-29 | 3.63 |
| H.M. Rowe | 54 | 3 | 269 | 9 | 29.88 | 5-55 | 4.98 |
| A.C. Kerr | 64 | 3 | 286 | 9 | 31.77 | 3-50 | 4.47 |
| J.M. Kerr | 54 | 5 | 222 | 5 | 44.40 | 2-36 | 4.11 |
| S.F.M. Devine | 11 | 0 | 60 | 1 | 60.00 | 1-27 | 5.45 |
| F.C. Jonas | 6 | 0 | 39 | 0 | - | - | 6.50 |

## WARM-UP GAMES

*27 February, 2022, Lincoln*
**New Zealand** 229 (A.E. Satterthwaite 80, M.L. Green 58, J.M. Kerr 34*, Nashra Sandhu 4-32) **lost to Pakistan** 233-6 (Aliya Riaz 62*, Nida Dar 54, Sidra Ameen 34, Omaima Sohail 31) by 4 wickets

*27 February, 2022, Lincoln*
**England** 182-6 lost to **West Indies** 183-4 by 6 wickets

*27 February, 2022, Rangiora*
**India** 244 defeated **South Africa** 242-7 by 2 runs

*28 February, 2022, Lincoln*
**England** 310-9 defeated **Bangladesh** 201 by 109 runs

*1 March, 2022, Rangiora*
**India** 258 defeated **West Indies** 177 by 81 runs

*1 March, 2022, Lincoln*
**Australia** 321 (M.M. Lanning 87, A.J. Healy 64, A.K. Gardner 60, B.L. Mooney 55, H.M. Rowe 4-49) lost to **New Zealand** 325-1 (S.F.M. Devine 161*, A.C. Kerr 92*, S.W. Bates 63) by 9 wickets

*2 March, 2022, Lincoln*
**Pakistan** 199-7 defeated **Bangladesh** 194 by 5 runs

*2 March, 2022, Rangiora*
**South Africa** 138-9 lost to **England** 139-4 by 6 wickets

## WORLD CUP

*5 March 2022, Hamilton*
**Australia** 310-3 **beat England** 298-8 by 12 runs

*5 March 2022, Dunedin*
**South Africa** 207 **beat Bangladesh** 175 by 32 runs

*6 March 2022, Mt Maunganui*
**India** 244-7 **beat Pakistan** 137 by 107 runs

*8 March 2022, Mt Maunganui*
**Pakistan** 190-6 **lost to Australia** 193-3 by 7 wickets

*9 March 2022, Dunedin*
**West Indies** 225-6 **beat England** 218 by 7 runs

*11 March 2022, Mt Maunganui*
**South Africa** 223-9 **beat Pakistan** 217 by 6 runs

*12 March 2022, Hamilton*
**India** 317-8 **beat West Indies** 162 by 155 runs

*14 March 2022, Hamilton*
**Bangladesh** 234-7 **defeated Pakistan** 225-9 by 9 runs

*14 March 2022, Mt Maunganui*
**England** 235-9 **lost to South Africa** 236-7 by 3 wickets

*15 March 2022, Wellington*
**West Indies** 131 **lost to Australia** 132-3 by 7 wickets

*16 March 2022, Mt Maunganui*
**India** 134 **lost to England** 136-6 by 4 wickets

*18 March 2022, Mt Maunganui*
**West Indies** 140-9 **defeated Bangladesh** 136 by 4 runs

*19 March 2022, Auckland*
**India** 277-7 **lost to Australia** 280-4 by 6 wickets

*21 March 2022, Hamilton*
**West Indies** 89-7 **lost to Pakistan** 90-2 by 8 wickets

*22 March 2022, Wellington*
**South Africa** 271-5 **lost to Australia** 272-5 by 5 wickets

*22 March 2022, Hamilton*
**India** 229-7 **defeated Bangladesh** 119 by 110 runs

*24 March 2022, Wellington*
**South Africa** 61-4 **v West Indies** no result

*24 March 2022, Christchurch*
**Pakistan** 105 **lost to England** 107-1 by 9 wickets

*25 March 2022, Wellington*
**Bangladesh** 135-6 **lost to Australia** 136-5 by 5 wickets

*27 March 2022, Wellington*
**England** 234-6 **defeated Bangladesh** 134 by 100 runs

*27 March 2022, Christchurch*
**India** 274-7 **lost to South Africa** 275-7 by 3 wickets

**Points:** Australia 14, South Africa 11, England 8, West Indies 7, India 6, New Zealand 6, Bangladesh 2, Pakistan 2.

### SEMI-FINALS

*30 March 2022, Wellington*
**Australia** 305-3 **beat West Indies** 148 by 157 runs

*31 March 2022, Christchurch*
**England** 293-8 **beat South Africa** 156 by 137 runs

### FINAL

*3 April 2022, Christchurch*
**Australia** 356-5 (A.J. Healy 170, R.L. Haynes 68, B.L. Mooney 62, A. Shrubsole 3-46)
**beat England** 285 (N.R. Sciver 148*, J.L. Jonassen 3-57, A.M. King 3-64) by 71 runs

# NEW ZEALAND v WEST INDIES                 World Cup

*at Bay Oval, Mt Maunganui on 4 March, 2022 (d/n)*
*Toss : New Zealand. Umpires : L. Agenbag & Sharfuddoula*
**West Indies won by 3 runs**

New Zealand won the toss and decided to field in the tournament opener. Matthews was the star of the West Indies' innings, reaching fifty from 55 balls, her century from 118 and going on to her highest score. Taylor, Campbelle and Nation all gave good support and West Indies reached 259-9.

New Zealand lost Bates to a deflection of the bowler and Amelia Kerr went at 47. Devine and Satterthwaite added 76 but wickets fell quickly and the home side were 162-6. Devine (fifty from 70 balls and a century from 117) was seventh out at 215 but Martin and Jess Kerr added 40 to put New Zealand in sight of the target.

Dottin, who had not bowled in the innings, came on to bowl the fiftieth over and dismissed Martin with her second ball. This left New Zealand needing five runs off four balls. Kerr went two balls later with four still required and Jonas was run out next ball as she attempted to steal a bye, leaving West Indies the winners by three runs.

## WEST INDIES

| | Runs | Mins | Balls | 6s | 4s |
|---|---|---|---|---|---|
| D.J.S.Dottin c Kerr J.M. | | | | | |
| b Tahuhu | 12 | 7 | 7 | - | 3 |
| H.K.Matthews c Rowe | | | | | |
| b Kerr J.M. | 119 | 171 | 128 | 1 | 16 |
| Kycia A.Knight c Jonas | | | | | |
| b Kerr J.M. | 5 | 13 | 9 | - | 1 |
| S.R.Taylor* c Martin b Tahuhu . | 30 | 60 | 47 | - | 3 |
| S.A.Campbelle† lbw b Kerr A.C. | 20 | 48 | 38 | - | 2 |
| C.N.Nation c Martin b Tahuhu .. | 36 | 59 | 46 | - | 4 |
| C.A.Henry c Green b Rowe | 8 | 15 | 10 | - | 1 |
| A.A.Alleyne run out | 2 | 8 | 3 | - | - |
| S.S.Connell not out | 4 | 12 | 6 | - | - |
| A.Mohammed run out | 11 | 6 | 6 | - | 2 |
| S.C.Selman | | | | | |
| Extras (lb 3, w 9) | 12 | | | | |
| **TOTAL** (50 overs) (9 wkts) . | **259** | 201 | | | |

## NEW ZEALAND

| | Runs | Mins | Balls | 6s | 4s |
|---|---|---|---|---|---|
| S.W.Bates run out | 3 | 13 | 6 | - | - |
| S.F.M.Devine* c & b Henry | 108 | 186 | 127 | - | 10 |
| A.C.Kerr lbw b Matthews | 13 | 33 | 19 | - | 2 |
| A.E.Satterthwaite | | | | | |
| lbw b Mohammed | 31 | 70 | 56 | - | 1 |
| L.M.M.Tahuhu b Mohammed | 6 | 8 | 5 | - | 1 |
| M.L.Green c Taylor b Selman | 9 | 14 | 11 | - | 1 |
| B.M.Halliday c Mohammed | | | | | |
| b Matthews | 3 | 9 | 7 | - | - |
| K.J.Martin† lbw b Dottin | 44 | 64 | 47 | - | 4 |
| J.M.Kerr c Henry b Dottin | 25 | 28 | 21 | - | 3 |
| H.M.Rowe not out | 1 | 4 | 2 | - | - |
| F.C.Jonas run out | 0 | 2 | 0 | - | - |
| Extras (lb 5, w 6, nb 2) | 13 | | | | |
| **TOTAL** (49.5 overs) | **256** | 218 | | | |

| Bowling | O | M | R | W |
|---|---|---|---|---|
| **NEW ZEALAND** | | | | |
| Tahuhu | 9 | 0 | 57 | 3 |
| Kerr J.M. | 10 | 0 | 43 | 2 |
| Rowe | 9 | 0 | 51 | 1 |
| Devine | 6 | 0 | 33 | 0 |
| Kerr A.C. | 10 | 1 | 33 | 1 |
| Jonas | 6 | 0 | 39 | 0 |
| **WEST INDIES** | | | | |
| Connell | 5 | 0 | 25 | 0 |
| Henry | 10 | 1 | 53 | 1 |
| Alleyne | 7 | 0 | 33 | 0 |
| Matthews | 10 | 1 | 41 | 2 |
| Selman | 7 | 0 | 37 | 1 |
| Mohammed | 10 | 0 | 60 | 2 |
| Dottin | 0.5 | 0 | 2 | 2 |

| Fall of Wickets | | |
|---|---|---|
| | WI | NZ |
| 1st | 16 | 14 |
| 2nd | 39 | 47 |
| 3rd | 105 | 123 |
| 4th | 165 | 131 |
| 5th | 220 | 152 |
| 6th | 234 | 162 |
| 7th | 243 | 215 |
| 8th | 246 | 255 |
| 9th | 259 | 256 |
| 10th | - | 256 |

**NZC**

# NEW ZEALAND v BANGLADESH

**World Cup**

*at University of Otago Oval, Dunedin on 7 March, 2022*
*Toss : New Zealand. Umpires : C.A. Polosak & P. Wilson*
**New Zealand won by 9 wickets**

Rain reduced this game to 27 overs per side, with New Zealand again winning the toss and bowling. The Bangladesh openers made a bright start and had reached 59 in the tenth over before Shamima was dismissed. Farzana reached fifty off 60 balls while wickets fell at the other end and Bangladesh ended with 140-8 after their 27 overs.

New Zealand lost Devine at 36 but were untroubled from then on. Bates, who was playing her first game for New Zealand in her home city in her long career, got to fifty from 51 balls and shared an unbroken stand of 108 with Amelia Kerr .

## BANGLADESH

| | Runs | Mins | Balls | 6s | 4s |
|---|---|---|---|---|---|
| Shamima Sultana† c Tahuhu b Mackay | 33 | 39 | 36 | - | 4 |
| Farzana Haque run out | 52 | 92 | 63 | - | 1 |
| Nigar Sultana* c Martin b Satterthwaite | 11 | 18 | 13 | - | 1 |
| Rumana Ahmed b Satterthwaite | 1 | 3 | 4 | - | - |
| Sobhana Mostary c Green b Jensen | 13 | 22 | 21 | - | 1 |
| Ritu Moni c Devine b Satterthwaite | 4 | 4 | 2 | - | 1 |
| Salma Khatun run out | 9 | 12 | 10 | - | - |
| Lata Mondal not out | 9 | 16 | 10 | - | - |
| Jahanara Alam run out | 2 | 6 | 3 | - | - |
| Naihida Akter not out | 0 | 1 | 0 | - | - |
| Fariha Trisna | | | | | |
| Extras (b 1, lb 1, w 4) | 6 | | | | |
| **TOTAL** (27 overs) (8 wkts) | **140** | 108 | | | |

## NEW ZEALAND

| | Runs | Mins | Balls | 6s | 4s |
|---|---|---|---|---|---|
| S.F.M.Devine* b Khatun | 14 | 28 | 16 | - | 1 |
| S.W.Bates not out | 79 | 89 | 68 | - | 8 |
| A.C.Kerr not out | 47 | 60 | 37 | - | 5 |
| A.E.Satterthwaite | | | | | |
| L.M.M.Tahuhu | | | | | |
| M.L.Green | | | | | |
| F.L.Mackay | | | | | |
| K.J.Martin† | | | | | |
| J.M.Kerr | | | | | |
| H.M.Rowe | | | | | |
| H.N.K.Jensen | | | | | |
| Extras (b 1, w 2, nb 1) | 4 | | | | |
| **TOTAL** (20 overs) (1 wkt) | **144** | 89 | | | |

| Bowling | O | M | R | W |
|---|---|---|---|---|
| **NEW ZEALAND** | | | | |
| Tahuhu | 2 | 0 | 19 | 0 |
| Kerr J.M. | 5 | 1 | 24 | 0 |
| Jensen | 3 | 0 | 18 | 1 |
| Kerr A.C. | 6 | 0 | 28 | 0 |
| Mackay | 6 | 0 | 24 | 1 |
| Satterthwaite | 5 | 0 | 25 | 3 |
| **BANGLADESH** | | | | |
| Jahanara | 3 | 0 | 25 | 0 |
| Trisna | 3 | 0 | 17 | 0 |
| Khatun | 4 | 0 | 34 | 1 |
| Nahida | 5 | 1 | 31 | 0 |
| Moni | 2 | 0 | 13 | 0 |
| Rumana | 2 | 0 | 14 | 0 |
| Mondal | 1 | 0 | 9 | 0 |

| Fall of Wickets | | |
|---|---|---|
| | B | NZ |
| 1st | 59 | 36 |
| 2nd | 79 | - |
| 3rd | 81 | - |
| 4th | 108 | - |
| 5th | 118 | - |
| 6th | 119 | - |
| 7th | 130 | - |
| 8th | 139 | - |
| 9th | - | - |
| 10th | - | - |

# NEW ZEALAND v INDIA

**World Cup**

*at Seddon Park, Hamilton on 10 March, 2022 (d/n)*
*Toss : India. Umpires : R.S.A. Palliyaguruge & S. Redfern*
**New Zealand won by 62 runs**

New Zealand were sent in and soon lost Bates to a run out. Amelia Kerr and Satterthwaite (fifties from 63 and 60 balls) put on 67 for the third wicket and Martin made a valuable 41 before being dismissed in the last over. Vastrakar finished with 4-34 from her ten overs.

India made a very slow start and were 26-2 after ten overs. Despite Kaur's half-century from 54 balls, India were always well behind the asking rate and the innings ended in the 47th over with wickets from successive deliveries from Jensen. New Zealand won by 62 runs with Tahuhu taking 3-17 from ten overs.

## NEW ZEALAND

| | Runs | Mins | Balls | 6s | 4s |
|---|---|---|---|---|---|
| S.W.Bates run out | 5 | 11 | 10 | - | 1 |
| S.F.M.Devine*c Ghosh b Vastrakar | 35 | 48 | 30 | - | 7 |
| A.C.Kerr lbw b Gayakwad | 50 | 81 | 64 | - | 5 |
| A.E.Satterthwaite c Raj b Vastrakar | 75 | 121 | 84 | - | 9 |
| M.L.Green c Mandhana b Sharma | 27 | 47 | 36 | - | 3 |
| K.J.Martin† b Goswami | 41 | 59 | 51 | - | 3 |
| H.N.K.Jensen b Gayakwad | 1 | 12 | 7 | - | - |
| L.M.M.Tahuhu b Vastrakar | 1 | 5 | 4 | - | - |
| J.M.Kerr b Vastrakar | 0 | 1 | 1 | - | - |
| F.L.Mackay not out | 13 | 16 | 11 | - | 1 |
| H.M.Rowe not out | 2 | 4 | 3 | - | - |
| Extras (b 1, lb 5, w 3, nb 1) | 10 | | | | |
| **TOTAL** (50 overs) (9 wkts) | **260** | 202 | | | |

## INDIA

| | Runs | Mins | Balls | 6s | 4s |
|---|---|---|---|---|---|
| Y.H.Bhatia c Mackay b Tahuhu | 28 | 77 | 59 | - | 2 |
| S.S.Mandhana c Bates b Kerr J.M. | 6 | 17 | 21 | - | - |
| D.B.Sharma lbw b Tahuhu | 5 | 20 | 13 | - | 1 |
| M.Raj* st Martin b Kerr A.C. | 31 | 79 | 56 | - | 1 |
| H.Kaur c Devine b Kerr A.C. | 71 | 98 | 63 | 2 | 6 |
| R.M.Ghosh† b Kerr A.C. | 0 | 2 | 1 | - | - |
| S.Rana c Martin b Tahuhu | 18 | 30 | 28 | - | 2 |
| P.Vastrakar c Bates b Rowe | 6 | 14 | 16 | - | - |
| J.N.Goswami b Jensen | 15 | 24 | 13 | 1 | 1 |
| Meghna Sing not out | 12 | 12 | 9 | - | 2 |
| R.S.Gayakwad c Martin b Jensen | 0 | 2 | 1 | - | - |
| Extras (lb 2, w 4) | 6 | | | | |
| **TOTAL** (46.4 overs) | **198** | 186 | | | |

| Bowling | O | M | R | W |
|---|---|---|---|---|
| **INDIA** | | | | |
| Goswami | 9 | 1 | 41 | 1 |
| Meghna | 8 | 0 | 49 | 0 |
| Gayakwad | 10 | 0 | 46 | 2 |
| Vastrakar | 10 | 0 | 34 | 4 |
| Sharma | 8 | 0 | 52 | 1 |
| Rana | 5 | 0 | 32 | 0 |
| **NEW ZEALAND** | | | | |
| Mackay | 8 | 1 | 25 | 0 |
| Kerr J.M. | 7 | 1 | 40 | 1 |
| Rowe | 6 | 1 | 28 | 1 |
| Tahuhu | 10 | 2 | 17 | 3 |
| Jensen | 6.4 | 0 | 30 | 2 |
| Kerr A.C. | 9 | 0 | 56 | 3 |

| Fall of Wickets | | |
|---|---|---|
| | NZ | I |
| 1st | 9 | 10 |
| 2nd | 54 | 26 |
| 3rd | 121 | 50 |
| 4th | 175 | 97 |
| 5th | 224 | 97 |
| 6th | 233 | 127 |
| 7th | 240 | 143 |
| 8th | 240 | 178 |
| 9th | 255 | 198 |
| 10th | - | 198 |

**NZC**

# NEW ZEALAND v AUSTRALIA

## World Cup

*at Basin Reserve, Wellington on 13 March, 2022*
*Toss : New Zealand. Umpires : L. Agenbag & L. Rusere*
**Australia won by 141 runs**

New Zealand won the toss and had Australia 56-3 in the sixteenth over. Perry (fifty from 74 balls) and Mooney took the score to 113 and McGrath (fifty from 47 balls) helped Perry in a century stand for the fifth wicket. Gardner then arrived at the crease and hit an unbeaten 48 off just 18 balls, with 40 runs coming in boundaries.

New Zealand lost wickets at 22, 23 and 24 and were 35-5 and then 86-8. Tahuhu hit out to take the score into three figures but the result was obvious by that stage. New Zealand were bowled out in the 31st over with Brown taking 3-22 from seven overs.

### AUSTRALIA

| | Runs | Mins | Balls | 6s | 4s |
|---|---|---|---|---|---|
| R.L.Haynes b Tahuhu | 30 | 62 | 44 | - | 4 |
| A.J.Healy† c Kerr A.C. b Mackay | 15 | 37 | 31 | - | 2 |
| M.M.Lanning* c Martin b Jensen | 5 | 19 | 15 | - | - |
| E.A.Perry c Green b Tahuhu | 68 | 114 | 86 | 1 | 6 |
| B.L.Mooney b Kerr A.C. | 30 | 50 | 44 | - | 2 |
| T.M.McGrath c Bates b Rowe | 57 | 66 | 56 | - | 8 |
| A.K.Gardner not out | 48 | 23 | 18 | 4 | 4 |
| A.M.King c Bates b Tahuhu | 2 | 4 | 5 | - | - |
| A-J.Wellington run out | 1 | 6 | 3 | - | - |
| M.L.Schutt not out | 0 | 3 | 0 | - | - |
| D.R.Brown | | | | | |
| Extras (lb 1, w 10, nb 2) | 13 | | | | |
| **TOTAL** (50 overs) (8 wkts) | **269** | 198 | | | |

### NEW ZEALAND

| | Runs | Mins | Balls | 6s | 4s |
|---|---|---|---|---|---|
| S.W.Bates c McGrath b Brown | 16 | 33 | 28 | - | 1 |
| S.F.M.Devine* b Perry | 6 | 18 | 6 | - | 1 |
| A.C.Kerr c Mooney b Brown | 1 | 3 | 3 | - | - |
| A.E.Satterthwaite c Lanning b Gardner | 44 | 97 | 67 | - | 5 |
| M.L.Green c Healy b McGrath | 3 | 12 | 10 | - | - |
| F.L.Mackay lbw b Brown | 1 | 3 | 2 | - | - |
| K.J.Martin† lbw b Wellington | 19 | 35 | 27 | - | 2 |
| H.N.K.Jensen c McGrath b Wellington | 0 | 1 | 1 | - | - |
| H.M.Rowe c Perry b Schutt | 6 | 8 | 8 | - | 1 |
| L.M.M.Tahuhu c Mooney b Gardner | 23 | 32 | 25 | 1 | 2 |
| J.M.Kerr not out | 6 | 7 | 5 | - | 1 |
| Extras (w 3) | 3 | | | | |
| **TOTAL** (30.2 overs) | **128** | 130 | | | |

| Bowling | O | M | R | W |
|---|---|---|---|---|
| **NEW ZEALAND** | | | | |
| Kerr J.M. | 8 | 1 | 34 | 0 |
| Rowe | 9 | 0 | 50 | 1 |
| Mackay | 7 | 0 | 34 | 1 |
| Jensen | 8 | 0 | 55 | 1 |
| Tahuhu | 9 | 0 | 53 | 3 |
| Kerr A.C. | 9 | 0 | 42 | 1 |
| **AUSTRALIA** | | | | |
| Perry | 5 | 0 | 18 | 1 |
| Brown | 7 | 1 | 22 | 3 |
| McGrath | 3 | 0 | 17 | 1 |
| Wellington | 6 | 0 | 34 | 2 |
| Schutt | 6 | 0 | 22 | 1 |
| Gardner | 3.2 | 0 | 15 | 2 |

| Fall of Wickets | A | NZ |
|---|---|---|
| 1st | 37 | 22 |
| 2nd | 54 | 23 |
| 3rd | 56 | 24 |
| 4th | 113 | 30 |
| 5th | 214 | 35 |
| 6th | 229 | 73 |
| 7th | 238 | 73 |
| 8th | 253 | 86 |
| 9th | - | 121 |
| 10th | - | 128 |

# NEW ZEALAND v SOUTH AFRICA
## World Cup

*at Seddon Park, Hamilton on 17 March, 2022 (d/n)*
*Toss : New Zealand. Umpires : Ahmed Shah & S. Redfern*
**South Africa won by 2 wickets**

New Zealand again won the toss but batted. Bates went early but Devine (fifty from 61 balls) and Amelia Kerr took the total to 87. Devine and Green added 80 for the fourth wicket but when Devine was dismissed in the 41st over, the innings fell away. Five further wickets fell in 7.3 overs for the addition of just 30 runs with Ismail and Khaka taking three wickets each.

South Africa were on top at 161-2 after a third wicket stand of 88 between Wolvaardt and Luus (fifties from 72 and 67 balls) but the innings then threatened to follow the same pattern as New Zealand's. Ismail was eighth out with twelve runs needed off ten balls but Kapp and Khaka were able to take their side to victory with three balls to spare.

### NEW ZEALAND

| | Runs | Mins | Balls | 6s | 4s |
|---|---|---|---|---|---|
| S.W.Bates b Ismail | 4 | 10 | 7 | - | - |
| S.F.M.Devine* b Khaka | 93 | 158 | 101 | 1 | 12 |
| A.C.Kerr lbw b Luus | 42 | 57 | 58 | - | 5 |
| A.E.Satterthwaite c Chetty b Khaka | 1 | 2 | 3 | - | - |
| M.L.Green run out | 30 | 57 | 58 | - | 1 |
| B.M.Halliday b Kapp | 24 | 44 | 29 | - | 1 |
| K.J.Martin† b Ismail | 9 | 8 | 8 | - | 1 |
| F.L.Mackay not out | 7 | 26 | 13 | - | - |
| H.M.Rowe c Chetty b Kapp | 0 | 2 | 1 | - | - |
| L.M.M.Tahuhu b Ismail | 0 | 4 | 3 | - | - |
| J.M.Kerr c Kapp b Khaka | 6 | 5 | 6 | - | 1 |
| Extras (b 1, lb 1, w 10) | 12 | | | | |
| **TOTAL** (47.5 overs) | **228** | 191 | | | |

### SOUTH AFRICA

| | Runs | Mins | Balls | 6s | 4s |
|---|---|---|---|---|---|
| L.Lee run out | 17 | 20 | 23 | - | 2 |
| L.Wolvaardt lbw b Kerr A.C. | 67 | 136 | 94 | - | 6 |
| T.Brits st Martin b Kerr A.C. | 18 | 50 | 38 | - | 3 |
| S.Luus* c Martin b Rowe | 51 | 80 | 73 | - | 4 |
| M.du Preez c Martin b Kerr A.C. | 1 | 6 | 5 | - | - |
| M.Kapp not out | 34 | 53 | 35 | - | 4 |
| C.L.Tryon c Kerr A.C. b Mackay | 14 | 19 | 17 | - | 1 |
| T.Chetty† c & b Mackay | 3 | 8 | 4 | - | - |
| S.Ismail b Devine | 4 | 8 | 5 | - | - |
| A.Khaka not out | 2 | 6 | 3 | - | - |
| M.M.Klaas | | | | | |
| Extras (b 1, lb 3, w 14) | 18 | | | | |
| **TOTAL** (49.3 overs) (8 wkts) | **229** | 197 | | | |

| Bowling | O | M | R | W |
|---|---|---|---|---|
| **SOUTH AFRICA** | | | | |
| Ismail | 9 | 1 | 27 | 3 |
| Kapp | 10 | 0 | 44 | 2 |
| Khaka | 8.5 | 1 | 31 | 3 |
| Klaas | 2 | 0 | 19 | 0 |
| Tryon | 10 | 0 | 57 | 0 |
| Luus | 8 | 0 | 48 | 1 |
| **NEW ZEALAND** | | | | |
| Mackay | 8.3 | 0 | 49 | 2 |
| Kerr J.M. | 7 | 0 | 23 | 0 |
| Rowe | 10 | 0 | 32 | 1 |
| Devine | 5 | 0 | 27 | 1 |
| Tahuhu | 9 | 0 | 44 | 0 |
| Kerr A.C. | 10 | 1 | 50 | 3 |

**Fall of Wickets**

| | NZ | SA |
|---|---|---|
| 1st | 6 | 25 |
| 2nd | 87 | 73 |
| 3rd | 88 | 161 |
| 4th | 168 | 166 |
| 5th | 198 | 170 |
| 6th | 210 | 198 |
| 7th | 220 | 211 |
| 8th | 220 | 217 |
| 9th | 221 | - |
| 10th | 228 | - |

**NZC**

# NEW ZEALAND v ENGLAND

**World Cup**

*at Eden Park, Auckland on 20 March, 2022*
*Toss : England. Umpires : R.S.A. Palliyaguruge & J.M. Williams*
**England won by 1 wicket**

England won the toss and fielded but some wayward bowling saw New Zealand off to a bright start before Bates went in the twelfth over. Devine retired hurt six runs later with a back injury but Amelia Kerr, Satterthwaite and Green had New Zealand handily placed at 130-2 after thirty overs. England struck back and the hosts were bowled out in the 49th over, having added just 73 further runs, which included 42 for the last two wickets.

England looked set for a comfortable victory at 176-4 but Mackay sparked a collapse and five wickets fell for 20 runs to leave England 196-9. Shrubsole took two singles, Dean held out for three balls and five runs were needed off three overs. Shrubsole hit Halliday for four to level the scores and a single gave England victory. Tahuhu had been unable to complete her fifth over and took no further part in the game. Mair fielded substitute for Devine throughout the England innings.

## NEW ZEALAND

| | Runs | Mins | Balls | 6s | 4s |
|---|---|---|---|---|---|
| S.W.Bates c Beaumont b Cross | 22 | 47 | 36 | - | 3 |
| S.F.M.Devine* c Dean b Cross. | 41 | 65 | 48 | - | 5 |
| A.C.Kerr c Shrubsole b Dean ... | 24 | 43 | 38 | - | 3 |
| A.E.Satterthwaite lbw b Dean ... | 24 | 55 | 42 | - | 3 |
| M.L.Green not out | 52 | 96 | 75 | 1 | 4 |
| B.M.Halliday run out | 2 | 7 | 10 | - | - |
| K.J.Martin† lbw b Cross | 6 | 17 | 15 | - | - |
| L.M.M.Tahuhu c Knight | | | | | |
| b Ecclestone | 0 | 4 | 3 | - | - |
| F.L.Mackay lbw b Ecclestone ..... | 1 | 3 | 2 | - | - |
| H.M.Rowe c Jones b Ecclestone | 5 | 16 | 11 | - | - |
| J.M.Kerr run out | 14 | 15 | 13 | - | 2 |
| Extras (lb 5, w 7) | 12 | | | | |
| **TOTAL** (48.5 overs) | **203** | 193 | | | |

## ENGLAND

| | Runs | Mins | Balls | 6s | 4s |
|---|---|---|---|---|---|
| T.T.Beaumont b Tahuhu | 25 | 41 | 36 | - | 4 |
| D.N.Wyatt c Rowe b Kerr J.M. . | 12 | 11 | 7 | - | 3 |
| H.C.Knight* lbw b Mackay | 42 | 82 | 53 | - | 4 |
| N.R.Sciver b Kerr J.M. | 61 | 134 | 108 | - | 5 |
| A.E.Jones† c Satterthwaite | | | | | |
| b Halliday | 1 | 12 | 5 | - | - |
| S.I.R.Dunkley b Mackay | 33 | 58 | 43 | 1 | 3 |
| K.H.Brunt run out | 6 | 23 | 11 | - | - |
| S.Ecclestone b Mackay | 0 | 4 | 5 | - | - |
| K.L.Cross lbw b Mackay | 2 | 2 | 3 | - | - |
| C.E.Dean not out | 0 | 16 | 3 | - | - |
| A.Shrubsole not out | 7 | 11 | 10 | - | 1 |
| Extras (b 4, w 11) | 15 | | | | |
| **TOTAL** (47.2 overs) (9 wkts) | **204** | 202 | | | |

| Bowling | O | M | R | W |
|---|---|---|---|---|
| **ENGLAND** | | | | |
| Brunt | 6.5 | 0 | 38 | 0 |
| Shrubsole | 3 | 0 | 21 | 0 |
| Cross | 10 | 0 | 35 | 3 |
| Sciver | 9 | 1 | 27 | 0 |
| Dean | 10 | 0 | 36 | 2 |
| Ecclestone | 10 | 1 | 41 | 3 |
| **NEW ZEALAND** | | | | |
| Kerr J.M. | 10 | 2 | 36 | 2 |
| Rowe | 10 | 1 | 53 | 0 |
| Tahuhu | 4.4 | 1 | 18 | 1 |
| Halliday | 3.4 | 1 | 18 | 1 |
| Kerr A.C. | 10 | 1 | 41 | 0 |
| Mackay | 9 | 0 | 34 | 4 |

**Fall of Wickets**

| | NZ | E |
|---|---|---|
| 1st | 61 | 17 |
| 2nd | 96 | 53 |
| 3rd | 134 | 98 |
| 4th | 137 | 106 |
| 5th | 150 | 176 |
| 6th | 155 | 187 |
| 7th | 160 | 192 |
| 8th | 161 | 194 |
| 9th | 184 | 196 |
| 10th | 203 | - |

*Devine retired hurt on 27\* at 67-1*
*and returned at 155-6*

# NEW ZEALAND v PAKISTAN

**World Cup**

*at Hagley Oval, Christchurch on 26 March, 2022*
*Toss : Pakistan. Umpires : C.A. Polosak & L. Rusere*
**New Zealand won by 71 runs**

Pakistan won the toss and batted in the final game for both sides. Bates dominated the New Zealand innings, reaching fifty from 54 balls and her twelfth one-day international century from 110 deliveries. Amelia Kerr, Green and Halliday assisted in fifty partnerships but the innings fell away until Martin and Mackay took 32 off the last two overs.

Pakistan made a bright start but then lost both openers and never threatened to reach their target. Nidar Dar followed up her three wickets with 50 off 53 balls but Pakistan's ninth wicket fell with nine overs still remaining. Sandhu and Amin batted out the remaining overs as New Zealand won by 71 runs. Rowe achieved her first five wicket haul for New Zealand.

## NEW ZEALAND

| | Runs | Mins | Balls | 6s | 4s |
|---|---|---|---|---|---|
| S.W.Bates b Sandhu | 126 | 167 | 135 | - | 14 |
| S.F.M.Devine* b Amin | 12 | 25 | 10 | 1 | 1 |
| A.C.Kerr c Ameen b Dar | 24 | 52 | 31 | - | 1 |
| A.E.Satterthwaite c Ameen b Dar | 0 | 2 | 1 | - | - |
| M.L.Green b Dar | 23 | 50 | 48 | - | - |
| B.M.Halliday b Fatima | 29 | 52 | 38 | - | 3 |
| K.J.Martin† not out | 30 | 34 | 26 | - | 4 |
| J.M.Kerr run out | 6 | 4 | 4 | - | 1 |
| H.M.Rowe run out | 1 | 3 | 2 | - | - |
| F.L.Mackay not out | 9 | 12 | 7 | - | 1 |
| R.A.Mair | | | | | |

Extras (b 1, lb 1, w 1, nb 2) ...... 5
**TOTAL** (50 overs) (8 wkts) . **265** 209

## PAKISTAN

| | Runs | Mins | Balls | 6s | 4s |
|---|---|---|---|---|---|
| Muneeba Ali c Devine b Mair | 29 | 42 | 45 | 1 | 3 |
| Sidra Ameen c Halliday b Mackay | 14 | 34 | 21 | - | 2 |
| Bismah Maroof* c Martin b Rowe | 38 | 91 | 66 | - | 2 |
| Omaima Sohail c Satterthwaite b Mackay | 14 | 27 | 26 | - | 2 |
| Nida Dar b Rowe | 50 | 72 | 53 | 1 | 5 |
| Aliya Riaz c Martin b Rowe | 1 | 5 | 7 | - | - |
| Sidra Nawaz† b Rowe | 10 | 18 | 12 | - | 1 |
| Fatima Sana c Rowe b Kerr A.C. | 0 | 8 | 7 | - | - |
| Diana Baig c Mair b Rowe | 6 | 9 | 6 | - | 1 |
| Nashra Sandhu not out | 10 | 33 | 34 | - | 1 |
| Anam Amin not out | 11 | 29 | 23 | - | 1 |

Extras (w 11) ........................... 11
**TOTAL** (50 overs) (9 wkts) . **194** 201

| Bowling | O | M | R | W |
|---|---|---|---|---|
| **PAKISTAN** | | | | |
| Baig | 5 | 0 | 23 | 0 |
| Amin | 9 | 1 | 58 | 1 |
| Fatima | 10 | 0 | 69 | 1 |
| Sandhu | 10 | 0 | 50 | 1 |
| Dar | 10 | 0 | 39 | 3 |
| Omaima | 6 | 0 | 24 | 0 |
| **NEW ZEALAND** | | | | |
| Kerr J.M. | 7 | 0 | 22 | 0 |
| Rowe | 10 | 1 | 55 | 5 |
| Mackay | 10 | 1 | 29 | 2 |
| Mair | 8 | 1 | 29 | 1 |
| Kerr A.C. | 10 | 0 | 36 | 1 |
| Satterthwaite | 5 | 0 | 23 | 0 |

| Fall of Wickets | | |
|---|---|---|
| | NZ | P |
| 1st | 31 | 39 |
| 2nd | 99 | 47 |
| 3rd | 100 | 73 |
| 4th | 160 | 155 |
| 5th | 211 | 157 |
| 6th | 223 | 158 |
| 7th | 229 | 165 |
| 8th | 231 | 173 |
| 9th | - | 174 |
| 10th | - | - |

# NEW ZEALAND INTERNATIONAL RECORDS

## REGISTER OF PLAYERS

| | Born | Died | Type | | Career |
|---|---|---|---|---|---|
| **Allan**<br>Elizabeth Patricia Norris | 6/11/1948<br>Auckland | | RHB | RM | 1971/72-1977/78 |
| **Anderson**<br>Kelly Sarah | 4/02/1983<br>Auckland | | RHB | RM | 2011 |
| **Anderson**<br>Trudy Lee | 26/08/1959<br>Dunedin | | RHB | RSM | 1992/93-1996/97 |
| **Astle**<br>Lisa Marie | 17/05/1973<br>Christchurch | | RHB | RM | 1993 |
| **Badham**<br>Eileen Anne | 2/11/1951<br>Mangakino | | RHB | LM | 1977/78-1981/82 |
| **Bailey**<br>Doris Lilian | 6/12/1916<br>Wellington | 30/11/2009<br>Waikanae | RHB | RM | 1948/49 |
| **Bastion**<br>Helen Rachel | 26/05/1976<br>Hamilton | | RHB | LM | 1996-1996/97 |
| **Bates**<br>Suzannah Wilson | 16/09/1987<br>Dunedin | | RHB | RM | 2005/06-2021/22 |
| **Batty**<br>Kathleen Elaine | 15/12/1920<br>Auckland | 16/12/2008<br>Auckland | RHB | RFM | 1948/49-1954 |
| **Bayliss**<br>Loretta Irene | 25/11/1939<br>Christchurch | 30/06/1966<br>Christchurch | LHB | LFM | 1960/61 |
| **Bermingham**<br>Erin Margaret | 18/04/1988<br>Greymouth | | RHB | RLB | 2009/10-2017 |
| **Bevege**<br>Barbara Lynette | 25/11/1942<br>Wellington | 29/04/1999<br>Wellington | RHB | RM | 1973-1981/82 |
| **Bezuidenhout**<br>Bernadine Michelle | 14/09/1993<br>Kimberley, South Africa | | RHB | WK | 2018-2019/20 |
| **Bishop**<br>Marjorie Claire | 3/01/1910<br>Christchurch | 26/01/1960<br>Christchurch | RHB | ROB | 1934/35 |
| **Blackie**<br>Esther Elizabeth | 29/01/1916<br>Invercargill | 9/03/1991<br>Invercargill | RHB | WK | 1948/49 |
| **Blackler**<br>Phyllis | 13/06/1919<br>Christchurch | 25/05/1975<br>Christchurch | RHB | RLB | 1947/48-1966 |
| **Bond**<br>Kirsty Elizabeth | 20/11/1967<br>Christchurch | | RHB | RM | 1988/89-1996 |
| **Brehaut**<br>Janet Catherine | 24/07/1988<br>Timaru | | RHB | RM | 2011 |
| **Brentnall**<br>Beverley Anne | 21/02/1936<br>Auckland | | RHB | WK | 1966-1973 |
| **Broadmore**<br>Kate Ellen | 11/11/1991<br>New Plymouth | | RHB | RM | 2009/10-2020/21 |
| **Brown**<br>Kelly Dianne | 8/07/1973<br>Hamilton | | RHB | RM | 1996-1997/98 |
| **Brown**<br>Susan Helen | 1/04/1958<br>Christchurch | | RHB | RM | 1978/79-1985/86 |
| **Browne**<br>Nancy Ariel | 5/09/1913<br>Auckland | 10/10/1996<br>Auckland | RHB | LM | 1934/35 |
| **Browne**<br>Nicola Jane | 14/09/1983<br>Matamata | | RHB | RM | 2001/02-2013/14 |
| **Brownlee**<br>Delwyn Karen | 10/01/1969<br>Christchurch | | RHB | | 1994/95 |
| **Buck**<br>Hilda Evelyn | 27/12/1914<br>Palmerston North | 10/05/1990<br>Wellington | RHB | WK | 1934/35 |
| **Bullen**<br>Saskia Mary | 20/07/1983<br>Auckland | | RHB | SLA | 2009-2009/10 |

| | Born | Died | Type | | Career |
|---|---|---|---|---|---|
| **Burke** | 2/01/1982 | | RHB | RM | 2002/03-2007/08 |
| Sarah Kate | Christchurch | | | | |
| **Burley** | 2/09/1942 | | RHB | RFM | 1966-1973 |
| Jocelyn Anne | Auckland | | | | |
| **Burrows** | 29/01/1977 | | LHB | RM | 2008/09-2009/10 |
| Abby Kirstyn | Whakatane | | | | |
| **Butler** | 26/05/1933 | 24/02/2009 | RHB | | 1954-1960/61 |
| Elizabeth Margaret | Dunedin | Dunedin | | | |
| **Caird** | 24/11/1958 | | RHB | ROB | 1984 |
| Susan Diana | Christchurch | | | | |
| **Campbell** | 20/07/1963 | | LHB | ROB | 1988/89-2000/01 |
| Catherine Anne | Christchurch | | | | |
| **Campbell** | 18/02/1982 | | RHB | RLB | 2009/10 |
| Emma Maree | Timaru | | | | |
| **Candy** | 23/07/1986 | | RHB | RM | 2007-2013/14 |
| Rachel Helen | Palmerston North | | | | |
| **Carrick** | 27/09/1941 | | RHB | RM | 1968/69-1977/78 |
| Patricia Frances | Dunedin | | | | |
| **Charteris** | 5/06/1981 | | RHB | ROB | 2006/07-2007 |
| Selena Eloise | Timaru | | | | |
| **Clark** | 14/03/1962 | | LHB | RSM | 1984-1991/92 |
| Jacqueline | New Plymouth | | | | |
| **Clothier** | 25/05/1922 | 14/06/2003 | RHB | WK | 1954-1960/61 |
| Ivy Joyce | Matamata | Auckland | | | |
| **Clough** | 24/07/1937 | | RHB | RFM | 1968/69 |
| Aletha Louise | Chatham Islands | | | | |
| **Coe** | 17/02/1942 | | RHB | RFM | 1966-1968/69 |
| Wendy Joy | Lower Hutt | | | | |
| **Corbin** | 24/10/1980 | | RHB | ROB | 2001/02-2006/07 |
| Anna Maree | Foxton | | | | |
| **Corby** | 25/10/1913 | 1/10/1993 | RHB | RM | 1934/35 |
| Mabel Cecilia | Wanganui | Wanganui | | | |
| **Costello** | 14/01/1960 | 4/08/2018 | RHB | RM | 1984/85 |
| Delwyn Anne | Christchurch | Christchurch | | | |
| **Coulston** | 8/10/1934 | 30/01/2001 | LHB | RM | 1954-1957/58 |
| Jean Marie | Petone | Lower Hutt | | | |
| **Coutts** | 13/07/1930 | 31/01/2010 | RHB | RM | 1954-1957/58 |
| Verna Reed | Inglewood | Auckland | | | |
| **Cowles** | 26/04/1939 | 5/03/2020 | RHB | RM | 1968/69-1976/77 |
| Shirley Dawn | Christchurch | Christchurch | | | |
| **Cronin-Knight** | 6/10/1977 | | RHB | | 2007/08 |
| Ingrid | Auckland | | | | |
| **Currie** | 4/11/1931 | 5/10/2012 | RHB | RFM | 1954-1957/58 |
| Margaret Joyce | Christchurch | Wellington | | | |
| **Curtis** | 28/10/1985 | | RHB | RLB | 2013/14-2017/18 |
| Samantha Rae Haereakau | Auckland | | | | |
| **Devine** | 1/09/1989 | | RHB | RM | 2006/07-2021/22 |
| Sophie Frances Monique | Wellington | | | | |
| **Dickson** | 11/09/1934 | 16/08/2012 | RHB | RM | 1957/58 |
| Evon Joan | Christchurch | Christchurch | | | |
| **Dodd** | 22/11/1992 | | RHB | WK | 2009/10-2020/21 |
| Natalie Claire | Hamilton | | | | |
| **Doolan** | 11/12/1987 | | RHB | ROB | 2007/08-2012/13 |
| Lucy Rose | Lower Hutt | | | | |
| **Doull** | 15/07/1937 | | RHB | | 1966-1974/75 |
| Judith Diana | Whakatane | | | | |
| **Down** | 7/05/1995 | | RHB | RM | 2017/18-2021/22 |
| Lauren Renee | Auckland | | | | |
| **Drumm** | 15/09/1974 | | RHB | RM | 1991/92-2005/06 |
| Emily Cecilia | Auckland | | | | |
| **Duncan** | 23/10/1932 | | LHB | RFM | 1956/57-1957/58 |
| Brenda Margaret | Gisborne | | | | |

NZC

| | Born | Died | Type | | Career |
|---|---|---|---|---|---|
| **Dunlop** | 4/01/1943 | | RHB | RM | 1973-1981/82 |
| Maureen Helen | Lower Hutt | | | | |
| **Dunning** | 4/03/1957 | | RHB | ROB | 1984-1987/88 |
| Jeanette Rose | Wellsford | | | | |
| **Early** | 11/05/1944 | | RHB | RM | 1971/72-1981/82 |
| Carol Elizabeth | Auckland | | | | |
| **Ell** | 17/01/1917 | 13/07/2003 | RHB | RM | 1934/35 |
| Agnes Elizabeth | Wellington | Wellington | | | |
| **Fahey** | 5/03/1984 | | LHB | ROB | 2003/04-2010 |
| Maria Frances | Timaru | | | | |
| **Farrell** | 20/08/1913 | 22/04/1989 | RHB | WK | 1947/48-1954 |
| Violet Maude Helen | London, England | Wellington | | | |
| **Flannery** | 27/05/1974 | | RHB | ROB | 1999/00-2004 |
| Paula Bernadette | Clyde | | | | |
| **Ford** | 5/02/1965 | | LHB | RM | 1988/89 |
| Deborah Lee | Christchurch | | | | |
| **Francis** | 9/09/1920 | 23/07/1961 | RHB | RFM | 1947/48-1954 |
| Joan Winifred | Wellington | Lower Hutt | | | |
| **Fraser** | 6/09/1980 | | RHB | RM | 2002 |
| Fiona Elizabeth | Wellington | | | | |
| **Fraser** | 30/10/1953 | | RHB | LM | 1981/82-1986/87 |
| Linda Mary | Napier | | | | |
| **Fruin** | 31/12/1961 | | RHB | WK | 1991/92-1997/98 |
| Michelle Kay | Pukekohe | | | | |
| **Fryer** | 8/10/1972 | | RHB | SLA | 1995/96-1997/98 |
| Justine Anne | Dunedin | | | | |
| **Fulford** | 21/08/1914 | 28/05/1987 | RHB | ROB | 1947/48 |
| Marjorie Joyce | Wellington | Wellington | | | |
| **Gilchrist** | 8/10/1958 | | RHB | RM | 1984-1984/85 |
| Shona Mary | Dunedin | | | | |
| **Gooder** | 22/03/1924 | 21/03/1983 | RHB | RSM | 1948/49 |
| Grace Patricia | Auckland | Auckland | | | |
| **Green** | 19/03/1984 | | RHB | RM | 2002/03-2004 |
| Amanda Jayne | Turangi | | | | |
| **Green** | 20/10/1992 | | RHB | ROB | 2011/12-2021/22 |
| Madeline Lee | Auckland | | | | |
| **Gruber** | 30/11/1974 | | RHB | ROB | 1999/00 |
| Paula Anne | Waiouru | | | | |
| **Gunn** | 12/05/1962 | | RHB | RSM | 1984/85-1993 |
| Karen Vivienne | Christchurch | | | | |
| **Gurrey** | 3/08/1995 | | RHB | | 2018/19 |
| Caitlin Ann | Wellington | | | | |
| **Guy** | 26/11/1993 | | RHB | ROB | 2014/15-2015 |
| Georgia Ann | Auckland | | | | |
| **Hadlee** | 26/12/1951 | | RHB | RFM | 1977/78 |
| Karen Ann | Whangarei | | | | |
| **Halliday** | 30/10/1995 | | LHB | RM | 2020/21-2021/22 |
| Brooke Maree | Hamilton | | | | |
| **Harford** | 25/03/1973 | | RHB | ROB | 1997/98 |
| Losalini Ravucake Vuetibau Stephi | Bridgetown, Barbados | | | | |
| **Harris** | 24/11/1960 | | RHB | RM | 1986/87-1996/97 |
| Julie Elizabeth | Lower Hutt | | | | |
| **Harris** | 27/01/1959 | | RHB | RFM | 1977/78 |
| Sheree Angela | Waikari | | | | |
| **Hatcher** | 4/11/1921 | 21/09/2006 | RHB | RM | 1947/48-1954 |
| Joan Constance | Wellington | Wellington | | | |
| **Heffernan** | 7/10/1999 | | RHB | LM | 2017/18 |
| Kate Alexandra | Invercargill | | | | |
| **Henshilwood** | 1/08/1952 | | RHB | ROB | 1976/77-1977/78 |
| Cheryl Elizabeth | Wellington | | | | |
| **Hockley** | 7/11/1962 | | RHB | RM | 1978/79-2000/01 |
| Deborah Ann | Christchurch | | | | |

| | Born | Died | Type | | Career |
|---|---|---|---|---|---|
| **Hollis** | 22/05/1915 | 31/08/1980 | RHB | RM | 1934/35 |
| Meryl | Dunedin | Dunedin | | | |
| **Huddleston** | 11/10/1987 | | RHB | RM | 2013/14-2020/21 |
| Holly Rachael | Springs, South Africa | | | | |
| **Illingworth** | 9/09/1963 | | RHB | WK | 1988/89-1996 |
| Sarah Louise | Lancaster, England | | | | |
| **Jagersma** | 8/05/1959 | | RHB | WK | 1984-1989/90 |
| Ingrid Catriena Petronella | Christchurch | | | | |
| **Jensen** | 7/10/1992 | | RHB | RM | 2013/14-2021/22 |
| Hayley Nicole Kayla | Christchurch | | | | |
| **Jonas** | 8/04/2004 | | RHB | SLA | 2020/21-2021/22 |
| Frances Cecilia | Auckland | | | | |
| **Kainuku** | 5/09/1967 | | RHB | RFM | 1991/92 |
| Yvonne Joan | Auckland | | | | |
| **Kasperek** | 15/02/1992 | | RHB | ROB | 2015-2021 |
| Leigh Megan | Edinburgh, Scotland | | | | |
| **Kember** | 28/01/1985 | | RHB | RLB | 2006/07-2007/08 |
| Rosamond Jane | Auckland | | | | |
| **Kerr** | 13/10/2000 | | RHB | RLBG | 2016/17-2021/22 |
| Amelia Charlotte | Wellington | | | | |
| **Kerr** | 18/01/1998 | | RHB | RM | 2019/20-2021/22 |
| Jessica Mackenzie | Wellington | | | | |
| **King** | 28/11/1980 | 11/09/2003 | RHB | RFM | 2001/02-2002/03 |
| Frances Sarah | Wellington | Wellington | | | |
| **Kinsella** | 14/08/1963 | | RHB | RLB | 1987/88-1994/95 |
| Penelope Dale | Palmerston North | | | | |
| **Lamason** | 2/05/1912 | 30/04/1994 | RHB | ROB | 1947/48-1954 |
| Ina Mabel | Palmerston North | Auckland | | | |
| **Lamason** | 19/12/1915 | 16/02/2012 | RHB | RM | 1947/48-1954 |
| Joyce Grace | Auckland | Porirua | | | |
| **Le Comber** | 5/07/1969 | | RHB | RM | 1996-1997/98 |
| Karen | Christchurch | | | | |
| **Legg** | 29/06/1964 | | RHB | RM | 1986/87-1989/90 |
| Brigit Jane | Christchurch | | | | |
| **Lewis** | 20/06/1970 | | RHB | RSM | 1991/92-2004/05 |
| Maia Ann Mereana | Christchurch | | | | |
| **Leydon-Davis** | 22/06/1994 | | RHB | RM | 2013/14-2015/16 |
| Felicity Carol | Hamilton | | | | |
| **Lind** | 15/05/1985 | | RHB | WK | 2009-2009/10 |
| Victoria Jayne | Auckland | | | | |
| **Lindsay** | 28/02/1950 | | RHB | RFM | 1977/78 |
| Linda Rose | Wellington | | | | |
| **Lord** | 1/08/1947 | | RHB | RLB | 1966-1981/82 |
| Jacqueline | Rochdale, England | | | | |
| **Lynch** | 16/10/1975 | | RHB | WK | 2002/03-2003/04 |
| Michelle Louise | Auckland | | | | |
| **Mackay** | 1/06/1990 | | RHB | ROB | 2011-2021/22 |
| Frances Louise | Christchurch | | | | |
| **Mair** | 7/11/1998 | | RHB | RM | 2018/19-2021/22 |
| Rosemary Alison | Napier | | | | |
| **Maker** | 10/12/1925 | 2/02/2004 | LHB | LM | 1966 |
| Elizabeth Jean | Melbourne, Australia | Wellington | | | |
| **Marks** | 5/01/1918 | 20/08/2014 | RHB | | 1934/35-1947/48 |
| Margaret Ellen | Christchurch | Christchurch | | | |
| **Martin** | 7/02/1985 | | RHB | WK | 2003/04-2021/22 |
| Katey Jane | Dunedin | | | | |
| **Mason** | 11/10/1982 | | LHB | ROB | 2001/02-2011 |
| Aimee Louise | New Plymouth | | | | |
| **McDonald** | 25/11/1980 | | RHB | SLA | 2000/01 |
| Erin Teresa | Lower Hutt | | | | |
| **McDonald** | 9/05/1967 | | RHB | | 1990/91-1991/92 |
| Kim Lorraine | Morrinsville | | | | |

| | Born | Died | Type | | Career |
|---|---|---|---|---|---|
| **McGlashan** Sara Jade | 28/03/1982 Napier | | RHB | WK | 2002-2015/16 |
| **McGregor** Vicki Louise | 24/01/1955 Christchurch | | RHB | RM | 1976/77-1981/82 |
| **McKelvey** Patricia Frances | 5/01/1942 Lower Hutt | | RHB | RM | 1966-1981/82 |
| **McKenna** Ann | 20/10/1943 Christchurch | | RHB | | 1968/68-1986/87 |
| **McKenzie** Rona Una | 20/08/1922 Takapau | 24/07/1999 Auckland | RHB | RM | 1954-1960/61 |
| **McLauchlan** Sarah | 6/04/1973 Christchurch | | RHB | RM | 1991/92-1997/98 |
| **McNeill** Beth Hannah | 10/11/1982 Wellington | | RHB | RM | 2003/04-2008/09 |
| **Milburn** Rowan Claire | 18/06/1977 Mosgiel | | RHB | WK | 2006/07-2007 |
| **Miller** Evelynn Luella | 3/01/1952 Auckland | | RHB | RSM | 1978/79 |
| **Miller** Helen Edith | 4/11/1915 Dunedin | 10/10/1972 Hamilton | RHB | RM | 1934/35 |
| **Milliken** Louise Elizabeth | 19/09/1983 Morrinsville | | RHB | RFM | 2001/02-2006/07 |
| **Molloy** Katrina Susan | 22/01/1962 Hamilton | | RHB | RM | 1984/85 |
| **Moore** Patricia Nellie | 13/08/1930 Christchurch | | LHB | RM | 1960/61-1966 |
| **Morris** Susan Rachel Margaret | 30/05/1958 Auckland | | RHB | RM | 1988/89 |
| **Musson** Karen Jane | 27/06/1967 Hastings | | RHB | RM | 1992/93-1995/96 |
| **Newton** Thamsyn Michelle Moupia | 3/06/1995 Paraparaumu | | RHB | RM | 2015/16-2021 |
| **Nicholson** Clare Maree | 20/09/1967 Auckland | | RHB | ROB | 1994/95-2000/01 |
| **Nielsen** Morna Jessie Godwin | 24/02/1990 Tauranga | | RHB | LM/SLA | 2009/10-2016/17 |
| **O'Leary** Anna Michelle | 12/05/1978 Dunedin | | RHB | | 1996-2001/02 |
| **Olson** Jennifer Betty | 28/01/1945 Christchurch | | RHB | RM | 1968/69-1973 |
| **Oyler** Carol Mary | 12/08/1947 Auckland | | RHB | RSM | 1966-1968/69 |
| **Page** Glenys Lynne | 11/08/1940 Auckland | 7/11/2012 Auckland | RHB | SLA | 1973 |
| **Paton** Eris Annie | 9/10/1926 Wellington | 23/11/2004 Invercargill | RHB | RM | 1954-1960/61 |
| **Payne** Nicola | 10/09/1969 Toronto, Canada | | RHB | RM | 1999/00-2002/03 |
| **Penfold** Molly Mae | 15/06/2001 London, England | | RHB | RM | 2021 |
| **Perkins** Katie Teresa | 7/07/1988 Auckland | | RHB | RM | 2011/12-2020/21 |
| **Perry** Elizabeth Cecelia | 22/11/1987 Taumarunui | | RHB | RM | 2010-2016/17 |
| **Peterson** Anna Michelle | 12/09/1990 Auckland | | RHB | ROB | 2011/12-2019/20 |
| **Plummer** Karen Vi | 14/09/1951 Auckland | | RHB | RM | 1981/82-1991/92 |
| **Powell** Lynda Myra | 12/03/1950 Taumarunui | | RHB | RSM | 1971/72-1974/75 |
| **Priest** Rachel Holly | 13/06/1985 New Plymouth | | RHB | WK | 2007-2019/20 |

| | Born | Died | Type | | Career |
|---|---|---|---|---|---|
| **Pulford** Katherine Louise | 27/08/1980 Nelson | | RHB | RM | 1998/99-2009/10 |
| **Pullar** Rachel Jane | 3/06/1977 Balclutha | | RHB | RFM | 1997/98-2004/05 |
| **Ramel** Kathryn Ann | 7/09/1973 Auckland | | RHB | RM | 1997/98-2002 |
| **Rattray** Susan Joy | 18/12/1953 Christchurch | | RHB | RLBG | 1974/75-1984/85 |
| **Robinson** Daphne Maureen May | 16/02/1932 Dunedin | 7/02/2008 Dunedin | LHB | RM | 1960/61 |
| **Robinson** Vera Esther | 14/01/1927 Patea | 21/09/2017 Auckland | RHB | SLA | 1947/48-1968/69 |
| **Rolls** Rebecca Jane | 22/08/1975 Napier | | RHB | WK | 1996/97-2006/07 |
| **Rouse** Ethna Frances | 29/12/1937 Christchurch | | LHB | | 1971/72-1973 |
| **Rouse** Mary Turns | 11/01/1926 Waipara | 27/01/1993 Christchurch | RHB | | 1954-1956/57 |
| **Rowe** Hannah Maree | 3/10/1996 Palmerston North | | RHB | RM | 2014/15-2021/22 |
| **Ruck** Sian Elizabeth Ansley | 8/12/1983 Auckland | | RHB | LM | 2009-2013/14 |
| **Russell** Justine Anne | 16/11/1969 Invercargill | | RHB | RM | 1994/95-1995/96 |
| **Ryan** Edna May | 8/12/1946 Auckland | | RHB | WK | 1974/75-1981/82 |
| **Satterthwaite** Amy Ella | 7/10/1986 Christchurch | | LHB | RM/ROB | 2007-2021/22 |
| **Saulbrey** Jillian Margaret | 22/02/1943 Lower Hutt | | RHB | LFM | 1966-1974/75 |
| **Savin** Pearl Hannah | 20/06/1914 Christchurch | 19/11/2000 Auckland | RHB | WK | 1934/35 |
| **Scripps** Natalee | 9/12/1978 Auckland | | RHB | RM | 2003/04-2004/05 |
| **Sexton** Vivian Sherill | 8/11/1953 Foxton | 5/09/2021 Taradale | RHB | RM | 1977/78 |
| **Shankland** Lesley Jean | 18/03/1956 Christchurch | | RHB | ROB | 1978/79-1989/90 |
| **Signal** Elizabeth Ann | 4/05/1962 Feilding | | RHB | RFM | 1984-1987/88 |
| **Signal** Rosemary Jill | 4/05/1962 Feilding | | RHB | RFM | 1984-1984/85 |
| **Simpson** Lois Jane | 11/06/1961 Feilding | | RHB | | 1984/85-1987/88 |
| **Sinton** Carolyn Marie | 23/01/1938 Auckland | | RHB | | 1957/58 |
| **Speight** Mary Averil | 9/04/1936 Dunedin | | RHB | ROB | 1956/57-1960/61 |
| **Stead** Janice Ellen | 1/11/1939 Christchurch | | RHB | | 1966-1971/72 |
| **Steele** Rebecca Jayne | 2/01/1985 Christchurch | | RHB | SLA | 2002/03-2004/05 |
| **Stonell** Jean Melva | 30/12/1928 Wellington | 27/07/2008 Wellington | RHB | RM | 1956/57-1966 |
| **Sutherland** Gwen Anne | 5/12/1917 Perth, Australia | 1/01/1985 Perth, Australia | RHB | RM/ROB | 1956/57-1957/58 |
| **Symons** Ruth Evelyn | 3/10/1913 Christchurch | 11/09/2004 Christchurch | RHB | RM | 1934/35 |
| **Tahuhu** Lea-Marie Maureen | 23/09/1990 Christchurch | | RHB | RFM | 2011-2021/22 |
| **Taylor** Margaret Jean | 19/02/1917 Christchurch | 22/07/2004 Christchurch | RHB | RM | 1934/35 |

**NZC**

| | Born | Died | Type | | Career |
|---|---|---|---|---|---|
| **Thompson**<br>Hilda Margaret | 26/03/1919<br>Wellington | 16/06/2004<br>Melbourne, Australia | LHB | LM | 1947/48 |
| **Thorner**<br>Betty Irene | 23/02/1938<br>Upper Hutt | | LHB | RFM | 1956/57-1960/61 |
| **Tiffen**<br>Haidee Maree | 4/09/1979<br>Timaru | | RHB | RM | 1998/99-2008/09 |
| **Travers**<br>Emily Anne | 29/07/1978<br>Hunterville | | RHB | WK | 2000/01 |
| **Trow**<br>Donna Marie | 13/07/1977<br>Napier | | RHB | RM | 1998/99 |
| **Tsukigawa**<br>Sarah Jane | 16/01/1982<br>Balclutha | | RHB | RM | 2005/06-2010/11 |
| **Tunupopo**<br>Munokoa Fellesite | 23/02/1984<br>Tokoroa | | RHB | RM | 1999/00 |
| **Turner**<br>Jennifer Ann | 5/09/1969<br>Lincoln | | RHB | RM | 1988/89-1993/94 |
| **Turner**<br>Nichola Joan | 25/12/1959<br>Christchurch | | RHB | RSM | 1981/82-1990/91 |
| **Watkin**<br>Jessica Marie | 7/05/1998<br>Wanganui | | RHB | ROB | 2018-2018/19 |
| **Watson**<br>Helen Maree | 17/02/1972<br>Ashburton | | RHB | RM | 1998/99-2007/08 |
| **White**<br>Elaine Grace | 9/07/1944<br>Auckland | | RHB | RSM | 1971/72 |
| **Wickham**<br>Una Katherine | 12/01/1923<br>Tauranga | 20/06/1983<br>Tauranga | RHB | RM | 1947/48-1948/49 |
| **Williams**<br>Nancy May | 4/03/1959<br>Christchurch | | RHB | ROB/RM | 1984/85-1991/92 |
| **Withers**<br>Katrina Marie | 24/02/1971<br>Christchurch | | RHB | RFM | 1994/95-2000/01 |
| **Woodbury**<br>Tania Lorraine | 6/07/1964<br>Lower Hutt | | RHB | LFM | 1991/92 |

# TEST CAREER RECORDS

| | M | In | NO | HS | Runs | Ave | 100 | 50 | Ct | st | Wkts | Runs | Ave | 5WI | 10WM | Best |
|---|---|---|---|---|---|---|---|---|---|---|---|---|---|---|---|---|
| E.P.N.Allan | 4 | 6 | 4 | 29* | 87 | 43.50 | - | - | 1 | - | 5 | 138 | 27.60 | - | - | 3-38 |
| T.L.Anderson | 2 | 3 | 0 | 63 | 108 | 36.00 | - | 1 | - | - | | | | | | |
| E.A.Badham | 3 | 6 | 1 | 42 | 121 | 24.20 | - | - | 7 | - | 10 | 275 | 27.50 | - | - | 4-46 |
| D.L.Bailey | 1 | 2 | 0 | 5 | 6 | 3.00 | - | - | - | - | | | | | | |
| H.R.Bastion | 1 | - | - | - | - | - | - | - | - | - | 0 | 59 | - | - | - | - |
| K.E.Batty | 4 | 7 | 1 | 24 | 67 | 11.16 | - | - | 6 | - | 2 | 78 | 39.00 | - | - | 1-18 |
| L.I.Bayliss | 1 | - | - | - | - | - | - | - | - | - | 5 | 70 | 14.00 | 1 | - | 5-28 |
| B.L.Bevege | 5 | 10 | 1 | 100* | 400 | 44.44 | 1 | 2 | 3 | - | 0 | 70 | - | - | - | - |
| M.C.Bishop | 1 | 2 | 0 | 27 | 27 | 13.50 | - | - | 2 | - | 0 | 33 | - | - | - | - |
| E.E.Blackie | 1 | 2 | 1 | 13* | 21 | 21.00 | - | - | 3 | 1 | | | | | | |
| P.Blackler | 12 | 21 | 0 | 68 | 371 | 17.66 | - | 1 | 5 | - | 18 | 527 | 29.27 | - | - | 4-22 |
| B.A.Brentnall | 10 | 16 | 2 | 84* | 301 | 21.50 | - | 1 | 16 | 12 | | | | | | |
| K.D.Brown | 3 | 2 | 2 | 50* | 52 | - | - | 1 | 4 | - | 7 | 160 | 22.85 | - | - | 3-47 |
| S.H.Brown | 6 | 9 | 3 | 19 | 59 | 9.83 | - | - | 1 | - | 9 | 432 | 48.00 | - | - | 3-64 |
| N.A.Browne | 1 | 2 | 2 | 5* | 5 | - | - | - | 1 | - | 0 | 77 | - | - | - | - |
| N.J.Browne | 2 | 2 | 0 | 24 | 23 | 12.00 | - | - | 2 | - | 1 | 83 | 83.00 | - | - | 1-43 |
| D.K.Brownlee | 1 | 2 | 0 | 12 | 17 | 8.50 | - | - | - | - | | | | | | |
| H.E.Buck | 1 | 2 | 0 | 16 | 16 | 8.00 | - | - | - | - | | | | | | |
| S.K.Burke | 1 | 1 | 1 | 1* | 1 | - | - | - | - | - | 1 | 57 | 57.00 | - | - | 1-57 |
| J.A.Burley | 6 | 9 | 0 | 46 | 110 | 12.22 | - | - | 3 | - | 21 | 553 | 26.33 | 1 | - | 7-41 |
| V.E.Burt | 3 | 5 | 0 | 15 | 40 | 8.00 | - | - | - | - | 0 | 28 | | | | |
| V.L.Burtt | 4 | 8 | 0 | 39 | 101 | 12.62 | - | - | 5 | - | | | | | | |
| C.A.Campbell | 9 | 5 | 1 | 29 | 55 | 13.75 | - | - | 2 | - | 18 | 720 | 40.00 | - | - | 4-94 |
| P.F.Carrick | 7 | 11 | 3 | 21 | 63 | 7.87 | - | - | 4 | - | 21 | 489 | 23.28 | 1 | - | 6-29 |
| J.Clark | 11 | 18 | 0 | 79 | 482 | 26.77 | - | 2 | 7 | - | 0 | 5 | - | - | - | - |
| A.L.Clough | 1 | 1 | 0 | 0 | 0 | 0.00 | - | - | - | - | 1 | 70 | 70.00 | - | - | 1-70 |
| W.J.Coe | 3 | 5 | 1 | 34 | 83 | 20.75 | - | - | - | - | 6 | 222 | 37.00 | - | - | 2-30 |
| M.C.Corby | 1 | 2 | 0 | 12 | 13 | 6.50 | - | - | - | - | 0 | 36 | - | - | - | - |
| D.A.Costello | 1 | 1 | 0 | 0 | 0 | 0.00 | - | - | - | - | 2 | 104 | 52.00 | - | - | 2-77 |
| J.M.Coulston | 5 | 8 | 1 | 24 | 76 | 10.85 | - | - | 3 | - | 19 | 341 | 17.94 | - | - | 4-38 |
| V.R.Coutts | 6 | 11 | 0 | 41 | 136 | 12.36 | - | - | 1 | - | | | | | | |
| S.D.Cowles | 7 | 14 | 0 | 46 | 324 | 23.14 | - | - | 6 | - | 0 | 13 | | | | |
| M.J.Currie | 3 | 5 | 2 | 3* | 7 | 2.33 | - | - | 2 | - | 3 | 170 | 56.66 | - | - | 3-30 |
| E.J.Dickson | 2 | 4 | 0 | 65 | 114 | 28.50 | - | 1 | - | - | | | | | | |
| J.D.Doull | 11 | 22 | 4 | 103 | 779 | 43.27 | 1 | 5 | 6 | - | 0 | 34 | | | | |
| E.C.Drumm | 5 | 6 | 3 | 161* | 433 | 144.33 | 2 | 2 | - | - | 2 | 175 | 87.50 | - | - | 1-24 |
| B.M.Duncan | 2 | 3 | 3 | 1* | 1 | - | - | - | 1 | - | 2 | 115 | 57.50 | - | - | 1-37 |
| M.H.Dunlop | 2 | 2 | 0 | 5 | 5 | 2.50 | - | - | - | - | 3 | 123 | 41.00 | - | - | 1-5 |
| J.R.Dunning | 6 | 12 | 2 | 71 | 320 | 32.00 | - | 2 | 5 | - | 6 | 170 | 28.33 | - | - | 2-10 |
| A.E.Ell | 1 | 2 | 0 | 1 | 2 | 1.00 | - | - | - | - | 0 | 55 | - | - | - | - |
| M.F.Fahey | 2 | 4 | 1 | 60* | 125 | 41.66 | - | 1 | 1 | - | | | | | | |
| V.H.M.Farrell | 3 | 4 | 0 | 5 | 12 | 3.00 | - | - | 5 | 3 | | | | | | |
| P.B.Flannery | 1 | 2 | 0 | 46 | 64 | 32.00 | - | - | - | - | 0 | 5 | - | - | - | - |
| K.E.Flavell | 6 | 7 | 0 | 204 | 473 | 67.57 | 1 | 2 | 2 | - | | | | | | |
| J.W.Francis | 5 | 7 | 1 | 19 | 46 | 7.66 | - | - | 2 | - | 14 | 362 | 25.85 | - | - | 4-72 |
| L.M.Fraser | 3 | - | - | - | - | - | - | - | - | - | 4 | 210 | 52.50 | - | - | 2-6 |
| M.K.Fruin | 6 | 8 | 0 | 80 | 188 | 23.50 | - | 2 | 3 | 1 | | | | | | |
| J.A.Fryer | 3 | 1 | 1 | 7* | 7 | - | - | - | 1 | - | 5 | 154 | 30.80 | - | - | 4-37 |
| M.J.Fulford | 1 | 2 | 0 | 10 | 12 | 6.00 | - | - | - | - | 2 | 46 | 23.00 | - | - | 2-46 |
| S.M.Gilchrist | 5 | 3 | 2 | 7* | 12 | 12.00 | - | - | 5 | - | 14 | 384 | 27.42 | - | - | 3-4. |
| G.P.Gooder | 1 | 2 | 0 | 11 | 11 | 5.50 | - | - | - | - | 8 | 73 | 9.12 | 1 | - | 6-42 |
| K.V.Gunn | 9 | 12 | 0 | 49 | 194 | 16.16 | - | - | 6 | 1 | 11 | 429 | 39.00 | - | - | 3-4. |
| J.E.Harris | 10 | 7 | 3 | 9 | 26 | 6.50 | - | - | 1 | - | 15 | 691 | 46.06 | - | - | 4-1. |
| J.C.Hatcher | 4 | 7 | 0 | 23 | 79 | 11.28 | - | - | - | - | | | | | | |
| C.E.Henshilwood | 1 | 2 | 0 | 41 | 48 | 24.00 | - | - | - | - | 0 | 14 | - | - | - | - |
| D.A.Hockley | 19 | 29 | 4 | 126* | 1301 | 52.04 | 4 | 7 | 9 | - | 5 | 146 | 29.20 | - | - | 2-9 |
| M.Hollis | 1 | 2 | 0 | 24 | 26 | 13.00 | - | - | - | - | 1 | 81 | 81.00 | - | - | 1-81 |
| S.L.Illingworth | 6 | 7 | 3 | 40* | 120 | 30.00 | - | - | 5 | 5 | | | | | | |
| I.C.P.Jagersma | 9 | 13 | 5 | 52 | 271 | 33.87 | - | 1 | 10 | 2 | 4 | 38 | 9.50 | - | - | 4-3. |
| Y.J.Kainuku | 1 | 1 | 1 | 23* | 23 | - | - | - | - | - | 1 | 50 | 50.00 | - | - | 1-50 |
| K.M.Keenan | 5 | 3 | 2 | 26* | 32 | 32.00 | - | - | 4 | - | 15 | 348 | 23.20 | 1 | - | 6-7. |
| P.D.Kinsella | 6 | 8 | 0 | 53 | 131 | 16.37 | - | 1 | 3 | - | | | | | | |
| I.M.Lamason | 4 | 6 | 2 | 37* | 86 | 21.50 | - | - | - | - | 2 | 136 | 68.00 | - | - | 2-2. |
| J.G.Lamason | 4 | 8 | 0 | 24 | 87 | 10.87 | - | - | - | - | 8 | 264 | 33.00 | - | - | 4-5 |
| B.J.Legg | 3 | 4 | 1 | 26 | 30 | 10.00 | - | - | - | - | 4 | 149 | 37.25 | - | - | 2-5. |
| M.A.M.Lewis | 9 | 12 | 0 | 65 | 252 | 21.00 | - | 2 | 6 | - | | | | | | |

**NZC**

| | M | In | NO | HS | Runs | Ave | 100 | 50 | Ct | st | Wkts | Runs | Ave | 5WI | 10WM | Best |
|---|---|---|---|---|---|---|---|---|---|---|---|---|---|---|---|---|
| J.Lord | 15 | 22 | 3 | 39* | 258 | 13.57 | - | - | 5 | - | 55 | 1049 | 19.07 | 4 | 1 | 6-119 |
| E.J.Maker | 3 | 4 | 0 | 5 | 10 | 2.50 | - | - | 1 | - | 5 | 156 | 31.20 | - | - | 3-34 |
| C.E.Marett | 7 | 13 | 4 | 49 | 304 | 33.77 | - | - | 3 | - | 9 | 268 | 29.77 | - | - | 2-16 |
| M.E.Marks | 2 | 4 | 1 | 23 | 30 | 10.00 | - | - | - | - | | | | | | |
| K.J.Martin | 1 | 2 | 0 | 46 | 49 | 24.50 | - | - | - | - | | | | | | |
| A.L.Mason | 2 | 2 | 0 | 14 | 15 | 7.50 | - | - | 2 | - | 3 | 105 | 35.00 | - | - | 2-68 |
| K.L.McDonald | 1 | 1 | 0 | 1 | 1 | 1.00 | - | - | - | - | | | | | | |
| S.J.McGlashan | 2 | 2 | 0 | 14 | 20 | 10.00 | - | - | - | - | | | | | | |
| P.F.McKelvey | 15 | 26 | 2 | 155* | 699 | 29.12 | 2 | 1 | 8 | - | | | | | | |
| A.McKenna | 7 | 14 | 1 | 97* | 465 | 35.76 | - | 3 | 7 | - | 0 | 6 | - | - | - | - |
| R.U.McKenzie | 7 | 13 | 0 | 61 | 295 | 22.69 | - | 2 | 3 | - | 8 | 214 | 26.75 | - | - | 4-18 |
| S.McLauchlan | 4 | 4 | 0 | 4 | 4 | 1.00 | - | - | 1 | - | 2 | 83 | 41.50 | - | - | 1-7 |
| E.L.Miller | 3 | 6 | 0 | 32 | 92 | 15.33 | - | - | 1 | - | | | | | | |
| H.E.Miller | 1 | 2 | 0 | 11 | 11 | 5.50 | - | - | - | - | 1 | 77 | 77.00 | - | - | 1-77 |
| L.E.Milliken | 2 | 2 | 0 | 6 | 10 | 5.00 | - | - | - | - | 2 | 73 | 36.50 | - | - | 2-49 |
| K.S.Molloy | 2 | 1 | 1 | 1* | 1 | - | - | - | 2 | - | 5 | 91 | 18.20 | - | - | 2-24 |
| P.N.Moore | 2 | 3 | 1 | 47* | 80 | 40.00 | - | - | 3 | - | 0 | 31 | - | - | - | - |
| L.J.Murdoch | 6 | 10 | 0 | 72 | 253 | 25.30 | - | 1 | 1 | - | | | | | | |
| K.J.Musson | 1 | - | - | - | - | - | - | - | - | - | | | | | | |
| C.M.Nicholson | 4 | 5 | 0 | 46 | 140 | 28.00 | - | - | 1 | - | 5 | 170 | 34.00 | - | - | 2-25 |
| A.M.O'Leary | 1 | 1 | 0 | 27 | 27 | 27.00 | - | - | 1 | - | | | | | | |
| J.B.Olson | 1 | 1 | 0 | 0 | 0 | 0.00 | - | - | - | - | 0 | 48 | - | - | - | - |
| C.M.Oyler | 5 | 8 | 2 | 67* | 212 | 35.33 | - | 1 | 2 | - | | | | | | |
| E.A.Paton | 4 | 8 | 1 | 77* | 180 | 25.71 | - | 1 | 4 | - | 9 | 160 | 17.77 | - | - | 4-35 |
| K.V.Plummer | 4 | 6 | 0 | 13 | 28 | 4.66 | - | - | 2 | - | | | | | | |
| I.J.Powell | 7 | 13 | 2 | 63 | 272 | 24.72 | - | 1 | 9 | 1 | | | | | | |
| L.M.Powell | 5 | 9 | 0 | 66 | 188 | 20.88 | - | 1 | 2 | - | 0 | 8 | - | - | - | - |
| K.L.Pulford | 1 | 2 | 0 | 0 | 0 | 0.00 | - | - | 1 | - | 2 | 15 | 7.50 | - | - | 2-15 |
| S.J.Rattray | 9 | 17 | 2 | 59 | 412 | 27.46 | - | 4 | 1 | - | 19 | 461 | 24.26 | 1 | - | 5-76 |
| D.M.M.Robinson | 1 | 1 | 1 | 2* | 2 | - | - | - | - | - | 1 | 16 | 16.00 | - | - | 1-16 |
| R.J.Rolls | 1 | 2 | 1 | 71 | 71 | 71.00 | - | 1 | 1 | - | | | | | | |
| E.F.Rouse | 1 | 2 | 0 | 35 | 36 | 18.00 | - | - | - | - | | | | | | |
| M.T.Rouse | 2 | 4 | 2 | 15* | 18 | 9.00 | - | - | - | - | | | | | | |
| J.A.Russell | 1 | 1 | 0 | 39 | 39 | 39.00 | - | - | - | - | 1 | 37 | 37.00 | - | - | 1-14 |
| E.M.Ryan | 5 | 8 | 4 | 10 | 38 | 9.50 | - | - | 3 | 11 | | | | | | |
| J.M.Saulbrey | 11 | 16 | 4 | 62 | 198 | 16.50 | - | 1 | 6 | - | 35 | 951 | 27.17 | 1 | - | 5-32 |
| P.H.Savin | 1 | 2 | 0 | 15 | 18 | 9.00 | - | - | - | - | | | | | | |
| N.Scripps | 1 | 1 | 1 | 10* | 10 | - | - | - | - | - | 0 | 57 | - | - | - | - |
| E.A.Signal | 6 | 6 | 0 | 55* | 82 | 20.50 | - | 1 | 3 | - | 8 | 325 | 40.62 | - | - | 2-34 |
| R.J.Signal | 1 | 2 | 1 | 8* | 8 | 8.00 | - | - | - | - | 0 | 21 | - | - | - | - |
| L.J.Simpson | 1 | 2 | 0 | 4 | 6 | 3.00 | - | - | - | - | | | | | | |
| E.M.Sinclair | 2 | 4 | 0 | 10 | 26 | 8.66 | - | - | 2 | - | | | | | | |
| C.M.Sinton | 1 | 2 | 0 | 10 | 14 | 7.00 | - | - | - | - | | | | | | |
| J.E.Stead | 9 | 18 | 2 | 95 | 433 | 27.06 | - | 3 | 3 | - | | | | | | |
| R.J.Steele | 2 | 3 | 0 | 12 | 16 | 5.33 | - | - | 3 | - | 8 | 141 | 17.62 | 1 | - | 5-79 |
| J.M.Stonell | 4 | 8 | 0 | 47 | 127 | 15.87 | - | - | 2 | - | | | | | | |
| G.A.Sutherland | 3 | 6 | 0 | 22 | 66 | 11.00 | - | - | 1 | - | 2 | 86 | 43.00 | - | - | 1-29 |
| R.E.Symons | 1 | 1 | 0 | 5 | 5 | 5.00 | - | - | 1 | - | 2 | 71 | 35.50 | - | - | 2-71 |
| M.J.Taylor | 1 | 2 | 0 | 3 | 3 | 1.50 | - | - | - | - | 1 | 62 | 62.00 | - | - | 1-62 |
| H.M.Thompson | 1 | 2 | 1 | 17* | 17 | 17.00 | - | - | 1 | - | 0 | 18 | - | - | - | - |
| B.I.Thorner | 3 | 6 | 1 | 37 | 76 | 15.20 | - | - | - | - | 4 | 78 | 19.50 | - | - | 2-33 |
| H.M.Tiffen | 2 | 4 | 3 | 66* | 124 | 124.00 | - | 1 | 1 | - | | | | | | |
| J.A.Turner | 6 | 8 | 1 | 11* | 30 | 4.28 | - | - | 2 | - | 19 | 469 | 24.68 | - | - | 3-42 |
| N.J.Turner | 6 | 9 | 2 | 65* | 208 | 29.71 | - | 2 | 1 | - | | | | | | |
| M.A.Webb | 4 | 8 | 0 | 42 | 110 | 13.75 | - | - | - | - | 6 | 66 | 11.00 | - | - | 3-32 |
| E.G.White | 3 | 5 | 0 | 17 | 33 | 6.60 | - | - | - | - | 2 | 85 | 42.50 | - | - | 1-5 |
| U.K.Wickham | 2 | 4 | 0 | 34 | 40 | 10.00 | - | - | - | - | 3 | 76 | 25.33 | - | - | 2-33 |
| N.M.Williams | 4 | 5 | 1 | 35* | 70 | 17.50 | - | - | 1 | - | 3 | 158 | 52.66 | - | - | 2-19 |
| T.L.Woodbury | 2 | 3 | 3 | 7* | 7 | - | - | - | - | - | 4 | 100 | 25.00 | - | - | 2-29 |

# TEAM RECORDS

## Highest Totals

| | | | |
|---|---|---|---|
| 517-8 | v England | Scarborough | 1996 |
| 403-8d | v India | Nelson | 1994/95 |
| 362-5d | v England | Guildford | 1996 |
| 359 | v Australia | Wellington | 1974/75 |
| 335 | v Australia | Melbourne | 1971/72 |

## Lowest Totals

| | | | |
|---|---|---|---|
| 44 | v England | Christchurch | 1934/35 |
| 61 | v England | Auckland | 1948/49 |
| 63 | v England | Worcester | 1954 |
| 78 | v Australia | Adelaide | 1978/79 |
| 87 | v Australia | Wellington | 1947/48 |

# INDIVIDUAL RECORDS

## Centuries

| | | |
|---|---|---|
| 204 | K.E. Flavell v England at Scarborough | 1996 |
| 161* | E.C. Drumm v Australia at Christchurch | 1994/95 |
| 155* | P.F. McKelvey v England at Wellington | 1968/69 |
| 126* | D.A. Hockley v Australia at Auckland | 1989/90 |
| 117* | P.F. McKelvey v South Africa at Cape Town | 1971/72 |
| 115 | D.A. Hockley v England at Worcester | 1996 |
| 112* | E.C. Drumm v England at Guildford | 1996 |
| 107* | D.A. Hockley v England at Canterbury | 1984 |
| 107 | D.A. Hockley v India at Nelson | 1994/95 |
| 103 | J.D. Doull v England at Christchurch | 1968/69 |
| 100* | B.L. Bevege v India at Dunedin | 1976/77 |

## Five Wickets in an Innings

| | | |
|---|---|---|
| 7-41 | J.A. Burley v England at The Oval | 1966 |
| 6-29 | P.F. Carrick v Australia at Melbourne | 1971/72 |
| 6-42 | G.P. Gooder v England at Auckland | 1948/49 |
| 6-73 | K.M. Keenan v England at Worcester | 1996 |
| 6-119 | J. Lord v Australia at Melbourne | 1978/79 |
| 5-24 | J. Lord v South Africa at Durban | 1971/72 |
| 5-28 | L.I. Bayliss v Australia at Dunedin | 1960/61 |
| 5-32 | J.M. Saulbrey v South Africa at Durban | 1971/72 |
| 5-40 | J. Lord v India at Dunedin | 1976/77 |
| 5-76 | S.J. Rattray v India at Cuttack | 1984/85 |
| 5-78 | J. Lord v Australia at Adelaide | 1978/79 |
| 5-79 | R.J. Steele v India at Vapi | 2003/04 |

## Ten Wickets in a Match

| | | |
|---|---|---|
| 10-137 | J. Lord v Australia at Melbourne | 1978/79 |

# Wicketkeeping

### DISMISSALS IN AN INNINGS

*(ct/st)*

| | | | | |
|---|---|---|---|---|
| 6 | (2/4) | B.A. Brentnall | v South Africa | Johannesburg | 1971/72 |
| 5 | (3/2) | B.A. Brentnall | v England | Auckland | 1968/69 |
| 4 | (1/3) | V.H.M. Farrell | v England | Worcester | 1954 |
| 4 | (4/0) | V.H.M. Farrell | v England | The Oval | 1954 |
| 4 | (1/3) | E.M. Ryan | v Australia | Melbourne | 1978/79 |

### DISMISSALS IN A MATCH

*(ct/st)*

| | | | | |
|---|---|---|---|---|
| 7 | (3/4) | B.A. Brentnall | v South Africa | Johannesburg | 1971/72 |
| 7 | (2/5) | E.M. Ryan | v Australia | Melbourne | 1978/79 |
| 6 | (4/2) | B.A. Brentnall | v England | Auckland | 1968/69 |
| 5 | (3/2) | B.A. Brentnall | v South Africa | Durban | 1971/72 |
| 5 | (2/3) | S.L. Illingworth | v England | Guildford | 1996 |

# Fielding

### CATCHES IN AN INNINGS

| | | | | |
|---|---|---|---|---|
| 3 | K.E. Batty | v England | Auckland | 1948/49 |
| 3 | P. N.Moore | v England | The Oval | 1966 |
| 3 | E.A. Badham | v Australia | Sydney | 1978/79 |
| 3 | M.A.M. Lewis | v England | Wanganui | 1991/92 |
| 3 | D.A. Hockley | v England | Scarborough | 1996 |

### CATCHES IN A MATCH

| | | | | |
|---|---|---|---|---|
| 4 | S.M. Gilchrist | v India | Ahmedabad | 1984/85 |
| 4 | M.A.M. Lewis | v England | Wanganui | 1991/92 |

# RECORD PARTNERSHIPS

| | | | | | |
|---|---|---|---|---|---|
| 1st | 150 | M.K. Fruin & D.A. Hockley | v England | Guildford | 1996 |
| 2nd | 146 | M.K. Fruin & K.E. Flavell | v England | Scarborough | 1996 |
| 3rd | 106 | K.E. Flavell & E.C. Drumm | v England | Guildford | 1996 |
| 4th | 94 | I.J. Powell & R.U. McKenzie | v Australia | Dunedin | 1960/61 |
| 5th | 94* | E.C. Drumm & D.A. Hockley | v England | Guildford | 1996 |
| 6th | 83 | D.A. Hockley & K.V. Gunn | v Australia | Christchurch | 1989/90 |
| 7th | 90 | B.A. Brentnall & J.A. Burley | v England | Birmingham | 1966 |
| 8th | 87 | C.E. Marett & J.M. Saulbrey | v Australia | Wellington | 1974/75 |
| 9th | 60* | K.E. Flavell & K.D. Brown | v England | Scarborough | 1996 |
| 10th | 55* | C.M. Oyler & J. Lord | v England | The Oval | 1966 |

# SUMMARY OF TEST CAREER RECORDS

## Most Matches

| | | | | | | | |
|---|---|---|---|---|---|---|---|
| D.A. Hockley | 19 | P. Blackler | 12 | J. Clark | 11 |
| P.F. McKelvey | 15 | J.D. Doull | 11 | J.E. Harris | 10 |
| J. Lord | 15 | J.M. Saulbrey | 11 | B.A. Brentnall | 10 |

## Most Runs

| | | | | | |
|---|---|---|---|---|---|
| D.A. Hockley | 1301 | K.E. Flavell | 473 | J.E. Stead | 433 |
| J.D. Doull | 779 | A. McKenna | 465 | S.J. Rattray | 412 |
| P.F. McKelvey | 699 | E.C. Drumm | 433 | B.L. Bevege | 400 |
| J. Clark | 482 | | | | |

## Most Wickets

| | | | | | |
|---|---|---|---|---|---|
| J. Lord | 55 | J.M. Coulston | 19 | P. Blackler | 18 |
| J.M. Saulbrey | 35 | J.A. Turner | 19 | K.M. Keenan | 15 |
| J.A. Burley | 21 | S.J. Rattray | 19 | J.E. Harris | 15 |
| P.F. Carrick | 21 | C.A. Campbell | 18 | | |

## Most Wicketkeeping Dismissals

| | Ct | St | Total |
|---|---|---|---|
| B.A. Brentnall | 15 | 12 | 27 |
| E.M. Ryan | 3 | 11 | 14 |
| I.C.P. Jagersma | 10 | 2 | 12 |
| S.L. Illingworth | 5 | 5 | 10 |

## Most Catches

| | |
|---|---|
| D.A. Hockley | 9 |
| P.F. McKelvey | 8 |
| E.A. Badham | 7 |
| A. McKenna | 7 |
| J. Clark | 7 |

# ONE-DAY INTERNATIONAL
# CAREER RECORDS

| | M | In | NO | HS | Runs | Ave | 100s | 50s | Ct | st | O | M | R | W | Ave | R/O | Best |
|---|---|---|---|---|---|---|---|---|---|---|---|---|---|---|---|---|---|
| E.P.N.Allan | 7 | 6 | 1 | 17 | 42 | 8.40 | - | - | 2 | - | 59 | 8 | 162 | 3 | 54.00 | 2.75 | 1-22 |
| K.S.Anderson | 6 | 5 | 2 | 9* | 22 | 7.33 | - | - | - | - | 38 | 2 | 187 | 5 | 37.40 | 4.92 | 3-45 |
| T.L.Anderson | 26 | 25 | 0 | 85 | 440 | 17.60 | - | 2 | 9 | - | | | | | | | |
| L.M.Astle | 1 | - | - | - | - | - | - | - | - | - | | | | | | | |
| E.A.Badham | 13 | 10 | 1 | 30 | 86 | 9.55 | - | - | - | 5 | - | 135.3 | 33 | 290 | 12 | 24.16 | 2.14 | 2-14 |
| H.R.Bastion | 3 | - | - | - | - | - | - | - | - | 1 | - | 20 | 2 | 57 | 2 | 28.50 | 2.85 | 1-12 |
| S.W.Bates | 142 | 136 | 13 | 168 | 5045 | 41.01 | 12 | 28 | 77 | - | 502.5 | 31 | 2488 | 75 | 33.17 | 4.95 | 4-7 |
| E.M.Bermingham | 34 | 21 | 5 | 35 | 187 | 11.68 | - | - | 10 | - | 260.5 | 19 | 1047 | 43 | 24.34 | 4.01 | 4-16 |
| B.L.Bevege | 16 | 16 | 1 | 101 | 488 | 32.53 | 1 | 3 | 3 | - | 22.2 | 7 | 48 | 3 | 16.00 | 2.15 | 3-17 |
| B.M.Bezuidenhout | 9 | 7 | 1 | 43 | 123 | 20.50 | - | - | 6 | 1 | | | | | | | |
| J.C.Brehaut | 3 | 3 | 1 | 23* | 40 | 20.00 | - | - | 3 | - | | | | | | | |
| B.A.Brentnall | 5 | 3 | 0 | 18 | 40 | 13.33 | - | - | 3 | 3 | | | | | | | |
| K.D.Brown | 14 | 6 | 3 | 9* | 19 | 6.33 | - | - | 4 | - | 86.4 | 14 | 252 | 10 | 25.20 | 2.91 | 2-8 |
| S.H.Brown | 18 | 9 | 4 | 17* | 59 | 11.80 | - | - | 5 | - | 170 | 63 | 308 | 19 | 16.21 | 1.81 | 2-3 |
| N.J.Browne | 125 | 102 | 28 | 63 | 2002 | 27.05 | - | 10 | 33 | - | 761.5 | 66 | 3005 | 88 | 34.14 | 3.94 | 4-20 |
| S.K.Burke | 36 | 18 | 9 | 10* | 73 | 8.11 | - | - | 3 | - | 256 | 27 | 1019 | 25 | 40.76 | 3.98 | 3-17 |
| J.A.Burley | 2 | 1 | 0 | 7 | 7 | 7.00 | - | - | - | - | 13 | 3 | 28 | 0 | - | 2.15 | - |
| A.K.Burrows | 9 | 5 | 3 | 3* | 5 | - | - | - | 2 | - | 56.1 | 3 | 267 | 7 | 38.14 | 4.75 | 3-27 |
| V.L.Burtt | 9 | 8 | 0 | 46 | 168 | 21.00 | - | - | 4 | - | 6 | 0 | 31 | 2 | 15.50 | 5.17 | 2-31 |
| S.D.Caird | 4 | 4 | 1 | 45 | 72 | 24.00 | - | - | - | - | | | | | | | |
| C.A.Campbell | 85 | 30 | 15 | 12 | 69 | 4.60 | - | - | 15 | - | 753 | 150 | 2018 | 78 | 25.87 | 2.68 | 3-15 |
| E.A.Campbell | 2 | 2 | 1 | 8* | 14 | 14.00 | - | - | 2 | - | 14 | 0 | 69 | 2 | 34.50 | 4.93 | 1-19 |
| R.H.Candy | 18 | 11 | 7 | 8 | 27 | 6.75 | - | - | 3 | - | 120 | 12 | 551 | 18 | 30.61 | 4.59 | 5-19 |
| P.F.Carrick | 3 | 2 | 1 | 6* | 7 | 7.00 | - | - | 1 | - | 29 | 1 | 106 | 6 | 17.66 | 3.66 | 3-43 |
| S.E.Charteris | 5 | 3 | 1 | 20* | 20 | 10.00 | - | - | - | - | 16 | 0 | 102 | 1 | 102.00 | 6.38 | 1-32 |
| J.Clark | 31 | 31 | 1 | 85 | 875 | 29.16 | - | 7 | 5 | - | | | | | | | |
| D.A.Costello | 7 | 2 | 1 | 1 | 1 | 1.00 | - | - | 1 | - | 56.4 | 8 | 139 | 2 | 69.50 | 2.45 | 2-37 |
| S.D.Cowles | 5 | 5 | 0 | 46 | 93 | 18.60 | - | - | 2 | - | 5 | 0 | 24 | 0 | - | 4.80 | - |
| S.R.H.Curtis | 20 | 18 | 3 | 55* | 346 | 23.06 | - | 2 | 5 | - | 10 | 0 | 54 | 2 | 27.00 | 5.40 | 1-15 |
| I.Cronin-Knight | 3 | 3 | 0 | 36 | 41 | 13.66 | - | - | - | - | | | | | | | |
| S.F.M.Devine | 128 | 115 | 11 | 145 | 3227 | 31.02 | 6 | 14 | 36 | - | 719.5 | 52 | 3222 | 87 | 37.03 | 4.48 | 3-24 |
| A.M.Dodd | 31 | 20 | 11 | 20* | 155 | 17.22 | - | - | 10 | - | 207.1 | 24 | 755 | 28 | 26.96 | 3.64 | 3-13 |
| N.C.Dodd | 18 | 17 | 0 | 52 | 224 | 13.17 | - | 1 | 6 | - | | | | | | | |
| L.R.Doolan | 40 | 36 | 5 | 76 | 674 | 21.74 | - | 1 | 18 | - | 214.3 | 21 | 1003 | 32 | 31.34 | 4.68 | 3-7 |
| J.D.Doull | 5 | 5 | 0 | 42 | 64 | 12.80 | - | - | 2 | - | | | | | | | |
| L.R.Down | 22 | 21 | 1 | 90 | 352 | 17.60 | - | 2 | 8 | - | | | | | | | |
| E.C.Drumm | 101 | 94 | 13 | 116 | 2844 | 35.11 | 2 | 19 | 24 | - | 257 | 53 | 778 | 37 | 21.02 | 3.03 | 4-31 |
| J.R.Dunning | 22 | 21 | 4 | 89 | 346 | 20.35 | - | 1 | 4 | - | 157 | 12 | 527 | 13 | 40.53 | 3.36 | 3-29 |
| K.E.Ebrahim | 31 | 25 | 8 | 24 | 181 | 10.64 | - | - | 7 | - | 183.1 | 18 | 735 | 20 | 36.75 | 4.01 | 3-33 |
| M.F.Fahey | 54 | 53 | 2 | 91 | 1403 | 27.50 | - | 14 | 15 | - | | | | | | | |
| P.B.Flannery | 17 | 17 | 2 | 49* | 258 | 17.20 | - | - | 3 | - | | | | | | | |
| K.E.Flavell | 38 | 33 | 9 | 54 | 719 | 29.95 | - | 2 | 5 | - | 70 | 15 | 156 | 7 | 22.28 | 2.23 | 2-5 |
| D.L.Ford | 3 | 2 | 0 | 35 | 46 | 23.00 | - | - | 1 | - | 6 | 0 | 32 | 0 | - | 5.33 | - |
| F.E.Fraser | 5 | 3 | 2 | 54* | 94 | 94.00 | - | 1 | 1 | - | | | | | | | |
| L.M.Fraser | 13 | 7 | 1 | 8 | 31 | 5.16 | - | - | 2 | - | 117 | 20 | 294 | 12 | 24.50 | 2.51 | 3-21 |
| M.K.Fruin | 23 | 23 | 4 | 51 | 385 | 20.26 | - | 1 | 4 | 1 | | | | | | | |
| J.A.Fryer | 7 | 1 | 1 | 1* | 1 | - | - | - | - | - | 33 | 9 | 115 | 10 | 11.50 | 3.48 | 3-8 |
| S.M.Gilchrist | 8 | 5 | 1 | 12 | 19 | 4.75 | - | - | 4 | - | 77 | 21 | 202 | 7 | 28.85 | 2.62 | 3-20 |
| A.J.Green | 14 | 8 | 5 | 17* | 23 | 7.66 | - | - | 3 | - | 108.3 | 17 | 392 | 12 | 32.66 | 3.61 | 5-15 |
| M.L.Green | 52 | 46 | 3 | 121 | 944 | 21.95 | 1 | 4 | 24 | - | 18.4 | 0 | 118 | 1 | 118.00 | 6.32 | 1-30 |
| P.A.Gruber | 2 | 1 | 0 | 0 | 0 | 0.00 | - | - | - | - | 10 | 3 | 35 | 0 | - | 3.50 | - |
| K.V.Gunn | 45 | 34 | 9 | 52 | 461 | 18.44 | - | 1 | 14 | - | 458.5 | 110 | 1113 | 53 | 21.00 | 2.43 | 5-22 |
| G.A.Guy | 7 | 5 | 4 | 2* | 2 | 2.00 | - | - | 1 | - | 48.1 | 5 | 177 | 9 | 19.66 | 3.67 | 3-23 |
| K.A.Hadlee | 1 | 1 | 0 | 14 | 14 | 14.00 | - | - | - | - | | | | | | | |
| B.M.Halliday | 17 | 16 | 0 | 60 | 356 | 22.25 | - | 2 | 5 | - | 11.4 | 2 | 58 | 3 | 19.33 | 4.97 | 1-17 |
| L.R.V.S.Harford | 3 | 3 | 0 | 9 | 20 | 6.66 | - | - | - | - | 7 | 0 | 30 | 0 | - | 4.29 | - |
| J.E.Harris | 45 | 24 | 12 | 19* | 99 | 8.25 | - | - | 9 | - | 414.2 | 98 | 1124 | 61 | 18.42 | 2.71 | 4-8 |
| S.A.Harris | 2 | 1 | 1 | 1* | 1 | - | - | - | - | - | 3 | 0 | 19 | 0 | - | 6.33 | - |
| C.E.Henshilwood | 2 | 1 | 1 | 15* | 15 | - | - | - | - | - | | | | | | | |
| D.A.Hockley | 118 | 115 | 18 | 117 | 4064 | 41.89 | 4 | 34 | 41 | - | 253.4 | 41 | 853 | 20 | 42.65 | 3.36 | 3-49 |
| H.R.Huddleston | 36 | 18 | 7 | 16* | 67 | 6.09 | - | - | 2 | - | 254.3 | 22 | 1118 | 46 | 24.30 | 4.39 | 5-25 |
| S.L.Illingworth | 37 | 29 | 7 | 51 | 342 | 15.54 | - | 1 | 27 | 21 | | | | | | | |
| I.C.P.Jagersma | 34 | 27 | 4 | 58* | 453 | 19.69 | - | 2 | 24 | 9 | 22 | 5 | 48 | 4 | 12.00 | 2.18 | 2-14 |
| H.N.K.Jensen | 30 | 25 | 1 | 53 | 286 | 11.91 | - | 1 | - | - | 175.5 | 8 | 869 | 24 | 36.20 | 4.95 | 3-32 |
| F.C.Jonas | 5 | 3 | 1 | 1* | 1 | 0.50 | - | - | 1 | - | 35 | 1 | 209 | 2 | 104.50 | 5.97 | 1-40 |
| Y.Kainuku | 2 | 2 | 0 | 4 | 4 | 2.00 | - | - | - | - | 12 | 0 | 49 | 0 | - | 4.08 | - |

| | M | In | NO | HS | Runs | Ave | 100s | 50s | Ct | st | O | M | R | W | Ave | R/O | Best |
|---|---|---|---|---|---|---|---|---|---|---|---|---|---|---|---|---|---|
| L.M.Kasperek | 39 | 25 | 8 | 113 | 299 | 17.58 | 1 | - | 11 | - | 317.2 | 32 | 1263 | 65 | 19.43 | 3.98 | 6-46 |
| K.M.Keenan | 55 | 36 | 9 | 57* | 348 | 12.88 | - | 1 | 9 | - | 452 | 72 | 1253 | 70 | 17.90 | 2.77 | 4-5 |
| R.J.Kember | 10 | 10 | 0 | 64 | 155 | 15.50 | - | 1 | 3 | - | | | | | | | |
| A.C.Kerr | 53 | 42 | 10 | 232* | 1240 | 38.75 | 2 | 6 | 31 | - | 447.3 | 18 | 2052 | 76 | 27.00 | 4.59 | 5-17 |
| J.M.Kerr | 20 | 18 | 5 | 28 | 134 | 10.30 | - | - | 3 | - | 147.1 | 13 | 627 | 22 | 28.50 | 4.26 | 4-35 |
| F.S.King | 15 | 10 | 3 | 31 | 81 | 11.57 | - | - | 2 | - | 108.1 | 14 | 404 | 21 | 19.23 | 3.73 | 4-24 |
| P.D.Kinsella | 20 | 20 | 3 | 57 | 443 | 26.05 | - | 2 | - | - | | | | | | | |
| K.Le Comber | 15 | 14 | 4 | 135* | 442 | 44.20 | 1 | 2 | 2 | - | | | | | | | |
| B.J.Legg | 18 | 13 | 3 | 17 | 79 | 7.90 | - | - | 2 | - | 199.4 | 62 | 394 | 20 | 19.70 | 1.97 | 3-4 |
| M.A.M.Lewis | 78 | 73 | 12 | 105 | 1372 | 22.49 | 1 | 4 | 30 | - | 5 | 0 | 32 | 0 | - | 6.40 | - |
| F.C.Leydon-Davis | 1 | 1 | 1 | 10* | 10 | - | - | - | - | - | 8.2 | 1 | 18 | 5 | 3.60 | 2.16 | 5-18 |
| V.J.Lind | 8 | 8 | 0 | 68 | 178 | 22.25 | - | 1 | 5 | - | | | | | | | |
| L.R.Lindsay | 2 | 1 | 0 | 27 | 27 | 27.00 | - | - | - | - | 13 | 0 | 42 | 2 | 21.00 | 3.23 | 2-26 |
| J.Lord | 15 | 13 | 0 | 25 | 101 | 7.76 | - | - | 2 | - | 132.3 | 25 | 318 | 25 | 12.72 | 2.40 | 6-10 |
| M.L.Lynch | 6 | 6 | 0 | 29 | 105 | 17.50 | - | - | - | - | | | | | | | |
| F.L.Mackay | 30 | 24 | 5 | 39* | 313 | 16.47 | - | - | 12 | - | 165.4 | 10 | 720 | 26 | 27.69 | 4.35 | 4-34 |
| R.A.Mair | 16 | 11 | 6 | 7* | 30 | 6.00 | - | - | 4 | - | 110 | 7 | 570 | 8 | 71.25 | 5.18 | 2-21 |
| C.E.Marett | 14 | 12 | 2 | 24 | 149 | 14.90 | - | - | - | - | 126.5 | 24 | 310 | 16 | 19.37 | 2.44 | 3-14 |
| K.J.Martin | 103 | 95 | 14 | 81 | 1794 | 22.14 | - | 7 | 63 | 19 | | | | | | | |
| E.T.McDonald | 3 | - | - | - | - | - | - | - | 1 | - | 24 | 4 | 50 | 5 | 10.00 | 2.08 | 2-17 |
| K.L.McDonald | 6 | 6 | 0 | 34 | 80 | 13.33 | - | - | 1 | - | | | | | | | |
| S.J.McGlashan | 134 | 125 | 16 | 97* | 2438 | 22.36 | - | 11 | 37 | - | | | | | | | |
| P.F.McKelvey | 15 | 14 | 4 | 42 | 214 | 21.40 | - | - | 2 | - | | | | | | | |
| A.McKenna | 14 | 13 | 0 | 39 | 214 | 16.46 | - | - | - | - | | | | | | | |
| S.McLauchlan | 29 | 21 | 5 | 34* | 137 | 8.56 | - | - | 6 | - | 227.5 | 47 | 665 | 19 | 35.00 | 2.92 | 2-6 |
| B.H.McNeill | 23 | 18 | 8 | 88* | 193 | 19.30 | - | 1 | 8 | - | 175.1 | 20 | 680 | 23 | 29.56 | 3.88 | 6-32 |
| R.C.Milburn | 15 | 14 | 1 | 71 | 237 | 18.23 | - | 1 | 7 | 5 | | | | | | | |
| L.E.Milliken | 48 | 18 | 8 | 21 | 110 | 11.00 | - | - | 13 | - | 370 | 45 | 1409 | 59 | 23.88 | 3.81 | 5-25 |
| K.S.Molloy | 5 | 2 | 1 | 0* | 0 | 0.00 | - | - | 2 | - | 36 | 8 | 99 | 4 | 24.75 | 2.75 | 2-16 |
| S.R.M.Morris | 8 | 1 | 0 | 5 | 5 | 5.00 | - | - | - | - | 69 | 12 | 175 | 7 | 25.00 | 2.54 | 2-13 |
| L.J.Murdoch | 25 | 22 | 3 | 69 | 417 | 21.94 | - | 1 | 4 | - | | | | | | | |
| K.J.Musson | 13 | 10 | 2 | 31 | 86 | 10.75 | - | - | 3 | - | 87.2 | 12 | 253 | 10 | 25.30 | 2.90 | 3-22 |
| T.M.M.Newton | 10 | 7 | 1 | 18* | 56 | 9.33 | - | - | 5 | - | 64 | 5 | 275 | 11 | 25.00 | 4.30 | 5-31 |
| C.M.Nicholson | 35 | 22 | 10 | 73* | 195 | 16.25 | - | 1 | 13 | - | 272.4 | 62 | 707 | 38 | 18.60 | 2.59 | 4-18 |
| M.J.G.Nielsen | 52 | 25 | 5 | 20 | 121 | 6.05 | - | - | 7 | - | 392 | 54 | 1418 | 53 | 26.75 | 3.62 | 5-21 |
| A.M.O'Leary | 19 | 18 | 3 | 91* | 497 | 33.13 | - | 3 | 3 | - | | | | | | | |
| J.B.Olson | 4 | 4 | 1 | 9* | 17 | 5.66 | - | - | - | - | 27 | 9 | 52 | 4 | 13.00 | 1.93 | 3-16 |
| G.L.Page | 2 | 1 | 0 | 5 | 5 | 5.00 | - | - | - | - | 17.2 | 3 | 46 | 6 | 7.66 | 2.65 | 6-20 |
| N.Payne | 65 | 64 | 7 | 93 | 1178 | 20.66 | - | 4 | 17 | - | 158 | 48 | 407 | 20 | 20.35 | 2.58 | 3-20 |
| M.M.Penfold | 2 | 1 | 1 | 0* | 0 | - | - | - | - | - | 17 | 1 | 85 | 2 | 42.50 | 5.00 | 2-42 |
| K.T.Perkins | 73 | 57 | 13 | 78 | 1198 | 27.22 | - | 4 | 35 | - | | | | | | | |
| E.C.Perry | 17 | 13 | 4 | 70 | 201 | 22.33 | - | 1 | 4 | - | 8 | 0 | 50 | 0 | - | 6.25 | - |
| M.H.Peters | 16 | 12 | 5 | 24 | 79 | 11.28 | - | - | 3 | - | 155.5 | 63 | 291 | 19 | 15.31 | 1.87 | 2-3 |
| A.M.Peterson | 32 | 21 | 4 | 46 | 279 | 16.41 | - | - | 9 | - | 137.4 | 13 | 482 | 27 | 17.85 | 3.50 | 4-25 |
| K.V.Plummer | 11 | 10 | 1 | 32 | 100 | 11.11 | - | - | 2 | - | 10 | 0 | 36 | 0 | - | 3.60 | - |
| L.M.Powell | 5 | 4 | 0 | 70 | 73 | 18.25 | - | 1 | 1 | - | | | | | | | |
| R.H.Priest | 87 | 74 | 14 | 157 | 1694 | 28.23 | 2 | 9 | 73 | 20 | | | | | | | |
| K.L.Pulford | 46 | 40 | 0 | 95 | 743 | 18.57 | - | 3 | 9 | - | 199.3 | 16 | 782 | 30 | 26.06 | 3.92 | 4-5 |
| R.J.Pullar | 51 | 32 | 11 | 27* | 253 | 12.04 | - | - | 14 | - | 430.1 | 80 | 1215 | 74 | 16.41 | 2.82 | 5-7 |
| K.A.Ramel | 47 | 37 | 7 | 41 | 519 | 17.30 | - | - | 13 | - | 204.3 | 26 | 729 | 35 | 20.82 | 3.56 | 3-26 |
| S.J.Rattray | 15 | 15 | 7 | 60* | 305 | 38.12 | - | 1 | 1 | - | 123.1 | 16 | 399 | 11 | 36.27 | 3.24 | 2-33 |
| R.J.Rolls | 104 | 91 | 3 | 114 | 2201 | 25.01 | 2 | 12 | 90 | 43 | | | | | | | |
| E.F.Rouse | 3 | 3 | 0 | 48 | 90 | 30.00 | - | - | - | - | | | | | | | |
| H.M.Rowe | 41 | 26 | 7 | 29* | 184 | 9.68 | - | - | 8 | - | 269.2 | 19 | 1226 | 43 | 28.51 | 4.55 | 5-55 |
| S.E.A.Ruck | 27 | 12 | 8 | 12* | 48 | 12.00 | - | - | 3 | - | 213.1 | 28 | 786 | 24 | 32.75 | 3.69 | 4-31 |
| J.A.Russell | 5 | 4 | 1 | 8* | 8 | 2.66 | - | - | - | - | 26 | 3 | 84 | 1 | 84.00 | 3.23 | 1-20 |
| E.M.Ryan | 15 | 5 | 1 | 6* | 17 | 4.25 | - | - | 13 | 8 | | | | | | | |
| J.M.Saulbrey | 5 | 5 | 3 | 22* | 75 | 37.50 | - | - | - | - | 43 | 12 | 100 | 4 | 25.00 | 2.33 | 2-32 |
| A.E.Satterthwaite | 145 | 138 | 17 | 137* | 4639 | 38.33 | 7 | 27 | 58 | - | 321.4 | 19 | 1486 | 50 | 29.72 | 4.62 | 4-13 |
| N.Scripps | 7 | 3 | 3 | 9* | 12 | - | - | - | - | - | 50.2 | 6 | 206 | 6 | 34.33 | 4.09 | 2-17 |
| V.S.Sexton | 2 | 2 | 0 | 9 | 12 | 6.00 | - | - | - | - | | | | | | | |
| E.A.Signal | 19 | 12 | 5 | 28* | 79 | 11.28 | - | - | 5 | - | 130.3 | 23 | 496 | 7 | 70.85 | 3.80 | 2-26 |
| R.J.Signal | 6 | 3 | 1 | 8 | 12 | 6.00 | - | - | 2 | - | 27 | 2 | 89 | 2 | 44.50 | 3.30 | 1-10 |
| L.J.Simpson | 12 | 11 | 1 | 23* | 99 | 9.50 | - | - | 1 | - | | | | | | | |
| R.J.Steele | 32 | 12 | 6 | 8* | 41 | 6.83 | - | - | 6 | - | 293 | 57 | 831 | 34 | 24.44 | 2.84 | 3-10 |
| L.M.M.Tahuhu | 83 | 54 | 16 | 26 | 339 | 8.92 | - | - | 23 | - | 628 | 41 | 2818 | 93 | 30.30 | 4.49 | 5-37 |
| H.M.Tiffen | 117 | 111 | 16 | 100 | 2919 | 30.72 | 1 | 18 | 32 | - | 276 | 43 | 955 | 49 | 19.48 | 3.46 | 4-43 |
| E.A.Travers | 3 | - | - | - | - | - | - | - | - | - | | | | | | | |
| D.M.Trow | 2 | 1 | 1 | 1* | 1 | - | - | - | 1 | - | 12 | 3 | 18 | 4 | 4.50 | 1.50 | 3-8 |
| S.J.Tsukigawa | 42 | 39 | 6 | 78* | 730 | 22.12 | - | 2 | 9 | - | 255.5 | 19 | 1121 | 35 | 32.02 | 4.38 | 4-43 |

| | M | In | NO | HS | Runs | Ave | 100s | 50s | Ct | st | O | M | R | W | Ave | R/O | Best |
|---|---|---|---|---|---|---|---|---|---|---|---|---|---|---|---|---|---|
| M.F.Tunupopo | 3 | - | - | - | - | - | - | - | 2 | - | 18 | 4 | 57 | 0 | - | 3.17 | - |
| J.A.Turner | 30 | 14 | 2 | 15 | 54 | 4.50 | - | - | 6 | - | 265.2 | 42 | 695 | 28 | 24.82 | 2.62 | 5-5 |
| N.J.Turner | 28 | 26 | 2 | 114 | 624 | 26.00 | 1 | 2 | 4 | - | | | | | | | |
| J.M.Watkin | 6 | 5 | 0 | 62 | 86 | 17.20 | - | 1 | - | - | 29.3 | 2 | 113 | 6 | 18.83 | 3.83 | 2-30 |
| A.L.Watkins | 103 | 94 | 7 | 111 | 1889 | 21.71 | 2 | 6 | 37 | - | 732 | 67 | 2860 | 92 | 31.08 | 3.91 | 4-2 |
| H.M.Watson | 66 | 48 | 10 | 115* | 580 | 15.26 | 1 | - | 21 | - | 414.3 | 67 | 1287 | 54 | 23.83 | 3.10 | 3-14 |
| N.M.Williams | 19 | 13 | 2 | 21* | 80 | 7.27 | - | - | 1 | - | 110.5 | 19 | 374 | 15 | 24.93 | 3.37 | 3-37 |

# TEAM RECORDS

## Highest Totals

| | | | |
|---|---|---|---|
| 490-4 | v Ireland | Dublin | 2018 |
| 455-5 | v Pakistan | Christchurch | 1996/97 |
| 440-3 | v Ireland | Dublin | 2018 |
| 418 | v Ireland | Dublin | 2018 |
| 373-7 | v Pakistan | Sydney | 2008/09 |

## Lowest Totals

| | | | |
|---|---|---|---|
| 58 | v Australia | Melbourne | 1984/85 |
| 59 | v West Indies | Kingston | 2013/14 |
| 61 | v Australia | Wellington | 1998/99 |
| 69 | v West Indies | Basseterre | 2014/15 |
| 72 | v England | Blackpool | 2007 |

# INDIVIDUAL RECORDS

## Centuries

| | | |
|---|---|---|
| 232* | A.C. Kerr v Ireland at Dublin | 2018 |
| 168 | S.W. Bates v Pakistan at Sydney | 2008/09 |
| 157 | R.H. Priest v Sri Lanka at Lincoln | 2015/16 |
| 151 | S.W. Bates v Ireland at Dublin | 2018 |
| 145 | S.F.M. Devine v South Africa at Cuttack | 2012/13 |
| 137* | A.E. Satterthwaite v Pakistan at Lincoln | 2016/17 |
| 135* | K. LeComber v Ireland at Dublin | 1996 |
| 126 | S.W. Bates v Pakistan at Christchurch | 2021/22 |
| 123 | A.E. Satterthwaite v Pakistan at Nelson | 2016/17 |
| 122* | S.W. Bates v Australia at Sydney | 2012/13 |
| 122 | S.W. Bates v India at Chennai | 2006/07 |
| 121 | M.L. Green v Ireland at Dublin | 2018 |
| 119* | A.E. Satterthwaite v England at Dunedin | 2020/21 |
| 119* | A.C. Kerr v India at Queenstown | 2021/22 |
| 117 | D.A. Hockley v England at Chester-le-Street | 1996 |
| 116 | E.C. Drumm v England at Oamaru | 2000/01 |
| 115* | H.M. Watson v Ireland at Dublin | 2004 |
| 115* | A.E. Satterthwaite v Pakistan at Lincoln | 2016/17 |
| 114 | N.J. Turner v Netherlands at Sydney | 1988/89 |
| 114 | R.J. Rolls v Australia at Lincoln | 2001/02 |
| 113 | L.M. Kasperek v Ireland at Dublin | 2018 |
| 111 | A.L. Mason v England at Blackpool | 2007 |
| 110 | S.W. Bates v West Indies at Kingston | 2013/14 |
| 110 | S.W. Bates v Australia at Mt Maunganui | 2015/16 |
| 109 | A.E. Satterthwaite v Australia at Sydney | 2012/13 |

| 108* | E.C. Drumm v South Africa at Lincoln | 2000/01 |
| 108 | R.H. Priest v Sri Lanka at Lincoln | 2015/16 |
| 108 | S.F.M. Devine v West Indies at Lincoln | 2017/18 |
| 108 | S.F.M. Devine v Ireland at Dublin | 2018 |
| 108 | S.F.M. Devine v West Indies at Mt Maunganui | 2021/22 |
| 106* | S.W. Bates v Sri Lanka at Bristol | 2017 |
| 106 | S.W. Bates v England at Mt Maunganui | 2014/15 |
| 106 | S.W. Bates v India at Queenstown | 2021/22 |
| 105 | M.A.M. Lewis v Pakistan at Christchurch | 1996/97 |
| 104* | R.J. Rolls v Australia at Chennai | 2006/07 |
| 103 | A.E. Satterthwaite v England at Mumbai | 2012/13 |
| 103 | S.F.M. Devine v Pakistan at Sharjah | 2017/18 |
| 102* | A.E. Satterthwaite v Australia at Auckland | 2016/17 |
| 102 | A.L. Mason v Australia at Darwin | 2007/08 |
| 102 | S.W. Bates v Australia at Cuttack | 2012/13 |
| 101* | S.W. Bates v West Indies at Lincoln | 2017/18 |
| 101 | B.L. Bevege v International XI at Auckland | 1981/82 |
| 100* | D.A. Hockley v Sri Lanka at Chandigarh | 1997/98 |
| 100 | D.A. Hockley v West Indies at Chandigarh | 1997/98 |
| 100 | D.A. Hockley v Australia  at Melbourne | 1999/00 |
| 100 | H.M. Tiffen v Pakistan at Sydney | 2008/09 |

## Five Wickets in an Innings

| 6-10 | J. Lord v India at Auckland | 1981/82 |
| 6-20 | G.L. Page v Trinidad & Tobago at St Albans | 1973 |
| 6-32 | B.H. McNeill v England at Lincoln | 2007/08 |
| 6-46 | L.M. Kasperek v Australia at Mt Maunganui | 2020/21 |
| 5-5 | J.A. Turner v Netherlands at Lindfield | 1993 |
| 5-7 | R.J. Pullar v South Africa at Hamilton | 1998/99 |
| 5-10 | R.J. Pullar v India at St Saviour | 2002 |
| 5-15 | A.J Green v Ireland at Dublin | 2004 |
| 5-17 | A.C Kerr v Ireland at Dublin | 2018 |
| 5-18 | F.C. Leydon-Davis v West Indies at Lincoln | 2013/14 |
| 5-19 | R.H. Candy v Pakistan at Cuttack | 2012/13 |
| 5-21 | M.J.G. Nielsen v Sri Lanka at Lincoln | 2015/16 |
| 5-22 | K.V. Gunn v Australia at Wellington | 1989/90 |
| 5-25 | L.E. Milliken v India, Pretoria | 2004/05 |
| 5-25 | H.R. Huddleston v South Africa at Kimberley | 2016/17 |
| 5-31 | T.M.M. Newton v Pakistan at Nelson | 2016/17 |
| 5-35 | H.R. Huddleston v Sri Lanka at Bristol | 2017 |
| 5-36 | H.R. Huddleston v West Indies at Lincoln | 2013/14 |
| 5-37 | L.M.M. Tahuhu v England at Leicester | 2021 |
| 5-39 | M.J.G. Nielsen v South Africa at Kimberley | 2016/17 |
| 5-39 | L.M. Kasperek v England at Leicester | 2018 |
| 5-55 | H.M. Rowe v Pakistan at Christchurch | 2021/22 |

## Hat-tricks

| 7.1-1-18-3 | J.E. Harris | v West Indies | Chiswick | 1993 |
| 8-2-22-3 | E.C. Drumm | v Australia | Adelaide | 1995/96 |

# Most Economical Bowling

| | | | | |
|---|---|---|---|---|
| 10-7-3-0 | C.A. Campbell | v Netherlands | Christchurch | 2000/01 |
| 12-9-4-3 | B.J. Legg | v Netherlands | Melbourne | 1988/89 |
| 12-9-5-3 | J.E. Harris | v Netherlands | Lindfield | 1993 |
| 11.2-7-5-5 | J.A. Turner | v Netherlands | Lindfield | 1993 |
| 10-6-5-4 | K.M. Keenan | v West Indies | Chandigarh | 1997/98 |

# Most Expensive Bowling

| | | | | |
|---|---|---|---|---|
| 10-1-74-1 | S.F. Devine | v England | Canterbury | 2021 |
| 10-0-70-0 | R.A. Mair | v Australia | Brisbane | 2020/21 |
| 10-1-69-1 | S.E.A. Ruck | v Australia | Sydney | 2012/13 |
| 9-1-68-1 | L.E. Milliken | v Australia | Auckland | 2003/04 |
| 10-0-67-0 | R.H. Candy | v Australia | Sydney | 2012/13 |
| 10-0-67-0 | L.M.M. Tahuhu | v Australia | Mt Maunganui | 2016/17 |
| 10-0-65-0 | L.R. Doolan | v England | Lincoln | 2011/12 |
| 10-0-65-2 | A.E. Satterthwaite | v Pakistan | Lincoln | 2016/17 |
| 10-1-65-2 | H.M. Rowe | v England | Canterbury | 2021 |

# Wicketkeeping

**DISMISSALS IN AN INNINGS**

*(ct/st)*

| | | | | |
|---|---|---|---|---|
| 6 | (4/2) | S.L. Illingworth | v Australia | Beckenham | 1993 |
| 5 | (4/1) | R.H. Priest | v Australia | Auckland | 2016/17 |

# Fielding

**CATCHES IN AN INNINGS**

| | | | | |
|---|---|---|---|---|
| 4 | A.C. Kerr | v India | Queenstown | 2021/22 |

# SUMMARY OF ONE-DAY INTERNATIONAL CAREER RECORDS

## Most Matches

| | | | | | |
|---|---|---|---|---|---|
| A.E. Satterthwaite | 145 | A.L. Watkins | 103 | H.M. Watson | 66 |
| S.W. Bates | 142 | K.J. Martin | 103 | K.M. Keenan | 55 |
| S.J. McGlashan | 134 | E.C. Drumm | 101 | M.F. Fahey | 54 |
| S.F.M. Devine | 128 | R.H. Priest | 87 | A.C. Kerr | 53 |
| N.J. Browne | 125 | C.A. Campbell | 85 | M.J.G. Nielsen | 52 |
| D.A. Hockley | 118 | L.M.M.Tahuhu | 83 | M.L. Green | 52 |
| H.M. Tiffen | 117 | M.A.M. Lewis | 78 | R.J. Pullar | 51 |
| R.J. Rolls | 104 | K.T. Perkins | 73 | | |

## Most Runs

| | | | | | |
|---|---|---|---|---|---|
| S.W. Bates | 5045 | S.J. McGlashan | 2438 | M.F. Fahey | 1403 |
| A.E. Satterthwaite | 4639 | R.J. Rolls | 2201 | M.A.M. Lewis | 1372 |
| D.A. Hockley | 4064 | N.J. Browne | 2002 | A.C. Kerr | 1240 |
| S.F.M. Devine | 3227 | A.L. Watkins | 1889 | K.T. Perkins | 1198 |
| H.M. Tiffen | 2919 | K.J. Martin | 1794 | N. Payne | 1178 |
| E.C. Drumm | 2844 | R.H. Priest | 1694 | | |

## Most Wickets

| | | | | | |
|---|---|---|---|---|---|
| L.M.M.Tahuhu | 93 | S.W. Bates | 75 | L.E. Milliken | 59 |
| A.L. Watkins | 92 | R.J. Pullar | 74 | H.M. Watson | 54 |
| N.J. Browne | 88 | K.M. Keenan | 70 | K.V. Gunn | 53 |
| S.F.M. Devine | 87 | L.M. Kasperek | 65 | M.J.G. Nielsen | 53 |
| C.A. Campbell | 78 | J.E. Harris | 61 | A.E. Satterthwaite | 50 |
| A.C Kerr | 76 | | | | |

## Most Wicketkeeping Dismissals

| | Ct | St | Total |
|---|---|---|---|
| R.J. Rolls | 90 | 43 | 133 |
| R.H. Priest | 73 | 20 | 93 |
| K.J. Martin | 56 | 19 | 75 |
| S.L. Illingworth | 26 | 21 | 47 |
| I.C.P. Jagersma | 24 | 9 | 33 |
| E.M. Ryan | 13 | 8 | 21 |

## Most Catches

| | |
|---|---|
| S.W. Bates | 77 |
| A.E.Satterthwaite | 58 |
| D.A. Hockley | 41 |
| A.L. Watkins | 37 |
| S.J. McGlashan | 36 |
| S.F.M. Devine | 36 |
| K.T. Perkins | 35 |

# RECORD PARTNERSHIPS

| | | | | | |
|---|---|---|---|---|---|
| 1st | 196 | S.W. Bates & R.H. Priest | v Sri Lanka | Lincoln | 2015/16 |
| 2nd | 295 | A.C. Kerr & L.M. Kasperek | v Ireland | Dublin | 2018 |
| 3rd | 150 | A.E.Satterthwaite & K.J. Martin | v Pakistan | Lincoln | 2016/17 |
| 4th | 172* | A.E.Satterthwaite & A.C Kerr | v England | Dunedin | 2020/21 |
| 5th | 108* | R.J. Rolls & S.J. Tsukigawa | v Australia | Chennai | 2006/07 |
| 6th | 139* | S.J. McGlashan & N.J. Browne | v South Africa | Bowral | 2008/09 |
| 7th | 104* | S.J. Tsukigawa & N.J. Browne | v England | Chennai | 2006/07 |
| 8th | 74 | A.E.Satterthwaite & L.R.Doolan | v Australia | Whangarei | 2008/09 |
| 9th | 58 | K.V. Gunn & S. McLauchlan | v Australia | Wellington | 1991/92 |
| 10th | 34 | A.E.Satterthwaite & L.M. Kasperek | v England | Bristol | 2021 |

# TWENTY20 INTERNATIONAL CAREER RECORDS

| | M | In | NO | HS | Runs | Ave | 100s | 50s | Ct | St | O | M | R | W | Ave | R/O | Best |
|---|---|---|---|---|---|---|---|---|---|---|---|---|---|---|---|---|---|
| K.S.Anderson | 2 | 1 | 1 | 1* | 1 | - | - | - | - | - | 4 | 0 | 17 | 3 | 5.66 | 4.25 | 3-17 |
| S.W.Bates | 126 | 123 | 9 | 124* | 3381 | 29.65 | 1 | 21 | 70 | - | 189.3 | 1 | 1276 | 50 | 25.52 | 6.73 | 4-26 |
| E.M.Bermingham | 31 | 17 | 4 | 20 | 74 | 5.69 | - | - | 3 | - | 105 | 3 | 569 | 33 | 17.24 | 5.42 | 2-12 |
| B.M.Bezuidenhout | 9 | 7 | 2 | 20* | 35 | 7.00 | - | - | 3 | 2 | | | | | | | |
| N.J.Browne | 54 | 46 | 12 | 34* | 547 | 16.08 | - | - | 24 | - | 146 | 4 | 814 | 47 | 17.31 | 5.58 | 4-15 |
| S.M.Bullen | 3 | - | - | - | - | - | - | - | - | - | 9 | 0 | 57 | 3 | 19.00 | 6.33 | 2-20 |
| S.K.Burke | 7 | 2 | 1 | 3* | 6 | 6.00 | - | - | - | - | 23 | 1 | 149 | 7 | 21.28 | 6.48 | 3-15 |
| R.H.Candy | 10 | 4 | 2 | 9* | 14 | 7.00 | - | - | 3 | - | 33 | 1 | 213 | 7 | 30.42 | 6.45 | 2-24 |
| S.E.Charteris | 2 | 1 | 1 | 5* | 5 | - | - | - | 1 | - | 4 | 0 | 17 | 1 | 17.00 | 4.25 | 1-17 |
| S.R.H.Curtis | 8 | 4 | 0 | 8 | 13 | 3.25 | - | - | - | - | | | | | | | |
| S.F.M.Devine | 102 | 99 | 12 | 105 | 2592 | 29.79 | 1 | 15 | 34 | - | 273 | 7 | 1733 | 98 | 17.68 | 6.35 | 4-22 |
| N.C.Dodd | 6 | 4 | 1 | 14 | 26 | 8.66 | - | - | - | - | | | | | | | |
| L.R.Doolan | 33 | 23 | 3 | 41 | 194 | 9.70 | - | - | 5 | - | 100 | 2 | 602 | 28 | 21.50 | 6.02 | 3-16 |
| L.R.Down | 6 | 4 | 1 | 12 | 35 | 11.66 | - | - | 4 | - | | | | | | | |
| K.E.Ebrahim | 39 | 20 | 9 | 27* | 91 | 8.27 | - | - | 8 | - | 96.4 | 3 | 595 | 22 | 27.04 | 6.16 | 3-9 |
| M.F.Fahey | 8 | 7 | 1 | 43 | 134 | 22.33 | - | - | 1 | - | | | | | | | |
| P.B.Flannery | 1 | 1 | 0 | 18 | 18 | 18.00 | - | - | - | - | | | | | | | |
| A.J.Green | 1 | 1 | 0 | 3 | 3 | 3.00 | - | - | - | - | 4 | 0 | 20 | 2 | 10.00 | 5.00 | 2-20 |
| M.L.Green | 57 | 45 | 8 | 29 | 440 | 11.89 | - | - | 19 | - | 9 | 0 | 58 | 1 | 58.00 | 6.44 | 1-6 |
| C.A.Gurrey | 2 | 2 | 0 | 15 | 19 | 9.50 | - | - | - | - | | | | | | | |
| G.A.Guy | 6 | 2 | 1 | 2 | 2 | 2.00 | - | - | - | - | 18 | 0 | 100 | 3 | 33.33 | 5.56 | 1-14 |
| B.M.Halliday | 10 | 9 | 4 | 25* | 73 | 14.60 | - | - | 1 | - | 2 | 0 | 11 | 1 | 11.00 | 5.50 | 1-11 |
| K.A.Heffernan | 2 | - | - | - | - | - | - | - | - | - | 6 | 0 | 29 | 1 | 29.00 | 4.83 | 1-14 |
| H.R.Huddleston | 16 | 3 | 1 | 10 | 15 | 7.50 | - | - | 7 | - | 44 | 4 | 238 | 13 | 18.30 | 5.41 | 2-9 |
| H.N.K.Jensen | 40 | 23 | 6 | 19 | 151 | 8.88 | - | - | 11 | - | 106 | 1 | 733 | 29 | 25.27 | 6.92 | 3-11 |
| L.M.Kasperek | 46 | 22 | 5 | 19 | 104 | 6.11 | - | - | 12 | - | 168.2 | 2 | 1060 | 75 | 14.13 | 6.30 | 4-7 |
| R.J.Kember | 3 | 3 | 0 | 15 | 22 | 7.33 | - | - | - | - | | | | | | | |
| A.C.Kerr | 42 | 24 | 9 | 36 | 234 | 15.60 | - | - | 20 | - | 150.3 | 1 | 892 | 41 | 21.75 | 5.93 | 3-16 |
| J.M.Kerr | 14 | 4 | 1 | 12* | 25 | 8.33 | - | - | 2 | - | 40.5 | 1 | 251 | 9 | 27.88 | 6.15 | 2-17 |
| M.A.M.Lewis | 1 | 1 | 0 | 25 | 25 | 25.00 | - | - | - | - | | | | | | | |
| F.C.Leydon-Davis | 8 | - | - | - | - | - | - | - | 2 | - | 22 | 0 | 120 | 4 | 30.00 | 5.45 | 2-15 |
| V.J.Lind | 2 | 2 | 0 | 20 | 29 | 14.50 | - | - | - | - | | | | | | | |
| F.L.Mackay | 30 | 22 | 5 | 51 | 332 | 19.52 | - | 1 | 6 | - | 87.4 | 1 | 576 | 25 | 23.04 | 6.57 | 3-18 |
| R.A.Mair | 17 | 5 | 4 | 13* | 18 | 18.00 | - | - | - | - | 48.2 | 0 | 321 | 13 | 24.69 | 6.64 | 2-17 |
| K.J.Martin | 95 | 77 | 22 | 65 | 996 | 18.10 | - | 4 | 34 | 24 | | | | | | | |
| S.J.McGlashan | 76 | 73 | 9 | 84 | 1164 | 18.18 | - | 2 | 30 | - | | | | | | | |
| B.H.McNeill | 2 | - | - | - | - | - | - | - | - | - | 5 | 0 | 30 | 0 | - | 6.00 | - |
| R.C.Milburn | 2 | 1 | 1 | 1* | 1 | - | - | - | - | 1 | | | | | | | |
| L.E.Milliken | 1 | - | - | - | - | - | - | - | - | - | 4 | 0 | 28 | 1 | 28.00 | 7.00 | 1-28 |
| T.M.M.Newton | 15 | 8 | 4 | 14 | 22 | 5.50 | - | - | 8 | - | 23 | 0 | 126 | 9 | 14.00 | 5.48 | 3-9 |
| M.J.G.Nielsen | 44 | 13 | 8 | 21* | 60 | 12.00 | - | - | 6 | - | 156.5 | 4 | 753 | 41 | 18.36 | 4.80 | 4-10 |
| K.T.Perkins | 55 | 42 | 16 | 34 | 448 | 17.23 | - | - | 15 | - | | | | | | | |
| E.C.Perry | 31 | 29 | 7 | 50* | 369 | 16.77 | - | 1 | 11 | - | | | | | | | |
| A.M.Peterson | 33 | 18 | 3 | 15 | 92 | 6.13 | - | - | 8 | - | 62 | 0 | 427 | 18 | 23.72 | 6.89 | 3-2 |
| R.H.Priest | 75 | 64 | 12 | 60 | 873 | 16.78 | - | 1 | 39 | 33 | | | | | | | |
| K.L.Pulford | 12 | 8 | 2 | 29 | 66 | 11.00 | - | - | 1 | - | 39 | 1 | 186 | 11 | 16.90 | 4.77 | 2-21 |
| R.J.Rolls | 2 | 2 | 0 | 41 | 80 | 40.00 | - | - | 2 | 1 | | | | | | | |
| H.M.Rowe | 25 | 9 | 5 | 14* | 48 | 12.00 | - | - | 7 | - | 43 | 1 | 299 | 12 | 24.91 | 6.95 | 3-18 |
| S.E.A.Ruck | 37 | 9 | 5 | 6 | 16 | 4.00 | - | - | 5 | - | 125 | 5 | 688 | 40 | 17.20 | 5.50 | 3-12 |
| A.E.Satterthwaite | 111 | 100 | 17 | 71* | 1784 | 21.49 | - | 1 | 36 | - | 85.3 | 0 | 609 | 26 | 23.42 | 7.12 | 6-17 |
| R.J.Steele | 1 | - | - | - | - | - | - | - | 2 | - | 4 | 0 | 14 | 0 | - | 3.50 | - |
| L.M.M.Tahuhu | 61 | 17 | 6 | 27 | 89 | 8.09 | - | - | 16 | - | 187.3 | 5 | 1124 | 53 | 21.20 | 5.99 | 3-17 |
| H.M.Tiffen | 9 | 8 | 1 | 30 | 121 | 17.28 | - | - | 6 | - | | | | | | | |
| S.J.Tsukigawa | 19 | 16 | 2 | 22 | 129 | 9.21 | - | - | 2 | - | 25 | 0 | 170 | 5 | 34.00 | 6.80 | 2-19 |
| J.M.Watkin | 9 | 8 | 1 | 77* | 118 | 16.85 | - | 1 | 2 | - | 20.3 | 0 | 132 | 7 | 18.85 | 6.44 | 3-9 |
| A.L.Watkins | 36 | 36 | 3 | 89* | 772 | 23.39 | - | 3 | 14 | - | 84.3 | 0 | 519 | 22 | 23.59 | 6.14 | 3-8 |
| H.M.Watson | 8 | 3 | 2 | 9* | 16 | 16.00 | - | - | - | - | 28 | 2 | 152 | 7 | 21.71 | 5.43 | 3-13 |

## Highest Totals

| | | | |
|---|---|---|---|
| 216-1 | v South Africa | Taunton | 2018 |
| 188-3 | v Sri Lanka | Christchurch | 2015/16 |
| 186-7 | v South Africa | Taunton | 2007 |
| 185-3 | v West Indies | Mt Maunganui | 2017/18 |
| 180-5 | v West Indies | Gros Islet | 2009/10 |

## Highest Individual Scores

| | | |
|---|---|---|
| 124* | S.W. Bates v South Africa at Taunton | 2018 |
| 105 | S.F.M. Devine v South Africa at Wellington | 2019/20 |
| 94* | S.W. Bates v Pakistan at Sylhet | 2013/14 |
| 89* | A.L. Watkins v India at Nottingham | 2009 |
| 84 | S.J. McGlashan v West Indies at Gros Islet | 2009/10 |
| 82 | S.W. Bates v Ireland at Mohali | 2015/16 |
| 77* | J.M. Watkin v Ireland at Dublin | 2018 |
| 77 | S.W. Bates v Australia at Brisbane | 2018/19 |
| 77 | S.F.M. Devine v South Africa at Wellington | 2019/20 |
| 75* | S.F.M. Devine v Sri Lanka at Perth | 2019/20 |

## Best Bowling in an Innings

| | | |
|---|---|---|
| 6-17 | A.E. Satterthwaite v England at Taunton | 2007 |
| 4-7 | L.M. Kasperek v Australia at Wellington | 2015/16 |
| 4-10 | M.J.G. Nielsen v England at Invercargill | 2011/12 |
| 4-15 | N.J. Browne v Pakistan at Basseterre | 2009/10 |
| 4-22 | S.F.M. Devine v West Indies at Mumbai | 2015/16 |
| 4-24 | A.E. Satterthwaite v West Indies at Kingstown | 2014/15 |
| 4-26 | S.W. Bates v Australia at Invercargill | 2010/11 |

## Hat-trick

| | | | | |
|---|---|---|---|---|
| 1-0-2-3 | A.N. Peterson | v Australia | Geelong | 2016/17 |

# RECORD PARTNERSHIPS

| | | | | | |
|---|---|---|---|---|---|
| 1st | 182 | S.W. Bates & S.F.M. Devine | v South Africa | Taunton | 2018 |
| 2nd | 142 | S.F.M. Devine & S.W. Bates | v South Africa | Wellington | 2019/20 |
| 3rd | 124 | K.J. Martin & A.E. Satterthwaite | v West Indies | Mt Maunganui | 2017/18 |
| 4th | 116* | K.J. Martin & A.E. Satterthwaite | v West Indies | Hamilton | 2017/18 |
| 5th | 62 | K.J. Martin & E.C. Perry | v India | Clifton | 2011 |
| 6th | 42* | K.J. Martin & B.M.Bezuidenhout | v Australia | Sydney | 2018/19 |
| 7th | 37 | K.J. Martin & L.M. Kasperek | v India | Providence | 2018/19 |
| 8th | 27 | L.M.M. Tahuhu & A.C. Kerr | v Pakistan | Nelson | 2016/17 |
| 9th | 32* | K.J. Martin & M.J.G. Nielsen | v Australia | Sydney | 2011/12 |
| 10th | 33 | M.L. Green & R.A. Mair | v England | Wellington | 2020/21 |

# PROVINCIAL COMPETITIONS

The symbol of supremacy in women's provincial cricket has been the Hallyburton Johnstone Shield (1935/36 to 1981/82), Hansells Cup (1982/83 to 1989/90), Pub Charities National Tournament (1990/91 to 1997/98), State Insurance Cup (1998/99 to 2000/01), State League (2001/02 to 2008/09), One-day Competition (2009/10 and from 2012/13 to 2016/17) and Action Cricket Cup (2010/11 to 2011/12). The Hallyburton Johnstone Shield was reinstated in 2017/18.

## WINNERS

| | | | | | |
|---|---|---|---|---|---|
| 1935/36 | Wellington | 1964/65 | Auckland | 1993/94 | Canterbury |
| 1936/37 | Wellington | 1965/66 | Auckland | 1994/95 | Canterbury |
| 1937/38 | Wellington | 1966/67 | Canterbury | 1995/96 | Canterbury |
| 1938/39 | Wellington | 1967/68 | Wellington | 1996/97 | Canterbury |
| 1939/40 | Auckland | 1968/69 | North Shore | 1997/98 | Canterbury |
| 1940/41 | Auckland | 1969/70 | Wellington | 1998/99 | Canterbury |
| 1941/42 | no competition | 1970/71 | North Shore | 1999/00 | Auckland |
| 1942/43 | Auckland | 1971/72 | North Shore | 2000/01 | Auckland |
| 1943/44 | Canterbury | 1972/73 | Canterbury | 2001/02 | Auckland |
| 1944/45 | Canterbury | 1973/74 | Wellington | 2002/03 | Auckland |
| 1945/46 | Canterbury | 1974/75 | Wellington | 2003/04 | Canterbury |
| 1946/47 | Auckland | 1975/76 | Canterbury | 2004/05 | Canterbury/Wellington |
| 1947/48 | Auckland | 1976/77 | Wellington | 2005/06 | Central Districts |
| 1948/49 | Auckland | 1977/78 | Wellington | 2006/07 | Canterbury |
| 1949/50 | Wellington | 1978/79 | Canterbury | 2007/08 | Canterbury |
| 1950/51 | Wellington | 1979/80 | Canterbury | 2008/09 | Canterbury |
| 1951/52 | Auckland | 1980/81 | Canterbury | 2009/10 | Central Districts |
| 1952/53 | Wellington | 1981/82 | Canterbury | 2010/11 | Canterbury |
| 1953/54 | Wellington | 1982/83 | Canterbury | 2011/12 | Auckland |
| 1954/55 | Auckland | 1983/84 | Canterbury | 2012/13 | Canterbury |
| 1955/56 | Canterbury | 1984/85 | Canterbury | 2013/14 | Otago |
| 1956/57 | Auckland | 1985/86 | Canterbury | 2014/15 | Auckland |
| 1957/58 | Auckland | 1986/87 | Canterbury | 2015/16 | Auckland |
| 1958/59 | Wellington | 1987/88 | Canterbury | 2016/17 | Canterbury |
| 1959/60 | Wellington | 1988/89 | Canterbury | 2017/18 | Auckland |
| 1960/61 | Canterbury | 1989/90 | Wellington | 2018/19 | Central Districts |
| 1961/62 | Canterbury | 1990/91 | Canterbury | 2019/20 | Auckland |
| 1962/63 | Otago | 1991/92 | Canterbury | 2020/21 | Canterbury |
| 1963/64 | Canterbury | 1992/93 | Canterbury | 2021/22 | Otago |

The women's Twenty20 competition was introduced in 2007/08 as the State League Twenty20 to 2008/09, Twenty20 Competition (2009/10 and from 2012/13 to 2017/18), Action Cricket Twenty20 (2010/11 to 2011/12), Burger King Super Smash in 2018/19 and Dream11 Super Smash from 2019/20.

## WINNERS

| | | | | | |
|---|---|---|---|---|---|
| 2007/08 | Canterbury | 2012/13 | Wellington | 2017/18 | Wellington |
| 2008/09 | Wellington | 2013/14 | Auckland | 2018/19 | Wellington |
| 2009/10 | Central Districts | 2014/15 | Wellington | 2019/20 | Wellington |
| 2010/11 | Canterbury | 2015/16 | Canterbury | 2020/21 | Canterbury |
| 2011/12 | Canterbury | 2016/17 | Otago | 2021/22 | Wellington |

# REGISTER OF PLAYERS

| | | *Born* | *At* | *Type* | |
|---|---|---|---|---|---|
| **Agafili** Carol Lora | ND | 20.11.02 | Auckland | RHB | RM |
| **Anderson** Kate Georgia | ND | 6. 5.96 | Invercargill | RHB | ROB |
| **Armstrong** Bella Grace | A | 16.11.99 | Auckland | RHB | RM |
| **Asmussen** Sarah Renee | C | 15. 7.00 | Christchurch | RHB | RLB |
| **Atkinson** Georgia Kate | CD | 23. 4.00 | Masterton | RHB | RLBG |
| **Baker** Emma Louise | ND | 28. 5.01 | Hamilton | RHB | RM |
| **Banks** Melissa Jane | C | 2.11.01 | Christchurch | RHB | RM |
| **Barnett** Jane Louise | A | 7. 7.93 | Palmerston North | RHB | RLB |
| **Bartlett** Ocean Jade Sadlier | CD | 27. 6.03 | Hamilton | RHB | RLBG |
| **Bates** Suzannah Wilson | O | 16. 9.87 | Dunedin | RHB | RM |
| **Black** Emma Jordan | O | 8. 8.01 | Dunedin | RHB | RM |
| **Blakely** Caitlin Grace | O | 7. 1.96 | Dunedin | RHB | RM |
| **Boivin** Olivia Ann | W | 18. 4.99 | Lower Hutt | RHB | RM |
| **Boucher** Lucy Frances | ND | 23.10.01 | Hamilton | RHB | RM |
| **Bowden** Skye Elizabeth | A | 23. 7.01 | Palmerston North | RHB | RM |
| **Browning** Anna Sophie | A | 24.10.03 | Auckland | RHB | ROB |
| **Bultitude** Sydney Jasmine | A | 14. 2.00 | Christchurch | RHB | ROB |
| **Burns** Rebecca Maureen | W | 30. 9.94 | Wellington | RHB | ROB |
| **Carnachan** Sarah Jane | A | 10.12.91 | Auckland | RHB | WK |
| **Carson** Eden Jean | O | 8. 8.01 | Dunedin | RHB | ROB |
| **Catton** Prue | A | 3. 7.03 | Auckland | RHB | RLBG |
| **Chandler** Katherine Mary | W | 2.11.06 | Wellington | RHB | RLBG |
| **Codyre** Natasha Emma | W | 29.10.03 | Lower Hutt | RHB | RM |
| **Cox** Natalie Bridget | C | 21. 8.94 | Dunedin | RHB | |
| **Cunningham** Emily Grace | CD | 5. 7.97 | Bury St Edmunds, England | | |
| | | | | RHB | RLB |
| **Curtis** Samantha Rae Haereakau | ND | 28.10.85 | Auckland | RHB | RLB |
| **Cuttance** Harriet Orla | O | 24.11.02 | Dunedin | RHB | RM |
| **Dean** Jodie | C | 7. 5.02 | Christchurch | RHB | RM |
| **Deerness** Chloe Maree | O | 23. 8.05 | Truro, England | RHB | RM |
| **Devine** Sophie Frances Monique | W, NZ | 1. 9.89 | Wellington | RHB | RM |
| **Dodd** Natalie Claire | CD | 22.11.92 | Hamilton | RHB | ROB |
| **Doughty** Deanna Mary | W | 7.12.93 | Porirua | RHB | RLB |
| **Down** Lauren Renee | A, NZ | 7. 5.95 | Auckland | RHB | RM |
| **Ebrahim** Kate Ellen | O | 11.11.91 | New Plymouth | RHB | RM |
| **Ewart** Annie May | ND | 27. 1.01 | Auckland | RHB | WK |
| **Gaging** Kate Jane | CD | 19. 7.01 | Ashford, England | RHB | WK |
| **Gain** Olivia Nicole | O | 2. 1.02 | Dunedin | RHB | WK |
| **Gaze** Isabella Charli | A | 8. 5.04 | Haarlem, Netherlands | RHB | WK |
| **Gerken** Abigale Grace | C | 12. 5.02 | Christchurch | RHB | RM |
| **Graham** Harriet May | C | 18. 3.04 | Cowra, Australia | LHB | ROB |
| **Green** Claudia Lauren | CD | 6.12.97 | Nelson | RHB | RM |
| **Green** Madeline Lee | W, NZ | 20.10.92 | Auckland | RHB | ROB |
| **Greig** Mikaela Jane | CD | 22. 4.95 | Palmerston North | RHB | ROB |
| **Gurrey** Caitlin Ann | ND | 3. 8.95 | Wellington | RHB | |
| **Halliday** Brooke Maree | ND, NZ | 30.10.95 | Hamilton | LHB | RM |
| **Hansen** Melissa Jane | CD | 2. 5.96 | Masterton | RHB | RM |
| **Harris** Georgina Ann | ND | 10.12.01 | Wellington | RHB | SLA |
| **Havill** Kirsty Jane | C | 10.12.96 | Greymouth | RHB | RLBG |
| **Heaps** Lauren Heather | ND | 13. 1.90 | Auckland | RHB | SLA |
| **Hucker** Amie Tareta | A | 28. 3.02 | Dunedin | RHB | RM |
| **Huddleston** Holly Rachael | A | 11.10.87 | Springs, South Africa | RHB | RM |
| **Hughes** Laura Ellen Victoria | C | 16.10.92 | Palmerston North | RHB | WK |
| **Hyde** Mereana Natasha | ND | 23 .9.95 | Waikari | RHB | RM |
| **Illing** Breearne Grace | A | 29. 9.03 | Auckland | LHB | LM |
| **Inglis** Polly Margot | O | 31. 5.96 | Dunedin | RHB | WK |
| **Irwin** Emma | A | 16. 5.04 | Auckland | RHB | RM |
| **James** Isabela Rose | O | 27. 1.99 | Timaru | RHB | |
| **Jensen** Hayley Nicole Kayla | O, NZ | 7.10.92 | Christchurch | RHB | RM |
| **Jetly** Xara Ange Rose | W | 29. 8.01 | Lower Hutt | RHB | ROB |
| **Jonas** Frances Cecilia | A, NZ | 8. 4.04 | Auckland | RHB | SLA |
| **Kasperek** Leigh Megan | W, NZ | 15. 2.92 | Edinburgh, Scotland | RHB | ROB |
| **Kelly** Arlene Nora | A | 8. 1.94 | Auckland | RHB | RM |
| **Kench** Emma Kate | C | 3. 7.99 | Christchurch | RHB | RM |
| **Kerr** Amelia Charlotte | W, NZ | 13.10.00 | Wellington | RHB | RLBG |
| **Kerr** Jessica Mackenzie | W, NZ | 18. 1.98 | Wellington | RHB | RM |

| | | *Born* | *At* | *Type* | |
|---|---|---|---|---|---|
| **King** Caitlin Rose | W | 5. 9.96 | Hastings | RHB | RM |
| **Knight** Kayley Alona | ND | 20.10.03 | Gisborne | RHB | RM |
| **Kumar** Ashtuti | CD | 14.12.94 | Suva, Fiji | RHB | RM |
| **Lamplough** Marina Buonocore Antonia | O | 28. 9.99 | Hong Kong, China | RHB | RM |
| **Loe** Molly Elizabeth | O | 25. 6.03 | Christchurch | RHB | RM |
| **Loggenberg** Paige Rachelle | O | 15.10.03 | Durban, South Africa | RHB | RM |
| **Mair** Rosemary Alison | CD, NZ | 7.11.98 | Napier | RHB | RM |
| **Martin** Katey Jane | O, NZ | 7. 2.85 | Dunedin | RHB | WK |
| **Mace-Cochrane** Alexandra Christine | C | 27. 8.97 | Christchurch | RHB | ROB |
| **McFadyen** Jessica Toihi | W | 5.10.91 | Wellington | RHB | WK |
| **Mackay** Frances Louise | C, NZ | 1. 6.90 | Christchurch | RHB | ROB |
| **Matthews** Naomi | ND | 4. 6.97 | Belfast, Ireland | RHB | ROB |
| **Molony** Bethany Clare | W | 31.10.00 | Wellington | RHB | RM |
| **Naidu** Shriya Ramesh | ND | 26.11.95 | Dubai | RHB | RM |
| **Nation** Kirsten Frances Glasson | C | 23.12.95 | Christchurch | RHB | RM |
| **Newton** Thamsyn Michelle Moupia | W, NZ | 3. 6.95 | Paraparaumu | RHB | RM |
| **Oldershaw** Sophie Alice | O | 20. 5.98 | Auckland | RHB | RLB |
| **Parr-Thomson** Amberly Jayne | A | 18. 3.98 | Auckland | RHB | RM |
| **Patel** Nensi Hiteshkumar | ND | 27. 5.02 | Bharuch, India | RHB | RM |
| **Pedersen** Cate Samantha | CD | 31. 7.02 | Rotorua | RHB | RM |
| **Penfold** Josie Olivia | A | 28. 6.99 | London, England | RHB | RM |
| **Penfold** Molly Mae | A, NZ | 15. 6.01 | London, England | RHB | RM |
| **Perkins** Katie Teresa | A | 7. 7.88 | Auckland | RHB | RM |
| **Peterson** Anna Michelle | A | 12. 9.90 | Auckland | RHB | ROB |
| **Plimmer** Georgia Ellen | W | 8. 2.04 | Wellington | RHB | RSM |
| **Prasad** Jesse Ellen Indira | A | 19. 1.99 | Auckland | RHB | RM |
| **Rees** Monique Sarah | CD | 29. 9.00 | Wellington | RHB | RM |
| **Richardson** Eimear Ann Jermyn | ND | 14. 9.86 | Dublin, Ireland | RHB | ROB |
| **Rout** Alisha Jane | ND | 17. 7.95 | Morrinsville | RHB | RM |
| **Rowe** Hannah Maree | CD, NZ | 3.10.96 | Palmerston North | RHB | RM |
| **Sarsfield** Charlotte Rose | ND | 22. 6.93 | Auckland | RHB | ROB |
| **Satterthwaite** Amy Ella | C, NZ | 7.11.86 | Christchurch | LHB | RM |
| **Savage** Jacinta Lynn | C | 17. 6.95 | Christchurch | RHB | RM |
| **Shahri** Saachi | A | 7.11.97 | Mumbai, India | RHB | RLB |
| **Sharp** Isobel Grace | C | 1.12.92 | Timaru | RHB | |
| **Simmons** Jessica Ann | C | 29. 4.00 | Christchurch | RHB | RM |
| **Sims** Gemma | CD | 27. 7.01 | Masterton | RHB | WK |
| **Sims** Kate Margaret | C | 27. 7.01 | Masterton | RHB | RM |
| **Singh** Maneka Pushpanjali | W | 18. 2.96 | Dunedin | RHB | LM |
| **Tahuhu** Lea-Marie Maureen | C, NZ | 23. 9.90 | Christchurch | RHB | RFM |
| **Templeton** Makayla Belle | ND | 10.10.02 | Redhill, England | RHB | RLB |
| **Tomlinson** Kerry-Anne | CD | 19. 1.90 | Gisborne | RHB | RM |
| **Topp** Holly Erole | ND | 21. 8.01 | Christchurch | RHB | WK |
| **Wakelin** Natasha Ann | ND | 9.12.05 | Gisborne | RHB | RM |
| **Watkin** Jessica Marie | CD | 7. 5.98 | Wanganui | RHB | ROB |
| **Wilson** Saffron Rose | O | 5.12.01 | Christchurch | RHB | RM |

# HALLYBURTON JOHNSTONE SHIELD

## 2021/22

The Hallyburton Johnstone Shield was won by Otago who defeated previously unbeaten Wellington by 138 runs in the final at Queenstown. Otago, coached by Craig Cumming, completed a remarkable turnaround after having lost all ten matches the previous season.

Otago's Kate Ebrahim was again the leading scorer with 451 runs followed by Northern Districts' Kate Anderson (306) and Wellington's Maddie Green (265). Suzie Bates, Abby Gerken, Lauren Down, Brooke Halliday, Katey Martin and Green scored centuries.

Northern Districts's Nensi Patel topped the wicket takers with 18 victims followed by Amelia Kerr *(Wellington)* and Eden Carson *(Otago)* with 14. Patel (6-25 against Auckland) had the season's best figures. Kerr (twice), Patel (twice), Carson, Emma Black *(Otago)* and Leigh Kasperek *(Wellington)* took five wickets in an innings.

Final points were:

|  | P | W | L | T | NR | Bonus | Points |
|---|---|---|---|---|---|---|---|
| Wellington | 10 | 5 | – | – | 5 | 2 | 32 |
| Otago | 10 | 3 | 2 | – | 5 | 3 | 25 |
| Northern Districts | 10 | 4 | 2 | 1 | 3 | 1 | 25 |
| Central Districts | 10 | 2 | 2 | – | 6 | 2 | 22 |
| Auckland | 10 | 1 | 5 | 1 | 3 | 1 | 13 |
| Canterbury | 10 | 1 | 5 | – | 4 | – | 12 |

---

## CENTRAL DISTRICTS v OTAGO — One-day Competition

*at Saxton Oval, Nelson on 30 October, 2021*
*Toss : Central Districts. Umpires : E.D. Sanders & G.M. Walklin*
**Otago won by 213 runs.** Points: Otago 5, Central Districts 0

### OTAGO

|  | Runs | Mins | Balls | 6s | 4s |
|---|---|---|---|---|---|
| S.W.Bates* c Pedersen b Green | 12 | 10 | 9 | - | 3 |
| K.E.Ebrahim not out | 96 | 191 | 130 | - | 7 |
| I.R.James c Watkin b Hansen .. | 53 | 105 | 87 | - | 7 |
| K.J.Martin† not out | 111 | 76 | 74 | 1 | 14 |
| C.G.Blakely | | | | | |
| P.M.Inglis | | | | | |
| H.N.K.Jensen | | | | | |
| E.J.Carson | | | | | |
| E.J.Black | | | | | |
| S.A.Oldershaw | | | | | |
| M.E.Loe | | | | | |
| Extras (lb 3, w 16) | 19 | | | | |
| **TOTAL** (50 overs) (2 wkts) . | **291** | 191 | | | |

### CENTRAL DISTRICTS

|  | Runs | Mins | Balls | 6s | 4s |
|---|---|---|---|---|---|
| J.M.Watkin* b Black | 1 | 9 | 5 | - | - |
| C.S.Pedersen c Martin b Loe ..... | 1 | 6 | 5 | - | - |
| K.A.Tomlinson c & b Loe | 5 | 25 | 15 | - | 1 |
| H.M.Rowe lbw b Black | 5 | 9 | 12 | - | 1 |
| G.Sims c Martin b Loe | 7 | 20 | 14 | - | 1 |
| M.J.Greig c Blakely b Jensen ... | 26 | 73 | 51 | - | 3 |
| K.L.Gaging† c Bates b Carson | 3 | 18 | 16 | - | - |
| G.K.Atkinson lbw b Black | 13 | 23 | 17 | - | 2 |
| M.J.Hansen c Bates b Black | 2 | 8 | 11 | - | - |
| M.S.Rees b Black | 0 | 7 | 7 | - | - |
| C.L.Green not out | 0 | 6 | 4 | - | - |
| Extras (w 15) | 15 | | | | |
| **TOTAL** (26.1 overs) | **78** | 105 | | | |

| Bowling | O | M | R | W |
|---|---|---|---|---|
| **CENTRAL DISTRICTS** | | | | |
| Green | 6 | 0 | 30 | 1 |
| Rowe | 6 | 1 | 21 | 0 |
| Hansen | 6 | 0 | 29 | 1 |
| Rees | 5 | 0 | 36 | 0 |
| Atkinson | 7 | 0 | 42 | 0 |
| Watkin | 10 | 0 | 58 | 0 |
| Greig | 10 | 0 | 72 | 0 |
| **OTAGO** | | | | |
| Black | 7 | 0 | 28 | 5 |
| Loe | 5 | 1 | 7 | 3 |
| Carson | 5 | 1 | 15 | 1 |
| Jensen | 5.1 | 0 | 20 | 1 |
| Oldershaw | 4 | 0 | 8 | 0 |

| Fall of Wickets | O | CD |
|---|---|---|
| 1st | 14 | 5 |
| 2nd | 132 | 5 |
| 3rd | - | 13 |
| 4th | - | 23 |
| 5th | - | 29 |
| 6th | - | 36 |
| 7th | - | 62 |
| 8th | - | 67 |
| 9th | - | 75 |
| 10th | - | 78 |

**NZC**

# CENTRAL DISTRICTS v OTAGO          One-day Competition

*at Saxton Oval, Nelson on 31 October, 2021*
*Toss : Otago.  Umpires : E.D. Sanders & G.M. Walklin*
**Otago won by 82 runs.** Points: Otago 5, Central Districts 0

### OTAGO

| | Runs | Mins | Balls | 6s | 4s |
|---|---|---|---|---|---|
| S.W.Bates* c & b Watkin | 6 | 27 | 24 | - | - |
| K.E.Ebrahim lbw b Green | 22 | 25 | 20 | - | 4 |
| C.G.Blakely c Hansen b Watkin | 34 | 78 | 59 | - | 2 |
| P.M.Inglis† c Hansen b Watkin | 68 | 91 | 72 | 1 | 7 |
| H.N.K.Jensen b Watkin | 7 | 7 | 8 | - | - |
| K.J.Martin not out | 49 | 77 | 51 | - | 4 |
| I.R.James c Watkin b Greig | 11 | 10 | 9 | - | 2 |
| E.J.Carson lbw b Hansen | 18 | 28 | 21 | - | 2 |
| E.J.Black st Gaging b Atkinson | 12 | 17 | 17 | - | 1 |
| S.A.Oldershaw b Hansen | 0 | 5 | 9 | - | - |
| M.E.Loe b Hansen | 2 | 6 | 6 | - | - |
| Extras (b 3, lb 4, w 29) | 36 | | | | |
| **TOTAL** (49.2 overs) | **265** | 188 | | | |

### CENTRAL DISTRICTS

| | Runs | Mins | Balls | 6s | 4s |
|---|---|---|---|---|---|
| J.M.Watkin* c Carson b Jensen | 17 | 16 | 17 | - | 4 |
| C.S.Pedersen b Oldershaw | 39 | 112 | 74 | - | 5 |
| K.A.Tomlinson b Carson | 14 | 41 | 48 | - | 1 |
| H.M.Rowe b Carson | 3 | 18 | 13 | - | - |
| G.Sims lbw b Carson | 36 | 48 | 41 | - | 6 |
| M.J.Greig not out | 33 | 58 | 39 | - | 3 |
| K.L.Gaging† lbw b Black | 2 | 4 | 3 | - | - |
| G.K.Atkinson c Bates b Black | 1 | 8 | 3 | - | - |
| M.J.Hansen b Black | 0 | 1 | 3 | - | - |
| A.Kumar b Erahim | 3 | 12 | 10 | - | - |
| C.L.Green run out | 12 | 19 | 17 | - | - |
| Extras (b 4, lb 5, w 14) | 23 | | | | |
| **TOTAL** (44.4 overs) | **183** | 170 | | | |

| Bowling | O | M | R | W |
|---|---|---|---|---|
| **CENTRAL DISTRICTS** | | | | |
| Green | 6 | 0 | 33 | 1 |
| Watkin | 10 | 1 | 33 | 4 |
| Rowe | 6 | 0 | 30 | 0 |
| Kumar | 9 | 0 | 61 | 0 |
| Hansen | 8.2 | 0 | 29 | 3 |
| Atkinson | 5 | 1 | 30 | 1 |
| Greig | 5 | 0 | 42 | 1 |
| **OTAGO** | | | | |
| Black | 10 | 2 | 23 | 3 |
| Loe | 7 | 0 | 37 | 0 |
| Jensen | 6 | 0 | 23 | 1 |
| Ebrahim | 7 | 0 | 33 | 1 |
| Carson | 10 | 1 | 31 | 3 |
| Oldershaw | 4.4 | 0 | 27 | 1 |

| Fall of Wickets | O | CD |
|---|---|---|
| 1st | 33 | 22 |
| 2nd | 33 | 50 |
| 3rd | 148 | 63 |
| 4th | 158 | 113 |
| 5th | 166 | 129 |
| 6th | 192 | 132 |
| 7th | 235 | 139 |
| 8th | 260 | 139 |
| 9th | 261 | 148 |
| 10th | 265 | 183 |

# CANTERBURY v WELLINGTON          One-day Competition

*at MainPower Oval, Rangiora on 6 November, 2021*
*Toss : Wellington.  Umpires : K.D. Cotton & S.J. Kannan*
**Wellington won by 39 runs.** Points: Wellington 4, Canterbury 0

### WELLINGTON

| | Runs | Mins | Balls | 6s | 4s |
|---|---|---|---|---|---|
| R.M.Burns b Sims | 47 | 76 | 59 | - | 10 |
| J.T.McFadyen† c Gerken b Satterthwaite | 40 | 90 | 69 | - | 3 |
| A.C.Kerr lbw b Satterthwaite | 15 | 28 | 19 | - | 1 |
| M.L.Green* not out | 87 | 105 | 75 | - | 11 |
| G.E.Plimmer st Hughes b Savage | 26 | 49 | 42 | - | 2 |
| L.M.Kasperek run out | 14 | 23 | 22 | - | - |
| T.M.M.Newton b Simmons | 0 | 2 | 3 | - | - |
| C.R.King b Simmons | 0 | 2 | 3 | - | - |
| N.E.Codyre run out | 6 | 13 | 8 | - | - |
| X.A.R.Jetly | | | | | |
| M.P.Singh | | | | | |
| Extras (lb 6, w 26) | 32 | | | | |
| **TOTAL** (50 overs) (8 wkts) . | **267** | 196 | | | |

### CANTERBURY

| | Runs | Mins | Balls | 6s | 4s |
|---|---|---|---|---|---|
| E.K.Kench b King | 9 | 35 | 40 | - | - |
| N.B.Cox c King b Singh | 7 | 5 | 17 | - | 1 |
| A.E.Satterthwaite* b Kerr | 87 | 138 | 94 | - | 8 |
| A.G.Gerken c Plimmer b Kasperek | 14 | 29 | 24 | - | 2 |
| J.L.Savage c & b Kerr | 40 | 71 | 59 | - | 4 |
| K.F.G.Nation b Codyre | 37 | 43 | 43 | - | 3 |
| L.E.V.Hughes† lbw b Kerr | 0 | 1 | 1 | - | - |
| M.J.Banks b Kerr | 5 | 8 | 6 | - | 1 |
| K.M.Sims b Kerr | 2 | 8 | 5 | - | - |
| J.A.Simmons not out | 5 | 16 | 11 | - | - |
| S.R.Asmussen | | | | | |
| Extras (lb 3, w 19) | 22 | | | | |
| **TOTAL** (50 overs) (9 wkts) . | **228** | 179 | | | |

| Bowling | O | M | R | W |
|---|---|---|---|---|
| **CANTERBURY** | | | | |
| Simmons | 10 | 1 | 44 | 2 |
| Savage | 10 | 0 | 43 | 1 |
| Asmussen | 8 | 0 | 52 | 0 |
| Banks | 9 | 0 | 50 | 0 |
| Sims | 3 | 0 | 31 | 1 |
| Satterthwaite | 10 | 0 | 41 | 2 |
| **WELLINGTON** | | | | |
| Singh | 10 | 0 | 37 | 1 |
| Codyre | 10 | 1 | 42 | 1 |
| Kasperek | 10 | 0 | 45 | 1 |
| King | 5 | 0 | 25 | 1 |
| Kerr | 10 | 0 | 40 | 5 |
| Jetly | 3 | 0 | 17 | 0 |
| Newton | 2 | 0 | 19 | 0 |

| Fall of Wickets | W | C |
|---|---|---|
| 1st | 94 | 13 |
| 2nd | 115 | 34 |
| 3rd | 130 | 62 |
| 4th | 200 | 165 |
| 5th | 238 | 177 |
| 6th | 238 | 177 |
| 7th | 238 | 189 |
| 8th | 267 | 202 |
| 9th | - | 228 |
| 10th | - | - |

## CANTERBURY v WELLINGTON       One-day Competition

*at MainPower Oval, Rangiora on 7 November, 2021*
*Toss : Canterbury.  Umpires : K.D. Cotton & S.J. Kannan*
**Wellington won by 2 wickets.** *Points: Wellington 4, Canterbury 0*

### CANTERBURY

| | Runs | Mins | Balls | 6s | 4s |
|---|---|---|---|---|---|
| F.L.Mackay* c McFadyen b Singh | 22 | 33 | 29 | - | 3 |
| E.K.Kench b Singh | 0 | 8 | 1 | - | - |
| A.E.Satterthwaite b Kasperek | 96 | 170 | 105 | - | 11 |
| N.B.Cox b King | 4 | 14 | 8 | - | 1 |
| J.L.Savage lbw b Kerr | 6 | 23 | 15 | - | - |
| A.G.Gerken b Kerr | 0 | 1 | 2 | - | - |
| K.F.G.Nation lbw b Kerr | 34 | 48 | 44 | - | 3 |
| L.E.V.Hughes† lbw b Kerr | 2 | 7 | 5 | - | - |
| M.J.Banks b Kerr | 14 | 23 | 22 | - | 1 |
| J.A.Simmons c McFadyen b Green | 5 | 17 | 20 | - | - |
| S.R.Asmussen not out | 0 | 8 | 9 | - | - |
| Extras (lb 3, w 20, nb 1) | 24 | | | | |
| **TOTAL** (43.1 overs) | **207** | 178 | | | |

### WELLINGTON

| | Runs | Mins | Balls | 6s | 4s |
|---|---|---|---|---|---|
| R.M.Burns lbw b Savage | 14 | 22 | 24 | - | 3 |
| J.T.McFadyen† c Satterthwaite b Banks | 12 | 52 | 33 | - | 1 |
| A.C.Kerr c Mackay b Asmussen | 41 | 67 | 58 | - | 7 |
| M.L.Green* c Cox b Mackay | 21 | 49 | 45 | - | 2 |
| G.E.Plimmer c Satterthwaite b Mackay | 29 | 31 | 32 | - | 5 |
| L.M.Kasperek not out | 30 | 77 | 56 | - | 1 |
| T.M.M.Newton lbw b Satterthwaite | 29 | 42 | 35 | | 3 |
| C.R.King lbw b Satterthwaite | 0 | 2 | 2 | - | - |
| N.E.Codyre c Cox b Satterthwaite | 0 | 1 | 1 | - | - |
| M.P.Singh not out | 2 | 10 | 10 | - | - |
| D.M.Doughty | | | | | |
| Extras (lb 2, w 16, nb 2) | 30 | | | | |
| **TOTAL** (49 overs) (8 wkts) | **208** | 179 | | | |

| Bowling | O | M | R | W |
|---|---|---|---|---|
| **WELLINGTON** | | | | |
| Singh | 9 | 1 | 33 | 2 |
| Codyre | 6 | 0 | 29 | 0 |
| Kasperek | 8.1 | 0 | 40 | 1 |
| King | 6 | 0 | 40 | 1 |
| Kerr | 10 | 1 | 36 | 5 |
| Doughty | 2 | 0 | 15 | 0 |
| Green | 2 | 0 | 11 | 1 |
| **CANTERBURY** | | | | |
| Simmons | 8 | 0 | 30 | 0 |
| Savage | 9 | 1 | 33 | 1 |
| Satterthwaite | 10 | 2 | 38 | 3 |
| Banks | 5 | 0 | 22 | 1 |
| Asmussen | 7 | 0 | 42 | 1 |
| Mackay | 10 | 1 | 31 | 2 |

| Fall of Wickets | | |
|---|---|---|
| | C | W |
| 1st | 10 | 24 |
| 2nd | 43 | 52 |
| 3rd | 63 | 104 |
| 4th | 79 | 117 |
| 5th | 79 | 148 |
| 6th | 147 | 201 |
| 7th | 157 | 201 |
| 8th | 189 | 201 |
| 9th | 204 | - |
| 10th | 207 | - |

## OTAGO v CENTRAL DISTRICTS       One-day Competition

*at University of Otago Oval, Dunedin on 13 November, 2021*
**Abandoned without a ball being bowled.** *Points: Otago 2, Central Districts 2*

## WELLINGTON v CANTERBURY       One-day Competition

*at Karori Park, Wellington on 13 November, 2021*
**Abandoned without a ball being bowled.** *Points: Wellington 2, Canterbury 2*

## OTAGO v CENTRAL DISTRICTS       One-day Competition

*at University of Otago Oval, Dunedin on 14 November, 2021*
**Abandoned without a ball being bowled.** *Points: Otago 2, Central Districts 2*

## WELLINGTON v CANTERBURY       One-day Competition

*at Karori Park, Wellington on 14 November, 2021*
**Abandoned without a ball being bowled.** *Points: Wellington 2, Canterbury 2*

**NZC**

## CANTERBURY v OTAGO
## One-day Competition

*at Hagley Oval, Christchurch on 20 November, 2021*
*Toss : Otago. Umpires : C.A. Black & D.J. Henderson*
**Otago won by 6 wickets.** *Points: Otago 5, Canterbury 0*

### CANTERBURY

| | Runs | Mins | Balls | 6s | 4s |
|---|---|---|---|---|---|
| F.L.Mackay* b Loe | 2 | 7 | 9 | - | - |
| A.G.Gerken c Martin b Jensen | 50 | 104 | 76 | - | 6 |
| A.E.Satterthwaite c Jensen b Black | 13 | 24 | 9 | - | 2 |
| N.B.Cox c Black b Jensen | 49 | 82 | 70 | 1 | 6 |
| J.L.Savage st Martin b Oldershaw | 6 | 28 | 21 | - | - |
| K.F.G.Nation c Jensen b Carson | 13 | 44 | 21 | - | 1 |
| L.M.M.Tahuhu c Bates b Loe | 24 | 30 | 26 | - | 3 |
| L.E.V.Hughes† c Blakely b Carson | 6 | 7 | 11 | - | - |
| M.J.Banks not out | 10 | 24 | 17 | - | - |
| J.A.Simmons c Martin b Carson | 2 | 6 | 7 | - | - |
| S.R.Asmussen lbw b Oldershaw | 0 | 14 | 5 | - | - |
| Extras (lb 2, w 18, nb 2) | 22 | | | | |
| **TOTAL** (45 overs) | **197** | 187 | | | |

### OTAGO

| | Runs | Mins | Balls | 6s | 4s |
|---|---|---|---|---|---|
| S.W.Bates* c Cox b Simmons | 0 | 2 | 4 | - | - |
| K.E.Ebrahim b Savage | 66 | 124 | 104 | - | 9 |
| I.R.James b Mackay | 26 | 49 | 41 | - | 5 |
| C.G.Blakely c Banks b Savage | 63 | 87 | 70 | - | 10 |
| K.J.Martin† not out | 20 | 22 | 12 | - | 3 |
| P.M.Inglis not out | 3 | 7 | 6 | - | - |
| H.N.K.Jensen | | | | | |
| E.J.Carson | | | | | |
| E.J.Black | | | | | |
| S.A.Oldershaw | | | | | |
| M.E.Loe | | | | | |
| Extras (b 2, w 17, nb 1) | 20 | | | | |
| **TOTAL** (39.1 overs) (4 wkts) | **198** | 147 | | | |

| Bowling | O | M | R | W |
|---|---|---|---|---|
| **OTAGO** | | | | |
| Black | 7 | 0 | 42 | 1 |
| Loe | 8 | 1 | 43 | 2 |
| Jensen | 10 | 1 | 33 | 2 |
| Ebrahim | 3 | 0 | 11 | 0 |
| Carson | 8 | 0 | 24 | 3 |
| Oldershaw | 9 | 1 | 42 | 2 |
| **CANTERBURY** | | | | |
| Simmons | 7 | 1 | 35 | 1 |
| Savage | 8.1 | 0 | 49 | 2 |
| Banks | 7 | 1 | 25 | 0 |
| Mackay | 8 | 0 | 35 | 1 |
| Satterthwaite | 5 | 0 | 24 | 0 |
| Asmussen | 4 | 0 | 28 | 0 |

| Fall of Wickets | C | O |
|---|---|---|
| 1st | 6 | 1 |
| 2nd | 40 | 57 |
| 3rd | 122 | 164 |
| 4th | 127 | 185 |
| 5th | 147 | - |
| 6th | 171 | - |
| 7th | 180 | - |
| 8th | 188 | - |
| 9th | 194 | - |
| 10th | 197 | - |

## CENTRAL DISTRICTS v NORTHERN DISTRICTS
## One-day

*at Donnelly Park, Levin on 20 November, 2021*
*Toss : Northern Districts. Umpires : T.R. Davies & P.J. Pasco*
**Central Districts won by 87 runs.** *Points: Canterbury 5, Northern Districts 0*

### CENTRAL DISTRICTS

| | Runs | Mins | Balls | 6s | 4s |
|---|---|---|---|---|---|
| N.C.Dodd*† b Knight | 0 | 1 | 2 | - | - |
| E.G.Cunningham c Boucher b Sarsfield | 58 | 73 | 58 | 1 | 8 |
| J.M.Watkin c Rout b Knight | 23 | 22 | 19 | - | 5 |
| C.S.Pedersen lbw b Sarsfield | 25 | 73 | 51 | - | 2 |
| H.M.Rowe c Patel b Boucher | 13 | 36 | 24 | - | 2 |
| K.A.Tomlinson run out | 0 | 3 | 1 | - | - |
| M.J.Greig run out | 65 | 93 | 78 | 1 | 5 |
| G.K.Atkinson c Hyde b Knight | 28 | 41 | 31 | - | 5 |
| M.S.Rees c Sarsfield b Hyde | 23 | 40 | 32 | - | 1 |
| M.J.Hansen not out | 3 | 4 | 4 | - | - |
| A.Kumar not out | 5 | 2 | 3 | - | 1 |
| Extras (lb 4, w 25, nb 3) | 32 | | | | |
| **TOTAL** (50 overs) (9 wkts) | **275** | 196 | | | |

### NORTHERN DISTRICTS

| | Runs | Mins | Balls | 6s | 4s |
|---|---|---|---|---|---|
| K.G.Anderson* c Hansen b Watkin | 26 | 29 | 21 | - | 6 |
| H.E.Topp† c Greig b Watkin | 19 | 49 | 35 | - | 3 |
| N.H.Patel b Greig b Watkin | 0 | 2 | 2 | - | - |
| S.R.H.Curtis c Greig b Kumar | 16 | 42 | 24 | - | 2 |
| N.Matthews b Atkinson | 23 | 54 | 36 | - | 4 |
| L.F.Boucher c Pedersen b Kumar | 6 | 17 | 16 | - | - |
| A.J.Rout b Hansen | 14 | 25 | 19 | - | 2 |
| M.N.Hyde c Tomlinson b Atkinson | 6 | 9 | 10 | - | 1 |
| C.R.Sarsfield not out | 25 | 73 | 48 | - | 2 |
| E.L.Baker c Cunningham b Watkin | 1 | 6 | 5 | - | - |
| K.A.Knight lbw b Hansen | 17 | 63 | 71 | - | 2 |
| Extras (b 4, lb 1, w 30) | 35 | | | | |
| **TOTAL** (47.5 overs) | **188** | 186 | | | |

| Bowling | O | M | R | W |
|---|---|---|---|---|
| **NORTHERN DISTRICTS** | | | | |
| Knight | 10 | 1 | 48 | 3 |
| Patel | 10 | 1 | 54 | 0 |
| Baker | 1 | 0 | 15 | 0 |
| Hyde | 10 | 1 | 44 | 1 |
| Sarsfield | 10 | 0 | 58 | 2 |
| Boucher | 6 | 0 | 28 | 1 |
| Anderson | 3 | 0 | 24 | 0 |
| **CENTRAL DISTRICTS** | | | | |
| Rowe | 8 | 1 | 38 | 0 |
| Hansen | 5.5 | 1 | 26 | 2 |
| Watkin | 10 | 4 | 28 | 4 |
| Rees | 5 | 0 | 22 | 0 |
| Atkinson | 7 | 0 | 29 | 2 |
| Kumar | 7 | 0 | 23 | 2 |
| Greig | 3 | 1 | 7 | 0 |
| Cunningham | 2 | 0 | 10 | 0 |

| Fall of Wickets | CD | ND |
|---|---|---|
| 1st | 0 | 49 |
| 2nd | 39 | 49 |
| 3rd | 107 | 66 |
| 4th | 128 | 89 |
| 5th | 128 | 107 |
| 6th | 139 | 128 |
| 7th | 201 | 136 |
| 8th | 266 | 137 |
| 9th | 267 | 144 |
| 10th | - | 188 |

## CANTERBURY v OTAGO                    One-day Competition

*at Hagley Oval, Christchurch on 21 November, 2021*
*Toss : Otago. Umpires : C.A. Black & D.J. Henderson*
**Canterbury won by 7 runs (D/L).** *Points: Canterbury 4, Otago 0*

### CANTERBURY

| | Runs | Mins | Balls | 6s | 4s |
|---|---|---|---|---|---|
| F.L.Mackay* c Bates b Jensen . | 25 | 31 | 32 | - | 4 |
| A.G.Gerken c Blakely b Ebrahim | 108 | 187 | 128 | - | 13 |
| A.E.Satterthwaite c Inglis b Oldershaw | 46 | 62 | 53 | - | 7 |
| N.B.Cox b Jensen | 0 | 5 | 2 | - | - |
| J.L.Savage st Inglis b Oldershaw | 61 | 73 | 65 | - | 9 |
| L.M.M.Tahuhu c Bates b Ebrahim | 22 | 13 | 11 | 2 | 1 |
| K.F.G.Nation not out | 1 | 4 | 1 | - | - |
| L.E.V.Hughes† b Ebrahim | 0 | 1 | 1 | - | - |
| M.J.Banks not out | 4 | 1 | 1 | - | 1 |
| S.R.Asmussen | | | | | |
| J.A.Simmons | | | | | |
| Extras (lb 6, w 9) | 15 | | | | |
| **TOTAL (49 overs) (7 wkts)** . | **282** | 190 | | | |

### OTAGO

| | Runs | Mins | Balls | 6s | 4s |
|---|---|---|---|---|---|
| S.W.Bates* c Savage b Satterthwaite | 62 | 80 | 69 | - | 10 |
| K.E.Ebrahim lbw b Savage | 56 | 132 | 78 | - | 2 |
| I.R.James b Satterthwaite | 0 | 3 | 3 | - | - |
| H.N.K.Jensen c Satterthwaite b Simmons | 76 | 114 | 73 | - | 9 |
| K.J.Martin not out | 60 | 82 | 65 | - | 8 |
| P.M.Inglis† c Nation b Satterthwaite | 2 | 8 | 3 | - | - |
| C.G.Blakely run out | 3 | 6 | 3 | - | - |
| E.J.Carson not out | 0 | 1 | 1 | - | - |
| E.J.Black | | | | | |
| S.A.Oldershaw | | | | | |
| M.E.Loe | | | | | |
| Extras(lb 1, w 17, nb 1) | 19 | | | | |
| **TOTAL (49 overs) (6 wkts)** . | **278** | 214 | | | |

| Bowling OTAGO | O | M | R | W |
|---|---|---|---|---|
| Black | 8 | 1 | 44 | 0 |
| Loe | 7 | 0 | 45 | 0 |
| Jensen | 10 | 1 | 36 | 2 |
| Carson | 7 | 0 | 44 | 0 |
| Oldershaw | 10 | 0 | 62 | 2 |
| Ebrahim | 7 | 0 | 45 | 3 |
| **CANTERBURY** | | | | |
| Simmons | 10 | 2 | 49 | 1 |
| Savage | 10 | 0 | 61 | 1 |
| Banks | 9 | 0 | 55 | 0 |
| Mackay | 6 | 0 | 32 | 0 |
| Satterthwaite | 9 | 0 | 43 | 3 |
| Asmussen | 5 | 0 | 37 | 0 |

| Fall of Wickets | C | O |
|---|---|---|
| 1st | 47 | 104 |
| 2nd | 123 | 107 |
| 3rd | 124 | 153 |
| 4th | 241 | 261 |
| 5th | 277 | 268 |
| 6th | 277 | 278 |
| 7th | 278 | - |
| 8th | - | - |
| 9th | - | - |
| 10th | - | - |

## CENTRAL DISTRICTS v NORTHERN DISTRICTS      One-day

*at Donnelly Park, Levin on 21 November, 2021*
*Toss : Northern Districts. Umpires : T.R. Davies & P.J. Pasco*
**Central Districts won by 86 runs.** *Points: Central Districts 5, Northern Districts 0*

### CENTRAL DISTRICTS

| | Runs | Mins | Balls | 6s | 4s |
|---|---|---|---|---|---|
| N.C.Dodd*† c Sarsfield b Boucher | 22 | 39 | 22 | - | 4 |
| E.G.Cunningham lbw b Knight ... | 8 | 11 | 12 | - | 1 |
| J.M.Watkin lbw b Anderson | 87 | 95 | 62 | 5 | 8 |
| K.A.Tomlinson run out | 26 | 57 | 51 | - | 3 |
| H.M.Rowe c Curtis b Hyde | 61 | 92 | 56 | 1 | 5 |
| G.Sims c Knight b Baker | 1 | 10 | 9 | - | - |
| M.J.Greig b Anderson | 21 | 42 | 40 | - | 2 |
| G.K.Atkinson b Hyde | 27 | 22 | 23 | - | 4 |
| M.S.Rees b Boucher | 13 | 18 | 14 | - | - |
| M.J.Hansen run out | 14 | 13 | 9 | - | 1 |
| A.Kumar not out | 3 | 3 | 2 | - | - |
| Extras (lb 1, w 10) | 11 | | | | |
| **TOTAL (50 overs)** | **294** | 203 | | | |

### NORTHERN DISTRICTS

| | Runs | Mins | Balls | 6s | 4s |
|---|---|---|---|---|---|
| K.G.Anderson* c Rowe b Kumar | 54 | 75 | 48 | - | 8 |
| H.E.Topp† lbw b Watkin | 6 | 24 | 17 | - | - |
| N.H.Patel c Kumar b Rowe | 36 | 71 | 52 | - | 3 |
| S.R.H.Curtis c Greig b Rees | 55 | 70 | 55 | - | 6 |
| N.Matthews lbw b Watkin | 0 | 3 | 1 | - | - |
| L.F.Boucher c Kumar b Watkin | 21 | 31 | 24 | - | 2 |
| M.N.Hyde c sub (C.S.Pedersen) b Rees | 4 | 7 | 3 | - | 1 |
| T.Wakelin b Rees | 4 | 1 | 2 | - | 1 |
| C.R.Sarsfield c Rowe b Kumar ... | 1 | 11 | 6 | - | - |
| K.A.Knight not out | 3 | 18 | 14 | - | - |
| E.L.Baker b Rowe | 4 | 11 | 7 | - | - |
| Extras (w 15, pen 5) | 20 | | | | |
| **TOTAL (38.1 overs)** | **208** | 164 | | | |

| Bowling CENTRAL DISTRICTS | O | M | R | W |
|---|---|---|---|---|
| Knight | 7 | 0 | 49 | 1 |
| Patel | 6 | 0 | 45 | 0 |
| Hyde | 8 | 0 | 48 | 2 |
| Boucher | 9 | 0 | 56 | 2 |
| Sarsfield | 4 | 1 | 30 | 0 |
| Anderson | 10 | 0 | 43 | 2 |
| Baker | 6 | 0 | 22 | 1 |
| **CENTRAL DISTRICTS** | | | | |
| Rowe | 8.1 | 0 | 33 | 2 |
| Hansen | 7 | 0 | 38 | 0 |
| Watkin | 10 | 1 | 55 | 3 |
| Rees | 5 | 0 | 27 | 3 |
| Kumar | 6 | 1 | 39 | 2 |
| Greig | 1 | 0 | 7 | 0 |
| Atkinson | 1 | 0 | 4 | 0 |

| Fall of Wickets | CD | ND |
|---|---|---|
| 1st | 15 | 34 |
| 2nd | 69 | 108 |
| 3rd | 146 | 127 |
| 4th | 155 | 127 |
| 5th | 161 | 185 |
| 6th | 208 | 191 |
| 7th | 257 | 195 |
| 8th | 269 | 198 |
| 9th | 290 | 199 |
| 10th | 294 | 208 |

## NORTHERN DISTRICTS v OTAGO         One-day Competition

*at Seddon Park, Hamilton on 4 December, 2021*
*Toss : Northern Districts. Umpires : L.R. Els & D.R. Morrow*
**No result.** *Points: Northern Districts 2, Otago 2*

| OTAGO | NORTHERN DISTRICTS |
|-------|-------------------|
| K.E.Ebrahim | K.G.Anderson* |
| S.W.Bates* | H.E.Topp† |
| I.R.James | S.R.H.Curtis |
| C.G.Blakely | N.H.Patel |
| O.N.Gain | M.B.Templeton |
| P.M.Inglis† | L.F.Boucher |
| S.R.Wilson | N.A.Wakelin |
| E.J.Carson | M.N.Hyde |
| E.J.Black | C.R.Sarsfield |
| S.A.Oldershaw | K.A.Knight |
| M.E.Loe | E.L.Baker |


## OTAGO v NORTHERN DISTRICTS       One-day Competition

*at University of Otago Oval, Dunedin on 11 December, 2021*
*Toss : Northern Districts. Umpires : S.B. Haig & N. Louw*
**No result.** *Points: Otago 2, Northern Districts 2*

| OTAGO | | | | | | NORTHERN DISTRICTS |
|-------|------|------|-----|----|----|-------------------|
| | Runs | Mins | Balls | 6s | 4s | |
| S.W.Bates* c Harris b Baker .. | 138 | 147 | 120 | - | 15 | K.G.Anderson* |
| K.E.Ebrahim c Sarsfield b Knight | 88 | 161 | 124 | - | 4 | H.E.Topp† |
| I.R.James not out .................... | 32 | 30 | 17 | - | 5 | N.H.Patel |
| C.G.Blakely run out .................. | 13 | 12 | 11 | - | 1 | S.R.H.Curtis |
| K.J.Martin† not out .................... | 5 | 3 | 4 | - | - | M.B.Templeton |
| P.M.Inglis | | | | | | L.F.Boucher |
| S.R.Wilson | | | | | | C.R.Sarsfield |
| E.J.Carson | | | | | | M.N.Hyde |
| E.J.Black | | | | | | K.A.Knight |
| S.A.Oldershaw | | | | | | E.L.Baker |
| M.E.Loe | | | | | | G.A.Harris |
| Extras (w 23) ......................... | 23 | | | | | |
| **TOTAL** (46 overs) (3 wkts). **299** | 276 | | | | | |

| Bowling | O | M | R | W | | Fall of Wickets | |
|---------|---|---|---|---|---|-----------------|---|
| NORTHERN DISTRICTS | | | | | | | O |
| Knight | 5 | 0 | 54 | 1 | | 1st | 235 |
| Patel | 3 | 0 | 29 | 0 | | 2nd | 260 |
| Boucher | 7 | 0 | 51 | 0 | | 3rd | 289 |
| Hyde | 6 | 0 | 40 | 0 | | 4th | - |
| Sarsfield | 7 | 0 | 32 | 0 | | 5th | - |
| Templeton | 6 | 0 | 35 | 0 | | 6th | - |
| Anderson | 3 | 0 | 16 | 0 | | 7th | - |
| Baker | 7 | 1 | 23 | 1 | | 8th | - |
| Harris | 2 | 0 | 19 | 0 | | 9th | - |
| | | | | | | 10th | - |

## NORTHERN DISTRICTS v AUCKLAND    One-day Competition

*at Seddon Park, Hamilton on 18 December, 2021*
*Toss : Auckland.  Umpires : J.M. Dempsey & M.A. Fernandes*
**Northern Districts won by 5 wickets.** Points: Northern Districts 4, Auckland 0

### AUCKLAND

| | Runs | Mins | Balls | 6s | 4s |
|---|---|---|---|---|---|
| L.R.Down* c Boucher b Patel ... | 67 | 99 | 74 | - | 7 |
| I.C.Gaze b Patel | 1 | 7 | 9 | - | - |
| A.N.Kelly c Sarsfield b Boucher | 12 | 35 | 26 | - | - |
| K.T.Perkins c Curtis b Patel | 59 | 90 | 72 | - | 4 |
| H.R.Huddleston not out | 53 | 94 | 66 | - | 4 |
| B.G.Armstrong c Topp b Halliday | 9 | 22 | 18 | - | 1 |
| J.E.I.Prasad c Topp b Halliday ... | 3 | 15 | 15 | - | - |
| S.J.Carnachan† b Boucher | 0 | 4 | 5 | - | - |
| M.M.Penfold c Naidu b Boucher . | 0 | 2 | 2 | - | - |
| F.C.Jonas run out | 5 | 14 | 13 | - | - |
| J.L.Barnett not out | 0 | 1 | 0 | - | - |
| Extras (b 1, lb 3, w 12) | 16 | | | | |
| **TOTAL** (50 overs) (9 wkts) . | **225** | 194 | | | |

| Bowling | O | M | R | W |
|---|---|---|---|---|
| **NORTHERN DISTRICTS** | | | | |
| Naidu | 4 | 0 | 20 | 0 |
| Patel | 10 | 2 | 40 | 3 |
| Boucher | 10 | 0 | 41 | 3 |
| Halliday | 10 | 1 | 27 | 2 |
| Sarsfield | 8 | 0 | 46 | 0 |
| Baker | 3 | 0 | 18 | 0 |
| Templeton | 5 | 0 | 29 | 0 |
| **AUCKLAND** | | | | |
| Kelly | 4 | 0 | 23 | 0 |
| Huddleston | 9.5 | 0 | 52 | 0 |
| Jonas | 10 | 2 | 34 | 3 |
| Penfold | 6 | 0 | 40 | 0 |
| Barnett | 9 | 0 | 49 | 0 |
| Prasad | 8 | 0 | 25 | 2 |

### NORTHERN DISTRICTS

| | Runs | Mins | Balls | 6s | 4s |
|---|---|---|---|---|---|
| K.G.Anderson c Perkins b Jonas | 50 | 62 | 42 | 1 | 7 |
| C.A.Gurrey b Jonas | 12 | 36 | 29 | - | 1 |
| B.M.Halliday* c Carnachan b Jonas | 24 | 37 | 26 | 1 | 2 |
| S.R.H.Curtis c Perkins b Prasad | 12 | 34 | 20 | - | 1 |
| N.H.Patel not out | 71 | 111 | 90 | - | 6 |
| H.E.Topp† lbw b Prasad | 5 | 26 | 21 | - | - |
| M.B.Templeton not out | 29 | 62 | 55 | - | 2 |
| L.F.Boucher | | | | | |
| S.R.Naidu | | | | | |
| C.R.Sarsfield | | | | | |
| E.L.Baker | | | | | |
| Extras (lb 6, w 18, nb 2) | 26 | | | | |
| **TOTAL** (46.5 overs) (5 wkts) | **229** | 185 | | | |

| Fall of Wickets | | |
|---|---|---|
| | A | ND |
| 1st | 4 | 55 |
| 2nd | 47 | 85 |
| 3rd | 111 | 97 |
| 4th | 160 | 123 |
| 5th | 181 | 157 |
| 6th | 202 | - |
| 7th | 203 | - |
| 8th | 203 | - |
| 9th | 223 | - |
| 10th | - | - |

## AUCKLAND v WELLINGTON    One-day Competition

*at Kennards Hire Community Oval, Auckland on 3 January, 2022*
*Toss : Auckland.  Umpires : S.J. Kannan & B.A. O'Brien*
**Wellington won by 8 wickets.** Points: Auckland 0, Wellington 4

### AUCKLAND

| | Runs | Mins | Balls | 6s | 4s |
|---|---|---|---|---|---|
| L.R.Down* c Newton b Kerr J.M. | 124 | 186 | 143 | 1 | 10 |
| I.C.Gaze run out | 0 | 9 | 5 | - | - |
| A.N.Kelly b Kerr A.C. | 22 | 62 | 47 | - | 1 |
| K.T.Perkins c McFadyen b King . | 3 | 12 | 12 | - | - |
| H.R.Huddleston c Kerr A.C. b Jetly | 2 | 13 | 9 | - | - |
| B.G.Armstrong c Burns b Jetly ... | 1 | 9 | 11 | - | - |
| J.E.I.Prasad b Kerr A.C. | 38 | 56 | 40 | - | 6 |
| S.J.Carnachan† run out | 1 | 10 | 6 | - | - |
| M.M.Penfold b Kerr A.C. | 0 | 4 | 3 | - | - |
| F.C.Jonas c Burns b Kerr J.M. ... | 5 | 16 | 12 | - | - |
| J.L.Barnett not out | 2 | 8 | 7 | - | - |
| Extras (b 5, lb 1, w 12, nb 3) .. | 21 | | | | |
| **TOTAL** (48.5 overs) | **219** | 195 | | | |

| Bowling | O | M | R | W |
|---|---|---|---|---|
| **WELLINGTON** | | | | |
| Kerr J.M. | 5.5 | 1 | 9 | 2 |
| Singh | 7 | 1 | 33 | 0 |
| Kasperek | 9 | 0 | 40 | 0 |
| Kerr A.C. | 10 | 1 | 47 | 3 |
| King | 5 | 1 | 31 | 1 |
| Jetly | 10 | 1 | 32 | 2 |
| Newton | 2 | 0 | 21 | 0 |
| **AUCKLAND** | | | | |
| Huddleston | 8.2 | 1 | 37 | 1 |
| Kelly | 6 | 0 | 32 | 0 |
| Penfold | 5 | 0 | 38 | 0 |
| Jonas | 10 | 1 | 35 | 1 |
| Barnett | 5 | 0 | 34 | 0 |
| Prasad | 4 | 0 | 26 | 0 |
| Armstrong | 3 | 0 | 15 | 0 |

### WELLINGTON

| | Runs | Mins | Balls | 6s | 4s |
|---|---|---|---|---|---|
| J.T.McFadyen† c Perkins b Jonas | 44 | 106 | 84 | - | 2 |
| R.M.Burns b Huddleston | 12 | 16 | 12 | - | 2 |
| A.C.Kerr not out | 93 | 155 | 96 | - | 8 |
| M.L.Green* not out | 51 | 66 | 56 | - | 6 |
| G.E.Plimmer | | | | | |
| L.M.Kasperek | | | | | |
| T.M.M.Newton | | | | | |
| J.M.Kerr | | | | | |
| C.R.King | | | | | |
| X.A.R.Jetly | | | | | |
| M.P.Singh | | | | | |
| Extras (lb 5, w 17) | 22 | | | | |
| **TOTAL** (41.2 overs) (2 wkts) | **222** | 172 | | | |

| Fall of Wickets | | |
|---|---|---|
| | A | W |
| 1st | 3 | 19 |
| 2nd | 64 | 107 |
| 3rd | 77 | - |
| 4th | 89 | - |
| 5th | 93 | - |
| 6th | 190 | - |
| 7th | 205 | - |
| 8th | 208 | - |
| 9th | 213 | - |
| 10th | 219 | - |

# AUCKLAND v WELLINGTON    One-day Competition

*at Kennards Hire Community Oval, Auckland on 4 January, 2022*
*Toss : Wellington. Umpires : S.J. Kannan & V. Mahna*
**Wellington won by 78 runs.** Points: Wellington 5, Auckland 0

## WELLINGTON

| | Runs | Mins | Balls | 6s | 4s |
|---|---|---|---|---|---|
| J.T.McFadyen† c Carnachan b Hucker | 25 | 50 | 35 | - | 1 |
| R.M.Burns c Gaze b Hucker ..... | 23 | 43 | 35 | - | 3 |
| A.C.Kerr st Carnachan b Prasad | 29 | 48 | 39 | - | 2 |
| M.L.Green* c Down b Kelly ..... | 106 | 128 | 94 | - | 13 |
| G.E.Plimmer c Perkins b Huddleston | 2 | 13 | 9 | - | - |
| L.M.Kasperek b Barnett ........... | 29 | 49 | 40 | - | 3 |
| T.M.M.Newton c Perkins b Jonas | 26 | 39 | 32 | - | 1 |
| J.M.Kerr not out ........................ | 20 | 18 | 13 | - | 2 |
| C.R.King st Carnachan b Jonas . | 0 | 1 | 1 | - | - |
| X.A.R.Jetly not out ..................... | 5 | 2 | 2 | - | 1 |
| M.P.Singh | | | | | |
| Extras (lb 3, w 9) ........................ | 12 | | | | |
| **TOTAL** (50 overs) (8 wkts) . | **277** | 198 | | | |

## AUCKLAND

| | Runs | Mins | Balls | 6s | 4s |
|---|---|---|---|---|---|
| L.R.Down* b Jetly ..................... | 15 | 26 | 28 | - | 2 |
| I.C.Gaze c Plimmer b Kerr A.C. | 14 | 47 | 24 | - | 2 |
| A.N.Kelly c Burns b Singh ........... | 2 | 4 | 5 | - | - |
| K.T.Perkins lbw b Kasperek ...... | 17 | 22 | 25 | - | 2 |
| H.R.Huddleston c Kerr J.M. b Kasperek | 36 | 96 | 59 | - | 2 |
| S.Shahri c Kerr A.C. b Kasperek | 53 | 81 | 67 | - | 7 |
| J.E.I.Prasad c Kerr J.M. b Kasperek | 4 | 1 | 2 | - | 1 |
| A.T.Hucker c Green b Kasperek | 8 | 22 | 16 | - | 1 |
| S.J.Carnachan† c Kerr J.M. b Singh | 18 | 30 | 30 | - | 3 |
| F.C.Jonas not out ..................... | 13 | 23 | 25 | - | - |
| J.L.Barnett lbw b Jetly ................. | 2 | 7 | 4 | - | - |
| Extras (lb 7, w 10) ................... | 17 | | | | |
| **TOTAL** (47.3 overs) ............ | **199** | 182 | | | |

| Bowling | O | M | R | W |
|---|---|---|---|---|
| **AUCKLAND** | | | | |
| Huddleston | 10 | 0 | 49 | 1 |
| Kelly | 10 | 0 | 48 | 1 |
| Jonas | 10 | 1 | 37 | 2 |
| Hucker | 5 | 0 | 44 | 2 |
| Barnett | 8 | 0 | 54 | 1 |
| Prasad | 7 | 0 | 42 | 1 |
| **WELLINGTON** | | | | |
| Kerr J.M. | 6 | 0 | 28 | 0 |
| Singh | 10 | 1 | 30 | 2 |
| Jetly | 6.3 | 0 | 36 | 2 |
| Kerr A.C. | 10 | 1 | 33 | 1 |
| Kasperek | 10 | 1 | 45 | 5 |
| King | 5 | 0 | 20 | 0 |

| Fall of Wickets | | |
|---|---|---|
| | W | A |
| 1st | 44 | 23 |
| 2nd | 50 | 27 |
| 3rd | 120 | 52 |
| 4th | 135 | 54 |
| 5th | 193 | 152 |
| 6th | 241 | 156 |
| 7th | 269 | 157 |
| 8th | 270 | 178 |
| 9th | - | 191 |
| 10th | - | 199 |

# NORTHERN DISTRICTS v AUCKLAND    One-day Competition

*at Seddon Park, Hamilton on 9 January, 2022*
*Toss : Northern Districts. Umpires : B.M. Davis & J.M. Dempsey*
**Northern Districts won by 8 wickets.** Points: Northern Districts 4, Auckland 0

## AUCKLAND

| | Runs | Mins | Balls | 6s | 4s |
|---|---|---|---|---|---|
| L.R.Down* c Rout b Heaps ....... | 55 | 116 | 89 | 2 | 4 |
| I.C.Gaze c Topp b Baker ........... | 8 | 35 | 29 | - | 1 |
| A.N.Kelly c Topp b Halliday ...... | 13 | 43 | 29 | - | 2 |
| K.T.Perkins b Sarsfield .............. | 5 | 17 | 13 | - | - |
| H.R.Huddleston st Topp b Sarsfield | 52 | 83 | 55 | - | 6 |
| S.Shahri c Naidu b Patel .......... | 10 | 27 | 22 | - | - |
| J.E.I.Prasad st Topp b Patel ..... | 46 | 51 | 46 | - | 5 |
| M.M.Penfold c Baker b Halliday | 21 | 10 | 12 | 1 | 2 |
| S.J.Carnachan† run out ......... | 9 | 6 | 3 | - | 2 |
| F.C.Jonas c Halliday b Patel ...... | 0 | 1 | 1 | - | - |
| J.L.Barnett not out ..................... | 0 | 1 | 1 | - | - |
| Extras (b 2, w 18) ................... | 20 | | | | |
| **TOTAL** (50 overs) .............. | **239** | 198 | | | |

## NORTHERN DISTRICTS

| | Runs | Mins | Balls | 6s | 4s |
|---|---|---|---|---|---|
| C.A.Gurrey c Perkins b Kelly .... | 14 | 30 | 30 | - | 1 |
| B.M.Halliday* not out ............... | 106 | 183 | 126 | 1 | 12 |
| S.R.H.Curtis b Penfold ............. | 65 | 125 | 98 | - | 6 |
| N.H.Patel not out ...................... | 37 | 28 | 17 | 1 | 6 |
| A.J.Rout | | | | | |
| L.F.Boucher | | | | | |
| H.E.Topp† | | | | | |
| S.R.Naidu | | | | | |
| E.L.Baker | | | | | |
| C.R.Sarsfield | | | | | |
| L.H.Heaps | | | | | |
| Extras (b 1, lb 2, w 12, nb 3) .. | 18 | | | | |
| **TOTAL** (46.2 overs) (2 wkts) | **240** | 183 | | | |

| Bowling | O | M | R | W |
|---|---|---|---|---|
| **NORTHERN DISTRICTS** | | | | |
| Naidu | 4 | 0 | 17 | 0 |
| Heaps | 10 | 1 | 28 | 1 |
| Baker | 6 | 0 | 38 | 1 |
| Patel | 10 | 0 | 46 | 3 |
| Halliday | 10 | 0 | 52 | 2 |
| Sarsfield | 10 | 0 | 56 | 2 |
| **AUCKLAND** | | | | |
| Huddleston | 8.2 | 1 | 30 | 0 |
| Kelly | 10 | 1 | 42 | 1 |
| Penfold | 6 | 0 | 51 | 1 |
| Jonas | 10 | 0 | 61 | 0 |
| Barnett | 3 | 0 | 17 | 0 |
| Prasad | 9 | 1 | 36 | 0 |

| Fall of Wickets | | |
|---|---|---|
| | A | ND |
| 1st | 29 | 29 |
| 2nd | 67 | 189 |
| 3rd | 82 | - |
| 4th | 104 | - |
| 5th | 129 | - |
| 6th | 197 | - |
| 7th | 226 | - |
| 8th | 239 | - |
| 9th | 239 | - |
| 10th | 239 | - |

# NORTHERN DISTRICTS v CANTERBURY One-day Competition

*at Seddon Park, Hamilton on 5 February, 2022*
*Toss : Canterbury.  Umpires : C. High & D.R. Morrow*
**Northern Districts won by 7 wickets.** Points: Northern Districts 4, Canterbury 0

## CANTERBURY

| | Runs | Mins | Balls | 6s | 4s |
|---|---|---|---|---|---|
| E.K.Kench lbw b Baker | 10 | 60 | 42 | - | - |
| A.G.Gerken c Heaps b Patel | 49 | 99 | 73 | - | 7 |
| J.L.Savage c Richardson b Patel | 3 | 21 | 9 | - | - |
| J.Dean c Baker b Patel | 38 | 75 | 68 | - | 3 |
| A.C.Mace-Cochrane c Naidu b Richardson | 14 | 35 | 30 | - | 1 |
| I.G.Sharp c Gurrey b Patel | 28 | 33 | 33 | 1 | 2 |
| L.E.V.Hughes*† not out | 29 | 32 | 29 | - | 3 |
| M.J.Banks c Agafili b Patel | 0 | 2 | 2 | - | - |
| K.J.Havill c Patel b Richardson | 10 | 10 | 9 | - | 2 |
| J.A.Simmons not out | 8 | 8 | 7 | - | 1 |
| S.R.Asmussen | | | | | |
| Extras (lb 3, w 35, nb 2) | 40 | | | | |
| **TOTAL** (50 overs) (8 wkts) . | **229** | 190 | | | |

## NORTHERN DISTRICTS

| | Runs | Mins | Balls | 6s | 4s |
|---|---|---|---|---|---|
| K.G.Anderson c Banks b Asmussen | 46 | 58 | 53 | - | 9 |
| C.A.Gurrey st Hughes b Havill | 58 | 111 | 79 | - | 6 |
| H.E.Topp† c Hughes b Havill | 47 | 71 | 67 | - | 5 |
| N.H.Patel not out | 33 | 38 | 32 | - | 4 |
| L.F.Boucher not out | 17 | 19 | 13 | - | 2 |
| E.A.J.Richardson* | | | | | |
| M.B.Templeton | | | | | |
| C.Agafili | | | | | |
| S.R.Naidu | | | | | |
| E.L.Baker | | | | | |
| L.H.Heaps | | | | | |
| Extras (lb 6, w 23) | 29 | | | | |
| **TOTAL** (40.4 overs) (3 wkts) | **230** | 149 | | | |

| Bowling | O | M | R | W |
|---|---|---|---|---|
| **NORTHERN DISTRICTS** | | | | |
| Naidu | 9 | 1 | 48 | 0 |
| Boucher | 4 | 0 | 28 | 0 |
| Heaps | 5 | 1 | 22 | 0 |
| Baker | 6 | 0 | 16 | 1 |
| Patel | 10 | 0 | 46 | 5 |
| Templeton | 6 | 1 | 20 | 0 |
| Richardson | 10 | 0 | 46 | 2 |
| **CANTERBURY** | | | | |
| Banks | 8.4 | 0 | 44 | 0 |
| Simmons | 5 | 0 | 37 | 0 |
| Savage | 6 | 0 | 28 | 0 |
| Asmussen | 10 | 0 | 58 | 1 |
| Dean | 4 | 0 | 20 | 0 |
| Havill | 6 | 0 | 32 | 2 |
| Mace-Cochrane | 1 | 0 | 5 | 0 |

| Fall of Wickets | | |
|---|---|---|
| | C | ND |
| 1st | 65 | 81 |
| 2nd | 79 | 161 |
| 3rd | 98 | 185 |
| 4th | 138 | - |
| 5th | 166 | - |
| 6th | 189 | - |
| 7th | 190 | - |
| 8th | 209 | - |
| 9th | - | - |
| 10th | - | - |

# CENTRAL DISTRICTS v AUCKLAND   One-day Competition

*at Pukekura Park, New Plymouth on 5 February, 2022*
**Abandoned without a ball being bowled.** Points: Central Districts 2, Auckland 2

# OTAGO v WELLINGTON   One-day Competition

*at Whitestone Contracting Stadium, Oamaru on 5 February, 2022*
**Abandoned without a ball being bowled.** Points: Otago 2, Wellington 2

# CENTRAL DISTRICTS v AUCKLAND   One-day Competition

*at Pukekura Park, New Plymouth on 6 February, 2022*
**Abandoned without a ball being bowled.** Points: Central Districts 2, Auckland 2

# NORTHERN DISTRICTS v CANTERBURY One-day Competition

*at Seddon Park, Hamilton on 6 February, 2022*
*Toss : Canterbury.  Umpires : C. High & D.R. Morrow*
**No result.** Points: Northern Districts 2, Canterbury 2

## NORTHERN DISTRICTS

| | Runs | Mins | Balls | 6s | 4s |
|---|---|---|---|---|---|
| K.G.Anderson b Savage | 56 | 81 | 57 | 1 | 6 |
| C.A.Gurrey run out | 22 | 46 | 30 | - | 3 |
| H.E.Topp† b Asmussen | 7 | 30 | 25 | - | - |
| E.A.J.Richardson* c Simmons b Dean | 23 | 22 | 18 | - | 4 |
| C.L.Agafili c & b Savage | 0 | 2 | 3 | - | - |
| L.F.Boucher c Asmussen b Simmons | 11 | 23 | 12 | - | 2 |
| N.H.Patel not out | 22 | 25 | 15 | - | 2 |
| M.B.Templeton not out | 19 | 17 | 14 | - | 2 |
| S.R.Naidu | | | | | |
| N.A.Wakelin | | | | | |
| C.R.Sarsfield | | | | | |
| Extras b 1, lb 2, w 8) | 11 | | | | |
| **TOTAL** (29 overs) (6 wkts) | **171** | 124 | | | |

## CANTERBURY

| | Runs | Mins | Balls | 6s | 4s |
|---|---|---|---|---|---|
| H.M.Graham not out | 16 | 31 | 21 | - | 2 |
| A.G.Gerken not out | 25 | 31 | 21 | - | 4 |
| J.L.Savage | | | | | |
| J.Dean | | | | | |
| A.C.Mace-Cochrane | | | | | |
| I.G.Sharp | | | | | |
| L.E.V.Hughes*† | | | | | |
| M.J.Banks | | | | | |
| K.J.Havill | | | | | |
| J.A.Simmons | | | | | |
| S.R.Asmussen | | | | | |
| Extras (lb 1, w 3) | 4 | | | | |
| **TOTAL** (7 overs) (0 wkts) | **45** | 31 | | | |

| Bowling | O | M | R | W |
|---|---|---|---|---|
| **CANTERBURY** | | | | |
| Simmons | 5 | 0 | 40 | 1 |
| Banks | 6 | 0 | 37 | 0 |
| Dean | 3 | 0 | 32 | 1 |
| Asmussen | 6 | 0 | 31 | 1 |
| Savage | 6 | 3 | 13 | 2 |
| Havill | 3 | 0 | 15 | 0 |
| **NORTHERN DISTRICTS** | | | | |
| Naidu | 3 | 0 | 18 | 0 |
| Boucher | 3 | 0 | 21 | 0 |
| Patel | 1 | 0 | 5 | 0 |

| Fall of Wickets | | |
|---|---|---|
| | ND | C |
| 1st | 69 | - |
| 2nd | 91 | - |
| 3rd | 95 | - |
| 4th | 95 | - |
| 5th | 120 | - |
| 6th | 135 | - |
| 7th | - | - |
| 8th | - | - |
| 9th | - | - |
| 10th | - | - |

# OTAGO v WELLINGTON                  One-day Competition

*at Whitestone Contracting Stadium, Oamaru on 6 February, 2022*
*Toss : Otago.  Umpires : M.A. Fernandes & D.J. Walker*
**Wellington won by 49 runs.** Points: Wellington 5, Otago 0

## WELLINGTON

| | Runs | Mins | Balls | 6s | 4s |
|---|---|---|---|---|---|
| J.T.McFadyen† not out | 76 | 135 | 90 | - | 2 |
| R.M.Burns lbw b Carson | 2 | 14 | 10 | - | - |
| L.M.Kasperek c Oldershaw b Lamplough | 11 | 31 | 20 | - | - |
| G.E.Plimmer st Inglis b Wilson | 38 | 37 | 40 | 1 | 3 |
| T.M.M.Newton b Wilson | 0 | 3 | 4 | - | - |
| C.R.King b Wilson | 8 | 23 | 17 | - | - |
| X.A.R.Jetly c Lamplough b Carson | 7 | 13 | 11 | - | - |
| K.M.Chandler c Deerness b Black | 2 | 10 | 7 | - | - |
| M.P.Singh not out | 0 | 1 | 0 | - | - |
| D.M.Doughty* | | | | | |
| N.E.Codyre | | | | | |
| Extras (lb 2, w 12, nb 1) | 15 | | | | |
| **TOTAL** (33 overs) (7 wkts) | **159** | 135 | | | |

## OTAGO

| | Runs | Mins | Balls | 6s | 4s |
|---|---|---|---|---|---|
| O.N.Gain run out | 20 | 31 | 28 | - | 2 |
| I.R..James c Burns b Jetly | 4 | 12 | 7 | - | - |
| K.E.Ebrahim* c Chandler b Kasperek | 31 | 83 | 62 | - | 1 |
| P.M.Inglis† c Newton b Codyre | 14 | 14 | 12 | - | 3 |
| S.R.Wilson b Jetly | 17 | 26 | 21 | - | 2 |
| M.B.Lamplough c & b Jetly | 0 | 1 | 1 | - | - |
| P.R.Loggenberg c Jetly b Kasperek | 11 | 19 | 22 | - | 1 |
| E.J.Carson c Codyre b Doughty | 1 | 5 | 6 | - | - |
| E.J.Black c Codyre b Kasperek | 6 | 12 | 7 | - | 1 |
| S.A.Oldershaw c King b Doughty | 2 | 7 | 10 | - | - |
| C.M.Deerness not out | 1 | 2 | 1 | - | - |
| Extras (lb 1, w 2) | 3 | | | | |
| **TOTAL** (29.3 overs) | **110** | 108 | | | |

| Bowling | O | M | R | W |
|---|---|---|---|---|
| **OTAGO** | | | | |
| Black | 5 | 0 | 24 | 1 |
| Carson | 7 | 0 | 28 | 2 |
| Lamplough | 6 | 0 | 26 | 1 |
| Ebrahim | 3 | 0 | 13 | 0 |
| Oldershaw | 5 | 0 | 24 | 0 |
| Wilson | 7 | 1 | 42 | 3 |
| **WELLINGTON** | | | | |
| Singh | 4 | 0 | 14 | 0 |
| Jetly | 6 | 0 | 19 | 3 |
| Kasperek | 5.3 | 0 | 22 | 3 |
| Codyre | 4 | 0 | 13 | 1 |
| King | 3 | 0 | 16 | 0 |
| Doughty | 7 | 0 | 25 | 2 |

| Fall of Wickets | | |
|---|---|---|
| | W | O |
| 1st | 15 | 18 |
| 2nd | 44 | 32 |
| 3rd | 94 | 54 |
| 4th | 94 | 80 |
| 5th | 121 | 80 |
| 6th | 141 | 100 |
| 7th | 157 | 101 |
| 8th | - | 101 |
| 9th | - | 108 |
| 10th | - | 110 |

## AUCKLAND v CANTERBURY     One-day Competition

*at Kennards Hire Community Oval, Auckland on 12 February, 2022*
*Toss : Canterbury. Umpires : C. High & E.D. Sanders*
**Auckland won by 92 runs.** *Points: Auckland 5, Canterbury 0*

<table>
<tr><td colspan="6" align="center">**AUCKLAND**</td><td colspan="6" align="center">**CANTERBURY**</td></tr>
<tr><td></td><td>*Runs*</td><td>*Mins*</td><td>*Balls*</td><td>*6s*</td><td>*4s*</td><td></td><td>*Runs*</td><td>*Mins*</td><td>*Balls*</td><td>*6s*</td><td>*4s*</td></tr>
<tr><td>S.Shahri c & b Asmussen</td><td>42</td><td>78</td><td>55</td><td>-</td><td>5</td><td>E.K.Kench lbw b Illing</td><td>6</td><td>41</td><td>24</td><td>-</td><td>-</td></tr>
<tr><td>A.S.Browning c & b Asmussen .</td><td>18</td><td>71</td><td>45</td><td>-</td><td>1</td><td>A.G.Gerken c Hucker b Kelly</td><td>3</td><td>6</td><td>7</td><td>-</td><td>-</td></tr>
<tr><td>A.N.Kelly c Gerken b Savage</td><td>3</td><td>10</td><td>8</td><td>-</td><td>-</td><td>J.L.Savage c Shahri b Penfold .</td><td>17</td><td>39</td><td>32</td><td>-</td><td>1</td></tr>
<tr><td>K.T.Perkins* not out</td><td>85</td><td>125</td><td>75</td><td>1</td><td>7</td><td>J.Dean run out</td><td>17</td><td>49</td><td>30</td><td>-</td><td>2</td></tr>
<tr><td>B.G.Armstrong b Dean</td><td>10</td><td>14</td><td>17</td><td>-</td><td>1</td><td>A.C.Mace-Cochrane c Gaze</td><td></td><td></td><td></td><td></td><td></td></tr>
<tr><td>I.C.Gaze† lbw b Asmussen</td><td>1</td><td>4</td><td>5</td><td>-</td><td>-</td><td>  b Penfold</td><td>14</td><td>10</td><td>8</td><td>-</td><td>3</td></tr>
<tr><td>J.E.I.Prasad c Havill b Dean</td><td>10</td><td>13</td><td>17</td><td>-</td><td>-</td><td>I.G.Sharp lbw b Armstrong</td><td>12</td><td>22</td><td>16</td><td>-</td><td>2</td></tr>
<tr><td>M.M.Penfold c Simmons</td><td></td><td></td><td></td><td></td><td></td><td>L.E.V.Hughes*† c Perkins b Prasad</td><td>18</td><td>35</td><td>30</td><td>-</td><td>3</td></tr>
<tr><td>  b Asmussen</td><td>1</td><td>4</td><td>5</td><td>-</td><td>-</td><td>M.J.Banks b Illing</td><td>29</td><td>49</td><td>33</td><td>-</td><td>4</td></tr>
<tr><td>A.T.Hucker run out</td><td>9</td><td>19</td><td>25</td><td>-</td><td>1</td><td>K.J.Havill b Penfold</td><td>16</td><td>42</td><td>27</td><td>-</td><td>1</td></tr>
<tr><td>S.J.Bultitude b Dean</td><td>40</td><td>58</td><td>48</td><td>-</td><td>4</td><td>J.A.Simmons c Illing b Penfold ...</td><td>2</td><td>6</td><td>7</td><td>-</td><td>-</td></tr>
<tr><td>B.G.Illing not out</td><td>2</td><td>3</td><td>2</td><td>-</td><td>-</td><td>S.R.Asmussen not out</td><td>4</td><td>10</td><td>9</td><td>-</td><td>-</td></tr>
<tr><td>  Extras (b 2, lb 3, w 21, nb 2) ..</td><td>28</td><td></td><td></td><td></td><td></td><td>  Extras (b 4, w 14, nb 1)</td><td>19</td><td></td><td></td><td></td><td></td></tr>
<tr><td>  **TOTAL** (50 overs) (9 wkts) .</td><td>**249**</td><td>203</td><td></td><td></td><td></td><td>  **TOTAL** (37 overs)</td><td>**157**</td><td>156</td><td></td><td></td><td></td></tr>
</table>

| Bowling | O | M | R | W |
|---|---|---|---|---|
| **CANTERBURY** | | | | |
| Simmons | 8 | 0 | 46 | 0 |
| Banks | 9 | 0 | 44 | 0 |
| Savage | 10 | 0 | 61 | 1 |
| Asmussen | 10 | 1 | 33 | 4 |
| Dean | 9 | 0 | 37 | 3 |
| Havill | 4 | 0 | 23 | 0 |
| **AUCKLAND** | | | | |
| Hucker | 7 | 0 | 22 | 0 |
| Kelly | 3 | 1 | 13 | 1 |
| Illing | 7 | 1 | 15 | 2 |
| Penfold | 8 | 0 | 42 | 4 |
| Bultitude | 4 | 0 | 22 | 0 |
| Armstrong | 4 | 0 | 17 | 1 |
| Prasad | 4 | 0 | 22 | 1 |

| Fall of Wickets | A | C |
|---|---|---|
| 1st | 72 | 5 |
| 2nd | 77 | 32 |
| 3rd | 79 | 33 |
| 4th | 94 | 50 |
| 5th | 95 | 80 |
| 6th | 116 | 93 |
| 7th | 118 | 117 |
| 8th | 135 | 147 |
| 9th | 245 | 150 |
| 10th | - | 157 |

## WELLINGTON v CENTRAL DISTRICTS     One-day Competition

*at Cello Basin Reserve, Wellington on 12 February, 2022*
**Abandoned without a ball being bowled.** *Points: Wellington 2, Central Districts 2*

## WELLINGTON v CENTRAL DISTRICTS     One-day Competition

*at Cello Basin Reserve, Wellington on 13 February, 2022*
**Abandoned without a ball being bowled.** *Points: Wellington 2, Central Districts 2*

## AUCKLAND v CANTERBURY     One-day Competition

*at Kennards Hire Community Oval, Auckland on 13 February, 2022*
*Toss : Canterbury. Umpires : C. High & E.D. Sanders*
**No result.** *Points: Auckland 2, Canterbury 2*

| CANTERBURY | AUCKLAND |
|---|---|
| E.K.Kench | S.Shahri |
| A.G.Gerken | E.Irwin |
| J.L.Savage | A.N.Kelly |
| J.Dean | K.T.Perkins * |
| A.C.Mace-Cochrane | B.G.Armstrong |
| I.G.Sharp | I.C.Gaze† |
| L.E.V.Hughes*† | J.E.I.Prasad |
| M.J.Banks | M.M.Penfold |
| K.J.Havill | A.T.Hucker |
| J.A.Simmons | J.L.Barnett |
| S.R.Asmussen | A.J.Parr-Thomson |

# NORTHERN DISTRICTS v AUCKLAND    One-day Competition

*at Seddon Park, Hamilton on 19 February, 2022*
*Toss : Northern Districts. Umpires : C. High & G.M. Walklin*
**Northern Districts won by 10 wickets.** *Points: Northern Districts 5, Auckland 0*

## AUCKLAND

| | Runs | Mins | Balls | 6s | 4s |
|---|---|---|---|---|---|
| S.Shahri b Naidu | 0 | 1 | 3 | - | - |
| E.Irwin b Naidu | 4 | 19 | 13 | - | - |
| A.N.Kelly c Naidu b Boucher | 12 | 44 | 37 | - | 1 |
| K.T.Perkins* b Patel | 42 | 105 | 65 | - | 3 |
| B.G.Armstrong c Templeton b Patel | 63 | 66 | 62 | - | 10 |
| I.C.Gaze† c Richardson b Templeton | 9 | 17 | 15 | - | 1 |
| J.E.I.Prasad st Ewart b Patel | 15 | 37 | 31 | - | 2 |
| A.J.Parr-Thomson c Curtis b Patel | 9 | 16 | 16 | 1 | - |
| A.T.Hucker b Patel | 4 | 7 | 6 | - | - |
| M.M.Penfold c Gurrey b Patel | 6 | 13 | 12 | - | - |
| B.G.Illing not out | 6 | 5 | 6 | - | 1 |
| Extras (lb 1, w 13, nb 1) | 15 | | | | |
| **TOTAL** (44.1 overs) | **185** | 168 | | | |

## NORTHERN DISTRICTS

| | Runs | Mins | Balls | 6s | 4s |
|---|---|---|---|---|---|
| C.A.Gurrey not out | 94 | 133 | 107 | - | 15 |
| S.R.H.Curtis not out | 77 | 133 | 102 | - | 10 |
| E.A.J.Richardson* | | | | | |
| N.H.Patel | | | | | |
| M.B.Templeton | | | | | |
| A.M.Ewart† | | | | | |
| L.F.Boucher | | | | | |
| S.R.Naidu | | | | | |
| E.L.Baker | | | | | |
| C.R.Sarsfield | | | | | |
| L.H.Heaps | | | | | |
| Extras (b 1, lb 5, w 10, nb 1) | 17 | | | | |
| **TOTAL** (34.4 overs) (0 wkts) | **188** | 133 | | | |

| Bowling | O | M | R | W |
|---|---|---|---|---|
| **NORTHERN DISTRICTS** | | | | |
| Naidu | 7 | 1 | 26 | 2 |
| Boucher | 6 | 3 | 9 | 1 |
| Heaps | 5 | 0 | 23 | 0 |
| Baker | 3 | 0 | 31 | 0 |
| Sarsfield | 4 | 1 | 20 | 0 |
| Templeton | 6 | 0 | 22 | 1 |
| Patel | 8.1 | 1 | 25 | 6 |
| Richardson | 5 | 0 | 28 | 0 |
| **AUCKLAND** | | | | |
| Hucker | 5.4 | 0 | 38 | 0 |
| Illing | 7 | 0 | 43 | 0 |
| Kelly | 6 | 2 | 10 | 0 |
| Armstrong | 3 | 0 | 29 | 0 |
| Penfold | 5 | 0 | 19 | 0 |
| Parr-Thomson | 6 | 0 | 30 | 0 |
| Prasad | 2 | 0 | 13 | 0 |

| Fall of Wickets | A | ND |
|---|---|---|
| 1st | 0 | - |
| 2nd | 8 | - |
| 3rd | 29 | - |
| 4th | 130 | - |
| 5th | 143 | - |
| 6th | 145 | - |
| 7th | 156 | - |
| 8th | 171 | - |
| 9th | 178 | - |
| 10th | 185 | - |

# NORTHERN DISTRICTS v AUCKLAND    One-day Competition

*at Seddon Park, Hamilton on 20 February, 2022*
*Toss : Northern Districts. Umpires : C. High & G.M. Walklin*
**Match tied (D/L).** *Points: Northern Districts 2, Auckland 2*

## AUCKLAND

| | Runs | Mins | Balls | 6s | 4s |
|---|---|---|---|---|---|
| S.Shahri c Boucher b Patel | 34 | 76 | 63 | - | 3 |
| P.Catton b Templeton | 46 | 87 | 72 | - | 6 |
| A.N.Kelly c Boucher b Richardson | 41 | 42 | 46 | - | 4 |
| K.T.Perkins* b Templeton | 12 | 19 | 7 | - | 1 |
| B.G.Armstrong not out | 20 | 19 | 12 | - | 2 |
| I.C.Gaze† not out | 5 | 6 | 4 | - | - |
| J.O.Penfold | | | | | |
| A.T.Hucker | | | | | |
| M.M.Penfold | | | | | |
| B.G.Illing | | | | | |
| J.L.Barnett | | | | | |
| Extras (w 9) | 9 | | | | |
| **TOTAL** (34 overs) (4 wkts) | **167** | 126 | | | |

## NORTHERN DISTRICTS

| | Runs | Mins | Balls | 6s | 4s |
|---|---|---|---|---|---|
| K.G.Anderson run out | 74 | 85 | 61 | - | 11 |
| C.A.Gurrey lbw b Hucker | 5 | 35 | 18 | - | - |
| S.R.H.Curtis c Catton b Penfold M.M. | 9 | 26 | 16 | - | - |
| M.B.Templeton run out | 25 | 49 | 33 | - | 3 |
| N.H.Patel run out | 37 | 64 | 43 | - | 1 |
| E.A.J.Richardson* c Penfold J.O. b Hucker | 11 | 19 | 11 | - | 2 |
| L.F.Boucher c Penfold M.M. b Illing | 15 | 22 | 16 | - | 1 |
| S.R.Naidu retired hurt | 1 | 4 | 3 | - | - |
| A.M.Ewart† lbw b Kelly | 0 | 6 | 1 | - | - |
| C.L.Agafili not out | 7 | 7 | 3 | 1 | - |
| C.R.Sarsfield not out | 5 | 2 | 2 | - | 1 |
| L.H.Heaps | | | | | |
| Extras (b 3, lb 4, w 13, nb 3) | 23 | | | | |
| **TOTAL** (34 overs) (8 wkts) | **212** | 162 | | | |

| Bowling | O | M | R | W |
|---|---|---|---|---|
| **NORTHERN DISTRICTS** | | | | |
| Naidu | 5 | 0 | 24 | 0 |
| Boucher | 6 | 0 | 34 | 0 |
| Richardson | 5 | 0 | 33 | 1 |
| Heaps | 3 | 0 | 11 | 0 |
| Patel | 7 | 1 | 31 | 1 |
| Templeton | 7 | 1 | 22 | 2 |
| Sarsfield | 1 | 0 | 12 | 0 |
| **AUCKLAND** | | | | |
| Hucker | 7 | 0 | 38 | 2 |
| Illing | 5 | 0 | 31 | 1 |
| Penfold M.M. | 7 | 0 | 46 | 1 |
| Kelly | 7 | 0 | 27 | 1 |
| Penfold J.O. | 2 | 0 | 23 | 0 |
| Armstrong | 4 | 0 | 25 | 0 |
| Barnett | 2 | 0 | 15 | 0 |

| Fall of Wickets | A | ND |
|---|---|---|
| 1st | 78 | 33 |
| 2nd | 87 | 65 |
| 3rd | 125 | 124 |
| 4th | 151 | 136 |
| 5th | - | 159 |
| 6th | - | 188 |
| 7th | - | 197 |
| 8th | - | 205 |
| 9th | - | - |
| 10th | - | - |

*Naidu retired hurt at 194-6*
*and was replaced by Agafili*
*as a concussion substutute*

# OTAGO v WELLINGTON          One-day Competition Final

*at John Davies Oval, Queenstown on 27 February, 2022*
*Toss : Otago.  Umpires : C.A. Black & J.M. Dempsey*
**Otago won by 138 runs**

## OTAGO

| | Runs | Mins | Balls | 6s | 4s |
|---|---|---|---|---|---|
| K.E.Ebrahim* run out | 92 | 178 | 138 | - | 5 |
| I.R.James c McFadyen b Jetly | 4 | 16 | 13 | - | - |
| C.G.Blakely lbw b Chandler | 57 | 89 | 82 | - | 6 |
| P.M.Inglis† lbw b Chandler | 1 | 6 | 7 | - | - |
| S.R.Wilson run out | 15 | 31 | 21 | - | 2 |
| M.B.Lamplough b Doughty | 2 | 2 | 2 | - | - |
| P.R.Loggenberg run out | 7 | 12 | 12 | - | 1 |
| E.J.Carson b Chandler | 9 | 8 | 11 | - | 1 |
| E.J.Black not out | 9 | 14 | 10 | - | - |
| S.A.Oldershaw st McFadyen b Jetly | 2 | 1 | 2 | - | - |
| H.O.Cuttance not out | 1 | 1 | 2 | - | - |

Extras (lb 2, w 19) .................. 21
**TOTAL** (50 overs) (9 wkts) . **220**  181

## WELLINGTON

| | Runs | Mins | Balls | 6s | 4s |
|---|---|---|---|---|---|
| J.T.McFadyen† c Ebrahim b Black | 3 | 20 | 12 | - | - |
| R.M.Burns c Inglis b Cuttance | 4 | 9 | 6 | - | 1 |
| K.M.Chandler b Black | 5 | 19 | 15 | - | - |
| T.M.M.Newton c Ebrahim b Carson | 15 | 41 | 32 | - | 3 |
| C.R.King lbw b Black | 3 | 8 | 8 | - | - |
| X.A.R.Jetly lbw b Carson | 1 | 11 | 12 | - | - |
| O.A.Boivin c Inglis b Carson | 7 | 28 | 20 | - | 1 |
| M.P.Singh c & b Carson | 3 | 23 | 18 | - | - |
| N.E.Codyre c Lamplough b Carson | 11 | 20 | 20 | - | 2 |
| D.M.Doughty* not out | 13 | 21 | 22 | - | 2 |
| B.C.Molony b Oldershaw | 0 | 9 | 8 | - | - |

Extras (b 2, lb 1, w 14) .......... 17
**TOTAL** (28.5 overs) .............. **82**  107

| Bowling | O | M | R | W |
|---|---|---|---|---|
| **WELLINGTON** | | | | |
| Jetly | 10 | 0 | 41 | 2 |
| Singh | 10 | 0 | 38 | 0 |
| Molony | 5 | 0 | 22 | 0 |
| Codyre | 3 | 0 | 10 | 0 |
| Doughty | 8 | 0 | 51 | 1 |
| King | 6 | 0 | 26 | 0 |
| Chandler | 8 | 0 | 30 | 3 |
| **OTAGO** | | | | |
| Black | 6 | 1 | 13 | 3 |
| Cuttance | 4 | 0 | 18 | 1 |
| Carson | 10 | 5 | 17 | 5 |
| Wilson | 4 | 0 | 16 | 0 |
| Oldershaw | 4.5 | 0 | 15 | 1 |

| Fall of Wickets | O | W |
|---|---|---|
| 1st | 16 | 12 |
| 2nd | 119 | 17 |
| 3rd | 123 | 23 |
| 4th | 165 | 29 |
| 5th | 167 | 32 |
| 6th | 180 | 44 |
| 7th | 191 | 54 |
| 8th | 214 | 63 |
| 9th | 216 | 76 |
| 10th | - | 82 |

# 2021/22 ONE-DAY AVERAGES

| | M | In | NO | HS | Runs | Ave | 100s | 50s | ct | st | O | M | R | W | Ave | R/O | Best |
|---|---|---|---|---|---|---|---|---|---|---|---|---|---|---|---|---|---|
| C.L.Agafili | 3 | 2 | 1 | 7* | 7 | 7.00 | - | - | 1 | - | | | | | | | |
| K.G.Anderson | 8 | 6 | 0 | 74 | 306 | 51.00 | - | 4 | - | - | 16 | 0 | 83 | 2 | 41.50 | 5.19 | 2-43 |
| B.G.Armstrong | 6 | 5 | 1 | 63 | 103 | 25.75 | - | 1 | - | - | 14 | 0 | 86 | 1 | 86.00 | 6.14 | 1-17 |
| S.R.Asmussen | 8 | 3 | 2 | 4* | 4 | 4.00 | - | - | 3 | - | 50 | 1 | 281 | 7 | 40.14 | 5.62 | 4-33 |
| G.K.Atkinson | 4 | 4 | 0 | 28 | 69 | 17.25 | - | - | - | - | 20 | 1 | 105 | 3 | 35.00 | 5.25 | 2-29 |
| E.L.Baker | 8 | 2 | 0 | 4 | 5 | 2.50 | - | - | 2 | - | 32 | 1 | 163 | 4 | 40.75 | 5.09 | 1-16 |
| M.J.Banks | 8 | 6 | 2 | 29 | 62 | 15.50 | - | - | 2 | - | 53.4 | 1 | 277 | 1 | 277.00 | 5.16 | 1-22 |
| J.L.Barnett | 6 | 4 | 3 | 2* | 4 | 4.00 | - | - | - | - | 27 | 0 | 169 | 1 | 169.00 | 6.26 | 1-54 |
| S.W.Bates | 6 | 5 | 0 | 138 | 218 | 43.60 | 1 | 1 | 6 | - | | | | | | | |
| E.J.Black | 8 | 3 | 1 | 12 | 27 | 13.50 | - | - | 1 | - | 43 | 4 | 174 | 13 | 13.38 | 4.05 | 5-28 |
| C.G.Blakely | 7 | 5 | 0 | 63 | 170 | 34.00 | - | 2 | 3 | - | | | | | | | |
| O.A.Boivin | 1 | 1 | 0 | 7 | 7 | 7.00 | - | - | - | - | | | | | | | |
| L.F.Boucher | 10 | 5 | 1 | 21 | 70 | 17.50 | - | - | 4 | - | 51 | 3 | 268 | 7 | 38.28 | 5.25 | 3-41 |
| A.S.Browning | 1 | 1 | 0 | 18 | 18 | 18.00 | - | - | - | - | | | | | | | |
| S.J.Bultitude | 1 | 1 | 0 | 40 | 40 | 40.00 | - | - | - | - | 4 | 0 | 22 | 0 | - | 5.50 | - |
| R.M.Burns | 6 | 6 | 0 | 47 | 102 | 17.00 | - | - | 4 | - | | | | | | | |
| S.J.Carnachan | 4 | 4 | 0 | 18 | 28 | 7.00 | - | - | 2 | 2 | | | | | | | |
| E.J.Carson | 8 | 4 | 1 | 18 | 28 | 9.33 | - | - | 2 | - | 47 | 7 | 159 | 14 | 11.35 | 3.38 | 5-17 |
| P.Catton | 1 | 1 | 0 | 46 | 46 | 46.00 | - | - | 1 | - | | | | | | | |
| K.M.Chandler | 2 | 2 | 0 | 5 | 7 | 3.50 | - | - | 1 | - | 8 | 0 | 30 | 3 | 10.00 | 3.75 | 3-30 |
| N.E.Codyre | 4 | 3 | 0 | 11 | 17 | 5.66 | - | - | 2 | - | 23 | 1 | 94 | 2 | 47.00 | 4.09 | 1-13 |
| N.B.Cox | 4 | 4 | 0 | 49 | 60 | 15.00 | - | - | 3 | - | | | | | | | |
| E.G.Cunningham | 2 | 2 | 0 | 58 | 66 | 33.00 | - | 1 | 1 | - | 2 | 0 | 10 | 0 | - | 5.00 | - |
| S.R.H.Curtis | 8 | 6 | 1 | 77* | 234 | 46.80 | - | 3 | 3 | - | | | | | | | |
| H.O.Cuttance | 1 | 1 | 1 | 1* | 1 | - | - | - | - | - | 4 | 0 | 18 | 1 | 18.00 | 4.50 | 1-18 |
| J.Dean | 4 | 2 | 0 | 38 | 55 | 27.50 | - | - | - | - | 16 | 0 | 89 | 4 | 22.25 | 5.56 | 3-37 |
| C.M.Deerness | 1 | 1 | 1 | 1* | 1 | - | - | - | 1 | - | | | | | | | |
| N.C.Dodd | 2 | 2 | 0 | 22 | 22 | 11.00 | - | - | - | - | | | | | | | |
| D.M.Doughty | 3 | 1 | 1 | 13* | 13 | - | - | - | - | - | 17 | 0 | 91 | 3 | 30.33 | 5.35 | 2-25 |
| L.R.Down | 4 | 4 | 0 | 124 | 261 | 65.25 | 1 | 2 | 4 | - | | | | | | | |
| K.E.Ebrahim | 8 | 7 | 1 | 96* | 451 | 75.16 | - | 5 | 2 | - | 20 | 0 | 102 | 4 | 25.50 | 5.10 | 3-45 |
| A.M.Ewart | 2 | 1 | 0 | 0 | 0 | 0.00 | - | - | - | 1 | | | | | | | |
| K.L.Gaging | 2 | 2 | 0 | 3 | 5 | 2.50 | - | - | - | 1 | | | | | | | |
| O.N.Gain | 2 | 1 | 0 | 20 | 20 | 20.00 | - | - | - | - | | | | | | | |
| I.C.Gaze | 8 | 7 | 1 | 14 | 38 | 6.33 | - | - | 2 | - | | | | | | | |
| A.G.Gerken | 8 | 7 | 1 | 108 | 249 | 41.50 | 1 | 1 | 2 | - | | | | | | | |
| H.M.Graham | 1 | 1 | 1 | 16* | 16 | - | - | - | - | - | | | | | | | |
| C.L.Green | 2 | 2 | 1 | 12 | 12 | 12.00 | - | - | - | - | 12 | 0 | 63 | 2 | 31.50 | 5.25 | 1-30 |
| M.L.Green | 4 | 4 | 2 | 106 | 265 | 132.50 | 1 | 2 | 1 | - | 2 | 0 | 11 | 1 | 11.00 | 5.50 | 1-11 |
| M.J.Greig | 4 | 4 | 1 | 65 | 145 | 48.33 | - | 1 | 4 | - | 19 | 1 | 128 | 2 | 128.00 | 6.74 | 1-42 |
| C.A.Gurrey | 6 | 6 | 1 | 94* | 205 | 41.00 | - | 2 | 2 | - | | | | | | | |
| B.M.Halliday | 2 | 2 | 1 | 106* | 130 | 130.00 | 1 | - | 1 | - | 20 | 1 | 79 | 4 | 19.75 | 3.95 | 2-27 |
| M.J.Hansen | 4 | 4 | 1 | 14 | 19 | 6.33 | - | - | 3 | - | 27.1 | 1 | 122 | 6 | 20.33 | 4.49 | 3-29 |
| G.A.Harris | 1 | - | - | - | - | - | - | - | 1 | - | 2 | 0 | 19 | 0 | - | 9.50 | - |
| K.J.Havill | 4 | 2 | 0 | 16 | 26 | 13.00 | - | - | 1 | - | 13 | 0 | 70 | 2 | 35.00 | 5.38 | 2-32 |
| L.H.Heaps | 4 | - | - | - | - | - | - | - | 1 | - | 23 | 2 | 84 | 1 | 84.00 | 3.65 | 1-28 |
| A.T.Hucker | 5 | 3 | 0 | 9 | 21 | 7.00 | - | - | 1 | - | 24.4 | 0 | 142 | 4 | 35.50 | 5.76 | 2-38 |
| H.R.Huddleston | 4 | 4 | 1 | 53* | 143 | 47.66 | - | 2 | - | - | 36.3 | 2 | 168 | 2 | 84.00 | 4.60 | 1-37 |
| L.E.V.Hughes | 8 | 6 | 1 | 29* | 55 | 11.00 | - | - | 1 | 2 | | | | | | | |
| M.N.Hyde | 4 | 2 | 0 | 6 | 10 | 5.00 | - | - | 1 | - | 24 | 1 | 132 | 3 | 44.00 | 5.50 | 2-48 |
| B.G.Illing | 3 | 2 | 2 | 6* | 8 | - | - | - | 1 | - | 19 | 1 | 89 | 3 | 29.66 | 4.68 | 2-15 |
| P.M.Inglis | 8 | 5 | 1 | 68 | 88 | 22.00 | - | 1 | 3 | 2 | | | | | | | |
| E.Irwin | 2 | 1 | 0 | 4 | 4 | 4.00 | - | - | - | - | | | | | | | |
| I.R.James | 8 | 7 | 1 | 53 | 130 | 21.66 | - | 1 | - | - | | | | | | | |
| H.N.K.Jensen | 4 | 2 | 0 | 76 | 83 | 41.50 | - | 1 | 2 | - | 31.1 | 2 | 112 | 6 | 18.66 | 3.59 | 2-33 |
| X.A.R.Jetly | 5 | 3 | 1 | 7 | 13 | 6.50 | - | - | 2 | - | 35.3 | 1 | 145 | 9 | 16.11 | 4.08 | 3-19 |
| F.C.Jonas | 4 | 4 | 1 | 13* | 23 | 7.66 | - | - | - | - | 40 | 4 | 167 | 6 | 27.83 | 4.18 | 3-34 |
| L.M.Kasperek | 5 | 4 | 1 | 30* | 84 | 28.00 | - | - | - | - | 42.4 | 1 | 192 | 10 | 19.20 | 4.50 | 5-45 |
| A.N.Kelly | 8 | 7 | 0 | 41 | 105 | 15.00 | - | - | - | - | 46 | 4 | 195 | 4 | 48.75 | 4.24 | 1-13 |
| E.K.Kench | 5 | 4 | 0 | 10 | 25 | 6.25 | - | - | - | - | | | | | | | |
| A.C.Kerr | 4 | 4 | 1 | 93* | 178 | 59.33 | - | 1 | 3 | - | 40 | 3 | 156 | 14 | 11.14 | 3.90 | 5-36 |
| J.M.Kerr | 2 | 1 | 1 | 20* | 20 | - | - | - | 3 | - | 11.5 | 1 | 37 | 2 | 18.50 | 3.13 | 2-9 |
| C.R.King | 6 | 5 | 0 | 8 | 11 | 2.20 | - | - | 2 | - | 30 | 1 | 158 | 3 | 52.66 | 5.27 | 1-25 |
| K.A.Knight | 4 | 2 | 1 | 17 | 20 | 20.00 | - | - | 1 | - | 22 | 1 | 151 | 5 | 30.20 | 6.86 | 3-48 |
| A.Kumar | 3 | 3 | 2 | 5* | 11 | 11.00 | - | - | 2 | - | 22 | 1 | 123 | 4 | 30.75 | 5.59 | 2-23 |

| | M | In | NO | HS | Runs | Ave | 100s | 50s | ct | st | O | M | R | W | Ave | R/O | Best |
|---|---|---|---|---|---|---|---|---|---|---|---|---|---|---|---|---|---|
| M.B.Lamplough | 2 | 2 | 0 | 2 | 2 | 1.00 | - | - | 2 | - | 6 | 0 | 26 | 1 | 26.00 | 4.33 | 1-26 |
| M.E.Loe | 6 | 1 | 0 | 2 | 2 | 2.00 | - | - | 1 | - | 27 | 2 | 132 | 5 | 26.40 | 4.89 | 3-7 |
| P.R.Loggenberg | 2 | 2 | 0 | 11 | 18 | 9.00 | - | - | - | - | | | | | | | |
| A.C.Mace-Cochrane | 4 | 2 | 0 | 14 | 28 | 14.00 | - | - | - | - | 1 | 0 | 5 | 0 | - | 5.00 | - |
| F.L.Mackay | 3 | 3 | 0 | 25 | 49 | 16.33 | - | - | 1 | - | 24 | 1 | 98 | 3 | 32.66 | 4.08 | 2-31 |
| K.J.Martin | 5 | 5 | 5 | 111* | 245 | - | 1 | 1 | 4 | 1 | | | | | | | |
| N.Matthews | 2 | 2 | 0 | 23 | 23 | 11.50 | - | - | - | - | | | | | | | |
| J.T.McFadyen | 6 | 6 | 1 | 76* | 200 | 40.00 | - | 1 | 4 | 1 | | | | | | | |
| B.C.Molony | 1 | 1 | 0 | 0 | 0 | 0.00 | - | - | - | - | 5 | 0 | 22 | 0 | - | 4.40 | - |
| S.R.Naidu | 6 | 1 | 1 | 1* | 1 | - | - | - | 4 | - | 32 | 2 | 153 | 2 | 76.50 | 4.78 | 2-26 |
| K.F.G.Nation | 4 | 4 | 1 | 37 | 85 | 28.33 | - | - | 1 | - | | | | | | | |
| T.M.M.Newton | 6 | 5 | 0 | 29 | 70 | 14.00 | - | - | 2 | - | 4 | 0 | 40 | 0 | - | 10.00 | - |
| S.A.Oldershaw | 8 | 3 | 0 | 2 | 4 | 1.33 | - | - | 1 | - | 37.3 | 1 | 178 | 6 | 29.66 | 4.74 | 2-42 |
| A.J.Parr-Thomson | 2 | 1 | 0 | 9 | 9 | 9.00 | - | - | - | - | 6 | 0 | 30 | 0 | - | 5.00 | - |
| N.H.Patel | 10 | 7 | 4 | 71* | 236 | 78.66 | - | 1 | 2 | - | 65.1 | 5 | 321 | 18 | 17.83 | 4.93 | 6-25 |
| C.S.Pedersen | 3 | 3 | 0 | 39 | 65 | 21.66 | - | - | 2 | - | | | | | | | |
| J.O.Penfold | 1 | - | - | - | - | - | - | - | 1 | - | 2 | 0 | 23 | 0 | - | 11.50 | - |
| M.M.Penfold | 7 | 5 | 0 | 21 | 28 | 5.60 | - | - | 1 | - | 37 | 0 | 236 | 6 | 39.33 | 6.38 | 4-42 |
| K.T.Perkins | 8 | 7 | 1 | 85* | 223 | 37.16 | - | 2 | 7 | - | | | | | | | |
| G.E.Plimmer | 5 | 4 | 0 | 38 | 95 | 23.75 | - | - | 2 | - | | | | | | | |
| J.E.I.Prasad | 7 | 6 | 0 | 46 | 116 | 19.33 | - | - | - | - | 34 | 1 | 164 | 4 | 41.00 | 4.82 | 2-25 |
| M.S.Rees | 3 | 3 | 0 | 23 | 36 | 12.00 | - | - | - | - | 15 | 0 | 85 | 3 | 28.33 | 5.67 | 3-27 |
| E.A.J.Richardson | 4 | 2 | 0 | 23 | 34 | 17.00 | - | - | 2 | - | 20 | 0 | 107 | 3 | 35.66 | 5.35 | 2-46 |
| A.J.Rout | 2 | 1 | 0 | 14 | 14 | 14.00 | - | - | 2 | - | | | | | | | |
| H.M.Rowe | 4 | 4 | 0 | 61 | 82 | 20.50 | - | 1 | 2 | - | 28.1 | 2 | 122 | 2 | 61.00 | 4.33 | 2-33 |
| C.R.Sarsfield | 9 | 3 | 2 | 25* | 31 | 31.00 | - | - | 4 | - | 44 | 2 | 254 | 4 | 63.50 | 5.77 | 2-56 |
| A.E.Satterthwaite | 4 | 4 | 0 | 96 | 242 | 60.50 | - | 2 | 3 | - | 34 | 2 | 146 | 8 | 18.25 | 4.29 | 3-38 |
| J.L.Savage | 8 | 6 | 0 | 61 | 133 | 22.16 | - | 1 | 2 | - | 59.1 | 4 | 288 | 8 | 36.00 | 4.87 | 2-13 |
| S.Shahri | 6 | 5 | 0 | 53 | 139 | 27.80 | - | 1 | 1 | - | | | | | | | |
| I.G.Sharp | 4 | 2 | 0 | 28 | 40 | 20.00 | - | - | - | - | | | | | | | |
| J.A.Simmons | 8 | 5 | 2 | 8* | 22 | 7.33 | - | - | 2 | - | 53 | 4 | 281 | 5 | 56.20 | 5.30 | 2-44 |
| G.Sims | 3 | 3 | 0 | 36 | 44 | 14.66 | - | - | - | - | | | | | | | |
| K.M.Sims | 1 | 1 | 0 | 2 | 2 | 2.00 | - | - | - | - | 3 | 0 | 31 | 1 | 31.00 | 10.33 | 1-31 |
| M.P.Singh | 6 | 3 | 2 | 3 | 5 | 5.00 | - | - | - | - | 50 | 3 | 185 | 5 | 37.00 | 3.70 | 2-30 |
| L.M.M.Tahuhu | 2 | 2 | 0 | 24 | 46 | 23.00 | - | - | - | - | | | | | | | |
| M.B.Templeton | 7 | 3 | 2 | 29* | 73 | 73.00 | - | - | 1 | - | 30 | 2 | 128 | 3 | 42.66 | 4.27 | 2-22 |
| K.A.Tomlinson | 4 | 4 | 0 | 26 | 45 | 11.25 | - | - | 1 | - | | | | | | | |
| H.E.Topp | 8 | 5 | 0 | 47 | 84 | 16.80 | - | 4 | 4 | 2 | | | | | | | |
| N.A.Wakelin | 3 | 1 | 0 | 4 | 4 | 4.00 | - | - | - | - | | | | | | | |
| J.M.Watkin | 4 | 4 | 0 | 87 | 128 | 32.00 | - | 1 | 3 | - | 40 | 6 | 174 | 11 | 15.81 | 4.35 | 4-28 |
| S.R.Wilson | 4 | 2 | 0 | 17 | 32 | 16.00 | - | - | - | - | 11 | 1 | 58 | 3 | 19.33 | 5.27 | 3-42 |

## HIGHEST STRIKE RATES *(qualification 100 runs)*

| | | Runs | Balls | S/R | | | | Runs | Balls | S/R |
|---|---|---|---|---|---|---|---|---|---|---|
| J.M.Watkin | CD | 128 | 103 | 124 | | A.E.Satterthwaite | C | 242 | 261 | 92 |
| K.J.Martin | O | 245 | 206 | 118 | | N.H.Patel | ND | 236 | 261 | 90 |
| K.G.Anderson | ND | 306 | 282 | 108 | | B.G.Armstrong | A | 103 | 120 | 85 |
| M.L.Green | W | 265 | 270 | 98 | | B.M.Halliday | ND | 130 | 152 | 85 |
| S.W.Bates | O | 218 | 226 | 98 | | A.C.Kerr | W | 178 | 212 | 83 |

## MOST ECONOMICAL BOWLING *(qualification 30 overs)*

| | | O | M | R | W | Ave | R/O |
|---|---|---|---|---|---|---|---|
| E.J.Carson | O | 47 | 7 | 159 | 14 | 11.35 | 3.38 |
| H.N.K.Jensen | O | 31.1 | 2 | 112 | 6 | 18.66 | 3.59 |
| M.P.Singh | W | 50 | 3 | 185 | 5 | 37.00 | 3.70 |
| A.C.Kerr | W | 40 | 3 | 156 | 14 | 11.14 | 3.90 |
| E.J.Black | ND | 43 | 4 | 174 | 13 | 13.38 | 4.05 |
| X.A.R.Jetly | W | 35.3 | 1 | 145 | 9 | 16.11 | 4.08 |
| F.C.Jonas | A | 40 | 4 | 167 | 6 | 27.83 | 4.18 |
| A.N.Kelly | A | 46 | 4 | 195 | 4 | 48.75 | 4.24 |
| M.B.Templeton | ND | 30 | 2 | 128 | 3 | 42.66 | 4.27 |
| A.E.Satterthwaite | C | 34 | 2 | 146 | 8 | 18.25 | 4.29 |

# CAREER RECORDS

| | M | In | NO | HS | Runs | Ave | 100s | 50s | ct | st | O | M | R | W | Ave | R/O | Best |
|---|---|---|---|---|---|---|---|---|---|---|---|---|---|---|---|---|---|
| C.L.Agafili | 3 | 2 | 1 | 7* | 7 | 7.00 | - | - | - | 1 | - | | | | | | |
| K.G.Anderson | 67 | 61 | 9 | 160* | 1615 | 31.05 | 2 | 7 | 18 | - | 301.2 | 7 | 1548 | 52 | 29.76 | 5.14 | 5-30 |
| B.G.Armstrong | 54 | 30 | 7 | 63 | 303 | 13.17 | - | 2 | 11 | - | 307.5 | 25 | 1255 | 60 | 20.91 | 4.08 | 7-18 |
| S.R.Asmussen | 32 | 10 | 5 | 8 | 22 | 4.40 | - | - | 7 | - | 218.1 | 10 | 1097 | 42 | 26.11 | 5.03 | 4-9 |
| G.K.Atkinson | 39 | 21 | 2 | 58 | 279 | 14.68 | - | 1 | 9 | - | 183.5 | 5 | 889 | 33 | 26.93 | 4.84 | 4-24 |
| E.L.Baker | 15 | 6 | 3 | 4* | 9 | 3.00 | - | - | 2 | - | 49.3 | 1 | 309 | 8 | 38.62 | 6.24 | 2-19 |
| M.J.Banks | 42 | 28 | 9 | 46* | 257 | 13.52 | - | - | 12 | - | 218.2 | 13 | 1062 | 16 | 66.37 | 4.86 | 2-5 |
| J.L.Barnett | 14 | 7 | 4 | 4 | 11 | 3.66 | - | - | 1 | - | 58 | 1 | 318 | 12 | 26.50 | 5.48 | 4-31 |
| S.W.Bates | 121 | 115 | 14 | 183* | 4547 | 45.01 | 9 | 26 | 48 | - | 883.1 | 94 | 3602 | 117 | 30.78 | 4.08 | 4-20 |
| E.J.Black | 40 | 27 | 5 | 36 | 183 | 8.31 | - | - | 4 | - | 276.2 | 15 | 1313 | 50 | 26.26 | 4.75 | 5-28 |
| C.G.Blakely | 81 | 72 | 7 | 78 | 1241 | 19.09 | - | 7 | 21 | - | 21 | 0 | 126 | 2 | 63.00 | 6.00 | 1-2 |
| O.A.Boivin | 6 | 6 | 2 | 13 | 43 | 10.75 | - | - | - | - | 13 | 0 | 64 | 0 | - | 4.92 | - |
| L.F.Boucher | 23 | 15 | 2 | 36* | 149 | 11.46 | - | - | 5 | - | 97 | 5 | 491 | 16 | 30.68 | 5.06 | 3-41 |
| A.S.Browning | 1 | 1 | 0 | 18 | 18 | 18.00 | - | - | - | - | | | | | | | |
| S.J.Bultitude | 1 | 1 | 0 | 40 | 40 | 40.00 | - | - | - | - | 4 | 0 | 22 | 0 | - | 5.50 | - |
| R.M.Burns | 68 | 64 | 2 | 72* | 1451 | 23.40 | - | 8 | 30 | - | 51 | 4 | 237 | 8 | 29.62 | 4.65 | 2-33 |
| S.J.Carnachan | 42 | 26 | 9 | 23 | 166 | 9.76 | - | - | 35 | 10 | | | | | | | |
| E.J.Carson | 36 | 27 | 7 | 51* | 257 | 12.85 | - | 1 | 7 | - | 214.4 | 11 | 1084 | 36 | 30.11 | 5.05 | 5-17 |
| P.Catton | 1 | 1 | 0 | 46 | 46 | 46.00 | - | - | 1 | - | | | | | | | |
| K.M.Chandler | 8 | 6 | 1 | 5 | 9 | 1.80 | - | - | 4 | - | 44.1 | 2 | 222 | 12 | 18.50 | 5.03 | 5-41 |
| N.E.Codyre | 15 | 11 | 3 | 11 | 36 | 4.50 | - | - | 3 | - | 84.4 | 2 | 391 | 7 | 55.85 | 4.62 | 3-50 |
| N.B.Cox | 66 | 49 | 10 | 65 | 833 | 21.35 | - | 4 | 17 | - | | | | | | | |
| E.G.Cunningham | 26 | 22 | 1 | 58 | 416 | 19.80 | - | 1 | 4 | - | 5 | 0 | 32 | 0 | - | 6.40 | - |
| S.R.H.Curtis | 111 | 99 | 10 | 95* | 2468 | 27.73 | - | 19 | 31 | - | 205 | 18 | 965 | 26 | 37.11 | 4.71 | 3-19 |
| H.O.Cuttance | 1 | 1 | 1 | 1* | 1 | - | - | - | - | - | 4 | 0 | 18 | 1 | 18.00 | 4.50 | 1-18 |
| J.Dean | 8 | 5 | 1 | 38 | 66 | 16.50 | - | - | 2 | - | 34 | 1 | 159 | 7 | 22.71 | 4.68 | 3-37 |
| C.M.Deerness | 1 | 1 | 1 | 1* | 1 | - | - | - | 1 | - | | | | | | | |
| N.C.Dodd | 121 | 112 | 17 | 142 | 4265 | 44.89 | 10 | 23 | 50 | 7 | 177.5 | 7 | 792 | 22 | 36.00 | 4.45 | 2-22 |
| D.M.Doughty | 82 | 39 | 12 | 26 | 165 | 6.11 | - | - | 11 | - | 657.4 | 71 | 2575 | 105 | 24.52 | 3.92 | 5-26 |
| L.R.Down | 80 | 70 | 5 | 124 | 2127 | 32.72 | 3 | 14 | 28 | - | 126.3 | 8 | 548 | 18 | 30.44 | 4.33 | 3-38 |
| K.E.Ebrahim | 131 | 118 | 22 | 115* | 3686 | 38.39 | 5 | 27 | 47 | - | 902.4 | 100 | 3366 | 129 | 26.09 | 3.73 | 4-11 |
| A.M.Ewart | 2 | 1 | 0 | 0 | 0 | 0.00 | - | - | - | 1 | | | | | | | |
| K.L.Gaging | 6 | 6 | 0 | 16 | 48 | 8.00 | - | - | 1 | 2 | | | | | | | |
| O.N.Gain | 29 | 28 | 1 | 60 | 295 | 10.92 | - | 1 | 4 | - | | | | | | | |
| I.C.Gaze | 12 | 9 | 1 | 16 | 61 | 7.62 | - | - | 3 | - | | | | | | | |
| A.G.Gerken | 9 | 8 | 1 | 108 | 258 | 36.85 | 1 | 1 | 2 | - | | | | | | | |
| H.M.Graham | 1 | 1 | 1 | 16* | 16 | - | - | - | - | - | | | | | | | |
| C.L.Green | 22 | 10 | 6 | 16 | 45 | 11.25 | - | - | 6 | - | 114.2 | 5 | 456 | 19 | 24.00 | 3.99 | 4-20 |
| M.L.Green | 87 | 81 | 15 | 106 | 2180 | 33.03 | 2 | 13 | 32 | - | 131.5 | 3 | 577 | 29 | 19.89 | 4.38 | 5-45 |
| M.J.Greig | 61 | 41 | 5 | 65 | 431 | 11.97 | - | 1 | 25 | - | 259.4 | 6 | 1306 | 47 | 27.78 | 5.03 | 7-56 |
| C.A.Gurrey | 67 | 66 | 5 | 123 | 1931 | 31.65 | 3 | 8 | 20 | - | | | | | | | |
| B.M.Halliday | 59 | 49 | 6 | 106* | 987 | 22.95 | 2 | 3 | 22 | - | 154 | 9 | 720 | 23 | 31.30 | 4.68 | 4-33 |
| M.J.Hansen | 60 | 47 | 8 | 62 | 467 | 11.97 | - | 1 | 16 | - | 276.3 | 15 | 1234 | 43 | 28.69 | 4.46 | 4-29 |
| G.A.Harris | 5 | 2 | 0 | 17 | 20 | 10.00 | - | - | 1 | - | 8 | 0 | 55 | 0 | - | 6.88 | - |
| K.J.Havill | 5 | 3 | 0 | 16 | 27 | 9.00 | - | - | 1 | - | 21 | 3 | 93 | 4 | 23.25 | 4.43 | 2-23 |
| L.H.Heaps | 17 | 6 | 5 | 6 | 9 | 9.00 | - | - | 6 | - | 107 | 5 | 438 | 15 | 29.20 | 4.09 | 4-34 |
| A.T.Hucker | 11 | 6 | 0 | 11 | 38 | 6.33 | - | - | 1 | - | 47.4 | 3 | 246 | 5 | 49.20 | 5.16 | 2-38 |
| H.R.Huddleston | 139 | 94 | 21 | 64 | 1547 | 21.19 | - | 4 | 26 | 1 | 877.5 | 92 | 3481 | 124 | 28.07 | 3.97 | 4-22 |
| L.E.V.Hughes | 56 | 37 | 6 | 51 | 360 | 11.61 | - | 1 | 32 | 10 | | | | | | | |
| M.N.Hyde | 49 | 26 | 6 | 49 | 205 | 10.25 | - | - | 7 | - | 206.1 | 14 | 1068 | 26 | 41.07 | 5.18 | 3-21 |
| B.G.Illing | 3 | 2 | 2 | 6* | 8 | - | - | - | 1 | - | 19 | 1 | 89 | 3 | 29.66 | 4.68 | 2-15 |
| P.M.Inglis | 79 | 68 | 4 | 83* | 1059 | 16.54 | - | 5 | 41 | 13 | | | | | | | |
| E.Irwin | 2 | 1 | 0 | 4 | 4 | 4.00 | - | - | - | - | | | | | | | |
| I.R.James | 51 | 45 | 3 | 60 | 595 | 14.16 | - | 3 | 14 | - | | | | | | | |
| H.N.K.Jensen | 68 | 57 | 8 | 83 | 1173 | 23.93 | - | 8 | 16 | - | 406.1 | 36 | 1608 | 65 | 24.73 | 3.96 | 5-40 |
| X.A.R.Jetly | 25 | 18 | 5 | 30 | 149 | 11.46 | - | - | 6 | - | 173.3 | 9 | 775 | 26 | 29.80 | 4.47 | 3-19 |
| F.C.Jonas | 19 | 13 | 5 | 13* | 41 | 5.12 | - | - | 3 | - | 142.5 | 10 | 557 | 26 | 21.42 | 3.90 | 4-41 |
| L.M.Kasperek | 69 | 62 | 4 | 95* | 1638 | 28.24 | - | 11 | 24 | - | 536 | 48 | 2228 | 112 | 19.89 | 4.16 | 6-8 |
| A.N.Kelly | 84 | 54 | 8 | 110 | 838 | 18.21 | 1 | 2 | 21 | - | 587.3 | 72 | 2250 | 60 | 37.50 | 3.83 | 4-34 |
| E.K.Kench | 29 | 25 | 2 | 33 | 240 | 10.43 | - | - | 6 | - | | | | | | | |
| A.C.Kerr | 49 | 42 | 8 | 119 | 1081 | 31.79 | 1 | 6 | 20 | - | 421.5 | 23 | 1706 | 84 | 20.30 | 4.04 | 5-36 |
| J.M.Kerr | 39 | 29 | 8 | 58 | 428 | 20.38 | - | 2 | 13 | - | 254.2 | 17 | 1060 | 43 | 24.65 | 4.17 | 5-44 |
| C.R.King | 36 | 27 | 2 | 53* | 304 | 12.16 | - | 1 | 9 | - | 30 | 1 | 158 | 3 | 52.66 | 5.27 | 1-25 |
| K.A.Knight | 9 | 5 | 4 | 17 | 22 | 22.00 | - | - | 1 | - | 47 | 4 | 290 | 10 | 29.00 | 6.17 | 3-48 |
| A.Kumar | 9 | 6 | 3 | 5* | 19 | 6.33 | - | - | 5 | - | 47 | 1 | 218 | 7 | 31.14 | 4.64 | 3-28 |

| | M | In | NO | HS | Runs | Ave | 100s | 50s | ct | st | | O | M | R | W | Ave | R/O | Best |
|---|---|---|---|---|---|---|---|---|---|---|---|---|---|---|---|---|---|---|
| M.B.Lamplough | 19 | 16 | 4 | 43 | 138 | 11.50 | - | - | 11 | - | | 97.3 | 2 | 578 | 3 | 192.66 | 5.93 | 1-15 |
| M.E.Loe | 15 | 9 | 6 | 16 | 41 | 13.66 | - | - | 3 | - | | 78 | 2 | 405 | 9 | 45.00 | 5.19 | 3-7 |
| P.R.Loggenberg | 2 | 2 | 0 | 11 | 18 | 9.00 | - | - | - | - | | | | | | | | |
| A.C.Mace-Cochrane | 36 | 28 | 5 | 84 | 391 | 17.00 | - | 2 | 6 | - | | 32 | 2 | 153 | 4 | 38.25 | 4.78 | 2-18 |
| F.L.Mackay | 118 | 113 | 12 | 145 | 4837 | 47.89 | 13 | 22 | 43 | - | | 926.1 | 73 | 3242 | 157 | 20.64 | 3.50 | 5-15 |
| K.J.Martin | 169 | 161 | 20 | 118* | 4594 | 32.58 | 7 | 27 | 109 | 69 | | 1 | 0 | 7 | 1 | 7.00 | 7.00 | 1-7 |
| N.Matthews | 2 | 2 | 0 | 23 | 23 | 11.50 | - | - | - | - | | | | | | | | |
| J.T.McFadyen | 54 | 48 | 11 | 153* | 1353 | 36.56 | 2 | 6 | 45 | 21 | | | | | | | | |
| B.C.Molony | 32 | 17 | 7 | 31 | 92 | 9.20 | - | - | 1 | - | | 176.1 | 5 | 788 | 17 | 46.35 | 4.47 | 3-25 |
| S.R.Naidu | 14 | 4 | 1 | 7 | 8 | 2.66 | - | - | 7 | - | | 64 | 3 | 304 | 5 | 60.80 | 4.75 | 2-26 |
| K.F.G.Nation | 54 | 45 | 5 | 40 | 567 | 14.17 | - | - | 16 | - | | 8.4 | 0 | 71 | 0 | - | 8.19 | - |
| T.M.M.Newton | 88 | 70 | 9 | 64 | 1177 | 19.29 | - | 6 | 36 | - | | 329.3 | 14 | 1593 | 40 | 39.82 | 4.83 | 3-23 |
| S.A.Oldershaw | 30 | 20 | 5 | 36* | 106 | 7.06 | - | - | 4 | - | | 162.4 | 5 | 813 | 30 | 27.10 | 5.00 | 5-19 |
| A.J.Parr-Thomson | 2 | 1 | 0 | 9 | 9 | 9.00 | - | - | - | - | | 6 | 0 | 30 | 0 | - | 5.00 | - |
| N.H.Patel | 35 | 25 | 11 | 71* | 373 | 26.64 | - | 2 | 8 | - | | 221.1 | 15 | 954 | 36 | 26.50 | 4.31 | 6-25 |
| C.S.Pedersen | 3 | 3 | 0 | 39 | 65 | 21.66 | - | - | 2 | - | | | | | | | | |
| J.O.Penfold | 1 | - | - | - | - | - | - | - | 1 | - | | 2 | 0 | 23 | 0 | - | 11.50 | - |
| M.M.Penfold | 15 | 11 | 2 | 21 | 47 | 5.22 | - | - | 2 | - | | 69.4 | 1 | 395 | 11 | 35.90 | 5.67 | 4-42 |
| K.T.Perkins | 125 | 115 | 29 | 101* | 3088 | 35.90 | 3 | 20 | 59 | - | | 13 | 0 | 96 | 1 | 96.00 | 7.38 | 1-26 |
| G.E.Plimmer | 20 | 17 | 2 | 38 | 232 | 15.46 | - | - | 3 | - | | | | | | | | |
| J.E.I.Prasad | 26 | 18 | 0 | 52 | 277 | 15.38 | - | 1 | 5 | - | | 126 | 11 | 553 | 24 | 23.04 | 4.39 | 3-47 |
| M.S.Rees | 29 | 17 | 7 | 24* | 142 | 14.20 | - | - | 3 | - | | 147.1 | 10 | 677 | 29 | 23.34 | 4.60 | 5-14 |
| E.A.J.Richardson | 98 | 85 | 4 | 102* | 1909 | 23.56 | 1 | 11 | 32 | - | | 675.2 | 33 | 3006 | 90 | 33.40 | 4.45 | 4-21 |
| A.J.Rout | 42 | 25 | 2 | 57 | 196 | 8.52 | - | 1 | 14 | - | | 100.2 | 1 | 620 | 10 | 62.00 | 6.18 | 3-72 |
| H.M.Rowe | 81 | 63 | 14 | 62 | 1106 | 22.57 | - | 2 | 24 | - | | 556.2 | 50 | 2265 | 89 | 25.44 | 4.07 | 4-15 |
| C.R.Sarsfield | 33 | 16 | 4 | 25* | 73 | 6.08 | - | - | 14 | - | | 165 | 7 | 816 | 21 | 38.85 | 4.95 | 3-29 |
| A.E.Satterthwaite | 150 | 131 | 30 | 136 | 4741 | 46.94 | 7 | 34 | 62 | - | | 841 | 75 | 3391 | 146 | 23.22 | 4.03 | 5-27 |
| J.L.Savage | 80 | 58 | 8 | 61 | 1033 | 20.66 | - | 5 | 37 | 4 | | 255.4 | 18 | 1243 | 37 | 33.59 | 4.86 | 6-18 |
| S.Shahri | 45 | 40 | 3 | 89 | 869 | 23.48 | - | 6 | 6 | - | | | | | | | | |
| I.G.Sharp | 4 | 2 | 0 | 28 | 40 | 20.00 | - | - | - | - | | | | | | | | |
| J.A.Simmons | 44 | 19 | 8 | 12 | 53 | 4.81 | - | - | 4 | - | | 288.5 | 24 | 1329 | 38 | 34.97 | 4.60 | 3-17 |
| J.A.Simpson | 4 | 3 | 0 | 8 | 16 | 5.33 | - | - | 1 | - | | 31 | 3 | 88 | 4 | 22.00 | 2.84 | 1-12 |
| K.M.Sims | 12 | 8 | 5 | 18* | 29 | 9.66 | - | - | 2 | - | | 45 | 4 | 237 | 10 | 23.70 | 5.27 | 3-19 |
| M.P.Singh | 55 | 35 | 12 | 47* | 259 | 11.26 | - | - | 1 | - | | 404.5 | 36 | 1560 | 48 | 32.50 | 3.85 | 4-11 |
| L.M.M.Tahuhu | 74 | 42 | 16 | 56 | 526 | 20.23 | - | 2 | 27 | - | | 511.4 | 44 | 2161 | 73 | 29.60 | 4.22 | 4-17 |
| M.B.Templeton | 20 | 12 | 3 | 29* | 158 | 17.55 | - | - | 3 | - | | 102 | 7 | 399 | 16 | 24.93 | 3.91 | 3-36 |
| K.A.Tomlinson | 130 | 106 | 13 | 67 | 1937 | 20.82 | - | 8 | 36 | 3 | | 110.4 | 8 | 662 | 11 | 60.18 | 5.98 | 2-13 |
| H.E.Topp | 10 | 6 | 1 | 47 | 113 | 22.60 | - | - | 6 | 2 | | | | | | | | |
| N.A.Wakelin | 3 | 1 | 0 | 4 | 4 | 4.00 | - | - | - | - | | | | | | | | |
| J.M.Watkin | 76 | 73 | 3 | 158 | 1727 | 24.67 | 1 | 11 | 27 | - | | 590.4 | 65 | 2258 | 94 | 24.02 | 3.82 | 4-13 |
| S.R.Wilson | 12 | 10 | 3 | 23* | 108 | 15.42 | - | - | - | - | | 42.2 | 1 | 256 | 8 | 32.00 | 6.05 | 3-42 |

# TEAM RECORDS

## Highest Totals

| | | | |
|---|---|---|---|
| 339-9 | Wellington v Northern Districts | Wellington | 2015/16 |
| 339-2 | Central Districts v Otago | Palmerston North | 2018/19 |
| 332-4 | Otago v Wellington | Lincoln | 2012/13 |
| 329-5 | Wellington v Otago | Dunedin | 2019/20 |
| 325-7 | Wellington v Northern Districts | Wellington | 2013/14 |
| 322-4 | Wellington v Northern Districts | Mt Maunganui | 2012/13 |
| 322-8 | Auckland v Wellington | Wellington | 2014/15 |
| 322-5 | Auckland v Northern Districts | Hamilton | 2019/20 |
| 321-4 | Canterbury v Otago | Oamaru | 2020/21 |
| 321-8 | Wellington v Otago | Wellington | 2020/21 |

## Lowest Totals

| | | | |
|---|---|---|---|
| 41 | Otago v Wellington | Upper Hutt | 2010/11 |
| 43 | Central Districts v Auckland | Wanganui | 1999/00 |
| 46 | Northern Districts v Wellington | Wellington | 1999/00 |
| 49 | Auckland v Central Districts | New Plymouth | 2020/21 |
| 51 | Northern Districts v Otago | Dunedin | 2004/05 |

# INDIVIDUAL RECORDS

## Highest Scores

| | | | | |
|---|---|---|---|---|
| 183* | S.W. Bates | Otago v Auckland | Auckland | 2005/06 |
| 169* | A. van Deventer | Central Districts v Otago | Palmerston North | 2018/19 |
| 164* | S.W. Bates | Otago v Wellington | Lincoln | 2012/13 |
| 162* | S.F.M. Devine | Wellington v Northern Districts | Wellington | 2015/16 |
| 160* | S.W. Bates | Otago v Canterbury | Rangiora | 2012/13 |
| 160* | K.G. Anderson | Northern Districts v Canterbury | Christchurch | 2018/19 |
| 158 | J.M. Watkin | Central Districts v Wellington | Wellington | 2019/20 |
| 153* | K.L. Pulford | Central Districts v Canterbury | Christchurch | 1999/00 |
| 153* | J.T. McFadyen | Wellington v Otago | Dunedin | 2019/20 |
| 150* | M.L.Lynch | Auckland v Canterbury | Auckland | 2009/10 |
| 150* | S.W. Bates | Otago v Central Districts | Lincoln | 2014/15 |

## Most Wickets in an Innings

| | | | | |
|---|---|---|---|---|
| 9-4-18-7 | B.G. Armstrong | Auckland v Otago | Auckland | 2019/20 |
| 7.1-1-19-7 | M.F. Tunupopo | Auckland v Central Districts | Wanganui | 1999/00 |
| 9-0-56-7 | M.J. Greig | Central Districts v Canterbury | Hastings | 2015/16 |
| 10-6-8-6 | R.J. Steele | Canterbury v Auckland | Auckland | 2005/06 |
| 5.1-3-8-6 | L.M. Kasperek | Otago v Canterbury | Mosgiel | 2013/14 |
| 10-6-9-6 | A.E. Cooper | Wellington v Otago | Wellington | 2008/09 |
| 10-3-18-6 | N. Scripps | Auckland v Northern Districts | Auckland | 2003/04 |
| 7.1-1-18-6 | J.L. Savage | Canterbury v Northern Districts | Whangarei | 2020/21 |
| 9.2-2-19-6 | N. Scripps | Auckland v Wellington | Auckland | 2002/03 |
| 9-1-20-6 | D.M. Trow | Central Districts v Northern Districts | Wanganui | 2003/04 |
| 8.1-1-25-6 | N.H. Patel | Northern Districts v Auckland | Hamilton | 2021/22 |
| 9.5-1-31-6 | B.H. McNeill | Canterbury v Auckland | Auckland | 2001/02 |

# RECORD PARTNERSHIPS

## AUCKLAND

| | | | | |
|---|---|---|---|---|
| 1st | 187 R.J. Rolls & R.J. Kember | v Otago | Auckland | 2005/06 |
| 2nd | 180 L.R. Down & A.N. Kelly | v Wellington | Wellington | 2020/21 |
| 3rd | 151* R.J. Rolls & I. Cronin-Knight | v Otago | Dunedin | 2006/07 |
| | 151* A.N. Kelly & R.S.M. Lili'i | v Central Districts | Auckland | 2019/20 |
| 4th † | 198* K.T. Perkins & A.M. Peterson | v Wellington | Wellington | 2019/20 |
| 5th | 120 R.J. Rolls & K. Perkins | v Northern Districts | Auckland | 2006/07 |
| 6th | 101* V.J. Lind & H.R. Huddleston | v Central Districts | Masterton | 2009/10 |
| 7th | 90 K.A. Ramel & A. Soma | v Wellington | Auckland | 1998/99 |
| 8th | 60 H.R. Huddleston & R.S.M. Lili'i | v Northern Districts | Whangarei | 2016/17 |
| 9th † | 110 K.T. Perkins & S.J. Bultitude | v Canterbury | Auckland | 2021/22 |
| 10th | 57* K.T. Perkins & N. Scripps | v Northern Districts | Whangarei | 2008/09 |

## CANTERBURY

| | | | | |
|---|---|---|---|---|
| 1st | 181 F.L. Mackay & A.E. Satterthwaite | v Otago | Christchurch | 2015/16 |
| 2nd | 227 D.A. Hockley & N. Payne | v Wellington | Christchurch | 1999/00 |
| 3rd | 240 F.L. Mackay & K.E. Ebrahim | v Otago | Oamaru | 2020/21 |
| 4th | 167 E.M. Bermingham & H.N.K. Jensen | v Otago | Alexandra | 2016/17 |
| 5th | 127 K.E. Ebrahim & A.C. Mace-Cochrane | v Northern Districts | Hamilton | 2018/19 |
| 6th | 114* A.E. Satterthwaite & L.M.M. Tahuhu | v Northern Districts | Hamilton | 2014/15 |
| 7th † | 128 E.M. Bermingham & L.M.M. Tahuhu | v Central Districts | Rangiora | 2014/15 |
| 8th | 53 H.M. Tiffen & E.M. Bermingham | v Northern Districts | Mt Maunganui | 2007/08 |
| 9th | 44* N.B. Cox & K.F.G. Nation | v Northern Districts | Rangiora | 2013/14 |
| 10th | 53 L.M.M. Tahuhu & G.E.S. Sullivan | v Otago | Christchurch | 2015/16 |

## CENTRAL DISTRICTS

| | | | | |
|---|---|---|---|---|
| 1st | 216 J.M. Watkin & N.C. Dodd | v Wellington | Wellington | 2019/20 |
| 2nd † | 328 N.C. Dodd & A. van Deventer | v Otago | P. North | 2018/19 |
| 3rd | 143 N.M. Thessman & A.L. Mason | v Wellington | Wanganui | 2005/06 |
| 4th | 152 S.J. McGlashan & A.L. Mason | v Auckland | P. North | 2007/08 |
| 5th | 112 A.L. Mason & Z.A. McWilliams | v Wellington | New Plymouth | 2007/08 |
| 6th | 120 K.C.R. Rangi & H.M. Rowe | v Northern Districts | Whangarei | 2015/16 |
| 7th | 111 H.M. Rowe & G.K. Atkinson | v Wellington | Levin | 2020/21 |
| 8th | 70 R.H. Priest & M.A. Frey | v Northern Districts | Mt Maunganui | 2008/09 |
| 9th | 67* N.M. Thessman & K.M. Sutherland | v Otago | Dunedin | 2001/02 |
| 10th † | 66 H.M. Rowe & K.E. Baxter | v Otago | New Plymouth | 2016/17 |

## NORTHERN DISTRICTS

| | | | | |
|---|---|---|---|---|
| 1st | 188* C.A. Gurrey & S.R.H. Curtis | v Auckland | Hamilton | 2021/22 |
| 2nd | 160 B.M. Halliday & S.R.H. Curtis | v Auckland | Hamilton | 2021/22 |
| 3rd † | 308* F.C. Leydon-Davis & K.G. Anderson | v Canterbury | Hamilton | 2018/19 |
| 4th | 137 E.C. Drumm & N.J. Browne | v Canterbury | Hamilton | 2005/06 |
| 5th | 101 N.C. Dodd & F.C. Leydon-Davis | v Canterbury | Hamilton | 2014/15 |
| 6th | 138* N.J. Browne & L.E. Milliken | v Auckland | Auckland | 2005/06 |
| 7th | 122 R.F. Vincent & M.J.G. Nielsen | v Otago | Lincoln | 2011/12 |
| 8th † | 81 L.S. Mulivai & B.M. Perry | v Central Districts | New Plymouth | 2018/19 |
| 9th | 69 N.J. Browne & K.A. Tomlinson | v Wellington | Wellington | 2007/08 |
| 10th | 52 H.R. Huddleston & M.A. Taylor | v Otago | Mt Maunganui | 2007/08 |

**OTAGO**

| 1st | † 235 | S.W. Bates & K.E. Ebrahim | v Northern Districts | Dunedin | 2021/22 |
|---|---|---|---|---|---|
| 2nd | 214 | S.W. Bates & L.M. Kasperek | v Northern Districts | Alexandra | 2014/15 |
| 3rd | 168 | K.J. Martin & L.M. Kasperek | v Central Districts | Alexandra | 2013/14 |
| 4th | 143 | S.W. Bates & V.L. Abbott | v Auckland | Auckland | 2013/14 |
| 5th | † 166 | L.M. Kasperek & B.A. Langston | v Central Districts | Oamaru | 2017/18 |
| 6th | 101 | K.J. Martin & V.L. Holden | v Auckland | Lincoln | 2016/17 |
| 7th | 106 | E.J. Scurr & S.W. Bates | v Auckland | Auckland | 2003/04 |
| 8th | 80 | C.E. Taylor & K.M. Spence | v Northern Districts | Hamilton | 2005/06 |
| 9th | 56 | S.K. Helmore & A.L. Kane | v Auckland | Auckland | 2003/04 |
| 10th | 53 | S.A. Oldershaw & M.E. Loe | v Northern Districts | Hamilton | 2020/21 |

**WELLINGTON**

| 1st | 153 | L.R. Doolan & R.J.M Moffitt | v Central Districts | Hastings | 2013/14 |
|---|---|---|---|---|---|
| 2nd | 173* | L.R.V.S. Harford & M.A.M. Lewis | v Auckland | Wellington | 2003/04 |
| 3rd | 185 | R.H. Priest & S.F.M. Devine | v Canterbury | Wellington | 2014/15 |
| 4th | 141 | L.R. Doolan & S.F.M Devine | v Northern Districts | Wellington | 2009/10 |
| 5th | 144* | E.C. Perry & J.T. McFadyen | v Otago | Wellington | 2018/19 |
| 6th | † 144* | M.A.M. Lewis & M.G. Wakefield | v Auckland | Auckland | 2002/03 |
| 7th | 92 | L.M. Kasperek & M.P. Singh | v Canterbury | Wellington | 2019/20 |
| 8th | 55 | A.E. Cooper & S.F.M Devine | v Auckland | Auckland | 2006/07 |
| 9th | 97 | A.C. Stockwell & M.D. Bunkall | v Canterbury | Wellington | 2012/13 |
| 10th | 44 | A.M. Corbin & A.J. Green | v Central Districts | Lower Hutt | 2000/01 |

† *record for all teams*

# Wicketkeeping

## MOST DISMISSALS IN AN INNINGS

| | (ct/st) | | | | |
|---|---|---|---|---|---|
| 6 | (6/0) | S.J. Hill | Wellington v Northern Districts | Hamilton | 2006/07 |
| 5 | (2/3) | R.J. Rolls | Auckland v Canterbury | Christchurch | 2000/01 |
| 5 | (4/1) | R.C. Milburn | Canterbury v Auckland | Auckland | 2003/04 |
| 5 | (0/5) | K.J. Martin | Otago v Wellington | Dunedin | 2007/08 |
| 5 | (5/0) | A.C. Stockwell | Wellington v Auckland | Auckland | 2008/09 |
| 5 | (3/2) | A.C. Stockwell | Wellington v Northern Districts | Upper Hutt | 2011/12 |
| 5 | (5/0) | K.C.R. Rangi | Central Districts v Northern Districts | Hastings | 2014/15 |
| 5 | (5/0) | B.M. Bezuidenhout | Northern Districts v Central Districts | Napier | 2016/17 |
| 5 | (5/0) | S.J. Carnachan | Auckland v Otago | Auckland | 2017/18 |
| 5 | (5/0) | T.I. Lamb | Auckland v Otago | Auckland | 2019/20 |
| 5 | (4/1) | J.T. McFadyen | Wellington v Canterbury | Christchurch | 2020/21 |

# Fielding

## MOST CATCHES IN AN INNINGS

| 4 | M.M. Graham | Central Districts v Northern Districts | Wanganui | 1999/00 |
|---|---|---|---|---|
| 4 | S.J. Tsukigawa | Otago v Canterbury | Dunedin | 2003/04 |
| 4 | E.C. Drumm | Auckland v Central Districts | Auckland | 2004/05 |

| WICKETKEEPING | ct | st | Total | FIELDING | ct |
|---|---|---|---|---|---|
| K.J. Martin | 102 | 69 | 171 | A.E. Satterthwaite | 62 |
| R.J. Rolls | 86 | 48 | 134 | E.C. Perry | 56 |
| R.H. Priest | 94 | 38 | 132 | K.T. Perkins | 59 |
| R.C. Milburn | 76 | 36 | 112 | H.M. Tiffen | 49 |
| V.J. Lind | 59 | 16 | 75 | A.L. Watkins | 49 |
| J.T. McFadyen | 40 | 19 | 59 | N.J. Browne | 49 |
| A.C. Stockwell | 44 | 14 | 58 | S.W. Bates | 48 |
| S.J. Hill | 35 | 21 | 56 | K.E. Ebrahim | 47 |

# CAREER RECORDS

| BATTING | M | In | NO | HS | Runs | Ave | 100s | 50s |
|---|---|---|---|---|---|---|---|---|
| F.L. Mackay | 118 | 113 | 12 | 145 | 4837 | 47.89 | 13 | 22 |
| A.E. Satterthwaite | 150 | 131 | 30 | 136 | 4741 | 46.94 | 7 | 34 |
| K.J. Martin | 169 | 161 | 20 | 118* | 4594 | 32.58 | 7 | 27 |
| S.J. McGlashan | 146 | 137 | 21 | 125 | 4553 | 39.25 | 5 | 31 |
| S.W. Bates | 121 | 115 | 14 | 183* | 4547 | 45.01 | 9 | 26 |
| N.C. Dodd | 121 | 112 | 17 | 142 | 4265 | 44.89 | 10 | 23 |
| N.J. Browne | 133 | 123 | 22 | 115 | 3893 | 38.54 | 4 | 28 |
| K.E. Ebrahim | 123 | 111 | 21 | 115* | 3235 | 35.94 | 5 | 22 |
| R.H. Priest | 127 | 121 | 14 | 136* | 3172 | 29.64 | 4 | 14 |
| K.T. Perkins | 125 | 115 | 29 | 101* | 3088 | 35.90 | 3 | 20 |
| E.C. Drumm | 80 | 78 | 16 | 118 | 2993 | 48.27 | 5 | 17 |
| S.F.M. Devine | 104 | 85 | 17 | 162* | 2859 | 42.04 | 6 | 14 |
| H.M. Tiffen | 104 | 96 | 25 | 97 | 2692 | 37.91 | - | 15 |
| R.J. Rolls | 90 | 88 | 7 | 118 | 2591 | 31.98 | 4 | 14 |
| E.C. Perry | 136 | 110 | 25 | 114 | 2543 | 29.91 | 2 | 16 |
| V.J. Lind | 118 | 107 | 14 | 91 | 2538 | 27.29 | - | 14 |
| S.R.H. Curtis | 111 | 99 | 10 | 95* | 2468 | 27.73 | - | 19 |
| L.R. Doolan | 98 | 96 | 4 | 102* | 2396 | 26.04 | 2 | 1 |
| K.L. Pulford | 89 | 86 | 11 | 153* | 2395 | 31.93 | 3 | 15 |
| S.J. Tsukigawa | 123 | 115 | 16 | 117* | 2381 | 24.05 | 2 | 12 |
| A.L. Watkins | 105 | 97 | 14 | 116 | 2361 | 28.44 | 1 | 10 |
| M.C. Godliman | 77 | 72 | 3 | 139 | 2223 | 32.21 | 1 | 18 |
| M.L. Green | 87 | 81 | 15 | 106 | 2180 | 33.03 | 2 | 13 |
| L.R. Down | 80 | 70 | 5 | 124 | 2127 | 32.72 | 3 | 14 |
| M.G. Wakefield | 91 | 83 | 11 | 120 | 2124 | 29.50 | 1 | 13 |
| M.F. Fahey | 96 | 90 | 11 | 91 | 2050 | 25.94 | - | 16 |

| BOWLING | M | O | M | R | W | Ave | R/O | Best |
|---|---|---|---|---|---|---|---|---|
| N. Scripps | 91 | 767.3 | 111 | 2499 | 158 | 15.81 | 3.26 | 6-18 |
| F.L. Mackay | 118 | 926.1 | 73 | 3242 | 157 | 20.64 | 3.50 | 5-15 |
| A.E. Satterthwaite | 150 | 841 | 75 | 3391 | 146 | 23.22 | 4.03 | 5-27 |
| N.J. Browne | 133 | 1020 | 81 | 4246 | 144 | 29.48 | 4.16 | 5-31 |
| S.F.M. Devine | 104 | 764.1 | 92 | 2733 | 129 | 21.18 | 3.58 | 5-15 |
| K.E. Ebrahim | 131 | 902.4 | 100 | 3366 | 129 | 26.09 | 3.73 | 4-11 |
| H.R. Huddleston | 139 | 877.5 | 92 | 3481 | 124 | 28.07 | 3.97 | 4-22 |
| B.H. McNeill | 94 | 714.2 | 95 | 2541 | 122 | 20.82 | 3.56 | 6-31 |
| E.M. Campbell | 71 | 548.1 | 49 | 2018 | 120 | 16.81 | 3.68 | 5-8 |
| A.L. Watkins | 105 | 812.4 | 97 | 2840 | 119 | 23.86 | 3.49 | 5-25 |
| L.R. Doolan | 98 | 689.4 | 54 | 2752 | 119 | 23.12 | 3.99 | 5-38 |
| S.W. Bates | 121 | 883.1 | 94 | 3602 | 117 | 30.78 | 4.08 | 4-20 |
| A.E. Cooper | 104 | 587.3 | 80 | 2204 | 114 | 19.33 | 3.75 | 6-9 |
| A.K. Burrows | 109 | 805.1 | 90 | 2908 | 112 | 25.96 | 3.61 | 5-39 |
| L.M. Kasperek | 69 | 536 | 48 | 2228 | 112 | 19.89 | 4.16 | 6-8 |
| H.M. Watson | 101 | 732.5 | 130 | 2263 | 110 | 20.57 | 3.09 | 5-18 |
| P.A. Gruber | 96 | 697.3 | 66 | 2361 | 106 | 22.27 | 3.38 | 4-15 |
| D.M. Doughty | 82 | 657.4 | 71 | 2575 | 105 | 24.52 | 3.92 | 5-26 |
| S.J. Tsukigawa | 123 | 728.3 | 83 | 2809 | 104 | 27.00 | 3.86 | 5-13 |
| S.K. Burke | 97 | 737.3 | 105 | 2528 | 103 | 24.54 | 3.43 | 4-28 |
| E.M. Bermingham | 102 | 713.3 | 71 | 2755 | 101 | 27.27 | 3.86 | 4-19 |

# DREAM11
# SUPER SMASH

*2021/22*

Wellington won their fourth Twenty20 title in five seasons after going unbeaten throughout the competition. They defeated Otago, who had finished second, in a one-sided final at Hamilton. Otago had defeated Auckland in the elimination final. Otago's Suzie Bates was the leading run scorer with 504, followed by Amelia Kerr (346) and Amy Satterthwaite (313). Wellington's Leigh Kasperek was the top wicket-taker with 20, followed by Jess Kerr (18) and Amelia Kerr and Eden Carson (17). Satterthwaite (114 for Canterbury against Northern Districts) recorded the only century.

Final points were:

| | P | W | L | NR | Points |
|---|---|---|---|---|---|
| Wellington | 10 | 10 | – | – | 40 |
| Otago | 10 | 8 | 2 | – | 32 |
| Auckland | 10 | 5 | 5 | – | 20 |
| Canterbury | 10 | 4 | 6 | – | 16 |
| Central Districts | 10 | 2 | 8 | – | 8 |
| Northern Districts | 10 | 1 | 9 | – | 4 |

## CANTERBURY v WELLINGTON                     Super Smash

*at Hagley Oval, Christchurch on 26 November, 2021*
*Toss : Canterbury.  Umpires : K.D. Cotton & T.J. Parlane*
**Wellington won by 44 runs.** *Points: Wellington 4, Canterbury 0*

### WELLINGTON

| | Runs | Mins | Balls | 6s | 4s |
|---|---|---|---|---|---|
| R.M.Burns c Savage b Banks | 1 | 8 | 3 | - | - |
| G.E.Plimmer c Banks b Mackay | 34 | 27 | 25 | - | 6 |
| A.C.Kerr c Cox b Satterthwaite | 71 | 67 | 55 | - | 8 |
| M.L.Green* c & b Asmussen | 7 | 4 | 6 | - | 1 |
| L.M.Kasperek st Hughes b Mackay | 28 | 39 | 26 | - | 3 |
| T.M.M.Newton st Hughes b Mackay | 0 | 2 | 1 | - | - |
| J.T.McFadyen† not out | 1 | 4 | 5 | - | - |
| C.R.King not out | 1 | 3 | 1 | - | - |
| X.A.R.Jetly | | | | | |
| N.E.Codyre | | | | | |
| M.P.Singh | | | | | |
| Extras (w 1, nb 1) | 2 | | | | |
| **TOTAL** (20 overs) (6 wkts) | **145** | 79 | | | |

### CANTERBURY

| | Runs | Mins | Balls | 6s | 4s |
|---|---|---|---|---|---|
| N.B.Cox c King b Jetly | 7 | 7 | 9 | - | 1 |
| A.G.Gerken b Singh | 0 | 1 | 1 | - | - |
| A.E.Satterthwaite b Kerr | 15 | 20 | 13 | - | 3 |
| F.L.Mackay* not out | 41 | 68 | 45 | - | 3 |
| J.L.Savage c & b Newton | 17 | 24 | 23 | - | 2 |
| L.M.M.Tahuhu b Kerr | 0 | 4 | 2 | - | - |
| M.J.Banks b Kerr | 1 | 2 | 2 | - | - |
| L.E.V.Hughes† c Singh b Newton | 0 | 3 | 2 | - | - |
| K.M.Sims b Kerr | 4 | 4 | 5 | - | 1 |
| J.A.Simmons c & b Jetly | 6 | 8 | 9 | - | - |
| S.R.Asmussen c Plimmer b Kasperek | 1 | 5 | 3 | - | - |
| Extras (b 4, lb 1, w 4) | 9 | | | | |
| **TOTAL** (19 overs) | **101** | 76 | | | |

| Bowling | O | M | R | W |
|---|---|---|---|---|
| **CANTERBURY** | | | | |
| Banks | 3 | 0 | 24 | 1 |
| Simmons | 2 | 0 | 19 | 0 |
| Savage | 4 | 0 | 31 | 0 |
| Satterthwaite | 4 | 0 | 26 | 1 |
| Asmussen | 3 | 0 | 22 | 1 |
| Mackay | 4 | 0 | 23 | 3 |
| **WELLINGTON** | | | | |
| Singh | 3 | 0 | 22 | 1 |
| Jetly | 4 | 0 | 20 | 2 |
| Kasperek | 4 | 1 | 16 | 1 |
| Kerr | 4 | 1 | 12 | 4 |
| Codyre | 2 | 0 | 15 | 0 |
| Newton | 2 | 0 | 11 | 2 |

| Fall of Wickets | | |
|---|---|---|
| | W | C |
| 1st | 22 | 3 |
| 2nd | 53 | 7 |
| 3rd | 62 | 31 |
| 4th | 143 | 68 |
| 5th | 143 | 70 |
| 6th | 143 | 72 |
| 7th | - | 73 |
| 8th | - | 80 |
| 9th | - | 95 |
| 10th | - | 101 |

## OTAGO v CENTRAL DISTRICTS          Super Smash

*at University of Otago Oval, Dunedin on 28 November, 2021*
*Toss : Central Districts. Umpires : S.B. Haig & S.J. Kannan*
**Otago won by 8 runs.** *Points: Otago 4, Central Districts 0*

### OTAGO

| | Runs | Mins | Balls | 6s | 4s |
|---|---|---|---|---|---|
| S.W.Bates* c & b Watkin | 64 | 62 | 52 | - | 6 |
| P.M.Inglis b Watkin | 9 | 20 | 11 | - | 1 |
| K.J.Martin† run out | 29 | 34 | 33 | - | 1 |
| K.E.Ebrahim c Cunningham | | | | | |
| b Rowe | 7 | 20 | 9 | - | - |
| H.N.K.Jensen b Hansen | 13 | 11 | 10 | - | 1 |
| C.G.Blakely run out | 7 | 6 | 4 | - | 1 |
| I.R.James not out | 1 | 6 | 1 | - | - |
| E.J.Carson not out | 0 | 2 | 0 | - | - |
| E.J.Black | | | | | |
| S.A.Oldershaw | | | | | |
| M.B.Lamplough | | | | | |
| Extras (lb 1, w 3) | 4 | | | | |
| **TOTAL** (20 overs) (6 wkts) | **134** | 79 | | | |

### CENTRAL DISTRICTS

| | Runs | Mins | Balls | 6s | 4s |
|---|---|---|---|---|---|
| N.C.Dodd† run out | 9 | 29 | 19 | - | 1 |
| J.M.Watkin* c Bates b Jensen | 32 | 37 | 24 | 1 | 5 |
| E.G.Cunningham b Oldershaw | 2 | 3 | 4 | - | - |
| H.M.Rowe b Oldershaw | 0 | 3 | 2 | - | - |
| M.J.Greig c Bates b Oldershaw | 7 | 17 | 13 | - | 1 |
| K.A.Tomlinson b Jensen | 24 | 39 | 25 | - | 2 |
| G.K.Atkinson c Lamplough | | | | | |
| b Jensen | 37 | 30 | 24 | - | 6 |
| O.J.S.Bartlett c & b Jensen | 0 | 2 | 1 | - | - |
| M.J.Hansen not out | 1 | 9 | 2 | - | - |
| A.Kumar c Carson b Ebrahim | 4 | 6 | 5 | - | - |
| C.L.Green b Ebrahim | 0 | 1 | 1 | - | - |
| Extras (lb 3, w 7) | 10 | | | | |
| **TOTAL** (20 overs) | **126** | 86 | | | |

| Bowling | O | M | R | W |
|---|---|---|---|---|
| **CENTRAL DISTRICTS** | | | | |
| Rowe | 4 | 0 | 28 | 1 |
| Green | 4 | 0 | 28 | 0 |
| Watkin | 4 | 0 | 22 | 2 |
| Hansen | 2 | 0 | 12 | 1 |
| Bartlett | 2 | 0 | 14 | 0 |
| Greig | 2 | 0 | 11 | 0 |
| Kumar | 2 | 0 | 18 | 0 |
| **OTAGO** | | | | |
| Jensen | 4 | 0 | 20 | 4 |
| Black | 4 | 0 | 29 | 0 |
| Ebrahim | 4 | 0 | 26 | 2 |
| Carson | 3 | 0 | 24 | 0 |
| Oldershaw | 4 | 0 | 16 | 3 |
| Lamplough | 1 | 0 | 8 | 0 |

| Fall of Wickets | | |
|---|---|---|
| | O | CD |
| 1st | 25 | 46 |
| 2nd | 97 | 48 |
| 3rd | 107 | 48 |
| 4th | 126 | 49 |
| 5th | 126 | 61 |
| 6th | 133 | 120 |
| 7th | - | 120 |
| 8th | - | 120 |
| 9th | - | 126 |
| 10th | - | 126 |

## NORTHERN DISTRICTS v OTAGO          Super Smash

*at Seddon Park, Hamilton on 3 December, 2021*
*Toss : Northern Districts. Umpires : C.M. Brown & D.R. Morrow*
**Otago won by 61 runs.** *Points: Otago 4, Northern Districts 0*

### OTAGO

| | Runs | Mins | Balls | 6s | 4s |
|---|---|---|---|---|---|
| S.W.Bates* not out | 76 | 81 | 59 | - | 8 |
| P.M.Inglis c Patel b Hyde | 18 | 17 | 16 | - | 3 |
| K.J.Martin† run out | 7 | 12 | 8 | - | - |
| K.E.Ebrahim b Templeton | 9 | 13 | 13 | - | - |
| C.G.Blakely c Anderson b Patel | 16 | 21 | 15 | - | 2 |
| I.R.James run out | 11 | 11 | 10 | - | - |
| M.B.Lamplough not out | 3 | 5 | 2 | - | - |
| E.J.Carson | | | | | |
| E.J.Black | | | | | |
| S.A.Oldershaw | | | | | |
| M.E.Loe | | | | | |
| Extras (b 5, lb 1, w 5, nb 3) | 14 | | | | |
| **TOTAL** (20 overs) (5 wkts) | **154** | 81 | | | |

### NORTHERN DISTRICTS

| | Runs | Mins | Balls | 6s | 4s |
|---|---|---|---|---|---|
| K.G.Anderson* b Black | 7 | 10 | 11 | - | 1 |
| L.F.Boucher lbw b Oldershaw | 22 | 33 | 23 | - | 2 |
| S.R.H.Curtis c & b Carson | 5 | 13 | 10 | - | - |
| N.H.Patel b Ebrahim | 18 | 25 | 19 | - | 2 |
| M.B.Templeton c Martin b Loe | 14 | 27 | 21 | - | 1 |
| G.A.Harris c James b Black | 9 | 23 | 16 | - | - |
| N.A.Wakelin c Martin b Loe | 1 | 7 | 7 | - | - |
| H.E.Topp† not out | 8 | 12 | 8 | - | 1 |
| M.N.Hyde run out | 0 | 2 | 0 | - | - |
| C.R.Sarsfield not out | 1 | 5 | 5 | - | - |
| K.A.Knight | | | | | |
| Extras (b 1, lb 2, w 5) | 8 | | | | |
| **TOTAL** (20 overs) (8 wkts) | **93** | 80 | | | |

| Bowling | O | M | R | W |
|---|---|---|---|---|
| **NORTHERN DISTRICTS** | | | | |
| Patel | 4 | 0 | 17 | 1 |
| Knight | 1 | 0 | 7 | 0 |
| Boucher | 1 | 0 | 10 | 0 |
| Hyde | 3 | 0 | 30 | 1 |
| Anderson | 2 | 0 | 22 | 0 |
| Sarsfield | 1 | 0 | 9 | 0 |
| Templeton | 4 | 0 | 27 | 1 |
| Harris | 4 | 0 | 26 | 0 |
| **OTAGO** | | | | |
| Black | 4 | 0 | 15 | 2 |
| Loe | 4 | 0 | 21 | 2 |
| Carson | 4 | 0 | 17 | 1 |
| Oldershaw | 4 | 0 | 17 | 1 |
| Lamplough | 2 | 0 | 10 | 0 |
| Ebrahim | 2 | 0 | 10 | 1 |

| Fall of Wickets | | |
|---|---|---|
| | O | ND |
| 1st | 35 | 12 |
| 2nd | 59 | 29 |
| 3rd | 77 | 45 |
| 4th | 126 | 64 |
| 5th | 145 | 76 |
| 6th | - | 80 |
| 7th | - | 84 |
| 8th | - | 84 |
| 9th | - | - |
| 10th | - | - |

# WELLINGTON v CENTRAL DISTRICTS — Super Smash

*at Cello Basin Reserve, Wellington on 5 December, 2021*
*Toss : Wellington. Umpires : T.R. Davies & S.B. Haig*
**Wellington won by 65 runs.** Points: Wellington 4, Central Districts 0

## WELLINGTON

| | Runs | Mins | Balls | 6s | 4s |
|---|---|---|---|---|---|
| R.M.Burns c Cunningham b Green | 14 | 20 | 15 | 1 | 1 |
| G.E.Plimmer c Dodd b Mair | 0 | 6 | 4 | - | - |
| A.C.Kerr c Cunningham b Hansen | 62 | 73 | 49 | - | 7 |
| M.L.Green* c Dodd b Rowe | 0 | 7 | 6 | - | - |
| L.M.Kasperek not out | 60 | 59 | 43 | - | 10 |
| T.M.M.Newton not out | 4 | 7 | 3 | - | - |
| J.T.McFadyen† | | | | | |
| C.R.King | | | | | |
| X.A.R.Jetly | | | | | |
| N.E.Codyre | | | | | |
| M.P.Singh | | | | | |
| Extras (b 3, w 1) | 4 | | | | |
| **TOTAL** (20 overs) (4 wkts) | **144** | 85 | | | |

## CENTRAL DISTRICTS

| | Runs | Mins | Balls | 6s | 4s |
|---|---|---|---|---|---|
| N.C.Dodd† c Green b King | 24 | 45 | 34 | - | 2 |
| J.M.Watkin* c Plimmer b Singh | 2 | 10 | 7 | - | - |
| E.G.Cunningham c King b Singh | 0 | 3 | 2 | - | - |
| H.M.Rowe c Jetly b Kasperek | 2 | 11 | 9 | - | - |
| M.J.Greig st McFadyen b Singh | 3 | 7 | 5 | - | - |
| K.A.Tomlinson b King | 5 | 8 | 5 | - | 1 |
| G.K.Atkinson b Kerr | 4 | 5 | 3 | - | 1 |
| R.A.Mair not out | 16 | 34 | 21 | - | 1 |
| O.J.S.Bartlett b King | 9 | 16 | 14 | - | 1 |
| M.J.Hansen st McFadyen b Kasperek | 5 | 8 | 5 | - | - |
| C.L.Green st McFadyen b Jetly | 2 | 8 | 4 | - | - |
| Extras (b 3, lb 1, w 2, nb 1) | 7 | | | | |
| **TOTAL** (18 overs) | **79** | 75 | | | |

### Bowling

| CENTRAL DISTRICTS | O | M | R | W |
|---|---|---|---|---|
| Watkin | 4 | 0 | 18 | 0 |
| Mair | 4 | 0 | 19 | 1 |
| Green | 3 | 0 | 23 | 1 |
| Rowe | 4 | 1 | 31 | 1 |
| Hansen | 3 | 0 | 21 | 1 |
| Bartlett | 2 | 0 | 29 | 0 |
| **WELLINGTON** | | | | |
| Singh | 4 | 0 | 13 | 3 |
| Jetly | 3 | 0 | 11 | 1 |
| Kasperek | 3 | 1 | 14 | 2 |
| King | 3 | 0 | 18 | 3 |
| Kerr | 4 | 0 | 11 | 1 |
| Codyre | 1 | 0 | 8 | 0 |

### Fall of Wickets

| | W | CD |
|---|---|---|
| 1st | 6 | 7 |
| 2nd | 22 | 7 |
| 3rd | 24 | 12 |
| 4th | 123 | 17 |
| 5th | - | 31 |
| 6th | - | 36 |
| 7th | - | 43 |
| 8th | - | 60 |
| 9th | - | 70 |
| 10th | - | 79 |

# CANTERBURY v CENTRAL DISTRICTS — Super Smash

*at Hagley Oval, Christchurch on 10 December, 2021*
*Toss : Central Districts. Umpires : C.M. Brown & P.J. Pasco*
**Canterbury won by 6 wickets.** Points: Canterbury 4, Central Districts 0

## CENTRAL DISTRICTS

| | Runs | Mins | Balls | 6s | 4s |
|---|---|---|---|---|---|
| J.M.Watkin* c Mackay b Banks | 7 | 14 | 18 | - | - |
| N.C.Dodd† st Gerken b Asmussen | 52 | 56 | 40 | - | 7 |
| G.K.Atkinson b Satterthwaite | 10 | 14 | 7 | - | 2 |
| M.J.Greig c Sims b Banks | 36 | 25 | 26 | 1 | 5 |
| H.M.Rowe c Cox b Asmussen | 6 | 12 | 9 | - | - |
| K.A.Tomlinson lbw b Mackay | 2 | 4 | 3 | - | - |
| R.A.Mair b Mackay | 0 | 1 | 2 | - | - |
| E.G.Cunningham not out | 9 | 10 | 7 | - | 1 |
| C.L.Green not out | 6 | 7 | 8 | - | - |
| O.J.S.Bartlett | | | | | |
| M.J.Hansen | | | | | |
| Extras (b 1, lb 2, w 6) | 9 | | | | |
| **TOTAL** (20 overs) (7 wkts) | **137** | 74 | | | |

## CANTERBURY

| | Runs | Mins | Balls | 6s | 4s |
|---|---|---|---|---|---|
| N.B.Cox not out | 63 | 83 | 53 | - | 7 |
| A.G.Gerken† lbw b Green | 0 | 1 | 3 | - | - |
| A.E.Satterthwaite c Hansen b Green | 9 | 17 | 14 | - | 1 |
| F.L.Mackay* c Bartlett b Watkin | 14 | 29 | 22 | - | 1 |
| J.L.Savage c Rowe b Mair | 13 | 15 | 12 | - | 2 |
| L.M.M.Tahuhu not out | 39 | 19 | 16 | 3 | 2 |
| A.C.Mace-Cochrane | | | | | |
| K.M.Sims | | | | | |
| M.J.Banks | | | | | |
| J.A.Simmons | | | | | |
| S.R.Asmussen | | | | | |
| Extras (w 2, nb 1) | 3 | | | | |
| **TOTAL** (19.5 overs) (4 wkts) | **141** | 83 | | | |

### Bowling

| CANTERBURY | O | M | R | W |
|---|---|---|---|---|
| Banks | 4 | 0 | 24 | 2 |
| Simmons | 2 | 0 | 15 | 0 |
| Sims | 1 | 0 | 11 | 0 |
| Savage | 2 | 0 | 21 | 0 |
| Satterthwaite | 3 | 0 | 21 | 1 |
| Mackay | 4 | 0 | 23 | 2 |
| Asmussen | 4 | 0 | 19 | 2 |
| **CENTRAL DISTRICTS** | | | | |
| Green | 4 | 0 | 9 | 2 |
| Mair | 4 | 1 | 21 | 1 |
| Rowe | 4 | 0 | 38 | 0 |
| Hansen | 2.5 | 0 | 32 | 0 |
| Watkin | 4 | 0 | 30 | 1 |
| Greig | 1 | 0 | 11 | 0 |

### Fall of Wickets

| | CD | C |
|---|---|---|
| 1st | 20 | 1 |
| 2nd | 48 | 12 |
| 3rd | 112 | 47 |
| 4th | 112 | 82 |
| 5th | 118 | - |
| 6th | 118 | - |
| 7th | 124 | - |
| 8th | - | - |
| 9th | - | - |
| 10th | - | - |

# OTAGO v NORTHERN DISTRICTS

**Super Smash**

*at University of Otago Oval, Dunedin on 12 December, 2021*
*Toss : Otago.  Umpires : C.A. Black & D.J. Walker*
**Otago won by 4 wickets.** *Points: Otago 4, Northern Districts 0*

## NORTHERN DISTRICTS

| | Runs | Mins | Balls | 6s | 4s |
|---|---|---|---|---|---|
| K.G.Anderson* run out | 52 | 64 | 49 | - | 6 |
| L.F.Boucher c Bates b Black | 15 | 10 | 10 | - | 2 |
| S.R.H.Curtis c Lamplough b Carson | 39 | 58 | 43 | - | 2 |
| N.H.Patel not out | 11 | 14 | 9 | - | 1 |
| G.A.Harris st Martin b Oldershaw | 2 | 5 | 3 | - | - |
| M.B.Templeton not out | 7 | 7 | 6 | - | - |
| H.E.Topp† | | | | | |
| N.A.Wakelin | | | | | |
| S.R.Naidu | | | | | |
| C.R.Sarsfield | | | | | |
| E.L.Baker | | | | | |
| Extras (b 6, lb 2, w 1) | 9 | | | | |
| **TOTAL** (20 overs) (4 wkts) | **135** | 78 | | | |

## OTAGO

| | Runs | Mins | Balls | 6s | 4s |
|---|---|---|---|---|---|
| S.W.Bates* c Sarsfield b Patel | 16 | 17 | 12 | - | 3 |
| P.M.Inglis lbw b Anderson | 31 | 60 | 31 | - | 4 |
| K.J.Martin† run out | 15 | 21 | 23 | - | 1 |
| K.E.Ebrahim not out | 38 | 51 | 32 | - | 2 |
| C.G.Blakely b Patel | 20 | 21 | 16 | - | 2 |
| I.R.James run out | 0 | 4 | 2 | - | - |
| M.B.Lamplough st Topp b Patel | 1 | 4 | 2 | - | - |
| E.J.Carson not out | 1 | 3 | 1 | - | - |
| E.J.Black | | | | | |
| S.A.Oldershaw | | | | | |
| M.E.Loe | | | | | |
| Extras (w 16, nb 1) | 17 | | | | |
| **TOTAL** (19.4 overs) (6 wkts) | **139** | 88 | | | |

| Bowling | O | M | R | W |
|---|---|---|---|---|
| **OTAGO** | | | | |
| Black | 4 | 0 | 22 | 1 |
| Loe | 4 | 0 | 33 | 0 |
| Carson | 4 | 0 | 21 | 1 |
| Ebrahim | 4 | 0 | 27 | 0 |
| Oldershaw | 4 | 0 | 24 | 1 |
| **NORTHERN DISTRICTS** | | | | |
| Naidu | 4 | 1 | 24 | 0 |
| Patel | 4 | 0 | 13 | 3 |
| Templeton | 1 | 0 | 9 | 0 |
| Baker | 3 | 0 | 31 | 0 |
| Sarsfield | 2 | 0 | 18 | 0 |
| Boucher | 3.4 | 0 | 29 | 0 |
| Anderson | 2 | 0 | 15 | 1 |

**Fall of Wickets**

| | ND | O |
|---|---|---|
| 1st | 17 | 27 |
| 2nd | 115 | 45 |
| 3rd | 117 | 91 |
| 4th | 121 | 131 |
| 5th | - | 131 |
| 6th | - | 133 |
| 7th | - | - |
| 8th | - | - |
| 9th | - | - |
| 10th | - | - |

# NORTHERN DISTRICTS v AUCKLAND

**Super Smash**

*at Seddon Park, Hamilton on 17 December, 2021*
*Toss : Auckland.  Umpires : J.M. Dempsey & L.R. Els*
**Auckland won by 48 runs.** *Points: Auckland 4, Northern Districts 0*

## AUCKLAND

| | Runs | Mins | Balls | 6s | 4s |
|---|---|---|---|---|---|
| A.M.Peterson c Halliday b Heaps | 14 | 17 | 11 | 1 | 1 |
| L.R.Down* c Gurrey b Boucher | 44 | 70 | 51 | - | 2 |
| B.G.Armstrong c Templeton b Patel | 3 | 9 | 9 | - | - |
| K.T.Perkins run out | 7 | 13 | 7 | - | - |
| H.R.Huddleston c Boucher b Halliday | 54 | 44 | 34 | 3 | 4 |
| A.N.Kelly not out | 6 | 12 | 6 | - | - |
| I.C.Gaze† not out | 4 | 4 | 2 | - | 1 |
| S.E.Bowden | | | | | |
| J.E.I.Prasad | | | | | |
| M.M.Penfold | | | | | |
| F.C.Jonas | | | | | |
| Extras (lb 1, w 9) | 10 | | | | |
| **TOTAL** (20 overs) (5 wkts) | **142** | 82 | | | |

## NORTHERN DISTRICTS

| | Runs | Mins | Balls | 6s | 4s |
|---|---|---|---|---|---|
| K.G.Anderson c Penfold b Kelly | 7 | 14 | 10 | - | - |
| C.A.Gurrey c Armstrong b Kelly | 0 | 5 | 2 | - | - |
| L.F.Boucher c Armstrong b Huddleston | 4 | 24 | 11 | - | - |
| B.M.Halliday* c Down b Huddleston | 7 | 7 | 5 | - | 1 |
| S.R.H.Curtis b Penfold | 13 | 23 | 19 | - | - |
| N.H.Patel b Jonas | 32 | 48 | 38 | - | 4 |
| M.B.Templeton c Down b Kelly | 14 | 30 | 25 | - | 1 |
| S.R.Naidu not out | 3 | 10 | 7 | - | - |
| A.M.Ewart† not out | 5 | 6 | 4 | - | 1 |
| C.R.Sarsfield | | | | | |
| L.H.Heaps | | | | | |
| Extras (lb 1, w 7, nb 1) | 9 | | | | |
| **TOTAL** (20 overs) (7 wkts) | **94** | 76 | | | |

| Bowling | O | M | R | W |
|---|---|---|---|---|
| **NORTHERN DISTRICTS** | | | | |
| Naidu | 2 | 0 | 22 | 0 |
| Heaps | 3 | 0 | 16 | 1 |
| Patel | 4 | 0 | 28 | 1 |
| Halliday | 4 | 0 | 19 | 1 |
| Sarsfield | 3 | 0 | 17 | 0 |
| Templeton | 2 | 0 | 23 | 0 |
| Boucher | 2 | 0 | 16 | 1 |
| **AUCKLAND** | | | | |
| Kelly | 4 | 0 | 21 | 3 |
| Huddleston | 3 | 0 | 14 | 2 |
| Peterson | 4 | 0 | 16 | 0 |
| Penfold | 2 | 0 | 7 | 1 |
| Jonas | 4 | 0 | 13 | 1 |
| Armstrong | 1 | 0 | 13 | 0 |
| Prasad | 2 | 0 | 9 | 0 |

**Fall of Wickets**

| | A | ND |
|---|---|---|
| 1st | 33 | 1 |
| 2nd | 38 | 9 |
| 3rd | 53 | 17 |
| 4th | 117 | 24 |
| 5th | 135 | 41 |
| 6th | - | 85 |
| 7th | - | 87 |
| 8th | - | - |
| 9th | - | - |
| 10th | - | - |

# CENTRAL DISTRICTS v OTAGO

**Super Smash**

*at McLean Park, Napier on 18 December, 2021*
*Toss : Central Districts.  Umpires : B.F. Bowden & W.R. Knights*
**Otago won by 7 wickets.** *Points: Otago 4, Central Districts 0*

| CENTRAL DISTRICTS | Runs | Mins | Balls | 6s | 4s |
|---|---|---|---|---|---|
| N.C.Dodd† c Martin b Ebrahim . | 16 | 38 | 25 | - | 1 |
| J.M.Watkin* lbw b Black | 0 | 4 | 2 | - | - |
| G.K.Atkinson c Bates b Loe | 12 | 15 | 13 | - | 1 |
| M.J.Greig st Martin b Ebrahim .. | 23 | 3 | 25 | 1 | 2 |
| H.M.Rowe c Black b Oldershaw . | 2 | 6 | 4 | - | - |
| K.A.Tomlinson b Bates | 2 | 11 | 5 | - | - |
| R.A.Mair run out | 4 | 10 | 6 | - | - |
| E.G.Cunningham c James b Loe | 8 | 20 | 15 | - | - |
| O.J.S.Bartlett b Carson | 0 | 6 | 6 | - | - |
| M.J.Hansen st Martin b Ebrahim | 2 | 6 | 4 | - | - |
| C.L.Green not out | 0 | 5 | 4 | - | - |
| Extras (w 6) | 6 | | | | |
| **TOTAL** (18.1 overs) | **75** | 74 | | | |

| OTAGO | Runs | Mins | Balls | 6s | 4s |
|---|---|---|---|---|---|
| S.W.Bates* run out | 14 | 28 | 16 | - | 2 |
| P.M.Inglis st Dodd b Bartlett | 27 | 45 | 34 | - | 2 |
| K.J.Martin† c Cunningham b Watkin | 7 | 10 | 9 | - | 1 |
| K.E.Ebrahim not out | 17 | 16 | 18 | - | 2 |
| C.G.Blakely not out | 5 | 10 | 8 | - | - |
| I.R.James | | | | | |
| O.N.Gain | | | | | |
| E.J.Carson | | | | | |
| E.J.Black | | | | | |
| S.A.Oldershaw | | | | | |
| M.E.Loe | | | | | |
| Extras (lb 5, w 4) | 9 | | | | |
| **TOTAL** (14 overs) (3 wkts) ... | **79** | 53 | | | |

| Bowling OTAGO | O | M | R | W |
|---|---|---|---|---|
| Black | 4 | 0 | 27 | 1 |
| Loe | 2.1 | 0 | 7 | 2 |
| Carson | 4 | 1 | 5 | 1 |
| Oldershaw | 4 | 0 | 19 | 1 |
| Ebrahim | 3 | 0 | 13 | 3 |
| Bates | 1 | 0 | 4 | 1 |
| **CENTRAL DISTRICTS** | | | | |
| Mair | 2 | 0 | 11 | 0 |
| Green | 2 | 0 | 10 | 0 |
| Rowe | 3 | 0 | 17 | 0 |
| Watkin | 4 | 0 | 18 | 1 |
| Bartlett | 2 | 0 | 12 | 1 |
| Atkinson | 1 | 0 | 6 | 0 |

| Fall of Wickets | CD | O |
|---|---|---|
| 1st | 1 | 43 |
| 2nd | 19 | 55 |
| 3rd | 41 | 59 |
| 4th | 50 | - |
| 5th | 58 | - |
| 6th | 62 | - |
| 7th | 65 | - |
| 8th | 68 | - |
| 9th | 75 | - |
| 10th | 75 | - |

# WELLINGTON v CANTERBURY

**Super Smash**

*at Cello Basin Reserve, Wellington on 19 December, 2021*
*Toss : Wellington.  Umpires : S.B. Haig & E.D. Sanders*
**Wellington won by 45 runs.** *Points: Wellington 4, Canterbury 0*

| WELLINGTON | Runs | Mins | Balls | 6s | 4s |
|---|---|---|---|---|---|
| R.M.Burns c Simmons b Savage | 32 | 52 | 38 | 1 | 1 |
| G.E.Plimmer run out | 11 | 15 | 12 | - | - |
| A.C.Kerr c Savage b Asmussen | 50 | 53 | 41 | - | 4 |
| M.L.Green* c Satterthwaite b Mackay | 2 | 9 | 3 | - | - |
| J.M.Kerr not out | 20 | 26 | 15 | - | 2 |
| L.M.Kasperek not out | 15 | 18 | 12 | - | 1 |
| T.M.M.Newton | | | | | |
| J.T.McFadyen† | | | | | |
| X.A.R.Jetly | | | | | |
| M.P.Singh | | | | | |
| D.M.Doughty | | | | | |
| Extras (b 2, lb 3, w 6, nb 1) | 12 | | | | |
| **TOTAL** (20 overs) (4 wkts) . | **142** | 85 | | | |

| CANTERBURY | Runs | Mins | Balls | 6s | 4s |
|---|---|---|---|---|---|
| N.B.Cox st McFadyen b Singh ... | 0 | 1 | 1 | - | - |
| A.E.Satterthwaite c McFadyen b Kerr J.M. | 2 | 18 | 16 | - | - |
| F.L.Mackay* not out | 55 | 83 | 47 | - | 8 |
| J.L.Savage c McFadyen b Kerr J.M. | 0 | 9 | 8 | - | - |
| A.G.Gerken† st McFadyen b Kasperek | 4 | 12 | 9 | - | - |
| L.M.M.Tahuhu c McFadyen b Kasperek | 15 | 17 | 15 | - | 1 |
| A.C.Mace-Cochrane c Doughty b Kasperek | 0 | 3 | 1 | - | - |
| K.M.Sims b Newton | 3 | 15 | 12 | - | - |
| M.J.Banks not out | 11 | 15 | 12 | - | 1 |
| J.A.Simmons | | | | | |
| S.R.Asmussen | | | | | |
| Extras (lb 1, w 5, nb 1) | 7 | | | | |
| **TOTAL** (20 overs) (7 wkts) ... | **97** | 85 | | | |

| Bowling CANTERBURY | O | M | R | W |
|---|---|---|---|---|
| Satterthwaite | 4 | 1 | 22 | 0 |
| Banks | 3 | 0 | 19 | 0 |
| Simmons | 3 | 0 | 27 | 0 |
| Savage | 2 | 0 | 23 | 1 |
| Mackay | 4 | 0 | 23 | 1 |
| Asmussen | 4 | 0 | 23 | 1 |
| **WELLINGTON** | | | | |
| Singh | 4 | 2 | 7 | 1 |
| Kerr J.M. | 4 | 0 | 17 | 2 |
| Kasperek | 4 | 0 | 21 | 3 |
| Doughty | 3 | 0 | 19 | 0 |
| Kerr A.C. | 3 | 0 | 15 | 0 |
| Newton | 2 | 0 | 17 | 1 |

| Fall of Wickets | W | C |
|---|---|---|
| 1st | 14 | 0 |
| 2nd | 89 | 7 |
| 3rd | 99 | 13 |
| 4th | 105 | 21 |
| 5th | - | 45 |
| 6th | - | 47 |
| 7th | - | 70 |
| 8th | - | - |
| 9th | - | - |
| 10th | - | - |

# AUCKLAND v NORTHERN DISTRICTS

**Super Smash**

*at Kennards Hire Community Oval, Auckland on 20 December, 2021*
*Toss : Northern Districts.  Umpires : B.F. Bowden & W.R. Knights*
**Auckland won by 4 wickets.** *Points: Auckland 4, Northern Districts 0*

## NORTHERN DISTRICTS

| | Runs | Mins | Balls | 6s | 4s |
|---|---|---|---|---|---|
| K.G.Anderson run out | 12 | 15 | 13 | - | 1 |
| C.A.Gurrey c Kelly b Peterson | 34 | 54 | 35 | - | 4 |
| L.F.Boucher c Huddleston b Peterson | 7 | 10 | 7 | - | 1 |
| B.M.Halliday* c Peterson b Jonas | 13 | 24 | 21 | - | - |
| S.R.H.Curtis b Penfold | 3 | 4 | 4 | - | - |
| N.H.Patel c Down b Peterson | 0 | 1 | 3 | - | - |
| S.R.Naidu run out | 14 | 23 | 18 | - | - |
| M.B.Templeton c Perkins b Jonas | 8 | 15 | 13 | - | 1 |
| H.E.Topp† not out | 3 | 15 | 4 | - | - |
| C.R.Sarsfield not out | 2 | 9 | 2 | - | - |
| L.H.Heaps | | | | | |
| Extras (lb 5, w 2) | 7 | | | | |
| **TOTAL** (20 overs) (8 wkts) | **103** | 80 | | | |

## AUCKLAND

| | Runs | Mins | Balls | 6s | 4s |
|---|---|---|---|---|---|
| L.R.Down* b Naidu | 10 | 9 | 8 | - | 1 |
| A.M.Peterson b Heaps | 13 | 13 | 10 | - | 2 |
| K.T.Perkins c Boucher b Halliday | 29 | 59 | 29 | - | 2 |
| B.G.Armstrong run out | 20 | 29 | 33 | - | 1 |
| H.R.Huddleston c & b Halliday | 0 | 4 | 4 | - | - |
| A.N.Kelly c Halliday b Patel | 15 | 14 | 15 | - | 1 |
| I.C.Gaze† not out | 10 | 16 | 11 | - | 2 |
| S.E.Bowden not out | 5 | 6 | 3 | - | 1 |
| J.E.I.Prasad | | | | | |
| M.M.Penfold | | | | | |
| F.C.Jonas | | | | | |
| Extras (w 3) | 3 | | | | |
| **TOTAL** (18.5 overs) (6 wkts) | **105** | 76 | | | |

| Bowling AUCKLAND | O | M | R | W |
|---|---|---|---|---|
| Kelly | 3 | 0 | 23 | 0 |
| Huddleston | 3 | 0 | 18 | 0 |
| Peterson | 4 | 0 | 14 | 3 |
| Penfold | 4 | 0 | 16 | 1 |
| Jonas | 4 | 0 | 17 | 2 |
| Prasad | 2 | 0 | 10 | 0 |
| **NORTHERN DISTRICTS** | | | | |
| Naidu | 2 | 0 | 15 | 1 |
| Heaps | 4 | 0 | 15 | 1 |
| Patel | 4 | 0 | 20 | 1 |
| Halliday | 3 | 0 | 14 | 2 |
| Sarsfield | 4 | 0 | 20 | 0 |
| Boucher | 1.5 | 0 | 21 | 0 |

| Fall of Wickets | ND | A |
|---|---|---|
| 1st | 17 | 16 |
| 2nd | 37 | 25 |
| 3rd | 66 | 58 |
| 4th | 73 | 58 |
| 5th | 74 | 82 |
| 6th | 74 | 92 |
| 7th | 92 | - |
| 8th | 100 | - |
| 9th | - | - |
| 10th | - | - |

# NORTHERN DISTRICTS v CANTERBURY

**Super Smash**

*at Bay Oval, Mt Maunganui on 23 December, 2021*
*Toss : Canterbury.  Umpires : C. High & W.R. Knights*
**Canterbury won by 16 runs.** *Points: Canterbury 4, Northern Districts 0*

## CANTERBURY

| | Runs | Mins | Balls | 6s | 4s |
|---|---|---|---|---|---|
| A.E.Satterthwaite c Naidu b Patel | 37 | 48 | 32 | - | 5 |
| N.B.Cox c Halliday b Heaps | 11 | 16 | 10 | - | 1 |
| F.L.Mackay* b Anderson | 43 | 66 | 47 | - | 4 |
| L.M.M.Tahuhu c Topp b Halliday | 22 | 11 | 9 | 1 | 3 |
| J.L.Savage run out | 19 | 27 | 19 | - | 2 |
| A.G.Gerken run out | 4 | 7 | 3 | - | - |
| M.J.Banks not out | 1 | 2 | 1 | - | - |
| S.R.Asmussen | | | | | |
| L.E.V.Hughes† | | | | | |
| E.K.Kench | | | | | |
| J.A.Simmons | | | | | |
| Extras (lb 1, w 3, nb 1) | 5 | | | | |
| **TOTAL** (20 overs) (6 wkts) | **142** | 88 | | | |

## NORTHERN DISTRICTS

| | Runs | Mins | Balls | 6s | 4s |
|---|---|---|---|---|---|
| K.G.Anderson c Asmussen b Savage | 49 | 62 | 42 | - | 4 |
| C.A.Gurrey run out | 29 | 39 | 30 | - | 4 |
| B.M.Halliday* c Satterthwaite b Simmons | 7 | 17 | 9 | - | - |
| S.R.H.Curtis c Hughes b Savage | 3 | 15 | 8 | - | - |
| L.F.Boucher c Banks b Satterthwaite | 11 | 12 | 10 | - | 2 |
| N.H.Patel run out | 3 | 10 | 4 | - | - |
| S.R.Naidu b Banks | 3 | 6 | 5 | - | - |
| H.E.Topp† c Tahuhu b Mackay | 4 | 8 | 4 | - | - |
| C.R.Sarsfield not out | 3 | 6 | 7 | - | - |
| M.B.Templeton not out | 1 | 1 | 1 | - | - |
| L.H.Heaps | | | | | |
| Extras (lb 2, w 11) | 13 | | | | |
| **TOTAL** (20 overs) (8 wkts) | **126** | 85 | | | |

| Bowling NORTHERN DISTRICTS | O | M | R | W |
|---|---|---|---|---|
| Naidu | 4 | 0 | 15 | 0 |
| Heaps | 2 | 0 | 14 | 1 |
| Patel | 4 | 0 | 32 | 1 |
| Halliday | 4 | 0 | 29 | 1 |
| Sarsfield | 2 | 0 | 21 | 0 |
| Templeton | 1 | 0 | 9 | 0 |
| Anderson | 2 | 0 | 10 | 1 |
| Boucher | 1 | 0 | 11 | 0 |
| **CANTERBURY** | | | | |
| Simmons | 3 | 0 | 18 | 1 |
| Banks | 4 | 0 | 25 | 1 |
| Satterthwaite | 4 | 0 | 30 | 1 |
| Savage | 4 | 0 | 25 | 2 |
| Mackay | 4 | 0 | 17 | 1 |
| Asmussen | 1 | 0 | 9 | 0 |

| Fall of Wickets | C | ND |
|---|---|---|
| 1st | 22 | 63 |
| 2nd | 65 | 91 |
| 3rd | 92 | 100 |
| 4th | 136 | 103 |
| 5th | 138 | 113 |
| 6th | 142 | 116 |
| 7th | - | 118 |
| 8th | - | 123 |
| 9th | - | - |
| 10th | - | - |

# WELLINGTON v AUCKLAND

**Super Smash**

*at Cello Basin Reserve, Wellington on 24 December, 2021*
*Toss : Wellington. Umpires : T.R. Davies & J.M. Dempsey*
**Wellington won by 40 runs.** *Points: Wellington 4, Auckland 0*

## WELLINGTON

| | Runs | Mins | Balls | 6s | 4s |
|---|---|---|---|---|---|
| G.E.Plimmer run out | 23 | 26 | 24 | - | 3 |
| R.M.Burns c Huddleston b Prasad | 42 | 50 | 31 | - | 7 |
| A.C.Kerr c Peterson b Huddleston | 42 | 48 | 43 | - | 5 |
| M.L.Green* c & b Peterson | 7 | 14 | 6 | - | 1 |
| T.M.M.Newton c Shahri | | | | | |
| b Huddleston | 10 | 17 | 8 | - | 1 |
| J.M.Kerr not out | 11 | 10 | 7 | - | 2 |
| L.M.Kasperek not out | 1 | 2 | 2 | - | - |
| J.T.McFadyen† | | | | | |
| X.A.R.Jetly | | | | | |
| M.P.Singh | | | | | |
| D.M.Doughty | | | | | |
| Extras (b 2, w 4, nb 1) | 7 | | | | |
| **TOTAL** (20 overs) (5 wkts) | **143** | 84 | | | |

| Bowling | O | M | R | W |
|---|---|---|---|---|
| **AUCKLAND** | | | | |
| Kelly | 3 | 0 | 21 | 0 |
| Huddleston | 3 | 0 | 23 | 2 |
| Peterson | 4 | 0 | 33 | 1 |
| Jonas | 4 | 0 | 21 | 0 |
| Penfold | 3 | 0 | 18 | 0 |
| Prasad | 3 | 0 | 25 | 1 |
| **WELLINGTON** | | | | |
| Singh | 3 | 0 | 17 | 0 |
| Kerr J.M. | 4 | 1 | 13 | 4 |
| Kasperek | 4 | 0 | 24 | 2 |
| Kerr A.C. | 4 | 0 | 22 | 0 |
| Jetly | 3 | 0 | 13 | 1 |
| Doughty | 2 | 0 | 11 | 1 |

## AUCKLAND

| | Runs | Mins | Balls | 6s | 4s |
|---|---|---|---|---|---|
| A.M.Peterson b Kerr J.M. | 5 | 16 | 12 | - | - |
| L.R.Down* c Kasperek b Kerr J.M. | 2 | 6 | 3 | - | - |
| K.T.Perkins c Kerr A.C. b Kerr J.M. | 0 | 1 | 2 | - | - |
| B.G.Armstrong c Newton b Doughty | 31 | 44 | 46 | - | 4 |
| H.R.Huddleston c Burns b Kerr J.M. | 0 | 6 | 2 | - | - |
| A.N.Kelly c Burns b Kasperek | 25 | 42 | 24 | - | 2 |
| I.C.Gaze† st McFadyen b Jetly | 2 | 5 | 6 | - | - |
| S.Shahri not out | 16 | 20 | 14 | - | - |
| M.M.Penfold c Jetly b Kasperek | 0 | 2 | 1 | - | - |
| J.E.I.Prasad not out | 11 | 10 | 10 | - | - |
| F.C.Jonas | | | | | |
| Extras (b 3, w 8) | 11 | | | | |
| **TOTAL** (20 overs) (8 wkts) | **103** | 78 | | | |

### Fall of Wickets

| | W | A |
|---|---|---|
| 1st | 42 | 4 |
| 2nd | 83 | 4 |
| 3rd | 111 | 14 |
| 4th | 122 | 24 |
| 5th | 136 | 59 |
| 6th | - | 65 |
| 7th | - | 78 |
| 8th | - | 79 |
| 9th | - | - |
| 10th | - | - |

# CANTERBURY v OTAGO

**Super Smash**

*at Hagley Oval, Christchurch on 26 December, 2021*
*Toss : Otago. Umpires : K.D. Cotton & T.J. Parlane*
**Otago won by 12 runs.** *Points: Otago 4, Canterbury 0*

## OTAGO

| | Runs | Mins | Balls | 6s | 4s |
|---|---|---|---|---|---|
| S.W.Bates* b Banks | 47 | 65 | 48 | - | 5 |
| P.M.Inglis st Hughes b Banks | 23 | 20 | 19 | - | 4 |
| K.J.Martin† b Savage | 38 | 32 | 32 | - | 5 |
| K.E.Ebrahim c Hughes b Banks | 1 | 4 | 4 | - | - |
| C.G.Blakely run out | 5 | 11 | 8 | - | - |
| I.R.James not out | 8 | 8 | 7 | - | 1 |
| O.N.Gain not out | 7 | 5 | 2 | 1 | - |
| E.J.Carson | | | | | |
| E.J.Black | | | | | |
| S.A.Oldershaw | | | | | |
| M.E.Loe | | | | | |
| Extras (lb 2, w 5) | 7 | | | | |
| **TOTAL** (20 overs) (5 wkts) | **136** | 74 | | | |

| Bowling | O | M | R | W |
|---|---|---|---|---|
| **CANTERBURY** | | | | |
| Satterthwaite | 4 | 0 | 31 | 0 |
| Banks | 4 | 0 | 22 | 3 |
| Savage | 3 | 0 | 25 | 1 |
| Dean | 3 | 0 | 20 | 0 |
| Mackay | 4 | 0 | 16 | 0 |
| Asmussen | 2 | 0 | 20 | 0 |
| **OTAGO** | | | | |
| Black | 4 | 0 | 31 | 2 |
| Loe | 4 | 0 | 33 | 1 |
| Carson | 4 | 0 | 17 | 3 |
| Oldershaw | 4 | 0 | 20 | 1 |
| Ebrahim | 3.4 | 0 | 23 | 3 |

## CANTERBURY

| | Runs | Mins | Balls | 6s | 4s |
|---|---|---|---|---|---|
| A.E.Satterthwaite st Martin | | | | | |
| b Carson | 23 | 21 | 19 | - | 4 |
| N.B.Cox b Ebrahim | 37 | 53 | 36 | - | 4 |
| F.L.Mackay* lbw b Loe | 2 | 6 | 3 | - | - |
| J.L.Savage c Gain b Oldershaw | 5 | 10 | 9 | - | 1 |
| K.F.G.Nation lbw b Carson | 9 | 27 | 11 | - | 1 |
| A.G.Gerken c Inglis b Black | 13 | 18 | 17 | - | 1 |
| M.J.Banks b Carson | 1 | 3 | 4 | - | - |
| L.E.V.Hughes† c Black b Ebrahim | 7 | 8 | 4 | - | 1 |
| E.K.Kench c Bates b Black | 1 | 3 | 3 | - | - |
| J.Dean lbw b Ebrahim | 12 | 12 | 8 | - | 2 |
| S.R.Asmussen not out | 6 | 8 | 6 | - | - |
| Extras (w 6, nb 2) | 8 | | | | |
| **TOTAL** (19.4 overs) | **124** | 87 | | | |

### Fall of Wickets

| | O | C |
|---|---|---|
| 1st | 36 | 42 |
| 2nd | 106 | 49 |
| 3rd | 107 | 60 |
| 4th | 120 | 79 |
| 5th | 121 | 94 |
| 6th | - | 97 |
| 7th | - | 97 |
| 8th | - | 100 |
| 9th | - | 107 |
| 10th | - | 124 |

# CENTRAL DISTRICTS v AUCKLAND          **Super Smash**

*at Fitzherbert Park, Palmerston North on 27 December, 2021*
*Toss : Central Districts.  Umpires : B.F. Bowden & C.M. Brown*
**Central Districts won by 14 runs.** *Points: Central Districts 4, Auckland 0*

| CENTRAL DISTRICTS | Runs | Mins | Balls | 6s | 4s |
|---|---|---|---|---|---|
| J.M.Watkin* c Penfold b Kelly .... | 5 | 11 | 7 | - | 1 |
| N.C.Dodd† c Jonas b Prasad ... | 57 | 76 | 55 | - | 7 |
| G.K.Atkinson c Armstrong | | | | | |
| b Peterson ............................ | 32 | 42 | 34 | - | 6 |
| M.J.Greig c Huddleston b Jonas | 10 | 10 | 9 | 1 | - |
| H.M.Rowe b Huddleston ............. | 1 | 6 | 3 | - | - |
| R.A.Mair not out ........................ | 12 | 13 | 7 | - | 2 |
| E.G.Cunningham not out ........... | 3 | 7 | 5 | - | - |
| K.L.Gaging | | | | | |
| O.J.S.Bartlett | | | | | |
| M.J.Hansen | | | | | |
| C.L.Green | | | | | |
| Extras (b 4, w 3) ...................... | 7 | | | | |
| **TOTAL** (20 overs) (5 wkts) . | **127** | 84 | | | |

| AUCKLAND | Runs | Mins | Balls | 6s | 4s |
|---|---|---|---|---|---|
| A.M.Peterson c Bartlett b Watkin | 0 | 1 | 1 | - | - |
| L.R.Down* c Hansen b Green .. | 14 | 27 | 18 | - | 3 |
| B.G.Armstrong c Cunningham | | | | | |
| b Green ................................ | 16 | 36 | 28 | - | 2 |
| K.T.Perkins c Rowe b Watkin ... | 33 | 40 | 34 | - | 2 |
| H.R.Huddleston c Watkin b Rowe | 22 | 41 | 26 | - | 2 |
| A.N.Kelly c Dodd b Mair ............. | 2 | 7 | 4 | - | - |
| I.C.Gaze† not out ...................... | 10 | 9 | 5 | - | 2 |
| S.Shahri not out .......................... | 6 | 5 | 5 | - | 1 |
| J.E.I.Prasad | | | | | |
| M.M.Penfold | | | | | |
| F.C.Jonas | | | | | |
| Extras (b 1, lb 4, w 4, nb 1) .... | 10 | | | | |
| **TOTAL** (20 overs) (6 wkts) . | **113** | 85 | | | |

| Bowling AUCKLAND | O | M | R | W |
|---|---|---|---|---|
| Kelly | 4 | 0 | 18 | 1 |
| Huddleston | 4 | 0 | 26 | 1 |
| Peterson | 4 | 0 | 23 | 1 |
| Jonas | 4 | 0 | 20 | 1 |
| Penfold | 2 | 0 | 16 | 0 |
| Prasad | 2 | 0 | 20 | 1 |
| **CENTRAL DISTRICTS** | | | | |
| Watkin | 4 | 0 | 16 | 2 |
| Mair | 4 | 0 | 28 | 1 |
| Green | 4 | 0 | 13 | 2 |
| Rowe | 4 | 0 | 21 | 1 |
| Bartlett | 2 | 0 | 16 | 0 |
| Atkinson | 1 | 0 | 11 | 0 |
| Hansen | 1 | 0 | 3 | 0 |

| Fall of Wickets | CD | A |
|---|---|---|
| 1st | 10 | 0 |
| 2nd | 77 | 31 |
| 3rd | 96 | 41 |
| 4th | 108 | 89 |
| 5th | 116 | 95 |
| 6th | - | 97 |
| 7th | - | - |
| 8th | - | - |
| 9th | - | - |
| 10th | - | - |

# OTAGO v WELLINGTON          **Super Smash**

*at John Davies Oval, Queenstown on 28 December, 2021*
*Toss : Wellington.  Umpires : S.B. Haig & D.J. Walker*
**Wellington won by 66 runs.** *Points: Wellington 4, Otago 0*

| WELLINGTON | Runs | Mins | Balls | 6s | 4s |
|---|---|---|---|---|---|
| G.E.Plimmer c Bates b Loe ...... | 19 | 8 | 10 | - | 2 |
| R.M.Burns c Carson b Ebrahim | 13 | 28 | 14 | 1 | - |
| A.C.Kerr b Oldershaw ............... | 56 | 64 | 50 | - | 6 |
| M.L.Green* c Martin b Black ...... | 7 | 10 | 6 | - | - |
| L.M.Kasperek run out ............... | 24 | 37 | 26 | - | - |
| T.M.M.Newton st Martin | | | | | |
| b Ebrahim ............................. | 3 | 9 | 4 | - | - |
| J.M.Kerr st Martin b Carson ........ | 7 | 5 | 5 | - | 1 |
| J.T.McFadyen† not out .............. | 4 | 5 | 1 | - | 1 |
| X.A.R.Jetly not out ..................... | 7 | 4 | 4 | - | - |
| M.P.Singh | | | | | |
| D.M.Doughty | | | | | |
| Extras (lb 3, w 14) .................. | 17 | | | | |
| **TOTAL** (20 overs) (7 wkts) . | **157** | 88 | | | |

| OTAGO | Runs | Mins | Balls | 6s | 4s |
|---|---|---|---|---|---|
| S.W.Bates* hit wicket b Kerr A.C. | 24 | 37 | 31 | - | 1 |
| P.M.Inglis b Kerr J.M. ................. | 1 | 4 | 4 | - | - |
| K.J.Martin† c Plimmer b Singh . | 40 | 47 | 34 | - | 6 |
| K.E.Ebrahim b Jetly ................... | 0 | 4 | 4 | - | - |
| C.G.Blakely c Plimmer b Kasperek | 9 | 15 | 13 | - | - |
| I.R.James c Plimmer b Singh ..... | 0 | 2 | 1 | - | - |
| O.N.Gain c Jetly b Kerr J.M. ....... | 7 | 7 | 8 | - | - |
| E.J.Carson b Kerr A.C. .............. | 0 | 12 | 3 | - | - |
| E.J.Black lbw b Jetly ................... | 0 | 2 | 1 | - | - |
| S.A.Oldershaw c Plimmer | | | | | |
| b Kasperek ........................... | 4 | 7 | 8 | - | - |
| M.E.Loe not out ........................ | 0 | 2 | 2 | - | - |
| Extras (b 2, w 4) ...................... | 6 | | | | |
| **TOTAL** (18.1 overs) ............... | **91** | 71 | | | |

| Bowling OTAGO | O | M | R | W |
|---|---|---|---|---|
| Black | 4 | 0 | 30 | 1 |
| Loe | 3 | 0 | 38 | 1 |
| Carson | 4 | 0 | 27 | 1 |
| Ebrahim | 4 | 0 | 34 | 2 |
| Oldershaw | 4 | 0 | 19 | 1 |
| Blakely | 1 | 0 | 6 | 0 |
| **WELLINGTON** | | | | |
| Singh | 4 | 0 | 22 | 2 |
| Kerr J.M. | 3 | 1 | 16 | 2 |
| Kasperek | 3.1 | 0 | 16 | 2 |
| Kerr A.C. | 4 | 0 | 17 | 2 |
| Jetly | 4 | 0 | 18 | 2 |

| Fall of Wickets | W | O |
|---|---|---|
| 1st | 23 | 2 |
| 2nd | 56 | 57 |
| 3rd | 70 | 60 |
| 4th | 135 | 76 |
| 5th | 137 | 77 |
| 6th | 146 | 80 |
| 7th | 146 | 85 |
| 8th | - | 86 |
| 9th | - | 91 |
| 10th | - | 91 |

# OTAGO v AUCKLAND

**Super Smash**

*at John Davies Oval, Queenstown on 29 December, 2021*
*Toss : Otago. Umpires : S.B. Haig & P.J. Pasco*
**Otago won by 45 runs.** *Points: Otago 4, Auckland 0*

## OTAGO

| | Runs | Mins | Balls | 6s | 4s |
|---|---|---|---|---|---|
| S.W.Bates* not out | 89 | 85 | 61 | - | 10 |
| P.M.Inglis† c Down b Jonas | 15 | 25 | 23 | - | 1 |
| K.J.Martin run out | 40 | 51 | 35 | - | 5 |
| K.E.Ebrahim not out | 1 | 8 | 1 | - | - |
| C.G.Blakely | | | | | |
| I.R.James | | | | | |
| O.N.Gain | | | | | |
| E.J.Carson | | | | | |
| E.J.Black | | | | | |
| S.A.Oldershaw | | | | | |
| M.E.Loe | | | | | |
| Extras (b 2, lb 1, w 5) | 8 | | | | |
| **TOTAL** (20 overs) (2 wkts) | **153** | 85 | | | |

## AUCKLAND

| | Runs | Mins | Balls | 6s | 4s |
|---|---|---|---|---|---|
| S.Shahri c Bates b Loe | 8 | 11 | 6 | - | 1 |
| L.R.Down* c Carson b Loe | 0 | 2 | 1 | - | - |
| K.T.Perkins b Black | 29 | 45 | 32 | - | 1 |
| B.G.Armstrong retired hurt | 20 | 28 | 26 | - | 1 |
| H.R.Huddleston b Blakely | 12 | 34 | 22 | - | - |
| A.N.Kelly c Bates b Black | 0 | 1 | 1 | - | - |
| I.C.Gaze† b Carson | 12 | 16 | 12 | - | 2 |
| J.E.I.Prasad b Carson | 12 | 15 | 10 | - | 1 |
| M.M.Penfold c Blakely b Carson | 11 | 9 | 6 | - | 2 |
| A.T.Hucker b Carson | 0 | 1 | 1 | - | - |
| F.C.Jonas not out | 1 | 2 | 3 | - | - |
| Extras (b 2, lb 1) | 3 | | | | |
| **TOTAL** (20 overs) | **108** | 83 | | | |

| Bowling | O | M | R | W |
|---|---|---|---|---|
| **AUCKLAND** | | | | |
| Kelly | 4 | 0 | 27 | 0 |
| Huddleston | 4 | 1 | 27 | 0 |
| Penfold | 2 | 0 | 25 | 0 |
| Jonas | 4 | 0 | 21 | 1 |
| Hucker | 3 | 0 | 23 | 0 |
| Prasad | 3 | 0 | 27 | 0 |
| **OTAGO** | | | | |
| Loe | 4 | 0 | 17 | 2 |
| Black | 4 | 1 | 25 | 2 |
| Ebrahim | 3 | 0 | 24 | 0 |
| Oldershaw | 4 | 0 | 19 | 0 |
| Carson | 4 | 0 | 12 | 4 |
| Blakely | 1 | 0 | 8 | 1 |

| Fall of Wickets | O | A |
|---|---|---|
| 1st | 34 | 1 |
| 2nd | 127 | 12 |
| 3rd | - | 58 |
| 4th | - | 58 |
| 5th | - | 77 |
| 6th | - | 92 |
| 7th | - | 107 |
| 8th | - | 107 |
| 9th | - | 108 |
| 10th | - | - |

*Armstrong retired hurt at 54-2*

# CENTRAL DISTRICTS v NORTHERN DISTRICTS  Super Smash

*at Pukekura Park, New Plymouth on 30 December, 2021*
*Toss : Northern Districts. Umpires : B.F. Bowden & G.M. Walklin*
**Northern Districts won by 3 runs.** *Points: Northern Districts 4, Central Districts 0*

## NORTHERN DISTRICTS

| | Runs | Mins | Balls | 6s | 4s |
|---|---|---|---|---|---|
| K.G.Anderson b Green | 1 | 7 | 5 | - | - |
| C.A.Gurrey lbw b Rees | 44 | 35 | 32 | - | 8 |
| B.M.Halliday* c Mair b Rees | 19 | 32 | 15 | - | 2 |
| S.R.H.Curtis c Dodd b Mair | 17 | 31 | 22 | - | - |
| N.H.Patel c Dodd b Rees | 0 | 1 | 1 | - | - |
| L.F.Boucher c Rowe b Watkin | 7 | 17 | 13 | - | - |
| S.R.Naidu c Dodd b Rowe | 9 | 12 | 12 | - | 1 |
| H.E.Topp† not out | 14 | 16 | 11 | - | 2 |
| C.R.Sarsfield b Mair | 1 | 3 | 3 | - | - |
| L.H.Heaps not out | 3 | 6 | 6 | - | - |
| K.A.Knight | | | | | |
| Extras (lb 1, w 7) | 8 | | | | |
| **TOTAL** (20 overs) (8 wkts) | **123** | 82 | | | |

## CENTRAL DISTRICTS

| | Runs | Mins | Balls | 6s | 4s |
|---|---|---|---|---|---|
| N.C.Dodd† c Patel b Halliday | 13 | 35 | 22 | - | 1 |
| E.G.Cunningham lbw b Naidu | 6 | 10 | 10 | - | 1 |
| G.K.Atkinson c Gurrey b Naidu | 0 | 1 | 1 | - | - |
| J.M.Watkin* run out | 21 | 19 | 14 | 1 | 3 |
| M.J.Greig st Topp b Sarsfield | 24 | 32 | 25 | - | 4 |
| R.A.Mair run out | 26 | 43 | 32 | - | 2 |
| H.M.Rowe b Halliday | 11 | 15 | 11 | 1 | - |
| M.S.Rees run out | 3 | 7 | 3 | - | - |
| A.Kumar run out | 0 | 2 | 0 | - | - |
| M.J.Hansen not out | 0 | 5 | 0 | - | - |
| C.L.Green not out | 1 | 1 | 3 | - | - |
| Extras (b 2, lb 3, w 9, nb 1) | 15 | | | | |
| **TOTAL** (20 overs) (9 wkts) | **120** | 88 | | | |

| Bowling | O | M | R | W |
|---|---|---|---|---|
| **CENTRAL DISTRICTS** | | | | |
| Mair | 4 | 0 | 25 | 2 |
| Green | 3 | 0 | 34 | 1 |
| Rowe | 4 | 0 | 16 | 1 |
| Watkin | 4 | 0 | 24 | 1 |
| Rees | 3 | 0 | 12 | 3 |
| Hansen | 1 | 0 | 6 | 0 |
| Atkinson | 1 | 0 | 5 | 0 |
| **NORTHERN DISTRICTS** | | | | |
| Naidu | 4 | 0 | 14 | 2 |
| Heaps | 2 | 0 | 11 | 0 |
| Patel | 3 | 0 | 21 | 0 |
| Knight | 3 | 0 | 19 | 0 |
| Halliday | 4 | 0 | 20 | 2 |
| Sarsfield | 4 | 0 | 30 | 1 |

| Fall of Wickets | ND | CD |
|---|---|---|
| 1st | 5 | 13 |
| 2nd | 68 | 13 |
| 3rd | 75 | 44 |
| 4th | 75 | 47 |
| 5th | 94 | 93 |
| 6th | 102 | 116 |
| 7th | 111 | 116 |
| 8th | 113 | 116 |
| 9th | - | 119 |
| 10th | - | - |

## CENTRAL DISTRICTS v CANTERBURY　　　Super Smash

*at Pukekura Park, New Plymouth on 31 December, 2021*
*Toss : Canterbury.　Umpires : J.A.K. Bromley & E.D. Sanders*
**Canterbury won by 5 wickets.** *Points: Canterbury 4, Central Districts 0*

### CENTRAL DISTRICTS

| | Runs | Mins | Balls | 6s | 4s |
|---|---|---|---|---|---|
| N.C.Dodd† c Mackay b Satterthwaite | 0 | 1 | 1 | - | - |
| K.L.Gaging b Banks | 2 | 16 | 9 | - | - |
| G.K.Atkinson b Banks | 6 | 18 | 16 | - | - |
| J.M.Watkin* c Hughes b Tahuhu | 15 | 15 | 11 | - | 3 |
| M.J.Greig c Satterthwaite | | | | | |
| b Asmussen | 29 | 49 | 36 | - | 3 |
| R.A.Mair c Banks b Savage | 4 | 5 | 3 | - | 1 |
| H.M.Rowe not out | 39 | 44 | 38 | - | 1 |
| M.S.Rees st Hughes b Mackay | 6 | 11 | 7 | - | - |
| M.J.Hansen not out | 1 | 1 | 1 | - | - |
| O.J.S.Bartlett | | | | | |
| C.L.Green | | | | | |
| Extras (lb 1, w 7, nb 2) | 10 | | | | |
| **TOTAL** (20 overs) (7 wkts) | **112** | 82 | | | |

### CANTERBURY

| | Runs | Mins | Balls | 6s | 4s |
|---|---|---|---|---|---|
| A.E.Satterthwaite c Hansen | | | | | |
| b Rees | 13 | 36 | 28 | - | - |
| N.B.Cox c Rowe b Watkin | 2 | 3 | 3 | - | - |
| F.L.Mackay* lbw b Mair | 5 | 14 | 12 | - | - |
| J.L.Savage c Rowe b Hansen | 28 | 49 | 34 | - | 1 |
| K.F.G.Nation c Greig b Rowe | 19 | 21 | 17 | 1 | - |
| L.M.M.Tahuhu not out | 29 | 19 | 10 | 2 | 3 |
| L.E.V.Hughes† not out | 9 | 9 | 7 | - | 2 |
| A.G.Gerken | | | | | |
| M.J.Banks | | | | | |
| J.A.Simmons | | | | | |
| S.R.Asmussen | | | | | |
| Extras (b 3, w 6) | 9 | | | | |
| **TOTAL** (18.3 overs) (5 wkts) | **114** | 76 | | | |

**Bowling**

| AUCKLAND | O | M | R | W |
|---|---|---|---|---|
| Satterthwaite | 4 | 0 | 20 | 1 |
| Simmons | 2 | 0 | 4 | 0 |
| Banks | 3 | 0 | 25 | 2 |
| Tahuhu | 2 | 0 | 14 | 1 |
| Savage | 3 | 0 | 14 | 1 |
| Mackay | 3 | 0 | 19 | 1 |
| Asmussen | 3 | 0 | 15 | 1 |
| **CENTRAL DISTRICTS** | | | | |
| Watkin | 4 | 0 | 21 | 1 |
| Green | 4 | 0 | 14 | 0 |
| Mair | 3.3 | 0 | 19 | 1 |
| Rowe | 3 | 0 | 18 | 1 |
| Rees | 3 | 0 | 17 | 1 |
| Hansen | 1 | 0 | 22 | 1 |

**Fall of Wickets**

| | CD | C |
|---|---|---|
| 1st | 0 | 5 |
| 2nd | 12 | 16 |
| 3rd | 14 | 31 |
| 4th | 34 | 65 |
| 5th | 39 | 77 |
| 6th | 93 | - |
| 7th | 111 | - |
| 8th | - | - |
| 9th | - | - |
| 10th | - | - |

## WELLINGTON v OTAGO　　　Super Smash

*at Cello Basin Reserve, Wellington on 6 January, 2022*
*Toss : Wellington.　Umpires : D.J. Walker & G.M. Walklin*
**Wellington won by 33 runs.** *Points: Wellington 4, Otago 0*

### WELLINGTON

| | Runs | Mins | Balls | 6s | 4s |
|---|---|---|---|---|---|
| G.E.Plimmer c Blakely b Loe | 7 | 4 | 4 | - | 1 |
| R.M.Burns c Bates b Ebrahim | 30 | 19 | 15 | 1 | 3 |
| A.C.Kerr c Bates b Ebrahim | 10 | 13 | 6 | - | 1 |
| M.L.Green* c Bates | | | | | |
| b Oldershaw | 30 | 32 | 19 | - | 4 |
| J.M.Kerr b Carson | 9 | 10 | 10 | - | - |
| T.M.M.Newton c Bates b Loe | 11 | 12 | 11 | - | - |
| L.M.Kasperek b Black | 1 | 5 | 2 | - | - |
| J.T.McFadyen† c James b Black | 0 | 1 | 1 | - | - |
| C.R.King not out | 5 | 3 | 4 | - | - |
| X.A.R.Jetly not out | 1 | 2 | 1 | - | - |
| M.P.Singh | | | | | |
| Extras (b 1, w 2, nb 1) | 4 | | | | |
| **TOTAL** (12 overs) (8 wkts) | **108** | 52 | | | |

### OTAGO

| | Runs | Mins | Balls | 6s | 4s |
|---|---|---|---|---|---|
| S.W.Bates* st McFadyen b Singh | 1 | 2 | 3 | - | - |
| P.M.Inglis c Kerr A.C. b Kasperek | 9 | 19 | 13 | - | 1 |
| K.J.Martin† c King b Jetly | 19 | 24 | 18 | - | 3 |
| K.E.Ebrahim hit wicket | | | | | |
| b Kerr A.C. | 29 | 33 | 21 | 1 | 2 |
| C.G.Blakely run out | 3 | 5 | 4 | - | - |
| I.R.James b Kerr A.C. | 0 | 1 | 1 | - | - |
| O.N.Gain run out | 0 | 2 | 0 | - | - |
| E.J.Carson b Jetly | 3 | 5 | 4 | - | - |
| E.J.Black run out | 1 | 2 | 2 | - | - |
| S.A.Oldershaw c King b Kerr J.M. | 1 | 3 | 2 | - | - |
| M.E.Loe not out | 3 | 5 | 4 | - | - |
| Extras (lb 1, w 5) | 6 | | | | |
| **TOTAL** (12 overs) | **75** | 53 | | | |

**Bowling**

| OTAGO | O | M | R | W |
|---|---|---|---|---|
| Carson | 3 | 0 | 23 | 1 |
| Loe | 2 | 0 | 19 | 2 |
| Black | 2 | 0 | 30 | 2 |
| Ebrahim | 2 | 0 | 15 | 2 |
| Oldershaw | 3 | 0 | 20 | 1 |
| **WELLINGTON** | | | | |
| Singh | 2 | 0 | 10 | 1 |
| Kerr J.M. | 3 | 0 | 20 | 1 |
| Kasperek | 2 | 0 | 15 | 1 |
| Kerr A.C. | 3 | 0 | 20 | 2 |
| Jetly | 2 | 0 | 9 | 2 |

**Fall of Wickets**

| | W | O |
|---|---|---|
| 1st | 11 | 5 |
| 2nd | 49 | 26 |
| 3rd | 49 | 37 |
| 4th | 69 | 44 |
| 5th | 90 | 44 |
| 6th | 102 | 44 |
| 7th | 102 | 56 |
| 8th | 103 | 58 |
| 9th | - | 64 |
| 10th | - | 75 |

# AUCKLAND v CANTERBURY                    Super Smash

*at Kennards Hire Community Oval, Auckland on 7 January, 2022*
*Toss : Auckland.  Umpires : J.M. Dempsey & A. Stanley*
**Auckland won by 1 run.** *Points: Auckland 4, Canterbury 0*

## AUCKLAND

| | Runs | Mins | Balls | 6s | 4s |
|---|---|---|---|---|---|
| L.R.Down* not out | 66 | 80 | 58 | - | 6 |
| I.C.Gaze† b Tahuhu | 6 | 19 | 10 | - | - |
| B.G.Armstrong b Tahuhu | 0 | 2 | 2 | - | - |
| K.T.Perkins b Mackay | 1 | 9 | 7 | - | - |
| H.R.Huddleston c Banks | | | | | |
| b Satterthwaite | 42 | 42 | 40 | - | 4 |
| A.N.Kelly not out | 7 | 6 | 4 | - | 1 |
| J.E.I.Prasad | | | | | |
| J.O.Penfold | | | | | |
| F.C.Jonas | | | | | |
| A.T.Hucker | | | | | |
| M.M.Penfold | | | | | |
| Extras (lb 2, w 10, nb 1) | 13 | | | | |
| **TOTAL** (20 overs) (4 wkts) . | **135** | 80 | | | |

## CANTERBURY

| | Runs | Mins | Balls | 6s | 4s |
|---|---|---|---|---|---|
| A.E.Satterthwaite c Gaze | | | | | |
| b Huddleston | 71 | 91 | 59 | - | 6 |
| N.B.Cox b Kelly | 0 | 3 | 4 | - | - |
| F.L.Mackay* c Penfold J.O. | | | | | |
| b Penfold M.M. | 34 | 56 | 41 | - | 3 |
| L.M.M.Tahuhu c Penfold J.O. | | | | | |
| b Penfold M.M. | 11 | 9 | 6 | 1 | - |
| J.L.Savage run out | 4 | 15 | 7 | - | - |
| K.F.G.Nation not out | 5 | 7 | 3 | - | - |
| A.G.Gerken | | | | | |
| J.Dean | | | | | |
| M.J.Banks | | | | | |
| L.E.V.Hughes† | | | | | |
| S.R.Asmussen | | | | | |
| Extras (lb 2, w 6, nb 1) | 9 | | | | |
| **TOTAL** (20 overs) (5 wkts) . | **134** | 91 | | | |

| Bowling | O | M | R | W |
|---|---|---|---|---|
| **CANTERBURY** | | | | |
| Satterthwaite | 4 | 0 | 35 | 1 |
| Tahuhu | 4 | 0 | 13 | 2 |
| Banks | 2 | 0 | 16 | 0 |
| Mackay | 4 | 0 | 21 | 1 |
| Asmussen | 3 | 0 | 21 | 0 |
| Savage | 2 | 0 | 15 | 0 |
| Dean | 1 | 0 | 12 | 0 |
| **AUCKLAND** | | | | |
| Kelly | 4 | 0 | 17 | 1 |
| Huddleston | 4 | 0 | 26 | 1 |
| Jonas | 4 | 0 | 28 | 0 |
| Penfold M.M. | 4 | 0 | 29 | 2 |
| Hucker | 4 | 0 | 32 | 0 |

| Fall of Wickets | A | C |
|---|---|---|
| 1st | 28 | 1 |
| 2nd | 28 | 82 |
| 3rd | 40 | 100 |
| 4th | 115 | 121 |
| 5th | - | 134 |
| 6th | - | - |
| 7th | - | - |
| 8th | - | - |
| 9th | - | - |
| 10th | - | - |

# CENTRAL DISTRICTS v WELLINGTON         Super Smash

*at Pukekura Park, New Plymouth on 8 January, 2022*
*Toss : Central Districts.  Umpires : B.F. Bowden & T.S. Shirriffs*
**Wellington won by 5 wickets.** *Points: Wellington 4, Central Districts 0*

## CENTRAL DISTRICTS

| | Runs | Mins | Balls | 6s | 4s |
|---|---|---|---|---|---|
| G.Sims† b Kerr J.M. | 2 | 7 | 8 | - | 2 |
| C.S.Pedersen c McFadyen | | | | | |
| b Kerr J.M. | 3 | 10 | 7 | - | - |
| G.K.Atkinson b Kerr J.M. | 2 | 10 | 12 | - | - |
| J.M.Watkin* c Jetly b Kerr J.M. | 70 | 53 | 45 | 6 | 5 |
| M.J.Greig c Green b Jetly | 7 | 26 | 20 | - | - |
| R.A.Mair c & b Kasperek | 1 | 3 | 2 | - | - |
| H.M.Rowe not out | 28 | 27 | 20 | 1 | 2 |
| E.G.Cunningham not out | 5 | 11 | 7 | - | - |
| M.J.Hansen | | | | | |
| C.L.Green | | | | | |
| M.S.Rees | | | | | |
| Extras (lb 1, w 3, nb 1) | 5 | | | | |
| **TOTAL** (20 overs) (6 wkts) . | **123** | 75 | | | |

## WELLINGTON

| | Runs | Mins | Balls | 6s | 4s |
|---|---|---|---|---|---|
| R.M.Burns c Greig b Mair | 7 | 4 | 7 | - | 1 |
| G.E.Plimmer c Hansen b Mair | 1 | 15 | 6 | - | - |
| A.C.Kerr c Sims b Rees | 26 | 36 | 28 | - | 2 |
| M.L.Green* st Sims b Atkinson | 28 | 41 | 27 | - | 3 |
| L.M.Kasperek c & b Watkin | 1 | 6 | 3 | - | - |
| T.M.M.Newton not out | 23 | 34 | 29 | - | 2 |
| J.M.Kerr not out | 25 | 24 | 15 | - | 4 |
| J.T.McFadyen† | | | | | |
| C.R.King | | | | | |
| X.A.R.Jetly | | | | | |
| M.P.Sing | | | | | |
| Extras (lb 2, w 14) | 16 | | | | |
| **TOTAL** (19.1 overs) (5 wkts) | **127** | 81 | | | |

| Bowling | O | M | R | W |
|---|---|---|---|---|
| **WELLINGTON** | | | | |
| Kerr J.M. | 4 | 1 | 18 | 4 |
| Singh | 4 | 0 | 13 | 0 |
| Kasperek | 4 | 0 | 28 | 1 |
| Kerr A.C. | 4 | 0 | 32 | 0 |
| Jetly | 4 | 0 | 31 | 1 |
| **CENTRAL DISTRICTS** | | | | |
| Green | 4 | 0 | 33 | 0 |
| Mair | 4 | 1 | 16 | 2 |
| Rowe | 4 | 0 | 31 | 0 |
| Watkin | 4 | 0 | 23 | 1 |
| Rees | 1 | 0 | 9 | 1 |
| Atkinson | 2 | 0 | 9 | 1 |
| Hansen | 0.1 | 0 | 4 | 0 |

| Fall of Wickets | CD | W |
|---|---|---|
| 1st | 7 | 9 |
| 2nd | 9 | 20 |
| 3rd | 10 | 59 |
| 4th | 50 | 64 |
| 5th | 62 | 82 |
| 6th | 98 | - |
| 7th | - | - |
| 8th | - | - |
| 9th | - | - |
| 10th | - | - |

## NORTHERN DISTRICTS v CENTRAL DISTRICTS  Super Smash

*at Bay Oval, Mt Maunganui on 14 January, 2022*
*Toss : Northern Districts.  Umpires : L.R. Els & D.J. Walker*
**Central Districts won by 4 wickets.** *Points: Central Districts 4, Northern Districts 0*

| NORTHERN DISTRICTS | Runs | Mins | Balls | 6s | 4s |
|---|---|---|---|---|---|
| C.A.Gurrey not out .................. | 58 | 85 | 50 | 1 | 5 |
| L.F.Boucher b Green ................. | 5 | 9 | 8 | - | 1 |
| B.M.Halliday* c Greig b Mair ...... | 1 | 7 | 7 | - | - |
| S.R.H.Curtis run out .................. | 4 | 18 | 12 | - | - |
| N.H.Patel b Mair ........................ | 4 | 13 | 17 | - | - |
| M.B.Templeton c Greig b Mair .... | 0 | 2 | 1 | - | - |
| H.E.Topp† c Sims b Rees .......... | 9 | 18 | 13 | - | 1 |
| S.R.Naidu run out ...................... | 3 | 9 | 9 | - | - |
| C.R.Sarsfield not out ................. | 7 | 6 | 3 | - | - |
| K.A.Knight | | | | | |
| L.H.Heaps | | | | | |
| Extras (b 6, w 13) .................... | 19 | | | | |
| **TOTAL** (20 overs) (7 wkts) | **110** | 85 | | | |

| CENTRAL DISTRICTS | Runs | Mins | Balls | 6s | 4s |
|---|---|---|---|---|---|
| E.G.Cunningham c Templeton | | | | | |
|   b Patel ..................................... | 28 | 39 | 29 | - | 5 |
| G.Sims† lbw b Heaps ................. | 1 | 13 | 4 | - | - |
| K.A.Tomlinson c Templeton b Heaps | 5 | 10 | 9 | - | 1 |
| J.M.Watkin* st Topp b Patel ..... | 16 | 10 | 10 | 1 | 2 |
| M.J.Greig st Topp b Sarsfield ... | 17 | 34 | 30 | - | 1 |
| R.A.Mair c Topp b Halliday ......... | 1 | 3 | 3 | - | - |
| H.M.Rowe not out ..................... | 27 | 35 | 25 | - | 3 |
| G.K.Atkinson not out .................. | 9 | 10 | 8 | - | 2 |
| M.S.Rees | | | | | |
| M.J.Hansen | | | | | |
| C.L.Green | | | | | |
| Extras (b 1, lb 2, w 6) .............. | 9 | | | | |
| **TOTAL** (19.4 overs) (6 wkts) | **113** | 78 | | | |

| Bowling | O | M | R | W |
|---|---|---|---|---|
| **CENTRAL DISTRICTS** | | | | |
| Green | 4 | 0 | 16 | 1 |
| Mair | 4 | 1 | 22 | 3 |
| Rowe | 4 | 0 | 13 | 0 |
| Watkin | 4 | 0 | 34 | 0 |
| Rees | 3 | 0 | 16 | 1 |
| Atkinson | 1 | 0 | 3 | 0 |
| **NORTHERN DISTRICTS** | | | | |
| Naidu | 2 | 0 | 15 | 0 |
| Heaps | 4 | 0 | 23 | 2 |
| Knight | 2 | 0 | 12 | 0 |
| Patel | 4 | 0 | 20 | 2 |
| Halliday | 4 | 0 | 15 | 1 |
| Sarsfield | 3.4 | 0 | 25 | 1 |

| Fall of Wickets | ND | CD |
|---|---|---|
| 1st | 18 | 22 |
| 2nd | 19 | 34 |
| 3rd | 40 | 56 |
| 4th | 53 | 59 |
| 5th | 54 | 61 |
| 6th | 87 | 96 |
| 7th | 97 | - |
| 8th | - | - |
| 9th | - | - |
| 10th | - | - |

## AUCKLAND v OTAGO  Super Smash

*at Kennards Hire Community Oval, Auckland on 15 January, 2022*
*Toss : Auckland.  Umpires : J.A.K. Bromley & J.M. Dempsey*
**Otago won by 10 wickets.** *Points: Otago 4, Auckland 0*

| AUCKLAND | Runs | Mins | Balls | 6s | 4s |
|---|---|---|---|---|---|
| K.T.Perkins c Bates b Jensen .... | 23 | 36 | 34 | - | 1 |
| L.R.Down* c Martin b Oldershaw | 49 | 57 | 40 | - | 5 |
| I.C.Gaze† lbw b Jensen .............. | 0 | 1 | 1 | - | - |
| H.R.Huddleston c Bates b Black .. | 6 | 25 | 13 | - | - |
| J.E.I.Prasad st Martin b Carson . | 13 | 22 | 17 | - | 1 |
| B.G.Armstrong c Bates b Jensen . | 1 | 4 | 2 | - | - |
| A.N.Kelly not out .......................... | 9 | 13 | 11 | - | - |
| S.E.Bowden not out ..................... | 1 | 2 | 2 | - | - |
| M.M.Penfold | | | | | |
| A.T.Hucker | | | | | |
| F.C.Jonas | | | | | |
| Extras (b 1, lb 1, w 2) ................ | 4 | | | | |
| **TOTAL** (20 overs) (6 wkts) ... | **106** | 81 | | | |

| OTAGO | Runs | Mins | Balls | 6s | 4s |
|---|---|---|---|---|---|
| S.W.Bates* not out ................... | 40 | 60 | 40 | - | 4 |
| P.M.Inglis not out ...................... | 61 | 60 | 58 | - | 8 |
| K.J.Martin† | | | | | |
| K.E.Ebrahim | | | | | |
| C.G.Blakely | | | | | |
| O.N.Gain | | | | | |
| E.J.Carson | | | | | |
| E.J.Black | | | | | |
| S.A.Oldershaw | | | | | |
| H.N.K.Jensen | | | | | |
| M.B.Lamplough | | | | | |
| Extras (lb 1, w 4, nb 1) ............. | 6 | | | | |
| **TOTAL** (16.1 overs) (0 wkts) | **107** | 60 | | | |

| Bowling | O | M | R | W |
|---|---|---|---|---|
| **OTAGO** | | | | |
| Jensen | 4 | 0 | 21 | 3 |
| Black | 4 | 0 | 17 | 1 |
| Ebrahim | 2 | 0 | 11 | 0 |
| Carson | 4 | 0 | 24 | 1 |
| Oldershaw | 4 | 0 | 21 | 1 |
| Lamplough | 2 | 0 | 10 | 0 |
| **AUCKLAND** | | | | |
| Kelly | 2 | 0 | 14 | 0 |
| Huddleston | 2 | 0 | 8 | 0 |
| Penfold | 3 | 0 | 22 | 0 |
| Jonas | 4 | 0 | 24 | 0 |
| Hucker | 1 | 0 | 10 | 0 |
| Prasad | 2.1 | 0 | 15 | 0 |
| Armstrong | 2 | 0 | 13 | 0 |

| Fall of Wickets | A | O |
|---|---|---|
| 1st | 59 | - |
| 2nd | 59 | - |
| 3rd | 79 | - |
| 4th | 85 | - |
| 5th | 87 | - |
| 6th | 102 | - |
| 7th | - | - |
| 8th | - | - |
| 9th | - | - |
| 10th | - | - |

# NORTHERN DISTRICTS v WELLINGTON          Super Smash

*at Cobham Oval, Whangarei on 16 January, 2022*
*Toss : Northern Districts.  Umpires : R. Allen & B.F. Bowden*
**Wellington won by 8 wickets.** *Points: Wellington 4, Northern Districts 0*

## NORTHERN DISTRICTS

| | Runs | Mins | Balls | 6s | 4s |
|---|---|---|---|---|---|
| C.A.Gurrey c Jetly b Kerr J.M. .... | 6 | 9 | 8 | - | 1 |
| B.M.Halliday* c Devine | | | | | |
| b Kerr A.C. ............................... | 10 | 25 | 15 | 1 | - |
| S.R.H.Curtis run out ................. | 22 | 39 | 36 | - | 2 |
| N.H.Patel c King b Kasperek ...... | 1 | 6 | 4 | - | - |
| L.F.Boucher b Kerr A.C. ............. | 0 | 1 | 1 | - | - |
| M.B.Templeton b Kerr A.C. ......... | 0 | 1 | 1 | - | - |
| H.E.Topp† c Green b Jetly ......... | 1 | 17 | 17 | - | - |
| E.L.Baker lbw b Jetly ................. | 0 | 9 | 4 | - | - |
| S.R.Naidu not out ...................... | 2 | 10 | 6 | - | - |
| C.R.Sarsfield b Jetly ................. | 0 | 2 | 2 | - | - |
| L.H.Heaps c Plimmer b Jetly ..... | 0 | 2 | 2 | - | - |
| Extras (lb 2, w 2) ...................... | 4 | | | | |
| **TOTAL** (16 overs) ................. | **46** | 62 | | | |

## WELLINGTON

| | Runs | Mins | Balls | 6s | 4s |
|---|---|---|---|---|---|
| S.F.M.Devine not out ................ | 20 | 27 | 14 | 1 | 2 |
| G.E.Plimmer b Baker ................. | 6 | 9 | 7 | - | - |
| T.M.M.Newton c Templeton | | | | | |
| b Baker ................................... | 12 | 8 | 11 | - | 2 |
| M.L.Green* not out ................... | 11 | 8 | 6 | - | 2 |
| A.C.Kerr | | | | | |
| L.M.Kasperek | | | | | |
| R.M.Burns | | | | | |
| J.M.Kerr | | | | | |
| J.T.McFadyen† | | | | | |
| C.R.King | | | | | |
| X.A.R.Jetly | | | | | |
| Extras (lb 1, w 1) ...................... | 2 | | | | |
| **TOTAL** (6.2 overs) (2 wkts) .. | **51** | 27 | | | |

| Bowling | O | M | R | W |
|---|---|---|---|---|
| **WELLINGTON** | | | | |
| Kerr J.M. | 3 | 0 | 18 | 1 |
| Devine | 3 | 0 | 9 | 0 |
| Kasperek | 3 | 0 | 7 | 1 |
| Kerr A.C. | 4 | 0 | 9 | 3 |
| Jetly | 3 | 2 | 1 | 4 |
| **NORTHERN DISTRICTS** | | | | |
| Naidu | 1 | 0 | 6 | 0 |
| Heaps | 1 | 0 | 5 | 0 |
| Baker | 2.2 | 0 | 17 | 2 |
| Patel | 1 | 0 | 11 | 0 |
| Templeton | 1 | 0 | 11 | 0 |

| Fall of Wickets | ND | W |
|---|---|---|
| 1st | 16 | 13 |
| 2nd | 27 | 31 |
| 3rd | 31 | - |
| 4th | 32 | - |
| 5th | 32 | - |
| 6th | 44 | - |
| 7th | 44 | - |
| 8th | 46 | - |
| 9th | 46 | - |
| 10th | 46 | - |

# CANTERBURY v AUCKLAND          Super Smash

*at Hagley Oval, Christchurch on 18 January, 2022*
*Toss : Canterbury.  Umpires : W.R. Knights & E.D. Sanders*
**Auckland won by 8 runs.** *Points: Auckland 4, Canterbury 0*

## AUCKLAND

| | Runs | Mins | Balls | 6s | 4s |
|---|---|---|---|---|---|
| L.R.Down* c Cox b Tahuhu ........ | 2 | 8 | 8 | - | - |
| K.T.Perkins b Simmons ............. | 29 | 54 | 37 | - | 4 |
| A.N.Kelly run out ....................... | 6 | 8 | 6 | - | 1 |
| J.E.I.Prasad c & b Simmons ....... | 0 | 5 | 3 | - | - |
| B.G.Armstrong c Hughes | | | | | |
| b Savage ............................... | 13 | 21 | 16 | - | 1 |
| I.C.Gaze† run out ..................... | 24 | 43 | 26 | - | 3 |
| S.Shahri c Asmussen b Savage | 26 | 19 | 15 | - | 6 |
| S.E.Bowden b Satterthwaite ...... | 3 | 4 | 5 | - | - |
| M.M.Penfold b Satterthwaite ...... | 0 | 1 | 1 | - | - |
| A.T.Hucker not out ................... | 10 | 7 | 5 | 1 | - |
| F.C.Jonas not out ..................... | 0 | 1 | 0 | - | - |
| Extras (lb 4, w 12, nb 2) ......... | 18 | | | | |
| **TOTAL** (20 overs) (9 wkts) . | **131** | 87 | | | |

## CANTERBURY

| | Runs | Mins | Balls | 6s | 4s |
|---|---|---|---|---|---|
| A.E.Satterthwaite c Down b Jonas | 22 | 39 | 34 | - | 2 |
| N.B.Cox c Shahri b Hucker ....... | 34 | 48 | 38 | 1 | 3 |
| F.L.Mackay* b Kelly .................. | 23 | 42 | 21 | - | 2 |
| L.M.M.Tahuhu c Armstrong | | | | | |
| b Penfold ............................... | 0 | 8 | 6 | - | - |
| J.L.Savage st Gaze b Prasad ... | 20 | 16 | 14 | - | 3 |
| K.F.G.Nation st Gaze b Kelly ...... | 8 | 11 | 9 | - | 1 |
| L.E.V.Hughes† not out .............. | 0 | 2 | 1 | - | - |
| A.G.Gerken | | | | | |
| M.J.Banks | | | | | |
| J.A.Simmons | | | | | |
| S.R.Asmussen | | | | | |
| Extras (b 7, lb 1, w 5, nb 3) .... | 16 | | | | |
| **TOTAL** (20 overs) (6 wkts) . | **123** | 84 | | | |

| Bowling | O | M | R | W |
|---|---|---|---|---|
| **CANTERBURY** | | | | |
| Tahuhu | 4 | 1 | 19 | 1 |
| Satterthwaite | 3 | 0 | 18 | 2 |
| Simmons | 4 | 0 | 26 | 2 |
| Banks | 2 | 0 | 7 | 0 |
| Mackay | 4 | 0 | 29 | 0 |
| Savage | 3 | 0 | 28 | 2 |
| **AUCKLAND** | | | | |
| Jonas | 4 | 0 | 29 | 1 |
| Kelly | 4 | 0 | 13 | 2 |
| Hucker | 4 | 0 | 15 | 1 |
| Armstrong | 4 | 0 | 31 | 0 |
| Penfold | 2 | 0 | 14 | 1 |
| Prasad | 2 | 0 | 13 | 1 |

| Fall of Wickets | A | C |
|---|---|---|
| 1st | 4 | 57 |
| 2nd | 22 | 71 |
| 3rd | 22 | 77 |
| 4th | 52 | 110 |
| 5th | 70 | 122 |
| 6th | 112 | 123 |
| 7th | 117 | - |
| 8th | 117 | - |
| 9th | 125 | - |
| 10th | - | - |

# AUCKLAND v WELLINGTON                    Super Smash

*at Kennards Hire Community Oval, Auckland on 20 January, 2022*
*Toss : Wellington. Umpires : C.A. Black & J.A.K. Bromley*
**Wellington won by 5 wickets.** *Points: Wellington 4, Auckland 0*

## AUCKLAND

| | Runs | Mins | Balls | 6s | 4s |
|---|---|---|---|---|---|
| K.T.Perkins b Kerr J.M. | 11 | 19 | 11 | - | 2 |
| L.R.Down* c Green b Kasperek | 10 | 25 | 17 | - | 1 |
| A.N.Kelly b Kerr A.C. | 3 | 10 | 8 | - | - |
| A.M.Peterson run out | 2 | 8 | 3 | - | - |
| B.G.Armstrong c Kasperek b Kerr A.C. | 6 | 13 | 13 | - | - |
| S.Shahri c Kerr A.C. b Kerr J.M. | 34 | 42 | 39 | - | 4 |
| I.C.Gazet c McFadyen b Devine | 3 | 12 | 7 | - | - |
| J.E.I.Prasad c Green b Kasperek | 0 | 1 | 1 | - | - |
| S.E.Bowden c Kasperek b Devine | 9 | 22 | 16 | - | - |
| M.M.Penfold c McFadyen b Devine | 0 | 2 | 2 | - | - |
| A.T.Hucker not out | 1 | 1 | 2 | - | - |
| Extras (lb 2, w 7, nb 1) | 10 | | | | |
| **TOTAL** (19.4 overs) | **89** | 80 | | | |

## WELLINGTON

| | Runs | Mins | Balls | 6s | 4s |
|---|---|---|---|---|---|
| S.F.M.Devine c Bowden b Kelly | 36 | 23 | 22 | 1 | 5 |
| G.E.Plimmer c Down b Peterson | 2 | 9 | 5 | - | - |
| A.C.Kerr run out | 0 | 3 | 0 | - | - |
| M.L.Green* not out | 39 | 44 | 32 | 1 | 5 |
| L.M.Kasperek c Armstrong b Kelly | 0 | 4 | 3 | - | - |
| T.M.M.Newton b Armstrong | 11 | 25 | 16 | - | 1 |
| R.M.Burns not out | 0 | 3 | 2 | - | - |
| J.M.Kerr | | | | | |
| J.T.McFadyen† | | | | | |
| C.R.King | | | | | |
| X.A.R.Jetly | | | | | |
| Extras (w 2) | 2 | | | | |
| **TOTAL** (13.2 overs) (5 wkts) | **90** | 56 | | | |

| Bowling | O | M | R | W |
|---|---|---|---|---|
| **WELLINGTON** | | | | |
| Kerr J.M. | 4 | 1 | 11 | 2 |
| Devine | 3.4 | 0 | 24 | 3 |
| Kasperek | 4 | 0 | 17 | 2 |
| Kerr A.C. | 4 | 0 | 13 | 2 |
| Jetly | 2 | 0 | 15 | 0 |
| King | 2 | 0 | 7 | 0 |
| **AUCKLAND** | | | | |
| Peterson | 4 | 0 | 33 | 1 |
| Kelly | 4 | 1 | 17 | 2 |
| Penfold | 2 | 0 | 17 | 0 |
| Hucker | 1 | 0 | 6 | 0 |
| Armstrong | 2 | 0 | 13 | 1 |
| Prasad | 0.2 | 0 | 4 | 0 |

### Fall of Wickets

| | A | W |
|---|---|---|
| 1st | 22 | 13 |
| 2nd | 26 | 23 |
| 3rd | 28 | 43 |
| 4th | 30 | 43 |
| 5th | 44 | 86 |
| 6th | 65 | - |
| 7th | 65 | - |
| 8th | 87 | - |
| 9th | 87 | - |
| 10th | 89 | - |

---

# CANTERBURY v NORTHERN DISTRICTS            Super Smash

*at Hagley Oval, Christchurch on 21 January, 2022*
*Toss : Northern Districts. Umpires : T.J. Parlane & P.J. Pasco*
**Canterbury won by 24 runs.** *Points: Canterbury 4, Northern Districts 0*

## CANTERBURY

| | Runs | Mins | Balls | 6s | 4s |
|---|---|---|---|---|---|
| A.E.Satterthwaite run out | 114 | 87 | 66 | 1 | 18 |
| N.B.Cox c Boucher b Heaps | 8 | 16 | 11 | - | 1 |
| F.L.Mackay* lbw b Halliday | 14 | 22 | 13 | - | 2 |
| J.L.Savage run out | 26 | 42 | 27 | - | 1 |
| L.M.M.Tahuhu not out | 1 | 5 | 3 | - | - |
| K.F.G.Nation | | | | | |
| L.E.V.Hughes† | | | | | |
| J.Dean | | | | | |
| M.J.Banks | | | | | |
| J.A.Simmons | | | | | |
| S.R.Asmussen | | | | | |
| Extras (lb 1, w 8) | 9 | | | | |
| **TOTAL** (20 overs) (4 wkts) | **172** | 87 | | | |

## NORTHERN DISTRICTS

| | Runs | Mins | Balls | 6s | 4s |
|---|---|---|---|---|---|
| K.G.Anderson b Banks | 5 | 5 | 4 | - | 1 |
| C.A.Gurrey b Banks | 10 | 23 | 11 | - | 2 |
| B.M.Halliday* c Hughes b Banks | 28 | 21 | 18 | 2 | 3 |
| L.F.Boucher c Asmussen b Banks | 6 | 11 | 8 | - | 1 |
| S.R.H.Curtis c Mackay b Satterthwaite | 31 | 20 | 16 | - | 6 |
| N.H.Patel b Simmons | 23 | 33 | 25 | - | 2 |
| E.A.J.Richardson c Nation b Tahuhu | 11 | 5 | 6 | - | 2 |
| H.E.Topp† c Banks b Simmons | 7 | 23 | 15 | - | - |
| S.R.Naidu not out | 11 | 14 | 14 | - | 1 |
| L.H.Heaps not out | 2 | 5 | 3 | - | - |
| C.R.Sarsfield | | | | | |
| Extras (lb 5, w 9) | 14 | | | | |
| **TOTAL** (20 overs) (8 wkts) | **148** | 82 | | | |

| Bowling | O | M | R | W |
|---|---|---|---|---|
| **NORTHERN DISTRICTS** | | | | |
| Naidu | 3 | 0 | 16 | 0 |
| Heaps | 2 | 0 | 19 | 1 |
| Patel | 4 | 0 | 37 | 0 |
| Richardson | 4 | 0 | 26 | 0 |
| Boucher | 2 | 0 | 33 | 0 |
| Halliday | 4 | 0 | 31 | 1 |
| Sarsfield | 1 | 0 | 9 | 0 |
| **CANTERBURY** | | | | |
| Tahuhu | 4 | 0 | 20 | 1 |
| Banks | 4 | 0 | 29 | 4 |
| Savage | 2 | 0 | 27 | 0 |
| Asmussen | 2 | 0 | 21 | 0 |
| Satterthwaite | 3 | 0 | 18 | 1 |
| Mackay | 2 | 0 | 11 | 0 |
| Simmons | 3 | 0 | 17 | 2 |

### Fall of Wickets

| | C | ND |
|---|---|---|
| 1st | 30 | 5 |
| 2nd | 63 | 46 |
| 3rd | 164 | 48 |
| 4th | 172 | 59 |
| 5th | - | 94 |
| 6th | - | 105 |
| 7th | - | 125 |
| 8th | - | 133 |
| 9th | - | - |
| 10th | - | - |

# AUCKLAND v CENTRAL DISTRICTS     Super Smash

at Eden Park, Auckland on 22 January, 2022
Toss : Central Districts. Umpires : W.R. Knights & A. Stanley
**Auckland won by 8 wickets.** Points: Auckland 4, Central Districts 0

## CENTRAL DISTRICTS

| | Runs | Mins | Balls | 6s | 4s |
|---|---|---|---|---|---|
| E.G.Cunningham b Huddleston .. | 8 | 13 | 13 | - | 1 |
| K.A.Tomlinson b Armstrong ...... | 40 | 53 | 44 | 1 | 3 |
| R.A.Mair b Armstrong ............... | 34 | 48 | 31 | - | 4 |
| M.J.Greig not out ...................... | 26 | 25 | 18 | - | 3 |
| H.M.Rowe* not out ................... | 21 | 17 | 14 | 1 | 1 |
| G.K.Atkinson | | | | | |
| M.J.Hansen | | | | | |
| C.L.Green | | | | | |
| G.Sims† | | | | | |
| O.J.S.Bartlett | | | | | |
| A.Kumar | | | | | |
| Extras (b 1, w 5) ....................... | 6 | | | | |
| **TOTAL** (20 overs) (3 wkts) . | **135** | 79 | | | |

## AUCKLAND

| | Runs | Mins | Balls | 6s | 4s |
|---|---|---|---|---|---|
| K.T.Perkins b Hansen ............... | 67 | 59 | 54 | 1 | 7 |
| L.R.Down* c Greig b Mair ......... | 36 | 63 | 38 | - | 4 |
| H.R.Huddleston not out .............. | 7 | 15 | 7 | - | 1 |
| S.Shahri not out ........................ | 14 | 11 | 12 | - | 2 |
| A.M.Peterson | | | | | |
| B.G.Armstrong | | | | | |
| I.C.Gaze† | | | | | |
| A.N.Kelly | | | | | |
| J.E.I.Prasad | | | | | |
| M.M.Penfold | | | | | |
| A.T.Hucker | | | | | |
| Extras (lb 2, w 10) .................. | 12 | | | | |
| **TOTAL** (18.3 overs) (2 wkts) | **136** | 75 | | | |

| Bowling | O | M | R | W |
|---|---|---|---|---|
| **AUCKLAND** | | | | |
| Huddleston | 4 | 0 | 24 | 1 |
| Kelly | 4 | 0 | 12 | 0 |
| Hucker | 3 | 0 | 24 | 0 |
| Peterson | 3 | 0 | 29 | 0 |
| Penfold | 3 | 0 | 21 | 0 |
| Armstrong | 3 | 0 | 24 | 2 |
| **CENTRAL DISTRICTS** | | | | |
| Green | 3 | 0 | 20 | 0 |
| Mair | 3.3 | 0 | 20 | 1 |
| Rowe | 4 | 0 | 27 | 0 |
| Kumar | 2 | 0 | 17 | 0 |
| Hansen | 3 | 0 | 29 | 1 |
| Bartlett | 2 | 0 | 13 | 0 |
| Atkinson | 1 | 0 | 8 | 0 |

| Fall of Wickets | | |
|---|---|---|
| | CD | A |
| 1st | 13 | 111 |
| 2nd | 83 | 115 |
| 3rd | 90 | - |
| 4th | - | - |
| 5th | - | - |
| 6th | - | - |
| 7th | - | - |
| 8th | - | - |
| 9th | - | - |
| 10th | - | - |

# OTAGO v CANTERBURY     Super Smash

at University of Otago Oval, Dunedin on 23 January, 2022
Toss : Canterbury. Umpires : S.B. Haig & N. Louw
**Otago won by 7 wickets.** Points: Otago 4, Canterbury 0

## CANTERBURY

| | Runs | Mins | Balls | 6s | 4s |
|---|---|---|---|---|---|
| A.E.Satterthwaite c Inglis b Jensen | 7 | 19 | 13 | - | - |
| K.F.G.Nation c Bates b Black ..... | 0 | 6 | 3 | - | - |
| F.L.Mackay* run out ................. | 11 | 33 | 21 | - | 1 |
| J.L.Savage c Inglis b Jensen ...... | 4 | 2 | 2 | - | 1 |
| A.G.Gerken c Black b Carson .. | 26 | 39 | 33 | - | 2 |
| L.M.M.Tahuhu c Lamplough | | | | | |
|   b Oldershaw ........................... | 31 | 16 | 15 | 2 | 3 |
| J.Dean not out .......................... | 17 | 22 | 16 | - | 2 |
| M.J.Banks lbw b Oldershaw ....... | 5 | 8 | 9 | - | - |
| L.E.V.Hughes† c Bates b Carson | 5 | 7 | 8 | - | - |
| J.A.Simmons not out .................. | 0 | 2 | 0 | - | - |
| S.R.Asmussen | | | | | |
| Extras (lb 1, w 4) ...................... | 5 | | | | |
| **TOTAL** (20 overs) (8 wkts) . | **111** | 79 | | | |

## OTAGO

| | Runs | Mins | Balls | 6s | 4s |
|---|---|---|---|---|---|
| S.W.Bates* c Banks b Tahuhu . | 55 | 51 | 49 | - | 8 |
| P.M.Inglis b Banks ...................... | 1 | 13 | 4 | - | - |
| K.J.Martin† c Dean b Savage ..... | 2 | 10 | 7 | - | - |
| K.E.Ebrahim not out .................. | 36 | 45 | 43 | - | 4 |
| H.N.K.Jensen not out ............... | 14 | 17 | 11 | - | 2 |
| C.G.Blakely | | | | | |
| O.N.Gain | | | | | |
| M.B.Lamplough | | | | | |
| E.J.Carson | | | | | |
| E.J.Black | | | | | |
| S.A.Oldershaw | | | | | |
| Extras (lb 2, w 4, nb 1) ............ | 7 | | | | |
| **TOTAL** (18.5 overs) (3 wkts) | **115** | 69 | | | |

| Bowling | O | M | R | W |
|---|---|---|---|---|
| **OTAGO** | | | | |
| Jensen | 4 | 0 | 15 | 2 |
| Black | 4 | 1 | 23 | 1 |
| Oldershaw | 4 | 0 | 23 | 2 |
| Ebrahim | 4 | 0 | 21 | 0 |
| Carson | 4 | 0 | 28 | 2 |
| **CANTERBURY** | | | | |
| Tahuhu | 4 | 0 | 14 | 1 |
| Banks | 3 | 0 | 30 | 1 |
| Savage | 1 | 0 | 9 | 1 |
| Simmons | 1 | 0 | 8 | 0 |
| Mackay | 2.5 | 0 | 19 | 0 |
| Satterthwaite | 4 | 0 | 17 | 0 |
| Asmussen | 3 | 0 | 16 | 0 |

| Fall of Wickets | | |
|---|---|---|
| | C | O |
| 1st | 3 | 17 |
| 2nd | 12 | 33 |
| 3rd | 16 | 83 |
| 4th | 41 | - |
| 5th | 81 | - |
| 6th | 84 | - |
| 7th | 93 | - |
| 8th | 101 | - |
| 9th | - | - |
| 10th | - | - |

# WELLINGTON v NORTHERN DISTRICTS          Super Smash

*at Cello Basin Reserve, Wellington on 24 January, 2022*
*Toss : Northern Districts.  Umpires : T.R. Davies & T.J. Parlane*
**Wellington won by 54 runs.** *Points: Wellington 4, Northern Districts 0*

## WELLINGTON

| | Runs | Mins | Balls | 6s | 4s |
|---|---|---|---|---|---|
| S.F.M.Devine c Baker b Boucher | 5 | 14 | 7 | - | - |
| G.E.Plimmer c Boucher b Richardson | 27 | 26 | 22 | - | 3 |
| A.C.Kerr c Topp b Baker | 9 | 18 | 11 | - | 1 |
| M.L.Green* c Patel b Richardson | 2 | 2 | 2 | - | - |
| L.M.Kasperek c Richardson b Halliday | 29 | 51 | 29 | - | 3 |
| T.M.M.Newton c Boucher b Halliday | 38 | 20 | 23 | - | 5 |
| R.M.Burns c Anderson b Patel | 1 | 8 | 7 | - | - |
| J.M.Kerr c Halliday b Patel | 20 | 16 | 9 | 1 | 2 |
| J.T.McFadyen† b Richardson | 2 | 8 | 4 | - | - |
| X.A.R.Jetly not out | 7 | 7 | 5 | - | 1 |
| M.P.Singh not out | 2 | 1 | 1 | - | - |
| Extras (b 4, lb 1, w 7) | 12 | | | | |
| **TOTAL (20 overs) (9 wkts)** | **154** | 88 | | | |

## NORTHERN DISTRICTS

| | Runs | Mins | Balls | 6s | 4s |
|---|---|---|---|---|---|
| K.G.Anderson c Devine b Singh | 37 | 62 | 42 | - | 4 |
| C.A.Gurrey c Plimmer b Devine | 7 | 21 | 19 | - | - |
| B.M.Halliday* c McFadyen b Devine | 9 | 8 | 8 | - | 1 |
| N.H.Patel run out | 13 | 16 | 18 | - | 1 |
| E.A.J.Richardson st McFadyen b Kerr A.C. | 10 | 11 | 8 | - | 2 |
| L.F.Boucher c Kerr J.M. b Kerr A.C. | 1 | 7 | 3 | - | - |
| M.B.Templeton lbw b Kerr J.M. | 3 | 20 | 5 | - | - |
| E.L.Baker c Burns b Kasperek | 5 | 17 | 7 | - | - |
| C.R.Sarsfield c Burns b Kasperek | 12 | 10 | 6 | - | 3 |
| H.E.Topp† not out | 0 | 9 | 0 | - | - |
| S.R.H.Curtis absent hurt | | | | | |
| Extras (lb 1, w 2) | 3 | | | | |
| **TOTAL (19.2 overs)** | **100** | 92 | | | |

| Bowling | O | M | R | W |
|---|---|---|---|---|
| **NORTHERN DISTRICTS** | | | | |
| Patel | 4 | 0 | 36 | 2 |
| Boucher | 4 | 0 | 32 | 1 |
| Richardson | 4 | 0 | 27 | 3 |
| Baker | 4 | 0 | 32 | 1 |
| Halliday | 4 | 0 | 22 | 2 |
| **WELLINGTON** | | | | |
| Kerr J.M. | 4 | 0 | 23 | 1 |
| Singh | 4 | 0 | 25 | 1 |
| Kasperek | 3.2 | 0 | 6 | 2 |
| Devine | 2 | 0 | 14 | 2 |
| Kerr A.C. | 4 | 0 | 20 | 2 |
| Jetly | 2 | 0 | 11 | 0 |

### Fall of Wickets

| | W | ND |
|---|---|---|
| 1st | 30 | 25 |
| 2nd | 47 | 40 |
| 3rd | 50 | 58 |
| 4th | 50 | 73 |
| 5th | 95 | 80 |
| 6th | 99 | 80 |
| 7th | 139 | 88 |
| 8th | 143 | 100 |
| 9th | 152 | 100 |
| 10th | - | - |

# OTAGO v AUCKLAND          Elimination Final

*at University of Otago Oval, Dunedin on 27 January, 2022*
*Toss : Otago.  Umpires : S.B. Haig & B.F. Bowden*
**Otago won by 29 runs**

## OTAGO

| | Runs | Mins | Balls | 6s | 4s |
|---|---|---|---|---|---|
| S.W.Bates* c Jonas b Hucker | 75 | 72 | 62 | 1 | 7 |
| P.M.Inglis c Gaze b Penfold | 19 | 23 | 17 | - | 2 |
| K.J.Martin† c Armstrong b Penfold | 17 | 22 | 15 | - | 3 |
| K.E.Ebrahim c Jonas b Kelly | 11 | 21 | 12 | - | 1 |
| H.N.K.Jensen c Armstrong b Jonas | 5 | 12 | 7 | - | - |
| C.G.Blakely not out | 11 | 8 | 7 | - | 1 |
| O.N.Gain not out | 0 | 2 | 0 | - | - |
| I.R.James | | | | | |
| E.J.Carson | | | | | |
| E.J.Black | | | | | |
| S.A.Oldershaw | | | | | |
| Extras (lb 1, w 4) | 5 | | | | |
| **TOTAL (20 overs) (5 wkts)** | **143** | 81 | | | |

## AUCKLAND

| | Runs | Mins | Balls | 6s | 4s |
|---|---|---|---|---|---|
| K.T.Perkins run out | 24 | 47 | 28 | - | 1 |
| L.R.Down* c Gain b Black | 2 | 8 | 7 | - | - |
| S.E.Bowden b Oldershaw | 8 | 21 | 17 | - | - |
| S.Shahri c Bates b Oldershaw | 15 | 24 | 19 | - | 1 |
| B.G.Armstrong run out | 10 | 11 | 9 | - | 1 |
| I.C.Gaze† c Oldershaw b Carson | 5 | 8 | 6 | - | 1 |
| A.N.Kelly not out | 28 | 23 | 21 | - | 2 |
| J.E.I.Prasad not out | 8 | 20 | 13 | - | - |
| M.M.Penfold | | | | | |
| A.T.Hucker | | | | | |
| F.C.Jonas | | | | | |
| Extras (b 11, lb 1, w 2) | 14 | | | | |
| **TOTAL (20 overs) (6 wkts)** | **114** | 82 | | | |

| Bowling | O | M | R | W |
|---|---|---|---|---|
| **AUCKLAND** | | | | |
| Kelly | 4 | 0 | 19 | 1 |
| Jonas | 4 | 0 | 34 | 1 |
| Hucker | 3 | 0 | 23 | 1 |
| Armstrong | 2 | 0 | 19 | 0 |
| Penfold | 4 | 0 | 27 | 2 |
| Prasad | 3 | 0 | 20 | 0 |
| **OTAGO** | | | | |
| Jensen | 4 | 0 | 11 | 0 |
| Black | 4 | 0 | 27 | 1 |
| Ebrahim | 4 | 0 | 26 | 0 |
| Carson | 4 | 0 | 21 | 1 |
| Oldershaw | 4 | 0 | 17 | 2 |

### Fall of Wickets

| | O | A |
|---|---|---|
| 1st | 43 | 4 |
| 2nd | 82 | 21 |
| 3rd | 118 | 47 |
| 4th | 128 | 55 |
| 5th | 137 | 68 |
| 6th | - | 71 |
| 7th | - | - |
| 8th | - | - |
| 9th | - | - |
| 10th | - | - |

# WELLINGTON v OTAGO

**Final**

*at Seddon Park, Hamilton on 29 January, 2022*
*Toss : Wellington.  Umpires : C.M. Brown & W.R. Knights*
**Wellington won by 75 runs**

## WELLINGTON

| | Runs | Mins | Balls | 6s | 4s |
|---|---|---|---|---|---|
| S.F.M.Devine c Blakely b Black | 92 | 81 | 62 | 5 | 10 |
| G.E.Plimmer c Bates b Jensen | 3 | 11 | 6 | - | - |
| A.C.Kerr lbw b Carson | 20 | 24 | 17 | - | 3 |
| M.L.Green* c Bates b Black | 55 | 49 | 35 | 2 | 5 |
| J.M.Kerr not out | 0 | 3 | 0 | - | - |
| L.M.Kasperek | | | | | |
| T.M.M.Newton | | | | | |
| R.M.Burns | | | | | |
| J.T.McFadyen† | | | | | |
| X.A.R.Jetly | | | | | |
| M.P.Singh | | | | | |
| Extras (lb 1, w 4) | 5 | | | | |
| **TOTAL** (20 overs) (4 wkts) | **175** | 85 | | | |

## OTAGO

| | Runs | Mins | Balls | 6s | 4s |
|---|---|---|---|---|---|
| S.W.Bates* c Newton b Kerr J.M. | 3 | 10 | 5 | - | - |
| P.M.Inglis c McFadyen b Singh | 13 | 8 | 8 | - | 3 |
| K.J.Martin† c Kerr J.M. b Devine | 16 | 23 | 14 | - | 2 |
| K.E.Ebrahim b Devine | 4 | 14 | 11 | - | - |
| H.N.K.Jensen c Kerr J.M. b Kerr A.C. | 4 | 12 | 8 | - | - |
| C.G.Blakely c & b Kasperek | 9 | 16 | 15 | - | - |
| O.N.Gain c Kerr A.C. b Kasperek | 10 | 10 | 9 | 1 | - |
| I.R.James not out | 13 | 26 | 16 | - | 1 |
| E.J.Carson c Kerr A.C. b Kasperek | 7 | 6 | 9 | - | 1 |
| E.J.Black run out | 16 | 14 | 9 | 1 | 1 |
| S.A.Oldershaw run out | 0 | 4 | 2 | - | - |
| Extras (lb 1, w 4) | 5 | | | | |
| **TOTAL** (17.3 overs) | **100** | 74 | | | |

| Bowling OTAGO | O | M | R | W |
|---|---|---|---|---|
| Jensen | 4 | 0 | 31 | 1 |
| Black | 4 | 0 | 36 | 2 |
| Carson | 4 | 0 | 50 | 1 |
| Oldershaw | 4 | 0 | 30 | 0 |
| Ebrahim | 4 | 0 | 27 | 0 |
| **WELLINGTON** | | | | |
| Kerr J.M. | 3 | 0 | 16 | 1 |
| Singh | 2 | 0 | 19 | 1 |
| Devine | 3.3 | 0 | 14 | 2 |
| Kerr A.C. | 4 | 0 | 21 | 1 |
| Kasperek | 3 | 0 | 23 | 3 |
| Jetly | 2 | 0 | 6 | 0 |

| Fall of Wickets | W | O |
|---|---|---|
| 1st | 20 | 18 |
| 2nd | 60 | 18 |
| 3rd | 170 | 36 |
| 4th | 175 | 43 |
| 5th | - | 47 |
| 6th | - | 64 |
| 7th | - | 64 |
| 8th | - | 72 |
| 9th | - | 98 |
| 10th | - | 100 |

# 2021/22 DREAM11 SUPER SMASH AVERAGES

| | M | In | NO | HS | Runs | Ave | 100s | 50s | Ct | St | O | M | R | W | Ave | R/O | Best |
|---|---|---|---|---|---|---|---|---|---|---|---|---|---|---|---|---|---|
| K.G.Anderson | 8 | 8 | 0 | 52 | 170 | 21.25 | - | 1 | 2 | - | 6 | 0 | 47 | 2 | 23.50 | 7.83 | 1-10 |
| B.G.Armstrong | 11 | 10 | 1 | 31 | 120 | 13.33 | - | - | 7 | - | 14 | 0 | 113 | 3 | 37.66 | 8.07 | 2-24 |
| S.R.Asmussen | 10 | 2 | 1 | 6* | 7 | 7.00 | - | - | 4 | - | 25 | 0 | 166 | 5 | 33.20 | 6.64 | 2-19 |
| G.K.Atkinson | 10 | 9 | 1 | 37 | 112 | 14.00 | - | - | - | - | 7 | 0 | 42 | 1 | 42.00 | 6.00 | 1-9 |
| E.L.Baker | 3 | 2 | 0 | 5 | 5 | 2.50 | - | - | 1 | - | 9.2 | 0 | 80 | 3 | 26.66 | 8.57 | 2-17 |
| M.J.Banks | 10 | 5 | 2 | 11* | 19 | 6.33 | - | - | 6 | - | 32 | 0 | 221 | 14 | 15.78 | 6.91 | 4-29 |
| O.J.S.Bartlett | 7 | 3 | 0 | 9 | 9 | 3.00 | - | - | 2 | - | 10 | 0 | 84 | 1 | 84.00 | 8.40 | 1-12 |
| S.W.Bates | 12 | 12 | 3 | 89* | 504 | 56.00 | - | 5 | 20 | - | 1 | 0 | 4 | 1 | 4.00 | 4.00 | 1-4 |
| E.J.Black | 12 | 3 | 0 | 16 | 17 | 5.66 | - | - | 3 | - | 46 | 2 | 312 | 16 | 19.50 | 6.78 | 2-15 |
| C.G.Blakely | 12 | 9 | 2 | 20 | 85 | 12.14 | - | - | 3 | - | 2 | 0 | 14 | 1 | 14.00 | 7.00 | 1-8 |
| L.F.Boucher | 10 | 10 | 0 | 22 | 78 | 7.80 | - | - | 5 | - | 15.3 | 0 | 152 | 2 | 76.00 | 9.81 | 1-16 |
| S.E.Bowden | 6 | 5 | 2 | 9 | 26 | 8.66 | - | - | 1 | - | | | | | | | |
| R.M.Burns | 11 | 9 | 1 | 42 | 140 | 17.50 | - | - | 4 | - | | | | | | | |
| E.J.Carson | 12 | 5 | 2 | 7 | 11 | 3.66 | - | - | 4 | - | 46 | 1 | 269 | 17 | 15.82 | 5.85 | 4-12 |
| N.E.Codyre | 2 | - | - | - | - | - | - | - | - | - | 3 | 0 | 23 | 0 | - | 7.67 | - |
| N.B.Cox | 9 | 9 | 1 | 63* | 162 | 20.25 | - | 1 | 3 | - | | | | | | | |
| E.G.Cunningham | 9 | 9 | 3 | 28 | 69 | 11.50 | - | - | 5 | - | | | | | | | |
| S.R.H.Curtis | 10 | 9 | 0 | 39 | 137 | 15.22 | - | - | - | - | | | | | | | |
| J.Dean | 4 | 2 | 1 | 17* | 29 | 29.00 | - | - | 1 | - | 4 | 0 | 32 | 0 | - | 8.00 | - |
| S.F.M.Devine | 4 | 4 | 1 | 92 | 153 | 51.00 | - | 1 | 2 | - | 12.1 | 0 | 61 | 7 | 8.71 | 5.01 | 3-24 |
| N.C.Dodd | 7 | 7 | 0 | 57 | 171 | 24.42 | - | 2 | 6 | 1 | | | | | | | |
| D.M.Doughty | 3 | - | - | - | - | - | - | - | 1 | - | 5 | 0 | 30 | 1 | 30.00 | 6.00 | 1-11 |
| L.R.Down | 11 | 11 | 1 | 66* | 235 | 23.50 | - | 1 | 6 | - | | | | | | | |
| K.E.Ebrahim | 12 | 11 | 4 | 38* | 153 | 21.85 | - | - | - | - | 39.4 | 0 | 257 | 13 | 19.76 | 6.48 | 3-13 |
| A.M.Ewart | 1 | 1 | 1 | 5* | 5 | - | - | - | - | - | | | | | | | |
| K.L.Gaging | 2 | 1 | 0 | 2 | 2 | 2.00 | - | - | - | - | | | | | | | |
| O.N.Gain | 9 | 5 | 2 | 10 | 24 | 8.00 | - | - | 2 | - | | | | | | | |
| I.C.Gaze | 11 | 10 | 3 | 24 | 76 | 10.85 | - | - | 2 | 2 | | | | | | | |
| A.G.Gerken | 9 | 6 | 0 | 26 | 47 | 7.83 | - | - | 1 | | | | | | | | |
| C.L.Green | 10 | 5 | 3 | 6* | 9 | 4.50 | - | - | - | - | 35 | 0 | 200 | 7 | 28.57 | 5.71 | 2-9 |
| M.L.Green | 11 | 11 | 2 | 55 | 188 | 20.88 | - | 1 | 5 | - | | | | | | | |
| M.J.Greig | 10 | 10 | 1 | 36 | 182 | 20.22 | - | - | 5 | - | 3 | 0 | 22 | 0 | - | 7.33 | - |
| C.A.Gurrey | 8 | 8 | 1 | 58* | 188 | 26.85 | - | 1 | 2 | - | | | | | | | |
| B.M.Halliday | 8 | 8 | 0 | 28 | 94 | 11.75 | - | - | 5 | - | 27 | 0 | 150 | 10 | 15.00 | 5.56 | 2-14 |
| M.J.Hansen | 10 | 5 | 3 | 5 | 9 | 4.50 | - | - | 4 | - | 14 | 0 | 129 | 4 | 32.25 | 9.21 | 1-12 |
| G.A.Harris | 2 | 2 | 0 | 9 | 11 | 5.50 | - | - | - | - | 4 | 0 | 26 | 0 | - | 6.50 | - |
| L.H.Heaps | 7 | 3 | 2 | 3* | 5 | 5.00 | - | - | - | - | 18 | 0 | 103 | 6 | 17.16 | 5.72 | 2-23 |
| A.T.Hucker | 7 | 3 | 2 | 10* | 11 | 11.00 | - | - | - | - | 19 | 0 | 133 | 2 | 66.50 | 7.00 | 1-15 |
| H.R.Huddleston | 8 | 8 | 1 | 54 | 143 | 20.42 | - | 1 | 3 | - | 27 | 1 | 166 | 7 | 23.71 | 6.15 | 2-14 |
| L.E.V.Hughes | 8 | 5 | 2 | 9* | 21 | 7.00 | - | - | 5 | 4 | | | | | | | |
| M.N.Hyde | 1 | 1 | 0 | 0 | 0 | 0.00 | - | - | - | - | 3 | 0 | 30 | 1 | 30.00 | 10.00 | 1-30 |
| P.M.Inglis | 12 | 12 | 1 | 61* | 227 | 20.63 | - | 1 | 3 | - | | | | | | | |
| I.R.James | 10 | 7 | 3 | 13* | 33 | 8.25 | - | - | 3 | - | | | | | | | |
| H.N.K.Jensen | 5 | 4 | 1 | 14* | 36 | 12.00 | - | - | 1 | - | 20 | 0 | 98 | 10 | 9.80 | 4.90 | 4-20 |
| X.A.R.Jetly | 11 | 3 | 3 | 7* | 15 | - | - | - | 6 | - | 29 | 2 | 135 | 13 | 10.38 | 4.66 | 4-1 |
| F.C.Jonas | 9 | 2 | 2 | 1* | 1 | - | - | - | 3 | - | 36 | 0 | 207 | 7 | 29.57 | 5.75 | 2-17 |
| L.M.Kasperek | 11 | 9 | 3 | 60* | 159 | 26.50 | - | 1 | 5 | - | 37.3 | 2 | 187 | 20 | 9.35 | 4.99 | 3-21 |
| A.N.Kelly | 11 | 10 | 4 | 28* | 101 | 16.83 | - | - | 1 | - | 40 | 1 | 202 | 10 | 20.20 | 5.05 | 3-21 |
| E.K.Kench | 2 | 1 | 0 | 1 | 1 | 1.00 | - | - | - | - | | | | | | | |
| A.C.Kerr | 11 | 10 | 0 | 71 | 346 | 34.60 | - | 4 | 5 | - | 42 | 1 | 192 | 17 | 11.29 | 4.57 | 4-12 |
| J.M.Kerr | 9 | 7 | 4 | 25* | 92 | 30.66 | - | - | 3 | - | 32 | 4 | 152 | 18 | 8.44 | 4.75 | 4-13 |
| C.R.King | 6 | 2 | 2 | 5* | 6 | - | - | - | 5 | - | 5 | 0 | 25 | 3 | 8.33 | 5.00 | 3-18 |
| K.A.Knight | 3 | - | - | - | - | - | - | - | - | - | 6 | 0 | 38 | 0 | - | 6.33 | - |
| A.Kumar | 3 | 2 | 0 | 4 | 4 | 2.00 | - | - | - | - | 4 | 0 | 35 | 0 | - | 8.75 | - |
| M.B.Lamplough | 5 | 2 | 1 | 3* | 4 | 4.00 | - | - | 3 | - | 5 | 0 | 28 | 0 | - | 5.60 | - |
| M.E.Loe | 7 | 2 | 2 | 3* | 3 | - | - | - | - | - | 23.1 | 0 | 168 | 10 | 16.80 | 7.25 | 2-7 |
| A.C.Mace-Cochrane | 2 | 1 | 0 | 0 | 0 | 0.00 | - | - | - | - | | | | | | | |
| F.L.Mackay | 10 | 10 | 2 | 55* | 242 | 30.25 | - | 1 | 3 | - | 35.5 | 0 | 201 | 9 | 22.33 | 5.61 | 3-23 |
| R.A.Mair | 9 | 9 | 2 | 34 | 98 | 14.00 | - | - | 1 | - | 33 | 3 | 181 | 12 | 15.08 | 5.48 | 3-22 |
| K.J.Martin | 12 | 11 | 0 | 40 | 230 | 20.90 | - | - | 5 | 7 | | | | | | | |
| J.T.McFadyen | 11 | 4 | 2 | 4* | 7 | 3.50 | - | - | 8 | 8 | | | | | | | |
| S.R.Naidu | 8 | 7 | 3 | 14 | 45 | 11.25 | - | - | 1 | - | 22 | 1 | 127 | 3 | 42.33 | 5.77 | 2-14 |
| K.F.G.Nation | 6 | 5 | 1 | 19 | 41 | 10.25 | - | - | 1 | - | | | | | | | |
| T.M.M.Newton | 11 | 9 | 2 | 38 | 112 | 16.00 | - | - | 3 | - | 4 | 0 | 28 | 3 | 9.33 | 7.00 | 2-11 |
| S.A.Oldershaw | 12 | 3 | 0 | 4 | 5 | 1.66 | - | - | 1 | - | 47 | 0 | 245 | 14 | 17.50 | 5.21 | 3-16 |
| N.H.Patel | 10 | 10 | 1 | 32 | 105 | 11.66 | - | - | 3 | - | 36 | 0 | 235 | 11 | 21.36 | 6.53 | 3-13 |

| | M | In | NO | HS | Runs | Ave | 100s | 50s | Ct | St | O | M | R | W | Ave | R/O | Best |
|---|---|---|---|---|---|---|---|---|---|---|---|---|---|---|---|---|---|
| C.S.Pedersen | 1 | 1 | 0 | 3 | 3 | 3.00 | - | - | - | - | | | | | | | |
| J.O.Penfold | 1 | - | - | - | - | | - | - | 2 | - | | | | | | | |
| M.M.Penfold | 11 | 4 | 0 | 11 | 11 | 2.75 | - | - | 2 | - | 31 | 0 | 212 | 7 | 30.28 | 6.84 | 2-27 |
| K.T.Perkins | 11 | 11 | 0 | 67 | 253 | 23.00 | - | 1 | 1 | - | | | | | | | |
| A.M.Peterson | 6 | 5 | 0 | 14 | 34 | 6.80 | - | - | 3 | - | 23 | 0 | 148 | 6 | 24.66 | 6.43 | 3-14 |
| G.E.Plimmer | 11 | 11 | 0 | 34 | 133 | 12.09 | - | - | 8 | - | | | | | | | |
| J.E.I.Prasad | 11 | 6 | 2 | 13 | 44 | 11.00 | - | - | - | - | 19.3 | 0 | 143 | 3 | 47.66 | 7.33 | 1-13 |
| M.S.Rees | 4 | 2 | 0 | 6 | 9 | 4.50 | - | - | - | - | 10 | 0 | 54 | 6 | 9.00 | 5.40 | 3-12 |
| E.A.J.Richardson | 2 | 2 | 0 | 11 | 21 | 10.50 | - | - | 1 | - | 8 | 0 | 53 | 3 | 17.66 | 6.63 | 3-27 |
| H.M.Rowe | 10 | 10 | 4 | 39* | 137 | 22.83 | - | - | 5 | - | 38 | 1 | 240 | 5 | 48.00 | 6.32 | 1-16 |
| C.R.Sarsfield | 10 | 7 | 4 | 12 | 26 | 8.66 | - | - | 1 | - | 20.4 | 0 | 149 | 2 | 74.50 | 7.21 | 1-25 |
| A.E.Satterthwaite | 10 | 10 | 0 | 114 | 313 | 31.30 | 1 | 1 | 3 | - | 37 | 1 | 238 | 8 | 29.75 | 6.43 | 2-18 |
| J.L.Savage | 10 | 10 | 0 | 28 | 136 | 13.60 | - | - | 2 | - | 26 | 0 | 218 | 8 | 27.25 | 8.38 | 2-25 |
| S.Shahri | 7 | 7 | 3 | 34 | 119 | 29.75 | - | - | 2 | - | | | | | | | |
| J.A.Simmons | 8 | 2 | 1 | 6 | 6 | 6.00 | - | - | 2 | - | 20 | 0 | 134 | 5 | 26.80 | 6.70 | 2-17 |
| G.Sims | 3 | 2 | 0 | 2 | 3 | 1.50 | - | - | 2 | 1 | | | | | | | |
| K.M.Sims | 3 | 2 | 0 | 4 | 7 | 3.50 | - | - | 1 | - | 1 | 0 | 11 | 0 | - | 11.00 | - |
| M.P.Singh | 9 | 1 | 1 | 2* | 2 | - | - | - | 1 | - | 30 | 2 | 148 | 10 | 14.80 | 4.93 | 3-13 |
| L.M.M.Tahuhu | 9 | 9 | 3 | 39* | 148 | 24.66 | - | - | 1 | - | 18 | 1 | 80 | 6 | 13.33 | 4.44 | 2-13 |
| M.B.Templeton | 8 | 8 | 2 | 14 | 47 | 7.83 | - | - | 4 | - | 9 | 0 | 79 | 1 | 79.00 | 8.78 | 1-27 |
| K.A.Tomlinson | 6 | 6 | 0 | 40 | 78 | 13.00 | - | - | - | - | | | | | | | |
| H.E.Topp | 9 | 8 | 4 | 14* | 46 | 11.50 | - | - | 3 | 4 | | | | | | | |
| N.A.Wakelin | 2 | 1 | 0 | 1 | 1 | 1.00 | - | - | - | - | | | | | | | |
| J.M.Watkin | 9 | 9 | 0 | 70 | 168 | 18.66 | - | 1 | 3 | - | 36 | 0 | 206 | 9 | 22.88 | 5.72 | 2-16 |

## HIGHEST STRIKE RATES *(qualification 100 runs)*

| | | Runs | Balls | S/R | | | Runs | Balls | S/R |
|---|---|---|---|---|---|---|---|---|---|
| L.M.M.Tahuhu | C | 148 | 82 | 180 | S.W.Bates | O | 504 | 438 | 115 |
| S.F.M.Devine | W | 153 | 105 | 145 | L.M.Kasperek | W | 159 | 146 | 108 |
| M.L.Green | W | 188 | 148 | 127 | S.Shahri | A | 119 | 110 | 108 |
| J.M.Watkin | CD | 168 | 138 | 121 | A.E.Satterthwaite | C | 313 | 294 | 106 |
| A.C.Kerr | W | 346 | 300 | 115 | G.E.Plimmer | W | 133 | 125 | 106 |

## MOST ECONOMICAL BOWLING *(qualification 20 overs)*

| | | O | M | R | W | Ave | R/O |
|---|---|---|---|---|---|---|---|
| A.C.Kerr | W | 42 | 1 | 192 | 17 | 11.29 | 4.57 |
| X.A.R.Jetly | W | 29 | 2 | 135 | 13 | 10.38 | 4.66 |
| J.M.Kerr | W | 32 | 4 | 152 | 18 | 8.44 | 4.75 |
| H.N.K.Jensen | O | 20 | 0 | 98 | 10 | 9.80 | 4.90 |
| M.P.Singh | W | 30 | 2 | 148 | 10 | 14.80 | 4.93 |
| L.M.Kasperek | W | 37.3 | 2 | 187 | 20 | 9.35 | 4.99 |
| A.N.Kelly | A | 40 | 1 | 202 | 10 | 20.20 | 5.05 |
| S.A.Oldershaw | O | 47 | 0 | 245 | 14 | 17.50 | 5.21 |
| R.A.Mair | CD | 33 | 3 | 181 | 12 | 15.08 | 5.48 |
| B.M.Halliday | ND | 27 | 0 | 150 | 10 | 15.00 | 5.56 |

# CAREER RECORDS

| | M | In | NO | HS | Runs | Ave | 100s | 50s | Ct | St | O | M | R | W | Ave | R/O | Best |
|---|---|---|---|---|---|---|---|---|---|---|---|---|---|---|---|---|---|
| K.G.Anderson | 60 | 51 | 4 | 52 | 687 | 14.61 | - | 2 | 18 | - | 81 | 0 | 561 | 21 | 26.71 | 6.93 | 3-22 |
| B.G.Armstrong | 52 | 39 | 10 | 39 | 376 | 12.96 | - | - | 17 | - | 133.3 | 1 | 869 | 34 | 25.55 | 6.51 | 3-18 |
| S.R.Asmussen | 25 | 6 | 2 | 6* | 11 | 2.75 | - | - | 4 | - | 52 | 0 | 385 | 11 | 35.00 | 7.40 | 2-19 |
| G.K.Atkinson | 40 | 25 | 4 | 37 | 196 | 9.33 | - | - | 3 | - | 49 | 0 | 358 | 10 | 35.80 | 7.31 | 2-20 |
| E.L.Baker | 4 | 2 | 0 | 5 | 5 | 2.50 | - | - | 1 | - | 11.2 | 0 | 97 | 4 | 24.25 | 8.56 | 2-17 |
| M.J.Banks | 40 | 14 | 6 | 11* | 47 | 5.87 | - | - | 14 | - | 72.1 | 0 | 516 | 27 | 19.11 | 7.15 | 4-29 |
| O.J.S.Bartlett | 8 | 3 | 0 | 9 | 9 | 3.00 | - | - | 2 | - | 10 | 0 | 84 | 1 | 84.00 | 8.40 | 1-12 |
| S.W.Bates | 81 | 81 | 11 | 106* | 2647 | 37.81 | 1 | 18 | 55 | - | 204.5 | 0 | 1249 | 55 | 22.70 | 6.10 | 5-15 |
| E.J.Black | 45 | 15 | 3 | 16 | 58 | 4.83 | - | - | 9 | - | 144.1 | 3 | 1009 | 48 | 21.02 | 7.00 | 4-14 |
| C.G.Blakely | 51 | 39 | 12 | 32* | 294 | 10.88 | - | - | 12 | - | 6.3 | 0 | 47 | 3 | 15.66 | 7.23 | 1-1 |
| L.F.Boucher | 22 | 22 | 1 | 41* | 174 | 8.28 | - | - | 9 | - | 28.3 | 0 | 275 | 5 | 55.00 | 9.65 | 3-21 |
| S.E.Bowden | 11 | 5 | 2 | 9 | 26 | 8.66 | - | - | 1 | - | 5 | 0 | 32 | 0 | - | 6.40 | - |
| R.M.Burns | 65 | 55 | 5 | 62 | 748 | 14.96 | - | 2 | 26 | - | 15 | 0 | 100 | 4 | 25.00 | 6.67 | 2-22 |
| E.J.Carson | 37 | 19 | 9 | 17* | 60 | 6.00 | - | - | 5 | - | 114.4 | 2 | 755 | 40 | 18.87 | 6.58 | 5-18 |
| N.E.Codyre | 2 | - | - | - | - | - | - | - | - | - | 3 | 0 | 23 | 0 | - | 7.67 | - |
| N.B.Cox | 57 | 43 | 9 | 63* | 496 | 14.58 | - | 1 | 14 | - | | | | | | | |
| E.G.Cunningham | 36 | 36 | 3 | 45 | 370 | 11.21 | - | - | 10 | - | 1.4 | 0 | 10 | 0 | - | 6.00 | - |
| S.R.H.Curtis | 82 | 79 | 16 | 69 | 1078 | 17.11 | - | 3 | 17 | - | 59.1 | 0 | 409 | 15 | 27.26 | 6.91 | 3-17 |
| J.Dean | 4 | 2 | 1 | 17* | 29 | 29.00 | - | - | 1 | - | 4 | 0 | 32 | 0 | - | 8.00 | - |
| S.F.M.Devine | 75 | 72 | 17 | 112 | 2644 | 48.07 | 3 | 16 | 35 | - | 212.1 | 3 | 1282 | 69 | 18.57 | 6.04 | 4-21 |
| N.C.Dodd | 97 | 88 | 14 | 70* | 1804 | 24.37 | - | 7 | 36 | 7 | 11 | 0 | 65 | 6 | 10.83 | 5.91 | 3-16 |
| D.M.Doughty | 67 | 4 | 2 | 6 | 6 | 3.00 | - | - | 7 | - | 229.4 | 4 | 1197 | 68 | 17.60 | 5.21 | 4-13 |
| L.R.Down | 70 | 59 | 8 | 92* | 974 | 19.09 | - | 3 | 24 | - | 31.2 | 0 | 220 | 9 | 24.44 | 7.02 | 2-17 |
| K.E.Ebrahim | 98 | 81 | 26 | 84* | 1640 | 29.81 | - | 6 | 15 | - | 285.2 | 6 | 1631 | 64 | 25.48 | 5.72 | 3-8 |
| A.M.Ewart | 8 | 6 | 1 | 8 | 19 | 3.80 | - | - | 1 | 3 | | | | | | | |
| K.L.Gaging | 6 | 4 | 1 | 28 | 41 | 13.66 | - | - | 1 | - | | | | | | | |
| O.N.Gain | 14 | 9 | 2 | 10 | 39 | 5.57 | - | - | 3 | - | | | | | | | |
| I.C.Gaze | 14 | 11 | 4 | 24 | 81 | 11.57 | - | - | 3 | 2 | | | | | | | |
| A.G.Gerken | 9 | 6 | 0 | 26 | 47 | 7.83 | - | - | - | 1 | | | | | | | |
| C.L.Green | 35 | 17 | 11 | 6* | 35 | 5.83 | - | - | 2 | - | 99.2 | 0 | 594 | 16 | 37.12 | 5.98 | 2-9 |
| M.L.Green | 94 | 88 | 19 | 74 | 1615 | 23.40 | - | 6 | 37 | - | 43.3 | 0 | 314 | 15 | 20.93 | 7.22 | 4-9 |
| M.J.Greig | 50 | 40 | 8 | 39* | 420 | 13.12 | - | - | 11 | - | 82.2 | 0 | 618 | 19 | 32.52 | 7.51 | 3-33 |
| C.A.Gurrey | 58 | 56 | 7 | 106* | 1526 | 31.14 | 1 | 10 | 8 | - | | | | | | | |
| B.M.Halliday | 54 | 45 | 8 | 43 | 546 | 14.75 | - | - | 16 | - | 76 | 0 | 496 | 25 | 19.84 | 6.53 | 2-3 |
| M.J.Hansen | 53 | 35 | 17 | 31* | 157 | 8.72 | - | - | 10 | - | 80.3 | 0 | 609 | 12 | 50.75 | 7.57 | 2-15 |
| G.A.Harris | 3 | 3 | 0 | 9 | 12 | 4.00 | - | - | - | - | 4 | 0 | 26 | 0 | - | 6.50 | - |
| L.H.Heaps | 25 | 6 | 4 | 3* | 12 | 6.00 | - | - | 5 | - | 63.3 | 1 | 430 | 19 | 22.63 | 6.77 | 3-32 |
| A.T.Hucker | 14 | 4 | 2 | 10* | 15 | 7.50 | - | - | 2 | - | 26 | 0 | 188 | 3 | 62.66 | 7.23 | 1-15 |
| H.R.Huddleston | 100 | 70 | 20 | 55* | 970 | 19.40 | - | 2 | 25 | - | 273.2 | 13 | 1571 | 65 | 24.16 | 5.75 | 3-8 |
| L.E.V.Hughes | 51 | 19 | 2 | 16 | 126 | 7.41 | - | - | 23 | 16 | | | | | | | |
| M.N.Hyde | 30 | 8 | 4 | 9 | 32 | 8.00 | - | - | 8 | - | 56 | 0 | 451 | 8 | 56.37 | 8.05 | 2-14 |
| P.M.Inglis | 57 | 51 | 8 | 62 | 728 | 16.93 | - | 2 | 14 | - | | | | | | | |
| I.R.James | 41 | 26 | 7 | 24 | 167 | 8.78 | - | - | 13 | - | | | | | | | |
| H.N.K.Jensen | 64 | 44 | 9 | 55 | 598 | 17.08 | - | 1 | 9 | - | 178.2 | 4 | 1061 | 46 | 23.06 | 5.95 | 4-20 |
| X.A.R.Jetly | 24 | 6 | 5 | 7* | 16 | 16.00 | - | - | 11 | - | 45 | 2 | 225 | 20 | 11.25 | 5.00 | 4-1 |
| F.C.Jonas | 28 | 5 | 4 | 5* | 6 | 6.00 | - | - | 4 | - | 100.2 | 0 | 595 | 21 | 28.33 | 5.93 | 2-17 |
| L.M.Kasperek | 69 | 56 | 16 | 60* | 850 | 21.25 | - | 2 | 18 | - | 235 | 2 | 1331 | 86 | 15.47 | 5.66 | 4-16 |
| A.N.Kelly | 68 | 39 | 13 | 41* | 324 | 12.46 | - | - | 8 | - | 234.5 | 7 | 1322 | 60 | 22.03 | 5.63 | 4-28 |
| E.K.Kench | 11 | 6 | 2 | 11 | 20 | 5.00 | - | - | 1 | - | | | | | | | |
| A.C.Kerr | 67 | 50 | 15 | 71 | 1253 | 35.80 | - | 9 | 16 | - | 248.4 | 3 | 1276 | 96 | 13.29 | 5.14 | 4-4 |
| J.M.Kerr | 54 | 26 | 11 | 25* | 230 | 15.33 | - | - | 15 | - | 168 | 6 | 935 | 62 | 15.08 | 5.57 | 4-13 |
| C.R.King | 27 | 10 | 6 | 13* | 31 | 7.75 | - | - | 8 | - | 5 | 0 | 25 | 3 | 8.33 | 5.00 | 3-18 |
| K.A.Knight | 3 | - | - | - | - | - | - | - | - | - | 6 | 0 | 38 | 0 | - | 6.33 | - |
| A.Kumar | 8 | 3 | 1 | 4 | 7 | 3.50 | - | - | 2 | - | 14 | 0 | 119 | 1 | 119.00 | 8.50 | 1-23 |
| M.B.Lamplough | 11 | 2 | 1 | 3* | 4 | 4.00 | - | - | 3 | - | 11 | 0 | 74 | 0 | - | 6.73 | - |
| M.E.Loe | 14 | 6 | 6 | 3* | 5 | - | - | - | 1 | - | 48.1 | 0 | 365 | 14 | 26.07 | 7.58 | 2-7 |
| A.C.Mace-Cochrane | 33 | 19 | 6 | 23 | 144 | 11.07 | - | - | 1 | - | 4 | 0 | 35 | 0 | - | 8.75 | - |
| F.L.Mackay | 104 | 97 | 22 | 97 | 2579 | 34.38 | - | 14 | 28 | - | 362.1 | 8 | 1884 | 106 | 17.77 | 5.20 | 4-10 |
| R.A.Mair | 47 | 36 | 11 | 36* | 304 | 12.16 | - | - | 1 | - | 141.2 | 9 | 801 | 37 | 21.64 | 5.67 | 3-22 |
| K.J.Martin | 103 | 102 | 9 | 94 | 2568 | 27.61 | - | 17 | 39 | 34 | | | | | | | |
| J.T.McFadyen | 49 | 24 | 6 | 28 | 180 | 10.00 | - | - | 21 | 26 | | | | | | | |
| S.R.Naidu | 11 | 8 | 4 | 14 | 45 | 11.25 | - | - | 1 | - | 27 | 1 | 164 | 3 | 54.66 | 6.07 | 2-14 |
| K.F.G.Nation | 52 | 39 | 5 | 91 | 492 | 14.47 | - | 1 | 9 | - | | | | | | | |
| T.M.M.Newton | 77 | 47 | 16 | 50* | 439 | 14.16 | - | 1 | 25 | - | 103.2 | 1 | 727 | 27 | 26.92 | 7.04 | 3-13 |
| S.A.Oldershaw | 31 | 7 | 1 | 6 | 12 | 2.00 | - | - | 3 | - | 87.3 | 0 | 508 | 26 | 19.53 | 5.81 | 3-16 |

| | M | In | NO | HS | Runs | Ave | 100s | 50s | Ct | St | O | M | R | W | Ave | R/O | Best |
|---|---|---|---|---|---|---|---|---|---|---|---|---|---|---|---|---|---|
| N.H.Patel | 29 | 19 | 5 | 32 | 182 | 13.00 | - | - | 4 | - | 80.1 | 0 | 489 | 28 | 17.46 | 6.10 | 4-19 |
| C.S.Pedersen | 1 | 1 | 0 | 3 | 3 | 3.00 | - | - | - | - | | | | | | | |
| J.O.Penfold | 1 | - | - | - | - | - | - | - | 2 | - | | | | | | | |
| M.M.Penfold | 14 | 6 | 0 | 11 | 12 | 2.00 | - | - | 2 | - | 36 | 0 | 253 | 7 | 36.14 | 7.03 | 2-27 |
| K.T.Perkins | 103 | 93 | 24 | 75* | 2147 | 31.11 | - | 9 | 34 | - | | | | | | | |
| A.M.Peterson | 91 | 85 | 9 | 68 | 1358 | 17.86 | - | 4 | 27 | - | 254.3 | 4 | 1589 | 78 | 20.37 | 6.24 | 4-11 |
| G.E.Plimmer | 22 | 13 | 0 | 34 | 137 | 10.53 | - | - | 8 | - | | | | | | | |
| J.E.I.Prasad | 27 | 10 | 4 | 18* | 67 | 11.16 | - | - | 3 | - | 51.1 | 0 | 363 | 14 | 25.92 | 7.09 | 3-19 |
| M.S.Rees | 22 | 11 | 3 | 7 | 26 | 3.25 | - | - | 3 | - | 31.1 | 0 | 255 | 10 | 25.50 | 8.18 | 3-12 |
| E.A.J.Richardson | 79 | 60 | 13 | 54* | 632 | 13.44 | - | 1 | 15 | - | 237.3 | 5 | 1457 | 62 | 23.50 | 6.13 | 5-17 |
| H.M.Rowe | 72 | 60 | 16 | 45 | 716 | 16.27 | - | - | 22 | - | 232.4 | 5 | 1591 | 44 | 36.15 | 6.84 | 3-27 |
| C.R.Sarsfield | 30 | 15 | 9 | 12 | 37 | 6.16 | - | - | 4 | - | 68.4 | 1 | 521 | 16 | 32.56 | 7.59 | 3-19 |
| A.E.Satterthwaite | 93 | 89 | 17 | 114 | 2549 | 35.40 | 1 | 15 | 41 | - | 224 | 2 | 1392 | 64 | 21.75 | 6.21 | 4-14 |
| J.L.Savage | 67 | 34 | 5 | 42 | 357 | 12.31 | - | - | 13 | 6 | 118.1 | 0 | 839 | 38 | 22.07 | 7.10 | 4-26 |
| S.Shahri | 34 | 27 | 8 | 40* | 375 | 19.73 | - | - | 4 | - | | | | | | | |
| J.A.Simmons | 31 | 8 | 5 | 9* | 23 | 7.66 | - | - | 8 | - | 81 | 1 | 540 | 14 | 38.57 | 6.67 | 2-14 |
| G.Sims | 4 | 3 | 0 | 2 | 5 | 1.66 | - | - | 2 | 1 | | | | | | | |
| K.M.Sims | 9 | 4 | 1 | 4 | 7 | 2.33 | - | - | 1 | - | 11 | 1 | 83 | 2 | 41.50 | 7.55 | 1-5 |
| M.P.Singh | 55 | 6 | 5 | 6 | 15 | 15.00 | - | - | 5 | - | 169.4 | 7 | 929 | 44 | 21.11 | 5.48 | 4-26 |
| L.M.M.Tahuhu | 75 | 42 | 20 | 39* | 390 | 17.72 | - | - | 12 | - | 224.4 | 8 | 1255 | 58 | 21.63 | 5.59 | 3-6 |
| M.B.Templeton | 11 | 10 | 3 | 31 | 80 | 11.42 | - | - | 4 | - | 19.3 | 0 | 138 | 3 | 46.00 | 7.08 | 2-15 |
| K.A.Tomlinson | 81 | 69 | 5 | 47 | 821 | 12.82 | - | - | 17 | 5 | 12 | 0 | 95 | 6 | 15.83 | 7.92 | 3-11 |
| H.E.Topp | 9 | 8 | 4 | 14* | 46 | 11.50 | - | - | 3 | 4 | | | | | | | |
| N.A.Wakelin | 2 | 1 | 0 | 1 | 1 | 1.00 | - | - | - | - | | | | | | | |
| J.M.Watkin | 62 | 59 | 4 | 95 | 1135 | 20.63 | - | 6 | 11 | - | 201.4 | 4 | 1247 | 44 | 28.34 | 6.18 | 4-22 |

# NEW ZEALAND DEVELOPMENT TEAM

A New Zealand development squad was selected for matches against a Wellington XI (fifty-over) and a Hutt Academy Boys XI (Twenty20). The squad was C.L. Agafili, B.G. Armstrong, S.R. Asmussen, G.K. Anderson, E.J. Carson, P. Catton, I.C. Gaze, C.L. Green, J.M. Hollard, B.G. Illing, A. Kumar, N.H. Patel, M.B. Templeton.

### WELLINGTON XI v NEW ZEALAND DEVELOPMENT XI
*At Karori Park, Wellington 12 March, 2022*
**Abandoned without a ball being bowled**

### HUTT CRICKET ACADEMY XI v NEW ZEALAND DEVELOPMENT XI
*At Hutt Recreation Ground, Lower Hutt 13 March, 2022*
**Hutt Cricket Academy XI** 96-9 (C.A. Pietersz 28, M.D. Bassett 26, A. Kumar 2-8, C.L. Agafili 2-14) defeated **New Zealand Development XI** 91-5 (B.G. Armstrong 48*) by 5 runs

# BATES XII v DEVINE XII

Twenty-four players selected from the Under 19 National Tournament were split into two teams and played three Twenty20 games at Lincoln in March.

### BATES XII v DEVINE XII
*At Lincoln Green 26 March, 2022*
**Bates XII** 104-6 (E.M.A. McLeod 32, H.M Graham 25*, A. Kumar 2-8, K.M. Chandler 2-17) lost to **Devine XII** 108-3 (I.G. Sharp 35*, E.R. Brosnahan 22) by 7 wickets

### BATES XII v DEVINE XII
*At Lincoln Green 26 March, 2022*
**Devine XII** 119-6 (A.S. Browning 25, I.G. Sharp 21, M.W. Downes 2-26) defeated **Bates XII** 88 (M.W. Downes 23*, A.B. Apperley 2-7, B.G. Illing 2-10, K.M. Chandler 2-17) by 31 runs

### BATES XII v DEVINE XII
*At Lincoln Green 27 March, 2022*
**Bates XII** 129-5 (A.S. Hamilton 41*, M.B. Templeton 24, A.B. Apperley 2-32) lost to **Devine XII** 133-7 (F.D.M. Devonshire 32, A. Kumar 29, M.W. Downes 2-20) by 7 wickets

# TEAM RECORDS

## Highest Totals

| | | | |
|---|---|---|---|
| 211-3 | Auckland v Northern Districts | Hamilton | 2017/18 |
| 204-5 | Auckland v Canterbury | Lincoln | 2019/20 |
| 201-5 | Wellington v Northern Districts | Mt Maunganui | 2019/20 |
| 196-5 | Wellington v Otago | Wellington | 2020/21 |
| 189-4 | Auckland v Northern Districts | Hamilton | 2013/14 |

## Lowest Totals

| | | | |
|---|---|---|---|
| 46 | Northern Districts v Wellington | Whangarei | 2021/22 |
| 56 | Central Districts v Wellington | Lincoln | 2019/20 |
| 59 | Central Districts v Wellington | Lincoln | 2017/18 |
| 63 | Auckland v Canterbury | Christchurch | 2010/11 |
| 65 | Central Districts v Wellington | Levin | 2017/18 |

# INDIVIDUAL RECORDS

## Centuries

| | | | | |
|---|---|---|---|---|
| 131* | S.J. McGlashan | Auckland v Northern Districts | Hamilton | 2013/14 |
| 114 | A.E. Satterthwaite | Canterbury v Northern Districts | Christchurch | 2021/22 |
| 112 | S.F.M. Devine | Wellington v Northern Districts | Mt Maunganui | 2019/20 |
| 108* | S.F.M. Devine | Wellington v Otago | Dunedin | 2020/21 |
| 106* | R.H. Priest | Central Districts v Otago | Dunedin | 2011/12 |
| 106* | S.F.M. Devine | Wellington v Auckland | Wellington | 2015/16 |
| 106* | S.W. Bates | Otago v Northern Districts | Lincoln | 2019/20 |
| 106* | C.A. Gurrey | Northern Districts v Central Districts | Lincoln | 2019/20 |

## Fastest Century

| *Balls* | | | | |
|---|---|---|---|---|
| 36 | S.F.M. Devine | Wellington v Otago | Dunedin | 2020/21 |

## Fastest Fifty

| *Balls* | | | | |
|---|---|---|---|---|
| 21 | S.F.M. Devine | Wellington v Otago | Dunedin | 2020/21 |

## Most Wickets in an Innings

| | | | | |
|---|---|---|---|---|
| 4-0-15-5 | S.W. Bates | Otago v Canterbury | Christchurch | 2010/11 |
| 4-0-17-5 | E.A.J. Richardson | Central Districts v Canterbury | Paraparaumu | 2010/11 |
| 4-0-18-5 | E.J. Carson | Otago v Central Districts | Napier | 2019/20 |

## Most Economical Bowling

| | | | | |
|---|---|---|---|---|
| 4-1-4-4 | A.C. Kerr | Wellington v Northern Districts | Lincoln | 2018/19 |
| 4-1-5-1 | E.J. Carson | Otago v Central Districts | Napier | 2021/22 |

## Most Expensive Bowling

| | | | | |
|---|---|---|---|---|
| 4-0-65-0 | M.N. Hyde | Northern Districts v Auckland | Hamilton | 2017/18 |
| 4-0-64-0 | M.P. Murphy | Auckland v Central Districts | Palmerston North | 2007/08 |
| 4-0-61-1 | C. Esterhuizen | Northern Districts v Wellington | Mt Maunganui | 2019/20 |

## Hat-tricks

| | | | | |
|---|---|---|---|---|
| 4-0-40-3 | A.E. Cooper | Wellington v Northern Districts | Mt Maunganui | 2008/09 |
| 4-0-10-4 | L.R. Doolan | Wellington v Canterbury | Upper Hutt | 2010/11 |
| 4-0-26-3 | R.H. Candy | Canterbury v Central Districts | Hastings | 2015/16 |
| 4-0-23-3 | A.C. Kerr | Wellington v Otago | Lincoln | 2018/19 |
| 4-0-27-3 | G.E.S. Sullivan | Canterbury v Wellington | Christchurch | 2019/20 |
| 4-0-19-3 | A.C.Kerr | Wellington v Canterbury | Wellington | 2020/21 |

## Wicketkeeping

**DISMISSALS**

*(ct/st)*

| | | | | | |
|---|---|---|---|---|---|
| 5 | (1/4) | R.H. Priest | Wellington v Central Districts | Lincoln | 2017/18 |
| 5 | (1/4) | J.T. McFadyen | Wellington v Northern Districts | Hamilton | 2018/19 |
| 5 | (3/2) | J.T. McFadyen | Wellington v Canterbury | Wellington | 2021/22 |

## Fielding

**CATCHES**

| | | | | |
|---|---|---|---|---|
| 4 | G.E. Plimmer | Wellington v Otago | Queenstown | 2021/22 |
| 4 | S.W. Bates | Otago v Wellington | Wellington | 2021/22 |

# RECORD PARTNERSHIPS

| | | | | | |
|---|---|---|---|---|---|
| 1st | 173* | C.A. Gurrey & B.M. Bezuidenhout | ND v CD | Lincoln | 2019/20 |
| 2nd | 153* | S.W. Bates & K.J. Martin | Otago v ND | Lincoln | 2019/20 |
| 3rd | 150 | A.L. Watkins & S.J. McGlashan | CD v Wellington | New Plymouth | 2007/08 |
| 4th | 119* | K.T. Perkins & V.J. Lind | Auckland v Otago | Lincoln | 2016/17 |
| 5th | 100* | K.E. Ebrahim & K.F.G. Nation | Canterbury v ND | Christchurch | 2020/21 |
| 6th | 91 | B.M. Halliday & L.F. Boucher | ND v Canterbury | Christchurch | 2019/20 |
| 7th | 66* | K.E. Ebrahim & L.M.M. Tahuhu | Canterbury v Wellington | Wellington | 2020/21 |
| 8th | 46 | P.A. Gruber & R.S.M Lili'i | Auckland v Canterbury | Christchurch | 2010/11 |
| 9th | 47* | M.J. Hansen & K.E. Baxter | CD v ND | Napier | 2016/17 |
| 10th | 17 | J. Dean & S.R. Asmussen | Canterbury v Otago | Christchurch | 2021/22 |

# DOMESTIC TWENTY20 CAREER RECORDS

**BATTING**

| | | M | In | NO | HS | Runs | Ave | 100s | 50s |
|---|---|---|---|---|---|---|---|---|---|
| S.W. Bates | O | 81 | 81 | 11 | 106* | 2647 | 37.81 | 1 | 18 |
| S.F.M. Devine | C, W | 75 | 72 | 17 | 112 | 2644 | 48.07 | 3 | 16 |
| F.L. Mackay | C | 104 | 97 | 22 | 97 | 2579 | 34.38 | – | 14 |
| K.J. Martin | O | 103 | 102 | 9 | 94 | 2568 | 27.61 | – | 17 |
| A.E. Satterthwaite | C | 93 | 89 | 17 | 114 | 2549 | 35.40 | 1 | 15 |
| K.T. Perkins | A | 103 | 93 | 24 | 75* | 2147 | 31.11 | – | 9 |
| N.C. Dodd | ND, CD | 97 | 88 | 14 | 70* | 1804 | 24.37 | – | 7 |
| K.E. Ebrahim | CD, C, O | 98 | 81 | 26 | 84* | 1640 | 29.81 | – | 6 |
| M.L. Green | A, W | 94 | 88 | 19 | 74 | 1615 | 23.40 | – | 6 |
| C.A. Gurrey | ND | 58 | 56 | 7 | 106* | 1526 | 31.14 | 1 | 10 |

**BOWLING**

| | | M | O | M | R | W | Ave | R/O | Best |
|---|---|---|---|---|---|---|---|---|---|
| F.L. Mackay | C | 104 | 362.1 | 8 | 1884 | 106 | 17.77 | 5.20 | 4-10 |
| A.C. Kerr | W | 67 | 248.4 | 3 | 1276 | 96 | 13.29 | 5.13 | 4-4 |
| L.M. Kasperek | W, O | 69 | 235 | 2 | 1331 | 86 | 15.47 | 5.66 | 4-16 |
| A.M. Peterson | ND, A | 91 | 254.3 | 4 | 1589 | 78 | 20.37 | 6.24 | 4-11 |
| S.F.M. Devine | C, W | 75 | 212.1 | 3 | 1282 | 69 | 18.57 | 6.04 | 4-21 |
| D.M. Doughty | W | 67 | 229.4 | 4 | 1197 | 68 | 17.60 | 5.21 | 4-13 |
| H.R. Huddleston | ND, A | 100 | 273.2 | 13 | 1571 | 65 | 24.16 | 5.75 | 3-8 |
| A.E. Satterthwaite | C | 93 | 224 | 2 | 1392 | 64 | 21.75 | 6.21 | 4-14 |
| K.E. Ebrahim | CD, C, O | 98 | 285.2 | 6 | 1631 | 64 | 25.48 | 5.72 | 3-8 |
| E.A.J. Richardson | CD, W, ND | 79 | 237.3 | 5 | 1457 | 62 | 23.50 | 6.13 | 5-17 |
| J.M. Kerr | W | 54 | 168 | 6 | 935 | 62 | 15.08 | 5.57 | 4-13 |

**WICKETKEEPING**

| | ct | st | Total |
|---|---|---|---|
| R.H. Priest | 35 | 53 | 88 |
| K.J. Martin | 35 | 34 | 69 |
| J.T. McFadyen | 19 | 26 | 45 |
| N.C. Dodd | 33 | 7 | 40 |
| L.E.V. Hughes | 23 | 16 | 39 |
| V.J. Lind | 20 | 19 | 39 |

**FIELDING**

| | ct |
|---|---|
| S.W. Bates | 55 |
| A.E. Satterthwaite | 41 |
| E.C. Perry | 39 |
| M.L. Green | 37 |
| S.F.M. Devine | 35 |
| K.T. Perkins | 34 |

# UNDER 19 TOURNAMENT

The Under 19 Tournament was held at Lincoln from 6 to 12 January, 2022. The tournament was made up of five rounds of fifty-over games and one round of Twenty20 matches. The tournament was won by Central Districts.

### FIRST ROUND

**Central Districts** 169 defeated **Auckland** 110 by 60 runs *(D/L)*
**Canterbury** 193-9 defeated **Northern Districts** 174-9 by 19 runs
**Wellington** 207-9 defeated **Otago** 144-9 by 63 runs

### SECOND ROUND

**Canterbury** 109 lost to **Auckland** 110-2 by 8 wickets
**Central Districts** 265-5 defeated **Otago** 118 by 147 runs
**Wellington** 200-7 defeated **Northern Districts** 184 by 16 runs

### THIRD ROUND

**Auckland** 213-9 defeated **Wellington** 209 by 4 runs
**Central Districts** 260-9 defeated **Canterbury** 126 by 134 runs
**Northern Districts** 109 lost to **Otago** 110-2 by 8 wickets

### FOURTH ROUND

**Otago** 193 lost to **Auckland** 195-7 by 3 wickets
**Wellington** 224-9 lost to **Canterbury** 227-7 by 3 wickets
**Central Districts** 141 lost to **Northern Districts** 144-9 by 1 wicket

### FIFTH ROUND

**Auckland** 251-2 defeated **Northern Districts** 212 by 39 runs
**Otago** 175 defeated **Canterbury** 137 by 38 runs
**Central Districts** 239-8 defeated **Wellington** 170 by 69 runs

### SIXTH ROUND

**Otago** 123-9 lost to **Central Districts** 124-5 by 5 wickets
**Canterbury** 122-7 defeated **Auckland** 97-9 by 25 runs
**Wellington** 124-5 lost to **Northern Districts** 125-2 by 8 wickets

**Final points:** Central Districts 23, Auckland 17, Canterbury 11, Otago 10, Wellington 9, Northern Districts 8.

# NEW ZEALAND
# FIRST-CLASS RECORDS

*to 1 July, 2022*

**FIRST-CLASS MATCH DEFINED**

The six countries represented at Imperial Cricket Conference on 19 May 1947 reached agreement in regard to definition of a first-class match. This did not have effect retrospectively.

A match of three or more days' duration between two sides of eleven players officially adjudged first-class shall be regarded as a first-class fixture. Matches in which either team has more than eleven players or which are scheduled for less than three days shall not be regarded as first-class. The governing body in each country shall decide the status of teams.

The records have been compiled on the following basis:

    (1)  Otago and Canterbury from 1863/64 to date

    (2)  Wellington and Auckland from 1873/74 to date

    (3)  Nelson from 1873/74 to 1891/92 inclusive

    (4)  West Coast (North Island) 1879/80

    (5)  Taranaki from 1882/83 to 1897/98 inclusive

    (6)  Hawke's Bay from 1883/84 to 1920/21 inclusive

    (7)  Southland from 1914/15 to 1920/21 inclusive

    (8)  Central Districts from 1950/51 to date

    (9)  Northern Districts from 1956/57 to date

**Notes:**

• Games played by the Melbourne Cricket Club teams of 1899/1900, 1905/1906 and 1926/27, are not treated as first-class in accordance with a decision of the New Zealand Cricket Council.

• Although set down for only two days each, the return matches played by A. Sims' Australian XI in 1913/14 against Canterbury and Wellington are included in these records; so is the match An Australian XI v Minor Associations, 1920/21, and MCC v Wellington, 1932/33.

• From 1933/34 season onwards, only games for which at least three days have been set down are treated as first-class.

• There have now been 2528 first-class matches in New Zealand.

• Unless otherwise stated, the first-class records relate to first-class matches in New Zealand and by New Zealand touring teams overseas. Apart from the games which have taken place in New Zealand, there are a further 639 played by New Zealand overseas as follows:

| | | |
|---|---|---|
| in Australia | 1898/99 to 2019/20 | 96 |
| in England | 1927 to 2022 | 314 |
| in South Africa | 1953/54 to 2016/17 | 59 |
| in Pakistan | 1955/56 to 2001/02 | 33 |
| in India | 1955/56 to 2021/22 | 54 |
| in West Indies | 1971/72 to 2014 | 32 |
| in Sri Lanka | 1983/84 to 2019/20 | 24 |
| in Zimbabwe | 1992/93 to 2016/17 | 15 |
| in Bangladesh | 2004/05 to 2013/14 | 6 |
| in United Arab Emirates | 2014/15 to 2018/19 | 6 |

plus four games by Young New Zealand in Zimbabwe in 1984/85, three games by New Zealand Young Internationals in Zimbabwe 1988/89, one match by Wellington in Australia 1990/91, one match by Canterbury in South Africa 1993/94, three matches by New Zealand Academy in South Africa 1997/98, seven games by New Zealand A in England 2000 and 2014, three matches by New Zealand A in South Africa in 2004/05, five matches by New Zealand A in Sri Lanka in 2005/06 and 2013/14, one match by New Zealand White in Australia 2006/07, six matches by New Zealand A in India in 2008/09, 2013/14 and 2017/18, three games by New Zealand A in Zimbabwe in 2010/11 and two games by New Zealand A in United Arab Emirates in 2018/19.

# GROUNDS

| Ground | No of matches | First and most recent match | | Highest and lowest team totals | | | | Highest Innings / Best Bowling | | | |
|---|---|---|---|---|---|---|---|---|---|---|---|
| South Dunedin Recreation Ground | 9 | O v C | 1863/64 | C | 272 | v O | 1875/76 | 75 | H.W. Moore | C v O | 1877/78 |
| | | O v C | 1877/78 | MCC | 34 | v O | 1863/64 | 8-28 | W. Hendley | O v C | 1869/70 |
| Hagley Park (old) Christchurch | 1 | C v O | 1864/65 | C | 80 | v O | 1864/65 | 22 | J. Fulton | O v C | 1864/65 |
| | | only match | | O | 61 | v C | 1864/65 | 5-17 | J.W. Stevens | C v O | 1864/65 |
| Hagley Park (new) * Christchurch | 71 | C v O | 1866/67 | NZ | 659-6d | v P | 2020/21 | 301* | P.G. Fulton | C v A | 2002/03 |
| | | NZ v SA | 2021/22 | C | 25 | v O | 1866/67 | 10-28 | A.E. Moss | C v W | 1889/90 |
| Basin Reserve Wellington | 457 | W v A | 1873/74 | NZ | 680-8d | v I | 2013/14 | 327* | D.P. Conway | W v C | 2019/20 |
| | | W v CD | 2021/22 | W | 22 | v C | 1903/04 | 9-43 | T. Eden | N v W | 1875/76 |
| Victory Square Nelson | 7 | N v W | 1874/75 | N | 150 | v A | 1882/83 | 31 | C.A. Knapp | W v N | 1874/75 |
| | | N v W | 1887/88 | W | 19 | v N | 1885/86 | 8-26 | F.H. Cooke | N v W | 1887/88 |
| Domain Auckland | 33 | A v C | 1877/78 | A | 579 | v O | 1909/10 | 151* | Harold B. Lusk | C v A | 1910/11 |
| | | A v C | 1912/13 | A | 13 | v C | 1877/78 | 9-75 | R. Neill | A v C | 1891/92 |
| Caledonian Ground Dunedin | 4 | O v C | 1879/80 | O | 297 | v W | 1904/05 | 88 | H.G. Seideberg | O v W | 1904/05 |
| | | O v W | 1904/05 | A | 48 | v O | 1889/90 | 8-36 | A.W. Rees | A v O | 1889/90 |
| Lancaster Park § Christchurch | 334 | C v A | 1882/83 | C | 777 | v O | 1996/97 | 385 | B. Sutcliffe | O v C | 1952/53 |
| | | NZ v SL | 2006/07 | O | 35 | v A | 1884/85 | 9-72 | F.H. Cooke | O v C | 1884/85 |
| Botanical Gardens Nelson | 1 | N v W | 1883/84 | N | 56 | v W | 1883/84 | 17 | L. Fowler | N v W | 1883/84 |
| | | only match | | W | 30 | v N | 1883/84 | 5-10 | G. Fowler | N v W | 1883/84 |
| Carisbrook Dunedin | 252 | O v Tas | 1883/84 | NSW | 752-8d | v O | 1923/24 | 355 | B. Sutcliffe | O v A | 1949/50 |
| | | O v C | 2007/08 | C | 27 | v O | 1906/07 | 9-50 | A.H. Fisher | O v Q'ld | 1896/97 |
| Recreation Ground Napier | 20½ | HB v W | 1884/85 | MCC | 394 | v HB | 1906/07 | 188 | C.G. Wilson | O v HB | 1908/09 |
| | | HB v A | 1912/13 | HB | 42 | v C | 1897/98 | 9-47 | T.H. Dent | HB v W | 1900/01 |
| Farndon Park Napier | 4½ | HB v T | 1891/92 | Q'ld | 492 | v HB | 1896/97 | 135 | O.W. Cowley | Q'ld v HB | 1896/97 |
| | | HB v Q'ld | 1896/97 | T | 39 | v HB | 1891/92 | 8-14 | S.W. Austin | NSW v HB | 1893/94 |
| King Edward Park Hawera | 2 | T v HB | 1891/92 | T | 135 | v Fiji | 1894/95 | 62 | Hugh B. Lusk | HB v T | 1891/92 |
| | | T v Fiji | 1894/95 | T | 29 | v HB | 1891/92 | 7-? | C.R. Smith | HB v T | 1891/92 |
| Bayly Park Hawera | 2 | T v HB | 1896/97 | C | 260 | v T | 1897/98 | 106 | W.J. Crawshaw | T v HB | 1896/97 |
| | | T v C | 1897/98 | HB | 100 | v T | 1896/97 | 6-43 | D. Reese | C v T | 1897/98 |
| Victoria Park Auckland | 3 | A v C | 1908/09 | A | 470 | v HB | 1910/11 | 88 | W. Carlton | C v A | 1909/10 |
| | | A v HB | 1910/11 | HB | 28 | v A | 1910/11 | 7-42 | A.E. Relf | A v C | 1908/09 |
| Nelson Cricket Ground Hastings | 3 | HB v W | 1913/14 | C | 337 | v HB | 1914/15 | 111 | V.S. Ransford | Aust v HB | 1913/14 |
| | | HB v C | 1914/15 | HB | 89 | v C | 1914/15 | 8-51 | A.A. Mailey | Aust v HB | 1913/14 |
| Eden Park Auckland | 237 | A v Aust | 1913/14 | A | 693-9d | v C | 1939/40 | 336* | W.R. Hammond | E v NZ | 1932/33 |
| | | NZ v E | 2017/18 | NZ | 26 | v E | 1954/55 | 9-36 | A.F. Wensley | A v O | 1929/30 |
| Rugby Park Invercargill | 5 | S v O | 1914/15 | Aust | 195 | v S | 1920/21 | 71 | A. Galland | O v S | 1919/20 |
| | | S v Aust | 1920/21 | C | 37 | v S | 1920/21 | 8-84 | D.J. McBeath | S v C | 1920/21 |
| Nelson Park Napier | 23 | HB v W | 1919/20 | A | 668-7d | v CD | 2014/15 | 281 | C. Munro | A v CD | 2014/15 |
| | | CD v ND | 2017/18 | CD | 99 | v ND | 2017/18 | 7-48 | S.C. Kuggeleijn | ND v CD | 2017/18 |
| Wellington College Ground | 1 | W v A | 1923/24 | W | 569 | v A | 1923/24 | 163 | J.S. Hiddleston | W v A | 1923/24 |
| | | only match | | A | 280 | v W | 1923/24 | 6-172 | S.G. Smith | A v W | 1923/24 |
| Sportsground † Palmerston North | 52 | CD v C | 1950/51 | W | 590-8d | v CD | 2004/05 | 236 | J.D. Ryder | W v CD | 2004/05 |
| | | CD v C | 2021/22 | A | 71 | v CD | 2001/02 | 7-31 | H.B. Cave | CD v A | 1952/53 |
| Pukekura Park New Plymouth | 55 | CD v A | 1950/51 | ND | 556-9d | v CD | 2014/15 | 334 | D.G. Brownlie | ND v CD | 2014/15 |
| | | CD v W | 2014/15 | CD | 59 | v A | 1958/59 | 9-100 | B.W. Yuile | CD v C | 1965/66 |
| McLean Park Napier | 92 | CD v O | 1951/52 | O | 624 | v CD | 2006/07 | 265 | M.D. Bell | W v CD | 2007/08 |
| | | CD v A | 2021/22 | Zim | 51 | v NZ | 2011/12 | 8-148 | T.D. Astle | C v CD | 2013/14 |
| Trafalgar Park Nelson | 28 | N v W | 1891/92 | CD | 448-3d | v O | 1968/69 | 202* | B.E. Congdon | C v O | 1968/69 |
| | | CD v ND | 1996/97 | CD | 65 | v W | 1995/96 | 7-23 | B.A. Bolton | C v CD | 1961/62 |
| Cook's Gardens Wanganui | 17 | CD v WI | 1955/56 | MCC | 376-7d | v CD | 1960/61 | 138 | M.G. Burgess | A v CD | 1976/77 |
| | | CD v YNZ | 1979/80 | CD | 71 | v ND | 1962/63 | 8-37 | D.B. Clarke | ND v CD | 1962/63 |

§ *was Jade Stadium and later AMI Stadium*    † *now Fitzherbert Park*    * *now Hagley Oval*

| Ground | No of matches | First and most recent match | | Highest and lowest team totals | | | Highest Innings Best Bowling | | | |
|---|---|---|---|---|---|---|---|---|---|---|
| 26 Seddon Park Hamilton | 192 | ND v A 1956/57 | NZ v WI 2020/21 | NZ 715-6d v Ban 2018/19 | ND 32 v A 1996/97 | | 251 9-48 | K.S. Williamson A.R. Tait | NZ v WI ND v A | 2020/ 1996/ |
| 27 Tauranga Domain Tauranga (*Inner*) | 1 | ND v CD 1965/66 | only match | CD 232 v ND 1965/66 | ND 163 v CD 1965/66 | | 64 5-41 | G.V. Giles B.W. Yuile | ND v CD CD v ND | 1965/ 1965/ |
| 28 Tauranga Domain Tauranga (*Outer*) | 6 | ND v C 1978/79 | ND v A 1985/86 | ND 370 v O 1982/83 | O 90 v ND 1982/83 | | 127 6-75 | J.G. Gibson D.A. Stirling | ND v C CD v ND | 1978/ 1981/ |
| 29 Cobham Oval Whangarei | 11 | ND v A 1966/67 | ND v C 2000/01 | ND 363 v CD 1983/84 | ND 127 v A 1966/67 | | 195 7-30 | J.M. Parker R.S. Cunis | ND v C A v ND | 1972/ 1966/ |
| 30 Queen Elizabeth Park Masterton | 12 | CD v A 1966/67 | CD v W 2002/03 | CD 414-7d v A 1998/99 | CD 86 v A 1966/67 | | 189 6-33 | M.S. Sinclair A.J. Penn | CD v W W v CD | 1996/ 2002/ |
| 31 Smallbone Park Rotorua | 17 | ND v O 1968/69 | ND v CD 1995/96 | CD 456 v ND 1995/96 | A 72 v ND 1991/92 | | 237* 7-74 | R.T. Latham G.D. Alabaster | C v ND O v ND | 1990/ 1968/ |
| 32 Cornwall Park Auckland | 3 | A v U23 1970/71 | A v W 2000/01 | A 274-8d v U23 1970/71 | A 274-9d v U23 1976/77 A 75 v W 2000/01 | | 102 8-75 | R.W. Morgan H.J. Howarth | A v U23 A v U23 | 1970/ 1976/ |
| 33 Horton Park Blenheim | 10 | CD v ND 1972/73 | CD v A 2002/03 | CD 538 v C 2000/01 | ND 100 v CD 2001/02 | | 212* 7-36 | D.P. Kelly A.M. Schwass | CD v C CD v ND | 2000/ 2001/ |
| 34 Harry Barker Reserve Gisborne | 28 | ND v O 1974/75 | ND v C 2013/14 | ND 516 v C 2006/07 | O 77 v ND 1999/00 | | 161* 6-32 | V.R. Brown S.B. Styris | C v ND ND v O | 1986/ 1999/ |
| 35 Eden Park No. 2 † Auckland | 133 | A v CD 1975/76 | A v W 2021/22 | A 662-5d v C 2008/09 | O 54 v A 2020/21 | | 269* 7-27 | C. Munro N.A. Mallender | A v W O v A | 2012/ 1984/ |
| 36 Queen's Park Invercargill | 22 | O v CD 1975/76 | O v A 2020/21 | W 487 v O 2013/14 | O 68 v C 1977/78 | | 196 8-31 | A.M. Ellis D.G. Sewell | C v O O v CD | 2016/ 1996/ |
| 37 Bledisloe Park Pukekohe | 2 | ND v A 1976/77 | ND v W 1989/90 | W 297-5d v ND 1989/90 | ND 152 v W 1989/90 | | 123 5-27 | R.H. Vance G.R. Larsen | W v ND W v ND | 1989/ 1989/ |
| 38 Hutt Recreation Ground Lower Hutt | 14 | W v ND 1976/77 | W v C 1985/86 | W 316 v O 1983/84 | W 93 v WI 1979/80 | | 145* 8-24 | J.G. Wright E.J. Chatfield | ND v W W v ND | 1978/ 1979/ |
| 39 Logan Park Dunedin | 3 | O v U23 1977/78 | O v C 1979/80 | O 313 v U23 1977/78 | O 127 v C 1979/80 | | 106 6-44 | J.M. Parker P.J. Petherick | ND v O O v U23 | 1978/ 1977/ |
| 40 Temuka Oval Temuka | 1 | YNZ v E 1977/78 | only match | E 310 v YNZ 1977/78 | YNZ 139 v E 1977/78 | | 104 6-71 | D.W. Randall G. Miller | E v YNZ E v YNZ | 1977/ 1977/ |
| 41 Molyneux Park Alexandra | 33 | O v CD 1978/79 | O v A 2021/22 | ND 553 v O 2021/22 | O 81 v CD 2001/02 | | 226 8-27 | G.R. Hay J.T.C. Vaughan | CD v O A v O | 2018/ 1996/ |
| 42 University Oval * Dunedin | 67 | O v Pak 1978/79 | O v W 2021/22 | O 651-9d v W 2012/13 | O 46 v Pak 1978/79 A 46 v O 2010/11 | | 239 7-46 | H.D. Rutherford N. Wagner | O v W O v W | 2011/ 2011/ |
| 43 Maidstone Park Upper Hutt | 1 | W v CD 1979/80 | only match | W 216 v CD 1979/80 | CD 50 v W 1979/80 | | 63 6-17 | B.R. Taylor J.V. Coney | W v CD W v CD | 1979/ 1979/ |
| 44 Dudley Park Rangiora | 15 | C v W 1984/85 | C v W 2002/03 | C 543-8d v CD 1996/97 | C 62 v A 1998/99 | | 251* 7-17 | C.Z. Harris S.J. Maguiness | C v CD W v C | 1996/ 1984/ |
| 45 Centennial Park Oamaru | 9 | O v CD 1984/85 | O v W 1998/99 | O 430 v CD 1984/85 | C 94 v O 1994/95 | | 182 6-36 | K.R. Rutherford S.W. Duff | O v W CD v O | 1987/ 1985/ |
| 46 Levin Domain Levin | 3 | CD v C 1985/86 | CD v W 1987/88 | W 435-5d v CD 1987/88 | C 68 v CD 1985/86 | | 205* 6-28 | E.B. McSweeney P.J. Visser | W v CD CD v C | 1987/ 1985/ |
| 47 Recreational Ground Morrinsville | 2 | ND v CD 1986/87 | ND v W 1988/89 | CD 368-3d v ND 1986/87 | ND 198 v CD 1986/87 | | 151 5-71 | M.D. Crowe K.W. Martin | CD v ND CD v ND | 1986/ 1986/ |
| 48 Albert Park Te Awamutu | 1 | ND v CD 1987/88 | only match | ND 259 v CD 1987/88 | CD 135 v ND 1987/88 | | 94 4-41 | B.A. Young B.J. Barrett | ND v CD ND v CD | 1987/ 1987/ |
| 49 Victoria Park Wanganui | 11 | CD v ND 1990/91 | CD v O 2002/03 | W 506-4d v CD 1993/94 | CC 103 v SC 1997/98 | | 203* 6-20 | M.S. Sinclair B.C. Strang | CD v ND Z v NZ XI | 1998/ 1995/ |
| 50 Burnside Park Christchurch | 1 | C v CD 1991/92 | only match | O 189-7 v CD 1991/92 | C 124 v CD 1991/92 | | 63 6-67 | T.E. Blain D.J. Leonard | CD v C CD v C | 1991/ 1991/ |
| 51 Petone Recreation Ground, Lower Hutt | 2 | W v O 1991/92 | W v A 1998/99 | O 300-8d v W 1991/92 | W 142 v O 1991/92 | | 107 5-37 | E.B. McSweeney N.A. Mallender | W v O O v W | 1991/ 1991/ |
| 52 Sunnyvale Dunedin | 1 | O v A 1992/93 | only match | O 193 v A 1992/93 | A 105 v O 1992/93 | | 51 4-21 | I.S. Billcliff N.A. Mallender | O v A O v A | 1992/ 1992/ |

† *now Kennards Hire Community Oval*    * *now University of Otago Oval*

NZC

| Ground | No of matches | First and most recent match | | Highest and lowest team totals | | | Highest Innings Best Bowling | | | |
|---|---|---|---|---|---|---|---|---|---|---|
| 53 Lincoln Green Lincoln | 5 | NZA v B 1997/98 NZA v SA 1998/99 | | NZA B | 459-8d v PkA 130 v NZA | 1998/99 1997/98 | 190 6-69 | M.E. Parlane Fazal-e-Akber | NZA v B Pk A v NZA | 1997/98 1998/99 |
| 54 Aorangi Park Timaru | 4 | C v Z 1997/98 C v O 2003/04 | | Z C | 422-8d v C 100 v Z | 1997/98 1997/98 | 196 6-56 | A.D.R. Campbell M.J. Mason | Z v C CD v C | 1997/98 2002/03 |
| 55 Owen Delany Park Taupo | 6 | ND v O 1998/99 ND v W 2002/03 | | WI A | 450 v NZ A 131 v ND | 1999/00 1999/00 | 216* 7-33 | S. Chanderpaul B.P. Martin | WI v NZ A ND v A | 1999/00 1999/00 |
| 56 Colin Maiden Park Auckland | 28 | A v ND 1998/99 A v W 2019/20 | | A O | 635-6d v CD 63 v A | 2009/10 2011/12 | 210 8-23 | J.M. Brodie M.J. McClenaghan | W v A A v O | 2011/12 2011/12 |
| 57 Queen Elizabeth II Park Christchurch | 31 | C v O 1998/99 C v A 2010/11 | | W C | 614-8 v C 114 v O | 2006/07 1998/99 | 235 9-13 | J.A.H. Marshall P.J. Wiseman | ND v C C v CD | 2001/02 2004/05 |
| 58 BIL Oval † Lincoln | 16 | NI v E A 1999/00 C v A 2021/22 | | A O | 627-7d v O 63 v CD | 2006/07 2011/12 | 205 6-20 | T.G. McIntosh M.J. Mason | A v O CD v O | 2006/07 2011/12 |
| 59 Queenstown Events Centre # | 18 | O v E 2001/02 NZA v WI 2020/21 | | NZ A C | 597-9d v SL A 114 v O | 2003/04 2005/06 | 246 6-32 | K.C. Brathwaite J.S. Patel | WI v NZA W v O | 2020/21 2004/05 |
| 60 North Harbour Stadium Auckland | 1 | A v O 2002/03 only match | | A O | 289 v O 185 v A | 2002/03 2002/03 | 157 4-34 | T.G. McIntosh S.B. O'Connor | A v O O v A | 2002/03 2002/03 |
| 61 Rangiora Recreation * Ground | 36 | C v CD 2003/04 C v O 2021/22 | | ND C | 726 v C 61 v ND | 2009/10 2011/12 | 226* 8-74 | L.J. Carter K.A. Jamieson | C v W C v A | 2019/20 2016/17 |
| 62 Cobham Oval (new) Whangarei | 26 | ND v A 2008/09 ND v W 2021/22 | | O ND | 576-8d v ND 93 v C | 2009/10 2010/11 | 209 7-45 | J.A. Raval S.C. Kuggeleijn | ND v CD ND v A | 2021/22 2020/21 |
| 63 Lincoln No.3 Lincoln | 1 | ND v W 2011/12 only match | | ND W | 608-9d v W 162 v N | 2011/12 2011/12 | 284* 7-37 | K.S. Williamson T.G. Southee | ND v W ND v W | 2011/12 2011/12 |
| 64 Saxton Oval Nelson | 18 | CD v C 2011/12 CD v O 2021/22 | | NZA CD | 481-7d v WIA 118 v C | 2020/21 2011/12 | 210 6-42 | D.A.J. Bracewell | NZA v WIA | 2015/16 2020/21 |
| 65 Karori Park Wellington | 6 | W v CD 2011/12 W v O 2014/15 | | W ND | 501-6d v CD 206 v W | 2011/12 2012/13 | 241* 5-69 | T.W.M. Latham T.G. Southee | W v C ND v W | 2013/14 2012/13 |
| 66 Bay Oval Mt Maunganui | 16 | ND v C 2014/15 NZ v B 2021/22 | | NZ C | 615-9d v E 82 v ND | 2019/20 2021/22 | 205 6-35 | B-J. Watling E.J. Nuttall | NZ v E C v ND | 2019/20 2014/15 |
| 67 Westpac Stadium § Wellington | 1 | W v O 2016/17 only match | | W O | 302-8d v O 98 v W | 2016/17 2016/17 | 118 4-19 | S.R. Wells H.K. Bennett | O v W O v W | 2016/17 2016/17 |

† *now Bert Sutcliffe Oval*      * *now MainPower Oval*      § *now Sky Stadium*      # *now John Davies Oval*

# PROVINCIAL CAREER RECORDS

Performances for the following teams are not included in the Provincial Career Records:

| Team | Opponent | |
|---|---|---|
| D. Reese's Canterbury XI | Wellington | 1913/14 |
| Canterbury/Otago | MCC | 1936/37 |
| Auckland/Wellington | MCC | 1936/37 |
| Auckland XI | New Zealand | 1957/58 |
| Northern Districts/Central Districts | MCC | 1958/59 |
| Otago Invitation XI | MCC | 1962/63 |
| Canterbury XI | New Zealand Touring Team | 1967/68 |

## Most Games for One Province

206 players have now represented their province on 50 or more occasions in first-class cricket.

| | | | | | | | | | |
|---|---|---|---|---|---|---|---|---|---|
| 143 | Woodcock L.J. | W | 88 | Franklin T.J. | A | 75 | Gaffaney C.B. | O |
| 134 | Patel J.S. | W | 88 | Priest M.W. | C | 74 | Coney J.V. | W |
| 127 | Marshall J.A.H. | ND | 88 | Stead G.R. | C | 74 | Sulzberger G.P. | CD |
| 121 | Fulton P.G. | C | 87 | Edgar B.A. | W | 74 | Redmond A.J. | O |
| 120 | Gray E.J. | W | 85 | Duff S.W. | CD | 74 | Worker G.H. | CD |
| 120 | Yovich J.A.F. | ND | 85 | Hart R.G. | ND | 73 | Sparling J.T. | A |
| 119 | Vance R.H. | W | 85 | Parlane M.E. | ND | 73 | Barnes A.C. | A |
| 119 | Sinclair M.S. | CD | 85 | Nicol R.J. | A | 73 | Raval J.A. | A |
| 119 | Aldridge G.W. | ND | 84 | Chatfield E.J. | W | 72 | Hastings B.F. | C |
| 115 | Bradburn G.E. | ND | 84 | Harris C.Z. | C | 72 | Troup G.B. | A |
| 108 | Lees W.K. | O | 83 | Blain T.E. | CD | 72 | Wells J.D. | W |
| 106 | Nevin C.J. | W | 82 | Dunning B. | ND | 71 | Rutherford H.D. | O |
| 105 | Ellis A.M. | C | 82 | Hadlee B.G. | C | 70 | Duffy J.A. | O |
| 105 | Astle T.D. | C | 82 | Kuggeleijn C.M. | ND | 69 | Alabaster G.D. | O |
| 104 | Roberts A.D.G. | ND | 82 | Griggs B.B.J. | CD | 69 | Reid J.F. | A |
| 103 | McEwan P.E. | C | 82 | Gillespie M.R. | W | 69* | Boyle D.J. | C |
| 102 | McSweeney E.B. | W | 81 | Blair W.L. | O | 69 | Papps M.H.W. | W |
| 102 | McIntosh T.G. | A | 81 | Briasco P.S. | CD | 68 | Burgess M.G. | A |
| 101 | Latham R.T. | C | 80 | Howarth H.J. | A | 68 | Cameron F.J. | O |
| 101 | Broom N.T. | O | 80 | Hoskin R.N. | O | 68 | Sinclair B.W. | W |
| 100 | Flynn D.R. | ND | 80 | Franklin J.E.C. | W | 68 | Rutherford K.R. | O |
| 99 | White D.J. | ND | 79 | Larsen G.R. | W | 68* | Bates M.D. | A |
| 99 | de Boorder D.C. | O | 79 | Jones R.A. | A | 68 | Young W.A. | CD |
| 97 | Shrimpton M.J.F. | CD | 79 | Parlane N.R. | W | 67 | Edwards G.N. | CD |
| 97 | Young R.A. | A | 79 | Mason M.J. | CD | 67 | Harris R.M. | A |
| 96 | Bell M.D. | W | 78 | Mallender N.A. | O | 67 | Patel D.N. | A |
| 96* | Stewart S.L. | C | 78 | Robertson G.K. | CD | 67 | McSkimming W.C. | O |
| 95 | Hart M.N. | ND | 78 | Bailey M.D. | ND | 67 | Bracewell D.A.J. | CD |
| 95 | Papps M.H.W. | C | 78 | Wilson B.S. | ND | 67* | Smith B.S. | CD |
| 95 | Cumming C.D. | O | 77 | McIntyre J.M. | A | 66 | Puna N. | ND |
| 93 | Young R.A. | ND | 77 | Stead D.W. | C | 66 | Lawson R.A. | O |
| 92 | How J.M. | CD | 77 | Martin B.P. | ND | 65 | Alabaster J.C. | O |
| 92 | Hay G.R. | CD | 77 | Ingram P.J. | CD | 65 | Brown V.R. | C |
| 91 | Watling B-J. | ND | 77 | de Grandhomme C.A | | 65 | Hunt A.J. | A |
| 90 | Blair B.R. | O | 76 | Germon L.K. | C | 65 | Webb P.N. | A |
| 90* | Dickeson C.W. | ND | 76 | Douglas M.W. | CD | 65* | Wright M.J.E. | ND |
| 90 | Morgan R.W. | A | 76 | Marshall H.J.H. | ND | 64 | Murray B.A.G. | W |
| 90 | McGregor S.N. | O | 76 | Murdoch S.J. | W | 64 | Mitchell D.J. | ND |
| 90 | O'Sullivan D.R. | CD | 76* | Baker J.D. | ND | 64 | Fletcher C.D. | C |
| 89 | Morrison J.F.M. | W | 75 | Parker J.M. | ND | 63 | Rutherford I.A. | O |
| 88 | Boock S.L. | O | 75* | McCullum S.J. | O | 63* | Stott L.W. | A |

| | | | | | | | | | |
|---|---|---|---|---|---|---|---|---|---|
| 63 | Wagner N. | O | 59 | Sodhi I.S. | ND | 55 | Carter J.F. | ND |
| 63 | Kuggeleijn S.C. | ND | 58 | Dowling G.T. | C | 54 | Bilby G.P. | W |
| 62 | Cunis R.S. | A | 58 | Howarth G.P. | ND | 54* | Crocker L.M. | ND |
| 62 | Hadlee R.J. | C | 58 | Patrick W.R. | C | 54 | Cromb I.B. | C |
| 62* | Smith C.J.P. | CD | 58 | Reid J.R. | W | 54 | McGirr H.M. | W |
| 62* | Cooper B.G. | ND | 58 | Ritchie T.D. | W | 54 | Moir A.M. | O |
| 62 | McCullum N.L. | O | 58 | Thomson K. | C | 54 | Sutton R.E. | A |
| 62 | Arnel B.J. | ND | 58 | Vivian G.E. | A | 54 | Ward J.T. | C |
| 62 | Blundell T.A. | W | 58 | Patel A.Y. | CD | 54 | Dobbs P.W. | O |
| 61 | Yuile B.W. | CD | 57 | Bull C.L. | C | 53 | Colquhoun I.A. | CD |
| 61 | Campbell K.O. | O | 57 | Burns K.J. | O | 53* | Pierce R.A. | CD |
| 61 | Greatbatch M.J. | CD | 57 | Petrie E.C. | ND | 53* | Schofield R.M. | CD |
| 61 | Walker B.G.K. | A | 57 | Hamilton L.J. | CD | 53 | Toynbee M.H. | CD |
| 61 | Wells S.R. | O | 57 | Elliott G.D. | W | 53 | Watson W. | A |
| 61* | O'Donnell R.R. | A | 57 | Bruce T.C. | CD | 53 | Devcich A.P. | ND |
| 60 | Milburn B.D. | O | 56 | Brice A.W.S. | W | 52* | Cederwall B.W. | W |
| 60 | Newdick G.A. | W | 56 | Motz R.C. | C | 52 | Popli B. | ND |
| 60 | Parsons A.E.W. | A | 56 | Canning T.K. | A | 51* | Knight A.R. | O |
| 60 | Sutcliffe B. | O | 56 | Adams A.R. | A | 51 | Brown S.W. | A |
| 60 | Roberts S.J. | C | 56* | McMillan J.M. | O | 51 | Thomson S.A. | ND |
| 60 | Cleaver D. | CD | 55 | Bradburn W.P. | ND | 51 | Thompson E.P. | CD |
| 59 | Blair R.W. | W | 55 | Congdon B.E. | CD | 51 | Kitchen A.K. | A |
| 59 | Crowe J.J. | A | 55 | Jordan A.B. | CD | 50 | Boxshall C. | C |
| 59 | Smith I.D.S. | CD | 55 | Mills G.H. | O | 50 | Butler L.C. | W |
| 59 | Turner G.M. | O | 55 | Snedden M.C. | A | 50 | Horne M.J. | A |
| 59 | Hartland B.R. | C | 55 | Sewell D.G. | O | 50 | Mills K.D. | A |
| 59 | Smith L.D. | O | 55 | Hopkins G.J. | A | 50 | Nicholls H.M. | C |
| 59 | McGlashan P.D. | ND | 55 | Bracewell M.G. | O | | *entire first-class career* | |

# Highest Averages for One Province

| 2000 RUNS/45.00 AVE | Province | M | In | NO | HS | Runs | Ave | 100 |
|---|---|---|---|---|---|---|---|---|
| Hick G.A. | ND | 17 | 30 | 4 | 211* | 2055 | 79.03 | 10 |
| Crowe M.D. | CD | 32 | 55 | 7 | 242 | 3299 | 68.72 | 13 |
| Conway D.P. | W | 22 | 39 | 8 | 327* | 2054 | 66.25 | 5 |
| Scott V.J. | A | 44 | 74 | 15 | 204 | 3546 | 60.10 | 11 |
| Sutcliffe B. | O | 60 | 110 | 8 | 385 | 6028 | 59.09 | 17 |
| Harris C.Z. | C | 84 | 125 | 31 | 251* | 5442 | 57.89 | 13 |
| Munro C. | A | 42 | 64 | 4 | 281 | 3440 | 57.33 | 13 |
| Williamson K.S. | ND | 25 | 41 | 4 | 284* | 2021 | 54.62 | 6 |
| Jones A.H. | W | 39 | 67 | 11 | 181* | 2978 | 53.17 | 7 |
| van Wyk C.F.K. | CD | 45 | 73 | 19 | 131 | 2854 | 52.85 | 3 |
| Myburgh J.G. | C | 25 | 46 | 4 | 199 | 2172 | 51.71 | 7 |
| Sinclair M.S. | CD | 119 | 203 | 26 | 243* | 9148 | 51.68 | 27 |
| Wallace W.M. | A | 47 | 73 | 5 | 211 | 3409 | 50.13 | 9 |
| Crowe J.J. | A | 59 | 95 | 9 | 156 | 4245 | 49.36 | 11 |
| Bruce T.C. | CD | 57 | 100 | 19 | 208* | 3919 | 48.38 | 6 |
| Reid J.R. | W | 58 | 102 | 8 | 296 | 4538 | 48.27 | 13 |
| Guptill M.J. | A | 42 | 73 | 6 | 195* | 3162 | 47.19 | 9 |
| Turner G.M. | O | 59 | 109 | 14 | 186* | 4439 | 46.72 | 13 |
| Hopkins G.J. | A | 55 | 82 | 12 | 201 | 3228 | 46.40 | 9 |
| Brownlie D.G. | C | 35 | 65 | 8 | 171 | 2635 | 46.22 | 6 |
| Hiddleston J.S. | W | 41 | 75 | 1 | 212 | 3413 | 46.12 | 8 |
| Ryder J.D. | W | 40 | 67 | 3 | 236 | 2908 | 45.43 | 8 |

# Most Runs for One Province

| | Province | M | In | NO | HS | Runs | Ave | 100 |
|---|---|---|---|---|---|---|---|---|
| Sinclair M.S. | CD | 119 | 203 | 26 | 243* | 9148 | 51.68 | 27 |
| Fulton P.G. | C | 121 | 224 | 22 | 301* | 8719 | 43.16 | 16 |
| Woodcock L.J. | W | 143 | 246 | 30 | 220* | 7719 | 35.73 | 11 |
| Papps M.H.W. | C | 95 | 172 | 14 | 192 | 6663 | 42.17 | 19 |
| Cumming C.D. | O | 95 | 167 | 15 | 173 | 6589 | 43.34 | 21 |
| Bell M.D. | W | 96 | 168 | 11 | 265 | 6565 | 41.81 | 20 |
| Edgar B.A. | W | 87 | 160 | 3 | 162 | 6494 | 44.17 | 15 |
| Vance R.H. | W | 119 | 205 | 18 | 254* | 6440 | 34.43 | 12 |
| Marshall J.A.H. | ND | 127 | 214 | 16 | 235 | 6418 | 32.41 | 11 |
| Hay G.R. | CD | 92 | 161 | 13 | 226 | 6269 | 42.35 | 15 |
| Flynn D.R. | ND | 100 | 175 | 9 | 241 | 6265 | 37.74 | 20 |
| Broom N.T. | O | 101 | 172 | 22 | 203* | 6085 | 40.56 | 15 |
| Sutcliffe B. | O | 60 | 110 | 8 | 385* | 6028 | 59.09 | 17 |
| McIntosh T.G. | A | 102 | 176 | 15 | 268 | 5980 | 37.14 | 17 |
| McEwan P.E. | C | 103 | 185 | 11 | 155 | 5940 | 34.13 | 11 |
| Latham R.T. | C | 101 | 176 | 17 | 237* | 5919 | 37.22 | 8 |
| Stewart S.L. | C | 96 | 173 | 18 | 227* | 5693 | 36.72 | 7 |
| How J.M. | CD | 92 | 167 | 16 | 207* | 5680 | 37.61 | 13 |
| Roberts A.D.G. | ND | 104 | 192 | 35 | 128* | 5533 | 35.24 | 7 |
| Watling B-J. | ND | 91 | 162 | 12 | 176 | 5479 | 36.52 | 9 |
| Harris C.Z. | C | 84 | 125 | 31 | 251* | 5442 | 57.89 | 13 |
| Ingram P.J. | CD | 77 | 140 | 8 | 247 | 5378 | 40.74 | 17 |
| Ellis A.M. | C | 105 | 167 | 21 | 171 | 5179 | 35.47 | 9 |
| Blair B.R. | O | 90 | 154 | 5 | 143 | 5057 | 33.93 | 7 |
| Franklin T.J. | A | 88 | 157 | 14 | 181 | 5051 | 35.25 | 12 |
| Rutherford K.R. | O | 68 | 121 | 7 | 226* | 5051 | 44.30 | 14 |
| Rutherford H.D. | O | 71 | 129 | 0 | 239 | 5027 | 38.96 | 12 |

# Most Wickets for One Province

| | Province | M | Wkts | Runs | Ave | 5WI | 10WM | Best |
|---|---|---|---|---|---|---|---|---|
| Chatfield E.J. | W | 84 | 403 | 7531 | 18.68 | 23 | 7 | 8-24 |
| Boock S.L. | O | 88 | 399 | 8235 | 20.63 | 28 | 5 | 8-57 |
| O'Sullivan D.R. | CD | 90 | 392 | 9560 | 24.38 | 21 | 3 | 6-40 |
| Gray E.J. | W | 120 | 357 | 9778 | 27.38 | 13 | 3 | 8-37 |
| Aldridge G.W. | ND | 119 | 355 | 10,052 | 28.31 | 14 | 1 | 6-41 |
| Gillespie M.R. | W | 82 | 344 | 9389 | 27.29 | 16 | 2 | 6-38 |
| Patel J.S. | W | 134 | 333 | 12,592 | 37.81 | 12 | 1 | 7-105 |
| Howarth H.J. | A | 80 | 332 | 7361 | 22.17 | 18 | 4 | 8-75 |
| Blair R.W. | W | 59 | 330 | 5004 | 15.16 | 30 | 10 | 9-72 |
| Astle T.D. | C | 105 | 303 | 9505 | 31.36 | 12 | 1 | 8-148 |
| Priest M.W. | C | 88 | 290 | 8501 | 29.31 | 12 | 3 | 9-95 |
| Downes A.D. | O | 44 | 287 | 3902 | 13.59 | 33 | 13 | 8-35 |
| Hadlee R.J. | C | 62 | 285 | 4600 | 16.14 | 19 | 2 | 7-49 |
| Moir A.M. | O | 54 | 282 | 5926 | 21.01 | 20 | 5 | 8-37 |
| Dickeson C.W. | ND | 90 | 282 | 8242 | 29.22 | 9 | 2 | 7-79 |
| Wagner N. | O | 63 | 277 | 7307 | 26.37 | 16 | 1 | 7-46 |
| Mallender N.A. | O | 78 | 268 | 5433 | 20.27 | 14 | 3 | 7-27 |
| Alabaster J.C. | O | 65 | 264 | 5738 | 21.73 | 14 | 3 | 6-39 |
| Mason M.J. | CD | 78 | 263 | 6387 | 24.28 | 12 | 1 | 6-20 |
| Cameron F.J. | O | 68 | 258 | 5204 | 20.17 | 9 | — | 6-21 |
| Yovich J.A.F. | ND | 110 | 255 | 8579 | 33.64 | 8 | 1 | 7-64 |
| Adams A.R. | A | 56 | 251 | 4729 | 18.84 | 14 | 3 | 6-25 |

# Most Centuries for One Province

| | Province | 100s | | Province | 100s | | Province | 100s |
|---|---|---|---|---|---|---|---|---|
| Sinclair M.S. | CD | 27 | Rutherford K.R. | O | 14 | Murdoch S.J. | W | 12 |
| Cumming C.D. | O | 21 | Reid J.R. | W | 13 | Rutherford H.D. | O | 12 |
| Bell M.D. | W | 20 | Turner G.M. | O | 13 | Scott V.J. | A | 11 |
| Flynn D.R. | ND | 20 | Crowe M.D. | CD | 13 | Crowe J.J. | A | 11 |
| Papps M.H.W. | C | 19 | Harris C.Z. | C | 13 | McEwan P.E. | C | 11 |
| Sutcliffe B. | O | 17 | How J.M. | CD | 13 | Parlane N.R. | W | 11 |
| McIntosh T.G. | A | 17 | Franklin J.E.C | W | 13 | Redmond A.J. | O | 11 |
| Ingram P.J. | CD | 17 | Munro C. | A | 13 | Marshall J.A.H. | ND | 11 |
| Fulton P.G. | C | 16 | Papps M.H.W. | W | 13 | Woodcock L.J. | W | 11 |
| Edgar B.A. | W | 15 | Raval J.A. | A | 13 | Hadlee W.A. | C | 10 |
| Broom N.T. | O | 15 | Vance R.H. | W | 12 | Burgess M.G. | A | 10 |
| Hay G.R. | CD | 15 | Franklin T.J. | A | 12 | Hick G.A. | ND | 10 |
| Greatbatch M.J. | CD | 14 | Jones R.A. | A | 12 | Stead G.R. | C | 10 |

# Most Dismissals for One Province

| WICKETKEEPING | Province | M | Caught | Stumped | Total |
|---|---|---|---|---|---|
| de Boorder D.C. | O | 99 | 322 | 22 | 344 |
| McSweeney E.B. | W | 102 | 289 | 39 | 328 |
| Nevin C.J. | W | 106 | 289 | 9 | 298 |
| Young R.A. | A | 97 | 245 | 5 | 250 |
| Lees W.K. | O | 108 | 208 | 36 | 244 |
| Hart R.G. | ND | 85 | 228 | 15 | 243 |
| Germon L.K. | C | 76 | 217 | 21 | 238 |
| Griggs B.B.J | CD | 82 | 225 | 7 | 232 |
| Fletcher C.D. | C | 64 | 205 | 12 | 217 |
| Young B.A. | ND | 93 | 179 | 11 | 190 |
| McGlashan P.D. | ND | 59 | 175 | 12 | 187 |
| Cleaver D. | CD | 60 | 162 | 11 | 173 |
| Hopkins G.J. | A | 55 | 165 | 7 | 172 |
| Milburn B.D. | O | 60 | 148 | 17 | 165 |
| Ward J.T. | C | 54 | 136 | 17 | 153 |
| Kelly P.J. | A | 48 | 140 | 12 | 152 |
| van Wyk C.F.K. | CD | 45 | 140 | 5 | 145 |
| Horne B.J. | A | 42 | 139 | 6 | 145 |
| Blundell T.A. | W | 62 | 139 | 5 | 144 |
| Blain T.E. | CD | 83 | 124 | 19 | 143 |
| Croy M.G. | O | 42 | 127 | 4 | 131 |
| Watling B-J. | ND | 91 | 129 | 2 | 131 |
| Colquhoun I.A. | CD | 53 | 102 | 28 | 130 |
| Smith I.D.S. | CD | 59 | 119 | 11 | 130 |
| Sigley M.A. | CD | 44 | 124 | 4 | 128 |
| Seifert T.L. | ND | 44 | 118 | 10 | 128 |
| Schofield R.M. | CD | 53 | 107 | 15 | 122 |
| Robinson S.A. | O | 45 | 117 | 5 | 122 |
| Wright M.J.E. | ND | 65 | 104 | 17 | 121 |
| Hopkins G.J. | O | 33 | 111 | 3 | 114 |
| Petrie E.C. | ND | 57 | 90 | 22 | 112 |
| Mills G.H. | O | 55 | 78 | 29 | 107 |
| Boxshall C. | C | 50 | 70 | 36 | 106 |
| van Wyk C.F.K. | C | 35 | 101 | 5 | 106 |
| Cachopa B. | A | 43 | 101 | 4 | 105 |
| Hopkins G.J. | C | 41 | 91 | 10 | 101 |
| Therkleson I.J. | W | 39 | 93 | 7 | 100 |

# Represented Most Provinces

| | | |
|---|---|---|
| 5 | Guy J.W. | CD, C, O, W, ND |
| 4 | Anderson R.W. | C, ND, O, CD |
| | Congdon B.E. | CD, W, O, C |
| | Crawshaw W.J. | O, C, W, T |
| | Hopkins G.J. | ND, C, O, A |
| | Hounsell A.R. | C, W, A, ND |
| | Howell L.G. | C, CD, A, ND |
| | McGregor P.B. | A, ND, W, CD |
| | Worker R.V. de R. | A, C, O, W |
| 3 | Alabaster G.D. | O, C, ND |
| | Allcott C.F.W. | HB, A, O |
| | Alpe S. | A, C, W |
| | Andrews B. | C, CD, O |
| | Beard D.D. | W, CD, ND |
| | Billcliff I.S. | O, W, A |
| | Bracewell B.P. | CD, O, ND |
| | Cairns B.L. | CD, O, ND |
| | Clark L.A. | W, O, A |
| | Collinge R.O. | CD, W, ND |
| | Crowe M.D. | A, CD, W |
| | D'Arcy J.W. | C, O, W |
| | Frith W. | C, O, W |
| | Hastings B.F. | W, CD, C |
| | Holland P.J. | CD, ND, W |
| | Hussey J.M. | HB, O, A |
| | Jones A.H. | CD, O, W |
| | King R.T. | O, A, CD |
| | Lane M.E.L. | W, CD, C |

| | | |
|---|---|---|
| 3 | Lusk Harold B. | A, C, W |
| | McBeath D.J. | O, C, S |
| | McEwan M.B. | C, W, A |
| | McGlashan P.D. | CD, O, ND |
| | Macleod D.N. | CD, W, C |
| | Mills G. | A, HB, O |
| | Moloney D.A.R. | O, W, C |
| | Neesham. J.D.S. | A, O, W |
| | Neutze P.S. | O, A, ND |
| | Nicol R.J. | A, C, O |
| | Parlane N.R. | ND, W, A |
| | Paterson J.L. | C, HB, A |
| | Raval J.A. | A, CD, ND |
| | Riley J.D. | C, W, A |
| | Ryder J.D. | CD, W, O |
| | Sampson H.C. | CD, O, C |
| | Salmon W.J. | W, HB, T |
| | Sherlock R.R. | CD, C, A |
| | Stephenson F.C. | O, W, C |
| | Sutcliffe B. | A, O, ND |
| | Todd G.R. | CD, O, A |
| | Tracy S.R. | A, C, O |
| | Twose R.G. | ND, CD, W |
| | Uttley K.F.M. | O, C, W |
| | Watson H.C. | O, C, W |
| | Wiseman P.J. | A, O, C |
| | Worker G.H. | CD, C, A |
| | Wright E. | A, W, C |
| | Wright J.G. | ND, C, A |

T *Taranaki*   S *Southland*   HB *Hawke's Bay*

# Longest Careers for One Province

| Seasons | | | |
|---|---|---|---|
| 34 | Read R.J. | Canterbury | 1904/05-1937/38 |
| 31 | Reese T.W. | Canterbury | 1887/88-1917/18 |
| 29 | Luckie M.M.F. | Wellington | 1891/92-1919/20 |
| 27 | Fowke J.N. | Canterbury | 1880/81-1906/07 |
| 27 | Downes A.D. | Otago | 1887/88-1913/14 |
| 27 | Dempster C.S. | Wellington | 1921/22-1947/48 |
| 26 | Reese D. | Canterbury | 1895/96-1920/21 |
| 26 | Knight A.R. | Otago | 1918/19-1943/44 |
| 25 | Moorhouse H.M. | Canterbury | 1883/84-1907/08 |
| 25 | Tucker K.H. | Wellington | 1895/96-1919/20 |
| 25 | Garrard D.R. | Auckland | 1917/18-1941/42 |

# PROVINCIAL RECORDS

## MOST WINS IN SUCCESSION

| | | |
|---|---|---|
| 8 | Canterbury | 1873/74 to 1880/81 |
| 7 | Canterbury | 1912/13 to 1913/14 |
| 7 | Wellington | 1960/61 to 1961/62 |
| 6 | Canterbury | 1910/11 to 1911/12 |
| 6 | Auckland | 1939/40 to 1943/44 |
| 6 | Wellington | 1962/63 to 1963/64 |
| 6 | Canterbury | 1996/97 |

## MOST LOSSES IN SUCCESSION

| | | |
|---|---|---|
| 10 | Otago | 1961/62 to 1963/64 |
| 8 | Otago | 1929/30 to 1931/32 |
| 7 | Otago | 1874/75 to 1880/81 |
| 7 | Otago | 1920/21 to 1922/23 |
| 7 | Otago | 1926/27 to 1927/28 |
| 7 | Auckland | 1997/98 to 1998/99 |
| 7 | Otago | 2001/02 |

## MOST DRAWS IN SUCCESSION

| | | |
|---|---|---|
| 9 | ND | 1974/75 to 1975/76 |
| 8 | Wellington | 1974/75 to 1975/76 |
| 7 | ND | 1968/69 to 1969/70 |
| 7 | CD | 1991/92 to 1992/93 |
| 7 | Wellington | 1992/93 |

## MOST GAMES WITHOUT A WIN

| | | |
|---|---|---|
| 38 | CD | 1973/74 to 1978/79 |
| 36 | Otago | 1960/61 to 1965/66 |
| 24 | ND | 1972/73 to 1975/76 |
| 21 | ND | 1966/67 to 1970/71 |

## MOST GAMES WITHOUT A LOSS

| | | |
|---|---|---|
| 24 | Wellington | 1984/85 to 1986/87 |
| 23 | Auckland | 1978/79 to 1981/82 |
| 22 | Auckland | 1934/35 to 1943/44 |
| 21 | Central Districts | 2016/17 to 2018/19 |
| 18 | Auckland | 1961/62 to 1964/65 |
| 18 | Canterbury | 1966/67 to 1969/70 |

## MOST GAMES WITHOUT A DRAW

| | | |
|---|---|---|
| 42 | Canterbury | 1896/97 to 1909/10 |
| 30 | Otago | 1894/95 to 1907/08 |
| 22 | Canterbury | 1869/70 to 1883/84 |
| 20 | Canterbury | 1919/20 to 1924/25 |

## Highest Individual Innings

*for and against the major sides in NZ*

| | For | | Against |
|---|---|---|---|
| **Auckland** | 290 | W.N. Carson v Otago at Dunedin, 1936/37 | 355 B. Sutcliffe for Otago at Dunedin, 1949/50 |
| **Canterbury** | 301* | P.G. Fulton v Auckland at Christchurch, 2002/03 | 385 B. Sutcliffe for Otago at Christchurch, 1952/53 |
| **Central Dist.** | 247 | P.J. Ingram v ND at Hamilton, 2008/09 | 334 D.G. Brownlie for ND at New Plymouth, 2014/15 |
| **Northern Dist.** | 334 | D.G. Brownlie v CD at New Plymouth, 2014/15 | 296 J.R. Reid for Wellington at Wellington, 1962/63 |
| **Otago** | 385 | B. Sutcliffe v Canterbury at Christchurch, 1952/53 | 290 W.N. Carson for Auckland at Dunedin, 1936/37 |
| **Wellington** | 327* | D.P. Conway v Canterbury at Wellington, 2019/20 | 284* K.S. Williamson v Wellington at Lincoln, 2011/12 |
| **MCC/England** | 336* | W.R. Hammond v NZ at Auckand, 1932/33 | 222 N.J. Astle for NZ at Christchurch, 2001/02 |
| **Australia** | 293 | V.T. Trumper v Canterbury at Christchurch 1913/14 | 198 W.A. Hadlee for Otago at Dunedin, 1945/46 |
| **South Africa** | 275* | D.J. Cullinan v NZ at Auckland, 1998/99 | 176 K.S. Williamson for NZ at Hamilton, 2016/17 |
| **West Indies** | 258 | S.M. Nurse v NZ at Christchurch, 1968/69 | 251 K.S. Williamson for NZ at Hamilton, 2020/21 |
| **Pakistan** | 271 | Javed Miandad v NZ at Auckland, 1988/89 | 238 K.S. Williamson for NZ at Christchurch, 2020/21 |
| **India** | 192 | M. Azharuddin v NZ at Auckland, 1989/90 | 302 B.B. McCullum for NZ at Wellington, 2013/14 |
| **Sri Lanka** | 267 | P.A. de Silva v NZ at Wellington, 1990/91 | 299 M.D. Crowe for NZ at Wellington, 1990/91 |
| **New Zealand** | 302 | B.B. McCullum v India at Wellington, 2013/14 | 336* W.R. Hammond for England at Auckland, 1932/33 |
| **Zimbabwe** | 196 | A.D.R. Campbell v Canterbury at Timaru, 1997/98 | 157 M.J. Horne for NZ at Auckland, 1997/98 |
| **Bangladesh** | 217 | Shakib Al Hasan v NZ at Wellington, 2016/17 | 252 T.W.M. Latham for NZ at Christchurch, 2021/22 |

# Best Bowling
*for and against the major sides in NZ*

| | For | | Against | |
|---|---|---|---|---|
| **Auckland** | 9-36 | A.F. Wensley v Otago at Auckland, 1929/30 | 9-48 | A.R. Tait v Auckland at Hamilton, 1996/97 |
| **Canterbury** | 10-28 | A.E. Moss v Wellington at Christchurch, 1889/90 | 9-72 | F.H. Cooke for Otago at Christchurch, 1884/85 |
| **Central Dist.** | 9-100 | B.W. Yuile v Canterbury at New Plymouth, 1965/66 | 9-13 | P.J. Wiseman for Canterbury at Christchurch, 2004/05 |
| **Northern Dist.** | 9-48 | A.R. Tait v Auckland at Hamilton, 1996/97 | 9-93 | P.J. Petherick for Otago at Dunedin, 1975/76 |
| **Otago** | 9-50 | A.H. Fisher v Queensland at Dunedin, 1896/97 | 9-36 | A.E. Wensley for Auckland at Auckland, 1929/30 |
| **Wellington** | 9-67 | A.W.S. Brice v Auckland at Wellington, 1918/19 | 10-28 | A.E. Moss for Canterbury at Christchurch, 1889/90 |
| **MCC/England** | 8-45 | F.S. Trueman v Otago at Dunedin, 1958/59 | 7-50 | H.W. Monaghan for Wellington at Wellington, 1906/07 |
| **Australia** | 8-27 | W.J. Whitty v Auckland at Auckland, 1909/10 | 8-66 | G.O. Rabone for Auckland at Auckland, 1956/57 |
| **South Africa** | 6-40 | K.A. Maharaj v NZ at Wellington, 2016/17 | 7-23 | M.J. Henry for NZ at Christchurch, 2021/22 |
| **West Indies** | 7-37 | C.A. Walsh v NZ at Wellington, 1994/95 | 7-27 | C.L. Cairns for NZ at Hamilton, 1999/00 |
| **Pakistan** | 7-16 | Farooq Hamid v Wellington at Wellington, 1964/65 | 7-95 | N.A. Huxford for Wellington at Wellington, 1964/65 |
| **India** | 8-76 | E.A.S. Prasanna v NZ at Auckland, 1975/76 | 7-23 | R.J. Hadlee for NZ at Wellington, 1975/76 |
| **Sri Lanka** | 6-79 | C.P.H. Ramanayake v Wellington at Wellington, 1990/91 | 7-130 | D.L. Vettori for NZ at Wellington, 2006/07 |
| **New Zealand** | 8-100 | G.F. Cresswell v Australia B at Dunedin, 1949/50 | 8-33 | H.S.T.L. Hendry for NSW at Wellington, 1923/24 |
| **Zimbabwe** | 6-20 | B.C. Strang v NZ XI at Wanganui, 1995/96 | 6-26 | C.S. Martin for NZ at Napier, 2011/12 |
| **Bangladesh** | 6-46 | Ebadot Hossain v NZ at Mt Maunganui, 2021/22 | 7-53 | C.L. Cairns for NZ at Hamilton, 2001/02 |

# Highest Totals
*for and against the major sides in NZ*

| | For | | Against | |
|---|---|---|---|---|
| **Auckland** | 693-9 dec | v Canterbury at Auckland, 1939/40 | 658 | by Australians at Auckland, 1913/14 |
| **Canterbury** | 777 | v Otago at Christchurch, 1996/97 | 726 | by Northern Districts at Rangiora, 2009/10 |
| **Central Dist.** | 650-8 dec | v Otago at Napier, 2015/16 | 668-7 dec | by Auckland at Napier, 2014/15 |
| **Northern Dist.** | 726 | v Canterbury at Rangiora, 2009/10 | 608-9 dec | by Wellington at Hamilton, 1998/99 |
| **Otago** | 651-9 dec | v Wellington at Dunedin, 2012/13 | 777 | by Canterbury at Christchurch, 1996/97 |
| **Wellington** | 614-8 | v Canterbury at Christchurch, 2006/07 | 658-9 dec | by Auckland at Auckland, 2012/13 |
| **MCC/England** | 653-5 dec | v New Zealand at Dunedin, 1935/36 | 615-9 dec | by New Zealand at Mt Maunganui, 2019/20 |
| **Australia** | 663 | v New Zealand at Auckland, 1920/21 | 484 | by New Zealand at Wellington, 1973/74 |
| **South Africa** | 621-5 dec | v New Zealand at Auckland, 1998/99 | 595 | by New Zealand at Auckland, 2003/04 |
| **West Indies** | 660-5 dec | v New Zealand at Wellington, 1994/95 | 609-9 dec | by New Zealand at Dunedin, 2013/14 |
| **Pakistan** | 616-5 dec | v New Zealand at Auckland, 1988/89 | 659-6 dec | by New Zealand at Christchurch, 2020/21 |
| **India** | 520 | v New Zealand at Hamilton, 2008/09 | 680-8 dec | by New Zealand at Wellington, 2013/14 |
| **Sri Lanka** | 498 | v New Zealand at Napier, 2004/05 | 671-4 | by New Zealand at Wellington, 1990/91 |
| **New Zealand** | 715-6 dec | v Bangladesh at Hamilton, 2018/19 | 663 | by Australia at Auckland, 1920/21 |
| **Zimbabwe** | 422-8 dec | v Canterbury at Timaru, 1997/98 | 495-7 dec | by New Zealand at Napier, 2011/12 |
| **Bangladesh** | 595-8 dec | v New Zealand at Wellington, 2016/17 | 715-6 dec | by New Zealand at Hamilton, 2018/19 |

# Lowest Totals
*for and against the major sides in NZ*

| | For | | Against | |
|---|---|---|---|---|
| **Auckland** | 13 | v Canterbury at Auckland, 1877/78 | 28 | by Hawke's Bay at Auckland, 1910/11 |
| **Canterbury** | 25 | v Otago at Christchurch, 1866/67 | 13 | by Auckland at Auckland, 1877/78 |
| **Central Dist.** | 50 | v Wellington at Upper Hutt, 1979/80 | 63 | by Otago at Lincoln, 2011/12 |
| **Northern Dist.** | 32 | v Auckland at Hamilton, 1996/97 | 51 | by Central Dist. at Hamilton, 1957/58 |
| **Otago** | 34 | v Wellington at Dunedin, 1956/57 | 25 | by Canterbury at Christchurch, 1866/67 |
| **Wellington** | 19 | v Nelson at Nelson, 1885/86 | 32 | by Hawke's Bay at Wellington, 1883/84 |
| **MCC/England** | 58 | v New Zealand at Auckland, 2017/18 | 26 | by New Zealand at Auckland, 1954/55 |
| **Australia** | 103 | v New Zealand at Auckland, 1985/86 | 42 | by New Zealand at Hamilton, 1945/46 |
| **South Africa** | 95 | v Canterbury at Christchurch, 2021/22 | 73 | by Canterbury at Christchurch, 1963/64 |
| **West Indies** | 77 | v New Zealand at Auckland, 1955/56 | 74 | by New Zealand at Dunedin, 1955/56 |
| **Pakistan** | 100 | v New Zealand A at Lincoln, 2000/01 | 46 | by Otago at Dunedin, 1978/79 |
| **India** | 81 | v New Zealand at Wellington, 1975/76 | 94 | by New Zealand at Hamilton, 2002/03 |
| **Sri Lanka** | 93 | v New Zealand at Wellington, 1982/83 | 109 | by New Zealand at Napier, 1994/95 |
| **New Zealand** | 26 | v England at Auckland, 1954/55 | 58 | by England at Auckland, 2017/18 |
| **Zimbabwe** | 51 | v New Zealand at Napier, 2011/12 | 100 | by Canterbury at Timaru, 1997/98 |
| **Bangladesh** | 108 | v New Zealand at Hamilton, 2001/02 | 169 | by New Zealand at Mt Maunganui, 2021/22 |

# AUCKLAND

## Highest Totals

| | | | |
|---|---|---|---|
| 693-9 dec | v Canterbury | Auckland | 1939/40 |
| 668-7 dec | v Central Districts | Napier | 2014/15 |
| 662-5 dec | v Central Districts | Auckland | 2008/09 |
| 658-9 dec | v Wellington | Auckland | 2012/13 |
| 643 | v Canterbury | Auckland | 1919/20 |
| 635-6 dec | v Central Districts | Auckland | 2009/10 |
| 627-7 dec | v Otago | Lincoln | 2006/07 |
| 598 | v Wellington | Wellington | 2015/16 |
| 590 | v Canterbury | Auckland | 1937/38 |
| 587-7 dec | v West Indies | Auckland | 2008/09 |

## Lowest Totals

| | | | |
|---|---|---|---|
| 13 | v Canterbury | Auckland | 1877/78 |
| 46 | v Otago | Dunedin | 2010/11 |
| 48 | v Otago | Dunedin | 1889/90 |
| 48 | v Wellington | Wellington | 1889/90 |
| 53 | v Wellington | Wellington | 1873/74 |
| 55 | v Otago | Dunedin | 1900/01 |
| 56 | v Canterbury | Auckland | 1931/32 |
| 62 | v Wellington | Wellington | 2017/18 |
| 69 | v Northern Districts | Auckland | 1963/64 |

## Most Appearances

| | | | | | | | |
|---|---|---|---|---|---|---|---|
| 102 | McIntosh T.G. | 69 | Reid J.F. | 59 | Crowe J.J. |
| 97 | Young R.A. | 68 | Burgess M.G. | 58 | Vivian G.E. |
| 90 | Morgan R.W. | 68 | Bates M.D. | 56 | Canning T.K. |
| 88 | Franklin T.J. | 67 | Harris R.M. | 56 | Adams A.R. |
| 85 | Nicol R.J. | 67 | Patel D.N. | 55 | Snedden M.C. |
| 80 | Howarth H.J. | 65 | Hunt A.J. | 55 | Hopkins G.J. |
| 79 | Jones R.A. | 65 | Webb P.N. | 54 | Sutton R.E. |
| 77 | McIntyre J.M. | 63 | Stott L.W. | 53 | Watson W. |
| 77 | de Grandhomme C. | 62 | Cunis R.S. | 51 | Brown S.W. |
| 73 | Sparling J.T. | 61 | Walker B.G.K. | 51 | Kitchen A.K. |
| 73 | Barnes A.C. | 61 | O'Donnell R.R. | 50 | Horne M.J. |
| 73 | Raval J.A. | 60 | Parsons A.E.W. | 50 | Mills K.D. |
| 72 | Troup G.B. | | | | |

## Longest Careers

| Seasons | | | | Seasons | | |
|---|---|---|---|---|---|---|
| 25 | Garrard D.R. | 1917/18-1941/42 | | 21 | Cleverley D.C. | 1930/31-1950/51 |
| 24 | Wallace W.M. | 1933/34-1956/57 | | 20 | Stemson W.I. | 1889/90-1908/09 |
| 22 | Anthony A. | 1909/10-1930/31 | | 20 | Horspool E. | 1909/10-1928/29 |
| 22 | McIntyre J.M. | 1961/62-1982-83 | | 20 | Weir G.L. | 1927/28-1946/47 |
| 21 | Yates R.J. | 1873/74-1893/94 | | 20 | Morgan R.W. | 1957/58-1976/77 |

## Benefits

| | | | | |
|---|---|---|---|---|
| Troup G.B. | 1986/87 | | Watson W. | 1994/95 |
| Snedden M.C. | 1989/90 | | Patel D.N. | 1995/96 |
| Crowe J.J. | 1990/91 | | Morrison D.K. | 1996/97 |
| Franklin T.J. | 1991/92 | | Pringle C. | 1998/99 |
| Hunt A.J. | 1992/93 | | Barnes A.C. | 2002/03 |

# Batting

| 2000 RUNS | Career | M | In | NO | HS | Runs | Ave | 100 |
|---|---|---|---|---|---|---|---|---|
| McIntosh T.G. | 1998/99-2013/14 | 102 | 176 | 15 | 268 | 5980 | 37.14 | 17 |
| Franklin T.J. | 1980/81-1992/93 | 88 | 157 | 14 | 181 | 5051 | 35.25 | 12 |
| Raval J.A. | 2008/09-2019/20 | 73 | 131 | 6 | 256 | 4796 | 38.36 | 13 |
| Jones R.A. | 1993/94-2009/10 | 79 | 137 | 8 | 201 | 4721 | 36.59 | 12 |
| Crowe J.J. | 1982/83-1991/92 | 59 | 95 | 9 | 156 | 4245 | 49.36 | 11 |
| Burgess M.G. | 1966/67-1979/80 | 68 | 116 | 13 | 146 | 4228 | 41.04 | 10 |
| Nicol R.J. | 2001/02-2016/17 | 85 | 136 | 15 | 160 | 4227 | 34.93 | 7 |
| Morgan R.W. | 1957/58-1976/77 | 90 | 154 | 8 | 166 | 4162 | 28.50 | 7 |
| de Grandhomme C. | 2006/07-2017/18 | 77 | 125 | 18 | 144* | 3980 | 37.19 | 9 |
| Reid J.F. | 1975/76-1987/88 | 69 | 117 | 17 | 173 | 3733 | 37.33 | 5 |
| Patel D.N. | 1985/86-1994/95 | 67 | 102 | 9 | 204 | 3648 | 39.22 | 8 |
| Harris R.M. | 1955/56-1973/74 | 67 | 119 | 4 | 157 | 3598 | 31.28 | 3 |
| O'Donnell R.R. | 2014/15-2021/22 | 61 | 105 | 7 | 223 | 3588 | 36.61 | 7 |
| Scott V.J. | 1937/38-1952/53 | 44 | 74 | 15 | 204 | 3546 | 60.10 | 11 |
| Munro C. | 2006/07-2017/18 | 42 | 64 | 4 | 281 | 3440 | 57.33 | 13 |
| Wallace W.M. | 1933/34-1956/57 | 47 | 73 | 5 | 211 | 3409 | 50.13 | 9 |
| Webb P.N. | 1976/77-1986/87 | 65 | 114 | 18 | 136 | 3307 | 34.44 | 5 |
| Hopkins G.J. | 2007/08-2013/14 | 55 | 82 | 12 | 201 | 3228 | 46.40 | 9 |
| Horne M.J. | 1992/93-2005/06 | 50 | 80 | 4 | 209* | 3184 | 41.89 | 9 |
| Guptill M.J. | 2005/06-2021/22 | 42 | 73 | 6 | 195* | 3162 | 47.19 | 9 |
| Young R.A. | 1998/99-2012/13 | 97 | 132 | 22 | 126* | 3056 | 27.78 | 5 |
| Sparling J.T. | 1956/57-1970/71 | 73 | 123 | 17 | 105 | 2977 | 28.08 | 2 |
| Barnes A.C. | 1993/94-2004/05 | 73 | 113 | 10 | 134* | 2893 | 28.08 | 4 |
| Kitchen A.K. | 2008/09-2014/15 | 51 | 90 | 11 | 132 | 2893 | 36.62 | 6 |
| Parsons A.E.W. | 1973/74-1982/83 | 60 | 113 | 8 | 132 | 2820 | 26.85 | 3 |
| Hemus L.G. | 1904/05-1921/22 | 39 | 71 | 4 | 148 | 2701 | 40.31 | 8 |
| Weir G.L. | 1927/28-1946/47 | 42 | 67 | 6 | 191 | 2625 | 43.03 | 7 |
| Whitelaw P.E. | 1928/29-1946/47 | 42 | 68 | 4 | 195 | 2417 | 37.76 | 5 |
| Jarvis T.W. | 1964/65-1976/77 | 46 | 80 | 3 | 118* | 2403 | 31.20 | 2 |
| Horne P.A. | 1979/80-1990/91 | 40 | 67 | 6 | 209 | 2380 | 39.01 | 4 |
| Vincent L. | 1997/98-2012/13 | 45 | 70 | 6 | 185* | 2345 | 36.64 | 4 |
| Vivian G.E. | 1966/67-1978/79 | 58 | 98 | 16 | 111* | 2327 | 28.37 | 2 |
| Guptill-Bunce M.L. | 2012/13-2018/19 | 38 | 71 | 1 | 189 | 2290 | 32.71 | 3 |
| Cachopa B. | 2010/11-2016/17 | 43 | 75 | 10 | 135* | 2278 | 35.04 | 3 |
| Vaughan J.T.C. | 1989/90-1996/97 | 48 | 81 | 14 | 127 | 2269 | 33.86 | 2 |
| Gedye S.G. | 1956/57-1964/65 | 40 | 73 | 4 | 104 | 2169 | 31.43 | 3 |
| Mills J.E. | 1925/26-1937/38 | 35 | 63 | 1 | 185 | 2126 | 34.29 | 3 |
| Phillips G.D. | 2016/17-2021/22 | 31 | 56 | 6 | 138* | 2122 | 42.44 | 4 |
| Hunt A.J. | 1981/82-1992/93 | 65 | 99 | 15 | 102* | 2069 | 24.63 | 1 |
| Canning T.K. | 1999/00-2006/07 | 56 | 82 | 10 | 115 | 2067 | 28.70 | 3 |
| Chapman M.S. | 2015/16-2021/22 | 32 | 56 | 5 | 146 | 2043 | 40.05 | 3 |
| Redmond R.E. | 1969/70-1975/76 | 29 | 55 | 4 | 141* | 2004 | 39.29 | 4 |

## CENTURY ON DEBUT FOR PROVINCE

| | | | | |
|---|---|---|---|---|
| † 112* | Brook-Smith W. | v Hawke's Bay | Auckland | 1904/05 |
| 157 | Relf A.E. | v Canterbury | Christchurch | 1907/08 |
| † 119 | Snedden C.A. | v Hawke's Bay | Auckland | 1920/21 |
| † 122 | Scott V.J. | v Canterbury | Auckland | 1937/38 |
| † 122 | Kerr A.C. | v Wellington | Auckland | 1941/42 |
| 174 | Patel D.N. | v Canterbury | Christchurch | 1985/86 |
| † 106* & 1 | Vaughan J.T.C. | v Wellington | Wellington | 1989/90 |
| † 141* & 4 | Hakaraia D.N. | v Northern Districts | Hamilton | 2012/13 |

† *indicates player was making his first-class debut*

**MOST RUNS IN A SEASON**

| | | Runs | Ave | | | | Runs | Ave |
|---|---|---|---|---|---|---|---|---|
| Crowe J.J. | 1991/92 | 1063 | 62.52 | | Cachopa B. | 2014/15 | 783 | 71.18 |
| Jones R.A. | 2009/10 | 953 | 59.56 | | Cachopa Craig | 2013/14 | 781 | 55.78 |
| Munro C. | 2014/15 | 899 | 56.18 | | Raval J.A. | 2015/16 | 780 | 55.71 |
| Raval J. | 2014/15 | 876 | 48.66 | | Crowe M.D. | 1982/83 | 736 | 52.57 |
| Guptill-Bunce M.L. | 2015/16 | 859 | 45.21 | | Patel D.N. | 1986/87 | 723 | 55.61 |
| McIntosh T.G. | 2002/03 | 820 | 58.57 | | O'Donnell R.R. | 2015/16 | 721 | 40.05 |
| Cachopa Craig | 2012/13 | 795 | 49.68 | | Jones R.A. | 2008/09 | 703 | 46.86 |

**HIGHEST INDIVIDUAL INNINGS**

| | | | | |
|---|---|---|---|---|
| 290 | Carson W.N. | v Otago | Dunedin | 1936/37 |
| 281 | Munro C. | v Central Districts | Napier | 2014/15 |
| 269* | Munro C. | v Wellington | Auckland | 2012/13 |
| 268 | McIntosh T.G. | v Canterbury | Auckland | 2007/08 |
| 256 | Smith S.G. | v Canterbury | Auckland | 1919/20 |
| 256 | Raval J.A. | v Central Districts | Auckland | 2008/09 |
| 223 | O'Donnell R.R. | v Canterbury | Auckland | 2021/22 |
| 211 | Wallace W.M. | v Canterbury | Auckland | 1939/40 |
| 209* | Brown S.W. | v Canterbury | Christchurch | 1990/91 |
| 209* | Horne M.J. | v Northern Districts | Auckland | 2003/04 |
| 209 | Horne P.A. | v Northern Districts | Auckland | 1988/89 |
| 205 | McIntosh T.G. | v Otago | Lincoln | 2006/07 |
| 204 | Scott V.J. | v Otago | Dunedin | 1947/48 |
| 204 | Patel D.N. | v Northern Districts | Auckland | 1991/92 |
| 203 | Cachopa C. | v Wellington | Auckland | 2013/14 |
| 202* | Raval J.A. | v Otago | Auckland | 2015/16 |
| 201 | Jones R.A. | v West Indies | Auckland | 2008/09 |
| 201 | Hopkins G.J. | v Central Districts | Auckland | 2009/10 |

**MOST CENTURIES IN A SEASON**

| | | |
|---|---|---|
| 4 | Franklin T.J. | 1987/88 |
| 4 | Crowe J.J. | 1991/92 |
| 4 | Jones R.A. | 2009/10 |
| 4 | Munro C. | 2016/17 |

**TOTAL NUMBER OF CENTURIES**      **391**

| | | |
|---|---|---|
| Most in one season | 18 | 2008/09 |
| 1st | Mills G. 106* v Wellington | 1895/96 |
| 100th | Playle W.R. 102* v Central Districts | 1957/58 |
| 200th | Crowe J.J. 102 v Otago | 1991/92 |
| 300th | Jones R.A. 123 v Central Districts | 2009/10 |

# Bowling

| 150 WICKETS | Career | M | Wkts | Runs | Ave | 5WI | 10WM | Best |
|---|---|---|---|---|---|---|---|---|
| Howarth H.J. | 1963/64-1978/79 | 80 | 332 | 7361 | 22.17 | 18 | 4 | 8-75 |
| Adams A.R. | 1997/98-2011/12 | 56 | 251 | 4729 | 18.84 | 14 | 3 | 6-25 |
| Sparling J.T. | 1956/57-1970/71 | 73 | 248 | 5327 | 21.47 | 17 | 3 | 7-49 |
| McIntyre J.M. | 1961/62-1982/83 | 77 | 238 | 5447 | 22.88 | 8 | 1 | 6-84 |
| Cunis R.S. | 1960/61-1973/74 | 62 | 229 | 4603 | 20.10 | 14 | 2 | 7-29 |
| Snedden M.C. | 1977/78-1989/90 | 55 | 217 | 4631 | 21.34 | 10 | 2 | 7-49 |
| Stott L.W. | 1969/70-1983/84 | 63 | 214 | 5341 | 24.95 | 8 | — | 6-68 |
| Troup G.B. | 1974/75-1986/87 | 72 | 200 | 5213 | 26.06 | 4 | — | 6-48 |
| Canning T.K. | 1999/00-2006/07 | 56 | 196 | 4822 | 24.60 | 6 | — | 6-44 |
| Bates M.D. | 2003/04-2015/16 | 68 | 193 | 5681 | 29.43 | 5 | — | 6-55 |
| Patel D.N. | 1985/86-1994/95 | 67 | 184 | 4298 | 23.35 | 8 | 2 | 7-83 |

| | Career | M | Wkts | Runs | Ave | 5WI | 10WM | Best |
|---|---|---|---|---|---|---|---|---|
| Watson W. | 1984/85-1994/95 | 53 | 176 | 4110 | 23.35 | 7 | — | 7-60 |
| Bracewell J.G. | 1982/83-1989/90 | 42 | 168 | 4189 | 24.93 | 8 | 2 | 7-65 |
| Morrison D.K. | 1985/86-1996/97 | 49 | 168 | 4034 | 24.01 | 7 | — | 7-82 |
| Nethula T.S. | 2008/09-2017/18 | 46 | 156 | 5483 | 35.14 | 7 | 2 | 6-36 |
| Cowie J. | 1932/33-1949/50 | 34 | 154 | 3379 | 21.94 | 6 | — | 6-44 |
| Sutton R.E. | 1958/59-1973/74 | 54 | 152 | 3364 | 22.13 | 6 | — | 7-64 |

## MOST WICKETS IN A SEASON

| | | Wkts | Ave | | | | Wkts | Ave |
|---|---|---|---|---|---|---|---|---|
| Canning T.K. | 2002/03 | 46 | 21.97 | Hayes J.A. | 1957/58 | | 42 | 11.38 |
| Bracewell J.G. | 1986/87 | 43 | 20.90 | Lankham W. | 1882/83 | | 41 | 6.31 |
| Nethula T.S. | 2016/17 | 43 | 30.06 | | | | | |

### BEST IN AN INNINGS

| | | | | |
|---|---|---|---|---|
| 9-36 | Wensley A.F. | v Otago | Auckland | 1929/30 |
| 9-75 | Neill R. | v Canterbury | Auckland | 1891/92 |
| 9-86 | Neill R. | v Canterbury | Auckland | 1897/98 |
| 8-23 | McClenaghan M.J. | v Otago | Auckland | 2011/12 |
| 8-27 | Vaughan J.T.C. | v Otago | Alexandra | 1996/97 |
| 8-36 | Rees A.W. | v Otago | Dunedin | 1889/90 |
| 8-51 | Neill R. | v Wellington | Auckland | 1895/96 |
| 8-51 | Garrard D.R. | v Canterbury | Auckland | 1921/22 |
| 8-55 | Smith S.G. | v Wellington | Auckland | 1919/20 |
| 8-65 | Smith S.G. | v Otago | Auckland | 1923/24 |
| 8-66 | Rabone G.O. | v Australia | Auckland | 1956/57 |
| 8-75 | Cleverley D.C. | v Wellington | Wellington | 1945/46 |
| 8-75 | Howarth H.J. | v NZ Under 23 XI | Auckland | 1976/77 |

### BEST IN A MATCH

| | | | | |
|---|---|---|---|---|
| 14-63 | Rees A.W. | v Otago | Dunedin | 1889/90 |
| 14-65 | Hayes J.A. | v Wellington | Auckland | 1957/58 |
| 14-94 | Howarth H.J. | v Otago | Dunedin | 1973/74 |
| 14-119 | Pringle C. | v Otago | Dunedin | 1993/94 |
| 13-35 | Lankham W. | v Taranaki | Auckland | 1882/83 |
| 13-85 | Cunis R.S. | v Canterbury | Christchurch | 1963/64 |
| 13-104 | Oliff C. | v Wellington | Auckland | 1912/13 |
| 13-107 | Smith S.G. | v Wellington | Auckland | 1919/20 |

## Wicketkeeping

| 100 DISMISSALS | Career | M | Caught | Stumped | Total |
|---|---|---|---|---|---|
| Young R.A. | 1998/99-2009/10 | 97 | 245 | 5 | 250 |
| Hopkins G.J. | 2007/08-2013/14 | 55 | 165 | 7 | 172 |
| Kelly P.J. | 1981/82-1988/89 | 48 | 140 | 12 | 152 |
| Horne B.J. | 2016/17-2021/22 | 42 | 139 | 6 | 145 |
| Cachopa B. | 2010/11-2016/17 | 43 | 101 | 4 | 105 |

### MOST DISMISSALS IN A SEASON

| | | | |
|---|---|---|---|
| 45 | (44ct/1st) | Cachopa B. | 2015/16 |
| 39 | (39ct) | Cachopa B. | 2014/15 |
| 35 | (33ct/2st) | Young R.A. | 2001/02 |
| 35 | (35ct) | Young R.A. | 2002/03 |
| 35 | (34ct/1st) | Hopkins G.J. | 2012/13 |

**MOST DISMISSALS IN A MATCH**

| | | | | |
|---|---|---|---|---|
| 9 | (9ct) | Horne B.J. v Central Districts | Auckland | 2018/19 |
| 8 | (2ct/6st) | Kent L.A.W. v Wellington | Wellington | 1944/45 |
| 8 | (8ct) | Smith I.D.S. v Central Districts | Nelson | 1988/89 |
| 8 | (8ct) | Vincent L. v Central Districts | Palmerston North | 2000/01 |
| 8 | (8ct) | Hopkins G.J. v Canterbury | Auckland | 2010/11 |
| 8 | (8ct) | Hopkins G.J. v Otago | Dunedin | 2013/14 |
| 8 | (8ct) | Cachopa B. v Otago | Auckland | 2014/15 |
| 8 | (8ct) | Cachopa B. v Otago | Dunedin | 2015/16 |
| 8 | (8ct) | Cachopa B. v Wellington | Wellington | 2015/16 |
| 8 | (8ct) | Horne B.J. v Northern Districts | Auckland | 2017/18 |
| 8 | (8ct) | Horne B.J. v Central Districts | Auckland | 2019/20 |

**MOST DISMISSALS IN AN INNINGS**

| | | | | |
|---|---|---|---|---|
| 6 | (6ct) | Young R.A.v Wellington | Wellington | 2002/03 |
| 6 | (6ct) | Hopkins G.J. v Northern Districts | Whangarei | 2011/12 |
| 6 | (6ct) | Hopkins G.J. v Otago | Auckland | 2011/12 |
| 6 | (6ct) | Cachopa B. v Wellington | Wellington | 2015/16 |
| 6 | (6ct) | Horne B.J. v Central Districts | Auckland | 2018/19 |

**MOST CATCHES IN A MATCH**

| | | | |
|---|---|---|---|
| 9 | Horne B.J. v Central Districts | Auckland | 2018/19 |
| 8 | Smith I.D.S. v Central Districts | Nelson | 1988/89 |
| 8 | Vincent L. v Central Districts | Palmerston North | 2000/01 |
| 8 | Hopkins G.J. v Canterbury | Auckland | 2010/11 |
| 8 | Hopkins G.J. v Otago | Dunedin | 2013/14 |
| 8 | Cachopa B. v Otago | Auckland | 2014/15 |
| 8 | Cachopa B. v Otago | Dunedin | 2015/16 |
| 8 | Cachopa B. v Wellington | Wellington | 2015/16 |
| 8 | Horne B.J. v Northern Districts | Auckland | 2017/18 |
| 8 | Horne B.J. v Central Districts | Auckland | 2019/20 |

**MOST CATCHES IN AN INNINGS**

| | | | |
|---|---|---|---|
| 6 | Young R.A.v Wellington | Wellington | 2002/03 |
| 6 | Hopkins G.J. v Northern Districts | Whangarei | 2011/12 |
| 6 | Hopkins G.J. v Otago | Auckland | 2011/12 |
| 6 | Cachopa B. v Wellington | Wellington | 2015/16 |
| 6 | Horne B.J. v Central Districts | Auckland | 2018/19 |

# Fielding

### MOST CATCHES IN A SEASON

| | | |
|---|---|---|
| 18 | Raval J.A. | 2014/15 |

**MOST CATCHES IN A MATCH**

| | | | |
|---|---|---|---|
| 6 | Williams N.T. v Hawke's Bay | Napier | 1894/95 |
| 6 | Jarvis T.W. v Northern Districts | Hamilton | 1968/69 |
| 6 | de Grandhomme C. v Canterbury | Christchurch | 2010/11 |

**MOST CATCHES IN AN INNINGS**

| | | | |
|---|---|---|---|
| 5 | Williams N.T. v Hawkes Bay | Napier | 1894/95 |
| 5 | Crowe J.J. v Canterbury | Auckland | 1988/89 |

# Record Partnerships

## FOR

| Wicket | Score | Batsmen | Against | At | Date |
|---|---|---|---|---|---|
| 1st | 286 | B. Sutcliffe & D.D. Taylor | Canterbury | Auckland | 1948/49 |
| 2nd | 241 | T.J. Franklin & J.J. Crowe | Wellington | Wellington | 1988/89 |
| 3rd | 445 | P.E. Whitelaw & W.N. Carson | Otago | Dunedin | 1936/37 |
| 4th | 280 | J.J. Crowe & D.N. Patel | ND | Auckland | 1991/92 |
| 5th | 347* | M.J. Horne & A.C. Barnes | ND | Auckland | 2003/04 |
| 6th | 377 | C. Munro & Craig Cachopa | Wellington | Auckland | 2012/13 |
| 7th | 224 | V.J. Scott & A.M. Matheson | Canterbury | Auckland | 1937/38 |
| 8th | 189 | W.N. Carson & A.M. Matheson | Wellington | Auckland | 1938/39 |
| 9th | 204 | B.J. Horne & D.K. Ferns | Otago | Auckland | 2020/21 |
| 10th | 139 | M.J. McClenaghan & R.S. Sandhu | ND | Auckland | 2016/17 |

## AGAINST

| Wicket | Score | Batsmen | For | At | Date |
|---|---|---|---|---|---|
| 1st | 432 | M.H.W. Papps & L.J. Woodcock | Wellington | Wellington | 2017/18 |
| 2nd | 301 | D.R. Flynn & B.S. Wilson | ND | Hamilton | 2012/13 |
| 3rd | 287 | D.P. Conway & M.G. Bracewell | Wellington | Wellington | 2020/21 |
| 4th | 252 | S.A. Thomson & B.A. Young | ND | Auckland | 1990/91 |
| 5th | 282 | J.E.C. Franklin & L.J. Woodcock | Wellington | Auckland | 2008/09 |
| 6th | 220 | M.H. Toynbee & I.D.S. Smith | CD | Napier | 1982/83 |
| 7th | 165 | R.K. Brown & M.E.L. Lane | CD | Palmerston Nth | 1993/94 |
| 8th | 166 | R.J. Hadlee & D.R. Hadlee | Canterbury | Christchurch | 1983/84 |
| 9th | 208 | W.C. McSkimming & B.E. Scott | Otago | Auckland | 2004/05 |
| 10th | 133 | G.A. Bartlett & I.A. Colquhoun | CD | Auckland | 1959/60 |

# CANTERBURY

## Highest Totals

| | | | |
|---|---|---|---|
| 777 | v Otago | Christchurch | 1996/97 |
| 613-7 dec | v Wellington | Christchurch | 2006/07 |
| 582 | v Central Districts | Napier | 2013/14 |
| 570-8 dec | v Wellington | Rangiora | 2019/20 |
| 559 | v Central Districts | Christchurch | 1993/94 |
| 558-4 dec | v Northern Districts | Rangiora | 2009/10 |
| 551-5 dec | v Central Districts | New Plymouth | 2009/10 |
| 549 | v Northern Districts | Christchurch | 1996/97 |
| 547-5 dec | v Wellington | Christchurch | 1953/54 |
| 543-8 dec | v Central Districts | Rangiora | 1996/97 |

## Lowest Totals

| | | | |
|---|---|---|---|
| 25 | v Otago | Christchurch | 1886/87 |
| 27 | v Otago | Dunedin | 1896/97 |
| 32 | v Otago | Christchurch | 1866/67 |
| 34 | v Otago | Dunedin | 1863/64 |
| 37 | v Southland | Invercargill | 1920/21 |
| 37 | v Wellington | Wellington | 1925/26 |
| 38 | v Otago | Dunedin | 1873/74 |
| 42 | v Otago | Dunedin | 1863/64 |
| 42 | v Otago | Dunedin | 1992/93 |
| 44 | v Otago | Dunedin | 1883/84 |

# Most Appearances

| | | | | | | | | |
|---|---|---|---|---|---|---|---|---|
| 121 | Fulton P.G. | | 82 | Hadlee B.G. | | 58 | Patrick W.R. |
| 105 | Ellis A.M. | | 77 | Stead D.W. | | 58 | Dowling G.T. |
| 105 | Astle T.D. | | 76 | Germon L.K. | | 58 | Thomson K. |
| 103 | McEwan P.E. | | 72 | Hastings B.F. | | 57 | Bull C.L. |
| 101 | Latham R.T. | | 69 | Boyle D.J. | | 56 | Motz R.C. |
| 96 | Stewart S.L. | | 65 | Brown V.R. | | 54 | Cromb I.B. |
| 95 | Papps M.H.W. | | 64 | Fletcher C.D. | | 54 | Ward J.T. |
| 88 | Stead G.R. | | 62 | Hadlee R.J. | | 50 | Boxshall C. |
| 88 | Priest M.W. | | 60 | Roberts S.J. | | 50 | Nicholls H.M. |
| 84 | Harris C.Z. | | 59 | Hartland B.R. | | | |

# Longest Careers

| *Seasons* | | | | *Seasons* | | |
|---|---|---|---|---|---|---|
| 34 | Read R.J. | 1904/05-1937/38 | | 21 | Stevens E.C.J. | 1863/64-1883/84 |
| 31 | Reese T.W. | 1887/88-1917/18 | | 21 | Wilding F. | 1881/82-1901/02 |
| 27 | Fowke J.N. | 1880/81-1906/07 | | 21 | Ridley A.E. | 1889/90-1909/10 |
| 26 | Reese D. | 1895/96-1920/21 | | 21 | Harris C.Z. | 1989/90-2009/10 |
| 25 | Moorhouse H.M. | 1883/84-1907/08 | | 20 | Harman T.D. | 1882/83-1901/02 |
| 22 | Wheatley J. | 1882/83-1903/04 | | 20 | Hadlee B.G. | 1961/62-1980/81 |
| 22 | Patrick W.R. | 1905/06-1926/27 | | | | |

# Benefits

| | | | | |
|---|---|---|---|---|
| McEwan P.E. | 1988/89 | | Germon L.K./Priest M.W. | 1997/98 |
| Hadlee R.J. | 1989/90 | | Harris C.Z. | 1998/99 |
| Latham R.T. | 1992/93 | | Cairns C.L. | 1999/00 |

# Batting

| **2000 RUNS** | Career | M | In | NO | HS | Runs | Ave | 100 |
|---|---|---|---|---|---|---|---|---|
| Fulton P.G. | 2000/01-2016/17 | 121 | 224 | 22 | 301* | 8719 | 43.16 | 16 |
| Papps M.H.W. | 1998/99-2010/11 | 95 | 172 | 14 | 192 | 6663 | 42.17 | 19 |
| McEwan P.E. | 1977/78-1990/91 | 103 | 185 | 11 | 155 | 5940 | 34.13 | 11 |
| Latham R.T. | 1980/81-1994/95 | 101 | 176 | 17 | 237* | 5919 | 37.22 | 8 |
| Stewart S.L. | 2001/02-2013/14 | 96 | 173 | 18 | 227* | 5693 | 36.72 | 7 |
| Harris C.Z. | 1989/90-2009/10 | 84 | 125 | 31 | 251* | 5442 | 57.89 | 13 |
| Ellis A.M. | 2002/03-2017/18 | 105 | 167 | 21 | 171 | 5179 | 35.47 | 9 |
| Hadlee B.G. | 1961/62-1980/81 | 82 | 151 | 11 | 163* | 4429 | 31.63 | 6 |
| Stead G.R. | 1993/94-2005/06 | 88 | 146 | 10 | 190 | 4410 | 32.42 | 10 |
| Astle T.D. | 2005/06-2019/20 | 105 | 172 | 20 | 195 | 4077 | 26.82 | 2 |
| Dowling G.T. | 1958/59-1971/72 | 58 | 100 | 7 | 206 | 3690 | 39.67 | 8 |
| Hastings B.F. | 1961/62-1976/77 | 72 | 122 | 8 | 226 | 3540 | 31.05 | 7 |
| Priest M.W. | 1984/85-1998/99 | 88 | 130 | 21 | 119 | 3457 | 31.71 | 4 |
| Boyle D.J. | 1980/81-1994/95 | 69 | 121 | 12 | 149 | 3216 | 29.50 | 3 |
| Hadlee W.A. | 1933/34-1951/52 | 44 | 80 | 7 | 194 | 3183 | 43.60 | 10 |
| Stead D.W. | 1969/70-1985/86 | 77 | 133 | 11 | 193* | 3169 | 25.97 | 1 |
| Latham T.W.M. | 2010/11-2021/22 | 45 | 76 | 5 | 261 | 3169 | 44.63 | 7 |
| Nicholls H.M. | 2011/12-2021/22 | 50 | 88 | 5 | 119 | 3000 | 36.14 | 3 |
| Cromb I.B. | 1929/30-1946/47 | 54 | 96 | 5 | 171 | 2986 | 31.05 | 3 |
| Fletcher C.D. | 2014/15-2021/22 | 64 | 100 | 20 | 157 | 2882 | 36.02 | 5 |
| Brown V.R. | 1978/79-1986/87 | 65 | 111 | 11 | 161* | 2872 | 28.72 | 5 |
| Patrick W.R. | 1905/06-1926/27 | 58 | 108 | 7 | 129* | 2803 | 27.75 | 2 |
| Hartland B.R. | 1986/87-1996/97 | 59 | 103 | 8 | 150 | 2771 | 29.16 | 5 |
| Brownlie D.G. | 2009/10-2013/14 | 35 | 65 | 8 | 171 | 2635 | 46.22 | 6 |
| Coman P.G. | 1968/69-1977/78 | 44 | 78 | 4 | 104 | 2603 | 35.17 | 2 |
| Thomson K. | 1959/60-1973/74 | 58 | 103 | 11 | 136* | 2543 | 27.64 | 4 |

| | Career | M | In | NO | HS | Runs | Ave | 100 |
|---|---|---|---|---|---|---|---|---|
| McClure K.J. | 2015/16-2021/22 | 46 | 78 | 8 | 210 | 2539 | 36.27 | 6 |
| Bowes C.J. | 2015/16-2021/22 | 48 | 84 | 5 | 155 | 2497 | 31.60 | 5 |
| Page M.L. | 1920/21-1936/37 | 41 | 75 | 2 | 206 | 2424 | 33.20 | 2 |
| Leggat J.G. | 1944/45-1955/56 | 35 | 66 | 6 | 166 | 2391 | 39.85 | 5 |
| Chapple M.E. | 1949/50-1960/61 | 44 | 79 | 9 | 165 | 2364 | 33.77 | 3 |
| McConchie C.E. | 2012/13-2021/22 | 48 | 78 | 5 | 187* | 2341 | 32.06 | 5 |
| Germon L.K. | 1987/88-1997/98 | 76 | 101 | 25 | 160* | 2336 | 30.73 | 3 |
| McMillan C.D. | 1994/95-2006/07 | 40 | 65 | 9 | 159 | 2332 | 41.64 | 6 |
| Kerr J.L. | 1929/30-1939/40 | 32 | 61 | 3 | 196 | 2228 | 38.41 | 3 |
| Carter L.J. | 2014/15-2021/22 | 43 | 72 | 6 | 226* | 2198 | 33.30 | 3 |
| Guillen S.C. | 1952/53-1960/61 | 42 | 73 | 5 | 197 | 2186 | 32.14 | 3 |
| Myburgh J.G. | 2007/08-2009/10 | 25 | 46 | 4 | 199 | 2172 | 51.71 | 7 |
| Reese D. | 1895/96-1920/21 | 47 | 85 | 4 | 111 | 2066 | 25.50 | 2 |
| Ryan M.L. | 1965/66-1978/79 | 45 | 78 | 8 | 129 | 2041 | 29.15 | 2 |
| Hadlee R.J. | 1971/72-1988/89 | 62 | 100 | 22 | 93 | 2012 | 25.79 | — |
| Roberts A.W. | 1927/28-1940/41 | 35 | 60 | 8 | 181 | 2004 | 38.53 | 2 |

## CENTURY ON DEBUT FOR PROVINCE

| † 175 | Watson G. | v Otago | Christchurch | 1880/81 |
|---|---|---|---|---|
| † 108 & 18 | Wood B.B. | v Wellington | Wellington | 1907/08 |
| † 105 | Talbot R.O. | v Otago | Dunedin | 1922/23 |
| 5 & 112* | Newman J.A. | v Otago | Christchurch | 1927/28 |
| 149 | Hastings B.F. | v Central Districts | Nelson | 1961/62 |
| 8 & 135 | Parker N.M. | v Wellington | Wellington | 1973/74 |
| 115 | Hopkins G.J. | v Central Districts | Christchurch | 1998/99 |
| 102 | Dravid R.S. | v Central Districts | Rangiora | 2008/09 |
| † 102 | McCone R.J. | v Otago | Christchurch | 2008/09 |
| † 112* | Brownlie D.G. | v Northern Districts | Rangiora | 2009/10 |

*† indicates player was making his first-class debut*

## HIGHEST INDIVIDUAL INNINGS

| 301* | Fulton P.G. | v Auckland | Christchurch | 2002/03 |
|---|---|---|---|---|
| 261 | Latham T.W.M. | v Central Districts | Napier | 2013/14 |
| 251* | Harris C.Z. | v Central Districts | Rangiora | 1996/97 |
| 241* | Latham T.W.M. | v Wellington | Wellington | 2013/14 |
| 237* | Latham R.T. | v Northern Districts | Rotorua | 1990/91 |
| 227* | Stewart S.L. | v Central Districts | New Plymouth | 2009/10 |
| 226* | Carter L.J. | v Wellington | Rangiora | 2019/20 |
| 226 | Hastings B.F. | v NZ Under 23 XI | Christchurch | 1964/65 |
| 224 | Latham T.W.M. | v Wellington | Wellington | 2019/20 |
| 221* | Fulton P.G. | v Otago | Dunedin | 2004/05 |
| 210 | McClure K.J. | v Auckland | Rangiora | 2017/18 |
| 209* | Fulton P.G. | v Central Districts | Christchurch | 2014/15 |
| 206 | Page M.L. | v Wellington | Wellington | 1931/32 |
| 206 | Dowling G.T. | v Wellington | Christchurch | 1962/63 |
| 206 | Harris C.Z. | v Central Districts | Blenheim | 1996/97 |
| 204 | Cox A. | v Otago | Christchurch | 1925/26 |

## MOST RUNS IN A SEASON

| | | Runs | Ave | | | Runs | Ave |
|---|---|---|---|---|---|---|---|
| Papps M.H.W. | 2006/07 | 1005 | 91.36 | Wright J.G. | 1986/87 | 780 | 60.00 |
| Latham T.W.M. | 2013/14 | 948 | 79.00 | Nicholls H.M. | 2014/15 | 778 | 43.22 |
| Papps M.H.W. | 2009/10 | 927 | 48.78 | McEwan P.E. | 1988/89 | 758 | 44.58 |
| Fulton P.G. | 2012/13 | 902 | 56.37 | Myburgh J.G. | 2009/10 | 758 | 50.53 |
| Fulton P.G. | 2014/15 | 879 | 54.93 | Latham R.T. | 1988/89 | 757 | 58.23 |

**NZC**

| | | Runs | Ave | | | | Runs | Ave |
|---|---|---|---|---|---|---|---|---|
| Ellis A.M. | 2014/15 | 853 | 53.31 | | Harris C.Z. | 1996/97 | 748 | 187.00 |
| Stead G.R. | 2000/01 | 852 | 50.11 | | Brownlie D.G. | 2012/13 | 743 | 43.70 |
| Fulton P.G. | 2004/05 | 828 | 69.00 | | Myburgh J.G. | 2008/09 | 739 | 61.58 |
| Broom N.T. | 2014/15 | 820 | 45.55 | | Brownlie D.G. | 2013/14 | 733 | 40.72 |
| Stewart S.L. | 2009/10 | 812 | 73.81 | | Englefield J.I. | 2000/01 | 724 | 38.10 |
| McMillan C.D. | 1996/97 | 809 | 73.54 | | Papps M.H.W. | 2008/09 | 719 | 59.91 |
| Papps M.H.W. | 2001/02 | 793 | 52.86 | | McEwan P.E. | 1983/84 | 713 | 59.41 |

## MOST CENTURIES IN A SEASON
| | | |
|---|---|---|
| 4 | Papps M.H.W. | 2006/07 |
| 4 | Papps M.H.W. | 2009/10 |

## TOTAL NUMBER OF CENTURIES

| | | | 373 |
|---|---|---|---|
| Most in one season | 14 | | 2009/10 |
| 1st | Watson G. 175 v Otago | | 1880/81 |
| 100th | Hastings B.F. 136 v Auckland | | 1964/65 |
| 200th | Germon L.K. 114 v Central Districts | | 1993/94 |
| 300th | Brownlie D.G. 153* v Auckland | | 2010/11 |

# Bowling

## 150 WICKETS

| | Career | M | Wkts | Runs | Ave | 5WI | 10WM | Best |
|---|---|---|---|---|---|---|---|---|
| Astle T.D. | 2005/06-2019/20 | 105 | 303 | 9505 | 31.36 | 12 | 1 | 8-148 |
| Priest M.W. | 1984/85-1998/99 | 88 | 290 | 8501 | 29.31 | 12 | 3 | 9-95 |
| Hadlee R.J. | 1971/72-1988/89 | 62 | 285 | 4600 | 16.14 | 19 | 2 | 7-49 |
| Ellis A.M. | 2003/04-2017/18 | 105 | 249 | 7356 | 29.54 | 6 | — | 6-35 |
| Burtt T.B. | 1943/44-1954/55 | 46 | 241 | 4991 | 20.70 | 16 | 3 | 8-35 |
| Motz R.C. | 1957/58-1968/69 | 56 | 239 | 4589 | 19.20 | 12 | 3 | 8-61 |
| Bennett J.H. | 1898/99-1919/20 | 40 | 205 | 3367 | 16.43 | 17 | 4 | 7-35 |
| Hadlee D.R. | 1969/70-1983/84 | 49 | 195 | 3918 | 20.09 | 10 | 3 | 7-55 |
| Roberts S.J. | 1985/86-1995/96 | 60 | 193 | 5738 | 29.73 | 6 | – | 5-56 |
| Read R.J. | 1904/05-1937/38 | 44 | 184 | 4704 | 25.56 | 11 | 1 | 7-24 |
| Henry M.J. | 2010/11-2021/22 | 42 | 181 | 4270 | 23.59 | 7 | — | 5-21 |
| Reese D. | 1895/96-1920/21 | 48 | 168 | 3040 | 18.09 | 10 | 1 | 6-43 |
| Stead D.W. | 1969/70-1985/86 | 77 | 167 | 5009 | 29.99 | 6 | — | 7-99 |
| Brown V.R. | 1978/79-1986/87 | 65 | 159 | 4393 | 27.62 | 4 | 2 | 7-28 |
| Merritt W.E. | 1926/27-1935/36 | 24 | 154 | 3559 | 23.11 | 15 | 4 | 8-105 |
| Wisneski W.A. | 1996/97-2003/04 | 44 | 154 | 4092 | 26.57 | 7 | — | 7-151 |
| Bennett H.K. | 2005/06-2015/16 | 48 | 154 | 4942 | 32.09 | 3 | — | 7-50 |
| Martin C.S. | 1997/98-2009/10 | 49 | 152 | 4445 | 29.24 | 3 | — | 5-40 |

## BEST IN AN INNINGS

| | | | | |
|---|---|---|---|---|
| 10-28 | Moss A.E. | v Wellington | Christchurch | 1889/90 |
| 9-13 | Wiseman P.J. | v Central Districts | Christchurch | 2004/05 |
| 9-56 | McBeath D.J. | v Auckland | Christchurch | 1918/19 |
| 9-95 | Priest M.W. | v Otago | Dunedin | 1989/90 |
| 9-98 | Robertson W. | v Wellington | Christchurch | 1894/95 |
| 8-18 | Frith W. | v Otago | Christchurch | 1880/81 |
| 8-33 | Callaway S.T. | v Hawkes Bay | Napier | 1903/04 |
| 8-35 | Burtt T.B. | v Otago | Dunedin | 1953/54 |
| 8-41 | Callaway S.T. | v Otago | Dunedin | 1900/01 |
| 8-59 | Robertson W. | v Auckland | Christchurch | 1893/94 |
| 8-61 | Mulcock E. | v Otago | Christchurch | 1937/38 |
| 8-61 | Motz R.C. | v Wellington | Christchurch | 1966/67 |
| 8-74 | Jamieson K.A. | v Auckland | Rangiora | 2016/17 |

| 8-75 | Edser H. | v Wellington | Wellington | 1883/84 |
| 8-96 | McBeath D.J. | v Auckland | Auckland | 1921/22 |
| 8-99 | Thomas A.W. | v Auckland | Auckland | 1914/15 |
| 8-105 | Merritt W.E. | v Auckland | Auckland | 1931/32 |
| 8-148 | Astle T.D. | v Central Districts | Napier | 2013/14 |

**BEST IN A MATCH**

| 15-60 | Callaway S.T. | v Hawkes Bay | Napier | 1903/04 |
| 15-168 | McBeath D.J. | v Auckland | Christchurch | 1918/19 |
| 14-59 | Read R.J. | v Southland | Invercargill | 1920/21 |
| 14-107 | Robertson W. | v Auckland | Christchurch | 1893/94 |
| 14-234 | Astle T.D. | v Central Districts | Napier | 2013/14 |
| 13-72 | Moss A.E. | v Wellington | Christchurch | 1889/90 |
| 13-82 | Howell W.B. | v Wellington | Christchurch | 1902/03 |
| 13-90 | Frankish F.S. | v Wellington | Wellington | 1901/02 |
| 13-140 | Edser H. | v Wellington | Wellington | 1883/84 |
| 13-163 | Robertson W. | v Wellington | Christchurch | 1894/95 |
| 13-181 | Merritt W.E. | v Otago | Wellington | 1935/36 |

## MOST WICKETS IN A SEASON

| | | Wkts | Ave | | | | Wkts | Ave |
|---|---|---|---|---|---|---|---|---|
| Boock S.L. | 1977/78 | 56 | 15.66 | Hadlee R.J. | 1981/82 | | 45 | 14.31 |
| Callaway S.T. | 1903/04 | 47 | 8.49 | Hadlee R.J. | 1986/87 | | 45 | 12.91 |

# Wicketkeeping

| **100 DISMISSALS** | *Career* | M | *Caught* | *Stumped* | *Total* |
|---|---|---|---|---|---|
| Germon L.K. | 1987/88-1997/98 | 76 | 217 | 21 | 238 |
| Fletcher C.D. | 2014/15-2021/22 | 64 | 205 | 12 | 217 |
| Ward J.T. | 1957/58-1970/71 | 54 | 136 | 17 | 153 |
| Boxshall C. | 1897/98-1914/15 | 50 | 70 | 36 | 106 |
| van Wyk C.F.K. | 2006/07-2009/10 | 35 | 101 | 5 | 106 |
| Hopkins G.J. | 1998/99-2002/03 | 41 | 91 | 10 | 101 |

### MOST DISMISSALS IN A SEASON
39  (37ct/2st)  Fletcher C.D. 2015/16
34  (31ct/3st)  Germon L.K. 1991/92

**MOST DISMISSALS IN A MATCH**
9  (9ct)  Germon L.K. v Northern Districts  Christchurch  1992/93

**MOST DISMISSALS IN AN INNINGS**
6  (6ct)  Germon L.K. v Northern Districts  Christchurch  1992/93
6  (5ct/1st)  Papps M.H.W. v Northern Districts  Gisborne  2004/05

### MOST CATCHES IN A MATCH
9  Germon L.K. v Northern Districts  Christchurch  1992/93

### MOST CATCHES IN AN INNINGS
6  Germon L.K. v Northern Districts  Christchurch  1992/93

# Fielding
## MOST CATCHES IN A SEASON
20  Fulton P.G.  2014/15

### MOST CATCHES IN A MATCH

| | | | |
|---|---|---|---|
| 6 | Cromb I.B. v Otago | Christchurch | 1937/38 |
| 6 | MacDonald G.K. v Pakistan | Christchurch | 1984/85 |
| 6 | Latham R.T. v Otago | Oamaru | 1994/95 |
| 6 | Myburgh J.G. v Auckland | Rangiora | 2008/09 |

### MOST CATCHES IN AN INNINGS

| | | | |
|---|---|---|---|
| 5 | MacDonald G.K. v Pakistan | Christchurch | 1984/85 |
| 5 | Harris C.Z. v England | Christchurch | 2001/02 |
| 5 | Myburgh J.G. v Auckland | Rangiora | 2008/09 |

## Record Partnerships

**FOR**

| Wicket | Score | Batsmen | Against | At | Date |
|---|---|---|---|---|---|
| 1st | 306 | L.A. Cuff & J.D. Lawrence | Auckland | Christchurch | 1893/94 |
| 2nd | 254* | M.H.W. Papps & J.G. Myburgh | CD | Napier | 2007/08 |
| 3rd | 394* | P.G. Kennedy & R.T. Latham | ND | Rotorua | 1990/91 |
| 4th | 278 | M.L. Page & A.W. Roberts | Wellington | Wellington | 1931/32 |
| 5th | 290 | G.R. Stead & C.Z. Harris | CD | Blenheim | 1996/97 |
| 6th | 379* | S.L. Stewart & C.F.K. van Wyk | CD | New Plymouth | 2009/10 |
| 7th | 265 | J.L. Powell & N. Dorreen | Otago | Christchurch | 1929/30 |
| 8th | 220 | P.J. Wiseman & B.C. Hiini | ND | Hamilton | 2005/06 |
| 9th | 182* | L.K. Germon & R.M. Ford | Wellington | Christchurch | 1989/90 |
| 10th | 160 | L.K. Germon & W.A. Wisneski | ND | Rangiora | 1997/98 |

**AGAINST**

| Wicket | Score | Batsmen | For | At | Date |
|---|---|---|---|---|---|
| 1st | 286 | B. Sutcliffe & D.D. Taylor | Auckland | Auckland | 1948/49 |
| 2nd | 317 | R.T. Hart & P.S. Briasco | CD | New Plymouth | 1983/84 |
| 3rd | 278 | T.J. Franklin & D.N. Patel | Auckland | Christchurch | 1985/86 |
| 4th | 282 | W.A.C. Wilkinson & A.P.F. Chapman | MCC | Christchurch | 1922/23 |
| 5th | 235* | G.P. Sulzberger & J.D. Ryder | CD | Napier | 2002/03 |
| 6th | 211 | M.J. Guptill & C. de Grandhomme | Auckland | Rangiora | 2011/12 |
| 7th | 261 | A.D.R. Campbell & P.A. Strang | Zimbabwe | Timaru | 1997/98 |
| 8th | 433 | A. Sims & V.T. Trumper | Australia | Christchurch | 1913/14 |
| 9th | 134 | J.W. Wilson & N.A. Mallender | Otago | Christchurch | 1992/93 |
| 10th | 184 | R.C. Blunt & W. Hawksworth | Otago | Christchurch | 1931/32 |

# CENTRAL DISTRICTS

## Highest Totals

| | | | |
|---|---|---|---|
| 650-8 dec | v Otago | Napier | 2015/16 |
| 594-8 dec | v Auckland | Auckland | 1995/96 |
| 584-8 dec | v Otago | Napier | 2018/19 |
| 549-8 dec | v Canterbury | Christchurch | 1998/99 |
| 542-4 dec | v Canterbury | Napier | 2002/03 |
| 538 | v Canterbury | Blenheim | 2000/01 |
| 531-7 dec | v Northern Districts | Napier | 2009/10 |
| 526 | v Otago | Napier | 1995/96 |
| 524 | v Auckland | Auckland | 2017/18 |
| 523 | v Wellington | Wellington | 2008/09 |

# Lowest Totals

| | | | |
|---|---|---|---|
| 50 | v Wellington | Upper Hutt | 1979/80 |
| 51 | v Northern Districts | Hamilton | 1957/58 |
| 59 | v Auckland | New Plymouth | 1958/59 |
| 61 | v Auckland | Auckland | 1996/97 |
| 61 | v Auckland | Auckland | 2007/08 |
| 63 | v Wellington | Napier | 2003/04 |
| 65 | v Wellington | Nelson | 1995/96 |
| 71 | v Northern Districts | Wanganui | 1962/63 |
| 72 | v Auckland | Palmerston North | 2001/02 |
| 74 | v Otago | Invercargill | 1996/97 |

# Most Appearances

| | | | | | | | |
|---|---|---|---|---|---|---|---|
| 119 | Sinclair M.S. | 76 | Douglas M.W. | 59 | Smith I.D.S. |
| 97 | Shrimpton M.J.F. | 74 | Sulzberger G.P. | 58 | Patel A.Y. |
| 92 | How J.M. | 74 | Worker G.H. | 57 | Hamilton L.J. |
| 92 | Hay G.R. | 68 | Young W.A. | 57 | Bruce T.C. |
| 90 | O'Sullivan D.R. | 67 | Edwards G.N. | 55 | Congdon B.E. |
| 85 | Duff S.W. | 67 | Bracewell D.A.J. | 55 | Jordan A.B. |
| 83 | Blain T.E. | 67 | Smith B.S. | 53 | Colquhoun I.A. |
| 82 | Griggs B.B.J. | 62 | Smith C.J.P. | 53 | Toynbee M.H. |
| 81 | Briasco P.S. | 61 | Greatbatch M.J. | 53 | Schofield R.M. |
| 79 | Mason M.J. | 61 | Yuile B.W. | 53 | Pierce R.A. |
| 78 | Robertson G.K. | 60 | Cleaver D. | 51 | Thompson E.P. |
| 77 | Ingram P.J. | | | | |

# Longest Careers

| *Seasons* | | | | *Seasons* | | |
|---|---|---|---|---|---|---|
| 19 | Shrimpton M.J.F. | 1961/62-1979/80 | | 16 | Snook I.R. | 1972/73-1987/88 |
| 19 | Taylor L.R.P.L. | 2002/03-2020/21 | | 16 | Ryder J.D. | 2002/03-2017/18 |
| 18 | Sinclair M.S. | 1995/96-2012/13 | | 16 | Hay G.R. | 2006/07-2021/22 |
| 17 | Jones A.H. | 1979/80-1995/96 | | 15 | Coutts P.J.C. | 1958/59-1972/73 |
| 16 | Chapple M.E. | 1950/51-1965/66 | | 15 | Mason M.J. | 1997/98-2011/12 |
| 16 | Schofield R.M. | 1959/60-1974/75 | | 15 | How J.M. | 2000/01-2014/15 |

# Benefits

| | | | | |
|---|---|---|---|---|
| O'Sullivan D.R. | 1984/85 | | Duff S.W. | 1995/96 |
| Robertson G.K. | 1989/90 | | Greatbatch M.J. | 1996/97 |
| Briasco P.S. | 1991/92 | | Douglas M.W. | 2000/01 |
| Blain T.E. | 1994/95 | | Sinclair M.S. | 2009/10 |

# Batting

| **2000 RUNS** | *Career* | *M* | *In* | *NO* | *HS* | *Runs* | *Ave* | *100* |
|---|---|---|---|---|---|---|---|---|
| Sinclair M.S. | 1995/96-2012/13 | 119 | 203 | 26 | 243* | 9148 | 51.68 | 27 |
| Hay G.R. | 2006/07-2021/22 | 92 | 161 | 13 | 226 | 6269 | 42.35 | 15 |
| How J.M. | 2000/01-2014/15 | 92 | 167 | 16 | 207* | 5680 | 37.61 | 13 |
| Ingram P.J. | 2001/02-2011/12 | 77 | 140 | 8 | 247 | 5378 | 40.74 | 17 |
| Shrimpton M.J.F. | 1961/62-1979/80 | 97 | 171 | 15 | 150 | 4551 | 29.17 | 5 |
| Blain T.E. | 1982/83-1994/95 | 83 | 145 | 15 | 161 | 4547 | 34.97 | 7 |
| Young W.A. | 2011/12-2021/22 | 68 | 118 | 12 | 162 | 4516 | 42.60 | 8 |
| Greatbatch M.J. | 1986/87-1999/00 | 61 | 107 | 8 | 202* | 4363 | 44.07 | 14 |
| Briasco P.S. | 1982/83-1991/92 | 81 | 146 | 16 | 157 | 4301 | 33.08 | 6 |
| Bruce T.C. | 2014/15-2021/22 | 57 | 100 | 19 | 208* | 3919 | 48.38 | 6 |
| Douglas M.W. | 1987/88-2000/01 | 76 | 132 | 19 | 144 | 3838 | 33.96 | 7 |

| | Career | M | In | NO | HS | Runs | Ave | 100 |
|---|---|---|---|---|---|---|---|---|
| Worker G.H. | 2007/08-2020/21 | 74 | 129 | 4 | 210 | 3730 | 29.84 | 7 |
| Edwards G.N. | 1973/74-1984/85 | 67 | 122 | 5 | 177* | 3709 | 31.70 | 5 |
| Sulzberger G.P. | 1995/96-2004/05 | 74 | 120 | 12 | 159 | 3505 | 32.45 | 8 |
| Cleaver D. | 2010/11-2021/22 | 60 | 102 | 12 | 201 | 3590 | 39.88 | 6 |
| Smith C.J.P. | 1983/84-1990/91 | 62 | 118 | 9 | 160* | 3499 | 32.10 | 7 |
| Smith B.S. | 2010/11-2021/22 | 67 | 114 | 8 | 244 | 3414 | 32.20 | 6 |
| Crowe M.D. | 1983/84-1989/90 | 32 | 55 | 7 | 242 | 3299 | 68.72 | 13 |
| Griggs B.B.J | 2000/01-2009/10 | 82 | 129 | 16 | 143 | 3144 | 27.82 | 2 |
| Duff S.W. | 1985/86-1995/96 | 85 | 129 | 29 | 164* | 3079 | 30.79 | 1 |
| Spearman C.M. | 1996/97-2003/04 | 44 | 76 | 3 | 144 | 2951 | 40.42 | 5 |
| van Wyk C.F.K. | 2010/11-2015/16 | 45 | 73 | 19 | 131 | 2854 | 52.85 | 3 |
| Congdon B.E. | 1960/61-1970/71 | 55 | 93 | 8 | 202* | 2807 | 33.02 | 3 |
| Taylor L.R.P.L. | 2002/03-2020/21 | 48 | 75 | 1 | 217 | 2783 | 37.60 | 4 |
| Bracewell D.A.J. | 2008/09-2021/22 | 67 | 101 | 15 | 105 | 2670 | 31.04 | 2 |
| Weston T.I. | 2005/06-2010/11 | 46 | 75 | 11 | 152 | 2577 | 40.26 | 2 |
| Payton D.H. | 1965/66-1976/77 | 49 | 92 | 4 | 145 | 2459 | 27.94 | 3 |
| Pierce R.A. | 1971/72-1984/85 | 53 | 98 | 5 | 100* | 2296 | 24.68 | 1 |
| Smith I.D.S. | 1977/78-1986/87 | 59 | 95 | 12 | 145 | 2265 | 27.28 | 3 |
| Hart R.T. | 1982/83-1990/91 | 37 | 68 | 3 | 207 | 2222 | 34.18 | 5 |
| Yuile B.W. | 1959/60-1971/72 | 61 | 90 | 10 | 146 | 2190 | 27.37 | 1 |
| Noema-Barnett K. | 2008/09-2018/19 | 47 | 73 | 9 | 108 | 2053 | 32.07 | 4 |

## CENTURY ON DEBUT FOR PROVINCE

| † 117 | Macleod D.N. | v Wellington | Wanganui | 1956/57 |
|---|---|---|---|---|
| † 25 & 119 | Sampson H.C. | v Wellington | Wellington | 1970/71 |
| 119 & 0 | Crowe M.D. | v Northern Districts | Whangarei | 1983/84 |
| 112 & 21 | Wilson S.W.J. | v Otago | Blenheim | 1990/91 |
| 124 & 7* | Smith B.F. | v Otago | Wanganui | 2000/01 |
| † 203 & 4 | Schmulian B.D. | v Northern Districts | Mt Maunganui | 2017/18 |
| † 133 & 9* | Wiggins B.L. | v Canterbury | Christchurch | 2021/22 |

† *indicates player was making his first-class debut*

## HIGHEST INDIVIDUAL INNINGS

| 247 | Ingram P.J. | v Northern Districts | Hamilton | 2008/09 |
|---|---|---|---|---|
| 245* | Ingram P.J. | v Wellington | Wellington | 2009/10 |
| 244 | Smith B.S. | v Otago | Napier | 2015/16 |
| 243* | Sinclair M.S. | v Otago | Napier | 2007/08 |
| 242 | Crowe M.D. | v Otago | New Plymouth | 1989/90 |
| 226 | Hay G.R. | v Otago | Alexandra | 2018/19 |
| 217 | Taylor L.R.P.L. | v Otago | Napier | 2006/07 |
| 212* | Kelly D.P. | v Canterbury | Blenheim | 2000/01 |
| 210 | Worker G.H. | v Wellington | Nelson | 2015/16 |
| 208* | Bruce T.C. | v Northern Districts | Whangarei | 2021/22 |
| 207* | How J.M. | v Otago | Nelson | 2013/14 |
| 207 | Hart R.T. | v Wellington | Wellington | 1985/86 |
| 204* | Bruce T.C. | v Auckland | Napier | 2021/22 |
| 203* | Sinclair M.S. | v Northern Districts | Wanganui | 1998/99 |
| 203 | Schmulian B.D. | v Northern Districts | Mt Maunganui | 2017/18 |
| 202* | Congdon B.E. | v Otago | Nelson | 1968/69 |
| 202* | Greatbatch M.J. | v Otago | Palmerston North | 1988/89 |
| 202* | Hay G.R. | v Canterbury | Rangiora | 2013/14 |
| 202 | Greatbatch M.J. | v Northern Districts | Rotorua | 1995/96 |
| 201* | Smith B.F. | v Canterbury | New Plymouth | 2001/02 |
| 201 | Cleaver D. | v Northern Districts | Napier | 2019/20 |

## MOST RUNS IN A SEASON

| | | Runs | Ave | | | | Runs | Ave |
|---|---|---|---|---|---|---|---|---|
| Crowe M.D. | 1986/87 | 1348 | 103.69 | | Hay G.R. | 2017/18 | 786 | 60.46 |
| Smith B.F. | 2000/01 | 939 | 58.68 | | Sinclair M.S. | 2009/10 | 778 | 59.64 |
| Smith B.S. | 2015/16 | 917 | 61.13 | | Raval J.A. | 2012/13 | 750 | 44.11 |
| Young W.A. | 2014/15 | 909 | 53.47 | | Young W.A. | 2015/16 | 733 | 45.81 |
| Sinclair M.S. | 2008/09 | 904 | 75.33 | | van Wyk C.F.K. | 2013/14 | 725 | 55.76 |
| Ingram P.J. | 2008/09 | 884 | 63.14 | | Sinclair M.S. | 2005/06 | 723 | 51.64 |
| Ingram P.J. | 2010/11 | 858 | 50.47 | | Sinclair M.S. | 1996/97 | 722 | 48.13 |
| Bruce T.C. | 2021/22 | 858 | 143.00 | | Douglas M.W. | 1991/92 | 714 | 44.62 |
| Ingram P.J. | 2009/10 | 855 | 77.72 | | Briasco P.S. | 1990/91 | 708 | 41.64 |
| Sinclair M.S. | 2011/12 | 809 | 53.93 | | How J.M. | 2012/13 | 706 | 41.52 |
| Cachopa C. | 2012/13 | 807 | 47.47 | | How J.M. | 2002/03 | 704 | 44.00 |

## MOST CENTURIES IN A SEASON
6   Crowe M.D.        1986/87

## TOTAL NUMBER OF CENTURIES                    295
| Most in one season | 12 | | 2008/09, 2011/12 |
|---|---|---|---|
| 1st | Hunter A.A. 108 v Otago | | 1951/52 |
| 100th | Blain T.E. 103* v Otago | | 1990/91 |
| 200th | Hay G.R. 131* v Canterbury | | 2008/09 |

# Bowling

| 150 WICKETS | Career | M | Wkts | Runs | Ave | 5WI | 10WM | Best |
|---|---|---|---|---|---|---|---|---|
| O'Sullivan D.R. | 1972/73-1984/85 | 90 | 392 | 9560 | 24.38 | 21 | 3 | 6-40 |
| Mason M.J. | 1997/98-2011/12 | 78 | 263 | 6387 | 24.28 | 12 | 1 | 6-20 |
| Yuile B.W. | 1959/60-1971/72 | 61 | 233 | 4485 | 19.24 | 11 | 2 | 9-100 |
| Robertson G.K. | 1979/80-1989/90 | 78 | 228 | 6573 | 28.78 | 8 | 1 | 6-47 |
| Patel A.Y. | 2012/13-2021/22 | 58 | 225 | 7072 | 31.43 | 16 | 3 | 6-48 |
| Bracewell D.A.J. | 2008/09-2021/22 | 67 | 217 | 6715 | 30.94 | 6 | — | 7-35 |
| Beard D.D. | 1950/51-1960/61 | 49 | 213 | 4531 | 21.27 | 8 | 2 | 7-56 |
| Duff S.W. | 1985/86-1995/96 | 85 | 208 | 6856 | 32.96 | 4 | 2 | 6-36 |
| Hamilton L.J. | 1996/97-2006/07 | 57 | 198 | 5104 | 25.77 | 7 | — | 6-32 |
| Thompson E.P. | 2000/01-2009/10 | 51 | 171 | 5140 | 30.05 | 6 | 1 | 7-55 |
| Jordan A.B. | 1968/69-1979/80 | 55 | 157 | 4431 | 28.22 | 7 | — | 7-82 |
| Tickner B.M. | 2014/15-2021/22 | 49 | 152 | 5359 | 35.25 | 5 | — | 5-23 |
| Cave H.B. | 1950/51-1958/59 | 37 | 150 | 2962 | 19.74 | 7 | 1 | 7-31 |

## BEST IN AN INNINGS
| | | | | |
|---|---|---|---|---|
| 9-100 | Yuile B.W. | v Canterbury | New Plymouth | 1965/66 |
| 7-28 | Yuile B.W. | v Northern Districts | Hamilton | 1967/68 |
| 7-35 | Bracewell D.A.J. | v Canterbury | Rangiora | 2012/13 |
| 7-31 | Cave H.B. | v Auckland | Palmerston North | 1952/53 |
| 7-33 | Cave H.B. | v Northern Districts | New Plymouth | 1956/57 |
| 7-36 | Yuile B.W. | v Otago | Nelson | 1962/63 |
| 7-36 | Schwass A.M. | v Northern Districts | Blenheim | 2001/02 |

## BEST IN A MATCH
| | | | | |
|---|---|---|---|---|
| 13-64 | Cave H.B. | v Auckland | Palmerston North | 1952/53 |
| 11-99 | Beard D.D. | v Otago | Dunedin | 1956/57 |
| 11-115 | Mason M.J. | v Canterbury | Timaru | 2002/03 |
| 11-134 | Robertson G.K. | v Northern Districts | Nelson | 1986/87 |
| 11-138 | Kay D.J. | v Canterbury | Palmerston North | 1976/77 |

## MOST WICKETS IN A SEASON

| | | Wkts | Ave | | | Wkts | Ave |
|---|---|---|---|---|---|---|---|
| O'Sullivan D.R. | 1978/79 | 52 | 19.01 | Patel A.Y. | 2015/16 | 43 | 33.69 |
| Patel A.Y. | 2017/18 | 48 | 21.52 | Blair R.W. | 1955/56 | 42 | 17.28 |
| Schwass A.M. | 2001/02 | 45 | 14.73 | Hamilton L.J. | 2001/02 | 42 | 18.40 |
| O'Sullivan D.R. | 1977/78 | 44 | 20.22 | O'Sullivan D.R. | 1980/81 | 40 | 22.00 |
| Patel A.Y | 2016/17 | 44 | 30.81 | Mason M.J. | 2002/03 | 40 | 19.67 |

# Wicketkeeping

| 100 DISMISSALS | Career | M | Caught | Stumped | Total |
|---|---|---|---|---|---|
| Griggs B.B.J | 2000/01-2009/10 | 82 | 225 | 7 | 232 |
| Cleaver D. | 2010/11-2021/22 | 60 | 162 | 11 | 173 |
| van Wyk C.F.K. | 2010/11-2015/16 | 45 | 140 | 5 | 145 |
| Blain T.E. | 1982/83-1994/95 | 83 | 124 | 19 | 143 |
| Colquhoun I.A. | 1953/54-1963/64 | 53 | 102 | 28 | 130 |
| Smith I.D.S. | 1977/78-1986/87 | 59 | 119 | 11 | 130 |
| Sigley M.A. | 1994/95-2002/03 | 44 | 124 | 4 | 128 |
| Schofield R.M. | 1959/60-1974/75 | 53 | 107 | 15 | 122 |

### MOST DISMISSALS IN A SEASON

| | | | |
|---|---|---|---|
| 40 | (39ct/1st)) | van Wyk C.F.K. | 2014/15 |
| 36 | (35ct/1st)) | Griggs B.B.J. | 2005/06 |

## MOST DISMISSALS IN A MATCH

| | | | | |
|---|---|---|---|---|
| 10 | (10ct) | van Wyk C.F.K. v Otago | Napier | 2014/15 |

## MOST DISMISSALS IN AN INNINGS

| | | | | |
|---|---|---|---|---|
| 7 | (7ct) | Schofield R.M. v Wellington | Wellington | 1964/65 |
| 7 | (7ct) | Griggs B.B.J. v Northern Districts | Hamilton | 2007/08 |

### MOST CATCHES IN A MATCH

| | | | |
|---|---|---|---|
| 10 | van Wyk C.F.K. v Otago | Napier | 2014/15 |

### MOST CATCHES IN AN INNINGS

| | | | |
|---|---|---|---|
| 7 | Schofield R.M. v Wellington | Wellington | 1964/65 |
| 7 | Griggs B.B.J. v Northern Districts | Hamilton | 2007/08 |

# Fielding

## MOST CATCHES IN A SEASON

| | | |
|---|---|---|
| 22 | Bruce T.C. | 2015/16 |

## MOST CATCHES IN A MATCH

| | | | |
|---|---|---|---|
| 5 | Congdon B.E. v Wellington | Wellington | 1964/65 |
| 5 | Congdon B.E. v Otago | New Plymouth | 1970/71 |
| 5 | Smith I.D.S. v Auckland | New Plymouth | 1978/79 |
| 5 | Edwards G.N. v Otago | Palmerston North | 1979/80 |
| 5 | Briasco P.S. v Canterbury | Christchurch | 1984/85 |
| 5 | Douglas M.W. v Otago | Palmerston North | 1988/89 |
| 5 | How J.M. v Canterbury | Palmerston North | 2003/04 |
| 5 | Sinclair M.S. v Canterbury | Napier | 2010/11 |
| 5 | Sinclair M.S. v Wellington | Wellington | 2010/11 |
| 5 | Sinclair M.S. v Auckland | Napier | 2012/13 |
| 5 | How J.M. v Wellington | Napier | 2013/14 |

## MOST CATCHES IN AN INNINGS

| | | | |
|---|---|---|---|
| 5 | Sinclair M.S. v Wellington | Wellington | 2010/11 |

# Record Partnerships

**FOR**

| Wicket | Score | Batsmen | Against | At | Date |
|--------|-------|---------|---------|-----|------|
| 1st | 428 | P.J. Ingram & J.M. How | Wellington | Wellington | 2009/10 |
| 2nd | 317 | R.T. Hart & P.S. Briasco | Canterbury | New Plymouth | 1983/84 |
| 3rd | 264 | P.J. Ingram & M.S. Sinclair | ND | Hamilton | 2008/09 |
| 4th | 276* | M.D. Crowe & P.S. Briasco | Canterbury | Christchurch | 1986/87 |
| 5th | 301 | J.I. Englefield & L.R.P.L. Taylor | Wellington | P. North | 2004/05 |
| 6th | 235 | M.S. Sinclair & B.B.J. Griggs | Wellington | Wellington | 2008/09 |
| 7th | 219 | B.W. Yuile & B.L. Hampton | Canterbury | Napier | 1967/68 |
| 8th | 173 | I.D.S. Smith & G.K. Robertson | ND | Hamilton | 1982/83 |
| 9th | 239 | H.B. Cave & I.B. Leggat | Otago | Dunedin | 1952/53 |
| 10th | 134 | G.H. Worker & A.W. Mathieson | Wellington | Nelson | 2015/16 |

**AGAINST**

| Wicket | Score | Batsmen | For | At | Date |
|--------|-------|---------|-----|-----|------|
| 1st | 334 | J.A. Raval & B. Popli | ND | Whangarei | 2021/22 |
| 2nd | 254* | M.H.W. Papps & J.G. Myburgh | Canterbury | Napier | 2007/08 |
| 3rd | 306 | S.B. Haig & N.T. Broom | Otago | Napier | 2009/10 |
| 4th | 310 | J.D. Ryder & N.R. Parlane | Wellington | P. North | 2004/05 |
| 5th | 341 | G.R. Larsen & E.B. McSweeney | Wellington | Levin | 1987/88 |
| 6th | 379* | S.L. Stewart & C.F.K. van Wyk | Canterbury | New Plymouth | 2009/10 |
| 7th | 192 | S.W. Brown & A.C. Parore | Auckland | Auckland | 1990/91 |
| 8th | 143 | C.M. Presland & C.W. Dickeson | ND | Whangarei | 1983/84 |
| 9th | 225 | L.J. Woodcock & M.J. Tugaga | Wellington | Wellington | 2009/10 |
| 10th | 89 | M.J.E. Wright & S.J. Scott | ND | Wanganui | 1978/79 |

# NORTHERN DISTRICTS

## Highest Totals

| | | | |
|---|---|---|---|
| 726 | v Canterbury | Rangiora | 2009/10 |
| 614-7 dec | v Auckland | Hamilton | 2012/13 |
| 608-9 dec | v Wellington | Lincoln | 2011/12 |
| 559-9 dec | v Otago | Hamilton | 2010/11 |
| 556-9 dec | v Central Districts | New Plymouth | 2014/15 |
| 553 | v Otago | Alexandra | 2021/22 |
| 546 | v Wellington | Whangarei | 2008/09 |
| 533-6 dec | v Otago | Hamilton | 2012/13 |
| 523-7 dec | v Otago | Hamilton | 2006/07 |
| 520-8 dec | v Otago | Hamilton | 1987/88 |

## Lowest Totals

| | | | |
|---|---|---|---|
| 32 | v Auckland | Hamilton | 1996/97 |
| 52 | v Canterbury | Hamilton | 1966/67 |
| 57 | v Wellington | Hamilton | 1961/62 |
| 59 | v Canterbury | Hamilton | 1960/61 |
| 64 | v Otago | Dunedin | 1971/72 |
| 64 | v Auckland | Auckland | 1987/88 |
| 69 | v Australia | Hamilton | 1973/74 |
| 69 | v England | Hamilton | 1996/97 |
| 77 | v Auckland | Auckland | 2000/01 |
| 79 | v Auckland | Auckland | 1989/90 |

**NZC**

## Most Appearances

| | | | | | | |
|---|---|---|---|---|---|---|
| 127 | Marshall J.A.H. | 82 | Kuggeleijn C.M. | 62 | Arnel B.J. |
| 120 | Yovich J.A.F. | 82 | Dunning B. | 62 | Cooper B.G. |
| 119 | Aldridge G.W. | 78 | Bailey M.D. | 59 | McGlashan P.D. |
| 115 | Bradburn G.E. | 78 | Wilson B.S. | 59 | Sodhi I.S. |
| 104 | Roberts A.D.G. | 77 | Martin B.P. | 58 | Howarth G.P. |
| 100 | Flynn D.R. | 76 | Marshall H.J.H. | 57 | Petrie E.C. |
| 99 | White D.J. | 76 | Baker J.D. | 55 | Bradburn W.P. |
| 95 | Hart M.N. | 75 | Parker J.M. | 55 | Carter J.F. |
| 93 | Young B.A. | 66 | Puna N. | 54 | Crocker L.M. |
| 91 | Watling B-J. | 65 | Wright M.J.E. | 53 | Devcich A.P. |
| 90 | Dickeson C.W. | 64 | Mitchell D.J. | 52 | Popli B. |
| 85 | Parlane M.E. | 63 | Kuggeleijn S.C. | 51 | Thomson S.A. |
| 85 | Hart R.G. | | | | |

## Longest Careers

| Seasons | | | | Seasons | | |
|---|---|---|---|---|---|---|
| 19 | Parlane M.E. | 1992/93-2010/11 | | 16 | Marshall J.A.H. | 1997/98-2012/13 |
| 18 | Vettori D.L. | 1996/97-2013/14 | | 16 | Flynn D.R. | 2004/05-2019/20 |
| 17 | Dunning B. | 1961/62-1977/78 | | 16 | Southee T.G. | 2006/07-2021/22 |
| 17 | Roberts A.D.G. | 1967/68-1983/84 | | 15 | Giles G.V. | 1961/62-1975/76 |
| 17 | Bradburn G.E. | 1985/86-2001/02 | | 15 | Cooper B.G. | 1980/81-1994/95 |
| 17 | Yovich J.A.F. | 1996/97-2012/13 | | 15 | Young B.A. | 1983/84-1997/98 |
| 17 | Aldridge G.W. | 1998/99-2014/15 | | 15 | Hart M.N. | 1990/91-2004/05 |
| 17 | Watling B-J. | 2004/05-2020/21 | | 15 | Devcich A.P. | 2004/05-2018/19 |
| 16 | Kuggeleijn C.M. | 1975/76-1990/91 | | | | |

## Benefits

| | |
|---|---|
| Kuggeleijn C.M. | 1990/91 |
| White D.J. | 1992/93 |
| Cooper B.G. | 1995/96 |
| Young B.A. | 1997/98 |

## Batting

| 2000 RUNS | Career | M | In | NO | HS | Runs | Ave | 100 |
|---|---|---|---|---|---|---|---|---|
| Marshall J.A.H. | 1997/98-2012/13 | 127 | 214 | 16 | 235 | 6418 | 32.41 | 11 |
| Flynn D.R. | 2004/05-2019/20 | 100 | 175 | 9 | 241 | 6265 | 37.74 | 20 |
| Roberts A.D.G. | 1967/68-1983/84 | 104 | 192 | 35 | 128* | 5533 | 35.24 | 7 |
| Watling B-J. | 2004/05-2020/21 | 91 | 162 | 12 | 176 | 5479 | 36.52 | 9 |
| Yovich J.A.F. | 1996/97-2012/13 | 120 | 189 | 29 | 144 | 4839 | 30.24 | 6 |
| White D.J. | 1979/80-1992/93 | 99 | 173 | 15 | 209 | 4656 | 29.46 | 7 |
| Bradburn G.E. | 1985/86-2001/02 | 115 | 188 | 23 | 148* | 4614 | 27.96 | 4 |
| Parker J.M. | 1972/73-1983/84 | 75 | 139 | 19 | 195 | 4611 | 38.42 | 7 |
| Parlane M.E. | 1992/93-2010/11 | 85 | 146 | 13 | 146 | 4258 | 32.01 | 7 |
| Wilson B.S. | 2004/05-2014/15 | 78 | 143 | 7 | 165 | 4171 | 30.66 | 8 |
| Marshall H.J.H. | 1998/99-2011/12 | 76 | 130 | 9 | 170 | 4093 | 33.82 | 6 |
| Dunning B. | 1961/62-1977/78 | 82 | 148 | 10 | 142 | 3898 | 28.24 | 3 |
| Young B.A. | 1983/84-1997/98 | 93 | 148 | 36 | 138* | 3853 | 34.40 | 5 |
| Bailey M.D. | 1989/90-2001/02 | 78 | 122 | 8 | 180* | 3468 | 30.42 | 6 |
| Kuggeleijn C.M. | 1975/76-1990/91 | 82 | 138 | 12 | 116 | 3457 | 27.43 | 3 |
| Mitchell D.J. | 2011/12-2019/20 | 64 | 107 | 14 | 170* | 3429 | 36.87 | 7 |
| Hart M.N. | 1990/91-2004/05 | 95 | 140 | 15 | 201* | 3398 | 27.18 | 4 |
| Wright J.G. | 1975/76-1983/84 | 43 | 84 | 3 | 145* | 3301 | 40.75 | 5 |
| Popli B. | 2013/14-2021/22 | 52 | 90 | 5 | 172 | 3154 | 37.10 | 4 |
| Carter J.F. | 2013/14-2021/22 | 55 | 98 | 4 | 169 | 3139 | 33.39 | 6 |

| | Career | M | In | NO | HS | Runs | Ave | 100 |
|---|---|---|---|---|---|---|---|---|
| Howarth G.P. | 1974/75-1985/86 | 58 | 105 | 6 | 151 | 3122 | 31.53 | 5 |
| Cooper B.G. | 1980/81-1994/95 | 62 | 110 | 4 | 116* | 2982 | 28.13 | 4 |
| Crocker L.M. | 1982/83-1988/89 | 54 | 100 | 3 | 126 | 2663 | 27.45 | 2 |
| Wright M.J.E. | 1972/73-1983/84 | 65 | 114 | 10 | 115 | 2632 | 25.30 | 1 |
| Devcich A.P. | 2004/05-2018/19 | 53 | 95 | 5 | 132 | 2606 | 28.95 | 4 |
| Gibson J.G. | 1968/69-1980/81 | 49 | 92 | 5 | 128 | 2580 | 29.65 | 4 |
| Thomson S.A. | 1987/88-1996/97 | 51 | 80 | 20 | 167 | 2530 | 42.16 | 5 |
| Seifert T.L. | 2014/15-2021/22 | 44 | 77 | 4 | 167* | 2488 | 34.05 | 5 |
| McGlashan P.D. | 2004/05-2011/12 | 59 | 85 | 6 | 115 | 2482 | 31.41 | 2 |
| Kuggeleijn S.C. | 2013/14-2021/22 | 63 | 104 | 20 | 112 | 2374 | 28.26 | 2 |
| Cooper H.R. | 2016/17-2021/22 | 38 | 67 | 2 | 200 | 2367 | 36.41 | 6 |
| Aldridge G.W. | 1998/99-2014/15 | 119 | 157 | 42 | 75 | 2327 | 20.23 | — |
| Brownlie D.G. | 2014/15-2019/20 | 33 | 60 | 3 | 334 | 2224 | 39.01 | 5 |
| Hart R.G. | 1992/93-2003/04 | 85 | 119 | 19 | 102* | 2135 | 21.35 | 1 |
| Hick G.A. | 1987/88-1988/89 | 17 | 30 | 4 | 211* | 2055 | 79.03 | 10 |
| Wealleans K.A. | 1988/89-1994/95 | 43 | 74 | 4 | 112* | 2053 | 29.33 | 4 |
| Williamson K.S. | 2007/08-2019/20 | 25 | 41 | 4 | 284* | 2021 | 54.62 | 6 |
| Bradburn W.P. | 1957/58-1968/69 | 55 | 103 | 5 | 107 | 2015 | 20.56 | 1 |
| Horsley N.K.W. | 2002/03-2007/08 | 35 | 60 | 3 | 159 | 2003 | 35.14 | 2 |

### CENTURY ON DEBUT FOR PROVINCE

| 118 | McGregor P.B. | v Auckland | Hamilton | 1962/63 |
|---|---|---|---|---|
| † 127* | Mitchell W.J. | v Pakistan | Hamilton | 1964/65 |
| 14 & 153* | Maynard M.P. | v Auckland | Hamilton | 1990/91 |

† *indicates player was making his first-class debut*

### HIGHEST INDIVIDUAL INNINGS

| 334 | Brownlie D.G. | v Central Districts | New Plymouth | 2014/15 |
|---|---|---|---|---|
| 284* | Williamson K.S. | v Wellington | Lincoln | 2011/12 |
| 241 | Flynn D.R. | v Otago | Hamilton | 2010/11 |
| 235 | Marshall J.A.H. | v Canterbury | Christchurch | 2001/02 |
| 212* | Styris S.B. | v Otago | Hamilton | 2001/02 |
| 211* | Hick G.A. | v Auckland | Auckland | 1988/89 |
| 209 | White D.J. | v Central Districts | Hamilton | 1985/86 |
| 209 | Raval J.A. | v Central Districts | Whangarei | 2021/22 |
| 201* | Hart M.N. | v Auckland | Auckland | 2002/03 |
| 200 | Cooper H.R. | v Otago | Alexandra | 2021/22 |

### MOST RUNS IN A SEASON

| | | Runs | Ave | | | Runs | Ave |
|---|---|---|---|---|---|---|---|
| Hick G.A. | 1988/89 | 1228 | 94.46 | Wilson B.S. | 2010/11 | 733 | 48.86 |
| Popli B. | 2015/16 | 1149 | 67.58 | Bradburn G.E. | 1989/90 | 726 | 36.30 |
| Maynard M.P. | 1991/92 | 893 | 68.69 | Wealleans K.A. | 1989/90 | 721 | 36.05 |
| Hick G.A. | 1987/88 | 827 | 63.61 | Mitchell D.J. | 2012/13 | 709 | 54.53 |
| Flynn D.R. | 2013/14 | 775 | 43.05 | Williamson K.S. | 2008/09 | 707 | 54.38 |
| Marshall H.J.H. | 2006/07 | 766 | 54.71 | Marshall J.A.H. | 2001/02 | 706 | 39.22 |
| Flynn D.R. | 2015/16 | 764 | 42.44 | Seifert T.L. | 2017/18 | 703 | 50.21 |
| Devcich A.P. | 2014/15 | 744 | 49.60 | | | | |

### MOST CENTURIES IN A SEASON

6   Hick G.A.   1988/89

| TOTAL NUMBER OF CENTURIES | | | **241** |
|---|---|---|---|
| Most in one season | 12 | | 2012/13 |
| 1st | Everest J.K. 104 v Canterbury | | 1956/57 |
| 100th | Parlane M.E. 132* v Canterbury | | 1995/96 |
| 200th | Santner M.J. 101 v Central Districts | | 2014/15 |

# Bowling

| 150 WICKETS | Career | M | Wkts | Runs | Ave | 5WI | 10WM | Best |
|---|---|---|---|---|---|---|---|---|
| Aldridge G.W. | 1998/99-2014/15 | 119 | 355 | 10052 | 28.31 | 14 | 1 | 6-41 |
| Dickeson C.W. | 1973/74-1986/87 | 90 | 282 | 8242 | 29.22 | 9 | 2 | 7-79 |
| Yovich J.A.F. | 1996/97-2012/13 | 110 | 255 | 8579 | 33.64 | 8 | 1 | 7-64 |
| Bradburn G.E. | 1985/86-2001/02 | 115 | 231 | 7302 | 31.61 | 3 | — | 6-56 |
| Arnel B.J. | 2005/06-2017/18 | 62 | 229 | 5432 | 23.97 | 10 | 1 | 6-18 |
| Puna N. | 1956/57-1968/69 | 66 | 224 | 5314 | 23.72 | 11 | — | 6-25 |
| Sodhi I.S. | 2012/13-2021/22 | 59 | 210 | 6160 | 29.33 | 14 | 2 | 7-30 |
| Kuggeleijn S.C. | 2013/14-2021/22 | 63 | 209 | 6323 | 30.25 | 8 | — | 7-45 |
| Baker J.D. | 2010/11-2020/21 | 76 | 201 | 5961 | 29.65 | 7 | 1 | 6-72 |
| Martin B.P. | 1999/00-2009/10 | 77 | 192 | 6889 | 35.88 | 12 | 2 | 7-33 |
| de Groen R.P. | 1990/91-1995/96 | 38 | 157 | 3320 | 21.14 | 8 | 2 | 7-50 |

### BEST IN AN INNINGS

| 9-48 | Tait A.R. | v Auckland | Hamilton | 1996/97 |
|---|---|---|---|---|
| 8-21 | Langdon M.C. | v Auckland | Auckland | 1963/64 |
| 8-27 | Southee T.G. | v Wellington | Hamilton | 2009/10 |
| 8-30 | Alabaster G.D. | v NZ Under 23 XI | Hamilton | 1962/63 |
| 8-37 | Clarke D.B. | v Central Districts | Wanganui | 1962/63 |
| 8-49 | Kennedy K.D. | v Central Districts | Hamilton | 1969/70 |

### BEST IN A MATCH

| 16-130 | Tait A.R. | v Auckland | Hamilton | 1996/97 |
|---|---|---|---|---|
| 13-99 | de Groen R.P. | v Otago | Alexandra | 1992/93 |
| 12-55 | Martin B.P. | v Auckland | Taupo | 1999/00 |
| 12-62 | Sodhi I.S. | v Wellington | Wellington | 2017/18 |
| 12-109 | Lissette A.F. | v Otago | Dunedin | 1959/60 |

### MOST WICKETS IN A SEASON

| | | Wkts | Ave | | | | Wkts | Ave |
|---|---|---|---|---|---|---|---|---|
| Tait A.R. | 1996/97 | 53 | 16.32 | | Aldridge G.W. | 2009/10 | 42 | 23.04 |
| de Groen R.P. | 1992/93 | 46 | 16.84 | | Yovich J.A.F. | 2001/02 | 40 | 26.45 |
| Arnel B.J. | 2012/13 | 45 | 24.84 | | Sodhi I.S. | 2016/17 | 40 | 25.92 |

# Wicketkeeping

| 100 DISMISSALS | Career | M | Caught | Stumped | Total |
|---|---|---|---|---|---|
| Hart R.G. | 1992/93-2003/04 | 85 | 228 | 15 | 243 |
| Young B.A. | 1983/84-1997/98 | 93 | 179 | 11 | 190 |
| McGlashan P.D. | 2004/05-2011/12 | 59 | 175 | 12 | 187 |
| Watling B-J. | 2004/05-2020/21 | 91 | 129 | 2 | 131 |
| Seifert T.L. | 2014/15-2021/22 | 44 | 118 | 10 | 128 |
| Wright M.J.E. | 1972/73-1983/84 | 65 | 104 | 17 | 121 |
| Petrie E.C. | 1956/57-1966/67 | 57 | 90 | 22 | 112 |

### MOST DISMISSALS IN A SEASON

| 41 | (37ct/4st) | McGlashan P.D. | | 2009/10 |
|---|---|---|---|---|

### MOST DISMISSALS IN A MATCH

| 12 | (12ct) | McGlashan P.D. v Central Districts | Whangarei | 2009/10 |
|---|---|---|---|---|

**MOST DISMISSALS IN AN INNINGS**

| | | | | |
|---|---|---|---|---|
| 7 | (7ct) | Young B.A. v Canterbury | Christchurch | 1986/87 |

**MOST CATCHES IN A MATCH**

| | | | |
|---|---|---|---|
| 12 | McGlashan P.D. v Central Districts | Whangarei | 2009/10 |

**MOST CATCHES IN AN INNINGS**

| | | | |
|---|---|---|---|
| 7 | Young B.A. v Canterbury | Christchurch | 1986/87 |

# Fielding

## MOST CATCHES IN A SEASON

| | | | | | |
|---|---|---|---|---|---|
| 15 | Mitchell D.J. | 2014/15 | 15 | Brownlie D.G. | 2015/16 |

**MOST CATCHES IN A MATCH**

| | | | |
|---|---|---|---|
| 6 | Young B.A. v Wellington | Wellington | 1995/96 |
| 6 | Vettori D.L. v Canterbury | Rangiora | 2011/12 |
| 6 | Anderson C.J. v Auckland | Auckland | 2015/16 |
| 6 | Brownlie D.G. v Canterbury | Christchurch | 2018/19 |

**MOST CATCHES IN AN INNINGS**

| | | | |
|---|---|---|---|
| 4 | Pairaudeau B.H. v Central Districts | Wanganui | 1962/63 |
| 4 | Harris S.J. (sub) v Otago | Dunedin | 1965/66 |
| 4 | Barton P.H. v Canterbury | Hamilton | 1974/75 |
| 4 | Young B.A. v Wellington | Wellington | 1995/96 |
| 4 | Bailey M.D. v Otago | Alexandra | 1996/97 |
| 4 | Vettori D.L. v Canterbury | Rangiora | 2011/12 |
| 4 | Mitchell D.J. v Auckland | Whangarei | 2014/15 |
| 4 | Brownlie D.G. v Canterbury | Christchurch | 2018/19 |
| 4 | Clarke K.D. v Wellington | Whangarei | 2021/22 |

# Record Partnerships

**FOR**

| Wicket | Score | Batsmen | Against | At | Date |
|---|---|---|---|---|---|
| 1st | 334 | J.A. Raval & B. Popli | CD | Whangarei | 2021/22 |
| 2nd | 317 | D.R. Flynn & B.S. Wilson | Auckland | Hamilton | 2012/13 |
| 3rd | 261* | M.P. Maynard & S.A. Thomson | Auckland | Hamilton | 1990/91 |
| 4th | 283 | D.R. Flynn & C.J. Anderson | Otago | Hamilton | 2012/13 |
| 5th | 226 | D.J. Mitchell & T.L. Seifert | Otago | Dunedin | 2016/17 |
| 6th | 322 | M.G. Orchard & J.A.F. Yovich | CD | Napier | 2005/06 |
| 7th | 174 | B. Popli & M.J. Santner | Wellington | Gisborne | 2013/14 |
| 8th | 163 | P.D.McGlashan & G.W.Aldridge | Canterbury | Hamilton | 2008/09 |
| 9th | 188 | N.R. Parlane & D.R. Tuffey | Wellington | Wellington | 1999/00 |
| 10th | 113* | P.D. McGlashan & G.W. Aldridge | Wellington | Wellington | 2005/06 |

**AGAINST**

| Wicket | Score | Batsmen | For | At | Date |
|---|---|---|---|---|---|
| 1st | 310 | R.H. Vance & B.A. Edgar | Wellington | Wellington | 1988/89 |
| 2nd | 263 | M.J. Greatbatch & M.D. Crowe | CD | Morrinsville | 1986/87 |
| 3rd | 394* | P.G. Kennedy & R.T. Latham | Canterbury | Rotorua | 1990/91 |
| 4th | 280 | J.J. Crowe & D.N. Patel | Auckland | Auckland | 1991/92 |
| 5th | 347* | M.J. Horne & A.C. Barnes | Auckland | Auckland | 2003/04 |
| 6th | 224 | B.D. Schmulian & D.A.J. Bracewell | CD | Mt Maunganui | 2017/18 |
| 7th | 205 | L.K. Germon & M.W. Priest | Canterbury | Christchurch | 1991/92 |
| 8th | 220 | P.J. Wiseman & B.C. Hiini | Canterbury | Hamilton | 2005/06 |
| 9th | 151 | R.A. Young & G.J. Morgan | Auckland | Auckland | 2007/08 |
| 10th | 160 | L.K. Germon & W.A. Wisneski | Canterbury | Rangiora | 1997/98 |

NZC

# OTAGO

## Highest Totals

| | | | |
|---|---|---|---|
| 651-9 dec | v Wellington | Dunedin | 2012/13 |
| 642-6 dec | v Central Districts | Dunedin | 2021/22 |
| 624 | v Central Districts | Napier | 2006/07 |
| 602-8 dec | v Canterbury | Dunedin | 1928/29 |
| 601-9 dec | v Canterbury | Christchurch | 2006/07 |
| 589 | v Canterbury | Christchurch | 1931/32 |
| 576-8 dec | v Northern Districts | Whangarei | 2009/10 |
| 571-8 | v Central Districts | Napier | 1995/96 |
| 569-8 dec | v Auckland | Dunedin | 2012/13 |
| 558-8 dec | v Auckland | Dunedin | 1949/50 |

## Lowest Totals

| | | | |
|---|---|---|---|
| 34 | v Wellington | Dunedin | 1956/57 |
| 35 | v Auckland | Christchurch | 1884/85 |
| 36 | v New South Wales | Dunedin | 1889/90 |
| 40 | v Canterbury | Dunedin | 1869/70 |
| 41 | v Auckland | Dunedin | 1873/74 |
| 42 | v Canterbury | Dunedin | 1871/72 |
| 43 | v Canterbury | Christchurch | 1872/73 |
| 44 | v Canterbury | Dunedin | 1904/05 |
| 46 | v Pakistan | Dunedin | 1978/79 |
| 47 | v Canterbury | Christchurch | 1888/89 |

## Most Appearances

| | | | | | |
|---|---|---|---|---|---|
| 108 | Lees W.K. | 71 | Rutherford H.D. | 60 | Sutcliffe B. |
| 101 | Broom N.T. | 70 | Duffy J.A. | 60 | Milburn B.D. |
| 99 | de Boorder D.C. | 69 | Alabaster G.D. | 59 | Smith L.D. |
| 95 | Cumming C.D. | 68 | Cameron F.J. | 59 | Turner G.M. |
| 90 | Blair B.R. | 68 | Rutherford K.R. | 57 | Burns K.J. |
| 90 | McGregor S.N. | 67 | McSkimming W.C. | 56 | McMillan J.M. |
| 88 | Boock S.L. | 66 | Lawson R.A. | 55 | Mills G.H. |
| 81 | Blair W.L. | 65 | Alabaster J.C. | 55 | Sewell D.G. |
| 80 | Hoskin R.N. | 63 | Rutherford I.A. | 55 | Bracewell M.G. |
| 78 | Mallender N.A. | 63 | Wagner N. | 54 | Moir A.M. |
| 75 | McCullum S.J. | 62 | McCullum N.L. | 54 | Dobbs P.W. |
| 75 | Gaffaney C.B. | 61 | Campbell K.O. | 51 | Knight A.R. |
| 74 | Redmond A.J. | 61 | Wells S.R. | | |

## Longest Careers

| Seasons | | | | Seasons | | | |
|---|---|---|---|---|---|---|---|
| 27 | Downes A.D. | 1887/88-1913/14 | | 22 | McGregor S.N. | 1947/48-1968/69 |
| 26 | Knight A.R. | 1918/19-1943/44 | | 21 | Groves L.J. | 1929/30-1949/50 |
| 24 | Siedeberg H.G. | 1898/99-1921/22 | | 21 | Alabaster G.D. | 1955/56-1975/76 |
| 24 | Blair W.L. | 1967/68-1990/91 | | 20 | Fisher A.H. | 1890/91-1909/10 |
| 23 | Torrance R.C. | 1905/06-1927/28 | | 20 | Watt L. | 1943/44-1962/63 |
| 23 | Smith L.D. | 1934/35-1956/57 | | 20 | Milburn B.D. | 1963/64-1982/83 |
| 23 | Mills G.H. | 1935/36-1957/58 | | | | |

## Benefits

| | | | | | |
|---|---|---|---|---|---|
| Lees W.K. | 1987/88 | Boock S.L. | 1989/90 | Mallender N.A. | 1992/93 |

# Batting

| 2000 RUNS | Career | M | In | NO | HS | Runs | Ave | 100 |
|---|---|---|---|---|---|---|---|---|
| Cumming C.D. | 2000/01-2011/12 | 95 | 167 | 15 | 173 | 6589 | 43.34 | 21 |
| Broom N.T. | 2005/06-2019/20 | 101 | 172 | 22 | 203* | 6085 | 40.56 | 15 |
| Sutcliffe B. | 1946/47-1961/62 | 60 | 110 | 8 | 385 | 6028 | 59.09 | 17 |
| Blair B.R. | 1977/78-1989/90 | 90 | 154 | 5 | 143 | 5057 | 33.93 | 7 |
| Rutherford K.R. | 1982/83-1994/95 | 68 | 121 | 7 | 226* | 5051 | 44.30 | 14 |
| Rutherford H.D. | 2008/09-2021/22 | 71 | 129 | 0 | 239 | 5027 | 38.96 | 12 |
| Redmond A.J. | 2004/05-2014/15 | 74 | 130 | 8 | 154 | 4795 | 39.30 | 11 |
| de Boorder D.C. | 2007/08-2017/18 | 99 | 154 | 25 | 146 | 4695 | 36.39 | 4 |
| Turner G.M. | 1964/65-1982/83 | 59 | 109 | 14 | 186* | 4439 | 46.72 | 13 |
| Gaffaney C.B. | 1995/96-2004/05 | 75 | 138 | 11 | 194 | 4326 | 34.06 | 7 |
| McGregor S.N. | 1947/48-1968/69 | 90 | 167 | 13 | 114* | 4259 | 27.65 | 3 |
| Lees W.K. | 1972/73-1987/88 | 108 | 179 | 31 | 124 | 3754 | 25.36 | 4 |
| Blair W.L. | 1967/68-1990/91 | 81 | 149 | 9 | 140 | 3654 | 26.10 | 2 |
| Hoskin R.N. | 1980/81-1992/93 | 80 | 138 | 6 | 157 | 3573 | 27.06 | 6 |
| Bracewell M.G. | 2010/11-2016/17 | 55 | 98 | 7 | 190 | 3266 | 35.89 | 7 |
| McCullum S.J. | 1976/77-1990/91 | 75 | 131 | 1 | 134 | 3174 | 24.41 | 2 |
| Rutherford I.A. | 1974/75-1983/84 | 63 | 115 | 3 | 222 | 3122 | 27.87 | 4 |
| Richardson M.H. | 1992/93-2000/01 | 49 | 89 | 10 | 166 | 3089 | 39.10 | 8 |
| Lawson R.A. | 1992/93-2003/04 | 66 | 120 | 5 | 200 | 2890 | 25.13 | 2 |
| Todd G.R. | 2004/05-2009/10 | 45 | 79 | 10 | 165 | 2774 | 40.20 | 4 |
| Burns K.J. | 1980/81-1991/92 | 57 | 98 | 6 | 136 | 2699 | 29.33 | 3 |
| Campbell K.O. | 1963/64-1978/79 | 61 | 108 | 17 | 111 | 2613 | 28.71 | 3 |
| Dobbs P.W. | 1988/89-1994/95 | 54 | 99 | 6 | 144* | 2606 | 28.02 | 3 |
| Wells S.R. | 2007/08-2016/17 | 61 | 95 | 10 | 118 | 2588 | 30.44 | 4 |
| Alabaster G.D. | 1955/56-1975/76 | 69 | 108 | 16 | 108 | 2340 | 25.43 | 3 |
| Kitchen A.K. | 2015/16-2021/22 | 41 | 77 | 2 | 207 | 2301 | 30.68 | 4 |
| Smith L.D. | 1934/35-1956/57 | 59 | 108 | 16 | 109 | 2277 | 24.75 | 1 |
| McCullum N.L. | 1999/00-2015/16 | 62 | 97 | 9 | 106* | 2270 | 25.79 | 1 |
| Knight A.R. | 1918/19-1943/44 | 51 | 97 | 3 | 152 | 2245 | 23.88 | 1 |
| Wilson B.S. | 2015/16-2018/19 | 33 | 61 | 2 | 126 | 2112 | 35.79 | 6 |

### CENTURY ON DEBUT FOR PROVINCE

|  |  |  |  |  |
|---|---|---|---|---|
| 107 & 38 | Patrick W.R. | v Canterbury | Christchurch | 1917/18 |
| † 157* | McMullan J.J.M. | v Southland | Dunedin | 1917/18 |
| 172 & 16 | Worker R.V.de R. | v Canterbury | Christchurch | 1923/24 |
| 35 & 133 | Blamires E.O. | v Canterbury | Christchurch | 1923/24 |
| † 15 & 105 | Watt D.G. | v Canterbury | Christchurch | 1943/44 |
| 157 | Hadlee W.A. | v Auckland | Dunedin | 1945/46 |
| 197 & 128 | Sutcliffe B. | v MCC | Dunedin | 1946/47 |
| 124 & 90 | Horne M.J. | v Central Districts | Wanganui | 1996/97 |
| † 119 | Broom D.J. | v Northern Districts | Whangarei | 2009/10 |
| 118 & 54* | ten Doeschate R.N. | v Central Districts | Dunedin | 2012/13 |
| 117 & 28 | Ryder J.D. | v Wellington | Wellington | 2013/14 |

*† indicates player was making his first-class debut*

### HIGHEST INDIVIDUAL INNINGS

|  |  |  |  |  |
|---|---|---|---|---|
| 385 | Sutcliffe B. | v Canterbury | Christchurch | 1952/53 |
| 355 | Sutcliffe B. | v Auckland | Dunedin | 1949/50 |
| 338* | Blunt R.C. | v Canterbury | Christchurch | 1931/32 |
| 275 | Sutcliffe B. | v Auckland | Auckland | 1950/51 |
| 264 | Sutcliffe B. | v Central Districts | Dunedin | 1959/60 |
| 241 | Horne M.J. | v Auckland | Auckland | 1997/98 |
| 239 | Rutherford H.D. | v Wellington | Dunedin | 2011/12 |

| 234* | Kelly N.F. | v Central Districts | Dunedin | 2021/22 |
|---|---|---|---|---|
| 226* | Rutherford K.R. | v India | Dunedin | 1989/90 |
| 222 | Rutherford I.A. | v Central Districts | New Plymouth | 1978/79 |
| 221 | Blunt R.C. | v Canterbury | Dunedin | 1928/29 |
| 207 | Kitchen A.K. | v Northern Districts | Dunedin | 2016/17 |
| 203* | Broom N.T. | v Northern Districts | Queenstown | 2010/11 |
| 201 | Reid J.R. | v Canterbury | Dunedin | 1957/58 |
| 201 | Sutcliffe B. | v Northern Districts | Hamilton | 1960/61 |
| 200 | Lawson R.A. | v Central Districts | Napier | 1995/96 |

## MOST RUNS IN A SEASON

| | | Runs | Ave | | | | Runs | Ave |
|---|---|---|---|---|---|---|---|---|
| Turner G.M. | 1975/76 | 1027 | 85.58 | | Cumming C.D. | 2002/03 | 751 | 46.93 |
| Redmond A.J. | 2012/13 | 941 | 55.35 | | Rutherford K.R. | 1989/90 | 747 | 67.90 |
| Cumming C.D. | 2009/10 | 924 | 61.60 | | Wilson B.S. | 2016/17 | 730 | 45.62 |
| Wilson B.S. | 2015/16 | 886 | 46.63 | | Bracewell M.G. | 2014/15 | 726 | 42.70 |
| Bracewell M.G. | 2013/14 | 845 | 52.81 | | Cumming C.D. | 2010/11 | 714 | 51.00 |
| Cumming C.D. | 2008/09 | 784 | 65.33 | | Sutcliffe B. | 1952/53 | 709 | 78.77 |
| Ryder J.D. | 2013/14 | 776 | 59.69 | | Turner G.M. | 1974/75 | 703 | 78.11 |
| Blair B.R. | 1989/90 | 759 | 47.43 | | | | | |

## MOST CENTURIES IN A SEASON

| 4 | Turner G.M. | 1974/75 |
|---|---|---|
| 4 | Turner G.M. | 1975/76 |
| 4 | Cumming C.D. | 2008/09 |
| 4 | Cumming C.D | 2009/10 |
| 4 | Ryder J.D. | 2013/14 |
| 4 | Bracewell M.G. | 2013/14 |
| 4 | Kitchen A.K. | 2016/17 |

## TOTAL NUMBER OF CENTURIES — 310

| Most in one season | 14 | | 2013/14 |
|---|---|---|---|
| 1st | Baker J.C. 103 v Hawke's Bay | | 1901/02 |
| 100th | Cairns B.L. 110 v Wellington | | 1979/80 |
| 200th | Hopkins G.J. 139* v Auckland | | 2006/07 |
| 300th | Rippon M.J.G. 106 v Auckland | | 2020/21 |

# Bowling

| 150 WICKETS | Career | M | Wkts | Runs | Ave | 5WI | 10WM | Best |
|---|---|---|---|---|---|---|---|---|
| Boock S.L. | 1973/74-1989/90 | 88 | 399 | 8235 | 20.63 | 28 | 5 | 8-57 |
| Downes A.D. | 1887/88-1913/14 | 44 | 287 | 3902 | 13.59 | 33 | 13 | 8-35 |
| Moir A.M. | 1949/50-1961/62 | 54 | 282 | 5926 | 21.01 | 20 | 5 | 8-37 |
| Wagner N. | 2008/09-2017/18 | 63 | 277 | 7307 | 26.37 | 16 | 1 | 7-46 |
| Mallender N.A. | 1983/84-1992/93 | 78 | 268 | 5433 | 20.27 | 14 | 3 | 7-27 |
| Alabaster J.C. | 1956/57-1971/72 | 65 | 264 | 5738 | 21.73 | 14 | 3 | 6-39 |
| Cameron F.J. | 1953/54-1966/67 | 68 | 258 | 5204 | 20.17 | 9 | — | 6-21 |
| McSkimming W.C. | 1999/00-2011/12 | 67 | 238 | 5808 | 24.40 | 11 | 2 | 6-39 |
| Alabaster G.D. | 1955/56-1975/76 | 69 | 205 | 4774 | 23.28 | 13 | 1 | 7-74 |
| Duffy J.A. | 2011/12-2021/22 | 70 | 200 | 6654 | 33.27 | 8 | — | 7-89 |
| Sewell D.G. | 1995/96-2005/06 | 55 | 178 | 5198 | 29.20 | 7 | 1 | 8-31 |
| Fisher A.H. | 1890/91-1909/10 | 40 | 176 | 2766 | 15.71 | 9 | 1 | 9-50 |
| O'Connor S.B. | 1994/95-2002/03 | 35 | 160 | 3321 | 20.75 | 11 | 2 | 6-31 |
| Scott B.E. | 2000/01-2015/16 | 49 | 158 | 3982 | 25.20 | 5 | — | 6-20 |

## BEST IN AN INNINGS

| | | | | |
|---|---|---|---|---|
| 9-50 | Fisher A.H. | v Queensland | Dunedin | 1896/97 |
| 9-72 | Cooke F.H. | v Canterbury | Christchurch | 1884/85 |
| 9-93 | Petherick P.J. | v Northern Districts | Dunedin | 1975/76 |
| 8-28 | Hendley W. | v Canterbury | Dunedin | 1869/70 |
| 8-31 | Sewell D.G. | v Central Districts | Invercargill | 1996/97 |
| 8-35 | Downes A.D. | v Canterbury | Dunedin | 1891/92 |
| 8-37 | Moir A.M. | v Northern Districts | Hamilton | 1958/59 |
| 8-46 | Cairns B.L. | v Wellington | Invercargill | 1978/79 |
| 8-55 | Moir A.M. | v Canterbury | Dunedin | 1951/52 |
| 8-57 | Boock S.L. | v Auckland | Dunedin | 1989/90 |
| 8-59 | Boock S.L. | v Wellington | Invercargill | 1978/79 |
| 8-61 | Cooke F.H. | v Canterbury | Christchurch | 1882/83 |
| 8-66 | Wiseman P.J. | v Wellington | Wellington | 1996/97 |
| 8-70 | Hay W.A. | v Southland | Dunedin | 1917/18 |
| 8-99 | Blunt R.C. | v Auckland | Dunedin | 1930/31 |
| 8-119 | Moir A.M. | v Central Districts | New Plymouth | 1953/54 |
| 8-136 | Shacklock F.J. | v Canterbury | Christchurch | 1903/04 |

## BEST IN A MATCH

| | | | | |
|---|---|---|---|---|
| 15-94 | Cooke F.H. | v Canterbury | Christchurch | 1882/83 |
| 15-104 | Boock S.L. | v Auckland | Dunedin | 1989/90 |
| 15-203 | Moir A.M. | v Central Districts | New Plymouth | 1953/54 |
| 14-93 | Torrance R.C. | v Hawke's Bay | Napier | 1908/09 |
| 14-103 | Downes A.D. | v Hawke's Bay | Dunedin | 1893/94 |
| 14-126 | Moir A.M. | v Canterbury | Dunedin | 1951/52 |
| 13-111 | Downes A.D. | v Hawke's Bay | Dunedin | 1901/02 |
| 13-144 | Boock S.L. | v Northern Districts | Whangarei | 1980/81 |

## MOST WICKETS IN A SEASON

| | | Wkts | Ave | | | | Wkts | Ave |
|---|---|---|---|---|---|---|---|---|
| Boock S.L. | 1978/79 | 54 | 18.51 | | Petherick P.J. | 1975/76 | 42 | 20.16 |
| Wagner N. | 2010/11 | 51 | 18.15 | | O'Connor S.B. | 2002/03 | 42 | 18.71 |
| Mallender N.A. | 1991/92 | 49 | 12.30 | | Moir A.M. | 1953/54 | 41 | 17.58 |
| Boock S.L. | 1986/87 | 48 | 15.48 | | Boock S.L. | 1980/81 | 41 | 18.46 |
| Wagner N. | 2011/12 | 46 | 26.32 | | Boock S.L. | 1987/88 | 41 | 21.82 |
| Petherick P.J. | 1977/78 | 45 | 17.15 | | Webb M.G. | 1973/74 | 40 | 14.65 |
| Duffy J.A. | 2014/15 | 45 | 24.06 | | Cairns B.L. | 1978/79 | 40 | 22.70 |

# Wicketkeeping

| 100 DISMISSALS | Career | M | Caught | Stumped | Total |
|---|---|---|---|---|---|
| de Boorder D.C. | 2007/08-2017/18 | 99 | 322 | 22 | 344 |
| Lees W.K. | 1972/73-1987/88 | 108 | 208 | 36 | 244 |
| Milburn B.D. | 1963/64-1982/83 | 60 | 148 | 17 | 165 |
| Croy M.G. | 1994/95-2001/02 | 42 | 127 | 4 | 131 |
| Robinson S.A. | 1984/85-1996/97 | 45 | 117 | 5 | 122 |
| Hopkins G.J. | 2003/04-2006/07 | 33 | 111 | 3 | 114 |
| Mills G.H. | 1935/36-1957/58 | 55 | 78 | 29 | 107 |

### MOST DISMISSALS IN A SEASON
44　(43ct/1st)　de Boorder D.C.　　　　　2012/13

### MOST DISMISSALS IN A MATCH
10　(10ct)　Hopkins G.J. v Canterbury　　　Dunedin　　2004/05

### MOST DISMISSALS IN AN INNINGS
8　(8ct)　de Boorder D.C. v Wellington　　Wellington　2009/10

**MOST CATCHES IN A MATCH**
10    Hopkins G.J. v Canterbury          Dunedin          2004/05

**MOST CATCHES IN AN INNINGS**
8     de Boorder D.C. v Wellington       Wellington       2009/10

# Fielding

### MOST CATCHES IN A SEASON
15        Blair W.L.                  1978/79

**MOST CATCHES IN A MATCH**
6     McCullum N.L. v Central Districts    Napier          2006/07

**MOST CATCHES IN AN INNINGS**
| | | | |
|---|---|---|---|
| 4 | Geddes A.E. v Canterbury | Christchurch | 1903/04 |
| 4 | Watson E.A. v Canterbury | Dunedin | 1953/54 |
| 4 | Campbell K.O. v Auckland | Dunedin | 1969/70 |
| 4 | Blair W.L. v Canterbury | Invercargill | 1977/78 |
| 4 | Blair W.L. v Northern Districts | Dunedin | 1978/79 |
| 4 | McCullum S.J. v Auckland | Dunedin | 1987/88 |
| 4 | Dobbs P.W. v India | Dunedin | 1989/90 |
| 4 | Burns K.J. v Northern Districts | Dunedin | 1990/91 |
| 4 | Gaffaney C.B. v Wellington | Wellington | 1996/97 |
| 4 | McCullum N.L. v Auckland | Dunedin | 2004/05 |
| 4 | McCullum N.L. v Central Districts | Napier | 2006/07 |
| 4 | Hicks S. v Auckland | Auckland | 2018/19 |
| 4 | Phillips D.N. v Central Districts | Dunedin | 2020/21 |

# Record Partnerships

**FOR**

| Wicket | Score | Batsmen | Against | At | Date |
|---|---|---|---|---|---|
| 1st | 373 | B. Sutcliffe & L. Watt | Auckland | Auckland | 1950/51 |
| 2nd | 254 | K.J. Burns & K.R. Rutherford | Wellington | Oamaru | 1987/88 |
| 3rd | 306 | S.B. Haig & N.T. Broom | CD | Napier | 2009/10 |
| 4th | 239 | N.B. Beard & N.T. Broom | Auckland | Dunedin | 2012/13 |
| 5th | 266 | B. Sutcliffe & W.S. Haig | Auckland | Dunedin | 1949/50 |
| 6th | 256 | N.F. Kelly & M.W. Chu | CD | Dunedin | 2021/22 |
| 7th | 190 | N.G. Smith & M.J.G. Rippon | ND | Dunedin | 2019/20 |
| 8th | 165* | J.N. Crawford & A.G. Eckhold | Wellington | Wellington | 1914/15 |
| 9th | 208 | W.C. McSkimming & B.E. Scott | Auckland | Auckland | 2004/05 |
| 10th | 184 | R.C. Blunt & W. Hawksworth | Canterbury | Christchurch | 1931/32 |

**AGAINST**

| Wicket | Score | Batsmen | For | At | Date |
|---|---|---|---|---|---|
| 1st | 299 | M.D. Bell & R.A. Jones | Wellington | Dunedin | 2001/02 |
| 2nd | 279 | M.D. Bell & M.E. Parlane | Wellington | Dunedin | 2006/07 |
| 3rd | 445 | P.E. Whitelaw & W.N. Carson | Auckland | Dunedin | 1936/37 |
| 4th | 283 | D.R. Flynn & C.J. Anderson | ND | Hamilton | 2012/13 |
| 5th | 258 | C.E. McConchie & A.M. Ellis | Canterbury | Invercargill | 2016/17 |
| 6th | 305 | L.J. Carter & C.D. Fletcher | Canterbury | Christchurch | 2020/21 |
| 7th | 265 | J.L. Powell & N. Dorreen | Canterbury | Christchurch | 1929/30 |
| 8th | 215 | J.R. Murray & A.C. Cummins | West Indies | Dunedin | 1994/95 |
| 9th | 239 | H.B. Cave & I.B. Leggat | CD | Dunedin | 1952/53 |
| 10th | 138 | K.C. James & A.W.S. Brice | Wellington | Wellington | 1926/27 |

# WELLINGTON

## Highest Totals

| | | | |
|---|---|---|---|
| 614-8 | v Canterbury | Christchurch | 2006/07 |
| 608-9 dec | v Northern Districts | Hamilton | 1998/99 |
| 595 | v Auckland | Wellington | 1927/28 |
| 590-8 dec | v Central Districts | Palmerston North | 2004/05 |
| 575-7 dec | v Otago | Wellington | 1951/52 |
| 569 | v Auckland | Wellington | 1923/24 |
| 560 | v Otago | Dunedin | 1923/24 |
| 553 | v Canterbury | Wellington | 1931/32 |
| 553-3 dec | v Auckland | Wellington | 2017/18 |
| 547-8 dec | v Auckland | Wellington | 2005/06 |

## Lowest Totals

| | | | |
|---|---|---|---|
| 19 | v Nelson | Nelson | 1885/86 |
| 22 | v Canterbury | Wellington | 1903/04 |
| 29 | v Nelson | Nelson | 1879/80 |
| 30 | v Nelson | Nelson | 1883/84 |
| 31 | v Nelson | Nelson | 1887/88 |
| 34 | v Canterbury | Wellington | 1886/87 |
| 35 | v Auckland | Wellington | 1873/74 |
| 36 | v Nelson | Nelson | 1885/86 |
| 37 | v Nelson | Nelson | 1876/77 |
| 42 | v New South Wales | Wellington | 1895/96 |
| 42 | v Otago | Wellington | 1945/46 |

## Most Appearances

| | | | | | | | |
|---|---|---|---|---|---|---|---|
| 143 | Woodcock L.J. | 80 | Franklin J.E.C. | 60 | Newdick G.A. |
| 134 | Patel J.S. | 79 | Larsen G.R. | 59 | Blair R.W. |
| 120 | Gray E.J. | 79 | Parlane N.R. | 58 | Reid J.R. |
| 119 | Vance R.H. | 76 | Murdoch S.J. | 58 | Ritchie T.D. |
| 106 | Nevin C.J. | 74 | Coney J.V. | 57 | Elliott G.D. |
| 102 | McSweeney E.B. | 72 | Wells J.D. | 56 | Brice A.W.S. |
| 96 | Bell M.D. | 69 | Papps M.H.W. | 54 | Bilby G.P. |
| 89 | Morrison J.F.M. | 68 | Sinclair B.W. | 54 | McGirr H.M. |
| 87 | Edgar B.A. | 64 | Murray B.A.G. | 52 | Cederwall B.W. |
| 84 | Chatfield E.J. | 62 | Blundell T.A. | 50 | Butler L.C. |
| 82 | Gillespie M.R. | | | | |

## Longest Careers

| Seasons | | | | Seasons | | |
|---|---|---|---|---|---|---|
| 29 | Luckie M.M.F. | 1891/92-1919/20 | | 22 | Collins D.C. | 1905/06-1926/27 |
| 27 | Dempster C.S. | 1921/22-1947/48 | | 22 | Reaney T.P.L. | 1927/28-1948/49 |
| 25 | Tucker K.H. | 1895/96-1919/20 | | 20 | McGirr H.M. | 1913/14-1932/33 |
| 24 | James K.C. | 1923/24-1946/47 | | 20 | Lamason J.R. | 1927/28-1946/47 |
| 22 | Hutchings J.H. | 1903/04-1924/25 | | 20 | Patel J.S. | 1999/00-2018/19 |

## Benefits

| | | | |
|---|---|---|---|
| Morrison J.F.M. | 1983/84 | Gray E.J. | 1989/90 |
| Chatfield E.J. | 1985/86 | Vance R.H. | 1990/91 |
| Coney J.V. | 1986/87 | McSweeney E.B. | 1991/92 |
| Edgar B.A. | 1987/88 | Larsen G.R. | 1996/97 |

# Batting

| 2000 RUNS | Career | M | In | NO | HS | Runs | Ave | 100 |
|---|---|---|---|---|---|---|---|---|
| Woodcock L.J. | 2001/02-2018/19 | 143 | 246 | 30 | 220* | 7719 | 35.73 | 11 |
| Bell M.D. | 1997/98-2010/11 | 96 | 168 | 11 | 265 | 6565 | 41.81 | 20 |
| Edgar B.A. | 1975/76-1989/90 | 87 | 160 | 13 | 162 | 6494 | 44.17 | 15 |
| Vance R.H. | 1976/77-1990/91 | 119 | 205 | 18 | 254* | 6440 | 34.43 | 12 |
| Nevin C.J. | 1995/96-2009/10 | 106 | 163 | 26 | 143* | 4882 | 35.63 | 4 |
| Murdoch S.J. | 2009/10-2017/18 | 76 | 140 | 6 | 171 | 4847 | 36.17 | 12 |
| Papps M.H.W. | 2011/12-2017/18 | 69 | 128 | 9 | 316* | 4837 | 40.64 | 13 |
| Morrison J.F.M. | 1967/68-1983/84 | 89 | 160 | 22 | 180* | 4694 | 34.01 | 6 |
| Parlane N.R. | 2002/03-2010/11 | 79 | 128 | 11 | 193 | 4654 | 39.77 | 11 |
| Franklin J.E.C. | 1998/99-2014/15 | 80 | 122 | 18 | 219 | 4595 | 44.18 | 13 |
| Reid J.R. | 1947/48-1964/65 | 58 | 102 | 8 | 296 | 4538 | 48.27 | 13 |
| McSweeney E.B. | 1981/82-1993/94 | 102 | 153 | 23 | 205* | 4296 | 33.04 | 5 |
| Gray E.J. | 1975/76-1991/92 | 120 | 181 | 38 | 128* | 4228 | 29.56 | 5 |
| Murray B.A.G. | 1958/59-1972/73 | 64 | 116 | 9 | 213 | 3753 | 35.07 | 3 |
| Sinclair B.W. | 1955/56-1970/71 | 68 | 116 | 14 | 148 | 3583 | 35.12 | 2 |
| Hiddleston J.S. | 1913/14-1928/29 | 41 | 75 | 1 | 212 | 3413 | 46.12 | 8 |
| Blundell T.A. | 2012/13-2021/22 | 62 | 106 | 15 | 153 | 3317 | 36.45 | 8 |
| Coney J.V. | 1971/72-1986/87 | 74 | 126 | 21 | 120* | 3251 | 30.96 | 4 |
| Newdick G.A. | 1970/71-1980/81 | 60 | 112 | 6 | 143 | 3236 | 30.52 | 4 |
| McGirr H.M. | 1913/14-1932/33 | 54 | 97 | 4 | 141 | 3032 | 32.60 | 5 |
| Wells J.D. | 1989/90-2000/01 | 72 | 113 | 18 | 115 | 3016 | 31.74 | 5 |
| Jones A.H. | 1985/86-1993/94 | 39 | 67 | 11 | 181* | 2978 | 53.17 | 7 |
| Larsen G.R. | 1984/85-1998/99 | 79 | 118 | 25 | 161 | 2938 | 31.59 | 2 |
| Ryder J.D. | 2004/05-2012/13 | 40 | 67 | 3 | 236 | 2908 | 45.43 | 8 |
| Elliott G.D. | 2005/06-2013/14 | 57 | 91 | 6 | 196* | 2907 | 34.20 | 7 |
| Bilby G.P. | 1962/63-1976/77 | 54 | 95 | 11 | 161 | 2852 | 33.95 | 3 |
| Patel J.S. | 1999/00-2018/19 | 134 | 174 | 42 | 99 | 2691 | 20.38 | — |
| Dempster C.S. | 1921/22-1947/48 | 40 | 76 | 3 | 154 | 2602 | 35.64 | 5 |
| Ritchie T.D. | 1982/83-1990/91 | 58 | 92 | 14 | 106 | 2494 | 31.97 | 3 |
| Tindill E.W.T. | 1932/33-1949/50 | 39 | 73 | 5 | 149 | 2442 | 35.91 | 6 |
| Parlane M.E. | 2003/04-2007/08 | 40 | 69 | 3 | 203 | 2598 | 38.20 | 7 |
| Jones R.A. | 2000/01-2003/04 | 36 | 63 | 4 | 188 | 2343 | 39.71 | 7 |
| Pollard M.A. | 2009/10-2016/17 | 45 | 85 | 7 | 166 | 2317 | 29.70 | 3 |
| Brodie J.M. | 2007/08-2013/14 | 42 | 73 | 2 | 210 | 2266 | 31.91 | 4 |
| Conway D.P. | 2017/18-2020/21 | 22 | 39 | 8 | 327* | 2054 | 66.25 | 5 |
| Burnett G.P. | 1987/88-1992/93 | 44 | 80 | 13 | 203* | 2029 | 30.28 | 1 |

## CENTURY ON DEBUT FOR PROVINCE

| 163 | Williams A.B. | v Canterbury | Christchurch | 1896/97 |
|---|---|---|---|---|
| 110 & 5* | Crawford J.N. | v Auckland | Auckland | 1917/18 |
| 113 & 53 | Kortlang H.H.L. | v Auckland | Wellington | 1922/23 |
| 117 & 6 | Bernau E.H.L. | v Auckland | Wellington | 1922/23 |
| † 106 & 0 | Tindill E.W.T. | v Auckland | Auckland | 1932/33 |
| † 110 | Ongley J.A. | v Otago | Wellington | 1938/39 |
| † 27 &141* | Smith K.F.H. | v Central Districts | Wellington | 1953/54 |
| † 132 & 2* | Bilby G.P. | v Central Districts | Wellington | 1962/63 |
| † 39 & 156* | Aiken J.M. | v Canterbury | Christchurch | 1989/90 |
| 115 | Fleming S.P. | v Central Districts | Wellington | 2001/02 |
| † 142* & 1 | Rhodes S.J. | v Otago | Queenstown | 2009/10 |
| 111 | Ronchi L. | v Central Districts | Wellington | 2011/12 |
| 102 & 0 | Borthwick S.G. | v Otago | Queenstown | 2015/16 |
| 179 & 6 | Nofal M.J. | v Central Districts | Wellington | 2017/18 |

† *indicates player was making his first-class debut*

## HIGHEST INDIVIDUAL INNINGS

| | | | | |
|---|---|---|---|---|
| 327* | Conway D.P. | v Canterbury | Wellington | 2019/20 |
| 316* | Papps M.H.W. | v Auckland | Wellington | 2017/18 |
| 296 | Reid J.R. | v Northern Districts | Wellington | 1962/63 |
| 283 | Reid J.R. | v Otago | Wellington | 1951/52 |
| 265 | Bell M.D. | v Central Districts | Napier | 2007/08 |
| 254* | Vance R.H. | v Northern Districts | Wellington | 1988/89 |
| 236 | Ryder J.D. | v Central Districts | Palmerston North | 2004/05 |
| 222* | Midlane F.A. | v Otago | Wellington | 1914/15 |
| 220* | Woodcock L.J. | v Central Districts | Wellington | 2009/10 |
| 219 | Bell M.D. | v Northern Districts | Hamilton | 1998/99 |
| 219 | Franklin J.E.C. | v Auckland | Auckland | 2008/09 |
| 216 | Bell M.D. | v Auckland | Auckland | 1997/98 |
| 214* | Kortlang H.H.L. | v Auckland | Wellington | 1921/26 |
| 213 | Murray B.A.G. | v Otago | Dunedin | 1968/69 |
| 212 | Hiddleston J.S. | v Canterbury | Wellington | 1925/26 |
| 210 | Brodie J.M. | v Auckland | Auckland | 2011/12 |
| 208 | Franklin J.E.C. | v Auckland | Wellington | 2005/06 |
| 206* | Papps M.H.W. | v Canterbury | Rangiora | 2012/13 |
| 205* | McSweeney E.B. | v Central Districts | Levin | 1987/88 |
| 204 | Hiddleston J.S. | v Auckland | Wellington | 1925/26 |
| 203* | Burnett G.P. | v Northern Districts | Hamilton | 1991/92 |
| 203* | Woodcock L.J. | v Auckland | Auckland | 2016/17 |
| 203* | Conway D.P. | v Otago | Wellington | 2018/19 |
| 203 | Parlane M.E. | v Auckland | Auckland | 2004/05 |
| 202 | Austen M.H. | v Central Districts | Wanganui | 1993/94 |

## MOST RUNS IN A SEASON

| | | Runs | Ave | | | Runs | Ave |
|---|---|---|---|---|---|---|---|
| Murdoch S.J. | 2014/15 | 998 | 52.52 | Edgar B.A. | 1988/89 | 762 | 63.50 |
| Woodcock L.J. | 2009/10 | 988 | 65.86 | Blundell T.A. | 2015/16 | 761 | 44.76 |
| Ronchi L. | 2012/13 | 898 | 64.14 | Woodcock L.J. | 2015/16 | 739 | 38.89 |
| Vance R.H. | 1988/89 | 888 | 80.72 | Papps M.H.W. | 2014/15 | 738 | 39.60 |
| Jones R.A. | 2000/01 | 849 | 47.16 | Bell M.D. | 2007/08 | 731 | 73.10 |
| Bell M.D. | 2000/01 | 844 | 52.75 | Edgar B.A. | 1978/79 | 728 | 45.50 |
| Papps M.H.W. | 2013/14 | 841 | 64.69 | Jones R.A. | 2002/03 | 726 | 45.37 |
| Murdoch S.J. | 2015/16 | 824 | 43.36 | Ryder J.D. | 2012/13 | 723 | 51.64 |
| Papps M.H.W. | 2017/18 | 814 | 50.87 | Franklin T.J. | 2013/14 | 721 | 65.54 |
| Papps M.H.W. | 2012/13 | 810 | 45.00 | Edgar B.A. | 1989/90 | 720 | 40.00 |
| Parlane N.R. | 2007/08 | 809 | 57.78 | Twose R.G. | 1994/95 | 720 | 80.00 |
| Merchant C.J. | 2009/10 | 764 | 40.21 | Jones A.H. | 1988/89 | 701 | 87.62 |
| Parlane N.R. | 2009/10 | 763 | 40.15 | Conway D.P. | 2019/20 | 701 | 87.62 |

## MOST CENTURIES IN A SEASON

| | | |
|---|---|---|
| 5 | Bell M.D. | 2000/01 |

## TOTAL NUMBER OF CENTURIES     383

| | | |
|---|---|---|
| Most in one season | 12 | 2012/13 |
| 1st | Heenan G.C. 146* v Hawke's Bay | 1886/87 |
| 100th | Sinclair B.W. 102* v Northern Districts | 1963/64 |
| 200th | Chandler P.J.B. 177 v Auckland | 1996/97 |
| 300th | Murdoch S.J. 103 v Central Districts | 2011/12 |

# Bowling

| 150 WICKETS | Career | M | Wkts | Runs | Ave | 5WI | 10WM | Best |
|---|---|---|---|---|---|---|---|---|
| Chatfield E.J. | 1973/74-1989/90 | 84 | 403 | 7531 | 18.68 | 23 | 7 | 8-24 |
| Gray E.J. | 1975/76-1991/92 | 120 | 357 | 9778 | 27.38 | 13 | 3 | 8-37 |
| Gillespie M.R. | 1999/00-2014/15 | 82 | 344 | 9389 | 27.29 | 16 | 2 | 6-38 |
| Patel J.S. | 1999/00-2018/19 | 134 | 333 | 12,592 | 37.81 | 12 | 1 | 7-105 |
| Blair R.W. | 1951/52-1964/65 | 59 | 330 | 5004 | 15.16 | 30 | 10 | 9-72 |
| Brice A.W.S. | 1902/03-1927/28 | 56 | 229 | 4684 | 20.45 | 17 | 7 | 9-67 |
| Upham E.F. | 1892/93-1909/10 | 40 | 227 | 3393 | 14.94 | 17 | 2 | 7-24 |
| Franklin J.E.C. | 1998/99-2014/15 | 80 | 206 | 5103 | 24.77 | 6 | 1 | 7-30 |
| O'Brien I.E. | 2000/01-2009/10 | 45 | 179 | 3976 | 22.21 | 10 | 1 | 8-55 |
| Reid J.R. | 1947/48-1964/65 | 58 | 172 | 3115 | 18.11 | 10 | — | 7-29 |
| McGirr H.M. | 1913/14-1932/33 | 54 | 166 | 4326 | 26.06 | 7 | 1 | 7-45 |
| Morrison B.D. | 1953/54-1964/65 | 45 | 163 | 3858 | 23.66 | 7 | 2 | 7-42 |

### BEST IN AN INNINGS

| | | | | |
|---|---|---|---|---|
| 9-67 | Brice A.W.S. | v Auckland | Wellington | 1918/19 |
| 9-72 | Blair R.W. | v Auckland | Wellington | 1956/57 |
| 9-75 | Blair R.W. | v Canterbury | Wellington | 1956/57 |
| 8-13 | Firth J.P. | v Hawke's Bay | Wellington | 1883/84 |
| 8-21 | Penn A.J. | v Canterbury | Wellington | 2001/02 |
| 8-24 | Chatfield E.J. | v Northern Districts | Lower Hutt | 1979/80 |
| 8-34 | Fisher F.E. | v Canterbury | Wellington | 1952/53 |
| 8-36 | Blair R.W. | v Otago | Dunedin | 1952/53 |
| 8-37 | Gray E.J. | v Canterbury | Lower Hutt | 1985/86 |
| 8-50 | Butler L.C. | v NZ Under 23 XI | Wellington | 1965/66 |
| 8-55 | O'Brien I.E. | v Auckland | Wellington | 2006/07 |
| 8-58 | Ashbolt F.L. | v Hawke's Bay | Napier | 1897/98 |
| 8-59 | Hiddleston J.S. | v Canterbury | Christchurch | 1918/19 |
| 8-64 | Collinge R.O. | v Auckland | Auckland | 1967/68 |
| 8-78 | Gray E.J. | v Auckland | Wellington | 1989/90 |
| 8-83 | Chatfield E.J. | v Otago | Dunedin | 1986/87 |

### BEST IN A MATCH

| | | | | |
|---|---|---|---|---|
| 14-136 | Blair R.W. | v Canterbury | Wellington | 1956/57 |
| 14-151 | Gray E.J. | v Canterbury | Lower Hutt | 1985/86 |
| 13-58 | Salmon I.J. | v Nelson | Wellington | 1873/74 |
| 13-86 | Chatfield E.J. | v West Indies | Lower Hutt | 1979/80 |
| 13-91 | Gore A.H. | v Hawke's Bay | Napier | 1886/87 |
| 13-92 | Middleton F.S. | v Hawke's Bay | Wellington | 1919/20 |
| 13-97 | Ashbolt F.L. | v Hawke's Bay | Napier | 1897/98 |
| 13-117 | O'Brien I.E. | v Auckland | Wellington | 2006/07 |
| 13-157 | Tucker K.H. | v Auckland | Wellington | 1900/01 |
| 13-176 | Brice A.W.S. | v Auckland | Wellington | 1920/21 |

## MOST WICKETS IN A SEASON

| | | Wkts | Ave | | | Wkts | Ave |
|---|---|---|---|---|---|---|---|
| Chatfield E.J. | 1979/80 | 49 | 10.51 | Gillespie M.R. | 2013/14 | 42 | 32.90 |
| Gray E.J. | 1984/85 | 48 | 21.75 | Saunders J.V. | 1913/14 | 41 | 17.58 |
| Chatfield E.J. | 1981/82 | 47 | 16.87 | Chatfield E.J. | 1976/77 | 41 | 19.48 |
| Blair R.W. | 1956/57 | 46 | 9.47 | O'Brien I.E. | 2000/01 | 41 | 19.68 |
| Walker M.D.J. | 2002/03 | 45 | 18.00 | Penn A.J. | 2001/02 | 40 | 18.30 |
| Gillespie M.R. | 2012/13 | 45 | 31.37 | van Beek L.V. | 2017/18 | 40 | 14.47 |
| Gillespie M.R. | 2005/06 | 43 | 23.16 | | | | |

# Wicketkeeping

| 100 DISMISSALS | Career | M | Caught | Stumped | Total |
|---|---|---|---|---|---|
| McSweeney E.B. | 1981/82-1993/94 | 102 | 289 | 39 | 328 |
| Nevin C.J. | 1995/95-2009/10 | 106 | 289 | 9 | 298 |
| Blundell T.A. | 2012/13-2021/22 | 62 | 139 | 5 | 144 |
| Therkleson I.J. | 1966/67-1973/74 | 39 | 93 | 7 | 100 |

### MOST DISMISSALS IN A SEASON
46   (46ct)      Nevin C.J.    2000/01

### MOST DISMISSALS IN A MATCH
| 10 | (10ct) | Nevin C.J. v Otago | Dunedin | 1995/96 |
|---|---|---|---|---|
| 10 | (10ct) | Blundell T.A. v Canterbury | Wellington | 2017/18 |

### MOST DISMISSALS IN AN INNINGS
| 6 | (6ct) | Vance R.H. v Otago | Wellington | 1977/78 |
|---|---|---|---|---|
| 6 | (5ct 1st) | Nevin C.J. v Central Districts | Nelson | 1995/96 |
| 6 | (6ct) | Austin-Smellie J. v Central Districts | Napier | 2010/11 |
| 6 | (6ct) | Ronchi L. v Northern Districts | Wellington | 2012/13 |
| 6 | (6ct) | Ronchi L. v Canterbury | Christchurch | 2016/17 |
| 6 | (6ct) | Blundell T.A. v Canterbury | Wellington | 2017/18 |

### MOST CATCHES IN A MATCH
| 10 | Nevin C.J. v Otago | Dunedin | 1995/96 |
|---|---|---|---|
| 10 | Blundell T.A. v Canterbury | Wellington | 2017/18 |

### MOST CATCHES IN AN INNINGS
| 6 | Vance R.H. v Otago | Wellington | 1977/78 |
|---|---|---|---|
| 6 | Austin-Smellie J. v Central Districts | Napier | 2010/11 |
| 6 | Ronchi L. v Northern Districts | Wellington | 2012/13 |
| 6 | Ronchi L. v Canterbury | Christchurch | 2016/17 |
| 6 | Blundell T.A. v Canterbury | Wellington | 2017/18 |

# Fielding

### MOST CATCHES IN A SEASON
18      Coney J.V.      1977/78

### MOST CATCHES IN A MATCH
| 7 | Morrison J.F.M. v Northern Districts | Wellington | 1980/81 |
|---|---|---|---|

### MOST CATCHES IN AN INNINGS
| 5 | Lamason J.R. v Otago | Dunedin | 1937/38 |
|---|---|---|---|
| 5 | Morrison J.F.M. v Northern Districts | Wellington | 1980/81 |
| 5 | Brodie J.M. v Otago | Wellington | 2008/09 |
| 5 | Bell M.D. v Northern Districts | Hamilton | 2009/10 |

# Record Partnerships

## FOR

| Wicket | Score | Batsmen | Against | At | Date |
|--------|-------|---------|---------|-----|------|
| 1st | 432 | M.H.W. Papps & L.J. Woodcock | Wellington | Wellington | 2017/18 |
| 2nd | 287 | M.D. Bell & J.D. Wells | Auckland | Auckland | 1997/98 |
| 3rd | 346 | G.P. Burnett & R.A. Verry | ND | Hamilton | 1991/92 |
| 4th | 310 | J.D. Ryder & N.R. Parlane | CD | P. North | 2004/05 |
| 5th | 341 | G.R. Larsen & E.B. McSweeney | CD | Levin | 1987/88 |
| 6th | 247 | L.J. Woodcock & M.J. Nofal | CD | Wellington | 2017/18 |
| 7th | 250 | C.J. Nevin & M.D.J. Walker | Otago | Wellington | 2003/04 |
| 8th | 180 | R.G. Twose & M.C. Goodson | Otago | Dunedin | 1994/95 |
| 9th | 225 | L.J. Woodcock & M.J. Tugaga | CD | Wellington | 2009/10 |
| 10th | 138 | K.C. James & A.W.S. Brice | Otago | Wellington | 1926/27 |

## AGAINST

| Wicket | Score | Batsmen | For | At | Date |
|--------|-------|---------|-----|-----|------|
| 1st | 428 | P.J. Ingram & J.M. How | CD | Wellington | 2009/10 |
| 2nd | 254 | K.J. Burns & K.R. Rutherford | Otago | Oamaru | 1987/88 |
| 3rd | 291 | M.G. Bracewell & N.T. Broom | Otago | Dunedin | 2012/13 |
| 4th | 278 | A.W. Roberts & M.L. Page | Canterbury | Wellington | 1931/32 |
| 5th | 301 | J.I. Englefield & L.R.P.L. Taylor | CD | P. North | 2004/05 |
| 6th | 377 | C. Munro & Craig Cachopa | Auckland | Auckland | 2012/13 |
| 7th | 241 | N.J. Astle & M.W. Priest | Canterbury | Christchurch | 1994/95 |
| 8th | 189 | W.N. Carson & A.M. Matheson | Auckland | Auckland | 1938/39 |
| 9th | 188 | N.R. Parlane & D.R. Tuffey | ND | Wellington | 1999/00 |
| 10th | 134 | G.H. Worker & A.W. Mathieson | CD | Nelson | 2015/16 |

# INTER-PROVINCIAL RECORDS

## AUCKLAND v CANTERBURY

| First match 1873/74 | Played 149 | Won by Auckland 54 | Won by Canterbury 48 | Drawn 47 |
|---|---|---|---|---|

| | | | | |
|---|---|---|---|---|
| **Highest totals** | A | 693-9 dec | Auckland | 1939/40 |
| | C | 514-6 dec | Christchurch | 2002/03 |
| **Lowest totals** | A | 13 | Auckland | 1877/78 |
| | C | 62 | Rangiora | 1998/99 |
| **Highest innings** | A | 268 T.G. McIntosh | Auckland | 2007/08 |
| | C | 301* P.G. Fulton | Christchurch | 2002/03 |
| **Best bowling** *(innings)* | A | 9-75 R. Neill | Auckland | 1891/92 |
| | C | 9-56 D.J. McBeath | Christchurch | 1918/19 |
| **Best bowling** *(match)* | A | 13-85 R.S. Cunis | Christchurch | 1963/64 |
| | C | 15-168 D.J. McBeath | Christchurch | 1918/19 |

## Record Partnerships

**AUCKLAND**

| 1st | 286 | B. Sutcliffe & D.D. Taylor | Auckland | 1948/49 |
|---|---|---|---|---|
| 2nd | 197 | T.G. McIntosh & R.A. Young | Rangiora | 2008/09 |
| 3rd | 278 | T.J. Franklin & D.N. Patel | Christchurch | 1985/86 |
| 4th | 241* | R.A. Jones & R.A. Young | Auckland | 2009/10 |
| 5th | 161* | B. Sutcliffe & D.D. Taylor | Auckland | 1946/47 |
| 6th | 211 | M.J. Guptill & C. de Grandhomme | Rangiora | 2011/12 |
| 7th | 224 | V.J. Scott & A.M. Matheson | Auckland | 1937/38 |
| 8th | 153 | R.J. Nicol & R.A. Young | Auckland | 2001/02 |
| 9th | 96 | C. Pringle & D.K. Morrison | Rangiora | 1995/96 |
| 10th | 83 | S.W. Brown & C. Pringle | Christchurch | 1990/91 |

**CANTERBURY**

| 1st | 306 | L.A. Cuff & J.D. Lawrence | Christchurch | 1893/94 |
|---|---|---|---|---|
| 2nd | 179 | B.G. Hadlee & N.M. Parker | Auckland | 1978/79 |
| 3rd | 183 | G.R. Stead & C.Z. Harris | Christchurch | 2000/01 |
| 4th | 200 | K.J. McClure & C.E. McConchie | Rangiora | 2017/18 |
| 5th | 183 | K.J. McClure & A.M. Ellis | Auckland | 2016/17 |
| 6th | 185 | K.J. McClure & C.D. Fletcher | Rangiora | 2017/18 |
| 7th | 142 | G.J. Hopkins & P.J. Wiseman | Auckland | 2002/03 |
| 8th | 166 | R.J. Hadlee & D.R. Hadlee | Christchurch | 1983/84 |
| 9th | 115 | G.J. Hopkins & A.M. Ellis | Auckland | 2002/03 |
| 10th | 83 | H.C. Wilson & H.W. Monaghan | Christchurch | 1913/14 |
| | 83 | M. Graham & A.P. Cobden | Auckland | 1935/36 |

# AUCKLAND v CENTRAL DISTRICTS

| First match 1950/51 | Played 101 | Won by Auckland 35 | Won by Central Districts 29 | Drawn 37 |
|---|---|---|---|---|

| Highest totals | A | 668-7 dec | Napier | 2014/15 |
|---|---|---|---|---|
| | CD | 594-8 dec | Auckland | 1995/96 |
| Lowest totals | A | 71 | Palmerston North | 2001/02 |
| | CD | 59 | New Plymouth | 1958/59 |
| Highest innings | A | 281 C. Munro | Napier | 2014/15 |
| | CD | 204* T.C. Bruce | Napier | 2021/22 |
| Best bowling (innings) | A | 7-29 R.S. Cunis | Auckland | 1961/62 |
| | CD | 7-31 H.B. Cave | Palmerston North | 1952/53 |
| Best bowling (match) | A | 12-146 K.W. Hough | Auckland | 1959/60 |
| | CD | 13-64 H.B. Cave | Palmerston North | 1952/53 |

## Record Partnerships

**AUCKLAND**

| | | | | |
|---|---|---|---|---|
| 1st | 172 | R.A. Jones & M.J. Horne | Auckland | 2004/05 |
| 2nd | 196 | J.A. Raval & R.R. O'Donnell | Auckland | 2015/16 |
| 3rd | 184 | R.A. Jones & A.K. Kitchen | Lincoln | 2008/09 |
| 4th | 278 | M.J. Guptill & R.R. O'Donnell | Auckland | 2021/22 |
| 5th | 234* | V.J. Scott & J.B. Morris | Auckland | 1951/52 |
| 6th | 165 | J.J. Crowe & J.G. Bracewell | Auckland | 1987/88 |
| 7th | 192 | S.W. Brown & A.C. Parore | Auckland | 1990/91 |
| 8th | 133 | C. Munro & M.D. Bates | Napier | 2012/13 |
| 9th | 104* | R.A. Young & C.J. Drum | Auckland | 2000/01 |
| 10th | 86* | L.J. Shaw & A.J. McKay | Auckland | 2007/08 |

**CENTRAL DISTRICTS**

| | | | | |
|---|---|---|---|---|
| 1st | 173 | J.M. How & J.A. Raval | Auckland | 2012/13 |
| 2nd | 207* | R.G. Twose & M.W. Douglas | Auckland | 1991/92 |
| 3rd | 224 | M.S. Sinclair & C.M. Spearman | Auckland | 2003/04 |
| 4th | 155 | R.T. Hart & T.E. Blain | Masterton | 1989/90 |
| 5th | 168 | B.B.J. Griggs & T.I. Weston | Auckland | 2006/07 |
| 6th | 220 | M.H. Toynbee & I.D.S. Smith | Napier | 1982/83 |
| 7th | 165 | R.K. Brown & M.E.L. Lane | Palmerston North | 1993/94 |
| 8th | 102 | D.A.J. Bracewell & J.F.A. Field | Auckland | 2020/21 |
| 9th | 82 | R.J. Schaw & G.J.T. Hegglun | Auckland | 2006/07 |
| 10th | 133 | G.A. Bartlett & I.A. Colquhoun | Auckland | 1959/60 |

# AUCKLAND v NORTHERN DISTRICTS

| First match 1956/57 | Played 96 | Won by Auckland 38 | Won by Northern Districts 21 | Drawn 37 |
|---|---|---|---|---|

| | | | | |
|---|---|---|---|---|
| **Highest totals** | A | 547-8 dec | Auckland | 2000/01 |
| | ND | 492 | Auckland | 1990/91 |
| **Lowest totals** | A | 69 | Auckland | 1963/64 |
| | ND | 32 | Hamilton | 1996/97 |
| **Highest innings** | A | 209 P.A. Horne | Auckland | 1988/89 |
| | | 209* M.J. Horne | Auckland | 2003/04 |
| | ND | 211* G.A. Hick | Auckland | 1988/89 |
| **Best bowling** (*innings*) | A | 7-28 K.P. Walmsley | Hamilton | 2004/05 |
| | ND | 9-48 A.R. Tait | Hamilton | 1996/97 |
| **Best bowling** (*match*) | A | 11-71 J.A. Hayes | Auckland | 1957/58 |
| | ND | 16-130 A.R. Tait | Hamilton | 1996/97 |

## Record Partnerships

### AUCKLAND

| | | | | |
|---|---|---|---|---|
| 1st | 197 | T.J. Franklin & P.A. Horne | Auckland | 1985/86 |
| 2nd | 190 | M.J. Guptill & S.M. Solia | Whangarei | 2018/19 |
| 3rd | 152 | T.J. Franklin & J.J. Crowe | Rotorua | 1983/84 |
| 4th | 280 | J.J. Crowe & D.N. Patel | Auckland | 1991/92 |
| 5th | 347* | M.J. Horne & A.C. Barnes | Auckland | 2003/04 |
| 6th | 205 | M.S. Chapman & B.J. Horne | Auckland | 2019/20 |
| 7th | 168 | Craig Cachopa & B.P. Martin | Auckland | 2012/13 |
| 8th | 93 | G.J. Hopkins & R.M. Hira | Gisborne | 2007/08 |
| 9th | 151 | R.A. Young & G.J. Morgan | Auckland | 2007/08 |
| 10th | 139 | M.J. McClenaghan & R.S. Sandhu | Auckland | 2016/17 |

### NORTHERN DISTRICTS

| | | | | |
|---|---|---|---|---|
| 1st | 156 | J.A.H. Marshall & N.K.W. Horsley | Auckland | 2003/04 |
| 2nd | 301 | D.R. Flynn & B.S. Wilson | Hamilton | 2012/13 |
| 3rd | 261* | M.P. Maynard & S.A. Thomson | Hamilton | 1990/91 |
| 4th | 252 | S.A. Thomson & B.A. Young | Auckland | 1990/91 |
| 5th | 142 | M.P. Maynard & B.A. Young | Auckland | 1991/92 |
| 6th | 146* | G.A. Hick & S.A. Thomson | Auckland | 1988/89 |
| 7th | 127 | C.M. Kuggeleijn & S.A. Thomson | Auckland | 1988/89 |
| 8th | 113* | S.C. Kuggeleijn & B.R. Hampton | Auckland | 2015/16 |
| 9th | 185 | M.P. Maynard & S.B. Doull | Auckland | 1991/92 |
| 10th | 82 | S.B. Doull & B.P. Martin | Taupo | 1999/00 |

# AUCKLAND v OTAGO

| First match 1873/74 | Played 141 | Won by Auckland 70 | Won by Otago 33 | Drawn 38 |
|---|---|---|---|---|

| | | | | |
|---|---|---|---|---|
| **Highest totals** | A | 627 | Lincoln | 2006/07 |
| | O | 569-8 dec | Dunedin | 2012/13 |
| **Lowest totals** | A | 46 | Dunedin | 2010/11 |
| | O | 35 | Christchurch | 1884/85 |
| **Highest innings** | A | 290 W.N. Carson | Dunedin | 1936/37 |
| | O | 355 B. Sutcliffe | Dunedin | 1949/50 |
| **Best bowling** (innings) | A | 9-36 A.F. Wensley | Auckland | 1929/30 |
| | O | 8-57 S.L. Boock | Dunedin | 1989/90 |
| **Best bowling** (match) | A | 14-63 A.W. Rees | Dunedin | 1889/90 |
| | O | 15-104 S.L. Boock | Dunedin | 1989/90 |

## Record Partnerships

**AUCKLAND**

| | | | | |
|---|---|---|---|---|
| 1st | 240 | T.G. McIntosh & M.J. Horne | Dunedin | 2001/02 |
| 2nd | 170 | L.G. Hemus & A.E. Relf | Auckland | 1909/10 |
| 3rd | 445 | P.E. Whitelaw & W.N. Carson | Dunedin | 1936/37 |
| 4th | 273 | T.G. McIntosh & R.J. Nicol | Lincoln | 2006/07 |
| 5th | 197 | C.C.R. Dacre & C.F.W. Allcott | Dunedin | 1926/27 |
| 6th | 209* | A.C. Parore & A.P. O'Dowd | Dunedin | 1991/92 |
| 7th | 177* | A.C. Barnes & J.M. Mills | Alexandra | 1995/96 |
| 8th | 140 | J.G. Kemp & J.M. McIntyre | Dunedin | 1969/70 |
| 9th | 204 | B.J. Horne & D.K. Ferns | Auckland | 2020/21 |
| 10th | 119 | W.N. Carson & J. Cowie | Auckland | 1937/38 |

**OTAGO**

| | | | | |
|---|---|---|---|---|
| 1st | 373 | B. Sutcliffe & L. Watt | Auckland | 1950/51 |
| 2nd | 227 | P.W. Dobbs & M.J. Lamont | Dunedin | 1990/91 |
| 3rd | 199 | W.S. Haig & B. Sutcliffe | Auckland | 1954/55 |
| 4th | 239 | N.B. Beard & N.T. Broom | Dunedin | 2012/13 |
| 5th | 266 | B. Sutcliffe & W.S. Haig | Dunedin | 1949/50 |
| 6th | 162* | N.T. Broom & L.J. Morgan | Auckland | 2009/10 |
| 7th | 164 | A. Galland & A.R. Knight | Auckland | 1925/26 |
| 8th | 93 | A.K. Kitchen & C. Viljoen | Dunedin | 2016/17 |
| 9th | 208 | W.C. McSkimming & B.E. Scott | Auckland | 2004/05 |
| 10th | 63 | R.M. Phillips & J.A. Duffy | Auckland | 2014/15 |

# AUCKLAND v WELLINGTON

| First match | Played | Won by Auckland | Won by Wellington | Drawn |
|---|---|---|---|---|
| 1873/74 | 159 | 62 | 42 | 55 |

| Highest totals | A | 658-9d | | Auckland | 2012/13 |
|---|---|---|---|---|---|
| | W | 595 | | Wellington | 1927/28 |
| Lowest totals | A | 48 | | Wellington | 1889/90 |
| | W | 35 | | Wellington | 1873/74 |
| Highest innings | A | 269* | C. Munro | Auckland | 2012/13 |
| | W | 316* | M.H.W. Papps | Wellington | 2017/18 |
| Best bowling | A | 8-51 | R. Neill | Auckland | 1895/96 |
| (innings) | W | 9-67 | A.W.S. Brice | Wellington | 1918/19 |
| Best bowling | A | 14-65 | J.A. Hayes | Auckland | 1957/58 |
| (match) | W | 13-117 | I.E. O'Brien | Wellington | 2006/07 |

## Record Partnerships

**AUCKLAND**

| 1st | 215 | M.L. Guptill-Bunce & J.A. Raval | Wellington | 2015/16 |
|---|---|---|---|---|
| 2nd | 241 | T.J. Franklin & J.J. Crowe | Wellington | 1988/89 |
| 3rd | 213 | S.M. Solia & R.R. O'Donnell | Auckland | 2021/22 |
| 4th | 180 | A.N.C. Snedden & C.C.R. Dacre | Wellington | 1922/23 |
| 5th | 174 | R.W. Morgan & J.G. Kemp | Auckland | 1967/68 |
| 6th | 377 | C. Munro & Craig Cachopa | Auckland | 2012/13 |
| 7th | 131 | G.L. Weir & C.C.R. Dacre | Wellington | 1927/28 |
| 8th | 189 | W.N. Carson & A.M. Matheson | Auckland | 1938/39 |
| 9th | 122 | H.T. Schuster & R.S. Cunis | Wellington | 1964/65 |
| 10th | 97 | A.C. Kerr & H.C. Nottman | Auckland | 1941/42 |

**WELLINGTON**

| 1st | 432 | M.H.W. Papps & L.J. Woodcock | Wellington | 2017/18 |
|---|---|---|---|---|
| 2nd | 287 | M.D. Bell & J.D. Wells | Auckland | 1997/98 |
| 3rd | 287 | D.P. Conway & M.G. Bracewell | Wellington | 2020/21 |
| 4th | 217 | M.G. Bracewell & T.A. Blundell | Auckland | 2020/21 |
| 5th | 282 | J.E.C. Franklin & L.J. Woodcock | Auckland | 2008/09 |
| 6th | 199 | J.E.C. Franklin & T.A. Blundell | Wellington | 2013/14 |
| 7th | 144 | J.R. Reid & P.T. Barton | Auckland | 1959/60 |
| 8th | 137 | F.L.H. Mooney & F.E. Fisher | Wellington | 1952/53 |
| 9th | 127 | F.L.H. Mooney & R.A. Buchan | Wellington | 1943/44 |
| 10th | 113 | F.L.H. Mooney & E.C.V. Knapp | Wellington | 1943/44 |

# CANTERBURY v CENTRAL DISTRICTS

| First match 1950/51 | Played 105 | Won by Canterbury 35 | Won by Central Districts 29 | Drawn 41 |
|---|---|---|---|---|

| | | | | | |
|---|---|---|---|---|---|
| **Highest totals** | C | 582 | | Napier | 2013/14 |
| | CD | 549-8 dec | | Christchurch | 1998/99 |
| **Lowest totals** | C | 68 | | Levin | 1985/86 |
| | CD | 86 | | Christchurch | 2016/17 |
| **Highest innings** | C | 261 | T.W.M. Latham | Napier | 2013/14 |
| | CD | 212* | D.P. Kelly | Blenheim | 2000/01 |
| **Best bowling** *(innings)* | C | 9-13 | P.J. Wiseman | Christchurch | 2004/05 |
| | CD | 9-100 | B.W. Yuile | New Plymouth | 1965/66 |
| **Best bowling** *(match)* | C | 14-234 | T.D. Astle | Napier | 2013/14 |
| | CD | 11-115 | M.J. Mason | Timaru | 2002/03 |

## Record Partnerships

**CANTERBURY**

| | | | | |
|---|---|---|---|---|
| 1st | 185 | B.R. Hartland & D.J. Murray | Palmerston North | 1994/95 |
| 2nd | 254* | M.H.W. Papps & J.G. Myburgh | Napier | 2007/08 |
| 3rd | 208 | M.H.W. Papps & C.D. McMillan | Christchurch | 2006/07 |
| 4th | 204 | T.W. Jarvis & K. Thomson | Wanganui | 1969/70 |
| 5th | 290 | C.Z. Harris & G.R. Stead | Blenheim | 1996/97 |
| 6th | 379* | S.L. Stewart & C.F.K. van Wyk | New Plymouth | 2009/10 |
| 7th | 184* | C.L. Bull & B.P. Isherwood | Nelson | 1971/72 |
| 8th | 138* | C.E. McConchie & F.W. Sheat | Palmerston North | 2021/22 |
| 9th | 113 | G.J. Hopkins & S.J. Cunis | Christchurch | 1998/99 |
| 10th | 85 | G.T. Dowling & A.F. Rapley | Christchurch | 1958/59 |

**CENTRAL DISTRICTS**

| | | | | |
|---|---|---|---|---|
| 1st | 188 | G.H. Worker & G.R. Hay | Christchurch | 2017/18 |
| 2nd | 317 | R.T. Hart & P.S. Briasco | New Plymouth | 1983/84 |
| 3rd | 197 | M.J. Greatbatch & M.D. Crowe | New Plymouth | 1986/87 |
| 4th | 276* | M.D. Crowe & P.S. Briasco | Christchurch | 1986/87 |
| 5th | 235* | G.P. Sulzberger & J.D. Ryder | Napier | 2002/03 |
| 6th | 142 | M.S. Sinclair & C.F.K. van Wyk | Napier | 2012/13 |
| 7th | 219 | B.W. Yuile & B.L. Hampton | Napier | 1967/68 |
| 8th | 159 | B.J. Diamanti & R.R. Sherlock | Napier | 2007/08 |
| 9th | 89 | S.W. Duff & D.J. Leonard | Christchurch | 1993/94 |
| 10th | 98 | I.A. Rutherford & D.J. Kay | Napier | 1977/78 |

# CANTERBURY v NORTHERN DISTRICTS

| First match 1956/57 | Played 95 | Won by Canterbury 37 | Won by Northern Districts 21 | Drawn 37 |
|---|---|---|---|---|

| | | | | |
|---|---|---|---|---|
| **Highest totals** | C | 558-4 dec | Rangiora | 2009/10 |
| | ND | 726 | Rangiora | 2009/10 |
| **Lowest totals** | C | 73 | Gisborne | 2013/14 |
| | ND | 52 | Hamilton | 1966/67 |
| **Highest innings** | C | 237* R.T. Latham | Rotorua | 1990/91 |
| | ND | 235 J.A.H. Marshall | Christchurch | 2001/02 |
| **Best bowling** *(innings)* | C | 7-24 J.W.F. Kiddey | Hamilton | 1960/61 |
| | ND | 7-58 R.P. de Groen | Hamilton | 1995/96 |
| **Best bowling** *(match)* | C | 12-81 R.J. Hadlee | Christchurch | 1986/87 |
| | ND | 11-129 R.P. de Groen | Hamilton | 1995/96 |

## Record Partnerships

**CANTERBURY**

| | | | | |
|---|---|---|---|---|
| 1st | 214 | B.A. Bolton & G.T. Dowling | Christchurch | 1959/60 |
| 2nd | 243 | M.H.W. Papps & S.L. Stewart | Hamilton | 2006/07 |
| 3rd | 394* | P.G. Kennedy & R.T. Latham | Rotorua | 1990/91 |
| 4th | 182 | H.M. Nicholls & C.E. McConchie | Christchurch | 2019/20 |
| 5th | 252* | R.T. Latham & M.W. Priest | Christchurch | 1988/89 |
| 6th | 175 | S.P. Fleming & L.K. Germon | Hamilton | 1993/94 |
| 7th | 205 | L.K. Germon & M.W. Priest | Christchurch | 1991/92 |
| 8th | 220 | P.J. Wiseman & B.C. Hiini | Hamilton | 2005/06 |
| 9th | 76 | C.R.W. Dickel & K.I. Ferries | Hamilton | 1974/75 |
| 10th | 160 | L.K. Germon & W.A. Wisneski | Rangiora | 1997/98 |

**NORTHERN DISTRICTS**

| | | | | |
|---|---|---|---|---|
| 1st | 278 | D.R. Flynn & H.R. Cooper | Whangarei | 2017/18 |
| 2nd | 237 | J.G. Gibson & C.M. Kuggeleijn | Hamilton | 1980/81 |
| 3rd | 198 | K.S. Williamson & H.J.H. Marshall | Rangiora | 2009/10 |
| 4th | 259 | G.E. Bradburn & M.E. Parlane | Christchurch | 1996/97 |
| 5th | 155* | J.A.H. Marshall & N.K.W. Horsley | Hamilton | 2005/06 |
| 6th | 180 | S.A. Thomson & M.N. Hart | Hamilton | 1992/93 |
| 7th | 174 | B. Popli & M.J. Santner | Gisborne | 2013/14 |
| 8th | 163 | P.D. McGlashan & G.W. Aldridge | Hamilton | 2008/09 |
| 9th | 69 | M.N. Hart & S.B. Doull | Rangiora | 2000/01 |
| 10th | 80 | D.J. Mitchell & T.C. Goodin | Hamilton | 2015/16 |

# CANTERBURY v OTAGO

| First match 1863/64 | Played 193 | Won by Canterbury 86 | Won by Otago 68 | Drawn 39 |
|---|---|---|---|---|

| Highest totals | C | 777 | | Christchurch | 1996/97 |
|---|---|---|---|---|---|
| | O | 602-8 dec | | Dunedin | 1928/29 |
| Lowest totals | C | 25 | | Christchurch | 1866/67 |
| | O | 40 | | Dunedin | 1869/70 |
| Highest innings | C | 221* | P.G. Fulton | Dunedin | 2004/05 |
| | O | 385 | B. Sutcliffe | Christchurch | 1952/53 |
| Best bowling (innings) | C | 9-95 | M.W. Priest | Dunedin | 1989/90 |
| | O | 9-72 | F.H. Cooke | Christchurch | 1884/85 |
| Best bowling (match) | C | 13-181 | W.E. Merritt | Christchurch | 1935/36 |
| | O | 15-94 | F.H. Cooke | Christchurch | 1882/83 |

## Record Partnerships

**CANTERBURY**

| 1st | 226* | W.A. Hadlee & J.G. Leggat | Christchurch | 1948/49 |
|---|---|---|---|---|
| 2nd | 210 | W.A. Hadlee & F.P. O'Brien | Christchurch | 1940/41 |
| 3rd | 216* | P.G. Fulton & K.J. McClure | Christchurch | 2015/16 |
| 4th | 187 | P.G. Fulton & J.G. Myburgh | Christchurch | 2007/08 |
| 5th | 258 | C.E. McConchie & A.M. Ellis | Invercargill | 2016/17 |
| 6th | 305 | L.J. Carter & C.D. Fletcher | Christchurch | 2020/21 |
| 7th | 265 | J.L. Powell & N. Dorreen | Christchurch | 1929/30 |
| 8th | 167 | C.F.K. van Wyk & R.J. McCone | Christchurch | 2008/09 |
| 9th | 112 | A.M. Ellis & R.J. McCone | Queenstown | 2010/11 |
| 10th | 104 | L.V. van Beek & W.S.A. Williams | Christchurch | 2015/16 |

**OTAGO**

| 1st | 209 | B. Sutcliffe & L. Watt | Dunedin | 1947/48 |
|---|---|---|---|---|
| 2nd | 170 | C.C. Hopkins & G.G. Austin | Christchurch | 1911/12 |
| 3rd | 221 | R.C. Blunt & J.J.M. McMullan | Dunedin | 1928/29 |
| 4th | 185* | N.T. Broom & S.R. Wells | Dunedin | 2013/14 |
| 5th | 147 | K.J. Burns & D.J. Walker | Christchurch | 1985/86 |
| 6th | 121 | J.D.S. Neesham & M.J.G. Rippon | Dunedin | 2017/18 |
| 7th | 182 | B. Sutcliffe & A.W. Gilbertson | Christchurch | 1952/53 |
| 8th | 146 | M.H. Austen & P.J. Wiseman | Christchurch | 1996/97 |
| 9th | 134 | J.W. Wilson & N.A. Mallender | Christchurch | 1992/93 |
| 10th | 184 | R.C. Blunt & W. Hawksworth | Christchurch | 1931/32 |

# CANTERBURY v WELLINGTON

| First match<br>1883/84 | Played<br>165 | Won by Canterbury<br>62 | Won by Wellington<br>59 | Drawn<br>43 | Tied<br>1 |
|---|---|---|---|---|---|

| | | | | |
|---|---|---|---|---|
| **Highest totals** | C | 613-7 dec | Christchurch | 2006/07 |
| | W | 614-8 | Christchurch | 2006/07 |
| **Lowest totals** | C | 37 | Wellington | 1925/26 |
| | W | 22 | Wellington | 1903/04 |
| **Highest innings** | C | 241* T.W.M. Latham | Wellington | 2013/14 |
| | W | 327* D.P. Conway | Wellington | 2019/20 |
| **Best bowling**<br>*(innings)* | C | 10-28 A.E. Moss | Christchurch | 1889/90 |
| | W | 9-75 R.W. Blair | Wellington | 1956/57 |
| **Best bowling**<br>*(match)* | C | 13-72 A.E. Moss | Christchurch | 1889/90 |
| | W | 14-136 R.W. Blair | Wellington | 1956/57 |

## Record Partnerships

**CANTERBURY**

| | | | | |
|---|---|---|---|---|
| 1st | 287 | B.R. Hartland & G.R. Stead | Christchurch | 1994/95 |
| 2nd | 174 | G.T. Dowling & J.W. Burtt | Wellington | 1967/68 |
| 3rd | 187* | C.D. McMillan & R.T. Latham | Christchurch | 1994/95 |
| 4th | 278 | M.L. Page & A.W. Roberts | Wellington | 1931/32 |
| 5th | 183 | C.Z. Harris & C.D. McMillan | Christchurch | 1996/97 |
| 6th | 209 | C.Z. Harris & A.J. Redmond | Rangiora | 2001/02 |
| 7th | 241 | N.J. Astle & M.W. Priest | Christchurch | 1994/95 |
| 8th | 114 | A.W. Thomas & H.B. Whitta | Christchurch | 1919/20 |
| 9th | 182* | L.K. Germon & R.M. Ford | Christchurch | 1989/90 |
| 10th | 85 | A.W. Hart & C.H. Thiele | Rangiora | 1984/85 |

**WELLINGTON**

| | | | | |
|---|---|---|---|---|
| 1st | 239 | C.S. Dempster & W.H. Dustin | Wellington | 1931/32 |
| 2nd | 209* | A.H. Jones & M.D. Crowe | Christchurch | 1992/93 |
| 3rd | 206 | A.H. Preston & J.E.F. Beck | Christchurch | 1955/56 |
| 4th | 187 | H.M. McGirr & T.C. Lowry | Christchurch | 1930/31 |
| 5th | 139 | M.H.W. Papps & L.J. Woodcock | Rangiora | 2013/14 |
| 6th | 184 | G.D. Elliott & S.M. Mills | Christchurch | 2006/07 |
| | 184 | T.A. Blundell & P.F. Younghusband | Christchurch | 2016/17 |
| 7th | 176 | S.M. Mills & C.J. Nevin | Christchurch | 2006/07 |
| 8th | 154 | K.C. James & F.T. Badcock | Christchurch | 1926/27 |
| 9th | 125 | S.G. Borthwick & I.G. McPeake | Christchurch | 2015/16 |
| 10th | 113 | A.J. McKay & M.R. Gillespie | Rangiora | 2012/13 |

# CENTRAL DISTRICTS v NORTHERN DISTRICTS

| First match 1956/57 | Played 97 | Won by Central Districts 28 | Won by Northern Districts 29 | Drawn 40 |
|---|---|---|---|---|

| Highest totals | CD | 531-7 dec | | Napier | 2009/10 |
|---|---|---|---|---|---|
| | ND | 556-9 dec | | New Plymouth | 2014/15 |
| Lowest totals | CD | 51 | | Hamilton | 1957/58 |
| | ND | 86 | | New Plymouth | 1956/57 |
| Highest innings | CD | 247 | P.J. Ingram | Hamilton | 2008/09 |
| | ND | 334 | D.G. Brownlie | New Plymouth | 2014/15 |
| Best bowling (innings) | CD | 7-28 | B.W. Yuile | Hamilton | 1967/68 |
| | ND | 8-37 | D.B. Clarke | Wanganui | 1962/63 |
| Best bowling (match) | CD | 11-134 | G.K. Robertson | Nelson | 1986/87 |
| | ND | 11-145 | G.W. Aldridge | Whangarei | 2009/10 |

## Record Partnerships

**CENTRAL DISTRICTS**

| | | | | |
|---|---|---|---|---|
| 1st | 215 | J.M. How & M.S. Sinclair | Napier | 2004/05 |
| | 215 | J.M. How & J.A. Raval | Nelson | 2012/13 |
| 2nd | 263 | M.J. Greatbatch & M.D. Crowe | Morrinsville | 1986/87 |
| 3rd | 264 | P.J. Ingram & M.S. Sinclair | Hamilton | 2008/09 |
| 4th | 176 | T.C. Bruce & D. Cleaver | Napier | 2016/17 |
| 5th | 222 | M.S. Sinclair & C.F.K van Wyk | Gisborne | 2011/12 |
| 6th | 224 | B.D. Schmulian & D.A.J. Bracewell | Mt Maunganui | 2017/18 |
| 7th | 179 | B.B.J. Griggs & C.J.M. Furlong | Hamilton | 2001/02 |
| 8th | 173 | I.D.S. Smith & G.K. Robertson | Hamilton | 1982/83 |
| 9th | 116 | V. Pollard & R.O. Collinge | Palmerston North | 1964/65 |
| 10th | 55 | B.S. Smith & A.F. Milne | Gisborne | 2012/13 |

**NORTHERN DISTRICTS**

| | | | | |
|---|---|---|---|---|
| 1st | 334 | J.A. Raval & B. Popli | Whangarei | 2021/22 |
| 2nd | 199 | R.E.W. Mawhinney & D.J. White | Hamilton | 1985/86 |
| 3rd | 258 | D.R. Flynn & B. Popli | Hamilton | 2015/16 |
| 4th | 169 | D.J. White & B.S. Oxenham | Wanganui | 1990/91 |
| 5th | 155 | C.J. Anderson & J.A.H. Marshall | Nelson | 2012/13 |
| 6th | 322 | M.G. Orchard & J.A.F. Yovich | Napier | 2005/06 |
| 7th | 136 | D.J. Nash & A.R. Tait | Masterton | 1997/98 |
| 8th | 143 | C.M. Presland & C.W. Dickeson | Whangarei | 1983/84 |
| 9th | 107 | R.G. Hart & A.R. Tait | Rotorua | 1995/96 |
| 10th | 89 | M.J.E. Wright & S.J. Scott | Wanganui | 1978/79 |

# CENTRAL DISTRICTS v OTAGO

| First match 1950/51 | Played 101 | Won by Central Districts 34 | Won by Otago 27 | Drawn 40 |
|---|---|---|---|---|

| Highest totals | CD | 650-8 dec | | Napier | 2015/16 |
|---|---|---|---|---|---|
| | O | 642-6 dec | | Dunedin | 2021/22 |
| Lowest totals | CD | 74 | | Invercargill | 1996/97 |
| | O | 63 | | Lincoln | 2011/12 |
| Highest innings | CD | 244 | B.S. Smith | Napier | 2015/16 |
| | O | 264 | B. Sutcliffe | Dunedin | 1959/60 |
| Best bowling (innings) | CD | 7-36 | B.W. Yuile | Nelson | 1962/63 |
| | O | 8-31 | D.G. Sewell | Invercargill | 1996/97 |
| Best bowling (match) | CD | 11-99 | D.D. Beard | Dunedin | 1956/57 |
| | O | 15-203 | A.M. Moir | New Plymouth | 1953/54 |

# Record Partnerships

## CENTRAL DISTRICTS

| | | | | |
|---|---|---|---|---|
| 1st | 202 | G.H. Worker & G.R. Hay | Napier | 2018/19 |
| 2nd | 242* | J.M. How & M.S. Sinclair | New Plymouth | 2005/06 |
| 3rd | 223 | C.J.P. Smith & S.W.J. Wilson | Blenheim | 1990/91 |
| 4th | 234 | B.S. Smith & G.H. Worker | Napier | 2015/16 |
| 5th | 205 | G.R. Hay & K. Noema-Barnett | Alexandra | 2018/19 |
| 6th | 184* | M.S. Sinclair & T.I. Lythe | Napier | 2007/08 |
| 7th | 123 | I.D.S. Smith & S.J. Gill | Napier | 1981/82 |
| 8th | 133 | T.S. Nethula & A.F. Milne | Napier | 2012/13 |
| 9th | 239 | H.B. Cave & I.B. Leggat | Dunedin | 1952/53 |
| 10th | 60* | B.L. Cairns & A.B. Jordan | Wanganui | 1975/76 |

## OTAGO

| | | | | |
|---|---|---|---|---|
| 1st | 305 | R.A. Lawson & M.G. Croy | Napier | 1995/96 |
| 2nd | 169 | G.M. Turner & R.W. Anderson | Dunedin | 1974/75 |
| 3rd | 306 | S.B. Haig & N.T. Broom | Napier | 2009/10 |
| 4th | 200 | B.R. Blair & G.J. Dawson | Dunedin | 1982/83 |
| 5th | 192 | M.H. Richardson & I.S. Billcliff | Napier | 1994/95 |
| 6th | 256 | N.F. Kelly & M.W. Chu | Dunedin | 2021/22 |
| 7th | 121* | W.K. Lees & B. Abernethy | Napier | 1981/82 |
| 8th | 119 | M.D. Craig & N. Wagner | Dunedin | 2012/13 |
| 9th | 92 | D.E.C. McKechnie & B.L. Cairns | Dunedin | 1976/77 |
| 10th | 78 | C.B. Gaffaney & D.G. Sewell | Palmerston North | 1999/00 |

# CENTRAL DISTRICTS v WELLINGTON

| First match 1950/51 | Played 99 | Won by Central Districts 22 | Won by Wellington 34 | Drawn 43 |
|---|---|---|---|---|

| | | | | |
|---|---|---|---|---|
| **Highest totals** | CD | 523 | Wellington | 2008/09 |
| | W | 590-8 dec | Palmerston North | 2004/05 |
| **Lowest totals** | CD | 50 | Upper Hutt | 1979/80 |
| | W | 88 | Wellington | 1991/92 |
| **Highest innings** | CD | 245*   P.J. Ingram | Wellington | 2009/10 |
| | W | 265   M.D. Bell | Napier | 2007/08 |
| **Best bowling** *(innings)* | CD | 7-55   E.P. Thompson | Napier | 2003/04 |
| | W | 7-30   J.E.C. Franklin | Wellington | 2005/06 |
| **Best bowling** *(match)* | CD | 11-149  E.P. Thompson | Napier | 2003/04 |
| | W | 10-103  B.D. Morrison | Wellington | 1955/56 |

## Record Partnerships

**CENTRAL DISTRICTS**

| | | | | |
|---|---|---|---|---|
| 1st | 428 | P.J. Ingram & J.M. How | Wellington | 2009/10 |
| 2nd | 204 | P.J. Ingram & B.S. Smith | Wellington | 2010/11 |
| 3rd | 224 | C. Cachopa & M.S. Sinclair | Napier | 2012/13 |
| 4th | 172* | P.S. Briasco & M.W. Douglas | Palmerston North | 1990/91 |
| 5th | 301 | J.I. Englefield & L.R.P.L. Taylor | Palmerston North | 2004/05 |
| 6th | 235 | M.S. Sinclair & B.B.J. Griggs | Wellington | 2008/09 |
| 7th | 187 | C.F.K. van Wyk & D.A.J. Bracewell | Napier | 2010/11 |
| 8th | 84 | P.M. Blackbourn & G.K. Robertson | Palmerston North | 1983/84 |
| 9th | 73 | G.R. Hay & E.J. McInnis | Napier | 2007/08 |
| 10th | 134 | G.H. Worker & A.W. Mathieson | Nelson | 2015/16 |

**WELLINGTON**

| | | | | |
|---|---|---|---|---|
| 1st | 316 | M.H. Austen & R.T. Hart | Wanganui | 1993/94 |
| 2nd | 215 | M.D. Bell & M.E. Parlane | Napier | 2004/05 |
| 3rd | 256 | M.H.W. Papps & J.D. Ryder | Wellington | 2012/13 |
| 4th | 310 | J.D. Ryder & N.R. Parlane | Palmerston North | 2004/05 |
| 5th | 341 | G.R. Larsen & E.B. McSweeney | Levin | 1987/88 |
| 6th | 247 | L.J. Woodcock & M.J. Nofal | Wellington | 2017/18 |
| 7th | 161 | S.P. Fleming & M.D.J. Walker | Wellington | 2001/02 |
| 8th | 135 | G.R. Larsen & J.E.C. Franklin | Wellington | 1998/99 |
| 9th | 225 | L.J. Woodcock & M.J. Tugaga | Wellington | 2009/10 |
| 10th | 81 | L.C. Butler & R.E. Reid | Wanganui | 1959/60 |

# NORTHERN DISTRICTS v OTAGO

| First match<br>1956/57 | Played<br>92 | Won by Northern Districts<br>33 | Won by Otago<br>23 | Drawn<br>36 |
|---|---|---|---|---|

| | | | | |
|---|---|---|---|---|
| **Highest totals** | ND | 559-9 dec | Hamilton | 2010/11 |
| | O | 576-8 dec | Whangarei | 2009/10 |
| **Lowest totals** | ND | 64 | Dunedin | 1971/72 |
| | O | 77 | Gisborne | 1999/00 |
| **Highest innings** | ND | 241  D.R. Flynn | Hamilton | 2010/11 |
| | O | 207  A.K. Kitchen | Dunedin | 2016/17 |
| **Best bowling**<br>*(innings)* | ND | 7-42  K. Treiber | Hamilton | 1985/86 |
| | O | 9-93  P.J. Petherick | Dunedin | 1975/76 |
| **Best bowling**<br>*(match)* | ND | 13-99  R.P. de Groen | Alexandra | 1992/93 |
| | O | 13-144  S.L. Boock | Whangarei | 1980/81 |

## Record Partnerships

**NORTHERN DISTRICTS**

| | | | | |
|---|---|---|---|---|
| 1st | 214 | D.G. Brownlie & B.S. Wilson | Hamilton | 2014/15 |
| 2nd | 222 | L.M. Crocker & C.M. Kuggeleijn | Hamilton | 1983/84 |
| 3rd | 199 | B-J. Watling & B. Popli | Whangarei | 2015/16 |
| 4th | 283 | D.R. Flynn & C.J. Anderson | Hamilton | 2012/13 |
| 5th | 226 | D.J. Mitchell & T.L. Seifert | Dunedin | 2016/17 |
| 6th | 191 | S.B. Styris & R.G. Hart | Hamilton | 2001/02 |
| 7th | 131 | D.R. Flynn & P.D. McGlashan | Gisborne | 2005/06 |
| 8th | 102 | J.A.F. Yovich & B.P. Martin | Dunedin | 2005/06 |
| 9th | 112 | J.A.F. Yovich & B.E. Scott | Dunedin | 2009/10 |
| 10th | 97 | R.G. Hart & G.L. West | Hamilton | 2002/03 |

**OTAGO**

| | | | | |
|---|---|---|---|---|
| 1st | 260 | R.A. Lawson & Mohammad Wasim | Dunedin | 2002/03 |
| 2nd | 247 | C.D. Cumming & D.J. Broom | Whangarei | 2009/10 |
| 3rd | 150 | K.B.K. Ibadulla & K.J. Burns | Gisborne | 1989/90 |
| 4th | 235 | K.J. Burns & R.N. Hoskin | Hamilton | 1987/88 |
| 5th | 252 | N.T. Broom & D.J. Broom | Queenstown | 2010/11 |
| 6th | 146 | G.J. Hopkins & N.L. McCullum | Dunedin | 2006/07 |
| 7th | 190 | N.G. Smith & M.J.G. Rippon | Dunedin | 2019/20 |
| 8th | 149 | N.T. Broom & M.D. Craig | Hamilton | 2012/13 |
| 9th | 85 | D.C. de Boorder & N.B. Beard | Queenstown | 2010/11 |
| 10th | 102 | M.D. Craig & J.A. Duffy | Dunedin | 2014/15 |

# NORTHERN DISTRICTS v WELLINGTON

| First match | Played | Won by Northern Districts | Won by Wellington | Drawn |
|:---:|:---:|:---:|:---:|:---:|
| 1956/57 | 97 | 24 | 39 | 34 |

| | | | | |
|:---|:---:|:---|:---|:---:|
| **Highest totals** | ND | 608-9 dec | Lincoln | 2011/12 |
| | W | 608-9 dec | Hamilton | 1998/99 |
| **Lowest totals** | ND | 57 | Hamilton | 1961/62 |
| | W | 58 | Hamilton | 2014/15 |
| **Highest innings** | ND | 284* K.S. Williamson | Lincoln | 2011/12 |
| | W | 296 J.R. Reid | Wellington | 1962/63 |
| **Best bowling** | ND | 8-27 T.G. Southee | Hamilton | 2009/10 |
| *(innings)* | W | 8-24 E.J. Chatfield | Lower Hutt | 1979/80 |
| **Best bowling** | ND | 12-62 I.S. Sodhi | Wellington | 2017/18 |
| *(match)* | W | 12-39 E.J. Chatfield | Lower Hutt | 1979/80 |

## Record Partnerships

**NORTHERN DISTRICTS**

| | | | | |
|:---|:---|:---|:---|:---|
| **1st** | 274 | B.S. Wilson & B-J. Watling | Whangarei | 2010/11 |
| **2nd** | 177 | B.S. Wilson & K.S. Williamson | Lincoln | 2011/12 |
| **3rd** | 169 | J.M. Parker & A.D.G. Roberts | Wellington | 1983/84 |
| **4th** | 208 | S.A. Thomson & M.P. Maynard | Hamilton | 1991/92 |
| **5th** | 180 | B. Popli & B-J. Watling | Hamilton | 2015/16 |
| **6th** | 170 | E.C. Petrie & R.J. McPherson | Hamilton | 1959/60 |
| **7th** | 166 | D.J. Mitchell & T.G. Southee | Wellington | 2012/13 |
| **8th** | 152 | J.A.H. Marshall & M.G. Orchard | Hamilton | 2006/07 |
| **9th** | 188 | N.R. Parlane & D.R. Tuffey | Wellington | 1999/00 |
| **10th** | 113* | P.D. McGlashan & G.W. Aldridge | Wellington | 2005/06 |

**WELLINGTON**

| | | | | |
|:---|:---|:---|:---|:---|
| **1st** | 310 | B.A. Edgar & R.H. Vance | Wellington | 1988/89 |
| **2nd** | 215 | M.D. Bell & J.D. Wells | Hamilton | 1998/99 |
| **3rd** | 346 | G.P. Burnett & R.A. Verry | Hamilton | 1991/92 |
| **4th** | 179 | P.T. Barton & J.R. Reid | Wellington | 1964/65 |
| **5th** | 158* | T.A. Blundell & T.M. Johnson | Wellington | 2020/21 |
| **6th** | 139 | J.F.M. Morrison & R.W. Smith | Wellington | 1972/73 |
| **7th** | 165 | G.D. Elliott & H.K.P. Boam | Wellington | 2010/11 |
| **8th** | 102 | L. Ronchi & J.S. Patel | Wellington | 2012/13 |
| **9th** | 87 | I.J. Therkleson & R.O. Collinge | Whangarei | 1973/74 |
| **10th** | 89 | M.H.W. Papps & B.J. Arnel | Mt Maunganui | 2016/17 |

# OTAGO v WELLINGTON

| First match 1892/93 | Played 137 | Won by Otago 37 | Won by Wellington 63 | Drawn 37 |
|---|---|---|---|---|

| | | | | |
|---|---|---|---|---|
| **Highest totals** | O | 651-9 dec | Dunedin | 2012/13 |
| | W | 575-7 dec | Wellington | 1951/52 |
| **Lowest totals** | O | 34 | Dunedin | 1956/57 |
| | W | 42 | Wellington | 1945/46 |
| **Highest innings** | O | 239 H.D. Rutherford | Dunedin | 2011/12 |
| | W | 283 J.R. Reid | Wellington | 1951/52 |
| **Best bowling** *(innings)* | O | 8-46 B.L. Cairns | Invercargill | 1978/79 |
| | W | 8-36 R.W. Blair | Dunedin | 1952/53 |
| **Best bowling** *(match)* | O | 12-277 A.W. Alloo | Dunedin | 1923/24 |
| | W | 12-87 E.J. Chatfield | Wellington | 1973/74 |

## Record Partnerships

**OTAGO**

| | | | | |
|---|---|---|---|---|
| 1st | 193 | M.H. Richardson & M.J. Horne | Wellington | 2000/01 |
| 2nd | 254 | K.J. Burns & K.R. Rutherford | Oamaru | 1987/88 |
| 3rd | 291 | M.G. Bracewell & N.T. Broom | Dunedin | 2012/13 |
| 4th | 211* | K.J. Burns & A.H. Jones | Wellington | 1984/85 |
| 5th | 134 | C.B. Gaffaney & G.J. Hopkins | Dunedin | 2003/04 |
| 6th | 216 | H.D. Rutherford & D.C. de Boorder | Dunedin | 2011/12 |
| 7th | 159 | D.C. de Boorder & M.D. Craig | Wellington | 2013/14 |
| 8th | 165* | J.N. Crawford & A.G. Eckhold | Wellington | 1914/15 |
| 9th | 130* | D.C. de Boorder & W.C. McSkimming | Queenstown | 2010/11 |
| 10th | 90 | B.L. Cairns & G.B. Thomson | Lower Hutt | 1979/80 |

**WELLINGTON**

| | | | | |
|---|---|---|---|---|
| 1st | 299 | M.D. Bell & R.A. Jones | Dunedin | 2001/02 |
| 2nd | 279 | M.D. Bell & M.E. Parlane | Dunedin | 2006/07 |
| 3rd | 246 | B.A.G. Murray & J.F.M. Morrison | Dunedin | 1968/69 |
| 4th | 274 | R.A. Jones & S.R. Mather | Wellington | 2000/01 |
| 5th | 255 | B.R. Taylor & J.V. Coney | Dunedin | 1972/73 |
| 6th | 184 | H.M. McGirr & D.C. Collins | Dunedin | 1923/24 |
| 7th | 250 | C.J. Nevin & M.D.J. Walker | Wellington | 2003/04 |
| 8th | 180 | R.G. Twose & M.C. Goodson | Dunedin | 1994/95 |
| 9th | 85 | A.T. Fletcher & I.G. McPeake | Dunedin | 2018/19 |
| 10th | 138 | K.C. James & A.W.S. Brice | Wellington | 1926/27 |

# PROVINCIAL COMPETITION

## Plunket Shield

*1921/22 — 1974/75*

Awarded by the Governor of New Zealand, Lord Plunket, the Shield was given to Canterbury as the association with the best record in the 1906/07 season. From 1907/08 to 1920/21 the trophy was competed for under a challenge system but thereafter on a competition basis.

| HOLDERS | Tenure | Challenges resisted |
|---|---|---|
| Canterbury | 17 December, 1907 | — |
| Auckland | 17 December, 1907 to 1 February, 1911 | 7 |
| Canterbury | 1 February, 1911 to 12 February, 1912 | 2 |
| Auckland | 12 February, 1912 to 31 January, 1913 | 1 |
| Canterbury | 31 January, 1913 to 27 December, 1918 | 9 |
| Wellington | 27 December, 1918 to 24 January, 1919 | — |
| Canterbury | 24 January, 1919 to 4 January, 1920 | 2 |
| Auckland | 4 January, 1920 to 10 January, 1921 | 3 |
| Wellington | 10 January, 1921 | — |

## Shell Series

*1975/76-2000/01*

In 1975/76, a new competition, sponsored by Shell, was established. For the first four seasons this was played under a two-stage system — the first round of 15 games (all teams playing each other) was for the Shell Cup*, while the second round (on a knock-out basis culminating in a final) carried the season's major prize, the Shell Trophy.

From 1979/80, only the Shell Trophy was competed for. The Shell Cup was reallocated to the limited-over competition in 1980/81, while the Plunket Shield was reserved for matches between the North and South Islands.

### WINNERS

| | | | | | |
|---|---|---|---|---|---|
| 1921/22 | Auckland | 1952/53 | Otago | 1977/78 | Auckland |
| 1922/23 | Canterbury | 1953/54 | Central Districts | | *Canterbury** |
| 1923/24 | Wellington | 1954/55 | Wellington | 1978/79 | Otago |
| 1924/25 | Otago | 1955/56 | Canterbury | | *Otago** |
| 1925/26 | Wellington | 1956/57 | Wellington | 1979/80 | Northern Districts |
| 1926/27 | Auckland | 1957/58 | Otago | 1980/81 | Auckland |
| 1927/28 | Wellington | 1958/59 | Auckland | 1981/82 | Wellington |
| 1928/29 | Auckland | 1959/60 | Canterbury | 1982/83 | Wellington |
| 1929/30 | Wellington | 1960/61 | Wellington | 1983/84 | Canterbury |
| 1930/31 | Canterbury | 1961/62 | Wellington | 1984/85 | Wellington |
| 1931/32 | Wellington | 1962/63 | Northern Districts | 1985/86 | Otago |
| 1932/33 | Otago | 1963/64 | Auckland | 1986/87 | Central Districts |
| 1933/34 | Auckland | 1964/65 | Canterbury | 1987/88 | Otago |
| 1934/35 | Canterbury | 1965/66 | Wellington | 1988/89 | Auckland |
| 1935/36 | Wellington | 1966/67 | Central Districts | 1989/90 | Wellington |
| 1936/37 | Auckland | 1967/68 | Central Districts | 1990/91 | Auckland |
| 1937/38 | Auckland | 1968/69 | Auckland | 1991/92 | Central Districts & |
| 1938/39 | Auckland | 1969/70 | Otago | | Northern Districts |
| 1939/40 | Auckland | 1970/71 | Central Districts | 1992/93 | Northern Districts |
| 1945/46 | Canterbury | 1971/72 | Otago | 1993/94 | Canterbury |
| 1946/47 | Auckland | 1972/73 | Wellington | 1994/95 | Auckland |
| 1947/48 | Otago | 1973/74 | Wellington | 1995/96 | Auckland |
| 1948/49 | Canterbury | 1974/75 | Otago | 1996/97 | Canterbury |
| 1949/50 | Wellington | 1975/76 | Canterbury | 1997/98 | Canterbury |
| 1950/51 | Otago | | *Canterbury** | 1998/99 | Central Districts |
| 1951/52 | Canterbury | 1976/77 | Otago | 1999/00 | Northern Districts |
| | | | *Northern Districts** | 2000/01 | Wellington |

# State Championship
*from 2001/02*

State Insurance took over the sponsorship of the competition in 2001/02.

### WINNERS

| | | |
|---|---|---|
| 2001/02 Auckland | 2002/03 Auckland | 2003/04 Wellington |
| 2004/05 Auckland | 2005/06 Central Districts | 2006/07 Northern Districts |
| 2007/08 Canterbury | 2008/09 Auckland | |

# Plunket Shield
*from 2009/10*

The Plunket Shield was reinstated at the conclusion of State Insurance's sponsorship term.

### WINNERS

| | | |
|---|---|---|
| 2009/10 Northern Districts | 2010/11 Canterbury | 2011/12 Northern Districts |
| 2012/13 Central Districts | 2013/14 Canterbury | 2014/15 Canterbury |
| 2015/16 Auckland | 2016/17 Canterbury | 2017/18 Central Districts |
| 2018/19 Central Districts | 2019/20 Wellington | 2020/21 Canterbury |
| 2021/22 Auckland | | |

# TEAM RECORDS

## Playing Record of the First-class Sides in New Zealand

| | P | W | L | D | | P | W | L | D |
|---|---|---|---|---|---|---|---|---|---|
| Canterbury | 760 | 283 | 254 | 223* | India A | 7 | — | — | 7 |
| Wellington | 740 | 261 | 241 | 238† | The Rest | 6 | 1 | 3 | 2 |
| Otago | 721 | 201 | 312 | 208 | Victoria | 6 | 1 | 1 | 4 |
| Auckland | 703 | 273 | 194 | 236 | Pakistan A | 6 | 1 | 1 | 4 |
| Central Districts | 530 | 145 | 168 | 217* | Young New Zealand | 5 | — | 2 | 3 |
| Northern Districts | 497 | 129 | 177 | 191 | Queensland | 5 | 3 | 1 | 1 |
| New Zealand | 286 | 79 | 87 | 120 | Tasmania | 4 | — | 3 | 1 |
| England/MCC | 140 | 63 | 12 | 65* | Shell XI | 3 | 1 | 1 | 1 |
| Australia | 113 | 63 | 7 | 43 | Emerging Players | 3 | — | 1 | 2 |
| Pakistan | 61 | 22 | 11 | 28 | Governor General's XI | 2 | 1 | 1 | — |
| Hawke's Bay | 53 | 9 | 34 | 10 | Commonwealth XI | 2 | 2 | — | — |
| West Indies | 49 | 11 | 16 | 22 | D.H. Robins' XI | 2 | — | — | 2 |
| India | 40 | 11 | 11 | 18 | NZ Major Association XI | 2 | — | — | 2 |
| New Zealand A | 30 | 12 | 2 | 16 | West Indies A | 2 | — | 2 | — |
| South Africa | 30 | 12 | 2 | 16 | U-Bix XI | 1 | — | — | 1 |
| Sri Lanka | 28 | 4 | 12 | 12 | West Coast (NI) | 1 | 1 | — | — |
| New South Wales | 24 | 16 | 2 | 6 | D. Reese's XI | 1 | — | 1 | — |
| Nelson | 17 | 9 | 6 | 2* | Minor Associations | 1 | — | 1 | — |
| North Island | 16 | 6 | 5 | 5 | Sir Julien Cahn's XI | 1 | — | — | 1 |
| Bangladesh | 16 | 1 | 15 | — | South Island Army | 1 | 1 | — | — |
| Fiji | 15 | 5 | 8 | 2 | North Island Army | 1 | — | 1 | — |
| South Island | 15 | 4 | 8 | 3 | New Zealand Army | 1 | 1 | — | — |
| New Zealand U23 XI | 12 | — | 9 | 3 | New Zealand Air Force | 1 | — | 1 | — |
| Zimbabwe | 11 | 2 | 4 | 5 | New Zealand Services | 1 | — | — | 1 |
| President's XI | 9 | — | 3 | 6 | Canterbury/Otago | 1 | — | — | 1 |
| NZ Academy XI | 9 | 3 | 3 | 3 | Auckland/Wellington | 1 | — | 1 | — |
| Southland | 8 | 1 | 5 | 2 | ND/CD | 1 | — | — | 1 |
| Taranaki | 8 | 1 | 6 | 1 | Auckland XI | 1 | — | — | 1 |
| Southern | 8 | 4 | 1 | 3 | Otago Invitation XI | 1 | — | 1 | — |
| Sri Lanka A | 8 | — | 6 | 2 | Canterbury XI | 1 | — | — | 1 |
| Northern | 7 | 2 | 1 | 4 | Board XI | 1 | — | 1 | — |
| Central | 7 | 2 | 3 | 2 | Australian Academy XI | 1 | 1 | — | — |
| England A | 7 | 3 | — | 4 | Western Australia | 1 | — | — | 1 |
| New Zealand XI | 7 | 1 | 3 | 3 | **TOTALS** | **5056** | **1650** | **1650** | **1756** |

*\* includes a tie    † includes two ties*

# Highest Match Aggregates

*Runs-Wickets*

| | | | |
|---|---|---|---|
| 1945-18 | Canterbury v Wellington | Christchurch | 1994/95 |
| 1905-40 | Otago v Wellington | Dunedin | 1923/24 |
| 1567-37 | Auckland v Wellington | Auckland | 1936/37 |
| 1554-40 | Wellington v Auckland | Wellington | 1922/23 |
| 1549-34 | Central Districts v Canterbury | New Plymouth | 2009/10 |
| 1549-36 | Auckland v Central Districts | Auckland | 2015/16 |
| 1531-39 | Wellington v Auckland | Wellington | 1923/24 |
| 1521-17 | Auckland v Northern Districts | Auckland | 2013/14 |
| 1513-34 | Central Districts v Otago | Napier | 2006/07 |
| 1511-31 | New Zealand v Bangladesh | Wellington | 2016/17 |
| 1505-25 | New Zealand v India | Auckland | 1989/90 |
| 1501-37 | Canterbury v Otago | Christchurch | 1931/32 |
| 1501-32 | New Zealand v Bangladesh | Hamilton | 2009/10 |
| 1501-31 | Central Districts v Northern Districts | Napier | 2009/10 |
| 1500-32 | Wellington v Canterbury | Wellington | 2019/20 |

# Highest Team Totals

| | | |
|---|---|---|
| 777 | Canterbury v Otago at Christchurch | 1996/97 |
| 752-8 dec | NSW v Otago at Dunedin | 1923/24 |
| 726 | Northern Districts v Canterbury at Rangiora | 2009/10 |
| 715-6 dec | New Zealand v Bangladesh at Hamilton | 2018/19 |
| 693-9 dec | Auckland v Canterbury at Auckland | 1939/40 |
| 680-8 dec | New Zealand v India at Wellington | 2013/14 |
| 671-4 | New Zealand v Sri Lanka at Wellington | 1990/91 |
| 668-7 dec | Auckland v Central Districts at Napier | 2014/15 |
| 663 | Australia v New Zealand at Auckland | 1920/21 |
| 662-5 dec | Auckland v Central Districts at Auckland | 2008/09 |
| 660-5 dec | West Indies v New Zealand at Wellington | 1994/95 |
| 659-6 dec | New Zealand v Pakistan at Christchurch | 2020/21 |
| 658 | Australians v Auckland at Auckland | 1913/14 |
| 658-9 dec | Auckland v Wellington at Auckland | 2012/13 |
| 653-5 dec | MCC v New Zealand at Dunedin | 1935/36 |
| 653 | Australians v Canterbury at Christchurch | 1913/14 |
| 651-9 dec | Otago v Wellington at Dunedin | 2012/13 |
| 650-8 dec | Central Districts v Otago at Napier | 2015/16 |
| 643 | Auckland v Canterbury at Auckland | 1919/20 |
| 642-6 dec | Otago v Central Districts at Dunedin | 2021/22 |
| 635-6 dec | Auckland v Central Districts at Auckland | 2009/10 |
| 627-7 dec | Auckland v Otago at Lincoln | 2006/07 |
| 624 | Otago v Central Districts at Napier | 2006/07 |
| 621-5 dec | South Africa v New Zealand at Auckland | 1998/99 |
| 619-9 dec | New Zealand v India at Napier | 2008/09 |
| 616-5 dec | Pakistan v New Zealand at Auckland | 1988/89 |
| 615-9 dec | New Zealand v England at Mt Maunganui | 2019/20 |
| 614-8 | Wellington v Canterbury at Christchurch | 2006/07 |
| 614-7 dec | Northern Districts v Auckland at Hamilton | 2012/13 |
| 613-7 dec | Canterbury v Wellington at Christchurch | 2006/07 |
| 610-6 dec | Australia v New Zealand at Auckland | 1913/14 |
| 609-9 dec | New Zealand v West Indies at Dunedin | 2013/14 |
| 608-9 dec | Wellington v Northern Districts at Hamilton | 1998/99 |
| 608-9 dec | Northern Districts v Wellington at Lincoln | 2011/12 |
| 602-8 dec | Otago v Canterbury at Dunedin | 1928/29 |
| 601-9 dec | Otago v Canterbury at Christchurch | 2006/07 |

## Most Runs in a Match by One Side

*Runs-Wickets*

| | | | | |
|---|---|---|---|---|
| 1025-20 | 560 & 465 | Wellington v Otago | Dunedin | 1923/24 |
| 973-6 | 498-2d & 475-4 | Wellington v Canterbury | Christchurch | 1994/95 |
| 972-12 | 496 & 476-2d | Canterbury v Wellington | Christchurch | 1994/95 |
| 971-14 | 511-6d & 460-8 | Australia v New Zealand | Wellington | 1973/74 |
| 948-20 | 569 & 379 | Wellington v Auckland | Wellington | 1923/24 |
| 903-17 | 534-9d & 369-8d | Otago v Wellington | Wellington | 2013/14 |

## Lowest Match Aggregates

*completed matches, i.e. not drawn*

*Runs-Wickets*

| | | | |
|---|---|---|---|
| 151-30 | Canterbury v Otago | Christchurch | 1866/67 |
| 153-31 | Otago v Canterbury | Dunedin | 1896/97 |
| 156-30 | Nelson v Wellington | Nelson | 1885/86 |
| 159-31 | Nelson v Wellington | Nelson | 1887/88 |
| 176-32 | Otago v Tasmania | Dunedin | 1883/84 |
| 183-40 | Nelson v Wellington | Nelson | 1883/84 |
| 192-30 | Taranaki v Hawke's Bay | Hawera | 1891/92 |

The lowest aggregates since 1900 are:

*Runs-Wickets*

| | | | |
|---|---|---|---|
| 241-30 | Otago v Southland | Dunedin | 1919/20 |
| 278-40 | Southland v Otago | Invercargill | 1918/19 |
| 295-28 | New Zealand v Australia | Wellington | 1945/46 |

## Lowest Match Aggregates by One Side

| | | | | |
|---|---|---|---|---|
| 55 | 36 & 19 | Wellington v Nelson | Nelson | 1885/86 |
| 57 | 25 & 32 | Canterbury v Otago | Christchurch | 1866/67 |
| 64 | 35 & 29 | Taranaki v Hawke's Bay | Hawera | 1891/92 |
| 72 | 30 & 42 | Wellington v Nelson | Nelson | 1883/84 |
| 76 | 34 & 42 | Canterbury v Otago | Dunedin | 1863/64 |
| 76 | 27 & 49 | Canterbury v Otago | Dunedin | 1896/97 |
| 79 | 31 & 48 | Wellington v Nelson | Nelson | 1887/88 |
| 80 | 51 & 29 | Wellington v Nelson | Nelson | 1879/80 |
| 87 | 40 & 47 | Tasmania v Otago | Dunedin | 1883/84 |
| 95 | 43 & 52 | Otago v Canterbury | Christchurch | 1872/73 |
| 96 | 41 & 55 | Southland v Otago | Invercargill | 1918/19 |
| 96 | 42 & 54 | New Zealand v Australia | Wellington | 1945/46 |
| 97 | 37 & 60 | Wellington v Nelson | Christchurch | 1876/77 |
| 99 | 65 & 34 | Wellington v Canterbury | Wellington | 1886/87 |

## Lowest Team Totals

| | | |
|---|---|---|
| 13 | Auckland v Canterbury at Auckland | 1877/78 |
| | *(included 8 extras)* | |
| 19 | Wellington v Nelson at Nelson | 1885/86 |
| 22 | Wellington v Canterbury at Wellington | 1903/04 |
| 25 | Canterbury v Otago at Christchurch | 1866/67 |
| 26 | New Zealand v England at Auckland | 1954/55 |
| 27 | Canterbury v Otago at Dunedin | 1896/97 |
| 28 | Hawke's Bay v Auckland at Auckland | 1910/11 |
| | *(included 13 extras)* | |
| 29 | Wellington v Nelson at Nelson | 1879/80 |
| 29 | Taranaki v Hawke's Bay at Hawera | 1891/92 |

## Highest Second Innings Totals

| | | | |
|---|---|---|---|
| 680-8 dec | New Zealand v India | Wellington | 2013/14 |
| 671-4 | New Zealand v Sri Lanka | Wellington | 1990/91 |
| 602-8 | Otago v Canterbury | Dunedin | 1928/29 |
| 598 | Auckland v Wellington | Wellington | 2015/16 |
| 589 | Otago v Canterbury | Christchurch | 1931/32 |
| 585-4 dec | New Zealand v Sri Lanka | Christchurch | 2018/19 |
| 575-7 dec | Wellington v Otago | Wellington | 1951/52 |
| 571-8 | Otago v Central Districts | Napier | 1995/96 |
| 551-5 dec | Canterbury v Central Districts | New Plymouth | 2009/10 |
| 539 | Auckland v Otago | Dunedin | 1926/27 |
| 537 | Auckland v Canterbury | Christchurch | 1930/31 |
| 537 | New Zealand v England | Wellington | 1983/84 |
| 533-6 dec | Northern Districts v Otago | Hamilton | 2012/13 |
| 531-7 dec | Central Districts v Northern Districts | Napier | 2009/10 |
| 526-8 dec | Canterbury v Wellington | Wellington | 1931/32 |
| 524-5 dec | New Zealand v Sri Lanka | Wellington | 2014/15 |
| 519 | Canterbury v Wellington | Christchurch | 1930/31 |
| 517 | Central Districts v Otago | Napier | 2009/10 |
| 511-8 dec | Australia v New Zealand | Hamilton | 2009/10 |
| 507 | West Indies v New Zealand | Dunedin | 2013/14 |

## Highest Fourth Innings Totals

| | | | |
|---|---|---|---|
| 495 | lost 145 runs | Otago v Wellington | Dunedin | 1923/24 |
| 475-4 | and won | Wellington v Canterbury | Christchurch | 1994/95 |
| 474 | lost 27 runs | Otago v Northern Districts | Dunedin | 2014/15 |
| 473-6 | and won | Canterbury v Auckland | Christchurch | 1930/31 |
| 459 | lost 10 runs | Wellington v Canterbury | Rangiora | 2013/14 |
| 458 | lost 276 runs | Auckland v Wellington | Wellington | 1927/28 |
| 453-8 | and won | Northern Districts v Wellington | Wellington | 1995/96 |
| 451 | lost 98 runs | New Zealand v England | Christchurch | 2001/02 |
| 450-7 | and won | Central Districts v Canterbury | New Plymouth | 2008/09 |
| 445-1 | and won | Central Districts v Wellington | Wellington | 2009/10 |
| 431 | lost 121 runs | New Zealand v England | Napier | 2007/08 |
| 429-8 | and won | Northern Districts v Central Districts | Lincoln | 2006/07 |
| 411-4 | and won | Northern Districts v Central Districts | Napier | 2009/10 |
| 409-4 | and won | Auckland v Northern Districts | Auckland | 2013/14 |
| 400-9 | and won | Northern Districts v Central Districts | Napier | 2004/05 |

## Highest Fourth Innings Totals without Loss for Victory

| | | | |
|---|---|---|---|
| 226-0 | Canterbury v Otago | Christchurch | 1948/49 |
| 175-0 | Otago v Central Districts | Masterton | 1971/72 |
| 174-0 | Otago v Northern Districts | Alexandra | 1985/86 |
| 147-0 | Wellington v Otago | Dunedin | 2005/06 |
| 138-0 | Auckland v Otago | Auckland | 1937/38 |
| 130-0 | Wellington v Otago | Wellington | 1921/22 |
| 130-0 | Canterbury v Auckland | Christchurch | 1951/52 |

# Large Victories

### BY AN INNINGS AND

| | | | |
|---|---|---|---|
| 364 runs | Sims' Australian XI defeated Canterbury | Christchurch | 1913/14 |
| 358 runs | Australia defeated New Zealand | Wellington | 1904/05 |
| 356 runs | Australia defeated Otago | Dunedin | 1949/50 |
| 354 runs | Auckland defeated Hawke's Bay | Auckland | 1920/21 |
| 332 runs | Wellington defeated Canterbury | Wellington | 1925/26 |
| 327 runs | NSW defeated Otago | Dunedin | 1923/24 |
| 322 runs | Wellington defeated Hawkes Bay | Wellington | 1905/06 |
| 322 runs | West Indies defeated New Zealand | Wellington | 1994/95 |
| 301 runs | New Zealand defeated Zimbabwe | Napier | 2011/12 |

### BY A RUNS MARGIN

| | | | |
|---|---|---|---|
| 512 runs | Wellington defeated Auckland | Wellington | 1925/26 |
| 446 runs | Wellington defeated Otago | Wellington | 1926/27 |
| 438 runs | Auckland defeated Wellington | Auckland | 1934/35 |
| 425 runs | Central Districts defeated Otago | Alexandra | 2001/02 |
| 423 runs | New Zealand defeated Sri Lanka | Christchurch | 2018/19 |
| 395 runs | Northern Districts defeated Wellington | Hamilton | 2014/15 |
| 382 runs | Auckland defeated Canterbury | Christchurch | 1920/21 |
| 365 runs | Wellington defeated Auckland | Wellington | 1923/24 |
| 355 runs | Wellington defeated Canterbury | Christchurch | 1926/27 |

# Tied Matches

| | | |
|---|---|---|
| Wellington v Nelson | Wellington | 1873/74 |
| New Zealand v T.N. Pearce's XI | Scarborough | 1958 |
| Central Districts v England XI | New Plymouth | 1977/78 |
| Victoria v New Zealand | Melbourne | 1982/83 |
| Wellington v Canterbury | Wellington | 1988/89 |

# Close Finishes

### VICTORY BY 1 WICKET

| | | |
|---|---|---|
| Canterbury defeated Tasmania | Christchurch | 1883/84 |
| Otago defeated Canterbury | Christchurch | 1890/91 |
| Wellington defeated Nelson | Nelson | 1891/92 |
| Auckland defeated Wellington | Wellington | 1893/94 |
| Canterbury defeated Wellington | Wellington | 1899/00 |
| Auckland defeated Wellington | Wellington | 1911/12 |
| Canterbury defeated Auckland | Auckland | 1914/15 |
| Wellington defeated Otago | Wellington | 1924/25 |
| Auckland defeated Otago | Auckland | 1946/47 |
| Fiji defeated Wellington | Wellington | 1947/48 |
| Otago defeated Wellington | Dunedin | 1948/49 |
| Auckland defeated Canterbury | Auckland | 1950/51 |
| Central Districts defeated Wellington | Wellington | 1951/52 |
| Otago defeated Wellington | Dunedin | 1952/53 |
| MCC defeated Canterbury | Christchurch | 1960/61 |
| Auckland defeated Canterbury | Christchurch | 1963/64 |
| Wellington defeated NZ Under-23 XI | Wellington | 1965/66 |
| Canterbury defeated Auckland | Auckland | 1974/75 |
| Northern Districts defeated Central Districts | Gisborne | 1979/80 |
| New Zealand defeated West Indies | Dunedin | 1979/80 |
| Otago defeated Wellington | Alexandra | 1980/81 |
| Otago defeated Canterbury | Christchurch | 1990/91 |

| | | |
|---|---|---|
| Otago defeated Wellington | Dunedin | 1991/92 |
| Central Districts defeated Auckland | Auckland | 1994/95 |
| Canterbury defeated Northern Districts | Christchurch | 1994/95 |
| Southern defeated Central | Wanganui | 1997/98 |
| Wellington defeated Northern Districts | Hamilton | 2001/02 |
| Northern Districts defeated Central Districts | Napier | 2004/05 |
| Central Districts defeated Canterbury | New Plymouth | 2009/10 |
| Central Districts defeated Northern Districts | Napier | 2018/19 |
| Auckland defeated Northern Districts | Auckland | 2019/20 |

**VICTORY BY 10 RUNS OR LESS**

| | | | |
|---|---|---|---|
| 1 run | Northern Districts defeated Central Districts | Rotorua | 1989/90 |
| 2 runs | Auckland defeated Canterbury | Auckland | 1903/04 |
| | Wellington defeated Canterbury | Wellington | 1935/36 |
| 3 runs | Otago defeated Wellington | Wellington | 1953/54 |
| | Central Districts defeated Wellington | Wellington | 1970/71 |
| | Central Districts defeated Otago | New Plymouth | 1970/71 |
| | Canterbury defeated Central Districts | Napier | 1979/80 |
| | Auckland defeated Otago | Dunedin | 2004/05 |
| 4 runs | Auckland defeated Nelson | Nelson | 1882/83 |
| | Canterbury defeated Otago | Christchurch | 1882/83 |
| | Auckland defeated Wellington | Auckland | 1977/78 |
| | New Zealand defeated Pakistan | Abu Dhabi | 2018/19 |
| 5 runs | Central Districts defeated Otago | New Plymouth | 1953/54 |
| | Northern Districts defeated Central Districts | Napier | 1976/77 |
| 6 runs | Canterbury defeated Tasmania | Christchurch | 1883/84 |
| | Auckland defeated Canterbury | Auckland | 1952/53 |
| | South Island XI defeated North Island XI | Wellington | 1957/58 |
| | Northern Districts defeated Central Districts | Hamilton | 1977/78 |
| | Northern Districts defeated Otago | Dunedin | 1978/79 |
| | Central Districts defeated Northern Districts | Napier | 1988/89 |
| | Canterbury defeated Auckland | Auckland | 2006/07 |
| 7 runs | Auckland defeated Canterbury | Christchurch | 1873/74 |
| 8 runs | Auckland defeated Wellington | Wellington | 1945/46 |
| | Auckland defeated Northern Districts | Auckland | 1963/64 |
| | Central Districts defeated Auckland | Napier | 1982/83 |
| | Auckland defeated Central Districts | Auckland | 1999/00 |
| | Canterbury defeated Northern Districts | Rangiora | 2017/18 |
| 9 runs | Central Districts defeated Auckland | Nelson | 1983/84 |
| 10 runs | Northern Districts defeated Canterbury | Hamilton | 1960/61 |
| | Wellington defeated Central Districts | New Plymouth | 1973/74 |
| | Otago defeated Auckland | Dunedin | 1975/76 |
| | Canterbury defeated Wellington | Rangiora | 2013/14 |
| | Auckland defeated Otago | Dunedin | 2015/16 |
| | Canterbury defeated Auckland | Rangiora | 2016/17 |

## Victory after Follow-on

| | | | |
|---|---|---|---|
| Auckland (180 & 302) | beat Canterbury (392 & 84) | Auckland | 1952/53 |
| Northern Districts (165 & 275) | beat Otago (320-9d & 105) | Dunedin | 1961/62 |
| Auckland (69 & 303) | beat Northern Districts (224 & 140) | Auckland | 1963/64 |
| Canterbury (166 & 360) | beat Auckland (351-9d & 149) | Christchurch | 1973/74 |
| Auckland (101 & 278) | beat Otago (268 & 108) | Dunedin | 2004/05 |

# Longest Matches in New Zealand
*before 1900*

### FOUR DAYS

| | | |
|---|---|---|
| Otago v Canterbury | Dunedin | 1875/76 |
| Canterbury v Tasmania | Christchurch | 1883/84 |
| Otago v Canterbury | Dunedin | 1884/85 |

*since 1900*

### SIX DAYS

| | | |
|---|---|---|
| New Zealand v England | Christchurch | 1974/75 |
| New Zealand v India | Christchurch | 1975/76 |
| * New Zealand v England | Auckland | 1977/78 |
| New Zealand v Pakistan | Napier | 1978/79 |
| New Zealand v West Indies | Auckland | 1979/80 |
| New Zealand v India | Christchurch | 1980/81 |

*\* the only match where play took place on all six days*
*The other instances involved the rest day being used after a day's play was lost*

### FIVE DAYS

| | | |
|---|---|---|
| Canterbury v Otago | Christchurch | 1911/12 |
| Canterbury v Wellington | Christchurch | 1922/23 |
| Otago v Wellington | Dunedin | 1923/24 |
| Canterbury v Auckland | Christchurch | 1924/25 |
| Wellington v Otago | Wellington | 1926/27 |
| Northern Districts v Auckland | Taupo | 1999/00 |
| Auckland v Wellington | Auckland | 2004/05 |
| Wellington v Central Districts | Wellington | 2005/06 |
| Northern Districts v Canterbury | Hamilton | 2006/07 |
| Wellington v Canterbury | Wellington | 2007/08 |
| Auckland v Central Districts | Lincoln | 2008/09 |

*All other matches of five days duration since 1926/27 have been test matches. A complete list of these up to 1993/94 is on pages 288 and 289 of the 1994 Almanack. The 1998/99 Shell Trophy final between Central Districts and Otago at Napier was scheduled for five days but completed in three.*

# Matches Abandoned without a Ball Being Bowled
*these matches are not included in any first-class records*

| | | |
|---|---|---|
| Hawke's Bay v Australia | Napier | 1909/10 |
| Central Districts v Northern Districts | Napier | 1970/71 |
| † Wellington v Australia | Wellington | 1973/74 |
| Central Districts v Australia | Napier | 1973/74 |
| † New Zealand v Pakistan | Dunedin | 1988/89 |
| † New Zealand President's XI v Australia | Nelson | 1992/93 |
| New Zealand A v Sri Lanka | Gisborne | 1996/97 |
| Wellington v Canterbury | Wellington | 1996/97 |
| † Northern v Pakistan A | Auckland | 1998/99 |
| † New Zealand v India | Dunedin | 1998/99 |
| Wellington v Canterbury | Wellington | 2010/11 |
| Wellington v Central Districts | Wellington | 2010/11 |
| New Zealand v Bangladesh | Christchurch | 2018/19 |
| Wellington v Canterbury | Wellington | 2018/19 |
| Otago v Auckland | Dunedin | 2019/20 |
| Central Districts v Auckland | Nelson | 2020/21 |
| Northern Districts v Auckland | Whangarei | 2021/22 |

*† replaced with a limited-overs match*
*The match between New Zealand A and Pakistan at Nelson, 2016/17 was abandoned without any play but as the toss had been made it counts as an official game and is included in all records.*

## Matches Completed in One Day

| | | |
|---|---|---|
| Otago v Canterbury | Dunedin | 11. 2.1868 |
| Wellington v Auckland | Wellington | 29.11.1874 |
| Nelson v Wellington | Nelson | 26.12.1887 |
| Otago v Auckland | Dunedin | 27.12.1889 |
| Hawke's Bay v Taranaki | Napier | 9. 1.1892 |
| Auckland v New South Wales* | Auckland | 20. 1.1894 |
| Ireland v New Zealand | Dublin | 11. 9.1937 |
| Auckland v Fiji† | Auckland | 9. 3.1954 |

*\* no play on first day       † after no play on first two days and three declarations on third*

## Most Extras in an Innings

| Extras | B | LB | NB | W | | | | |
|---|---|---|---|---|---|---|---|---|
| 67 | 26 | 34 | 6 | 1 | New Zealand (523) | v England | Lord's | 2015 |
| † 66 | 2 | 9 | 54 | 1 | NZ Academy XI (459-8d) | v Pakistan A | Lincoln | 1998/99 |
| 64 | 27 | 8 | 12 | 17 | New Zealand (659-6d) | v Pakistan | Christchurch | 2020/21 |
| 62 | 25 | 21 | 13 | 3 | England (562) | v New Zealand | Leeds | 2004 |
| † 60 | 18 | 17 | 20 | 5 | Central Districts (460-4d) | v Wellington | Wellington | 1997/98 |
| 58 | 41 | 14 | 3 | — | Wellington (380-5) | v Auckland | Wellington | 1929/30 |
| † 58 | 6 | 14 | 30 | 8 | Auckland (322-4d) | v Wellington | Auckland | 1993/94 |
| 58 | 4 | 12 | 33 | 9 | New Zealand (563) | v Pakistan | Hamilton | 2003/04 |
| 57 | 31 | 16 | 10 | — | New Zealand (387) | v England | Auckland | 1929/30 |
| 54 | 35 | 14 | 1 | 4 | Auckland (200-8d) | v Wellington | Auckland | 1973/74 |
| 54 | 5 | 16 | 33 | — | New Zealand A (597-9d) | v Sri Lanka A | Queenstown | 2003/04 |
| 53 | 26 | 10 | 17 | — | Canterbury (473-6) | v Auckland | Christchurch | 1930/31 |
| † 53 | 4 | 2 | 46 | 1 | Wellington (498-2d) | v Canterbury | Christchurch | 1994/95 |
| 52 | 40 | 11 | — | 1 | Wellington (370) | v Canterbury | Christchurch | 1922/23 |
| 52 | 12 | 7 | 33 | — | New Zealand (468) | v Pakistan | Karachi | 1976/77 |
| 52 | 1 | 27 | 33 | 1 | Auckland (423-7d) | v Wellington | Wellington | 1992/93 |
| † 52 | 1 | 15 | 32 | 4 | Canterbury (537) | v Central Districts | Blenheim | 1996/97 |
| 52 | 21 | 28 | 3 | 1 | New Zealand (630-6d) | v India | Mohali | 2003/04 |
| 52 | 7 | 9 | 28 | 8 | Central Districts (499) | v Canterbury | N.Plymouth | 2004/05 |
| 52 | 7 | 15 | 7 | 23 | Central Districts (476) | v Otago | Napier | 2012/13 |
| 51 | 10 | 11 | 30 | — | Auckland (369) | v West Indies | Auckland | 1999/00 |
| 51 | 5 | 23 | 13 | 10 | New Zealand (393) | v Bangladesh | Wellington | 2007/08 |
| 51 | 7 | 16 | 15 | 13 | Northern Districts (334) | v Auckland | Auckland | 2016/17 |
| 50 | 26 | 12 | 11 | 1 | Otago (602-8d) | v Canterbury | Dunedin | 1928/29 |
| 50 | 13 | 24 | 11 | 2 | Wellington (356) | v Canterbury | Wellington | 1981/82 |
| † 50 | 3 | 11 | 36 | — | Southern (554) | v Pakistan A | Christchurch | 1998/99 |
| 50 | 12 | 22 | 9 | 7 | Northern Districts (438) | v Auckland | Auckland | 2019/20 |

*† no balls counted as two extras, regardless of whether runs were scored from the bat*

# INDIVIDUAL RECORDS
## BATTING
### Highest Individual Scores

| | | | | |
|---|---|---|---|---|
| 385 | Sutcliffe B. | Otago v Canterbury | Christchurch | 1952/53 |
| 355 | Sutcliffe B. | Otago v Auckland | Dunedin | 1949/50 |
| 338* | Blunt R.C. | Otago v Canterbury | Christchurch | 1931/32 |
| 336* | Hammond W.R. | England v New Zealand | Auckland | 1932/33 |
| 334 | Brownlie D.G. | Northern Districts v Central Districts | New Plymouth | 2014/15 |
| 327* | Conway D.P. | Wellington v Canterbury | Wellington | 2019/20 |
| 317 | Rutherford K.R. | New Zealand v D.B. Close's XI | Scarborough | 1986 |
| 316* | Papps M.H.W. | Wellington v Auckland | Wellington | 2017/18 |
| 306 | Richardson M.H. | New Zealand v Zimbabwe A | Kwekwe | 2000/01 |
| 302 | McCullum B.B. | New Zealand v India | Wellington | 2013/14 |
| 301* | Fulton P.G. | Canterbury v Auckland | Christchurch | 2002/03 |
| 299 | Crowe M.D. | New Zealand v Sri Lanka | Wellington | 1990/91 |
| 296 | Reid J.R. | Wellington v Northern Districts | Wellington | 1962/63 |
| 293 | Trumper V.T. | Sims' Australian XI v Canterbury | Christchurch | 1913/14 |
| 290 | Carson W.N. | Auckland v Otago | Dunedin | 1936/37 |
| 290 | Taylor L.R.P.L. | New Zealand v Australia | Perth | 2015/16 |
| 284* | Williamson K.S. | Northern Districts v Wellington | Lincoln | 2011/12 |
| 284 | Woodfull W.M. | Australia v New Zealand | Auckland | 1927/28 |
| 283 | Reid J.R. | Wellington v Otago | Wellington | 1951/52 |
| 281 | Munro C. | Auckland v Central Districts | Napier | 2014/15 |
| 275* | Cullinan D.J. | South Africa v New Zealand | Auckland | 1998/99 |
| 275 | Sutcliffe B. | Otago v Auckland | Auckland | 1950/51 |
| 274* | Fleming S.P. | New Zealand v Sri Lanka | Colombo | 2002/03 |
| 271 | Javed Miandad | Pakistan v New Zealand | Auckland | 1988/89 |
| 269* | Munro C. | Auckland v Wellington | Auckland | 2012/13 |
| 268 | Sinclair M.S. | New Zealand A v South Africa A | Potchefstroom | 2004/05 |
| 268 | McIntosh T.G. | Auckland v Canterbury | Auckland | 2007/08 |
| 267* | Young B.A. | New Zealand v Sri Lanka | Dunedin | 1996/97 |
| 267 | de Silva P.A. | Sri Lanka v New Zealand | Wellington | 1990/91 |
| 265 | Bell M.D. | Wellington v Central Districts | Napier | 2007/08 |
| 264* | Latham T.W.M. | New Zealand v Sri Lanka | Wellington | 2018/19 |
| 264 | Sutcliffe B. | Otago v Central Districts | Dunedin | 1959/60 |
| 262 | Fleming S.P. | New Zealand v South Africa | Cape Town | 2005/06 |
| 261 | Latham T.W.M. | Canterbury v Central Districts | Napier | 2013/14 |
| 259 | Turner G.M. | New Zealand v Guyana | Georgetown | 1971/72 |
| 259 | Turner G.M. | New Zealand v West Indies | Georgetown | 1971/72 |
| 258 | Nurse S.M. | West Indies v New Zealand | Christchurch | 1968/69 |
| 256 | Smith S.G. | Auckland v Canterbury | Auckland | 1919/20 |
| 256 | Raval J.A. | Auckland v Central Districts | Auckland | 2008/09 |
| 255* | McGlew D.J. | South Africa v New Zealand | Wellington | 1952/53 |
| 254* | Vance R.H. | Wellington v Northern Districts | Wellington | 1988/89 |
| 252 | Latham T.W.M. | New Zealand v Bangladesh | Christchurch | 2021/22 |
| 251* | Harris C.Z. | Canterbury v Central Districts | Rangiora | 1996/97 |
| 251 | Williamson K.S. | New Zealand v West Indies | Hamilton | 2020/21 |
| 250 | Walters K.D. | Australia v New Zealand | Christchurch | 1976/77 |
| 247* | Chappell G.S. | Australia v New Zealand | Wellington | 1973/74 |
| 247 | Ingram P.J. | Central Districts v Northern Districts | Hamilton | 2008/09 |
| 246 | Brathwaite K.C. | West Indies v New Zealand A | Queenstown | 2020/21 |
| 245* | Ingram P.J. | Central Districts v Wellington | Wellington | 2009/10 |
| 244 | Smith B.S. | Central Districts v Otago | Napier | 2015/16 |

| 243* | Sinclair M.S. | Central Districts v Otago | Napier | 2007/08 |
|---|---|---|---|---|
| 243 | Sutcliffe B. | New Zealand v Essex | Southend | 1949 |
| 242* | Crowe M.D. | New Zealand v South Australia | Adelaide | 1985/86 |
| 242* | Williamson K.S. | New Zealand v Sri Lanka | Wellington | 2014/15 |
| 242 | Crowe M.D. | Central Districts v Otago | New Plymouth | 1989/90 |
| 241* | Latham T.W.M. | Canterbury v Wellington | Wellington | 2013/14 |
| 241 | Horne M.J. | Otago v Auckland | Auckland | 1997/98 |
| 241 | Flynn D.R. | Northern Districts v Otago | Hamilton | 2010/11 |
| 239 | Dowling G.T. | New Zealand v India | Christchurch | 1967/68 |
| 239 | Rutherford H.D. | Otago v Wellington | Dunedin | 2011/12 |
| 239 | Voges A.C. | Australia v New Zealand | Wellington | 2015/16 |
| 238 | Williamson K.S. | New Zealand v Pakistan | Christchurch | 2020/21 |
| 237* | Latham R.T. | Canterbury v Northern Districts | Rotorua | 1990/91 |
| 236 | Ryder J.D. | Wellington v Central Districts | Palmerston North | 2004/05 |
| 235 | Marshall J.A.H. | Northern Districts v Canterbury | Christchurch | 2001/02 |
| 234* | Kelly N.F. | Otago v Central Districts | Dunedin | 2021/22 |
| 230* | Sutcliffe B. | New Zealand v India | New Delhi | 1955/56 |
| 227* | Stewart S.L. | Canterbury v Central Districts | New Plymouth | 2009/10 |
| 227 | Hammond W.R. | England v New Zealand | Christchurch | 1932/33 |
| 226* | Rutherford K.R. | Otago v India | Dunedin | 1989/90 |
| 226* | Carter L.J. | Canterbury v Wellington | Rangiora | 2019/20 |
| 226 | Hastings B.F. | Canterbury v NZ Under 23 XI | Christchurch | 1964/65 |
| 226 | Hay G.R. | Central Districts v Otago | Alexandra | 2018/19 |
| 226 | Root J.E. | England v New Zealand | Hamilton | 2019/20 |
| 225* | Blunt R.C. | New Zealand v Gentlemen | Eastbourne | 1931 |
| 225 | McCullum B.B. | New Zealand v India | Hyderabad | 2010/11 |
| 224 | Vincent L. | New Zealand v Sri Lanka | Wellington | 2004/05 |
| 224 | McCullum B.B. | New Zealand v India | Auckland | 2013/14 |
| 224 | Latham T.W.M. | Canterbury v Wellington | Wellington | 2019/20 |
| 223* | Turner G.M. | New Zealand v West Indies | Kingston | 1971/72 |
| 223 | Astle N.J. | New Zealand v Queensland | Brisbane | 2001/02 |
| 223 | O'Donnell R.R. | Auckland v Canterbury | Auckland | 2021/22 |
| 222* | Midlane F.A. | Wellington v Otago | Wellington | 1914/15 |
| 222 | Rutherford I.A. | Otago v Central Districts | New Plymouth | 1978/79 |
| 222 | Astle N.J. | New Zealand v England | Christchurch | 2001/02 |
| 221* | Fulton P.G. | Canterbury v Otago | Dunedin | 2004/05 |
| 221 | Macartney C.G. | NSW v Canterbury | Christchurch | 1923/24 |
| 221 | Blunt R.C. | Otago v Canterbury | Dunedin | 1928/29 |
| 220* | Woodcock L.J. | Wellington v Central Districts | Wellington | 2009/10 |
| 219 | Bell M.D. | Wellington v Northern Districts | Hamilton | 1998/99 |
| 219 | Franklin J.E.C. | Wellington v Auckland | Auckland | 2008/09 |
| 218 | Bravo D.M. | West Indies v New Zealand | Dunedin | 2013/14 |
| 217* | Taylor L.R.P.L. | New Zealand v West Indies | Dunedin | 2013/14 |
| 217 | Taylor L.R.P.L. | Central Districts v Otago | Napier | 2006/07 |
| 217 | Shakib Al Hasan | Bangladesh v New Zealand | Wellington | 2016/17 |
| 216 | Fletcher K.W.R. | England v New Zealand | Auckland | 1974/75 |
| 216 | Bell M.D. | Wellington v Auckland | Auckland | 1997/98 |
| 216* | Chanderpaul S. | West Indies v New Zealand A | Taupo | 1999/00 |
| 214* | Kortlang H.H.L. | Wellington v Auckland | Wellington | 1925/26 |
| 214* | Booth B.C. | Australia B v Central Districts | Palmerston North | 1966/67 |
| 214 | Sinclair M.S. | New Zealand v West Indies | Wellington | 1999/00 |
| 213 | Murray B.A.G. | Wellington v Otago | Dunedin | 1968/69 |
| 213 | Trimble S.C. | Australia B v New Zealand | Wellington | 1969/70 |
| 213 | Greenidge C.G. | West Indies v New Zealand | Auckland | 1986/87 |
| 212* | Woodfull W.M. | Victoria v Canterbury | Christchurch | 1924/25 |
| 212* | Richardson M.H. | New Zealand A v Sussex | Hove | 2000 |

| 212* | Kelly D.P. | Central Districts v Canterbury | Blenheim | 2000/01 |
|---|---|---|---|---|
| 212* | Styris S.B. | Northern Districts v Otago | Hamilton | 2001/02 |
| 212 | Hiddleston J.S. | Wellington v Canterbury | Wellington | 1925/26 |
| 212 | Dempster C.S. | New Zealand v Essex | Leyton | 1931 |
| 211* | Hick G.A. | Northern Districts v Auckland | Auckland | 1988/89 |
| 211* | Gibbs H.H. | South Africa v New Zealand | Christchurch | 1998/99 |
| 211 | Warner P.F. | Lord Hawke's XI v Otago | Dunedin | 1902/03 |
| 211 | Wallace W.M. | Auckland v Canterbury | Auckland | 1939/40 |
| 210 | Brodie J.M. | Wellington v Auckland | Auckland | 2011/12 |
| 210 | Worker G.H. | Central Districts v Wellington | Nelson | 2015/16 |
| 210 | McClure K.J. | Canterbury v Auckland | Rangiora | 2017/18 |
| 209* | Brown S.W. | Auckland v Canterbury | Christchurch | 1990/91 |
| 209* | Horne M.J. | Auckland v Northern Districts | Auckland | 2003/04 |
| 209* | Fulton P.G. | Canterbury v Central Districts | Christchurch | 2014/15 |
| 209 | White D.J. | Northern Districts v Central Districts | Hamilton | 1985/86 |
| 209 | Horne P.A. | Auckland v Northern Districts | Auckland | 1988/89 |
| 209 | Raval J.A. | Northern Districts v Central Districts | Whangarei | 2021/22 |
| 208* | Sutcliffe B. | North Island v South Island | Dunedin | 1947/48 |
| 208* | Bruce T.C. | Central Districts v Northern Districts | Whangarei | 2021/22 |
| 208 | Franklin J.E.C. | Wellington v Auckland | Wellington | 2005/06 |
| 207* | How J.M. | Central Districts v Otago | Nelson | 2013/14 |
| 207 | Hart R.T. | Central Districts v Wellington | Wellington | 1985/86 |
| 207 | Kitchen A.K. | Otago v Northern Districts | Dunedin | 2016/17 |
| 206* | Papps M.H.W. | Wellington v Canterbury | Rangiora | 2012/13 |
| 206 | Page M.L. | Canterbury v Wellington | Wellington | 1931/32 |
| 206 | Donnelly M.P. | New Zealand v England | Lord's | 1949 |
| 206 | Dowling G.T. | Canterbury v Wellington | Christchurch | 1962/63 |
| 206 | Harris C.Z | Canterbury v Central Districts | Blenheim | 1996/97 |
| 205* | Lloyd C.H. | West Indies v South Island | Dunedin | 1968/69 |
| 205* | McSweeney E.B. | Wellington v Central Districts | Levin | 1987/88 |
| 205 | McIntosh T.G. | Auckland v Otago | Lincoln | 2006/07 |
| 205 | Watling B-J. | New Zealand v England | Mt Maunganui | 2019/20 |
| 204* | Sinclair M.S. | New Zealand v Pakistan | Christchurch | 2000/01 |
| 204* | Gill S. | India A v New Zealand A | Christchurch | 2019/20 |
| 204* | Bruce T.C. | Central Districts v Auckland | Napier | 2021/22 |
| 204 | Cox A. | Canterbury v Otago | Christchurch | 1925/26 |
| 204 | Hiddleston J.S. | Wellington v Auckland | Wellington | 1925/26 |
| 204 | Scott V.J. | Auckland v Otago | Dunedin | 1947/48 |
| 204 | Patel D.N. | Auckland v Northern Districts | Auckland | 1991/92 |
| 203* | Burnett G.P. | Wellington v Northern Districts | Hamilton | 1991/92 |
| 203* | Sinclair M.S. | Central Districts v Northern Districts | Wanganui | 1998/99 |
| 203* | Broom N.T. | Otago v Northern Districts | Queenstown | 2010/11 |
| 203* | Woodcock L.J. | Wellington v Auckland | Auckland | 2016/17 |
| 203* | Conway D.P. | Wellington v Otago | Wellington | 2018/19 |
| 203 | Scott V.J. | New Zealand v Combined Services | Gillingham | 1949 |
| 203 | Reid J.R. | New Zealand v Western Province | Cape Town | 1961/62 |
| 203 | Edgar B.A. | Young New Zealand v Zimbabwe | Bulawayo | 1984/85 |
| 203 | Parlane M.E. | Wellington v Auckland | Auckland | 2004/05 |
| 203 | Cachopa C. | Auckland v Wellington | Auckland | 2013/14 |
| 203 | Sangakkara K.C. | Sri Lanka v New Zealand | Wellington | 2014/15 |
| 203 | Schmulian B.D. † | Central Districts v Northern Districts | Mt Maunganui | 2017/18 |
| 202* | Congdon B.E. | Central Districts v Otago | Nelson | 1968/69 |
| 202* | Greatbatch M.J. | Central Districts v Otago | Palmerston North | 1988/89 |
| 202* | Hay G.R. | Central Districts v Canterbury | Rangiora | 2013/14 |
| 202* | Raval J.A. | Auckland v Otago | Auckland | 2015/16 |
| 202 | Turner G.M. | New Zealand v President's XI | Montego Bay | 1971/72 |

| 202 | Austen M.H. | Wellington v Central Districts | Wanganui | 1993/94 |
| 202 | Greatbatch M.J. | Central Districts v Northern Districts | Rotorua | 1995/96 |
| 202 | Fleming S.P. | New Zealand v Bangladesh | Chittagong | 2004/05 |
| 202 | McCullum B.B. | New Zealand v Pakistan | Sharjah | 2014/15 |
| 201* | Hart M.N. | Northern Districts v Auckland | Auckland | 2002/03 |
| 201* | Smith B.F. | Central Districts v Canterbury | New Plymouth | 2001/02 |
| 201 | Reid J.R. | Otago v Canterbury | Dunedin | 1957/58 |
| 201 | Sutcliffe B. | Otago v Northern Districts | Hamilton | 1960/61 |
| 201 | Mushtaq Mohammad | Pakistan v New Zealand | Dunedin | 1972/73 |
| 201 | Jones R.A. | Auckland v West Indies | Auckland | 2008/09 |
| 201 | Ryder J.D. | New Zealand v India | Napier | 2008/09 |
| 201 | Hopkins G.J. | Auckland v Central Districts | Auckland | 2009/10 |
| 201 | Cleaver D. | Central Districts v Northern Districts | Napier | 2019/20 |
| 200* | MacLaren A.C. | MCC v New Zealand | Wellington | 1922/23 |
| 200* | Bardsley W. | NSW v Auckland | Auckland | 1923/24 |
| 200* | Thorpe G.P. | England v New Zealand | Christchurch | 2001/02 |
| 200* | Williamson K.S. | New Zealand v Bangladesh | Hamilton | 2018/19 |
| 200 | Lawson R.A. | Otago v Central Districts | Napier | 1995/96 |
| 200 | Taylor L.R.P.L. | New Zealand v Bangladesh | Wellington | 2018/19 |
| 200 | Conway D.P. | New Zealand v England | Lord's | 2021 |
| 200 | Cooper H.R. | Northern Districts v Otago | Alexandra | 2021/22 |

† *on first-class debut*

## Most Runs in a Season in New Zealand

| | | M | I | NO | HS | Runs | Ave | 100 |
|---|---|---|---|---|---|---|---|---|
| Crowe M.D. | 1986/87 | 11 | 21 | 3 | 175* | 1676 | 93.11 | 8 |
| Fulton P.G. | 2012/13 | 12 | 23 | 2 | 136 | 1249 | 59.47 | 5 |
| Turner G.M. | 1975/76 | 11 | 20 | 4 | 177* | 1244 | 77.75 | 5 |
| Hick G.A. | 1988/89 | 8 | 16 | 3 | 211* | 1228 | 94.46 | 6 |
| Popli B. | 2015/16 | 10 | 17 | 0 | 172 | 1149 | 67.58 | 3 |
| Bell M.D. | 2000/01 | 13 | 21 | 0 | 134 | 1092 | 52.00 | 6 |
| Rutherford H.D. | 2012/13 | 13 | 23 | 0 | 171 | 1077 | 46.82 | 2 |
| Crowe J.J. | 1991/92 | 10 | 19 | 2 | 142* | 1063 | 62.52 | 4 |
| Brownlie D.G. | 2012/13 | 16 | 28 | 2 | 135* | 1057 | 40.65 | 4 |
| Vance R.H. | 1988/89 | 10 | 18 | 2 | 254* | 1037 | 64.81 | 4 |
| Richardson M.H. | 2000/01 | 11 | 19 | 2 | 166 | 1035 | 60.88 | 2 |
| Wright J.G. | 1986/87 | 11 | 21 | 2 | 192 | 1019 | 53.63 | 3 |
| Bell M.D. | 2007/08 | 12 | 21 | 2 | 265 | 1016 | 53.47 | 3 |
| Raval J.A. | 2015/16 | 10 | 19 | 2 | 202* | 1016 | 59.76 | 4 |
| Papps M.H.W. | 2006/07 | 7 | 11 | 0 | 188 | 1005 | 91.36 | 4 |
| Sinclair M.S. | 1999/00 | 14 | 26 | 2 | 214 | 1004 | 41.83 | 3 |

## Most Runs in a Season for New Zealand

| | | M | I | NO | HS | Runs | Ave | 100 |
|---|---|---|---|---|---|---|---|---|
| Sutcliffe B. | 1949 | 29 | 49 | 5 | 243 | 2627 | 59.70 | 7 |
| Donnelly M.P. | 1949 | 29 | 45 | 8 | 206 | 2287 | 61.81 | 5 |
| Reid J.R. | *1961/62 | 20 | 36 | 2 | 203 | 2083 | 61.26 | 7 |

* *includes South Africa & Australia*

# Most Runs in Season of First-class Debut

| | | | M | I | NO | HS | Runs | Ave |
|---|---|---|---|---|---|---|---|---|
| Carter J.F. | *ND* | 2013/14 | 9 | 16 | 1 | 95 | 674 | 44.93 |
| McClure K.J. | *Canterbury* | 2015/16 | 8 | 13 | 2 | 193* | 667 | 60.63 |
| Bruce T.C. | *CD* | 2014/15 | 7 | 12 | 1 | 112* | 632 | 57.45 |
| Hay G.R. | *CD* | 2006/07 | 8 | 14 | 1 | 106 | 593 | 45.61 |
| Cooper B.G. | *ND* | 1980/81 | 7 | 13 | 0 | 105 | 520 | 40.00 |
| Briasco P.S. | *CD* | 1982/83 | 8 | 15 | 1 | 95 | 519 | 37.07 |
| Cachopa B. | *Auckland* | 2010/11 | 10 | 18 | 1 | 71 | 509 | 29.94 |
| Carson W.N. | *Auckland* | 1936/37 | 3 | 4 | 0 | 290 | 500 | 125.00 |

# Highest Average in a Season in New Zealand

| | | M | I | NO | HS | Runs | Ave | 100 |
|---|---|---|---|---|---|---|---|---|
| Hammond W.R. | 1932/33 | 3 | 3 | 1 | 336* | 621 | 310.50 | 2 |
| Woodfull W.M. | 1924/25 | 6 | 9 | 5 | 212* | 710 | 177.50 | 3 |
| Williamson K.S. | 2020/21 | 3 | 4 | 0 | 251 | 639 | 159.75 | 3 |
| Greatbatch M.J. | 1995/96 | 5 | 6 | 2 | 202 | 623 | 155.75 | 4 |
| Javed Miandad | 1988/89 | 4 | 5 | 1 | 271 | 597 | 149.25 | 3 |
| Bruce T.C. | 2021/22 | 8 | 13 | 7 | 208* | 858 | 143.00 | 2 |
| Harris C.Z. | 1996/97 | 5 | 7 | 1 | 251* | 835 | 139.16 | 3 |
| Woodfull W.M. | 1927/28 | 6 | 9 | 3 | 284 | 781 | 130.16 | 3 |
| Carson W.N. | 1936/37 | 3 | 4 | 0 | 290 | 500 | 125.00 | 2 |
| Bardsley W. | 1923/24 | 6 | 7 | 2 | 200* | 623 | 124.60 | 1 |
| Munro C. | 2012/13 | 4 | 6 | 1 | 269* | 623 | 124.60 | 3 |
| Cullinan D.J. | 1998/99 | 5 | 7 | 2 | 275* | 553 | 110.60 | 3 |
| Hiddleston J.S. | 1925/26 | 3 | 5 | 0 | 212 | 537 | 107.40 | 2 |
| Weekes E. de C. | 1955/56 | 8 | 10 | 1 | 156 | 940 | 104.44 | 6 |
| Williamson K.S. | 2011/12 | 5 | 7 | 2 | 284* | 517 | 103.40 | 2 |
| Sutcliffe B. | 1946/47 | 6 | 8 | 1 | 197 | 722 | 103.14 | 3 |
| Parker J.M. | 1981/82 | 7 | 13 | 7 | 117 | 618 | 103.00 | 2 |
| Sutcliffe B. | 1947/48 | 5 | 10 | 1 | 208* | 911 | 101.22 | 4 |

*minimum 500 runs*

# Centuries

George Watson registered the first century in New Zealand first-class cricket on 24 February, 1881 when he made 175 for Canterbury v Otago at Hagley Park, Christchurch.

To date, 2700 centuries have been scored in New Zealand with 92 in 2009/10 being the record for one season. A further 428 have been recorded for New Zealand teams overseas. The following New Zealand players have made 20 or more centuries during their first-class careers:

| | | | | | |
|---|---|---|---|---|---|
| Turner G.M. | 103 | Howarth G.P. | 32 | Donnelly M.P. | 23 |
| Crowe M.D. | 71 | Marshall H.J.H. | 31 | Congdon B.E. | 23 |
| Wright J.G. | 59 | Spearman C.M. | 30 | Cumming C.D. | 23 |
| Sutcliffe B. | 44 | Taylor L.R.P.L. | 27 | Latham T.W.M. | 23 |
| Reid J.R. | 39 | Patel D.N. | 26 | Crowe J.J. | 22 |
| Sinclair M.S. | 36 | Ryder J.D. | 25 | Parker J.M. | 21 |
| Dempster C.S. | 35 | Dacre C.C.R. | 24 | Franklin J.E.C. | 21 |
| Rutherford K.R. | 35 | Edgar B.A. | 24 | Flynn D.R. | 21 |
| Fleming S.P. | 35 | Greatbatch M.J. | 24 | Conway D.P. | 21 |
| Williamson K.S. | 34 | Horne M.J. | 24 | Burgess M.G. | 20 |
| Papps M.H.W. | 33 | Bell M.D. | 24 | Richardson M.H. | 20 |

## Most Centuries in a Season in New Zealand

| | | | | | | |
|---|---|---|---|---|---|---|
| 8 | Crowe M.D. | 1986/87 | | 6 | Bell M.D. | 2000/01 |
| 6 | Weekes E. de C. | 1955/56 | | 5 | Turner G.M. | 1975/76 |
| 6 | Hick G.A. | 1988/89 | | 5 | Fulton P.G. | 2012/13 |

## Five Centuries in Consecutive Innings

| | | | | |
|---|---|---|---|---|
| Weekes E. de C. | 156 | West Indies v Auckland | Auckland | 1955/56 |
| | 148 | West Indies v Canterbury | Auckland | |
| | 123 | West Indies v New Zealand | Dunedin | |
| | 119* | West Indies v Wellington | Wellington | |
| | 103 | West Indies v New Zealand | Christchurch | |

## Three Centuries in Consecutive Innings

| | | | | |
|---|---|---|---|---|
| Macartney C.G. | 120 | NSW v Wellington | Wellington | 1923/24 |
| | 120 | NSW v Otago | Dunedin | |
| | 221 | NSW v Canterbury | Christchurch | |
| Sutcliffe B. | 103 | Otago v Auckland | Auckland | 1947/48 |
| | 118 }<br>125 } | Otago v Canterbury | Dunedin | |
| Sutcliffe B. | 141 }<br>135 } | Auckland v Canterbury | Auckland | 1948/49 |
| | 140 | New Zealand XI v The Rest | Christchurch | |
| Reid J.R. | 101 }<br>118* } | New Zealand v Orange Free State | Bloemfontein | 1961/62 |
| | 165 | New Zealand v South African Colts XI | East London | |
| Chappell I.M. | 128 | Australia v Northern Districts | Hamilton | 1973/74 |
| | 145 }<br>121 } | Australia v New Zealand | Wellington | |
| Crowe M.D. | 151 | Central Districts v Northern Districts | Morrinsville | 1986/87 |
| | 144 }<br>151 } | Central Districts v Canterbury | New Plymouth | |
| Hick G.A. | 211* | Northern Districts v Auckland | Auckland | 1988/89 |
| | 144 }<br>132 } | Northern Districts v Wellington | Morrinsville | |

| Jones A.H. | 186 | New Zealand v Sri Lanka | Wellington | 1990/91 |
|---|---|---|---|---|
| | 122 100* } | New Zealand v Sri Lanka | Hamilton | |
| Maynard M.P. | 142 | Northern Districts v Otago | Hamilton | 1991/92 |
| | 195 110 } | Northern Districts v Auckland | Auckland | |
| Greatbatch M.J. | 115 | Central Districts v Canterbury | Christchurch | 1995/96 |
| | 202 | Central Districts v Northern Districts | Rotorua | |
| | 162* | Central Districts v Auckland | Auckland | |
| Campbell S.L. | 112 109* } | West Indies v Auckland | Auckland | 1999/00 |
| | 170 | West Indies v New Zealand | Hamilton | |
| Wells J.D. | 143 | Wellington v Canterbury | Wellington | 1999/00 |
| | 107 132* } | Wellington v Central Districts | New Plymouth | |
| How J.M. | 105 108* } | Central Districts v Otago | Queenstown | 2004/05 |
| | 121 | Central Districts v Northern Districts | Napier | |
| Sinclair M.S. | 121 103* } | Central Districts v Otago | New Plymouth | 2005/06 |
| | 101 | Central Districts v Auckland | Palmerston North | |
| Ingram P.J. | 119 166* } | Central Districts v Canterbury | Christchurch | 2006/07 |
| | 105 | Central Districts v Auckland | Napier | |
| Franklin J.E.C. | 116 | Wellington v Otago | Invercargill | 2013/14 |
| | 108* | Wellington v Canterbury | Wellington | |
| | 120* | Wellington v Auckland | Wellington | |
| Ryder J.D. | 109* | Central Districts v Canterbury | Nelson | 2016/17 |
| | 175 106* } | Central Districts v Auckland | Nelson | 2017/18 |

## Century on First-class Debut

| † Watson G. | 175 | Canterbury v Otago | Christchurch | 1880/81 |
|---|---|---|---|---|
| Brook-Smith W. | 112* | Auckland v Hawke's Bay | Auckland | 1904/05 |
| † Wood B.B. | 108 & 18 | Canterbury v Wellington | Wellington | 1907/08 |
| McMullan J.J.M. | 157* | Otago v Southland | Dunedin | 1917/18 |
| † Snedden C.A. | 119 | Auckland v Hawke's Bay | Auckland | 1920/21 |
| Talbot R.O. | 105 | Canterbury v Otago | Dunedin | 1922/23 |
| Tindill E.W.T. | 106 & 0 | Wellington v Auckland | Auckland | 1932/33 |
| Scott V.J. | 122 | Auckland v Canterbury | Auckland | 1937/38 |
| † Ongley J.A. | 110 | Wellington v Otago | Wellington | 1938/39 |
| † Kerr A.C. | 122 | Auckland v Wellington | Auckland | 1941/42 |
| † Watt D.G. | 15 & 105 | Otago v Canterbury | Christchurch | 1943/44 |
| Smith K.F.H. | 27 & 141* | Wellington v Central Districts | Wellington | 1953/54 |
| Macleod D.N. | 117 | Central Districts v Wellington | Wanganui | 1956/57 |
| Bilby G.P. | 132 & 2* | Wellington v Central Districts | Wellington | 1962/63 |
| † Mitchell W.J. | 127* | Northern Districts v Pakistan | Hamilton | 1964/65 |
| † Sampson H.C. | 25 & 119 | Central Districts v Wellington | Wellington | 1970/71 |
| Vaughan J.T.C. | 106* & 1 | Auckland v Wellington | Wellington | 1989/90 |
| Aiken J.M. | 39 & 156* | Wellington v Canterbury | Christchurch | 1989/90 |
| † McCone R.J. | 102 | Canterbury v Otago | Christchurch | 2008/09 |
| Rhodes S.J. | 142* & 1 | Wellington v Otago | Queenstown | 2009/10 |
| Brownlie D.G. | 112* | Canterbury v Northern Districts | Rangiora | 2009/10 |
| Broom D.J. | 119 | Otago v Northern Districts | Whangarei | 2009/10 |

| † Hakaraia D.N. | 141* & 4 | Auckland v Northern Districts | Hamilton | 2012/13 |
| Schmulian B.D. | 203 & 4 | Central Districts v Northern Districts | Mt Maunganui | 2017/18 |
| † Wiggins B.L. | 133 & 9* | Central Districts v Canterbury | Christchurch | 2021/22 |

† *only century in first-class cricket*

*B.R. Williams scored 103\* in his fourth first-class match, not having batted in his first three matches, for Wellington v Central Districts at Wellington, 1989/90.*

## Century on First-class Debut in Other Countries

### In ENGLAND

| Dacre C.C.R. | 107 | New Zealand v MCC | Lord's | 1927 |
| Crowe M.D. | 104 | D.B. Close's XI v Pakistan | Scarborough | 1982 |
| Horne M.J. | 133 | New Zealand v British Universities | Oxford | 1999 |
| Spearman C.M. | 111 | Gloucestershire v Worcestershire | Worcester | 2002 |
| Adams A.R. | 124 | Essex v Leicestershire | Leicester | 2004 |
| Marshall H.J.H. | 102 | Gloucestershire v Worcestershire | Bristol | 2006 |
| Conway D.P. | 200 | New Zealand v England | Lord's | 2021 |
| Ravindra R. | 217 | Durham v Worcestershire | Chester-le-Street | 2022 |

*J.D.P. Oram scored 103\* for New Zealand v Worcestershire at Worcester in 2004 in his first innings in England after not batting in his first game*

### In AUSTRALIA

| Sutcliffe B. | 142 | New Zealand v Western Australia | Perth | 1953/54 |
| Miller L.S.M. | 142 | New Zealand v South Australia | Adelaide | 1953/54 |
| Patel D.N. | 105 | New Zealand v Western Australia | Perth | 1987/88 |
| How J.M. | 170 | New Zealand v New South Wales | Sydney | 2008/09 |
| Blundell T.A. | 121 | New Zealand v Australia | Melbourne | 2019/20 |

### In SOUTH AFRICA

| Reid J.R. | 111 | New Zealand v Western Province | Cape Town | 1953/54 |
| Kasper R.J. | 122* | Natal B v Transvaal B | Pietermaritzburg | 1970/71 |
| Harris C.Z. | 118* | Canterbury v Eastern Province | Grahamstown | 1993/94 |
| Richardson M.H. | 173* | New Zealand v Boland | Paarl | 2000/01 |
| McCullum B.B. | 101 | New Zealand v Rest of South Africa | Benoni | 2005/06 |
| Brownlie D.G. | 109 | New Zealand v South Africa | Cape Town | 2012/13 |

### In WEST INDIES

| Hastings B.F. | 100* | New Zealand v Jamaica | Kingston | 1971/72 |
| Crowe M.D. | 118 | New Zealand v Shell Award XI | Kingston | 1984/85 |
| Styris S.B. | 107 | New Zealand v West Indies | St George's | 2001/02 |
| Neesham J.D.S. | 107 | New Zealand v West Indies | Kingston | 2014 |

### In INDIA

| Taylor B.R. | 105 | New Zealand v India | Calcutta | 1964/65 |
| Burgess M.G. | 102 | Prime Minister's XI v President's XI | Bombay | 1967/68 |
| Parker J.M. | 104 | New Zealand v India | Bombay | 1976/77 |
| Wright J.G. | 104 | New Zealand v West Zone | Rajkot | 1988/89 |
| Crowe M.D. | 101* | New Zealand v President's XI | Rajkot | 1995/96 |
| Oram J.D.P. | 101* | New Zealand v India A | Rajkot | 2003/04 |
| Ryder J.D. | 103 | New Zealand v India | Ahmedabad | 2010/11 |
| Williamson K.S. | 131 | New Zealand v India | Ahmedabad | 2010/11 |
| Anderson C.J. | 100 | New Zealand A v India A | Visakhapatnam | 2013/14 |
| Devcich A.P. | 115 | New Zealand A v India A | Visakhapatnam | 2013/14 |

*M.H. Richardson scored 128\* for New Zealand v India at Rajkot in 2003/04 in his first innings in India after not batting in his first game.*

### In PAKISTAN

| | | | | |
|---|---|---|---|---|
| Reid J.R. | 105* | NZ v Chief Commissioner's XI | Karachi | 1955/56 |
| Anderson R.W. | 103* | NZ v NWFP Chief Minister's XI | Peshawar | 1976/77 |

### In SRI LANKA

| | | | | |
|---|---|---|---|---|
| Dempster C.S. | 112* | Sir Julien Cahn's XI v Ceylon | Colombo | 1936/37 |
| Rutherford K.R. | 108 | New Zealand v Board President's XI | Galle | 1986/87 |
| Fulton P.G. | 101 | New Zealand A v Sri Lanka A | Kandy | 2005/06 |
| Cachopa Carl | 104 | New Zealand A v Sri Lanka A | Pallekele | 2013/14 |

### In ZIMBABWE

| | | | | |
|---|---|---|---|---|
| Franklin T.J. | 153* | Young New Zealand v Zimbabwe | Harare | 1984/85 |
| Horne M.J. | 181 | New Zealand v Mashonaland | Harare | 1997/98 |
| Sinclair M.S. | 100* | New Zealand v President's XI | Mutare | 2000/01 |
| Flynn D.R. | 162 | New Zealand A v Zimbabwe A | Harare | 2010/11 |
| Latham T.W.M. | 105 | New Zealand v Zimbabwe | Bulawayo | 2016/17 |

### In BANGLADESH

| | | | | |
|---|---|---|---|---|
| McCullum B.B. | 143 | New Zealand v Bangladesh | Dhaka | 2004/05 |
| Williamson K.S. | 114 | New Zealand v Bangladesh | Chittagong | 2013/14 |
| Watling B-J. | 103 | New Zealand v Bangladesh | Chittagong | 2013/14 |

### In UNITED ARAB EMIRATES

| | | | | |
|---|---|---|---|---|
| Latham T.W.M. | 103 | New Zealand v Pakistan | Abu Dhabi | 2014/15 |

## Century in Last First-class Match

| | | | | |
|---|---|---|---|---|
| † Phillips J. | 110* | Canterbury v Wellington | Christchurch | 1898/99 |
| Board J.H. | 63 & 134 | Hawke's Bay v Wellington | Wellington | 1914/15 |
| Midlane F.A. | 126 & 4 | Auckland v Wellington | Wellington | 1918/19 |
| † Beechey E.M. | 180 & 5 | Wellington vAuckland | Wellington | 1918/19 |
| MacLaren A.C | 200* | MCC v New Zealand | Wellington | 1922/23 |
| † Watt D.G. | 15 & 105 | Otago v Canterbury | Christchurch | 1943/44 |
| Redmond R.E. | 103 & 22 | Auckland v Otago | Auckland | 1975/76 |
| Wadsworth K.J. | 117 | Canterbury v Otago | Christchurch | 1975/76 |
| Parker J.M. | 1* & 110 | Northern Districts v Wellington | Wellington | 1983/84 |
| † Snook I.R. | 100* | Central Dists v Northern Dists | Palmerston North | 1987/88 |
| Dempsey D.A. | 121 & 44 | Canterbury v Otago | Dunedin | 1987/88 |
| Reid J.F. | 112 | Auckland v Northern Districts | Hamilton | 1987/88 |
| Mawhinney R.E.W. | 9* & 108 | Otago v Canterbury | Christchurch | 1990/91 |
| Austen M.H. | 15 & 100 | Otago v Canterbury | Christchurch | 1996/07 |
| Twose R.G. | 108 & 6 | Wellington v Auckland | Wellington | 2000/01 |
| Douglas M.W. | 134 & 22 | Central Districts v Otago | Alexandra | 2000/01 |
| Nash D.J. | 118 & 11* | Auckland v Otago | Dunedin | 2001/02 |
| Evans A.W. | 29 & 104* | Northern Districts v Canterbury | Hamilton | 2006/07 |
| Jones R.A. | 89 & 170* | Auckland v Canterbury | Auckland | 2009/10 |
| Ingram P.J. | 39 & 139 | Central Districts v Auckland | Auckland | 2011/12 |
| Marshall J.A.H. | 54 & 156* | Northern Dists v Central Dists | Nelson | 2012/13 |
| McCullum B.B. | 145 & 25 | New Zealand v Australia | Christchurch | 2015/16 |
| Marshall H.J.H. | 25 & 105* | Wellington v Canterbury | Christchurch | 2016/17 |
| Noema-Barnett K. | 0 & 101 | Central Dists v Northern Dists | Hamilton | 2018/19 |

† only first-class century of career. D.G. Watt was making his only appearance in first-class cricket.
J. Phillips was playing his 124th first-class match and 203rd innings.
J.D. Riley scored 34, 121*, 26 and 94 (run out) in his final two first-class matches, for Auckland in 1976/77.

# Century in Each Innings of a Match

| | | | | |
|---|---|---|---|---|
| Dacre C.C.R. | 127* & 101* | Auckland v Victoria | Auckland | 1924/25 |
| † Whitelaw P.E. | 115 & 155 | Auckland v Wellington | Auckland | 1934/35 |
| Uttley K.F.M. | 132 & 138 | Otago v Auckland | Auckland | 1937/38 |
| Sutcliffe B. | 197 & 128 | Otago v MCC | Dunedin | 1946/47 |
| Sutcliffe B. | 118 & 125 | Otago v Canterbury | Dunedin | 1947/48 |
| Sutcliffe B. | 141 & 135 | Auckland v Canterbury | Auckland | 1948/49 |
| Sutcliffe B. | 243 & 100* | New Zealand v Essex | Southend | 1949 |
| Reid J.R. | 101 & 118* | New Zealand v Orange Free State | Bloemfontein | 1961/62 |
| † Gedye S.G. | 104 & 101 | Auckland v Central Districts | Auckland | 1963/64 |
| † Thomson K. | 102 & 102* | Canterbury v Otago | Dunedin | 1966/67 |
| Chappell G.S. | 247* & 133 | Australia v New Zealand | Wellington | 1973/74 |
| Chappell I.M. | 145 & 121 | Australia v New Zealand | Wellington | 1973/74 |
| Turner G.M. | 101 & 110* | New Zealand v Australia | Christchurch | 1973/74 |
| Turner G.M. | 135 & 108 | Otago v Northern Districts | Gisborne | 1974/75 |
| Turner G.M. | 105 & 186* | Otago v Central Districts | Dunedin | 1974/75 |
| Howarth G.P. | 122 & 102 | New Zealand v England | Auckland | 1977/78 |
| Wright J.G. | 113 & 105 | Northern Districts v Auckland | Auckland | 1981/82 |
| Parker J.M. | 117 & 102* | Northern Districts v Central Districts | Tauranga | 1981/82 |
| Rutherford K.R. | 105 & 104* | Otago v Northern Districts | Alexandra | 1985/86 |
| Border A.R. | 140 & 114* | Australia v New Zealand | Christchurch | 1985/86 |
| Cooper B.G. | 105 & 100 | Northern Districts v Canterbury | Gisborne | 1986/87 |
| Crowe M.D. | 144 & 151 | Central Districts v Canterbury | New Plymouth | 1986/87 |
| Vance R.H. | 116* & 123 | Wellington v Central Districts | New Plymouth | 1988/89 |
| Hick G.A. | 144 & 132 | Northern Districts v Wellington | Morrinsville | 1988/89 |
| Jones A.H. | 122 & 100* | New Zealand v Sri Lanka | Hamilton | 1990/91 |
| Gurusinha A.P. | 119 & 102 | Sri Lanka v New Zealand | Hamilton | 1990/91 |
| Maynard M.P. | 195 & 110 | Northern Districts v Auckland | Auckland | 1991/92 |
| Crowe M.D. | 152 & 137* | Wellington v Canterbury | Christchurch | 1992/93 |
| Dravid R.S. | 190 & 103* | India v New Zealand | Hamilton | 1998/99 |
| Rhodes J.N. | 101* & 106* | South Africa v New Zealand A | Lincoln | 1998/99 |
| Campbell S.L. | 112 & 109* | West Indies v Auckland | Auckland | 1999/00 |
| Wells J.D. | 107 & 132* | Wellington v Central Districts | New Plymouth | 1999/00 |
| Spearman C.M. | 100 & 115 | New Zealand v North West | Potchefstroom | 2000/01 |
| Hopkins G.J. | 113 & 175* | Canterbury v Auckland | Auckland | 2002/03 |
| Horne M.J. | 118 & 209* | Auckland v Northern Districts | Auckland | 2003/04 |
| How J.M. | 105 & 108* | Central Districts v Otago | Queenstown | 2004/05 |
| Sinclair M.S. | 121 & 103* | Central Districts v Otago | New Plymouth | 2005/06 |
| Ingram P.J. | 119 & 166* | Central Districts v Canterbury | Christchurch | 2006/07 |
| Jones R.A. | 143 & 120 | Auckland v Central Districts | Auckland | 2006/07 |
| Todd G.R. | 110 & 165 | Otago v Wellington | Wellington | 2007/08 |
| Myburgh J.G. | 199 & 101* | Canterbury v Central Districts | New Plymouth | 2008/09 |
| Papps M.H.W. | 104 & 180 | Canterbury v Auckland | Auckland | 2009/10 |
| Cumming C.D. | 127* & 127 | Otago v Canterbury | Queenstown | 2010/11 |
| Redmond A.J. | 122 & 115 | Otago v Northern Districts | Hamilton | 2010/11 |
| Ingram P.J. | 135 & 143 | Central Districts v Wellington | Wellington | 2010/11 |
| † Rutherford H.D. | 107 & 118 | Otago v Northern Districts | Hamilton | 2011/12 |
| Redmond A.J. | 133 & 123 | Otago v Canterbury | Rangiora | 2012/13 |
| Ryder J.D. | 117* & 174 | Wellington v Central Districts | Napier | 2012/13 |
| Fulton P.G. | 102 & 108 | Canterbury v Otago | Dunedin | 2012/13 |
| Ronchi L. | 113 & 108 | Wellington v Northern Districts | Wellington | 2012/13 |
| Fulton P.G. | 136 & 110 | New Zealand v England | Auckland | 2012/13 |
| Wilson B.S. | 111 & 117* | Otago v Central Districts | Nelson | 2016/17 |
| Munro C. | 146 & 142 | Auckland v Central Districts | Auckland | 2016/17 |
| Ryder J.D. | 175 & 106* | Central Districts v Auckland | Nelson | 2017/18 |
| Carter J.F. | 169 & 120 | Northern Districts v Auckland | Auckland | 2019/20 |

| Chapman M.S. | 143 & 146 | Auckland v Northern Districts | Auckland | 2019/20 |
|---|---|---|---|---|
| Bracewell M.G. | 105 & 119 | Wellington v Auckland | Auckland | 2020/21 |
| † O'Donnell W.T. | 117 & 137* | Auckland v Wellington | Auckland | 2020/21 |

† *maiden first-class century*

## Highest Maiden Centuries

| 301* | Fulton P.G. | Canterbury v Auckland | Christchurch | 2002/03 |
|---|---|---|---|---|
| 290 | Carson W.N. | Auckland v Otago | Dunedin | 1936/37 |
| 256 | Raval J.A. | Auckland v Central Districts | Auckland | 2008/09 |
| 209 | White D.J. | Northern Districts v Central Districts | Hamilton | 1985/86 |
| 204 | Cox A. | Canterbury v Otago | Christchurch | 1925/26 |
| 203* | Burnett G.P. | Wellington v Northern Districts | Hamilton | 1991/92 |
| 203 | Schmulian B.D. | Central Districts v Northern Districts | Mt Maunganui | 2017/18 |
| 196 | Kerr J.L. | Canterbury v Wellington | Christchurch | 1932/33 |
| 194 | Gaffaney C.B. | Otago v Auckland | Dunedin | 1996/97 |
| 193* | Stead D.W. | Canterbury v Central Districts | Christchurch | 1980/81 |
| 193* | McClure K.J. | Canterbury v Otago | Invercargill | 2015/16 |
| 190 | Moloney D.A.R. | Wellington v Auckland | Auckland | 1936/37 |
| 190 | Bracewell M.G. | Otago v Wellington | Dunedin | 2012/13 |
| 189 | Sinclair M.S. | Central Districts v Wellington | Masterton | 1996/97 |
| 188 | Beard N.B. | Otago v Auckland | Dunedin | 2012/13 |
| 184 | Taylor L.R.P.L. | Central Districts v Wellington | Palmerston North | 2004/05 |
| 183 | Gillespie H.D. | Auckland v Canterbury | Auckland | 1929/30 |
| 182 | McIntosh T.G. | Auckland v Canterbury | Christchurch | 2000/01 |
| 180 | Beechey E.M. | Wellington v Auckland | Wellington | 1918/19 |
| 180 | Dempster C.S. | New Zealand v Warwickshire | Birmingham | 1927 |
| 180 | Mooney F.L.H. | Wellington v Auckland | Wellington | 1943/44 |
| 180* | Andrew G.M. | Canterbury v Auckland | Auckland | 2012/13 |
| 179 | Ormiston R.W. | Wellington v Central Districts | New Plymouth | 1982/83 |
| 179 | Nofal M.J. | Wellington v Central Districts | Wellington | 2017/18 |
| 177 | Chandler P.J.B. | Wellington v Auckland | Wellington | 1996/97 |
| 176 | Cuff L.A. | Canterbury v Auckland | Christchurch | 1893/94 |
| 175 | Watson G. | Canterbury v Otago | Christchurch | 1880/81 |
| 175 | Astle N.J. | Canterbury v Northern Districts | Hamilton | 1994/95 |
| 175 | Orchard M.G. | Northern Districts v Central Districts | Napier | 2005/06 |
| 172 | Worker R.V. de R. | Otago v Canterbury | Dunedin | 1923/24 |
| 172 | Englefield J.I. | Canterbury v Central Districts | Blenheim | 2000/01 |
| 171 | Mills S.M. | Wellington v Canterbury | Christchurch | 2006/07 |
| 167* | Hart R.T. | Central Districts v Canterbury | New Plymouth | 1983/84 |
| 167 | Lawrence J.D. | Canterbury v Auckland | Christchurch | 1893/94 |
| 167 | Anderson C.J. | Northern Districts v Otago | Hamilton | 2012/13 |
| 167 | O'Donnell R.R. | Auckland v Wellington | Auckland | 2015/16 |
| 166 | Cachopa C. | Auckland v Wellington | Auckland | 2012/13 |
| 165 | Redgrave W.P. | Wellington v Hawkes Bay | Wellington | 1905/06 |
| 165 | Chapple M.E. | Canterbury v South Africans | Christchurch | 1952/53 |
| 165 | Truscott P.B. | NZ Under-23 v Auckland | Auckland | 1963/64 |
| 164* | Duff S.W. | Central Districts v Auckland | Wanganui | 1991/92 |
| 164 | Powell J.L. | Canterbury v Otago | Christchurch | 1929/30 |
| 163* | How J.M. | Central Districts v Northern Districts | Hamilton | 2002/03 |
| 163 | Menzies R.E.J. | Canterbury v Wellington | Christchurch | 1938/39 |
| 163 | Williams A.B. | Wellington v Canterbury | Christchurch | 1896/97 |
| 163 | Reade L.B. | Central Districts v Northern Districts | Palmerston North | 1960/61 |
| 161 | Larsen G.R. | Wellington v Central Districts | Levin | 1987/88 |
| 159* | Kennedy P.G. | Canterbury v Northern Districts | Rotorua | 1990/91 |
| 159 | Vincent L. | Auckland v Northern Districts | Auckland | 1998/99 |
| 158* | Papps M.H.W. | Canterbury v Otago | Christchurch | 2001/02 |

| 158 | Harford N.S. | New Zealand v Oxford University | Oxford | 1958 |
|---|---|---|---|---|
| 157* | McMullan J.J.M. | Otago v Southland | Dunedin | 1917/18 |
| 157 | Briasco P.S. | Central Districts v Canterbury | New Plymouth | 1983/84 |
| 156* | Aiken J.M. | Wellington v Canterbury | Christchurch | 1989/90 |
| 156 | Southee T.G. | Northern Districts v Wellington | Wellington | 2012/13 |
| 155* | James V. | Canterbury v Otago | Dunedin | 1940/41 |
| 155* | Parore A.C. | Auckland v Otago | Dunedin | 1991/92 |
| 155 | Badcock F.T. | Wellington v Canterbury | Christchurch | 1926/27 |
| 155 | Oram J.D.P. | Central Districts v Canterbury | Christchurch | 1998/99 |
| 154 | Meuli E.M. | Central Districts v Auckland | Palmerston North | 1952/53 |
| 153 | Watling B-J. | Northern Districts v Otago | Dunedin | 2006/07 |
| 152 | Knight A.R. | Otago v Canterbury | Dunedin | 1940/41 |
| 152 | Kemp R.J. | Wellington v Auckland | Auckland | 1947/48 |
| 152 | Coutts P.J.C. | Central Districts v Canterbury | Christchurch | 1966/67 |
| 152 | Lees W.K. | New Zealand v Pakistan | Karachi | 1976/77 |
| 152 | Brown S.W. | Auckland v Central Districts | Auckland | 1990/91 |
| 152 | Weston T.I. | Central Districts v Auckland | Auckland | 2006/07 |
| 151 | Petrie E.C. | Auckland v Wellington | Auckland | 1953/54 |
| 151* | Cleaver D. | Central Districts v Wellington | Napier | 2015/16 |
| 150 | Crowe M.D. | Auckland v Central Districts | New Plymouth | 1981/82 |

*Watson, McMullan and Aiken scored their centuries on their debut in first-class cricket. Beechey was playing in his last first-class game. Carson (aged 20 years 168 days) and Cox (21 years 19 days) were both playing only their second first-class innings. Carson is the youngest player to score a double-century in New Zealand first-class cricket.*

## One Hundred Runs before Lunch

| Runs | Mins | | | | |
|---|---|---|---|---|---|
| * 110 | 120 | Smith S.G. | Auckland v Canterbury | Auckland | 1919/20 |
| 100 | 120 | Richardson V.Y. | Australia v New Zealand | Auckland | 1920/21 |
| * 106 | 120 | Blunt R.C. | Canterbury v MCC | Christchurch | 1922/23 |
| 112 | 113 | Macartney C.G. | NSW v Wellington | Wellington | 1923/24 |
| * 116 | 120 | † Punch A.T.E. | NSW v Otago | Dunedin | 1923/24 |
| * 101 | 91 | Macartney C.G. | NSW v Otago | Dunedin | 1923/24 |
| * 108 | 120 | Macartney C.G. | NSW v Canterbury | Christchurch | 1923/24 |
| * 100 | 120 | Bardsley W. | NSW v Auckland | Auckland | 1923/24 |
| 103 | 110 | Hiddleston J.S. | Wellington v Canterbury | Wellington | 1925/26 |
| 105 | 102 | Dacre C.C.R. | Auckland v Otago | Dunedin | 1926/27 |
| 103 | 103 | † Vorrath W. | Otago v Wellington | Dunedin | 1927/28 |
| * 106 | 120 | Blunt R.C. | Otago v Canterbury | Christchurch | 1928/29 |
| 164 | 130 | † Powell J.L. | Canterbury v Otago | Christchurch | 1929/30 |
| 105 | 105 | Badcock F.T. | Otago v Canterbury | Christchurch | 1931/32 |
| * 111 | 120 | Hammond W.R. | England v New Zealand | Auckland | 1932/33 |
| 102 | 120 | Whitelaw P.E. | Auckland v Wellington | Auckland | 1934/35 |
| 115 | 110 | Wallace W.M. | New Zealand v Somerset | Taunton | 1937 |
| * 110 | 120 | Wallace W.M. | New Zealand v Sussex | Hove | 1937 |
| * 103 | 120 | Smith F.B. | Canterbury v Auckland | Auckland | 1948/49 |
| 100 | 117 | Sutcliffe B. | New Zealand v Essex | Southend | 1949 |
| * 100 | 120 | Reid J.R. | Wellington v Otago | Wellington | 1951/52 |
| * 122 | 111 | Guillen S.C. | Canterbury v Fiji | Christchurch | 1953/54 |
| * 100 | 126 | Smith K.F.H. | Central Districts v Wellington | Wanganui | 1959/60 |
| * 108 | 131 | Sutcliffe B. | Otago v Central Districts | Dunedin | 1959/60 |
| * 100 | 140 | Sutcliffe B. | Otago v Northern Districts | Hamilton | 1960/61 |
| * 174 | 140 | Reid J.R. | Wellington v Northern Districts | Wellington | 1962/63 |
| 120 | 125 | Reid J.R. | Wellington v Northern Districts | Wellington | 1964/65 |
| 103 | 120 | Murray B.A.G. | New Zealand v President's XI | Rawalpindi | 1969/70 |
| * 109 | 141 | Dunning B. | Northern Dist. v Central Dist. | Blenheim | 1972/73 |
| 111 | 150 | Dempsey D.A. | Canterbury v Otago | Christchurch | 1980/81 |
| 102 | 147 | † Crowe M.D. | Auckland v Central Districts | New Plymouth | 1981/82 |

| | Runs | Mins | | | | |
|---|------|------|---|---|---|---|
| * | 100 | 107 | Chappell G.S. | Australia v New Zealand | Christchurch | 1981/82 |
| * | 100 | 150 | Crowe J.J. | Auckland v Northern Districts | Rotorua | 1983/84 |
| | 101 | 103 | Rutherford K.R. | New Zealand v DB Close's XI | Scarborough | 1986 |
| * | 101 | 144 | Jones A.H. | Wellington v Otago | Wellington | 1986/87 |
| * | 112 | 149 | McSweeney E.B. | Wellington v Central Districts | Levin | 1987/88 |
| * | 122 | 150 | Crowe J.J. | Auckland v Wellington | Wellington | 1988/89 |
| * | 117 | 160 | Greatbatch M.J. | Central Districts v Otago | Palmerston North | 1988/89 |
| | 101 | 127 | Blain T.E. | Central Districts v Wellington | New Plymouth | 1988/89 |
| | 107 | 136 | † Reid R.B. | Auckland v Central Districts | Masterton | 1989/90 |
| * | 116 | 136 | Thomson S.A. | Northern Districts v Auckland | Auckland | 1990/91 |
| | 141 | 144 | Maynard M.P. | Northern Districts v Auckland | Auckland | 1991/92 |
| * | 139 | 92 | Patel D.N. | Auckland v Northern Districts | Auckland | 1991/92 |
| | 104 | 140 | Spearman C.M. | Central Districts v Wellington | Wellington | 1997/98 |
| | 101 | 137 | Cairns C.L. | Southern v Central | Wellington | 1998/99 |
| | 103 | 140 | How J.M. | Central Districts v Northern Districts | Napier | 2004/05 |
| | 105 | 140 | Fulton P.G. | Canterbury v Otago | Christchurch | 2004/05 |
| | 106 | 122 | Taylor L.R.P.L. | Central Districts v Northern Districts | Napier | 2007/08 |
| * | 100 | 120 | Watling B-J. | Northern Districts v Auckland | Auckland | 2009/10 |
| * | 104 | 150 | Sinclair M.S. | Central Districts v Otago | Invercargill | 2009/10 |
| | 104 | 120 | Papps M.H.W. | Canterbury v Auckland | Auckland | 2009/10 |
| | 121 | 120 | Munro C. | Auckland v Central Districts | Auckland | 2016/17 |

\* *batsman had been not out overnight*
† *maiden first-class hundred. Punch, Vorrath, Powell and Reid did not score another century in first-class cricket*

## Scores of Ninety-nine

| | | | | |
|---|---|---|---|---|
| | Johnson P.R. | MCC v New Zealand | Christchurch | 1906/07 |
| † | Snedden A.N.C. | Auckland v Canterbury | Auckland | 1921/22 |
| § | Elmes C.J. | New Zealand v MCC | Auckland | 1935/36 |
| * | Whitelaw P.E. | Auckland/Wellington v MCC | Auckland | 1936/37 |
| | Sutcliffe B. | Otago v Auckland | Dunedin | 1947/48 |
| | Taylor D.D. | Auckland v Canterbury | Auckland | 1948/49 |
| † | Leggat J.G. | Canterbury v Auckland | Christchurch | 1951/52 |
| | Rae A.F. | West Indies v New Zealand | Auckland | 1951/52 |
| | O'Malley P.W. | Canterbury v Wellington | Christchurch | 1953/54 |
| † | Beck J.E.F. | New Zealand v South Africa | Cape Town | 1953/54 |
| | Hunter A.A. | Central Districts v Auckland | Auckland | 1953/54 |
| † | Leggat J.G. | Canterbury v MCC | Christchurch | 1954/55 |
| | Sutcliffe B. | Rest v New Zealand XI | Christchurch | 1957/58 |
| | Sutcliffe B. | New Zealand v Sussex | Hove | 1958 |
| §* | Bartlett G.A. | Central Districts v Auckland | Auckland | 1959/60 |
| | McGregor S.N. | Otago v Canterbury | Christchurch | 1963/64 |
| † | Cunis R.S. | Auckland v Wellington | Wellington | 1966/67 |
| | Surti R.F. | India v New Zealand | Auckland | 1967/68 |
| | Turner G.M. | New Zealand v Tasmania | Hobart | 1969/70 |
| | Burtt J.W. | Canterbury v Central Districts | Christchurch | 1970/71 |
| | Dowling G.T. | Canterbury v Northern Districts | Hamilton | 1970/71 |
| | Murray B.A.G. | Wellington v Northern Districts | Wellington | 1970/71 |
| | Dowling G.T. | New Zealand v Western Australia | Perth | 1970/71 |
| §* | O'Keeffe K.J. | Australia v Auckland | Auckland | 1973/74 |
| | Edwards G.N. | Central Districts v Australia | Nelson | 1976/77 |
| | Blair W.L. | Otago v Auckland | Auckland | 1978/79 |
| | Crowe M.D. | Auckland v Northern Districts | Auckland | 1981/82 |
| | Hadlee R.J. | New Zealand v England | Christchurch | 1983/84 |
| † | Lees W.K. | Otago v Northern Districts | Hamilton | 1983/84 |

| | | | |
|---|---|---|---|
| Vance R.H. | Wellington v Canterbury | Wellington | 1984/85 |
| Coney J.V. | New Zealand v President's XI | St Lucia | 1984/85 |
| Jones A.H. | Wellington v Auckland | Auckland | 1985/86 |
| §* Robertson G.K. | Central Districts v Otago | Oamaru | 1985/86 |
| Wright J.G. | New Zealand v Australia | Melbourne | 1987/88 |
| Crocker L.M. | Northern Districts v Wellington | Hamilton | 1987/88 |
| Moxon M.D. | England v New Zealand | Auckland | 1987/88 |
| McEwan P.E. | Canterbury v Wellington | Christchurch | 1988/89 |
| Hart R.T. | Central Districts v Auckland | Masterton | 1989/90 |
| Wright J.G. | New Zealand v Worcestershire | Worcester | 1990 |
| † Patel D.N. | New Zealand v England | Christchurch | 1991/92 |
| + Wright J.G. | New Zealand v England | Christchurch | 1991/92 |
| Douglas M.W. | Central Districts v Auckland | Wanganui | 1991/92 |
| McSweeney E.B. | Wellington v Canterbury | Wellington | 1993/94 |
| Twose R.G. | Central Districts v Auckland | Palmerston North | 1993/94 |
| † Jones R.A. | Auckland v Otago | Dunedin | 1996/97 |
| * Sinclair M.S. | Central Districts v Northern Districts | Hamilton | 1996/97 |
| Twose R.G. | Wellington v India | Wellington | 1998/99 |
| Yovich J.A.F. | Northern Districts v Auckland | Taupo | 1999/00 |
| Richardson M.H. | New Zealand v Zimbabwe | Harare | 2000/01 |
| Fleming S.P. | New Zealand v South Africa | Bloemfontein | 2000/01 |
| Gaffaney C.B. | Otago v Auckland | Auckland | 2000/01 |
| Nevin C.J. | Wellington v Otago | Wellington | 2000/01 |
| Sinclair M.S. | Central Districts v South Africa | Napier | 2003/04 |
| Gaffaney C.B. | Otago v Wellington | Wellington | 2004/05 |
| McCullum B.B. | New Zealand v Sri Lanka | Napier | 2004/05 |
| Redmond A.J. | Otago v Northern Districts | Gisborne | 2005/06 |
| Guptill M.J. | Auckland v Wellington | Auckland | 2005/06 |
| Marshall H.J.H. | Northern Districts v Auckland | Auckland | 2006/07 |
| Marshall J.A.H. | Northern Districts v Central Districts | Gisborne | 2006/07 |
| Vettori D.L. | New Zealand v SA Inviation XI | Bloemfontein | 2007/08 |
| Marshall J.A.H. | Northern Districts v Central Districts | Hamilton | 2007/08 |
| Hay G.R. | Central Districts v Northern Districts | Hamilton | 2007/08 |
| Hopkins G.J. | Auckland v Northern Districts | Gisborne | 2007/08 |
| Vettori D.L. | New Zealand v Pakistan | Dunedin | 2009/10 |
| Merchant C.J. | Wellington v Canterbury | Wellington | 2009/10 |
| Misbah-ul-Haq | Pakistan v New Zealand | Wellington | 2010/11 |
| Watling B-J. | Northern Districts v Central Districts | Whangarei | 2010/11 |
| Weston T.I. | Central Districts v Northern Districts | Whangarei | 2010/11 |
| Patel J.S. | Wellington v Northern Districts | Whangarei | 2010/11 |
| Stewart S.L. | Canterbury v Wellington | Rangiora | 2010/11 |
| Rutherford H.D. | New Zealand A v India A | Lincoln | 2012/13 |
| * de Grandhomme C. | Auckland v Wellington | Wellington | 2012/13 |
| Young W.A. | Central Districts v Otago | Dunedin | 2013/14 |
| Grobbelaar D.J. | Auckland v Canterbury | Rangiora | 2014/15 |
| Jayasundera M.D.U.S. | Sri Lanka A v New Zealand A | Christchurch | 2015/16 |
| McConchie C.E. | Canterbury v Auckland | Rangiora | 2017/18 |
| Rutherford H.D. | Otago v Central Districts | Napier | 2018/19 |
| Cleaver D. | Central Districts v Otago | Dunedin | 2020/21 |

*\* not out    † batsman was run out    + batsman was stumped    § highest score in first-class cricket*

## Carried Bat Through a Complete Innings

| | Score | Total | | | |
|---|---|---|---|---|---|
| Harris L.M. | 41* | 65 | Otago v Tasmania | Dunedin | 1883/84 |
| Gatehouse G.H. | 54* | 146 | Tasmania v Otago | Dunedin | 1883/84 |
| Mills I. | 88* | 156 | Auckland v Otago | Dunedin | 1893/94 |

| | Score | Total | | | |
|---|---|---|---|---|---|
| † Collins J.C. | 128* | 187 | Fiji v Hawke's Bay | Napier | 1894/95 |
| Cobcroft L.T. | 85* | 239 | NSW v Wellington | Wellington | 1895/96 |
| Mills G. | 106* | 235 | Auckland v Wellington | Auckland | 1895/96 |
| Collins D.C. | 53* | 131 | Wellington v Canterbury | Christchurch | 1906/07 |
| § Midlane F.A. | 14* | 60 | Wellington v Canterbury | Christchurch | 1910/11 |
| Gibbes W.R.L. | 75* | 193 | Wellington v Canterbury | Christchurch | 1911/12 |
| † Midlane F.A. | 222* | 498 | Wellington v Otago | Wellington | 1914/15 |
| Blunt R.C. | 137* | 336 | Canterbury v Wellington | Wellington | 1919/20 |
| † Bardsley W. | 200* | 352 | NSW v Auckland | Auckland | 1923/24 |
| Blunt R.C. | 131* | 204 | Otago v Canterbury | Dunedin | 1926/27 |
| Dempster C.S. | 167* | 345 | New Zealand v Glamorgan | Cardiff | 1927 |
| Kerr J.L. | 146* | 243 | Canterbury v MCC | Christchurch | 1935/36 |
| Whitelaw P.E. | 99* | 183 | Auckland/Wellington v MCC | Auckland | 1936/37 |
| Tindill E.W.T. | 47* | 111 | Wellington v Otago | Dunedin | 1946/47 |
| † Miller L.S.M. | 81* | 154 | Wellington v Otago | Dunedin | 1956/57 |
| Playle W.R. | 89* | 139 | Auckland v Northern Districts | Auckland | 1959/60 |
| Bradburn W.P. | 45* | 87 | Northern Districts v Wellington | Wellington | 1960/61 |
| Bradburn W.P. | 37* | 57 | Northern Districts v Wellington | Hamilton | 1961/62 |
| Holloway R.A. | 61* | 122 | Otago v Central Districts | Nelson | 1962/63 |
| Turner G.M. | 43* | 131 | New Zealand v England | Lord's | 1969 |
| Turner G.M. | 223* | 386 | New Zealand v West Indies | Kingston | 1971/72 |
| Redpath I.R. | 159* | 346 | Australia v New Zealand | Auckland | 1973/74 |
| Wettimuny S. | 63* | 144 | Sri Lanka v New Zealand | Christchurch | 1982/83 |
| † Franklin T.J. | 153* | 311 | Young NZ v Zimbabwe | Harare | 1984/85 |
| Rutherford K.R. | 89* | 241 | Otago v Auckland | Dunedin | 1984/85 |
| Boon D.C. | 58* | 103 | Australia v New Zealand | Auckland | 1985/86 |
| Wright J.G. | 149* | 307 | Canterbury v Auckland | Auckland | 1988/89 |
| Smith C.J.P. | 90* | 154 | Central Dists v Northern Dists | Rotorua | 1989/90 |
| Murray D.J. | 106* | 233 | Canterbury v Northern Dists | Hamilton | 1992/93 |
| Dobbs P.W. | 81* | 177 | Otago v Canterbury | Oamaru | 1994/95 |
| Atherton M.A. | 94* | 228 | England v New Zealand | Christchurch | 1996/97 |
| Kelly D.P. | 212* | 538 | Central Districts v Canterbury | Blenheim | 2000/01 |
| Ingram P.J. | 105* | 201 | Central Districts v Auckland | Auckland | 2003/04 |
| † How J.M. § | 190* | 430 | New Zealand A v England Lions | Queenstown | 2008/09 |
| Imran Farhat | 117* | 223 | Pakistan v New Zealand | Napier | 2009/10 |
| † Cumming C.D. | 106* | 199 | Otago v Canterbury | Rangiora | 2010/11 |
| Guptill M.J. | 195* | 381 | Auckland v Canterbury | Rangiora | 2011/12 |
| Papps M.H.W. | 183* | 459 | Wellington v Canterbury | Rangiora | 2013/14 |
| Duffy R.M. | 90* | 177 | Otago v Auckland | Dunedin | 2015/16 |
| † Latham T.W.M. | 264* | 578 | New Zealand v Sri Lanka | Wellington | 2018/19 |

† *player was on the field for every ball of the match*   § *one man absent*

## Longest Individual Batting in a Match

| Mins | Runs | | | | |
|---|---|---|---|---|---|
| 954 | 274* & 69* | Fleming S.P. | New Zealand v Sri Lanka | Colombo | 2002/03 |
| 876 | 76 & 146* | Greatbatch M.J. | New Zealand v Australia | Perth | 1989/90 |
| 835 | 122 & 102 | Howarth G.P. | New Zealand v England | Auckland | 1977/78 |
| 828 | 75 & 138 | Wright J.G. | New Zealand v West Indies | Wellington | 1986/87 |
| 818 | 8 & 302 | McCullum B.B. | New Zealand v India | Wellington | 2013/14 |
| 813 | 93 & 101 | Richardson M.H. | New Zealand v England | Lord's | 2004 |
| 811 | 69 & 242* | Williamson K.S. | New Zealand v Sri Lanka | Wellington | 2014/15 |
| 772 | 140 & 89 | Elgar D. | South Africa v New Zealand | Dunedin | 2016/17 |
| 770 | 166* & 82 | Congdon B.E. | New Zealand v West Indies | Port-of-Spain | 1971/72 |

# Longest Individual Innings

| Mins | Runs | | | | |
|------|------|--|--|--|--|
| 775 | 302 | McCullum B.B. | New Zealand v India | Wellington | 2013/14 |
| 741 | 306 | Richardson M.H. | New Zealand v Zimbabwe A | Kwekwe | 2000/01 |
| 720 | 163 | Shoaib Mohammad | Pakistan v New Zealand | Wellington | 1988/89 |
| 704 | 259 | Turner G.M. | New Zealand v West Indies | Georgetown | 1971/72 |
| 694 | 264* | Latham T.W.M. | New Zealand v Sri Lanka | Wellington | 2018/19 |
| 685 | 180 | Reid J.F. | New Zealand v Sri Lanka | Colombo | 1983/84 |
| 671 | 212* | Richardson M.H. | New Zealand A v Sussex | Hove | 2000 |
| 667 | 205 | Watling B-J. | England v New Zealand | Mt Maunganui | 2019/20 |
| 659 | 211* | Gibbs H.H. | South Africa v New Zealand | Christchurch | 1998/99 |
| 658 | 275* | Cullinan D.J. | South Africa v New Zealand | Auckland | 1998/99 |
| 655 | 146* | Greatbatch M.J. | New Zealand v Australia | Perth | 1989/90 |
| 655 | 274* | Fleming S.P. | New Zealand v Sri Lanka | Colombo | 2002/03 |
| 648 | 158 | Radley C.T. | England v New Zealand | Auckland | 1977/78 |
| 647 | 251* | Harris C.Z. | Canterbury v Central Districts | Rangiora | 1996/97 |
| 643 | 137 | Gambhir G. | India v New Zealand | Napier | 2008/09 |
| 636 | 170* | Jones A.H. | New Zealand v India | Auckland | 1989/90 |
| 635 | 226 | Root J.E. | England v New Zealand | Hamilton | 2019/20 |
| 625 | 222 | Rutherford I.A. | Otago v Central Districts | New Plymouth | 1978/79 |
| 624 | 251 | Williamson K.S. | New Zealand v West Indies | Hamilton | 2020/21 |
| 623 | 242* | Williamson K.S. | New Zealand v Sri Lanka | Wellington | 2014/15 |
| 621 | 226 | Hay G.R. | Central Districts v Otago | Alexandra | 2018/19 |
| 610 | 299 | Crowe M.D. | New Zealand v Sri Lanka | Wellington | 1990/91 |
| 609 | 120* | Crowe J.J. | New Zealand v Sri Lanka | Colombo | 1986/87 |
| 606 | 241* | Latham T.W.M. | Canterbury v Wellington | Wellington | 2013/14 |
| 605 | 267* | Young B.A. | New Zealand v Sri Lanka | Dunedin | 1996/97 |
| 603 | 259 | Turner G.M. | New Zealand v Guyana | Georgetown | 1971/72 |
| 603 | 256 | Raval J.A. | Auckland v Central Districts | Auckland | 2008/09 |

## Fastest Fifties
### (by time)

| Mins | Balls | | | | |
|------|-------|--|--|--|--|
| 15 | | Dacre C.C.R. | New Zealand v Gloucestershire | Cheltenham | 1927 |
| 24 | 32 | Cooper B.G. | Northern Districts v Canterbury | Gisborne | 1986/87 |
| 25 | | Reid J.R. | New Zealand v Orange Free State | Bloemfontein | 1961/62 |

## Fastest Fifties
### (by balls faced)

| Balls | Mins | | | | |
|-------|------|--|--|--|--|
| 20 | 30 | Adams A.R. | Auckland v Otago | Auckland | 1997 98 |
| 21 | | Adams A.R. | Auckland v Canterbury | Auckland | 2006/07 |
| 21 | 33 | Phillips G.D. | Auckland v Otago | Dunedin | 2021/22 |
| 22 | 31 | Cairns B.L. | Otago v Wellington | Lower Hutt | 1979/80 |
| 22 | 36 | Maguiness S.J. | Wellington v Canterbury | Christchurch | 1985/86 |
| 22 | | Twose R.G. | Wellington v Otago | Dunedin | 2000/01 |
| 22 | 26 | Astle T.D. | Canterbury v Otago | Christchurch | 2006/07 |
| 23 | 30 | Bates M.D. | Auckland v Northern Districts | Whangarei | 2009/10 |
| 25 | 37 | Ellis A.M. | Canterbury v Wellington | Wellington | 2015/16 |

## Slowest Fifties
### (by time)

| Mins | Balls | | | | |
|------|-------|--|--|--|--|
| 333 | 229 | Young B.A. | New Zealand v South Africa | Durban | 1994/95 |
| 312 | 234 | Crowe J.J. | New Zealand v Sri Lanka | Colombo | 1986/87 |
| 311 | | Pringle M.R. | Auckland v Northern Districts | Hamilton | 1987/88 |

| Mins | Balls | | | | |
|------|-------|--|--|--|--|
| 310 | 241 | Edgar B.A. | New Zealand v Australia | Wellington | 1981/82 |
| 310 | 241 | Austen M.H. | Otago v Canterbury | Christchurch | 1996/97 |
| 310 | 226 | Yovich J.A.F. | Northern Districts v Canterbury | Hamilton | 2008/09 |

## Slowest Fifties
*(by balls faced)*

| Balls | Mins | | | | |
|-------|------|--|--|--|--|
| 264 | 294 | Smith C.L. | England v New Zealand | Auckland | 1983/84 |
| 251 | 298 | James H.T.G. | Canterbury v Zimbabwe | Timaru | 1997/98 |
| 241 | 310 | Edgar B.A. | New Zealand v Australia | Wellington | 1981/82 |
| 241 | 310 | Austen M.H. | Otago v Canterbury | Christchurch | 1996/97 |
| 239 | 296 | Pocock B.A. | New Zealand v England | Wellington | 1996/97 |
| 234 | 312 | Crowe J.J. | New Zealand v Sri Lanka | Colombo | 1986/87 |
| 231 | | Pollard V. | New Zealand v England | Lord's | 1965 |
| 230 | 254 | Bailey T.E. | England v New Zealand | Christchurch | 1950/51 |
| 230 | 242 | Turner G.M. | New Zealand v England | Christchurch | 1970/71 |

## Fastest Centuries
*(by time)*

| Mins | Balls | | | | |
|------|-------|--|--|--|--|
| 52 | 45 | Cairns B.L. | Otago v Wellington | Lower Hutt | 1979/80 |
| 52 | 66 | Cooper B.G. | Northern Districts v Canterbury | Gisborne | 1986/87 |
| 53 | 63 | Motz R.C. | Canterbury v Otago | Christchurch | 1967/68 |

## Fastest Centuries
*(by balls faced)*

| Balls | Mins | | | | |
|-------|------|--|--|--|--|
| 45 | 52 | Cairns B.L. | Otago v Wellington | Lower Hutt | 1979/80 |
| 54 | | McCullum B.B. | New Zealand v Australia | Christchurch | 2015/16 |
| 60 | | Munro C. | Auckland v Central Districts | Auckland | 2016/17 |

## Slowest Centuries
*(by time)*

| Mins | Balls | | | | |
|------|-------|--|--|--|--|
| 516 | 331 | Crowe J.J. | New Zealand v Sri Lanka | Colombo | 1986/87 |
| 487 | 397 | Radley C.T. | England v New Zealand | Auckland | 1977/78 |
| 464 | 390 | Austen M.H. | Otago v Canterbury | Christchurch | 1996/97 |
| 462 | 341 | Greatbatch M.J. | New Zealand v Australia | Perth | 1989/90 |
| 461 | 265 | Crowe M.D. | New Zealand v Pakistan | Lahore | 1990/91 |
| 458 | 341 | Astle N.J. | New Zealand v Zimbabwe | Wellington | 2000/01 |
| 455 | 307 | Howarth G.P. | New Zealand v England | Auckland | 1977/78 |

## Slowest Centuries
*(by balls faced)*

| Balls | Mins | | | | |
|-------|------|--|--|--|--|
| 399 | 414 | Wright J.G. | New Zealand v India | Auckland | 1980/81 |
| 397 | 487 | Radley C.T. | England v New Zealand | Auckland | 1977/78 |
| 390 | 464 | Austen M.H. | Otago v Canterbury | Christchurch | 1996/97 |
| 380 | 434 | Reid J.F. | Auckland v Northern Districts | Hamilton | 1987/88 |
| 371 | 363 | Jarvis T.W. | New Zealand v West Indies | Guyana | 1971/72 |
| 368 | 375 | Turner G.M. | New Zealand v Pakistan | Dacca | 1969/70 |
| 368 | 427 | Burns K.J. | Otago v Northern Districts | Hamilton | 1987/88 |
| 358 | 386 | Hart R.T. | Central Districts v Wellington | Wanganui | 1993/94 |
| 357 | 337 | Rabone G.O. | New Zealand v South Africa | Durban | 1953/54 |
| 350 | 356 | Reid J.F. | New Zealand v India | Christchurch | 1980/81 |

# Most Boundaries in an Innings

| 6s | 4s | | | Runs | | | |
|----|----|----|----|------|----|----|----|
| 53 | 8 | 45 | Rutherford K.R. | 317 | New Zealand v D.B. Close's XI | Scarborough | 1986 |
| 53 | 5 | 48 | Conway D.P. | 327* | Wellington v Canterbury | Wellington | 2019/20 |
| 52 | 1 | 51 | Papps M.H.W. | 316* | Wellington v Auckland | Wellington | 2017/18 |
| 50 | 15 | 35 | Reid J.R. | 296 | Wellington v Northern Districts | Wellington | 1962/63 |
| 49 | 3 | 46 | Sutcliffe B. | 385 | Otago v Canterbury | Christchurch | 1952/53 |
| 48 | 3 | 45 | Fulton P.G. | 301* | Canterbury v Auckland | Christchurch | 2002/03 |
| 48 | 8 | 40 | Brownlie D.G. | 334 | Northern Districts v Central Districts | New Plymouth | 2014/15 |
| 47 | 3 | 44 | Trumper V.T. | 293 | Sims' Australian XI v Canterbury | Christchurch | 1913/14 |
| 45 | 2 | 43 | Raval J.A. | 256 | Auckland v Central Districts | Auckland | 2008/09 |
| 44 | 10 | 34 | Hammond W.R. | 336* | England v New Zealand | Auckland | 1932/33 |
| 43 | — | 43 | Richardson M.H. | 306 | New Zealand v Zimbabwe A | Kwekwe | 2000/01 |
| 43 | 3 | 40 | McIntosh T.G. | 268 | Auckland v Canterbury | Auckland | 2007/08 |
| 43 | — | 43 | Taylor L.R.P.L. | 290 | New Zealand v Australia | Perth | 2015/16 |
| 42 | 1 | 41 | Reid J.R. | 283 | Wellington v Otago | Wellington | 1951/52 |
| 42 | 1 | 41 | Crowe M.D. | 242* | New Zealand v South Australia | Adelaide | 1985/86 |
| 42 | 3 | 39 | Crowe M.D. | 242 | Central Districts v Otago | New Plymouth | 1989/90 |
| 41 | — | 41 | Blunt R.C. | 338* | Otago v Canterbury | Christchurch | 1931/32 |
| 41 | 14 | 27 | Munro C. | 269* | Auckland v Wellington | Auckland | 2012/13 |
| 40 | — | 40 | de Silva P.A. | 267 | Sri Lanka v New Zealand | Wellington | 1990/91 |
| 40 | 23 | 17 | Munro C. | 281 | Auckland v Central Districts | Napier | 2014/15 |

# Most Sixes in an Innings

| Sixes | | Runs | | | |
|-------|----|------|----|----|----|
| 23 | Munro C. | 281 | Auckland v Central Districts | Napier | 2014/15 |
| 16 | Ryder J.D. | 175 | New Zealand v Australia A | Brisbane | 2011/12 |
| 15 | Reid J.R. | 296 | Wellington v Northern Districts | Wellington | 1962/63 |
| 14 | Munro C. | 269* | Auckland v Wellington | Auckland | 2012/13 |
| 12 | Patel D.N. | 204 | Auckland v Northern Districts | Auckland | 1991/92 |
| 11 | Astle N.J. | 222 | New Zealand v England | Christchurch | 2001/02 |
| 11 | Spearman C.M. | 133 | Central Districts v Auckland | Auckland | 2003/04 |
| 11 | McCullum B.B. | 202 | New Zealand v Pakistan | Sharjah | 2014/15 |
| 11 | McCullum B.B. | 195 | New Zealand v Sri Lanka | Christchurch | 2014/15 |
| 10 | Hammond W.R. | 336* | England v New Zealand | Auckland | 1932/33 |
| 10 | Robinson R.T. | 166 | England XI v Northern Districts | Hamilton | 1987/88 |
| 10 | Styris S.B. | 212* | Northern Districts v Otago | Hamilton | 2001/02 |
| 9 | Cairns B.L. | 110 | Otago v Wellington | Lower Hutt | 1979/80 |
| 9 | Botham I.T. | 80 | England XI v Central Districts | Palmerston North | 1983/84 |
| 9 | Cairns C.L. | 120 | New Zealand v Zimbabwe | Auckland | 1995/96 |
| 9 | Southee T.G. | 77* | New Zaland v England | Napier | 2007/08 |
| 9 | Flynn D.R. | 241 | Northern Districts v Otago | Hamilton | 2010/11 |
| 9 | Cachopa C. | 203 | Auckland v Wellington | Auckland | 2013/14 |
| 9 | Kitchen A.K. | 207 | Otago v Northern Districts | Dunedin | 2016/17 |
| 9 | Kelly N.F. | 234* | Otago v Central Districts | Dunedin | 2021/22 |
| 9 | O'Donnell R.R. | 223 | Auckland v Canterbury | Auckland | 2021/22 |
| 8 | Taylor L.R.P.L. | 152 | Central Districts v Northern Districts | Napier | 2007/08 |
| 8 | Dacre C.C.R. | 176 | New Zealand v Derbyshire | Derby | 1927 |
| 8 | Bula I.L. | 102 | Fiji v Canterbury | Christchurch | 1953/54 |
| 8 | Rutherford K.R. | 317 | New Zealand v DB Close's XI | Scarborough | 1986 |
| 8 | Germon L.K. | 160* | Canterbury v Wellington | Christchurch | 1989/90 |
| 8 | Parore A.C. | 111* | Auckland v Wellington | Auckland | 1997/98 |
| 8 | Horne M.J. | 209* | Auckland v Northern Districts | Auckland | 2003/04 |
| 8 | Adams A.R. | 117* | Auckland v Otago | Lincoln | 2006/07 |

| Sixes | | Runs | | | |
|---|---|---|---|---|---|
| 8 | Franklin J.E.C. | 219 | Wellington v Auckland | Auckland | 2008/09 |
| 8 | Fulton P.G. | 122 | Canterbury v Northern Districts | Christchurch | 2008/09 |
| 8 | de Grandhomme C. | 103* | Auckland v Central Districts | Auckland | 2008/09 |
| 8 | Brownlie D.G. | 334 | Northern Districts v Central Districts | New Plymouth | 2014/15 |
| 8 | Ellis A.M. | 143 | Canterbury v Northern Districts | Hamilton | 2015/16 |
| 8 | Cleaver D. | 201 | Central Districts v Northern Districts | Napier | 2019/20 |

## Five Sixes off Consecutive Balls

Germon L.K.        off Vance R.H.        Canterbury v Wellington        Christchurch        1989/90
*(Full tosses and deliberate no-balls were provided for him to hit).*

## Four Sixes off Consecutive Balls

Rutherford K.R.    off Doshi D.R.    New Zealand v DB Close's XI    Scarborough    1986
McMillan C.D.      off Styris S.B.    Canterbury v Northern Districts Christchurch    1996/97

## Three Sixes off Consecutive Balls

| Hill C. | off Ollivier K.M. | Australia v New Zealand | Wellington | 1904/05 |
|---|---|---|---|---|
| Hammond W.R. | off Newman J. | England v New Zealand | Auckland | 1932/33 |
| McRae D.A.N. | off Burke C. | Canterbury v Auckland | Auckland | 1937/38 |
| Pritchard T.L. | off Groves L.J. | Wellington v Otago | Dunedin | 1937/38 |
| Edwards R.M. | off Carew M.C. | Governor General's XI v West Indies | Auckland | 1968/69 |
| Burgess M.G. | off Anderson R.W. | Auckland v Central Districts | Wanganui | 1977/78 |
| Stirling D.A. | off Brown V.R. | Central Districts v Canterbury | New Plymouth | 1986/87 |
| Thomson S.A. | off Bracewell J.G. | Northern Districts v Auckland | Auckland | 1987/88 |
| Hick G.A. | off Duff S.W. | England XI v Central Districts | New Plymouth | 1991/92 |
| Astle N.J. | off Wells J.D. | Canterbury v Wellington | Christchurch | 1994/95 |
| Vincent L. | off Vettori D.L. | Auckland v Northern Districts | Auckland | 1998/99 |
| Astle N.J. | off Caddick A.R. | New Zealand v England | Christchurch | 2001/02 |
| Spearman C.M. | off Nicol R.J. | Central Districts v Auckland | Auckland | 2003/04 |
| Adams A.R. | off Bowden D.J. | Auckland v Wellington | Wellington | 2005/06 |
| Nicol R.J. | off Worker G.H. | Auckland v Central Districts | Auckland | 2008/09 |
| Taylor L.R.P.L. | off Hauritz N.M. | New Zealand v Australia | Hamilton | 2009/10 |
| Southee T.G. | off Zulfiqar Babar | New Zealand v Pakistan | Dubai | 2014/15 |
| Boult T.A. | off Craig M.D. | Northern Districts v Otago | Mt Maunganui | 2018/19 |
| de Grandhomme C. | off Rae M.D. | Northern Districts v Otago | Mt Maunganui | 2020/21 |
| Shepherd R.* | off McConchie C.E. | West Indies A v New Zealand A | Mt Maunganui | 2020/21 |

*\* Shepherd had also hit a six from the previous ball he had faced (from I.S. Sodhi)*

# Most Ducks in Succession

| | | | |
|---|---|---|---|
| 5 | Hayes J.A. | (C, NZ 1954/55) | 17,0 / dnb / 0,0 / 0,0 |
| 5 | Bateman S.N. | (C 1982/83) | 5*,0 / 0,0 / 0,0 |
| 4 | Frith W. | (C 1882/83-1887/88) | 0,0 / 0,0 |
| 4 | Silver R.C.D. | (O 1936/37-1937/38) | 12,0 / 0,0 / 0,11 |
| *4 | Langdon M.C. | (ND 1957/58) | 25,0 / 0,0 / 0,5 |
| 4 | Hastings B.F. | (C 1963/64) | 1,0 / 0,0 / 0,35 |
| 4 | Steele H.K.C. | (A 1974/75) | 0,0 / 0,0 |
| 4 | Bracewell B.P. | (NZ 1978) | 0 / dnb / 0,0 / 0,0* |
| 4 | Bradburn G.E. | (ND 1987/88) | 0 / 0,0 / 0 |
| 4 | Morrison D.K. | (NZ 1993/94) | 0 / 0,0 / 0,20* |
| 4 | Davis H.T. | (NZ, W 1997/98) | 7*,0 / 0,0 / 0,21 |
| 4 | Young R.A. | (A 1999/00) | 0,0 / 0,0 |
| 4 | Martin C.S. | (C NZ 2000/01) | 5,0 / 0,0 / 0 |
| 4 | Gaffaney C.B. | (O 2001/02) | 31,0 / 0,0 / 0,56 |
| 4 | Hamilton L.J. | (CD 2004/05) | 11,0 / 0,0 / 0,2 |
| 4 | Astle T.D. | (C 2008/09) | 18,0 / 0,0 / 0,1 |
| 4 | McPeake I.G. | (W 2020/21) | 0,0 / 0,0 |

*\* first three games in first-class cricket*

# Most Scoreless Innings in Succession

| | | | |
|---|---|---|---|
| 10 | Visser P.J. | (CD 1984/85-1985/86) | 0 / 0,0 / 0*,0 / 0*,0* / 0,0 / 0 |
| 9 | Martin C.S. | (NZ 2008, War 2008, NZ 2008/09) | 0* / 0,0* / 0*,0 / 0 / 0 / 0*,0* |
| 7 | Hamilton L.J. | (CD 1999/00) | 0,0* / 0 / 0*,0 / 0 / 0 |
| 6 | Hayes J.A. | (C, NZ 1954/55-1955/56) | 17,0 / 0,0 / 0,0 / 0* |
| 6 | de Groen R.P. | (A 1988/89-1989/90) | 1,0* / 0,0 / 0* / 0*,0* |
| 6 | Martin C.S. | (NZ, NZW, A 2005/06 - 2006/07) | 1,0 / 0*,0 / 0* / 0* / 0*,4* |
| 6 | Martin C.S. | (NZ, NZ A 2008/09)) | 0,0 / 0*,0* / 0*,0* |
| 5 | Frith W. | (O, C 1881/82-1887/8) | 1,0* / 0,0 / 0,0 |
| *5 | Moss A.E. | (C 1889/90) | 0,0* / 0,0 / 0*,4* |
| 5 | Burrows J.T. | (C 1932/33) | 0*,0* / 0* / 0*,0* |
| 5 | Hill J. | (O 1961/62-1962/63) | 0*,0* / 0* / 0*,0* |
| 5 | Unka H. | (ND 1968/69-1971/72) | 0* / 0*,0* / 0*,0 |
| 5 | Bracewell B.P. | (NZ 1978) | 0 / 0,0 / 0,0* |
| 5 | Webb R.J. | (O 1980/81) | 1,0 / 0 / 0* / 0,0* |
| 5 | Troup G.B. | (A, NZ 1980/81-1981/82) | 0,0* / 0,0 / 0 |
| 5 | Bateman S.N. | (C 1982/83) | 5*,0 / 0,0 / 0,0 |
| 5 | Arnel B.J. | (ND 2012/13) | 0*,0 / 0, / 0* / 0,4* |
| †5 | McMillan J.M. | (O 2012/13-2013/14) | 0 / 0 / 0* / 0* / 0 |

*\* first five innings in first-class cricket*

*† last five innings in first-class cricket*

# UNUSUAL DISMISSALS

**HANDLED THE BALL**

| | | | |
|---|---|---|---|
| Benson E.T. | MCC v Auckland | Auckland | 1929/30 |
| Gilbertson A.W. | Otago v Auckland | Auckland | 1952/53 |
| Vaughan J.T.C. | NZ Emerging Players v England XI | Hamilton | 1991/92 |
| Williams W.S.A. | Canterbury v Otago | Dunedin | 2012/13 |

**OBSTRUCTING THE FIELD**

| | | | |
|---|---|---|---|
| Hayes J.A. | Canterbury v Central Districts | Christchurch | 1954/55 |
| Blundell T.A. | Wellington v Otago | Wellington | 2020/21 |

*(prior to a change in the laws in 2017, Blundell would have been given out handled the ball)*

**RUN OUT BY THE BOWLER** *(while backing up before the ball had been bowled)*

| | | | |
|---|---|---|---|
| Wilson W.C. by Hendley W. | Canterbury v Otago | Christchurch | 1864/65 |
| Powys R.A.N. by Hendley W. | Canterbury v Otago | Dunedin | 1865/66 |
| Reese T.W. by Downes A.D. | Canterbury v Otago | Christchurch | 1894/95 |
| Smith J. by Allen R. | Canterbury v Wellington | Wellington | 1943/44 |
| Randall D.W. by Chatfield E.J. | England v New Zealand | Christchurch | 1977/78 |

**STUMPED BY A SUBSTITUTE**

| | | | |
|---|---|---|---|
| Pervez Sajjad by Congdon B.E. | Pakistan v New Zealand | Lahore | 1964/65 |
| Congdon B.E. by Burge P.J.P. | Central Districts v Australia | Palmerston North | 1966/67 |
| Latham T.W.M. by Bharat K.S. | New Zealand v India | Kanpur | 2021/22 |

**RETIRED (out)**

| | | | |
|---|---|---|---|
| Ransford V.S. | Australia v Hawke's Bay | Napier | 1920/21 |
| Chappell G.S. | Australia v Wellington | Wellington | 1976/77 |
| Saeed Anwar | Pakistan v New Zealand XI | Napier | 1993/94 |
| Basit Ali | Pakistan v New Zealand XI | Napier | 1993/94 |
| Inzamam-ul-Haq | Pakistan v New Zealand XI | Napier | 1993/94 |
| Spearman C.M. | New Zealand v North West | Potchefstroom | 2000/01 |
| Strauss A.J. | England v Major Association XI | Dunedin | 2007/08 |
| Taylor L.R.P.L. | New Zealand v Northamptonshire | Northampton | 2008 |
| How J.M. | Central Districts v Northern Districts | Napier | 2009/10 |

# REPRESENTED TWO PROVINCES IN ONE SEASON

| | | |
|---|---|---|
| Sutcliffe B. | Auckland and Otago | 1946/47 |
| Sutcliffe B. | Otago and Auckland | 1947/48 |
| Clark L.A. | Otago and Auckland | 1959/60 |
| Andrews B. | Canterbury and Central Districts | 1966/67 |
| Ave M.T.M.M.J. | Central Districts and Otago | 2021/22 |

*Ave was a loan player to Otago in a Plunket Shield match. On the other occasions, the second province was represented in a match against a non-provincial side.*

# REPLACEMENT PLAYERS

| Substitute | Player replaced | | | |
|---|---|---|---|---|
| Lawrence J. | Bell F.H.D. | Wellington v Nelson | Wellington | 1873/74 |
| Cotterill C.N. | White G. | Hawke's Bay v NSW | Napier | 1893/94 |
| unknown | Epeli V. | Fiji v Auckland | Auckland | 1894/95 |
| Kilgour W.A. | *Wilson C.G. | Otago v Auckland | Auckland | 1907/08 |
| Bryden J.S. | *Siedeberg H.G. | Otago v Canterbury | Dunedin | 1913/14 |
| Graham W.H. | Middleton F.S. | Auckland v Wellington | Wellington | 1917/18 |
| Whitta H.B. | *Foster P.S. | Canterbury v Wellington | Christchurch | 1919/20 |
| Samuels B. | *Brice A.W.S. | Wellington v Auckland | Auckland | 1919/20 |
| Wilson E.S. | Eastman L.C. | Otago v Wellington | Wellington | 1927/28 |
| Kubunavanua P. | Logavatu I.T. | Fiji v Canterbury | Christchurch | 1947/48 |
| Abernethy B. | Webb R.J. | Otago v Auckland | Dunedin | 1982/83 |
| Neutze P.S. | Brown V.R. | Auckland v Wellington | Auckland | 1987/88 |
| Brown R.K. | Greatbatch M.J. | Central Districts v Otago | Palmerston North | 1991/92 |
| Lee C.D. | Larsen G.R. | Wellington v Northern Dists | Hamilton | 1991/92 |
| Fleming S.P. | Harris C.Z. | Canterbury v Auckland | Auckland | 1991/92 |
| Lee C.D. | *Patel D.N. | Auckland v Otago | Dunedin | 1994/95 |
| Garner C.D. | Spearman C.M. | Central Dists v Northern Dists | Nelson | 1996/97 |
| Cooper D.M. | Howell L.G. | Central Dists v Northern Dists | Nelson | 1996/97 |
| Lamont M.J. | Horne M.J. | Otago v Auckland | Dunedin | 1996/97 |
| Morland N.D. | Wiseman P.J. | Otago v Auckland | Dunedin | 1996/97 |
| Sewell D.G. | Kennedy R.J. | Otago v Auckland | Dunedin | 1996/97 |
| Irving R.J.R. | Mills J.M. | Auckland v Otago | Dunedin | 1996/97 |
| Weenink S.W. | Chandler P.J.B. | Wellington v Canterbury | Christchurch | 1996/97 |
| Jonas G.R. | Davis H.T. | Wellington v Canterbury | Christchurch | 1996/97 |
| Hartland B.R. | Murray D.J. | Canterbury v Wellington | Christchurch | 1996/97 |
| Frew R.M. | Harris C.Z. | Canterbury v Wellington | Christchurch | 1996/97 |
| Sharpe M.F. | Allott G.I. | Canterbury v Wellington | Christchurch | 1996/97 |
| Hotter S.J. | Davis H.T. | Wellington v Central Districts | Masterton | 1996/97 |
| Muir G.A. | Priest M.W. | Canterbury v Zimbabwe | Timaru | 1997/98 |
| Pawson S.J. | Priest M.W. | Canterbury v Otago | Dunedin | 1997/98 |
| Dry L.R. | Bell M.D. | Wellington v Northern Dists | Hamilton | 1998/99 |
| Morland N.D. | *Wiseman P.J. | Otago v Auckland | Dunedin | 1999/00 |
| Spearman C.M. | Sinclair M.S. | Central Districts v Otago | Palmerston North | 1999/00 |
| Todd G.R. | Oram J.D.P. | Central Districts v Wellington | Napier | 2000/01 |
| McCullum N.L. | Wiseman P.J. | Otago v Canterbury | Alexandra | 2000/01 |
| Robinson G.G. | *Marshall J.A.H. | Northern Dists v Canterbury | Gisborne | 2004/05 |
| O'Brien I.E. | Rasmussen S. | Wellington v Otago | Dunedin | 2006/07 |
| Hitchcock P.A. | *Hopkins G.J. | Auckland v Wellington | Auckland | 2008/09 |
| Houghton M.V. | Patel J.S. | Wellington v Auckland | Auckland | 2008/09 |
| Shaw L.J. | McIntosh T.G. | Auckland v West Indies | Auckland | 2008/09 |
| Boult J.J. | Martin B.P. | Northern Districts v Auckland | Whangarei | 2008/09 |
| Robertson I.A. | Thompson E.P. | N.Zealand A v England Lions | Lincoln | 2008/09 |
| Raval J.A. | McIntosh T.G. | Auckland v Otago | Queenstown | 2008/09 |
| Shaw L.J. | Martin C.S. | Auckland v Otago | Queenstown | 2008/09 |
| Davis T.T. | Arnel B.J. | Northern Dists v Canterbury | Christchurch | 2008/09 |
| Scott B.E. | Flynn D.R. | Northern Dists v Canterbury | Christchurch | 2008/09 |
| Boam H.K.P. | Franklin J.E.C. | Wellington v Central Districts | Napier | 2008/09 |
| Croft S.J. | Mills K.D. | Auckland v Central Districts | Auckland | 2008/09 |
| Patel J.S. | Burns M. | Wellington v Northern Dists | Hamilton | 2009/10 |
| Milne A.F. | *Mason M.J. | Central Districts v Canterbury | New Plymouth | 2009/10 |
| van Beek L.V. | Stewart S.L. | Canterbury v Central Districts | New Plymouth | 2009/10 |
| Kitchen A.K. | *Hopkins G.J. | Auckland v Otago | Dunedin | 2009/10 |
| Gillespie M.R. | Patel J.S. | Wellington v Central Districts | Napier | 2009/10 |

| Substitute | Player replaced | | | |
|---|---|---|---|---|
| Astle T.D. | Martin C.S. | Canterbury v Otago | Queenstown | 2009/10 |
| Tuffey D.R. | Munro C. | Auckland v Canterbury | Christchurch | 2010/11 |
| van Beek L.V. | *Lonsdale W.M. | Canterbury v Auckland | Christchurch | 2010/11 |
| Styris S.B. | Scott B.E. | Northern Districts v Otago | Queenstown | 2010/11 |
| McCullum N.L. | Butler I.G. | Otago v Northern Districts | Queenstown | 2010/11 |
| Henry M.J. | Ellis A.M. | Canterbury v Wellington | Rangiora | 2010/11 |
| Latham T.W.M. | Astle T.D. | Canterbury v Wellington | Rangiora | 2010/11 |
| Verma A. | Watling B-J. | Northern Districts v Otago | Dunedin | 2011/12 |
| Johnston T.G. | Latham T.W.M. | Canterbury v Northern Dists | Rangiora | 2011/12 |
| Tuffey D.R. | Martin C.S. | Auckland v Central Districts | Napier | 2011/12 |
| Young W.A. | *Taylor L.R.P.L. | Central Districts v Auckland | Napier | 2011/12 |
| de Terte J.W. | van Wyk C.F.K. | Central Districts v Auckland | Napier | 2011/12 |
| Devcich A.P. | Vettori D.L. | Northern Districts v Otago | Hamilton | 2011/12 |
| Hiini B.C. | *Arnel B.J. | Northern Districts v Otago | Hamilton | 2011/12 |
| Santner M.J. | *Boult T.A. | Northern Districts v Otago | Hamilton | 2011/12 |
| Arnel B.J. | Boult T.A. | Northern Districts v Auckland | Auckland | 2011/12 |
| Mitchell D.J. | Flynn D.R. | Northern Districts v Auckland | Auckland | 2011/12 |
| Wagner N. | Duffy J.A. | Otago v Auckland | Auckland | 2012/13 |
| Martin C.S. | Bartlett D.J. | Auckland v Otago | Auckland | 2012/13 |
| Astle T.D. | *Hira R.M. | Canterbury v Northern Dists | Hamilton | 2012/13 |
| Wagner N. | Soper B.E. | Otago v Northern Districts | Queenstown | 2012/13 |
| Elliott G.D. | Boam H.K.P. | Wellington v Canterbury | Wellington | 2012/13 |
| Boam H.K.P. | Ronchi L. | Wellington v Canterbury | Wellington | 2012/13 |
| Fulton D.H. | Latham T.W.M. | Canterbury v Wellington | Wellington | 2012/13 |
| Bates M.D. | *Ferguson L.H. | Auckland v Wellington | Wellington | 2012/13 |
| Ronchi L. | Blundell T.A. | Wellington v Auckland | Wellington | 2012/13 |
| Latham T.W.M. | Fulton D.H. | Canterbury v Northern Dists | Christchurch | 2012/13 |
| Walker J.G. | Sodhi I.S. | Northern Dists v Central Dists | Napier | 2015/16 |
| van Beek L.V. | Henry M.J. | Canterbury v Auckland | Rangiora | 2016/17 |
| Cooper H.R. | Brownlie D.G. | Northern Dists v Central Dists | Napier | 2016/17 |
| Rance S.H.A. | Bracewell D.A.J. | Central Dists v Northern Dists | Napier | 2016/17 |
| Younghusband P.F. | Patel J.S. | Wellington v Canterbury | Wellington | 2016/17 |
| Ronchi L. | Taylor M.J. | Wellington v Otago | Wellington | 2016/17 |
| Hampton B.R. | Kuggeleijn S.C. | Northern Districts v Wellington | Mt Maunganui | 2016/17 |
| Rae M.D. | *Hicks S. | Otago v Wellington | Dunedin | 2017/18 |
| Conway D.P. | Blundell T.A. | Wellington v Otago | Dunedin | 2017/18 |
| Ridley A.D. | Woodcock L.J. | Wellington v Central Districts | Wellington | 2017/18 |
| van Woerkom T.F. | McClure K.J. | Canterbury v Northern Dists | Christchurch | 2018/19 |
| Brown J.A. | McEwan M.B. | Auckland v Northern Dists | Auckland | 2018/19 |
| Astle T.D. | *van Woerkom T.F. | Canterbury v Auckland | Rangiora | 2018/19 |
| Young W.A. | Smith B.S. | Central Dists v Northern Dists | Napier | 2018/19 |
| Kuggeleijn S.C | Rutherford H.D. | New Zealand A v England | Whangarei | 2019/20 |
| Rae M.D. | Tickner B.M. | New Zealand A v India A | Lincoln | 2019/20 |
| Lister B.G. | Sodhi I.S. | New Zealand A v India A | Lincoln | 2019/20 |
| Walker J.G. | *Sodhi I.S. | Northern Dists v Central Dists | Hamilton | 2020/21 |
| Lister B.G. | †Chapman M.S. | Auckland v Otago | Auckland | 2020/21 |
| Bacon M.B. | Chu M.W. | Otago v Northern Districts | Mt Maunganui | 2020/21 |
| Fletcher A.T. | Sears B.V. | Wellington v Otago | Wellington | 2020/21 |
| Boyle J.C.T. | Carter L.J. | Canterbury v Auckland | Auckland | 2020/21 |
| O'Donnell W.T. | Solia S.M. | Auckland v Canterbury | Auckland | 2021/22 |
| Smith N.G. | Neesham J.D.S. | Wellington v Northern Dists | Whangarei | 2021/22 |
| Muller T. | Gibson J.M. | Otago v Canterbury | Rangiora | 2021/22 |

*\* indicates player did not bat or bowl before being replaced*

*† Lister began the game as a Covid subsitute for Chapman who subsequently replaced him*

# BOWLING

## Ten Wickets in an Innings

| | Overs | Maidens | Runs | Wickets | | | |
|---|---|---|---|---|---|---|---|
| * Moss A.E. | 21.3 | 10 | 28 | 10 | Canterbury v Wellington | Christchurch | 1889/90 |
| Patel A.Y. | 47.5 | 12 | 119 | 10 | New Zealand v India | Mumbai | 2021/22 |

*\* on debut — the only instance in first-class cricket*

## Nine Wickets in an Innings

| | Overs | Maidens | Runs | Wickets | | | |
|---|---|---|---|---|---|---|---|
| Wiseman P.J. | 16.4 | 9 | 13 | 9 | Canterbury v Central Districts | Christchurch | 2004/05 |
| Wensley A.F. | 24 | 13 | 36 | 9 | Auckland v Otago | Auckland | 1929/30 |
| Eden T.G. | 15.2 | 0 | 43 | 9 | Nelson v Wellington | Wellington | 1875/76 |
| Dent T.H. | 28 | 11 | 47 | 9 | Hawke's Bay v Wellington | Napier | 1900/01 |
| Tait A.R. | 24.5 | 8 | 48 | 9 | Northern Districts v Auckland | Hamilton | 1996/97 |
| Fisher A.H. | 25.2 | 4 | 50 | 9 | Otago v Queensland | Dunedin | 1896/97 |
| Hadlee R.J. | 23.4 | 4 | 52 | 9 | New Zealand v Australia | Brisbane | 1985/86 |
| Hadlee R.J. | 24 | 5 | 55 | 9 | New Zealand v West Zone | Rajkot | 1988/89 |
| McBeath D.J. | 24 | 7 | 56 | 9 | Canterbury v Auckland | Christchurch | 1918/19 |
| Brice A.W.S. | 25.5 | 5 | 67 | 9 | Wellington v Auckland | Wellington | 1918/19 |
| Blair R.W. | 35 | 9 | 72 | 9 | Wellington v Auckland | Wellington | 1956/57 |
| Cooke F.H. | 56 | 24 | 73 | 9 | Otago v Canterbury | Christchurch | 1884/85 |
| Neill R. | 31 | 7 | 75 | 9 | Auckland v Canterbury | Auckland | 1891/92 |
| Blair R.W. | 29.5 | 9 | 75 | 9 | Wellington v Canterbury | Wellington | 1956/57 |
| Neill R. | 24.2 | 1 | 86 | 9 | Auckland v Canterbury | Auckland | 1897/98 |
| Petherick P.J. | 35 | 10 | 93 | 9 | Otago v Northern Districts | Dunedin | 1975/76 |
| Priest M.W. | 28.5 | 5 | 95 | 9 | Canterbury v Otago | Dunedin | 1989/90 |
| Robertson W. | 39.3 | 8 | 98 | 9 | Canterbury v Wellington | Christchurch | 1894/95 |
| Yuile B.W. | 45 | 19 | 100 | 9 | Central Districts v Canterbury | New Plymouth | 1965/66 |

## Sixteen Wickets in a Match

| | | | | |
|---|---|---|---|---|
| 16-130 | Tait A.R. | 24.5-8-48-9/38.4-13-82-7 | Northern Dists v Auckland, Hamilton | 1996/97 |

## Fifteen Wickets in a Match

| | | | | |
|---|---|---|---|---|
| 15-60 | Callaway S.T. | 23.3-10-33-8/17-7-27-7 | Canterbury v Hawke's Bay, Napier | 1903/04 |
| 15-94 | Cooke F.H. | 40.3-16-61-8/33.3-14-33-7 | Otago v Canterbury, Christchurch | 1882/83 |
| 15-104 | Boock S.L. | 29.3-13-47-7/34.3-16-57-8 | Otago v Auckland, Dunedin | 1989/90 |
| 15-123 | Hadlee R.J. | 23.4-4-52-9/28.5-9-71-6 | New Zealand v Australia, Brisbane | 1985/86 |
| 15-168 | McBeath D.J. | 24-7-56-9/37-4-112-6 | Canterbury v Auckland, Christchurch | 1918/19 |
| 15-175 | Callaway S.T. | 35-14-77-7/43.4-11-98-8 | NSW v New Zealand, Christchurch | 1895/96 |
| 15-203 | Moir A.M. | 24.1-4-84-7/35.1-3-119-8 | Otago v Central Dists, New Plymouth | 1953/54 |

## Fourteen Wickets in a Match

| | | | | |
|---|---|---|---|---|
| 14-59 | Read R.J. | 13-3-35-7/14-5-24-7 | Canterbury v Southland, Invercargill | 1920/21 |
| 14-63 | Eden T.G. | 15.2-0-43-9/15.5-7-20-5 | Nelson v Wellington, Wellington | 1875/76 |
| * 14-63 | Rees A.W. | 13-4-27-6/15.3-3-36-8 | Auckland v Otago, Dunedin | 1889/90 |
| 14-65 | Callaway S.T. | 36.3-18-47-7/18.2-7-18-7 | NSW v Wellington, Wellington | 1895/96 |
| 14-65 | Hayes J.A. | 18.2-6-28-7/12.1-3-37-7 | Auckland v Wellington, Auckland | 1957/58 |
| 14-93 | Torrance R.C. | 23-6-51-7/19-5-42-7 | Otago v Hawke's Bay, Napier | 1908/09 |
| 14-94 | Howarth H.J. | 22.1-5-42-7/23-6-52-7 | Auckland v Otago, Auckland | 1973/74 |
| 14-103 | Downes A.D. | 30-12-32-7/30-8-71-7 | Otago v Hawke's Bay, Dunedin | 1893/94 |
| * 14-107 | Robertson W. | 28.2-8-59-8/20.4-7-48-6 | Canterbury v Auckland, Christchurch | 1893/94 |
| 14-119 | Pringle C. | 27.4-10-63-7/23.5-5-56-7 | Auckland v Otago, Dunedin | 1993/94 |
| 14-126 | Moir A.M. | 18-1-55-8/25-6-71-6 | Otago v Canterbury, Dunedin | 1951/52 |

| 14-136 | Blair R.W. | 29.5-9-75-9/26-8-61-5 | Wellington v Canterbury, Wellington | 1956/57 |
| 14-151 | Gray E.J. | 50-19-114-6/26.1-12-37-8 | Wellington v Canterbury, Lower Hutt | 1985/86 |
| 14-225 | Patel A.Y. | 47.5-12-119-10/26-5-106-4 | New Zealand v India, Mumbai | 2021/22 |
| 14-234 | Astle T.D. | 51.4-9-148-8/35-7-86-6 | Canterbury v Central Districts, Napier | 2013/14 |

* on debut

## Four Wickets with Consecutive Balls

| Downes A.D. | Otago v Auckland | Dunedin | 1893/94 |
| Wagner N. | Otago v Wellington | Queenstown | 2010/11 |

* Wagner achieved the unique feat of taking five wickets in one over

## Hat Tricks

| Salmon I.J. | Wellington v Nelson | Wellington | 1873/74 |
| Lankham W. | Auckland v Taranaki | Auckland | 1882/83 |
| Frith C. | Otago v Canterbury | Dunedin | 1884/85 |
| Fannin H.A. | Hawkes Bay v Taranaki | Napier | 1897/98 |
| Barclay F. | Auckland v Canterbury | Auckland | 1903/04 |
| Orchard S.A. | Canterbury v Auckland | Auckland | 1909/10 |
| Bennett J.H. | Canterbury v Wellington | Wellington | 1911/12 |
| Olliff C. | Auckland v Wellington | Auckland | 1912/13 |
| Middleton F.S. | Wellington v Hawke's Bay | Wellington | 1919/20 |
| Allom M.J.C.* | England v New Zealand | Christchurch | 1929/30 |
| Mulcock E. | Canterbury v Otago | Christchurch | 1937/38 |
| Overton G.W.F. | Otago v Canterbury | Christchurch | 1946/47 |
| Murray R.M. | Wellington v Otago | Wellington | 1949/50 |
| Moir A.M. | Otago v Canterbury | Christchurch | 1950/51 |
| Jones J.F. | Wellington v Central Districts | Wellington | 1953/54 |
| Reid R.E. | Wellington v Otago | Dunedin | 1958/59 |
| Bartlett G.A. | Central Districts v Northern Districts | Hamilton | 1959/60 |
| Cameron F.J. | Otago v Northern Districts | Hamilton | 1962/63 |
| Blair R.W. | Wellington v Northern Districts | Wellington | 1962/63 |
| Alabaster G.D. | Northern Districts v Canterbury | Hamilton | 1962/63 |
| Furlong B.D.M. | NZ Under 23 XI v Canterbury | Christchurch | 1964/65 |
| Hadlee R.J. | Canterbury v Central Districts | Nelson | 1971/72 |
| Petherick P.J. | New Zealand v Pakistan | Lahore | 1976/77 |
| Toynbee M.H. | Central Districts v Northern Districts | Gisborne | 1979/80 |
| Visser P.J. | Central Districts v Auckland | Nelson | 1983/84 |
| Maguiness S.J. | Wellington v Northern Districts | Wellington | 1983/84 |
| Beard D.A. | Northern Districts v Central Districts | Nelson | 1989/90 |
| Gale A.J. | Otago v Canterbury | Dunedin | 1992/93 |
| Harris C.Z. | New Zealand v Orange Free State | Bloemfontein | 1994/95 |
| Hayes R.L. | Northern Districts v Central Districts | Rotorua | 1995/96 |
| Hotter S.J. | Wellington v Otago | Wellington | 1996/97 |
| Anderson T.R. | Central Districts v Auckland | Masterton | 1998/99 |
| Canning T.K. | Auckland v Central Districts | Auckland | 1999/00 |
| Orchard M.G. | Northern Districts v Canterbury | Gisborne | 2003/04 |
| Franklin J.E.C. | New Zealand v Bangladesh | Dhaka | 2004/05 |
| Sidebottom R.J. | England v New Zealand | Hamilton | 2007/08 |
| McClenaghan M.J. | Central Districts v Canterbury | Rangiora | 2008/09 |
| Aldridge G.W. | Northern Districts v Central Districts | Whangarei | 2010/11 |
| Noema-Barnett K. | Central Districts v Otago | Nelson | 2013/14 |
| Hutchinson D.S. | Wellington v Northern Districts | Hamilton | 2015/16 |
| Tickner B.M. | Central Districts v Wellington | Nelson | 2017/18 |
| van Beek L.V.† | Wellington v Canterbury | Christchurch | 2017/18 |
| McEwan M.B.† | Auckland v Northern Districts | Auckland | 2017/18 |

| Lister B.G. | Auckland v Otago | Auckland | 2018/19 |
| Jamieson K.A. | Auckland v Central Districts | Auckland | 2020/21 |
| Delport L.J. | Auckland v Northern Districts | Whangarei | 2020/21 |
| Rae M.D. | Otago v Central Districts | Dunedin | 2020/21 |

*\* Allom took 4 wickets with 5 balls in the same over † van Beek and McEwan performed their hat-tricks on the same day*

## Most Wickets in a Single Day's Play in New Zealand

| 14 | Rees A.W. | Auckland v Otago | Dunedin | 1889/90 |
| 13 | Lankham W. | Auckland v Taranaki | Auckland | 1882/83 |
| 13 | Smith C.R. | Hawke's Bay v Taranaki | Hawera | 1891/92 |
| 13 | Cave H.B. | Central Districts v Auckland | Palmerston North | 1952/53 |

## Outstanding Analyses

**TEN WICKETS IN AN INNINGS**

| 21.3 | 11 | 28 | 10 | Moss A.E. | Canterbury v Wellington | Christchurch | 1889/90 |

**NINE WICKETS IN AN INNINGS**

| 16.4 | 9 | 13 | 9 | Wiseman P.J. | Canterbury v Central Districts | Christchurch | 2004/05 |
| 24 | 13 | 36 | 9 | Wensley A.F. | Auckland v Otago | Auckland | 1929/30 |
| 15.2 | 0 | 43 | 9 | Eden T.G. | Nelson v Wellington | Wellington | 1875/76 |
| 28 | 11 | 47 | 9 | Dent T.H. | Hawke's Bay v Wellington | Napier | 1900/01 |

**EIGHT WICKETS IN AN INNINGS**

| 13 | 6 | 13 | 8 | Firth J.P. | Wellington v Hawke's Bay | Wellington | 1883/84 |
| 19 | 12 | 14 | 8 | Austin S.W. | NSW v Hawke's Bay | Napier | 1893/94 |
| 29 | 21 | 18 | 8 | Frith W. | Canterbury v Otago | Christchurch | 1880/81 |
| 14.5 | 7 | 19 | 8 | Fannin H.A. | Hawke's Bay v Auckland | Auckland | 1897/98 |

**SEVEN WICKETS IN AN INNINGS**

| 10.1 | 6 | 9 | 7 | Bracewell J.G. | Otago v Canterbury | Dunedin | 1981/82 |
| 13 | 9 | 11 | 7 | Fisher A.H. | Otago v Canterbury | Christchurch | 1896/97 |
| 25.3 | 16 | 12 | 7 | Downes A.D. | Otago v Canterbury | Dunedin | 1896/97 |
| 16 | 8 | 12 | 7 | Tuffey D.R. | Northern Districts v Wellington | Hamilton | 2000/01 |
| 32.1 | 24 | 13 | 7 | Lankham W. | Auckland v Taranaki | Auckland | 1882/83 |
| 10.4 | 5 | 16 | 7 | Farooq Hamid | Pakistan v Wellington | Wellington | 1964/65 |
| 17 | 10 | 17 | 7 | Armstrong W.W. | Australia v Wellington | Wellington | 1913/14 |
| 14.2 | 7 | 17 | 7 | Maguiness S.J. | Wellington v Canterbury | Rangiora | 1984/85 |
| 18.2 | 7 | 18 | 7 | Callaway S.T. | NSW v Wellington | Wellington | 1895/96 |

**SIX WICKETS IN AN INNINGS**

| 8 | 5 | 3 | 6 | Cowie J. | New Zealand v Ireland | Dublin | 1937 |
| 8 | 5 | 4 | 6 | Callaway S.T. | Canterbury v Wellington | Wellington | 1903/04 |
| 9.2 | 3 | 5 | 6 | Bennett A.P. | Nelson v Wellington | Nelson | 1885/86 |
| 16 | 11 | 6 | 6 | Haskell W.J.R. | Wellington v Otago | Wellington | 1967/68 |
| 14 | 10 | 7 | 6 | Dunlop D.E.L. | Canterbury v Wellington | Wellington | 1886/87 |
| 18 | 14 | 7 | 6 | Hampton B.L. | Central Districts v Otago | Dunedin | 1963/64 |
| 15 | 10 | 8 | 6 | Downes W.F. | Otago v Canterbury | Christchurch | 1866/67 |
| 11.2 | 6 | 9 | 6 | Fowler G. | Nelson v Wellington | Nelson | 1887/88 |
| 9.3 | 6 | 10 | 6 | Pearson F.A. | Auckland v Hawke's Bay | Auckland | 1910/11 |

**FIVE WICKETS IN AN INNINGS**

| 15.2 | 13 | 2 | 5 | Ashby D.A. | Canterbury v Auckland | Auckland | 1877/78 |
| 5 | 3 | 3 | 5 | Allcott C.F.W. | New Zealand v Somerset | Taunton | 1927 |
| 10.3 | 6 | 5 | 5 | Bright R.J. | Australia v Central Districts | Nelson | 1976/77 |
| 9 | 6 | 6 | 5 | Parker T.S. | Otago v Canterbury | Christchurch | 1866/67 |
| 21 | 18 | 8 | 5 | Frith C. | Otago v Tasmania | Dunedin | 1883/84 |
| 4 | 2 | 8 | 5 | Burnup C.J. | Lord Hawke's XI v NZ | Wellington | 1902/03 |
| 8 | 4 | 8 | 5 | McBeath D.J. | Southland v Canterbury | Invercargill | 1920/21 |

| 5.4 | 1 | 8 | 5 | Solia S.M. | Auckland v Otago | Auckland | 2020/21 |
| 9 | 3 | 9 | 5 | Bennett J.H. | Canterbury v Wellington | Christchurch | 1910/11 |
| 12 | 5 | 9 | 5 | Butterfield L.A. | South Island v North Island | Auckland | 1944/45 |
| 9.1 | 5 | 9 | 5 | Boock S.L. | New Zealand v Middlesex | Lord's | 1978 |

## FOUR WICKETS IN AN INNINGS

| 3.2 | 2 | 1 | 4 | Snedden C.A. | Auckland v Hawke's Bay | Auckland | 1920/21 |
| 6.4 | 5 | 2 | 4 | Puna N. | Northern Dists v Central Dists | Hamilton | 1957/58 |
| 7 | 6 | 3 | 4 | Carrington S.M. | Northern Districts v Otago | Tauranga | 1982/83 |
| 6.5 | 5 | 3 | 4 | Woodcock L.J. | Wellington v Otago | Wellington | 2001/02 |

## THREE WICKETS IN AN INNINGS

| 3 | 3 | 0 | 3 | Smith K.F.H. | Central Districts v Canterbury | Nelson | 1959/60 |
| 2.1 | 2 | 0 | 3 | Barnes S.G. | Australia v Canterbury | Christchurch | 1945/46 |
| 5 | 5 | 0 | 3 | Gray E.J. | Wellington v Canterbury | Christchurch | 1985/86 |
| 1.4 | 0 | 1 | 3 | Bolton B.A. | Canterbury v Central Districts | Christchurch | 1958/59 |
| 2 | 1 | 1 | 3 | Thomson S.A. | Northern Districts v Canterbury | Christchurch | 1992/93 |
| 1.4 | 0 | 2 | 3 | Anthony A. | Canterbury v Wellington | Christchurch | 1908/09 |
| 3.3 | 1 | 2 | 3 | Thomas A.W. | Canterbury v Otago | Christchurch | 1917/18 |
| 4 | 2 | 2 | 3 | Sparling J.T. | Auckland v Wellington | Auckland | 1957/58 |
| 5 | 4 | 2 | 3 | Bennett H.K. | Wellington v Auckland | Wellington | 2017/18 |
| 5 | 2 | 3 | 3 | Cowlishaw W.P. | Canterbury v Otago | Christchurch | 1864/65 |
| 15 | 12 | 3 | 3 | Frith W. | Canterbury v Auckland | Auckland | 1877/78 |
| 2.3 | 1 | 3 | 3 | Richardson G.R. | Nelson v Wellington | Wellington | 1886/87 |
| 3 | 2 | 3 | 3 | Dowson E.M. | Lord Hawke's XI v Otago | Dunedin | 1902/03 |
| 5 | 2 | 3 | 3 | Pollard V. | New Zealand v England | Auckland | 1965/66 |

## Seven Wickets in an Innings on First-class Debut

| 10-28 | | Moss A.E. | Canterbury v Wellington | Christchurch | 1889/90 |
| 8-35 | | Wilson R. | Queensland v Auckland | Auckland | 1896/97 |
| † 8-36 | | Rees A.W. | Auckland v Otago | Dunedin | 1889/90 |
| 8-37 | | Hole H.W. | Nelson v Wellington | Nelson | 1874/75 |
| 8-48 | | O'Connell W.J. | Hawke's Bay v Wellington | Wellington | 1919/20 |
| 8-59 | | Robertson W. | Canterbury v Auckland | Christchurch | 1893/94 |
| 8-70 | | Hay W.A. | Otago v Southland | Dunedin | 1917/18 |
| 7-31 | | Lynch D.J.F. | Auckland v Canterbury | Auckland | 1877/78 |
| 7-36 | | Mills G. | Auckland v Wellington | Auckland | 1886/87 |
| 7-39 | | Lankham W. | Auckland v Canterbury | Christchurch | 1882/83 |
| † 7-42 | | Morrison B.D. | Wellington v Otago | Wellington | 1953/54 |
| † 7-46 | | Stephens W.B. | Auckland v Otago | Auckland | 1899/00 |
| 7-46 | | Doig J.A. | Southland v Otago | Invercargill | 1914/15 |
| † 7-50 | | Badcock F.T. | Wellington v Canterbury | Christchurch | 1924/25 |
| † 7-54 | | Turnbull J.A. | Auckland v Central Districts | Auckland | 1955/56 |
| 7-61 | | Merrin R.C. | Canterbury XI v NZ Touring Team | Christchurch | 1967/68 |
| † 7-95 | | Noonan D.J. | New South Wales v Canterbury | Christchurch | 1895/96 |
| 7-95 | | Huxford N.A. | Wellington v Pakistan | Wellington | 1964/65 |

† 2nd innings

## Ten Wickets in a Match on First-class Debut

| 14-63 | Rees A.W. | Auckland v Otago | Dunedin | 1889/90 |
| 14-107 | Robertson W. | Canterbury v Auckland | Christchurch | 1893/94 |
| 13-72 | Moss A.E. | Canterbury v Wellington | Christchurch | 1889/90 |
| 12-18 | Bennett A.P. | Nelson v Wellington | Nelson | 1885/86 |
| 12-90 | Mills W. | Taranaki v Fiji | Hawera | 1894/95 |
| 12-118 | Hay W.A. | Otago v Southland | Dunedin | 1917/18 |
| 11-43 | Fuller E.T.A. | Canterbury v Otago | Christchurch | 1872/73 |
| 11-97 | Wilson R. | Queensland v Auckland | Auckland | 1896/97 |

| 11-99 | Lankham W. | Auckland v Canterbury | Christchurch | 1882/83 |
| 11-112 | Morrison B.D. | Wellington v Otago | Wellington | 1953/54 |
| 11-126 | Noonan D.J. | New South Wales v Canterbury | Christchurch | 1895/96 |
| 10-30 | Lawson H.W. | Wellington v Nelson | Nelson | 1883/84 |
| 10-31 | MacDonald F. | Otago v Canterbury | Dunedin | 1863/64 |
| 10-39 | Holderness H.V.A. | Otago v Southland | Invercargill | 1918/19 |
| 10-61 | Hole H.W. | Nelson v Wellington | Nelson | 1874/75 |
| 10-70 | Mills G. | Auckland v Wellington | Auckland | 1886/87 |
| 10-71 | Lawton J.C. | Otago v Canterbury | Christchurch | 1890/91 |
| 10-90 | Brown C.M. | Auckland v Canterbury | Rangiora | 1993/94 |
| 10-105 | Frame W.D. | Otago v Canterbury | Dunedin | 1955/56 |
| 10-122 | Badcock F.T. | Wellington v Canterbury | Christchurch | 1924/25 |
| 10-133 | Leonard D.J. | Central Districts v Northern Districts | Rotorua | 1989/90 |

## Ten Wickets in Last First-class Match

| † 10-31 | MacDonald F. | Otago v Canterbury | Dunedin | 1863/64 |
| † 10-61 | Hole H.W. | Nelson v Wellington | Nelson | 1874/75 |
| 10-91 | Downes W.F. | Otago v Canterbury | Dunedin | 1875/76 |
| 12-114 | Lankham W. | Auckland v Canterbury | Auckland | 1883/84 |
| 13-140 | Edser H. | Canterbury v Wellington | Wellington | 1883/84 |
| 11-25 | Fowler G. | Nelson v Wellington | Nelson | 1887/88 |
| 11-77 | Carson W. | Otago v Canterbury | Dunedin | 1887/88 |
| † 10-39 | Holderness H.V.A. | Otago v Southland | Invercargill | 1918/19 |
| 10-108 | Vivian H.G. | Auckland v Wellington | Auckland | 1938/39 |
| 11-129 | de Groen R.P. | Northern Districts v Canterbury | Hamilton | 1995/96 |

† *this was the players only first-class appearance*

## Most Wickets in a Season

| | | Matches | Wkts | Runs | Ave | 5WI | 10WM | Best |
|---|---|---|---|---|---|---|---|---|
| Boock S.L. | 1977/78 | 13 | 66 | 1088 | 16.48 | 6 | — | 7-57 |
| Hadlee R.J. | 1986/87 | 11 | 62 | 935 | 15.08 | 8 | 1 | 7-49 |
| Hadlee R.J. | 1981/82 | 10 | 59 | 867 | 14.69 | 7 | — | 6-26 |
| Boock S.L. | 1978/79 | 12 | 58 | 1238 | 21.34 | 4 | 1 | 8-59 |
| Thompson G.J. | 1902/03 | 7 | 57 | 668 | 11.71 | 6 | 3 | 8-124 |
| Boock S.L. | 1986/87 | 10 | 55 | 920 | 16.72 | 6 | 1 | 6-62 |
| Callaway S.T. | 1903/04 | 5 | 54 | 474 | 8.77 | 8 | 4 | 8-33 |
| Blair R.W. | 1956/57 | 8 | 53 | 784 | 14.79 | 6 | 4 | 9-72 |
| Tait A.R. | 1996/97 | 9 | 53 | 865 | 16.32 | 4 | 1 | 9-48 |
| Drum C.J. | 2001/02 | 9 | 53 | 827 | 15.60 | 3 | 2 | 6-34 |
| Martin C.S. | 2003/04 | 12 | 53 | 1144 | 21.58 | 6 | 1 | 6-76 |
| Austin S.W. | 1893/94 | 7 | 52 | 606 | 11.65 | 6 | 1 | 8-14 |
| Armstrong W.W. | 1913/14 | 8 | 52 | 789 | 15.17 | 7 | 1 | 7-17 |
| O'Sullivan D.R. | 1978/79 | 9 | 52 | 989 | 19.01 | 3 | — | 6-51 |
| Arnel B.J. | 2012/13 | 12 | 52 | 1341 | 25.78 | 2 | — | 5-55 |
| Chatfield E.J. | 1981/82 | 10 | 51 | 868 | 17.01 | 2 | — | 5-29 |
| Wagner N. | 2010/11 | 9 | 51 | 926 | 18.15 | 4 | 1 | 6-36 |
| Wagner N. | 2012/13 | 12 | 51 | 1454 | 28.50 | 1 | — | 5-54 |
| Douglas J.W.H.T. | 1906/07 | 9 | 50 | 663 | 13.26 | 5 | 1 | 7-49 |
| Hadlee R.J. | 1978/79 | 10 | 50 | 909 | 18.18 | 4 | — | 6-28 |
| Gillespie M.R. | 2012/13 | 10 | 50 | 1611 | 32.22 | 2 | 1 | 6-83 |

## Most Wickets in a Season for New Zealand Overseas

| | | Matches | Wkts | Runs | Ave | 5WI | 10WM | Best |
|---|---|---|---|---|---|---|---|---|
| Burtt T.B. | 1949 | 27 | 128 | 2929 | 22.28 | 11 | 2 | 7-102 |
| Cowie J. | 1937 | 24 | 114 | 2275 | 19.95 | 6 | 1 | 6-3 |
| Merritt W.E. | 1927 | 25 | 107 | 2530 | 23.64 | 5 | 1 | 6-38 |

## Most Wickets in a Season of First-class Debut

|  |  |  | Overs | Mdns | Runs | Wkts | Ave |
|---|---|---|---|---|---|---|---|
| Robertson W. | *Canterbury & NZ* | 1893/94 | *1534 | balls | 570 | 47 | 12.12 |
| Gillespie S.R. | *Northern Districts* | 1979/80 | 384.5 | 98 | 998 | 45 | 22.17 |
| Petherick P.J. | *Otago* | 1975/76 | 286 | 57 | 847 | 42 | 20.16 |
| Lankham W. | *Auckland* | 1882/83 | †1006 | balls | 259 | 41 | 6.31 |
| O'Brien I.E. | *Wellington* | 2000/01 | 319.1 | 81 | 807 | 41 | 19.68 |

*\* Robertson bowled 222.2 6-ball overs and 40 5-ball overs   † Lankham bowled 96.2 5-ball overs and 131 4-ball overs*

## Most Balls Bowled in an Innings

| 444 | Howarth H.J. | 74-24-138-2 | New Zealand v West Indies | Bridgetown | 1971/72 |
|---|---|---|---|---|---|
| 426 | Tufnell P.C.R. | 71-22-147-2 | England v New Zealand | Wellington | 1991/92 |
| 426 | Vettori D.L. | 71-24-171-2 | New Zealand v India | Mohali | 1999/00 |
| 420 | Howarth H.J. | 70-24-144-4 | New Zealand v England | Lord's | 1973 |
| 420 | Boock S.L. | 70-10-229-1 | New Zealand v Pakistan | Auckland | 1988/89 |
| 417† | O'Sullivan D.R. | 52.1-15-125-4 | Central Districts v Otago | New Plymouth | 1978/79 |
| 414 | Doshi D.R. | 69-34-79-2 | India v New Zealand | Auckland | 1980/81 |
| 414 | Tauseef Ahmed | 69-28-106-1 | Pakistan v New Zealand | Auckland | 1988/89 |
| 414 | Hick G.A. | 69-27-126-4 | England v New Zealand | Wellington | 1991/92 |
| 414 | Donnelly J.P.T. | 69-10-257-4 | Canterbury v Northern Dists | Rangiora | 2009/10 |
| 408† | Morgan H.A. | 51-16-108-3 | Wellington v Otago | Dunedin | 1968/69 |
| 408 | Wiseman P.J. | 68-21-123-4 | Otago v Northern Districts | Hamilton | 1995/96 |
| 407 | Boock S.L. | 67.5-31-75-4 | Otago v Central Districts | Alexandra | 1988/89 |
| 399 | Cook N.G.B. | 66.3-26-153-3 | England v New Zealand | Wellington | 1983/84 |
| 396 | Puna N. | 66-23-131-4 | Northern Dists v Auckland | Hamilton | 1964/65 |
| 396 | Nadkarni R.G. | 66-34-114-2 | India v New Zealand | Christchurch | 1967/68 |
| 390 | Chatfield E.J. | 65-14-158-1 | New Zealand v Pakistan | Auckland | 1988/89 |

*† eight-ball overs*

## Most Balls Bowled in a Match

| 629 | Badcock F.T. | 104.5-44-178-9 | Otago v Canterbury | Christchurch | 1933/34 |
|---|---|---|---|---|---|
| 624 | Dickeson C.W. | 104-45-142-11 | Northern Dists v Wellington | Hamilton | 1979/80 |
| 618 | Gray E.J. | 103-39-214-6 | Wellington v Otago | Wellington | 1984/85 |
| 600† | Allcott C.F.W. | 75-23-161-5 | Auckland v Canterbury | Christchurch | 1924/25 |
| 600 | Butler L.C. | 100-46-122-4 | Wellington v Auckland | Auckland | 1965/66 |

*† eight-ball overs*

## Most Runs Conceded in a Match

| 304 | 2-173, 0-131 | Dickinson G.R. | Otago v Wellington | Dunedin | 1923/24 |
|---|---|---|---|---|---|
| 300 | 6-172, 4-128 | Smith S.G. | Auckland v Wellington | Wellington | 1923/24 |
| 277 | 6-136, 6-141 | Alloo A.W. | Otago v Wellington | Dunedin | 1923/24 |
| 266 | 6-185, 2-81 | Merritt W.E. | New Zealand v Kent | Canterbury | 1927 |
| 266 | 1-104, 2-162 | Southee T.G. | New Zealand v England | Lord's | 2015 |
| 257 | 4-257 | Donnelly J.P.T. | Canterbury v Northern Districts | Rangiora | 2009/10 |
| 251 | 1-105, 1-146 | Schaw R.J. | Central Districts v Canterbury | Napier | 2007/08 |
| 246 | 2-246 | Mehidy Hasan | Bangladesh v New Zealand | Hamilton | 2018/19 |
| 243 | 6-128, 7-115 | Grimmett C.V. | Australia v Canterbury | Christchurch | 1927/28 |
| 243 | 1-58, 3-185 | Lythe T.I. | Central Districts v Wellington | Napier | 2007/08 |
| 241 | 2-99, 5-142 | Brice A.W.S. | Wellington v Otago | Dunedin | 1923/24 |
| 241 | 3-123, 1-118 | Prabhakar M. | India v New Zealand | Auckland | 1989/90 |
| 240 | 1-90, 4-150 | Donnelly J.P.T. | Canterbury v Central Districts | New Plymouth | 2009/10 |
| 239 | 6-112, 3-127 | McBeath D.J. | Otago v Auckland | Dunedin | 1922/23 |
| 239 | 1-60, 4-179 | Lambert H.N. | Wellington v Canterbury | Wellington | 1931/32 |
| 237 | 0-99, 0-138 | Bracewell J.G. | New Zealand v Sussex | Hove | 1990 |

| 237 | 4-158, 0-79 | Vettori D.L. | New Zealand v South Africa | Hamilton | 2003/04 |
| 236 | 2-83, 2-153 | Newman J.A. | Canterbury v Otago | Dunedin | 1928/29 |
| 234 | 3-86, 4-148 | Merritt W.E. | Canterbury v Otago | Dunedin | 1928/29 |
| 234 | 4-165, 2-69 | Vettori D.L. | New Zealand v Zimbabwe | Bulawayo | 1997/98 |
| 234 | 8-148, 6-86 | Astle T.D. | Canterbury v Central Districts | Napier | 2013/14 |

## Most Runs Conceded in an Innings

| 69 | 10 | 257 | 4 | Donnelly J.P.T. | Canterbury v Northern Districts | Rangiora | 2009/10 |
| 49 | 2 | 246 | 2 | Mehidy Hasan | Bangladesh v New Zealand | Hamilton | 2018/19 |
| 56 | 6 | 230 | 3 | Martin B.P. | Auckland v Northern Districts | Hamilton | 2012/13 |
| 70 | 10 | 229 | 1 | Boock S.L. | New Zealand v Pakistan | Auckland | 1988/89 |
| 23.2 | 0 | 218 | 5 | Merritt W.E. | New Zealand v NSW | Sydney | 1927/28 |
| 34 | 1 | 206 | 1 | Alloo A.W. | Otago v NSW | Dunedin | 1923/24 |
| 59 | 12 | 204 | 4 | Furlong C.J.M. | Central Districts v Canterbury | Palmerston Nth | 1994/95 |
| 42 | 3 | 204 | 3 | Worker G.H. | Central Districts v Auckland | Auckland | 2009/10 |
| 57 | 5 | 200 | 4 | Vettori D.L. | New Zealand v India | Ahmedabad | 1999/00 |
| 51.2 | 11 | 198 | 5 | Pringle C. | Auckland v Central Districts | Auckland | 1995/96 |
| 41 | 3 | 194 | 3 | Callaway S.T. | New Zealand v Australia | Wellington | 1904/05 |
| 59 | 8 | 187 | 6 | Martin B.P. | Auckland v Wellington | Auckland | 2011/12 |
| 32 | 1 | 186 | 2 | Torrance R.C. | Otago v NSW | Dunedin | 1923/24 |
| 43.1 | 1 | 185 | 6 | Merritt W.E. | New Zealand v Kent | Canterbury | 1927 |
| 38.3 | 6 | 185 | 3 | Lythe T.I. | Central Districts v Wellington | Napier | 2007/08 |
| 46 | 4 | 181 | 0 | Hart M.N. | New Zealand v West Indies | Wellington | 1994/95 |
| 34 | 2 | 180 | 5 | O'Connell W.J. | Hawke's Bay v Auckland | Auckland | 1920/21 |

## Most Runs Off One Over

| † 77 | Vance R.H. | Germon L.K. & Ford R.M. | | | |
| | | | Wellington v Canterbury | Christchurch | 1989/90 |
| § 35 | Davis H.T. | Reinholds A.T. | Wellington v Auckland | Auckland | 1995/96 |
| * 34 | Edwards R.M. | Carew M.C. | Gov-General's XI v West Indies | Auckland | 1968/69 |
| 32 | Snook I.R. | Botham I.T. | Central Districts v England | P.North | 1983/84 |
| * 30 | Anderson R.W. | Burgess M.G. | Central Districts v Auckland | Wanganui | 1977/78 |
| 28 | Holland P.J. | Cairns B.L. | Wellington v Northern Districts | Tauranga | 1983/84 |

*† Full tosses and deliberate no-balls were provided for the players to hit*

*§ Davis bowled six no-balls which counted as two extras each in addition to any runs scored off the bat. The total also included 4 byes*

*\* Eight-ball overs*

# ALL ROUND CRICKET

## 500 Runs and 25 Wickets in the Same Season

| | | *Runs* | *Ave* | *Wkts* | *Ave* |
|---|---|---|---|---|---|
| Reid J.R. | 1954/55 | 505 | 38.84 | 30 | 16.53 |
| Sparling J.T. | 1959/60 | 705 | 37.11 | 36 | 19.50 |
| Reid J.R. | 1960/61 | 549 | 34.31 | 37 | 14.78 |
| Pollard V. | 1967/68 | 537 | 31.58 | 31 | 24.74 |
| Taylor B.R. | 1968/69 | 518 | 39.84 | 30 | 28.06 |
| Cairns B.L. | 1975/76 | 538 | 41.38 | 27 | 25.66 |
| Hadlee R.J. | 1981/82 | 500 | 33.33 | 59 | 14.69 |
| Brown V.R. | 1984/85 | 540 | 38.57 | 31 | 31.35 |
| Gray E.J. | 1985/86 | 545 | 49.54 | 34 | 22.00 |
| Priest M.W. | 1988/89 | 603 | 43.07 | 28 | 40.14 |
| Bradburn G.E. | 1989/90 | 842 | 38.27 | 30 | 30.93 |
| Patel D.N. | 1990/91 | 679 | 52.23 | 41 | 28.09 |
| Patel D.N. | 1991/92 | 574 | 44.15 | 32 | 26.78 |
| Duff S.W. | 1991/92 | 559 | 46.58 | 28 | 27.64 |
| Styris S.B. | 2001/02 | 662 | 44.13 | 28 | 17.03 |
| Wiseman P.J. | 2003/04 | 535 | 38.21 | 31 | 31.00 |
| de Grandhomme C. | 2013/14 | 629 | 48.38 | 30 | 20.80 |
| Ellis A.M. | 2014/15 | 853 | 53.31 | 29 | 32.93 |
| Ellis A.M. | 2015/16 | 518 | 37.00 | 33 | 18.57 |
| Ellis A.M | 2016/17 | 652 | 40.75 | 27 | 24.59 |
| Astle T.D. | 2016/17 | 522 | 37.28 | 31 | 26.87 |

## A Century and Five Wickets in Each Innings of the Same Match

| | | | | | |
|---|---|---|---|---|---|
| Armstrong W.W. | 126* | 5-27 & 5-25 | Australia v New Zealand | Christchurch | 1904/05 |
| Crawford J.N. | 110 & 4* | 5-90 & 5-53 | Wellington v Auckland | Auckland | 1917/18 |

## A Century and Ten Wickets in the Same Match
*but not five in each innings*

| | | | | | |
|---|---|---|---|---|---|
| Woolley F.E. | 132 | 6-50 & 4-38 | MCC v Otago | Dunedin | 1929/30 |
| Patel D.N. | 6 & 204 | 6-117 & 4-116 | Auckland v ND | Auckland | 1991/92 |

## A Century and Five Wickets in One Innings of the Same Match

| | | | | | |
|---|---|---|---|---|---|
| Wilding F. | 104 | 6-55 & 0-4 | Canterbury v Auckland | Christchurch | 1884/85 |
| Redgrave W.P. | 165 | 5-37 | Wellington v Hawke's Bay | Wellington | 1905/06 |
| Relf A.E. | 157 | 6-64 & 2-48 | Auckland v Canterbury | Christchurch | 1907/08 |
| Armstrong W.W. | 110* | 6-47 & 0-25 | Australia v New Zealand | Auckland | 1913/14 |
| Crawford J.N. | 6 & 178* | 5-149 | Otago v Wellington | Wellington | 1914/15 |
| Snedden A.N.C. | 139 | 5-13 & 2-21 | Auckland v Hawke's Bay | Auckland | 1920/21 |
| Andrews T.J.E. | 111* | 5-41 | NSW v Canterbury | Christchurch | 1923/24 |
| McGirr H.M. | 106 | 5-17 & 0-22 | Wellington v Canterbury | Wellington | 1925/26 |
| Bellamy F.W.J. | 113 & 22* | 5-31 & 1-39 | Canterbury v Wellington | Christchurch | 1934/35 |
| Cromb I.B. | 171 | 5-66 & 0-56 | Canterbury v Wellington | Wellington | 1939/40 |
| Reid J.R. | 0 & 283 | 5-35 & 1-34 | Wellington v Otago | Wellington | 1951/52 |
| Reid J.R. | 150* | 7-28 & 1-15 | NZ v Chief Comm XI | Karachi | 1955/56 |
| Sutcliffe B. | 152* | 5-102 | Otago v ND | Hamilton | 1956/57 |
| Sparling J.T. | 105 & 51 | 7-98 & 2-13 | Auckland v Canterbury | Christchurch | 1959/60 |
| Reid J.R. | 165 | 5-50 & 1-28 | Wellington v Auckland | Auckland | 1959/60 |
| Butler L.C. | 101* | 5-34 | Wellington v CD | New Plymouth | 1961/62 |
| Alabaster G.D. | 108 & 35 | 1-34 & 5-49 | Otago v CD | Wanganui | 1964/65 |
| Taylor B.R. | 105 & 0* | 5-86 | New Zealand v India | Calcutta | 1964/65 |

| Pollard V. | 146 & 16* | 3-66 & 6-53 | CD v Otago | Dunedin | 1967/68 |
|---|---|---|---|---|---|
| Motz R.C. | 103* | 3-41 & 6-57 | Canterbury v Otago | Christchurch | 1967/68 |
| Yuile B.W. | 146 | 6-68 & 1-13 | CD v Canterbury | Napier | 1967/68 |
| Inverarity R.J. | 108 | 5-28 | Australia B v Otago | Dunedin | 1969/70 |
| Morgan R.W. | 102 & 52 | 5-42 & 3-48 | Auckland v NZ U23 XI | Auckland | 1970/71 |
| Taylor B.R. | 10 & 129* | 5-37 & 2-34 | Wellington v Canterbury | Wellington | 1971/72 |
| Mushtaq Mohammad | 201 | 2-15 & 5-49 | Pakistan v New Zealand | Dunedin | 1972/73 |
| Morrison J.F.M. | 8 & 106 | 0-4 & 5-69 | Wellington v Auckland | Auckland | 1977/78 |
| Botham I.T. | 103 & 30* | 5-73 & 3-38 | England v New Zealand | Christchurch | 1977/78 |
| Hadlee R.J. | 48 & 103 | 5-61 & 1-76 | New Zealand v Queensland | Brisbane | 1980/81 |
| Stead D.W. | 2 & 193* | 6-79 & 1-67 | Canterbury v CD | New Plymouth | 1980/81 |
| Crowe M.D. | 17 & 151 | 0-20 & 5-18 | CD v Auckland | Auckland | 1983/84 |
| Botham I.T. | 138 | 5-59 & 1-137 | England v New Zealand | Wellington | 1983/84 |
| Crowe M.D. | 20 & 143 | 1-54 & 5-51 | CD v ND | New Plymouth | 1984/85 |
| Gray E.J. | 108 | 5-54 & 4-52 | NZ v Minor Counties | Norwich | 1986 |
| Rutherford K.R. | 11 & 146 | 5-72 | Otago v Wellington | Wellington | 1989/90 |
| Astle N.J. | 160 | 6-22 & 0-45 | Canterbury v Otago | Christchurch | 1996/97 |
| Nash D.J. | 135* & 62 | 7-39 & 0-22 | New Zealand v Hampshire | Southampton | 1999 |
| Bradburn G.E. | 35 & 104 | 5-114 | ND v Wellington | Wellington | 2000/01 |
| Canning T.K. | 115 | 6-44 & 2-28 | Auckland v ND | Hamilton | 2004/05 |
| Diamanti B.J. | 0 & 135* | 5-74 | CD v Canterbury | Rangiora | 2008/09 |
| Southee T.G. | 156 | 5-69 & 2-75 | ND v Wellington | Wellington | 2012/13 |
| Wells S.R. | 7 & 100* | 2-46 & 5-74 | Otago v Canterbury | Dunedin | 2013/14 |
| van Beek L.V. | 111* | 2-13 & 6-57 | Canterbury v Otago | Christchurch | 2015/16 |
| Ravindra R. | 144* & 22 | 0-56 & 6-89 | NZ A v West Indies A | Nelson | 2020/21 |

# WICKETKEEPING

## Most Dismissals in a Season

| | | | | | | | | | |
|---|---|---|---|---|---|---|---|---|---|
| 49 | 49/0 | Nevin C.J. | 2000/01 | | 37 | 36/1 | de Boorder D.C. | 2014/15 |
| 45 | 44/1 | Cachopa B. | 2015/16 | | 37 | 36/1 | de Boorder D.C. | 2015/16 |
| 44 | 43/1 | de Boorder D.C. | 2012/13 | | 36 | 32/4 | Smith I.D.S. | 1990/91 |
| 43 | 41/2 | Watling B-J. | 2013/14 | | 36 | 35/1 | Griggs B.B.J. | 2005/06 |
| 41 | 31/10 | McSweeney E.B. | 1984/85 | | 36 | 35/1 | Watling B-J. | 2014/15 |
| 41 | 35/6 | McSweeney E.B. | 1989/90 | | 36 | 34/2 | de Boorder D.C | 2017/18 |
| 41 | 37/4 | McGlashan P.D. | 2009/10 | | 36 | 33/3 | Fletcher C.D. | 2020/21 |
| 41 | 39/2 | Fletcher C.D. | 2015/16 | | 35 | 30/5 | Smith I.D.S. | 1979/80 |
| 41 | 39/2 | Blundell T.A. | 2017/18 | | 35 | 33/2 | Young R.A. | 2001/02 |
| 40 | 39/1 | van Wyk C.F.K. | 2014/15 | | 35 | 35/0 | Young R.A. | 2002/03 |
| 39 | 37/2 | Ronchi L. | 2012/13 | | 35 | 33/2 | Griggs B.B.J. | 2007/08 |
| 39 | 39/0 | Cachopa B. | 2014/15 | | 35 | 31/4 | de Boorder D.C. | 2009/10 |
| 38 | 37/1 | Hopkins G.J. | 2004/05 | | 35 | 34/1 | Hopkins G.J. | 2012/13 |
| 38 | 36/2 | de Boorder D.C. | 2011/12 | | 35 | 33/2 | van Wyk C.F.K. | 2013/14 |
| 38 | 38/0 | Watling B-J. | 2016/17 | | 35 | 33/2 | Cleaver D. | 2019/20 |
| 38 | 38/0 | Watling B-J. | 2019/20 | | | | | |

## Most Dismissals in a Match

| | | | | |
|---|---|---|---|---|
| 12 | 12/0 | McGlashan P.D., Northern Districts v Central Districts | Whangarei | 2009/10 |
| 10 | 10/0 | Nevin C.J., Wellington v Otago | Wellington | 1995/96 |
| | 10/0 | Gilchrist A.C., Australia v New Zealand | Hamilton | 1999/00 |
| | 10/0 | Hopkins G.J., Otago v Canterbury | Dunedin | 2004/05 |
| | 8/2 | Hopkins G.J., New Zealand A v Sri Lanka A | Kandy | 2005/06 |
| | 9/1 | McCullum B.B., New Zealand v S.African Invitation XI | Bloemfontein | 2007/08 |
| | 9/1 | de Boorder D.C., Otago v Wellington | Wellington | 2009/10 |

| | | | | |
|---|---|---|---|---|
| | 10/0 | McGlashan P.D., Northern Districts v Auckland | Auckland | 2010/11 |
| | 10/0 | van Wyk C.F.K., Central Districts v Otago | Napier | 2014/15 |
| | 10/0 | Blundell T.A., Wellington v Canterbury | Wellington | 2017/18 |
| 9 | 9/0 | Schofield R.M., Central Districts v Wellington | Wellington | 1964/65 |
| | 9/0 | Vance R.H., Wellington v Otago | Wellington | 1977/78 |
| | 8/1 | McSweeney E.B., Wellington v Otago | Lower Hutt | 1983/84 |
| | 9/0 | Young B.A., Northern Districts v Canterbury | Christchurch | 1986/87 |
| | 9/0 | Germon L.K., Canterbury v Northern Districts | Christchurch | 1992/93 |
| | 9/0 | Rashid Latif., Pakistan v New Zealand | Auckland | 1993/94 |
| | 9/0 | Hopkins G.J., Otago v Wellington | Queenstown | 2004/05 |
| | 9/0 | Hopkins G.J., Otago v Northern Districts | Dunedin | 2005/06 |
| | 9/0 | de Boorder D.C., Otago v Northern Districts | Hamilton | 2012/13 |
| | 9/0 | Watling B-J., New Zealand v India | Auckland | 2013/14 |
| | 9/0 | Watling B.J., New Zealand v Sri Lanka | Dunedin | 2015/16 |
| | 9/0 | Ronchi L., Wellington v Canterbury | Christchurch | 2016/17 |
| | 9/0 | de Boorder D.C., Otago v Auckland | Auckland | 2017/18 |
| | 9/0 | Horne B.J., Auckland v Central Districts | Auckland | 2018/19 |
| | 8/1 | Cleaver D., Central Districts v Northern Districts | Napier | 2019/20 |
| | 8/1 | McLachlan C.R., Wellington v Canterbury | Wellington | 2021/22 |
| 8 | 3/5 | James K.C., New Zealand v Derbyshire | Derby | 1927 |
| | 1/7 | Jackman C.K.Q., Canterbury v Wellington | Wellington | 1935/36 |
| | 2/6 | Kent L.A.W., Auckland v Wellington | Wellington | 1944/45 |
| | 8/0 | Curtis W.M., North Island XI v South Island XI | Wellington | 1957/58 |
| | 8/0 | Petrie E.C., New Zealand v Sussex | Hove | 1958 |
| | 5/3 | Dick A.E., NZ v Griqualand West | Kimberley | 1961/62 |
| | 8/0 | Parks J.M., England v New Zealand | Christchurch | 1965/66 |
| | 7/1 | Therkleson, I.J., Wellington v Northern Districts | Whangarei | 1973/74 |
| | 8/0 | Marsh R.W., Australia v New Zealand | Christchurch | 1976/77 |
| | 8/0 | Lees W.K., New Zealand v Sri Lanka | Wellington | 1982/83 |
| | 4/4 | McSweeney E.B., Wellington v Northern Districts | Wellington | 1984/85 |
| | 8/0 | Smith I.D.S., Auckland v Central Districts | Nelson | 1988/89 |
| | 8/0 | Smith I.D.S., New Zealand v Sri Lanka | Hamilton | 1990/91 |
| | 7/1 | Hart R.G., Northern Districts v Canterbury | Hamilton | 1994/95 |
| | 7/1 | Germon L.K., Canterbury v Central Districts | Palmerston North | 1994/95 |
| | 7/1 | Nevin C.J., Wellington v Central Districts | Nelson | 1995/96 |
| | 8/0 | Vincent L., Auckland v Central Districts | Palmerston North | 2000/01 |
| | 8/0 | Howell G.A., Wellington v Northern Districts | Hamilton | 2001/02 |
| | 7/1 | McCullum B.B., Canterbury v Northern Districts | Christchurch | 2003/04 |
| | 7/1 | Papps M.W.H., Canterbury v Northern Districts | Gisborne | 2004/05 |
| | 8/0 | van Wyk C.F.K., Canterbury v Auckland | Auckland | 2006/07 |
| | 8/0 | McGlashan P.D., Northern Districts v Auckland | Auckland | 2006/07 |
| | 8/0 | Griggs B.B.J., Central Districts v Northern Districts | Hamilton | 2007/08 |
| | 8/0 | Griggs B.B.J., Central Districts v Canterbury | Rangiora | 2009/10 |
| | 8/0 | Hopkins G.J., Auckland v Canterbury | Auckland | 2010/11 |
| | 8/0 | Adnan Akmal, Pakistan v New Zealand | Wellington | 2010/11 |
| | 8/0 | Ronchi L., Wellington v Northern Districts | Wellington | 2012/13 |
| | 8/0 | Watling B-J., Northern Districts v Canterbury | Christchurch | 2012/13 |
| | 8/0 | Latham T.W.M., Canterbury v Auckland | Christchurch | 2012/13 |
| | 8/0 | Watling B-J., New Zealand v West Indies | Hamilton | 2013/14 |
| | 8/0 | Fletcher C.D., Northern Districts v Otago | Whangarei | 2013/14 |
| | 8/0 | Hopkins G.J., Auckland v Otago | Dunedin | 2013/14 |
| | 8/0 | Watling B-J., New Zealand v West Indies | Kingston | 2014 |
| | 8/0 | Cachopa B., Auckland v Otago | Auckland | 2014/15 |
| | 8/0 | de Boorder D.C., Otago v Northern Districts | Dunedin | 2015/16 |
| | 8/0 | Cachopa B., Auckland v Otago | Dunedin | 2015/16 |
| | 8/0 | Cachopa B., Auckland v Wellington | Wellington | 2015/16 |

| 7/1 | Fletcher C.D., Canterbury v Northern Districts | Christchurch | 2015/16 |
| 8/0 | Fletcher C.D., Canterbury v Wellington | Wellington | 2015/16 |
| 8/0 | Horne B.J., Auckland v Northern Districts | Auckland | 2017/18 |
| 7/1 | Cleaver D., Central Districts v Canterbury | Napier | 2017/18 |
| 7/1 | Blundell T.A., Wellington v Auckland | Auckland | 2017/18 |
| 8/0 | Cleaver D., Central Districts v Northern Districts | Napier | 2018/19 |
| 8/0 | Horne B.J., Auckland v Central Districts | Auckland | 2019/20 |
| 8/0 | Watling B-J., New Zealand v Pakistan | Mt Maunganui | 2020/21 |
| 7/1 | Bocock P.D., Northern Districts v Otago | Dunedin | 2020/21 |
| 8/0 | Blundell T.A., New Zealand v England | Birmingham | 2021 |

## Most Dismissals in an Innings

| 8 | 8/0 | de Boorder D.C., Otago v Wellington | Wellington | 2009/10 |
| 7 | 7/0 | Schofield R.M., Central Districts v Wellington | Wellington | 1964/65 |
| | 7/0 | Wasim Bari, Pakistan v New Zealand | Auckland | 1978/79 |
| | 7/0 | Young B.A., Northern Districts v Canterbury | Christchurch | 1986/87 |
| | 7/0 | Smith I.D.S., New Zealand v Sri Lanka | Hamilton | 1990/91 |
| | 7/0 | Croy M.G., Otago v Auckland | Auckland | 2001/02 |
| | 7/0 | Hopkins G.J., New Zealand A v South Africa A | Centurion | 2004/05 |
| | 5/2 | Hopkins G.J., New Zealand A v Sri Lanka A | Kandy | 2005/06 |
| | 7/0 | Griggs B.B.J., Central Districts v Northern Districts | Hamilton | 2007/08 |
| 6 | 4/2 | Mooney F.L.H., New Zealand v Warwickshire | Birmingham | 1949 |
| | 5/1 | Wadsworth K.J., New Zealand v Surrey | The Oval | 1973 |
| | 6/0 | Downes L.W., Central Districts v Canterbury | Nelson | 1975/76 |
| | 5/1 | Kirmani S.M.H., India v New Zealand | Christchurch | 1975/76 |
| | 6/0 | Vance R.H., Wellington v Otago | Wellington | 1977/78 |
| | 6/0 | Downton P.R., England XI v Otago | Dunedin | 1977/78 |
| | 6/0 | Germon L.K., Canterbury v Northern Districts | Christchurch | 1992/93 |
| | 5/1 | Hart R.G., Northern Districts v Canterbury | Hamilton | 1994/95 |
| | 5/1 | Nevin C.J., Wellington v Central Districts | Nelson | 1995/96 |
| | 6/0 | Parore A.C., New Zealand A v Pakistan A | Hamilton | 1998/99 |
| | 6/0 | Young R.A., Auckland v Wellington | Wellington | 2002/03 |
| | 6/0 | Hopkins G.J., Otago v Canterbury | Dunedin | 2004/05 |
| | 5/1 | Papps M.H.W., Canterbury v Northern Districts | Gisborne | 2004/05 |
| | 6/0 | McGlashan P.D., Northern Districts v Auckland | Auckland | 2006/07 |
| | 6/0 | Watling B-J., Northern Districts v Central Districts | Gisborne | 2006/07 |
| | 6/0 | Dhoni M.S., India v New Zealand | Wellington | 2008/09 |
| | 6/0 | McGlashan P.D., Northern Districts v Central Districts | Whangarei | 2009/10 |
| | 6/0 | McGlashan P.D., Northern Districts v Central Districts | Whangarei | 2009/10 |
| | 6/0 | Austin-Smellie J., Wellington v Central Districts | Napier | 2010/11 |
| | 6/0 | McGlashan P.D., Northern Districts v Auckland | Auckland | 2010/11 |
| | 6/0 | Adnan Akmal, Pakistan v New Zealand | Wellington | 2010/11 |
| | 6/0 | Hopkins G.J., Auckland v Northern Districts | Whangarei | 2011/12 |
| | 6/0 | Hopkins G.J., Auckland v Otago | Auckland | 2011/12 |
| | 6/0 | de Boorder D.C., Otago v Northern Districts | Hamilton | 2012/13 |
| | 6/0 | Ronchi L.,Wellington v Northern Districts | Wellington | 2012/13 |
| | 6/0 | Watling B-J., New Zealand v India | Auckland | 2013/14 |
| | 6/0 | van Wyk C.F.K., Central Districts v Otago | Napier | 2014/15 |
| | 6/0 | Cachopa B., Auckland v Wellington | Wellington | 2015/16 |
| | 6/0 | Watling B-J., New Zealand v Sri Lanka | Dunedin | 2015/16 |
| | 6/0 | Ronchi L., Wellington v Canterbury | Christchurch | 2016/17 |
| | 6/0 | Blundell T.A., Wellington v Canterbury | Wellington | 2017/18 |
| | 6/0 | Horne B.J., Auckland v Central Districts | Auckland | 2018/19 |
| | 5/1 | Bocock P.D., Northern Districts v Otago | Dunedin | 2020/21 |

## Most Catches in a Season

| | | | | | | |
|---|---|---|---|---|---|---|
| 49 | Nevin C.J. | 2000/01 | | 37 | Hopkins G.J. | 2004/05 |
| 44 | Cachopa B. | 2015/16 | | 37 | McGlashan P.D. | 2009/10 |
| 43 | de Boorder D.C. | 2012/13 | | 37 | Ronchi L. | 2012/13 |
| 41 | Watling B-J. | 2013/14 | | 37 | de Boorder D.C. | 2015/16 |
| 41 | Fletcher C.D. | 2015/16 | | 36 | de Boorder D.C. | 2011/12 |
| 39 | van Wyk C.F.K. | 2014/15 | | 36 | de Boorder D.C. | 2014/15 |
| 39 | Cachopa B. | 2014/15 | | 35 | McSweeney E.B. | 1989/90 |
| 39 | Blundell T.A. | 2017/18 | | 35 | Young R.A. | 2002/03 |
| 38 | Watling B-J | 2016/17 | | 35 | Griggs B.B.J. | 2005/06 |
| 38 | Watling B-J | 2019/20 | | 35 | Watling B-J. | 2014/15 |

## Most Catches in a Match

| | | | |
|---|---|---|---|
| 12 | McGlashan P.D., Northern Districts v Central Districts | Whangarei | 2009/10 |
| 10 | Nevin C.J., Wellington v Otago | Wellington | 1995/96 |
| | Gilchrist A.C., Australia v New Zealand | Hamilton | 1999/00 |
| | Hopkins G.J., Otago v Canterbury | Dunedin | 2004/05 |
| | McGlashan P.D., Northern Districts v Auckland | Auckland | 2010/11 |
| | van Wyk C.F.K., Central Districts v Otago | Napier | 2014/15 |
| | Blundell T.A., Wellington v Canterbury | Wellington | 2017/18 |
| 9 | Schofield R.M., Central Districts v Wellington | Wellington | 1964/65 |
| | Vance R.H., Wellington v Otago | Wellington | 1977/78 |
| | Young B.A., Northern Districts v Canterbury | Christchurch | 1986/87 |
| | Germon L.K., Canterbury v Northern Districts | Christchurch | 1992/93 |
| | Rashid Latif., Pakistan v New Zealand | Auckland | 1993/94 |
| | Hopkins G.J., Otago v Wellington | Queenstown | 2004/05 |
| | Hopkins G.J., Otago v Northern Districts | Dunedin | 2005/06 |
| | McCullum B.B., New Zealand v South African Invitation XI | Bloemfontein | 2007/08 |
| | de Boorder D.C., Otago v Wellington | Wellington | 2009/10 |
| | de Boorder D.C., Otago v Northern Districts | Hamilton | 2012/13 |
| | Watling B-J., New Zealand v India | Auckland | 2013/14 |
| | de Boorder D.C., Otago v Auckland | Auckland | 2017/18 |
| | Horne B.J., Auckland v Central Districts | Auckland | 2018/19 |
| 8 | Curtis W.M., North Island XI v South Island XI | Wellington | 1957/58 |
| | Petrie E.C., New Zealand v Sussex | Hove | 1958 |
| | Parks J.M., England v New Zealand | Christchurch | 1965/66 |
| | Marsh R.W., Australia v New Zealand | Christchurch | 1976/77 |
| | Lees W.K., New Zealand v Sri Lanka | Wellington | 1982/83 |
| | McSweeney E.B., Wellington v Otago | Lower Hutt | 1983/84 |
| | Smith I.D.S., Auckland v Central Districts | Nelson | 1988/89 |
| | Smith I.D.S., New Zealand v Sri Lanka | Hamilton | 1990/91 |
| | Vincent L., Auckland v Central Districts | Palmerston North | 2000/01 |
| | Howell G.A., Wellington v Northern Districts | Hamilton | 2001/02 |
| | Hopkins G.J., New Zealand A v Sri Lanka A | Kandy | 2005/06 |
| | van Wyk C.F.K., Canterbury v Auckland | Auckland | 2006/07 |
| | McGlashan P.D., Northern Districts v Auckland | Auckland | 2006/07 |
| | Griggs B.B.J., Central Districts v Northern Districts | Hamilton | 2007/08 |
| | Griggs B.B.J., Central Districts v Canterbury | Rangiora | 2009/10 |
| | Hopkins G.J., Auckland v Canterbury | Auckland | 2010/11 |
| | Adnan Akmal, Pakistan v New Zealand | Wellington | 2010/11 |
| | Ronchi L., Wellington v Northern Districts | Wellington | 2012/13 |
| | Watling B-J., Northern Districts v Canterbury | Christchurch | 2012/13 |

| | | |
|---|---|---|
| Latham T.W.M., Canterbury v Auckland | Christchurch | 2012/13 |
| Watling B-J., New Zealand v West Indies | Hamilton | 2013/14 |
| Fletcher C.D., Northern Districts v Otago | Whangarei | 2013/14 |
| Hopkins G J., Auckland v Otago | Dunedin | 2013/14 |
| Watling B-J., New Zealand v West Indies | Kingston | 2014 |
| Cachopa B., Auckland v Otago | Auckland | 2014/15 |
| de Boorder D.C., Otago v Northern Districts | Dunedin | 2015/16 |
| Cachopa B., Auckland v Otago | Dunedin | 2015/16 |
| Cachopa B., Auckland v Wellington | Wellington | 2015/16 |
| Fletcher C.D., Canterbury v Wellington | Wellington | 2015/16 |
| Ronchi L., Wellington v Canterbury | Wellington | 2016/17 |
| Horne B.J., Auckland v Northern Districts | Auckland | 2017/18 |
| Cleaver D., Central Districts v Northern Districts | Napier | 2018/19 |
| Cleaver D., Central Districts v Northern Districts | Napier | 2019/20 |
| Horne B.J., Auckland v Central Districts | Auckland | 2019/20 |
| Watling B-J., New Zealand v Pakistan | Mt Maunganui | 2020/21 |
| Blundell T.A., New Zealand v England | Birmingham | 2021 |
| McLachlan C.R., Wellington v Canterbury | Wellington | 2021/22 |

## Most Catches in an Innings

| | | | |
|---|---|---|---|
| 8 | de Boorder D.C., Otago v Wellington | Wellington | 2009/10 |
| 7 | Schofield R.M., Central Districts v Wellington | Wellington | 1964/65 |
| | Wasim Bari, Pakistan v New Zealand | Auckland | 1978/79 |
| | Young B.A., Northern Districts v Canterbury | Christchurch | 1986/87 |
| | Smith I.D.S., New Zealand v Sri Lanka | Hamilton | 1990/91 |
| | Croy M.G., Otago v Auckland | Auckland | 2001/02 |
| | Hopkins G.J., New Zealand A v South Africa A | Centurion | 2004/05 |
| | Griggs B.B.J., Central Districts v Northern Districts | Hamilton | 2007/08 |
| 6 | Downes L.W., Central Districts v Canterbury | Nelson | 1975/76 |
| | Vance R.H., Wellington v Otago | Wellington | 1977/78 |
| | Downton P.R., England XI v Otago | Dunedin | 1977/78 |
| | Germon L.K., Canterbury v Northern Districts | Christchurch | 1992/93 |
| | Parore A.C., New Zealand A v Pakistan A | Hamilton | 1998/99 |
| | Young R.A., Auckland v Wellington | Wellington | 2002/03 |
| | Hopkins G.J., Otago v Canterbury | Dunedin | 2004/05 |
| | McGlashan P.D., Northern Districts v Auckland | Auckland | 2006/07 |
| | Watling B-J., Northern Districts v Central Districts | Gisborne | 2006/07 |
| | Dhoni M.S., India v New Zealand | Wellington | 2008/09 |
| | McGlashan P.D., Northern Districts v Central Districts *(1st)* | Whangarei | 2009/10 |
| | McGlashan P.D., Northern Districts v Central Districts *(2nd)* | Whangarei | 2009/10 |
| | Austin-Smellie J., Wellington v Central Districts | Napier | 2010/11 |
| | McGlashan P.D., Northern Districts v Auckland | Auckland | 2010/11 |
| | Adnan Akmal, Pakistan v New Zealand | Wellington | 2010/11 |
| | Hopkins G.J., Auckland v Northern Districts | Whangarei | 2011/12 |
| | Hopkins G.J., Auckland v Otago | Auckland | 2011/12 |
| | de Boorder D.C., Otago v Northern Districts | Hamilton | 2012/13 |
| | Ronchi L.,Wellington v Northern Districts | Wellington | 2012/13 |
| | Watling B-J., New Zealand v India | Auckland | 2013/14 |
| | van Wyk C.F.K., Central Districts v Otago | Napier | 2014/15 |
| | Cachopa B., Auckland v Wellington | Wellington | 2015/16 |
| | Watling B-J., New Zealand v Sri Lanka | Dunedin | 2015/16 |
| | Ronchi L., Wellington v Canterbury | Wellington | 2016/17 |
| | Blundell T.A., Wellington v Canterbury | Wellington | 2017/18 |
| | Horne B.J., Auckland v Central Districts | Auckland | 2018/19 |

## Most Stumpings in a Season

| 13 | Jackman C.K.Q. | 1935/36 | | 13 | Kent L.A.W. | 1944/45 |

### Most Stumpings in a Match

| 7 | Jackman C.K.Q., Canterbury v Wellington | Wellington | 1935/36 |
| 6 | Kent L.A.W., Auckand v Wellington | Wellington | 1944/45 |
| 5 | James K.C., NZ v Surrey | The Oval | 1927 |
| | James K.C., NZ v Derbyshire | Derby | 1927 |
| | Burns R.C., Canterbury v Otago | Dunedin | 1928/29 |
| | Mills A.S., Otago v Fiji | Dunedin | 1947/48 |

### Most Stumpings in an Innings

| 4 | Jackman C.K.Q., Canterbury v Wellington | Wellington | 1935/36 |
| | Tindill E.W.T., NZ v Glamorgan | Cardiff | 1937 |
| | Kent L.A.W., Auckland v Wellington | Wellington | 1944/45 |
| | Mills A.S., Otago v Fiji | Dunedin | 1947/48 |
| | McSweeney E.B., Wellington v Northern Districts | Wellington | 1984/85 |

# FIELDING

## Most Catches in a Season

| 23 | Murray B.A.G. | 1967/68 | | 18 | Brownlie D.G. | 2015/16 |
| 22 | Coney J.V. | 1977/78 | | 18 | Fulton P.G. | 2016/17 |
| 22 | Bruce T.C. | 2015/16 | | 18 | Taylor L.R.P.L. | 2020/21 |
| 20 | Howarth H.J. | 1973/74 | | 17 | Blair W.L. | 1978/79 |
| 20 | Fulton P.G. | 2014/15 | | 17 | Crowe M.D. | 1986/87 |
| 19 | Fulton P.G. | 2015/16 | | 17 | Boyle D.J. | 1990/91 |
| 18 | Sinclair M.S. | 2001/02 | | 17 | Parlane N.R. | 2002/03 |
| 18 | Sinclair M.S. | 2008/09 | | 17 | Raval J.A. | 2012/13 |
| 18 | Sinclair M.S. | 2010/11 | | 17 | Brownlie D.G. | 2012/13 |
| 18 | Raval J.A. | 2014/15 | | 17 | Papps M.H.W. | 2014/15 |

## Most Catches in a Match

| 7 | Morrison J.F.M., Wellington v Northern Districts | Wellington | 1980/81 |
| | Fleming S.P., New Zealand v Zimbabwe | Harare | 1997/98 |
| 6 | Marchant J.W.A., Wellington v Nelson | Wellington | 1873/74 |
| | Williams N.T., Auckland v Hawke's Bay | Napier | 1894/95 |
| | Cromb I.B., Canterbury v Otago | Christchurch | 1937/38 |
| | Ikin J.T., MCC v Auckland | Auckland | 1946/47 |
| | Reid J.R., New Zealand v South Zone | Bangalore | 1955/56 |
| | Jarvis T.W., Auckland v Northern Districts | Hamilton | 1968/69 |
| | Anderson R.W., Rest v New Zealand | New Plymouth | 1974/75 |
| | MacDonald G.K., Canterbury v Pakistan | Christchurch | 1984/85 |
| | Young B.A., New Zealand v Pakistan | Auckland | 1993/94 |
| | Latham R.T., Canterbury v Otago | Oamaru | 1994/95 |
| | Young B.A., Northern Districts v Wellington | Wellington | 1995/96 |
| | Chandler P.J.B., New Zealand A v England | Wanganui | 1996/97 |
| | McHardy D.S., Wellington v Northern Districts | Hamilton | 1996/97 |
| | Fleming S.P., New Zealand v Australia | Brisbane | 1997/98 |
| | Bell M.D., Wellington v Canterbury | Wellington | 2003/04 |

| | | |
|---|---|---|
| Fleming S.P., New Zealand v West Indies | Wellington | 2005/06 |
| McCullum N.L., Otago v Central Districts | Napier | 2006/07 |
| Myburgh J.G., Canterbury v Auckland | Rangiora | 2008/09 |
| de Grandhomme C., Auckland v Canterbury | Christchurch | 2010/11 |
| Vettori D.L., Northern Districts v Canterbury | Rangiora | 2011/12 |
| Sinclair M.S., Central Districts v Auckland | Napier | 2012/13 |
| de Grandhomme C., Auckland v Otago | Auckland | 2012/13 |
| Papps M.H.W., Wellington v Otago | Invercargill | 2013/14 |
| Anderson C.J., Northern Districts v Auckland | Auckland | 2015/16 |
| Papps M.H.W., Wellington v Auckland | Wellington | 2015/16 |
| Brownlie D.G., Northern Districts v Canterbury | Christchurch | 2018/19 |
| Latham T.W.M., New Zealand v Bangladesh | Christchurch | 2021/22 |

# Most Catches in an Innings

| | | | |
|---|---|---|---|
| 5 | Williams N.T., Auckand v Hawke's Bay | Napier | 1894/95 |
| | Lamason J.R., Wellington v Otago | Dunedin | 1937/38 |
| | Lamason J.R., North Island Army v South Island Army | Wellington | 1942/43 |
| | Ikin J.T., MCC v Auckland | Auckland | 1946/47 |
| | Rabone G.O., New Zealand v Oxford University | Oxford | 1949 |
| | Reid J.R., New Zealand v South Zone | Bangalore | 1955/56 |
| | Morrison J.F.M., Wellington v Northern Districts | Wellington | 1980/81 |
| | MacDonald G.K., Canterbury v Pakistan | Christchurch | 1984/85 |
| | Crowe J.J., Auckland v Canterbury | Auckland | 1988/89 |
| | Fleming S.P., New Zealand v Zimbabwe | Harare | 1997/98 |
| | Harris C.Z., Canterbury v England | Christchurch | 2001/02 |
| | Myburgh J.G., Canterbury v Auckland | Rangiora | 2008/09 |
| | Brodie J.M., Wellington v Otago | Wellington | 2008/09 |
| | Bell M.D., Wellington v Northern Districts | Hamilton | 2009/10 |
| | Sinclair M.S., Central Districts v Wellington | Wellington | 2010/11 |

# OLDEST PLAYERS

| AGE Years/days | | | |
|---|---|---|---|
| 52/189 | Boxshall C. | Canterbury v Wellington | 1914/15 |
| 52/66 | Luckie M.M.F. | Wellington v Hawke's Bay | 1919/20 |
| 52/1 | Spring J.P. | Otago v Auckland | 1884/85 |
| 51/216 | Read R.J. | Canterbury v Auckland | 1937/38 |
| 51/203 | Lyttelton C.J. † | Governor-General's XI v MCC | 1960/61 |
| 51/87 | Wilson C.G. | Wellington v Hawke's Bay | 1919/20 |
| 51/32 | MacLaren A.C. | MCC v New Zealand | 1922/23 |
| 50/286 | Alpe S. | Wellington v Auckland | 1884/85 |
| 50/284 | Wilson E.S. | Otago v Wellington | 1927/28 |
| 50/269 | Hay T.D.B. | New Zealand v Royal Navy | 1927 |
| 50/184 | Reese T.W. | Canterbury v Otago | 1917/18 |
| 50/86 | Dufaur F.E. | Auckland v Wellington | 1882/83 |
| 49/88 | Allcott C.F.W. | Otago v Auckland | 1945/46 |
| 49/48 | Wilding F. | Canterbury v Hawke's Bay | 1901/02 |
| 48/96 | Hartley J.C. | MCC v Auckland | 1922/23 |
| 48/40 | Hallamore R.G. | Southland v Otago | 1918/19 |
| 48/26 | Badcock F.T. | New Zealanders v H.D.G. Leveson-Gower's XI | 1945 |
| 47/357 | Board J.H. | Hawke's Bay v Wellington | 1914/15 |
| 47/325 | Rowntree R.W. | Auckland v South Africa | 1931/32 |
| 47/177 | Fox R.H. | New Zealand v Civil Service | 1927 |
| 47/151 | Jones S.P. | Auckland v Otago | 1908/09 |
| 47/114 | Hughes W.J. | Hawke's Bay v Wellington | 1905/06 |
| 47/98 | Brice A.W.S. | Wellington v Australia | 1927/28 |
| 47/70 | Fowke J.N. | Canterbury v MCC | 1906/07 |
| 46/319 | Kortlang H.H.L. | Wellington v Auckland | 1926/27 |
| 46/149 | Stevens E.C.J. | Canterbury v Otago | 1883/84 |
| 46/125 | Allen R. | Wellington v Fiji | 1953/54 |
| 46/14 | Downes A.D. | Otago v Canterbury | 1913/14 |
| 45/364 | Blackie D.D. | Australia v New Zealand | 1927/28 |
| 45/292 | Handford A. | Southland v Otago | 1914/15 |
| 45/270 | Wynyard E.G. | MCC v Wellington | 1906/07 |
| 45/241 | Blamires E.O. | Otago v Canterbury | 1926/27 |
| 45/39 | Smith S.G. | Auckland v Wellington | 1925/26 |
| 45/6 | Beard D.D. | Northern Districts v Wellington | 1964/65 |
| 44/349 | Levers W.C.S. | Hawke's Bay v Wellington | 1908/09 |
| 44/338 | Knight A.R. | Otago v Canterbury | 1943/44 |
| 44/308 | Chadwick C.S. | Otago v Auckland | 1924/25 |
| 44/226 | Tucker K.H. | Wellington v Hawke's Bay | 1919/20 |
| 44/182 | Anthony A. | Auckland v Wellington | 1930/31 |
| 44/178 | Siedeberg H.G. | Otago v Wellington | 1921/22 |
| 44/126 | Garrard D.R. | Auckland v Wellington | 1941/42 |
| 44/105 | Newman J.A. | Canterbury v Otago | 1928/29 |
| 44/75 | Cate W.A. | New Zealand v MCC | 1922/23 |
| 44/70 | Wallace W.M. | Governor General's XI v MCC | 1960/61 |
| 44/59 | Dempster C.S. | Wellington v Auckland | 1947/48 |
| 44/7 | Wheatley J. | Canterbury v Hawke's Bay | 1903/04 |

† *Lord Cobham*

# YOUNGEST PLAYERS

AGE
*Years/days*

| | | | |
|---|---|---|---|
| 15/224 | Dacre C.C.R. | Auckland v Wellington | 1914/15 |
| 15/273 | Midlane F.A. | Wellington v Hawke's Bay | 1898/99 |
| 15/321 | Ollivier A.M. | Canterbury v Otago | 1866/67 |
| 16/50 | Hartland J.F. | Canterbury v Otago | 1877/78 |
| 16/84 | Broad C.H. | Nelson v Wellington | 1888/89 |
| 16/86 | McGregor S.N. | Otago v Fiji | 1947/48 |
| 16/87 | Dacre L.M. | Auckland v Wellington | 1912/13 |
| 16/89 | Anderson C.J. | Canterbury v Central Districts | 2006/07 |
| 16/130 | Coutts H.D. | Taranaki v Auckland | 1882/83 |
| 16/147 | Puna K.N. | New Zealand Under 23 XI v Otago | 1971/72 |
| 16/173 | Aaqib Javed | Pakistan v President's XI | 1988/89 |
| 16/242 | Collins J.U. | Nelson v Wellington | 1884/85 |
| 16/250 | Taylor L.G. | Auckland v Hawke's Bay | 1910/11 |
| 16/273 | Tendulkar S.R. | India v President's XI | 1989/90 |
| 16/285 | Reese D. | Canterbury v Wellington | 1895/96 |
| 16/312 | Hale H. | Tasmania v Otago | 1883/84 |
| 16/325 | Morgan R.W. | Auckland v Northern Districts | 1957/58 |
| 16/330 | Maunder P.A. | Central Districts v Auckland | 1961/62 |
| 17/4 | Wallace W.M. | Auckland v Wellington | 1933/34 |
| 17/5 | Frater R.E. | Auckland v Wellington | 1918/19 |
| 17/12 | Bell M.D. | Northern Districts v New Zealand Academy XI | 1993/94 |
| 17/49 | Williams A.B. | Otago v Canterbury | 1886/87 |
| 17/52 | Blunt R.C. | Canterbury v Otago | 1917/18 |
| 17/65 | Mitchell W.J. | Northern Districts v Pakistan | 1964/65 |
| 17/66 | Wilding A.F. | Canterbury v Auckland | 1900/01 |
| 17/77 | Clarke D.B. | Auckland v Central Districts | 1950/51 |
| 17/93 | Hay T.D.B. | Auckland v Wellington | 1893/94 |
| 17/107 | Rutherford K.R. | Otago v Auckland | 1982/83 |
| 17/110 | Cooke F.H. | Otago v Canterbury | 1879/80 |
| 17/112 | Barron J.R. | Otago v Canterbury | 1917/18 |
| 17/119 | Crowe M.D. | Auckland v Canterbury | 1979/80 |
| 17/124 | MacNeil H. | Otago v Canterbury | 1877/78 |
| 17/124 | Williamson K.S. | Northern Districts v Auckland | 2007/08 |
| 17/152 | Butler L.C. | Wellington v Auckland | 1951/52 |
| 17/174 | McIntyre J.M. | Auckland v Canterbury | 1961/62 |
| 17/179 | Rutherford I.A. | Otago v Canterbury | 1974/75 |
| 17/182 | Robin T.P. | Central Districts v Canterbury | 1999/00 |
| 17/185 | Robinson S.A. | Otago v Northern Districts | 1984/85 |
| 17/213 | Turner G.M. | Otago v Canterbury | 1964/65 |
| 17/222 | Hemi R.C. | Auckland v Wellington | 1950/51 |
| 17/237 | Duffy J.A. | Otago v Wellington | 2011/12 |
| 17/244 | Ghulam Abbas | Pakistan v Auckland | 1964/65 |
| 17/258 | Rose G.A. | Central Districts v Northern Districts | 1958/59 |
| 17/259 | Smith N.G. | Otago v Northern Districts | 2015/16 |
| 17/268 | Snedden A.N.C. | Auckland v Wellington | 1909/10 |
| 17/268 | Beuth J.A. | Northern Districts v New Zealand Under 23 XI | 1962/63 |
| 17/274 | Ashbolt F.L. | Wellington v Auckland | 1893/94 |
| 17/276 | Collinge R.O. | Central Districts v Auckland | 1963/64 |
| 17/278 | Nicholls J.G. | Otago v Canterbury | 1876/77 |
| 17/286 | Hickmott R.G. | Canterbury v Wellington | 1911/12 |
| 17/291 | Bennett J.H. | Canterbury v Otago | 1898/99 |

*Years/days*

| 17/294 | Cairns A.E. | Otago v Canterbury | 1867/68 |
|--------|-------------|--------------------|---------|
| 17/305 | Gill M.F. | Central Districts v Wellington | 1974/75 |
| 17/307 | Currie E.W. | Otago v New South Wales | 1893/94 |
| 17/307 | Hastings B.F. | Wellington v Canterbury | 1957/58 |
| 17/325 | Bartlett G.A. | Central Districts v Northern Districts | 1958/59 |
| 17/326 | Milne A.F. | Central Districts v Canterbury | 2009/10 |
| 17/328 | Cushen J.A.J. | Otago v Canterbury | 1967/68 |
| 17/329 | West R.M. | Central Districts v Northern Districts | 1996/97 |
| 17/332 | Gadsdon S.R. | Northern Districts v Auckland | 2008/09 |
| 17/336 | Lambert H.N. | Wellington v Canterbury | 1917/18 |
| 17/352 | Motz R.C. | Canterbury v Northern Districts | 1957/58 |
| 17/355 | Tarrant D.R. | Central Districts v Auckland | 1954/55 |
| 17/362 | Vettori D.L. | Northern Districts v England | 1996/97 |

# CAREER RECORDS

The following career records cover the complete first-class careers of New Zealand players.
Matches for other than New Zealand teams e.g. county sides, are included.
To qualify for inclusion a player must have appeared in first-class cricket in New Zealand
while a bona fide resident of the country — professional coaches and the like thus being excluded.

## Batting

| **3000 RUNS** | *Career* | *M* | *In* | *NO* | *HS* | *Runs* | *Ave* | *100* |
|---|---|---|---|---|---|---|---|---|
| Turner G.M. | 1964/65-1982/83 | 455 | 792 | 101 | 311* | 34,346 | 49.70 | 103 |
| Wright J.G. | 1975/76-1992/93 | 366 | 636 | 46 | 192 | 25,073 | 42.35 | 59 |
| Crowe M.D. | 1979/80-1995/96 | 247 | 412 | 62 | 299 | 19,608 | 56.02 | 71 |
| Sutcliffe B. | 1941/42-1965/66 | 233 | 407 | 39 | 385 | 17,447 | 47.41 | 44 |
| Howarth G.P. | 1968/69-1985/86 | 338 | 584 | 42 | 183 | 17,294 | 31.90 | 32 |
| Fleming S.P. | 1991/92-2007/08 | 247 | 406 | 32 | 274* | 16,409 | 43.87 | 35 |
| Reid J.R. | 1947/48-1965 | 246 | 418 | 28 | 296 | 16,128 | 41.35 | 39 |
| Patel D.N. | 1976-1996/97 | 358 | 558 | 51 | 204 | 15,188 | 29.95 | 26 |
| Marshall H.J.H. | 1998/99-2016/17 | 264 | 434 | 29 | 170 | 14,820 | 36.59 | 31 |
| Rutherford K.R. | 1982/83-1999/00 | 220 | 383 | 33 | 317 | 13,974 | 39.92 | 35 |
| Sinclair M.S. | 1995/96-2012/13 | 188 | 319 | 37 | 268 | 13,717 | 48.64 | 36 |
| Congdon B.E. | 1960/61-1978 | 241 | 416 | 40 | 202* | 13,101 | 34.84 | 23 |
| Spearman C.M. | 1993/94-2009 | 201 | 360 | 16 | 341 | 13,021 | 37.85 | 30 |
| Hitchcock R.E. | 1947/48-1964 | 323 | 519 | 71 | 153* | 12,473 | 27.84 | 13 |
| Taylor L.R.P.L. | 2002/03-2021/22 | 192 | 323 | 27 | 290 | 12,369 | 41.78 | 27 |
| Papps M.H.W. | 1998/99-2017/18 | 188 | 344 | 26 | 316* | 12,294 | 38.66 | 33 |
| Dacre C.C.R. | 1914/15-1936 | 269 | 439 | 20 | 223 | 12,230 | 29.18 | 24 |
| Williamson K.S. | 2007/08-2022 | 156 | 267 | 21 | 284* | 12,179 | 49.50 | 34 |
| Dempster C.S. | 1921/22-1947/48 | 184 | 306 | 36 | 212 | 12,145 | 44.98 | 35 |
| Hadlee R.J. | 1971/72-1990 | 342 | 473 | 93 | 210* | 12,052 | 31.71 | 14 |
| Edgar B.A. | 1975/76-1989/90 | 175 | 307 | 26 | 203 | 11,304 | 40.22 | 24 |
| Parker J.M. | 1971-1983/84 | 207 | 362 | 39 | 195 | 11,254 | 34.84 | 21 |
| Smith S.G. | 1899/00-1925/26 | 211 | 379 | 30 | 256 | 10,920 | 31.28 | 14 |
| Cairns C.L. | 1988-2005/06 | 217 | 341 | 38 | 158 | 10,702 | 35.32 | 13 |
| Fulton P.G. | 2000/01-2016/17 | 162 | 288 | 23 | 301* | 10,569 | 39.88 | 19 |
| Burgess M.G. | 1963/64-1980/81 | 192 | 322 | 35 | 146 | 10,281 | 35.82 | 20 |
| Crowe J.J. | 1977/78-1991/92 | 180 | 304 | 34 | 159 | 10,233 | 37.90 | 22 |
| Watling B-J. | 2004/05-2021 | 178 | 297 | 36 | 205 | 10,034 | 38.44 | 18 |
| Richardson M.H. | 1989/90-2004/05 | 157 | 264 | 31 | 306 | 9994 | 42.89 | 20 |
| Greatbatch M.J. | 1982/83-1999/00 | 170 | 292 | 31 | 202* | 9890 | 37.89 | 24 |
| Bell M.D. | 1993/94-2010/11 | 171 | 293 | 18 | 265 | 9881 | 35.93 | 24 |
| Twose R.G. | 1989-2000/01 | 178 | 300 | 35 | 277* | 9802 | 36.98 | 18 |
| Franklin J.E.C. | 1998/99-2017 | 206 | 321 | 46 | 219 | 9780 | 35.56 | 22 |
| Latham T.W.M. | 2010/11-2022 | 137 | 236 | 15 | 264* | 9497 | 42.97 | 23 |
| Lowry T.C. | 1917/18-1937/38 | 198 | 322 | 20 | 181 | 9421 | 31.19 | 18 |
| Dowling G.T. | 1958/59-1971/72 | 158 | 282 | 13 | 239 | 9399 | 34.94 | 16 |
| Astle N.J. | 1991/92-2006/07 | 171 | 272 | 24 | 223 | 9321 | 37.58 | 19 |
| Donnelly M.P. | 1936/37-1960/61 | 131 | 221 | 26 | 208* | 9250 | 47.43 | 23 |
| McCullum B.B. | 1999/00-2015/16 | 150 | 261 | 13 | 302 | 9210 | 37.13 | 17 |
| Jones A.H. | 1979/80-1995/96 | 145 | 254 | 33 | 186 | 9180 | 41.53 | 16 |
| Cumming C.D. | 1995/96-2011/12 | 147 | 260 | 21 | 187 | 9142 | 38.25 | 23 |
| Ryder J.D. | 2002/03-2017/18 | 131 | 214 | 19 | 236 | 8784 | 45.04 | 25 |
| Horne M.J. | 1992/93-2005/06 | 128 | 219 | 11 | 241 | 8501 | 40.87 | 24 |
| Broom N.T. | 2002/03-2019/20 | 149 | 252 | 26 | 203* | 8457 | 37.42 | 18 |
| Raval J.A. | 2008/09-2021/22 | 132 | 232 | 11 | 256 | 8323 | 37.66 | 18 |
| Conway D.P. | 2008/09-2022 | 120 | 195 | 23 | 327* | 8169 | 47.49 | 21 |

| | Career | M | In | NO | HS | Runs | Ave | 100 |
|---|---|---|---|---|---|---|---|---|
| Arnold P.A. | 1953/54-1960 | 174 | 306 | 15 | 122 | 8013 | 27.53 | 7 |
| Blunt R.C. | 1917/18-1935 | 123 | 209 | 15 | 338* | 7953 | 40.99 | 15 |
| Coney J.V. | 1970/71-1986/87 | 165 | 272 | 48 | 174* | 7872 | 35.14 | 8 |
| McMillan C.D. | 1994/95-2007 | 138 | 226 | 27 | 168* | 7817 | 39.28 | 16 |
| Flynn D.R. | 2004/05-2019/20 | 135 | 238 | 15 | 241 | 7815 | 35.04 | 21 |
| Woodcock L.J. | 2001/02-2018/19 | 147 | 250 | 31 | 220* | 7811 | 35.66 | 11 |
| Franklin T.J. | 1980/81-1992/93 | 148 | 254 | 20 | 181 | 7794 | 33.30 | 15 |
| Wallace W.M. | 1933/34-1960/61 | 121 | 192 | 17 | 211 | 7757 | 44.32 | 17 |
| Guptill M.J. | 2005/06-2021/22 | 118 | 214 | 13 | 227 | 7747 | 38.54 | 17 |
| Hastings B.F. | 1957/58-1976/77 | 163 | 273 | 32 | 226 | 7685 | 31.89 | 15 |
| Rutherford H.D. | 2008/09-2021/22 | 122 | 212 | 3 | 239 | 7683 | 36.76 | 17 |
| How J.M. | 2000/01-2014/15 | 131 | 231 | 20 | 207* | 7647 | 36.24 | 16 |
| Hopkins G.J. | 1997/98-2013/14 | 158 | 245 | 39 | 201 | 7550 | 36.65 | 17 |
| Hadlee W.A. | 1933/34-1951/52 | 117 | 203 | 17 | 198 | 7523 | 40.44 | 18 |
| Young B.A. | 1983/84-1998/99 | 163 | 276 | 43 | 267* | 7489 | 32.14 | 10 |
| Marshall J.A.H. | 1997/98-2012/13 | 148 | 250 | 17 | 235 | 7422 | 31.85 | 13 |
| Harris C.Z. | 1989/90-2009/10 | 131 | 204 | 42 | 251* | 7377 | 45.53 | 15 |
| Parlane M.E. | 1992/93-2010/11 | 139 | 238 | 16 | 203 | 7354 | 33.12 | 15 |
| Jones R.A. | 1993/94-2009/10 | 124 | 215 | 12 | 201 | 7254 | 35.73 | 19 |
| Redmond A.J. | 1999/00-2014/15 | 129 | 225 | 13 | 154 | 7248 | 34.18 | 15 |
| McIntosh T.G. | 1998/99-2013/14 | 131 | 229 | 19 | 268 | 7169 | 33.58 | 19 |
| Vance R.H. | 1976/77-1990/91 | 135 | 230 | 18 | 254* | 6955 | 32.80 | 12 |
| Myburgh J.G. | 1997/98-2016 | 108 | 190 | 23 | 203 | 6841 | 40.53 | 16 |
| Parore A.C. | 1988/89-2001/02 | 163 | 252 | 43 | 155* | 6826 | 32.66 | 10 |
| van Wyk C.F.K. | 2000/01-2015/16 | 138 | 217 | 47 | 178* | 6733 | 39.60 | 7 |
| Vettori D.L. | 1996/97-2014/15 | 174 | 257 | 31 | 140 | 6695 | 29.62 | 9 |
| McEwan P.E. | 1976/77-1990/91 | 115 | 206 | 15 | 155 | 6677 | 34.95 | 12 |
| de Grandhomme C. | 2005/06-2022 | 126 | 202 | 29 | 174* | 6592 | 38.10 | 15 |
| McGregor S.N. | 1947/48-1968/69 | 148 | 274 | 16 | 114* | 6573 | 25.47 | 5 |
| Patel J.S. | 1999/00-2019 | 289 | 385 | 77 | 120 | 6573 | 21.34 | 3 |
| James K.C. | 1923/24-1946/47 | 204 | 330 | 41 | 109* | 6413 | 22.19 | 7 |
| Hay G.R. | 2006/07-2021/22 | 94 | 165 | 13 | 226 | 6367 | 41.88 | 15 |
| Young W.A. | 2011/12-2022 | 100 | 166 | 13 | 162 | 6333 | 41.39 | 13 |
| Nicol R.J. | 2001/02-2017/18 | 130 | 218 | 25 | 160 | 6319 | 32.74 | 10 |
| Latham R.T. | 1980/81-1994/95 | 108 | 189 | 19 | 237* | 6298 | 37.05 | 9 |
| Wilson B.S. | 2004/05-2018/19 | 111 | 204 | 9 | 165 | 6283 | 32.22 | 14 |
| Murray B.A.G. | 1958/59-1972/73 | 102 | 187 | 11 | 213 | 6257 | 35.55 | 6 |
| Brownlie D.G. | 2009/10-2019/20 | 94 | 169 | 14 | 334 | 6208 | 40.05 | 14 |
| Morrison J.F.M. | 1965/66-1983/84 | 126 | 225 | 25 | 180* | 6142 | 30.71 | 7 |
| Sinclair B.W. | 1955/56-1970/71 | 118 | 204 | 18 | 148 | 6114 | 32.87 | 6 |
| Nicholls H.M. | 2011/12-2022 | 103 | 168 | 12 | 174 | 6072 | 38.92 | 13 |
| Styris S.B. | 1994/95-2010/11 | 128 | 213 | 20 | 212* | 6048 | 31.33 | 10 |
| Blair B.R. | 1977/78-1989/90 | 110 | 190 | 6 | 143 | 5995 | 32.58 | 7 |
| Morgan R.W. | 1957/58-1976/77 | 136 | 229 | 13 | 166 | 5940 | 27.50 | 8 |
| Roberts A.D.G. | 1967/68-1983/84 | 112 | 206 | 37 | 128* | 5865 | 34.70 | 7 |
| Page M.L. | 1920/21-1942/43 | 132 | 213 | 17 | 206 | 5857 | 29.88 | 9 |
| Shrimpton M.J.F. | 1961/62-1979/80 | 122 | 218 | 23 | 150 | 5812 | 29.80 | 7 |
| Blain T.E. | 1982/83-1994/95 | 118 | 199 | 30 | 161 | 5749 | 34.02 | 8 |
| Stewart S.L. | 2001/02-2013/14 | 96 | 173 | 18 | 227* | 5693 | 36.72 | 7 |
| Reid J.F. | 1975/76-1987/88 | 101 | 170 | 22 | 180 | 5650 | 38.17 | 11 |
| Ingram P.J. | 2001/02-2011/12 | 82 | 149 | 8 | 247 | 5623 | 39.87 | 17 |
| Scott V.J. | 1937/38-1952/53 | 80 | 130 | 17 | 204 | 5620 | 49.73 | 16 |
| Ronchi L. | 2002/03-2016/17 | 100 | 158 | 15 | 148 | 5614 | 39.25 | 16 |
| Anderson R.W. | 1967/68-1981/82 | 111 | 197 | 14 | 155 | 5609 | 30.65 | 8 |
| Parlane N.R. | 1996/97-2011/12 | 103 | 170 | 14 | 193 | 5602 | 35.91 | 12 |

| | Career | M | In | NO | HS | Runs | Ave | 100 |
|---|---|---|---|---|---|---|---|---|
| Smith I.D.S. | 1977/78-1991/92 | 178 | 250 | 42 | 173 | 5570 | 26.77 | 6 |
| Murdoch S.J. | 2009/10-2019/20 | 87 | 158 | 9 | 171 | 5551 | 37.25 | 13 |
| Gray E.J. | 1975/76-1991/92 | 162 | 241 | 51 | 128* | 5472 | 28.80 | 6 |
| Worker G.H. | 2007/08-2021/22 | 110 | 199 | 7 | 210 | 5451 | 28.39 | 9 |
| Bracewell M.G. | 2010/11-2022 | 98 | 175 | 13 | 190 | 5358 | 32.55 | 11 |
| Chapple M.E. | 1949/50-1971/72 | 119 | 201 | 16 | 165 | 5344 | 28.88 | 4 |
| Pollard V. | 1964/65-1974/75 | 130 | 207 | 33 | 146 | 5314 | 30.54 | 6 |
| Ellis A.M. | 2002/03-2017/18 | 106 | 169 | 21 | 196 | 5221 | 35.27 | 9 |
| Kitchen A.K. | 2008/09-2021/22 | 92 | 167 | 13 | 207 | 5194 | 33.72 | 10 |
| Vincent L. | 1997/98-2012/13 | 98 | 162 | 12 | 224 | 5184 | 34.56 | 10 |
| Nevin C.J. | 1995/96-2009/10 | 112 | 172 | 26 | 143* | 5058 | 34.64 | 4 |
| Mills J.E. | 1925/26-1937/38 | 97 | 161 | 8 | 185 | 5025 | 32.84 | 11 |
| Graham H. | 1892/93-1906/07 | 113 | 200 | 9 | 124 | 5023 | 26.29 | 7 |
| Weir G.L. | 1927/28-1946/47 | 107 | 172 | 16 | 191 | 5022 | 32.19 | 10 |
| Mitchell D.J. | 2011/12-2022 | 88 | 141 | 18 | 190 | 4987 | 40.54 | 13 |
| Stead G.R. | 1991/92-2005/06 | 101 | 165 | 10 | 190 | 4984 | 32.15 | 10 |
| Bradburn G.E. | 1985/86-2001/02 | 127 | 206 | 27 | 148* | 4978 | 27.81 | 4 |
| McSweeney E.B. | 1979/80-1993/94 | 121 | 177 | 30 | 205* | 4947 | 33.65 | 6 |
| Lees W.K. | 1970/71-1987/88 | 146 | 243 | 43 | 152 | 4932 | 24.66 | 5 |
| Pairaudeau B.H. | 1946/47-1966/67 | 89 | 159 | 5 | 163 | 4930 | 32.01 | 11 |
| White D.J. | 1979/80-1993/94 | 106 | 187 | 17 | 209 | 4926 | 28.98 | 7 |
| de Boorder D.C. | 2007/08-2017/18 | 103 | 160 | 28 | 146 | 4858 | 36.80 | 4 |
| Yovich J.A.F. | 1996/97-2012/13 | 121 | 190 | 29 | 144 | 4839 | 30.05 | 6 |
| Kerr J.L. | 1929/30-1942/43 | 89 | 157 | 7 | 196 | 4829 | 32.19 | 8 |
| Douglas M.W. | 1987/88-2000/01 | 94 | 160 | 23 | 144 | 4808 | 35.09 | 9 |
| Miller L.S.M. | 1950/51-1959/60 | 82 | 142 | 15 | 144 | 4777 | 37.61 | 5 |
| Grimmett C.V. | 1911/12-1940/41 | 248 | 321 | 54 | 71* | 4720 | 17.67 | — |
| Gaffaney C.B. | 1995/96-2004/05 | 83 | 152 | 11 | 194 | 4711 | 33.41 | 8 |
| Pocock B.A. | 1990/91-2000/01 | 100 | 176 | 16 | 167 | 4699 | 29.36 | 10 |
| Jarvis T.W. | 1964/65-1976/77 | 97 | 167 | 8 | 182 | 4666 | 29.34 | 6 |
| Blundell T.A. | 2012/13-2022 | 86 | 145 | 19 | 153 | 4636 | 36.79 | 11 |
| Young R.A. | 1998/99-2012/13 | 126 | 183 | 30 | 126* | 4633 | 30.28 | 8 |
| Sparling J.T. | 1956/57-1970/71 | 127 | 215 | 26 | 105 | 4606 | 24.11 | 2 |
| Edwards G.N. | 1973/74-1984/85 | 92 | 164 | 8 | 177* | 4589 | 29.41 | 5 |
| Taylor B.R. | 1963/64-1979/80 | 141 | 210 | 25 | 173 | 4579 | 24.75 | 4 |
| Adams A.R. | 1997/98-2015 | 173 | 237 | 24 | 124 | 4540 | 21.31 | 3 |
| Hadlee B.G. | 1961/62-1980/81 | 84 | 155 | 11 | 163* | 4539 | 31.52 | 6 |
| Vivian H.G. | 1930/31-1938/39 | 85 | 143 | 15 | 165 | 4443 | 34.71 | 6 |
| Hart M.N. | 1990/91-2004/05 | 135 | 198 | 26 | 201* | 4418 | 25.68 | 4 |
| Briasco P.S. | 1982/83-1991/92 | 83 | 148 | 16 | 157 | 4390 | 33.25 | 6 |
| Bracewell J.G. | 1978/79-1990 | 149 | 208 | 40 | 110* | 4354 | 25.91 | 4 |
| Astle T.D. | 2005/06-2019/20 | 119 | 190 | 22 | 195 | 4345 | 25.86 | 2 |
| Wiseman P.J. | 1991/92-2008 | 186 | 254 | 51 | 130 | 4254 | 20.95 | 2 |
| Thomson S.A. | 1987/88-1996/97 | 90 | 148 | 38 | 167 | 4209 | 38.26 | 6 |
| Cairns B.L. | 1971/72-1988 | 148 | 226 | 25 | 110 | 4165 | 20.72 | 1 |
| McGirr H.M. | 1913/14-1932/33 | 88 | 146 | 7 | 141 | 3992 | 28.71 | 5 |
| Oram J.D.P. | 1997/98-2009/10 | 85 | 136 | 18 | 155 | 3992 | 33.83 | 8 |
| Cleaver D. | 2010/11-2021/22 | 66 | 109 | 12 | 201 | 3991 | 41.14 | 7 |
| Bruce T.C. | 2014/15-2021/22 | 59 | 104 | 20 | 208* | 3959 | 47.13 | 6 |
| Cromb I.B. | 1929/30-1946/47 | 88 | 148 | 12 | 171 | 3950 | 29.04 | 3 |
| Priest M.W. | 1984/85-1998/99 | 109 | 154 | 25 | 119 | 3945 | 30.58 | 4 |
| Bracewell D.A.J. | 2008/09-2021/22 | 114 | 171 | 23 | 105 | 3930 | 26.55 | 3 |
| Dunning B. | 1961/62-1977/78 | 83 | 150 | 10 | 142 | 3929 | 28.06 | 3 |
| Guy J.W. | 1953/54-1972/73 | 90 | 165 | 13 | 115 | 3923 | 25.80 | 3 |
| Elliott G.D. | 1996/97-2013/14 | 83 | 134 | 7 | 196* | 3883 | 30.57 | 8 |

| | Career | M | In | NO | HS | Runs | Ave | 100 |
|---|---|---|---|---|---|---|---|---|
| Bailey M.D. | 1989/90-2001/02 | 89 | 138 | 9 | 180* | 3882 | 30.09 | 8 |
| Harris R.M. | 1955/56-1973/74 | 73 | 130 | 5 | 157 | 3863 | 30.90 | 3 |
| Yuile B.W. | 1959/60-1971/72 | 123 | 187 | 31 | 146 | 3850 | 24.67 | 1 |
| Parsons A.E.W. | 1971/72-1982/83 | 82 | 156 | 10 | 141 | 3847 | 26.34 | 4 |
| Sulzberger G.P. | 1995/96-2004/05 | 83 | 135 | 12 | 159 | 3836 | 31.18 | 8 |
| Hiddleston J.S. | 1909/10-1928/29 | 52 | 97 | 1 | 212 | 3818 | 39.77 | 8 |
| Rutherford I.A. | 1974/75-1983/84 | 79 | 144 | 4 | 222 | 3794 | 27.10 | 5 |
| Taylor D.D. | 1946/47-1960/61 | 95 | 168 | 6 | 143 | 3772 | 23.28 | 1 |
| Hartland B.R. | 1986/87-1996/97 | 83 | 150 | 8 | 150 | 3753 | 26.42 | 5 |
| Kuggeleijn C.M. | 1975/76-1990/91 | 89 | 151 | 15 | 116 | 3747 | 27.55 | 4 |
| MacGibbon A.R. | 1947/48-1961/62 | 124 | 206 | 20 | 94 | 3699 | 19.88 | — |
| Blair W.L. | 1967/68-1990/91 | 82 | 151 | 9 | 140 | 3698 | 26.04 | 2 |
| Webb P.N. | 1976/77-1986/87 | 75 | 130 | 19 | 136 | 3671 | 33.07 | 5 |
| Wadsworth K.J. | 1968/69-1975/76 | 118 | 164 | 23 | 117 | 3664 | 25.98 | 2 |
| Roberts A.W. | 1927/28-1950/51 | 84 | 135 | 17 | 181 | 3645 | 30.88 | 3 |
| Leggat J.G. | 1944/45-1955/56 | 57 | 106 | 9 | 166 | 3634 | 37.46 | 7 |
| Austen M.H. | 1982/83-1996/97 | 66 | 120 | 8 | 202* | 3619 | 32.31 | 6 |
| Munro C. | 2006/07-2017/18 | 48 | 74 | 4 | 281 | 3611 | 51.58 | 13 |
| O'Donnell R.R. | 2014/15-2021/22 | 61 | 105 | 7 | 223 | 3588 | 36.61 | 7 |
| Howell L.G. | 1990/91-2004/05 | 83 | 143 | 16 | 181 | 3586 | 28.23 | 3 |
| Hoskin R.N. | 1980/81-1992/93 | 81 | 140 | 7 | 157 | 3580 | 26.91 | 6 |
| Nash D.J. | 1990/91-2001/02 | 120 | 168 | 37 | 135* | 3555 | 27.13 | 5 |
| Patrick W.R. | 1905/06-1926/27 | 74 | 138 | 8 | 143 | 3536 | 27.20 | 4 |
| Bowes C.J. | 2010/11-2021/22 | 79 | 130 | 8 | 155 | 3532 | 28.95 | 6 |
| Smith C.J.P. | 1983/84-1990/91 | 62 | 118 | 9 | 160* | 3499 | 32.10 | 7 |
| Motz R.C. | 1957/58-1969 | 142 | 225 | 21 | 103* | 3494 | 17.12 | 1 |
| Larsen G.R. | 1984/85-1998/99 | 103 | 157 | 35 | 161 | 3491 | 28.61 | 2 |
| Brown V.R. | 1978/79-1989/90 | 83 | 136 | 17 | 161* | 3485 | 29.28 | 6 |
| Rabone G.O. | 1940/41-1960/61 | 82 | 135 | 14 | 125 | 3425 | 28.30 | 3 |
| Smith B.S. | 2010/11-2021/22 | 67 | 114 | 8 | 244 | 3414 | 32.20 | 6 |
| Todd G.R. | 2000/01-2011/12 | 64 | 114 | 15 | 165 | 3368 | 34.02 | 4 |
| Pritchard T.L. | 1937/38-1956 | 200 | 293 | 41 | 81 | 3363 | 13.34 | — |
| Newdick G.A. | 1970/71-1980/81 | 61 | 114 | 6 | 143 | 3292 | 30.48 | 4 |
| Lawson R.A. | 1992/93-2003/04 | 73 | 133 | 6 | 200 | 3278 | 25.81 | 3 |
| Vivian G.E. | 1964/65-1978/79 | 88 | 140 | 25 | 137* | 3259 | 28.33 | 3 |
| Wagner N. | 2005/06-2022 | 191 | 250 | 55 | 70 | 3260 | 16.71 | — |
| Neesham J.D.S. | 2009/10-2021/22 | 67 | 112 | 10 | 147 | 3249 | 31.85 | 5 |
| Noema-Barnett K. | 2008/09-2018/19 | 87 | 131 | 19 | 108 | 3243 | 28.95 | 4 |
| Moloney D.A.R. | 1929/30-1940/41 | 64 | 119 | 7 | 190 | 3219 | 28.74 | 2 |
| Boyle D.J. | 1980/81-1994/95 | 69 | 121 | 12 | 149 | 3216 | 29.50 | 3 |
| Carter J.F. | 2013/14-2021/22 | 58 | 102 | 4 | 169 | 3206 | 32.71 | 6 |
| Stead D.W. | 1968/69-1985/86 | 80 | 139 | 11 | 193* | 3205 | 25.03 | 1 |
| Alabaster G.D. | 1955/56-1975/76 | 96 | 154 | 20 | 108 | 3200 | 23.88 | 3 |
| Reese D. | 1895/96-1920/21 | 72 | 134 | 8 | 148 | 3186 | 25.28 | 4 |
| Fletcher C.D. | 2012/13-2021/22 | 72 | 113 | 23 | 157 | 3179 | 35.32 | 6 |
| McCullum S.J. | 1976/77-1990/91 | 75 | 131 | 1 | 134 | 3174 | 24.41 | 2 |
| Duff S.W. | 1985/86-1995/96 | 88 | 134 | 29 | 164* | 3167 | 30.16 | 1 |
| Vaughan J.T.C. | 1989/90-1996/97 | 70 | 120 | 20 | 127 | 3159 | 31.59 | 2 |
| Griggs B.B.J. | 2000/01-2009/10 | 83 | 130 | 16 | 143 | 3155 | 27.67 | 2 |
| Popli B. | 2013/14-2021/22 | 53 | 90 | 5 | 172 | 3154 | 37.10 | 4 |
| Harford N.S. | 1953/54-1966/67 | 74 | 122 | 8 | 158 | 3149 | 27.62 | 3 |
| Merritt W.E. | 1926/27-1946 | 125 | 191 | 33 | 87 | 3147 | 19.91 | — |
| Mooney F.L.H. | 1941/42-1954/55 | 91 | 150 | 14 | 180 | 3143 | 23.11 | 2 |
| Redmond R.E. | 1963/64-1975/76 | 53 | 100 | 7 | 141* | 3134 | 33.69 | 5 |
| Thomson K. | 1959/60-1973/74 | 71 | 125 | 14 | 136* | 3134 | 28.23 | 5 |

| | Career | M | In | NO | HS | Runs | Ave | 100 |
|---|---|---|---|---|---|---|---|---|
| Tindill E.W.T. | 1932/33-1949/50 | 69 | 116 | 13 | 149 | 3127 | 30.35 | 6 |
| Harris P.G.Z. | 1949/50-1964/65 | 69 | 120 | 9 | 118 | 3126 | 28.16 | 5 |
| Germon L.K. | 1987/88-2001/02 | 103 | 142 | 35 | 160* | 3123 | 29.18 | 4 |
| Englefield J.I. | 1998/99-2005/06 | 55 | 97 | 7 | 172 | 3113 | 34.58 | 3 |
| Kuggeleijn S.C. | 2011/12-2021/22 | 87 | 134 | 23 | 142* | 3105 | 27.97 | 3 |
| Wells J.D. | 1989/90-2000/01 | 73 | 115 | 18 | 143 | 3058 | 31.52 | 5 |
| Ryan M.L. | 1965/66-1978/79 | 66 | 113 | 9 | 129 | 3023 | 29.06 | 3 |
| Barnes A.C. | 1993/94-2004/05 | 78 | 121 | 10 | 134* | 3006 | 27.08 | 4 |

## Bowling

| 200 WICKETS | Career | M | Wkts | Runs | Ave |
|---|---|---|---|---|---|
| Hadlee R.J. | 1971/72-1990 | 342 | 1490 | 26,998 | 18.11 |
| Grimmett C.V. | 1911/12-1940/41 | 248 | 1424 | 31,740 | 22.28 |
| Smith S.G. | 1899/00-1925/26 | 211 | 955 | 17,272 | 18.08 |
| Patel J.S. | 1999/00-2019 | 293 | 892 | 29,239 | 32.77 |
| Pritchard T.L. | 1937/38-1956 | 200 | 818 | 19,062 | 23.30 |
| Wagner N. | 2005/06-2022 | 191 | 783 | 20,996 | 26.81 |
| Adams A.R. | 1997/98-2015 | 173 | 692 | 16,581 | 23.96 |
| Patel D.N. | 1976-1996/97 | 358 | 654 | 21,737 | 33.23 |
| Cairns C.L. | 1988-2005/06 | 217 | 647 | 18,322 | 28.31 |
| Boock S.L. | 1973/74-1989/90 | 164 | 640 | 14,314 | 22.36 |
| Martin C.S. | 1997/98-2012/13 | 192 | 599 | 19,070 | 31.83 |
| Chatfield E.J. | 1973/74-1989/90 | 157 | 587 | 13,429 | 22.87 |
| Vettori D.L. | 1996/97-2014/15 | 174 | 565 | 17,981 | 31.82 |
| Saunders J.V. | 1899/00-1913/14 | 107 | 553 | 12,065 | 21.81 |
| Howarth H.J. | 1962/63-1978/79 | 145 | 541 | 13,674 | 25.27 |
| Blair R.W. | 1951/52-1964/65 | 119 | 537 | 9961 | 18.54 |
| Merritt W.E. | 1926/27-1946 | 125 | 536 | 13,669 | 25.50 |
| Collinge R.O. | 1963/64-1978 | 163 | 524 | 12,793 | 24.41 |
| O'Sullivan D.R. | 1971-1984/85 | 136 | 523 | 13,554 | 25.91 |
| Bracewell J.G. | 1978/79-1990 | 149 | 522 | 13,919 | 26.66 |
| Motz R.C. | 1957/58-1969 | 142 | 518 | 11,769 | 22.72 |
| Southee T.G. | 2006/07-2022 | 129 | 511 | 13,680 | 26.77 |
| Alabaster J.C. | 1955/56-1971/72 | 143 | 500 | 12,688 | 25.37 |
| Franklin J.E.C. | 1998/99-2017 | 206 | 479 | 13,504 | 28.19 |
| Cairns B.L. | 1971/72-1988 | 148 | 473 | 12,544 | 26.52 |
| Reid J.R. | 1947/48-1965 | 246 | 466 | 10,535 | 22.60 |
| Wiseman P.J. | 1991/92-2008 | 186 | 466 | 15,727 | 33.74 |
| Cameron F.J. | 1952/53-1966/67 | 119 | 447 | 9658 | 21.60 |
| Gray E.J. | 1975/76-1991/92 | 162 | 444 | 12,522 | 28.20 |
| Morrison D.K. | 1985/86-1996/97 | 142 | 440 | 13,298 | 30.22 |
| Boult T.A. | 2008/09-2022 | 113 | 433 | 11,634 | 26.86 |
| Taylor B.R. | 1963/64-1979/80 | 141 | 422 | 10,605 | 25.13 |
| Burtt T.B. | 1943/44-1954/55 | 84 | 408 | 9054 | 22.19 |
| Arnel B.J | 2005/06-2017/18 | 111 | 394 | 10,598 | 26.89 |
| Snedden M.C. | 1977/78-1990 | 118 | 387 | 9918 | 25.62 |
| Cunis R.S. | 1960/61-1976/77 | 132 | 386 | 10,287 | 26.65 |
| Gillespie M.R. | 1999/00-2014/15 | 94 | 385 | 10,769 | 27.97 |
| Yuile B.W. | 1959/60-1971/72 | 123 | 375 | 8209 | 21.89 |
| Moir A.M. | 1949/50-1961/62 | 97 | 368 | 9040 | 24.56 |
| Aldridge G.W. | 1998/99-2014/15 | 123 | 364 | 10,299 | 28.29 |
| Cave H.B. | 1945/46-1958/59 | 117 | 362 | 8663 | 23.93 |
| Cowie J. | 1932/33-1949/50 | 86 | 359 | 8002 | 22.28 |
| MacGibbon A.R. | 1947/48-1961/62 | 124 | 356 | 9301 | 26.12 |

| | *Career* | *M* | *Wkts* | *Runs* | *Ave* |
|---|---|---|---|---|---|
| Martin B.P. | 1999/00-2013/14 | 131 | 355 | 13,345 | 37.59 |
| Hadlee D.R. | 1966/67-1983/84 | 111 | 351 | 8853 | 25.22 |
| Henry M.J. | 2010/11-2022 | 81 | 351 | 8700 | 24.78 |
| Bracewell D.A.J. | 2008/09-2021/22 | 114 | 348 | 11,301 | 32.47 |
| McIntyre J.M. | 1961/62-1982/83 | 113 | 336 | 7917 | 23.56 |
| Astle T.D. | 2005/06-2019/20 | 119 | 334 | 10,746 | 32.17 |
| Priest M.W. | 1984/85-1998/99 | 109 | 329 | 10,478 | 31.84 |
| O'Brien I.E. | 2000/01-2010 | 91 | 322 | 8392 | 26.06 |
| Callaway S.T. | 1888/89-1906/07 | 62 | 320 | 5460 | 17.06 |
| Sparling J.T. | 1956/57-1970/71 | 127 | 318 | 7226 | 22.72 |
| Downes A.D. | 1888/89-1913/14 | 51 | 311 | 4564 | 14.67 |
| Hayes J.A. | 1946/47-1960/61 | 78 | 292 | 6759 | 23.14 |
| Tuffey D.R. | 1996/97-2011/12 | 91 | 288 | 7705 | 26.75 |
| Mason M.J. | 1997/98-2011/12 | 91 | 288 | 7240 | 25.13 |
| Dickeson C.W. | 1973/74-1986/87 | 90 | 282 | 8242 | 29.22 |
| Sodhi I.S. | 2012/13-2021/22 | 88 | 279 | 8410 | 33.72 |
| Beard D.D. | 1945/46-1964/65 | 66 | 278 | 6000 | 21.58 |
| O'Connor S.B. | 1994/95-2002/03 | 73 | 278 | 6582 | 23.67 |
| Alabaster G.D. | 1955/56-1975/76 | 96 | 275 | 6388 | 23.22 |
| Patel A.Y. | 2012/13-2022 | 74 | 273 | 8759 | 32.08 |
| Troup G.B. | 1974/75-1986/87 | 100 | 272 | 7541 | 27.72 |
| Watson W. | 1984/85-1994/95 | 93 | 272 | 7485 | 27.52 |
| Kuggeleijn S.C. | 2011/12-2021/22 | 87 | 270 | 8676 | 32.13 |
| Upham E.F. | 1892/93-1909/10 | 49 | 265 | 4414 | 16.65 |
| Bennett H.K. | 2005/06-2020/21 | 79 | 261 | 7437 | 28.49 |
| Nash D.J. | 1990/91-2001/02 | 120 | 255 | 7165 | 28.09 |
| Yovich J.A.F. | 1996/97-2012/13 | 102 | 255 | 8579 | 33.64 |
| Walmsley K.P | 1994/95-2005/06 | 67 | 253 | 6302 | 24.90 |
| Robertson G.K. | 1979/80-1989/90 | 88 | 252 | 7469 | 29.59 |
| Penn A.J. | 1994/95-2003/04 | 66 | 252 | 5806 | 23.03 |
| Bradburn G.E. | 1985/86-2001/02 | 127 | 250 | 8174 | 32.69 |
| Doull S.B. | 1989/90-2001/02 | 99 | 250 | 7233 | 28.93 |
| Ellis A.M. | 2002/03-2017/18 | 106 | 249 | 7416 | 29.78 |
| Wisneski W.A. | 1992/93-2003/04 | 71 | 248 | 6467 | 26.07 |
| Brice A.W.S. | 1902/03-1927/28 | 61 | 247 | 5260 | 21.29 |
| Nethula T.S. | 2008/09-2017/18 | 80 | 245 | 9040 | 36.89 |
| Bennett J.H. | 1898/99-1919/20 | 52 | 241 | 4476 | 18.58 |
| McSkimming W.C. | 1999/00-2011/12 | 69 | 240 | 5850 | 24.37 |
| McGirr H.M. | 1913/14-1932/33 | 88 | 239 | 6571 | 27.49 |
| Puna N. | 1956/57-1968/69 | 70 | 229 | 5597 | 24.44 |
| Dunning J.A. | 1923/24-1937/38 | 60 | 228 | 6290 | 27.58 |
| Bond S.E. | 1996/97-2009/10 | 60 | 225 | 5478 | 24.34 |
| Viljoen C. | 2009/10-2018/19 | 80 | 225 | 6075 | 27.00 |
| Pollard V. | 1964/65-1974/75 | 130 | 224 | 6931 | 30.94 |
| Vivian H.G. | 1930/31-1938/39 | 85 | 223 | 6160 | 27.62 |
| Cromb I.B. | 1929/30-1946/47 | 88 | 222 | 6152 | 27.71 |
| Badcock F.T. | 1924/25-1945 | 53 | 221 | 5211 | 23.57 |
| Allcott C.F.W. | 1920/21-1945/46 | 82 | 220 | 5882 | 26.73 |
| Sewell D.G. | 1995/96-2005/06 | 67 | 218 | 6260 | 28.71 |
| Duffy J.A. | 2011/12-2022 | 78 | 218 | 7328 | 33.61 |
| Duff S.W. | 1985/86-1995/96 | 88 | 217 | 7051 | 32.49 |
| Davis H.T. | 1991/92-2003/04 | 71 | 215 | 6693 | 31.13 |
| Blunt R.C. | 1917/18-1935 | 123 | 214 | 6638 | 31.01 |
| Stott L.W. | 1969/70-1983/84 | 63 | 214 | 5341 | 24.95 |
| Hart M.N. | 1990/91-2004/05 | 135 | 212 | 7424 | 35.01 |

| | Career | M | Wkts | Runs | Ave |
|---|---|---|---|---|---|
| Hamilton L.J. | 1996/97-2006/07 | 60 | 212 | 5391 | 25.42 |
| de Groen R.P. | 1987/88-1995/96 | 60 | 210 | 5266 | 25.07 |
| Stirling D.A. | 1981/82-1991/92 | 84 | 206 | 6948 | 33.72 |
| Canning T.K. | 1998/99-2006/07 | 61 | 206 | 5042 | 24.47 |
| de Grandhomme C. | 2005/06-2022 | 126 | 205 | 6070 | 29.60 |
| Congdon B.E. | 1960/61-1978 | 241 | 204 | 6125 | 30.02 |
| Styris S.B. | 1994/95-2010/11 | 128 | 204 | 6440 | 31.56 |
| Mills K.D. | 1998/99-2013/14 | 76 | 204 | 6083 | 29.81 |
| Butler I.G. | 2001/02-2014 | 72 | 204 | 6315 | 30.95 |
| Roberts S.J. | 1985/86-1995/96 | 63 | 203 | 6001 | 29.56 |
| Baker J.D. | 2010/11-2020/21 | 76 | 201 | 5961 | 29.65 |

## Leading Career Averages

| **BATTING** *(qualification 3000 runs)* | M | In | NO | HS | Runs | Ave |
|---|---|---|---|---|---|---|
| Crowe M.D. | 247 | 412 | 62 | 299 | 19,608 | 56.02 |
| Munro C. | 48 | 74 | 4 | 281 | 3611 | 51.58 |
| Scott V.J. | 80 | 130 | 17 | 204 | 5620 | 49.73 |
| Turner G.M. | 455 | 792 | 101 | 311* | 34,346 | 49.70 |
| Williamson K.S. | 156 | 267 | 21 | 284* | 12,179 | 49.50 |
| Sinclair M.S. | 188 | 319 | 37 | 268 | 13,717 | 48.64 |
| Conway D.P. | 120 | 195 | 23 | 327* | 8169 | 47.49 |
| Sutcliffe B. | 233 | 407 | 39 | 385 | 17,447 | 47.41 |
| Bruce T.C. | 59 | 104 | 20 | 208* | 3959 | 47.13 |
| Harris C.Z. | 131 | 204 | 42 | 251* | 7377 | 45.53 |
| Ryder J.D. | 131 | 214 | 19 | 236 | 8784 | 45.04 |
| Dempster C.S. | 184 | 306 | 36 | 212 | 12,145 | 44.98 |
| Wallace W.M. | 121 | 192 | 17 | 211 | 7757 | 44.32 |
| Fleming S.P. | 247 | 406 | 32 | 274* | 16,409 | 43.87 |
| Latham T.W.M. | 137 | 236 | 15 | 264* | 9497 | 42.97 |
| Richardson M.H. | 157 | 264 | 31 | 306 | 9994 | 42.89 |
| Wright J.G. | 366 | 636 | 44 | 192 | 25,073 | 42.35 |
| Hay G.R. | 94 | 165 | 13 | 226 | 6367 | 41.88 |
| Taylor L.R.P.L. | 192 | 323 | 27 | 290 | 12,369 | 41.78 |
| Jones A.H. | 145 | 254 | 33 | 186 | 9180 | 41.53 |
| Young W.A. | 100 | 166 | 13 | 162 | 6333 | 41.39 |
| Reid J.R. | 246 | 418 | 28 | 296 | 16,128 | 41.35 |
| Cleaver D. | 66 | 109 | 12 | 201 | 3991 | 41.14 |
| Blunt R.C. | 123 | 209 | 15 | 338* | 7953 | 40.99 |
| Horne M.J. | 128 | 219 | 11 | 241 | 8501 | 40.87 |
| Mitchell D.J. | 88 | 141 | 18 | 190 | 4987 | 40.54 |
| Myburgh J.G. | 108 | 190 | 23 | 203 | 6841 | 40.53 |
| Hadlee W.A. | 117 | 203 | 17 | 198 | 7523 | 40.44 |
| Broom N.T. | 116 | 197 | 22 | 203* | 7060 | 40.34 |
| Edgar B.A. | 175 | 307 | 26 | 203 | 11,304 | 40.22 |
| Brownlie D.G. | 94 | 169 | 14 | 334 | 6208 | 40.05 |

| **BOWLING** *(qualification 200 wickets)* | M | Wkts | Runs | Ave |
|---|---|---|---|---|
| Downes A.D. | 51 | 311 | 4564 | 14.67 |
| Upham E.F. | 49 | 265 | 4414 | 16.65 |
| Callaway S.T. | 62 | 320 | 5460 | 17.06 |
| Smith S.G. | 211 | 955 | 17,272 | 18.08 |
| Hadlee R.J. | 342 | 1490 | 26,998 | 18.11 |
| Blair R.W. | 119 | 537 | 9961 | 18.54 |
| Bennett J.H. | 52 | 241 | 4476 | 18.58 |

**NZC**

# Wicketkeeping

| 100 DISMISSALS | Career | M | Caught | Stumped | Total |
|---|---|---|---|---|---|
| Hopkins G.J. | 1997/98-2013/14 | 158 | 429 | 26 | 455 |
| van Wyk C.F.K. | 2000/01-2015/16 | 138 | 414 | 21 | 435 |
| Smith I.D.S. | 1977/78-1991/92 | 178 | 390 | 36 | 426 |
| James K.C. | 1923/24-1946/47 | 204 | 310 | 112 | 422 |
| Watling B-J. | 2004/05-2021 | 178 | 407 | 10 | 417 |
| McSweeney E.B. | 1979/80-1993/94 | 121 | 340 | 45 | 385 |
| Parore A.C. | 1988/89-2001/02 | 163 | 358 | 24 | 382 |
| Ronchi L. | 2002/03-2016/17 | 100 | 339 | 17 | 356 |
| de Boorder D.C. | 2007/08-2017/18 | 103 | 332 | 22 | 354 |
| Lees W.K. | 1970/71-1987/88 | 146 | 292 | 44 | 336 |
| Young R.A. | 1998/99-2012/13 | 126 | 315 | 5 | 320 |
| Hart R.G. | 1992/93-2003/04 | 110 | 298 | 17 | 315 |
| Nevin C.J. | 1995/96-2009/10 | 112 | 299 | 9 | 308 |
| Wadsworth K.J. | 1968/69-1975/76 | 118 | 256 | 26 | 282 |
| Germon L.K. | 1987/88-2001/02 | 103 | 256 | 26 | 282 |
| McCullum B.B. | 1999/00-2015/16 | 150 | 259 | 19 | 278 |
| Ward J.T. | 1957/58-1970/71 | 95 | 227 | 27 | 254 |
| Fletcher C.D. | 2012/13-2021/22 | 72 | 233 | 13 | 246 |
| Griggs B.B.J. | 2000/01-2009/10 | 83 | 231 | 7 | 238 |
| Petrie E.C. | 1950/51-1966/67 | 115 | 194 | 37 | 231 |
| Mooney F.L.H. | 1941/42-1954/55 | 91 | 164 | 54 | 218 |
| Blain T.E. | 1982/83-1994/95 | 118 | 190 | 26 | 216 |
| McGlashan P.D. | 2000/01-2011/12 | 71 | 194 | 13 | 207 |
| Croy M.G. | 1994/95-2001/02 | 65 | 183 | 14 | 197 |
| Young B.A. | 1983/84-1997/98 | 163 | 185 | 11 | 196 |
| Milburn B.D. | 1963/64-1982/83 | 75 | 176 | 19 | 195 |
| Blundell T.A. | 2012/13-2022 | 86 | 187 | 8 | 195 |
| Cleaver D. | 2010/11-2021/22 | 66 | 179 | 11 | 190 |
| Dick A.E. | 1956/57-1968/69 | 78 | 133 | 21 | 154 |
| Kelly P.J. | 1980/81-1988/89 | 49 | 140 | 13 | 153 |
| Horne B.J. | 2016/17-2021/22 | 42 | 139 | 6 | 145 |
| Cachopa B. | 2010/11-2016/17 | 58 | 131 | 7 | 138 |
| Colquhoun I.A. | 1953/54-1963/64 | 57 | 108 | 28 | 136 |
| Seifert T.L. | 2014/15-2022 | 55 | 124 | 12 | 136 |
| Guillen S.C. | 1947/48-1960/61 | 66 | 100 | 34 | 134 |
| Sigley M.A. | 1994/95-2002/03 | 44 | 124 | 4 | 128 |
| Boxshall C. | 1897/98-1914/15 | 65 | 81 | 43 | 124 |
| Schofield R.M. | 1964/65-1974/75 | 53 | 107 | 15 | 122 |
| Robinson S.A. | 1984/85-1996/97 | 45 | 117 | 5 | 122 |
| Wright M.J.E. | 1972/73-1983/84 | 65 | 104 | 17 | 121 |
| Mills G.H. | 1935/36-1957/58 | 59 | 85 | 34 | 119 |
| Tindill E.W.T. | 1932/33-1949/50 | 69 | 85 | 33 | 118 |
| Edwards G.N. | 1973/74-1984/85 | 92 | 88 | 16 | 104 |
| Therkleson I.J. | 1966/67-1973/74 | 39 | 93 | 7 | 100 |

# HIGHEST PARTNERSHIPS

## FIRST WICKET

| | | | | | |
|---|---|---|---|---|---|
| 432 | Papps M.H.W. | Woodcock L.J. | Wellington v Auckland | Wellington | 2017/18 |
| 428 | Ingram P.J. | How J.M. | Central Districts v Wellington | Wellington | 2009/10 |
| 387 | Turner G.M. | Jarvis T.W. | New Zealand v West Indies | Georgetown | 1971/72 |
| 373 | Sutcliffe B. | Watt L. | Otago v Auckland | Auckland | 1950/51 |
| 334 | Raval J.A. | Popli B. | Northern Districts v Central Districts | Whangarei | 2021/22 |
| 333 | Edgar B.A. | Jones A.H. | Wellington v Auckland | Wellington | 1988/89 |
| 316 | Austen M.H. | Hart R.T. | Wellington v Central Districts | Wanganui | 1993/94 |
| 310 | Edgar B.A. | Vance R.H. | Wellington v Northern Districts | Wellington | 1988/89 |
| 306 | Cuff L.A. | Lawrence J.D. | Canterbury v Auckland | Christchurch | 1893/94 |
| 305 | Lawson R.A. | Croy M.G. | Otago v Central Districts | Napier | 1995/96 |
| 299 | Bell M.D. | Jones R.A. | Wellington v Otago | Dunedin | 2001/02 |
| 287 | Hartland B.R. | Stead G.R. | Canterbury v Wellington | Christchurch | 1994/95 |
| 286 | Sutcliffe B. | Taylor D.D. | Auckland v Canterbury | Auckland | 1948/49 |
| 278 | Flynn D.R. | Cooper H.R. | Northern Districts v Canterbury | Whangarei | 2017/18 |
| 276 | Dempster C.S. | Mills J.E. | New Zealand v England | Wellington | 1929/30 |
| 276 | Griffith A.F.G. | Campbell S.L. | West Indies v New Zealand | Hamilton | 1999/00 |
| 274 | Wilson B.S. | Watling B-J. | Northern Districts v Wellington | Whangarei | 2010/11 |
| 268 | Turner G.M. | Dowling G.T. | New Zealand v President's XI | Montego Bay | 1971/72 |
| 260 | Lawson R.A. | Mohammad Wasim | Otago v Northern Districts | Dunedin | 2002/03 |
| 259 | Austen M.H. | Aiken J.M. | Wellington v Otago | Wellington | 1994/95 |
| 254 | Raval J.A. | Latham T.W.M. | New Zealand v Bangladesh | Hamilton | 2018/19 |
| 253 | Bell M.D. | Woodcock L.J. | Wellington v Central Districts | Napier | 2007/08 |
| 252 | Sutcliffe B. | Scott V.J. | New Zealand v Rest | Christchurch | 1948/49 |
| 251 | Rutherford H.D. | Renwick M. | Otago v Central Districts | Dunedin | 2021/22 |
| 250 | Hart R.T. | Smith C.J.P. | Central Districts v Wellington | Wellington | 1985/86 |
| 247 | Sutcliffe B. | Scott V.J. | New Zealand v Combined Services | Gillingham | 1949 |
| 244 | Richardson M.H. | Papps M.H.W. | New Zealand v Kent | Canterbury | 2004 |
| 240 | McIntosh T.G. | Horne M.J. | Auckland v Otago | Dunedin | 2001/02 |
| 239 | Dempster C.S. | Dustin W.H. | Wellington v Canterbury | Wellington | 1931/32 |
| 239 | Smith D. | Parks J.H. | MCC v Otago | Dunedin | 1935/36 |
| 236 | Brodie J.M. | Papps M.H.W. | Wellington v Auckland | Auckland | 2011/12 |
| 235 | Hadlee W.A. | Page M.L. | Canterbury v Wellington | Christchurch | 1936/37 |
| 235 | Woodcock L.J. | Papps M.H.W. | Wellington v Otago | Wellington | 2015/16 |
| 231 | Richardson M.H. | Vincent L. | New Zealand v India | Mohali | 2003/04 |
| 231 | Cook A.N. | Compton N.R.D. | England v New Zealand | Dunedin | 2012/13 |
| 230 | Murray B.A.G. | Turner G.M. | New Zealand v President's XI | Rawalpindi | 1969/70 |
| 229 | Sutcliffe B. | Scott V.J. | New Zealand v Surrey | Oval | 1949 |
| 227 | Rutherford H.D. | Wilson B.S. | Otago v Central Districts | Nelson | 2016/17 |
| 226* | Hadlee W.A. | Leggat J.G. | Canterbury v Otago | Christchurch | 1948/49 |
| 226 | Phillips G.D. | Seifert T.L. | New Zealand A v West Indies A | Mt Maunganui | 2020/21 |
| 226 | Georgeson L.I. | Ravindra R. | Wellington v Northern Districts | Wellington | 2020/21 |
| 225 | Richardson P.E. | Watson W. | MCC v Wellington | Wellington | 1958/59 |
| 225 | Greenidge C.G. | Haynes D.L. | West Indies v New Zealand | Christchurch | 1979/80 |
| 223 | Latham T.W.M. | Bowes C.J. | Canterbury v Wellington | Wellington | 2021/22 |
| 220 | Sutcliffe B. | Taylor D.D. | Auckland v Canterbury | Auckland | 1948/49 |
| 220 | Bell M.D. | Jones R.A. | Wellington v Canterbury | Christchurch | 2000/01 |
| 219* | Edgar B.A. | Vance R.H. | Wellington v Central Districts | Wellington | 1987/88 |
| 218 | Hadlee W.A. | Leggat J.G. | Canterbury v Wellington | Christchurch | 1947/48 |
| 218 | Dempsey D.A. | Hadlee B.G. | Canterbury v Otago | Christchurch | 1980/81 |
| 215 | Sinclair M.S. | How J.M. | Central Districts v Northern Districts | Napier | 2004/05 |
| 215 | Raval J.A. | How J.M. | Central Districts v Northern Districts | Nelson | 2012/13 |
| 215 | Guptill-Bunce M.L. | Raval J.A. | Auckland v Wellington | Wellington | 2015/16 |
| 214 | Woodfull W.M. | Ponsford W.H. | Australia v Otago | Dunedin | 1927/28 |
| 214 | Bolton B.A. | Dowling G.T. | Canterbury v Northern Districts | Christchurch | 1959/60 |
| 214 | Spearman C.M. | Twose R.G. | New Zealand v Zimbabwe | Auckland | 1995/96 |
| 214 | Brownlie D.G. | Wilson B.S. | Northern Districts v Otago | Hamilton | 2014/15 |
| 213 | Lawson R.A. | Bell M.D. | NZ Academy XI v Zimbabwe | Whangarei | 1995/96 |
| 213 | Gaffaney C.B. | Parlane M.E. | NZ Academy XI v Bangladesh | Christchurch | 1997/98 |
| 211 | Turner G.M. | Parker J.M. | New Zealand v MCC | Lord's | 1973 |

| 211 | Bell M.D. | Donaldson G.T. | Wellington v Central Districts | Wellington | 2003/04 |
| 211 | Brodie J.M. | Papps M.H.W. | Wellington v Canterbury | Rangiora | 2012/13 |
| 209 | Sutcliffe B. | Watt L. | Otago v Canterbury | Dunedin | 1947/48 |
| 209 | Harris B.Z. | Boyle D.J. | Canterbury v Otago | Christchurch | 1991/92 |
| 208 | Blunt R.C. | Worker R.V. de R. | Canterbury v MCC | Christchurch | 1922/23 |
| 208 | Athey C.W.J. | Robinson R.T. | England XI v Northern Districts | Hamilton | 1987/88 |
| 207 | Sadiq Mohammad | Zaheer Abbas | Pakistan v Wellington | Wellington | 1972/73 |
| 202 | Worker G.H. | Hay G.R. | Central Districts v Otago | Napier | 2018/19 |
| 201 | Anthony A. | Horspool E. | Auckland v Wellington | Auckland | 1924/25 |
| 201 | Astle T.D. | Papps M.H.W. | Canterbury v Wellington | Christchurch | 2006/07 |

## SECOND WICKET

| 317 | Hart R.T. | Briasco P.S. | Central Districts v Canterbury | New Plymouth | 1983/84 |
| 315* | Gibbs H.H. | Kallis J.H. | South Africa v New Zealand | Christchurch | 1998/99 |
| 303 | Dempster C.S. | Allcott C.F.W. | New Zealand v Warwickshire | Birmingham | 1927 |
| 301 | Flynn D.R. | Wilson B.S. | Northern Districts v Auckland | Hamilton | 2012/13 |
| 287 | Bell M.D. | Wells J.D. | Wellington v Auckland | Auckland | 1997/98 |
| 279 | Bell M.D. | Parlane M.E. | Wellington v Otago | Dunedin | 2006/07 |
| 263 | Greatbatch M.J. | Crowe M.D. | Central Districts v Northern Districts | Morrinsville | 1986/87 |
| 256 | Anderson R.W. | Edgar B.A. | New Zealand v Scotland | Dundee | 1978 |
| 254* | Papps M.H.W. | Myburgh J.G. | Canterbury v Central Districts | Napier | 2007/08 |
| 254 | Burns K.J. | Rutherford K.R. | Otago v Wellington | Oamaru | 1987/88 |
| 252 | Baker W.A. | Beechey E.M. | Wellington v Auckland | Wellington | 1918/19 |
| 251 | Parlane N.R. | Merchant C.J. | Wellington v Otago | Wellington | 2009/10 |
| 250 | Bell M.D. | Sinclair M.S. | New Zealand A v Sri Lanka A | Queenstown | 2003/04 |
| 248 | Horne M.J. | Fleming S.P. | Southern v Pakistan A | Christchurch | 1998/99 |
| 247 | Cumming C.D. | Broom D.J. | Otago v Northern Districts | Whangarei | 2009/10 |
| 245 | Horne M.J. | Fleming S.P. | New Zealand v British Universities | Oxford | 1999 |
| 244 | Spearman C.M. | Sinclair M.S. | Central Districts v Northern Districts | Wanganui | 1998/99 |
| 243 | Papps M.H.W. | Stewart S.L. | Canterbury v Northern Districts | Hamilton | 2006/07 |
| 242* | How J.M. | Sinclair M.S. | Central Districts v Otago | New Plymouth | 2005/06 |
| 241 | Franklin T.J. | Crowe J.J. | Auckland v Wellington | Wellington | 1988/89 |
| 241 | Wright J.G. | Jones A.H. | New Zealand v England | Wellington | 1991/92 |
| 237 | Gibson J.G. | Kuggeleijn C.M. | Northern Districts v Canterbury | Hamilton | 1980/81 |
| 232 | O'Donnell W.T. | O'Donnell R.R. | Auckland v Wellington | Auckland | 2020/21 |
| 231 | Carew M.C. | Nurse S.M. | West Indies v New Zealand | Christchurch | 1968/69 |
| 229 | Hemus L.G. | Midlane F.A. | Auckland v Wellington | Wellington | 1918/19 |
| 227 | Baker W.A. | Kortlang H.H.L. | Wellington v Otago | Dunedin | 1923/24 |
| 227 | Dobbs P.W. | Lamont M.J. | Otago v Auckland | Dunedin | 1990/91 |
| 223 | McIntosh T.G. | Jones R.A. | Auckland v West Indies | Auckland | 2008/09 |
| 222 | Warner P.F. | Fane F.L. | Lord Hawke's XI v Otago | Dunedin | 1902/03 |
| 222 | Crocker L.M. | Kuggeleijn C.M. | Northern Districts v Otago | Hamilton | 1983/84 |
| 222 | McCullum B.B. | Cumming C.D. | Otago v Auckland | Dunedin | 2001/02 |
| 220 | Macartney C.G. | Punch A.T.E. | NSW v Otago | Dunedin | 1923/24 |
| 220 | Richardson M.H. | Cumming C.D. | Otago v Northern Districts | Hamilton | 2000/01 |
| 217 | Redmond A.J. | Bracewell M.G. | Otago v Wellington | Wellington | 2013/14 |
| 215 | Bell M.D. | Wells J.D. | Wellington v Northern Districts | Hamilton | 1998/99 |
| 215 | Bell M.D. | Parlane M.E. | Wellington v Central Districts | Napier | 2004/05 |
| 215 | Latham T.W.M. | Conway D.P. | New Zealand v Bangladesh | Christchurch | 2021/22 |
| 213 | Barnett G.E.F. | Sinclair M.S. | Central Districts v Otago | New Plymouth | 2005/06 |
| 212 | Horspool E. | Snedden A.N.C. | Auckland v Victoria | Auckland | 1924/25 |
| 212 | McIntosh T.G. | Jones R.A. | Auckland v Wellington | Auckland | 2009/10 |
| 212 | Flynn D.R. | Carter J.F. | Northern Districts v Auckland | Auckland | 2013/14 |
| 210 | Hadlee W.A. | O'Brien F.P. | Canterbury v Otago | Christchurch | 1940/41 |
| 210 | Howarth G.P. | Crowe J.J. | New Zealand v West Indies | Kingston | 1984/85 |
| 210 | Compton N.R.D. | Trott I.J.L. | England v New Zealand | Wellington | 2012/13 |
| 209* | Jones A.H. | Crowe M.D. | Wellington v Canterbury | Christchurch | 1992/93 |
| 209 | Wilson B.S. | Flynn D.R. | Northern Districts v Canterbury | Christchurch | 2008/09 |
| 207* | Twose R.G. | Douglas M.W. | Central Districts v Auckland | Auckland | 1991/92 |
| 207 | Mills J.E. | Blunt R.C. | New Zealand v H.D.G.Leveson-Gower's XI | Scarborough | 1927 |
| 207 | Vaughan M.P. | Hussain N. | England v Canterbury | Christchurch | 2001/02 |
| 206 | Raman W.V. | Gursharan Singh | India v Otago | Dunedin | 1989/90 |

| 204 | Gavaskar S.M. | Amarnath S. | India v New Zealand | Auckland | 1975/76 |
|---|---|---|---|---|---|
| 204 | Ingram P.J. | Smith B.S. | Central Districts v Wellington | Wellington | 2010/11 |
| 202 | Naushad Ali | Saeed Ahmed | Pakistan v Canterbury | Christchurch | 1964/65 |
| 200 | Smith R.W. | Bilby G.P. | Wellington v Northern Districts | Whangarei | 1973/74 |

**THIRD WICKET**

| 467 | Jones A.H. | Crowe M.D. | New Zealand v Sri Lanka | Wellington | 1990/91 |
|---|---|---|---|---|---|
| 445 | Whitelaw P.E. | Carson W.N. | Auckland v Otago | Dunedin | 1936/37 |
| 394* | Kennedy P.G. | Latham R.T. | Canterbury v Northern Districts | Rotorua | 1990/91 |
| 346 | Burnett G.P. | Verry R.A. | Wellington v Northern Districts | Hamilton | 1991/92 |
| 306 | Haig S.B. | Broom N.T. | Otago v Central Districts | Napier | 2009/10 |
| 291 | Bracewell M.G. | Broom N.T. | Otago v Wellington | Dunedin | 2012/13 |
| 289 | Burns J.A. | Smith S.P.D. | Australia v New Zealand | Christchurch | 2015/16 |
| 287 | Conway D.P. | Bracewell M.G. | Wellington v Auckland | Wellington | 2020/21 |
| 278 | Franklin T.J. | Patel D.N. | Auckland v Canterbury | Christchurch | 1985/86 |
| 265 | Horne M.J. | Barnes A.C. | Auckland v Bangladesh | Auckland | 2001/02 |
| 264 | Chappell I.M. | Chappell G.S. | Australia v New Zealand | Wellington | 1973/74 |
| 264 | Ingram P.J. | Sinclair M.S. | Central Districts v Northern Districts | Hamilton | 2008/09 |
| 261* | Maynard M.P. | Thomson S.A. | Northern Districts v Auckland | Hamilton | 1990/91 |
| 259 | Papps M.H.W. | Fulton P.G. | Canterbury v Northern Districts | Christchurch | 2008/09 |
| 258 | Flynn D.R. | Popli B. | Northern Districts v Central Districts | Hamilton | 2015/16 |
| 256 | Papps M.H.W. | Ryder J.D. | Wellington v Central Districts | Wellington | 2012/13 |
| 255 | Lloyd C.H. | Davis C.A. | West Indies v South Island | Dunedin | 1968/69 |
| 252* | Howarth G.P. | Roberts A.D.G. | Northern Districts v Pakistan | Gisborne | 1978/79 |
| 248 | Shoaib Mohammad | Javed Miandad | Pakistan v New Zealand | Auckland | 1988/89 |
| 246 | Rabone G.O. | Reid J.R. | New Zealand v Nottinghamshire | Nottingham | 1949 |
| 246 | Murray B.A.G. | Morrison J.F.M. | Wellington v Otago | Dunedin | 1968/69 |
| 246 | Parlane N.R. | Elliott G.D. | Wellington v Auckland | Auckland | 2007/08 |
| 246 | McIntosh T.G. | Raval J.A. | Auckland v Otago | Dunedin | 2013/14 |
| 245 | Crowe M.D. | Coney J.V. | New Zealand v South Australia | Adelaide | 1985/86 |
| 244 | Nicol R.J. | Vincent L. | Auckland v Otago | Auckland | 2004/05 |
| 241 | Wright J.G. | Crowe M.D. | New Zealand v West Indies | Wellington | 1986/87 |
| 229 | Miller L.S.M. | Sutcliffe B. | New Zealand v South Australia | Adelaide | 1953/54 |
| 227 | Rutherford K.R. | Blair B.R. | Otago v Central Districts | Alexandra | 1988/89 |
| 226 | Haynes D.L. | Richardson R.B. | West Indies v Shell XI | Napier | 1986/87 |
| 224 | Reid J.F. | Crowe M.D. | New Zealand v Australia | Brisbane | 1985/86 |
| 224 | Sinclair M.S. | Spearman C.M. | Central Districts v Auckland | Auckland | 2003/04 |
| 224 | Cachopa Carl | Sinclair M.S. | Central Districts v Wellington | Napier | 2012/13 |
| 223 | Smith C.J.P. | Wilson S.W.J. | Central Districts v Otago | Blenheim | 1990/91 |
| 222* | Sutcliffe B. | Reid J.R. | New Zealand v India | New Delhi | 1955/56 |
| 222 | Snedden A.N.C. | Smith S.G. | Auckland v Hawke's Bay | Auckland | 1920/21 |
| 221 | Blunt R.C. | McMullan J.J.M. | Otago v Canterbury | Dunedin | 1928/29 |
| 221 | Lara B.C. | Adams J.C. | West Indies v New Zealand | Wellington | 1994/95 |
| 220 | Shoaib Mohammad | Javed Miandad | Pakistan v New Zealand | Wellington | 1988/89 |
| 218 | Woodfull W.M. | Schneider K.J. | Australia v New Zealand | Auckland | 1927/28 |
| 218 | Schmulian B.D. | Bruce T.C. | Central Districts v Northern Districts | Whangarei | 2021/22 |
| 217 | Dobbs P.W. | Rutherford K.R. | Otago v Central Districts | Blenheim | 1990/91 |
| 216* | Fulton P.G. | McClure K.J. | Canterbury v Otago | Christchurch | 2015/16 |
| 216 | Hemus L.G. | Smith S.G. | Auckland v Canterbury | Auckland | 1919/20 |
| 214 | Anthony A. | Gillespie H.D. | Auckland v Canterbury | Auckland | 1929/30 |
| 213* | Williamson K.S. | Taylor L.R.P.L. | New Zealand v England | Hamilton | 2019/20 |
| 213 | Turner G.M. | Congdon B.E. | Otago v Wellington | Dunedin | 1972/73 |
| 213 | Jones A.H. | Crowe M.D. | New Zealand v Australia | Adelaide | 1987/88 |
| 213 | Solia S.M. | O'Donnell R.R. | Auckland v Wellington | Auckland | 2021/22 |
| 212 | Booth B.C. | Burge P.J.P. | Australia B v New Zealand | Auckland | 1966/67 |
| 211 | McIntosh T.G. | Kitchen A.K. | Auckland v Canterbury | Auckland | 2011/12 |
| 210 | Howarth G.P. | Crowe M.D. | New Zealand v Essex | Chelmsford | 1983 |
| 210 | Edgar G.A. | Crowe M.D. | New Zealand v England | Lord's | 1986 |
| 210 | Smith B.F. | Douglas M.W. | Central Districts v Northern Districts | Taupo | 2000/01 |
| 209 | McCosker R.G. | Chappell G.S. | Australia v Wellington | Wellington | 1976/77 |
| 208 | Papps M.H.W. | McMillan C.D. | Canterbury v Central Districts | Christchurch | 2006/07 |
| 206 | Preston A.H. | Beck J.E.F. | Wellington v Canterbury | Christchurch | 1955/56 |

| 204 | Harford N.S. | Reid J.R. | New Zealand v Oxford University | Oxford | 1958 |
| 204 | Twose R.G. | Crowe M.D. | New Zealand v Indian Colts XI | Hyderabad | 1995/96 |
| 204 | Fleming S.P. | Styris S.B. | New Zealand v Bangladesh | Chittagong | 2004/05 |
| 204 | Wilson B.S. | Broom N.T. | Otago v Central Districts | Napier | 2015/16 |
| 203* | Pocock B.A. | Parore A.C. | Auckland v Wellington | Auckland | 1997/98 |
| 201 | McLeod E.G. | Lamason J.R. | Wellington v Auckland | Wellington | 1935/36 |
| 201 | Raval J.A. | Munro C. | Auckland v Wellington | Auckland | 2014/15 |
| 200 | Smith G.C. | Kallis J.H. | South Africa v New Zealand | Dunedin | 2011/12 |
| 200 | Petersen A.N. | Duminy J.P. | South Africa v New Zealand | Wellington | 2011/12 |

## FOURTH WICKET

| 369 | Williamson K.S. | Nicholls H.M. | New Zealand v Pakistan | Christchurch | 2020/21 |
| 350 | Mushtaq Mohammad | Asif Iqbal | Pakistan v New Zealand | Dunedin | 1972/73 |
| 324 | Reid J.R. | Wallace W.M. | New Zealand v Cambridge University | Cambridge | 1949 |
| 310 | Ryder J.D. | Parlane N.R. | Wellington v Central Districts | Palmerston North | 2004/05 |
| 299 | Wallace W.M. | Donnelly M.P. | New Zealand v Leicestershire | Leicester | 1949 |
| 283 | Flynn D.R. | Anderson C.J. | Northern Districts v Otago | Hamilton | 2012/13 |
| 282 | Wilkinson W.A.C. | Chapman A.P.F. | MCC v Canterbury | Christchurch | 1922/23 |
| 280 | Crowe J.J. | Patel D.N. | Auckland v Northern Districts | Auckland | 1991/92 |
| 278 | Roberts A.W. | Page M.L. | Canterbury v Wellington | Wellington | 1931/32 |
| 278 | Guptill M.J. | O'Donnell R.R. | Auckland v Canterbury | Auckland | 2021/22 |
| 276* | Crowe M.D. | Briasco P.S. | Central Districts v Canterbury | Christchurch | 1986/87 |
| 274* | Mendis B.K.G. | Mathews A.D. | Sri Lanka v New Zealand | Wellington | 2018/19 |
| 274 | Jones R.A. | Mather S.R. | Wellington v Otago | Wellington | 2000/01 |
| 273 | McIntosh T.G. | Nicol R.J. | Auckland v Otago | Lincoln | 2006/07 |
| 271 | Taylor L.R.P.L. | Ryder J.D. | New Zealand v India | Napier | 2008/09 |
| 266 | Denness M.H. | Fletcher K.W.R. | England v New Zealand | Auckland | 1974/75 |
| 259 | Bradburn G.E. | Parlane M.E. | Northern Districts v Canterbury | Christchurch | 1996/97 |
| 254 | Reid J.R. | Miller L.S.M. | New Zealand v Natal | Durban | 1953/54 |
| 252 | Thomson S.A. | Young B.A. | Northern Districts v Auckland | Auckland | 1990/91 |
| 243 | Horne M.J. | Astle N.J. | New Zealand v Zimbabwe | Auckland | 1997/98 |
| 241* | Jones R.A. | Young R.A. | Auckland v Canterbury | Auckland | 2009/10 |
| 240 | Fleming S.P. | McMillan C.D. | New Zealand v Sri Lanka | Colombo | 1997/98 |
| 239 | Beard N.B. | Broom N.T. | Otago v Auckland | Dunedin | 2012/13 |
| 238 | Pollard M.A. | Franklin J.E.C. | Wellington v Otago | Invercargill | 2013/14 |
| 235 | Burns K.J. | Hoskin R.N. | Otago v Northern Districts | Hamilton | 1987/88 |
| 234 | Smith B.S. | Worker G.H. | Central Districts v Otago | Napier | 2015/16 |
| 229 | Congdon B.E. | Hastings B.F. | New Zealand v Australia | Wellington | 1973/74 |
| 222* | Gill S. | Vihari G.H. | India A v New Zealand A | Christchurch | 2019/20 |
| 221 | Williamson K.S. | McCullum B.B. | New Zealand v India | Auckland | 2013/14 |
| 221 | McClure K.J. | Carter L.J. | Canterbury v Wellington | Rangiora | 2019/20 |
| 219 | Vivian H.G. | Page M.L. | New Zealand v Oxford University | Oxford | 1931 |
| 218 | Crowe J.J. | Coney J.V. | New Zealand v Glamorgan | Swansea | 1986 |
| 217 | Bracewell M.G. | Blundell T.A. | Wellington v Auckland | Auckland | 2020/21 |
| 216 | Taylor L.R.P.L. | Nicholls H.M. | New Zealand v Bangladesh | Wellington | 2018/19 |
| 214 | Ransford V.S. | Lampard A.W. | Australia v New Zealand | Auckland | 1920/21 |
| 214* | Papps M.H.W. | Kuggeleijn S.C. | Wellington v Central Districts | Wellington | 2012/13 |
| 214 | Munro C. | O'Donnell R.R. | Auckland v Central Districts | Napier | 2014/15 |
| 214 | Latham T.W.M. | Nicholls H.M. | New Zealand v Sri Lanka | Christchurch | 2018/19 |
| 211* | Jones A.H. | Burns K.J. | Otago v Wellington | Wellington | 1984/85 |
| 211 | White D.J. | Young B.A. | Northern Districts v Auckland | Auckland | 1992/93 |
| 210 | Nicol R.J. | Munro C. | Auckland v Central Districts | Auckland | 2016/17 |
| 208 | Thomson S.A. | Maynard M.P. | Northern Districts v Wellington | Hamilton | 1991/92 |
| 207 | Midlane F.A. | Richardson C.A. | Wellington v Otago | Wellington | 1899/00 |
| 207 | Badcock F.T. | Lowry T.C. | Wellington v Auckland | Wellington | 1927/28 |
| 207 | Sulzberger G.P. | Penn A.J. | Central Districts v Otago | Napier | 1995/96 |
| 206 | McCullum S.J. | Dawson G.J. | Otago v Northern Districts | Dunedin | 1983/84 |
| 206 | Stewart A.J. | Hussain N. | England v New Zealand XI | Palmerston North | 1996/97 |
| 206 | McIntosh T.G. | Vincent L. | Auckland v Canterbury | Christchurch | 2000/01 |
| 204 | Harvey R.N. | Simpson R.B. | Australia B v Otago | Dunedin | 1956/57 |
| 204 | Jarvis T.W. | Thomson K. | Canterbury v Central Districts | Wanganui | 1969/70 |
| 204 | Redmond A.J. | Broom N.T. | Otago v Northern Districts | Hamilton | 2006/07 |

| | | | | | |
|---|---|---|---|---|---|
| 203 | Thomson S.A. | Maynard M.P. | Northern Districts v Otago | Hamilton | 1991/92 |
| 200 | Blair B.R. | Dawson G.J. | Otago v Central Districts | Dunedin | 1982/83 |
| 200 | McClure K.J. | McConchie C.E. | Canterbury v Auckland | Rangiora | 2017/18 |

**FIFTH WICKET**

| | | | | | |
|---|---|---|---|---|---|
| 359 | Shakib Al Hasan | Mushfiqur Rahim | Bangladesh v New Zealand | Wellington | 2016/17 |
| 347* | Horne M.J. | Barnes A.C. | Auckland v Northern Districts | Auckland | 2003/04 |
| 341 | Larsen G.R. | McSweeney E.B. | Wellington v Central Districts | Levin | 1987/88 |
| 319 | Rutherford K.R. | Gray E.J. | NZ v DB Close's XI | Scarborough | 1986 |
| 318 | Mandeep Singh | Menaria A.L. | India A v New Zealand A | Lincoln | 2012/13 |
| 301 | Englefield J.I. | Taylor L.R.P.L. | Central Districts v Wellington | Palmerston North | 2004/05 |
| 290 | Harris C.Z. | Stead G.R. | Canterbury v Central Districts | Blenheim | 1996/97 |
| 282 | Franklin J.E.C. | Woodcock L.J. | Wellington v Auckland | Auckland | 2008/09 |
| 266 | Sutcliffe B. | Haig W.S. | Otago v Auckland | Dunedin | 1949/50 |
| 258 | Salim Malik | Inzamam-ul-Haq | Pakistan v New Zealand | Wellington | 1993/94 |
| 258 | McConchie C.E. | Ellis A.M. | Canterbury v Otago | Invercargill | 2016/17 |
| 255 | Taylor B.R. | Coney J.V. | Wellington v Otago | Dunedin | 1972/73 |
| 253 | Clarke M.J. | North M.J. | Australia v New Zealand | Wellington | 2009/10 |
| 252* | Latham R.T. | Priest M.W. | Canterbury v Northern Districts | Christchurch | 1988/89 |
| 252 | Broom N.T. | Broom D.J. | Otago v Northern Districts | Queenstown | 2010/11 |
| 244 | Reid J.R. | Chapple M.E. | New Zealand v Western Province | Cape Town | 1962/63 |
| 242 | Hammond W.R. | Ames L.E.G. | England v New Zealand | Christchurch | 1932/33 |
| 236* | Stewart S.L. | Brownlie D.G. | Canterbury v Northern Districts | Rangiora | 2009/10 |
| 236 | Harris C.Z. | Astle N.J. | Canterbury v Otago | Christchurch | 1996/97 |
| 236 | Mitchell D.J. | Blundell T.A. | New Zealand v England | Nottingham | 2022 |
| 235* | Woodfull W.M. | Ransford V.S. | Victoria v New Zealand | Christchurch | 1924/25 |
| 235* | Sulzberger G.P. | Ryder J.D. | Central Districts v Canterbury | Napier | 2002/03 |
| 235 | McClure K.J. | Ellis A.M. | Canterbury v Northern Districts | Hamilton | 2015/16 |
| 235 | Soumya Sarkar | Mahmudullah | Bangladesh v New Zealand | Hamilton | 2018/19 |
| 234* | Scott V.J. | Morris J.B. | Auckland v Central Districts | Auckland | 1951/52 |
| 233 | Moloney D.A.R. | Kerr J.L. | New Zealand v England XI | Folkestone | 1937 |
| 228 | Raval J.A. | Hopkins G.J. | Auckland v Central Districts | Auckland | 2008/09 |
| 226 | Mitchell D.J. | Seifert T.L. | Northern Districts v Otago | Dunedin | 2016/17 |
| 222 | Astle N.J. | McMillan C.D. | New Zealand v Zimbabwe | Wellington | 2000/01 |
| 222 | Sinclair M.S. | van Wyk C.F.K. | Central Districts v Northern Districts | Gisborne | 2011/12 |
| 219 | Broom N.T. | Hopkins G.J. | Otago v Auckland | Lincoln | 2006/07 |
| 216 | Parlane N.R. | Franklin J.E.C. | Wellington v Auckland | Wellington | 2005/06 |
| 215 | Fawad Alam | Rohail Nazir | Pakistan A v New Zealand A | Whangarei | 2020/21 |
| 213 | Ritchie G.M. | Matthews G.R.J. | Australia v New Zealand | Wellington | 1985/86 |
| 213 | de Boorder D.C. | Kitchen A.K. | Otago v Northern Districts | Dunedin | 2016/17 |
| 206 | Hopkins G.J. | Kitchen A.K. | Auckland v Central Districts | Auckland | 2009/10 |
| 205 | Hay G.R. | Noema-Barnett K. | Central Districts v Otago | Alexandra | 2018/19 |
| 203 | Booth B.C. | Davies G.R. | Australia B v Central Districts | Palmerston North | 1966/67 |
| 201 | Alexander W.C. | Richardson V.Y. | Australia v Auckland | Auckland | 1927/28 |
| 201 | Burgess M.G. | Jarvis T.W. | Auckland v Central Districts | Auckland | 1971/72 |

**SIXTH WICKET**

| | | | | | |
|---|---|---|---|---|---|
| 379* | Stewart S.L. | van Wyk C.F.K. | Canterbury v Central Districts | New Plymouth | 2009/10 |
| 377 | Munro C. | Cachopa Craig | Auckland v Wellington | Auckland | 2012/13 |
| 365* | Williamson K.S. | Watling B-J. | New Zealand v Sri Lanka | Wellington | 2014/15 |
| 352 | McCullum B.B. | Watling B-J. | New Zealand v India | Wellington | 2013/14 |
| 339 | Guptill M.J. | McCullum B.B. | New Zealand v Bangladesh | Hamilton | 2009/10 |
| 322 | Orchard M.G. | Yovich J.A.F. | Northern Districts v Central Districts | Napier | 2005/06 |
| 305 | Carter L.J. | Fletcher C.D. | Canterbury v Otago | Christchurch | 2020/21 |
| 293* | Fulton P.G. | Broom N.T. | Canterbury v Otago | Dunedin | 2004/05 |
| 281 | Thorpe G.P. | Flintoff A. | England v New Zealand | Christchurch | 2001/02 |
| 269 | Trumper V.T. | Hill C. | Australia v New Zealand | Wellington | 1904/05 |
| 268 | Chapman M.S. | Cleaver D. | New Zealand A v India A | Christchurch | 2019/20 |
| 256 | Martyn D.R. | Gilchrist A.C. | Australia v New Zealand | Wellington | 2004/05 |
| 256 | Kelly N.F. | Chu M.W. | Otago v Central Districts | Dunedin | 2021/22 |
| 247 | Cachopa Craig | Hopkins G.J. | Auckland v Wellington | Auckland | 2013/14 |
| 247 | Woodcock L.J. | Nofal M.J. | Wellington v Central Districts | Wellington | 2017/18 |

| 246* | Crowe J.J. | Hadlee R.J. | New Zealand v Sri Lanka | Colombo | 1986/87 |
|---|---|---|---|---|---|
| 240 | Parfitt P.H. | Knight B.R. | England v New Zealand | Auckland | 1962/63 |
| 238 | McDonald R. | Cowley O.W. | Queensland v Hawke's Bay | Napier | 1896/97 |
| 235 | Sinclair M.S. | Griggs B.B.J. | Central Districts v Wellington | Wellington | 2008/09 |
| 233 | Crawford J.N. | Armstrong W.W. | Australia v New Zealand | Auckland | 1913/14 |
| 232 | Botham I.T. | Randall D.W. | England v New Zealand | Wellington | 1983/84 |
| 230 | Worker G.H. | Cleaver D. | Central Districts v Wellington | Napier | 2015/16 |
| 226 | Gray E.J. | Ormiston R.W. | Wellington v Central Districts | Wellington | 1981/82 |
| 224 | Schmulian B.D. | Bracewell D.A.J. | Central Districts v Northern Districts | Mt Maunganui | 2017/18 |
| 220 | Turner G.M. | Wadsworth K.J. | New Zealand v West Indies | Kingston | 1971/72 |
| 220 | Toynbee M.H. | Smith I.D.S. | Central Districts v Auckland | Napier | 1982/83 |
| 218 | Trego P.D. | van Wyk C.F.K. | Central Districts v Auckland | Napier | 2013/14 |
| 217 | Brownlie D.G. | Santner M.J. | Northern Districts v Central Districts | New Plymouth | 2014/15 |
| 216 | Hart M.N. | Marshall H.J.H. | Northern Districts v Central Districts | Napier | 2004/05 |
| 216 | Rutherford H.D. | de Boorder D.C. | Otago v Wellington | Dunedin | 2011/12 |
| 212* | McMillan C.D. | Parore A.C. | New Zealand v President's XI | Jodhpur | 1999/00 |
| 211 | Guptill M.J. | de Grandhomme C. | Auckland v Canterbury | Rangiora | 2011/12 |
| 209* | Parore A.C. | O'Dowd A.P. | Auckland v Otago | Dunedin | 1991/92 |
| 209 | Harris C.Z. | Redmond A.J. | Canterbury v Wellington | Rangiora | 2001/02 |
| 205 | Chapman M.S. | Horne B.J. | Auckland v Northern Districts | Auckland | 2019/20 |
| 203 | Ormiston R.W. | Coney J.V. | Wellington v Central Districts | New Plymouth | 1982/83 |
| 202 | de Grandhomme C. | Munro C. | Auckland v Canterbury | Auckland | 2011/12 |
| 201 | Harris C.Z. | Parore A.C | New Zealand v Orange Free State | Bloemfontein | 1994/95 |
| 201 | Tendulkar S.R. | Mongia N.R. | India v Central Districts | Napier | 1998/99 |
| 201 | Neesham J.D.S. | Watling B-J. | New Zealand v West Indies | Kingston | 2014 |
| 200 | Chanderpaul S. | Ramdin D. | West Indies v New Zealand | Hamilton | 2013/14 |

## SEVENTH WICKET

| 265 | Powell J.L. | Dorreen N. | Canterbury v Otago | Christchurch | 1929/30 |
|---|---|---|---|---|---|
| 261 | Watling B-J. | Santner M.J. | New Zealand v England | Mt Maunganui | 2019/20 |
| 261 | Campbell A.D.R. | Strang P.A. | Zimbabwe v Canterbury | Timaru | 1997/98 |
| 250 | Nevin C.J. | Walker M.D.J. | Wellington v Otago | Wellington | 2003/04 |
| 248 | Yousuf Youhana | Saqlain Mushtaq | Pakistan v New Zealand | Christchurch | 2000/01 |
| 246 | McGlew D.J. | Murray A.R.A. | South Africa v New Zealand | Wellington | 1952/53 |
| 244 | Patrick W.R. | Allcott C.F.W. | New Zealand v NSW | Sydney | 1925/26 |
| 241 | Astle N.J. | Priest M.W. | Canterbury v Wellington | Christchurch | 1994/95 |
| 229 | Schneider K.J. | Oldfield W.A.S. | Australia v Canterbury | Christchurch | 1927/28 |
| 225 | Cairns C.L. | Oram J.D.P. | New Zealand v South Africa | Auckland | 2003/04 |
| 224 | Scott V.J. | Matheson A.M. | Auckland v Canterbury | Auckland | 1937/38 |
| 219 | Yuile B.W. | Hampton B.L. | Central Districts v Canterbury | Napier | 1967/68 |
| 217 | Walters K.D. | Gilmour G.J. | Australia v New Zealand | Christchurch | 1976/77 |
| 212 | Katich S.M. | Gilchrist A.C. | Australia v New Zealand | Christchurch | 2004/05 |
| 205 | Germon L.K. | Priest M.W. | Canterbury v Northern Districts | Christchurch | 1991/92 |
| 205* | Hay G.R. | Diamanti B.J. | Central Districts v Canterbury | Rangiora | 2008/09 |
| 192 | Brown S.W. | Parore A.C. | Auckland v Central Districts | Auckland | 1990/91 |
| 191 | Wright J.G. | Smith I.D.S. | New Zealand v Western Australia | Perth | 1989/90 |
| 190 | Smith N.G. | Rippon M.J.G. | Otago v Northern Districts | Dunedin | 2019/20 |
| 187 | vanWyk C.F.K. | Bracewell D.A.J. | Central Districts v Wellington | Napier | 2010/11 |
| 186 | Lees W.K. | Hadlee R.J. | New Zealand v Pakistan | Karachi | 1976/77 |
| 186 | Leggat R.I. | Hadlee D.R. | Canterbury v Sri Lanka | Christchurch | 1982/83 |
| 186 | Ryder J.D. | Vettori D.L. | New Zealand v India | Hamilton | 2008/09 |
| 184* | Bull C.L. | Isherwood B.P. | Canterbury v Central Districts | Nelson | 1971/72 |
| 183 | Oram J.D.P. | Vettori D.L. | New Zealand v South Africa | Centurion | 2005/06 |
| 183 | Wiggins B.L. | Wheeler B.M. | Central Districts v Canterbury | Christchurch | 2021/22 |
| 182 | Sutcliffe B. | Gilbertson A.W. | Otago v Canterbury | Christchurch | 1952/53 |
| 182 | Weston T.I. | Thompson E.P. | Central Districts v Canterbury | Christchurch | 2005/06 |
| 179 | Griggs B.B.J. | Furlong C.J.M. | Central Districts v Northern Districts | Hamilton | 2001/02 |
| 179 | McCullum B.B. | Neesham J.D.S. | New Zealand v India | Wellington | 2013/14 |
| 178 | Ellis A.M. | Anderson F.G. | Canterbury v Wellington | Wellington | 2014/15 |
| 177* | Barnes A.C. | Mills J.M. | Auckland v Otago | Alexandra | 1995/96 |
| 177 | Bruce T.C. | Small B.J. | Central Districts v Northern Districts | Hamilton | 2015/16 |
| 176 | Rabone G.O. | Mooney F.L.H. | New Zealand v MCC | Lord's | 1949 |
| 176 | Mills S.M. | Nevin C.J. | Wellington v Canterbury | Christchurch | 2006/07 |

## EIGHTH WICKET

| 433† | Trumper V.T. | Sims A. | Sims' Australian XI v Canterbury | Christchurch | 1913/14 |
|---|---|---|---|---|---|
| 256 | Fleming S.P. | Franklin J.E.C. | New Zealand v South Africa | Cape Town | 2005/06 |
| 253 | Astle N.J. | Parore A.C. | New Zealand v Australia | Perth | 2001/02 |
| 220 | Wiseman P.J. | Hiini B.C. | Canterbury v Northern Districts | Hamilton | 2005/06 |
| 215 | Murray J.R. | Cummins A.C. | West Indies v Otago | Dunedin | 1994/95 |
| 210 | Stead G.R. | Bond S.E. | Canterbury v Northern Districts | Christchurch | 2004/05 |
| 199 | Reifer R.A. | Shepherd R. | West Indies A v New Zealand A | Mt Maunganui | 2020/21 |
| 190* | Mills J.E. | Allcott C.F.W. | New Zealand v Civil Service | Chiswick | 1927 |
| 189 | Carson W.N. | Matheson A.M. | Auckland v Wellington | Auckland | 1938/39 |
| 185 | Nash D.J. | Mills K.D. | Auckland v Wellington | Wellington | 2000/01 |
| 180 | Twose R.G. | Goodson M.C. | Wellington v Otago | Dunedin | 1994/95 |
| 173 | Smith I.D.S. | Robertson G.K. | Central Districts v Northern Districts | Hamilton | 1982/83 |
| 172* | Walker B.G.K. | Mills K.D. | Auckland v Wellington | Auckland | 1999/00 |
| 167 | van Wyk C.F.K. | McCone R.J. | Canterbury v Otago | Christchurch | 2008/09 |
| 166 | Hadlee R.J. | Hadlee D.R. | Canterbury v Auckland | Christchurch | 1983/84 |
| 165* | Eckhold A.G. | Crawford J.N. | Otago v Wellington | Wellington | 1914/15 |
| 163 | McGlashan P.D. | Aldridge G.W. | Northern Districts v Canterbury | Hamilton | 2008/09 |
| 161 | McSweeney E.B. | Snedden M.C. | Shell XI v West Indies | Napier | 1986/87 |
| 159 | Diamanti B.J. | Sherlock R.R. | Central Districts v Canterbury | Napier | 2007/08 |
| 157 | McLaren A.C. | McLean J.F. | MCC v New Zealand | Wellington | 1922/23 |
| 154 | James K.C. | Badcock F.T. | Wellington v Canterbury | Christchurch | 1926/27 |
| 153 | Nicol R.J. | Young R.A. | Auckland v Canterbury | Auckland | 2001/02 |
| 152 | Bradburn G.E. | Doull S.B. | Northern Districts v Canterbury | Christchurch | 1991/92 |
| 152 | Marshall J.A.H. | Orchard M.G. | Northern Districts v Wellington | Hamilton | 2006/07 |

† *world record*

## NINTH WICKET

| 239 | Cave H.B. | Leggat I.B. | Central Districts v Otago | Dunedin | 1952/53 |
|---|---|---|---|---|---|
| 225 | Woodcock L.J. | Tugaga M.J. | Wellington v Central Districts | Wellington | 2009/10 |
| 209 | Wiseman P.J. | Martin B.P. | New Zealand A v Sri Lanka A | Christchurch | 2003/04 |
| 208 | McSkimming W.C. | Scott B.E. | Otago v Auckland | Auckland | 2004/05 |
| 204 | Horne B.J. | Ferns D.K. | Auckland v Otago | Auckland | 2020/21 |
| 188 | Parlane N.R. | Tuffey D.R. | Northern Districts v Wellington | Wellington | 1999/00 |
| 185 | Maynard M.P. | Doull S.B. | Northern Districts v Auckland | Auckland | 1991/92 |
| 182* | Germon L.K. | Ford R.M. | Canterbury v Wellington | Christchurch | 1989/90 |
| 170* | Hart M.N. | Yovich J.A.F. | Northern Districts v South Africa | Hamilton | 1998/99 |
| 163* | Cowdrey M.C. | Smith A.C. | England v New Zealand | Wellington | 1962/63 |
| 162 | Bracewell D.A.J. | Sodhi I.S. | New Zealand A v India A | Visakhapatnam | 2013/14 |
| 151 | Young R.A. | Morgan G.J. | Auckland v Northern Districts | Auckland | 2007/08 |
| 139 | Hart R.G. | Tait A.R. | Northern Districts v Wellington | Gisborne | 1996/97 |
| 138* | McConchie C.E. | Sheat F.W. | Canterbury v Central Districts | Palmerston North | 2021/22 |
| 136 | Smith I.D.S. | Snedden M.C. | New Zealand v India | Auckland | 1989/90 |
| 135 | Hart R.G. | Penn A.J. | Central v Northern | Rangiora | 1998/99 |
| 134 | Wilson J.W. | Mallender N.A. | Otago v Canterbury | Christchurch | 1992/93 |
| 130* | de Boorder D.C. | McSkimming W.C. | Otago v Wellington | Queenstown | 2010/11 |
| 127 | Mooney F.L.H. | Buchan R.A. | Wellington v Auckland | Wellington | 1943/44 |
| 125 | Borthwick S.G. | McPeake I.G. | Wellington v Canterbury | Christchurch | 2015/16 |
| 122 | Schuster H.T. | Cunis R.S. | Auckland v Wellington | Wellington | 1964/65 |
| 121 | Cheetham J.E. | Murray A.R.A. | South Africa v Canterbury | Christchurch | 1952/53 |
| 118 | Coney J.V. | Cairns B.L. | New Zealand v England | Wellington | 1983/84 |
| 116 | Nevin C.J. | Davis H.T. | Wellington v Auckland | Auckland | 1995/96 |
| 115 | Robertson G.K. | Hart R.T. | Central Districts v Otago | Oamaru | 1985/86 |
| 115 | Hopkins G.J. | Ellis A.M. | Canterbury v Auckland | Auckland | 2002/03 |

## TENTH WICKET

| 184 | Blunt R.C. | Hawksworth W. | Otago v Canterbury | Christchurch | 1931/32 |
|---|---|---|---|---|---|
| 160 | Germon L.K. | Wisneski W.A. | Canterbury v Northern Districts | Rangiora | 1997/98 |
| 151 | Hastings B.F. | Collinge R.O. | New Zealand v Pakistan | Auckland | 1972/73 |
| 139 | McClenaghan M.J. | Sandhu R.S. | Auckland v Northern Districts | Auckland | 2016/17 |
| 138 | James K.C. | Brice A.W.S. | Wellington v Otago | Wellington | 1926/27 |
| 134 | Worker G.H. | Mathieson A.M. | Central Districts v Wellington | Nelson | 2015/16 |

| 133 | Bartlett G.A. | Colquhoun I.A. | Central Districts v Auckland | Auckland | 1959/60 |
|---|---|---|---|---|---|
| 127 | Watling B-J. | Boult T.A. | New Zealand v Bangladesh | Chittagaong | 2013/14 |
| 124 | Bracewell J.G. | Boock S.L. | New Zealand v Australia | Sydney | 1985/86 |
| 123 | Brice A.W.S. | Beard T. | Wellington v Otago | Wellington | 1927/28 |
| 119 | Carson W.N. | Cowie J. | Auckland v Otago | Auckland | 1937/38 |
| 118 | Astle N.J. | Cairns C.L. | New Zealand v England | Christchurch | 2001/02 |
| 113* | McGlashan P.D. | Aldridge G.W. | Northern Districts v Wellington | Wellington | 2005/06 |
| 113 | Mooney F.L.H. | Knapp E.C.V. | Wellington v Auckland | Wellington | 1943/44 |
| 113 | McKay A.J. | Gillespie M.R. | Wellington v Canterbury | Rangiora | 2012/13 |
| 107 | Motz R.C. | Cameron F.J. | New Zealand v Worcestershire | Worcester | 1965 |
| 106* | Astle N.J. | Morrison D.K. | New Zealand v England | Auckland | 1996/97 |
| 105 | Cherry R.W. | Torrance R.C. | Otago v Canterbury | Christchurch | 1925/26 |
| 104 | James K.C. | Massey H.B. | Wellington v Australia | Wellington | 1927/28 |
| 104 | van Beek L.V. | Williams W.S.A. | Canterbury v Otago | Christchurch | 2015/16 |
| 103 | Kelly P.J. | Troup G.B. | Auckland v Northern Districts | Auckland | 1985/86 |
| 102 | Craig M.D. | Duffy J.A. | Otago v Northern Districts | Dunedin | 2014/15 |
| 101 | Astle N.J. | Owens M.B. | Canterbury v Northern Districts | Hamilton | 1994/95 |

# HIGHEST PARTNERSHIPS BY WICKET

| 1st | 432 | Papps M.H.W. & Woodcock L.J. | Wellington v Auckland | Wellington | 2017/18 |
|---|---|---|---|---|---|
| 2nd | 317 | Hart R.T. & Briasco P.S. | Central Districts v Canterbury | New Plymouth | 1983/84 |
| 3rd | 467 | Jones A.H. & Crowe M.D. | New Zealand v Sri Lanka | Wellington | 1990/91 |
| 4th | 369 | Williamson K.S. & Nicholls H.M. | New Zealand v Pakistan | Christchurch | 2020/21 |
| 5th | 359 | Shakib Al Hasan & Mushfiqur Rahim | Bangladesh v New Zealand | Wellington | 2016/17 |
| 6th | 379* | Stewart S.L. & van Wyk C.F.K. | Canterbury v Central Districts | New Plymouth | 2009/10 |
| 7th | 265 | Powell J.L. & Dorreen N. | Canterbury v Otago | Christchurch | 1929/30 |
| 8th | 433 | Trumper V.T. & Sims A. | Sims' Australian XI v Canterbury | Christchurch | 1913/14 |
| 9th | 239 | Cave H.B. & Leggat I.B. | Central Districts v Otago | Dunedin | 1952/53 |
| 10th | 184 | Blunt R.C. & Hawksworth W. | Otago v Canterbury | Christchurch | 1931/32 |

# HIGHEST PARTNERSHIPS BY RUNS

| | wkt | | | | |
|---|---|---|---|---|---|
| 467 | 3rd | Jones A.H. & Crowe M.D. | New Zealand v Sri Lanka | Wellington | 1990/91 |
| 445 | 3rd | Whitelaw P.E. & Carson W.N. | Auckland v Otago | Dunedin | 1936/37 |
| 433 | 8th | Trumper V.T. & Sims A. | Sims' Australian XI v Canterbury | Christchurch | 1913/14 |
| 432 | 1st | Papps M.H.W. & Woodcock L.J. | Wellington v Auckland | Wellington | 2017/18 |
| 428 | 1st | Ingram P.J. & How J.M. | Central Districts v Wellington | Wellington | 2009/10 |
| 394* | 3rd | Kennedy P.G. & Latham R.T. | Canterbury v Northern Districts | Rotorua | 1990/91 |
| 387 | 1st | Turner G.M. & Jarvis T.W. | New Zealand v West Indies | Georgetown | 1971/72 |
| 379* | 6th | Stewart S.L. & van Wyk C.F.K. | Canterbury v Central Districts | New Plymouth | 2009/10 |
| 377 | 6th | Munro C. & Cachopa Craig | Auckland v Wellington | Auckland | 2012/13 |
| 373 | 1st | Sutcliffe B. & Watt L. | Otago v Auckland | Auckland | 1950/51 |

# Hundred Partnership for the First Wicket in Both Innings

| 154 & 155 | Shepherd J.S.F. | Worker R.V. de.R. | Otago v Wellington | Dunedin | 1923/24 |
|---|---|---|---|---|---|
| 220 & 286 | Taylor D.D. | Sutcliffe B. | Auckland v Canterbury | Auckland | 1948/49 |
| 102 & 155 | Blair W.L. | Turner G.M. | Otago v Auckland | Auckland | 1972/73 |
| 172 & 148 | Briasco P.S. | Smith C.J.P. | Central Districts v Auckland | New Plymouth | 1985/86 |
| 107 | { Broad B.C. | Moxon M.D. | England XI v Northern Districts | Hamilton | 1987/88 |
| 208 | { Athey C.W.J. | Robinson R.T. | | | |
| 109 & 111 | Wealleans K.A. | White D.J. | Northern Districts v India | Hamilton | 1989/90 |
| 116 & 102 | Greatbatch M.J. | Latham R.T. | New Zealand v Zimbabwe | Bulawayo | 1992/93 |
| 145 & 131 | Lawson R.A. | Gaffaney C.B. | Otago v Wellington | Wellington | 1996/97 |
| 118* & 179 | Twose R.G. | Bell M.D. | Wellington v Central Districts | Wellington | 1997/98 |
| 102 & 112 | Spearman C.M. | Kelly D.P. | Central Districts v Wellington | New Plymouth | 1999/00 |
| 220 | { Bell M.D. | Jones R.A. | Wellington v Canterbury | Christchurch | 2000/01 |
| 127 | { Nevin C.J. | Jones R.A. | | | |
| 141 | { Cumming C.D. | Mohammad Wasim | Otago v Wellington | Wellington | 2002/03 |
| 147 | { Gaffaney C.B. | Cumming C.D. | | | |
| 104 & 118 | Richardson M.H. | McIntosh T.G. | Auckland v Northern Districts | Auckland | 2002/03 |
| 169 & 121* | Raval J.A. | McIntosh T.G. | Auckland v Wellington | Auckland | 2009/10 |
| 227 & 133 | Rutherford H.D. | Wilson B.S. | Otago v Central Districts | Nelson | 2016/17 |

# FAMILIES IN FIRST-CLASS CRICKET

## Four Generations

Snedden A.N.C. (A)     Snedden W.N. (A)     Snedden M.C. (A)     Snedden M.W. (W)

## Great-grandfather and Great-grandson

Orchard S.A. (C)          Orchard M.G. (ND)

## Three Generations

| | | | | | | |
|---|---|---|---|---|---|---|
| Anderson W.M. | (C) | Anderson R.W. | (C, ND, O, CD) | Anderson T.R. | | (CD) |
| *Blair J.R. | (O) | Blair R.A.J. | (O) | { Blair W.L. | | (O) |
| | | | | { Blair B.R. | | (O, ND) |
| Burton H.G.E.L. | (W) | Burton H.E.L. | (W, A) | Burton J.E.L. | | (W) |
| *Burtt N.V. | (C) | Burtt J.W. | (C, CD) | Burtt L.M. | | (C) |
| Smith F.A. | (C) | Smith F.B. | (C) | Smith G.B. | | (C) |
| *Carson W. | (O) | Carson W.N. | (A) | Carson J.R. | | (A, ND) |

*\* J.R. Blair is the uncle of R.A.J. Blair. The Carsons are uncles and nephews. J.W. Burtt is the uncle of L.M. Burtt.*

## Grandfather and Grandson

| | | | |
|---|---|---|---|
| Anderson I.P. | (C) | Anderson F.G. | (C) |
| Dowker R.T. | (C) | Wheeler B.M. | (CD) |
| Guillen S.C. | (C) | van Beek L.V. | (C, W) |
| Milnes L.A. | (O) | Milnes G.S. | (CD) |
| Pritchard T.L. | (W) | Meiring D.T. | (CD) |
| Roberts H. | (W) | du Chateau V.H. | (W) |
| Rapley A.F. | (C) | Sheat F.W. | (C) |

## Father and Three Sons

| | | | | | | | |
|---|---|---|---|---|---|---|---|
| Cotterill A.J. | (C) | Cotterill A.K. | (HB) | Cotterill B.W. | (HB) | Cotterill G.R. | (HB) |
| Hadlee W.A. | (C, O) | Hadlee B.G. | (C) | Hadlee D.R. | (C) | Hadlee R.J. | (C) |

## Father and Two Sons

| | | | | | |
|---|---|---|---|---|---|
| Blacklock J.W. | (W) | Blacklock C.P. | (W) | Blacklock J.P. | (W) |
| Blair R.A.J. | (O) | Blair W.L. | (O) | Blair B.R. | (O, ND) |
| Crowe D.W. | (W,C) | Crowe M.D. | (A, CD, W) | Crowe J.J. | (A, SA) |
| Garrard C.W. | (C) | Garrard W.R. | (A) | Garrard D.R. | (A) |
| Furlong B.D.M. | (CD) | Furlong J.B.M. | (CD) | Furlong C.J.M. | (CD) |
| Harris P.G.Z. | (C) | Harris B.Z. | (C, O) | Harris C.Z. | (C) |
| Howell J.H. | (CD) | Howell L.G. | (C, CD, A, ND) | Howell G.A. | (C, W) |
| McCullum S.J. | (O) | McCullum B.B. | (O, C) | McCullum N.L. | (O) |
| McVicar A.C. | (Minor Assocs) | McVicar S.A. | (W) | McVicar C.C. | (CD) |
| Puna N. | (ND) | Puna K.N. | (ND) | Puna A. | (ND) |
| Reaney P.S. | (HB) | Reaney H.E.I. | (W) | Reaney T.P.L. | (W, CD) |

## Father and One Son

| | | | |
|---|---|---|---|
| Airey W.F. | (W) | Airey D.M.L. | (W) |
| Aldridge C.W. | (C) | Aldridge G.W. | (ND) |
| Allen R. | (W) | Allen G.S. | (W) |
| Alpe S. | (A, C, W) | Alpe F.G. | (W) |
| Andrews S. | (C) | Andrews B. | (C, CD, O) |
| Astle A.M. | (CD) | Astle T.D. | (C) |
| Baker J.C. | (O) | Clark J.B. | (O) |

| | | | |
|---|---|---|---|
| Barclay W.S. | (W) | Barclay C.W. | (CD) |
| Barton P.H. | (ND, O) | Barton H.D. | (A, C) |
| Beard D.D. | (W, CD, ND) | Beard D.A. | (ND) |
| Blackmore J.H. | (ND) | Blackmore S.J. | (W) |
| Boyle J.G. | (C) | Boyle J.C.T. | (C) |
| Bracewell B.P. | (CD, O, ND) | Bracewell D.A.J. | (CD) |
| Bracewell M.A. | (O) | Bracewell M.G. | (O, W) |
| Bradburn W.P. | (ND) | Bradburn G.E. | (ND) |
| Burgess G.C. | (A) | Burgess M.G. | (A) |
| Burtt N.V. | (C) | Burtt J.W. | (C, CD) |
| Cairns B.L. | (CD, O, ND) | Cairns C.L. | (ND, C) |
| Campbell K.O. | (O) | Campbell P.A. | (O) |
| Carter R.M. | (C) | Carter L.J. | (C) |
| Child E.L. | (A, ND) | Child M.J. | (ND) |
| Clark L.G. | (O) | Clark L.A. | (W, O, A) |
| Collins W.E. | (W) | Collins D.C. | (W) |
| Cooper B.G. | (ND) | Cooper H.R. | (ND) |
| Cuff L.A. | (C, A) | Cuff A.G. | (Tasmania) |
| Cumming C.D. | (C, O) | Cumming J.M. | (O) |
| Cunis R.S. | (A, ND) | Cunis S.J. | (C) |
| Dawson G.J. | (O) | Dawson G.J. | (C) |
| Douglas G.W. | (CD) | Douglas M.W. | (CD, W) |
| Edgar A.J. | (W) | Edgar B.A. | (W) |
| Freeman T.A. | (O) | Freeman B.T. | (O) |
| Fulton F. | (O, HB) | Fulton P.R. | (HB) |
| Gasson E.A. snr | (C) | Gasson E.A. jnr | (C) |
| Gearry G.N. | (C) | Gearry R.M. | (C, CD) |
| Gedye A.E. | (W) | Gedye S.G. | (A) |
| Gilbertson J. | (S) | Gilbertson A.W. | (O) |
| Greenfield A. | (N) | Greenfield F.E. | (N) |
| Hartland I.R. | (C) | Hartland B.R. | (C) |
| Hartshorn D.J. | (C, CD) | Hartshorn J.W. | (W) |
| Hastings B.F. | (W, CD, C) | Hastings M.A. | (C) |
| Hay W.P.C. | (A) | Hay S.C. | (A) |
| Hill A.J. | (CD) | Hill J.V. | (CD) |
| Hill J. | (O) | Hill R.J. | (O) |
| Hoar F.R. | (W) | Hoar N.R. | (W) |
| Holden W.J. | (O) | Holden A.C. | (O) |
| Horne P.A. | (A) | Horne B.J. | (A) |
| Howden C.E. | (O) | Howden C.P. | (O) |
| Ibadulla K. | (O) | Ibadulla K.B.K. | (O) |
| Jefferson R.G. | (O, W) | Jefferson M.R. | (W, ND) |
| Kelly J.W.H. | (W) | Kelly P.J. | (A) |
| Kerr A.C. | (A) | Kerr A.C. | (A) |
| Kuggeleijn C.M. | (ND) | Kuggeleijn S.C. | (W, ND) |
| Lankham G. | (A) | Lankham W. | (A) |
| Latham R.T. | (C) | Latham T.W.M. | (C) |
| Lowry T.H. | (HB) | Lowry T.C. | (A, W) |
| McEwan P.E. | (C) | McEwan M.B. | (C, W, A) |
| McGirr W.P. | (W) | McGirr H.M. | (W) |
| McKnight S.G. | (O) | McKnight K.J. | (O) |
| McKenzie N.M. | (O) | McKenzie M.N. | (C, O) |
| Mills G. | (A, HB, O) | Mills J.E. | (A) |
| Monaghan H.W. | (W, C) | Monaghan D.W. | (SI Army) |
| Morgan H.A. | (W) | Morgan R.G. | (ND, A) |
| Murdoch D.H. | (O) | Murdoch G.H. | (O) |

| | | | |
|---|---|---|---|
| Newman A. | (W) | Newman P.A. | (CD) |
| North T.H. | (C) | North R.H. | (WC) |
| Nuttall A.J. | (C) | Nuttall E.J. | (C) |
| O'Brien J.J. | (HB) | O'Brien M.A. | (W) |
| O'Rourke P.W. | (W) | O'Rourke W.P. | (C) |
| Oakley J.H. | (W) | Oakley D.F. | (W) |
| Ollivier A.M. | (C) | Ollivier K.M. | (C) |
| Ongley A.M. | (HB) | Ongley J.A. | (W, CD) |
| Parker N.M. | (O, C) | Parker M.M. | (O) |
| Postles A.J. | (A) | Postles B.J. | (A) |
| Pringle M.R. | (A) | Pringle O.M.R. | (A) |
| Redmond R.E. | (W, A) | Redmond A.J. | (C, O) |
| Rees W.L. | (A) | Rees A.W. | (A, HB) |
| Reese T.W. | (C) | Reese D.W. | (C) |
| Reid J.R. | (W, O) | Reid R.B. | (W, A) |
| Roberts A. | (W) | Roberts S.A. | (A) |
| Roberts H. | (W) | Roberts E.J. | (W) |
| Rutherford K.R. | (O) | Rutherford H.D. | (O) |
| Sale E.V. | (A) | Sale V.S. | (A) |
| Sears M.J. | (W) | Sears B.V. | (W) |
| Standidge J.A. | (W) | Standidge P.H. | (W) |
| Stead D.W. | (C) | Stead G.R. | (C) |
| Stoyanoff P.A. | (U23) | Stoyanoff B.P. | (CD) |
| Tindill E.W.T. | (W) | Tindill P. | (W) |
| Tuke C.L. | (HB) | Tuke H.L. | (HB) |
| Vance R.A. | (W) | Vance R.H. | (W) |
| Vivian H.G. | (A) | Vivian G.E. | (A) |
| Wallace W.M. | (A) | Wallace G.M. | (A) |
| Ward J.T. | (C) | Ward B.J. | (C) |
| Wilding F. | (C) | Wilding A.F. | (C) |
| Wright G.T. | (C) | Wright J.G. | (ND, C, A) |

## Father and Son in Same First-class Match

| | | | |
|---|---|---|---|
| Reese T.W. & Reese D.W. | Canterbury v Otago | Dunedin | 1917/18 |

## Five Brothers

Cotterill A.J. (C)   Cotterill C.N. (HB)   Cotterill E.J. (C, A)   Cotterill H. (C)   Cotterill W.J. (C)

## Four Brothers

| | | | | | | | |
|---|---|---|---|---|---|---|---|
| Bayly A. | (T) | Bayly F. | (T) | Bayly G.T. | (T) | Bayly H. | (T) |
| Bracewell B.P. | | Bracewell D.W. | | Bracewell J.G. | | Bracewell M.A. | |
| | (CD, O, ND) | | (CD, C) | | (O, A) | | (O) |
| Mills E. | (A) | Mills G. (A, HB, O) | | Mills I. | (A) | Mills W. | (T, A) |

## Three Brothers

| | | | | | |
|---|---|---|---|---|---|
| Alloo A.P. | (O) | Alloo A.W. | (O) | Alloo H.C. | (O) |
| Blacklock A. | (W) | Blacklock J.W. | (W) | Blacklock R.V. | (W) |
| Cachopa B. | (A, C) | Cachopa Carl | (A, CD) | Cachopa Craig | (W, A) |
| Carlton W. | (A, C) | Carlton A.R. | (Vic) | Carlton J. | (Vic) |
| Cotterill A.K. | (HB) | Cotterill B.W. | (HB) | Cotterill G.R. | (HB) |
| Eden J. | (N) | Eden T.G. | (N) | Eden W. | (N) |
| Fowler G. | (N) | Fowler L.A. | (N) | Fowler S. | (N) |

| | | | | | |
|---|---|---|---|---|---|
| Gore A.H. | (W, HB) | Gore C.S. | (W) | Gore R. | (W) |
| Hadlee B.G. | (C) | Hadlee D.R. | (C) | Hadlee R.J. | (C) |
| Harman A.F.G. | (C) | Harman R.D. | (C) | Harman T.D. | (C) |
| Knapp C.H. | (N) | Knapp K.J. | (N) | Knapp W.H. | (N) |
| Lusk Hugh B. | (A, HB) | Lusk R.B. | (T) | Lusk W.N.B. | (A) |
| Mace C. | (O) | Mace H. | (W) | Mace J. | (O) |
| McCormick A.D. | (O) | McCormick C.E. | (A) | McCormick E. | (A) |
| Meldrum A.L. | (A) | Meldrum D. | (A) | Meldrum W. | (A) |
| Newman A. | (W) | Newman J. | (C, W) | Newman S. | (W) |
| Parker K.J. | (A) | Parker J.M. | (ND) | Parker N.M. | (O, C) |
| Reese D. | (C) | Reese J.B. | (C) | Reese T.W. | (C) |
| Ridley A.E. | (C) | Ridley H.C. | (C) | Ridley R.A. | (C) |
| Salmon I.J. | (W) | Salmon J.A.N. | (W) | Salmon W.J. | (W, HB, T) |
| Tucker K.H. | (W) | Tucker S.J. | (W) | Tucker W.C. | (T) |
| Williams A.M. | (HB) | Williams G.C. | (HB) | Williams N.T. | (A) |

## Two Brothers

| | | | |
|---|---|---|---|
| Aberhart D.C. | (CD, C) | Aberhart W.M. | (W) |
| Alabaster G.D. | (O, C, ND) | Alabaster J.C. | (O) |
| Austin G.G. | (O) | Austin T.T.L. | (O) |
| Baker E.G.H. | (W) | Baker W.A. | (W) |
| Bannerman J.W.H. | (S) | Bannerman W.E. | (O) |
| Barton P.H. | (ND, O) | Barton R.H. | (ND) |
| Beal C.E. | (O, C) | Beal W.M. | (O) |
| Beuth D. | (CD) | Beuth A.J. | (ND) |
| Bigg-Wither A. | (N) | Bigg-Wither J. | (N) |
| Billcliff I.S. | (O, W, A) | Billcliff M.R. | (O) |
| Bishop H.A. | (HB, C) | Bishop R.E. | (HB) |
| Blacklock C.P. | (W) | Blacklock J.P. | (W) |
| Blair B.R. | (O, ND) | Blair W.L. | (O) |
| Blakely D.J. | (O) | Blakely J.W. | (O) |
| Blamires E.O. | (W, O) | Blamires H.L. | (HB) |
| Boddington E.R. | (N, W) | Boddington H.A. | (N, O) |
| Boult J.J. | (ND) | Boult T.A. | (ND) |
| Boyle D.J. | (C) | Boyle J.G. | (W, C) |
| Broad C.H. | (N) | Broad E.W. | (N) |
| Broom D.J. | (O) | Broom N.T. | (C, O) |
| Burtt N.V. | (C) | Burtt T.B. | (C) |
| Cairns A.E. | (O) | Cairns H.W. | (O) |
| Cameron D.S. | (O) | Cameron H.R. | (O) |
| Cederwall B.W. | (W) | Cederwall G.N. | (W) |
| Chadwick C.S. | (O) | Chadwick L.N. | (O) |
| Clarke D.B. | (A, ND) | Clarke D.S. | (ND) |
| Collins J.U. | (N, C) | Collins W.E. | (W) |
| Coney C.J. | (W) | Coney J.V. | (W) |
| Cornelius C.J. | (C) | Cornelius W.A. | (C) |
| Cresswell A.E. | (W, CD) | Cresswell G.F. | (W, CD) |
| Cross C.S. | (N, W) | Cross W.H.S. | (N) |
| Crowe J.J. | (A, South Australia) | Crowe M.D. | (A, CD, W, Somerset) |
| Cummings E.M. | (O) | Cummings G.B. | (O) |
| Dacre C.C.R. | (A) | Dacre L.M. | (A) |
| Doull L.J. | (W) | Doull S.B. | (ND) |
| Dryden C.H. | (W) | Dryden W.E. | (W) |
| Dufaur E.T. | (A) | Dufaur P.P.R. | (A) |
| Duffy J.A. | (O) | Duffy R.M. | (O) |
| Farrant A.J. | (C) | Farrant D.G. | (C) |

| | | | |
|---|---|---|---|
| Fenwick F.F. | (O) | Fenwick H.S. | (C) |
| Findlay J.L. | (C) | Findlay J.W. | (W) |
| Fisher A.H. | (O) | Fisher R.L. | (C) |
| Frankish E.H. | (C) | Frankish F.S. | (C) |
| Frith C. | (C, O) | Frith W. | (C, O, W) |
| Fulton F. | (O, HB) | Fulton J.C. | (O) |
| Fulton D.H. | (C) | Fulton P.G. | (C) |
| Furlong C.J.M. | (CD) | Furlong J.B.M. | (CD) |
| Garrard D.R. | (A) | Garrard W.R. | (A) |
| Gatenby D.J. | (C) | Gatenby P.R. | (Tasmania) |
| Gilbertson J. | (S) | Gilbertson J.H. | (S) |
| Godby H.E. | (O) | Godby M.J. | (O, C) |
| Graham A.C. | (O) | Graham C.G. | (O) |
| Hamilton A.J. | (S) | Hamilton D.C. | (S) |
| Hampton B.L. | (CD) | Hampton I.R. | (CD) |
| Harris B.Z. | (C, O) | Harris C.Z. | (C) |
| Hart M.N. | (ND) | Hart R.G. | (ND) |
| Hatch R.K. | (W) | Hatch R.J. | (W) |
| Hatwell B.J. | (ND) | Hatwell J.G. | (ND) |
| Hay T.D.B. | (A) | Hay W.P.C. | (A) |
| Hewat D.F. | (W) | Hewat R. | (O) |
| Hickson H.C. | (W) | Hickson W.R.S. | (W) |
| Hindmarsh H.S.W. | (HB) | Hindmarsh J.S. | (HB) |
| Holdship A.R. | (W) | Holdship W.E.J. | (Middlesex) |
| Horne M.J. | (A, O) | Horne P.A. | (A) |
| Howarth G.P. | (A, ND, Surrey) | Howarth H.J. | (A) |
| Howell L.G. | (C, CD, A, ND) | Howell G.A. | (C, W) |
| Howden A.M. | (A) | Howden C.E. | (O) |
| Labatt A.B.M. | (C, A) | Labatt F.H.D. | (C) |
| Lash E.G. | (T) | Lash F.W. | (W) |
| Lynch D.J.F. | (A) | Lynch R.F. | (W) |
| Lynch R.K. | (A) | Lynch S.M. | (A) |
| McCullum B.B. | (O, C) | McCullum N.L. | (O) |
| McVicar S.A. | (W) | McVicar C.C. | (CD) |
| Marshall J.M. | (T) | Marshall P. | (A) |
| Marshall J.A.H. | (ND) | Marshall H.J.H. | (ND, Glos, W) |
| Martin J.H. | (HB) | Martin H. | (HB) |
| Matthias H.R. | (C) | Matthias R.B. | (C) |
| Morris J.B. | (A) | Morris P.P.W. | (A) |
| Naughton D.O. | (W) | Naughton M.P. | (W) |
| Neill R. | (A) | Neill T. | (A) |
| Nicholson C.R. | (C, O) | Nicholson K.A. | (O) |
| O'Donnell R.R. | (A) | O'Donnell W.T. | (A) |
| O'Rourke M.H. | (A) | O'Rourke P.W. | (W) |
| Ogier H.J. | (W) | Ogier P.H.W. | (C) |
| Ollivier A.M. | (C) | Ollivier F.M. | (C) |
| Ormiston I.W. | (W) | Ormiston R.W. | (CD, W) |
| Papps M.H.W. | (C, W) | Papps T.J.T. | (C) |
| Parlane M.E. | (ND, W) | Parlane N.R. | (ND, W, A) |
| Perry A. | (C) | Perry C.T.H. | (C) |
| Phillips D.N. | (O) | Phillips G.D. | (A) |
| Powell J.L. | (C) | Powell R.F.J. | (C) |
| Powys A.L. | (C) | Powys R.A.N. | (C) |
| Puna A. | (ND) | Puna K.N. | (ND) |
| Reaney H.E.I. | (W) | Reaney T.P.L. | (W, CD) |
| Richardson C.A. | (W) | Richardson W.A. | (NSW) |

| | | | |
|---|---|---|---|
| Ritchie A.W. | (A) | Ritchie D.C. | (A) |
| Robertson G.K. | (CD) | Robertson S.P. | (CD) |
| Rutherford I.A. | (O, CD) | Rutherford K.R. | (O) |
| Schofer J.W.J. | (W) | Schofer P.J. | (W) |
| Scott A.H. | (A) | Scott V.J. | (A) |
| Shaw G.S. | (A, O) | Shaw L.J. | (A) |
| Snedden A.N.C. | (A) | Snedden Cyril A. | (A) |
| Snedden Colin A. | (A) | Snedden W.N. | (A) |
| Sorenson B.J. | (A) | Sorenson R.G. | (A) |
| Stevens G.R. | (HB) | Stevens J.A.M. | (HB) |
| Studholme E.C | (C) | Studholme W.P. | (C) |
| ter Braak D.J. | (Netherlands) | ter Braak R.M. | (A) |
| Toomey C.D.G. | (O) | Toomey F.J. | (O) |
| Thomson K. | (C) | Thomson W.A. | (C) |
| Turnbull A.J. | (O) | Turnbull P.J. | (O) |
| Wallace G.F. | (A) | Wallace W.M. | (A) |
| Walker F.L. | (ND) | Walker J.G. | (ND) |
| Watson E.A. | (O) | Watson L.F. | (O) |
| Watson G. | (C) | Watson F.E. | (WC) |
| Watson H.C. | (O) | Watson L.C. | (O) |
| Webb M.G. | (O, C) | Webb R.J. | (O) |
| Weir A.F. | (A) | Weir G.L. | (A) |
| West G.L. | (CD, ND) | West R.M. | (CD, W) |
| Westbrook K.R. | (Tasmania) | Westbrook R.A. | (O, Tasmania) |
| White N.M. | (HB) | White P.C. | (HB) |
| Williams P.F.C. | (Gloucestershire) | Williams J.N. | (HB) |
| Wilson A.C. | (C) | Wilson W.C. | (C) |
| Wilkie J.L. | (O) | Wilkie R.A. | (O) |
| Wyatt I.E. | (A) | Wyatt J.L. | (ND) |

## Uncle and Nephew

*instances not included in previous lists*

| | | | |
|---|---|---|---|
| Bailey J.F. | (ND) | Bailey M.D. | (ND) |
| Burtt J.W. | (C, CD) | Burtt L.M. | (C) |
| Carlton W. | (A, C) | Carlton T.A. | (C, O) |
| Carson W. | (O) | Carson W.N. | (A) |
| Carson W.N. | (A) | Carson J.R. | (A, ND) |
| Crawford C.G. | (C) | Playle W.R. | (A) |
| Cunningham W.H.R. | (C) | Anderson G.F. | (C) |
| Dacre C.C.R. (A) & Dacre L.M. | (A) | Coleman D.D. | (A) |
| Fulton J. | (O) | Fulton F. (O, HB) & Fulton J.C. | (O) |
| Fulton R.W. | (C, ND) | Fulton D.H. & Fulton P.G. | (C) |
| Griffiths B.G. | (W) | Maguiness S.J. | (W) |
| Pocock M.G. | (ND) | Pocock B.A. | (A, ND) |
| Roberts B.L. | (ND) | Cairns C.L. | (ND, C) |
| Westbrook N.R. | (Tasmania) | Westbrook R.A. | (O, Tasmania) |
| Wilson R.S. | (O) | Paul J.M. | (O) |
| Wilson T.J. | (O) | Wilson J.W. | (O) |

## Cousins

| | | | |
|---|---|---|---|
| Bateman G.C. | (C) | Bateman S.N. | (C) |
| Bracewell D.A.J. | (CD) | Bracewell M.G. | (O, W) |
| Gibson J.M. | (O) | Gibson Z.N | (ND) |
| Hoskin R.N. | (O) | Lamont M.J. | (O) |
| Hotter S.J. | (W) | Verry R.A. | (W) |
| Leggat I.B. | (CD) | Leggat J.G. | (C) |

| | | | |
|---|---|---|---|
| Lusk Harold B. | (A, C, W) | ⎧ Lusk Hugh B. | (A, HB) |
| | | ⎨ Lusk R.B. | (T) |
| | | ⎩ Lusk W.N.B. | (A) |
| McMillan C.D. | (C) | McMillan J.M. | (O) |
| Pringle M.R. | (A) | Webb P.N. | (A) |
| Reid B.A. | (WA) | Reid J.F. | (A) |
| Studholme E.C. | (C) | Studholme W.P. | (C) |
| Talbot G.L. | (C) | Talbot R.O. | (C, O) |
| Vettori D.L. | (ND) | Hill J.V. | (CD) |
| Williamson K.S. | (ND) | Cleaver D. | (CD) |

## Miscellaneous

C.R.W. Dickel (O, C) is son of first cousin of T.H.V. Dickel (O).

G.A.W. Blakely (O) is son of first cousin of D.J. and J.W. Blakely (O).

A. Barron (C, W) and J.R. Barron (O) — fathers were first cousins.

D.W. Lamason (CD) is grandson of first cousin of J.R. Lamason (W).

W.H. Cooper (A) is great-uncle of B.G. Cooper (ND).

W.J. Pocock (NSW, C) and W.L. Rees (Vic, A) were related to the Graces and other first-class cricketers as follows:

W.R. Gilbert (Middx, Glos) and G.H.B. Gilbert (Middx, NSW) were half-brothers. They had the same father and their mothers were sisters (Pococks). W.J. Pocock (NSW, C), W.L. Rees (Vic, A) W.G. Rees (NSW) and the Graces all had a (different) parent who was a brother or sister of the two Pocock sisters.

**NB:** *Only instances where relationships have been verified have been included in these lists.*
*There are numerous other possibilities and we would welcome any additional information on this subject.*

# REDPATH CUP

*Presented by Mr David Redpath*

Awarded to the New Zealand batsman whose performances in first-class cricket have been, in the opinion of the Board of Control, the most meritorious since the award was last made.

## HOLDERS

*Season's first-class figures*

|  |  | Team | In | NO | HS | Runs | Ave |
|---|---|---|---|---|---|---|---|
| 1920/21 | Anthony A. | Auckland | 5 | 1 | 113 | 251 | 62.75 |
| 1921/22 | Hiddleston J.S. | Wellington | 8 | 1 | 118 | 396 | 56.57 |
| 1922/23 | Blunt R.C. | Canterbury | 12 | 1 | 174 | 583 | 53.00 |
| 1923/24 | Hiddleston J.S. | Wellington | 12 | 0 | 163 | 619 | 51.58 |
| 1924/25 | Worker R.V. de R. | Otago | 12 | 2 | 121* | 491 | 49.10 |
| 1925/26 | Allcott C.F.W. | Auckland | 9 † | 2 | 116 | 359 | 51.28 |
| 1926/27 | Blunt R.C. | Otago | 12 § | 1 | 187 | 758 | 69.80 |
| 1927/28 | Dempster C.S. | Wellington | 12 | 1 | 145 | 616 | 56.00 |
| 1928/29 | Weir G.L. | Auckland | 4 | 2 | 106* | 262 | 131.00 |
| 1929/30 | Dempster C.S. | Wellington | 10 | 4 | 141* | 559 | 93.16 |
| 1930/31 | Dempster C.S. | Wellington | 42 † | 6 | 212 | 1901 | 52.80 |
| 1931/32 | Roberts A.W. | Canterbury | 10 | 1 | 181 | 476 | 52.88 |
| 1932/33 | Dempster C.S. | Wellington | 9 | 2 | 83* | 336 | 48.00 |
| 1933/34 | Vivian H.G. | Auckland | 5 | 0 | 64 | 263 | 52.60 |
| 1934/35 | Whitelaw P.E. | Auckland | 7 | 0 | 155 | 472 | 67.42 |
| 1935/36 | Kerr J.L. | Canterbury | 13 † | 2 | 146 | 655 | 59.54 |
| 1936/37 | Whitelaw P.E. | Auckland | 6 | 1 | 195 | 410 | 82.00 |
| 1937/38 | Uttley K.F.M. | Otago | 6 | 0 | 138 | 420 | 70.00 |
| 1938/39 | Wallace W.M. | Auckland | 6 | 1 | 105 | 270 | 54.00 |
| 1939/40 | Donnelly M.P. | Canterbury | 5 | 1 | 104 | 302 | 75.50 |
| 1940-45 | no award | | | | | | |
| 1945/46 | Hadlee W.A. | Otago | 7 | 0 | 198 | 449 | 66.14 |
| 1946/47 | Sutcliffe B. | Auckland & Otago | 8 | 1 | 197 | 722 | 103.14 |
| 1947/48 | Sutcliffe B. | Otago | 10 | 1 | 208* | 911 | 101.22 |
| 1948/49 | Sutcliffe B. | Auckland | 6 | 0 | 141 | 511 | 85.16 |
| 1949/50 | Sutcliffe B. | Otago | 9 | 0 | 355 | 695 | 77.55 |
| 1950/51 | Sutcliffe B. | Otago | 12 | 0 | 275 | 798 | 66.50 |
| 1951/52 | Scott V.J. | Auckland | 10 | 2 | 151* | 459 | 57.37 |
| 1952/53 | Miller L.S.M. | Central Districts | 9 | 3 | 128* | 545 | 90.83 |
| 1953/54 | Sutcliffe B. | Otago | 34 † | 2 | 196 | 1691 | 52.84 |
| 1954/55 | Reid J.R. | Wellington | 15 | 2 | 106 | 505 | 38.84 |
| 1955/56 | Reid J.R. | New Zealand | 33 † | 6 | 150* | 1227 | 45.44 |
| 1956/57 | Miller L.S.M. | Wellington | 13 | 3 | 83 | 559 | 55.90 |
| 1957/58 | Miller L.S.M. | Wellington | 14 | 1 | 95 | 549 | 42.23 |
| 1958/59 | Pairaudeau B.H. | Northern Districts | 11 | 1 | 80 | 456 | 45.60 |
| 1959/60 | Reid J.R. | Wellington | 16 | 1 | 165 | 724 | 48.26 |
| 1960/61 | Harris P.G.Z. | Canterbury | 14 | 2 | 108 | 597 | 49.75 |
| 1961/62 | Reid J.R. | Wellington | 40 † | 2 | 203 | 2188 | 57.57 |
| 1962/63 | Reid J.R. | Wellington | 14 | 1 | 296 | 681 | 52.38 |
| 1963/64 | Sinclair B.W. | Wellington | 15 | 1 | 138 | 641 | 45.78 |
| 1964/65 | Pollard V. | Central Districts | 43 † | 6 | 85 | 1081 | 29.21 |
| 1965/66 | Sinclair B.W. | Wellington | 17 | 2 | 114 | 700 | 56.66 |
| 1966/67 | Dowling G.T. | Canterbury | 18 | 2 | 102* | 871 | 46.66 |
| 1967/68 | Dowling G.T. | Canterbury | 18 | 1 | 239 | 968 | 56.94 |
| 1968/69 | Hastings B.F. | Canterbury | 15 | 4 | 117* | 872 | 79.27 |
| 1969/70 | Murray B.A.G. | Wellington | 51 † | 3 | 157 | 2079 | 43.31 |

|  |  | Team | In | NO | HS | Runs | Ave |
|---|---|---|---|---|---|---|---|
| 1970/71 | Dowling G.T. | Canterbury | 16 | 1 | 102 | 667 | 44.66 |
| 1971/72 | Turner G.M. | Otago | 27 † | 5 | 259 | 1708 | 77.63 |
| 1972/73 | Congdon B.E. | Otago | 38 † | 6 | 126 | 1728 | 54.00 |
| 1973/74 | Turner G.M. | Otago | 17 † | 2 | 110* | 714 | 47.60 |
| 1974/75 | Turner G.M. | Otago | 15 | 1 | 186* | 838 | 59.85 |
| 1975/76 | Turner G.M. | Otago | 20 | 4 | 177* | 1244 | 77.75 |
| 1976/77 | Burgess M.G. | Auckland | 28 † | 1 | 138 | 1064 | 39.40 |
| 1977/78 | Howarth G.P. | Northern Districts | 22 | 1 | 122 | 685 | 32.61 |
| 1978/79 | Howarth G.P. | Northern Districts | 11 | 1 | 147* | 505 | 50.50 |
| 1979/80 | Howarth G.P. | Northern Districts | 22 | 2 | 151 | 767 | 38.35 |
| 1980/81 | Reid J.F. | Auckland | 18 | 4 | 173 | 817 | 58.35 |
| 1981/82 | Edgar B.A. | Wellington | 19 | 1 | 161 | 934 | 51.88 |
| 1982/83 | Edgar B.A. | Wellington | 30 † | 5 | 146 | 1116 | 44.64 |
| 1983/84 | Coney J.V. | Wellington | 19 † | 4 | 174* | 736 | 49.06 |
| 1984/85 | Coney J.V. | Wellington | 26 † | 4 | 111* | 877 | 39.86 |
| 1985/86 | Crowe M.D. | Central Districts | 31 † | 9 | 242* | 1667 | 75.77 |
| 1986/87 | Crowe M.D. | Central Districts | 22 † | 3 | 175* | 1703 | 89.63 |
| 1987/88 | Crowe M.D. | Central Districts | 16 † | 2 | 144 | 1064 | 76.00 |
| 1988/89 | Jones A.H. | Wellington | 25 † | 2 | 181* | 1079 | 46.91 |
| 1989/90 | Wright J.G. | Auckland | 32 † | 5 | 185 | 1641 | 60.77 |
| 1990/91 | Crowe M.D. | Wellington | 15 † | 3 | 299 | 847 | 70.58 |
| 1991/92 | Wright J.G. | Auckland | 14 | 0 | 116 | 518 | 37.00 |
| 1992/93 | Rutherford K.R. | Otago | 26 † | 3 | 105 | 907 | 39.43 |
| 1993/94 | Jones A.H. | Wellington | 20 † | 0 | 143 | 934 | 46.70 |
| 1994/95 | Parore A.C. | New Zealand | 36 † | 7 | 127* | 1050 | 36.20 |
| 1995/96 | Twose R.G. | New Zealand | 10 † | 2 | 119* | 452 | 56.50 |
| 1996/97 | Fleming S.P. | Canterbury | 16 † | 1 | 129 | 629 | 41.93 |
| 1997/98 | Horne M.J. | Otago | 22 † | 1 | 241 | 1114 | 53.04 |
| 1998/99 | Horne M.J. | Otago | 19 | 2 | 132 | 887 | 52.17 |
| 1999/00 | Cairns C.L. | New Zealand | 26 † | 3 | 109 | 903 | 39.26 |
| 2000/01 | Richardson M.H. | Otago | 45 † | 5 | 306 | 2672 | 66.80 |
| 2001/02 | Astle N.J. | Canterbury | 15 † | 3 | 223 | 899 | 74.91 |
| 2002/03 | Richardson M.H. | Auckland | 25 † | 2 | 113 | 885 | 38.47 |
| 2003/04 | Styris S.B. | Northern Districts | 17 † | 1 | 170 | 663 | 41.43 |
| 2004/05 | Marshall H.J.H. | Northern Districts | 16 † | 0 | 160 | 730 | 45.62 |
| 2005/06 | Sinclair M.S. | Central Districts | 18 † | 2 | 121 | 848 | 53.00 |
| 2006/07 | Papps M.H.W. | Canterbury | 18 † | 0 | 188 | 1141 | 63.38 |
| 2007/08 | Taylor L.R.P.L. | Central Districts | 19 † | 0 | 152 | 717 | 42.17 |
| 2008/09 | Ryder J.D. | Wellington | 18 † | 2 | 201 | 777 | 48.56 |
| 2009/10 | Taylor L.R.P.L. | Central Districts | 17 † | 0 | 138 | 852 | 50.12 |
| 2010/11 | Ingram P.J. | Central Districts | 21 † | 0 | 143 | 969 | 46.14 |
| 2011/12 | Guptill M.J. | Auckland | 23 † | 1 | 195* | 927 | 42.13 |
| 2012/13 | Fulton P.G. | Canterbury | 23 | 2 | 136 | 1249 | 59.47 |
| 2013/14 | Taylor L.R.P.L. | Central Districts | 17 † | 4 | 217* | 861 | 66.23 |
| 2014/15 | Williamson K.S. | Northern Districts | 15 † | 3 | 242* | 1070 | 89.16 |
| 2015/16 | Williamson K.S. | Northern Districts | 19 † | 2 | 166 | 1068 | 62.82 |
| 2016/17 | Williamson K.S. | Northern Districts | 21 † | 3 | 176 | 1079 | 59.94 |
| 2017/18 | Taylor L.R.P.L. | Central Districts | 8 | 1 | 107* | 375 | 53.57 |
| 2018/19 | Williamson K.S. | Northern Districts | 13 † | 2 | 200* | 885 | 80.45 |
| 2019/20 | Latham T.W.M. | Canterbury | 20 † | 1 | 224 | 875 | 46.05 |
| 2020/21 | Williamson K.S. | Northern Districts | 4 | 0 | 251 | 639 | 159.75 |
| 2021/22 | Conway D.P. | Wellington | 12 † | 0 | 200 | 767 | 63.91 |

† *including matches for New Zealand teams overseas*
§ *these figures include Blunt's scores for Otago and New Zealand against the Melbourne Cricket Club*

# WINSOR CUP

*Presented by Sir Arthur Donnelly to perpetuate the memory of Mr W.H. Winsor*

Presented to the New Zealand bowler whose performances in first-class cricket have been, in the opinion of the Board of Control, the most meritorious since the award was last made.

## HOLDERS

*Season's first-class figures*

|         |               | Team                | Matches | O     | M   | R    | W   | Ave   |
|---------|---------------|---------------------|---------|-------|-----|------|-----|-------|
| 1938/39 | Cowie J.      | Auckland            | 4       | 150   | 20  | 444  | 21  | 21.14 |
| 1939/40 | Pritchard T.L.| Wellington          | 3       | 113.3 | 9   | 404  | 23  | 17.56 |
| 1940-45 | no award      |                     |         |       |     |      |     |       |
| 1945/46 | Cowie J.      | Auckland            | 5       | 209   | 69  | 433  | 24  | 18.04 |
| 1946/47 | Cowie J.      | Auckland            | 5       | 257.4 | 61  | 578  | 26  | 22.23 |
| 1947/48 | Burtt T.B.    | Canterbury          | 4       | 256   | 57  | 666  | 26  | 25.61 |
| 1948/49 | Cresswell A.E.| Wellington          | 4       | 152   | 27  | 343  | 22  | 15.59 |
| 1949/50 | Cresswell G.F.| Wellington          | 4       | 235   | 111 | 304  | 20  | 15.20 |
| 1950/51 | Burtt T.B.    | Canterbury          | 6       | 363.2 | 151 | 673  | 44  | 15.29 |
| 1951/52 | Burtt T.B.    | Canterbury          | 6       | 317   | 120 | 643  | 37  | 17.37 |
| 1952/53 | Rabone G.O.   | Auckland            | 5       | 174   | 44  | 405  | 23  | 17.60 |
| 1953/54 | MacGibbon A.R.| Canterbury†         | 17      | 463.7 | 98  | 1271 | 63  | 20.17 |
| 1954/55 | Reid J.R.     | Wellington          | 8       | 279.1 | 121 | 496  | 30  | 16.53 |
| 1955/56 | Cave H.B.     | Central Districts*  | 18      | 673.4 | 271 | 1259 | 50  | 25.18 |
| 1956/57 | Cave H.B.     | Central Districts   | 9       | 358.3 | 138 | 685  | 41  | 16.70 |
| 1957/58 | Hayes J.A.    | Auckland            | 6       | 244.3 | 49  | 568  | 48  | 11.83 |
| 1958/59 | Hough K.W.    | Auckland            | 8       | 411.3 | 151 | 701  | 46  | 15.23 |
| 1959/60 | Alabaster J.C.| Otago               | 9       | 313   | 78  | 824  | 47  | 17.53 |
| 1960/61 | Alabaster J.C.| Otago               | 10      | 426.3 | 125 | 964  | 49  | 19.61 |
| 1961/62 | Blair R.W.    | Wellington          | 6       | 252   | 96  | 535  | 44  | 12,15 |
| 1962/63 | Blair R.W.    | Wellington          | 7       | 244.2 | 77  | 562  | 32  | 17.56 |
| 1963/64 | Blair R.W.    | Wellington          | 9       | 408.1 | 135 | 856  | 49  | 17.46 |
| 1964/65 | Motz R.C.     | Canterbury*         | 26      | 890   | 272 | 2179 | 93  | 23.43 |
| 1965/66 | Puna N.       | Northern Districts  | 8       | 338   | 126 | 706  | 38  | 18.57 |
| 1966/67 | Pollard V.    | Central Districts   | 11      | 345.4 | 141 | 672  | 41  | 16.39 |
| 1967/68 | Motz R.C.     | Canterbury          | 10      | 369.2 | 115 | 907  | 47  | 19.29 |
| 1968/69 | Motz R.C.     | Canterbury          | 9       | 265.2 | 54  | 880  | 40  | 22.00 |
| 1969/70 | Howarth H.J.  | Auckland*           | 24      | 991.4 | 355 | 2173 | 100 | 21.73 |
| 1970/71 | Collinge R.O. | Wellington          | 9       | 230.6 | 46  | 677  | 37  | 18.29 |
| 1971/72 | Taylor B.R.   | Wellington*         | 15      | 560.5 | 118 | 1474 | 69  | 21.36 |
| 1972/73 | Collinge R.O. | Wellington*         | 23      | 659.2 | 149 | 1806 | 83  | 21.75 |
| 1973/74 | Hadlee D.R.   | Canterbury*         | 13      | 336.3 | 35  | 1451 | 38  | 38.18 |
| 1974/75 | Alabaster G.D.| Otago               | 6       | 182.2 | 26  | 684  | 34  | 20.11 |
| 1975/76 | Collinge R.O. | Northern Districts  | 9       | 215.3 | 39  | 623  | 43  | 14.48 |
| 1976/77 | Hadlee R.J.   | Canterbury          | 15      | 418.2 | 41  | 1768 | 49  | 36.08 |
| 1977/78 | Hadlee R.J.   | Canterbury          | 10      | 266.1 | 56  | 860  | 42  | 20.47 |
| 1978/79 | Hadlee R.J.   | Canterbury          | 10      | 299.1 | 56  | 909  | 50  | 18.18 |
| 1979/80 | Hadlee R.J.   | New Zealand         | 3       | 161.3 | 50  | 361  | 19  | 19.00 |
| 1980/81 | Hadlee R.J.   | New Zealand*        | 8       | 349   | 89  | 855  | 37  | 23.10 |
| 1981/82 | Hadlee R.J.   | Canterbury          | 10      | 424.2 | 135 | 868  | 59  | 14.74 |
| 1982/83 | Hadlee R.J.   | Canterbury*         | 12      | 498   | 147 | 1132 | 59  | 19.18 |
| 1983/84 | Hadlee R.J.   | Canterbury*         | 10      | 310.4 | 111 | 587  | 48  | 12.22 |
| 1984/85 | Hadlee R.J.   | Canterbury*         | 12      | 429.5 | 119 | 1061 | 53  | 20.01 |
| 1985/86 | Hadlee R.J.   | Canterbury*         | 11      | 553.1 | 129 | 1314 | 72  | 18.25 |
| 1986/87 | Hadlee R.J.   | Canterbury*         | 12      | 446.1 | 116 | 1047 | 66  | 15.86 |
| 1987/88 | Chatfield E.J.| Wellington*         | 9       | 355.1 | 114 | 672  | 24  | 28.00 |

NZC

| | | Team | Matches | O | M | R | W | Ave |
|---|---|---|---|---|---|---|---|---|
| 1988/89 | Hadlee R.J. | Canterbury* | 7 | 247.5 | 59 | 541 | 34 | 15.91 |
| 1989/90 | Hadlee R.J. | New Zealand* | 9 | 349 | 71 | 1014 | 43 | 23.58 |
| 1990/91 | Watson W. | New Zealand | 8 | 333.3 | 92 | 807 | 26 | 31.03 |
| 1991/92 | Cairns C.L. | Canterbury | 8 | 294 | 67 | 872 | 42 | 20.76 |
| 1992/93 | Morrison D.K. | Auckland | 8 | 263.2 | 66 | 598 | 38 | 15.73 |
| 1993/94 | Morrison D.K. | Auckland* | 9 | 327.3 | 59 | 1021 | 28 | 36.46 |
| 1994/95 | Morrison D.K. | Auckland* | 11 | 368.5 | 82 | 1016 | 40 | 25.40 |
| 1995/96 | Cairns C.L. | New Zealand* | 8 | 232.4 | 62 | 631 | 26 | 24.26 |
| 1996/97 | Doull S.B. | New Zealand* | 8 | 255.3 | 67 | 715 | 33 | 21.66 |
| 1997/98 | Cairns C.L. | Canterbury* | 12 | 399 | 113 | 1124 | 51 | 22.03 |
| 1998/99 | Penn A.J. | Central Districts | 9 | 288 | 76 | 763 | 40 | 19.07 |
| 1999/00 | Cairns C.L. | New Zealand* | 17 | 508.5 | 124 | 1541 | 67 | 23.00 |
| 2000/01 | Tuffey D.R. | Northern Districts* | 12 | 396.5 | 118 | 1104 | 54 | 20.44 |
| 2001/02 | Drum C.J. | Auckland | 9 | 317.3 | 96 | 827 | 53 | 15.60 |
| 2002/03 | Bond S.E. | Canterbury* | 6 | 183.5 | 44 | 600 | 30 | 20.00 |
| 2003/04 | Martin C.S. | Canterbury | 12 | 448 | 141 | 1144 | 53 | 21.68 |
| 2004/05 | Vettori D.L. | Northern Districts* | 8 | 395.5 | 102 | 1052 | 40 | 26.30 |
| 2005/06 | Martin C.S. | Auckland* | 13 | 386.3 | 90 | 1199 | 50 | 23.98 |
| 2006/07 | Martin C.S. | Auckland* | 13 | 452 | 94 | 1424 | 52 | 27.38 |
| 2007/08 | Martin C.S. | Auckland* | 9 | 311.2 | 74 | 975 | 38 | 25.65 |
| 2008/09 | Vettori D.L. | Northern Districts* | 10 | 457.3 | 106 | 1071 | 40 | 26.77 |
| 2009/10 | Vettori D.L. | New Zealand* | 8 | 433.1 | 112 | 1176 | 32 | 36.75 |
| 2010/11 | Martin C.S. | Auckland* | 15 | 521.2 | 131 | 1536 | 60 | 25.60 |
| 2011/12 | Bracewell D.A.J. | Central Districts* | 10 | 301.3 | 54 | 977 | 41 | 23.82 |
| 2012/13 | Southee T.G. | Northern Districts* | 8 | 315 | 71 | 928 | 42 | 22.09 |
| 2013/14 | Southee T.G. | Northern Districts* | 9 | 320 | 60 | 967 | 48 | 20.14 |
| 2014/15 | Boult T.A. | Northern Districts* | 9 | 327 | 77 | 882 | 35 | 25.20 |
| 2015/16 | Boult T.A. | Northern Districts* | 10 | 418 | 72 | 1443 | 43 | 33.55 |
| 2016/17 | Wagner N. | Otago* | 15 | 550.2 | 118 | 1541 | 70 | 22.01 |
| 2017/18 | Wagner N. | Otago | 10 | 372.1 | 89 | 1090 | 43 | 25.34 |
| 2018/19 | Boult T.A. | Northern Districts* | 8 | 283.2 | 76 | 844 | 35 | 24.11 |
| 2019/20 | Southee T.G. | Northern Districts* | 9 | 341.5 | 84 | 915 | 41 | 22.31 |
| 2020/21 | Jamieson K.A. | Auckland | 7 | 230.1 | 77 | 548 | 47 | 11.65 |
| 2021/22 | Southee T.G. | Northern Districts* | 9 | 357.3 | 83 | 949 | 42 | 22.59 |

† *including 16 matches for New Zealand overseas*
\* *includes matches for New Zealand teams overseas*

# SUTCLIFFE MEDAL

For outstanding services to cricket.

| | | | |
|---|---|---|---|
| 1997/98 | Morrison B.D. | 2009/10 | Horton M.J. |
| | Curtis W.H.M. | 2010/11 | Renwick C. |
| 1998/99 | Neely D.O. | 2011/12 | Bull C.L. |
| 1999/00 | Gallaway I.W. | 2012/13 | no award |
| 2000/01 | Hadlee W.A. | 2013/14 | Astle A.M. |
| 2001/02 | Reid J.R. | 2014/15 | Dykes R.A. |
| 2002/03 | Cameron F.J. | 2015/16 | Smith R. |
| 2003/04 | Dowling G.T. | 2016/17 | Sulzberger L.N. |
| 2004/05 | Wallace W.M. | 2017/18 | Malcon P.J. |
| 2005/06 | Sharp P.A. | 2018/19 | Chatfield E.J. |
| 2006/07 | Shrimpton M.J.F. | 2019/20 | Smith I.D.S. |
| 2007/08 | Sir Richard Hadlee | 2020/21 | Crowe J.J. |
| 2008/09 | Whimp A.D. | 2021/22 | Kinsella P.D. |

# TOURING TEAMS IN NEW ZEALAND

| | | FIRST-CLASS MATCHES | | | | ALL MATCHES | | | |
|---|---|---|---|---|---|---|---|---|---|
| | | P | W | L | D | P | W | L | D |
| 1863/64 | G. Parr's England Team | — | — | — | — | 4 | 3 | — | 1 |
| 1876/77 | J. Lillywhite's England Team | — | — | — | — | 8 | 6 | — | 2 |
| 1877/78 | Australia | — | — | — | — | 7 | 5 | 1 | 1 |
| 1880/81 | Australia | — | — | — | — | 10 | 6 | 1 | 3 |
| 1881/82 | A. Shaw's England Team | — | — | — | — | 7 | 5 | — | 2 |
| 1883/84 | Tasmania | 4 | — | 3 | 1 | 7 | 2 | 3 | 2 |
| 1886/87 | Australia | — | — | — | — | 5 | 2 | — | 3 |
| 1887/88 | C.A. Smith's England Team | — | — | — | — | 3 | — | — | 3 |
| 1888/89 | English Footballers | — | — | — | — | 1 | — | — | 1 |
| 1889/90 | New South Wales | 5 | 4 | — | 1 | 7 | 6 | — | 1 |
| 1893/94 | New South Wales | 7 | 4 | 1 | 2 | 8 | 4 | 1 | 3 |
| 1894/95 | Fiji | 6 | 2 | 2 | 2 | 8 | 4 | 2 | 2 |
| 1895/96 | New South Wales | 5 | 3 | 1 | 1 | 5 | 3 | 1 | 1 |
| 1896/97 | Australia | — | — | — | — | 5 | 3 | — | 2 |
| 1896/97 | Queensland | 5 | 3 | 1 | 1 | 8 | 4 | 1 | 3 |
| 1899/00 | Melbourne Cricket Club | — | — | — | — | 7 | 6 | — | 1 |
| 1902/03 | Lord Hawke's England Team | 7 | 7 | — | — | 18 | 18 | — | — |
| 1904/05 | Australia | 4 | 3 | — | 1 | 6 | 4 | — | 2 |
| 1905/06 | Melbourne Cricket Club | — | — | — | — | 10 | 8 | — | 2 |
| 1906/07 | MCC | 11 | 6 | 2 | 3 | 16 | 10 | 2 | 4 |
| 1909/10 | Australia | 6 | 5 | — | 1 | 9 | 7 | — | 2 |
| 1913/14 | A. Sims' Australian Team | 8 | 6 | — | 2 | 16 | 8 | — | 8 |
| 1920/21 | Australia | 9 | 6 | — | 3 | 15 | 12 | — | 3 |
| 1922/23 | MCC | 8 | 6 | — | 2 | 14 | 11 | — | 3 |
| 1923/24 | New South Wales | 6 | 5 | — | 1 | 12 | 8 | — | 4 |
| 1924/25 | Victoria | 6 | 1 | 1 | 4 | 12 | 4 | 1 | 7 |
| 1926/27 | Melbourne Cricket Club | — | — | — | — | 13 | 5 | — | 8 |
| 1927/28 | Australia | 6 | 4 | — | 2 | 13 | 6 | — | 7 |
| 1929/30 | MCC | 8 | 2 | — | 6 | 17 | 9 | — | 8 |
| 1930/31 | West Indies | — | — | — | — | 1 | — | — | 1 |
| 1931/32 | South Africa | 3 | 3 | — | — | 3 | 3 | — | — |
| 1932/33 | MCC | 3 | — | — | 3 | 3 | — | — | 3 |
| 1935/36 | MCC | 8 | 2 | 1 | 5 | 18 | 5 | 1 | 12 |
| 1936/37 | MCC | 3 | 1 | — | 2 | 3 | 1 | — | 2 |
| 1938/39 | Sir Julien Cahn's XI | 1 | — | — | 1 | 10 | 2 | — | 8 |
| 1945/46 | Australia | 5 | 5 | — | — | 5 | 5 | — | — |
| 1946/47 | MCC | 4 | 2 | — | 2 | 4 | 2 | — | 2 |
| 1947/48 | Fiji | 5 | 2 | 3 | — | 17 | 6 | 3 | 8 |
| 1949/50 | Australia B | 5 | 3 | — | 2 | 14 | 9 | — | 5 |
| 1950/51 | MCC | 4 | 3 | — | 1 | 4 | 3 | — | 1 |
| 1951/52 | West Indies | 4 | 2 | — | 2 | 5 | 3 | — | 2 |
| 1952/53 | South Africa | 4 | 1 | — | 3 | 5 | 1 | — | 4 |
| 1953/54 | Fiji | 4 | 1 | 3 | — | 17 | 8 | 6 | 3 |
| 1954/55 | MCC | 4 | 4 | — | — | 4 | 4 | — | — |
| 1955/56 | West Indies | 8 | 6 | 1 | 1 | 15 | 11 | 1 | 3 |
| 1956/57 | Australia B | 7 | 5 | — | 2 | 12 | 7 | — | 5 |
| 1958/59 | MCC | 5 | 3 | — | 2 | 5 | 3 | — | 2 |
| 1959/60 | Australia B | 6 | 2 | — | 4 | 9 | 4 | — | 5 |

NZC

| | | FIRST-CLASS MATCHES | | | | ALL MATCHES | | | |
|---|---|---|---|---|---|---|---|---|---|
| | | P | W | L | D | P | W | L | D |
| 1960/61 | MCC | 10 | 4 | 1 | 5 | 21 | 11 | 1 | 9 |
| 1961/62 | Fiji | — | — | — | — | 22 | 9 | 9 | 4 |
| 1961/62 | R.A. Roberts' Commonwealth XI | 2 | 2 | — | — | 3 | 2 | — | 1 |
| 1962/63 | MCC | 4 | 4 | — | — | 4 | 4 | — | — |
| 1963/64 | South Africa | 4 | 1 | — | 3 | 7 | 1 | — | 6 |
| 1964/65 | Pakistan | 10 | 2 | — | 8 | 12 | 4 | — | 8 |
| 1965/66 | MCC | 4 | — | — | 4 | 4 | — | — | 4 |
| 1966/67 | Australia B | 9 | 1 | 2 | 6 | 10 | 2 | 2 | 6 |
| 1967/68 | Fiji | — | — | — | — | 25 | 12 | 7 | 6 |
| 1967/68 | India | 6 | 4 | 1 | 1 | 6 | 4 | 1 | 1 |
| 1968/69 | West Indies | 6 | 1 | 2 | 3 | 7 | 1 | 2 | 4 |
| 1969/70 | Australia B | 8 | 2 | — | 6 | 8 | 2 | — | 6 |
| 1970/71 | MCC | 2 | 1 | — | 1 | 5 | 3 | 1 | 1 |
| 1972/73 | Pakistan | 8 | 5 | 1 | 2 | 11 | 6 | 3 | 2 |
| 1973/74 | Australia | 7 | 2 | 1 | 4 | 11 | 6 | 1 | 4 |
| 1974/75 | MCC | 3 | 1 | — | 2 | 5 | 1 | — | 4 |
| 1975/76 | India | 6 | 3 | 1 | 2 | 9 | 3 | 4 | 2 |
| 1976/77 | Australia | 6 | 5 | — | 1 | 8 | 5 | 2 | 1 |
| 1977/78 | Fiji | — | — | — | — | 15 | 5 | 4 | 6 |
| 1977/78 | England | 8 | 3 | 1 | 4 † | 9 | 4 | 1 | 4 † |
| 1978/79 | Pakistan | 8 | 5 | — | 3 | 10 | 6 | 1 | 3 |
| 1979/80 | West Indies | 5 | — | 2 | 3 | 8 | 2 | 3 | 3 |
| 1979/80 | D.H. Robins' XI | 2 | — | — | 2 | 8 | 5 | 1 | 2 |
| 1980/81 | India | 5 | 1 | 1 | 3 | 7 | 1 | 3 | 3 |
| 1981/82 | Australia | 5 | 1 | 1 | 3 | 11 | 4 | 4 | 3 |
| 1982/83 | England | — | — | — | — | 3 | — | 3 | — |
| 1982/83 | Sri Lanka | 4 | — | 3 | 1 | 9 | 1 | 7 | 1 |
| 1983/84 | England | 7 | 1 | 1 | 5 | 11 | 4 | 2 | 5 |
| 1984/85 | Pakistan | 5 | 1 | 2 | 2 | 9 | 1 | 5 | 3 |
| 1985/86 | Australia | 5 | 1 | 1 | 3 | 11 | 5 | 3 | 3 |
| 1986/87 | West Indies | 5 | 1 | 1 | 3 | 9 | 5 | 1 | 3 |
| 1987/88 | England | 7 | 2 | 1 | 4 | 12 | 5 | 3 | 4 |
| 1988/89 | Pakistan | 5 | 1 | — | 4 | 12 | 2 | 5 | 5 |
| 1989/90 | India | 6 | 1 | 1 | 4 | 10 | 2 | 4 | 4 |
| 1989/90 | Australia | 1 | — | 1 | — | 6 | 5 | 1 | — |
| 1990/91 | Sri Lanka | 7 | 1 | — | 6 | 10 | 1 | 3 | 6 |
| 1990/91 | England | — | — | — | — | 3 | 1 | 2 | — |
| 1991/92 | England | 7 | 4 | — | 3 | 11 | 8 | — | 3 |
| 1991/92 | Zimbabwe | — | — | — | — | 3 | 1 | 2 | — |
| 1991/92 | Australia | — | — | — | — | 1 | 1 | — | — |
| 1991/92 | Sri Lanka | — | — | — | — | 1 | 1 | — | — |
| 1992/93 | Pakistan | 1 | 1 | — | — | 4 | 2 | 2 | — |
| 1992/93 | Australia | 4 | 2 | 1 | 1 | 10 | 5 | 4 | 1 |
| 1993/94 | Pakistan | 5 | 2 | 1 | 2 | 11 | 6 | 2 | 3 † |
| 1993/94 | India | 3 | — | — | 3 | 7 | 2 | 2 | 3 |
| 1994/95 | West Indies | 3 | 1 | — | 2 | 8 | 6 | — | 2 |
| 1994/95 | Australia | — | — | — | — | 4 | 3 | 1 | — |
| 1994/95 | South Africa | 2 | 2 | — | — | 6 | 3 | 2 | 1 † |
| 1994/95 | India | — | — | — | — | 4 | 2 | 2 | — |
| 1994/95 | Sri Lanka | 4 | 2 | — | 2 | 9 | 4 | 2 | 3 |
| 1994/95 | Australian Academy | 1 | 1 | — | — | 5 | 5 | — | — |

|  |  | FIRST-CLASS MATCHES | | | | ALL MATCHES | | | |
|---|---|---|---|---|---|---|---|---|---|
|  |  | P | W | L | D | P | W | L | D |
| 1995/96 | Pakistan | 1 | 1 | — | — | 5 | 3 | 2 | — |
| 1995/96 | Zimbabwe | 4 | 1 | — | 3 | 8 | 3 | 2 | 3 |
| 1996/97 | England | 6 | 4 | 1 | 1 | 12 | 6 | 3 | 3 † |
| 1996/97 | Sri Lanka | 2 | — | 2 | — | 6 | 2 | 3 | 1 |
| 1997/98 | Bangladesh | 4 | — | 4 | — | 7 | — | 6 | 1 |
| 1997/98 | Zimbabwe | 4 | 1 | 3 | — | 10 | 3 | 7 | — |
| 1998/99 | Pakistan A | 5 | — | 1 | 4 | 10 | 1 | 4 | 5 |
| 1998/99 | India | 4 | 1 | 2 | 1 | 10 | 3 | 5 | 2 |
| 1998/99 | South Africa | 5 | 1 | — | 4 | 13 | 5 | 2 | 6 |
| 1999/00 | England A | 5 | 3 | — | 2 | 10 | 7 | — | 3 |
| 1999/00 | West Indies | 4 | — | 2 | 2 | 10 | — | 8 | 2 |
| 1999/00 | Australia | 5 | 4 | — | 1 | 11 | 8 | 1 | 2 |
| 2000/01 | Zimbabwe | 2 | — | — | 2 | 6 | 3 | 1 | 2 |
| 2000/01 | Sri Lanka | — | — | — | — | 6 | 4 | 2 | — |
| 2000/01 | Pakistan | 5 | 1 | 2 | 2 | 10 | 3 | 5 | 2 |
| 2001/02 | Bangladesh | 3 | — | 3 | — | 4 | — | 3 | 1 |
| 2001/02 | England | 5 | 1 | 1 | 3 | 12 | 4 | 5 | 3 |
| 2002/03 | India | 3 | — | 2 | 1 | 11 | 2 | 8 | 1 |
| 2003/04 | Pakistan | 3 | 1 | — | 2 | 9 | 3 | 4 | 2 |
| 2003/04 | South Africa | 4 | 1 | 1 | 2 | 11 | 3 | 6 | 2 |
| 2003/04 | Sri Lanka A | 4 | — | 3 | 1 | 6 | — | 5 | 1 |
| 2004/05 | Sri Lanka | 3 | — | 1 | 2 | 5 | — | 2 | 3 |
| 2004/05 | FICA World XI | — | — | — | — | 3 | 1 | 2 | — |
| 2004/05 | Australia | 3 | 2 | — | 1 | 9 | 8 | — | 1 |
| 2005/06 | Australia | — | — | — | — | 3 | 2 | 1 | — |
| 2005/06 | Sri Lanka | — | — | — | — | 4 | 1 | 3 | — |
| 2005/06 | West Indies | 3 | — | 2 | 1 | 9 | 1 | 7 | 1 |
| 2006/07 | Sri Lanka | 2 | 1 | 1 | — | 10 | 4 | 4 | 2 |
| 2006/07 | Australia | — | — | — | — | 3 | — | 3 | — |
| 2007/08 | Bangladesh | 2 | — | 2 | — | 9 | 1 | 7 | 1 |
| 2007/08 | England | 4 | 2 | 1 | 1 | 14 | 7 | 4 | 3 † |
| 2008/09 | West Indies | 3 | — | — | 3 | 10 | 2 | 3 | 5 |
| 2008/09 | India | 3 | 1 | — | 2 | 10 | 4 | 3 | 3 |
| 2008/09 | England Lions | 2 | — | — | 2 | 7 | — | 3 | 4 |
| 2009/10 | Pakistan | 3 | 1 | 1 | 1 | 4 | 1 | 1 | 2 |
| 2009/10 | Bangladesh | 1 | — | 1 | — | 5 | — | 5 | — |
| 2009/10 | Australia | 2 | 2 | — | — | 9 | 6 | 3 | — |
| 2010/11 | Pakistan | 2 | 1 | — | 1 | 13 | 5 | 5 | 3 |
| 2011/12 | Zimbabwe | 1 | — | 1 | — | 7 | — | 6 | 1 |
| 2011/12 | South Africa | 3 | 1 | — | 2 | 10 | 7 | 1 | 2 |
| 2012/13 | India A | 2 | — | — | 2 | 6 | 1 | 1 | 4 |
| 2012/13 | England | 4 | — | 1 | 3 | 13 | 5 | 4 | 4 |
| 2013/14 | West Indies | 3 | — | 2 | 1 | 10 | 2 | 6 | 2 |
| 2013/14 | India | 2 | — | 1 | 1 | 8 | — | 5 | 3 † |
| 2014/15 | Afghanistan | — | — | — | — | 4 | 1 | 3 | — |
| 2014/15 | Scotland | — | — | — | — | 4 | 1 | 3 | — |
| 2014/15 | Ireland | — | — | — | — | 4 | — | 3 | 1 |
| 2014/15 | Sri Lanka | 2 | — | 2 | — | 12 | 2 | 8 | 2 |
| 2014/15 | Zimbabwe | — | — | — | — | 5 | 4 | — | 1 |
| 2014/15 | South Africa | — | — | — | — | 2 | 1 | 1 | — |
| 2015/16 | Sri Lanka A | 2 | — | 1 | 1 | 8 | 2 | 5 | 1 |

| | | FIRST-CLASS MATCHES | | | | ALL MATCHES | | | |
|---|---|---|---|---|---|---|---|---|---|
| | | P | W | L | D | P | W | L | D |
| 2015/16 | Sri Lanka | 2 | — | 2 | — | 10 | 1 | 7 | 2 |
| 2015/16 | Pakistan | — | — | — | — | 5 | 1 | 4 | — |
| 2015/16 | Australia | 2 | 2 | — | — | 5 | 3 | 2 | — |
| 2016/17 | Pakistan | 3 | — | 2 | 1 | 3 | — | 2 | 1 |
| 2016/17 | Bangladesh | 2 | — | 2 | — | 9 | — | 9 | — |
| 2016/17 | Australia | — | — | — | — | 2 | — | 2 | — |
| 2016/17 | South Africa | 3 | 1 | — | 2 | 9 | 5 | 2 | 2 |
| 2017/18 | West Indies | 2 | — | 2 | — | 10 | — | 8 | 2 |
| 2017/18 | Pakistan | — | — | — | — | 9 | 3 | 6 | — |
| 2017/18 | Australia | — | — | — | — | 1 | — | 1 | — |
| 2017/18 | England | 2 | — | 1 | 1 | 11 | 4 | 4 | 3 |
| 2018/19 | Sri Lanka | 2 | — | 1 | 1 | 7 | — | 5 | 2 |
| 2018/19 | India | — | — | — | — | 8 | 5 | 3 | — |
| 2018/19 | Bangladesh | 2 | — | 2 | — | 7 | — | 6 | 1 |
| 2019/20 | England | 3 | — | 1 | 2 | 11 | 4 | 4 | 3 |
| 2019/20 | India | 2 | — | 2 | — | 11 | 5 | 5 | 1 |
| 2020/21 | West Indies | 3 | — | 2 | 1 | 7 | — | 4 | 3 |
| 2020/21 | West Indies A | 2 | — | 2 | — | 2 | — | 2 | — |
| 2020/21 | Pakistan A | 1 | 1 | — | — | 6 | 3 | 3 | — |
| 2020/21 | Pakistan | 2 | — | 2 | — | 5 | 1 | 4 | — |
| 2020/21 | Australia | — | — | — | — | 5 | 2 | 3 | — |
| 2020/21 | Bangladesh | — | — | — | — | 6 | — | 6 | — |
| 2021/22 | Bangladesh | 2 | 1 | 1 | — | 3 | 1 | 1 | 1 |
| 2021/22 | South Africa | 2 | 1 | 1 | — | 2 | 1 | 1 | — |
| 2021/22 | Netherlands | — | — | — | — | 5 | — | 5 | — |

† *includes a tie*

**NB:** From 1900 the basis for inclusion is any of the following:

a) First-class matches were played.

b) The touring side was its country's official team.

c) The touring side played an official New Zealand team.

d) Matches in the 1992 and 2015 World Cups are not included, although preliminary games played by Zimbabwe, Australia and Sri Lanka in 1992 and by Zimbabwe, South Africa and Sri Lanka in 2015 are.

# NEW ZEALAND TOURING TEAMS

| | | FIRST-CLASS MATCHES | | | | ALL MATCHES | | | |
|---|---|---|---|---|---|---|---|---|---|
| | | P | W | L | D | P | W | L | D |
| 1898/99 | Australia | 2 | — | 2 | — | 4 | 1 | 2 | 1 |
| 1913/14 | Australia | 4 | 1 | 2 | 1 | 9 | 5 | 2 | 2 |
| 1925/26 | Australia | 4 | — | 1 | 3 | 9 | 3 | 1 | 5 |
| 1927 | Great Britain | 26 | 7 | 5 | 14 | 38 | 12 | 5 | 21 |
| | Ceylon | — | — | — | — | 1 | — | — | 1 |
| 1927/28 | Australia | 1 | — | 1 | — | 1 | — | 1 | — |
| 1931 | Great Britain | 32 | 6 | 3 | 23 | 36 | 7 | 3 | 26 |
| 1937 | Great Britain | 32 | 9 | 9 | 14 | 38 | 14 | 9 | 15 |
| | Ceylon | — | — | — | — | 1 | — | — | 1 |
| 1937/38 | Australia | 3 | — | 3 | — | 3 | — | 3 | — |
| 1949 | Great Britain | 32 | 13 | 1 | 18 | 35 | 14 | 1 | 20 |
| | West Germany | — | — | — | — | 1 | 1 | — | — |
| 1953/54 | South Africa | 16 | 3 | 4 | 9 | 17 | 3 | 4 | 10 |
| | Australia | 3 | 2 | — | 1 | 3 | 2 | — | 1 |
| 1955/56 | Pakistan | 6 | 1 | 3 | 2 | 6 | 1 | 3 | 2 |
| | India | 10 | 2 | 3 | 5 | 10 | 2 | 3 | 5 |
| 1958 | Great Britain | 31 | 7 | 6 | 18 † | 35 | 7 | 6 | 22 |
| 1961/62 | South Africa | 18 | 5 | 2 | 11 | 24 | 7 | 2 | 15 |
| | Australia | 3 | — | 2 | 1 | 3 | — | 2 | 1 |
| 1964/65 | India | 4 | — | 1 | 3 | 4 | — | 1 | 3 |
| | Pakistan | 3 | — | 2 | 1 | 3 | — | 2 | 1 |
| 1965 | Great Britain | 19 | 3 | 6 | 10 | 21 | 4 | 6 | 11 |
| | Holland | — | — | — | — | 1 | — | — | 1 |
| | Bermuda | — | — | — | — | 2 | — | — | 2 |
| | USA | — | — | — | — | 1 | 1 | — | — |
| 1967/68 | Australia | 4 | — | 2 | 2 | 7 | 2 | 2 | 3 |
| 1969 | Great Britain | 18 | 4 | 3 | 11 | 22 | 5 | 4 | 13 |
| 1969/70 | India | 5 | 1 | 1 | 3 | 5 | 1 | 1 | 3 |
| 1969/70 | Pakistan | 4 | 1 | — | 3 | 4 | 1 | — | 3 |
| 1969/70 | Australia | 3 | — | — | 3 | 8 | 3 | — | 5 |
| 1970/71 | Australia | 1 | — | — | 1 | 2 | — | 1 | 1 |
| 1971/72* | Australia | — | — | — | — | 2 | 1 | — | 1 |
| 1971/72 | West Indies | 13 | 1 | — | 12 | 16 | 4 | — | 12 |
| 1972/73 | Australia | 1 | — | — | 1 | 3 | 2 | — | 1 |
| 1973 | Great Britain | 19 | 3 | 2 | 14 | 23 | 4 | 3 | 16 |
| 1973/74 | Australia | 9 | 2 | 5 | 2 | 13 | 5 | 6 | 2 |
| 1974/75 | Australia | — | — | — | — | 3 | 3 | — | — |
| 1975 | England *(Prudential Cup)* | — | — | — | — | 4 | 2 | 2 | — |
| 1976/77 | Pakistan | 6 | 1 | 3 | 2 | 7 | 2 | 3 | 2 |
| | India | 3 | — | 2 | 1 | 3 | — | 2 | 1 |
| 1978 | Great Britain | 16 | 5 | 4 | 7 | 20 | 5 | 8 | 7 |
| 1979 | Great Britain *(Prudential Cup)* | — | — | — | — | 4 | 2 | 2 | — |
| 1980/81 | Australia | 7 | 1 | 2 | 4 | 29 | 14 | 9 | 6 |
| 1982/83 | Australia | 2 | — | — | 2 † | 4 | 1 | 1 | 2 † |
| 1982/83 | Australia | — | — | — | — | 18 | 12 | 6 | — |
| 1983 | England | 13 | 7 | 3 | 3 | 21 | 11 | 6 | 4 |
| 1983/84 | Sri Lanka | 5 | 2 | — | 3 | 8 | 4 | 1 | 3 |
| 1984/85 | Sri Lanka | — | — | — | — | 2 | 1 | 1 | — |
| | Pakistan | 5 | — | 2 | 3 | 9 | 1 | 5 | 3 |
| 1984/85 | Australia *(WCC)* | — | — | — | — | 4 | 1 | 2 | 1 |
| 1984/85 | West Indies | 7 | — | 2 | 5 | 12 | — | 7 | 5 |
| 1985/86 | Australia | 6 | 2 | 1 | 3 | 8 | 2 | 1 | 5 |

| | | FIRST-CLASS MATCHES | | | | ALL MATCHES | | | |
|---|---|---|---|---|---|---|---|---|---|
| | | *P* | *W* | *L* | *D* | *P* | *W* | *L* | *D* |
| 1985/86 | Australia | — | — | — | — | 11 | 3 | 6 | 2 |
| 1985/86 ⌠ | Sri Lanka | — | — | — | — | 2 | 1 | 1 | — |
| ⎨ | Sharjah | — | — | — | — | 2 | — | 2 | — |
| ⌡ | Hong Kong | — | — | — | — | 2 | 2 | — | — |
| 1986 ⌠ | England | 15 | 4 | — | 11 | 18 | 5 | 1 | 12 |
| ⌡ | Holland | — | — | — | — | 2 | 1 | 1 | — |
| 1986/87 | Sri Lanka | 2 | — | — | 2 | 2 | — | — | 2 |
| 1987/88 | India *(Reliance World Cup)* | — | — | — | — | 6 | 2 | 4 | — |
| 1987/88 | Australia | 6 | 1 | 2 | 3 | 19 | 8 | 8 | 3 |
| 1987/88 | Sharjah | — | — | — | — | 4 | 2 | 2 | — |
| 1988/89 | India | 6 | 1 | 2 | 3 | 10 | 1 | 6 | 3 |
| 1988/89 | Australia | — | — | — | — | 1 | — | 1 | — |
| 1989/90 | Australia | 3 | — | — | 3 | 4 | — | 1 | 3 |
| 1990 ⌠ | Sharjah | — | — | — | — | 3 | 1 | 2 | — |
| ⌡ | England | 12 | 4 | 2 | 6 | 19 | 8 | 5 | 6 |
| 1990/91 | Pakistan | 5 | — | 3 | 2 | 8 | — | 6 | 2 |
| 1990/91 | Australia | — | — | — | — | 10 | 3 | 7 | — |
| 1991/92 | Australia | — | — | — | — | 6 | 4 | 2 | — |
| 1992/93 ⌠ | Zimbabwe | 3 | 2 | — | 1 | 6 | 5 | — | 1 |
| ⌡ | Sri Lanka | 2 | — | 1 | 1 | 7 | — | 5 | 2 |
| 1993/94 | Australia | 7 | 2 | 3 | 2 | 16 | 5 | 9 | 2 |
| 1994 ⌠ | Sharjah | — | — | — | — | 3 | 1 | 2 | — |
| ⌡ | Great Britain | 12 | 1 | 3 | 8 | 21 | 8 | 5 | 8 |
| 1994/95 ⌠ | India | — | — | — | — | 4 | — | 3 | 1 |
| ⌡ | South Africa | 7 | 2 | 3 | 2 | 16 | 3 | 9 | 4 |
| 1995/96 | India | 6 | — | 1 | 5 | 11 | 2 | 4 | 5 |
| 1995/96 ⌠ | India & Pakistan *(Wills World Cup)* | — | — | — | — | 6 | 3 | 3 | — |
| 1995/96 ⌡ | West Indies | 4 | 1 | 2 | 1 | 13 | 7 | 5 | 1 |
| 1996/97 ⌠ | Sharjah | — | — | — | — | 5 | 1 | 3 | 1 † |
| 1996/97 ⌡ | Pakistan | 3 | 1 | 1 | 1 | 6 | 2 | 3 | 1 |
| 1996/97 | India *(Independence Cup)* | — | — | — | — | 3 | 1 | 2 | — |
| 1997/98 ⌠ | Kenya | — | — | — | — | 3 | 2 | — | 1 |
| ⌡ | Zimbabwe | 3 | — | — | 3 | 7 | 2 | 1 | 4 † |
| 1997/98 | Australia | 6 | — | 5 | 1 | 21 | 5 | 13 | 3 † |
| 1997/98 | Sharjah | — | — | — | — | 4 | 1 | 3 | — |
| 1997/98 | Sri Lanka | 5 | 1 | 2 | 2 | 11 | 3 | 4 | 4 |
| 1998 | Malaysia *(Commonwealth Games)* | — | — | — | — | 5 | 4 | 1 | — |
| 1998/99 | Bangladesh *(Wills International Cup)* | — | — | — | — | 2 | 1 | 1 | — |
| 1999 | England | 10 | 5 | 2 | 3 | 26 | 14 | 8 | 4 |
| 1999/00 | India | 6 | — | 2 | 4 | 11 | 2 | 5 | 4 |
| 2000/01 ⌠ | Singapore | — | — | — | — | 2 | — | 2 | — |
| 2000/01 ⎨ | Zimbabwe | 4 | 2 | — | 2 | 8 | 4 | 2 | 2 |
| 2000/01 ⎨ | Kenya | — | — | — | — | 3 | 3 | — | — |
| 2000/01 ⌡ | South Africa | 6 | 2 | 2 | 2 | 14 | 4 | 7 | 3 |
| 2000/01 | Sharjah | — | — | — | — | 4 | 1 | 3 | — |
| 2001/02 | Sri Lanka | — | — | — | — | 7 | 3 | 4 | — |
| 2001/02 | Australia | 5 | — | 1 | 4 | 21 | 6 | 8 | 7 |
| 2001/02 ⌠ | Sharjah | — | — | — | — | 4 | 1 | 3 | — |
| 2001/02 ⌡ | Pakistan | 1 | — | 1 | — | 4 | — | 4 | — |
| 2001/02 | West Indies | 2 | 1 | — | 1 | 8 | 3 | 3 | 2 |
| 2002/03 ⌠ | Australia | — | — | — | — | 4 | 4 | — | — |
| 2002/03 ⌡ | Sri Lanka *(ICC Champions Trophy)* | — | — | — | — | 4 | 2 | 2 | — |
| 2002/03 | South Africa *(World Cup)* | — | — | — | — | 11 | 7 | 4 | — |
| 2002/03 | Sri Lanka | 2 | — | — | 2 | 9 | 3 | 2 | 4 |

| | | FIRST-CLASS MATCHES | | | | ALL MATCHES | | | |
|---|---|---|---|---|---|---|---|---|---|
| | | P | W | L | D | P | W | L | D |
| 2003/04 | India | 4 | — | — | 4 | 10 | 1 | 4 | 5 |
| 2003/04 | Pakistan | — | — | — | — | 5 | — | 5 | — |
| 2004 | England | 7 | 1 | 4 | 2 | 16 | 7 | 5 | 4 |
| 2004 | England *(ICC Champions Trophy)* | — | — | — | — | 2 | 1 | 1 | — |
| 2004/05 | Bangladesh | 2 | 2 | — | — | 6 | 5 | — | 1 |
| 2004/05 | Australia | 3 | — | 3 | — | 6 | 2 | 4 | — |
| 2005/06 ⌠ | Namibia | — | — | — | — | 2 | 2 | — | — |
| 2005/06 ⌡ | Zimbabwe | 2 | 2 | — | — | 8 | 7 | 1 | — |
| 2005/06 | South Africa | — | — | — | — | 8 | 3 | 4 | 1 |
| 2005/06 | South Africa | 4 | — | 2 | 2 | 4 | — | 2 | 2 |
| 2006/07 | India *(ICC Champions Trophy)* | — | — | — | — | 6 | 4 | 2 | — |
| 2006/07 | Australia | — | — | — | — | 8 | 2 | 6 | — |
| 2006/07 | West Indies *(ICC World Cup)* | — | — | — | — | 12 | 8 | 4 | — |
| 2007/08 | South Africa *(Twenty20 World Championship)* | — | — | — | — | 6 | 3 | 3 | — |
| 2007/08 ⌠ | South Africa | 4 | 1 | 3 | — | 8 | 2 | 6 | — |
| 2007/08 ⌡ | Australia | — | — | — | — | 5 | — | 4 | 1 |
| 2008 | England | 7 | 1 | 2 | 4 | 17 | 4 | 4 | 6 |
| 2008/09 | Bangladesh | 2 | 1 | — | 1 | 5 | 3 | 1 | 1 |
| 2008/09 | Australia | 3 | — | 3 | — | 3 | — | 3 | — |
| 2008/09 | Australia | — | — | — | — | 7 | 2 | 4 | 1 |
| 2009 | England *(ICC World Twenty20)* | — | — | — | — | 5 | 2 | 3 | — |
| 2009/10 | Sri Lanka | 4 | — | 2 | 2 | 9 | 2 | 5 | 2 |
| 2009/10 | South Africa *(ICC Champions Trophy)* | — | — | — | — | 5 | 3 | 2 | — |
| 2009/10 | United Arab Emirates | — | — | — | — | 5 | 2 | 3 | — |
| 2009/10 | West Indies *(ICC World Twenty20)* | — | — | — | — | 5 | 3 | 2 | — |
| 2009/10 | United States of America | — | — | — | — | 2 | 1 | 1 | — |
| 2010/11 | Sri Lanka | — | — | — | — | 6 | 3 | 2 | 1 |
| 2010/11 | Bangladesh | — | — | — | — | 4 | — | 4 | — |
| 2010/11 | India | 3 | — | 1 | 2 | 8 | — | 6 | 2 |
| 2010/11 | India, Sri Lanka, Bangladesh *(ICC World Cup)* | — | — | — | — | 10 | 6 | 4 | — |
| 2011/12 | Zimbabwe | 1 | 1 | — | — | 7 | 5 | 1 | 1 |
| 2011/12 | Australia | 3 | 1 | 1 | 1 | 3 | 1 | 1 | 1 |
| 2012 ⌠ | United States of America | — | — | — | — | 2 | — | 2 | — |
| 2012 ⌡ | West Indies | 3 | — | 2 | 1 | 8 | 1 | 6 | 1 |
| 2012/13 | India | 2 | — | 2 | — | 4 | 1 | 2 | 1 |
| 2012/13 | Sri Lanka *(ICC World Twenty20)* | — | — | — | — | 5 | 1 | 4 | — |
| 2012/13 | Sri Lanka | 2 | 1 | 1 | — | 8 | 1 | 4 | 3 |
| 2012/13 | South Africa | 2 | — | 2 | — | 10 | 4 | 5 | 1 |
| 2013 | England | 4 | 1 | 2 | 1 | 12 | 5 | 4 | 3 |
| 2013/14 ⌠ | Bangladesh | 2 | — | — | 2 | 6 | 1 | 3 | 2 |
| 2013/14 ⌡ | Sri Lanka | — | — | — | — | 4 | 1 | 1 | 2 |
| 2013/14 | Bangladesh *(ICC World Twenty20)* | — | — | — | — | 4 | 2 | 2 | — |
| 2013/14 | West Indies | 3 | 2 | 1 | — | 7 | 4 | 2 | 1 |
| 2014/15 | Pakistan *(played in United Arab Emirates)* | 3 | 1 | 1 | 1 | 11 | 5 | 4 | 2 |
| 2015 | England | 3 | 2 | 1 | — | 11 | 6 | 5 | — |
| 2015/16 ⌠ | Zimbabwe | — | — | — | — | 4 | 3 | 1 | — |
| 2015/16 ⌡ | South Africa | — | — | — | — | 7 | 4 | 3 | — |
| 2015/16 | Australia | 4 | — | 2 | 2 | 7 | 1 | 2 | 4 |
| 2015/16 | India *(ICC World Twenty20)* | — | — | — | — | 5 | 4 | 1 | — |
| 2015/16 ⌠ | Zimbabwe | 2 | 2 | — | — | 3 | 3 | — | — |
| 2015/16 ⌡ | South Africa | 2 | — | 1 | 1 | 2 | — | 1 | 1 |
| 2016/17 | India | 3 | — | 3 | — | 9 | 2 | 6 | 1 |
| 2016/17 | Australia | — | — | — | — | 3 | — | 3 | — |

| | | FIRST-CLASS MATCHES | | | | ALL MATCHES | | | |
|---|---|---|---|---|---|---|---|---|---|
| | | P | W | L | D | P | W | L | D |
| 2017 | Ireland | — | — | — | — | 4 | 3 | 1 | — |
| 2017 | England *(ICC Champions Trophy)* | — | — | — | — | 5 | 1 | 3 | 1 |
| 2017/18 | India | — | — | — | — | 8 | 3 | 5 | — |
| 2018/19 | United Arab Emirates | 3 | 2 | 1 | — | 10 | 4 | 5 | 1 |
| 2019 | England *(ICC World Cup)* | — | — | — | — | 12 | 7 | 5 | — |
| 2019/20 | Sri Lanka | 2 | 1 | 1 | — | 7 | 4 | 2 | 1 |
| 2019/20 | Australia | 3 | — | 3 | — | 4 | — | 3 | 1 |
| 2019/20 | Australia | — | — | — | — | 1 | — | 1 | — |
| 2021 | England | 3 | 2 | — | 1 | 3 | 2 | — | 1 |
| 2012/22 ⎰ | Bangladesh | — | — | — | — | 5 | 2 | 3 | — |
| ⎱ | Pakistan | — | — | — | — | — | — | — | — |
| 2021/22 | United Arab Emirates | — | — | — | — | 10 | 7 | 3 | — |
| | *(ICC Twenty20 World Cup)* | | | | | | | | |
| 2021/22 | India | 2 | — | 1 | 1 | 5 | — | 4 | 1 |
| 2022 | England | 3 | — | 3 | — | 5 | — | 4 | 1 |

† *includes a tie*

**NB:** 1) All tours refer to those undertaken by official New Zealand sides. Unofficial practice matches have not been included in the totals.

2) The first team from New Zealand to tour overseas was Canterbury who visited Victoria and Tasmania in 1878/79. This was the first tour ever undertaken by a domestic association from any country. (None of the games are ranked as first-class.)

3) Where countries are bracketed it indicates this represented a single tour. Where there is more than one entry for the same season but countries are not bracketed, the tours were not connected.

4) The 1974/75, second 1982/83, 1990/91, 1993/94 and 1997/98 tours to Australia included a return trip after the teams had come back to New Zealand. They are all listed as single tours for the purposes of this article.

5) The 1986/87 tour to Sri Lanka was scheduled for 8 matches. The team returned home after 2 matches due to unrest in Sri Lanka.

6) One match played in Australia as part of the Trans-Tasman Twenty20 Tri-Series in 2017/18 is not regarded as a tour.

A total of 135 official New Zealand sides have toured overseas since the first in February, 1899. The teams were as follows:

1) **1898/99 to Australia**
L.T. Cobcroft *(captain)*, F.L. Ashbolt, J.C. Baker, C. Boxshall, A.D. Downes, A.H. Fisher, F.S. Frankish, Hugh B. Lusk, G. Mills, I. Mills, D. Reese, A. Sims, E.F. Upham.

2) **1913/14 to Australia**
D. Reese *(captain)*, J.H. Bennett, C. Boxshall, T.A. Carlton, L.G. Hemus, R.G. Hickmott, W.R. Patrick, C.W. Robinson, D.M. Sandman, A.N.C. Snedden, R.C. Somervell, L.G. Taylor, H.J. Tattersall, B.J. Tuckwell.

3) **1925/26 to Australia**
W.R. Patrick *(captain)*, C.F.W. Allcott, A.W. Alloo, R.C. Blunt, C.G. Crawford, W.H.R. Cunningham, C.C.R. Dacre, H.D. Gillespie, R.W. Hope, K.C. James, T.C. Lowry, D.J. McBeath, C.J. Oliver, R.V. de R. Worker.

4) **1927 to Great Britain, Ceylon and Australia**
T.C. Lowry *(captain)*, C.F.W. Allcott, E.H.L. Bernau, E.D. Blundell*, R.C. Blunt, W.H.R. Cunningham, C.C.R. Dacre, C.S. Dempster, R.H. Fox*, T.D.B. Hay*, M. Henderson, K.C. James, H.M. McGirr, W.E. Merritt, J.E. Mills, C.J. Oliver, M.L. Page.

5) **1931 to Great Britain**
T.C. Lowry *(captain)*, C.F.W. Allcott, R.C. Blunt, I.B. Cromb, C.S. Dempster, K.C. James, J.L. Kerr, A.M. Matheson, W.E. Merritt, J.E. Mills, M.L. Page, R.O. Talbot, H.G. Vivian, G.L. Weir.

6) **1937 to Great Britain, Ceylon and Australia**
M.L. Page *(captain)*, W.N. Carson, J. Cowie, M.P. Donnelly, J.A. Dunning, N. Gallichan, W.A. Hadlee, J.L. Kerr, J.R. Lamason, T.C. Lowry, D.A.R. Moloney, C.K. Parsloe*, A.W. Roberts, E.W.T. Tindill, H.G. Vivian, W.M. Wallace, G.L. Weir.

7) **1949 to Great Britain and West Germany**
W.A. Hadlee *(captain)*, C. Burke, T.B. Burtt, H.B. Cave, J. Cowie, G.F. Cresswell, M.P. Donnelly, J.A. Hayes, F.L.H. Mooney, G.O. Rabone, J.R. Reid, V.J. Scott, F.B. Smith, B. Sutcliffe, W.M. Wallace.

8) **1953/54 to South Africa and Australia**
G.O. Rabone *(captain)*, J.E.F. Beck, W. Bell, R.W. Blair, M.E. Chapple, E.W. Dempster, I.B. Leggat, J.G. Leggat*, A.R. MacGibbon, L.S.M. Miller, F.L.H. Mooney, G.W.F. Overton, M.B. Poore, J.R. Reid, B. Sutcliffe.

9) **1955/1956 to Pakistan and India**
H.B. Cave *(captain)*, J.C. Alabaster, J.W. Guy, N.S. Harford, J.A. Hayes, P.G.Z. Harris, J.G. Leggat, A.R. MacGibbon, S.N. McGregor, T.G. McMahon, A.M. Moir, E.C. Petrie, M.B. Poore, J.R. Reid, B. Sutcliffe.

10) **1958 to Great Britain**
J.R. Reid *(captain)*, J.C. Alabaster, R.W. Blair, H.B. Cave, J.W. D'Arcy, N.S. Harford, J.A. Hayes, A.R. MacGibbon, T. Meale, L.S.M. Miller, A.M. Moir, E.C. Petrie, W.R. Playle, J.T. Sparling, B. Sutcliffe, J.T. Ward.

11) **1961/62 to South Africa and Australia**
J.R. Reid *(captain)*, J.C. Alabaster, G.A. Bartlett, P.T. Barton, F.J. Cameron, M.E. Chapple, A.E. Dick, G.T. Dowling, J.W. Guy, P.G.Z. Harris, S.N. McGregor, R.C. Motz, J.T. Sparling, J.T. Ward, B.W. Yuile.

12) **1964/65 to India, Pakistan, Great Britain, Holland, Bermuda and USA**
J.R. Reid *(captain)*, F.J. Cameron, R.O. Collinge, B.E. Congdon, A.E. Dick*, G.T. Dowling, T.W. Jarvis, R.W. Morgan, R.C. Motz, V. Pollard, B.W. Sinclair, B. Sutcliffe, B.R. Taylor, G.E. Vivian, J.T. Ward, B.W. Yuile.

13) **1967/68 to Australia**
B.W. Sinclair *(captain)*, J.C. Alabaster, M.G. Burgess, R.O. Collinge, B.E. Congdon, R.I. Harford, T.W. Jarvis, R.C. Motz, B.A.G. Murray, V. Pollard, B.R. Taylor, K. Thomson, B.W. Yuile.

14) **1969 to Great Britain, India and Pakistan**
G.T. Dowling *(captain)*, M.G. Burgess, R.O. Collinge, B.E. Congdon, R.S. Cunis, D.R. Hadlee, B.F. Hastings, H.J. Howarth, B.D. Milburn, B.A.G. Murray, V. Pollard, B.R. Taylor, D.G. Trist*, G.M. Turner, K.J. Wadsworth, B.W. Yuile.

15) **1969/70 to Australia**
G.T. Dowling *(captain)*, M.G. Burgess, R.O. Collinge, B.E. Congdon, R.S. Cunis, D.R. Hadlee, B.F. Hastings, H.J. Howarth, R.W. Morgan*, B.W. Sinclair, G.M. Turner, G.E. Vivian, K.J. Wadsworth.

16) **1970/1971 to Australia**
G.T. Dowling *(captain)*, M.G. Burgess, R.O. Collinge, B.E. Congdon, R.S. Cunis, H.J. Howarth, T.W. Jarvis, R.W. Morgan, B.R. Taylor, G.M. Turner, G.E. Vivian, K.J. Wadsworth.

17) **1971/72 to Australia**
R.W. Morgan *(captain)*, R.W. Anderson, B. Andrews, B. Dunning, B.G. Hadlee, R.J. Hadlee, W.A. Greenstreet, G.A. Newdick, R.E. Redmond, M.L. Ryan, M.J.F. Shrimpton, D.G. Trist.

18) **1971/72 to West Indies**
G.T. Dowling *(captain)*, J.C. Alabaster, M.G. Burgess, K.O. Campbell, M.E. Chapple*, R.O. Collinge, B.E. Congdon, R.S. Cunis, B.F. Hastings, H.J. Howarth, T.W. Jarvis, R.W. Morgan*, B.R. Taylor, G.M. Turner, G.E. Vivian, K.J. Wadsworth, M.G. Webb.

19) **1972/73 to Australia**
B.E. Congdon *(captain)*, B. Andrews, R.S. Cunis, B. Dunning, R.J. Hadlee, B.F. Hastings, A.B. Jordan, D.R. O'Sullivan, R.E. Redmond, G.M. Turner, G.E. Vivian, K.J. Wadsworth.

20) **1973 to Great Britain**
B.E. Congdon *(captain)*, R.W. Anderson, M.G. Burgess, R.O. Collinge, E.K. Gillott,
D.R. Hadlee, R.J. Hadlee, B.F. Hastings, H.J. Howarth, J.M. Parker, V. Pollard, R.E. Redmond,
B.R. Taylor, G.M. Turner, K.J. Wadsworth.

21) **1973/74 to Australia**
B.E. Congdon *(captain)*, G.D. Alabaster, B. Andrews, B.L. Cairns, K.O. Campbell, J.V. Coney*,
D.R. Hadlee, R.J. Hadlee, B.F. Hastings, J.F.M. Morrison, D.R. O'Sullivan, J.M. Parker,
M.J.F. Shrimpton, G.M. Turner, K.J. Wadsworth.

22) **1974/75 to Australia**
B.E. Congdon *(captain)*, B.L. Cairns, E.J. Chatfield, R.O. Collinge, G.N. Edwards,
D.R. Hadlee, B.F. Hastings, G.P. Howarth, H.J. Howarth, J.F.M. Morrison, J.M. Parker,
G.M. Turner, K.J. Wadsworth.

23) **1975 to England** *(World Cup)*
G.M. Turner *(captain)*, B.L. Cairns, R.O. Collinge, B.G. Hadlee, D.R. Hadlee, R.J. Hadlee,
B.F. Hastings, G.P. Howarth, H.J. Howarth, B.J. McKechnie, J.F.M. Morrison, D.R. O'Sullivan,
J.M. Parker, K.J. Wadsworth.

24) **1976/77 to Pakistan and India**
G.M. Turner *(captain)*, R.W. Anderson, M.G. Burgess, B.L. Cairns, R.O. Collinge, R.J. Hadlee,
G.P. Howarth, W.K. Lees, J.F.M. Morrison, D.R. O'Sullivan, J.M. Parker, N.M. Parker,
P.J. Petherick, A.D.G. Roberts, G.B. Troup.

25) **1978 to Great Britain**
M.G. Burgess *(captain)*, R.W. Anderson, S.L. Boock, B.P. Bracewell, B.L. Cairns,
R.O. Collinge*, B.E. Congdon, B.A. Edgar, G.N. Edwards, D.R. Hadlee,
R.J. Hadlee, G.P. Howarth, J.M. McIntyre, J.M. Parker, G.B. Thomson, G.B. Troup*, J.G. Wright.

26) **1979 to England** *(World Cup)*
M.G. Burgess *(captain)*, B.L. Cairns, E.J. Chatfield, J.V. Coney, B.A. Edgar, R.J. Hadlee,
G.P. Howarth, W.K. Lees, B.J. McKechnie, J.F.M. Morrison, L.W. Stott, G.B. Troup, G.M. Turner,
J.G. Wright.

27) **1980/81 to Australia**
G.P. Howarth *(captain)*, S.L. Boock, B.P. Bracewell*, J.G. Bracewell, M.G. Burgess, B.L. Cairns,
E.J. Chatfield, J.V. Coney, B.A. Edgar, R.J. Hadlee, W.K. Lees, P.E. McEwan, B.J. McKechnie*,
J.M. Parker, I.D.S. Smith, M.C. Snedden, G.B. Troup, J.G. Wright.

28) **1982/83 to Australia**
G.P. Howarth *(captain)*, B.R. Blair, S.M. Carrington, E.J. Chatfield, J.V. Coney, M.D. Crowe,
B.A. Edgar, W.K. Lees, J.F.M. Morrison, J.F. Reid, G.K. Robertson, M.C. Snedden, G.B. Troup.

29) **1982/83 to Australia**
G.P. Howarth *(captain)*, B.L. Cairns, E.J. Chatfield, J.V. Coney, J.J. Crowe, M.D. Crowe*,
B.A. Edgar, T.J. Franklin*, R.J. Hadlee, W.K. Lees, J.F.M. Morrison, M.C. Snedden, G.B. Troup,
G.M. Turner, P.N. Webb, R.J. Webb*, J.G. Wright.

30) **1983 to England**
G.P. Howarth *(captain)*, J.G. Bracewell, B.L. Cairns, E.J. Chatfield, J.V. Coney, J.J. Crowe,
M.D. Crowe, B.A. Edgar, T.J. Franklin, E.J. Gray, R.J. Hadlee, W.K. Lees, I.D.S. Smith,
M.C. Snedden, S.R. Tracy*, G.M. Turner, J.G. Wright.

31) **1983/84 to Sri Lanka**
G.P. Howarth *(captain)*, S.L. Boock, J.G. Bracewell, B.L. Cairns, E.J. Chatfield, J.V. Coney,
J.J. Crowe, M.D. Crowe, B.A. Edgar, R.J. Hadlee, J.F. Reid, I.D.S. Smith, D.A. Stirling,
J.G. Wright.

32) **1984/85 to Pakistan and Sri Lanka**
J.V. Coney *(captain)*, S.L. Boock, J.G. Bracewell, B.L. Cairns, E.J. Chatfield, J.J. Crowe,
M.D. Crowe, B.A. Edgar, E.J. Gray, P.E. McEwan, J.F. Reid, I.D.S. Smith, M.C. Snedden,
D.A. Stirling, J.G. Wright.

33) **1984/85 to Australia** *(World Championship of Cricket)*
G.P. Howarth *(captain)*, B.P. Bracewell, J.G. Bracewell, B.L. Cairns, E.J. Chatfield, J.V. Coney,
J.J. Crowe, M.D. Crowe, R.J. Hadlee, P.E. McEwan, J.F. Reid, I.D.S. Smith, M.C. Snedden,
J.G. Wright.

34) **1984/85 to West Indies**
G.P. Howarth *(captain)*, S.L. Boock, J.G. Bracewell, B.L. Cairns, E.J. Chatfield, J.V. Coney, J.J. Crowe, M.D. Crowe, R.J. Hadlee, R.T. Hart, K.R. Rutherford, I.D.S. Smith, D.A. Stirling, G.B. Troup, J.G. Wright.

35) **1985/86 to Australia**
J.V. Coney *(captain)*, S.L. Boock, J.G. Bracewell*, V.R. Brown, B.L. Cairns, E.J. Chatfield, J.J. Crowe, M.D. Crowe, B.A. Edgar, T.J. Franklin, R.J. Hadlee, E.B. McSweeney*, J.F. Reid, I.D.S. Smith, M.C. Snedden, J.G. Wright.

36) **1985/86 to Australia**
J.V. Coney *(captain)*, B.R. Blair, S.L. Boock, J.G. Bracewell, E.J. Chatfield, J.J. Crowe, M.D. Crowe, B.A. Edgar, S.R. Gillespie, R.J. Hadlee, E.B. McSweeney, J.F. Reid, M.C. Snedden, J.G. Wright.

37) **1985/86 to Sri Lanka, Sharjah and Hong Kong**
J.G. Wright *(captain)*, T.E. Blain, B.R. Blair, J.G. Bracewell, E.J. Chatfield, J.J. Crowe, M.D. Crowe, E.J. Gray, E.B. McSweeney, G.K. Robertson, K.R. Rutherford, M.C. Snedden, W. Watson.

38) **1986 to England and Holland**
J.V. Coney *(captain)*, B.J. Barrett, T.E. Blain, J.G. Bracewell, E.J. Chatfield, J.J. Crowe, M.D. Crowe, B.A. Edgar, T.J. Franklin, E.J. Gray, R.J. Hadlee, K.R. Rutherford, I.D.S. Smith, D.A. Stirling, W. Watson, J.G. Wright.

39) **1986/87 to Sri Lanka**
J.J. Crowe *(captain)*, J.G. Bracewell, E.J. Chatfield, M.D. Crowe, E.J. Gray, R.J. Hadlee, P.A. Horne, A.H. Jones, E.B. McSweeney, D.K. Morrison, D.N. Patel, K.R. Rutherford, I.D.S. Smith, M.C. Snedden.

40) **1987/88 to India** *(World Cup)*
J.J. Crowe *(captain)*, S.L. Boock, J.G. Bracewell, E.J. Chatfield, M.D. Crowe, P.A. Horne, A.H. Jones, D.K. Morrison, D.N. Patel, K.R. Rutherford, I.D.S. Smith, M.C. Snedden, W. Watson, J.G. Wright.

41) **1987/88 to Australia**
J.J. Crowe *(captain)*, T.E. Blain*, J.G. Bracewell, V.R. Brown*, E.J. Chatfield, M.D. Crowe, S.R. Gillespie*, E.J. Gray, R.J. Hadlee, P.A. Horne, A.H. Jones, D.K. Morrison, D.N. Patel, K.R. Rutherford, I.D.S. Smith, M.C. Snedden, W. Watson, J.G. Wright.

42) **1987/88 to Sharjah**
J.G. Wright *(captain)*, T.E. Blain, E.J. Chatfield, M.J. Greatbatch, R.J. Hadlee, A.H. Jones, C.M. Kuggeleijn, D.K. Morrison, D.N. Patel, K.R. Rutherford, I.D.S. Smith, R.H. Vance, W. Watson.

43) **1988/89 to India**
J.G. Wright *(captain)*, T.E. Blain, J.G. Bracewell, E.J. Chatfield, T.J. Franklin, E.J. Gray, M.J. Greatbatch, R.J. Hadlee, A.H. Jones, C.M. Kuggeleijn, D.K. Morrison, K.R. Rutherford, I.D.S. Smith, M.C. Snedden, R.H. Vance, W. Watson*.

44) **1988/89 to Australia**
J.G. Wright *(captain)*, E.J. Chatfield, J.J. Crowe, M.D. Crowe, M.J. Greatbatch, A.H. Jones, C.M. Kuggeleijn, D.K. Morrison, I.D.S. Smith, M.C. Snedden, R.H. Vance, W. Watson.

45) **1989/90 to Australia**
J.G. Wright *(captain)*, B.P. Bracewell, J.G. Bracewell, C.L. Cairns*, J.J. Crowe, M.D. Crowe, M.J. Greatbatch, A.H. Jones, D.K. Morrison, D.N. Patel*, G.K. Robertson, I.D.S. Smith, M.C. Snedden, R.H. Vance, W. Watson.

46) **1990 to Sharjah and England**
J.G. Wright *(captain)*, J.G. Bracewell, J.J. Crowe, M.D. Crowe, T.J. Franklin, M.J. Greatbatch, Sir R.J. Hadlee, A.H. Jones, J.P. Millmow, D.K. Morrison, A.C. Parore, M.W. Priest, C. Pringle*, K.R. Rutherford, I.D.S. Smith, M.C. Snedden, S.A. Thomson, W. Watson*.

47) **1990/91 to Pakistan**
M.D. Crowe *(captain)*, G.E. Bradburn, T.J. Franklin, M.J. Greatbatch, P.A. Horne, D.K. Morrison, A.C. Parore, D.N. Patel, M.W. Priest, C. Pringle, S.J. Roberts, K.R. Rutherford, I.D.S. Smith, W. Watson, D.J. White.

48) **1990/91 to Australia**
M.D. Crowe *(captain)*, G.E. Bradburn, M.J. Greatbatch, C.Z. Harris, A.H. Jones, G.R. Larsen*,
R.T. Latham, D.K. Morrison, R.G. Petrie, C. Pringle, R.B. Reid*, K.R. Rutherford, I.D.S. Smith,
W. Watson, J.G. Wright, B.A. Young.

49) **1991/92 to Australia**
M.D. Crowe *(captain)*, G.E. Bradburn, C.L. Cairns, T.J. Franklin, M.J. Greatbatch, C.Z. Harris,
A.H. Jones, D.K. Morrison, A.C. Parore, D.N. Patel, C. Pringle, I.D.S. Smith, S.A. Thomson,
W. Watson, K.A. Wealleans.

50) **1992/93 to Zimbabwe and Sri Lanka**
M.D. Crowe *(captain)*, G.E. Bradburn*, S.B. Doull, M.J. Greatbatch, C.Z. Harris, B.R.
Hartland, M.J. Haslam, A.H. Jones, G.R. Larsen, R.T. Latham, D.J. Nash, M.B. Owens*, A.C.
Parore, D.N. Patel, C. Pringle*, K.R. Rutherford, M.L. Su'a, J.T.C. Vaughan*, W. Watson,
J.G. Wright*.

51) **1993/94 to Australia**
M.D. Crowe *(captain)*, T.E. Blain, C.L. Cairns, S.B. Doull, R.P. de Groen*, M.J. Greatbatch,
C.Z. Harris*, M.J. Haslam, A.H. Jones, G.R. Larsen*, R.T. Latham*, D.K. Morrison,
D.N. Patel, B.A. Pocock, C. Pringle*, K.R. Rutherford, M.L. Su'a, S.A. Thomson*, W. Watson,
D.J. White*, B.A. Young.

52) **1994 to Sharjah and England**
K.R. Rutherford *(captain)*, M.D. Crowe, H.T. Davis, M.W. Douglas, S.B. Doull, S.P. Fleming,
M.J. Greatbatch, C.Z. Harris, M.N. Hart, B.R. Hartland, G.R. Larsen, D.K. Morrison,
D.J. Nash, M.B. Owens*, A.C. Parore, B.A. Pocock, C. Pringle, S.J. Roberts*, S.A. Thomson,
B.A. Young. (Harris and Douglas were selected only for Sharjah but Douglas re-appeared as
an additional player during the England tour. Larsen captained the team in Sharjah as Rutherford
was not available for that part of the tour).

53) **1994/95 to India and South Africa**
K.R. Rutherford *(captain)*, M.D. Crowe, R.P. de Groen, S.B. Doull, S.P. Fleming, L.K. Germon,
C.Z. Harris, M.N. Hart, B.R. Hartland, D.K. Morrison*, D.J. Murray, D.J. Nash, A.C. Parore,
M.W. Priest*, C. Pringle, M.L. Su'a, S.A. Thomson, B.A. Young.

54) **1995/96 to India**
L.K. Germon *(captain)*, N.J. Astle*, C.L. Cairns, M.D. Crowe, S.B. Doull, S.P. Fleming,
A.J. Gale, M.J. Greatbatch, M.N. Hart, M.J. Haslam, G.R. Larsen*, D.K. Morrison, D.J. Nash,
A.C. Parore, S.A. Thomson, R.G. Twose, B.A. Young.

55) **1995/96 to India and Pakistan** *(World Cup)*
L.K. Germon *(captain)*, N.J. Astle, C.L. Cairns, S.P. Fleming, C.Z. Harris, R.J. Kennedy,
G.R. Larsen, D.K. Morrison, D.J. Nash, A.C. Parore, D.N. Patel, C.M. Spearman,
S.A. Thomson, R.G. Twose.

56) **1995/96 to West Indies**
L.K. Germon *(captain)*, N.J. Astle, M.D. Bailey*, C.L. Cairns, S.P. Fleming, C.Z. Harris,
M.J. Haslam*, R.J. Kennedy, G.R. Larsen, D.K. Morrison, D.J. Nash, A.C. Parore, D.N. Patel,
C.M. Spearman, S.A. Thomson, R.G. Twose, J.T.C. Vaughan*.

57) **1996/97 to Sharjah and Pakistan**
L.K. Germon *(captain)*, N.J. Astle, C.L. Cairns, S.B. Doull, S.P. Fleming, M.J. Greatbatch,
C.Z. Harris, M.N. Hart*, M.J. Haslam, G.R. Jonas*, R.J. Kennedy*, G.R. Larsen,
D.K. Morrison, A.C. Parore, D.N. Patel, C.M. Spearman, J.T.C. Vaughan, P.J. Wiseman*,
B.A. Young.

58) **1996/97 to India** *(Independence Cup)*
S.P. Fleming *(captain)*, N.J. Astle, C.L. Cairns, H.T. Davis, C.Z. Harris, M.J. Horne,
G.R. Larsen, C.D. McMillan, S.B. O'Connor, A.C. Parore, D.N. Patel, A.J. Penn, D.L. Vettori,
B.A. Young.

59) **1997/98 to Kenya and Zimbabwe**
S.P. Fleming *(captain)*, N.J. Astle, C.L. Cairns, H.T. Davis, C.Z. Harris, M.J. Horne,
G.R. Larsen, C.D. McMillan, S.B. O'Connor, A.C. Parore, B.A. Pocock, D.G. Sewell,
C.M. Spearman, D.L. Vettori, P.J. Wiseman.

60) **1997/98 to Australia**
S.P. Fleming *(captain)*, G.I. Allott, N.J. Astle, C.L. Cairns, H.T. Davis, S.B. Doull, C.J. Drum*, C.Z. Harris*, M.J. Horne, G.R. Larsen*, C.D. McMillan, D.J. Nash*, S.B. O'Connor, A.C. Parore, B.A. Pocock, C.M. Spearman*, R.G. Twose*, D.L. Vettori, B.A. Young.

61) **1997/98 to Sharjah**
S.P. Fleming *(captain)*, N.J. Astle, C.L. Cairns, S.B. Doull, C.Z. Harris, M.J. Horne, L.G. Howell, C.D. McMillan, D.J. Nash, S.B. O'Connor, A.C. Parore, M.W. Priest, P.J. Wiseman.

62) **1997/98 to Sri Lanka**
S.P. Fleming *(captain)*, N.J. Astle, C.L. Cairns, S.B. Doull, C.Z. Harris, M.J. Horne, C.D. McMillan, D.J. Nash, S.B. O'Connor, A.C. Parore, M.W. Priest, C.M. Spearman, A.R. Tait*, D.L. Vettori, P.J. Wiseman, B.A. Young.

63) **1998 to Malaysia** *(Commonwealth Games)*
S.P. Fleming *(captain)*, G.I. Allott, N.J. Astle, M.D. Bailey, M.D. Bell, C.J. Drum, C.Z. Harris, M.J. Horne, C.D. McMillan, S.B. O'Connor, A.C. Parore, A.R. Tait, D.L. Vettori, P.J. Wiseman.

64) **1998/99 to Bangladesh** *(Wills International Cup)*
S.P. Fleming *(captain)*, G.I. Allott, N.J. Astle, M.D. Bailey, M.D. Bell, S.B. Doull, C.Z. Harris, M.J. Horne, C.D. McMillan, S.B. O'Connor, A.C. Parore, A.R. Tait, D.L. Vettori, P.J. Wiseman.

65) **1999 to England**
S.P. Fleming *(captain)*, G.I. Allott, N.J. Astle, M.D. Bell*, C.E. Bulfin, C.L. Cairns, M.G. Croy*, S.B. Doull, C.Z. Harris, M.N. Hart, M.J. Horne, G.R. Larsen, C.D. McMillan, D.J. Nash, S.B. O'Connor*, A.C. Parore, A.J. Penn*, R.G. Twose, D.L. Vettori, B.G.K. Walker*.

66) **1999/00 to India**
S.P. Fleming *(captain)*, N.J. Astle, M.D. Bell, C.L. Cairns, C.J. Drum, C.Z. Harris, M.J. Horne, C.D. McMillan, D.J. Nash, S.B. O'Connor, A.C. Parore, A.J. Penn, C.M. Spearman, G.R. Stead*, S.B. Styris*, A.R. Tait*, R.G. Twose*, D.L. Vettori, P.J. Wiseman.

67) **2000/01 to Singapore, Zimbabwe, Kenya and South Africa**
S.P. Fleming *(captain)*, G.I. Allott, N.J. Astle, C.L. Cairns, C.Z. Harris, M.J. Horne, C.D. McMillan, H.J.H. Marshall, C.S. Martin, D.J. Nash, C.J. Nevin, S.B. O'Connor, A.C. Parore, A.J. Penn, M.H. Richardson, M.S. Sinclair, C.M. Spearman, S.B. Styris, G.P. Sulzberger, D.R. Tuffey, R.G. Twose, D.L. Vettori, B.G.K. Walker, K.P. Walmsley, P.J. Wiseman. (Apart from a number of players being replaced because of injury, this party was reselected and changed several times depending on the nature of the matches being played).

68) **2000/01 to Sharjah**
C.D. McMillan *(captain)*, A.R. Adams, M.D. Bell, G.E. Bradburn, J.E.C. Franklin, C.Z. Harris, K.D. Mills, C.J. Nevin, J.D.P. Oram, M.S. Sinclair, D.R.Tuffey, L. Vincent, B.G.K. Walker.

69) **2001/02 to Sri Lanka**
S.P. Fleming *(captain)*, N.J. Astle, G.E. Bradburn, J.E.C. Franklin, C.Z. Harris, K.D. Mills, C.D. McMillan, D.J. Nash, J.D.P. Oram, A.C. Parore, M.S. Sinclair, D.R.Tuffey, D.L. Vettori, L. Vincent.

70) **2001/02 to Australia**
S.P. Fleming *(captain)*, A.R. Adams, N.J. Astle, M.D. Bell, S.E. Bond*, C.L. Cairns, C.J. Drum*, J.E.C. Franklin, C.Z. Harris, B.B. McCullum, C.D. McMillan, C.S. Martin, D.J. Nash, S.B. O'Çonnor, A.C. Parore, M.H. Richardson, M.S. Sinclair, S.B. Styris, G.P. Sulzberger, D.R. Tuffey, D.L. Vettori, L. Vincent, P.J. Wiseman*.

71) **2001/02 to Sharjah and Pakistan**
S.P. Fleming *(captain)*, A.R. Adams, N.J. Astle, I.G. Butler, J.E.C. Franklin, C.Z. Harris, R.G. Hart, M.J. Horne, C.D. McMillan, C.S. Martin, C.J. Nevin, J.D.P. Oram, M.H. Richardson, M.S. Sinclair, S.B. Styris, D.R. Tuffey, D.L. Vettori, L. Vincent, B.G.K. Walker.

72) **2001/02 to West Indies**
S.P. Fleming *(captain)*, N.J. Astle, S.E. Bond, I.G. Butler, C.Z. Harris, M.N. Hart, R.G. Hart, P.A. Hitchcock, M.J. Horne, C.D. McMillan, C.S. Martin, C.J. Nevin, J.D.P. Oram, M.H. Richardson, S.B. Styris, D.R. Tuffey, D.L. Vettori, L. Vincent.

73) **2002/03 to Australia and Sri Lanka** *(ICC Champions Trophy)*
S.P. Fleming *(captain)*, N.J. Astle, S.E. Bond, I.G. Butler*, C.Z. Harris, M.N. Hart*, P.A. Hitchcock, M.J. Horne*, C.D. McMillan*, K.D. Mills, C.J. Nevin, J.D.P. Oram, M.S. Sinclair, S.B. Styris, G.P. Sulzberger, D.R. Tuffey, D.L. Vettori, L. Vincent, B.G.K. Walker*, J.A.F. Yovich*.

74) **2002/03 to South Africa** *(World Cup)*
S.P. Fleming *(captain)*, A.R. Adams, N.J. Astle, S.E. Bond, C.L. Cairns, C.Z. Harris, B.B. McCullum, C.D. McMillan, K.D. Mills, J.D.P. Oram, M.S. Sinclair, S.B. Styris, D.R. Tuffey, D.L. Vettori, L. Vincent.

75) **2002/03 to Sri Lanka**
S.P. Fleming *(captain)*, A.R. Adams, S.E. Bond, I.G. Butler, C.L. Cairns, C.Z. Harris, R.G. Hart, M.J. Horne, R.A. Jones, B.B. McCullum, K.D. Mills, C.J. Nevin, J.D.P. Oram, M.H. Richardson, M.S. Sinclair, S.B. Styris, D.R. Tuffey, D.L. Vettori, L. Vincent, P.J. Wiseman.

76) **2003/04 to India**
S.P. Fleming *(captain)*, N.J. Astle, I.G. Butler, C.L. Cairns*, C.Z. Harris*, R.G. Hart, P.A. Hitchcock*, R.A. Jones, B.B. McCullum*. C.D. McMillan, M.J. Mason, K.D. Mills*, C.J. Nevin*, J.D.P. Oram, M.H. Richardson, S.B. Styris, D.R. Tuffey, D.L. Vettori, L. Vincent, P.J. Wiseman.

77) **2003/04 to Pakistan**
C.L. Cairns *(captain)*, T.K. Canning, C.D. Cumming, C.Z. Harris, P.A. Hitchcock, R.A. Jones, B.B. McCullum, H.J.H. Marshall, M.J. Mason, J.D.P. Oram, M.S. Sinclair, D.R. Tuffey, D.L. Vettori, M.D.J. Walker, K.P. Walmsley.

78) **2004 to England**
S.P. Fleming *(captain)*, A.R. Adams*, N.J. Astle, S.E. Bond, I.G. Butler*, C.L. Cairns, J.E.C. Franklin*, C.Z. Harris*, G.J. Hopkins*, B.B. McCullum, C.D. McMillan, H.J.H Marshall*, C.S. Martin, K.D. Mills, J.D.P. Oram, M.H.W Papps, M.H. Richardson, S.B. Styris, D.R. Tuffey, D.L. Vettori.

79) **2004 to England** *(Champions Trophy)*
S.P. Fleming *(captain)*, N.J. Astle, I.G. Butler, C.L. Cairns, C.Z. Harris, B.B. McCullum, C.D. McMillan, H.J.H. Marshall, K.D. Mills, J.D.P Oram, M.H.W. Papps, S.B. Styris, D.R. Tuffey, D.L. Vettori.

80) **2004/05 to Bangladesh**
S.P. Fleming *(captain)*, A.R. Adams*, N.J. Astle, I.G. Butler, C.L. Cairns*, J.E.C. Franklin, P.G.Fulton*, C.Z. Harris*, B.B. McCullum, C.D. McMillan*, H.J.H. Marshall, C.S. Martin, K.D. Mills, J.D.P. Oram, M.H. Richardson, M.S. Sinclair, S.B. Styris, D.L. Vettori, P.J. Wiseman.

81) **2004/05 to Australia**
S.P. Fleming *(captain)*, A.R. Adams*, N.J. Astle, I.G. Butler, C.L. Cairns*, T.K. Canning*, J.E.C. Franklin, C.Z. Harris*, G.J.Hopkins*, B.B. McCullum, C.D. McMillan*, H.J.H. Marshall, C.S. Martin, K.D. Mills, J.D.P.Oram, M.H. Richardson, M.S. Sinclair, S.B. Styris, D.L. Vettori, P.J. Wiseman.

82) **2005/06 to Namibia and Zimbabwe**
S.P. Fleming *(captain)*, A.R. Adams*, N.J. Astle, S.E. Bond, C.L. Cairns*, C.D. Cumming, J.E.C. Franklin, B.B. McCullum, C.D. McMillan*, H.J.H. Marshall, J.A.H. Marshall, C.S. Martin, K.D. Mills, J.D.P. Oram, J.S. Patel*, S.B. Styris, D.L. Vettori, L. Vincent, P.J. Wiseman.

83) **2005/06 to South Africa**
S.P. Fleming *(captain)*, A.R. Adams, N.J. Astle, S.E. Bond, J.E.C. Franklin, H.J.H. Marshall, J.A.H. Marshall, B.B. McCullum, C.D. McMillan, K.D. Mills, J.D.P. Oram, J.S. Patel, S.B. Styris, D.L. Vettori, L. Vincent.

84) **2005/06 to South Africa**
S.P. Fleming *(captain)*, N.J. Astle, S.E. Bond, J.E.C. Franklin, P.G. Fulton, J.M. How, B.B. McCullum, H.J.H Marshall, C.S. Martin, M.J. Mason*, K.D. Mills, J.D.P. Oram, M.H.W. Papps, J.S. Patel, S.B. Styris, D.L. Vettori

85) **2006/07 to India** *(ICC Champions Trophy)*
S.P. Fleming *(captain)*, N.J. Astle, S.E. Bond, J.E.C. Franklin, P.G. Fulton, M.R. Gillespie, B.B. McCullum, H.J.H. Marshall, K.D. Mills, J.D.P. Oram, J.S. Patel, S.B. Styris, L.R.P.L. Taylor*, D.L. Vettori, L. Vincent.

86) **2006/07 to Australia**
S.P. Fleming *(captain)*, A.R. Adams, N.J. Astle, S.E. Bond, J.E.C. Franklin, P.G. Fulton, M.R. Gillespie, B.B. McCullum, C.D. McMillan, H.J.H. Marshall, M.J. Mason, K.D. Mills*, J.D.P. Oram*, J.S. Patel, S.B. Styris*, L.R.P.L. Taylor, D.L. Vettori, L. Vincent*.

87) **2006/07 to West Indies** *(World Cup)*
S.P. Fleming *(captain)*, S.E. Bond, J.E.C. Franklin, P.G. Fulton, M.R. Gillespie, B.B. McCullum, C.D. McMillan, H.J.H. Marshall*, C.S. Martin*, M.J. Mason, J.D.P. Oram, J.S. Patel, S.B. Styris, L.R.P.L. Taylor, D.R. Tuffey, D.L. Vettori, L. Vincent.

88) **2007/08 to South Africa** *(Twenty20 World Championship)*
D.L. Vettori *(captain)*, S.E. Bond, P.G. Fulton, M.R. Gillespie, G.J. Hopkins, B.B. McCullum, N.L. McCullum, C.D. McMillan, C.S. Martin, J.D.P. Oram, J.S. Patel, B.E. Scott, S.B. Styris, L.R.P.L. Taylor, L. Vincent.

89) **2007/08 to South Africa and Australia**
D.L. Vettori *(captain)*, S.E. Bond, C.D.Cumming, S.P. Fleming, M.R. Gillespie, G.J. Hopkins*, J.M. How*, B.B. McCullum, C.S. Martin, M.J. Mason, K.D. Mills*, I.E. O'Brien, J.D.P. Oram, M.H.W. Papps, J.S. Patel, M.S. Sinclair*, S.B. Styris, L.R.P.L. Taylor, L. Vincent.

90) **2008 to England**
D.L. Vettori *(captain)*, G.D. Elliott*, D.R. Flynn, P.G. Fulton, M.R. Gillespie*, G.J. Hopkins, J.M. How, B.B. McCullum, J.A.H. Marshall, C.S. Martin, M.J. Mason, K.D. Mills, I.E. O'Brien, J.D.P. Oram, J.S. Patel, A.J. Redmond, T.G. Southee, S.B. Styris*, L.R.P.L. Taylor.

91) **2008/09 to Bangladesh**
D.L. Vettori *(captain)*, G.D. Elliott, D.R. Flynn, M.R. Gillespie, G.J. Hopkins, J.M. How, B.B. McCullum, M.J. Mason, K.D. Mills, I.E. O'Brien*, J.D.P. Oram, J.S. Patel, A.J. Redmond*, J.D. Ryder, T.G. Southee, S.B. Styris, L.R.P.L. Taylor.

92) **2008/09 to Australia**
D.L. Vettori *(captain)*, G.D. Elliott, D.R. Flynn, P.G. Fulton, M.R. Gillespie, G.J. Hopkins, J.M. How, B.B. McCullum, C.S. Martin, K.D. Mills, I.E. O'Brien, J.S. Patel*, A.J. Redmond, J.D. Ryder, T.G. Southee, L.R.P.L. Taylor.

93) **2008/09 to Australia**
D.L. Vettori *(captain)*, T.A. Boult, N.T. Broom, I.G. Butler*, C.D. Cumming, B.J. Diamanti, G.D. Elliott, J.E.C. Franklin*, P.G. Fulton, M.J. Guptill, G.J. Hopkins*, B.B. McCullum, N.L. McCullum*, P.D. McGlashan*, K.D. Mills, I.E. O'Brien, J.S. Patel, T.G. Southee, L.R.P.L. Taylor.

94) **2009 to England** *(ICC World Twenty20)*
D.L. Vettori *(captain)*, N.T. Broom, I.G. Butler, B.J. Diamanti, J.E.C. Franklin, M.J. Guptill, B.B. McCullum, N.L. McCullum, P.D. McGlashan, K.D. Mills, I.E. O'Brien, J.D.P. Oram, A.J. Redmond*, J.D. Ryder, S.B. Styris, L.R.P.L. Taylor.

95) **2009/10 to Sri Lanka**
D.L. Vettori *(captain)*, S.E. Bond, N.T. Broom, I.G. Butler, C.D. Cumming, B.J. Diamanti, G.D. Elliott, D.R. Flynn, M.J. Guptill, G.J. Hopkins, B.B. McCullum, N.L. McCullum, P.D. McGlashan, T.G. McIntosh, C.S. Martin, K.D. Mills, I.E. O'Brien, J.D.P. Oram, J.S. Patel, J.D. Ryder, L.R.P.L. Taylor, D.R. Tuffey.

96) **2009/10 to South Africa** *(ICC Champions Trophy)*
D.L. Vettori *(captain)*, S.E. Bond, N.T. Broom, I.G. Butler, B.J. Diamanti, G.D. Elliott, J.E.C. Franklin*, M.J. Guptill, G.J. Hopkins, B.B. McCullum, K.D. Mills, I.E. O'Brien*, J.D.P. Oram, J.S. Patel, A.J. Redmond*, J.D. Ryder, S.B. Styris*, L.R.P.L. Taylor, D.R. Tuffey.

97) **2009/10 to United Arab Emirates**
D.L. Vettori *(captain)*, S.E. Bond, N.T. Broom, I.G. Butler, J.E.C. Franklin, M.J. Guptill, B.B. McCullum, N.L. McCullum, K.D. Mills, J.D.P. Oram, A.J. Redmond, T.G. Southee, S.B. Styris, L.R.P.L. Taylor, B-J. Watling.

98) **2009/10 to West Indies** *(ICC World Twenty20)*
D.L. Vettori *(captain)*, S.E. Bond, I.G. Butler, M.J. Guptill, G.J. Hopkins, B.B. McCullum, N.L. McCullum, K.D. Mills, R.J. Nicol, J.D.P. Oram, A.J. Redmond, J.D. Ryder, T.G. Southee, S.B. Styris, L.R.P.L. Taylor.

99) **2009/10 to United States of America**
D.L. Vettori *(captain)*, I.G. Butler, M.J. Guptill, G.J. Hopkins, B.B. McCullum, N.L. McCullum, A.J. McKay, K.D. Mills, R.J. Nicol, J.D.P. Oram, A.J. Redmond, T.G. Southee, S.B. Styris, L.R.P.L. Taylor.

100) **2010/11 to Sri Lanka**
L.R.P.L. Taylor *(captain)*, G.D. Elliott, M.J. Guptill, G.J. Hopkins, P.J. Ingram, N.L. McCullum A.J. McKay, K.D. Mills, J.D.P. Oram, J.S. Patel, T.G. Southee, S.B. Styris, D.R. Tuffey, B-J. Watling, K.S. Williamson.

101) **2010/11 to Bangladesh**
D.L. Vettori *(captain)*, H.K. Bennett, G.D. Elliott, B.B. McCullum, N.L. McCullum, A.J. McKay, K.D. Mills, A.J. Redmond, J.D. Ryder, T.G. Southee, S.L. Stewart, L.R.P.L. Taylor, D.R. Tuffey, B-J. Watling, K.S. Williamson.

102) **2010/11 to India**
D.L. Vettori *(captain)*, B.J. Arnel, H.K. Bennett, G.D. Elliott, J.E.C. Franklin*, M.J. Guptill, G.J. Hopkins, J.M. How, B.B. McCullum, N.L. McCullum, T.G. McIntosh, A.J. McKay, C.S. Martin, K.D. Mills, J.S. Patel, J.D. Ryder, T.G. Southee, S.B. Styris, L.R.P.L. Taylor, D.R. Tuffey, B-J. Watling, K.S. Williamson.

103) **2010/11 to India, Sri Lanka and Bangladesh** *(ICC World Cup)*
D.L. Vettori *(captain)*, H.K. Bennett, J.E.C. Franklin, M.J. Guptill, J.M. How, B.B. McCullum, N.L. McCullum, A.J. McKay*, K.D. Mills, J.D.P. Oram, J.D. Ryder, T.G. Southee, S.B. Styris, L.R.P.L. Taylor, D.R. Tuffey*, K.S. Williamson, L.J. Woodcock.

104) **2011/12 to Zimbabwe**
L.R.P.L. Taylor *(captain)*, G.W. Aldridge, D.A.J. Bracewell, D.G. Brownlie, J.E.C. Franklin, M.J. Guptill, B.B. McCullum, N.L. McCullum, A.J. McKay, C.S. Martin, K.D. Mills, R.J. Nicol, J.D.P. Oram, J.S. Patel, J.D. Ryder, D.L. Vettori, B-J. Watling, K.S. Williamson, L.J. Woodcock, R.A. Young.

105) **2011/12 to Australia**
L.R.P.L. Taylor *(captain)*, B.J. Arnel*, T.A. Boult, D.A.J. Bracewell, D.G. Brownlie, M.J. Guptill, B.B. McCullum, C.S. Martin, J.D. Ryder, T.G. Southee, D.L. Vettori, B-J. Watling, K.S. Williamson, R.A. Young.

106) **2012 to United States of America and West Indies**
L.R.P.L. Taylor *(captain)*, T.A. Boult, D.A.J. Bracewell, D.G. Brownlie, A.M. Ellis, D.R. Flynn, M.J. Guptill, R.M. Hira, T.W.M. Latham, B.B. McCullum, N.L. McCullum, C.S. Martin, K.D. Mills, T.S. Nethula, R.J.Nicol, J.D.P. Oram, T.G. Southee, C.F.K. van Wyk, D.L. Vettori, N. Wagner, B-J. Watling, K.S. Williamson.

107) **2012/13 to India**
L.R.P.L. Taylor *(captain)*, T.A. Boult, D.A.J. Bracewell, D.R. Flynn, J.E.C. Franklin, M.J. Guptill, R.M. Hira, B.B. McCullum, N.L. McCullum, C.S. Martin, K.D. Mills, A.F. Milne, T.S. Nethula, R.J. Nicol, J.D.P. Oram, J.S. Patel, T.G. Southee, C.F.K. van Wyk, D.L. Vettori, N. Wagner, B-J. Watling, K.S. Williamson.

108) **2012/13 to Sri Lanka** *(ICC World Twenty20)*
L.R.P.L. Taylor *(captain)*, D.A.J. Bracewell, J.E.C. Franklin, M.J. Guptill, R.M. Hira, B.B. McCullum, N.L. McCullum, K.D. Mills, A.F. Milne, R.J. Nicol, J.D.P. Oram, T.G. Southee, D.L. Vettori, B-J. Watling, K.S. Williamson.

109) **2012/13 to Sri Lanka**
L.R.P.L. Taylor *(captain)*, T.D. Astle, T.A. Boult, D.A.J. Bracewell, A.M. Ellis, D.R. Flynn, J.E.C. Franklin, M.J. Guptill, R.M. Hira, T.W.M. Latham, B.B. McCullum, N.L. McCullum, K.D. Mills, A.F. Milne, R.J. Nicol, J.D.P. Oram, J.S. Patel, T.G. Southee, C.F.K. van Wyk, B-J. Watling, K.S. Williamson.

110) **2012/13 to South Africa**
B.B. McCullum *(captain)*, C.J. Anderson, M.D. Bates, T.A. Boult, D.A.J. Bracewell, D.G. Brownlie, D.C. de Boorder, G.D. Elliott, D.R. Flynn, J.E.C. Franklin, P.G. Fulton, M.J. Guptill, R.M. Hira, M.J. McClenaghan, N.L. McCullum, B.P. Martin, C.S. Martin, K.D. Mills, C. Munro, J.D.S. Neesham, R.J. Nicol, J.S. Patel, N. Wagner, B-J. Watling, K.S. Williamson.

111) **2013 to England**
B.B. McCullum *(captain)*, T.A. Boult, D.A.J. Bracewell, D.G. Brownlie, I.G. Butler, G.D. Elliott, J.E.C. Franklin, P.G. Fulton, M.R. Gillespie, M.J. Guptill, R.M. Hira, T.W.M. Latham, N.L. McCullum, B.P. Martin, K.D. Mills, C. Munro, L. Ronchi, H.D. Rutherford, T.G. Southee, L.R.P.L. Taylor, D.L. Vettori, N. Wagner, B-J. Watling, K.S. Williamson.

112) **2013/14 to Bangladesh and Sri Lanka**
B.B. McCullum *(captain)*, C.J. Anderson, T.A. Boult, D.A.J. Bracewell, N.T. Broom*,
D.G. Brownlie, A.P. Devcich, G.D. Elliott, A.M. Ellis*, P.G. Fulton, M.R. Gillespie,
T.W.M. Latham, M.J. McClenaghan. N.L. McCullum, B.P. Martin, K.D. Mills, A.F. Milne,
C. Munro, J.D.S. Neesham, R.J. Nicol*, L. Ronchi, H.D. Rutherford, I.S. Sodhi, T.G. Southee,
L.R.P.L. Taylor, N. Wagner, B-J. Watling, K.S. Williamson.

113) **2013/14 to Bangladesh** *(ICC World Twenty20)*
B.B. McCullum *(captain)*, C.J. Anderson, T.A. Boult, A.P. Devcich, M.J. Guptill, R.M. Hira,
M.J. McClenaghan. N.L. McCullum, K.D. Mills, C. Munro, J.D.S. Neesham, L. Ronchi,
T.G. Southee, L.R.P.L. Taylor, K.S. Williamson.

114) **2014 to West Indies**
B.B. McCullum *(captain)*, C.J. Anderson, T.A. Boult, M.D. Craig, P.G. Fulton,
T.W.M. Latham, J.D.S. Neesham, L. Ronchi, H.D. Rutherford, I.S. Sodhi, T.G. Southee,
L.R.P.L. Taylor, N. Wagner, B-J. Watling, K.S. Williamson.

115) **2014/15 to United Arab Emirates**
B.B. McCullum *(captain)*, C.J. Anderson, T.A. Boult, D.A.J. Bracewell, D.G. Brownlie,
M.D. Craig, A.P. Devcich, M.P. Guptill, M.J. Henry, T.W.M. Latham, M.J. McClenaghan,
N.L. McCullum, K.D. Mills, A.F. Milne, J.D.S. Neesham, L. Ronchi, H.D. Rutherford,
I.S. Sodhi, T.G. Southee, L.R.P.L. Taylor, D.L. Vettori, N. Wagner, B-J. Watling,
K.S. Williamson.

116) **2015 to England**
B.B. McCullum *(captain)*, C.J. Anderson, T.A. Boult, D.A.J. Bracewell, M.D. Craig,
J.A. Duffy*, G.D. Elliott, M.J. Guptill, M.J. Henry, T.W.M. Latham, M.J. McClenaghan,
N.L. McCullum, A.W. Mathieson*, C. Munro*, L. Ronchi, H.D. Rutherford, M.J. Santner,
T.G. Southee, L.R.P.L. Taylor, N. Wagner, B-J. Watling, B.M. Wheeler*, K.S. Williamson.

117) **2015/16 to Zimbabwe and South Africa**
K.S. Williamson *(captain)*, D.A.J. Bracewell, G.D. Elliott, M.J. Guptill, M.J. Henry,
T.W.M. Latham, M.J. McClenaghan, N.L. McCullum, A.F. Milne, C. Munro, J.D.S. Neesham,
L. Ronchi, I.S. Sodhi, L.R.P.L. Taylor, B.M. Wheeler, G.H. Worker.

118) **2015/16 to Australia**
B.B. McCullum *(captain)*, T.A. Boult, D.A.J. Bracewell, M.D. Craig, M.J. Guptill,
M.J. Henry, T.W.M. Latham, M.J. McClenaghan*, J.D.S. Neesham, L. Ronchi,
H.D. Rutherford, M.J. Santner, T.G. Southee, L.R.P.L. Taylor, N.Wagner*, B-J. Watling,
K.S. Williamson.

119) **2015/16 to India** *(ICC World Twenty20)*
K.S. Williamson *(captain)*, C.J. Anderson, T.A. Boult, G.D. Elliott, M.J. Guptill,
M.J. McClenaghan, N.L. McCullum, A.F. Milne, C. Munro, H.M. Nicholls, L. Ronchi,
M.J. Santner, I.S. Sodhi, T.G. Southee, L.R.P.L. Taylor.

120) **2016/17 to Zimbabwe and South Africa**
K.S. Williamson *(captain)*, T.A. Boult, D.A.J. Bracewell, M.D. Craig, M.J. Guptill,
M.J. Henry, T.W.M. Latham, H.M. Nicholls, J.A. Raval, L. Ronchi, M.J. Santner, I.S. Sodhi,
T.G. Southee, L.R.P.L. Taylor, N. Wagner, B-J. Watling.

121) **2016/17 to India**
K.S. Williamson *(captain)*, C.J. Anderson, T.A. Boult, D.A.J. Bracewell, M.D. Craig,
A.P. Devcich, M.J. Guptill, M.J. Henry*, T.W.M. Latham, J.D.S. Neesham, H.M. Nicholls,
J.S. Patel*, L. Ronchi, M.J. Santner, I.S. Sodhi, T.G. Southee, L.R.P.L. Taylor, N. Wagner,
B-J. Watling.

122) **2016/17 to Australia**
K.S. Williamson *(captain)*, T.D. Astle, T.A. Boult, C. de Grandhomme, L.H. Ferguson,
M.J. Guptill, M.J. Henry, T.W.M. Latham, C. Munro, J.D.S. Neesham, H.M. Nicholls,
M.J. Santner, T.G. Southee, B-J. Watling.

123) **2017 to Ireland**
T.W.M. Latham *(captain)*, C.J. Anderson*, H.K. Bennett, N.T. Broom, M.J. Henry*,
S.C. Kuggeleijn, A.F. Milne*, C. Munro, J.D.S. Neesham, H.M. Nicholls, J.S. Patel,
S.H.A. Rance, L. Ronchi, M.J. Santner, I.S. Sodhi, L.R.P.L. Taylor, N. Wagner, G.H. Worker.

124) **2017 to England** *(ICC Champions Trophy)*
K.S. Williamson *(captain)*, C.J. Anderson, T.A. Boult, N.T. Broom, C. de Grandhomme, M.J. Guptill, T.W.M. Latham, M.J. McClenaghan, A.F. Milne, J.D.S. Neesham, J.S. Patel, L. Ronchi, M.J. Santner, T.G. Southee, L.R.P.L. Taylor.

125) **2017/18 to India**
K.S. Williamson *(captain)*, T.D. Astle, T.A. Boult, T.C. Bruce, C. de Grandhomme, M.J. Guptill, M.J. Henry, T.W.M. Latham, A.F. Milne, C. Munro, H.M. Nicholls, G.D. Phillips, M.J. Santner, I.S. Sodhi, T.G. Southee, L.R.P.L. Taylor, G.H. Worker.

126) **2018/19 to United Arab Emirates**
K.S. Williamson *(captain)*, C.J. Anderson, T.A. Blundell, T.A. Boult, M.S. Chapman, C. de Grandhomme, L.H. Ferguson, M.J. Henry, T.W.M. Latham, A.F. Milne, C. Munro, H.M. Nicholls, A.Y. Patel, G.D. Phillips, S.H.A. Rance, J.A. Raval, T.L. Seifert, I.S. Sodhi, W.E.R. Somerville, T.G. Southee, L.R.P.L. Taylor, N. Wagner, B-J. Watling, G.H. Worker.

127) **2019 to England** *(ICC World Cup)*
K.S. Williamson *(captain)*, T.A. Blundell, T.A. Boult, C. de Grandhomme, L.H. Ferguson, M.J. Guptill, M.J. Henry, T.W.M. Latham, C. Munro, J.D.S. Neesham, H.M. Nicholls, M.J. Santner, I.S. Sodhi, T.G. Southee, L.R.P.L. Taylor.

128) **2019/20 to Sri Lanka**
K.S. Williamson *(captain)*, T.D. Astle, T.A. Blundell, T.A. Boult, T.C. Bruce, C. de Grandhomme, L.H. Ferguson, M.J. Guptill, S.C. Kuggeleijn, T.W.M. Latham, D.J. Mitchell, C. Munro, H.M. Nicholls, A.Y. Patel, S.H.A. Rance, J.A. Raval, H.D. Rutherford*, M.J. Santner, T.L. Seifert, I.S.Sodhi, W.E.R. Somerville, T.G. Southee, L.R.P.L. Taylor, N. Wagner, B-J. Watling.

129) **2019/20 to Australia**
K.S. Williamson *(captain)*, T.D. Astle, T.A. Blundell, T.A. Boult, C. de Grandhomme, L.H. Ferguson, M.J. Henry, K.A. Jamieson*, T.W.M. Latham, H.M. Nicholls, G.D. Phillips*, J.A. Raval, M.J. Santner, W.E.R. Somerville*, T.G. Southee, L.R.P.L. Taylor, N. Wagner, B-J. Watling.

130) **2019/20 to Australia**
K.S.Williamson *(captain)*, T.A. Blundell, T.A. Boult, C. de Grandhomme, L.H. Ferguson, M.J. Guptill, M.J. Henry, K.A. Jamieson, T.W.M. Latham, J.D.S. Neesham, H.M. Nicholls, M.J Santner, I.S. Sodhi, T.G. Southee, L.R.P.L. Taylor.

131) **2021 to England**
K.S.Williamson *(captain)*, T.A. Blundell, T.A. Boult, D.A.J. Bracewell, D.P. Conway, C. de Grandhomme, J.A. Duffy, M.J. Henry, K.A. Jamieson, T.W.M. Latham, D.J. Mitchell, H.M. Nicholls, A.Y. Patel, R. Ravindra, M.J. Santner, T.G. Southee, L.R.P.L. Taylor, N. Wagner, B-J. Watling, W.A. Young.

132) **2021/22 to Bangladesh and Pakistan**
T.W.M. Latham *(captain)*, F.H. Allen, T.D. Astle, H.K. Bennett, T.A. Blundell, D.A.J. Bracewell, M.S. Chapman, C. de Grandhomme, J.A. Duffy, M.J. Guptill, M.J. Henry, S.C. Kuggeleijn, C.E. McConchie, D.J. Mitchell, H.M. Nicholls, A.Y. Patel, R. Ravindra, B.V. Sears, I.S. Sodhi, B.M. Tickner, W.A. Young.

133) **2021/22 to United Arab Emirates** *(ICC Twenty20 World Cup)*
K.S. Williamson *(captain)*, T.D. Astle, T.A. Boult, M.S. Chapman, D.P. Conway, L.H. Ferguson, M.J. Guptill, K.A. Jamieson, A.F. Milne, D.J. Mitchell, J.D.S. Neesham, G.D. Phillips, M.J. Santner, T.L. Seifert, I.S. Sodhi, T.G. Southee.

134) **2021/22 to India**
K.S. Williamson *(captain)*, T.D. Astle, T.A. Blundell, T.A. Boult, M.S. Chapman, L.H. Ferguson, M.J. Guptill, K.A. Jamieson, T.W.M. Latham, A.F. Milne, D.J. Mitchell, J.D.S. Neesham, H.M. Nicholls, A.Y. Patel, G.D. Phillips, R. Ravindra, M.J. Santner, T.L. Seifert, I.S. Sodhi, W.E.R. Somerville, T.G. Southee, L.R.P.L. Taylor, N. Wagner, W.A. Young.

135) **2022 to England**
K.S. Williamson *(captain)*, T.A. Blundell, T.A. Boult, M.G. Bracewell, D. Cleaver*, D.P. Conway, C. de Grandhomme, J.A. Duffy, C.D. Fletcher, M.J. Henry, K.A. Jamieson, T.W.M. Latham, D.J. Mitchell, H.M. Nicholls, A.Y. Patel, R. Ravindra, H.D. Rutherford, T.G. Southee, B.M. Tickner, N. Wagner, W.A. Young.

* *replacement or temporary addition to the touring party*

# NEW ZEALAND TEST RECORDS

## REGISTER OF PLAYERS

| | Born | Died | Type | | Test Career |
|---|---|---|---|---|---|
| **Adams**<br>Andre Ryan | 17/7/1975<br>Auckland | | RHB | RFM | 2001/02 |
| **Alabaster**<br>John Chaloner | 11/7/1930<br>Invercargill | | RHB | RLB | 1955/56-1971/72 |
| **Allcott**<br>Cyril Francis Walter | 7/10/1896<br>Lower Moutere | 19/11/1973<br>Auckland | LHB | LM | 1929/30-1931/32 |
| **Allott**<br>Geoffrey Ian | 24/12/1971<br>Christchurch | | RHB | LFM | 1995/96-1999 |
| **Anderson**<br>Corey James | 13/12/1990<br>Christchurch | | LHB | LFM | 2013/14-2015/16 |
| **Anderson**<br>Robert Wickham | 2/10/1948<br>Christchurch | | RHB | RLB | 1976/77-1978 |
| **Anderson**<br>William McDougall | 8/10/1919<br>Westport | 21/12/1979<br>Christchurch | LHB | RLBG | 1945/46 |
| **Andrews**<br>Bryan | 4/4/1945<br>Christchurch | | RHB | RFM | 1973/74 |
| **Arnel**<br>Brent John | 3/1/1979<br>Hamilton | | RHB | RFM | 2009/10-2011/12 |
| **Astle**<br>Nathan John | 15/9/1971<br>Christchurch | | RHB | RM | 1995/96-2006/07 |
| **Astle**<br>Todd Duncan | 24/9/1986<br>Palmerston North | | RHB | RLB | 2012/13-2019/20 |
| **Badcock**<br>Frederick Theodore | 9/8/1897<br>Abbottabad, India | 19/9/1982<br>Perth | RHB | RM | 1929/30-1932/33 |
| **Barber**<br>Richard Trevor | 3/6/1925<br>Otaki | 7/8/2015<br>Christchurch | RHB | WK | 1955/56 |
| **Bartlett**<br>Gary Alex | 3/2/1941<br>Blenheim | | RHB | RF | 1961/62-1967/68 |
| **Barton**<br>Paul Thomas | 9/10/1935<br>Wellington | | RHB | SLA | 1961/62-1962/63 |
| **Beard**<br>Donald Derek | 14/1/1920<br>Palmerston North | 15/7/1982<br>Lancaster | RHB | RM | 1951/52-1955/56 |
| **Beck**<br>John Edward Francis | 1/8/1934<br>Wellington | 23/4/2000<br>Waikanae | LHB | | 1953/54-1955/56 |
| **Bell**<br>Matthew David | 25/2/1977<br>Dunedin | | RHB | | 1998/99-2007/08 |
| **Bell**<br>William | 5/9/1931<br>Dunedin | 23/7/2002<br>Auckland | RHB | RLB | 1953/54 |
| **Bennett**<br>Hamish Kyle | 22/2/1987<br>Timaru | | LHB | RF | 2010/11 |
| **Bilby**<br>Grahame Paul | 7/5/1941<br>Wellington | | RHB | | 1965/66 |
| **Blain**<br>Tony Elston | 17/2/1962<br>Nelson | | RHB | WK | 1986-1993/94 |
| **Blair**<br>Robert William | 23/6/1932<br>Petone | | RHB | RFM | 1952/53-1963/64 |
| **Blundell**<br>Thomas Ackland | 1/9/1990<br>Wellington | | RHB | WK | 2017/18- 2022 |
| **Blunt**<br>Roger Charles | 3/11/1900<br>Durham, England | 22/6/1966<br>London | RHB | RLBG | 1929/30-1931/32 |
| **Bolton**<br>Bruce Alfred | 31/5/1935<br>Christchurch | | RHB | RLB | 1958/59 |
| **Bond**<br>Shane Edward | 7/6/1975<br>Christchurch | | RHB | RF | 2001/02-2009/10 |
| **Boock**<br>Stephen Lewis | 20/9/1951<br>Dunedin | | RHB | SLA | 1977/78-1988/89 |
| **Boult**<br>Trent Alexander | 22/7/1989<br>Rotorua | | RHB | LFM | 2011/12-2022 |

| | Born | Died | Type | | Test Career |
|---|---|---|---|---|---|
| **Bracewell**<br>Brendon Paul | 14/9/1959<br>Auckland | | RHB | RFM | 1978-1984/85 |
| **Bracewell**<br>Douglas Andrew John | 28/9/1990<br>Tauranga | | RHB | RFM | 2011/12-2016/17 |
| **Bracewell**<br>John Garry | 15/4/1958<br>Auckland | | RHB | ROB | 1980/81-1990 |
| **Bracewell**<br>Michael Gordon | 14/2/1991<br>Masterton | | LHB | ROB | 2022 |
| **Bradburn**<br>Grant Eric | 26/5/1966<br>Hamilton | | RHB | ROB | 1990/91-2000/01 |
| **Bradburn**<br>Wynne Pennell | 24/11/1938<br>Thames | 25/9/2008<br>Hamilton | RHB | RSM | 1963/64 |
| **Broom**<br>Neil Trevor | 20/11/1983<br>Christchurch | | RHB | | 2016/17 |
| **Brown**<br>Vaughan Raymond | 3/11/1959<br>Christchurch | | LHB | ROB | 1985/86 |
| **Brownlie**<br>Dean Graham | 30/7/1984<br>Perth, Australia | | RHB | RM | 2011/12-2013 |
| **Burgess**<br>Mark Gordon | 17/7/1944<br>Auckland | | RHB | ROB | 1967/68-1980/81 |
| **Burke**<br>Cecil | 22/3/1914<br>Auckland | 4/8/1997<br>Auckland | RHB | RLB | 1945/46 |
| **Burtt**<br>Thomas Browning | 22/1/1915<br>Christchurch | 24/5/1988<br>Christchurch | RHB | SLA | 1946/47-1952/53 |
| **Butler**<br>Ian Gareth | 24/11/1981<br>Auckland | | RHB | RF | 2001/02-2004/05 |
| **Butterfield**<br>Leonard Arthur | 29/8/1913<br>Christchurch | 5/7/1999<br>Christchurch | RHB | RM | 1945/46 |
| **Cairns**<br>Bernard Lance | 10/10/1949<br>Picton | | RHB | RM | 1973/74-1985/86 |
| **Cairns**<br>Christopher Lance | 13/6/1970<br>Picton | | RHB | RFM | 1989/90-2004 |
| **Cameron**<br>Francis James | 1/6/1932<br>Dunedin | | RHB | RFM | 1961/62-1965 |
| **Cave**<br>Henry Butler | 10/10/1922<br>Wanganui | 15/9/1989<br>Wanganui | RHB | RM | 1949-1958 |
| **Chapple**<br>Murray Ernest | 25/7/1930<br>Christchurch | 31/7/1985<br>Hamilton | RHB | SLA | 1952/53-1965/66 |
| **Chatfield**<br>Ewen John | 3/7/1950<br>Dannevirke | | RHB | RM | 1974/75-1988/89 |
| **Cleverley**<br>Donald Charles | 23/12/1909<br>Oamaru | 16/2/2004<br>Southport, Aust. | LHB | RFM | 1931/32-1945/46 |
| **Collinge**<br>Richard Owen | 2/4/1946<br>Wellington | | RHB | LFM | 1964/65-1978 |
| **Colquhoun**<br>Ian Alexander | 8/6/1924<br>Wellington | 26/2/2005<br>Paraparaumu Beach | RHB | WK | 1954/55 |
| **Coney**<br>Jeremy Vernon | 21/6/1952<br>Wellington | | RHB | RSM | 1973/74-1986/87 |
| **Congdon**<br>Bevan Ernest | 11/2/1938<br>Motueka | 10/2/2018<br>Auckland | RHB | RM | 1964/65-1978 |
| **Conway**<br>Devon Philip | 8/7/1991<br>Johannesburg, South Africa | | LHB | WK | 2021-2022 |
| **Cowie**<br>John | 30/3/1912<br>Auckland | 3/6/1994<br>Lower Hutt | RHB | RFM | 1937-1949 |
| **Craig**<br>Mark Donald | 23/3/1987<br>Auckland | | LHB | ROB | 2014-2016/17 |
| **Cresswell**<br>George Fenwick | 22/3/1915<br>Wanganui | 10/1/1966<br>Blenheim | LHB | RM | 1949-1950/51 |
| **Cromb**<br>Ian Burns | 25/6/1905<br>Christchurch | 6/3/1984<br>Christchurch | RHB | RM | 1931-1931/32 |
| **Crowe**<br>Jeffrey John | 14/9/1958<br>Auckland | | RHB | | 1982/83-1989/90 |
| **Crowe**<br>Martin David | 22/9/1962<br>Auckland | 3/3/2016<br>Auckland | RHB | RM | 1981/82-1995/96 |

| | Born | Died | Type | | Test Career |
|---|---|---|---|---|---|
| **Cumming**<br>Craig Derek | 31/8/1975<br>Timaru | | RHB | RM | 2004/05-2007/08 |
| **Cunis**<br>Robert Smith | 5/1/1941<br>Whangarei | 9/8/2008<br>Whangarei | RHB | RFM | 1963/64-1971/72 |
| **D'Arcy**<br>John William | 23/4/1936<br>Christchurch | | RHB | | 1958 |
| **de Grandhomme**<br>Colin | 22/7/1986<br>Harare, Zimbabwe | | RHB | RM | 2016/17-2022 |
| **de Groen**<br>Richard Paul | 5/8/1962<br>Otorohanga | | RHB | RM | 1993/94-1994/95 |
| **Davis**<br>Heath Te-Ihi-O-Te-Rangi | 30/11/1971<br>Lower Hutt | | RHB | RF | 1994-1997/98 |
| **Dempster**<br>Charles Stewart | 15/11/1903<br>Wellington | 12/2/1974<br>Wellington | RHB | | 1929/30-1932/33 |
| **Dempster**<br>Eric William | 25/1/1925<br>Wellington | 15/8/2011<br>Dunedin | LHB | SLA | 1952/53-1953/54 |
| **Dick**<br>Arthur Edward | 10/10/1936<br>Middlemarch | | RHB | WK | 1961/62-1965 |
| **Dickinson**<br>George Ritchie | 11/3/1903<br>Dunedin | 17/3/1978<br>Lower Hutt | RHB | RF | 1929/30-1931/32 |
| **Donnelly**<br>Martin Paterson | 17/10/1917<br>Ngaruawahia | 22/10/1999<br>Sydney | LHB | SLA | 1937-1949 |
| **Doull**<br>Simon Blair | 6/8/1969<br>Pukekohe | | RHB | RM | 1992/93-1999/00 |
| **Dowling**<br>Graham Thorne | 4/3/1937<br>Christchurch | | RHB | | 1961/62-1971/72 |
| **Drum**<br>Christopher James | 10/7/1974<br>Auckland | | RHB | RFM | 2000/01-2001/02 |
| **Dunning**<br>John Angus | 6/2/1903<br>Omaha | 24/6/1971<br>Adelaide | RHB | RM | 1932/33-1937 |
| **Edgar**<br>Bruce Adrian | 23/11/1956<br>Wellington | | LHB | WK | 1978-1986 |
| **Edwards**<br>Graham Neil | 27/5/1955<br>Nelson | 6/4/2020<br>Nelson | RHB | WK | 1976/77-1980/81 |
| **Elliott**<br>Grant David | 21/3/1979<br>Johanesburg, S. Africa | | RHB | RM | 2007/08-2009/10 |
| **Emery**<br>Raymond William George | 28/3/1915<br>Auckland | 18/12/1982<br>Auckland | RHB | RM | 1951/52 |
| **Ferguson**<br>Lachlan Hammond | 13/9/1991<br>Auckland | | RHB | RF | 2019/20 |
| **Fisher**<br>Frederick Eric | 28/7/1924<br>Johnsonville | 19/6/1996<br>Palmerston North | RHB | LM | 1952/53 |
| **Fleming**<br>Stephen Paul | 1/4/1973<br>Christchurch | | LHB | | 1993/94-2007/08 |
| **Flynn**<br>Daniel Raymond | 16/4/1985<br>Rotorua | | LHB | SLA | 2008-2012 |
| **Foley**<br>Henry | 28/1/1906<br>Wellington | 16/10/1948<br>Brisbane | LHB | | 1929/30 |
| **Franklin**<br>James Edward Charles | 7/11/1980<br>Wellington | | LHB | LFM | 2000/01-2012/13 |
| **Franklin**<br>Trevor John | 18/3/1962<br>Auckland | | RHB | RM | 1983-1990/91 |
| **Freeman**<br>Douglas Linford | 8/9/1914<br>Sydney, Australia | 31/5/1994<br>Sydney | RHB | RLBG | 1932/33 |
| **Fulton**<br>Peter Gordon | 1/2/1979<br>Christchurch | | RHB | RM | 2005/06-2014 |
| **Gallichan**<br>Norman | 3/6/1906<br>Palmerston North | 25/3/1969<br>Taupo | RHB | SLA | 1937 |
| **Gedye**<br>Sidney Graham | 2/5/1929<br>Otahuhu | 10/8/2014<br>Auckland | RHB | | 1963/64-1964/65 |
| **Germon**<br>Lee Kenneth | 4/11/1968<br>Christchurch | | RHB | WK | 1995/96-1996/97 |
| **Gillespie**<br>Mark Raymond | 17/10/1979<br>Wanganui | | RHB | RFM | 2007/08-2011/12 |

| | Born | Died | Type | | Test Career |
|---|---|---|---|---|---|
| **Gillespie** Stuart Ross | 2/3/1957 Wanganui | | RHB | RFM | 1985/86 |
| **Gray** Evan John | 18/11/1954 Wellington | | RHB | SLA | 1983-1988/89 |
| **Greatbatch** Mark John | 11/12/1963 Auckland | | LHB | | 1987/88-1996/97 |
| **Guillen** Simpson Clairmonte | 24/9/1924 Port of Spain, Trinidad | 1/3/2013 Christchurch | RHB | WK | 1955/56 |
| **Guptill** Martin James | 30/9/1986 Auckland | | RHB | ROB | 2008/09-2016/17 |
| **Guy** John William | 29/8/1934 Nelson | | LHB | | 1955/56-1961/62 |
| **Hadlee** Dayle Robert | 6/1/1948 Christchurch | | RHB | RM | 1969-1977/78 |
| **Hadlee** Richard John | 3/7/1951 Christchurch | | LHB | RFM | 1972/73-1990 |
| **Hadlee** Walter Arnold | 4/6/1915 Lincoln | 29/9/2006 Christchurch | RHB | | 1937-1950/51 |
| **Harford** Noel Sherwin | 30/8/1930 Winton | 30/3/1981 Auckland | RHB | RM | 1955/56-1958 |
| **Harford** Roy Ivan | 30/5/1936 London, England | | LHB | WK | 1967/68 |
| **Harris** Chris Zinzan | 20/11/1969 Christchurch | | LHB | RM | 1992/93-2001/02 |
| **Harris** Parke Gerald Zinzan | 18/7/1927 Christchurch | 1/12/1991 Christchurch | RHB | ROB | 1955/56-1964/65 |
| **Harris** Roger Meredith | 27/7/1933 Otahuhu | | RHB | RM | 1958/59 |
| **Hart** Matthew Norman | 16/5/1972 Hamilton | | LHB | SLA | 1993/94-1995/96 |
| **Hart** Robert Garry | 2/12/1974 Hamilton | | RHB | WK | 2001/02-2003/04 |
| **Hartland** Blair Robert | 22/10/1966 Christchurch | | RHB | | 1991/92-1994 |
| **Haslam** Mark James | 26/9/1972 Bury, England | | LHB | SLA | 1992/93-1995/96 |
| **Hastings** Brian Frederick | 23/3/1940 Wellington | | RHB | | 1968/69-1975/76 |
| **Hayes** John Arthur | 11/1/1927 Auckland | 25/12/2007 Auckland | RHB | RF | 1950/51-1958 |
| **Henderson** Matthew | 2/8/1895 Auckland | 17/6/1970 Wellington | LHB | LFM | 1929/30 |
| **Henry** Matthew James | 14/12/1991 Christchurch | | RHB | RFM | 2015-2022 |
| **Hopkins** Gareth James | 24/11/1976 Lower Hutt | | RHB | WK | 2008-2010/11 |
| **Horne** Matthew Jeffery | 5/12/1970 Auckland | | RHB | RM | 1996/97-2002/03 |
| **Horne** Philip Andrew | 21/1/1960 Upper Hutt | | LHB | | 1986/87-1990/91 |
| **Hough** Kenneth William | 24/10/1928 Sydney, Australia | 20/9/2009 Gladstone | RHB | RM | 1958/59 |
| **How** Jamie Michael | 19/5/1981 New Plymouth | | RHB | ROB | 2005/06-2008/09 |
| **Howarth** Geoffrey Philip | 29/3/1951 Auckland | | RHB | ROB | 1974/75-1984/85 |
| **Howarth** Hedley John | 25/12/1943 Auckland | 7/11/2008 Auckland | LHB | SLA | 1969-1976/77 |
| **Ingram** Peter John | 25/10/1978 Hawera | | RHB | | 2009/10 |
| **James** Kenneth Cecil | 12/3/1904 Wellington | 21/8/1976 Palmerston North | RHB | WK | 1929/30-1932/33 |
| **Jamieson** Kyle Alex | 30/12/1994 Auckland | | RHB | RFM | 2019/20-2022 |

| | *Born* | *Died* | *Type* | | | *Test Career* |
|---|---|---|---|---|---|---|
| **Jarvis** <br> Terrence Wayne | 29/7/1944 <br> Auckland | | RHB | | | 1964/65-1972/73 |
| **Jones** <br> Andrew Howard | 9/5/1959 <br> Wellington | | RHB | ROB | | 1986/87-1994/95 |
| **Jones** <br> Richard Andrew | 22/10/1973 <br> Auckland | | RHB | | | 2003/04 |
| **Kennedy** <br> Robert John | 3/6/1972 <br> Dunedin | | RHB | RFM | | 1995/96 |
| **Kerr** <br> John Lambert | 28/12/1910 <br> Dannevirke | 27/5/2007 <br> Christchurch | RHB | | | 1931-1937 |
| **Kuggeleijn** <br> Christopher Mary | 10/5/1956 <br> Auckland | | RHB | ROB | | 1988/89 |
| **Larsen** <br> Gavin Rolf | 27/9/1962 <br> Wellington | | RHB | RM | | 1994-1995/96 |
| **Latham** <br> Rodney Terry | 12/6/1961 <br> Christchurch | | RHB | | | 1991/92-1992/93 |
| **Latham** <br> Thomas William Maxwell | 2/4/1992 <br> Christchurch | | LHB | WK | | 2013/14-2022 |
| **Lees** <br> Warren Kenneth | 19/3/1952 <br> Dunedin | | RHB | WK | | 1976/77-1983 |
| **Leggat** <br> Ian Bruce | 7/6/1930 <br> Invercargill | | RHB | RM | | 1953/54 |
| **Leggat** <br> John Gordon | 27/5/1926 <br> Wellington | 9/3/1973 <br> Christchurch | RHB | | | 1951/52-1955/56 |
| **Lissette** <br> Allen Fisher | 6/11/1919 <br> Morrinsville | 24/1/1973 <br> Hamilton | RHB | SLA | | 1955/56 |
| **Loveridge** <br> Greg Riaka | 15/1/1975 <br> Palmerston North | | RHB | RLB | | 1995/96 |
| **Lowry** <br> Thomas Coleman | 17/2/1898 <br> Fernhill | 20/7/1976 <br> Hastings | RHB | ROB | WK | 1929/30-1931 |
| **McCullum** <br> Brendon Barrie | 27/9/1981 <br> Dunedin | | RHB | | WK | 2003/04-2015/16 |
| **McEwan** <br> Paul Ernest | 19/12/1953 <br> Christchurch | | RHB | RM | | 1979/80-1984/85 |
| **MacGibbon** <br> Anthony Roy | 28/8/1924 <br> Christchurch | 6/4/2010 <br> Christchurch | RHB | RFM | | 1950/51-1958 |
| **McGirr** <br> Herbert Mendelson | 5/11/1891 <br> Wellington | 14/4/1964 <br> Nelson | RHB | RFM | | 1929/30 |
| **McGregor** <br> Spencer Noel | 18/12/1931 <br> Dunedin | 21/11/2007 <br> Christchurch | RHB | | | 1954/55-1964/65 |
| **McIntosh** <br> Timothy Gavin | 4/12/1979 <br> Auckland | | LHB | | | 2008/09-2010/11 |
| **McKay** <br> Andrew John | 17/4/1980 <br> Auckland | | RHB | LF | | 2010/11 |
| **McLeod** <br> Edwin George | 14/10/1900 <br> Auckland | 14/9/1989 <br> Wellington | LHB | RLB | | 1929/30 |
| **McMahon** <br> Trevor George | 8/11/1929 <br> Wellington | | RHB | WK | | 1955/56 |
| **McMillan** <br> Craig Douglas | 13/9/1976 <br> Christchurch | | RHB | RM | | 1997/98-2004/05 |
| **McRae** <br> Donald Alexander Noel | 25/12/1912 <br> Christchurch | 10/8/1986 <br> Christchurch | LHB | LM | | 1945/46 |
| **Marshall** <br> Hamish John Hamilton | 15/2/1979 <br> Warkworth | | RHB | RM | | 2000/01-2005/06 |
| **Marshall** <br> James Andrew Hamilton | 15/2/1979 <br> Warkworth | | RHB | RM | | 2004/05-2008 |
| **Martin** <br> Bruce Philip | 25/4/1980 <br> Whangarei | | RHB | SLA | | 2012/13-2013/14 |
| **Martin** <br> Christopher Stewart | 10/12/1974 <br> Christchurch | | RHB | RFM | | 2000/01-2012 |
| **Mason** <br> Michael James | 27/8/1974 <br> Carterton | | RHB | RFM | | 2003/04 |
| **Matheson** <br> Alexander Malcolm | 27/2/1906 <br> Omaha | 31/12/1985 <br> Auckland | RHB | RFM | | 1929/30-1931 |

**NZC**

| | *Born* | *Died* | *Type* | | *Test Career* |
|---|---|---|---|---|---|
| **Meale**<br>Trevor | 11/11/1928<br>Auckland | 21/5/2010<br>Auckland | LHB | | 1958 |
| **Merritt**<br>William Edward | 18/8/1908<br>Sumner | 9/6/1977<br>Christchurch | RHB | RLBG | 1929/30-1931 |
| **Meuli**<br>Edgar Milton | 20/2/1926<br>Hawera | 15/4/2007<br>Auckland | RHB | RLB | 1952/53 |
| **Milburn**<br>Barry Douglas | 24/11/1943<br>Dunedin | | RHB | WK | 1968/69 |
| **Miller**<br>Lawrence Somerville Martin | 31/3/1923<br>New Plymouth | 17/12/1996<br>Paraparaumu | LHB | LSM | 1952/53-1958 |
| **Mills**<br>John Ernest | 3/9/1905<br>Dunedin | 11/12/1972<br>Hamilton | LHB | | 1929/30-1932/33 |
| **Mills**<br>Kyle David | 15/3/1979<br>Auckland | | RHB | RFM | 2004-2008/09 |
| **Mitchell**<br>Daryl Joseph | 20/5/1991<br>Hamilton | | RHB | RM | 2019/20-2022 |
| **Moir**<br>Alexander McKenzie | 17/7/1919<br>Dunedin | 17/6/2000<br>Dunedin | RHB | RLB | 1950/51-1958/59 |
| **Moloney**<br>Denis Andrew Robert | 11/8/1910<br>Dunedin | 15/7/1942<br>El Alamein | RHB | RLB | 1937 |
| **Mooney**<br>Francis Leonard Hugh | 26/5/1921<br>Wellington | 8/3/2004<br>Wellington | RHB | WK | 1949-1953/54 |
| **Morgan**<br>Ross Winston | 12/2/1941<br>Auckland | | RHB | ROB | 1964/65-1971/72 |
| **Morrison**<br>Bruce Donald | 17/12/1933<br>Lower Hutt | | LHB | RM | 1962/63 |
| **Morrison**<br>Daniel Kyle | 3/2/1966<br>Auckland | | RHB | RFM | 1987/88-1996/97 |
| **Morrison**<br>John Francis MacLean | 27/8/1947<br>Wellington | | RHB | SLA | 1973/74-1981/82 |
| **Motz**<br>Richard Charles | 12/1/1940<br>Christchurch | 29/4/2007<br>Christchurch | RHB | RFM | 1961/62-1969 |
| **Munro**<br>Colin | 11/3/1987<br>Durban, South Africa | | LHB | RM | 2012/13 |
| **Murray**<br>Bruce Alexander Grenfell | 18/9/1940<br>Wellington | | RHB | RLB | 1967/68-1970/71 |
| **Murray**<br>Darrin James | 4/9/1967<br>Christchurch | | RHB | | 1994/95 |
| **Nash**<br>Dion Joseph | 20/11/1971<br>Auckland | | RHB | RFM | 1992/93-2001/02 |
| **Neesham**<br>James Douglas Sheahan | 17/9/1990<br>Auckland | | LHB | RFM | 2013/14-2016/17 |
| **Newman**<br>Jack | 3/7/1902<br>Brightwater | 23/9/1996<br>Nelson | RHB | LM | 1931/32-1932/33 |
| **Nicholls**<br>Henry Michael | 15/11/1991<br>Christchurch | | LHB | WK | 2015/16-2022 |
| **Nicol**<br>Robert James | 28/5/1983<br>Auckland | | RHB | ROB | 2011/12 |
| **O'Brien**<br>Iain Edward | 10/7/1976<br>Lower Hutt | | RHB | RM | 2004/05-2009/10 |
| **O'Connor**<br>Shayne Barry | 15/11/1973<br>Hastings | | LHB | LFM | 1997/98-2001/02 |
| **Oram**<br>Jacob David Philip | 28/7/1978<br>Palmerston North | | LHB | RM | 2002/03-2009/10 |
| **O'Sullivan**<br>David Robert | 16/11/1944<br>Palmerston North | | RHB | SLA | 1972/73-1976/77 |
| **Overton**<br>Guy William Fitzroy | 8/6/1919<br>Dunedin | 7/9/1993<br>Winton | LHB | RFM | 1953/54 |
| **Owens**<br>Michael Barry | 11/11/1969<br>Christchurch | | RHB | RFM | 1992/93-1994 |
| **Page**<br>Milford Laurenson | 8/5/1902<br>Lyttelton | 13/2/1987<br>Christchurch | RHB | ROB | 1929/30-1937 |
| **Papps**<br>Michael Hugh William | 2/7/1979<br>Christchurch | | RHB | | 2003/04-2007/08 |

| | *Born* | *Died* | *Type* | | | *Test Career* |
|---|---|---|---|---|---|---|
| **Parker**<br>John Morton | 21/2/1951<br>Dannevirke | | RHB | WK | | 1972/73-1980/81 |
| **Parker**<br>Norman Murray | 28/8/1948<br>Dannevirke | | RHB | RLB | | 1976/77 |
| **Parore**<br>Adam Craig | 23/1/1971<br>Auckland | | RHB | WK | | 1990-2001/02 |
| **Patel**<br>Ajaz Yunus | 21/10/1988<br>Bombay, India | | LHB | SLA | | 2018/19-2022 |
| **Patel**<br>Dipak Narshibhai | 25/10/1958<br>Nairobi, Kenya | | RHB | ROB | | 1986/87-1996/97 |
| **Patel**<br>Jeetan Shashi | 7/5/1980<br>Wellington | | RHB | ROB | | 2005/06-2016/17 |
| **Petherick**<br>Peter James | 25/9/1942<br>Ranfurly | 7/6/2015<br>Perth, Australia | RHB | ROB | | 1976/77 |
| **Petrie**<br>Eric Charlton | 22/5/1927<br>Ngaruawahia | 14/8/2004<br>Omokoroa | RHB | WK | | 1955/56-1965/66 |
| **Phillips**<br>Glenn Dominic | 6/12/1996<br>East London, South Africa | | RHB | ROB | WK | 2019/20 |
| **Playle**<br>William Rodger | 1/12/1938<br>Palmerston North | 27/2/2019<br>Coffs Harbour, Australia | RHB | | | 1958-1962/63 |
| **Pocock**<br>Blair Andrew | 18/6/1971<br>Papakura | | RHB | | | 1993/94-1997/98 |
| **Pollard**<br>Victor | 7/9/1945<br>Burnley, England | | RHB | ROB | | 1964/65-1973 |
| **Poore**<br>Matt Beresford | 1/6/1930<br>Christchurch | 11/6/2020<br>Auckland | RHB | ROB | | 1952/53-1955/56 |
| **Priest**<br>Mark Wellings | 12/8/1961<br>Greymouth | | LHB | SLA | | 1990-1997/98 |
| **Pringle**<br>Christopher | 26/1/1968<br>Auckland | | RHB | RFM | | 1990/91-1994/95 |
| **Puna**<br>Narotam | 28/10/1929<br>Surat, India | 7/6/1996<br>Hamilton | RHB | ROB | | 1965/66 |
| **Rabone**<br>Geoffrey Osborne | 6/11/1921<br>Gore | 19/1/2006<br>Auckland | RHB | ROB | | 1949-1954/55 |
| **Raval**<br>Jeet Ashok | 22/5/1988<br>Ahmedabad, India | | LHB | RLB | | 2016/17-2019/20 |
| **Ravindra**<br>Rachin | 18/11/1999<br>Wellington | | LHB | SLA | | 2021/22 |
| **Redmond**<br>Aaron James | 23/9/1979<br>Auckland | | RHB | RLB | | 2008-2013/14 |
| **Redmond**<br>Rodney Ernest | 29/12/1944<br>Whangarei | | LHB | SLA | | 1972/73 |
| **Reid**<br>John Fulton | 3/3/1956<br>Auckland | 28/12/2020<br>Christchurch | LHB | RLB | WK | 1978/79-1985/86 |
| **Reid**<br>John Richard | 3/6/1928<br>Auckland | 19/10/2020<br>Auckland | RHB | RFM | WK | 1949-1965 |
| **Richardson**<br>Mark Hunter | 11/6/1971<br>Hastings | | LHB | SLA | | 2000/01-2004/05 |
| **Roberts**<br>Andrew Duncan Glenn | 6/5/1947<br>Te Aroha | 26/10/1989<br>Wellington | RHB | RM | | 1975/76-1976/77 |
| **Roberts**<br>Albert William | 20/8/1909<br>Christchurch | 13/5/1978<br>Clyde | RHB | RM | | 1929/30-1937 |
| **Robertson**<br>Gary Keith | 15/7/1960<br>New Plymouth | | RHB | RFM | | 1985/86 |
| **Ronchi**<br>Luke | 23/4/1981<br>Dannevirke | | RHB | | WK | 2015-2016/17 |
| **Rowe**<br>Charles Gordon | 30/6/1915<br>Glasgow, Scotland | 9/6/1995<br>Palmerston North | RHB | | | 1945/46 |
| **Rutherford**<br>Hamish Duncan | 27/4/1989<br>Dunedin | | LHB | | | 2012/13-2014/15 |
| **Rutherford**<br>Kenneth Robert | 26/10/1965<br>Dunedin | | RHB | RM | | 1984/85-1994/95 |
| **Ryder**<br>Jesse Daniel | 6/8/1984<br>Masterton | | LHB | RM | | 2008/09-2011/12 |

| | Born | Died | Type | | Test Career |
|---|---|---|---|---|---|
| **Santner**<br>Mitchell Josef | 5/2/1992<br>Hamilton | | LHB | SLA | 2015/16-2021 |
| **Scott**<br>Roy Hamilton | 6/3/1917<br>Clyde | 5/8/2005<br>Christchurch | RHB | RM | 1946/47 |
| **Scott**<br>Verdun John | 31/7/1916<br>Devonport | 2/8/1980<br>Devonport | RHB | RM | 1945/46-1951/52 |
| **Sewell**<br>David Graham | 20/10/1977<br>Christchurch | | RHB | LFM | 1997/98 |
| **Shrimpton**<br>Michael John Froud | 23/6/1940<br>Feilding | 13/6/2015<br>Hastings | RHB | RLBG | 1962/63-1973/74 |
| **Sinclair**<br>Barry Whitley | 23/10/1936<br>Wellington | 10/7/2022<br>Auckland | RHB | | 1962/63-1967/68 |
| **Sinclair**<br>Ian McKay | 1/6/1933<br>Rangiora | 25/8/2019<br>Tauranga | LHB | ROB | 1955/56 |
| **Sinclair**<br>Mathew Stuart | 9/11/1975<br>Katherine, Australia | | RHB | | 1999/00-2009/10 |
| **Smith**<br>Frank Brunton | 13/3/1922<br>Rangiora | 6/7/1997<br>Christchurch | | RHB | 1946/47-1951/52 |
| **Smith**<br>Horace Dennis | 8/1/1913<br>Toowoomba, Australia | 25/1/1986<br>Christchurch | RHB | RFM | 1932/33 |
| **Smith**<br>Ian David Stockley | 28/2/1957<br>Nelson | | RHB | WK | 1980/81-1991/92 |
| **Snedden**<br>Colin Alexander | 7/1/1918<br>Auckland | 23/4/2011<br>Auckland | RHB | ROB | 1946/47 |
| **Snedden**<br>Martin Colin | 23/11/1958<br>Auckland | | LHB | RFM | 1980/81-1990 |
| **Sodhi**<br>Inderbir Singh | 31/10/1992<br>Ludhiana, India | | RHB | RLB | 2013/14-2018/19 |
| **Somerville**<br>William Edgar Richard | 9/8/1984<br>Wellington | | RHB | ROB | 2018/19-2021/22 |
| **Southee**<br>Timothy Grant | 11/12/1988<br>Whangarei | | RHB | RFM | 2007/08-2022 |
| **Sparling**<br>John Trevor | 24/7/1938<br>Auckland | | RHB | ROB | 1958-1963/64 |
| **Spearman**<br>Craig Murray | 4/7/1972<br>Auckland | | RHB | | 1995/96-2000/01 |
| **Stead**<br>Gary Raymond | 9/1/1972<br>Christchurch | | RHB | RLB | 1998/99-1999/00 |
| **Stirling**<br>Derek Alexander | 5/10/1961<br>Upper Hutt | | RHB | RFM | 1984/85-1986 |
| **Styris**<br>Scott Bernard | 10/7/1975<br>Brisbane, Australia | | RHB | RM | 2001/02-2007/08 |
| **Su'a**<br>Murphy Logo | 7/11/1966<br>Wanganui | | LHB | LFM | 1991/92-1994/95 |
| **Sutcliffe**<br>Bert | 17/11/1923<br>Auckland | 20/4/2001<br>Auckland | LHB | SLA | 1946/47-1965 |
| **Taylor**<br>Bruce Richard | 12/7/1943<br>Timaru | 6/2/2021<br>Lower Hutt | LHB | RFM | 1964/65-1973 |
| **Taylor**<br>Donald Dougald | 2/3/1923<br>Auckland | 5/12/1980<br>Auckland | RHB | RLBG | 1946/47-1955/56 |
| **Taylor**<br>Luteru Ross Poutoa Lote | 8/3/1984<br>Lower Hutt | | RHB | ROB | 2007/08-2021/22 |
| **Thomson**<br>Keith | 26/2/1941<br>Methven | | RHB | | 1967/68 |
| **Thomson**<br>Shane Alexander | 27/1/1969<br>Hamilton | | RHB | ROB | 1989/90-1995/96 |
| **Tindill**<br>Eric William Thomas | 18/12/1910<br>Nelson | 1/8/2010<br>Wellington | LHB | WK | 1937-1946/47 |
| **Troup**<br>Gary Bertram | 3/10/1952<br>Taumarunui | | RHB | LFM | 1976/77-1985/86 |
| **Truscott**<br>Peter Bennetts | 14/8/1941<br>Pahiatua | | RHB | | 1964/65 |
| **Tuffey**<br>Daryl Raymond | 11/6/1978<br>Milton | | RHB | RFM | 1999/00-2009/10 |

| | Born | Died | Type | | Test Career |
|---|---|---|---|---|---|
| **Turner**<br>Glenn Maitland | 26/5/1947<br>Dunedin | | RHB | | 1968/69-1982/83 |
| **Twose**<br>Roger Graham | 17/4/1968<br>Torquay, England | | LHB | RM | 1995/96-1999 |
| **Vance**<br>Robert Howard | 31/3/1955<br>Wellington | | RHB | | 1987/88-1989/90 |
| **van Wyk**<br>Cornelius Francoius Kruger | 7/2/1980<br>Wolmaransstad, South Africa | | RHB | WK | 2011/12-2012/13 |
| **Vaughan**<br>Justin Thomas Caldwell | 30//8/1967<br>Hereford, England | | LHB | RM | 1992/93-1996/97 |
| **Vettori**<br>Daniel Luca | 27/1/1979<br>Auckland | | LHB | SLA | 1996/97-2014/15 |
| **Vincent**<br>Lou | 11/11/1978<br>Warkworth | | RHB | WK | 2001/02-2007/08 |
| **Vivian**<br>Graham Ellery | 28/2/1946<br>Auckland | | LHB | RLB | 1964/65-1971/72 |
| **Vivian**<br>Henry Gifford | 4/11/1912<br>Auckland | 12/8/1983<br>Auckland | LHB | SLA | 1931-1937 |
| **Wadsworth**<br>Kenneth John | 30/11/1946<br>Nelson | 19/8/1976<br>Nelson | RHB | WK | 1969-1975/76 |
| **Wagner**<br>Neil | 13/3/1986<br>Pretoria, South Africa | | LHB | LFM | 2012-2022 |
| **Walker**<br>Brooke Graeme Keith | 25/3/1977<br>Auckland | | RHB | RLB | 2000/01-2001/02 |
| **Wallace**<br>Walter Mervyn | 19/12/1916<br>Auckland | 21/3/2008<br>Auckland | RHB | | 1937-1952/53 |
| **Walmsley**<br>Kerry Peter | 23/8/1973<br>Dunedin | | RHB | RFM | 1994/95-2000/01 |
| **Ward**<br>John Thomas | 11/3/1937<br>Timaru | 12/1/2021<br>Timaru | RHB | WK | 1963/64-1967/68 |
| **Watling**<br>Bradley-John | 9/7/1985<br>Durban, South Africa | | RHB | WK | 2009/10-2021 |
| **Watson**<br>William | 31/8/1965<br>Auckland | | RHB | RFM | 1986-1993/94 |
| **Watt**<br>Leslie | 17/9/1924<br>Waitati | 15/11/1996<br>Dunedin | RHB | | 1954/55 |
| **Webb**<br>Murray George | 22/6/1947<br>Invercargill | | RHB | RFM | 1970/71-1973/74 |
| **Webb**<br>Peter Neil | 14/7/1957<br>Auckland | | RHB | WK | 1979/80 |
| **Weir**<br>Gordon Lindsay | 2/6/1908<br>Auckland | 31/10/2003<br>Auckland | RHB | RM | 1929/30-1937 |
| **White**<br>David John | 26/6/1961<br>Gisborne | | RHB | ROB | 1990/91 |
| **Whitelaw**<br>Paul Erskine | 10/2/1910<br>Auckland | 28/8/1988<br>Auckland | RHB | | 1932/33 |
| **Williamson**<br>Kane Stuart | 8/8/1990<br>Tauranga | | RHB | ROB | 2010/11-2022 |
| **Wiseman**<br>Paul John | 4/5/1970<br>Auckland | | RHB | ROB | 1997/98-2004/05 |
| **Wright**<br>John Geoffrey | 5/7/1954<br>Darfield | | LHB | RM | 1977/78-1992/93 |
| **Young**<br>Bryan Andrew | 3/11/1964<br>Whangarei | | RHB | WK | 1993/94-1998/99 |
| **Young**<br>Reece Alan | 15/9/1979<br>Auckland | | RHB | WK | 2010/11-2011/12 |
| **Young**<br>William Alexander | 22/12/1992<br>New Plymouth | | RHB | | 2020/21-2022 |
| **Yuile**<br>Bryan William | 29/10/1941<br>Palmerston North | | RHB | SLA | 1962/63-1969/70 |

# TEST UMPIRES

The following is the complete list of New Zealand test umpires:

| | | | | | | | |
|---|---|---|---|---|---|---|---|
| Bowden B.F. | 84 * | Pengelly M.F. | 4 | Currie R.G. | 2 |
| Gaffaney C.B. | 41 * | Harris J.C. | 4 | Clark L.G. | 2 |
| Hill A.L. | 40 * | Morris G.C. | 4 | Dumbleton D.P. | 2 |
| Dunne R.S. | 39 * | Knights W.R. | 4 | Page W.P. | 1 |
| Aldridge B.L. | 26 * | Cobcroft L.T. | 3 | Burgess T.W. | 1 |
| Goodall F.R. | 24 | McLellan J.M. | 3 | Torrance R.C. | 1 |
| Woodward S.J. | 24 | Pearce T.M. | 3 | Gourlay H.W. | 1 |
| Cowie D.B. | 22 * | Cowie J. | 3 | Montgomery O.R. | 1 |
| Martin W.T. | 15 | Gwynne W.J.C. | 3 | Brook E.G. | 1 |
| Copps D.E.A. | 13 | Kinsella D.A. | 3 | Vine B.W. | 1 |
| Gardiner W.R.C. | 9 | McHarg R.L. | 3 | Jelley A.E. | 1 |
| Shortt R.W.R. | 9 | King C.E. | 3 | Tindill E.W.T. | 1 |
| MacKintosh E.C.A. | 8 | Watkin E.A. | 3 | Johnston L.C. | 1 |
| Hastie J.B.R. | 7 | Butler W.P. | 2 | Burns D.C. | 1 |
| Cave K.H. | 6 | Forrester J.T. | 2 | Cassie H.B. | 1 |
| Monteith R.L. | 6 | Brown J.M.A. | 2 | Bricknell B.A. | 1 |
| Quested D.M. | 5 | Tomkinson S.B. | 2 | Higginson I.C. | 1 |
| Brown C.M. | 5 | | | | |

*\* includes test matches overseas*

The following overseas umpires have stood in test matches in New Zealand:

| | | | | | | |
|---|---|---|---|---|---|
| Harper D.J. *(Aus)* | 13 | Dharmasena H.P.D.K. *(SL)* | 4 | Erasmus M. *(SA)* | 2 |
| Tucker R.J. *(Aust)* | 11 | Randell S.G. *(Aus)* | 3 | Palliyaguruge R.S.A. *(SL)* | 1 |
| Reiffel P.R. *(Aus)* | 10 | Orchard D.L. *(SA)* | 3 | Robinson I.D. *(Zim)* | 1 |
| Koertzen R.E. *(SA)* | 10 | Tiffin R.B. *(Zim)* | 3 | Nicholls E.A. *(WI)* | 1 |
| Kettleborough R.A. *(Eng)* | 9 | Shepherd D.R. *(Eng)* | 3 | Plews N.T. *(Eng)* | 1 |
| Llong N.J. *(England)* | 8 | Benson M.R. *(Eng)* | 3 | Riazuddin *(Pak)* | 1 |
| Davis S.J. *(Aus)* | 7 | Venkataraghavan S. *(Ind)* | 3 | Jayaprakash A.V. *(Ind)* | 1 |
| Gould I.J. *(England)* | 7 | Gough M.A. *(Eng)* | 3 | Khizar Hayat *(Pak)* | 1 |
| Aleem Dar *(Pak)* | 7 | Ramaswamy V.K. *(Ind)* | 2 | Elliott C.S. *(Eng)* | 1 |
| Oxenford B.N.J. *(Aust)* | 7 | Cooray B.C. *(SL)* | 2 | Barker L.H. *(WI)* | 1 |
| de Silva E.A.R. *(SL)* | 6 | Francis K.T. *(SL)* | 2 | Lloyds J.W. *(Eng)* | 1 |
| Taufel S.J.A. *(Aus)* | 6 | Mahboob Shah *(Pak)* | 2 | Howell I.L *(SA)* | 1 |
| Hair D.B. *(Aus)* | 5 | Bird H.D. *(Eng)* | 2 | Enamul Haq *(Ban)* | 1 |
| Doctrove B.R. *(WI)* | 5 | Jerling B.G. *(SA)* | 2 | Martinesz R.E.J. *(SL)* | 1 |
| Bucknor S.A. *(WI)* | 4 | Parker P.D. *(Aus)* | 2 | Fry S.D. *(Aus)* | 1 |
| Asad Rauf *(Pak)* | 4 | Saheba A.M. *(India)* | 2 | Wilson J.S. *(WI)* | 1 |
| Illingworth R.K. *(Eng)* | 4 | Ravi S. *(India)* | 2 | Wilson P. *(Aus)* | 1 |

The following pairs of umpires have stood together in the most tests:

| | | | |
|---|---|---|---|
| Goodall F.R. & Woodward S.J. | 10 | MacKintosh E.C.A. & Shortt R.W.R. | 4 |
| Aldridge B.L. & Dunne R.S. | 7 | Harris J.C. & Pearce T.M. | 3 |
| Aldridge B.L. & Woodward S.J. | 6 | MacKintosh E.C.A. & Martin W.T. | 3 |
| Copps D.E.A. & Gardiner W.R.C. | 5 | Cobcroft L.T. & Cave K.H. | 3 |
| Copps D.E.A. & Martin W.T. | 4 | Dunne R.S. & Woodward S.J. | 3 |

These umpires have stood in every test of a series *(minimum 3 matches):*

| | | |
|---|---|---|
| Cave K. (4) | v England | 1929/30 |
| Martin W.T. (3) | v England | 1965/66 |
| MacKintosh E.C.A. (3) | v West Indies | 1968/69 |
| Goodall F.R. (3) | v England | 1983/84 |
| Woodward S.J. (3) | v England | 1983/84 |
| Aldridge B.L. (3) | v Sri Lanka | 1990/91 |
| Aldridge B.L. (3) | v England | 1991/92 |
| Dunne R.S. (3) | v England | 1991/92 |
| Aldridge B.L. (3) | v Australia | 1992/93 |

The following pairs stood in three tests during a series:

| | | |
|---|---|---|
| Cobcroft L.T. & Cave K. | v England | 1929/30 *(4 test series)* |
| Copps D.E.A. & Martin W.T. | v India | 1967/68 *(4 test series)* |
| Goodall F.R. & Woodward S.J. | v England | 1983/84 *(3 test series)* |
| Aldridge B.L. & Dunne R.S. | v England | 1991/92 *(3 test series)* |

*Woodward S.J. was appointed to all three tests v Pakistan 1988/89 but stood in only two as the first test was abandoned.*

**NZC**

# TEAM RECORDS

## New Zealand's Test Victories

1) **v West Indies** at Auckland 1955/56
NZ 255 & 157-9d WI 145 & 77
*NZ won by 190 runs*

2) **v South Africa** at Cape Town 1961/62
NZ 385 & 212-9d SA 190 & 335
*NZ won by 72 runs*

3) **v South Africa** at Port Elizabeth 1961/62
NZ 275 & 228 SA 190 & 273
*NZ won by 40 runs*

4) **v India** at Christchurch 1967/68
NZ 502 & 88-4 I 288 & 301
*NZ won by 6 wickets*

5) **v West Indies** at Wellington 1968/69
WI 297 & 148 NZ 282 & 166-4
*NZ won by 6 wickets*

6) **v India** at Nagpur 1969/70
NZ 319 & 214 I 257 & 109
*NZ won by 167 runs*

7) **v Pakistan** at Lahore 1969/70
P114 & 208 NZ 241 & 82-5
*NZ won by 5 wickets*

8) **v Australia** at Christchurch 1973/74
A 223 & 259 NZ 255 & 230-5
*NZ won by 5 wickets*

9) **v India** at Wellington 1975/76
I 220 & 81 NZ 334
*NZ won by an innings and 33 runs*

10) **v England** at Wellington 1977/78
NZ 228 & 123 E 215 & 64
*NZ won by 72 runs*

11) **v West Indies** at Dunedin 1979/80
WI 140 & 212 NZ 249 & 104-9
*NZ won by 1 wicket*

12) **v India** at Wellington 1980/81
NZ 375 & 100 I 233 & 190
*NZ won by 62 runs*

13) **v Australia** at Auckland 1981/82
A 210 & 280 NZ 387 & 109-5
*NZ won by 5 wickets*

14) **v Sri Lanka** at Christchurch 1982/83
NZ 344 SL 144 & 175
*NZ won by an innings and 25 runs*

15) **v Sri Lanka** at Wellington 1982/83
SL 240 & 93 NZ 201 & 134-4
*NZ won by 6 wickets*

16) **v England** at Leeds 1983
E 225 & 252 NZ 377 & 103-5
*NZ won by 5 wickets*

17) **v England** at Christchurch 1983/84
NZ 307 E 82 & 93
*NZ won by an innings and 132 runs*

18) **v Sri Lanka** at Kandy 1983/84
NZ 276 & 201-8d SL 215 & 97
*NZ won by 165 runs*

19) **v Sri Lanka** at Colombo 1983/84
SL 225 & 142 NZ 459
*NZ won by an innings and 61 runs*

20) **v Pakistan** at Auckland 1984/85
P 169 & 183 NZ 451-9d
*NZ won by an innings and 99 runs*

21) **v Pakistan** at Dunedin 1984/85
P274 & 223 NZ 220 & 278-8
*NZ won by 2 wickets*

22) **v Australia** at Brisbane 1985/86
A 179 & 333 NZ 553-7d
*NZ won by an innings and 41 runs*

23) **v Australia** at Perth 1985/86
A 203 & 259 NZ 299 & 164-4
*NZ won by 6 wickets*

24) **v Australia** at Auckland 1985/86
A 314 & 103 NZ 258 & 160-2
*NZ won by 8 wickets*

25) **v England** at Nottingham 1986
E 256 & 230 NZ 413 & 77-2
*NZ won by 8 wickets*

26) **v West Indies** at Christchurch 1986/87
WI 100 & 264 NZ 332-9d & 33-5
*NZ won by 5 wickets*

27) **v India** at Bombay 1988/89
NZ 236 & 279 I 234 & 145
*NZ wonby 136 runs*

28) **v India** at Christchurch 1989/90
NZ 459 & 2-0 I 164 & 296
*NZ won by 10 wickets*

29) **v Australia** at Wellington 1989/90
A 110 & 269 NZ 202 & 181-1
*NZ won by 9 wickets*

30) **v Zimbabwe** at Harare 1992/93
NZ 335 & 262-5d Z 283-9d & 137
*NZ won by 177 runs*

31) **v Australia** at Auckland 1992/93
A 139 & 285 NZ 224 & 201-5
*NZ won by 5 wickets*

32) **v Pakistan** at Christchurch 1993/94
P 344 & 179 NZ 200 & 324-5
*NZ won by 5 wickets*

33) **v South Africa** at Johannesburg 1994/95
NZ 411 & 194 SA 179 & 289
*NZ won by 137 runs*

34) **v Pakistan** at Lahore 1996/97
NZ 155 & 311 P 191 & 231
*NZ won by 44 runs*

35) **v Sri Lanka** at Dunedin 1996/97
NZ 586-7d SL 222 & 328
*NZ won by an innings & 36 runs*

36) **v Sri Lanka** at Hamilton 1996/97
NZ 222 & 273 SL 170 & 205
*NZ won by 120 runs*

37) **v Zimbabwe** at Wellington 1997/98
Z 180 & 250 NZ 411 & 20-0
*NZ won by 10 wickets*

38) **v Zimbabwe** at Auckland 1997/98
Z 170 & 277 NZ 460
*NZ won by an innings and 13 runs*

39) **v Sri Lanka** at Colombo 1997/98
NZ 305 & 444-6d SL 285 & 297
*NZ won by 167 runs*

40) **v India** at Wellington 1998/99
I 208 & 356 NZ 352 & 215-6
*NZ won by 4 wickets*

41) **v England** at Lord's 1999
E 186 & 229 NZ 358 & 60-1
*NZ won by 9 wickets*

42) **v England** at The Oval 1999
NZ 236 & 162 E 153 & 162
*NZ won by 83 runs*

43) **v West Indies** at Hamilton 1999/00
WI 365 & 97 NZ 393 & 70-1
*NZ won by 9 wickets*

44) **v West Indies** at Wellington 1999/00
NZ 518-9d WI 179 & 234
*NZ won by an innings and 105 runs*

45) **v Zimbabwe** at Bulawayo 2000/01
Z 350 & 119 NZ 338 & 132-3
*NZ won by 7 wickets*

46) **v Zimbabwe** at Harare 2000/01
NZ 465 & 74-2 Z 166 & 370
*NZ won by 8 wickets*

47) **v Pakistan** at Hamilton 2000/01
P 104 & 118 NZ 407-4d
*NZ won by an innings & 185 runs*

48) **v Bangladesh** at Hamilton 2001/02
NZ 365-9d B 205 & 108
*NZ won by an innings and 52 runs*

49) **v Bangladesh** at Wellington 2001/02
B 132 & 135 NZ 341-6d
*NZ won by an innings and 74 runs*

50) **v England** at Auckland 2001/02
NZ 202 & 269-9d E 160 & 233
*NZ won by 78 runs*

51) **v West Indies** at Bridgetown 2001/02
NZ 337 & 243 WI 107 & 269
*NZ won by 204 runs*

52) **v India** at Wellington 2002/03
I 161 & 121 NZ 247 & 36-0
*NZ won by 10 wickets*

53) **v India** at Hamilton 2002/03
I 99 & 154 NZ 94 & 160-6
*NZ won by 4 wickets*

54) **v South Africa** at Auckland 2003/04
SA 296 & 349 NZ 595 & 53-1
*NZ won by 9 wickets*

55) **v Bangladesh** at Dhaka 2004/05
B 177 & 126 NZ 402
*NZ won by an innings and 99 runs*

56) **v Bangladesh** at Chittagong 2004/05
NZ 545-6d B 182 & 262
*NZ won by an innings and 101 runs*

57) **v Sri Lanka** at Wellington 2004/05
SL 211 & 273 NZ 522-9d
*NZ won by an innings and 38 runs*

58) **v Zimbabwe** at Harare 2005/06
NZ 452-9d Z 59 & 99
*NZ won by an innings and 294 runs*

59) **v Zimbabwe** at Bulawayo 2005/06
Z 231 & 207 NZ 484
*NZ won by an innings and 46 runs*

60) **v West Indies** at Auckland 2005/06
NZ 275 & 272 WI 257 & 263
*NZ won by 27 runs*

61) **v West Indies** at Wellington 2005/06
WI 192 & 215 NZ 372 & 37-0
*NZ won by 10 wickets*

62) **v Sri Lanka** at Christchurch 2006/07
SL 154 & 179 NZ 206 & 119-5
*NZ won by 5 wickets*

63) **v Bangladesh** at Dunedin 2007/08
B 137 & 254 NZ 357 & 39-1
*NZ won by 9 wickets*

64) **v Bangladesh** at Wellington 2007/08
B 143 & 113 NZ 393
*NZ won by an innings and 137 runs*

65) **v England** at Hamilton 2007/08
NZ 470 & 177-9d E 348 & 110
*NZ won by 189 runs*

66) **v Bangladesh** at Chittagong 2008/09
B 245 & 242 NZ 171 and 317-7
*NZ won by 3 wickets*

67) **v Pakistan** at Dunedin 2009/10
NZ 429 & 153 P 332 & 128
*NZ won by 32 runs*

68) **v Bangladesh** at Hamilton 2009/10
NZ 553-7d & 258-5d B 408 & 282
*NZ won by 121 runs*

69) **v Zimbabwe** at Bulawayo 2011/12
NZ 426 & 252-8d Z 313 & 331
*NZ won by 34 runs*

70) **v Australia** at Hobart 2011/12
NZ 150 & 226 A 136 & 233
*NZ won by 7 runs*

71) **v Zimbabwe** at Napier 2011/12
NZ 495-7d Z 51 & 143
*NZ won by an innings and 301 runs*

72) **v Sri Lanka** at Colombo 2012/13
NZ 412 & 194-9d SL 244 & 195
*NZ won by 167 runs*

73) **v West Indies** at Wellington 2013/14
NZ 441 WI 193 & 175
*NZ won by an innings and 73 runs*

74) **v West Indies** at Hamilton 2013/14
WI 367 & 103 NZ 349 & 124-2
*NZ won by 8 wickets*

75) **v India** at Auckland 2013/14
NZ 503 & 105 I 202 & 366
*NZ won by 40 runs*

76) **v West Indies** at Kingston 2014
NZ 508-7d & 156-8d WI 262 & 216
*NZ won by 186 runs*

77) **v West Indies** at Bridgetown 2013/14
NZ 293 & 331-7d WI 317 & 254
*NZ won by 53 runs*

78) **v Pakistan** at Sharjah 2014/15
P 351 & 259 NZ 690
*NZ won by an innings and 80 runs*

79) **v Sri Lanka** at Christchurch 2014/15
NZ 441 & 107-2 SL 138 & 407
*NZ won by 8 wickets*

80) **v Sri Lanka** at Wellington 2014/15
NZ 221 & 524-5d SL 356 & 196
*NZ won by 193 runs*

81) **v England** at Leeds 2015
NZ 350 & 454-8d E 350 & 255
*NZ won by 199 runs*

82) **v Sri Lanka** at Dunedin 2015/16
NZ 431 & 267-3d SL 294 & 282
*NZ won by 122 runs*

83) **v Sri Lanka** at Hamilton 2015/16
SL 292 & 133 NZ 237 & 189-5
*NZ won by 5 wickets*

84) **v Zimbabwe** at Bulawayo 2016/17
Z 164 & 295 NZ 576-6d
*NZ won by an innings and 117 runs*

85) **v Zimbabwe** at Bulawayo 2016/17
NZ 582-4d & 166-2d Z 362 & 132
*NZ won by 254 runs*

86) **v Pakistan** at Christchurch 2016/17
P 133 & 171 NZ 200 & 108-2
*NZ won by 7 wickets*

87) **v Pakistan** at Hamilton 2016/17
NZ 271 & 313-5d P 216 & 230
*NZ won by 138 runs*

88) **v Bangladesh** at Wellington 2016/17
B 595-8d & 160 NZ 539 & 217-3
*NZ won by 7 wickets*

89) **v Bangladesh** at Christchurch 2016/17
B 289 & 173 NZ 354 & 111-1
*NZ won by 9 wickets*

90) **v West Indies** at Wellington 2017/18
WI 134 & 319 NZ 520-9d
*NZ won by an innings and 67 runs*

91) **v West Indies** at Hamilton 2017/18
NZ 373 & 281-8d WI 221 & 293
*NZ won by 140 runs*

92) **v England** at Auckland 2017/18
E 58 & 320 NZ 427-9d
*NZ won by an innings and 49 runs*

93) **v Pakistan** at Abu Dhabi 2018/19
NZ 153 & 249 P 227 & 171
*NZ won by 4 runs*

94) **v Pakistan** at Abu Dhabi 2018/19
NZ 274 & 353-7d P 348 & 156
*NZ won by 123 runs*

95) **v Sri Lanka** at Christchurch 2018/19
NZ 178 & 585-4d SL 104 & 236
*NZ won by 423 runs*

96) **v Bangladesh** at Hamilton 2018/19
B 234 & 429 NZ 715-6d
*NZ won by an innings & 52 runs*

97) **v Bangladesh** at Wellington 2018/19
B 211 & 209 NZ 432-6d
*NZ won by an innings & 12 runs*

98) **v Sri Lanka** at Colombo 2019/20
SL 244 & 122 NZ 431-6d
*NZ won by an innings and 65 runs*

99) **v England** at Mt Maunganui 2019/20
E 353 & 197 NZ 615-9d
*NZ won by an innings and 65 runs*

100) **v India** at Wellington 2019/20
I 165 & 191 NZ 348 & 9-0
*NZ won by 10 wickets*

101) **v India** at Christchurch 2019/20
I 242 & 124 NZ 235 & 132-3
*NZ won by 7 wickets*

102) **v West Indies** at Hamilton 2020/21
NZ 519-7d WI 138 & 247
*NZ won by an innings and 134 runs*

103) **v West Indies** at Wellington 2020/21
NZ 460 WI 131 & 317
*NZ won by an innings and 12 runs*

104) **v Pakistan** at Mt Maunganui 2020/21
NZ 431 & 180-5d P 239 & 271
*NZ won by 101 runs*

105) **v Pakistan** at Christchurch 2020/21
P 297 & 186 NZ 659-6d
*NZ won by an innings and 176 runs*

106) **v England** at Birmingham 2021
E 303 & 122 NZ 388 & 41-2
*NZ won by 8 wickets*

107) **v India** at Southampton 2021
I 217 & 170 NZ 249 & 140-2
*NZ won by 8 wickets*

108) **v Bangladesh** at Christchurch 2021/22
NZ 521-6d B 126 & 278
*NZ won by an innings and 117 runs*

109) v **South Africa** at Christchurch 2021/22
SA 95 & 111 NZ 482
*NZ won by an innings and 276 runs*

# Test Record by Series

*Cumulative*

| Season | Opponent | TOTAL | | | BY OPPONENT | | | | | |
|--------|----------|-----|------|-------|-----|------|-------|-----|------|-------|
| | | Won | Lost | Drawn | Won | Lost | Drawn | Won | Lost | Drawn |
| 1929/30 | England* | — | 1 | 3 | — | 1 | 3 | — | 1 | 3 |
| 1931 | England | — | 1 | 2 | — | 2 | 5 | — | 2 | 5 |
| 1931/32 | South Africa* | — | 2 | — | — | 4 | 5 | — | 2 | — |
| 1932/33 | England* | — | — | 2 | — | 4 | 7 | — | 2 | 7 |
| 1937 | England | — | 1 | 2 | — | 5 | 9 | — | 3 | 9 |
| 1945/46 | Australia* | — | 1 | — | — | 6 | 9 | — | 1 | — |
| 1946/47 | England* | — | — | 1 | — | 6 | 10 | — | 3 | 10 |
| 1949 | England | — | — | 4 | — | 6 | 14 | — | 3 | 14 |
| 1950/51 | England* | — | 1 | 1 | — | 7 | 15 | — | 4 | 15 |
| 1951/52 | West Indies* | — | 1 | 1 | — | 8 | 16 | — | 1 | 1 |
| 1952/53 | South Africa* | — | 1 | 1 | — | 9 | 17 | — | 3 | 1 |
| 1953/54 | South Africa | — | 4 | 1 | — | 13 | 18 | — | 7 | 2 |
| 1954/55 | England* | — | 2 | — | — | 15 | 18 | — | 6 | 15 |
| 1955/56 | Pakistan | — | 2 | 1 | — | 17 | 19 | — | 2 | 1 |
| 1955/56 | India | — | 2 | 3 | — | 19 | 22 | — | 2 | 3 |
| 1955/56 | West Indies* | 1 | 3 | — | 1 | 22 | 22 | 1 | 4 | 1 |
| 1958 | England | — | 4 | 1 | 1 | 26 | 23 | — | 10 | 16 |
| 1958/59 | England* | — | 1 | 1 | 1 | 27 | 24 | — | 11 | 17 |
| 1961/62 | South Africa | 2 | 2 | 1 | 3 | 29 | 25 | 2 | 9 | 3 |
| 1962/63 | England* | — | 3 | — | 3 | 32 | 25 | — | 14 | 17 |
| 1963/64 | South Africa* | — | — | 3 | 3 | 32 | 28 | 2 | 9 | 6 |
| 1964/65 | Pakistan* | — | — | 3 | 3 | 32 | 31 | — | 2 | 4 |
| 1964/65 | India | — | 1 | 3 | 3 | 33 | 34 | — | 3 | 6 |
| 1964/65 | Pakistan | — | 2 | 1 | 3 | 35 | 35 | — | 4 | 5 |
| 1965 | England | — | 3 | — | 3 | 38 | 35 | — | 17 | 17 |
| 1965/66 | England* | — | — | 3 | 3 | 38 | 38 | — | 17 | 20 |
| 1967/68 | India* | 1 | 3 | — | 4 | 41 | 38 | 1 | 6 | 6 |
| 1968/69 | West Indies* | 1 | 1 | 1 | 5 | 42 | 39 | 2 | 5 | 2 |
| 1969 | England | — | 2 | 1 | 5 | 44 | 40 | — | 19 | 21 |
| 1969/70 | India | 1 | 1 | 1 | 6 | 45 | 41 | 2 | 7 | 7 |
| 1969/70 | Pakistan | 1 | — | 2 | 7 | 45 | 43 | 1 | 4 | 7 |
| 1970/71 | England* | — | 1 | 1 | 7 | 46 | 44 | — | 20 | 22 |
| 1971/72 | West Indies | — | — | 5 | 7 | 46 | 49 | 2 | 5 | 7 |
| 1972/73 | Pakistan* | — | 1 | 2 | 7 | 47 | 51 | 1 | 5 | 9 |
| 1973 | England | — | 2 | 1 | 7 | 49 | 52 | — | 22 | 23 |
| 1973/74 | Australia | — | 2 | 1 | 7 | 51 | 53 | — | 3 | 1 |
| 1973/74 | Australia* | 1 | 1 | 1 | 8 | 52 | 54 | 1 | 4 | 2 |
| 1974/75 | England* | — | 1 | 1 | 8 | 53 | 55 | — | 23 | 24 |
| 1975/76 | India* | 1 | 1 | 1 | 9 | 54 | 56 | 3 | 8 | 8 |
| 1976/77 | Pakistan | — | 2 | 1 | 9 | 56 | 57 | 1 | 7 | 10 |
| 1976/77 | India | — | 2 | 1 | 9 | 58 | 58 | 3 | 10 | 9 |
| 1976/77 | Australia* | — | 1 | 1 | 9 | 59 | 59 | 1 | 5 | 3 |
| 1977/78 | England* | 1 | 1 | 1 | 10 | 60 | 60 | 1 | 24 | 25 |
| 1978 | England | — | 3 | — | 10 | 63 | 60 | 1 | 27 | 25 |
| 1978/79 | Pakistan* | — | 1 | 2 | 10 | 64 | 62 | 1 | 8 | 12 |
| 1979/80 | West Indies* | 1 | — | 2 | 11 | 64 | 64 | 3 | 5 | 9 |
| 1980/81 | Australia | — | 2 | 1 | 11 | 66 | 65 | 1 | 7 | 4 |
| 1980/81 | India* | 1 | — | 2 | 12 | 66 | 67 | 4 | 10 | 11 |
| 1981/82 | Australia* | 1 | 1 | 1 | 13 | 67 | 68 | 2 | 8 | 5 |
| 1982/83 | Sri Lanka* | 2 | — | — | 15 | 67 | 68 | 2 | — | — |

Cumulative

| | | TOTAL | | | | | | | BY OPPONENT | | |
|---|---|---|---|---|---|---|---|---|---|---|---|
| *Season* | *Opponent* | *Won* | *Lost* | *Drawn* | | *Won* | *Lost* | *Drawn* | | *Won* | *Lost* | *Drawn* |
| 1983 | England | 1 | 3 | — | | 16 | 70 | 68 | | 2 | 30 | 25 |
| 1983/84 | England* | 1 | — | 2 | | 17 | 70 | 70 | | 3 | 30 | 27 |
| 1983/84 | Sri Lanka | 2 | — | 1 | | 19 | 70 | 71 | | 4 | — | 1 |
| 1984/85 | Pakistan | — | 2 | 1 | | 19 | 72 | 72 | | 1 | 10 | 13 |
| 1984/85 | Pakistan* | 2 | — | 1 | | 21 | 72 | 73 | | 3 | 10 | 14 |
| 1984/85 | West Indies | — | 2 | 2 | | 21 | 74 | 75 | | 3 | 7 | 11 |
| 1985/86 | Australia | 2 | 1 | — | | 23 | 75 | 75 | | 4 | 9 | 5 |
| 1985/86 | Australia* | 1 | — | 2 | | 24 | 75 | 77 | | 5 | 9 | 7 |
| 1986 | England | 1 | — | 2 | | 25 | 75 | 79 | | 4 | 30 | 29 |
| 1986/87 | West Indies* | 1 | 1 | 1 | | 26 | 76 | 80 | | 4 | 8 | 12 |
| 1986/87 | Sri Lanka | — | — | 1 | | 26 | 76 | 81 | | 4 | — | 2 |
| 1987/88 | Australia | — | 1 | 2 | | 26 | 77 | 83 | | 5 | 10 | 9 |
| 1987/88 | England* | — | — | 3 | | 26 | 77 | 86 | | 4 | 30 | 32 |
| 1988/89 | India | 1 | 2 | — | | 27 | 79 | 86 | | 5 | 12 | 11 |
| 1988/89 | Pakistan* | — | — | 2 | | 27 | 79 | 88 | | 3 | 10 | 16 |
| 1989/90 | Australia | — | — | 1 | | 27 | 79 | 89 | | 5 | 10 | 10 |
| 1989/90 | India* | 1 | — | 2 | | 28 | 79 | 91 | | 6 | 12 | 13 |
| 1989/90 | Australia* | 1 | — | — | | 29 | 79 | 91 | | 6 | 10 | 10 |
| 1990 | England | — | 1 | 2 | | 29 | 80 | 93 | | 4 | 41 | 34 |
| 1990/91 | Pakistan | — | 3 | — | | 29 | 83 | 93 | | 3 | 13 | 16 |
| 1990/91 | Sri Lanka* | — | — | 3 | | 29 | 83 | 96 | | 4 | — | 5 |
| 1991/92 | England* | — | 2 | 1 | | 29 | 85 | 97 | | 4 | 33 | 35 |
| 1992/93 | Zimbabwe | 1 | — | 1 | | 30 | 85 | 98 | | 1 | — | 1 |
| 1992/93 | Sri Lanka | — | 1 | 1 | | 30 | 86 | 99 | | 4 | 1 | 6 |
| 1992/93 | Pakistan* | — | 1 | — | | 30 | 87 | 99 | | 3 | 14 | 16 |
| 1992/93 | Australia* | 1 | 1 | 1 | | 31 | 88 | 100 | | 7 | 11 | 11 |
| 1993/94 | Australia | — | 2 | 1 | | 31 | 90 | 101 | | 7 | 13 | 12 |
| 1993/94 | Pakistan* | 1 | 2 | — | | 32 | 92 | 101 | | 4 | 16 | 16 |
| 1993/94 | India* | — | — | 1 | | 32 | 92 | 102 | | 6 | 12 | 14 |
| 1994 | England | — | 1 | 2 | | 32 | 93 | 104 | | 4 | 34 | 37 |
| 1994/95 | South Africa | 1 | 2 | — | | 33 | 95 | 104 | | 3 | 11 | 6 |
| 1994/95 | West Indies* | — | 1 | 1 | | 33 | 96 | 105 | | 4 | 9 | 13 |
| 1994/95 | South Africa* | — | 1 | — | | 33 | 97 | 105 | | 3 | 12 | 6 |
| 1994/95 | Sri Lanka* | — | 1 | 1 | | 33 | 98 | 106 | | 4 | 2 | 7 |
| 1995/96 | India | — | 1 | 2 | | 33 | 99 | 108 | | 6 | 13 | 16 |
| 1995/96 | Pakistan* | — | 1 | — | | 33 | 100 | 108 | | 4 | 17 | 16 |
| 1995/96 | Zimbabwe* | — | — | 2 | | 33 | 100 | 110 | | 1 | — | 3 |
| 1995/96 | West Indies | — | 1 | 1 | | 33 | 101 | 111 | | 4 | 10 | 14 |
| 1996/97 | Pakistan | 1 | 1 | — | | 34 | 102 | 111 | | 5 | 18 | 16 |
| 1996/97 | England* | — | 2 | 1 | | 34 | 104 | 112 | | 4 | 36 | 38 |
| 1996/97 | Sri Lanka* | 2 | — | — | | 36 | 104 | 112 | | 6 | 2 | 7 |
| 1997/98 | Zimbabwe | — | — | 2 | | 36 | 104 | 114 | | 1 | — | 5 |
| 1997/98 | Australia | — | 2 | 1 | | 36 | 106 | 115 | | 7 | 15 | 13 |
| 1997/98 | Zimbabwe* | 2 | — | — | | 38 | 106 | 115 | | 3 | — | 5 |
| 1997/98 | Sri Lanka | 1 | 2 | — | | 39 | 108 | 115 | | 7 | 4 | 7 |
| 1998/99 | India* | 1 | — | 1 | | 40 | 108 | 116 | | 7 | 13 | 17 |
| 1998/99 | South Africa* | — | 1 | 2 | | 40 | 109 | 118 | | 3 | 13 | 8 |
| 1999 | England | 2 | 1 | 1 | | 42 | 110 | 119 | | 6 | 37 | 39 |
| 1999/00 | India | — | 1 | 2 | | 42 | 111 | 121 | | 7 | 14 | 19 |
| 1999/00 | West Indies* | 2 | — | — | | 44 | 111 | 121 | | 6 | 10 | 14 |
| 1999/00 | Australia* | — | 3 | — | | 44 | 114 | 121 | | 7 | 18 | 13 |
| 2000/01 | Zimbabwe | 2 | — | — | | 46 | 114 | 121 | | 5 | — | 5 |

| Season | Opponent | TOTAL | | | Cumulative | | | BY OPPONENT | | |
|---|---|---|---|---|---|---|---|---|---|---|
| | | Won | Lost | Drawn | Won | Lost | Drawn | Won | Lost | Drawn |
| 2000/01 | South Africa | — | 2 | 1 | 46 | 116 | 122 | 3 | 15 | 9 |
| 2000/01 | Zimbabwe* | — | — | 1 | 46 | 116 | 123 | 5 | — | 6 |
| 2000/01 | Pakistan* | 1 | 1 | 1 | 47 | 117 | 124 | 6 | 19 | 17 |
| 2001/02 | Australia | — | — | 3 | 47 | 117 | 127 | 7 | 18 | 16 |
| 2001/02 | Bangladesh* | 2 | — | — | 49 | 117 | 127 | 2 | — | — |
| 2001/02 | England* | 1 | 1 | 1 | 50 | 118 | 128 | 7 | 38 | 40 |
| 2001/02 | Pakistan | — | 1 | — | 50 | 119 | 128 | 6 | 20 | 17 |
| 2001/02 | West Indies | 1 | — | 1 | 51 | 119 | 129 | 7 | 10 | 15 |
| 2002/03 | India* | 2 | — | — | 53 | 119 | 129 | 9 | 14 | 19 |
| 2002/03 | Sri Lanka | — | — | 2 | 53 | 119 | 131 | 7 | 4 | 9 |
| 2003/04 | India | — | — | 2 | 53 | 119 | 133 | 9 | 14 | 21 |
| 2003/04 | Pakistan* | — | 1 | 1 | 53 | 120 | 134 | 6 | 21 | 18 |
| 2003/04 | South Africa* | 1 | 1 | 1 | 54 | 121 | 135 | 4 | 16 | 10 |
| 2004 | England | — | 3 | — | 54 | 124 | 135 | 7 | 41 | 40 |
| 2004/05 | Bangladesh | 2 | — | — | 56 | 124 | 135 | 4 | — | — |
| 2004/05 | Australia | — | 2 | — | 56 | 126 | 135 | 7 | 20 | 16 |
| 2004/05 | Australia* | — | 2 | 1 | 56 | 128 | 136 | 7 | 22 | 17 |
| 2004/05 | Sri Lanka* | 1 | — | 1 | 57 | 128 | 137 | 8 | 4 | 10 |
| 2005/06 | Zimbabwe | 2 | — | — | 59 | 128 | 137 | 7 | — | 6 |
| 2005/06 | West Indies* | 2 | — | 1 | 61 | 128 | 138 | 9 | 10 | 16 |
| 2005/06 | South Africa | — | 2 | 1 | 61 | 130 | 139 | 4 | 18 | 11 |
| 2006/07 | Sri Lanka* | 1 | 1 | — | 62 | 131 | 139 | 9 | 5 | 10 |
| 2007/08 | South Africa | — | 2 | — | 62 | 133 | 139 | 4 | 20 | 11 |
| 2007/08 | Bangladesh* | 2 | — | — | 64 | 133 | 139 | 6 | — | — |
| 2007/08 | England* | 1 | 2 | — | 65 | 135 | 139 | 8 | 43 | 40 |
| 2008 | England | — | 2 | 1 | 65 | 137 | 140 | 8 | 45 | 41 |
| 2008/09 | Bangladesh | 1 | — | 1 | 66 | 137 | 141 | 7 | — | 1 |
| 2008/09 | Australia | — | 2 | — | 66 | 139 | 141 | 7 | 24 | 17 |
| 2008/09 | West Indies* | — | — | 2 | 66 | 139 | 143 | 9 | 10 | 18 |
| 2008/09 | India* | — | 1 | 2 | 66 | 140 | 145 | 9 | 15 | 23 |
| 2009/10 | Sri Lanka | — | 2 | — | 66 | 142 | 145 | 9 | 7 | 10 |
| 2009/10 | Pakistan† | 1 | 1 | 1 | 67 | 143 | 146 | 7 | 22 | 19 |
| 2009/10 | Bangladesh* | 1 | — | — | 68 | 143 | 146 | 8 | — | 1 |
| 2009/10 | Australia* | — | 2 | — | 68 | 145 | 146 | 7 | 26 | 17 |
| 2010/11 | India | — | 1 | 2 | 68 | 146 | 148 | 9 | 16 | 25 |
| 2010/11 | Pakistan* | — | 1 | 1 | 68 | 147 | 149 | 7 | 23 | 20 |
| 2011/12 | Zimbabwe | 1 | — | — | 69 | 147 | 149 | 8 | — | 6 |
| 2011/12 | Australia | 1 | 1 | — | 70 | 148 | 149 | 8 | 27 | 17 |
| 2011/12 | Zimbabwe* | 1 | — | — | 71 | 148 | 149 | 9 | — | 6 |
| 2011/12 | South Africa* | — | 1 | 2 | 71 | 149 | 151 | 4 | 21 | 13 |
| 2012 | West Indies | — | 2 | — | 71 | 151 | 151 | 9 | 12 | 18 |
| 2012/13 | India | — | 2 | — | 71 | 153 | 151 | 9 | 18 | 25 |
| 2012/13 | Sri Lanka | 1 | 1 | — | 72 | 154 | 151 | 10 | 8 | 10 |
| 2012/13 | South Africa | — | 2 | — | 72 | 156 | 151 | 4 | 23 | 13 |
| 2012/13 | England* | — | — | 3 | 72 | 156 | 154 | 8 | 45 | 44 |
| 2013 | England | — | 2 | — | 72 | 158 | 154 | 8 | 47 | 44 |
| 2013/14 | Bangladesh | — | — | 2 | 72 | 158 | 156 | 8 | — | 3 |
| 2013/14 | West Indies* | 2 | — | 1 | 74 | 158 | 157 | 11 | 12 | 19 |
| 2013/14 | India* | 1 | — | 1 | 75 | 158 | 158 | 10 | 18 | 26 |
| 2014 | West Indies | 2 | 1 | — | 77 | 159 | 158 | 13 | 13 | 19 |
| 2014/15 | Pakistan+ | 1 | 1 | 1 | 78 | 160 | 159 | 8 | 24 | 21 |
| 2014/15 | Sri Lanka* | 2 | — | — | 80 | 160 | 159 | 12 | 8 | 10 |

| Season | Opponent | TOTAL | | | Cumulative | | | BY OPPONENT | | |
|--------|----------|-----|------|-------|-----|------|-------|-----|------|-------|
| | | Won | Lost | Drawn | Won | Lost | Drawn | Won | Lost | Drawn |
| 2015 | England | 1 | 1 | — | 81 | 161 | 159 | 9 | 48 | 44 |
| 2015/16 | Australia | — | 2 | 1 | 81 | 163 | 160 | 8 | 29 | 18 |
| 2015/16 | Sri Lanka* | 2 | — | — | 83 | 163 | 160 | 14 | 8 | 10 |
| 2015/16 | Australia* | — | 2 | — | 83 | 165 | 160 | 8 | 31 | 18 |
| 2016/17 | Zimbabwe | 2 | — | — | 85 | 165 | 160 | 11 | — | 6 |
| 2016/17 | South Africa | — | 1 | 1 | 85 | 166 | 161 | 4 | 24 | 14 |
| 2016/17 | India | — | 3 | — | 85 | 169 | 161 | 10 | 21 | 26 |
| 2016/17 | Pakistan* | 2 | — | — | 87 | 169 | 161 | 10 | 24 | 21 |
| 2016/17 | Bangladesh* | 2 | — | — | 89 | 169 | 161 | 10 | — | 3 |
| 2016/17 | South Africa* | — | 1 | 2 | 89 | 170 | 163 | 4 | 25 | 16 |
| 2017/18 | West Indies* | 2 | — | — | 91 | 170 | 163 | 15 | 13 | 19 |
| 2017/18 | England* | 1 | — | 1 | 92 | 170 | 164 | 10 | 48 | 45 |
| 2018/19 | Pakistan+ | 2 | 1 | — | 94 | 171 | 164 | 12 | 25 | 21 |
| 2018/19 | Sri Lanka* | 1 | — | 1 | 95 | 171 | 165 | 15 | 8 | 11 |
| 2018/19 | Bangladesh* | 2 | — | — | 97 | 171 | 165 | 12 | — | 3 |
| 2019/20 | Sri Lanka | 1 | 1 | — | 98 | 172 | 165 | 16 | 9 | 11 |
| 2019/20 | England* | 1 | — | 1 | 99 | 172 | 166 | 11 | 48 | 46 |
| 2019/20 | Australia | — | 3 | — | 99 | 175 | 166 | 8 | 34 | 18 |
| 2019/20 | India* | 2 | — | — | 101 | 175 | 166 | 12 | 21 | 26 |
| 2020/21 | West Indies* | 2 | — | — | 103 | 175 | 166 | 17 | 13 | 19 |
| 2020/21 | Pakistan* | 2 | — | — | 105 | 175 | 166 | 14 | 25 | 21 |
| 2021 | England | 1 | — | 1 | 106 | 175 | 167 | 12 | 48 | 47 |
| 2021 | India | 1 | — | — | 107 | 175 | 167 | 13 | 21 | 26 |
| 2021/22 | India | — | 1 | 1 | 107 | 176 | 168 | 13 | 22 | 27 |
| 2021/22 | Bangladesh* | 1 | 1 | — | 108 | 177 | 168 | 13 | 1 | 3 |
| 2021/22 | South Africa* | 1 | 1 | — | 109 | 178 | 168 | 5 | 26 | 16 |
| 2022 | England | — | 3 | — | 109 | 181 | 168 | 12 | 51 | 47 |

\* *home series*

† *scheduled as a Pakistan home series but was played in New Zealand*

+ *scheduled as a Pakistan home series but was played in United Arab Emirates*

## Summary of Results

| | Played | Won | Lost | Drawn |
|---|--------|-----|------|-------|
| v England | 110 | 12 | 51 | 47 |
| v India | 62 | 13 | 22 | 27 |
| v Australia | 60 | 8 | 34 | 18 |
| v Pakistan | 60 | 14 | 25 | 21 |
| v West Indies | 49 | 17 | 13 | 19 |
| v South Africa | 47 | 5 | 26 | 16 |
| v Sri Lanka | 36 | 16 | 9 | 11 |
| v Zimbabwe | 17 | 11 | — | 6 |
| v Bangladesh | 17 | 13 | 1 | 3 |
| **Total** | **458** | **109** | **181** | **168** |

## Highest Totals

**For**

| | | | |
|---|---|---|---|
| 715-6d | v Bangladesh | Hamilton | 2018/19 |
| 690 | v Pakistan | Sharjah | 2014/15 |
| 680-8d | v India | Wellington | 2013/14 |
| 671-4 | v Sri Lanka | Wellington | 1990/91 |
| 659-6d | v Pakistan | Christchurch | 2020/21 |
| 630-6d | v India | Mohali | 2003/04 |

| 624 | v Australia | Perth | 2015/16 |
| 619-9d | v India | Napier | 2008/09 |
| 615-9d | v England | Mt Maunganui | 2019/20 |
| 609-9d | v West Indies | Dunedin | 2013/14 |
| 595 | v South Africa | Auckland | 2003/04 |
| 593-8d | v South Africa | Cape Town | 2005/06 |
| 586-7d | v Sri Lanka | Dunedin | 1996/97 |
| 585-4d | v Sri Lanka | Christchurch | 2018/19 |
| 582-4d | v Zimbabwe | Bulawayo | 2016/17 |
| 578 | v Sri Lanka | Wellington | 2018/19 |
| 576-6d | v Zimbabwe | Bulawayo | 2016/17 |
| 563 | v Pakistan | Hamilton | 2003/04 |
| 561 | v Sri Lanka | Napier | 2004/05 |
| 553-7d | v Australia | Brisbane | 1985/86 |
| 553-7d | v Bangladesh | Hamilton | 2009/10 |
| 553 | v England | Nottingham | 2022 |
| 551-9d | v England | Lord's | 1973 |
| 545-6d | v Bangladesh | Chittagong | 2004/05 |
| 543-3d | v West Indies | Georgetown | 1971/72 |
| 539 | v Bangladesh | Wellington | 2016/17 |
| 537 | v England | Wellington | 1983/84 |
| 534-9d | v Australia | Perth | 2001/02 |
| 524-5d | v Sri Lanka | Wellington | 2014/15 |
| 523 | v England | Lord's | 2015 |
| 522-9d | v Sri Lanka | Wellington | 2004/05 |
| 521-6d | v Bangladesh | Christchurch | 2021/22 |
| 520-9d | v West Indies | Wellington | 2017/18 |
| 519-7d | v West Indies | Hamilton | 2020/21 |
| 518-9d | v West Indies | Wellington | 1999/00 |
| 515-7d | v Sri Lanka | Colombo | 2002/03 |
| 512-6d | v England | Wellington | 1987/88 |
| 509 | v South Africa | Hamilton | 2003/04 |
| 508-7d | v West Indies | Kingston | 2014 |
| 505 | v South Africa | Cape Town | 1953/54 |
| 503 | v India | Auckland | 2013/14 |
| 502 | v India | Christchurch | 1967/68 |

**Against**

| 660-5d | by West Indies | Wellington | 1994/95 |
| 643 | by Pakistan | Lahore | 2001/02 |
| 621-5d | by South Africa | Auckland | 1998/99 |
| 616-5d | by Pakistan | Auckland | 1988/89 |
| 607-6d | by Australia | Brisbane | 1993/94 |
| 595-8d | by Bangladesh | Wellington | 2016/17 |
| 593-6d | by England | Auckland | 1974/75 |
| 585 | by Australia | Brisbane | 2004/05 |
| 583-7d | by India | Ahmedabad | 1999/00 |
| 580-9d | by England | Christchurch | 1991/92 |
| 575-8d | by Australia | Adelaide | 2004/05 |
| 571-8d | by Pakistan | Christchurch | 2000/01 |
| 570-8d | by Australia | Wellington | 2004/05 |
| 567-8d | by England | Nottingham | 1994 |
| 566-8d | by India | Nagpur | 2010/11 |
| 566-3d | by Pakistan | Abu Dhabi | 2014/15 |
| 565-9d | by Pakistan | Karachi | 1976/77 |
| 564-8 | by West Indies | Bridgetown | 1971/72 |
| 562-7d | by England | Auckland | 1962/63 |

| | | | |
|---|---|---|---|
| 562 | by Australia | Wellington | 2015/16 |
| 561 | by Pakistan | Lahore | 1955/56 |
| 560-8d | by England | Christchurch | 1932/33 |
| 559-9d | by Australia | Perth | 2015/16 |
| 558-8d | by Australia | Hobart | 2001/02 |
| 557-5d | by India | Indore | 2016/17 |
| 556 | by Australia | Brisbane | 2015/16 |
| 552 | by Australia | Christchurch | 1976/77 |
| 550 | by England | Christchurch | 1950/51 |

## Lowest Totals

**For**

| | | | |
|---|---|---|---|
| 26 | v England | Auckland | 1954/55 |
| 42 | v Australia | Wellington | 1945/46 |
| 45 | v South Africa | Cape Town | 2012/13 |
| 47 | v England | Lord's | 1958 |
| 54 | v Australia | Wellington | 1945/46 |
| 62 | v India | Mumbai | 2021/22 |
| 65 | v England | Christchurch | 1970/71 |
| 67 | v England | Leeds | 1958 |
| 67 | v England | Lord's | 1978 |
| 68 | v England | Lord's | 2013 |
| 70 | v Pakistan | Dacca | 1955/56 |
| 73 | v Pakistan | Lahore | 2001/02 |
| 74 | v West Indies | Dunedin | 1955/56 |
| 74 | v England | Lord's | 1958 |
| 76 | v Australia | Brisbane | 2004/05 |
| 79 | v South Africa | Johannesburg | 1953/54 |
| 79 | v Pakistan | Rawalpindi | 1964/65 |
| 85 | v England | Manchester | 1958 |
| 89 | v England | Auckland | 1962/63 |
| 90 | v Pakistan | Dubai | 2018/19 |
| 93 | v Pakistan | Hamilton | 1992/93 |
| 94 | v England | Birmingham | 1958 |
| 94 | v West Indies | Bridgetown | 1984/85 |
| 94 | v India | Hamilton | 2002/03 |
| 97 | v England | Nottingham | 1973 |

**Against**

| | | | |
|---|---|---|---|
| 51 | by Zimbabwe | Napier | 2011/12 |
| 58 | by England | Auckland | 2017/18 |
| 59 | by Zimbabwe | Harare | 2005/06 |
| 64 | by England | Wellington | 1977/78 |
| 77 | by West Indies | Auckland | 1955/56 |
| 81 | by India | Wellington | 1975/76 |
| 82 | by England | Christchurch | 1983/84 |
| 83 | by India | Mohali | 1999/00 |
| 88 | by India | Bombay | 1964/65 |
| 89 | by India | Hyderabad | 1969/70 |
| 93 | by Sri Lanka | Wellington | 1982/83 |
| 93 | by England | Christchurch | 1983/84 |
| 95 | by South Africa | Christchurch | 2021/22 |
| 97 | by Sri Lanka | Kandy | 1983/84 |
| 97 | by West Indies | Hamilton | 1999/00 |
| 99 | by India | Hamilton | 2002/03 |
| 99 | by Zimbabwe | Harare | 2005/06 |

# Longest Innings

| Mins | Runs | | | |
|------|------|---|---|---|
| 904 | 680-8d | v India | Wellington | 2013/14 |
| 851 | 671-4 | v Sri Lanka | Wellington | 1990/91 |
| 845 | 615-9d | v England | Mt Maunganui | 2019/20 |
| 815 | 459 | v Sri Lanka | Colombo | 1983/84 |
| 802 | 630-6d | v India | Mohali | 2003/04 |
| 790 | 406-5 | v Sri Lanka | Colombo | 1986/87 |
| 784 | 512-6d | v England | Wellington | 1987/88 |
| 780 | 543-3d | v West Indies | Georgetown | 1971/72 |

# Largest First Innings Leads

| | | | |
|---|---|---|---|
| *481 | v Bangladesh | Hamilton | 2018/19 |
| *444 | v Zimbabwe | Napier | 2011/12 |
| *412 | v Zimbabwe | Bulawayo | 2016/17 |
| 396 | v West Indies | Dunedin | 2013/14 |
| *395 | v Bangladesh | Christchurch | 2021/22 |
| *393 | v Zimbabwe | Harare | 2005/06 |
| *387 | v South Africa | Christchurch | 2021/22 |
| *386 | v West Indies | Wellington | 2017/18 |
| *381 | v West Indies | Hamilton | 2020/21 |
| *374 | v Australia | Brisbane | 1985/86 |
| *369 | v England | Auckland | 2017/18 |
| *364 | v Sri Lanka | Dunedin | 1996/97 |
| *363 | v Bangladesh | Chittagong | 2004/05 |
| *362 | v Pakistan | Christchurch | 2020/21 |

*\* New Zealand won the match*

# Opposition Following-on

| | | |
|---|---|---|
| South Africa | Cape Town | 1953/54 |
| India | Bombay | 1964/65 |
| *India | Christchurch | 1967/68 |
| *Sri Lanka | Christchurch | 1982/83 |
| *England | Christchurch | 1983/84 |
| *India | Christchurch | 1989/90 |
| *Sri Lanka | Dunedin | 1996/97 |
| *West Indies | Wellington | 1999/00 |
| *Zimbabwe | Harare | 2000/01 |
| *Bangladesh | Hamilton | 2001/02 |
| India | Mohali | 2003/04 |
| *Bangladesh | Chittagong | 2004/05 |
| *Zimbabwe | Harare | 2005/06 |
| India | Napier | 2008/09 |
| *Zimbabwe | Napier | 2011/12 |
| West Indies | Dunedin | 2013/14 |
| *West Indies | Wellington | 2013/14 |
| *Sri Lanka | Christchurch | 2014/15 |
| *West Indies | Hamilton | 2020/21 |
| *West Indies | Wellington | 2020/21 |
| *Bangladesh | Christchurch | 2021/22 |

*\* New Zealand won the match*

**NB:** *New Zealand did not enforce the follow-on v South Africa at Cape Town, 1961/62, v West Indies at Bridgetown, 2001/02, v India at Auckland, 2013/14 and v Zimbabwe at Bulawayo, 2016/17 although they could have done so. They eventually won all four games.*

# GROUNDS
## Results by Grounds

| In New Zealand | P | W | L | D |
|---|---|---|---|---|
| Eden Park, Auckland | 50 | 11 | 15 | 24 |
| Lancaster Park, Christchurch | 40 | 8 | 16 | 16 |
| Basin Reserve, Wellington | 65 | 21 | 20 | 24 |
| Carisbrook, Dunedin | 10 | 3 | 4 | 3 |
| McLean Park, Napier | 10 | 1 | 2 | 7 |
| Seddon Park, Hamilton | 27 | 13 | 6 | 8 |
| University of Otago Oval, Dunedin | | | | |
| | 8 | 3 | — | 5 |
| Hagley Oval, Christchurch | 11 | 8 | 2 | 1 |
| Bay Oval, Mt Maunganui | 3 | 2 | 1 | — |
| **Total** | **224** | **70** | **66** | **88** |

| In Australia | P | W | L | D |
|---|---|---|---|---|
| Melbourne Cricket Ground | 4 | — | 2 | 2 |
| Sydney Cricket Ground | 3 | — | 2 | 1 |
| Adelaide Oval | 5 | — | 4 | 1 |
| WACA Ground, Perth | 7 | 1 | 2 | 4 |
| Woolloongabba, Brisbane | 10 | 1 | 8 | 1 |
| Bellerive Oval, Hobart | 4 | 1 | 1 | 2 |
| Optus Stadium, Perth | 1 | — | 1 | — |
| **Total** | **34** | **3** | **20** | **11** |

| In Bangladesh | | | | |
|---|---|---|---|---|
| National Stadium, Dhaka | 1 | 1 | — | — |
| Chittagong Stadium | 1 | 1 | — | — |
| Chittagong Divisional Stadium | 2 | 1 | — | 1 |
| National Stadium, Mirpur | 2 | — | — | 2 |
| **Total** | **6** | **3** | **—** | **3** |

| In England | | | | |
|---|---|---|---|---|
| Lord's, London | 19 | 1 | 9 | 9 |
| The Oval, London | 9 | 1 | 4 | 4 |
| Headingley, Leeds | 9 | 2 | 6 | 1 |
| Trent Bridge, Nottingham | 10 | 1 | 7 | 2 |
| Old Trafford, Manchester | 7 | — | 3 | 4 |
| Edgbaston, Birmingham | 5 | 1 | 4 | — |
| Rose Bowl, Southampton | 1 | 1 | — | — |
| **Total** | **60** | **7** | **33** | **20** |

| In Pakistan | P | W | L | D |
|---|---|---|---|---|
| National Stadium, Karachi | 6 | — | 3 | 3 |
| Bagh-e-Jinnah, Lahore | 1 | — | 1 | — |
| Dacca Stadium, Dacca | 2 | — | — | 2 |
| Niaz Stadium, Hyderabad | 2 | — | 2 | — |
| Rawalpindi Club Ground | 1 | — | 1 | — |
| Lahore (Gaddafi) Stadium | 7 | 2 | 4 | 1 |
| Iqbal Stadium, Faisalabad | 1 | — | 1 | — |
| Rawalpindi Cricket Stadium | 1 | — | 1 | — |
| **Total** | **21** | **2** | **13** | **6** |

| In India | | | | |
|---|---|---|---|---|
| Brabourne Stadium, Bombay | 3 | — | 2 | 1 |
| Wankhede Stadium, Bombay | 3 | 1 | 2 | — |
| Fateh Maidan, (Lal Bahadur Stadium) Hyderabad | 3 | — | 1 | 2 |
| Feroz Shah Kotla, Delhi | 2 | — | 1 | 1 |
| Eden Gardens, Calcutta | 3 | — | 1 | 2 |
| Corporation Stadium, Madras | 2 | — | 1 | 1 |
| Chepauk, (Chidambaram Stadium) Madras | 2 | — | 1 | 1 |
| VCA Ground, Nagpur | 1 | 1 | — | — |
| Green Park, Kanpur | 4 | — | 2 | 2 |
| Chinnaswamy Stadium, Bangalore | 3 | — | 3 | — |
| Barabati Stadium, Cuttack | 1 | — | — | 1 |
| Punjab C.A. Stadium, Mohali | 2 | — | — | 2 |
| VCA Stadium, Nagpur | 1 | — | 1 | — |
| Sardar Patel Stadium, Ahmedabad | 3 | — | — | 3 |
| Rajiv Gandhi International Stadium, Hyderabad | 2 | — | 1 | 1 |
| Holkar Stadium, Indore | 1 | — | 1 | — |
| **Total** | **36** | **2** | **17** | **17** |

| In South Africa | P | W | L | D |
|---|---|---|---|---|
| Kingsmead, Durban | 4 | — | 3 | 1 |
| Ellis Park, Johannesburg | 2 | — | 2 | — |
| New Wanderers, Johannesburg | 6 | 1 | 3 | 2 |
| Newlands, Cape Town | 5 | 1 | 2 | 2 |
| St George's Park, Port Elizabeth | 4 | 1 | 3 | — |
| Goodyear Park, Bloemfontein | 1 | — | 1 | — |
| SuperSport Park, Centurion | 3 | — | 3 | — |
| **Total** | **25** | **3** | **17** | **5** |

| In Sri Lanka | | | | |
|---|---|---|---|---|
| Asgiriya Stadium, Kandy | 2 | 1 | — | 1 |
| Sinhalese Sports Club Ground, Colombo | 4 | — | 3 | 1 |
| Colombo C.C. Ground | 2 | 1 | — | 1 |
| Tyrone Fernando Stadium, Moratuwa | 1 | — | — | 1 |
| R. Premadasa Stadium, Colombo | 1 | 1 | — | — |
| Galle International Stadium | 4 | — | 4 | — |
| P. Saravanamuttu Stadium, Colombo | 3 | 2 | — | 1 |
| **Total** | **17** | **5** | **7** | **5** |

**In West Indies**

| | | | | |
|---|---|---|---|---|
| Queen's Park Oval, Port of Spain | 4 | — | 1 | 3 |
| Sabina Park, Kingston | 4 | 1 | 2 | 1 |
| Kensington Oval, Bridgetown | 5 | 2 | 2 | 1 |
| Bourda, Georgetown | 2 | — | — | 2 |
| St Johns Recreation Ground, Antigua | 1 | — | — | 1 |
| Queen's Park, Grenada | 1 | — | — | 1 |
| Sir Vivian Richards Stadium, Antigua | 1 | — | 1 | — |
| **Total** | **18** | **3** | **6** | **9** |

**In United Arab Emirates**

| | | | | |
|---|---|---|---|---|
| Sheikh Zayed Stadium, Abu Dhabi | 3 | 2 | 1 | — |
| Dubai International Cricket Stadium | 2 | — | 1 | 1 |
| Sharjah Cricket Stadium | 1 | 1 | — | — |
| **Total** | **6** | **3** | **2** | **1** |

**In Zimbabwe**

| | | | | |
|---|---|---|---|---|
| Bulawayo Athletic Club | 1 | — | — | 1 |
| Harare Sports Club, Harare | 4 | 3 | — | 1 |
| Queens Sports Club, Bulawayo | 6 | 5 | — | 1 |
| **Total** | **11** | **8** | **—** | **3** |

# Record Performances in Tests on Each NZ Ground v All Countries

| Venue | Highest Total by NZ v NZ | Lowest Total by NZ v NZ | Highest Individual Innings by NZ v NZ | Best Bowling by NZ v NZ |
|---|---|---|---|---|
| **Eden Park, Auckland** 50 Tests | 595 2003/04 v South Africa 621-5d 1998/99 by South Africa | 26 1954/55 v England 58 2017/18 by England | 224 McCullum B.B. 2013/14 v India 336* Hammond W.R. 1932/33 for England | 7-87 Vettori D.L. 1999/00 v Australia 8-76 Prasanna E.A.S. 1975/76 for India |
| **Lancaster Park, Christchurch** 40 Tests | 502 1967/68 v India 580-9d 1991/92 by England | 65 1970/71 v England 82 1983/84 by England | 239 Dowling G.T. 1967/68 v India 258 Nurse S.M. 1968/69 for West Indies | 7-116 Hadlee R.J. 1985/86 v Australia 7-47 Tufnell P.C.R. 1991/92 for England |
| **Carisbrook, Dunedin** 10 Tests | 586-7d 1996/97 v Sri Lanka 507-6d 1972/73 by Pakistan | 74 1955/56 v West Indies 140 1979/80 by West Indies | 267* Young B.A. 1996/97 v Sri Lanka 201 Mushtaq Mohammad 1972/73 for Pakistan | 6-51 Hadlee R.J. 1984/85 v Pakistan 7-52 Intikhab Alam 1972/73 for Pakistan |
| **Basin Reserve, Wellington** 65 Tests | 680-8d 2013/14 v India 660-5d 1994/95 by West Indies | 42 1945/46 v Australia 64 1977/78 by England | 302 McCullum B.B. 2013/14 v India 267 de Silva P.A. 1990/91 for Sri Lanka | 7-23 Hadlee R.J. 1975/76 v India 7-37 Walsh C.A. 1994/95 for West Indies |
| **McLean Park, Napier** 10 Tests | 619-9d 2008/09 v India 498 2004/05 by Sri Lanka | 109 1994/95 v Sri Lanka 51 2011/12 by Zimbabwe | 201 Ryder J.D. 2008/09 v India 197 Gayle C.H. 2008/09 for West Indies | 6-26 Martin C.S. 2011/12 v Zimbabwe 7-47 Sidebottom R.J. 2007/08 for England |
| **Seddon Park, Hamilton** 27 Tests | 715-6d 2018/19 v Bangladesh 520 2008/09 by India | 93 1992/93 v Pakistan 97 1999/00 by West Indies | 251 Williamson K.S. 2020/21 v West Indies 226 Root J.E. 2019/20 for England | 7-27 Cairns C.L. 1999/00 v West Indies 6-49 Sidebottom R.J. 2007/08 for England |
| **University of Otago Oval, Dunedin** 8 Tests | 609-9d 2013/14 v West Indies 507 2013/14 by West Indies | 153 2009/10 v Pakistan 137 2008/09 by Bangladesh | 217* Taylor L.R.P.L. 2013/14 v West Indies 218 Bravo D.M. 2013/14 for West Indies | 6-56 Vettori D.L. 2008/09 v West Indies 5-94 Maharaj K.A. 2016/17 for South Africa |
| **Hagley Oval, Christchurch** 11 Tests | 659-6d 2020/21 v Pakistan 505 2015/16 by Australia | 200 2016/17 v Pakistan 95 2021/22 by South Africa | 252 Latham T.W.M. 2021/22 v Bangladesh 170 Burns J.A. 2015/16 for Australia | 7-23 Henry M.J. 2021/22 v South Africa 6-54 Broad S.C.J. 2017/18 for England |
| **Bay Oval, Mt Maunganui** 3 Tests | 615-9d 2019/20 v England 458 2021/22 by Bangladesh | 169 2021/22 v Bangladesh 197 2019/20 by England | 205 Watling B-J. 2019/20 v England 102 Fawad Alam 2020/21 for Pakistan | 5-44 Wagner N. 2019/20 v England 6-46 Ebadot Hossain 2021/22 for Bangladesh |
| **ALL TESTS IN NZ** 224 Tests | 715-6d 2018/19 v Bangladesh Hamilton 660-5d 1994/95 by West Indies Wellington | 26 1954/55 v England Auckland 51 2011/12 by Zimbabwe Napier | 302 McCullum B.B. 2013/14 v India Wellington 336* Hammond W.R. 1932/33 for England Auckland | 7-23 Hadlee R.J. 1975/76 v India Wellington 7-23 Henry M.J. 2021/22 v South Africa Christchurch 8-76 Prasanna E.A.S. 1975/76 for India Auckland |

# Record Performances in Tests v All Opponents

| Opponent | Highest Total by NZ / v NZ | Lowest Total by NZ / v NZ | Highest Individual Innings by NZ / v NZ | Best Bowling by NZ / v NZ |
|---|---|---|---|---|
| **England** | 615-9d Mt Maunganui 2019/20<br>593-6 Auckland 1974/75 | 26 Auckland 1954/55<br>58 Auckland 2017/18 | 222 Astle N.J. Christchurch, 2001/02<br>336* Hammond W.R. Auckland, 1932/33 | 7-74 Cairns B.L. Leeds, 1983<br>7-32 Underwood D.L. Lord's, 1969 |
| **Australia** | 624 Perth 2015/16<br>607-6d Brisbane 1993/94 | 42 Wellington 1945/46<br>103 Auckland 1985/86 | 290 Taylor L.R.P.L. Perth, 2015/16<br>250 Walters K.D. Christchurch, 1977/78 | 9-52 Hadlee R.J. Brisbane, 1985/86<br>6-31 Warne S.K. Hobart 1993/94 |
| **South Africa** | 595 Auckland 2003/04<br>621-5d Auckland 1998/99 | 45 Cape Town 2012/13<br>148 Johannesburg 1953/54 | 262 Fleming S.P. Cape Town, 2005/06<br>275* Cullinan D.J. Auckland, 1998/99 | 6-60 Reid J.R. Dunedin, 1963/64<br>8-53 Lawrence G.B. Johannesburg, 1961/62 |
| **West Indies** | 609-9d Dunedin 2013/14<br>660-5d Wellington 1994/95 | 74 Dunedin 1955/56<br>77 Auckland 1955/56 | 259 Turner G.M. Georgetown, 1971/72<br>258 Nurse S.M. Christchurch, 1968/69 | 7-27 Cairns C.L. Hamilton, 1999/00<br>7-37 Walsh C.A. Wellington, 1994/95 |
| **India** | 680-8d Wellington 2013/14<br>583-7d Ahmedabad 1999/00 | 62 Mumbai 2020/21<br>81 Wellington 1975/76 | 302 McCullum B.B. Wellington, 2013/14<br>231 Mankad M.H. Madras, 1955/56 | 10-119 Patel A.Y. Mumbai, 2020/21<br>8-72 Venkataraghavan S. Delhi, 1964/65 |
| **Pakistan** | 690 Sharjah 2014/15<br>643 Lahore 2001/02 | 70 Dacca 1955/56<br>102 Faisalabad 1990/91 | 238 Williamson K.S. Christchurch, 2020/21<br>329 Inzamam-ul-Haq Lahore, 2001/02 | 7-52 Pringle C. Faisalabad 1990/91<br>8-41 Yasir Shah Dubai, 2018/19 |
| **Sri Lanka** | 671-4 Wellington 1990/91<br>498 Napier 2004/05 | 102 Colombo 1992/93<br>93 Wellington 1982/83 | 299 Crowe M.D. Wellington, 1990/91<br>267 de Silva P.A. Wellington, 1990/91 | 7-130 Vettori D.L. Wellington 2006/07<br>6-43 Herath H.M.R.K.B. Galle, 2012/13 |
| **Zimbabwe** | 582-4d Bulawayo 2016/17<br>461 Bulawayo 1997/98 | 207 Harare 1997/98<br>51 Napier 2011/12 | 173* Taylor L.R.P.L. Bulawayo, 2016/17<br>203* Whittall G.J. Bulawayo, 1997/98 | 6-26 Martin C.S. Napier, 2011/12<br>8-109 Strang P.A. Bulawayo, 2000/01 |
| **Bangladesh** | 715-6d Hamilton 2018/19<br>595-8d Wellington 2016/17 | 169 Mt Maunganui 2021/22<br>108 Hamilton 2001/02 | 252 Latham T.W.M. Christchurch, 2021/22<br>217 Shakib Al Hasan Wellington, 2016/17 | 7-53 Cairns C.L. Hamilton, 2001/02<br>7-36 Shakib Al Hasan Chittagong, 2008/09 |

# INDIVIDUAL RECORDS

## BATTING

### Test Centuries
*(317 instances)*

| | | |
|---|---|---|
| 302 | McCullum B.B. v India at Wellington | 2013/14 |
| 299 | Crowe M.D. v Sri Lanka at Wellington | 1990/91 |
| 290 | Taylor L.R.P.L. v Australia at Perth | 2015/16 |
| 274* | Fleming S.P. v Sri Lanka at Colombo | 2002/03 |
| 267* | Young B.A. v Sri Lanka at Dunedin | 1996/97 |
| 264* | Latham T.W.M. v Sri Lanka at Wellington | 2018/19 |
| 262 | Fleming S.P. v South Africa at Cape Town | 2005/06 |
| 259 | Turner G.M. v West Indies at Georgetown | 1971/72 |
| 252 | Latham T.W.M. v Bangladesh at Christchurch | 2021/22 |
| 251 | Williamson K.S. v West Indies at Hamilton | 2020/21 |
| 242* | Williamson K.S. v Sri Lanka at Wellington | 2014/15 |
| 239 | Dowling G.T. v India at Christchurch | 1967/68 |
| 238 | Williamson K.S. v Pakistan at Christchurch | 2020/21 |
| 230* | Sutcliffe B. v India at New Delhi | 1955/56 |
| 225 | McCullum B.B. v India at Hyderabad | 2010/11 |
| 224 | Vincent L. v Sri Lanka at Wellington | 2004/05 |
| 224 | McCullum B.B. v India at Auckland | 2013/14 |
| 223* | Turner G.M. v West Indies at Kingston | 1971/72 |
| 222 | Astle N.J. v England at Christchurch | 2001/02 |
| 217* | Taylor L.R.P.L. v West Indies at Dunedin | 2013/14 |
| 214 | Sinclair M.S. v West Indies at Wellington | 1999/00 |
| 206 | Donnelly M.P. v England at Lord's | 1949 |
| 205 | Watling B-J. v England at Mount Maunganui | 2019/20 |
| 204* | Sinclair M.S. v Pakistan at Christchurch | 2000/01 |
| 202 | Fleming S.P. v Bangladesh at Chittagong | 2004/05 |
| 202 | McCullum B.B. v Pakistan at Sharjah | 2014/15 |
| 201 | Ryder J.D. v India at Napier | 2008/09 |
| 200* | Williamson K.S. v Bangladesh at Hamilton | 2018/19 |
| 200 | Taylor L.R.P.L. v Bangladesh at Wellington | 2018/19 |
| 200 | Conway D.P. v England at Lord's | 2021 |
| 195 | McCullum B.B. v Sri Lanka at Christchurch | 2014/15 |
| 192 | Fleming S.P. v Pakistan at Hamilton | 2003/04 |
| 192 | Williamson K.S. v Pakistan at Sharjah | 2014/15 |
| 190 | Mitchell D.J. v England at Nottingham | 2022 |
| 189 | Guptill M.J. v Bangladesh at Hamilton | 2009/10 |
| 188 | Crowe M.D. v West Indies at Georgetown | 1984/85 |
| 188 | Crowe M.D. v Australia at Brisbane | 1985/86 |
| 186 | Jones A.H. v Sri Lanka at Wellington | 1990/91 |
| 185 | Wright J.G. v India at Christchurch | 1989/90 |
| 185 | McCullum B.B. v Bangladesh at Hamilton | 2009/10 |
| 182 | Jarvis T.W. v West Indies at Georgetown | 1971/72 |
| 180 | Reid J.F. v Sri Lanka at Colombo | 1983/84 |
| 177 | Latham T.W.M. v Bangladesh at Wellington | 2016/17 |
| 176 | Congdon B.E. v England at Nottingham | 1973 |
| 176 | Williamson K.S. v South Africa at Hamilton | 2016/17 |
| 176 | Latham T.W.M. v Sri Lanka at Christchurch | 2018/19 |
| 175 | Congdon B.E. v England at Lord's | 1973 |
| 174* | Coney J.V. v England at Wellington | 1983/84 |

| 174* | Fleming S.P. v Sri Lanka at Colombo | 1997/98 |
| 174 | Crowe M.D. v Pakistan at Wellington | 1988/89 |
| 174 | Nicholls H.M. v West Indies at Wellington | 2020/21 |
| 173* | Taylor L.R.P.L v Zimbabwe at Bulawayo | 2016/17 |
| 173 | Smith I.D.S. v India at Auckland | 1989/90 |
| 171 | Rutherford H.D. v England at Dunedin | 2012/13 |
| 170* | Jones A.H. v India at Auckland | 1989/90 |
| 170 | Styris S.B. v South Africa at Auckland | 2003/04 |
| 166* | Congdon B.E. v West Indies at Port of Spain | 1971/72 |
| 166 | Williamson K.S. v Australia at Perth | 2015/16 |
| 162* | Nicholls H.M. v Sri Lanka at Christchurch | 2018/19 |
| 161* | Williamson K.S. v West Indies at Bridgetown | 2014 |
| 161 | Edgar B.A. v Australia at Auckland | 1981/82 |
| 161 | Latham T.W.M. v Bangladesh at Hamilton | 2018/19 |
| 160 | Marshall H.J.H. v Sri Lanka at Napier | 2004/05 |
| 158* | Reid J.F. v Pakistan at Auckland | 1984/85 |
| 158 | Cairns C.L. v South Africa at Auckland | 2003/04 |
| 157 | Horne M.J. v Zimbabwe at Auckland | 1997/98 |
| 157 | Nicholls H.M. v Pakistan at Christchurch | 2020/21 |
| 156* | Astle N.J. v Australia at Perth | 2001/02 |
| 156 | Guptill M.J. v Sri Lanka at Dunedin | 2015/16 |
| 154* | Taylor L.R.P.L. v England at Manchester | 2008 |
| 154 | Latham T.W.M. v Sri Lanka at Colombo | 2019/20 |
| 152 | Lees W.K. v Pakistan at Karachi | 1976/77 |
| 151* | Sutcliffe B. v India at Calcutta | 1964/65 |
| 151* | Hadlee R.J. v Sri Lanka at Colombo | 1986/87 |
| 151 | Taylor L.R.P.L. v India at Napier | 2008/09 |
| 150 | Jones A.H. v Australia at Adelaide | 1987/88 |
| 150 | Sinclair M.S. v South Africa at Port Elizabeth | 2000/01 |
| 148 | Reid J.F. v Pakistan at Wellington | 1984/85 |
| 147 | Howarth G.P. v West Indies at Christchurch | 1979/80 |
| 146* | Greatbatch M.J. v Australia at Perth | 1989/90 |
| 146 | Marshall H.J.H. v Australia at Christchurch | 2004/05 |
| 145* | Nicholls H.M. v England at Auckland | 2017/18 |
| 145 | Richardson M.H. v India at Mohali | 2003/04 |
| 145 | McCullum B.B. v Australia at Christchurch | 2015/16 |
| 143 | Dowling G.T. v India at Dunedin | 1967/68 |
| 143 | Crowe M.D. v England at Wellington | 1987/88 |
| 143 | Jones A.H. v England at Wellington | 1991/92 |
| 143 | Jones A.H. v Australia at Perth | 1993/94 |
| 143 | Richardson M.H. v Bangladesh at Hamilton | 2001/02 |
| 143 | McCullum B.B. v Bangladesh at Dhaka | 2004/05 |
| 142* | Watling B-J. v Sri Lanka at Wellington | 2014/15 |
| 142 | Reid J.R. v South Africa at Johannesburg | 1961/62 |
| 142 | Crowe M.D. v England at Lord's | 1994 |
| 142 | McMillan C.D. v Sri Lanka at Colombo | 1997/98 |
| 142 | McMillan C.D. v Zimbabwe at Wellington | 2000/01 |
| 142 | Taylor L.R.P.L. v Sri Lanka at Colombo | 2012/13 |
| 141 | Wright J.G. v Australia at Christchurch | 1981/82 |
| 141 | Astle N.J. v Zimbabwe at Wellington | 2000/01 |
| 140 | Crowe M.D. v Zimbabwe at Harare | 1992/93 |
| 140 | Vettori D.L. v Sri Lanka at Colombo | 2009/10 |
| 140 | Williamson K.S. v Australia at Brisbane | 2015/16 |
| 139 | McMillan C.D. v Zimbabwe at Wellington | 1997/98 |
| 139 | Williamson K.S. v Pakistan at Abu Dhabi | 2018/19 |
| 138 | Sinclair B.W. v South Africa at Auckland | 1963/64 |

| | | |
|---|---|---|
| 138 | Wright J.G. v West Indies at Wellington | 1986/87 |
| 138 | Taylor L.R.P.L. v Australia at Hamilton | 2009/10 |
| 137* | Sutcliffe B. v India at Hyderabad | 1955/56 |
| 137* | Howarth G.P. v India at Wellington | 1980/81 |
| 137* | Vettori D.L. v Pakistan at Hamilton | 2003/04 |
| 137* | Neesham J.D.S. v India at Wellington | 2013/14 |
| 137 | Crowe M.D. v Australia at Christchurch | 1985/86 |
| 137 | Crowe M.D. v Australia at Adelaide | 1987/88 |
| 137 | Latham T.W.M. v Pakistan at Dubai | 2014/15 |
| 136 | Dempster C.S. v England at Wellington | 1929/30 |
| 136 | McIntosh T.G. v West Indies at Napier | 2008/09 |
| 136 | Fulton P.G. v England at Auckland | 2012/13 |
| 136 | Latham T.W.M. v Zimbabwe at Bulawayo | 2016/17 |
| 135 | Reid J.R. v South Africa at Cape Town | 1953/54 |
| 135 | Williamson K.S. v Sri Lanka at Colombo | 2012/13 |
| 134 | Vettori D.L. v Pakistan at Napier | 2009/10 |
| 133 | Greatbatch M.J. v Pakistan at Hamilton | 1992/93 |
| 133 | Horne M.J. v Australia at Hobart | 1997/98 |
| 133 | Oram J.D.P. v South Africa at Centurion | 2005/06 |
| 132 | Congdon B.E. v Australia at Wellington | 1973/74 |
| 132 | Williamson K.S. v England at Lord's | 2015 |
| 132 | Raval J.A. v Bangladesh at Hamilton | 2018/19 |
| 131 | Williamson K.S. v India at Ahmedabad | 2010/11 |
| 131 | Taylor L.R.P.L. v West Indies at Hamilton | 2013/14 |
| 130 | Sinclair B.W. v Pakistan at Lahore | 1964/65 |
| 130 | Wright J.G. v England at Auckland | 1983/84 |
| 130 | Fleming S.P. v West Indies at Bridgetown | 2001/02 |
| 130 | Williamson K.S. v South Africa at Dunedin | 2016/17 |
| 129 | Dowling G.T. v India at Bombay | 1964/65 |
| 129 | Edgar B.A. v Pakistan at Christchurch | 1978/79 |
| 129 | Fleming S.P. v England at Auckland | 1996/97 |
| 129 | Taylor L.R.P.L. v West Indies at Wellington | 2013/14 |
| 129 | Williamson K.S. v Pakistan at Mt Maunganui | 2020/21 |
| 128 | Reid J.R. v Pakistan at Karachi | 1964/65 |
| 128 | Crowe J.J. v England at Auckland | 1983/84 |
| 128 | Astle N.J. v Zimbabwe at Bulawayo | 2005/06 |
| 127 | Edgar B.A. v West Indies at Auckland | 1979/80 |
| 127 | Vettori D.L. v Zimbabwe at Harare | 2005/06 |
| 126* | Oram J.D.P. v Australia at Brisbane | 2004/05 |
| 126* | Nicholls H.M. v Pakistan at Abu Dhabi | 2018/19 |
| 126 | Congdon B.E. v West Indies at Bridgetown | 1971/72 |
| 126 | Cairns C.L. v India at Hamilton | 1998/99 |
| 126 | Santner M.J. v England at Mount Maunganui | 2019/20 |
| 125 | Astle N.J. v West Indies at Bridgetown | 1995/96 |
| 124* | Taylor L.R.P.L. v Zimbabwe at Bulawayo | 2016/17 |
| 124 | Taylor B.R. v West Indies at Auckland | 1968/69 |
| 124 | Cairns C.L. v Zimbabwe at Harare | 2000/01 |
| 124 | Watling B-J. v India at Wellington | 2013/14 |
| 123* | Reid J.F. v India at Christchurch | 1980/81 |
| 123 | Howarth G.P. v England at Lord's | 1978 |
| 122* | Franklin J.E.C. v South Africa at Cape Town | 2005/06 |
| 122* | Taylor L.R.P.L. v Zimbabwe at Napier | 2011/12 |
| 122 | Howarth G.P. v England at Auckland | 1977/78 |
| 122 | Jones A.H. v Sri Lanka at Hamilton | 1990/91 |
| 122 | Conway D.P. v Bangladesh at Mt Maunganui | 2021/22 |
| 121 | Parker J.M. v England at Auckland | 1974/75 |

| 121 | Blundell T.A. v Australia at Melbourne | 2019/20 |
| 120* | Crowe J.J. v Sri Lanka at Colombo | 1986/87 |
| 120* | Thomson S.A. v Pakistan at Christchurch | 1993/94 |
| 120* | de Grandhomme C. v South Africa at Christchurch | 2021/22 |
| 120 | Dempster C.S. v England at Lord's | 1931 |
| 120 | Reid J.R. v India at Calcutta | 1955/56 |
| 120 | Young B.A. v Pakistan at Christchurch | 1993/94 |
| 120 | Cairns C.L. v Zimbabwe at Auckland | 1995/96 |
| 120 | Taylor L.R.P.L. v England at Hamilton | 2007/08 |
| 120 | Watling B-J. v England at Leeds | 2015 |
| 119* | Reid J.R. v India at Delhi | 1955/56 |
| 119* | Burgess M.G. v Pakistan at Dacca | 1969/70 |
| 119* | Oram J.D.P. v South Africa at Hamilton | 2003/04 |
| 119 | Wright J.G. v England at The Oval | 1986 |
| 119 | Crowe M.D. v West Indies at Wellington | 1986/87 |
| 119 | Latham R.T. v Zimbabwe at Bulawayo | 1992/93 |
| 119 | Styris S.B. v India at Mohali | 2003/04 |
| 118 | Vettori D.L. v India at Hamilton | 2008/09 |
| 118 | Nicholls H.M. v South Africa at Wellington | 2016/17 |
| 117* | Hastings B.F. v West Indies at Christchurch | 1968/69 |
| 117* | Wright J.G. v Australia at Wellington | 1989/90 |
| 117 | Mills J.E. v England at Wellington | 1929/30 |
| 117 | Morrison J.F.M. v Australia at Sydney | 1973/74 |
| 117 | Turner G.M. v India at Christchurch | 1975/76 |
| 117 | Fleming S.P. v England at Nottingham | 2004 |
| 117 | Oram J.D.P. v Bangladesh at Dunedin | 2007/08 |
| 116 | Hadlee W.A. v England at Christchurch | 1946/47 |
| 116 | Sutcliffe B. v England at Christchurch | 1950/51 |
| 116 | Pollard V. v England at Nottingham | 1973 |
| 116 | Wright J.G. v England at Wellington | 1991/92 |
| 116 | Anderson C.J. v Bangladesh at Mirpur | 2013/14 |
| 115 | Crowe M.D. v England at Manchester | 1994 |
| 115 | McCullum B.B. v India at Napier | 2008/09 |
| 114 | Sinclair B.W. v England at Auckland | 1965/66 |
| 114 | Howarth G.P. v Pakistan at Napier | 1978/79 |
| 114 | Astle N.J. v Zimbabwe at Auckland | 1997/98 |
| 114 | Astle N.J. v Sri Lanka at Napier | 2004/05 |
| 114 | Williamson K.S. v Bangladesh at Chittagong | 2013/14 |
| 113* | Smith I.D.S. v England at Auckland | 1983/84 |
| 113* | Wright J.G. v India at Napier | 1989/90 |
| 113 | Turner G.M. v India at Kanpur | 1976/77 |
| 113 | Crowe M.D. v India at Auckland | 1989/90 |
| 113 | Taylor L.R.P.L. v India at Bangalore | 2012/13 |
| 113 | McCullum B.B. v West Indies at Dunedin | 2013/14 |
| 113 | Williamson K.S. v India at Auckland | 2013/14 |
| 113 | Williamson K.S. v West Indies at Kingston | 2014 |
| 113 | Williamson K.S. v Zimbabwe at Bulawayo | 2016/17 |
| 112 | Crowe J.J. v West Indies at Kingston | 1984/85 |
| 112 | Spearman C.M. v Zimbabwe at Auckland | 1995/96 |
| 111* | Coney J.V. v Pakistan at Dunedin | 1984/85 |
| 111 | McGregor S.N. v Pakistan at Lahore | 1955/56 |
| 111 | Burgess M.G. v Pakistan at Lahore | 1976/77 |
| 111 | McCullum B.B. v Zimbabwe at Harare | 2005/06 |
| 110* | Turner G.M. v Australia at Christchurch | 1973/74 |
| 110 | Turner G.M. v Pakistan at Dacca | 1969/70 |
| 110 | Hastings B.F. v Pakistan at Auckland | 1972/73 |

| | | |
|---|---|---|
| 110 | Wright J.G. v India at Auckland | 1980/81 |
| 110 | Bracewell J.G. v England at Nottingham | 1986 |
| 110 | Horne M.J. v Zimbabwe at Bulawayo | 2000/01 |
| 110 | Parore A.C. v Australia at Perth | 2001/02 |
| 110 | Vettori D.L. v Pakistan at Wellington | 2010/11 |
| 110 | Fulton P.G. v England at Auckland | 2012/13 |
| 109* | Latham T.W.M. v Sri Lanka at Dunedin | 2015/16 |
| 109 | Barton P.T. v South Africa at Port Elizabeth | 1961/62 |
| 109 | Cairns C.L. v Australia at Wellington | 1999/00 |
| 109 | Guptill M.J. v Zimbabwe at Bulawayo | 2011/12 |
| 109 | Brownlie D.G. v South Africa at Cape Town | 2012/13 |
| 109 | Conway D.P. v Bangladesh at Christchurch | 2021/22 |
| 109 | Mitchell D.J. v England at Leeds | 2022 |
| 108* | Crowe M.D. v Pakistan at Lahore | 1990/91 |
| 108* | Williamson K.S. v Sri Lanka at Hamilton | 2015/16 |
| 108 | Parker J.M. v Australia at Sydney | 1973/74 |
| 108 | Reid J.F. v Australia at Brisbane | 1985/86 |
| 108 | Styris S.B. v England at Nottingham | 2004 |
| 108 | Mitchell D.J. v England at Lord's | 2022 |
| 107* | Congdon B.E. v Australia at Christchurch | 1976/77 |
| 107* | Greatbatch M.J. v England at Auckland | 1987/88 |
| 107* | Rutherford K.R. v England at Wellington | 1987/88 |
| 107* | McMillan C.D. v England at Manchester | 1999 |
| 107* | Blundell T.A. v West Indies at Wellington | 2017/18 |
| 107* | Taylor L.R.P.L. v West Indies at Hamilton | 2017/18 |
| 107 | Rabone G.O. v South Africa at Durban | 1953/54 |
| 107 | Redmond R.E. v Pakistan at Auckland | 1972/73 |
| 107 | Wright J.G. v Pakistan at Karachi | 1984/85 |
| 107 | Crowe M.D. v Sri Lanka at Colombo | 1992/93 |
| 107 | Styris S.B. v West Indies at St George's | 2001/02 |
| 107 | Bell M.D. v Bangladesh at Dunedin | 2007/08 |
| 107 | Taylor L.R.P.L. v India at Wellington | 2008/09 |
| 107 | Neesham J.D.S. v West Indies at Kingston | 2014 |
| 107 | Watling B-J. v Zimbabwe at Bulawayo | 2016/17 |
| 107 | Nicholls H.M. v Bangladesh at Wellington | 2018/19 |
| 106 | Reid J.F. v Pakistan at Hyderabad | 1984/85 |
| 106 | Crowe M.D. v England at Lord's | 1986 |
| 106 | Richardson M.H. v Pakistan at Hamilton | 2000/01 |
| 106 | McMillan C.D. v Bangladesh at Hamilton | 2001/02 |
| 106 | Vincent L. v India at Mohali | 2003/04 |
| 106 | Blundell T.A. v England at Nottingham | 2022 |
| 105* | Pollard V. v England at Lord's | 1973 |
| 105* | Watling B-J. v Sri Lanka at Colombo | 2019/20 |
| 105* | Taylor L.R.P.L. v England at Hamilton | 2019/20 |
| 105 | Taylor B.R. v India at Calcutta | 1964/65 |
| 105 | Hastings B.F. v West Indies at Bridgetown | 1971/72 |
| 105 | Burgess M.G. v England at Lord's | 1973 |
| 105 | Rutherford K.R. v Sri Lanka at Moratuwa | 1992/93 |
| 105 | Bell M.D. v Pakistan at Hamilton | 2000/01 |
| 105 | Fleming S.P. v Australia at Perth | 2001/02 |
| 105 | Latham T.W.M. v Zimbabwe at Bulawayo | 2016/17 |
| 105 | de Grandhomme C. v West Indies at Wellington | 2017/18 |
| 105 | Latham T.W.M. v England at Hamilton | 2019/20 |
| 105 | Nicholls H.M. v South Africa at Christchurch | 2021/22 |
| 104* | Williamson K.S. v Bangladesh at Wellington | 2016/17 |

| 104* | Williamson K.S. v England at Hamilton | 2019/20 |
| 104 | Page M.L. v England at Lord's | 1931 |
| 104 | Congdon B.E. v England at Christchurch | 1965/66 |
| 104 | Burgess M.G. v England at Auckland | 1970/71 |
| 104 | Parker J.M. v India at Bombay | 1976/77 |
| 104 | Crowe M.D. v West Indies at Auckland | 1986/87 |
| 104 | Vincent L. v Australia at Perth | 2001/02 |
| 104 | McCullum B.B. v Australia at Wellington | 2009/10 |
| 104 | Taylor L.R.P.L. v Pakistan at Dubai | 2014/15 |
| 103* | Styris S.B. v West Indies at Auckland | 2005/06 |
| 103 | Hadlee R.J. v West Indies at Christchurch | 1979/80 |
| 103 | Wright J.G. v England at Auckland | 1987/88 |
| 103 | Astle N.J. v West Indies at St John's | 1995/96 |
| 103 | Astle N.J. v India at Ahmedabad | 2003/04 |
| 103 | Ryder J.D. v India at Ahmedabad | 2010/11 |
| 103 | Watling B-J. v Bangladesh at Chittagong | 2013/14 |
| 103 | Latham T.W.M. v Pakistan at Abu Dhabi | 2014/15 |
| 102* | Astle N.J. v England at Auckland | 1996/97 |
| 102* | Watling B-J. v Zimbabwe at Napier | 2011/12 |
| 102* | Williamson K.S. v South Africa at Wellington | 2011/12 |
| 102* | Taylor L.R.P.L. v Pakistan at Hamilton | 2016/17 |
| 102* | Mitchell D.J. v Pakistan at Christchurch | 2020/21 |
| 102 | Guy J.W. v India at Hyderabad | 1955/56 |
| 102 | Howarth G.P. v England at Auckland | 1977/78 |
| 102 | Rutherford K.R. v Australia at Christchurch | 1992/93 |
| 102 | Ryder J.D. v India at Hamilton | 2008/09 |
| 102 | McIntosh T.G. v India at Hyderabad | 2010/11 |
| 102 | Williamson K.S. v England at Auckland | 2017/18 |
| 101* | Coney J.V. v Australia at Wellington | 1985/86 |
| 101 | Sutcliffe B. v England at Manchester | 1949 |
| 101 | Harris P.G.Z. v South Africa at Cape Town | 1961/62 |
| 101 | Burgess M.G. v West Indies at Kingston | 1971/72 |
| 101 | Hastings B.F. v Australia at Wellington | 1973/74 |
| 101 | Turner G.M. v Australia at Christchurch | 1973/74 |
| 101 | Franklin T.J. v England at Lord's | 1990 |
| 101 | Wright J.G. v Sri Lanka at Hamilton | 1990/91 |
| 101 | Astle N.J. v England at Manchester | 1999 |
| 101 | Richardson M.H. v England at Lord's | 2004 |
| 101 | Oram J.D.P. v England at Lord's | 2008 |
| 100* | Jones A.H. v Sri Lanka at Hamilton | 1990/91 |
| 100* | Parore A.C. v West Indies at Christchurch | 1994/95 |
| 100* | McMillan C.D. v India at Mohali | 2003/04 |
| 100 | Vivian H.G. v South Africa at Wellington | 1931/32 |
| 100 | Reid J.R. v England at Christchurch | 1962/63 |
| 100 | Crowe M.D. v England at Wellington | 1983/84 |
| 100 | Horne M.J. v England at Lord's | 1999 |

## Century on Test Debut

| 117 & 7 | Mills J.E. v England at Wellington | 1929/30 |
| 105 & 0* | Taylor B.R. v India at Calcutta | 1964/65 |
| 107 & 56 | Redmond R.E. v Pakistan at Auckland | 1972/73 |
| 11 & 107* | Greatbatch M.J. v England at Auckland | 1987/88 |
| 214 | Sinclair M.S. v West Indies at Wellington | 1999/00 |
| 104 & 54 | Vincent L. v Australia at Perth | 2001/02 |

| 107 & 69* | Styris S.B. v West Indies at St George's | 2001/02 |
| 131 | Williamson K.S. v India at Ahmedabad | 2010/11 |
| 171 | Rutherford H.D. v England at Dunedin | 2012/13 |
| 137* | Neesham J.D.S. v India at Wellington | 2013/14 |
| 107* | Blundell T.A. v West Indies at Wellington | 2017/18 |
| 200 & 23 | Conway D.P. v England at Lord's | 2021 |

## Centuries in Both Innings of a Test

| 101 & 110* | Turner G.M. v Australia at Christchurch | 1973/74 |
| 122 & 102 | Howarth G.P. v England at Auckland | 1977/78 |
| 122 & 100* | Jones A.H. v Sri Lanka at Hamilton | 1990/91 |
| 136 & 110 | Fulton P.G. v England at Auckland | 2012/13 |

**NB:** *In the same match that Jones achieved this feat A.P. Gurusinha (119 & 102) also scored a century in each innings. This is only the second occasion that a player from each side has scored centuries in each innings of a test (A.R. Morris and D.C.S. Compton, Australia v England, Adelaide, 1946/47).*

## A Century and a Fifty in a Test

| 136 & 80* | Dempster C.S. v England at Wellington | 1929/30 |
| 52 & 120 | Dempster C.S. v England at Lord's | 1931 |
| 100 & 73 | Vivian H.G. v South Africa at Wellington *(aged 19)* | 1931/32 |
| 107 & 68 | Rabone G.O. v South Africa at Durban | 1953/54 |
| 60 & 142 | Reid J.R. v South Africa at Johannesburg | 1961/62 |
| 74 & 100 | Reid J.R. v England at Christchurch | 1962/63 |
| 128 & 76 | Reid J.R. v Pakistan at Karachi | 1964/65 |
| 59 & 119* | Burgess M.G. v Pakistan at Dacca | 1969/70 |
| 166* & 82 | Congdon B.E. v West Indies at Port of Spain | 1971/72 |
| 107 & 56 | Redmond R.E. v Pakistan at Auckland | 1972/73 |
| 75 & 138 | Wright J.G. v West Indies at Wellington | 1986/87 |
| 150 & 64 | Jones A.H. v Australia at Adelaide | 1987/88 |
| 76 & 146* | Greatbatch M.J. v Australia at Perth | 1989/90 |
| 140 & 61 | Crowe M.D. v Zimbabwe at Harare | 1992/93 |
| 105 & 53 | Rutherford K.R. v Sri Lanka at Moratuwa | 1992/93 |
| 57 & 102 | Rutherford K.R. v Australia at Christchurch | 1992/93 |
| 70 & 115 | Crowe M.D. v England at Manchester | 1994 |
| 57 & 120 | Cairns C.L. v Zimbabwe at Auckland | 1995/96 |
| 54 & 125 | Astle N.J. v West Indies at Bridgetown | 1995/96 |
| 78 & 174* | Fleming S.P. v Sri Lanka at Colombo | 1997/98 |
| 109 & 69 | Cairns C.L. v Australia at Wellington | 1999/00 |
| 141 & 51* | Astle N.J. v Zimbabwe at Wellington | 2000/01 |
| 204 & 50* | Sinclair M.S. v Pakistan at Christchurch | 2000/01 |
| 104 & 54 | Vincent L. v Australia at Perth | 2001/02 |
| 107 & 69* | Styris S.B. v West Indies at St George's | 2001/02 |
| 274* & 69* | Fleming S.P. v Sri Lanka at Colombo | 2002/03 |
| 103 & 51 | Astle N.J. v India at Ahmedabad | 2003/04 |
| 93 & 101 | Richardson M.H. v England at Lord's | 2004 |
| 189 & 56* | Guptill M.J. v Bangladesh at Hamilton | 2009/10 |
| 142 & 74 | Taylor L.R.P.L. v Sri Lanka at Colombo | 2012/13 |
| 114 & 74 | Williamson K.S. v Bangladesh at Chittagong | 2013/14 |
| 69 & 242* | Williamson K.S. v Sri Lanka at Wellington | 2014/15 |
| 140 & 59 | Williamson K.S. v Australia at Brisbane | 2015/16 |
| 113 & 68* | Williamson K.S. v Zimbabwe at Bulawayo | 2016/17 |
| 124* & 67* | Taylor L.R.P.L. v Zimbabwe at Bulawayo | 2016/17 |
| 53 & 104* | Williamson K.S. v Bangladesh at Wellington | 2016/17 |
| 89 & 139 | Williamson K.S. v Pakistan at Abu Dhabi | 2018/19 |

| 53 & 105* | Taylor L.R.P.L. v England at Hamilton | 2019/20 |
| 190 & 62* | Mitchell D.J. v England at Nottingham | 2022 |
| 109 & 56 | Mitchell D.J. v England at Leeds | 2022 |

*Redmond's feat of scoring a century and a fifty in his only test is unique. Only he and A.G. Ganteaume (112 WI v England, Port of Spain 1947/48) have made a century in their only test.*

## Centuries in Three Successive Test Innings
Jones A.H. 186, Wellington, 122 and 100* Hamilton v Sri Lanka 1990/91

## Centuries in Two Successive Test Innings
Reid J.R. 119*, Delhi and 120, Calcutta v India 1955/56
Burgess M.G. 119*, Dacca v Pakistan 1969/70 and 104, Auckland v England 1970/71
Congdon B.E. 176, Nottingham and 175, Lord's v England 1973
Pollard V. 116, Nottingham and 105*, Lord's v England 1973
Turner G.M. 101 and 110*, Christchurch v Australia 1973/74
Howarth G.P. 122 and 102, Auckland v England 1977/78 – 94 v England, Oval 1978
Crowe M.D. 143, Wellington v England 1987/88 and 174, Wellington v Pakistan 1988/89
Wright J.G. 185, Christchurch and 113* Napier v India 1989/90
Astle N.J. 125, Bridgetown and 103, St Johns v West Indies 1995/96
Fulton P.G. 136 and 110, Auckland v England 2012/13
Taylor L.R.P.L. 129, Wellington and 131, Hamilton v West Indies 2013/14
Neesham J.D.S. 137*, Wellington v West Indies 2013/14 and 107, Kingston v West Indies 2014
Williamson K.S. 242* v Sri Lanka at Wellington 2014/15 and 132 v England at Lords 2015
Latham T.W.M. 105 and 136, Bulawayo v Zimbabwe 2016/17
Taylor L.R.P.L. 173* and 124*, Bulawayo v Zimbabwe 2016/17
Latham T.W.M. 176 v Sri Lanka at Christchurch and 161 v Bangladesh at Hamilton 2018/19
Watling B-J. 105* v Sri Lanka at Colombo and 205 v England at Mt Maunganui 2019/20
Williamson K.S. 251 v West Indies at Hamilton 2020/21 and 129 v Pakistan at Mt Maunganui 2020/21
Mitchell D.J. 108, Lord's and 190, Trent Bridge v England 2022

*M.G. Burgess scored centuries in three successive tests — all played in different countries. He followed the two centuries above with 15 & 101 v West Indies at Kingston, 1971/72.*
*L.R.P.L. Taylor scored centuries in three successive tests against West Indies in 2013/14 — 217* & 16* at Dunedin, 129 at Wellington and 131 & 2* at Hamilton.*
*T.W.M. Latham scored centuries in three successive tests. 264* and 10 & 176 v Sri Lanka at Wellington and Christchurch and 161 v Bangladesh at Hamilton, 2018/19.*
*K.S. Williamson scored centuries in three successive tests. 251 v West Indies at Hamilton, 129 & 21 v Pakistan at Mt Maunganui and 238 v Pakistan at Christchurch in 2020/21.*
*D.J. Mitchell score centuries in three successive tests against England in 2022 — 13 & 108 at Lord's, 109 & 62* at Nottingham and 109 & 56 at Leeds.*
*J.F. Reid scored 106 & 21 at Hyderabad, 97 at Karachi, 148 & 3 at Wellington and 158* at Auckland in successive tests v Pakistan in 1984/85.*
*G.T. Dowling scored 143 & 10 at Dunedin and 239 & 5 at Christchurch in successive tests v India in 1967/68.*
*B.E. Congdon scored 166* & 82 at Port of Spain and 126 at Bridgetown in successive tests v West Indies in 1971/72.*
*M.D Crowe scored 142 & 9 at Lord's and 70 & 115 at Manchester in successive tests v England in 1994.*
*B.B. McCullum scored 224 & 1 at Auckland and 8 & 302 at Wellington in successive tests v India 2013/14.*
*K.S. Williamson scored 140 & 59 at Brisbane and 166 & 32* at Adelaide in successive tests v Australia 2015/16.*
*D.P. Conway scored 122 & 13 at Mt Maunganui and 109 at Christchurch in successive tests v Bangladesh in 2021/22.*

## Fifty on Test Debut
| 3 & 51 | Vivian H.G. v England at The Oval *(aged 18)* | 1931 |
| 52 & 56 | Wallace W.M. v England at Lord's | 1937 |
| 64 & 0 | Moloney D.A.R. v England at Lord's | 1937 |
| 58 | Sutcliffe B. v England at Christchurch | 1946/47 |
| 50 & 25 | Reid J.R. v England at Manchester | 1949 |
| 93 & 64 | Harford N.S. v Pakistan at Lahore | 1955/56 |
| 54 & 23 | Barton P.T. v South Africa at Durban | 1961/62 |

| 74 & 58 | Dowling G.T. v South Africa at Johannesburg | 1961/62 |
| 64 & 1 | Yuile B.W. v England at Auckland | 1962/63 |
| 10 & 52 | Gedye S.G. v South Africa at Wellington | 1963/64 |
| 66 & 5 | Morgan R.W. v Pakistan at Auckland | 1964/65 |
| 17 & 54 | Murray B.A.G. v India at Dunedin | 1967/68 |
| 50 & 39 | Burgess M.G. v India at Dunedin | 1967/68 |
| 69 & 0* | Thomson K. v India at Christchurch | 1967/68 |
| 6 & 51* | Howarth G.P. v England at Auckland | 1974/75 |
| 14 & 92 | Anderson R.W. v Pakistan at Lahore | 1976/77 |
| 55 & 19 | Wright J.G. v England at Wellington | 1977/78 |
| 56 & 0* | Harris C.Z. v Sri Lanka at Moratuwa | 1992/93 |
| 38 & 53 | Young B.A. v Australia at Brisbane | 1993/94 |
| 16 & 92 | Fleming S.P. v India at Hamilton | 1993/94 |
| 54 & 0 | McMillan C.D. v Australia at Brisbane | 1997/98 |
| 59 & 12 | Papps M.H.W. v South Africa at Hamilton | 2003/04 |
| 57 & 19* | McCullum B.B. v South Africa at Hamilton | 2003/04 |
| 74 & 7 | Cumming C.D. v Australia at Christchurch | 2004/05 |
| 5 & 77* | Southee T.G. v England at Napier | 2007/08 |
| 18 & 60* | Watling B-J. v Pakstan at Napier | 2009/10 |
| 63 & 9 | Brownlie D.G. v Zimbabwe at Bulawayo | 2011/12 |
| 88 & 31 | Ronchi L. v England at Leeds | 2015 |
| 8 & 59 | Nicholls H.M. v Australia at Wellington | 2015/16 |
| 55 & 36* | Raval J.A. v Pakistan at Christchurch | 2016/17 |
| 73 | Mitchell D.J. v England at Hamilton | 2019/20 |
| 51 & 0 | Phillips G.D. v Australia at Sydney | 2019/20 |

*H.M. McGirr scored 51 in his first (and only) test innings but it was his second test appearance*

## Two Fifties in a Test

| 52 & 56 | †Wallace W.M. v England at Lord's | 1937 |
| 58 & 50 | Vivian H.G. v England at Old Trafford | 1937 |
| 96 & 54* | Smith F.B. v England at Headingley | 1949 |
| 75 & 80 | Donnelly M.P. v England at Old Trafford | 1949 |
| 88 & 54 | Sutcliffe B. v England at The Oval | 1949 |
| 55 & 58 | Wallace W.M. v England at The Oval | 1949 |
| 93 & 64 | †Harford N.S. v Pakistan at Lahore | 1955/56 |
| 74 & 58 | †Dowling G.T. v South Africa at Johannesburg | 1961/62 |
| 55 & 55 | Pollard V. v England at Lord's *(aged 19)* | 1965 |
| 66 & 60 | Burgess M.G. v India at Wellington | 1967/68 |
| 58 & 58 | Morrison J.F.M. v England at Auckland | 1974/75 |
| 54 & 54 | Congdon B.E. v India at Auckland | 1975/76 |
| 55 & 54 | Edwards G.N. v England at Auckland | 1977/78 |
| 62 & 76 | Edgar B.A. v England at Nottingham | 1983 |
| 62 & 60 | Howarth G.P. v Sri Lanka at Kandy | 1983/84 |
| 57 & 84 | Crowe M.D. v Pakistan at Dunedin | 1984/85 |
| 50 & 52 | Edgar B.A. v Australia at Sydney | 1985/86 |
| 56 & 59 | Wright J.G. v Australia at Auckland | 1985/86 |
| 82 & 79 | Crowe M.D. v Australia at Melbourne | 1987/88 |
| 87 & 88 | Greatbatch M.J. v Zimbabwe at Bulawayo | 1992/93 |
| 74 & 89 | Rutherford K.R. v Zimbabwe at Harare | 1992/93 |
| 63 & 59 | Rutherford K.R. v India at Hamilton | 1993/94 |
| 79 & 53 | Fleming S.P. v South Africa at Cape Town | 1994/95 |
| 59 & 51* | Twose R.G. v Pakistan at Christchurch | 1995/96 |
| 57 & 52 | Cairns C.L. v England at Christchurch | 1996/97 |
| 92 & 84 | McMillan C.D. v India at Hamilton | 1998/99 |
| 93 & 60 | Horne M.J. v South Africa at Auckland | 1998/99 |

| 57 & 99 | Fleming S.P. v South Africa at Bloemfontein | 2000/01 |
| 57 & 71 | Vincent L. v England at Wellington | 2001/02 |
| 95 & 71 | Richardson M.H. v West Indies at St George's | 2001/02 |
| 55 & 55 | Richardson M.H. v Sri Lanka at Kandy | 2002/03 |
| 54 & 83* | McMillan C.D. v India at Ahmedabad | 2003/04 |
| 53 & 55 | Taylor L.R.P.L. v England at Wellington | 2007/08 |
| 59 & 66 | Fleming S.P. v England at Napier | 2007/08 |
| 55 & 76* | Vettori D.L. v Bangladesh at Chittagong | 2008/09 |
| 57 & 59* | Ryder J.D. v West Indies at Napier | 2008/09 |
| 94 & 59 | Taylor L.R.P.L. v Pakistan at Dunedin | 2009/10 |
| 78 & 52 | Taylor L.R.P.L. v Pakistan at Wellington | 2010/11 |
| 76 & 76 | Taylor L.R.P.L. v Zimbabwe at Bulawayo | 2011/12 |
| 97 & 67 | Guptill M.J. v West Indies at North Sound | 2012 |
| 63 & 63 | Watling B-J. v South Africa at Port Elizabeth | 2012/13 |
| 73 & 59 | Fulton P.G. v Bangladesh at Chittagong | 2013/14 |
| 58 & 56 | Williamson K.S. v West Indies at Hamilton | 2013/14 |
| 83 & 73 | Latham T.W.M. v West Indies at Kingston | 2014 |
| 78 & 51 | Neesham J.D.M. v West Indies at Bridgetown | 2014 |
| 61* & 59 | Watling B-J. v England at Lord's | 2015 |
| 88 & 71 | Williamson K.S. v Sri Lanka at Dunedin | 2015/16 |
| 52 & 52 | Latham T.W.M. v India at Christchurch | 2019/20 |
| 95 & 52 | Latham T.W.M. v India at Kanpur | 2021/22 |
| 52 & 69 | Young W.A. v Bangladesh at Mt Maunganui | 2021/22 |
| 55 & 88* | Blundell T.A. v England at Leeds | 2022 |

† *on debut*

## Fifties in Successive Test Innings

Mitchell D.J. reached 50 in five successive test innings:
    108, 190, 62*, 109, 56 v England, 2022

The following reached 50 in four successive test innings:

    Donnelly M.P. 62, 206, 75 & 80 v England, 1949
    Sutcliffe B. 101, 88, 54 v England 1949 and 116 v England 1950/51
    Congdon B.E. 166*, 82, 126 and 61* v West Indies 1971/72
      54, 54, 58 & 52 v India 1975/76
    Coney J.V. 101*, 98, 93 v Australia 1985/86 and 51 v England 1986
    Rutherford K.R. 74, 89 v Zimbabwe and 105, 53 v Sri Lanka 1992/93
    Ryder J.D. 89, 57, 59* v West Indies and 102 v India 2008/09
    Taylor L.R.P.L. 78, 52 v Pakistan 2010/11 and 76, 76 v Zimbabwe 2011/12
    Williamson K.S. 97 v Australia 2015/16 and 91, 113 and 68* v Zimbabwe 2016/17
    Watling B-J. 77, 105* v Sri Lanka and 205, 55 v England 2019/20

## Highest Score in Each Batting Position

| Position | | | | | |
|---|---|---|---|---|---|
| 1/2 | 267* | Young B.A. | v Sri Lanka | Dunedin | 1996/97 |
| 3 | 274* | Fleming S.P. | v Sri Lanka | Colombo | 2002/03 |
| 4 | 299 | Crowe M.D. | v Sri Lanka | Wellington | 1990/91 |
| 5 | 302 | McCullum B.B. | v India | Wellington | 2013/14 |
| 6 | 205 | Watling B-J. | v England | Mt Maunganui | 2019/20 |
| 7 | 185 | McCullum B.B. | v Pakistan | Dunedin | 2009/10 |
| 8 | 140 | Vettori D.L. | v Sri Lanka | Colombo | 2009/10 |
| 9 | 173 | Smith I.D.S. | v India | Auckland | 1989/90 |
| 10 | 83* | Bracewell J.G. | v Australia | Sydney | 1985/86 |
| 11 | 68* | Collinge R.O. | v Pakistan | Auckland | 1972/73 |

# Century Partnership for The First Wicket

| | | | | | *Final innings total* |
|---|---|---|---|---|---|
| 276 | Dempster C.S. / Mills J.E. | v England | Wellington | 1929/30 | 440 |
| 133 | Sutcliffe B. / Hadlee W.A. | v England | Christchurch | 1946/47 | 345-9d |
| 112 | Sutcliffe B. / Scott V.J | v England | Leeds | 1949 | 195-2 |
| 121 | Sutcliffe B. / Scott V.J. | v England | The Oval | 1949 | 345 |
| 126 | Rabone G.O. / Chapple M.E. | v South Africa | Cape Town | 1953/54 | 505 |
| 101 | McGregor S.N. / Leggat J.G. | v India | Delhi | 1955/56 | 112-1 |
| 136 | Dowling G.T. / Jarvis T.W. | v Pakistan | Lahore | 1964/65 | 482-6d |
| 126 | Dowling G.T. / Murray B.A.G. | v India | Christchurch | 1967/68 | 502 |
| 112 | Dowling G.T. / Turner G.M. | v West Indies | Auckland | 1968/69 | 297-8d |
| 115 | Dowling G.T. / Turner G.M. | v West Indies | Christchurch | 1968/69 | 367-6 |
| 106 | Dowling G.T. / Murray B.A.G. | v India | Hyderabad | 1969/70 | 181 |
| 387 | Turner G.M. / Jarvis T.W. | v West Indies | Georgetown | 1971/72 | 543-3d |
| 159 | Redmond R.E. / Turner G.M. | v Pakistan | Auckland | 1972/73 | 402 |
| 107 | Parker J.M. / Turner G.M. | v Australia | Auckland | 1973/74 | 158 |
| 100 | Wright J.G. / Edgar B.A. | v Australia | Sydney | 1985/86 | 193 |
| 117 | Wright J.G. / Franklin T.J. | v England | Auckland | 1987/88 | 350-7d |
| 149 | Wright J.G. / Franklin T.J. | v India | Napier | 1989/90 | 178-1 |
| 185 | Wright J.G. / Franklin T.J. | v England | Lord's | 1990 | 462-9d |
| 134 | Franklin T.J. / Wright J.G. | v Sri Lanka | Wellington | 1990/91 | 671-4 |
| 161 | Franklin T.J. / Wright J.G. | v Sri Lanka | Hamilton | 1990/91 | 374-6d |
| 116 | Greatbatch M.J. / Latham R.T. | v Zimbabwe | Bulawayo | 1992/93 | 325-3d |
| 102 | Greatbatch M.J. / Latham R.T. | v Zimbabwe | Bulawayo | 1992/93 | 222-5d |

| 110 | { Hartland B.R.<br>Wright J.G. | v Sri Lanka | Moratuwa | 1992/93 | 195-5 |
|---|---|---|---|---|---|
| 110 | { Greatbatch M.J.<br>Hartland B.R. | v Pakistan | Hamilton | 1992/93 | 264 |
| 111 | { Greatbatch M.J.<br>Wright J.G. | v Australia | Wellington | 1992/93 | 329 |
| 214 | { Spearman C.M.<br>Twose R.G. | v Zimbabwe | Auckland | 1995/96 | 441-5d |
| 107 | { Young B.A.<br>Horne M.J. | v South Africa | Christchurch | 1998/99 | 127-1 |
| 131 | { Horne M.J.<br>Stead G.R. | v India | Ahmedabad | 1999/00 | 252-2 |
| 102 | { Richardson M.H.<br>Bell M.D. | v Pakistan | Christchurch | 2000/01 | 476 |
| 181 | { Richardson M.H.<br>Bell M.D. | v Pakistan | Hamilton | 2000/01 | 407-4d |
| 104 | { Richardson M.H.<br>Horne M.J. | v Bangladesh | Wellington | 2001/02 | 341-6d |
| 117 | { Richardson M.H.<br>Vincent L. | v West Indies | St George's | 2001/02 | 256-5 |
| 231 | { Richardson M.H.<br>Vincent L. | v India | Mohali | 2003/04 | 630-6d |
| 163 | { Richardson M.H.<br>Fleming S.P. | v England | Nottingham | 2004 | 384 |
| 125 | { McIntosh T.G.<br>McCullum B.B. | v India | Hyderabad | 2010/11 | 448-8d |
| 120 | { Guptill M.J.<br>McCullum B.B. | v Pakistan | Wellington | 2010/11 | 356 |
| 124 | { McCullum B.B.<br>Guptill M.J. | v Zimbabwe | Napier | 2011/12 | 495-7d |
| 158 | { Fulton P.G.<br>Rutherford H.D. | v England | Dunedin | 2012/13 | 460-9d |
| 148 | { Guptill M.J.<br>Latham T.W.M. | v England | Lord's | 2015 | 523 |
| 169 | { Guptill M.J.<br>Latham T.W.M. | v Zimbabwe | Bulawayo | 2016/17 | 582-4d |
| 118 | { Guptill M.J.<br>Latham T.W.M. | v India | Indore | 2016/17 | 299 |
| 121 | { Raval J.A.<br>Latham T.W.M. | v Sri Lanka | Christchurch | 2018/19 | 585-4d |
| 254 | { Raval J.A.<br>Latham T.W.M. | v Bangladesh | Hamilton | 2018/19 | 715-6d |
| 103 | { Latham T.W.M.<br>Blundell T.A. | v India | Christchurch | 2019/20 | 132-3 |
| 111 | { Latham T.W.M.<br>Blundell T.A. | v Pakistan | Mt Maunganui | 2020/21 | 180-5d |

| 151 | { Latham T.W.M. <br> { Young W.A. | v India | Kanpur | 2021/22 | 296 |
| 148 | { Latham T.W.M. <br> { Young W.A. | v Bangladesh | Christchurch | 2021/22 | 521-6d |

# Pairs in Test Matches Involving New Zealand

**By New Zealand**

| | |
|---|---|
| *James K.C. v England at Christchurch | 1929/30 |
| *Badcock F.T. v England at Christchurch | 1929/30 |
| Cowie J. v England at Manchester | 1937 |
| *Rowe C.G. v Australia at Wellington | 1945/46 |
| *Butterfield L.A. v Australia at Wellington | 1945/46 |
| Miller L.S.M. v South Africa at Johannesburg | 1953/54 |
| Poore M.B. v England at Auckland | 1954/55 |
| Colquhoun I.A. v England at Auckland | 1954/55 |
| Hayes J.A. v England at Auckland | 1954/55 |
| Blair R.W. v West Indies at Dunedin | 1955/56 |
| Cave H.B. v West Indies at Dunedin | 1955/56 |
| MacGibbon A.R. v India at Madras | 1955/56 |
| Harford N.S. v England at Leeds | 1958 |
| Motz R.C. v South Africa at Cape Town | 1961/62 |
| Blair R.W. v England at Christchurch | 1962/63 |
| Blair R.W. v South Africa at Auckland | 1963/64 |
| Shrimpton M.J.F. v South Africa at Auckland | 1963/64 |
| Dick A.E. v Pakistan at Rawalpindi | 1964/65 |
| Bartlett G.A. v England at Christchurch | 1965/66 |
| Jarvis T.W. v Pakistan at Wellington | 1972/73 |
| Lees W.K. v England at Christchurch | 1977/78 |
| *Bracewell B.P. v England at The Oval | 1978 |
| Cairns B.L. v Australia at Brisbane | 1980/81 |
| Edgar B.A. v Australia at Perth | 1980/81 |
| Troup G.B. v India at Wellington | 1980/81 |
| Coney J.V. v Australia at Christchurch | 1981/82 |
| Smith I.D.S. v Australia at Christchurch | 1981/82 |
| Bracewell J.G. v Pakistan at Hyderabad | 1984/85 |
| *Rutherford K.R. v West Indies at Port of Spain | 1984/85 |
| Wright J.G. v England at Lord's | 1986 |
| Morrison D.K. v Australia at Melbourne | 1987/88 |
| *Kuggeleijn C.M. v India at Bangalore | 1988/89 |
| Snedden M.C. v India at Hyderabad | 1988/89 |
| Morrison D.K. v Sri Lanka at Hamilton | 1990/91 |
| Hartland B.R. v England at Auckland | 1991/92 |
| Su'a M.L. v Pakistan at Hamilton | 1992/93 |
| Morrison D.K. v Australia at Hobart | 1993/94 |
| Doull S.B. v West Indies at Wellington | 1994/95 |
| Nash D.J. v Sri Lanka at Napier | 1994/95 |
| Harris C.Z. v West Indies at Bridgetown | 1995/96 |
| Patel D.N. v England at Auckland | 1996/97 |
| Doull S.B. v England at Wellington | 1996/97 |
| Fleming S.P. v Australia at Hobart | 1997/98 |
| Vettori D.L. v Sri Lanka at Galle | 1997/98 |
| Wiseman P.J. v India at Wellington | 1998/99 |
| Twose R.G. v England at Edgbaston | 1999 |
| Wiseman P.J. v India at Kanpur | 1999/00 |
| O'Connor S.B. v Australia at Hamilton | 1999/00 |
| *Franklin J.E.C. v Pakistan at Auckland | 2000/01 |
| Martin C.S. v Pakistan at Auckland | 2000/01 |
| Martin C.S. v Pakistan at Lahore | 2001/02 |
| Martin C.S. v Australia at Brisbane | 2004/05 |
| Martin C.S. v West Indies at Auckland | 2005/06 |
| Martin C.S. v South Africa at Johannesburg | 2007/08 |

| *Gillespie M.R. v South Africa at Centurion | 2007/08 |
|---|---|
| O'Brien I.E. v South Africa at Centurion | 2007/08 |
| O'Brien I.E. v Australia at Adelaide | 2008/09 |
| Martin C.S. v Australia at Adelaide | 2008/09 |
| McIntosh T.G. v India at Ahmedabad | 2010/11 |
| Bracewell D.A.J. v South Africa at Hamilton | 2011/12 |
| Martin C.S. v India at Hyderabad | 2012/13 |
| van Wyk C.F.K. v Sri Lanka at Colombo | 2012/13 |
| Flynn D.R. v South Africa at Port Elizabeth | 2012/13 |
| Boult T.A. v Pakistan at Dubai | 2018/19 |
| Southee T.G. v India at Mumbai | 2021/22 |
| Henry M.J. v South Africa at Christchurch | 2021/22 |

* on debut

### Against New Zealand

| Javed Burki for Pakistan at Wellington | 1964/65 |
|---|---|
| Jaisimha M.L. for India at Hyderabad | 1969/70 |
| Knott A.P.E. for England at Lord's | 1973 |
| Stackpole K.R. for Australia at Auckland | 1973/74 |
| Chandrasekhar B.S. for India at Wellington | 1975/76 |
| Hendrick M. for England at Wellington | 1977/78 |
| Kallicharran A.I. for West Indies at Dunedin | 1979/80 |
| Wood G.M. for Australia at Perth | 1980/81 |
| Holland R.G. for Australia at Brisbane | 1985/86 |
| *Patel R.G. for India at Bombay | 1988/89 |
| Malcolm D.E. for England at Birmingham | 1990 |
| Waqar Younis for Pakistan at Faisalabad | 1990/91 |
| Aamer Sohail for Pakistan at Hamilton | 1992/93 |
| Langer J.L. for Australia at Auckland | 1992/93 |
| Streak H.H. for Zimbabwe at Harare | 1997/98 |
| Rennie G.J. for Zimbabwe at Auckland | 1997/98 |
| Mbangwa M. for Zimbabwe at Auckland | 1997/98 |
| Walsh C.A. for West Indies at Wellington | 1999/00 |
| Nkala M.L. for Zimbabwe at Harare | 2000/01 |
| Monjurul Islam for Bangladesh at Wellington | 2001/02 |
| Dillon M. for West Indies at Bridgetown | 2001/02 |
| Laxman V.V.S. for India at Wellington | 2002/03 |
| Khan Z. for India at Hamilton | 2002/03 |
| Tareq Aziz for Bangladesh at Dhaka | 2004/05 |
| Mohammad Ashraful for Bangladesh at Chittagong | 2004/05 |
| Mpofu C.B. for Zimbabwe at Harare | 2005/06 |
| *Silva L.P.C. for Sri Lanka at Christchurch | 2006/07 |
| Malinga S.L. for Sri Lanka at Wellington | 2006/07 |
| Muralitharan M. for Sri Lanka at Wellington | 2006/07 |
| Aftab Ahmed for Bangladesh at Dunedin | 2007/08 |
| Shahadat Hossain for Bangladesh at Dunedin | 2007/08 |
| Mohammad Asif for Pakistan at Napier | 2009/10 |
| Rubel Hossain for Bangladesh at Hamilton | 2009/10 |
| Johnson M.G. for Australia at Hamilton | 2009/10 |
| Mpofu C.B. for Zimbabwe at Bulawayo | 2011/12 |
| Masakadza H. for Zimbabwe at Napier | 2011/12 |
| Vitori B.V. for Zimbabwe at Napier | 2011/12 |
| Finn S.T. for England at Auckland | 2012/13 |
| Prior M.J. for England at Lord's | 2013 |
| Sammy D.J.G. for West Indies at Wellington | 2013/14 |
| Gabriel S.T. for West Indies at Wellington | 2013/14 |

| Samuels M.N. for West Indies at Kingston | 2014 |
| Wahab Riaz for Pakistan at Hamilton | 2016/17 |
| Powell K.O.A. for West Indies at Hamilton | 2017/18 |
| Perera M.D.K.J. for Sri Lanka at Colombo | 2019/20 |
| Chase R.L. for West Indies at Wellington | 2020/21 |
| Shan Masood for Pakistan at Christchurch | 2020/21 |
| Bumrah J.J. for India at Southampton | 2021 |
| Rabada K. for South Africa at Christchurch | 2021/22 |

\* *on debut*

# BOWLING

## Ten Wickets in a Match

*(27 instances)*

| 15-123 | Hadlee R.J. v Australia at Brisbane | 1985/86 |
| 14-225 | Patel A.Y. v India at Mumbai | 2021/22 |
| 12-149 | Vettori D.L. v Australia at Auckland | 1999/00 |
| 12-170 | Vettori D.L. v Bangladesh at Chittagong | 2004/05 |
| 11-58 | Hadlee R.J. v India at Wellington | 1975/76 |
| 11-102 | Hadlee R.J. v West Indies at Dunedin | 1979/80 |
| 11-117 | Jamieson K.A. v Pakistan at Christchurch | 2020/21 |
| 11-152 | Pringle C. v Pakistan at Faisalabad | 1990/91 |
| 11-155 | Hadlee R.J. v Australia at Perth | 1985/86 |
| 11-169 | Nash D.J. v England at Lord's | 1994 |
| 11-180 | Martin C.S. v South Africa at Auckland | 2003/04 |
| 10-80 | Boult T.A. v West Indies at Wellington | 2013/14 |
| 10-88 | Hadlee R.J. v India at Bombay | 1988/89 |
| 10-99 | Bond S.E. v Zimbabwe at Bulawayo | 2005/06 |
| 10-100 | Hadlee R.J. v England at Wellington | 1977/78 |
| 10-100 | Cairns C.L. v West Indies at Hamilton | 1999/00 |
| 10-102 | Hadlee R.J. v Sri Lanka at Colombo | 1983/84 |
| 10-106 | Bracewell J.G. v Australia at Auckland | 1985/86 |
| 10-108 | Southee T.G. v England at Lord's | 2013 |
| 10-124 | Chatfield E.J. v West Indies at Port of Spain | 1984/85 |
| 10-140 | Cowie J. v England at Manchester | 1937 |
| 10-140 | Hadlee R.J. v England at Nottingham | 1986 |
| 10-144 | Cairns B.L. v England at Leeds | 1983 |
| 10-166 | Troup G.B. v West Indies at Auckland | 1979/80 |
| 10-176 | Hadlee R.J. v Australia at Melbourne | 1987/88 |
| 10-183 | Vettori D.L. v Sri Lanka at Wellington | 2006/07 |
| 10-203 | Craig M.D. v Pakistan at Sharjah | 2014/15 |

## Five Wickets in an Innings

*(225 instances)*

| 10-119 | Patel A.Y. v India at Mumbai | 2021/22 |
| 9-52 | Hadlee R.J. v Australia at Brisbane | 1985/86 |
| 7-23 | Hadlee R.J. v India at Wellington | 1975/76 |
| 7-23 | Henry M.J. v South Africa at Christchurch | 2021/22 |
| 7-27 | Cairns C.L. v West Indies at Hamilton | 1999/00 |
| 7-39 | Wagner N. v West Indies at Wellington | 2017/18 |
| 7-52 | Pringle C. v Pakistan at Faisalabad | 1990/91 |
| 7-53 | Cairns C.L. v Bangladesh at Hamilton | 2001/02 |
| 7-64 | Southee T.G. v India at Bangalore | 2012/13 |
| 7-65 | Doull S.B. v India at Wellington | 1998/99 |
| 7-74 | Taylor B.R. v West Indies at Bridgetown | 1971/72 |

| 7-74 | Cairns B.L. v England at Leeds | 1983 |
| 7-87 | Boock S.L. v Pakistan at Hyderabad | 1984/85 |
| 7-87 | Vettori D.L. v Australia at Auckland | 1999/00 |
| 7-89 | Morrison D.K. v Australia at Wellington | 1992/93 |
| 7-94 | Craig M.D. v Pakistan at Sharjah | 2014/15 |
| 7-116 | Hadlee R.J. v Australia at Christchurch | 1985/86 |
| 7-130 | Vettori D.L. v Sri Lanka at Wellington | 2006/07 |
| 7-143 | Cairns B.L. v England at Wellington | 1983/84 |
| 6-26 | Hadlee R.J. v England at Wellington | 1977/78 |
| 6-26 | Martin C.S. v Zimbabwe at Napier | 2011/12 |
| 6-27 | Nash D.J. v India at Mohali | 1999/00 |
| 6-28 | Vettori D.L. v Bangladesh at Dhaka | 2004/05 |
| 6-30 | Boult T.A. v Sri Lanka at Christchurch | 2018/19 |
| 6-32 | Bracewell J.G. v Australia at Auckland | 1985/86 |
| 6-32 | Boult T.A. v England at Auckland | 2017/18 |
| 6-37 | Morrison D.K. v Australia at Auckland | 1992/93 |
| 6-38 | Bartlett G.A. v India at Christchurch | 1967/68 |
| 6-40 | Cowie J. v Australia at Wellington | 1945/46 |
| 6-40 | Bracewell D.A.J. v Australia at Hobart | 2011/12 |
| 6-40 | Boult T.A. v West Indies at Wellington | 2013/14 |
| 6-41 | Wagner N. v Zimbabwe at Bulawayo | 2016/17 |
| *6-41 | de Grandhomme C. v Pakistan at Christchurch | 2016/17 |
| 6-43 | Southee T.G. v England at Lord's | 2021 |
| 6-46 | Butler I.G. v Pakistan at Wellington | 2003/04 |
| 6-49 | Jamieson K.A. v Pakistan at Christchurch | 2020/21 |
| 6-49 | Hadlee R.J. v India at Bombay | 1988/89 |
| 6-50 | Hadlee R.J. v West Indies at Christchurch | 1986/87 |
| 6-50 | Patel D.N. v Zimbabwe at Harare | 1992/93 |
| 6-50 | Southee T.G. v England at Lord's | 2013 |
| 6-51 | Hadlee R.J. v Pakistan at Dunedin | 1984/85 |
| 6-51 | Bracewell J.G. v India at Bombay | 1988/89 |
| 6-51 | Bond S.E. v Zimbabwe at Bulawayo | 2005/06 |
| 6-52 | Cairns C.L. v England at Auckland | 1991/92 |
| 6-53 | Hadlee R.J. v England at The Oval | 1983 |
| 6-54 | Tuffey D.R. v England at Auckland | 2001/02 |
| 6-54 | Martin C.S. v Sri Lanka at Wellington | 2004/05 |
| 6-56 | Vettori D.L. v West Indies at Dunedin | 2008/09 |
| 6-57 | Hadlee R.J. v Australia at Melbourne | 1980/81 |
| 6-60 | Reid J.R. v South Africa at Dunedin | 1963/64 |
| 6-62 | Southee T.G. v England at Christchurch | 2017/18 |
| 6-63 | Motz R.C. v India at Christchurch | 1967/68 |
| 6-63 | Collinge R.O. v India at Christchurch | 1975/76 |
| 6-64 | Vettori D.L. v Sri Lanka at Colombo | 1997/98 |
| 6-67 | Cowie J. v England at Manchester | 1937 |
| 6-68 | Rabone G.O. v South Africa at Cape Town | 1953/54 |
| 6-68 | Hadlee R.J. v West Indies at Dunedin | 1979/80 |
| 6-68 | Boult T.A. v England at Auckland | 2012/13 |
| 6-68 | Southee T.G. v Sri Lanka at Wellington | 2018/19 |
| 6-69 | Motz R.C. v West Indies at Wellington | 1968/69 |
| 6-69 | Morrison D.K. v West Indies at Christchurch | 1994/95 |
| 6-70 | Vettori D.L. v Bangladesh at Chittagong | 2004/05 |
| 6-71 | Hadlee R.J. v Australia at Brisbane | 1985/86 |
| 6-73 | Chatfield E.J. v West Indies at Port of Spain | 1984/85 |
| 6-75 | O'Brien I.E. v West Indies at Napier | 2008/09 |
| 6-76 | Cunis R.S. v England at Auckland | 1970/71 |
| 6-76 | Nash D.J. v England at Lord's | 1994 |

| 6-76 | Martin C.S. v South Africa at Auckland | 2003/04 |
| 6-77 | Cairns C.L. v England at Lord's | 1999 |
| 6-78 | Watson W. v Pakistan at Lahore | 1990/91 |
| 6-80 | Hadlee R.J. v England at Lord's | 1986 |
| 6-80 | Hadlee R.J. v England at Nottingham | 1986 |
| 6-80 | Southee T.G. v Pakistan at Hamilton | 2016/17 |
| 6-83 | Cowie J. v England at Christchurch | 1946/47 |
| 6-85 | Cairns B.L. v West Indies at Christchurch | 1979/80 |
| 6-85 | Bracewell J.G. v Australia at Wellington | 1989/90 |
| 6-87 | Vettori D.L. v Australia at Perth | 2001/02 |
| 6-90 | Hadlee R.J. v Australia at Perth | 1985/86 |
| 6-95 | Troup G.B. v West Indies at Auckland | 1979/80 |
| 6-100 | Hadlee R.J. v Australia at Christchurch | 1981/82 |
| 6-100 | Vettori D.L. v Bangladesh at Chittagong | 2004/05 |
| 6-105 | Hadlee R.J. v West Indies at Auckland | 1986/87 |
| 6-106 | Wagner N. v Australia at Christchurch | 2015/16 |
| 6-113 | Patel D.N. v Zimbabwe at Bulawayo | 1992/93 |
| 6-113 | Gillespie M.R. v South Africa at Wellington | 2011/12 |
| 6-119 | Franklin J.E.C v Australia at Auckland | 2004/05 |
| 6-127 | Vettori D.L. v India at Kanpur | 1999/00 |
| *6-155 | Moir A.M. v England at Christchurch | 1950/51 |
| 6-162 | Burtt T.B. v England at Manchester | 1949 |
| *6-168 | Cresswell G.F. v England at The Oval | 1949 |
| 5-26 | Taylor B.R. v India at Bombay | 1964/65 |
| 5-28 | Hadlee R.J. v England at Christchurch | 1983/84 |
| 5-28 | Boock S.L. v Sri Lanka at Kandy | 1983/84 |
| 5-28 | Franklin J.E.C v Bangladesh at Dhaka | 2004/05 |
| 5-29 | Hadlee R.J. v Sri Lanka at Colombo | 1983/84 |
| 5-31 | Cairns C.L. v England at The Oval | 1999 |
| 5-31 | Cairns C.L. v Zimbabwe at Bulawayo | 2000/01 |
| 5-31 | Jamieson K.A. v India at Southampton | 2021 |
| 5-32 | Southee T.G. v West Indies at Wellington | 2020/21 |
| 5-33 | Cairns B.L. v India at Wellington | 1980/81 |
| 5-34 | Cameron F.J. v Pakistan at Auckland | 1964/65 |
| 5-34 | Howarth H.J. v India at Nagpur | 1969/70 |
| 5-34 | Hadlee R.J. v West Indies at Dunedin | 1979/80 |
| 5-34 | Jamieson K.A. v West Indies at Wellington | 2020/21 |
| 5-35 | Southee T.G. v South Africa at Christchurch | 2021/22 |
| 5-37 | Martin C.S. v South Africa at Johannesburg | 2005/06 |
| 5-39 | Hadlee R.J. v Australia at Wellington | 1989/90 |
| 5-41 | Taylor B.R. v West Indies at Port of Spain | 1971/72 |
| 5-41 | Morrison D.K. v Pakistan at Hamilton | 1992/93 |
| 5-43 | Boult T.A. v Bangladesh at Christchurch | 2021/22 |
| 5-44 | Cairns C.L. v West Indies at Wellington | 1999/00 |
| 5-44 | Wagner N. v England at Mt Maunganui | 2019/20 |
| 5-45 | Wagner N. v Bangladesh at Wellington | 2018/19 |
| 5-45 | Jamieson K.A. v India at Christchurch | 2019/20 |
| 5-46 | Doull S.B. v Pakistan at Lahore | 1996/97 |
| 5-47 | Hadlee R.J. v India at Christchurch | 1980/81 |
| 5-47 | Wagner N. v Bangladesh at Hamilton | 2018/19 |
| 5-48 | Cameron F.J. v South Africa at Cape Town | 1961/62 |
| 5-50 | Cairns C.L. v Zimbabwe at Harare | 1997/98 |
| 5-51 | O'Connor S.B. v Australia at Hamilton | 1999/00 |
| 5-53 | Hadlee R.J. v England at Birmingham | 1990 |
| 5-53 | Franklin J.E.C. v West Indies at Wellington | 2005/06 |

| | | |
|---|---|---|
| 5-55 | Cairns B.L. v India at Madras | 1976/77 |
| 5-55 | Martin C.S. v South Africa at Wellington | 2003/04 |
| *5-55 | Southee T.G. v England at Napier | 2007/08 |
| 5-57 | Boult T.A. v England at Leeds | 2013 |
| 5-58 | Doull S.B. v Sri Lanka at Dunedin | 1996/97 |
| 5-59 | Vettori D.L. v Bangladesh at Chittagong | 2008/09 |
| 5-59 | Gillespie M.R. v South Africa at Hamilton | 2011/12 |
| *5-59 | Patel A.Y. v Pakistan at Abu Dhabi | 2018/19 |
| 5-60 | Boult T.A. v Australia at Adelaide | 2015/16 |
| 5-61 | Morrison D.K. v West Indies at St Johns | 1995/96 |
| 5-61 | Southee T.G. v India at Wellington | 2019/20 |
| 5-62 | Moir A.M. v England at Auckland | 1954/55 |
| 5-62 | Hadlee R.J. v Pakistan at Christchurch | 1978/79 |
| 5-62 | Cairns C.L. v Sri Lanka at Colombo | 1997/98 |
| 5-62 | Vettori D.L. v Australia at Auckland | 1999/00 |
| 5-62 | Southee T.G. v Sri Lanka at Colombo | 2012/13 |
| 5-63 | Hadlee R.J. v Australia at Auckland | 1981/82 |
| 5-63 | Chatfield E.J. v Sri Lanka at Colombo | 1983/84 |
| 5-63 | Davis H.T. v Sri Lanka at Hamilton | 1996/97 |
| 5-63 | Martin C.S. v India at Ahmedabad | 2010/11 |
| 5-64 | MacGibbon A.R. v England at Birmingham | 1958 |
| 5-64 | Wagner N. v Bangladesh at Mirpur | 2013/14 |
| 5-65 | Congdon B.E. v India at Auckland | 1975/76 |
| 5-65 | Hadlee R.J. v Australia at Sydney | 1985/86 |
| 5-65 | Hadlee R.J. v Australia at Perth | 1985/86 |
| 5-65 | Hadlee R.J. v India at Bangalore | 1988/89 |
| 5-65 | Martin C.S. v Bangladesh at Wellington | 2007/08 |
| 5-66 | Doull S.B. v Pakistan at Auckland | 1993/94 |
| 5-66 | Vettori D.L. v England at Manchester | 2008 |
| 5-66 | Vettori D.L. v Bangaldesh at Mirpur | 2008/09 |
| 5-67 | Boock S.L. v England at Auckland | 1977/78 |
| 5-67 | Hadlee R.J. v Australia at Melbourne | 1987/88 |
| 5-68 | Snedden M.C. v West Indies at Christchurch | 1986/87 |
| 5-68 | Hadlee R.J. v Australia at Adelaide | 1987/88 |
| 5-69 | Burtt T.B. v West Indies at Christchurch | 1951/52 |
| 5-69 | Morrison D.K. v England at Christchurch | 1987/88 |
| 5-69 | Bond S.E. v West Indies at Auckland | 2005/06 |
| 5-69 | Vettori D.L. v England at Lord's | 2008 |
| 5-69 | Southee T.G. v Australia at Perth | 2019/20 |
| 5-69 | Jamieson K.A. v Pakistan at Christchurch | 2020/21 |
| 5-69 | Southee T.G. v India at Kanpur | 2021/22 |
| 5-71 | Martin C.S. v Zimbabwe at Wellington | 2000/01 |
| 5-73 | Hadlee R.J. v Sri Lanka at Colombo | 1983/84 |
| 5-73 | Su'a M.L. v Pakistan at Hamilton | 1992/93 |
| 5-73 | Doull S.B. v South Africa at Durban | 1994/95 |
| 5-74 | Collinge R.O. v England at Leeds | 1973 |
| 5-75 | Bracewell J.G. v India at Auckland | 1980/81 |
| 5-75 | Morrison D.K. v India at Christchurch | 1989/90 |
| 5-75 | Cairns C.L. v Sri Lanka at Auckland | 1990/91 |
| 5-75 | Doull S.B. v England at Wellington | 1996/97 |
| 5-77 | Hart M.N. v South Africa at Johannesburg | 1994/95 |
| 5-78 | Bond S.E. v West Indies at Bridgetown | 2001/02 |
| 5-79 | Cairns C.L. v England at Nottingham | 2004 |
| 5-80 | Howarth H.J. v Pakistan at Karachi | 1969/70 |
| 5-82 | Collinge R.O. v Australia at Auckland | 1973/74 |

| | | |
|---|---|---|
| *5-82 | Wiseman P.J. v Sri Lanka at Colombo | 1997/98 |
| 5-83 | Cameron F.J. v South Africa at Johannesburg | 1961/62 |
| 5-84 | Hadlee R.J. v England at Lord's | 1978 |
| 5-84 | Vettori D.L. v Sri Lanka at Hamilton | 1996/97 |
| 5-85 | Su'a M.L. v Zimbabwe at Harare | 1992/93 |
| 5-85 | Bracewell D.A.J. v Zimbabwe at Bulawayo | 2011/12 |
| 5-85 | Boult T.A. v England at Lord's | 2015 |
| *5-86 | Taylor B.R. v India at Calcutta | 1964/65 |
| 5-86 | Motz R.C. v India at Dunedin | 1967/68 |
| 5-86 | Wagner N. v Zimbabwe at Bulawayo | 2016/17 |
| 5-87 | Cairns B.L. v Australia at Brisbane | 1980/81 |
| 5-87 | Hadlee R.J. v Australia at Perth | 1980/81 |
| 5-87 | Tuffey D.R. v Pakistan at Hamilton | 2003/04 |
| 5-89 | Patel A.Y. v Sri Lanka at Galle | 2019/20 |
| 5-90 | Wiseman P.J. v Zimabwe at Bulawayo | 2000/01 |
| 5-93 | Hadlee R.J. v England at Lord's | 1983 |
| 5-93 | Patel D.N. v Australia at Auckland | 1992/93 |
| 5-93 | Nash D.J. v England at Lord's | 1994 |
| 5-94 | Southee T.G. v Bangladesh at Christchurch | 2016/17 |
| 5-95 | Chatfield E.J. v England at Leeds | 1983 |
| 5-97 | Burtt T.B. v England at Leeds | 1949 |
| 5-98 | Morrison D.K. v India at Napier | 1989/90 |
| 5-104 | Hadlee R.J. v Pakistan at Auckland | 1978/79 |
| 5-104 | Bond S.E. v West Indies at St George's | 2001/02 |
| 5-104 | Martin C.S. v South Africa at Auckland | 2003/04 |
| 5-106 | Vettori D.L. v Australia at Christchurch | 2004/05 |
| 5-106 | Boult T.A. v England at Nottingham | 2022 |
| 5-107 | Bond S.E. v Pakistan at Dunedin | 2009/10 |
| 5-108 | Motz R.C. v England at Birmingham | 1965 |
| 5-109 | Hadlee R.J. v Australia at Melbourne | 1987/88 |
| 5-109 | Vettori D.L. v Zimbabwe at Bulawayo | 2011/12 |
| 5-110 | Patel J.S. v West Indies at Napier | 2008/09 |
| 5-113 | Motz R.C. v West Indies at Christchurch | 1968/69 |
| 5-117 | Boock S.L. v Pakistan at Wellington | 1984/85 |
| 5-121 | Hadlee R.J. v Pakistan at Lahore | 1976/77 |
| 5-123 | Boult T.A. v Bangladesh at Hamilton | 2018/19 |
| 5-124 | Wagner N. v England at Hamilton | 2019/20 |
| 5-127 | Cowie J. v England at Leeds | 1949 |
| 5-135 | Vettori D.L. v India at Hyderabad | 2010/11 |
| *5-136 | Gillespie M.R. v South Africa at Centurion | 2007/08 |
| 5-137 | Cairns C.L. v Pakistan at Rawalpindi | 1996/97 |
| 5-138 | Vettori D.L. v Australia at Hobart | 2001/02 |
| 5-145 | Morrison D.K. v India at Auckland | 1989/90 |
| 5-146 | Cairns C.L. v Australia at Brisbane | 2001/02 |
| 5-148 | O'Sullivan D.R. v Australia at Adelaide | 1973/74 |
| 5-152 | Martin C.S. v Australia at Brisbane | 2004/05 |
| 5-152 | Vettori D.L. v Australia at Adelaide | 2004/05 |
| 5-153 | Morrison D.K. v Sri Lanka at Wellington | 1990/91 |

* *on debut*

# Hat-tricks

| | | |
|---|---|---|
| *Petherick P.J. v Pakistan at Lahore | 1976/77 |
| Franklin J.E.C. v Bangladesh at Dhaka | 2004/05 |

* *on debut*

# ALL-ROUND CRICKET

| | |
|---|---|
| Rabone G.O. 56 and 6-68 & 1-16 v South Africa at Cape Town | 1953/54 |
| *Taylor B.R. 105 & 0* and 5-86 v India at Calcutta | 1964/65 |
| Congdon B.E. 54 & 54 and 5-65 v India at Auckland | 1975/76 |
| Hadlee R.J. 54* & 5 and 5-104 & 0-8 v Pakistan at Auckland | 1978/79 |
| Hadlee R.J. 51 & 17 and 5-34 & 6-68 v West Indies at Dunedin | 1979/80 |
| Hadlee R.J. 84 & 11 and 6-53 & 2-99 v England at The Oval | 1983 |
| Cairns B.L. 3 & 64 and 7-143 v England at Wellington | 1983/84 |
| Hadlee R.J. 99 and 3-16 & 5-28 v England at Christchurch | 1983/84 |
| Hadlee R.J. 54 and 9-52 & 6-71 v Australia at Brisbane | 1985/86 |
| Hadlee R.J. 68 and 6-80 & 4-60 v England at Nottingham | 1986 |
| Bracewell J.G. 52 & 32 and 2-81 & 6-51 v India at Bombay | 1988/89 |
| Patel D.N. 6 & 58* and 2-81 & 6-50 v Zimbabwe at Harare | 1992/93 |
| Nash D.J. 56 and 6-76 & 5-93 v England at Lord's | 1994 |
| Cairns C.L. 12 & 71* and 5-50 & 0-44 v Zimbabwe at Harare | 1997/98 |
| Cairns C.L. 11 & 80 and 5-31 & 1-50 v England at The Oval | 1999 |
| Cairns C.L. 72 and 3-73 & 7-27 v West Indies at Hamilton | 1999/00 |
| Cairns C.L. 61 & 43 and 5-146 & 1-29 v Australia at Brisbane | 2001/02 |
| Vettori D.L. 20 & 59 and 5-152 & 1-35 v Australia at Adelaide | 2004/05 |
| Vettori D.L. 0 & 51 and 3-53 & 7-130 v Sri Lanka at Wellington | 2006/07 |
| *Southee T.G. 5 & 77* and 5-55 & 0-84 v England at Napier | 2007/08 |
| Vettori D.L. 55 & 76* and 5-59 & 4-74 v Bangladesh at Chittagong | 2008/09 |
| Craig M.D. 65 and 7-94 & 3-109 v Pakistan at Sharjah | 2014/15 |
| Southee T.G. 50 & 0* and 6-62 & 1-65 v England at Christchurch | 2017/18 |

* On debut. Taylor is the only player from any country to score a century and take five wickets in an innings on debut.

# WICKETKEEPING AND FIELDING

### MOST DISMISSALS IN AN INNINGS BY A WICKETKEEPER

| | | |
|---|---|---|
| 7* | Smith I.D.S. v Sri Lanka at Hamilton *(all caught)* | 1990/91 |
| 6 | Watling B-J. v India at Auckland *(all caught)* | 2013/14 |
| 6 | Watling B-J. v Sri Lanka at Dunedin *(all caught)* | 2015/16 |
| 5 | Harford R.I. v India at Wellington *(all caught)* | 1967/68 |
| 5 | Wadsworth K.J. v Pakistan at Auckland *(all caught)* | 1972/73 |
| 5 | Lees W.K. v Sri Lanka at Wellington *(all caught)* | 1982/83 |
| 5 | Smith I.D.S. v England at Auckland *(4ct 1st)* | 1983/84 |
| 5 | Smith I.D.S. v Sri Lanka at Auckland *(all caught)* | 1990/91 |
| 5 | Parore A.C. v England at Auckland *(all caught)* | 1991/92 |
| 5 | Parore A.C. v Sri Lanka at Colombo *(4ct 1st)* | 1992/93 |
| 5 | Parore A.C. v Zimbabwe at Harare *(all caught)* | 2000/01 |
| 5 | Parore A.C. v Pakistan at Auckland *(all caught)* | 2000/01 |
| 5 | McCullum B.B. v England at Hamilton *(all caught)* | 2007/08 |
| 5 | McCullum B.B. v West Indies at Napier *(all caught)* | 2008/09 |
| 5 | McCullum B.B. v Pakistan at Napier *(all caught)* | 2009/10 |
| 5 | McCullum B.B. v England at Leeds *(all caught)* | 2013 |
| 5 | Watling B-J. v West Indies at Hamilton *(all caught)* | 2013/14 |
| 5 | Watling B-J. v India at Wellington *(all caught)* | 2013/14 |
| 5 | Watling B-J. v West Indies at Kingston *(all caught)* | 2014 |
| 5 | Watling B-J. v Sri Lanka at Wellington *(4ct 1st)* | 2014/15 |
| 5 | Watling B-J. v Sri Lanka at Wellington *(all caught)* | 2018/19 |
| 5 | Watling B-J. v Sri Lanka at Colombo *(all caught)* | 2019/20 |

* equals world test record

## MOST DISMISSALS IN A MATCH BY A WICKETKEEPER

| | | |
|---|---|---|
| 9 | McCullum B.B. v Pakistan at Napier *(8ct, 1st)* | 2009/10 |
| 9 | Watling B-J. v India at Auckland *(all caught)* | 2013/14 |
| 9 | Watling B-J. v Sri Lanka at Dunedin *(all caught)* | 2015/16 |
| 8 | Lees W.K. v Sri Lanka at Wellington *(all caught)* | 1982/83 |
| 8 | Smith I.D.S. v Sri Lanka at Hamilton *(all caught)* | 1990/91 |
| 8 | Watling B-J. v West Indies at Hamilton *(all caught)* | 2013/14 |
| 8 | Watling B-J. v West Indies at Kingston *(all caught)* | 2014 |
| 8 | Watling B-J. v Pakistan at Mt Maunganui *(all caught)* | 2020/21 |
| 8 | Blundell T.A. v England at Birmingham *(all caught)* | 2021 |
| 7 | Dick A.E. v South Africa at Durban *(6ct 1st)* | 1961/62 |
| 7 | Harford R.I. v India at Wellington *(all caught)* | 1967/68 |
| 7 | Smith I.D.S. v India at Wellington *(all caught)* | 1980/81 |
| 7 | Smith I.D.S. v England at Leeds *(all caught)* | 1983 |
| 7 | Parore A.C. v Pakistan at Auckland *(all caught)* | 2000/01 |
| 7 | Parore A.C. v Pakistan at Hamilton *(all caught)* | 2000/01 |
| 7 | McCullum B.B. v Australia at Brisbane *(all caught)* | 2008/09 |
| 7 | Watling B-J. v Sri Lanka at Wellington *(6ct 1st)* | 2014/15 |
| 7 | Watling B-J. v Australia at Perth *(5ct 2st)* | 2015/16 |
| 7 | Watling B-J. v Bangladesh at Christchurch *(all caught)* | 2016/17 |
| 7 | Watling B-J. v India at Wellington *(all caught)* | 2019/20 |

## MOST STUMPINGS IN AN INNINGS

| | | |
|---|---|---|
| 2 | Mooney F.L.H. v England at Leeds | 1949 |
| 2 | Milburn B.D. v West Indies at Christchurch | 1968/69 |
| 2 | Lees W.K. v Pakistan at Hyderabad | 1976/77 |
| 2 | Lees W.K. v Pakistan at Karachi | 1976/77 |
| 2 | Lees W.K. v India at Madras | 1976/77 |
| 2 | Watling B-J. v Australia at Perth | 2015/16 |

## MOST STUMPINGS IN A MATCH

| | | |
|---|---|---|
| 2 | Mooney F.L.H. v England at Leeds | 1949 |
| 2 | Milburn B.D. v West Indies at Christchurch | 1968/69 |
| 2 | Lees W.K. v Pakistan at Hyderabad | 1976/77 |
| 2 | Lees W.K. v Pakistan at Karachi | 1976/77 |
| 2 | Lees W.K. v India at Madras | 1976/77 |
| 2 | Smith I.D.S. v Australia at Sydney | 1985/86 |
| 2 | Parore A.C. v Australia at Auckland | 1999/00 |
| 2 | McCullum B.B. v Zimbabwe at Harare | 2005/06 |
| 2 | McCullum B.B. v Banladesh at Chittagong | 2008/09 |
| 2 | Watling B-J. v Australia at Perth | 2015/16 |

## MOST CATCHES IN AN INNINGS BY A FIELDER

| | | |
|---|---|---|
| 5* | Fleming S.P. v Zimbabwe at Harare | 1997/98 |
| 4 | Crowe J.J. v West Indies at Bridgetown | 1984/85 |
| 4 | Crowe M.D. v West Indies at Kingston | 1984/85 |
| 4 | Fleming S.P. v Australia at Brisbane | 1997/98 |
| 4 | Fleming S.P. v Zimbawe at Harare | 2005/06 |
| 4 | Fleming S.P. v West Indies at Wellington | 2005/06 |
| 4 | Brownlie D.G. v Zimbabwe at Napier | 2011/12 |
| 4 | Latham T.W.M. v Bangladesh at Christchurch | 2021/22 |

* *equals world test record*

## MOST CATCHES IN A MATCH BY A FIELDER

| | | |
|---|---|---|
| 7 | Fleming S.P. v Zimbabwe at Harare | 1997/98 |
| 6 | Young B.A. v Pakistan at Auckland | 1993/94 |
| 6 | Fleming S.P. v Australia at Brisbane | 1997/98 |
| 6 | Fleming S.P. v West Indies at Wellington | 2005/06 |
| 6 | Latham T.W.M. v Bangladesh at Christchurch | 2021/22 |
| 5 | Harris C.Z. v Zimbabwe at Bulawayo | 1997/98 |
| 5 | Fleming S.P. v India at Wellington | 1998/99 |
| 5 | Sinclair M.S. v Bangladesh at Chittagong | 2004/05 |
| 5 | Guptill M.J. v Pakistan at Napier | 2009/10 |
| 5 | Brownlie D.G. v Zimbabwe at Napier | 2011/12 |
| 5 | Williamson K.S. v Sri Lanka at Colombo | 2011/12 |
| 5 | Latham T.W.M. v India at Southampton | 2021 |

## REPLACEMENT WICKETKEEPERS IN TEST MATCHES

| Wicketkeeper | Replacement | Dismissal | | | |
|---|---|---|---|---|---|
| Mooney F.L.H. | Sutcliffe B. | — | v South Africa | Port Elizabeth | 1953/54 |
| Petrie E.C. | Reid J.R. | Richardson P.E. *(st)* | v England | Manchester | 1958 |
| Petrie E.C. | Reid J.R. | — | v England | Christchurch | 1958/59 |
| Ward J.T. | Morgan R.W. | Jaisimha M.L. *(c)* | v India | Calcutta | 1964/65 |
| Ward J.T. | Congdon B.E. | Hanumant Singh *(c)* | v India | Delhi | 1964/65 |
| Dick A.E. | Reid J.R. | — | v Pakistan | Lahore | 1964/65 |
| Dick A.E. | Congdon B.E. *(sub)* | Pervez Sajjad *(st)* | v Pakistan | Lahore | 1964/65 |
| Lees W.K. | Anderson R.W. | — | v Pakistan | Hyderabad | 1976/77 |
| Smith I.D.S. | Edgar B.A. | Laird B.M. *(c)* | v Australia | Christchurch | 1981/82 |
| Smith I.D.S. | Crowe M.D. | — | v West Indies | Kingston | 1984/85 |
| Smith I.D.S. | Horne P.A. | — | v Australia | Melbourne | 1987/88 |
| Smith I.D.S. | Blain T.E. | — | v India | Hyderabad | 1988/89 |
| Smith I.D.S. | Horne P.A. | — | v Pakistan | Faisalabad | 1990/91 |
| Smith I.D.S. | Parore A.C. *(sub)* | Shoaib Mohammad *(c)* Aaqib Javed *(c)* | v Pakistan | Faisalabad | 1990/91 |
| McCullum B.B. | Sinclair M.S. | Jayawardene D.P.M.D. *(c)* | v Sri Lanka | Wellington | 2006/07 |
| McCullum B.B. | Young R.A. *(sub)* | — | v Sri Lanka | Galle | 2009/10 |
| van Wyk C.F.K. | McCullum B.B. | — | v India | Bangalore | 2012/13 |
| Watling B-J. | McCullum B.B. | Swann G.P. *(c)* | v England | Lord's | 2013 |
| Watling B-J. | Latham T.W.M. | Root J.E. *(c)* Ali M.M. *(c)* Broad S.J.C. *(c)* Cook A.N. *(c)* Bell I.R. *(c)* Buttler J.C. *(c)* | v England | Lord's | 2015 |
| Watling B-J. | Latham T.W.M. | Sikandar Raza *(c)* | v Zimbabwe | Bulawayo | 2016/17 |
| Watling B-J. | Ronchi L. | Sharma R.G. *(c)* | v India | Calcutta | 2016/17 |
| Watling B-J. | Latham T.W.M. | — | v Pakistan | Abu Dhabi | 2018/19 |
| Watling B-J. | Bocock P.D. *(sub)* | — | v Bangladesh | Wellington | 2018/19 |
| Watling B-J. | Latham T.W.M. | — | v England | Mt Maunganui | 2019/20 |
| Watling B-J. | Blundell T.A. *(sub)* | — | v India | Southampton | 2021 |
| Blundell T.A. | Latham T.W.M. | — | v India | Mumbai | 2021/22 |

# RECORD PARTNERSHIPS

## NEW ZEALAND v ALL COUNTRIES

**For**

| | | | | |
|---|---|---|---|---|
| 1st | 387 | Turner G.M. & Jarvis T.W. v West Indies | Georgetown | 1971/72 |
| 2nd | 297 | McCullum B.B. & Williamson K.S. v Pakistan | Sharjah | 2014/15 |
| 3rd | 467 | Jones A.H. & Crowe M.D. v Sri Lanka | Wellington | 1990/91 |
| 4th | 369 | Williamson K.S. & Nicholls H.M. v Pakistan | Christchurch | 2020/21 |
| 5th | 236 | Mitchell D.J. & Blundell T.A. v England | Nottingham | 2022 |
| 6th | 365* | Williamson K.S.& Watling B-J. v Sri Lanka | Wellington | 2014/15 |
| 7th | 261 | Watling B-J. & Santner M.J. v England | Mt Maunganui | 2019/20 |
| 8th | 256 | Fleming S.P. & Franklin J.E.C. v South Africa | Cape Town | 2005/06 |
| 9th | 136 | Smith I.D.S. & Snedden M.C. v India | Auckland | 1989/90 |
| 10th | 151 | Hastings B.F. & Collinge R.O. v Pakistan | Auckland | 1972/73 |

**Against**

| | | | | |
|---|---|---|---|---|
| 1st | 413 | Mankad M.H. & Roy P. for India | Madras | 1955/56 |
| 2nd | 369 | Edrich J.H. & Barrington K.F. for England | Leeds | 1965 |
| 3rd | 330 | Amla H.M. & Kallis J.H. for South Africa | Johannesburg | 2007/08 |
| 4th | 365 | Kohli V. & Rahane A. for India | Indore | 2016/17 |
| 5th | 359 | Shakib Al Hasan & Mushfiqur Rahim for Bangladesh | Wellington | 2016/17 |
| 6th | 281 | Thorpe G.P. & Flintoff A. for England | Christchurch | 2001/02 |
| 7th | 308 | Waqar Hassan & Imtiaz Ahmed for Pakistan | Lahore | 1955/56 |
| 8th | 246 | Ames L.E.G. & Allen G.O.B. for England | Lord's | 1931 |
| 9th | 163* | Cowdrey M.C. & Smith A.C. for England | Wellington | 1962/63 |
| 10th | 114 | Gillespie J.N. & McGrath G.D. for Australia | Brisbane | 2004/05 |

## NEW ZEALAND v ENGLAND

**New Zealand**

| | | | | |
|---|---|---|---|---|
| 1st | 276 | Dempster C.S. & Mills J.E. | Wellington | 1929/30 |
| 2nd | 241 | Wright J.G. & Jones A.H. | Wellington | 1991/92 |
| 3rd | 213* | Williamson K.S. & Taylor L.R.P.L. | Hamilton | 2019/20 |
| 4th | 174 | Conway D.P. & Nicholls H.M. | Lord's | 2021 |
| 5th | 236 | Mitchell D.J. & Blundell T.A. | Nottingham | 2022 |
| 6th | 142 | Watling B-J. & de Grandhomme C. | Christchurch | 2017/18 |
| 7th | 261 | Watling B-J. & Santner M.J. v England | Mt Maunganui | 2019/20 |
| 8th | 104 | Roberts A.W. & Moloney D.A.R. | Lord's | 1937 |
| 9th | 118 | Coney J.V. & Cairns B.L. | Wellington | 1983/84 |
| 10th | 118 | Astle N.J. & Cairns C.L. | Christchurch | 2001/02 |

**England**

| | | | | |
|---|---|---|---|---|
| 1st | 231 | Cook A.N. & Compton N.R.D. | Dunedin | 2012/13 |
| 2nd | 369 | Edrich J.H. & Barrington K.F. | Leeds | 1965 |
| 3rd | 245 | Hammond W.R. & Hardstaff J. | Lord's | 1937 |
| 4th | 266 | Denness M.H. & Fletcher K.W.R. | Auckland | 1974/75 |
| 5th | 242 | Hammond W.R. & Ames L.E.G. | Christchurch | 1932/33 |
| 6th | 281 | Thorpe G.P. & Flintoff A. | Christchurch | 2001/02 |
| 7th | 241 | Bairstow J.M. & Overton J. | Leeds | 2022 |
| 8th | 246 | Ames L.E.G. & Allen G.O.B. | Lord's | 1931 |
| 9th | 163* | Cowdrey M.C. & Smith A.C. | Wellington | 1962/63 |
| 10th | 59 | Knott A.P.E. & Gifford N. | Nottingham | 1973 |

## NEW ZEALAND v AUSTRALIA

**New Zealand**

| | | | | |
|---|---|---|---|---|
| 1st | 111 | Greatbatch M.J. & Wright J.G. | Wellington | 1992/93 |
| 2nd | 132 | Horne M.J. & Parore A.C. | Hobart | 1997/98 |
| 3rd | 265 | Williamson K.S. & Taylor L.R.P.L. | Perth | 2015/16 |
| 4th | 229 | Congdon B.E. & Hastings B.F. | Wellington | 1973/74 |
| 5th | 179 | McCullum B.B. & Anderson C.J. | Christchurch | 2015/16 |
| 6th | 158 | Brownlie D.G. & Vettori D.L. | Brisbane | 2011/12 |
| 7th | 132* | Coney J.V. & Hadlee R.J. | Wellington | 1985/86 |
| 8th | 253 | Astle N.J. & Parore A.C. | Perth | 2001/02 |
| 9th | 73 | Howarth H.J. & Hadlee D.R. | Christchurch | 1976/77 |
| 10th | 124 | Bracewell J.G. & Boock S.L. | Sydney | 1985/86 |

**Australia**

| | | | | |
|---|---|---|---|---|
| 1st | 237 | Burns J.A. & Warner D.A. | Brisbane | 2015/16 |
| 2nd | 302 | Warner D.A. & Khawaja U.T. | Perth | 2015/16 |
| 3rd | 289 | Burns J.A. & Smith S.P.D. | Christchurch | 2015/16 |
| 4th | 184 | Langer J.L. & Lehmann D.S. | Adelaide | 2004/05 |
| 5th | 253 | Clarke M.J. & North M.J. | Wellington | 2009/10 |
| 6th | 256 | Martyn D.R. & Gilchrist A.C. | Wellington | 2004/05 |
| 7th | 217 | Walters K.D. & Gilmour G.J. | Christchurch | 1976/77 |
| 8th | 135 | Gilchrist A.C. & Lee B. | Brisbane | 2001/02 |
| 9th | 74 | Gilchrist A.C. & Kasprowicz M.S. | Auckland | 2004/05 |
| | 74 | Nevill P.M. & Lyon N.M. | Adelaide | 2015/16 |
| 10th | 114 | Gillespie J.N. & McGrath G.D. | Brisbane | 2004/05 |

## NEW ZEALAND v SOUTH AFRICA

**New Zealand**

| | | | | |
|---|---|---|---|---|
| 1st | 126 | Rabone G.O. & Chapple M.E. | Cape Town | 1953/54 |
| 2nd | 190 | Raval J.A. & Williamson K.S. | Hamilton | 2016/17 |
| 3rd | 125 | Richardson M.H. & Styris S.B. | Auckland | 2003/04 |
| 4th | 171 | Sinclair B.W. & McGregor S.N. | Auckland | 1963/64 |
| 5th | 176 | Reid J.R. & Beck J.E.F. | Cape Town | 1953/54 |
| 6th | 133 | Mitchell D.J. & de Grandhomme C. | Christchurch | 2021/22 |
| 7th | 225 | Cairns C.L. & Oram J.D.P. | Auckland | 2003/04 |
| 8th | 256 | Fleming S.P. & Franklin J.E.C. | Cape Town | 2005/06 |
| 9th | 87 | Oram J.D.P. & Wiseman P.J. | Hamilton | 2003/04 |
| 10th | 94 | Blundell T.A. & Henry M.J.. | Christchurch | 2021/22 |

**South Africa**

| | | | | |
|---|---|---|---|---|
| 1st | 196 | Mitchell B. & Christy J.A.H. | Christchurch | 1931/32 |
| 2nd | 315* | Gibbs H.H. & Kallis J.H. | Christchurch | 1998/99 |
| 3rd | 330 | Amla H.M. & Kallis J.H. | Johannesburg | 2007/08 |
| 4th | 171 | Smith G.C. & Kirsten G. | Wellington | 2003/04 |
| 5th | 141 | Cullinan D.J. & Rhodes J.N. | Auckland | 1998/99 |
| 6th | 131 | du Plessis F. & Elgar D. | Port Elizabeth | 2012/13 |
| 7th | 246 | McGlew D.J. & Murray A.R.A. | Wellington | 1952/53 |
| 8th | 136 | McKenzie N.D. & Boje N. | Port Elizabeth | 2000/01 |
| 9th | 62 | Jansen M. & Maharaj K.A. | Christchurch | 2021/22 |
| 10th | 57 | Philander V.D. & Morkel M. | Wellington | 2016/17 |

## NEW ZEALAND v WEST INDIES

**New Zealand**

| | | | | |
|---|---|---|---|---|
| 1st | 387 | Turner G.M. & Jarvis T.W. | Georgetown | 1971/72 |
| 2nd | 210 | Howarth G.P. & Crowe J.J. | Kingston | 1984/85 |
| 3rd | 241 | Wright J.G. & Crowe M.D. | Wellington | 1986/87 |
| 4th | 195 | Taylor L.R.P.L. & McCullum B.B. | Dunedin | 2013/14 |
| 5th | 144 | Astle N.J. & Vaughan J.T.C. | Bridgetown | 1995/96 |
| 6th | 220 | Turner G.M. & Wadsworth K.J. | Kingston | 1971/72 |
| 7th | 148 | de Grandhomme C. & Blundell T.A. | Wellington | 2017/18 |
| 8th | 136 | Congdon B.E. & Cunis R.S. | Port of Spain | 1971/72 |
| 9th | 99 | Watling B-J. & Craig M.D. | Port of Spain | 2014 |
| 10th | 78* | Blundell T.A. & Boult T.A. | Wellington | 2017/18 |

**West Indies**

| | | | | |
|---|---|---|---|---|
| 1st | 276 | Griffith A.F.G. & Campbell S.L. | Hamilton | 1999/00 |
| 2nd | 269 | Fredericks R.C. & Rowe L.G. | Kingston | 1971/72 |
| 3rd | 221 | Lara B.C. & Adams J.C. | Wellington | 1994/95 |
| 4th | 182 | Brathwaite K.C. & Bravo D.M. | Port of Spain | 2014 |
| 5th | 189 | Worrell F.M.M. & Walcott C.L. | Auckland | 1951/52 |
| 6th | 254 | Sobers G.S. & Davis C.A. | Bridgetown | 1971/72 |
| 7th | 155 | Blackwood J. & Joseph A.S. | Hamilton | 2020/21 |
| 8th | 83 | Richards I.V.A. & Marshall M.D. | Bridgetown | 1984/85 |
| 9th | 70 | Marshall M.D. & Garner J. | Bridgetown | 1984/85 |
| 10th | 82 | Benn S.J. & Shillingford S. | Kingston | 2014 |

## NEW ZEALAND v INDIA

**New Zealand**

| | | | | |
|---|---|---|---|---|
| 1st | 231 | Richardson M.H. & Vincent L. | Mohali | 2003/04 |
| 2nd | 155 | Dowling G.T. & Congdon B.E. | Dunedin | 1967/68 |
| 3rd | 222* | Sutcliffe B. & Reid J.R. | New Delhi | 1955/56 |
| 4th | 271 | Taylor L.R.P.L. & Ryder J.D. | Napier | 2008/09 |
| 5th | 194 | Ryder J.D. & Williamson K.S. | Ahmedabad | 2010/11 |
| 6th | 352 | McCullum B.B. & Watling B-J. | Wellington | 2013/14 |
| 7th | 186 | Ryder J.D. & Vettori D.L. | Hamilton | 2008/09 |
| 8th | 137 | Nash D.J. & Vettori D.L. | Wellington | 1998/99 |
| 9th | 136 | Smith I.D.S. & Snedden M.C. | Auckland | 1989/90 |
| 10th | 61 | Ward J.T. & Collinge R.O. | Madras | 1964/65 |

**India**

| | | | | |
|---|---|---|---|---|
| 1st | 413 | Mankad M.H. & Roy P. | Madras | 1955/56 |
| 2nd | 237 | Sehwag V. & Dravid R.S. | Ahmedabad | 2010/11 |
| 3rd | 238 | Umrigar P.R. & Manjrekar V.L. | Hyderabad | 1955/56 |
| 4th | 365 | Kohli V. & Rahane A. | Indore | 2016/17 |
| 5th | 182 | Dravid R.S. & Ganguly S.C. | Ahmedabad | 2003/04 |
| 6th | 193* | Sardesai D.N. & Hanumant Singh | Bombay | 1964/65 |
| | 193 | Dravid R.S. & Dhoni M.S. | Nagpur | 2010/11 |
| 7th | 163 | Laxman V.V.S. & Harbhajan Singh | Ahmedabad | 2010/11 |
| 8th | 144 | Dravid R.S. & Srinath J. | Hamilton | 1998/99 |
| 9th | 105 | Kirmani S.M.H. & Bedi B.S. | Bombay | 1976/77 |
| | 105 | Kirmani S.M.H. & Yadav N.S. | Auckland | 1980/81 |
| 10th | 105 | Harbhajan Singh & Sreesanth S. | Hyderabad | 2010/11 |

## NEW ZEALAND v PAKISTAN

**New Zealand**

| | | | | |
|---|---|---|---|---|
| 1st | 181 | Richardson M.H. & Bell M.D. | Hamilton | 2000/01 |
| 2nd | 297 | McCullum B.B. & Williamson K.S. | Sharjah | 2014/15 |
| 3rd | 178 | Sinclair B.W. & Reid J.R. | Lahore | 1964/65 |
| 4th | 369 | Williamson K.S. & Nicholls H.M. | Christchurch | 2020/21 |
| 5th | 212 | Williamson K.S. & Nicholls H.M. | Abu Dhabi | 2018/19 |
| 6th | 176 | Vettori D.L. & McCullum B.B. | Napier | 2009/10 |
| 7th | 186 | Lees W.K. & Hadlee R.J. | Karachi | 1976/77 |
| 8th | 125 | Fleming S.P. & Vettori D.L. | Hamilton | 2003/04 |
| 9th | 99 | Vettori D.L. & Tuffey D.R. | Hamilton | 2003/04 |
| 10th | 151 | Hastings B.F. & Collinge R.O. | Auckland | 1972/73 |

**Pakistan**

| | | | | |
|---|---|---|---|---|
| 1st | 178 | Mohammad Hafeez & Ahmed Shehzad | Abu Dhabi | 2014/15 |
| 2nd | 262 | Saeed Anwar & Ijaz Ahmed | Rawalpindi | 1996/97 |
| 3rd | 248 | Shoaib Mohammad & Javed Miandad | Auckland | 1988/89 |
| 4th | 350 | Mushtaq Mohammad & Asif Iqbal | Dunedin | 1972/73 |
| 5th | 281 | Javed Miandad & Asif Iqbal | Lahore | 1976/77 |
| 6th | 217 | Hanif Mohammad & Majid Khan | Lahore | 1964/65 |
| 7th | 308 | Waqar Hassan & Imtiaz Ahmed | Lahore | 1955/56 |
| 8th | 89 | Anil Dalpat & Iqbal Qasim | Karachi | 1984/85 |
| 9th | 78 | Inzamam-ul-Haq & Shoaib Akhtar | Lahore | 2001/02 |
| | 78 | Asad Shafiq & Rahat Ali | Sharjah | 2014/15 |
| 10th | 81 | Sarfraz Ahmed & Rahat Ali | Dubai | 2014/15 |

## NEW ZEALAND v SRI LANKA

**New Zealand**

| | | | | |
|---|---|---|---|---|
| 1st | 161 | Franklin T.J. & Wright J.G. | Hamilton | 1990/91 |
| 2nd | 173 | Guptill M.J. & Williamson K.S. | Dunedin | 2015/16 |
| 3rd | 467 | Jones A.H. & Crowe M.D. | Wellington | 1990/91 |
| 4th | 240 | Fleming S.P. & McMillan C.D. | Colombo | 1997/98 |
| 5th | 153 | McCullum B.B. & Neesham J.D.S. | Christchurch | 2014/15 |
| 6th | 365* | Williamson K.S. & Watling B-J. | Wellington | 2014/15 |
| 7th | 124 | Oram J.D.P. & Vettori D.L. | Colombo | 2009/10 |
| 8th | 98 | Vincent L. & Mills K.D. | Wellington | 2004/05 |
| 9th | 69 | Vettori D.L. & O'Brien I.E. | Colombo | 2009/10 |
| 10th | 52 | Lees W.K. & Chatfield E.J. | Christchurch | 1982/83 |

**Sri Lanka**

| | | | | |
|---|---|---|---|---|
| 1st | 161 | Karunaratne F.D.M. & Thirimanne H.D.R.L. | Galle | 2019/20 |
| 2nd | 137 | Mahanama R.S. & Gurusinha A.P. | Moratuwa | 1992/93 |
| 3rd | 184 | Atapattu M.S. & Jayawardene D.P.M.D. | Napier | 2004/05 |
| 4th | 274* | Mendis B.K.G. & Mathews A.D. | Wellington | 2018/19 |
| 5th | 138 | Mathews A.D. & Siriwardana T.A.M. | Hamilton | 2015/16 |
| 6th | 156 | Jayawardene D.P.M.D. & Mathews A.D. | Galle | 2012/13 |
| 7th | 137 | Kaluwitharana R.S. & Vaas W.P.J.U.C. | Dunedin | 1996/97 |
| 8th | 89 | Samaraweera T.T. & Chandana U.D.U. | Wellington | 2004/05 |
| 9th | 67 | Sangakkara K.C. & Lakmal R.A.S. | Wellington | 2014/15 |
| 10th | 71 | Kaluwitharana R.S. & Muralitharan M. | Colombo | 1997/98 |

## NEW ZEALAND v ZIMBABWE

**New Zealand**

| | | | | |
|---|---|---|---|---|
| 1st | 214 | Spearman C.M. & Twose R.G. | Auckland | 1995/96 |
| 2nd | 160 | Latham T.W.M. & Williamson K.S. | Bulawayo | 2016/17 |
| 3rd | 140* | Williamson K.S. & Taylor L.R.P.L. | Bulawayo | 2016/17 |
| 4th | 243 | Horne M.J. & Astle N.J. | Auckland | 1997/98 |
| 5th | 222 | Astle N.J. & McMillan C.D. | Wellington | 2000/01 |
| 6th | 253 | Taylor L.R.P.L. & Watling B-J | Bulawayo | 2016/17 |
| 7th | 108 | McMillan C.D. & Nash D.J. | Wellington | 1997/98 |
| 8th | 144 | Cairns C.L. & Nash D.J. | Harare | 2000/01 |
| 9th | 78 | Parore A.C. & Vettori D.L. | Bulawayo | 2000/01 |
| 10th | 27 | McMillan C.D. & Doull S.B. | Auckland | 1997/98 |

**Zimbabwe**

| | | | | |
|---|---|---|---|---|
| 1st | 156 | Rennie G.J. & Flower G.W. | Harare | 1997/98 |
| 2nd | 107 | Arnott K.J. & Campbell A.D.R. | Harare | 1992/93 |
| 3rd | 96 | Mawoyo T.M.K. & Taylor B.R.M. | Bulawayo | 2011/12 |
| 4th | 130 | Rennie G.J. & Flower A. | Wellington | 2000/01 |
| 5th | 131 | Flower A. & Whittall G.J. | Harare | 2000/01 |
| 6th | 151 | Whittall G.J. & Streak H.H. | Harare | 2000/01 |
| 7th | 118 | Cremer A.G. & Williams S.C. | Bulawayo | 2016/17 |
| 8th | 94 | Campbell A.D.R. & Streak H.H. | Wellington | 1997/98 |
| 9th | 85 | Masvaure P.S. & Tiripano D.T. | Bulawayo | 2016/17 |
| 10th | 40 | Whittall G.J. & Matambanadzo E. | Bulawayo | 1997/98 |

## NEW ZEALAND v BANGLADESH

**New Zealand**

| | | | | |
|---|---|---|---|---|
| 1st | 254 | Raval J.A & Latham T.W.M. | Hamilton | 2018/19 |
| 2nd | 215 | Latham T.W.M. & Conway D.P. | Christchurch | 2021/22 |
| 3rd | 204 | Fleming S P & Styris S B | Chittagong | 2004/05 |
| 4th | 216 | Taylor L.R.P.L. & Nicholls H.M. | Wellington | 2018/19 |
| 5th | 190 | Richardson M.H. & McMillan C.D. | Hamilton | 2001/02 |
| 6th | 339 | Guptill M.J. & McCullum B.B. | Hamilton | 2009/10 |
| 7th | 110* | Williamson K.S. & de Grandhomme C. | Hamilton | 2018/19 |
| 8th | 57 | McCullum B.B. & Franklin J.E.C. | Dhaka | 2004/05 |
| | 57 | Watling B-J. & Bracewell DA.J. | Chittagong | 2013/14 |
| 9th | 93 | Anderson C.J. & Sodhi I.S. | Mirpur | 2013/14 |
| 10th | 127 | Watling B-J. & Boult T.A. | Chittagong | 2013/14 |

**Bangladesh**

| | | | | |
|---|---|---|---|---|
| 1st | 161 | Tamim Iqbal & Zunaed Siddique | Dunedin | 2007/08 |
| 2nd | 104 | Mahmudul Hasan & Nazmul Hossain | Mt Maunganui | 2021/22 |
| 3rd | 157 | Tamim Iqbal & Mominul Haque | Mirpur | 2013/14 |
| 4th | 115 | Rajin Saleh & Mohammad Ashraful | Dhaka | 2004/05 |
| 5th | 359 | Shakib Al Hasan & Mushfiqur Rahim | Wellington | 2016/17 |
| 6th | 101 | Liton Das & Nurul Hasan | Christchurch | 2021/22 |
| 7th | 145 | Shakib Al Hasan & Mahmudullah | Hamilton | 2009/10 |
| 8th | 39 | Mushfiqur Rahman & Mohammad Rafique | Chittagong | 2004/05 |
| 9th | 105 | Sohag Gazi & Robiul Islam | Chittagong | 2013/14 |
| 10th | 45 | Tapash Baisya & Enamul Haque | Chittagong | 2004/05 |

# CAREER RECORDS
## Averages

| | M | I | NO | HS | Runs | Ave | 100 | 50 | Ct | St | Wkts | Runs | Ave | Best | 5WI | 10WM |
|---|---|---|---|---|---|---|---|---|---|---|---|---|---|---|---|---|
| Adams A.R. | 1 | 2 | 0 | 11 | 18 | 9.00 | — | — | 1 | — | 6 | 105 | 17.50 | 3-44 | — | — |
| Alabaster J.C. | 21 | 34 | 6 | 34 | 272 | 9.71 | — | — | 7 | — | 49 | 1863 | 38.02 | 4-46 | — | — |
| Allcott C.F.W. | 6 | 7 | 2 | 33 | 113 | 22.60 | — | — | 3 | — | 6 | 541 | 90.17 | 2-102 | — | — |
| Allott G.I. | 10 | 15 | 7 | 8* | 27 | 3.37 | — | — | 2 | — | 19 | 1111 | 58.47 | 4-74 | — | — |
| Anderson C.J. | 13 | 22 | 1 | 116 | 683 | 32.52 | 1 | 4 | 7 | — | 16 | 659 | 41.18 | 3-47 | — | — |
| Anderson R.W. | 9 | 18 | 0 | 92 | 423 | 23.50 | — | 3 | 1 | — | — | — | — | — | — | — |
| Anderson W.M. | 1 | 2 | 0 | 4 | 5 | 2.50 | — | — | 1 | — | — | — | — | — | — | — |
| Andrews B. | 2 | 3 | 2 | 17 | 22 | 22.00 | — | — | 1 | — | 2 | 154 | 77.00 | 2-40 | — | — |
| Arnel B.J. | 6 | 12 | 4 | 8* | 45 | 5.62 | — | — | 3 | — | 9 | 566 | 62.88 | 4-95 | — | — |
| Astle N.J. | 81 | 137 | 10 | 222 | 4702 | 37.02 | 11 | 24 | 70 | — | 51 | 2143 | 42.01 | 3-27 | — | — |
| Astle T.D. | 5 | 6 | 1 | 35 | 98 | 19.60 | — | — | 3 | — | 7 | 368 | 52.57 | 3-39 | — | — |
| Badcock F.T. | 7 | 9 | 2 | 64 | 137 | 19.57 | — | 2 | 1 | — | 16 | 610 | 38.13 | 4-80 | — | — |
| Barber R.T. | 1 | 2 | 0 | 12 | 17 | 8.50 | — | — | 1 | — | — | — | — | — | — | — |
| Bartlett G.A. | 10 | 18 | 1 | 40 | 263 | 15.47 | — | — | 8 | — | 24 | 792 | 33.00 | 6-38 | 1 | — |
| Barton P.T. | 7 | 14 | 0 | 109 | 285 | 20.36 | 1 | 1 | 4 | — | — | — | — | — | — | — |
| Beard D.D. | 4 | 7 | 2 | 31 | 101 | 20.20 | — | — | 2 | — | 9 | 302 | 33.56 | 3-22 | — | — |
| Beck J.E.F. | 8 | 15 | 0 | 99 | 394 | 26.27 | — | 3 | — | — | — | — | — | — | — | — |
| Bell M.D. | 18 | 32 | 2 | 107 | 729 | 24.30 | 2 | 3 | 19 | — | — | — | — | — | — | — |
| Bell W. | 2 | 3 | 3 | 21* | 21 | — | — | — | 1 | — | 2 | 235 | 117.50 | 1-54 | — | — |
| Bennett H.K. | 1 | 1 | 0 | 4 | 4 | 4.00 | — | — | — | — | 0 | 47 | — | — | — | — |
| Bilby G.P. | 2 | 4 | 0 | 28 | 55 | 13.75 | — | — | 3 | — | — | — | — | — | — | — |
| *Blain T.E. | 11 | 20 | 3 | 78 | 456 | 26.82 | — | 2 | 19 | 2 | — | — | — | — | — | — |
| Blair R.W. | 19 | 34 | 6 | 64* | 189 | 6.75 | — | 1 | 5 | — | 43 | 1515 | 35.23 | 4-85 | — | — |
| *Blundell T.A. | 20 | 33 | 4 | 121 | 1192 | 41.10 | 3 | 7 | 49 | 2 | 0 | 13 | — | — | — | — |
| Blunt R.C. | 9 | 13 | 1 | 96 | 330 | 27.50 | — | 1 | 5 | — | 12 | 472 | 39.33 | 3-17 | — | — |
| Bolton B.A. | 2 | 3 | 0 | 33 | 59 | 19.67 | — | — | 1 | — | — | — | — | — | — | — |
| Bond S.E. | 18 | 20 | 7 | 41* | 168 | 12.92 | — | — | 8 | — | 87 | 1922 | 22.09 | 6-51 | 5 | 1 |
| Boock S.L. | 30 | 41 | 8 | 37 | 207 | 6.27 | — | — | 14 | — | 74 | 2564 | 34.64 | 7-87 | 4 | — |
| Boult T.A. | 78 | 94 | 46 | 52* | 759 | 15.81 | — | 1 | 43 | — | 317 | 8717 | 27.49 | 6-30 | 10 | 1 |
| Bracewell B.P. | 6 | 12 | 2 | 8 | 24 | 2.40 | — | — | 1 | — | 14 | 585 | 41.78 | 3-110 | — | — |
| Bracewell D.A.J. | 27 | 45 | 4 | 47 | 568 | 13.85 | — | — | 10 | — | 72 | 2796 | 38.83 | 6-40 | 2 | — |
| Bracewell J.G. | 41 | 60 | 11 | 110 | 1001 | 20.42 | 1 | 4 | 31 | — | 102 | 3653 | 35.81 | 6-32 | 4 | 1 |
| Bracewell M.G. | 2 | 4 | 0 | 49 | 96 | 24.00 | — | — | — | — | 5 | 285 | 57.00 | 3-62 | — | — |
| Bradburn G.E. | 7 | 10 | 2 | 30* | 105 | 13.12 | — | — | 6 | — | 6 | 460 | 76.66 | 3-134 | — | — |
| Bradburn W.P. | 2 | 4 | 0 | 32 | 62 | 15.50 | — | — | 2 | — | — | — | — | — | — | — |
| Broom N.T. | 2 | 3 | 0 | 20 | 32 | 10.66 | — | — | — | — | — | — | — | — | — | — |
| Brown V.R. | 2 | 3 | 1 | 36* | 51 | 25.50 | — | — | 3 | — | 1 | 176 | 176.00 | 1-17 | — | — |
| Brownlie D.G. | 14 | 25 | 1 | 109 | 711 | 29.62 | 1 | 4 | 17 | — | 1 | 52 | 52.00 | 1-13 | — | — |
| Burgess M.G. | 50 | 92 | 6 | 119* | 2684 | 31.21 | 5 | 14 | 34 | — | 6 | 212 | 35.33 | 3-23 | — | — |
| Burke C. | 1 | 2 | 0 | 3 | 4 | 2.00 | — | — | — | — | 2 | 30 | 15.00 | 2-30 | — | — |
| Burtt T.B. | 10 | 15 | 3 | 42 | 252 | 21.00 | — | — | 2 | — | 33 | 1170 | 35.45 | 6-162 | 3 | — |
| Butler I.G. | 8 | 10 | 2 | 26 | 76 | 9.50 | — | — | 4 | — | 24 | 884 | 36.83 | 6-46 | 1 | — |
| Butterfield L.A. | 1 | 2 | 0 | 0 | 0 | 0.00 | — | — | — | — | 0 | 24 | — | — | — | — |
| Cairns B.L. | 43 | 65 | 8 | 64 | 928 | 16.28 | — | 2 | 30 | — | 130 | 4279 | 32.91 | 7-74 | 6 | 1 |
| Cairns C.L. | 62 | 104 | 5 | 158 | 3320 | 33.53 | 5 | 22 | 14 | — | 218 | 6410 | 29.40 | 7-27 | 13 | 1 |
| Cameron F.J. | 19 | 30 | 20 | 27* | 116 | 11.60 | — | — | 2 | — | 62 | 1849 | 29.82 | 5-34 | 3 | — |
| Cave H.B. | 19 | 31 | 5 | 22* | 229 | 8.81 | — | — | 8 | — | 34 | 1467 | 43.15 | 4-21 | — | — |
| Chapple M.E. | 14 | 27 | 1 | 76 | 497 | 19.12 | — | 3 | 10 | — | 1 | 84 | 84.00 | 1-24 | — | — |
| Chatfield E.J. | 43 | 54 | 33 | 21* | 180 | 8.57 | — | — | 7 | — | 123 | 3958 | 32.17 | 6-73 | 3 | 1 |

| | M | I | NO | HS | Runs | Ave | 100 | 50 | Ct | St | Wkts | Runs | Ave | Best | 5WI | 10WM |
|---|---|---|---|---|---|---|---|---|---|---|---|---|---|---|---|---|
| Cleverley D.C. | 2 | 4 | 3 | 10* | 19 | 19.00 | — | — | — | — | 0 | 130 | — | — | — | — |
| Collinge R.O. | 35 | 50 | 13 | 68* | 533 | 14.41 | — | 2 | 10 | — | 116 | 3393 | 29.25 | 6-63 | 3 | — |
| †Colquhoun I.A. | 2 | 4 | 2 | 1* | 1 | 0.50 | — | — | 4 | — | — | — | — | — | — | — |
| Coney J.V. | 52 | 85 | 14 | 174* | 2668 | 37.57 | 3 | 16 | 64 | — | 27 | 966 | 35.77 | 3-28 | — | — |
| *Congdon B.E. | 61 | 114 | 7 | 176 | 3448 | 32.22 | 7 | 19 | 44* | — | 59 | 2154 | 36.51 | 5-65 | 1 | — |
| Conway D.P. | 10 | 18 | 0 | 200 | 918 | 51.00 | 3 | 4 | 1 | — | — | — | — | — | — | — |
| Cowie J. | 9 | 13 | 4 | 45 | 90 | 10.00 | — | — | 3 | — | 45 | 969 | 21.53 | 6-40 | 4 | 1 |
| Craig M D. | 15 | 25 | 9 | 67 | 589 | 36.81 | — | 3 | 14 | — | 50 | 2326 | 46.52 | 7-94 | 1 | 1 |
| Cresswell G.F. | 3 | 5 | 3 | 12* | 14 | 7.00 | — | — | — | — | 13 | 292 | 22.46 | 6-168 | 1 | — |
| Cromb I.B. | 5 | 8 | 2 | 51* | 123 | 20.50 | — | 1 | 1 | — | 8 | 442 | 55.25 | 3-113 | — | — |
| Crowe J.J. | 39 | 65 | 4 | 128 | 1601 | 26.24 | 3 | 6 | 41 | — | 0 | 9 | — | — | — | — |
| Crowe M.D. | 77 | 131 | 11 | 299 | 5444 | 45.36 | 17 | 18 | 71 | — | 14 | 676 | 48.28 | 2-25 | — | — |
| Cumming C.D. | 11 | 19 | 2 | 74 | 441 | 25.94 | — | 1 | 3 | — | — | — | — | — | — | — |
| Cunis R.S. | 20 | 31 | 8 | 51 | 295 | 12.83 | — | 1 | 1 | — | 51 | 1887 | 37.00 | 6-76 | 1 | — |
| D'Arcy J.W. | 5 | 10 | 0 | 33 | 136 | 13.60 | — | — | — | — | — | — | — | — | — | — |
| de Grandhomme C. | 29 | 44 | 7 | 120* | 1432 | 38.70 | 2 | 8 | 19 | — | 49 | 1615 | 32.95 | 6-41 | 1 | — |
| de Groen R.P. | 5 | 10 | 4 | 26 | 45 | 7.50 | — | — | — | — | 11 | 505 | 45.90 | 3-40 | — | — |
| Davis H.T. | 5 | 7 | 4 | 8* | 20 | 6.66 | — | — | 4 | — | 17 | 499 | 29.35 | 5-63 | 1 | — |
| Dempster C.S. | 10 | 15 | 4 | 136 | 723 | 65.73 | 2 | 5 | 2 | — | 0 | 10 | — | — | — | — |
| Dempster E.W. | 5 | 8 | 2 | 47 | 106 | 17.67 | — | — | 1 | — | 2 | 219 | 109.50 | 1-24 | — | — |
| †Dick A.E. | 17 | 30 | 4 | 50* | 370 | 14.73 | — | 1 | 47 | 4 | — | — | — | — | — | — |
| Dickinson G.R. | 3 | 5 | 0 | 11 | 31 | 6.20 | — | — | 3 | — | 8 | 245 | 30.63 | 3-66 | — | — |
| Donnelly M.P. | 7 | 12 | 1 | 206 | 582 | 52.91 | 1 | 4 | 7 | — | 0 | 20 | — | — | — | — |
| Doull S.B. | 32 | 50 | 11 | 46 | 570 | 14.61 | — | — | 16 | — | 98 | 2872 | 29.30 | 7-65 | 6 | — |
| Dowling G.T. | 39 | 77 | 3 | 239 | 2306 | 31.16 | 3 | 11 | 23 | — | 1 | 19 | 19.00 | 1-19 | — | — |
| Drum C.J. | 5 | 5 | 2 | 4 | 10 | 3.33 | — | — | 4 | — | 16 | 482 | 30.12 | 3-36 | — | — |
| Dunning J.A. | 4 | 6 | 1 | 19 | 38 | 7.60 | — | — | 2 | — | 5 | 493 | 98.60 | 2-35 | — | — |
| *Edgar B.A. | 39 | 68 | 4 | 161 | 1958 | 30.59 | 3 | 12 | 14* | — | 0 | 3 | — | — | — | — |
| *Edwards G.N. | 8 | 15 | 0 | 55 | 377 | 25.13 | — | 3 | 7* | — | — | — | — | — | — | — |
| Elliott G.D. | 5 | 9 | 1 | 25 | 86 | 10.75 | — | — | 2 | — | 4 | 140 | 35.00 | 2-8 | — | — |
| Emery R.W.G. | 2 | 4 | 0 | 28 | 46 | 11.50 | — | — | — | — | 2 | 52 | 26.00 | 2-52 | — | — |
| Ferguson L.H. | 1 | 2 | 2 | 1* | 1 | — | — | — | — | — | 0 | 47 | — | — | — | — |
| Fisher F.E. | 1 | 2 | 0 | 14 | 23 | 11.50 | — | — | — | — | 1 | 78 | 78.00 | 1-78 | — | — |
| Fleming S.P. | 111 | 189 | 10 | 274* | 7172 | 40.06 | 9 | 46 | 172 | — | — | — | — | — | — | — |
| Flynn D.R. | 24 | 45 | 5 | 95 | 1038 | 25.95 | — | 6 | 10 | — | 0 | 0 | — | — | — | — |
| Foley H. | 1 | 2 | 0 | 2 | 4 | 2.00 | — | — | — | — | — | — | — | — | — | — |
| Franklin J.E.C. | 31 | 46 | 7 | 122* | 808 | 20.71 | 1 | 2 | 12 | — | 82 | 2786 | 33.97 | 6-119 | 3 | — |
| Franklin T.J. | 21 | 37 | 1 | 101 | 828 | 23.00 | 1 | 4 | 8 | — | — | — | — | — | — | — |
| Freeman D.L. | 2 | 2 | 0 | 1 | 2 | 1.00 | — | — | — | — | 1 | 169 | 169.00 | 1-91 | — | — |
| Fulton P.G. | 23 | 39 | 1 | 136 | 967 | 25.44 | 2 | 5 | 25 | — | — | — | — | — | — | — |
| Gallichan N. | 1 | 2 | 0 | 30 | 32 | 16.00 | — | — | 1 | — | 3 | 113 | 37.67 | 3-99 | — | — |
| Gedye S.G. | 4 | 8 | 0 | 55 | 193 | 24.13 | — | 2 | — | — | — | — | — | — | — | — |
| †Germon L.K. | 12 | 21 | 3 | 55 | 382 | 21.22 | — | 1 | 27 | 2 | — | — | — | — | — | — |
| Gillespie M.R. | 5 | 8 | 1 | 27 | 76 | 10.85 | — | — | 1 | — | 22 | 631 | 28.68 | 6-113 | 3 | — |
| Gillespie S.R. | 1 | 1 | 0 | 28 | 28 | 28.00 | — | — | — | — | 1 | 79 | 79.00 | 1-79 | — | — |
| Gray E.J. | 10 | 16 | 0 | 50 | 248 | 15.50 | — | 1 | 6 | — | 17 | 886 | 52.11 | 3-73 | — | — |
| Greatbatch M.J. | 41 | 71 | 5 | 146* | 2021 | 30.62 | 3 | 10 | 27 | — | 0 | 0 | — | — | — | — |
| †Guillen S.C. | 3 | 6 | 0 | 41 | 98 | 16.33 | — | — | 4 | 1 | — | — | — | — | — | — |
| Guptill M.J. | 47 | 89 | 1 | 189 | 2586 | 29.38 | 3 | 17 | 50 | — | 8 | 298 | 37.25 | 3-11 | — | — |
| Guy J.W. | 12 | 23 | 2 | 102 | 440 | 20.95 | 1 | 3 | 2 | — | — | — | — | — | — | — |
| Hadlee D.R. | 26 | 42 | 5 | 56 | 530 | 14.32 | — | 1 | 8 | — | 71 | 2389 | 33.65 | 4-30 | — | — |
| Hadlee R.J. | 86 | 134 | 19 | 151* | 3124 | 27.16 | 2 | 15 | 39 | — | 431 | 9611 | 22.29 | 9-52 | 36 | 9 |
| Hadlee W.A. | 11 | 19 | 1 | 116 | 543 | 30.17 | 1 | 2 | 6 | — | — | — | — | — | — | — |
| Harford N.S. | 8 | 15 | 0 | 93 | 229 | 15.27 | — | 2 | — | — | — | — | — | — | — | — |

| | M | I | NO | HS | Runs | Ave | 100 | 50 | Ct | St | Wkts | Runs | Ave | Best | 5WI | 10WM |
|---|---|---|---|---|---|---|---|---|---|---|---|---|---|---|---|---|
| †Harford R.I. | 3 | 5 | 2 | 6 | 7 | 2.33 | — | — | 11 | — | — | — | — | — | — | — |
| Harris C.Z. | 23 | 42 | 4 | 71 | 777 | 20.44 | — | 5 | 14 | — | 16 | 1170 | 73.12 | 2-16 | — | — |
| Harris P.G.Z. | 9 | 18 | 1 | 101 | 378 | 22.24 | 1 | 1 | 6 | — | 0 | 14 | — | — | — | — |
| Harris R.M. | 2 | 3 | 0 | 13 | 31 | 10.33 | — | — | — | — | — | — | — | — | — | — |
| Hart M.N. | 14 | 24 | 4 | 45 | 353 | 17.65 | — | — | 9 | — | 29 | 1438 | 49.58 | 5-77 | 1 | — |
| †Hart R.G. | 11 | 19 | 3 | 57* | 260 | 16.25 | — | 1 | 29 | 1 | — | — | — | — | — | — |
| Hartland B.R. | 9 | 18 | 0 | 52 | 303 | 16.83 | — | 1 | 5 | — | — | — | — | — | — | — |
| Haslam M.J. | 4 | 2 | 1 | 3 | 4 | 4.00 | — | — | 2 | — | 2 | 245 | 122.50 | 1-33 | — | — |
| Hastings B.F. | 31 | 56 | 6 | 117* | 1510 | 30.20 | 4 | 7 | 23 | — | 0 | 9 | — | — | — | — |
| Hayes J.A. | 15 | 22 | 7 | 19 | 73 | 4.87 | — | — | 3 | — | 30 | 1217 | 40.57 | 4-36 | — | — |
| Henderson M. | 1 | 2 | 1 | 6 | 8 | 8.00 | — | — | 1 | — | 2 | 64 | 32.00 | 2-38 | — | — |
| Henry M.J. | 17 | 22 | 5 | 66 | 312 | 18.35 | — | 2 | 7 | — | 53 | 2133 | 40.14 | 7-23 | 1 | — |
| †Hopkins G.J. | 4 | 7 | 1 | 15 | 71 | 11.83 | — | — | 9 | — | — | — | — | — | — | — |
| Horne M.J. | 35 | 65 | 2 | 157 | 1788 | 28.38 | 4 | 5 | 17 | — | 0 | 26 | — | — | — | — |
| Horne P.A. | 4 | 7 | 0 | 27 | 71 | 10.14 | — | — | 3 | — | — | — | — | — | — | — |
| Hough K.W. | 2 | 3 | 2 | 31* | 62 | 62.00 | — | — | 1 | — | 6 | 175 | 29.17 | 3-79 | — | — |
| How J.M. | 19 | 35 | 1 | 92 | 772 | 22.70 | — | 4 | 18 | — | 0 | 4 | — | — | — | — |
| Howarth G.P. | 47 | 83 | 5 | 147 | 2531 | 32.44 | 6 | 11 | 29 | — | 3 | 271 | 90.33 | 1-13 | — | — |
| Howarth H.J. | 30 | 42 | 18 | 61 | 291 | 12.13 | — | 1 | 33 | — | 86 | 3178 | 36.95 | 5-34 | 2 | — |
| Ingram P.J. | 2 | 4 | 0 | 42 | 61 | 15.25 | — | — | — | — | — | — | — | — | — | — |
| †James K.C. | 11 | 13 | 2 | 14 | 52 | 4.73 | — | — | 11 | 5 | — | — | — | — | — | — |
| Jamieson K.A. | 16 | 22 | 3 | 51* | 372 | 19.57 | — | 1 | 5 | — | 72 | 1401 | 19.45 | 6-48 | 5 | 1 |
| Jarvis T.W. | 13 | 22 | 1 | 182 | 625 | 29.76 | 1 | 2 | 3 | — | 0 | 3 | — | — | — | — |
| Jones A.H. | 39 | 74 | 8 | 186 | 2922 | 44.27 | 7 | 11 | 25 | — | 1 | 194 | 194.00 | 1-40 | — | — |
| Jones R.A. | 1 | 2 | 0 | 16 | 23 | 11.50 | — | — | — | — | — | — | — | — | — | — |
| Kennedy R.J. | 4 | 5 | 1 | 22 | 28 | 7.00 | — | — | 2 | — | 6 | 380 | 63.33 | 3-28 | — | — |
| Kerr J.L. | 7 | 12 | 1 | 59 | 212 | 19.27 | — | 1 | 4 | — | — | — | — | — | — | — |
| Kuggeleijn C.M. | 2 | 4 | 0 | 7 | 7 | 1.75 | — | — | 1 | — | 1 | 67 | 67.00 | 1-50 | — | — |
| Larsen G.R. | 8 | 13 | 4 | 26* | 127 | 14.11 | — | — | 5 | — | 24 | 689 | 28.70 | 3-57 | — | — |
| Latham R.T. | 4 | 7 | 0 | 119 | 219 | 31.28 | 1 | — | 5 | — | 0 | 6 | — | — | — | — |
| *Latham T.W.M. | 68 | 119 | 5 | 264* | 4623 | 40.55 | 12 | 23 | 76 | — | — | — | — | — | — | — |
| †Lees W.K. | 21 | 37 | 4 | 152 | 778 | 23.57 | 1 | 1 | 52 | 7 | 0 | 4 | — | — | — | — |
| Leggat I.B. | 1 | 1 | 0 | 0 | 0 | 0.00 | — | — | 2 | — | 0 | 6 | — | — | — | — |
| Leggat J.G. | 9 | 18 | 2 | 61 | 351 | 21.94 | — | 2 | — | — | — | — | — | — | — | — |
| Lissette A.F. | 2 | 4 | 2 | 1* | 2 | 1.00 | — | — | 1 | — | 3 | 124 | 41.33 | 2-73 | — | — |
| Loveridge G.R. | 1 | 1 | 1 | 4* | 4 | — | — | — | — | — | — | — | — | — | — | — |
| Lowry T.C. | 7 | 8 | 0 | 80 | 223 | 27.88 | — | 2 | 8 | — | 0 | 5 | — | — | — | — |
| *McCullum B.B. | 101 | 176 | 9 | 302 | 6453 | 38.64 | 12 | 31 | 198 | 11 | 1 | 88 | 88.00 | 1-1 | — | — |
| McEwan P.E. | 4 | 7 | 1 | 40* | 96 | 16.00 | — | — | 5 | — | 0 | 13 | — | — | — | — |
| MacGibbon A.R. | 26 | 46 | 5 | 66 | 814 | 19.85 | — | 3 | 13 | — | 70 | 2160 | 30.86 | 5-64 | 1 | — |
| McGirr H.M. | 2 | 1 | 0 | 51 | 51 | 51.00 | — | 1 | — | — | 1 | 115 | 115.00 | 1-65 | — | — |
| McGregor S.N. | 25 | 47 | 2 | 111 | 892 | 19.82 | 1 | 3 | 9 | — | — | — | — | — | — | — |
| McIntosh T.G. | 17 | 33 | 2 | 136 | 854 | 27.54 | 2 | 4 | 10 | — | — | — | — | — | — | — |
| McKay A.J. | 1 | 2 | 1 | 20* | 25 | 25.00 | — | — | — | — | 1 | 120 | 120.00 | 1-120 | — | — |
| McLeod E.G. | 1 | 2 | 1 | 16 | 18 | 18.00 | — | — | — | — | 0 | 5 | — | — | — | — |
| †McMahon T.G. | 5 | 7 | 4 | 4* | 7 | 2.33 | — | — | 7 | 1 | — | — | — | — | — | — |
| McMillan C.D. | 55 | 91 | 10 | 142 | 3116 | 38.46 | 6 | 19 | 22 | — | 28 | 1257 | 44.89 | 3-48 | — | — |
| McRae D.A.N. | 1 | 2 | 0 | 8 | 8 | 4.00 | — | — | — | — | 0 | 44 | — | — | — | — |
| Marshall H.J.H. | 13 | 19 | 2 | 160 | 652 | 38.35 | 2 | 2 | 1 | — | 0 | 4 | — | — | — | — |
| Marshall J.A.H. | 7 | 11 | 0 | 52 | 218 | 19.81 | — | 1 | 5 | — | — | — | — | — | — | — |
| Martin B.P. | 5 | 6 | 1 | 41 | 74 | 14.80 | — | — | — | — | 12 | 646 | 53.33 | 4-43 | — | — |
| Martin C.S. | 71 | 104 | 52 | 12* | 123 | 2.36 | — | — | 14 | — | 233 | 7878 | 33.81 | 6-26 | 10 | 1 |
| Mason M.J. | 1 | 2 | 0 | 3 | 3 | 1.50 | — | — | — | — | 0 | 105 | — | — | — | — |
| Matheson A.M. | 2 | 1 | 0 | 7 | 7 | 7.00 | — | — | 2 | — | 2 | 136 | 68.00 | 2-7 | — | — |

| | M | I | NO | HS | Runs | Ave | 100 | 50 | Ct | St | Wkts | Runs | Ave | Best | 5WI | 10WM |
|---|---|---|---|---|---|---|---|---|---|---|---|---|---|---|---|---|
| **Meale** T. | 2 | 4 | 0 | 10 | 21 | 5.25 | — | — | — | — | — | — | — | — | — | — |
| **Merritt** W.E. | 6 | 8 | 1 | 19 | 73 | 10.43 | — | — | 2 | — | 12 | 617 | 51.42 | 4-104 | — | — |
| **Meuli** E.M. | 1 | 2 | 0 | 23 | 38 | 19.00 | — | — | — | — | — | — | — | — | — | — |
| †**Milburn** B.D. | 3 | 3 | 2 | 4* | 8 | 8.00 | — | — | 6 | 2 | — | — | — | — | — | — |
| **Miller** L.S.M. | 13 | 25 | 0 | 47 | 346 | 13.84 | — | — | 1 | — | 0 | 1 | — | — | — | — |
| **Mills** J.E. | 7 | 10 | 1 | 117 | 241 | 26.78 | 1 | — | 1 | — | — | — | — | — | — | — |
| **Mills** K.D. | 19 | 30 | 5 | 57 | 289 | 11.56 | — | 1 | 4 | — | 44 | 1453 | 33.02 | 4-16 | — | — |
| **Mitchell** D.J. | 12 | 17 | 2 | 190 | 941 | 62.73 | 4 | 5 | 17 | — | 2 | 184 | 92.00 | 1-7 | — | — |
| **Moir** A.M. | 17 | 30 | 8 | 41* | 327 | 14.86 | — | — | 2 | — | 28 | 1418 | 50.64 | 6-155 | 2 | — |
| **Moloney** D.A.R. | 3 | 6 | 0 | 64 | 156 | 26.00 | — | 1 | 3 | — | 0 | 9 | — | — | — | — |
| †**Mooney** F.L.H. | 14 | 22 | 2 | 46 | 343 | 17.15 | — | — | 22 | 8 | 0 | 0 | — | — | — | — |
| ***Morgan** R.W. | 20 | 34 | 1 | 97 | 734 | 22.24 | — | 5 | 12* | — | 5 | 609 | 121.80 | 1-16 | — | — |
| **Morrison** B.D. | 1 | 2 | 0 | 10 | 10 | 5.00 | — | — | 1 | — | 2 | 129 | 64.50 | 2-129 | — | — |
| **Morrison** D.K. | 48 | 71 | 26 | 42 | 379 | 8.42 | — | — | 14 | — | 160 | 5549 | 34.68 | 7-89 | 10 | — |
| **Morrison** J.F.M. | 17 | 29 | 0 | 117 | 656 | 22.62 | 1 | 3 | 9 | — | 2 | 71 | 35.50 | 2-52 | — | — |
| **Motz** R.C. | 32 | 56 | 3 | 60 | 612 | 11.55 | — | 3 | 9 | — | 100 | 3148 | 31.48 | 6-63 | 5 | — |
| **Munro** C. | 1 | 2 | 0 | 15 | 15 | 7.50 | — | — | — | — | 2 | 40 | 20.00 | 2-40 | — | — |
| **Murray** B.A.G. | 13 | 26 | 1 | 90 | 598 | 23.92 | — | 5 | 21 | — | 1 | 0 | 0.00 | 1-0 | — | — |
| **Murray** D.J. | 8 | 16 | 1 | 52 | 303 | 20.20 | — | 1 | 6 | — | — | — | — | — | — | — |
| **Nash** D.J. | 32 | 45 | 14 | 89* | 729 | 23.51 | — | 4 | 13 | — | 93 | 2649 | 28.48 | 6-27 | 3 | 1 |
| **Neesham** J.D.S. | 12 | 22 | 1 | 137* | 709 | 33.76 | 2 | 4 | 12 | — | 14 | 675 | 48.21 | 3-42 | — | — |
| **Newman** J. | 3 | 4 | 0 | 19 | 33 | 8.25 | — | — | — | — | 2 | 254 | 127.00 | 2-76 | — | — |
| **Nicholls** H.M. | 48 | 73 | 6 | 174 | 2603 | 38.85 | 8 | 12 | 29 | — | — | — | — | — | — | — |
| **Nicol** R.J. | 2 | 4 | 0 | 19 | 28 | 7.00 | — | — | 2 | — | 0 | 13 | — | — | — | — |
| **O'Brien** I.E. | 22 | 34 | 5 | 31 | 219 | 7.55 | — | — | 7 | — | 73 | 2429 | 33.27 | 6-75 | 1 | — |
| **O'Connor** S.B. | 19 | 27 | 9 | 20 | 105 | 5.83 | — | — | 6 | — | 53 | 1724 | 32.52 | 5-51 | 1 | — |
| **O'Sullivan** D.R. | 11 | 21 | 4 | 23* | 158 | 9.29 | — | — | 2 | — | 18 | 1221 | 67.83 | 5-148 | 1 | — |
| **Oram** J.D.P. | 33 | 59 | 10 | 133 | 1780 | 36.32 | 5 | 6 | 15 | — | 60 | 1983 | 33.05 | 4-41 | — | — |
| **Overton** G.W.F. | 3 | 6 | 1 | 3* | 8 | 1.60 | — | — | 1 | — | 9 | 258 | 28.67 | 3-65 | — | — |
| **Owens** M.B. | 8 | 12 | 6 | 8* | 16 | 2.66 | — | — | 3 | — | 17 | 585 | 34.44 | 4-99 | — | — |
| **Page** M.L. | 14 | 20 | 0 | 104 | 492 | 24.60 | 1 | 2 | 6 | — | 5 | 231 | 46.20 | 2-21 | — | — |
| **Papps** M.H.W. | 8 | 16 | 1 | 86 | 246 | 16.40 | — | 2 | 11 | — | — | — | — | — | — | — |
| **Parker** J.M. | 36 | 63 | 2 | 121 | 1498 | 24.56 | 3 | 5 | 30 | — | 1 | 24 | 24.00 | 1-24 | — | — |
| **Parker** N.M. | 3 | 6 | 0 | 40 | 89 | 14.83 | — | — | 2 | — | — | — | — | — | — | — |
| ***Parore** A.C. | 78 | 128 | 19 | 110 | 2865 | 26.28 | 2 | 14 | 197 | 7 | — | — | — | — | — | — |
| **Patel** A.Y. | 12 | 17 | 7 | 20 | 91 | 9.10 | — | — | 6 | — | 43 | 1189 | 27.65 | 10-119 | 3 | 1 |
| **Patel** D.N. | 37 | 66 | 8 | 99 | 1200 | 20.68 | — | 5 | 15 | — | 75 | 3154 | 42.05 | 6-50 | 3 | — |
| **Patel** J.S. | 24 | 38 | 8 | 47 | 381 | 12.70 | — | — | 13 | — | 65 | 3078 | 47.35 | 5-110 | 1 | — |
| **Petherick** P.J. | 6 | 11 | 4 | 13 | 34 | 4.86 | — | — | 4 | — | 16 | 685 | 42.81 | 3-90 | — | — |
| †**Petrie** E.C. | 14 | 25 | 5 | 55 | 258 | 12.90 | — | 1 | 25 | — | — | — | — | — | — | — |
| **Phillips** G.D. | 1 | 2 | 0 | 52 | 52 | 26.00 | — | 1 | 1 | — | — | — | — | — | — | — |
| **Playle** W.R. | 8 | 15 | 0 | 65 | 151 | 10.07 | — | 1 | 4 | — | — | — | — | — | — | — |
| **Pocock** B.A. | 15 | 29 | 0 | 85 | 665 | 22.93 | — | 6 | 5 | — | 0 | 20 | — | — | — | — |
| **Pollard** V. | 32 | 59 | 7 | 116 | 1266 | 24.35 | 2 | 7 | 19 | — | 40 | 1853 | 46.33 | 3-3 | — | — |
| **Poore** M.B. | 14 | 24 | 1 | 45 | 355 | 15.43 | — | — | 1 | — | 9 | 367 | 40.78 | 2-28 | — | — |
| **Priest** M.W. | 3 | 4 | 0 | 26 | 56 | 14.00 | — | — | — | — | 3 | 158 | 52.66 | 2-42 | — | — |
| **Pringle** C. | 14 | 21 | 4 | 30 | 175 | 10.29 | — | — | 3 | — | 30 | 1389 | 46.30 | 7-52 | 1 | 1 |
| **Puna** N. | 3 | 5 | 3 | 18* | 31 | 15.50 | — | — | 1 | — | 4 | 240 | 60.00 | 2-40 | — | — |
| **Rabone** G.O. | 12 | 20 | 2 | 107 | 562 | 31.22 | 1 | 2 | 5 | — | 16 | 635 | 36.69 | 6-68 | 1 | — |
| **Raval** J.A. | 24 | 39 | 1 | 132 | 1143 | 30.07 | 1 | 7 | 21 | — | 1 | 34 | 34.00 | 1-33 | — | — |
| **Ravindra** R. | 3 | 6 | 1 | 18* | 73 | 14.60 | — | — | 2 | — | 3 | 188 | 62.66 | 3-56 | — | — |
| **Redmond** A.J. | 8 | 16 | 1 | 83 | 325 | 21.66 | — | 2 | 5 | — | 3 | 80 | 26.66 | 2-47 | — | — |
| **Redmond** R.E. | 1 | 2 | 0 | 107 | 163 | 81.50 | 1 | 1 | — | — | — | — | — | — | — | — |
| **Reid** J.F. | 19 | 31 | 3 | 180 | 1296 | 46.28 | 6 | 2 | 9 | — | 0 | 7 | — | — | — | — |

| | M | I | NO | HS | Runs | Ave | 100 | 50 | Ct | St | Wkts | Runs | Ave | Best | 5WI | 10WM |
|---|---|---|---|---|---|---|---|---|---|---|---|---|---|---|---|---|
| *Reid J.R. | 58 | 108 | 5 | 142 | 3428 | 33.28 | 6 | 22 | 43* | 1 | 85 | 2835 | 33.35 | 6-60 | 1 | — |
| Richardson M.H. | 38 | 65 | 3 | 145 | 2776 | 44.77 | 4 | 19 | 26 | — | 1 | 21 | 21.00 | 1-16 | — | — |
| Roberts A.D.G. | 7 | 12 | 1 | 84* | 254 | 23.09 | — | 1 | 4 | — | 4 | 182 | 45.50 | 1-12 | — | — |
| Roberts A.W. | 5 | 10 | 1 | 66* | 248 | 27.56 | — | 3 | 4 | — | 7 | 209 | 29.86 | 4-101 | — | — |
| Robertson G.K. | 1 | 1 | 0 | 12 | 12 | 12.00 | — | — | — | — | 1 | 91 | 91.00 | 1-91 | — | — |
| *Ronchi L. | 4 | 8 | 0 | 88 | 319 | 39.87 | — | 2 | 5 | — | — | — | — | — | — | — |
| Rowe C.G. | 1 | 2 | 0 | 0 | 0 | 0.00 | — | — | 1 | — | — | — | — | — | — | — |
| Rutherford H.D. | 14 | 25 | 1 | 171 | 650 | 27.08 | 1 | 1 | 10 | — | — | — | — | — | — | — |
| Rutherford K.R. | 56 | 99 | 8 | 107* | 2465 | 27.08 | 3 | 18 | 32 | — | 1 | 161 | 161.00 | 1-38 | — | — |
| Ryder J.D. | 18 | 33 | 2 | 201 | 1269 | 40.93 | 3 | 6 | 12 | — | 5 | 280 | 56.00 | 2-7 | — | — |
| Santner M.J. | 24 | 32 | 1 | 126 | 766 | 24.70 | 1 | 2 | 16 | — | 41 | 1871 | 45.63 | 3-53 | — | — |
| Scott R.H. | 1 | 1 | 0 | 18 | 18 | 18.00 | — | — | — | — | 1 | 74 | 74.00 | 1-74 | — | — |
| Scott V.J. | 10 | 17 | 1 | 84 | 458 | 28.63 | — | 3 | 7 | — | 0 | 14 | — | — | — | — |
| Sewell D.G. | 1 | 1 | 1 | 1* | 1 | — | — | — | — | — | 0 | 90 | — | — | — | — |
| Shrimpton M.J.F. | 10 | 19 | 0 | 46 | 265 | 13.95 | — | — | 2 | — | 5 | 158 | 31.60 | 3-35 | — | — |
| Sinclair B.W. | 21 | 40 | 1 | 138 | 1148 | 29.44 | 3 | 3 | 8 | — | 2 | 32 | 16.00 | 2-32 | — | — |
| Sinclair I.M. | 2 | 4 | 1 | 18* | 25 | 8.33 | — | — | 1 | — | 1 | 120 | 120.00 | 1-79 | — | — |
| *Sinclair M.S. | 33 | 56 | 5 | 214 | 1635 | 32.05 | 3 | 4 | 31 | — | 0 | 14 | — | — | — | — |
| Smith F.B. | 4 | 6 | 1 | 96 | 237 | 47.40 | — | 2 | 1 | — | — | — | — | — | — | — |
| Smith H.D. | 1 | 1 | 0 | 4 | 4 | 4.00 | — | — | — | — | 1 | 113 | 113.00 | 1-113 | — | — |
| †Smith I.D.S. | 63 | 88 | 17 | 173 | 1815 | 25.56 | 2 | 6 | 168 | 8 | 0 | 5 | — | — | — | — |
| Snedden C.A. | 1 | — | — | — | — | — | — | — | — | — | 0 | 46 | — | — | — | — |
| Snedden M.C. | 25 | 30 | 8 | 33* | 327 | 14.86 | — | — | 7 | — | 58 | 2199 | 37.91 | 5-68 | 1 | — |
| Sodhi I.S. | 17 | 25 | 4 | 63 | 448 | 21.33 | — | 3 | 11 | — | 41 | 1992 | 48.58 | 4-60 | — | — |
| Somerville W.E.R. | 4 | 10 | 2 | 40* | 115 | 14.37 | — | — | — | — | 15 | 724 | 48.26 | 4-75 | — | — |
| Southee T.G. | 88 | 126 | 11 | 77* | 1855 | 16.13 | — | 5 | 69 | — | 347 | 10061 | 28.99 | 7-64 | 14 | 1 |
| Sparling J.T. | 11 | 20 | 2 | 50 | 229 | 12.72 | — | 1 | 3 | — | 5 | 327 | 65.40 | 1-9 | — | — |
| Spearman C.M. | 19 | 37 | 2 | 112 | 922 | 26.34 | 1 | 3 | 20 | — | — | — | — | — | — | — |
| Stead G.R. | 5 | 8 | 0 | 78 | 278 | 34.75 | — | 2 | 2 | — | 0 | 1 | — | — | — | — |
| Stirling D.A. | 6 | 9 | 2 | 26 | 108 | 15.42 | — | — | 1 | — | 13 | 601 | 46.23 | 4-88 | — | — |
| Styris S.B. | 29 | 48 | 4 | 170 | 1586 | 36.04 | 5 | 6 | 23 | — | 20 | 1015 | 50.75 | 3-28 | — | — |
| Su'a M.L. | 13 | 18 | 5 | 44 | 165 | 12.69 | — | — | 8 | — | 36 | 1377 | 38.25 | 5-73 | 2 | — |
| Sutcliffe B. | 42 | 76 | 8 | 230* | 2727 | 40.10 | 5 | 15 | 20 | — | 4 | 344 | 86.00 | 2-38 | — | — |
| Taylor B.R. | 30 | 50 | 6 | 124 | 898 | 20.41 | 2 | 2 | 10 | — | 111 | 2953 | 26.60 | 7-74 | 4 | — |
| Taylor D.D. | 3 | 5 | 0 | 77 | 159 | 31.80 | — | 1 | 2 | — | — | — | — | — | — | — |
| Taylor L.R.P.L. | 112 | 196 | 24 | 290 | 7683 | 44.66 | 19 | 35 | 163 | — | 3 | 48 | 16.00 | 2-4 | — | — |
| Thomson K. | 2 | 4 | 1 | 69 | 94 | 31.33 | — | 1 | — | — | 1 | 9 | 9.00 | 1-9 | — | — |
| Thomson S.A. | 19 | 35 | 4 | 120* | 958 | 30.90 | 1 | 5 | 7 | — | 19 | 953 | 50.15 | 3-63 | — | — |
| †Tindill E.W.T. | 5 | 9 | 1 | 37* | 73 | 9.13 | — | — | 6 | 1 | — | — | — | — | — | — |
| Troup G.B. | 15 | 18 | 6 | 13* | 55 | 4.58 | — | — | 2 | — | 39 | 1454 | 37.28 | 6-95 | 1 | 1 |
| Truscott P.B. | 1 | 2 | 0 | 26 | 29 | 14.50 | — | — | 1 | — | — | — | — | — | — | — |
| Tuffey D.R. | 26 | 36 | 10 | 80* | 427 | 16.42 | — | 1 | 15 | — | 77 | 2445 | 31.75 | 6-54 | 2 | — |
| Turner G.M. | 41 | 73 | 6 | 259 | 2991 | 44.64 | 7 | 14 | 42 | — | 0 | 5 | — | — | — | — |
| Twose R.G. | 16 | 27 | 2 | 94 | 628 | 25.12 | — | 6 | 5 | — | 3 | 130 | 43.33 | 2-36 | — | — |
| Vance R.H. | 4 | 7 | 0 | 68 | 207 | 29.57 | — | 1 | — | — | — | — | — | — | — | — |
| †van Wyk C.F.K. | 9 | 17 | 1 | 71 | 341 | 21.31 | — | 1 | 23 | 1 | — | — | — | — | — | — |
| Vaughan J.T.C. | 6 | 12 | 1 | 44 | 201 | 18.27 | — | — | 4 | — | 11 | 450 | 40.90 | 4-27 | — | — |
| Vettori D.L. | 113 | 174 | 23 | 140 | 4531 | 30.00 | 6 | 23 | 58 | — | 362 | 12441 | 34.36 | 7-87 | 20 | 3 |
| Vincent L. | 23 | 40 | 1 | 224 | 1332 | 34.15 | 3 | 9 | 19 | — | 0 | 2 | — | — | — | — |
| Vivian G.E. | 5 | 6 | 0 | 43 | 110 | 18.33 | — | — | 3 | — | 1 | 107 | 107.00 | 1-14 | — | — |
| Vivian H.G. | 7 | 10 | 0 | 100 | 421 | 42.10 | 1 | 5 | 4 | — | 17 | 633 | 37.24 | 4-58 | — | — |
| †Wadsworth K.J. | 33 | 51 | 4 | 80 | 1010 | 21.49 | — | 5 | 92 | 4 | — | — | — | — | — | — |
| Wagner N. | 59 | 76 | 21 | 66* | 779 | 14.16 | — | 1 | 15 | — | 246 | 6572 | 26.71 | 7-39 | 9 | — |

| | M | I | NO | HS | Runs | Ave | 100 | 50 | Ct | St | Wkts | Runs | Ave | Best | 5WI | 10WM |
|---|---|---|---|---|---|---|---|---|---|---|---|---|---|---|---|---|
| **Walker** B.G.K. | 5 | 8 | 2 | 27* | 118 | 19.66 | — | — | — | — | 5 | 399 | 79.80 | 2-92 | — | — |
| **Wallace** W.M. | 13 | 21 | 0 | 66 | 439 | 20.90 | — | 5 | 5 | — | 0 | 5 | — | — | — | — |
| **Walmsley** K.P. | 3 | 5 | 0 | 5 | 13 | 2.60 | — | — | — | — | 9 | 391 | 43.44 | 3-70 | — | — |
| †**Ward** J.T. | 8 | 12 | 6 | 35* | 75 | 12.50 | — | — | 16 | 1 | — | — | — | — | — | — |
| *****Watling** B-J. | 75 | 117 | 16 | 205 | 3790 | 37.52 | 8 | 19 | 267 | 8 | — | — | — | — | — | — |
| **Watson** W. | 15 | 18 | 6 | 11 | 60 | 5.00 | — | — | 4 | — | 40 | 1387 | 34.67 | 6-78 | 1 | — |
| **Watt** L. | 1 | 2 | 0 | 2 | 2 | 1.00 | — | — | — | — | — | — | — | — | — | — |
| **Webb** M.G. | 3 | 2 | 0 | 12 | 12 | 6.00 | — | — | — | — | 4 | 471 | 117.75 | 2-114 | — | — |
| **Webb** P.N. | 2 | 3 | 0 | 5 | 11 | 3.67 | — | — | 2 | — | — | — | — | — | — | — |
| **Weir** G.L. | 11 | 16 | 2 | 74* | 416 | 29.71 | — | 3 | 3 | — | 7 | 209 | 29.86 | 3-38 | — | — |
| **White** D.J. | 2 | 4 | 0 | 18 | 31 | 7.75 | — | — | — | — | 0 | 5 | — | — | — | — |
| **Whitelaw** P.E. | 2 | 4 | 2 | 30 | 64 | 32.00 | — | — | — | — | — | — | — | — | — | — |
| **Williamson** K.S. | 88 | 154 | 14 | 251 | 7368 | 52.62 | 24 | 33 | 74 | — | 30 | 1207 | 40.23 | 4-44 | — | — |
| **Wiseman** P.J. | 25 | 34 | 8 | 36 | 366 | 14.07 | — | — | 11 | — | 61 | 2903 | 47.59 | 5-82 | 2 | — |
| **Wright** J.G. | 82 | 148 | 7 | 185 | 5334 | 37.82 | 12 | 23 | 38 | — | 0 | 5 | — | — | — | — |
| **Young** B.A. | 35 | 68 | 4 | 267* | 2034 | 31.78 | 2 | 12 | 54 | — | — | — | — | — | — | — |
| †**Young** R.A. | 5 | 10 | 3 | 57 | 169 | 24.14 | — | 1 | 8 | — | — | — | — | — | — | — |
| **Young** W.A. | 12 | 20 | 0 | 89 | 572 | 28.60 | — | 6 | 6 | — | — | — | — | — | — | — |
| **Yuile** B.W. | 17 | 33 | 6 | 64 | 481 | 17.81 | — | 1 | 12 | — | 34 | 1213 | 35.68 | 4-43 | — | — |

**Note:** There have been 81 dismissals made by substitutes: M.J. Greatbatch (5), J.G. Bracewell, J.J. Crowe, T.W. Jarvis (4), C.Z. Harris (3), J.M. How, J.A.H. Marshall, D.R. O'Sullivan, A.C. Parore, K.R. Rutherford, G.E. Vivian, M.J. Guptill, T.G. Southee (2), J.C. Alabaster, R.W. Anderson, T.A. Blundell, S.E. Bond, S.L. Boock, G.E. Bradburn, C. Burke, Carl Cachopa, R.O. Collinge, B.E. Congdon, D.P. Conway, M.D. Crowe, H.T. Davis, C.J. Drum, E.W. Dempster, G.T. Dowling, S.W. Eathorne, B.A. Edgar, G.N. Edwards, S.G. Gedye, M.N. Hart, M.A. Hastings, M.J. Henry, N.K.W. Horsley, I.B. Leggat, T.G. McMahon, P.E. McEwan, M.N. McKenzie, H.J.H. Marshall, M.J. Mason, S.M. Mills, D.J. Mitchell, R.C. Motz, J.D.S. Neesham, S.B. O'Connor, N.M. Parker, J.S. Patel, M.W. Priest, T.D. Ritchie, M.J. Santner, L. Vincent, B.G.K. Walker, W.A. Young, B-J. Watling catches and B.E. Congdon a stumping. The latter is one of only two instances in tests of a substitute making a stumping.

† *all test appearances were as wicketkeeper. A.C. Parore had 67 tests as wicketkeeper, B-J. Watling 67, B.B. McCullum 52, T.E. Blain 9, G.N. Edwards 4, T.A. Blundell 4, B.A. Edgar, J.R. Reid and L. Ronchi one each.*

\* *record includes catches taken while keeping wicket as follows: B-J. Watling 257, A.C. Parore 194, B.B. McCullum 168, T.A. Blundell 48, T.E. Blain 18, T.W.M. Latham 7, B.A. Edgar 4, J.R. Reid 2 and B.E. Congdon, R.W. Morgan and M.S. Sinclair one each. Edwards' and Ronchi's catches were all made while keeping wicket.*

*Vettori's record includes one match for ICC World XI.*

# SUMMARY OF TEST CAREER RECORDS

## Most Matches

| | | | | | |
|---|---|---|---|---|---|
| Vettori D.L. | 113 | Astle N.J. | 81 | Cairns C.L. | 62 |
| Taylor L.R.P.L. | 112 | Parore A.C. | 78 | Congdon B.E. | 61 |
| Fleming S.P. | 111 | Boult T.A. | 78 | Wagner N. | 59 |
| McCullum B.B. | 101 | Crowe M.D. | 77 | Reid J.R. | 58 |
| Southee T.G. | 88 | Watling B-J. | 75 | Rutherford K.R. | 56 |
| Williamson K.S. | 88 | Martin C.S. | 71 | McMillan C.D | 55 |
| Hadlee R.J. | 86 | Latham T.W.M. | 68 | Coney J.V. | 52 |
| Wright J.G. | 82 | Smith I.D.S. | 63 | Burgess M.G. | 50 |

## Most Runs

| | | | | | |
|---|---|---|---|---|---|
| Taylor L.R.P.L. | 7683 | Congdon B.E. | 3448 | Burgess M.G. | 2684 |
| Williamson K.S. | 7368 | Reid J.R. | 3428 | Coney J.V. | 2668 |
| Fleming S.P. | 7172 | Cairns C.L. | 3320 | Nicholls H.M. | 2603 |
| McCullum B.B. | 6453 | Hadlee R.J. | 3124 | Guptill M.J. | 2586 |
| Crowe M.D. | 5444 | McMillan C.D. | 3116 | Howarth G.P. | 2531 |
| Wright J.G. | 5334 | Turner G.M. | 2991 | Rutherford K.R. | 2465 |
| Astle N.J. | 4702 | Jones A.H. | 2922 | Dowling G.T. | 2306 |
| Latham T.W.M. | 4623 | Parore A.C. | 2865 | Young B.A. | 2034 |
| Vettori D.L. | 4531 | Richardson M.H. | 2776 | Greatbatch M.J. | 2021 |
| Watling B-J. | 3790 | Sutcliffe B. | 2727 | | |

## Most Wickets

| | | | | | |
|---|---|---|---|---|---|
| Hadlee R.J. | 431 | Martin C.S. | 233 | Collinge R.O. | 116 |
| Vettori D.L. | 362 | Cairns C.L. | 218 | Taylor B.R. | 111 |
| Southee T.G. | 347 | Morrison D.K. | 160 | Bracewell J.G. | 102 |
| Boult T.A. | 317 | Cairns B.L. | 130 | Motz R.C. | 100 |
| Wagner N. | 246 | Chatfield E.J. | 123 | | |

## Most Catches

| | | | | | |
|---|---|---|---|---|---|
| Fleming S.P. | 172 | Astle N.J. | 70 | Vettori D.L. | 58 |
| Taylor L.R.P.L. | 163 | Southee T.G. | 69 | Young B.A. | 54 |
| Williamson K.S. | 74 | Latham T.W.M | 69 | Guptill M.J. | 50 |
| Crowe M.D. | 71 | Coney J.V. | 64 | | |

## Most Wicketkeeping Dismissals

| | Ct | St | Total |
|---|---|---|---|
| Watling B-J. | 257 | 8 | 265 |
| Parore A.C. | 194 | 7 | 201 |
| McCullum B.B. | 168 | 11 | 179 |
| Smith I.D.S. | 168 | 8 | 176 |
| Wadsworth K.J. | 92 | 4 | 96 |
| Lees W.K. | 52 | 7 | 59 |
| Dick A.E. | 47 | 4 | 51 |

# Test Captains

| | | RESULTS | | | | TOSS | |
|---|---|---|---|---|---|---|---|
| | | **P** | **W** | **L** | **D** | **W** | **L** |
| Fleming S.P. | 1996/97 to 2006/07 | 80 | 28 | 27 | 25 | 37 | 43 |
| Williamson K.S. | 2016/17 to 2022 | 40 | 22 | 8 | 10 | 22 | 18 |
| Reid J.R. | 1955/56 to 1965 | 34 | 3 | 18 | 13 | 17 | 17 |
| Vettori D.L. | 2007/08 to 2010/11 | 32 | 6 | 16 | 10 | 17 | 15 |
| McCullum B.B. | 2012/13 to 2015/16 | 31 | 11 | 11 | 9 | 12 | 19 |
| Howarth G.P. | 1979/80 to 1984/85 | 30 | 11 | 7 | 12 | 17 | 13 |
| Dowling G.T. | 1967/68 to 1971/72 | 19 | 4 | 7 | 8 | 10 | 9 |
| Rutherford K.R. | 1992/93 to 1994/95 | 18 | 2 | 11 | 5 | 12 | 6 |
| Congdon B.E. | 1971/72 to 1974/75 | 17 | 1 | 7 | 9 | 4 | 13 |
| Crowe M.D. | 1990/91 to 1993/94 | 16 | 2 | 7 | 7 | 8 | 8 |
| Coney J.V. | 1984/85 to 1986/87 | 15 | 5 | 4 | 6 | 8 | 7 |
| Wright J.G. | 1987/88 to 1990 | 14 | 3 | 3 | 8 | 8 | 6 |
| Taylor L.R.P.L. | 2011/12 to 2016/17 | 14 | 4 | 8 | 2 | 8 | 6 |
| Germon L.K. | 1995/96 to 1996/97 | 12 | 1 | 5 | 6 | 6 | 6 |
| Turner G.M. | 1975/76 to 1976/77 | 10 | 1 | 6 | 3 | 2 | 8 |
| Burgess M.G. | 1977/78 to 1980/81 | 10 | 1 | 6 | 3 | 4 | 6 |
| Cave H.B. | 1955/56 | 9 | 0 | 5 | 4 | 5 | 4 |
| Latham T.W.M. | 2019/20 to 2022 | 9 | 4 | 5 | 0 | 1 | 8 |
| Hadlee W.A. | 1945/46 to 1950/51 | 8 | 0 | 2 | 6 | 4 | 4 |
| Lowry T.C. | 1929/30 to 1931 | 7 | 0 | 2 | 5 | 5 | 2 |
| Page M.L. | 1931/32 to 1937 | 7 | 0 | 3 | 4 | 4 | 3 |
| Crowe J.J. | 1986/87 to 1987/88 | 6 | 0 | 1 | 5 | 3 | 3 |
| Rabone G.O. | 1953/54 to 1954/55 | 5 | 0 | 4 | 1 | 2 | 3 |
| Sutcliffe B. | 1951/52 to 1953/54 | 4 | 0 | 3 | 1 | 4 | 0 |
| Sinclair B.W. | 1965/66 to 1967/68 | 3 | 0 | 1 | 2 | 3 | 0 |
| Nash D.J. | 1998/99 | 3 | 0 | 1 | 2 | 3 | 0 |
| Wallace W.M. | 1952/53 | 2 | 0 | 1 | 1 | 0 | 2 |
| Chapple M.E. | 1965/66 | 1 | 0 | 0 | 1 | 0 | 1 |
| Parker J.M. | 1976/77 | 1 | 0 | 0 | 1 | 0 | 1 |
| Smith I.D.S. | 1990/91 | 1 | 0 | 0 | 1 | 1 | 0 |
| **Totals** | | **458** | **109** | **181** | **168** | **227** | **231** |

# Test Debuts

New Zealand has now played 458 test matches. In 273 there have been no new test caps. In the other 185 the records are:

> 11 players making debut 1929/30 v England at Christchurch (NZ's first test match)
> 6 players making debut 1937 v England at Lord's (NZ's first test since 1932/33)
> 6 players making debut 1945/46 v Australia at Wellington
> 6 players making debut 1946/47 v England at Christchurch (test after one above)
> 5 players making debut 1961/62 v South Africa at Durban

Of the 12 players who made their debuts in the 1945/46 and 1946/47 tests above, seven did not appear again. In eight successive tests at least one player made his test debut — South Africa 1963/64 (3), Pakistan 1964/65 (3), India 1964/65 (3). In nine successive tests there were no new caps — England 1969 (2), India 1969/70 (3), Pakistan 1969/70 (3), England 1970/71 (1) and South Africa 1998/99 (1), England 1999 (4), India 1999/00 (3), West Indies 1999/00 (1).

# Youngest/Oldest Test Players

## YOUNGEST PLAYERS

| | | | *Bat* | *Bowl* |
|---|---|---|---|---|
| 18 years 10 days | Vettori D.L. v England at Wellington | 1996/97 | 3* & 2* | 2-98 |
| 18 years 197 days | Freeman D.L. v England at Christchurch | 1932/33 | 1 | 0-78 |
| 18 years 267 days | Vivian H.G. v England at The Oval | 1931 | 3 & 51 | 2-96 |
| 18 years 295 days | Collinge R.O. v Pakistan at Wellington | 1964/65 | 0* | 2-51 & 3-43 |
| 18 years 316 days | Bracewell B.P. v England at The Oval | 1978 | 0 & 0 | 2-46 & 1-26 |
| 19 years 5 days | Vivian G.E. v India at Calcutta | 1964/65 | 1 & 43 | 0-37 & 1-14 |
| 19 years 102 days | Southee T.G. v England at Napier | 2007/08 | 5 & 77* | 5-55 & 0-84 |
| 19 years 145 days | Beck J.E.F. v South Africa at Johannesburg | 1953/54 | 16 & 7 | |
| 19 years 154 days | Rutherford K.R. v West Indies at Port of Spain | 1984/85 | 0 & 0 | |
| 19 years 157 days | Crowe M.D. v Australia at Wellington | 1981/82 | 9 | 0-14 |
| 19 years 163 days | Parore A.C. v England at Birmingham | 1990 | 12* & 20 | 4ct/1st |
| 19 years 164 days | Cairns C.L. v Australia at Perth | 1989/90 | 1 & 28 | 0-60 |
| 19 years 173 days | Pollard V. v India at Madras | 1964/65 | 3 | 3-90 & 1-32 |
| 19 years 186 days | Playle W.R. v England at Birmingham | 1958 | 4 & 8 | |
| 19 years 252 days | Donnelly M.P. v England at Lord's | 1937 | 0 & 21 | |
| 19 years 340 days | Sewell D.G. v Zimbabwe at Bulawayo | 1997/98 | 1* | 0-81 & 0-9 |
| 19 years 344 days | Sparling J.T. v England at Leeds | 1958 | 9* & 18 | 1-78 |

## OLDEST PLAYERS *(age on last day of final test)*

| | | | | |
|---|---|---|---|---|
| 41 years 247 days | Alabaster J.C. v West Indies at Port of Spain | 1971/72 | 18 | 0-49 & 1-5 |
| 41 years 196 days | Sutcliffe B. v England at Birmingham | 1965 | 4* & 53 | |
| 40 years 198 days | Congdon B.E. v England at Lord's | 1978 | 2 & 3 | 0-12 |

## OLDEST PLAYER ON DEBUT

| | | | | |
|---|---|---|---|---|
| 38 years 101 days | McGirr H.M.† v England at Auckland | 1929/30 | | 0-46 |

† *he made 51 in his first test innings in his second test*

## YOUNGEST CENTURY MAKERS

| | | |
|---|---|---|
| 19 years 121 days† | Vivian H.G. 100 v South Africa at Wellington | 1931/32 |
| 20 years 91 days | Williamson K.S. 131 v India at Ahmedabad | 2010/11 |

† *world record at that time*

## OLDEST CENTURY MAKERS

| | | |
|---|---|---|
| 41 years 109 days | Sutcliffe B. 151* v India at Calcutta | 1964/65 |
| 39 years 12 days | Congdon B.E. 107* v Australia at Christchurch | 1976/77 |

## YOUNGEST CAPTAINS

| | | | |
|---|---|---|---|
| 23 years 319 days | Fleming S.P. v England at Christchurch | 1996/97 | 62 & 11 |
| 25 years 252 days | Parker J.M. v Pakistan at Karachi | 1976/77 | 24 & 16 |
| 25 years 355 days | Williamson K.S. v Zimbabwe at Bulawayo | 2016 | 91 |

## OLDEST CAPTAINS *(age on last day of final test)*

| | | | | |
|---|---|---|---|---|
| 37 years 40 days | Reid J.R. v England at Leeds | 1965 | 54 & 5 | |
| 37 years 22 days | Congdon B.E. v England at Christchurch | 1974/75 | 38 | 0-27 |
| 36 years 150 days | Burgess M.G. v Australia at Perth | 1980/81 | 43 & 18 | |
| 36 years 88 days | Wallace W.M. v South Africa at Auckland | 1952/53 | 23 | |

## LONGEST INTERVAL BETWEEN TEST APPEARANCES

| | |
|---|---|
| 14 years 28 days | Cleverley D.C. — v South Africa at Christchurch 1/3/1932 |
| | v Australia at Wellington 29/3/1946 |

*Only A.J. Traicos (22 years 222 days), G. Gunn (17 years 316 days), Younis Ahmed (17 years 111 days) and J.M.M. Commaille (14 years 95 days) have a longer interval between tests but Cleverley is unique in that the above matches were his only two tests.*

# NEW ZEALAND
# LIMITED-OVERS RECORDS

This section of the *Almanack* is devoted to limited-overs matches in New Zealand (other than one-day internationals) and has been compiled from the following games:

1.  1121 matches in national competitions (Shell Cup, State Shield, Ford Trophy etc) from 1971/72 to 2021/22.

2.  55 matches between provincial sides and overseas teams from 1970/71 to 2007/08.

| | |
|---|---|
| 1970/71 | Wellington v MCC |
| | Otago v MCC |
| | Central Districts v MCC |
| 1972/73 | Central Districts v Pakistan |
| 1973/74 | Wellington v Australia |
| | Central Districts v Australia |
| 1975/76 | Wellington v India |
| 1977/78 | Northern Districts v England XI |
| 1978/79 | Auckland v Pakistan |
| | Canterbury v Pakistan |
| 1979/80 | Auckland XI v West Indies |
| | Central Districts v West Indies |
| 1981/82 | Northern Districts v Australia |
| | Central Districts v Australia |
| 1983/84 | Otago v England XI |
| 1984/85 | Wellington v New South Wales |
| 1985/86 | Auckland v Australia |
| 1986/87 | Auckland v West Indies |
| | Central Districts v South Australia *(4 matches)* |
| 1987/88 | Wellington v England |
| | Auckland v Victoria *(2 matches)* |
| | Wellington v Queensland |
| | Canterbury v Queensland |
| | Otago v Queensland |
| 1988/89 | Auckland v Pakistan |
| 1991/92 | Auckland v England |
| | Auckland v Australia |
| | Northern Districts v Zimbabwe *(2 matches)* |
| 1993/94 | Canterbury v New South Wales |
| 1994/95 | Auckland v West Indies |
| | Central Districts v India |
| | Wellington v South Africa |
| | Canterbury v Sri Lanka |
| 1996/97 | Central Districts v Sri Lanka |
| 1997/98 | Canterbury v Bangladesh |
| 1998/99 | Northern v Pakistan A |
| 2000/01 | Wellington v New South Wales |
| | Canterbury v Zimbabwe |
| 2001/02 | Northern Districts v England *(2 matches)* |
| 2003/04 | Wellington v Pakistan |
| | Northern Districts v South Africa |
| 2004/05 | Central Districts v Sri Lanka |
| 2007/08 | Northern Districts v Bangladesh *(2 matches)* |
| | Auckland v Bangladesh |
| | Canterbury v England *(2 matches)* |

3.  Three matches in the Data General competition in 1986/87.

4.  Six matches in the Shell Shield competition in 1997/98.

5. 39 other matches not involving provincial sides.

| | |
|---|---|
| 1972/73 | New Zealand Under 23 XI v Pakistan |
| 1976/77 | Australia v Invitation XIs *(2 matches)* |
| 1981/82 | North Island v South Island |
| 1982/83 | Sri Lanka v NZ Minor Associations *(2 matches)* |
| 1992/93 | New Zealand President's XI v Australia |
| 1993/94 | North Island v South Island |
| | Sir Ron Brierley XI v Pakistan |
| 1994/95 | North Island v South Island |
| | Sir Ron Brierley XI v West Indies |
| | New Zealand Academy XI v Sri Lanka |
| | New Zealand Academy XI v Australian Academy XI |
| 1996/97 | New Zealand Academy XI v England |
| 1997/98 | New Zealand Academy XI v Zimbabwe |
| 1998/99 | New Zealand A v Pakistan A *(3 matches)* |
| | New Zealand Academy XI v South Africa |
| 1999/00 | New Zealand Academy XI v England A *(2 matches)* |
| | New Zealand A v England A *(3 matches)* |
| 2000/01 | North Island Selection XI v Sri Lanka |
| 2003/04 | South Island v North Island |
| | New Zealand A v Sri Lanka A *(2 matches)* |
| 2004/05 | New Zealand v FICA World XI *(3 matches)* |
| | North Island v South Island |
| 2008/09 | New Zealand A v England Lions *(2 matches)* |
| 2017/18 | New Zealand XI v Pakistan |
| 2018/19 | New Zealand A v India A *(3 matches)* |
| 2019/20 | New Zealand XI v India A *(2 matches)* |
| | New Zealand A v India A *(3 matches)* |

# TEAM RECORDS

## Highest Totals

| | | | |
|---|---|---|---|
| 427-8 | Wellington v Otago | Wellington | 2020/21 |
| 417-6 | Central Districts v Northern Districts | Hamilton | 2012/13 |
| 410-5 | Canterbury v Otago | Timaru | 2009/10 |
| 407-4 | Otago v Central Districts | Dunedin | 2019/20 |
| 405 | Central Districts v Canterbury | New Plymouth | 2014/15 |
| 405-6 | Central Districts v Canterbury | Timaru | 2014/15 |
| 405-6 | Central Districts v Canterbury | New Plymouth | 2015/16 |
| 401-8 | Central Districts v Northern Districts | New Plymouth | 2016/17 |
| 401-8 | Auckland v Canterbury | Christchurch | 2019/20 |

## Lowest Totals

| | | | |
|---|---|---|---|
| 48 | Pakistan v Auckland | Auckland | 1988/89 |
| 58 | Central Districts v Wellington | Wellington | 2001/02 |
| 64 | Otago v Wellington | Alexandra | 1984/85 |
| 64 | Otago v Central Districts | Invercargill | 2004/05 |
| 66 | Wellington v Canterbury | Wellington | 1996/97 |
| 67 | Otago v Central Districts | Invercargill | 2000/01 |
| 67 | Central Districts v Canterbury | Christchurch | 2002/03 |
| 70 | Auckland v Northern Districts | Pukekohe | 1977/78 |

**NZC**

## Most Extras in an Innings

| | | | |
|---|---|---|---|
| 55 | Northern Districts (271-8) v Wellington (228) | Hamilton | 2002/03 |
| 51 | NZ Academy XI (183)  v England A (184-4) | Lincoln | 1999/00 |
| 48 | Wellington (211-7)  v Otago (208-8) | Wellington | 1996/97 |
| 45 | Wellington (251-8)  v Otago (250-6) | Alexandra | 1997/98 |
| 45 | England A (219-7)  v New Zealand A (216) | Auckland | 1999/00 |

## Fewest Extras in an Innings

| | | | |
|---|---|---|---|
| 1 | Canterbury (205-6) | v Wellington (203) | Timaru | 1986/87 |
| 1 | New Zealand A (299-9) | v India A (300-5) | Mt Maunganui | 2018/19 |
| 2 | Pakistan (216-4) | v NZ Under 23 XI | Rotorua | 1972/73 |
| 2 | Otago (114) | v Canterbury (113) | Christchurch | 1979/80 |
| 2 | Auckland (163-4) | v Otago (162) | Oamaru | 1981/82 |
| 2 | Auckland (105) | v Otago (214-9) | Dunedin | 1993/94 |
| 2 | Otago (279-5) | v Central Districts (275-7) | Palmerston North | 2006/07 |
| 2 | Wellington (149) | v Auckland (230) | Auckland | 2009/10 |
| 2 | Canterbury (300-5) | v Wellington (299-7) | Christchurch | 2009/10 |
| 2 | Otago (222-7) | v Canterbury (221-9) | Rangiora | 2017/18 |

## Tied Matches

| | | |
|---|---|---|
| Wellington v South Africa | Wellington | 1994/95 |
| Northern Districts v Auckland | Hamilton | 2005/06 |
| Auckland v Canterbury | Auckland | 2009/10 |
| Northern Districts v Otago | Whangarei | 2010/11 |
| Wellington v Otago *(D/L)* | Wellington | 2015/16 |

## Close Finishes

**RUNS** *(winning team listed first)*

| | | | |
|---|---|---|---|
| 1 | Northern Districts v Canterbury | Hamilton | 1982/83 |
| 1 | Northern Districts v Zimbabwe | Pukekohe | 1991/92 |
| 1 | Auckland v Central Districts | Auckland | 1994/95 |
| 1 | Otago v Auckland | Alexandra | 1995/96 |
| 1 | Central Districts v Wellington | Wellington | 1996/97 |
| 1 | Northern Districts v Wellington *(D/L)* | Taupo | 2004/05 |
| 1 | Otago v Northern Districts | Taupo | 2005/06 |
| 1 | Canterbury v Northern Districts | Christchurch | 2019/20 |
| 1 | Otago v Northern Districts | Whangarei | 2021/22 |

**ONE WICKET** *(winning team listed first)*

| | | |
|---|---|---|
| Wellington v Auckland | Wellington | 1973/74 |
| Otago v Canterbury | Christchurch | 1979/80 |
| Central Districts v Australia | New Plymouth | 1981/82 |
| Canterbury v Central Districts | Christchurch | 1986/87 |
| Otago v Northern Districts | Gisborne | 1986/87 |
| Auckland v Northern Districts | Hamilton | 1989/90 |
| Otago v Auckland | Auckland | 1990/91 |
| Wellington v Otago | Alexandra | 1992/93 |
| Central Districts v Wellington | Masterton | 1993/94 |
| Wellington v Northern Districts | Wellington | 1996/97 |
| Central Districts v Canterbury | Napier | 1996/97 |
| Wellington v Northern Districts | Whangarei | 1999/00 |
| Auckland v Northern Districts | Auckland | 1999/00 |
| Otago v Wellington | Dunedin | 2000/01 |
| Central Districts v Wellington | Waikanae | 2000/01 |

| Canterbury v Auckland | Auckland | 2001/02 |
|---|---|---|
| Otago v Northern Districts | Invercargill | 2003/04 |
| Northern Districts v Wellington | Wellington | 2008/09 |
| Wellington v Otago | Invercargill | 2008/09 |
| Northern Districts v Central Districts | Palmerston North | 2010/11 |
| Auckland v Northern Districts | Auckland | 2014/15 |
| Northern Districts v Wellington | Wellington | 2019/20 |
| Wellington v Northern Districts | Wellington | 2020/21 |

**SCORES LEVEL** *(won by team listed first, having lost fewer wickets)*

| Otago (223-5) v Wellington (223-9) | Dunedin | 1979/80 |
|---|---|---|
| Canterbury (182-7) v Auckland (182-9) | Christchurch | 1983/84 |
| Canterbury (136-9) v Auckland (136) | Ashburton | 1985/86 |
| Queensland (174-8) v Wellington (174) | Wellington | 1987/88 |
| Wellington (227-8) v Auckland (227) | Wellington | 1995/96 |
| Canterbury (238-6) v Auckland (238-7) | Auckland | 1995/96 |

# Large Victories

**RUNS** *(winning team listed first)*

| 227 | Central Districts v Northern Districts | New Plymouth | 2016/17 |
|---|---|---|---|
| 222 | Otago v Northern Districts | Alexandra | 2014/15 |
| 221 | Otago v Wellington | Invercargill | 2015/16 |
| 219 | Auckland v Canterbury | Auckland | 2021/22 |
| 217 | Central Districts v Canterbury | New Plymouth | 2014/15 |
| 216 | Canterbury v Auckland | Rangiora | 2020/21 |
| 211 | Auckland v Central Districts | Auckland | 2012/13 |
| 210 | Otago v Auckland | Dunedin | 2019/20 |
| 200 | Central Districts v Otago | Hastings | 1998/99 |
| 200 | Central Districts v Otago | Invercargill | 2004/05 |
| 200 | Central Districts v Otago | Dunedin | 2021/22 |

**TEN WICKETS** *(winning team listed first)*

| Northern Districts (71-0) v Auckland (70) | Pukekohe | 1977/78 |
|---|---|---|
| West Indies (132-0) v Central Districts (130) | New Plymouth | 1979/80 |
| Canterbury (120-0) v Auckland (119) | Christchurch | 1987/88 |
| Auckland (81-0) v Central Districts (78) | New Plymouth | 1988/89 |
| Wellington (205-0) v Canterbury (202-7) | Wellington | 1994/95 |
| Auckland (164-0) v Central Districts (163) | Auckland | 1998/99 |
| Canterbury (97-0) v Central Districts (94) | Christchurch | 2013/14 |

# Most Run Outs

**INNINGS**

| 5 | Wellington v Auckland | Wellington | 1974/75 |
|---|---|---|---|
| 5 | Northern Districts v Wellington | Hamilton | 1992/93 |
| 5 | Central Districts v Northern Districts | Hamilton | 2000/01 |
| 5 | Otago v Canterbury | Alexandra | 2004/05 |

**MATCH**

| 7 | Wellington v Auckland | Wellington | 1974/75 |
|---|---|---|---|
| 7 | Auckland v Canterbury | Auckland | 1999/00 |

# INDIVIDUAL RECORDS
## Highest Scores

| | | | | |
|---|---|---|---|---|
| 222 | How J.M. | Central Districts v Northern Districts | Hamilton | 2012/13 |
| 194 | Worker G.H. | Central Districts v Canterbury | Timaru | 2014/15 |
| 181 | Worker G.H. | Central Districts v Northern Districts | New Plymouth | 2016/17 |
| 178 | Nicholls H.M. | Canterbury v Wellington | Wellington | 2014/15 |
| 177 | Pyke J.K. | South Australia v Central Districts | Palmerston North | 1986/87 |
| 177 | How J.M. | Central Districts v Canterbury | New Plymouth | 2014/15 |
| 174* | Munro C. | Auckland v Canterbury | Auckland | 2017/18 |
| 171* | Nicol R. J. | Canterbury v Northern Districts | Mt Maunganui | 2012/13 |
| 170 | McCullum B.B. | Otago v Auckland | Auckland | 2007/08 |
| 167 | Munro C. | Auckland v Canterbury | Christchurch | 2019/20 |
| 164 | Broom N.T. | Otago v Canterbury | Timaru | 2009/10 |
| 162* | Papps M.H.W | Wellington v Otago | Wellington | 2012/13 |
| 161 | Hartland B.R. | Canterbury v Northern Districts | Timaru | 1993/94 |
| 161 | McIntosh T.G. | Auckland v Otago | Auckland | 2010/11 |
| 159* | Vincent L. | Auckland v Canterbury | Christchurch | 2010/11 |
| 159 | Worker G.H. | Central Districts v Canterbury | New Plymouth | 2015/16 |
| 157 | Chapman M.S. | Auckland v Central Districts | Auckland | 2015/16 |
| 156 | Guptill M.J. | Auckland v Canterbury | Christchurch | 2009/10 |
| 156 | How J.M. | Central Districts v Auckland | Auckland | 2013/14 |
| 156 | Phillips G.D. | Auckland v Otago | Lincoln | 2019/20 |
| 155 | Rutherford H.D. | Otago v Central Districts | Dunedin | 2019/20 |
| 154 | Papps M.H.W | Wellington v Central Districts | Wellington | 2012/13 |
| 154 | Rutherford H.D. | Otago v Canterbury | Dunedin | 2018/19 |
| 153 | Vincent L. | Auckland v Canterbury | Christchurch | 2010/11 |
| 152* | Marshall J.A.H. | Northern Districts v Canterbury | Christchurch | 2006/07 |
| 152 | Solia S.M. | Auckland v Northern Districts | Auckland | 2016/17 |
| 151 | Munro C. | Auckland v Canterbury | Auckland | 2012/13 |
| 151 | Blundell T.A. | Wellington v Otago | Wellington | 2020/21 |
| 150 | Papps M.H.W. | Canterbury v Central Districts | Rangiora | 2009/10 |

## Fastest Centuries

| Balls | | | | |
|---|---|---|---|---|
| 49 | Taylor L.R.P.L. | Central Districts v Wellington | New Plymouth | 2021/22 |
| 50 | Fulton P.G. | Canterbury v Wellington | Rangiora | 2016/17 |
| 50 | Allen F.H. | Wellington v Otago | Wellington | 2020/21 |
| 52 | McCullum B.B. | Otago v Auckland | Auckland | 2007/08 |
| 54 | Fleming S.P. | New Zealand v FICA World XI | Christchurch | 2004/05 |
| 57 | Munro C. | Auckland v Canterbury | Christchurch | 2019/20 |
| 58 | Munro C. | Auckland v Otago | Auckland | 2019/20 |
| 59 | Kitchen A.K. | Otago v Northern Districts | Dunedin | 2016/17 |
| 60 | How J.M. | Central Districts v Northern Districts | Hamilton | 2012/13 |
| 61 | How J.M. | Central Districts v Canterbury | New Plymouth | 2014/15 |
| 63 | Latham T.W.M. | Canterbury v Auckland | Rangiora | 2020/21 |
| 65 | de Silva P.A. | Auckland v Canterbury | Auckland | 1996/97 |
| 65 | Munro C. | Auckland v Northern Districts | Lincoln | 2018/19 |
| 65 | Worker G.H. | Central Districts v Otago | New Plymouth | 2020/21 |
| 67 | Cooper H.R. | Northern Districts v Wellington | Hamilton | 2020/21 |
| 69 | Munro C. | Auckland v Otago | Alexandra | 2015/16 |
| 70 | Munro C. | Auckland v Canterbury | Auckland | 2012/13 |

# Fastest Fifties

**Balls**

| 16 | Bruce T.C. | Central Districts v Canterbury | New Plymouth | 2015/16 |
| 18 | Milne A.F. | Central Districts v Otago | Dunedin | 2021/22 |
| 19 | McGlashan P.D. | Northern Districts v Auckland | Hamilton | 2007/08 |
| 19 | Stewart S.L. | Canterbury v Otago | Timaru | 2009/10 |
| 20 | Cairns C.L. | Canterbury v Northern Districts | Timaru | 2002/03 |
| 20 | Napier G.R. | Central Districts v Northern Districts | Palmerston North | 2009/10 |
| 20 | Marshall H.J.H. | Wellington v Canterbury | Rangiora | 2016/17 |
| 20 | Carter L.J. | Canterbury v Northern Districts | Hamilton | 2021/22 |
| 21 | Rutherford H.R. | Otago v Central Districts | New Plymouth | 2020/21 |
| 22 | Maynard M.P. | Otago v Auckland | Alexandra | 1997/98 |
| 22 | Napier G.R. | England Lions v New Zealand A | Palmerston North | 2008/09 |
| 22 | Styris S.B. | Auckland v Otago | Oamaru | 2009/10 |
| 22 | Anderson C.J. | Northern Districts v Wellington | Wellington | 2011/12 |
| 22 | Bracewell D.A.J. | Central Districts v Auckland | Auckland | 2015/16 |
| 23 | Greatbatch M.J. | Central Districts v Otago | New Plymouth | 1996/97 |
| 23 | Butler I.G. | Otago v Canterbury | Timaru | 2009/10 |
| 23 | Bracewell D.A.J. | Central Districts v Canterbury | New Plymouth | 2014/15 |
| 23 | How J.M. | Central Districts v Wellington | Nelson | 2014/15 |
| 23 | Noema-Barnett K | Central Districts v Northern Districts | Gisborne | 2014/15 |
| 23 | Colson F.J. | Wellington v Central Districts | Wellington | 2019/20 |
| 24 | Ryder J.D. | Wellington v Otago | Invercargill | 2012/13 |
| 24 | van Beek L.V. | Wellington v Northern Districts | Wellington | 2017/18 |
| 24 | Bruce T.C. | Central Districts v Canterbury | Palmerston North | 2019/20 |
| 25 | Mascarenhas A.D. | Otago v Central Districts | New Plymouth | 2008/09 |

*Note: I.D.S. Smith reached fifty from 24 balls for Auckland v Central Districts at Auckland, 1989/90 but the game was abandoned and restarted the following day and none of the performances in the game are included in any records.*

# Most Wickets in an Innings

| 7-0-23-7 | Watson W. | Auckland v Otago | Auckland | 1984/85 |
| 8-1-28-7 | Penn A.J. | Wellington v Northern Districts | Mt Maunganui | 2000/01 |
| 10-1-35-7 | Rae M.D. | Otago v Auckland | Auckland | 2020/21 |
| 7.1-0-49-7 | Marshall E.J. | Otago v Auckland | Dunedin | 1993/94 |
| 10-5-12-6 | Barrett B.J. | Northern Districts v Otago | Gisborne | 1986/87 |
| 5.5-0-12-6 | Cairns C.L. | New Zealand v FICA World XI | Hamilton | 2004/05 |
| 10-2-19-6 | McCone R.J. | Canterbury v Northern Districts | Christchurch | 2013/14 |
| 9-2-20-6 | Thompson E.P. | Central Districts v Canterbury | New Plymouth | 2009/10 |
| 9.3-1-25-6 | Mason M.J. | Central Districts v Auckland | Auckland | 2003/04 |
| 9.5-3-26-6 | Vaughan J.T.C. | Auckland v Otago | Auckland | 1995/96 |
| 8-2-27-6 | Ferguson L.J. | Auckland v Northern Districts | Auckland | 2016/17 |
| 10-2-26-6 | Su'a M.L. | Auckland v Central Districts | New Plymouth | 1995/96 |
| 10-1-30-6 | Davey S.B. | Canterbury v Wellington | Christchurch | 2020/21 |
| 7.7-2-31-6 | Intikhab Alam | Pakistan v NZ Under 23 XI | Rotorua | 1972/73 |
| 8-2-34-6 | Ferguson L.H. | Auckland v Northern Districts | Auckland | 2021/22 |
| 10-1-35-6 | Duffy J.A. | Otago v Canterbury | Christchurch | 2018/19 |
| 10-1-37-6 | Cairns C.L. | Canterbury v Wellington | Christchurch | 1996/97 |
| 8.3-0-38-6 | Gillespie M.R. | Wellington v Northern Districts | Wellington | 2012/13 |
| 9.3-0-41-6 | McClenaghan M.J. | Auckland v Wellington | Auckland | 2011/12 |
| 9.3-0-43-6 | Wisneski W.A. | Canterbury v Auckland | Christchurch | 1996/97 |
| 10-1-45-6 | Bennett H.K. | Canterbury v Auckland | Auckland | 2007/08 |
| 10-0-45-6 | Henry M.J. | Canterbury v Auckland | Auckland | 2012/13 |
| 10-1-49-6 | Penn A.J. | Central Districts v Northern Districts | Napier | 1996/97 |
| 9.3-0-51-6 | Lister B.G. | Auckland v Northern Districts | Whangarei | 2019/20 |

# Most Expensive Bowling

| | | | | |
|---|---|---|---|---|
| 10-0-97-5 | Ellis A.M. | Canterbury v Central Districts | New Plymouth | 2014/15 |
| 10-0-97-2 | Ellis A.M. | Canterbury v Central Districts | New Plymouth | 2015/16 |
| 10-0-95-1 | Kuggeleijn S.C. | Northern Districts v Otago | Dunedin | 2016/17 |
| 10-0-93-2 | Presland C.M. | Northern Districts v Auckland | Gisborne | 1982/83 |
| 10-3-92-1 | Yasir Arafat | Otago v Auckland | Oamaru | 2009/10 |
| 10-1-92-0 | Arnel B.J. | Northern Districts v Canterbury | Mt Maunganui | 2012/13 |
| 10-0-90-1 | Ellis A.M. | Canterbury v Central Districts | Timaru | 2014/15 |
| 10-0-90-0 | Arnel B.J. | Wellington v Canterbury | Wellington | 2014/15 |

**ALSO NOTE** *(8-ball overs)*

| | | | | |
|---|---|---|---|---|
| 1-0-18-0 | Payton D.H. | Central Districts v Wellington | Wellington | 1973/74 |
| 1-0-18-1 | Redpath I.R. | Australia v Central Districts | New Plymouth | 1973/74 |
| 2-0-29-0 | Child M.J. | Northern Districts v Central Districts | Palmerston North | 1975/76 |
| 3-0-37-0 | Dunning B. | Northern Districts v Canterbury | Christchurch | 1977/78 |
| 4-0-42-1 | Maingay C.T. | Auckland v Wellington | Wellington | 1971/72 |
| 5-0-48-0 | Coles M.J. | Wellington v Canterbury | Christchurch | 1975/76 |
| 6-0-56-0 | Cater S.B. | Wellington v Auckland | Auckland | 1977/78 |
| 6-0-56-0 | Gilmour G.J. | Australia v Invitation XI | Christchurch | 1976/77 |
| 7-0-68-1 | Aldridge C.W. | Northern Districts v Auckland | Auckland | 1978/79 |

**ALSO NOTE** *(6-ball overs)*

| | | | | |
|---|---|---|---|---|
| 1-0-22-0 | Pryor C.R. | Auckland v Wellington | Wellington | 1998/99 |
| 1-0-22-0 | Solia S.M. | Auckland v Northern Districts | Lincoln | 2018/19 |
| 1.5-0-27-0 | Houghton M.V. | Wellington v Auckland | Auckland | 2007/08 |
| 2-0-33-0 | Sears B.V. | Wellington v Central Districts | New Plymouth | 2021/22 |
| 3-0-42-1 | McMillan C.D. | Canterbury v Central Districts | Napier | 1996/97 |
| 3.1-0-57-0 | Muralitharan M. | FICA World XI v New Zealand | Christchurch | 2004/05 |
| 4-0-53-0 | Toole R.L. | Central Districts v Otago | New Plymouth | 2020/21 |
| 5-0-63-1 | de Grandhomme C. | Northern Districts v Canterbury | Hamilton | 2021/22 |
| 6-0-81-1 | McKay J.D. | Otago v Central Districts | Dunedin | 2021/22 |
| 8-0-81-0 | Hutchinson D.S. | Wellington v Central Districts | Palmerston North | 2015/16 |

# Most Economical Bowling

| | | | | |
|---|---|---|---|---|
| 10-7-5-2 | Boock S.L. | Otago v Central Districts | Alexandra | 1986/87 |
| 10-5-6-2 | Larsen G.R. | Wellington v Otago | Alexandra | 1992/93 |
| *8-3-7-2 | Williams J.C. | Auckland v Northern Districts | Auckland | 1971/72 |
| 10-6-8-1 | Hills P.W. | Otago v Auckland | Oamaru | 1981/82 |
| 10-6-8-2 | Nuttall A.J. | Canterbury v Wellington | Christchurch | 1988/89 |
| 10-4-8-0 | Duff S.W. | Central Districts v Wellington | New Plymouth | 1989/90 |
| 10-5-8-3 | Vaughan J.T.C. | Auckland v Central Districts | Waikanae | 1993/94 |
| 10-5-8-1 | Harris C.Z. | Canterbury v Auckland | Christchurch | 1995/96 |
| *7-0-9-0 | Dunning B. | Northern Districts v Canterbury | Christchurch | 1976/77 |
| 10-6-9-1 | Boock S.L. | Otago v Canterbury | Christchurch | 1979/80 |
| 10-4-9-1 | de Mel A.L.F. | Sri Lanka v Minor Associations | Wanganui | 1982/83 |
| 10-5-9-2 | Astle N.J. | Canterbury v Northern Districts | Christchurch | 1991/92 |
| 10-4-9-2 | Astle N.J. | Canterbury v Wellington | Christchurch | 1993/94 |
| 10-3-9-1 | de Groen R.P. | Northern Districts v Central Districts | Levin | 1995/96 |
| 10-6-9-2 | McCullum N.J. | Otago v Auckland | Auckland | 2000/01 |
| *7-1-10-2 | Kirk C.M. | Canterbury v Otago | Christchurch | 1973/74 |
| 10-5-10-3 | McIntyre J.M. | Auckland v Canterbury | Auckland | 1980/81 |
| 10-4-10-2 | Pigott A.C.S. | Wellington v Northern Districts | Tauranga | 1983/84 |
| 10-6-10-0 | Bracewell J.G. | Auckland v Canterbury | Auckland | 1986/87 |
| 10-7-10-4 | Duers K.G. | Zimbabwe v Northern Districts | Cambridge | 1991/92 |

| 10-3-10-2 | Williams B.R. | Wellington v Northern Districts | Gisborne | 1993/94 |
| 10-3-10-3 | Larsen G.R. | Wellington v Canterbury | Rangiora | 1994/95 |

\* 8-ball overs

*(Note: C.M. Brown had figures of 10-5-6-2 for Auckland v Otago at Dunedin, 1993/94 but the game was abandoned and none of the performances in the game are included in any records).*

## Hat-tricks

| 7-0-23-7 | Watson W. | Auckland v Otago | Auckland | 1984/85 |
| 10-0-48-4 | Briasco P.S. | Central Districts v Auckland | Napier | 1989/90 |
| 10-1-40-3 | Walker M.D.J. | Wellington v Otago | Dunedin | 2000/01 |

## Wicketkeeping

### DISMISSALS

| | *(ct/st)* | | | | |
|---|---|---|---|---|---|
| 7 | (7/0) | Johns L.R. | Wellington v Canterbury | Wellington | 2018/19 |
| 6 | (5/1) | Murray D.A. | West Indies v Central Districts | New Plymouth | 1979/80 |
| 6 | (6/0) | McSweeney E.B. | Wellington v Auckland | Wellington | 1982/83 |
| 6 | (6/0) | McSweeney E.B. | Wellington v Northern Districts | Wellington | 1988/89 |
| 6 | (6/0) | McRae G.P. | Central Districts v Wellington | Masterton | 1994/95 |
| 6 | (6/0) | Hopkins G.J. | Auckland v Central Districts | Auckland | 2012/13 |

### THREE STUMPINGS IN AN INNINGS

| Milburn B.D. | Otago v Wellington | Alexandra | 1982/83 |
| Rixon S.J. | NSW v Wellington | Wellington | 1984/85 |
| Dyer G.C. | NSW v Wellington | Wellington | 1986/87 |

## Fielding

### CATCHES

| 5 | Wilson J.W. | Otago v Auckland | Dunedin | 1993/94 |
| 4 | Redmond R.E. | Auckland v Otago | Auckland | 1972/73 |
| 4 | Sampson H.C. | Otago v Canterbury | Christchurch | 1974/75 |
| 4 | Howarth G.P. | Invitation XI v Australia | Auckland | 1976/77 |
| 4 | Wiltshire J.R. | Auckland v Northern Districts | Auckland | 1978/79 |
| 4 | Dickeson C.W. | Northern Districts v Canterbury | Hamilton | 1980/81 |
| 4 | Cooper B.G. | Northern Districts v Central Districts | Palmerston North | 1982/83 |
| 4 | Hore A.J. | Otago v Canterbury | Christchurch | 1998/99 |
| 4 | Brownlie D.G. | Northern Districts v Central Districts | New Plymouth | 2014/15 |
| 4 | Beghin G.K. | Auckland v Canterbury | Christchurch | 2017/18 |
| 4 | Raval J.A. | Northern Districts v Otago | Whangarei | 2021/22 |

# HISTORY OF THE LIMITED-OVER COMPETITION IN NEW ZEALAND

2021/22 was the 51st season of limited over competition among the six New Zealand first-class sides. In that time there have been several changes both in sponsorship and format.

For the first six seasons a knock-out competition was sponsored by the New Zealand Motor Corporation. Each innings was limited to 40 eight-ball overs during the initial two seasons, reduced to 35 thereafter. In 1977/78 and 1978/79 the sponsors changed and the teams competed for the Gillette Cup. In the first season 30 eight-ball overs were used but the limit reverted to 35 the following year. There was no sponsorship for the competition in 1979/80, known simply as the National Knock-out, where 50 six-ball overs was the limit for each innings.

In 1980/81, the Shell Cup, previously contested for as part of the first-class season, became the limited-over prize and the contest was run on a league basis for the first time with each side playing the other once.

In keeping with the previous limited-over competitions, a final was arranged, this time between the top two teams of the league table, points gained being disregarded at this stage. Fifty six-ball overs was the limit on each innings.

From 1985/86 the competition was held, in its entirety, prior to the Shell Trophy series with no final. From 1989/90 the top four teams in the league table went on to semi-final play-offs, previous points being disregarded. The top two teams gained home ground advantage, the venue for the final being decided in a similar manner.

From 1993/94 to 1998/99 the top two sides played each other, with the winner going into the grand final. The loser then played the winner of the game between third and fourth to find the other finalist. From 1999/00, the leading team after the round robin went straight to the final with the second and third-placed sides meeting in a semi-final to find the other finalist. The finals became a best-of-three series.

From 2001/02 to 2008/09 the competition was known as the State Shield and the format remained unaltered except the final reverted to a single game. In 2009/10 and 2010/11, with no sponsor, the tournament was reduced to eight games but the semi-finals were increased to three games with the top four sides taking part. In 2011/12 it became the Ford Trophy, played under the same conditions.

From 2018/19 the competition was played over two full rounds (ten games each) with the top-placed side after the round robin qualifying to host the final and the second and third teams playing in an eliminator to determine the other finalist.

## Winners of Limited-over Competitions

**NEW ZEALAND MOTOR CORPORATION KNOCK-OUT**

| | |
|---|---|
| 1971/72 | Canterbury |
| 1972/73 | Auckland |
| 1973/74 | Wellington |
| 1974/75 | Wellington |
| 1975/76 | Canterbury |
| 1976/77 | Canterbury |

**GILLETTE CUP**

| | |
|---|---|
| 1977/78 | Canterbury |
| 1978/79 | Auckland |

**NATIONAL KNOCK-OUT**

| | |
|---|---|
| 1979/80 | Northern Districts |

**SHELL CUP**

| | |
|---|---|
| 1980/81 | Auckland |
| 1981/82 | Wellington |
| 1982/83 | Auckland |
| 1983/84 | Auckland |
| 1984/85 | Central Districts |
| 1985/86 | Canterbury |
| 1986/87 | Auckland |
| 1987/88 | Otago |
| 1988/89 | Wellington |
| 1989/90 | Auckland |
| 1990/91 | Wellington |
| 1991/92 | Canterbury |
| 1992/93 | Canterbury |
| 1993/94 | Canterbury |
| 1994/95 | Northern Districts |
| 1995/96 | Canterbury |

| | |
|---|---|
| 1996/97 | Canterbury |
| 1997/98 | Northern Districts |
| 1998/99 | Canterbury |
| 1999/00 | Canterbury |
| 2000/01 | Central Districts |

**STATE SHIELD**

| | |
|---|---|
| 2001/02 | Wellington |
| 2002/03 | Northern Districts |
| 2003/04 | Central Districts |
| 2004/05 | Northern Districts |
| 2005/06 | Canterbury |
| 2006/07 | Auckland |
| 2007/08 | Otago |
| 2008/09 | Northern Districts |

**ONE-DAY COMPETITION**

| | |
|---|---|
| 2009/10 | Northern Districts |
| 2010/11 | Auckland |

**FORD TROPHY**

| | |
|---|---|
| 2011/12 | Central Districts |
| 2012/13 | Auckland |
| 2013/14 | Wellington |
| 2014/15 | Central Districts |
| 2015/16 | Central Districts |
| 2016/17 | Canterbury |
| 2017/18 | Auckland |
| 2018/19 | Wellington |
| 2019/20 | Auckland |
| 2020/21 | Canterbury |
| 2021/22 | Auckland |

## Table of Results

*1971/72 — 2021/22*

|  | P | W | L | T | NR |
|---|---|---|---|---|---|
| Auckland | 390 | 191 | 173 | 2 | 24 |
| Canterbury | 392 | 206 | 159 | 1 | 26 |
| Central Districts | 371 | 159 | 181 | – | 31 |
| Northern Districts | 379 | 175 | 188 | 2 | 14 |
| Otago | 365 | 140 | 201 | 2 | 22 |
| Wellington | 381 | 195 | 164 | 1 | 21 |

*The Auckland and Central Districts totals include a match won by the toss of a coin against Central Districts and Northern Districts respectively.*

# INTER-PROVINCIAL RECORDS

|  | Highest Score | Lowest Score | Highest Individual Score | Best Bowling |
|---|---|---|---|---|
| **Auckland** | 401-8 v Canterbury 2019/20 | 70 v ND 1977/78 | C. Munro 174* v Canterbury 2017/18 | W. Watson 7-0-23-7 v Otago 1984/85 |
| **Canterbury** | 410-5 v Otago 2009/10 | 75 v Otago 1973/74 | H.M. Nicholls 178 v Wellington 2014/15 | R.J. McCone 10-2-19-6 v ND 2013/14 |
| **Central Districts** | 417-6 v ND 2012/13 | 58 v Wellington 2001/02 | J.M. How 222 v ND 2012/13 | E.P. Thompson 9-2-20-6 v Canterbury 2009/10 |
| **Northern Districts** | 398 v CD 2012/13 | 76 v CD 1987/88 | J.A.H. Marshall 152* v Canterbury 2006/07 | B.J. Barrett 10-5-12-6 v Otago 1986/87 |
| **Otago** | 407-4 v CD 2019/20 | 64 v Wellington 1984/85 v CD 2004/05 | B.B. McCullum 170* v Auckland 2007/08 | M.D. Rae 10-1-35-7 v Auckland 2020/21 |
| **Wellington** | 427-8 v Otago 2020/21 | 66 v Canterbury 1996/97 | M.H.W. Papps 162* v Otago 2012/13 | A.J. Penn 8-1-28-7 v ND 2000/01 |

|  | *Most Economical Bowling* | *Most Expensive Bowling* | *Most Dismissals in an Innings* |
|---|---|---|---|
| **Auckland** | J.T.C. Vaughan 10-5-8-3 v CD 1993/94 J.C. Williams 8-3-7-2 v ND 1971/72* | L.H. Ferguson 10-0-87-0 v CD 2015/16 | G.J. Hopkins 6c v CD 2012/13 |
| **Canterbury** | A.J. Nuttall 10-6-8-2 v Wellington 1988/89 C.Z. Harris 10-5-8-1 v Auckland 1995/96 | A.M.Ellis 10-0-97-5 v CD 2014/15 A.M.Ellis 10-0-97-2 v CD 2015/16 | L.K. Germon 5c v Otago 1988/89 |
| **Central Districts** | S.W. Duff 10-4-8-0 v Wellington 1989/90 | B.M. Wheeler 8-0-89-1 v ND 2012/13 | G.P. McRae 6c v Wellington 1994/95 |
| **Northern Districts** | R.P. de Groen 10-3-9-1 v CD 1995/96 | S.C. Kuggeleijn 10-0-95-1 v Otago 2016/17 | M.J.E. Wright 5c v Auckland 1982/83 |
| **Otago** | S.L. Boock 10-7-5-2 v C.D. 1986/87 | Yasir Arafat 10-3-92-1 v Canterbury 2009/10 | B.D. Milburn 5c v CD 1982/83 J.W. Wilson 5c v Auckland 1993/94 |
| **Wellington** | G.R. Larsen 10-5-6-2 v Otago 1992/93 | B.J.Arnel 10-0-90-0 v Canterbury 2014/15 | L.R. Johns 7c v Canterbury 2018/19 |

* *8-ball overs*

# RECORD PARTNERSHIPS

## AUCKLAND

| | | | | | |
|---|---|---|---|---|---|
| 1st | 260 | Guptill M.J. & Worker G.H. | v Otago | Auckland | 2021/22 |
| 2nd | 237 | Worker G.H. & Chapman M.S. | v Wellington | Wellington | 2021/22 |
| 3rd | 242 | Jones R.A. & Nicol R.J. | v Northern Districts | Auckland | 2007/08 |
| 4th | 185 | Worker G.H. & O'Donnell R.R. | v Northern Districts | Auckland | 2021/22 |
| 5th † | 229 | Munro C. & de Grandhomme C. | v Canterbury | Auckland | 2012/13 |
| 6th | 116 | Munro C. & Grobbelaar D.J. | v Canterbury | Auckland | 2012/13 |
| 7th | 126 | Chapman M.S. & Grobbelaar D.J. | v Central Districts | Auckland | 2015/16 |
| 8th | 121 | Canning T.K. & Morgan R.G. | v Otago | Alexandra | 2000/01 |
| 9th | 81 | Grobbelaar D.J. & Bates M.D. | v Central Districts | Auckland | 2014/15 |
| 10th | 65* | Bates M.D. & Quinn M.R. | v Canterbury | Timaru | 2014/15 |

## CANTERBURY

| | | | | | |
|---|---|---|---|---|---|
| 1st | 168 | Papps M.H.W. & Astle N.J. | v Wellington | Timaru | 2004/05 |
| 2nd † | 291 | Nicholls H.M. & Broom N.T. | v Wellington | Wellington | 2014/15 |
| 3rd | 174 | McMillan C.D. & Latham R.T. | v Central Districts | Christchurch | 1994/95 |
| 4th † | 221 | Howell L.G. & Stead G.R. | v Otago | Oamaru | 1997/98 |
| 5th | 198 | Cairns C.L. & Germon L.K. | v Wellington | Christchurch | 1992/93 |
| 6th | 142 | Cairns C.L. & Fleming S.P. | v Central Districts | Napier | 1993/94 |
| 7th | 124 | Ellis A.M. & Jamieson K.A. | v Central Districts | Palmerston Nth | 2017/18 |
| 8th | 91 | Harris C.Z. & Wiseman P.J. | v Central Districts | Christchurch | 2003/04 |
| 9th | 62 | van Beek L.V. & Henry M.J. | v Auckland | Auckland | 2012/13 |
| 10th | 57* | Williams W.S.A. & Sheat F.W. | v Auckland | Auckland | 2017/18 |

## CENTRAL DISTRICTS

| | | | | | |
|---|---|---|---|---|---|
| 1st † | 321 | Raval J.A. & How J.M. | v Northern Districts | Hamilton | 2012/13 |
| 2nd | 224 | Worker G.H. & Smith B.S. | v Otago | Nelson | 2019/20 |
| 3rd | 231 | Robinson D.S. & Sinclair M.S. | v Canterbury | Rangiora | 2011/12 |
| 4th | 147 | Young W.A. & Bruce T.C. | v Northern Districts | New Plymouth | 2015/16 |
| 5th | 211 | Young W.A. & Clarkson J.A. | v Auckland | Auckland | 2017/18 |
| 6th | 115 | Cleaver D. & Schmulian B.D. | v Northern Districts | Lincoln | 2019/20 |
| 7th † | 163 | Ryder J.D. & Wheeler B.M. | v Canterbury | Christchurch | 2015/16 |
| 8th | 105 | Wheeler B.M. & McCone R.J. | v Wellington | Lincoln | 2018/19 |
| 9th | 92 | Loveridge G.R. & Penn A.J. | v Canterbury | Napier | 1996/97 |
| 10th | 50 | Garner C.D. & Alcock A.J. | v Otago | Oamaru | 1993/94 |

## NORTHERN DISTRICTS

| | | | | | |
|---|---|---|---|---|---|
| 1st | 181 | Flynn D.R. & Devcich A P | v Otago | Mt Maunganui | 2012/13 |
| 2nd | 240 | Watling B-J. & Flynn D.R. | v Wellington | Whangarei | 2007/08 |
| 3rd | 210 | Flynn D.R. & Marshall J.A.H. | v Canterbury | Christchurch | 2007/08 |
| 4th | 155 | Mitchell D.J. & Marshall J.A.H. | v Central Districts | Nelson | 2012/13 |
| 5th | 157 | Brownlie D.G. & Mitchell D.J. | v Wellington | Wellington | 2017/18 |
| 6th † | 196 | Williamson K.S. & McGlashan P.D. | v Canterbury | Hamilton | 2008/09 |
| 7th | 119 | Devcich A.P. & Hiini B.C. | v Otago | Hamilton | 2011/12 |
| 8th | 93* | Southee T.G. & Aldridge G.W. | v Auckland | Hamilton | 2012/13 |
| 9th † | 117 | Mitchell D.J. & Baker J.D. | v Central Districts | New Plymouth | 2015/16 |
| 10th | 62 | Aldridge G.W. & Butler I.G. | v Canterbury | Hamilton | 2003/04 |

NZC

**OTAGO**

| | | | | | |
|---|---|---|---|---|---|
| 1st | 189 | Rutherford H.D. & Renwick M. | v Central Districts | Dunedin | 2019/20 |
| 2nd | 158 | Bracewell M.G. & Broom N.T. | v Auckland | Invercargill | 2015/16 |
| 3rd | 194 | McCullum B.B. & Cumming C.D. | v Auckland | Auckland | 2007/08 |
| 4th | 190 | Trott I.J.L. & Broom N.T. | v Northern Districts | Hamilton | 2005/06 |
| 5th | 150 | McCullum N.L. & Robertson I.A. | v Wellington | Queenstown | 2014/15 |
| 6th | 165* | Broom D.J. & de Boorder D.C. | v Northern Districts | Queenstown | 2010/11 |
| 7th | 122* | Kitchen A.K. & Muller T. | v Auckland | Auckland | 2021/22 |
| 8th † | 146 | Rippon M.J.G. & Viljoen C. | v Wellington | Dunedin | 2018/19 |
| 9th | 59 | Wagner N. & Scott B.E. | v Central Districts | Dunedin | 2014/15 |
| | 59 | Wagner N. & Scott B.E. | v Canterbury | Alexandra | 2015/16 |
| 10th † | 67 | Smith N.G. & Rae M.D. | v Wellington | Wellington | 2020/21 |

**WELLINGTON**

| | | | | | |
|---|---|---|---|---|---|
| 1st | 222 | Fletcher A.T. & Ravindra R. | v Auckland | Lincoln | 2019/20 |
| 2nd | 273 | Papps M.H.W. & Murdoch S.J. | v Otago | Wellington | 2012/13 |
| 3rd † | 244* | Fleming S.P. & Twose R.G. | v Otago | Wellington | 2000/01 |
| 4th | 162 | Parlane N.R. & Elliott G.D. | v Northern Districts | Wellington | 2008/09 |
| 5th | 137 | Blundell T.A. & Neesham J.D.S. | v Canterbury | Wellington | 2019/20 |
| 6th | 122 | Franklin J.E.C. & Woodcock L.J. | v Northern Districts | Wellington | 2012/13 |
| 7th | 130* | Bell M.D. & Mather S.R. | v Northern Districts | Mt Maunganui | 1997/98 |
| 8th | 98* | Taylor B.R. & Collinge R.O. | v Central Districts | Lower Hutt | 1971/72 |
| 9th | 98 | Doull L.J. & Williams B.R. | v Otago | Alexandra | 1993/94 |
| 10th | 42 | Woodcock L.J. & O'Brien I.E. | v Canterbury | Christchurch | 2008/09 |
| | 42 | Gillespie M.R. & McKay A.J. | v Auckland | Wellington | 2010/11 |

† *record for all teams*

# DOMESTIC ONE-DAY CAREER RECORDS

| **BATTING** | | *M* | *In* | *NO* | *HS* | *Runs* | *Ave* | *100s* | *50s* |
|---|---|---|---|---|---|---|---|---|---|
| Papps M.H.W. | *C, W* | 141 | 140 | 9 | 162* | 5163 | 39.41 | 11 | 28 |
| Worker G.H. | *CD, C, A* | 117 | 116 | 9 | 194 | 5069 | 47.37 | 16 | 27 |
| Broom N.T. | *C, O* | 137 | 127 | 13 | 164 | 4644 | 40.73 | 9 | 30 |
| Sinclair M.S. | *CD* | 143 | 137 | 22 | 123 | 4398 | 38.24 | 3 | 36 |
| Parlane M.E. | *ND, W* | 153 | 152 | 10 | 132 | 4225 | 29.75 | 5 | 23 |
| Harris C.Z. | *C* | 145 | 133 | 45 | 107 | 3893 | 44.23 | 1 | 23 |
| Nicol R.J. | *A, C, O* | 121 | 119 | 10 | 171* | 3864 | 35.44 | 5 | 24 |
| Marshall J.A.H. | *ND* | 120 | 114 | 10 | 152* | 3755 | 36.10 | 5 | 25 |
| Stewart S.L. | *C* | 108 | 107 | 9 | 120 | 3432 | 35.02 | 4 | 18 |
| Hopkins G.J. | *ND, C, O, A* | 156 | 139 | 22 | 142 | 3401 | 29.06 | 4 | 13 |
| Cumming C.D. | *C , O* | 124 | 117 | 8 | 123 | 3379 | 31.00 | 4 | 19 |
| Nevin C.J. | *W* | 136 | 129 | 10 | 149 | 3339 | 28.05 | 5 | 15 |
| Watling B-J. | *ND* | 90 | 89 | 11 | 145* | 3288 | 42.15 | 7 | 22 |
| Astle N.J. | *C* | 99 | 90 | 12 | 131 | 3285 | 42.11 | 8 | 16 |
| Fulton P.G. | *C* | 113 | 104 | 9 | 116* | 3274 | 34.46 | 3 | 25 |
| Kitchen A.K. | *A, O* | 115 | 111 | 11 | 143* | 3193 | 31.93 | 5 | 15 |
| How J.M. | *CD* | 105 | 103 | 4 | 222 | 3159 | 31.90 | 3 | 20 |
| Bell M.D. | *ND, W* | 130 | 124 | 10 | 124 | 3058 | 26.82 | 4 | 14 |
| Howell L.G. | *C. CD, A, ND* | 105 | 105 | 14 | 134* | 3022 | 33.20 | 5 | 22 |

## BOWLING

| | | M | O | M | R | W | Ave | R/O | Best |
|---|---|---|---|---|---|---|---|---|---|
| Aldridge G.W. | ND | 131 | 1002.4 | 66 | 4844 | 178 | 27.21 | 4.83 | 5-34 |
| Martin C.S. | C, A | 103 | 854.2 | 73 | 4125 | 150 | 27.50 | 4.83 | 5-21 |
| Harris C.Z. | C | 145 | 1153.4 | 72 | 4336 | 138 | 31.42 | 3.76 | 4-28 |
| Gillespie M.R. | W | 81 | 674.1 | 42 | 3491 | 137 | 25.48 | 5.18 | 6-38 |
| Mason M.J. | CD | 96 | 771.4 | 85 | 3305 | 136 | 24.30 | 4.28 | 6-25 |
| Ellis A.M. | C | 109 | 750.1 | 44 | 3903 | 133 | 29.34 | 5.20 | 5-17 |
| Tait A.R. | ND | 90 | 757.4 | 75 | 3138 | 128 | 24.51 | 4.14 | 4-29 |
| Arnel B.J. | ND, W | 92 | 774 | 54 | 3949 | 128 | 30.85 | 5.10 | 4-26 |
| Hitchcock P.A. | A, W | 89 | 706.5 | 38 | 3441 | 127 | 27.09 | 4.87 | 5-10 |
| Tuffey D.R. | ND, A | 100 | 824.5 | 63 | 3750 | 120 | 31.25 | 4.55 | 4-33 |
| Petrie R.G. | C, W | 100 | 736 | 58 | 3146 | 119 | 26.43 | 4.27 | 5-24 |
| Yovich J.A.F. | ND | 111 | 588.2 | 26 | 3172 | 119 | 26.65 | 5.39 | 4-44 |
| Scott B.E. | O, ND | 98 | 790.4 | 42 | 3978 | 116 | 34.29 | 5.03 | 4-63 |
| Bennett H.K. | C, W | 82 | 586.1 | 34 | 3025 | 112 | 27.00 | 5.16 | 6-45 |
| Duffy J.A. | O | 60 | 482.4 | 25 | 2667 | 109 | 24.46 | 5.53 | 6-35 |
| McSkimming W.C. | O | 89 | 718.5 | 61 | 3413 | 108 | 31.60 | 4.75 | 5-9 |
| Styris S.B. | ND, A | 100 | 672.3 | 50 | 2883 | 108 | 26.69 | 4.29 | 4-19 |
| Priest M.W. | C | 89 | 724.5 | 69 | 2668 | 106 | 25.16 | 3.68 | 5-26 |
| Wagner N. | O, ND | 66 | 549.4 | 38 | 3007 | 106 | 28.36 | 5.47 | 5-34 |
| Kuggeleijn S.C. | W, ND | 71 | 589.5 | 36 | 3285 | 106 | 30.99 | 5.57 | 5-24 |
| Adams A.R. | A | 66 | 573.1 | 42 | 2473 | 104 | 23.77 | 4.31 | 5-7 |
| Cairns C.L. | ND, C | 91 | 587.2 | 39 | 2412 | 103 | 23.41 | 4.11 | 6-37 |
| Astle N.J. | C | 99 | 728.2 | 86 | 2479 | 102 | 24.30 | 3.40 | 4-14 |
| Mills K.D. | A | 76 | 636 | 64 | 2693 | 101 | 26.66 | 4.23 | 4-40 |
| Thompson E.P. | CD | 63 | 518.1 | 40 | 2364 | 100 | 23.64 | 4.56 | 6-20 |

## MOST ECONOMICAL BOWLING *(qualification 100 overs)*

| | | O | M | R | W | Ave | R/O |
|---|---|---|---|---|---|---|---|
| Hadlee R.J. | C | 174.4 | 33 | 440 | 29 | 15.17 | 2.52 |
| Boock S.L. | O | 338.2 | 74 | 947 | 47 | 20.12 | 2.80 |
| McIntyre J.M. | A | 118 | 25 | 335 | 15 | 22.33 | 2.84 |
| Webb R.J. | O | 117.4 | 16 | 344 | 20 | 17.20 | 2.92 |
| Mallender N.A. | O | 458.4 | 83 | 1356 | 72 | 18.83 | 2.96 |
| Chatfield E.J. | W | 305 | 68 | 902 | 50 | 18.04 | 2.96 |

## FIELDING

| | | Ct | St | Total |
|---|---|---|---|---|
| Hopkins G.J. | ND, C, O, A | 171 | 26 | 197 |
| Nevin C.J. | W | 163 | 13 | 176 |
| Hart R.G. | ND | 117 | 30 | 147 |
| de Boorder D.C. | O | 116 | 14 | 130 |
| McSweeney E.B. | CD, W | 97 | 26 | 123 |
| Griggs B.B.J. | CD | 108 | 6 | 114 |
| van Wyk C.F.K. | C, CD | 95 | 12 | 107 |
| Germon L.K. | C, O | 88 | 18 | 106 |
| McGlashan P.D. | CD, O, ND | 81 | 15 | 96 |
| Young R.A. | A, C | 78 | 13 | 91 |
| Sinclair M.S. | CD | 82 | 1 | 83 |
| Papps M.H.W. | C, W | 78 | 3 | 81 |
| Blain T.E. | CD, C | 62 | 15 | 77 |
| Fletcher C.D. | ND, C | 70 | 10 | 80 |
| Harris C.Z. | C | 74 | — | 74 |
| Croy M.G. | O | 64 | 9 | 73 |
| Vincent L. | A | 68 | 3 | 71 |
| Cleaver D. | CD | 61 | 9 | 70 |

# NEW ZEALAND ONE-DAY INTERNATIONAL RECORDS

## TEAM RECORDS

### Results

| 1972/73 | Pakistan | Christchurch | NZ 187 | P | 165 | NZ won by 22 runs |
|---------|----------|--------------|--------|---|-----|-------------------|
| **1973** | England | Swansea | NZ 158 | E | 159-3 | England won by 7 wickets |
| | England | Manchester | E 167-8 | | | abandoned |
| **1973/74** | Australia | Dunedin | NZ 194-9 | A | 195-3 | Australia won by 7 wickets |
| | Australia | Christchurch | A 265-5 | NZ | 234-6 | Australia won by 31 runs |
| **1974/75** | England | Dunedin | E 136 | NZ | 15-0 | abandoned |
| | England | Wellington | NZ 227 | E | 35-1 | abandoned |
| **1975** | East Africa | Birmingham | NZ 309-5 | EA | 128-8 | NZ won by 181 runs |
| *World* | England | Nottingham | E 266-6 | NZ | 186 | England won by 80 runs |
| *Cup* | India | Manchester | I 230-9 | NZ | 233-6 | NZ won by 4 wickets |
| | West Indies | The Oval | NZ 158 | WI | 159-5 | West Indies won by 5 wickets |
| **1975/76** | India | Christchurch | I 154 | NZ | 155-1 | NZ won by 9 wickets |
| | India | Auckland | NZ 236-8 | I | 156 | NZ won by 80 runs |
| **1976/77** | Pakistan | Sialkot | NZ 198-8 | P | 197-9 | NZ won by 1 run |
| **1978** | England | Scarborough | E 206-8 | NZ | 187-8 | England won by 19 runs |
| | England | Manchester | E 278-5 | NZ | 152 | England won by 126 runs |
| **1979** | Sri Lanka | Nottingham | SL 189 | NZ | 190-1 | NZ won by 9 wickets |
| *World* | India | Leeds | I 182 | NZ | 183-2 | NZ won by 8 wickets |
| *Cup* | West Indies | Nottingham | WI 244-7 | NZ | 212-9 | West Indies won by 32 runs |
| | England | Manchester | E 221-8 | NZ | 212-9 | England won by 9 runs |
| **1979/80** | West Indies | Christchurch | WI 203-7 | NZ | 207-9 | NZ won by 1 wicket |
| **1980/81** | Australia | Adelaide | A 217-9 | NZ | 219-7 | NZ won by 3 wickets |
| | Australia | Sydney | A 289-3 | NZ | 195 | Australia won by 94 runs |
| | Australia | Melbourne | NZ 156 | A | 159-6 | Australia won by 4 wickets |
| | India | Perth | I 162 | NZ | 157 | India won by 5 runs |
| | India | Brisbane | I 204 | NZ | 205-7 | NZ won by 3 wickets |
| | India | Adelaide | I 230-7 | NZ | 224 | India won by 6 runs |
| | India | Melbourne | I 112-9 | NZ | 113-0 | NZ won by 10 wickets |
| | Australia | Sydney | NZ 220-8 | A | 219-7 | NZ won by 1 run |
| | India | Brisbane | NZ 242-9 | I | 220 | NZ won by 22 runs |
| | Australia | Sydney | A 180 | NZ | 23-1 | abandoned |
| | Australia | Sydney | NZ 233-6 | A | 155 | NZ won by 78 runs |
| | Australia | Melbourne | NZ 126 | A | 130-3 | Australia won by 7 wickets |
| | Australia | Melbourne | A 235-4 | NZ | 229-8 | Australia won by 6 runs |
| | Australia | Sydney | NZ 215-8 | A | 218-4 | Australia won by 6 wickets |
| **1980/81** | India | Auckland | NZ 218-6 | I | 140-9 | NZ won by 78 runs |
| | India | Hamilton | NZ 210-8 | I | 153 | NZ won by 57 runs |

| 1981/82 | Australia | Auckland | NZ 240-6 | A 194 | *NZ won by 46 runs* |
|---|---|---|---|---|---|
| | Australia | Dunedin | NZ 159-9 | A 160-4 | *Australia won by 6 wickets* |
| | Australia | Wellington | NZ 74 | A 75-2 | *Australia won by 8 wickets* |
| 1982/83 | Australia | Melbourne | NZ 181 | A 182-2 | *Australia won by 8 wickets* |
| | England | Melbourne | NZ 239-8 | E 237-8 | *NZ won by 2 runs* |
| | England | Brisbane | E 267-6 | NZ 213 | *England won by 54 runs* |
| | Australia | Sydney | NZ 226-8 | A 179 | *NZ won by 47 runs* |
| | England | Sydney | NZ 199 | E 200-2 | *England won by 8 wickets* |
| | Australia | Melbourne | NZ 246-6 | A 188 | *NZ won by 58 runs* |
| | England | Adelaide | E 296-5 | NZ 297-6 | *NZ won by 4 wickets* |
| | Australia | Adelaide | NZ 200-9 | A 153 | *NZ won by 47 runs* |
| | England | Perth | E 88-7 | NZ 89-3 | *NZ won by 7 wickets* |
| | Australia | Perth | A 191-9 | NZ 164 | *Australia won by 27 runs* |
| | Australia | Sydney | NZ 193-7 | A 155-4 | *Australia won on faster scoring rate* |
| | Australia | Melbourne | A 302-8 | NZ 153 | *Australia won by 149 runs* |
| 1982/83 | England | Auckland | E 184 | NZ 187-4 | *NZ won by 6 wickets* |
| | England | Wellington | NZ 295-6 | E 192 | *NZ won by 103 runs* |
| | England | Christchurch | NZ 211-8 | E 127 | *NZ won by 84 runs* |
| | Sri Lanka | Dunedin | NZ 183-8 | SL 118-9 | *NZ won by 65 runs* |
| | Australia | Sydney | NZ 138-8 | A 124 | *NZ won by 14 runs* |
| | Sri Lanka | Napier | SL 167-8 | NZ 168-3 | *NZ won by 7 wickets* |
| | Sri Lanka | Auckland | NZ 304-5 | SL 188-6 | *NZ won by 116 runs* |
| 1983 *World Cup* | England | The Oval | E 322-6 | NZ 216 | *England won by 106 runs* |
| | Pakistan | Birmingham | NZ 238-9 | P 186 | *NZ won by 52 runs* |
| | Sri Lanka | Bristol | SL 206 | NZ 209-5 | *NZ won by 5 wickets* |
| | England | Birmingham | E 234 | NZ 238-8 | *NZ won by 2 wickets* |
| | Sri Lanka | Derby | NZ 181 | SL 184-7 | *Sri Lanka won by 3 wickets* |
| | Pakistan | Nottingham | P 261-3 | NZ 250 | *Pakistan won by 11 runs* |
| 1983/84 | England | Christchurch | E 188-9 | NZ 134 | *England won by 54 runs* |
| | England | Wellington | NZ 135 | E 139-4 | *England won by 6 wickets* |
| | England | Auckland | E 209-9 | NZ 210-3 | *NZ won by 7 wickets* |
| 1983/84 | Sri Lanka | Colombo | NZ 234-6 | SL 130 | *NZ won by 104 runs* |
| | Sri Lanka | Moratuwa | SL 157-8 | NZ 116 | *Sri Lanka won by 41 runs* |
| | Sri Lanka | Colombo | NZ 201-8 | SL 115 | *NZ won by 86 runs* |
| 1984/85 | Sri Lanka | Colombo | NZ 171-6 | SL 174-6 | *Sri Lanka won by 4 wickets* |
| | Sri Lanka | Moratuwa | SL 114-9 | NZ 118-3 | *NZ won by 7 wickets* |
| | Pakistan | Peshawar | P 191-5 | NZ 145 | *Pakistan won by 46 runs* |
| | Pakistan | Faisalabad | P 157-5 | NZ 152-7 | *Pakistan won by 5 runs* |
| | Pakistan | Sialkot | NZ 187-9 | P 153-8 | *NZ won by 34 runs* |
| | Pakistan | Multan | NZ 213-8 | P 214-9 | *Pakistan won by 1 wicket* |
| 1984/85 | Pakistan | Napier | NZ 277-6 | P 167-9 | *NZ won by 110 runs* |
| | Pakistan | Hamilton | P 221-4 | NZ 222-6 | *NZ won by 4 wickets* |
| | Pakistan | Christchurch | NZ 264-8 | P 251 | *NZ won by 13 runs* |
| | Pakistan | Auckland | P 189 | | *abandoned* |
| 1984/85 *World Championship of Cricket* | West Indies | Sydney | NZ 57-2 | | *abandoned* |
| | Sri Lanka | Melbourne | NZ 223 | SL 172 | *NZ won by 51 runs* |
| | India | Sydney | NZ 206 | I 207-3 | *India won by 7 wickets* |
| | West Indies | Sydney | NZ 138-9 | WI 139-4 | *West Indies won by 6 wickets* |

| 1984/85 | West Indies | Antigua | WI 231-8 | NZ 208-8 | *West Indies won by 23 runs* |
|---|---|---|---|---|---|
|  | West Indies | Port of Spain | NZ 51-3 | WI 55-4 | *West Indies won by 6 wickets* |
|  | West Indies | Berbice | WI 259-5 | NZ 129 | *West Indies won by 130 runs* |
|  | West Indies | Port of Spain | NZ 116 | WI 117-0 | *West Indies won by 10 wickets* |
|  | West Indies | Bridgetown | WI 265-3 | NZ 153-8 | *West Indies won by 112 runs* |
| 1985/86 | Australia | Melbourne | NZ 161-7 |  | *abandoned* |
|  | India | Brisbane | NZ 259-9 | I 263-5 | *India won by 5 wickets* |
|  | Australia | Sydney | NZ 152 | A 153-6 | *Australia won by 4 wickets* |
|  | India | Perth | I 113 | NZ 115-7 | *NZ won by 3 wickets* |
|  | Australia | Perth | NZ 159-6 | A 161-6 | *Australia won by 4 wickets* |
|  | India | Melbourne | I 238-8 | NZ 239-5 | *NZ won by 5 wickets* |
|  | India | Adelaide | NZ 172 | I 174-5 | *India won by 5 wickets* |
|  | Australia | Adelaide | NZ 276-7 | A 70 | *NZ won by 206 runs* |
|  | Australia | Sydney | A 239-7 | NZ 140 | *Australia won by 99 runs* |
|  | India | Launceston | I 202-9 | NZ 168-9 | *India won by 21 runs (target adjusted)* |
| 1985/86 | Australia | Dunedin | NZ 186-6 | A 156 | *NZ won by 30 runs* |
|  | Australia | Christchurch | NZ 258-7 | A 205 | *NZ won by 53 runs* |
|  | Australia | Wellington | NZ 229-9 | A 232-7 | *Australia won by 3 wickets* |
|  | Australia | Auckland | A 231 | NZ 187-9 | *Australia won by 44 runs* |
| 1985/86 | Sri Lanka | Colombo | SL 137-9 | NZ 140-4 | *NZ won by 6 wickets* |
|  | Pakistan | Colombo | NZ 214-8 | P 217-6 | *Pakistan won by 4 wickets* |
|  | India | Sharjah | NZ 132-8 | I 134-7 | *India won by 3 wickets* |
|  | Pakistan | Sharjah | NZ 64 | P 66-0 | *Pakistan won by 10 wickets* |
| 1986 | England | Leeds | NZ 217-8 | E 170 | *NZ won by 47 runs* |
|  | England | Manchester | NZ 284-5 | E 286-4 | *England won by 6 wickets* |
| 1986/87 | West Indies | Dunedin | WI 237-9 | NZ 142 | *West Indies won by 95 runs* |
|  | West Indies | Auckland | NZ 213 | WI 217-4 | *West Indies won by 6 wickets* |
|  | West Indies | Wellington | *abandoned without a ball being bowled* |  |  |
|  | West Indies | Christchurch | NZ 191-9 | WI 192-0 | *West Indies won by 10 wickets* |
| 1987/88 *World Cup* | Zimbabwe | Hyderabad | NZ 242-7 | Z 239 | *NZ won by 3 runs* |
|  | India | Bangalore | I 252-7 | NZ 236-8 | *India won by 16 runs* |
|  | Australia | Indore | A 199-4 | NZ 196-9 | *Australia won by 3 runs* |
|  | Zimbabwe | Calcutta | Z 227-5 | NZ 228-6 | *NZ won by 4 wickets* |
|  | Australia | Chandigarh | A 251-8 | NZ 234 | *Australia won by 17 runs* |
|  | India | Nagpur | NZ 221-9 | I 224-1 | *India won by 9 wickets* |
| 1987/88 | Australia | Perth | NZ 232-9 | A 231 | *NZ won by 1 run* |
|  | Sri Lanka | Sydney | SL 174 | NZ 178-4 | *NZ won by 6 wickets* |
|  | Australia | Melbourne | A 216 | NZ 210-9 | *Australia won by 6 runs* |
|  | Sri Lanka | Adelaide | SL 241 | NZ 242-6 | *NZ won by 4 wickets* |
|  | Sri Lanka | Hobart | NZ 199-7 | SL 200-6 | *Sri Lanka won by 4 wickets* |
|  | Sri Lanka | Brisbane | SL 164-8 | NZ 167-6 | *NZ won by 4 wickets* |
|  | Australia | Brisbane | NZ 176-5 | A 177-5 | *Australia won by 5 wickets* |
|  | Australia | Sydney | A 221-8 | NZ 143 | *Australia won by 78 runs* |
|  | Australia | Melbourne | NZ 177 | A 180-2 | *Australia won by 8 wickets* |
|  | Australia | Sydney | NZ 168-5 | A 169-4 | *Australia won by 6 wickets* |

| 1987/88 | England | Dunedin | NZ 204 | E 207-5 | *England won by 5 wickets* |
|---|---|---|---|---|---|
| | England | Christchurch | NZ 186-8 | E 188-4 | *England won by 6 wickets* |
| | England | Napier | E 219 | NZ 223-3 | *NZ won by 7 wickets* |
| | England | Auckland | E 208 | NZ 211-6 | *NZ won by 4 wickets* |
| 1987/88 | India | Sharjah | I 267-6 | NZ 194-8 | *India won by 73 runs* |
| | Sri Lanka | Sharjah | NZ 258-8 | SL 159 | *NZ won by 99 runs* |
| | Sri Lanka | Sharjah | NZ 249-7 | SL 206-9 | *NZ won by 43 runs* |
| | India | Sharjah | I 250-7 | NZ 198 | *India won by 52 runs* |
| 1988/89 | India | Visakhapatnam | NZ 196-9 | I 197-6 | *India won by 4 wickets* |
| | India | Cuttack | NZ 160-7 | I 161-5 | *India won by 5 wickets* |
| | India | Indore | I 222-6 | NZ 169-9 | *India won by 53 runs* |
| | India | Baroda | NZ 278-3 | I 282-8 | *India won by 2 wickets* |
| | India | Jammu | *abandoned without a ball being bowled* | | |
| 1988/89 | Pakistan | Dunedin | P 170-9 | NZ 174-2 | *NZ won by 8 wickets* |
| | Pakistan | Christchurch | P 170-7 | NZ 171-3 | *NZ won by 7 wickets* |
| | Pakistan | Wellington | P 253-6 | NZ 254-4 | *NZ won by 6 wickets* |
| | Pakistan | Auckland | NZ 249 | P 251-3 | *Pakistan won by 7 wickets* |
| | Pakistan | Hamilton | P 138-9 | NZ 139-3 | *NZ won by 7 wickets* |
| 1989/90 | India | Dunedin | NZ 246-6 | I 138 | *NZ won by 108 runs* |
| | Australia | Christchurch | A 244-8 | NZ 94 | *Australia won by 150 runs* |
| | India | Wellington | I 221 | NZ 220 | *India won by 1 run* |
| | Australia | Auckland | A 239-6 | NZ 167-2 | *Australia won on faster scoring rate* |
| | Australia | Auckland | NZ 162 | A 164-2 | *Australia won by 8 wickets* |
| 1989/90 | Australia | Sharjah | A 258-5 | NZ 195-7 | *Australia won by 63 runs* |
| | Bangladesh | Sharjah | NZ 338-4 | B 177-5 | *NZ won by 161 runs* |
| | Pakistan | Sharjah | NZ 74 | P 75-2 | *Pakistan won by 8 wickets* |
| 1990 | England | Leeds | E 295-6 | NZ 298-6 | *NZ won by 4 wickets* |
| | England | The Oval | NZ 212-6 | E 213-4 | *England won by 6 wickets* |
| 1990/91 | Pakistan | Lahore | P 196-8 | NZ 177 | *Pakistan won by 19 runs* |
| | Pakistan | Peshawar | NZ 127 | P 128-2 | *Pakistan won by 8 wickets* |
| | Pakistan | Sialkot | P 223-2 | NZ 118 | *Pakistan won by 105 runs* |
| 1990/91 | Australia | Sydney | A 236-9 | NZ 174-7 | *Australia won by 61 runs target reduced* |
| | England | Adelaide | NZ 199-6 | E 192-9 | *NZ won by 7 runs* |
| | Australia | Adelaide | NZ 208-7 | A 210-4 | *Australia won by 6 wickets* |
| | England | Perth | NZ 158 | E 161-6 | *England won by 4 wickets* |
| | Australia | Melbourne | A 263-7 | NZ 224-8 | *Australia won by 39 runs* |
| | England | Sydney | E 194 | NZ 161 | *England won by 33 runs* |
| | England | Brisbane | E 203-6 | NZ 204-2 | *NZ won by 8 wickets* |
| | Australia | Hobart | NZ 194-6 | A 193 | *NZ won by 1 run* |
| | Australia | Sydney | NZ 199-7 | A 202-4 | *Australia won by 6 wickets* |
| | Australia | Melbourne | NZ 208-6 | A 209-3 | *Australia won by 7 wickets* |
| 1990/91 | Sri Lanka | Napier | SL 177-8 | NZ 178-5 | *NZ won by 5 wickets* |
| | Sri Lanka | Auckland | NZ 242-5 | SL 201 | *NZ won by 41 runs* |
| | Sri Lanka | Dunedin | NZ 272-6 | SL 165 | *NZ won by 107 runs* |
| | England | Christchurch | E 230-7 | NZ 216-8 | *England won by 14 runs* |
| | England | Wellington | NZ 196-8 | E 187 | *NZ won by 9 runs* |
| | England | Auckland | NZ 224-7 | E 217 | *NZ won by 7 runs* |

| | | | | | | |
|---|---|---|---|---|---|---|
| **1991/92** | England | Auckland | NZ 178-7 | E 179-3 | *England won by 7 wickets* |
| | England | Dunedin | NZ 186-7 | E 188-7 | *England won by 3 wickets* |
| | England | Christchurch | E 255-7 | NZ 184-8 | *England won by 71 runs* |
| **1991/92** | Australia | Auckland | NZ 248-6 | A 211 | *NZ won by 37 runs* |
| *World* | Sri Lanka | Hamilton | SL 206-9 | NZ 210-4 | *NZ won by 6 wickets* |
| *Cup* | South Africa | Auckland | SA 190-7 | NZ 191-3 | *NZ won by 7 wickets* |
| | Zimbabwe | Napier | NZ 163-3 | Z 105-7 | *NZ won by 49 runs target reduced* |
| | West Indies | Auckland | WI 203-7 | NZ 206-5 | *NZ won by 5 wickets* |
| | India | Dunedin | I 230-6 | NZ 231-6 | *NZ won by 4 wickets* |
| | England | Wellington | E 200-8 | NZ 201-3 | *NZ won by 7 wickets* |
| | Pakistan | Christchurch | NZ 166 | P 167-3 | *Pakistan won by 7 wickets* |
| | Pakistan | Auckland | NZ 262-7 | P 264-6 | *Pakistan won by 4 wickets* |
| **1992/93** | Zimbabwe | Bulawayo | NZ 244-7 | Z 222-9 | *NZ won by 22 runs* |
| | Zimbabwe | Harare | Z 271-6 | NZ 272-6 | *NZ won by 4 wickets* |
| **1992/93** | Sri Lanka | Colombo | NZ 166-9 | SL 41-2 | *abandoned* |
| | Sri Lanka | Colombo | NZ 190-7 | SL 192-2 | *SL won by 8 wickets* |
| | Sri Lanka | Colombo | SL 262-6 | NZ 231 | *SL won by 31 runs* |
| **1992/93** | Pakistan | Wellington | P 158-8 | NZ 108 | *Pakistan won by 50 runs* |
| | Pakistan | Napier | P 136-8 | NZ 137-4 | *NZ won by 6 wickets* |
| | Pakistan | Auckland | P 139 | NZ 140-4 | *NZ won by 6 wickets* |
| **1992/93** | Australia | Dunedin | A 258-4 | NZ 129 | *Australia won by 129 runs* |
| | Australia | Christchurch | NZ 196-8 | A 197-9 | *Australia won by 1 wicket* |
| | Australia | Wellington | NZ 214 | A 126 | *NZ won by 88 runs* |
| | Australia | Hamilton | A 247-7 | NZ 250-7 | *NZ won by 3 wickets* |
| | Australia | Auckland | A 232-8 | NZ 229-8 | *Australia won by 3 runs* |
| **1993/94** | South Africa | Adelaide | *abandoned without a ball being bowled* | | |
| | Australia | Adelaide | NZ 135 | A 136-2 | *Australia won by 8 wickets* |
| | Australia | Melbourne | A 202-5 | NZ 199-9 | *Australia won by 3 runs* |
| | South Africa | Hobart | SA 147-7 | NZ 148-6 | *NZ won by 4 wickets* |
| | South Africa | Brisbane | NZ 256-7 | SA 219-8 | *NZ won by 9 runs target reduced* |
| | Australia | Sydney | NZ 198-9 | A 185 | *NZ won by 13 runs* |
| | South Africa | Perth | NZ 150 | SA 151-5 | *SA won by 5 wickets* |
| | Australia | Melbourne | A 217-3 | NZ 166 | *Australia won by 51 runs* |
| **1993/94** | Pakistan | Dunedin | NZ 122-9 | P 123-5 | *Pakistan won by 5 wickets* |
| | Pakistan | Auckland | P 146 | NZ 110 | *Pakistan won by 36 runs* |
| | Pakistan | Wellington | P 213-6 | NZ 202-8 | *Pakistan won by 11 runs* |
| | Pakistan | Auckland | P 161-9 | NZ 161 | *Tie* |
| | Pakistan | Christchurch | P 145-9 | NZ 146-3 | *NZ won by 7 wickets* |
| | India | Napier | NZ 240-5 | I 212-9 | *NZ won by 28 runs* |
| | India | Auckland | NZ 142 | I 143-3 | *India won by 7 wickets* |
| | India | Wellington | I 255-5 | NZ 243-9 | *India won by 12 runs* |
| | India | Christchurch | I 222-6 | NZ 223-4 | *NZ won by 6 wickets* |
| **1993/94** | Australia | Sharjah | NZ 207-9 | A 208-3 | *Australia won by 7 wickets* |
| | Sri Lanka | Sharjah | NZ 217-8 | SL 215-9 | *NZ won by 2 runs* |
| | Pakistan | Sharjah | P 328-2 | NZ 266-7 | *Pakistan won by 62 runs* |
| **1994** | England | Birmingham | E 224-8 | NZ 182 | *England won by 42 runs* |
| | England | Lord's | *abandoned without a ball being bowled* | | |

| 1994/95 | West Indies | Goa | WI 123 | NZ 25-1 | *abandoned* |
|---|---|---|---|---|---|
| | India | Baroda | NZ 269-4 | I 271-3 | *India won by 7 wickets* |
| | West Indies | Guwahati | WI 306-6 | NZ 171-9 | *West Indies won by 135 runs* |
| | India | Delhi | I 289-3 | NZ 182 | *India won by 107 runs* |
| 1994/95 | South Africa | Cape Town | SA 203-8 | NZ 134 | *South Africa won by 69 runs* |
| | Sri Lanka | Bloemfontein | SL 288-4 | NZ 66-1 | *abandoned* |
| | South Africa | Verwoerdburg | SA 314-7 | NZ 233 | *South Africa won by 81 runs* |
| | Pakistan | Port Elizabeth | NZ 201 | P 206-5 | *Pakistan won by 5 wickets* |
| | Sri Lanka | East London | NZ 255-4 | SL 257-5 | *Sri Lanka won by 5 wickets* |
| | Pakistan | East London | NZ 172 | P 175-5 | *Pakistan won by 5 wickets* |
| 1994/95 | West Indies | Auckland | NZ 167-6 | WI 149-1 | *West Indies won by 9 wickets target reduced* |
| | West Indies | Wellington | WI 246-7 | NZ 205 | *West Indies won by 41 runs* |
| | West Indies | Christchurch | NZ 146 | WI 149-1 | *West Indies won by 9 wickets* |
| 1994/95 | India | Napier | I 160 | NZ 162-6 | *NZ won by 4 wickets* |
| | Australia | Auckland | A 254-5 | NZ 227-9 | *Australia won by 27 runs* |
| | South Africa | Christchurch | NZ 249-7 | SA 203 | *NZ won by 46 runs* |
| | Australia | Auckland | NZ 137-9 | A 138-4 | *Australia won by 6 wickets* |
| 1994/95 | Sri Lanka | Christchurch | NZ 271-6 | SL 238 | *NZ won by 33 runs* |
| | Sri Lanka | Hamilton | NZ 280-6 | SL 117-6 | *NZ won by 57 runs target reduced* |
| | Sri Lanka | Auckland | SL 250-6 | NZ 199 | *Sri Lanka won by 51 runs* |
| 1995/96 | India | Jamshedpur | I 236 | NZ 237-2 | *NZ won by 8 wickets* |
| | India | Amritsar | NZ 145 | I 146-4 | *India won by 6 wickets* |
| | India | Goa | *abandoned without a ball being bowled* | | |
| | India | Pune | NZ 235-6 | I 236-5 | *India won by 5 wickets* |
| | India | Nagpur | NZ 348-8 | I 249 | *NZ won by 99 runs* |
| | India | Bombay | NZ 126 | I 128-4 | *India won by 6 wickets* |
| 1995/96 | Pakistan | Dunedin | P 189-9 | NZ 169 | *Pakistan won by 20 runs* |
| | Pakistan | Christchurch | P 232-9 | NZ 236-9 | *NZ won by 1 wicket* |
| | Pakistan | Wellington | P 261-4 | NZ 207 | *Pakistan won by 54 runs* |
| | Pakistan | Auckland | NZ 244-8 | P 212 | *NZ won by 32 runs* |
| 1995/96 | Zimbabwe | Auckland | NZ 278-5 | Z 204 | *NZ won by 74 runs* |
| | Zimbabwe | Wellington | Z 181-9 | NZ 184-4 | *NZ won by 6 wickets* |
| | Zimbabwe | Napier | Z 267-7 | NZ 246 | *Zimbabwe won by 21 runs* |
| 1995/96 *World Cup* | England | Ahmedabad | NZ 239-6 | E 228-9 | *NZ won by 11 runs* |
| | Holland | Baroda | NZ 307-8 | H 188-7 | *NZ won by 119 runs* |
| | South Africa | Faisalabad | NZ 177-9 | SA 178-5 | *Sth Africa won by 5 wickets* |
| | UAE | Faisalabad | NZ 276-8 | UAE 167-9 | *NZ won by 109 runs* |
| | Pakistan | Lahore | P 281-5 | NZ 235 | *Pakistan won by 46 runs* |
| | Australia | Madras | NZ 286-9 | A 289-4 | *Australia won by 6 wickets* |
| 1995/96 | West Indies | Kingston | NZ 243 | WI 247-9 | *West Indies won by 1 wicket* |
| | West Indies | Port of Spain | WI 238-7 | NZ 239-6 | *NZ won by 4 wickets* |
| | West Indies | Port of Spain | NZ 219-8 | WI 225-3 | *West Indies won by 7 wickets* |
| | West Indies | Georgetown | NZ 158 | WI 154 | *NZ won by 4 runs* |
| | West Indies | Arnos Vale | NZ 241-8 | WI 242-3 | *West Indies won by 7 wickets* |
| 1996/97 | Sri Lanka | Sharjah | NZ 206-8 | SL 177 | *NZ won by 29 runs* |
| | Pakistan | Sharjah | NZ 197 | P 198-6 | *Pakistan won by 4 wickets* |
| | Sri Lanka | Sharjah | NZ 169-8 | SL 169 | *Tie* |
| | Pakistan | Sharjah | NZ 192 | P 196-6 | *Pakistan won by 4 wickets* |
| | Pakistan | Sharjah | P 160 | NZ 119 | *Pakistan won by 41 runs* |

| | | | | | |
|---|---|---|---|---|---|
| **1996/97** | Pakistan | Gujranwala | P 228-8 | NZ 217 | *Pakistan won by 11 runs* |
| | Pakistan | Sialkot | P 277-9 | NZ 231 | *Pakistan won by 46 runs* |
| | Pakistan | Karachi | P 234-4 | NZ 235-3 | *NZ won by 7 wickets* |
| **1996/97** | England | Christchurch | NZ 222-6 | E 226-6 | *England won by 4 wickets* |
| | England | Auckland | NZ 253-8 | E 134-4 | *England won by 6 wickets target reduced* |
| | England | Napier | NZ 237 | E 237-8 | *Tie* |
| | England | Auckland | NZ 153 | E 144 | *NZ won by 9 runs* |
| | England | Wellington | NZ 228-8 | E 200 | *NZ won by 28 runs* |
| **1996/97** | Sri Lanka | Auckland | *abandoned without a ball being bowled* | | |
| | Sri Lanka | Christchurch | NZ 201-9 | SL 202-4 | *Sri Lanka won by 6 wickets* |
| | Sri Lanka | Wellington | NZ 201 | SL 132 | *NZ won by 69 runs* |
| **1996/97** | Pakistan | Mohali | NZ 285-7 | P 263-9 | *NZ won by 22 runs* |
| | India | Bangalore | NZ 220-9 | I 221-2 | *India won by 8 wickets* |
| | Sri Lanka | Hyderabad | SL 214 | NZ 162 | *Sri Lanka won by 52 runs* |
| **1997/98** | Zimbabwe | Bulawayo | Z 233-8 | NZ 233-9 | *Tie* |
| | Zimbabwe | Harare | NZ 185-7 | Z 188-7 | *Zimbabwe won by 3 wickets* |
| | Zimbabwe | Harare | NZ 294-7 | Z 211 | *NZ won by 83 runs* |
| **1997/98** | South Africa | Adelaide | NZ 224-6 | SA 177 | *NZ won by 47 runs* |
| | Australia | Adelaide | NZ 260-7 | A 263-7 | *Australia won by 3 wickets* |
| | South Africa | Hobart | SA 174-9 | NZ 173-7 | *South Africa won by 1 run* |
| | Australia | Melbourne | NZ 141 | A 142-4 | *Australia won by 6 wickets* |
| | South Africa | Brisbane | SA 300-6 | NZ 298-9 | *South Africa won by 2 runs* |
| | Australia | Sydney | A 250 | NZ 119 | *Australia won by 131 runs* |
| | South Africa | Perth | SA 233-7 | NZ 166 | *South Africa won by 67 runs* |
| | Australia | Melbourne | A 251-4 | NZ 253-6 | *NZ won by 4 wickets* |
| **1997/98** | Zimbabwe | Hamilton | NZ 248-7 | Z 208 | *NZ won by 40 runs* |
| | Zimbabwe | Wellington | Z 138 | NZ 139-2 | *NZ won by 8 wickets* |
| | Australia | Christchurch | NZ 212-7 | A 215-3 | *Australia won by 7 wickets* |
| | Australia | Wellington | A 297-6 | NZ 231 | *Australia won by 66 runs* |
| | Australia | Napier | A 236 | NZ 240-3 | *NZ won by 7 wickets* |
| | Australia | Auckland | NZ 223-7 | A 193 | *NZ won by 30 runs* |
| | Zimbabwe | Christchurch | Z 228-7 | NZ 227-9 | *Zimbabwe won by 1 run* |
| | Zimbabwe | Napier | Z 207-8 | NZ 211-1 | *NZ won by 9 wickets* |
| | Zimbabwe | Auckland | NZ 231-9 | Z 229-9 | *NZ won by 2 runs* |
| **1997/98** | India | Sharjah | I 220-9 | NZ 205 | *India won by 15 runs* |
| | Australia | Sharjah | NZ 159 | A 160-4 | *Australia won by 6 wickets* |
| | India | Sharjah | I 181 | NZ 183-6 | *NZ won by 4 wickets* |
| | Australia | Sharjah | NZ 259-5 | A 261-5 | *Australia won by 5 wickets* |
| **1997/98** | Sri Lanka | Colombo | NZ 200-9 | SL 201-3 | *Sri Lanka won by 7 wickets* |
| | India | Colombo | NZ 219-8 | I 131-3 | *abandoned* |
| | Sri Lanka | Galle | *abandoned without a ball being bowled* | | |
| | India | Galle | *abandoned without a ball being bowled* | | |
| | India | Colombo | NZ 128-5 | | *abandoned* |
| | Sri Lanka | Colombo | SL 293-4 | NZ 206 | *Sri Lanka won by 87 runs* |
| **1998/99** | Zimbabwe | Dhaka | Z 258-7 | NZ 260-5 | *NZ won by 5 wickets* |
| *ICC Knockout* | Sri Lanka | Dhaka | NZ 188 | SL 191-5 | *Sri Lanka won by 5 wickets* |

| 1998/99 | India | Taupo | I 257-5 | NZ 200-5 | *NZ won by 5 wickets (D/L)* |
| | India | Napier | NZ 213 | I 214-8 | *India won by 2 wickets* |
| | India | Wellington | I 208-4 | NZ 89-2 | *abandoned* |
| | India | Auckland | NZ 207-7 | I 208-5 | *India won by 5 wickets* |
| | India | Christchurch | NZ 300-8 | I 230 | *NZ won by 70 runs* |
| **1998/99** | South Africa | Dunedin | SA 211 | NZ 215-7 | *NZ won by 3 wickets* |
| | South Africa | Christchurch | NZ 220-9 | SA 224-3 | *SA won by 7 wickets* |
| | South Africa | Auckland | SA 212-7 | NZ 215-3 | *NZ won by 7 wickets* |
| | South Africa | Napier | NZ 257-8 | SA 10-0 | *abandoned* |
| | South Africa | Napier | NZ 191 | SA 194-8 | *SA won by 2 wickets* |
| | South Africa | Auckland | SA 290-5 | NZ 147 | *SA won by 143 runs* |
| | South Africa | Wellington | SA 249-4 | | *abandoned* |
| **1999**<br>*World*<br>*Cup* | Bangladesh | Chelmsford | B 116 | NZ 117-4 | *NZ won by 6 wickets* |
| | Australia | Cardiff | A 213-8 | NZ 214-5 | *NZ won by 5 wickets* |
| | West Indies | Southampton | NZ 156 | WI 158-3 | *WI won by 7 wickets* |
| | Pakistan | Derby | P 269-8 | NZ 207-8 | *Pakistan won by 62 runs* |
| | Scotland | Edinburgh | S 121 | NZ 123-4 | *NZ won by 6 wickets* |
| | Zimbabwe | Leeds | Z 175 | NZ 70-3 | *abandoned* |
| | South Africa | Birmingham | SA 287-5 | NZ 213-8 | *SA won by 74 runs* |
| | India | Nottingham | I 251-6 | NZ 253-5 | *NZ won by 5 wickets* |
| | Pakistan | Manchester | NZ 241-7 | P 242-1 | *Pakistan won by 9 wickets* |
| **1999/00** | India | Rajkot | NZ 349-9 | I 306 | *NZ won by 43 runs* |
| | India | Hyderabad | I 376-2 | NZ 202 | *India won by 174 runs* |
| | India | Gwalior | I 261-5 | NZ 247-8 | *India won by 14 runs* |
| | India | Guwahati | NZ 236-9 | I 188 | *NZ won by 48 runs* |
| | India | Delhi | NZ 179-9 | I 181-3 | *India won by 7 wickets* |
| **1999/00** | West Indies | Auckland | WI 268-7 | NZ 250-7 | *NZ won by 3 wickets (D/L)* |
| | West Indies | Taupo | WI 192 | NZ 194-3 | *NZ won by 7 wickets* |
| | West Indies | Napier | WI 159 | NZ 160-6 | *NZ won by 4 wickets* |
| | West Indies | Wellington | WI 171-9 | NZ 172-2 | *NZ won by 8 wickets* |
| | West Indies | Christchurch | NZ 302-6 | WI 282 | *NZ won by 20 runs* |
| **1999/00** | Australia | Wellington | A 119-1 | NZ | *abandoned* |
| | Australia | Auckland | NZ 122 | A 123-5 | *Australia won by 5 wickets* |
| | Australia | Dunedin | A 310-4 | NZ 260 | *Australia won by 50 runs* |
| | Australia | Christchurch | A 349-6 | NZ 301-9 | *Australia won by 48 runs* |
| | Australia | Napier | NZ 243-9 | A 245-5 | *Australia won by 5 wickets* |
| | Australia | Auckland | A 191 | NZ 194-3 | *NZ won by 7 wickets* |
| **2000/01** | Pakistan | Singapore | P 191-6 | NZ 179 | *Pakistan won by 12 runs* |
| | South Africa | Singapore | NZ 158 | SA 159-2 | *SA won by 8 wickets* |
| **2000/01** | Zimbabwe | Harare | Z 183-8 | NZ 184-3 | *NZ won by 7 wickets* |
| | Zimbabwe | Bulawayo | Z 273-5 | NZ 252 | *Zimbabwe won by 21 runs* |
| | Zimbabwe | Bulawayo | NZ 264-8 | Z 268-4 | *Zimbabwe won by 6 wkts* |
| **2000/01**<br>*ICC Knockout* | Zimbabwe | Nairobi | NZ 265-7 | Z 201 | *NZ won by 64 runs* |
| | Pakistan | Nairobi | P 252 | NZ 255-6 | *NZ won by 4 wickets* |
| | India | Nairobi | I 264-6 | NZ 265-6 | *NZ won by 4 wickets* |
| **2000/01** | South Africa | Potchefstroom | SA 191-2 | NZ | *abandoned* |
| | South Africa | Benoni | NZ 194-8 | SA 197-4 | *SA won by 6 wkts* |
| | South Africa | Centurion | SA 324-4 | NZ 189 | *SA won by 115 runs (D/L)* |
| | South Africa | Kimberley | NZ 287-6 | SA 289-5 | *SA won by 5 wickets* |
| | South Africa | Durban | NZ 114-5 | SA 158-4 | *SA won by 6 wickets(D/L)* |
| | South Africa | Cape Town | NZ 256-9 | SA 258-7 | *SA won by 3 wickets* |

| | | | | | |
|---|---|---|---|---|---|
| **2000/01** | Zimbabwe | Taupo | Z 300-7 | NZ 210 | *Zimbabwe won by 70 runs (D/L)* |
| | Zimbabwe | Wellington | Z 236-7 | NZ 237-2 | *NZ won by 8 wickets* |
| | Zimbabwe | Auckland | NZ 273-9 | Z 274-9 | *Zimbabwe won by 1 wicket* |
| **2000/01** | Sri Lanka | Napier | SL 213-8 | NZ 152 | *Sri Lanka won by 61 runs* |
| | Sri Lanka | Wellington | NZ 205-8 | SL 209-7 | *Sri Lanka won by 3 wickets* |
| | Sri Lanka | Auckland | NZ 181 | SL 182-1 | *Sri Lanka won by 9 wickets* |
| | Sri Lanka | Hamilton | NZ 182-9 | SL 155-5 | *Sri Lanka won by 3 runs (D/L)* |
| | Sri Lanka | Christchurch | NZ 282-6 | SL 269 | *NZ won by 13 runs* |
| **2000/01** | Pakistan | Auckland | NZ 149 | P 150-4 | *Pakistan won by 6 wickets* |
| | Pakistan | Napier | P 135 | NZ 136-4 | *NZ won by 6 wickets* |
| | Pakistan | Wellington | P 243-9 | NZ 215 | *Pakistan won by 28 runs* |
| | Pakistan | Christchurch | NZ 284-5 | P 146 | *NZ won by 138 runs* |
| | Pakistan | Dunedin | P 285 | NZ 290-6 | *NZ won by 4 wickets* |
| **2000/01** | Sri Lanka | Sharjah | SL 269-9 | NZ 163 | *Sri Lanka won by 106 runs* |
| | Pakistan | Sharjah | NZ 266-7 | P 270-2 | *Pakistan won by 8 wickets* |
| | Pakistan | Sharjah | NZ 127 | P 131-3 | *Pakistan won by 7 wickets* |
| | Sri Lanka | Sharjah | NZ 248-6 | SL 169-8 | *NZ won by 79 runs* |
| **2001/02** | Sri Lanka | Colombo | SL 220 | NZ 204-9 | *Sri Lanka won by 16 runs* |
| | India | Colombo | NZ 211-8 | I 127 | *NZ won by 84 runs* |
| | Sri Lanka | Colombo | NZ 236-8 | SL 240-5 | *Sri Lanka won by 5 wickets* |
| | India | Colombo | NZ 200 | I 133 | *NZ won by 67 runs* |
| | Sri Lanka | Colombo | SL 221-6 | NZ 115-9 | *Sri Lanka won by 106 runs* |
| | India | Colombo | NZ 264-7 | I 267-3 | *India won by 7 wickets* |
| **2001/02** | Australia | Melbourne | NZ 199-8 | A 176 | *NZ won by 23 runs* |
| | South Africa | Hobart | SA 257-7 | NZ 231-9 | *SA won by 26 runs* |
| | Australia | Sydney | NZ 235-9 | A 212 | *NZ won by 23 runs* |
| | South Africa | Brisbane | SA 241 | NZ 244-6 | *NZ won by 4 wickets* |
| | Australia | Adelaide | NZ 242-5 | A 165 | *NZ won by 77 runs* |
| | South Africa | Adelaide | SA 253-5 | NZ 160 | *SA won by 93 runs* |
| | Australia | Melbourne | NZ 245-8 | A 248-8 | *Australia won by 2 wickets* |
| | South Africa | Perth | SA 270-5 | NZ 203-8 | *SA won by 67 runs* |
| | South Africa | Melbourne | NZ 190 | SA 191-2 | *SA won by 8 wickets* |
| | South Africa | Sydney | NZ 175 | SA 173-4 | *SA won by 6 wickets (D/L)* |
| **2001/02** | England | Christchurch | E 196 | NZ 198-6 | *NZ won by 4 wickets* |
| | England | Wellington | NZ 244-8 | E 89 | *NZ won by 155 runs* |
| | England | Napier | E 244-5 | NZ 201 | *England won by 43 runs* |
| | England | Auckland | E 193-6 | NZ 189 | *England won by 33 runs (D/L)* |
| | England | Dunedin | E 218-5 | NZ 223-5 | *NZ won by 5 wickets* |
| **2001/02** | Sri Lanka | Sharjah | NZ 218-8 | SL 207 | *NZ won by 11 runs* |
| | Pakistan | Sharjah | P 288-6 | NZ 237-8 | *Pakistan won by 51 runs* |
| | Sri Lanka | Sharjah | SL 243-9 | NZ 197-9 | *Sri Lanka won by 46 runs* |
| | Pakistan | Sharjah | NZ 213-9 | P 217-2 | *Pakistan won by 8 wickets* |
| **2001/02** | Pakistan | Karachi | P 275-6 | NZ 122 | *Pakistan won by 153 runs* |
| | Pakistan | Rawalpindi | NZ 277-5 | P 278-7 | *Pakistan won by 3 wickets* |
| | Pakistan | Lahore | P 278-5 | NZ 212 | *Pakistan won by 66 runs* |
| **2001/02** | West Indies | Kingston | NZ 176 | WI | *abandoned* |
| | West Indies | Gros Islet | NZ 248-7 | WI 250-4 | *West Indies won by 6 wickets* |
| | West Indies | Gros Islet | NZ 210-7 | WI 211-3 | *West Indies won by 7 wickets* |
| | West Indies | Port of Spain | NZ 212-5 | WI 202-9 | *NZ won by 9 runs (D/L)* |
| | West Indies | Arnos Vale | NZ 291-8 | WI 292-6 | *West Indies won by 4 wickets* |

| 2002/03 | Australia | Colombo | A 296-7 | NZ 132 | *Australia won by 164 runs* |
| *Champions Trophy* | Bangladesh | Colombo | NZ 244-9 | B 77 | *NZ won by 167 runs* |
| **2002/03** | India | Auckland | I 108 | NZ 109-7 | *NZ won by 3 wickets* |
| | India | Napier | NZ 254-9 | I 219 | *NZ won by 35 runs* |
| | India | Christchurch | I 108 | NZ 109-5 | *NZ won by 5 wickets* |
| | India | Queenstown | I 122 | NZ 123-3 | *NZ won by 7 wickets* |
| | India | Wellington | NZ 168 | I 169-8 | *India won by 2 wickets* |
| | India | Auckland | NZ 199-9 | I 200-9 | *India won by 1 wicket* |
| | India | Hamilton | I 122 | NZ 125-4 | *NZ won by 6 wickets* |
| **2002/03** | Sri Lanka | Bloemfontein | SL 272-7 | NZ 225 | *Sri Lanka won by 47 runs* |
| *World* | West Indies | Port Elizabeth | NZ 241-7 | WI 221 | *NZ won by 20 runs* |
| *Cup* | South Africa | Johannesburg | SL 306-6 | NZ 229-1 | *NZ won by 9 wickets (D/L)* |
| | Kenya | Nairobi | | | *NZ forfeited the match* |
| | Bangladesh | Kimberley | B 198-7 | NZ 199-3 | *NZ won by 7 wickets* |
| | Canada | Benoni | C 196 | NZ 197-5 | *NZ won by 5 wickets* |
| | Zimbabwe | Bloemfontein | Z 252-7 | NZ 253-4 | *NZ won by 6 wickets* |
| | Australia | Port Elizabeth | A 208-9 | NZ 112 | *Australia won by 96 runs* |
| | India | Centurion | NZ 146 | I 150-3 | *India won by 7 wickets* |
| **2002/03** | Pakistan | Dambulla | P 116 | NZ 117-3 | *NZ won by 7 wickets* |
| | Sri Lanka | Dambulla | NZ 139 | SL 143-5 | *Sri Lanka won by 5 wickets* |
| | Sri Lanka | Dambulla | NZ 156-8 | SL 147 | *NZ won by 9 runs* |
| | Pakistan | Dambulla | P 203-9 | NZ 181 | *Pakistan won by 22 runs* |
| | Pakistan | Dambulla | P 198 | NZ 200-6 | *NZ won by 4 wickets* |
| **2003/04** | India | Chennai | I 141-3 | NZ | *abandoned* |
| | Australia | Faridabad | NZ 97 | A 101-2 | *Australia won by 8 wickets* |
| | Australia | Pune | NZ 258-9 | A 259-8 | *Australia won by 2 wickets* |
| | India | Cuttack | I 246-6 | NZ 249-6 | *NZ won by 4 wickets* |
| | Australia | Guwahati | A 225-7 | NZ 181 | *Australia won by 44 runs* |
| | India | Hyderabad | I 353-5 | NZ 208 | *India won by 145 runs* |
| **2003/04** | Pakistan | Lahore | NZ 291-5 | P 292-7 | *Pakistan won by 3 wickets* |
| | Pakistan | Lahore | P 281-6 | NZ 157 | *Pakistan won by 124 runs* |
| | Pakistan | Faisalabad | P 314-7 | NZ 263-7 | *Pakistan won by 51 runs* |
| | Pakistan | Rawalpindi | NZ 183 | P 184-3 | *Pakistan won by 7 wickets* |
| | Pakistan | Rawalpindi | P 277-4 | NZ 228-6 | *Pakistan won by 49 runs* |
| **2003/04** | Pakistan | Auckland | P 229-7 | NZ 230-6 | *NZ won by 4 wickets* |
| | Pakistan | Queenstown | NZ 235-8 | P 236-4 | *Pakistan won by 6 wickets* |
| | Pakistan | Christchurch | P 255-9 | NZ 259-3 | *NZ won by 7 wickets* |
| | Pakistan | Napier | P 126 | NZ 127-2 | *NZ won by 8 wickets* |
| | Pakistan | Wellington | NZ 307-8 | P 303 | *NZ won by 4 runs* |
| **2003/04** | South Africa | Auckland | NZ 225-8 | SA 226-5 | *SA won by 5 wickets* |
| | South Africa | Christchurch | SA 253-8 | NZ 255-5 | *NZ won by 5 wickets* |
| | South Africa | Wellington | NZ 254-5 | SA 249-7 | *NZ won by 5 runs* |
| | South Africa | Dunedin | SA 259-7 | NZ 264-4 | *NZ won by 6 wickets* |
| | South Africa | Auckland | NZ 193-8 | SA 175-5 | *NZ won by 2 runs (D/L)* |
| | South Africa | Napier | SA 186-9 | NZ 190-5 | *NZ won by 5 wickets* |
| **2004** | England | Manchester | *abandoned without a ball being bowled* | | |
| | West Indies | Birmingham | WI 122-4 | NZ 97-2 | *abandoned* |
| | England | Chester-le-Street | E 101 | NZ 103-3 | *NZ won by 7 wickets* |
| | West Indies | Cardiff | WI 216 | NZ 220-5 | *NZ won by 5 wickets* |
| | England | Bristol | E 237-7 | NZ 241-4 | *NZ won by 6 wickets* |
| | West Indies | Southampton | *abandoned without a ball being bowled* | | |
| | West Indies | Lord's | NZ 266 | WI 159 | *NZ won by 107 runs* |

| 2004 | USA | The Oval | NZ 347-4 | USA 137 | *NZ won by 210 runs* |
|---|---|---|---|---|---|
| *Champions Trophy* | Australia | The Oval | NZ 198 | A 199-3 | *Australia won by 7 wickets* |
| **2004/05** | Bangladesh | Chittagong | NZ 224 | B 86 | *NZ won by 138 runs* |
| | Bangladesh | Dhaka | B 146 | NZ 148-7 | *NZ won by 3 wickets* |
| | Bangladesh | Dhaka | NZ 250-7 | B 167-7 | *NZ won by 83 runs* |
| **2004/05** | Australia | Melbourne | A 246-9 | NZ 247-6 | *NZ won by 4 wickets* |
| | Australia | Sydney | A 261-7 | NZ 244 | *Australia won by 17 runs* |
| | Australia | Brisbane | *abandoned without a ball being bowled* | | |
| **2004/05** | Sri Lanka | Auckland | SL 141 | NZ 144-3 | *NZ won by 7 wickets* |
| **2004/05** | Australia | Wellington | A 236-7 | NZ 226 | *Australia won by 10 runs* |
| | Australia | Christchurch | A 314-6 | NZ 208 | *Australia won by 106 runs* |
| | Australia | Auckland | A 264-5 | NZ 178 | *Australia won by 86 runs* |
| | Australia | Wellington | NZ 233 | A 236-3 | *Australia won by 7 wickets* |
| | Australia | Napier | A 347-5 | NZ 225-8 | *Australia won by 122 runs* |
| **2005/06** | Zimbabwe | Bulawayo | NZ 397-5 | Z 205 | *NZ won by 192 runs* |
| | India | Bulawayo | NZ 215 | I 164 | *NZ won by 51 runs* |
| | Zimbabwe | Harare | NZ 238 | Z 211 | *NZ won by 27 runs* |
| | India | Harare | NZ 278-9 | I 279-4 | *India won by 6 wickets* |
| | India | Harare | I 276 | NZ 278-4 | *NZ won by 6 wickets* |
| **2005/06** | South Africa | Bloemfontein | NZ 249-8 | SA 250-8 | *SA won by 2 wickets* |
| | South Africa | Cape Town | SA 201-9 | NZ 182 | *SA won by 19 runs* |
| | South Africa | Port Elizabeth | NZ 243-9 | SA 245-6 | *SA won by 4 wickets* |
| | South Africa | Durban | SA 79-2 | NZ | *abandoned* |
| | South Africa | Centurion | NZ 215 | SA 140-5 | *SA won by 5 wickets (D/L)* |
| **2005/06** | Australia | Auckland | A 252-8 | NZ 105 | *Australia won by 147 runs* |
| | Australia | Wellington | A 322-5 | NZ 320 | *Australia won by 2 runs* |
| | Australia | Christchurch | A 331-7 | NZ 332-8 | *NZ won by 2 wickets* |
| **2005/06** | Sri Lanka | Queenstown | SL 164 | NZ 166-3 | *NZ won by 7 wickets* |
| | Sri Lanka | Christchurch | SL 255-7 | NZ 256-5 | *NZ won by 5 wickets* |
| | Sri Lanka | Wellington | NZ 224-9 | SL 203 | *NZ won by 21 runs* |
| | Sri Lanka | Napier | SL 273-6 | NZ 253 | *Sri Lanka won by 20 runs* |
| **2005/06** | West Indies | Wellington | NZ 288-9 | WI 207 | *NZ won by 81 runs* |
| | West Indies | Queenstown | WI 200-9 | NZ 204-7 | *NZ won by 3 wickets* |
| | West Indies | Christchurch | NZ 276-6 | WI 255 | *NZ won by 21 runs* |
| | West Indies | Napier | NZ 324-6 | WI 233-8 | *NZ won by 91 runs* |
| | West Indies | Auckland | NZ 233 | WI 234-7 | *West Indies won by 3 wickets* |
| **2006/07** | South Africa | Mumbai | NZ 195 | SA 108 | *NZ won by 87 runs* |
| *Champions Trophy* | Sri Lanka | Mumbai | NZ 165 | SL 166-3 | *Sri Lanka won by 7 wkts* |
| | Pakistan | Chandigarh | NZ 274-7 | P 223 | *NZ won by 51 runs* |
| | Australia | Chandigarh | A 240-9 | NZ 206 | *Australia won by 34 runs* |
| **2006/07** | Sri Lanka | Napier | NZ 285-8 | SL 289-3 | *Sri Lanka won by 7 wickets* |
| | Sri Lanka | Queenstown | SL 224-7 | NZ 228-9 | *NZ won by 1 wicket* |
| | Sri Lanka | Christchurch | SL 112 | NZ 110-6 | *NZ won by 4 wickets (D/L)* |
| | Sri Lanka | Auckland | SL 262-6 | NZ 73 | *Sri Lanka won by 189 runs* |
| | Sri Lanka | Hamilton | *abandoned without a ball being bowled* | | |
| **2006/07** | Australia | Hobart | A 289-8 | NZ 184 | *Australia won by 105 runs* |
| | England | Hobart | NZ 205-9 | E 206-7 | *England won by 3 wickets* |
| | Australia | Sydney | NZ 218 | A 224-8 | *Australia won by 2 wickets* |
| | England | Adelaide | NZ 210 | E 120 | *NZ won by 90 runs* |
| | Australia | Perth | A 343-5 | NZ 335-5 | *Australia won by 8 runs* |

| | | | | | |
|---|---|---|---|---|---|
| | England | Perth | NZ 318-7 | E 260-8 | *NZ won by 58 runs* |
| | Australia | Melbourne | NZ 290-7 | A 291-5 | *Australia won by 5 wickets* |
| | England | Brisbane | E 270-7 | NZ 256-8 | *England won by 14 runs* |
| **2006/07** | Australia | Wellington | A 148 | NZ 149-0 | *NZ won by 10 wickets* |
| | Australia | Auckland | A 336-4 | NZ 340-5 | *NZ won by 5 wickets* |
| | Australia | Hamilton | A 346-5 | NZ 350-9 | *NZ won by 1 wicket* |
| **2006/07** | England | Gros Islet | E 209-7 | NZ 210-4 | *NZ won by 6 wickets* |
| *World Cup* | Kenya | Gros Islet | NZ 331-7 | K 183 | *NZ won by 148 runs* |
| | Canada | Gros Islet | NZ 363-5 | C 249 | *NZ won by 114 runs* |
| | West Indies | Antigua | WI 177 | NZ 179-3 | *NZ won by 7 wickets* |
| | Bangladesh | Antigua | B 174 | NZ 178-1 | *NZ won by 9 wickets* |
| | Ireland | Guyana | NZ 263-8 | I 134 | *NZ won by 129 runs* |
| | Sri Lanka | Grenada | NZ 219-7 | SL 222-4 | *Sri Lanka won by 6 wickets* |
| | South Africa | Grenada | SA 193-7 | NZ 196-5 | *NZ won by 5 wickets* |
| | Australia | Grenada | A 348-6 | NZ 133 | *Australia won by 215 runs* |
| | Sri Lanka | Kingston | SL 289-5 | NZ 208 | *Sri Lanka won by 81 runs* |
| **2007/08** | South Africa | Durban | NZ 248-6 | SA 249-8 | *South Africa won by 2 wickets* |
| | South Africa | Port Elizabeth | SA 209-9 | NZ 210-3 | *NZ won by 7 wickets* |
| | South Africa | Cape Town | NZ 238-8 | SA 242-5 | *South Africa won by 5 wickets* |
| **2007/08** | Australia | Adelaide | NZ 254-7 | A 255-3 | *Australia won by 7 wickets* |
| | Australia | Sydney | NZ 30-3 | | *abandoned* |
| | Australia | Hobart | A 282-6 | NZ 168 | *Australia won by 114 runs* |
| **2007/08** | Bangladesh | Auckland | B 201 | NZ 203-4 | *NZ  won by 6 wickets* |
| | Bangladesh | Napier | NZ 335-5 | B 181-6 | *NZ won by 102 runs ( D/L)* |
| | Bangladesh | Queenstown | B 93 | NZ 95-0 | *NZ won by 10 wickets* |
| **2007/08** | England | Wellington | E 130 | NZ 131-4 | *NZ won by 6 wickets* |
| | England | Hamilton | E 158 | NZ 165-0 | *NZ won by 10 wickets (D/L)* |
| | England | Auckland | NZ 234-9 | E 229-4 | *England won by 6 wickets (D/L)* |
| | England | Napier | E 340-6 | NZ 340-7 | *Tie* |
| | England | Christchurch | E 242-7 | NZ 213-6 | *NZ won by 34 runs (D/L)* |
| **2008** | England | Chester-le-Street | E 307-5 | NZ 193 | *England won by 114 runs* |
| | England | Birmingham | E 162 | NZ 127-2 | *abandoned* |
| | England | Bristol | NZ 182 | E 160 | *NZ won by 22 runs* |
| | England | The Oval | E 245 | NZ 246-9 | *NZ won by 1 wicket* |
| | England | Lord's | NZ 266-5 | E 215 | *NZ won by 51 runs* |
| | Ireland | Aberdeen | NZ 402-2 | I 112 | *NZ won by 290 runs* |
| | Scotland | Aberdeen | S 101 | NZ 102-2 | *NZ won by 8 wickets* |
| **2008/09** | Bangladesh | Mirpur | NZ 201-9 | B 202-3 | *Bangladesh won by 7 wickets* |
| | Bangladesh | Mirpur | NZ 212-9 | B 137 | *NZ won by 75 runs* |
| | Bangladesh | Chittagong | NZ 249-7 | B 170-8 | *NZ won by 79 runs* |
| **2008/09** | West Indies | Queenstown | WI 129-5 | | *abandoned* |
| | West Indies | Christchurch | NZ 152-8 | WI 158-5 | *West Indies by 5 wks (D/L)* |
| | West Indies | Wellington | WI 128 | NZ 129-3 | *NZ won by 7 wickets* |
| | West Indies | Auckland | NZ 275-4 | WI 64-0 | *abandoned* |
| | West Indies | Napier | WI 293-9 | NZ 211-5 | *NZ won by 9 runs (D/L)* |
| **2008/09** | Australia | Perth | A 181 | NZ 182-8 | *NZ won by 2 wickets* |
| | Australia | Melbourne | A 225-5 | NZ 226-4 | *NZ won by 6 wickets* |
| | Australia | Sydney | A 301-9 | NZ 269 | *Australia won by 32 runs* |
| | Australia | Adelaide | NZ 244-8 | A 247-4 | *Australia won by 6 wickets* |
| | Australia | Brisbane | A 168-4 | NZ 123-6 | *abandoned* |

| 2008/09 | India | Napier | I 273-4 | NZ 162-9 | *India won by 53 runs (D/L)* |
| | India | Wellington | I 188-4 | | *abandoned* |
| | India | Christchurch | I 392-4 | NZ 334 | *India won by 58 runs* |
| | India | Hamilton | NZ 270-5 | I 201-0 | *India won by 84 runs (D/L)* |
| | India | Auckland | I 149 | NZ 151-2 | *NZ won by 8 wickets* |
| 2009/10 | Sri Lanka | Colombo | SL 216-7 | NZ 119 | *Sri Lanka won by 97 runs* |
| | India | Colombo | NZ 155 | I 156-4 | *India won by 6 wickets* |
| 2009/10 | South Africa | Centurion | NZ 214 | SA 217-5 | *South Africa won by 5 wickets* |
| *Champions Trophy* | Sri Lanka | Johannesburg | NZ 315-7 | SL 277 | *NZ won by 38 runs* |
| | England | Johannesburg | E 146 | NZ 147-6 | *NZ won by 4 wickets* |
| | Pakistan | Johannesburg | P 233-9 | NZ 234-5 | *NZ won by 5 wickets* |
| | Australia | Centurion | NZ 200-9 | A 206-4 | *Australia won by 6 wickets* |
| 2009/10 | Pakistan | Abu Dhabi | P 287-9 | NZ 149 | *Pakistan won by 138 runs* |
| | Pakistan | Abu Dhabi | NZ 303-8 | P 239 | *NZ won by 64 runs* |
| | Pakistan | Abu Dhabi | NZ 211 | P 204 | *NZ won by 7 runs* |
| 2009/10 | Bangladesh | Napier | NZ 336-9 | B 190 | *NZ won by 146 runs* |
| | Bangladesh | Dunedin | B 183-8 | NZ 185-5 | *NZ won by 5 wickets* |
| | Bangladesh | Christchurch | B 241-9 | NZ 244-7 | *NZ won by 3 wickets* |
| 2009/10 | Australia | Napier | A 275-8 | NZ 281-8 | *NZ won by 2 wickets* |
| | Australia | Auckland | A 273-7 | NZ 253 | *Australia won by 12 runs (D/L)* |
| | Australia | Hamilton | NZ 245 | A 248-4 | *Australia won by 6 wickets* |
| | Australia | Auckland | NZ 238 | A 202-4 | *Australia won by 6 wickets (D/L)* |
| | Australia | Wellington | NZ 241-9 | A 190 | *NZ won by 51 runs* |
| 2010/11 | India | Dambulla | NZ 288 | I 88 | *NZ won by 200 runs* |
| | Sri Lanka | Dambulla | NZ 192 | SL 195-7 | *Sri Lanka won by 3 wickets* |
| | Sri Lanka | Dambulla | SL 203-3 | | *abandoned* |
| | India | Dambulla | I 223 | NZ 118 | *India won by 105 runs* |
| 2010/11 | Bangladesh | Mirpur | B 228 | NZ 200-8 | *Bangladesh won by 9 runs (D/L)* |
| | Bangladesh | Mirpur | *abandoned without a ball being bowled* | | |
| | Bangladesh | Mirpur | NZ 173 | B 177-3 | *Bangladesh won by 7 wickets* |
| | Bangladesh | Mirpur | B 241 | NZ 232 | *Bangladesh won by 9 runs* |
| | Bangladesh | Mirpur | B 174 | NZ 171 | *Bangladesh won by 3 runs* |
| 2010/11 | India | Guwahati | I 276 | NZ 236 | *India won by 40 runs* |
| | India | Jaipur | NZ 258-8 | I 259-2 | *India won by 8 wickets* |
| | India | Vadodara | NZ 224-9 | I 229-1 | *India won by 9 wickets* |
| | India | Bangalore | NZ 315-7 | I 321-5 | *India won by 5 wickets* |
| | India | Chennai | NZ 103 | I 107-2 | *India won by 8 wickets* |
| 2010/11 | Pakistan | Wellington | P 124 | NZ 125-1 | *NZ won by 9 wickets* |
| | Pakistan | Queenstown | P 31-0 | | *abandoned* |
| | Pakistan | Christchurch | P 293-7 | NZ 250-9 | *Pakistan won by 43 runs* |
| | Pakistan | Napier | NZ 262-7 | P 264-8 | *Pakistan won by 2 wickets* |
| | Pakistan | Hamilton | P 268-9 | NZ 227 | *Pakistan won by 41 runs* |
| | Pakistan | Auckland | NZ 311-7 | P 254 | *NZ won by 57 runs* |
| 2010/11 | Kenya | Chennai | K 69 | NZ 72-0 | *NZ won by 10 wickets* |
| *World Cup* | Australia | Nagpur | NZ 206 | A 207-3 | *Australia won by 7 wickets* |
| | Zimbabwe | Ahmedabad | Z 162 | NZ 166-0 | *NZ won by 10 wickets* |
| | Pakistan | Pallekele | NZ 302-7 | P 192 | *NZ won by 110 runs* |
| | Canada | Mumbai | NZ 358-6 | C 261-9 | *NZ won by 97 runs* |
| | Sri Lanka | Mumbai | SL 265-9 | NZ 153 | *Sri Lanka won by 112 runs* |
| | South Africa | Mirpur | NZ 221-8 | SA 172 | *NZ won by 49 runs* |
| | Sri Lanka | Colombo | NZ 217 | SL 220-5 | *Sri Lanka won by 5 wickets* |

| 2011/12 | Zimbabwe | Harare | Z 231-6 | NZ 232-1 | *NZ won by 9 wickets* |
|---|---|---|---|---|---|
| | Zimbabwe | Harare | Z 259-8 | NZ 261-6 | *NZ won by 4 wickets* |
| | Zimbabwe | Bulawayo | NZ 328-5 | Z 329-9 | *Zimbabwe won by 1 wicket* |
| 2011/12 | Zimbabwe | Dunedin | NZ 248 | Z 158 | *NZ won by 90 runs* |
| | Zimbabwe | Whangarei | NZ 372-6 | Z 231-8 | *NZ won by 141 runs* |
| | Zimbabwe | Napier | NZ 373-8 | Z 171 | *NZ won by 202 runs* |
| 2011/12 | South Africa | Wellington | NZ 253-9 | SA 254-4 | *South Africa won by 6 wickets* |
| | South Africa | Napier | NZ 230 | SA 231-4 | *South Africa won by 6 wickets* |
| | South Africa | Auckland | NZ 206 | SA 208-5 | *South Africa won by 5 wickets* |
| 2012 | West Indies | Kingston | NZ 190-9 | WI 136-1 | *West Indies won by 9 wkts (D/L)* |
| | West Indies | Kingston | WI 315-5 | NZ 260 | *West Indies won by 55 runs* |
| | West Indies | Basseterre | NZ 249-9 | WI 161 | *New Zealand won by 88 runs* |
| | West Indies | Basseterre | WI 264 | NZ 240 | *West Indies won by 24 runs* |
| | West Indies | Basseterre | WI 241-9 | NZ 221 | *West Indies won by 20 runs* |
| 2012/13 | Sri Lanka | Pallakele | *abandoned without a ball being bowled* | | |
| | Sri Lanka | Pallakele | NZ 250-6 | SL 118-3 | *Sri Lanka won by 14 runs (D/L)* |
| | Sri Lanka | Pallakele | NZ 188-6 | SL 200-3 | *Sri Lanka won by 7 wkts (D/L)* |
| | Sri Lanka | Hambantota | NZ 131-8 | SL 131-3 | *Sri Lanka won by 7 wkts (D/L)* |
| | Sri Lanka | Hambantota | SL 123-8 | NZ | *abandoned* |
| 2012/13 | South Africa | Paarl | SA 208 | NZ 209-9 | *NZ won by 1 wicket* |
| | South Africa | Kimberley | NZ 279-8 | SA 252 | *NZ won by 27 runs* |
| | South Africa | Potchefstroom | NZ 260-9 | SA 264-9 | *South Africa won by 1 wicket* |
| 2012/13 | England | Hamilton | E 258 | NZ 259-7 | *NZ won by 3 wickets* |
| | England | Napier | NZ 269 | E 270-2 | *England won by 8 wickets* |
| | England | Auckland | NZ 185 | E 186-5 | *England won by 5 wickets* |
| 2013 | England | Lord's | E 227-9 | NZ 231-5 | *NZ won by 5 wickets* |
| | England | Southampton | NZ 359-3 | E 273 | *NZ won by 86 runs* |
| | England | Nottingham | E 287-6 | NZ 253 | *England won by 34 runs* |
| 2013 | Sri Lanka | Cardiff | SL 138 | NZ 139-9 | *NZ won by 1 wicket* |
| *Champions Trophy* | Australia | Birmingham | A 243-8 | NZ 51-2 | *abandoned* |
| | England | Cardiff | E 169 | NZ 159-8 | *England won by 10 runs* |
| 2013/14 | Bangladesh | Mirpur | B 265 | NZ 162 | *Bangladesh won by 43 runs (D/L)* |
| | Bangladesh | Mirpur | B 247 | NZ 207 | *Bangladesh won by 40 runs* |
| | Bangladesh | Fatullah | NZ 307-5 | B 309-6 | *Bangladesh won by 4 wickets* |
| 2013/14 | Sri Lanka | Hambantota | SL 288-9 | NZ 13-1 | *abandoned* |
| | Sri Lanka | Hambantota | SL 138-1 | NZ 203-6 | *NZ won by 4 wickets (D/L)* |
| | Sri Lanka | Dambulla | SL 211-8 | NZ 126-6 | *Sri Lanka won by 36 runs (D/L)* |
| 2013/14 | West Indies | Auckland | NZ 156 | WI 157-8 | *West Indies won by 2 wickets* |
| | West Indies | Napier | *abandoned without a ball being bowled* | | |
| | West Indies | Queenstown | NZ 283-4 | WI 124-5 | *NZ won by 159 runs* |
| | West Indies | Nelson | NZ 285-6 | WI 134-5 | *NZ won by 58 runs (D/L)* |
| | West Indies | Hamilton | WI 363-4 | NZ 160 | *West Indies won by 203 runs* |
| 2013/14 | India | Napier | NZ 292-7 | I 268 | *NZ won by 24 runs* |
| | India | Hamilton | NZ 271-7 | I 277-9 | *NZ won by 15 runs (D/L)* |
| | India | Auckland | NZ 314 | I 314-9 | *Tied* |
| | India | Hamilton | I 278-5 | NZ 280-3 | *NZ won by 7 wickets* |
| | India | Wellington | NZ 303-5 | I 216 | *NZ won by 87 runs* |
| 2014/15 | South Africa | Mt Maunganui | NZ 230 | SA 236-4 | *South Africa won by 6 wickets* |
| | South Africa | Mt Maunganui | SA 282-9 | NZ 210 | *South Africa won by 72 runs* |
| | South Africa | Hamilton | SA 157-3 | | *abandoned* |

| | | | | | |
|---|---|---|---|---|---|
| **2014/15** | Pakistan | Dubai | NZ 246-7 | P 250-7 | *Pakistan won by 3 wickets* |
| | Pakistan | Sharjah | P 252 | NZ 255-6 | *NZ won by 4 wickets* |
| | Pakistan | Sharjah | P 364-7 | NZ 217 | *Pakistan won by 147 runs* |
| | Pakistan | Abu Dhabi | NZ 299-5 | P 292-8 | *NZ won by 7 runs* |
| | Pakistan | Abu Dhabi | NZ 275-4 | P 207 | *NZ won by 68 runs* |
| **2014/15** | Sri Lanka | Christchurch | SL 218-9 | NZ 219-7 | *NZ won by 3 wickets* |
| | Sri Lanka | Hamilton | NZ 248 | SL 252-4 | *Sri Lanka won by 6 wickets* |
| | Sri Lanka | Auckland | NZ 145-3 | | *abandoned* |
| | Sri Lanka | Nelson | SL 276 | NZ 280-6 | *NZ won by 4 wickets* |
| | Sri Lanka | Dunedin | NZ 360-5 | SL 252 | *NZ won by 108 runs* |
| | Sri Lanka | Dunedin | NZ 315-8 | SL 195 | *NZ won by 120 runs* |
| | Sri Lanka | Wellington | SL 287-6 | NZ 253 | *Sri Lanka won by 34 runs* |
| **2014/15** | Pakistan | Wellington | P 210 | NZ 213-3 | *NZ won by 7 wickets* |
| | Pakistan | Napier | NZ 369-5 | P 250 | *NZ won by 119 runs* |
| **2014/15** | Sri Lanka | Christchurch | NZ 331-6 | SL 233 | *NZ won by 98 runs* |
| *World Cup* | Scotland | Dunedin | S 142 | NZ 146-7 | *NZ won by 3 wickets* |
| | England | Wellington | E 123 | NZ 125-2 | *NZ won by 8 wickets* |
| | Australia | Auckland | A 151 | NZ 152-9 | *NZ won by 1 wicket* |
| | Afghanistan | Napier | A 186 | NZ 188-4 | *NZ won by 6 wickets* |
| | Bangladesh | Hamilton | B 288-7 | NZ 290-7 | *NZ won by 3 wickets* |
| | West Indies | Wellington | NZ 393-6 | WI 250 | *NZ won by 143 runs* |
| | South Africa | Auckland | SA 281-5 | NZ 299-6 | *NZ won by 4 wickets (D/L)* |
| | Australia | Melbourne | NZ 183 | A 186-3 | *Australia won by 7 wickets* |
| **2015** | England | Birmingham | E 408-9 | NZ 198 | *England won by 210 runs* |
| | England | The Oval | NZ 398-5 | E 365-9 | *NZ won by 13 runs (D/L)* |
| | England | Southampton | E 302 | NZ 306-7 | *NZ won by 3 wickets* |
| | England | Nottingham | NZ 349-7 | E 350-3 | *England won by 3 wickets* |
| | England | Durham | NZ 283-9 | E 192-7 | *England won by 3 wickets (D/L)* |
| **2015/16** | Zimbabwe | Harare | NZ 303-4 | Z 304-3 | *Zimbabwe won by 7 wickets* |
| | Zimbabwe | Harare | Z 235-9 | NZ 236-0 | *NZ won by 10 wickets* |
| | Zimbabwe | Harare | NZ 273-6 | Z 235 | *NZ won by 38 runs* |
| **2015/16** | South Africa | Centurion | SA 304-7 | NZ 284 | *South Africa won by 20 runs* |
| | South Africa | Potchefstroom | SA 204 | NZ 207-2 | *NZ won by 8 wickets* |
| | South Africa | Durban | SA 283-7 | NZ 221 | *South Africa won by 62 runs* |
| **2015/16** | Sri Lanka | Christchurch | SL 188 | NZ 191-3 | *NZ won by 7 wickets* |
| | Sri Lanka | Christchurch | SL 117 | NZ 118-0 | *NZ won by 10 wickets* |
| | Sri Lanka | Nelson | NZ 276-8 | SL 277-2 | *Sri Lanka won by 8 wickets* |
| | Sri Lanka | Nelson | NZ 75-3 | | *abandoned* |
| | Sri Lanka | Mt Maunganui | NZ 294-5 | SL 258 | *NZ won by 36 runs* |
| **2015/16** | Pakistan | Wellington | NZ 280-8 | P 210 | *NZ won by 70 runs* |
| | Pakistan | Napier | *abandoned without a ball being bowled* | | |
| | Pakistan | Auckland | P 290 | NZ 265-7 | *NZ won by 3 wickets (D/L)* |
| **2015/16** | Australia | Auckland | NZ 307-8 | A 148 | *NZ won by 159 runs* |
| | Australia | Wellington | NZ 281-9 | A 283-6 | *Australia won by 4 wickets* |
| | Australia | Hamilton | NZ 246 | A 191 | *NZ won by 55 runs* |
| **2016/17** | India | Dharamsala | NZ 190 | I 194-4 | *India won by 6 wickets* |
| | India | Delhi | NZ 242-9 | I 236 | *NZ won by 6 runs* |
| | India | Mohali | NZ 285 | I 289-3 | *India won by 7 wickets* |
| | India | Ranchi | NZ 260-7 | I 241 | *NZ won by 19 runs* |
| | India | Visakhapatnam | I 269-6 | NZ 79 | *India won by 190 runs* |

| 2016/17 | Australia | Sydney | A 324-8 | NZ 256 | *Australia won by 68 runs* |
|---|---|---|---|---|---|
| | Australia | Canberra | A 378-5 | NZ 262 | *Australia won by 116 runs* |
| | Australia | Melbourne | A 264-8 | NZ 147 | *Australia won by 117 runs* |
| 2016/17 | Bangladesh | Christchurch | NZ 341-7 | B 264 | *NZ won by 77 runs* |
| | Bangladesh | Nelson | NZ 251 | B 184 | *NZ won by 67 runs* |
| | Bangladesh | Nelson | B 236-9 | NZ 239-2 | *NZ won by 8 wickets* |
| 2016/17 | Australia | Auckland | NZ 286-9 | A 280 | *NZ won by 6 runs* |
| | Australia | Napier | *abandoned without a ball being bowled* | | |
| | Australia | Hamilton | NZ 281-9 | A 257 | *NZ won by 24 runs* |
| 2016/17 | South Africa | Hamilton | NZ 207-7 | SA 210-6 | *South Africa won by 4 wickets* |
| | South Africa | Christchurch | NZ 289-4 | SA 283-9 | *NZ won by 6 runs* |
| | South Africa | Wellington | SA 271-8 | NZ 112 | *South Africa won by 159 runs* |
| | South Africa | Hamilton | SA 279-8 | NZ 280-3 | *NZ won by 7 wickets* |
| | South Africa | Auckland | NZ 149 | SA 150-4 | *South Africa won by 6 wickets* |
| 2017 | Ireland | Dublin | NZ 289-7 | I 238 | *NZ won by 51 runs* |
| | Bangladesh | Dublin | B 257-9 | NZ 258-6 | *NZ won by 4 wickets* |
| | Ireland | Dublin | NZ 344-6 | I 154 | *NZ won by 190 runs* |
| | Bangladesh | Dublin | NZ 270-8 | B 271-5 | *Bangladesh won by 5 wickets* |
| 2017 *Champions Trophy* | Australia | Birmingham | NZ 291 | A 53-3 | *abandoned* |
| | England | Cardiff | E 310 | NZ 223 | *England won by 87 runs* |
| | Bangladesh | Cardiff | NZ 265-8 | B 268-5 | *Bangladesh won by 5 wickets* |
| 2017/18 | India | Mumbai | I 280-8 | NZ 284-4 | *NZ won by 6 wickets* |
| | India | Pune | NZ 230-9 | I 232-4 | *India won by 6 wickets* |
| | India | Kanpur | I 337-6 | NZ 331-7 | *India won by 6 runs* |
| 2017/18 | West Indies | Whangarei | WI 248-9 | NZ 249-5 | *NZ won by 5 wickets* |
| | West Indies | Christchurch | NZ 325-6 | WI 121 | *NZ won by 204 runs* |
| | West Indies | Christchurch | NZ 131-4 | WI 99-9 | *NZ won by 66 runs (D/L)* |
| 2017/18 | Pakistan | Wellington | NZ 315-7 | P 166-6 | *NZ won by 61 runs (D/L)* |
| | Pakistan | Nelson | P 246-9 | NZ 151-2 | *NZ won by 8 wickets (D/L)* |
| | Pakistan | Dunedin | NZ 257 | P 74 | *NZ won by 183 runs* |
| | Pakistan | Hamilton | P 262-8 | NZ 263-5 | *NZ won by 5 wickets* |
| | Pakistan | Wellington | NZ 271-7 | P 256 | *NZ won by 15 runs* |
| 2017/18 | England | Hamilton | E 284-8 | NZ 287-7 | *NZ won by 3 wickets* |
| | England | Mt Maunganui | NZ 223 | E 225-4 | *England won by 6 wickets* |
| | England | Wellington | E 234 | NZ 230-8 | *England won by 4 runs* |
| | England | Dunedin | E 335-9 | NZ 339-5 | *NZ won by 5 wickets* |
| | England | Christchurch | NZ 223 | E 229-3 | *England won by 7 wickets* |
| 2018/19 | Pakistan | Abu Dhabi | NZ 266-9 | P 219 | *NZ won by 47 runs* |
| | Pakistan | Abu Dhabi | NZ 209-9 | P 212-4 | *Pakistan won by 6 wickets* |
| | Pakistan | Dubai | P 279-8 | NZ 35-1 | *abandoned* |
| 2018/19 | Sri Lanka | Mt Maunganui | NZ 371-7 | SL 326 | *NZ won by 45 runs* |
| | Sri Lanka | Mt Maunganui | NZ 319-7 | SL 298 | *NZ won by 21 runs* |
| | Sri Lanka | Nelson | NZ 364-4 | SL 249 | *NZ won by 115 runs* |
| 2018/19 | India | Napier | NZ 157 | I 156-2 | *India won by 8 wickets (D/L)* |
| | India | Mt Maunganui | I 324-4 | NZ 234 | *India won by 90 runs* |
| | India | Mt Maunganui | NZ 243 | I 245-3 | *India won by 7 wickets* |
| | India | Hamilton | I 92 | NZ 93-2 | *NZ won by 8 wickets* |
| | India | Wellington | I 252 | NZ 217 | *India won by 35 runs* |
| 2018/19 | Bangladesh | Napier | B 232 | NZ 233-2 | *NZ won by 8 wickets* |
| | Bangladesh | Christchurch | B 226 | NZ 229-2 | *NZ won by 8 wickets* |
| | Bangladesh | Dunedin | NZ 330-6 | B 242 | *NZ won by 88 runs* |

| | | | | | |
|---|---|---|---|---|---|
| **2019** | Sri Lanka | Cardiff | SL 136 | NZ 137-0 | *NZ won by 10 wickets* |
| *World Cup* | Bangladesh | The Oval | B 244 | NZ 248-8 | *NZ won by 2 wickets* |
| | Afghanistan | Taunton | A 172 | NZ 173-3 | *NZ won by 7 wickets* |
| | India | Nottingham | *abandoned without a ball being bowled* | | |
| | South Africa | Birmingham | SA 241-6 | NZ 245-6 | *NZ won by 4 wickets* |
| | West Indies | Manchester | NZ 291-8 | WI 286 | *NZ won by 5 runs* |
| | Pakistan | Birmingham | NZ 237-6 | P 241-4 | *Pakistan won by 6 wickets* |
| | Australia | Lord's | A 243-9 | NZ 157 | *Australia won by 86 runs* |
| | England | Chester-le-Street | E 305-8 | NZ 186 | *England won by 119 runs* |
| | India | Manchester | NZ 239-8 | I 221 | *NZ won by 18 runs* |
| | England | Lord's | NZ 241-8 | E 241 | *England won on countback* |
| **2019/20** | India | Hamilton | I 347-4 | NZ 348-6 | *NZ won by 4 wickets* |
| | India | Auckland | NZ 273-8 | I 251 | *NZ won by 22 runs* |
| | India | Mt Maunganui | I 296-7 | NZ 300-5 | *NZ won by 5 wickets* |
| **2019/20** | Australia | Sydney | A 258-7 | NZ 187 | *Australia won by 71 runs* |
| **2020/21** | Bangladesh | Dunedin | B 131 | NZ 132-2 | *NZ won by 8 wickets* |
| | Bangladesh | Christchurch | B 271-6 | NZ 275-5 | *NZ won by 5 wickets* |
| | Bangladesh | Wellington | NZ 318-6 | B 154 | *NZ won by 164 runs* |
| **2021/22** | Netherlands | Mt Maunganui | N 202 | NZ 204-3 | *NZ won by 7 wickets* |
| | Netherlands | Hamilton | NZ 264-9 | N 146 | *NZ won by 118 runs* |
| | Netherlands | Hamilton | NZ 333-8 | N 218 | *NZ won by 115 runs* |

# Summary of Results

|  | Played | Won | Lost | Tie | Abandoned |
|---|---|---|---|---|---|
| v Australia | 138 | 39 | 98 | — | 7 |
| v India | 110 | 49 | 55 | 1 | 5 |
| v Pakistan | 107 | 48 | 55 | 1 | 3 |
| v Sri Lanka | 99 | 49 | 41 | 1 | 8 |
| v England | 91 | 43 | 42 | 2 | 4 |
| v South Africa | 71 | 25 | 41 | — | 5 |
| v West Indies | 65 | 28 | 30 | — | 7 |
| v Zimbabwe | 38 | 27 | 9 | 1 | 1 |
| v Bangladesh | 38 | 28 | 10 | — | — |
| v Ireland | 4 | 4 | — | — | — |
| v Netherlands | 4 | 4 | — | — | — |
| v Canada | 3 | 3 | — | — | — |
| v Scotland | 3 | 3 | — | — | — |
| v Kenya | 2 | 2 | — | — | — |
| v Afghanistan | 2 | 2 | — | — | — |
| v East Africa | 1 | 1 | — | — | — |
| v UAE | 1 | 1 | — | — | — |
| v USA | 1 | 1 | — | — | — |
| **TOTALS** | **778** | **357** | **375** | **6** | **40** |

*In addition, New Zealand forfeited their match against Kenya, at Nairobi, 2002/03*

# One-day International Captains

|  |  | Results | | | | | Toss | |
|---|---|---|---|---|---|---|---|---|
|  |  | P | W | L | Tie | NR | W | L |
| Fleming S.P. | 1996/97 to 2006/07 | 218 | 98 | 106 | 1 | 13 | 106 | 112 |
| Vettori D.L. | 2004/05 to 2010/11 | 82 | 41 | 33 | 1 | 7 | 46 | 36 |
| Williamson K.S. | 2012 to 2019/20 | 79 | 42 | 35 | — | 2 | 37 | 42 |
| McCullum B.B. | 2008/09 to 2015/16 | 62 | 36 | 22 | 1 | 3 | 28 | 34 |
| Howarth G.P. | 1979/80 to 1984/85 | 60 | 31 | 26 | — | 3 | 23 | 37 |
| Crowe M.D. | 1989/90 to 1992/93 | 44 | 21 | 22 | — | 1 | 28 | 16 |
| Rutherford K.R. | 1993/94 to 1994/95 | 37 | 10 | 24 | 1 | 2 | 18 | 19 |
| Germon L.K. | 1995/96 to 1996/97 | 36 | 15 | 19 | 2 | — | 17 | 19 |
| Wright J.G. | 1982/83 to 1990 | 31 | 16 | 15 | — | — | 21 | 10 |
| Coney J.V. | 1984/85 to 1986/87 | 25 | 8 | 16 | — | 1 | 13 | 12 |
| Taylor L.R.P.L | 2009/10 to 2012/13 | 20 | 6 | 12 | — | 2 | 10 | 10 |
| Latham T.W.M. | 2017-2021/22 | 18 | 16 | 1 | — | 1 | 8 | 10 |
| Crowe J.J. | 1985/86 to 1987/88 | 16 | 4 | 12 | — | — | 5 | 11 |
| Burgess M.G. | 1978 to 1980/81 | 8 | 2 | 6 | — | — | 6 | 2 |
| McMillan C.D. | 2000/01 to 2001/02 | 8 | 2 | 6 | — | — | 3 | 5 |
| Congdon B.E. | 1972/73 to 1974/75 | 7 | 1 | 3 | — | 3 | 5 | 2 |
| Turner G.M. | 1974/75 to 1976/77 | 7 | 5 | 2 | — | — | 4 | 3 |
| Nash D.J. | 1998/99 | 7 | 3 | 3 | — | 1 | 4 | 3 |
| Cairns C.L. | 2001/02 to 2003/04 | 7 | 1 | 6 | — | — | 3 | 4 |
| Mills K.D. | 2013/14 | 4 | 1 | 2 | — | 1 | 2 | 2 |
| Larsen G.R. | 1993/94 | 3 | 1 | 2 | — | — | 2 | 1 |
| Jones A.H. | 1992/93 | 2 | — | 2 | — | — | 1 | 1 |
| Southee T.G. | 2017/18 | 1 | — | 1 | — | — | — | 1 |
| **TOTAL** |  | **778** | **357** | **375** | **6** | **40** | **388** | **390** |

# Other One-day Internationals Played in New Zealand

| | | | | | | | |
|---|---|---|---|---|---|---|---|
| **1989/90** | Christchurch | A | 187-9 | I | 169 | *Australia won by 18 runs* |
| | Hamilton | I | 211-8 | A | 212-3 | *Australia won by 7 wickets* |
| **1991/92** | New Plymouth | Z | 312-4 | SL | 313-7 | *Sri Lanka won by 3 wickets* |
| *World* | Wellington | SA | 195 | SL | 198-7 | *Sri Lanka won by 3 wickets* |
| *Cup* | Christchurch | SA | 200-8 | WI | 136 | *South Africa won by 64 runs* |
| | Hamilton | I | 203-7 | Z | 104-1 | *India won by 55 runs\** |
| | Wellington | I | 197 | WI | 195-5 | *West Indies won by 5 wickets\** |
| **1994/95** | Wellington | SA | 123 | A | 124-7 | *Australia won by 3 wickets* |
| | Hamilton | SA | 223-6 | I | 209-9 | *South Africa won by 14 runs* |
| | Dunedin | A | 250-6 | I | 252-5 | *India won by 5 wickets* |
| **2014/15** | Hamilton | SA | 339-4 | Z | 277 | *South Africa won by 52 runs* |
| *World* | Nelson | WI | 304-7 | IRE | 307-6 | *Ireland won by 4 wickets* |
| *Cup* | Nelson | UAE | 258-7 | Z | 286-6 | *Zimbabwe won by 4 wickets* |
| | Christchurch | WI | 310-6 | P | 160 | *West Indies won by 150 runs* |
| | Dunedin | AFG | 232 | SL | 236-6 | *Sri Lanka won by 4 wickets* |
| | Christchurch | E | 303-8 | SCO | 184 | *England won by 119 runs* |
| | Dunedin | SCO | 210 | AFG | 211-9 | *Afghanistan won by 1 wicket* |
| | Wellington | E | 309-6 | SL | 312-1 | *Sri Lanka won by 9 wickets* |
| | Napier | P | 339-6 | UAE | 210-8 | *Pakistan won by 129 runs* |
| | Nelson | SCO | 318-8 | B | 322-4 | *Bangladesh won by 6 wickets* |
| | Auckland | P | 222 | SA | 202 | *Pakistan won by 29 runs (D/L)* |
| | Hamilton | IRE | 259 | I | 260-2 | *India won by 8 wickets* |
| | Wellington | SA | 341-6 | UAE | 195 | *South Africa won by 146 runs* |
| | Auckland | Z | 287 | I | 288-4 | *India won by 6 wickets* |
| | Napier | UAE | 175 | WI | 176-4 | *West Indies won by 6 wickets* |

*\* target reduced*

## Highest Totals

**For**

| | | | |
|---|---|---|---|
| 402-2 | v Ireland | Aberdeen | 2008 |
| 398-5 | v England | The Oval | 2015 |
| 397-5 | v Zimbabwe | Bulawayo | 2005/06 |
| 393-6 | v West Indies | Wellington | 2014/15 |
| 373-8 | v Zimbabwe | Napier | 2011/12 |
| 372-6 | v Zimbabwe | Whangarei | 2011/12 |
| 371-7 | v Sri Lanka | Mt Maunganui | 2018/19 |
| 369-5 | v Pakistan | Napier | 2014/15 |
| 364-4 | v Sri Lanka | Nelson | 2018/19 |
| 363-5 | v Canada | Gros Islet | 2006/07 |
| 360-5 | v Sri Lanka | Dunedin | 2014/15 |
| 359-3 | v England | Southampton | 2013 |
| 358-6 | v Canada | Mumbai | 2010/11 |
| 350-9 | v Australia | Hamilton | 2006/07 |

**Against**

| | | | |
|---|---|---|---|
| 408-9 | by England | Birmingham | 2015 |
| 392-4 | by India | Christchurch | 2008/09 |
| 378-5 | by Australia | Canberra | 2016/17 |
| 376-2 | by India | Hyderabad | 1999/00 |
| 365-9 | by England | The Oval | 2015 |
| 364-7 | by Pakistan | Sharjah | 2014/15 |
| 363-4 | by West Indies | Hamilton | 2013/14 |

| 353-5 | by India | Hyderabad | 2003/04 |
| 350-3 | by England | Nottingham | 2015 |

## Lowest Totals

**For**

| 64 | v Pakistan | Sharjah | 1985/86 |
| 73 | v Sri Lanka | Auckland | 2006/07 |
| 74 | v Australia | Wellington | 1981/82 |
| 74 | v Pakistan | Sharjah | 1989/90 |
| 79 | v India | Visakhapatnam | 2016/17 |
| 94 | v Australia | Christchurch | 1989/90 |
| 97 | v Australia | Faridabad | 2003/04 |

**Against**

| 69 | by Kenya | Chennai | 2010/11 |
| 70 | by Australia | Adelaide | 1985/86 |
| 77 | by Bangladesh | Colombo | 2002/03 |
| 86 | by Bangladesh | Chittagong | 2004/05 |
| 88 | by India | Dambulla | 2010/11 |
| 89 | by England | Wellington | 2001/02 |
| 92 | by India | Hamilton | 2018/19 |
| 93 | by Bangladesh | Queenstown | 2007/08 |

## Highest Match Aggregates

| 763 | New Zealand v England | The Oval | 2015 |
| 726 | New Zealand v India | Christchurch | 2008/09 |
| 699 | England v New Zealand | Nottingham | 2015 |
| 697 | New Zealand v Sri Lanka | Mt Maunganui | 2018/19 |
| 696 | New Zealand v Australia | Hamilton | 2006/07 |
| 695 | New Zealand v India | Hamilton | 2019/20 |
| 680 | New Zealand v England | Napier | 2007/08 |
| 678 | Australia v New Zealand | Perth | 2006/07 |
| 676 | New Zealand v Australia | Auckland | 2006/07 |
| 674 | New Zealand v England | Dunedin | 2017/18 |
| 668 | India v New Zealand | Kanpur | 2017/18 |
| 663 | New Zealand v Australia | Christchurch | 2005/06 |
| 657 | Zimbabwe v New Zealand | Bulawayo | 2011/12 |
| 655 | India v New Zealand | Rajkot | 1999/00 |
| 650 | New Zealand v Australia | Christchurch | 1999/00 |

## Lowest Match Aggregates

| 130 | New Zealand v Pakistan | Sharjah | 1985/86 |
| 141 | New Zealand v Kenya | Chennai | 2010/11 |
| 149 | New Zealand v Australia | Wellington | 1981/82 |
| 149 | New Zealand v Pakistan | Sharjah | 1989/90 |
| 185 | New Zealand v India | Hamilton | 2018/19 |
| 188 | New Zealand v Bangladesh | Queenstown | 2007/08 |
| 198 | New Zealand v Australia | Faridabad | 2003/04 |

# INDIVIDUAL RECORDS

## Centuries

| | | | | |
|---|---|---|---|---|
| 237* | Guptill M.J. | v West Indies | Wellington | 2014/15 |
| 189* | Guptill M.J. | v England | Southampton | 2013 |
| 181* | Taylor L.R.P.L. | v England | Dunedin | 2017/18 |
| 180* | Guptill M.J. | v South Africa | Hamilton | 2016/17 |
| 172 | Vincent L. | v Zimbabwe | Bulawayo | 2005/06 |
| 171* | Turner G.M. | v East Africa | Birmingham | 1975 |
| 170* | Ronchi L. | v Sri Lanka | Dunedin | 2014/15 |
| 166 | McCullum B.B. | v Ireland | Aberdeen | 2008 |
| 161 | Marshall J.A.H. | v Ireland | Aberdeen | 2008 |
| 148 | Williamson K.S. | v West Indies | Manchester | 2019 |
| 146 | Nicol R.J. | v Zimbabwe | Whangarei | 2011/12 |
| 145* | Astle N.J. | v USA | The Oval | 2004 |
| 145* | Williamson K.S. | v South Africa | Kimberley | 2012/13 |
| 141 | Styris S.B. | v Sri Lanka | Bloemfontein | 2002/03 |
| 140* | Latham T.W.M. | v Netherlands | Hamilton | 2021/22 |
| 140 | Turner G.M. | v Sri Lanka | Auckland | 1982/83 |
| 139 | How J.M. | v England | Napier | 2007/08 |
| 138 | Guptill M.J. | v Sri Lanka | Mt Maunganui | 2018/19 |
| 137 | Latham T.W.M. | v Bangladesh | Christchurch | 2016/17 |
| 137 | Taylor L.R.P.L. | v Sri Lanka | Nelson | 2018/19 |
| 134* | Fleming S.P. | v South Africa | Johannesburg | 2002/03 |
| 131* | Taylor L.R.P.L. | v Pakistan | Pallekele | 2010/11 |
| 131* | Anderson C.J. | v West Indies | Queenstown | 2013/14 |
| 131 | McCullum B.B. | v Pakistan | Abu Dhabi | 2009/10 |
| 130 | Harris C.Z. | v Australia | Madras | 1995/96 |
| 128* | Taylor L.R.P.L. | v Sri Lanka | Napier | 2006/07 |
| 126 | Conway D.P. | v Bangladesh | Wellington | 2020/21 |
| 124* | Nicholls H.M. | v Sri Lanka | Nelson | 2018/19 |
| 123 | Williamson K.S. | v Pakistan | Abu Dhabi | 2014/15 |
| 122* | Astle N.J. | v England | Dunedin | 2001/02 |
| 122* | Guptill M.J. | v West Indies | Auckland | 2008/09 |
| 120 | Astle N.J. | v Zimbabwe | Auckland | 1995/96 |
| 120 | Astle N.J. | v India | Rajkot | 1999/00 |
| 120 | Young W.A. | v Netherlands | Hamilton | 2021/22 |
| 119* | Taylor L.R.P.L. | v England | The Oval | 2015 |
| 119 | Astle N.J. | v Pakistan | Dunedin | 2000/01 |
| 119 | Taylor L.R.P.L. | v Zimbabwe | Bulawayo | 2011/12 |
| 119 | McCullum B.B. | v Zimbabwe | Napier | 2011/12 |
| 118* | Sinclair M.S. | v Sri Lanka | Sharjah | 2000/01 |
| 118* | Astle N.J. | v West Indies | Christchurch | 2005/06 |
| 118 | Williamson K.S. | v England | Southampton | 2015 |
| 118 | Williamson K.S. | v India | Delhi | 2016/17 |
| 118 | Guptill M.J. | v Bangladesh | Christchurch | 2018/19 |
| 117* | Guptill M.J. | v Bangladesh | Napier | 2018/19 |
| 117 | Astle N.J. | v Pakistan | Mohali | 1996/97 |
| 117 | Sinclair M.S. | v Pakistan | Sharjah | 2000/01 |
| 117 | Astle N.J. | v India | Colombo | 2001/02 |
| 117 | Taylor L.R.P.L. | v Australia | Auckland | 2006/07 |
| 117 | McMillan C.D. | v Australia | Hamilton | 2006/07 |
| 117 | McCullum B.B. | v Sri Lanka | Hamilton | 2014/15 |
| 116* | Fleming S.P. | v Australia | Melbourne | 1997/98 |
| 116* | Guptill M.J. | v Zimbabwe | Harare | 2015/16 |

| 115* | Fleming S.P. | v Pakistan | Christchurch | 2003/04 |
|---|---|---|---|---|
| 115* | Astle N.J. | v India | Harare | 2005/06 |
| 115 | Cairns C.L. | v India | Christchurch | 1998/99 |
| 115 | Elliott G.D. | v Australia | Sydney | 2008/09 |
| 115 | Williamson K.S. | v Pakistan | Wellington | 2017/18 |
| 114* | Turner G.M. | v India | Manchester | 1975 |
| 114 | Astle N.J. | v India | Nagpur | 1995/96 |
| 114 | Guptill M.J. | v Australia | Sydney | 2016/17 |
| 113 | Taylor L.R.P.L. | v England | Hamilton | 2017/18 |
| 112* | Taylor L.R.P.L. | v India | Hamilton | 2013/14 |
| 112* | Taylor L.R.P.L. | v Zimbabwe | Harare | 2015/16 |
| 112* | Williamson K.S. | v England | Wellington | 2017/18 |
| 112 | Fulton P.G. | v Sri Lanka | Napier | 2005/06 |
| 112 | Williamson K.S. | v Pakistan | Napier | 2014/15 |
| 111* | Fleming S.P. | v Australia | Napier | 1997/98 |
| 111* | Styris S.B. | v Sri Lanka | Grenada | 2006/07 |
| 111 | Greatbatch M.J. | v England | The Oval | 1990 |
| 111 | Guptill M.J. | v India | Auckland | 2013/14 |
| 110* | Latham T.W.M. | v Zimbabwe | Harare | 2015/16 |
| 110* | Latham T.W.M. | v Bangladesh | Christchurch | 2020/21 |
| 110 | Taylor L.R.P.L. | v West Indies | Basseterre | 2012 |
| 110 | Taylor L.R.P.L. | v England | Southampton | 2015 |
| 109* | Taylor L.R.P.L. | v India | Hamilton | 2019/20 |
| 109 | Broom N.T. | v Bangladesh | Nelson | 2016/17 |
| 108* | Nicol R.J. | v Zimbabwe | Harare | 2011/12 |
| 108 | Rutherford K.R. | v India | Baroda | 1994/95 |
| 108 | Parore A.C. | v South Africa | Verwoerdburg | 1994/95 |
| 108 | Astle N.J. | v India | Colombo | 2001/02 |
| 108 | Fleming S.P. | v South Africa | Christchurch | 2003/04 |
| 108 | Williamson K.S. | v Bangladesh | Mirpur | 2010/11 |
| 107* | Crowe M.D. | v India | Jamshedpur | 1995/96 |
| 107* | Taylor L.R.P.L. | v Bangladesh | Fatullah | 2013/14 |
| 107 | Ryder J.D. | v Pakistan | Auckland | 2010/11 |
| 107 | Taylor L.R.P.L. | v Australia | Hamilton | 2016/17 |
| 106* | Fleming S.P. | v West Indies | Port of Spain | 1995/96 |
| 106* | Williamson K.S. | v South Africa | Birmingham | 2019 |
| 106 | Fleming S.P. | v England | Brisbane | 2006/07 |
| 106 | Guptill M.J. | v Netherlands | Hamilton | 2021/22 |
| 105* | Crowe M.D. | v England | Auckland | 1983/84 |
| 105* | Taylor L.R.P.L. | v Pakistan | Dubai | 2014/15 |
| 105 | McMillan C.D. | v Pakistan | Rawalpindi | 2001/02 |
| 105 | Ryder J.D. | v India | Christchurch | 2008/09 |
| 105 | Guptill M.J. | v Zimbabwe | Harare | 2011/12 |
| 105 | Guptill M.J. | v Bangladesh | Hamilton | 2014/15 |
| 104* | Astle N.J. | v Zimbabwe | Napier | 1997/98 |
| 104* | McMillan C.D. | v Pakistan | Christchurch | 2000/01 |
| 104* | Elliott G.D. | v Sri Lanka | Dunedin | 2014/15 |
| 104 | Wadsworth K.J. | v Australia | Christchurch | 1973/74 |
| 104 | Crowe M.D. | v India | Dunedin | 1989/90 |
| 104 | Astle N.J. | v Australia | Napier | 1999/00 |
| 104 | Ryder J.D. | v West Indies | Queenstown | 2013/14 |
| 104 | Latham T.W.M. | v Ireland | Dublin | 2017 |
| 103* | Guptill M.J. | v England | Lord's | 2013 |
| 103* | Guptill M.J. | v South Africa | Potchefstroom | 2015/16 |
| 103* | Latham T.W.M. | v India | Mumbai | 2017/18 |
| 103* | Young W.A. | v Netherlands | Mt Maunganui | 2021/22 |

| 103 | Cairns C.L. | v India | Pune | 1995/96 |
|-----|-----|-----|-----|-----|
| 103 | Twose R.G. | v South Africa | Cape Town | 2000/01 |
| 103 | Taylor L.R.P.L. | v Bangladesh | Chittagong | 2008/09 |
| 103 | Williamson K.S. | v Sri Lanka | Nelson | 2014/15 |
| 102* | Edgar B.A. | v Australia | Melbourne | 1980/81 |
| 102* | Greatbatch M.J. | v England | Leeds | 1990 |
| 102* | Rutherford K.R. | v Sri Lanka | East London | 1994/95 |
| 102* | Cairns C.L. | v India | Nairobi | 2000/01 |
| 102* | Cairns C.L. | v South Africa | Brisbane | 2001/02 |
| 102* | Astle N.J. | v Zimbabwe | Bloemfontein | 2002/03 |
| 102* | Fleming S.P. | v Bangladesh | Antigua | 2006/07 |
| 102* | Taylor L.R.P.L. | v Sri Lanka | Napier | 2014/15 |
| 102* | Taylor L.R.P.L. | v South Africa | Christchurch | 2016/17 |
| 102 | Vincent L. | v West Indies | Napier | 2005/06 |
| 102 | Taylor L.R.P.L. | v India | Wellington | 2013/14 |
| 102 | Guptill M.J. | v Sri Lanka | Mt Maunganui | 2015/16 |
| 101* | Marshall H.J.H. | v Pakistan | Faisalabad | 2003/04 |
| 101* | Styris S.B. | v Pakistan | Auckland | 2003/04 |
| 101* | Oram J.D.P. | v Australia | Perth | 2006/07 |
| 101 | Congdon B.E. | v England | Wellington | 1974/75 |
| 101 | Wright J.G. | v England | Napier | 1987/88 |
| 101 | Astle N.J. | v England | Ahmedabad | 1995/96 |
| 101 | Styris S.B. | v Australia | Christchurch | 2005/06 |
| 101 | Vincent L. | v Canada | Gros Islet | 2006/07 |
| 101 | McCullum B.B. | v Canada | Mumbai | 2010/11 |
| 100* | Crowe M.D. | v Australia | Auckland | 1991/92 |
| 100* | Astle N.J. | v South Africa | Auckland | 1998/99 |
| 100* | Williamson K.S. | v Zimbabwe | Bulawayo | 2011/12 |
| 100* | Mitchell D.J. | v Bangladesh | Wellington | 2020/21 |
| 100 | Taylor L.R.P.L. | v England | Napier | 2012/13 |
| 100 | Williamson K.S. | v Australia | Birmingham | 2017 |
| 100 | Guptill M.J. | v Pakistan | Wellington | 2017/18 |

## Successive Centuries

| | |
|---|---|
| Taylor L.R.P.L. (3) 112* and 102 v India and 105* v Pakistan | 2013/14 & 2014/15 |
| Greatbatch M.J. (2) 102* and 111 v England | 1990 |
| Taylor L.R.P.L. (2) 119 v Zimbabwe and 110 v West Indies | 2011/12 |
| Guptill M.J. (2) 103* and 189* v England | 2013 |
| Guptill M.J. (2) 105 v Bangladesh and 237* v West Indies | 2014/15 |
| Taylor L.R.P.L. (2) 119* and 110 v England | 2015 |
| Guptill M.J. (2) 117* and 118 v Bangladesh | 2018/19 |
| Williamson K.S. (2) 106* v South Africa and 148 v West Indies | 2019 |

## Most Successive Fifties

| | | |
|---|---|---|
| Jones A.H. (6) | 57 v India and 55*, 62*, 67, 82, 63* v Pakistan | 1988/89 |
| Taylor L.R.P.L. (6) | 181* v England, 80 and 86 v Pakistan, | |
| | 54, 90 and 137 v Sri Lanka | 2017/18 & 2018/19 |

## Five Wickets in an Innings

| | | | | |
|---|---|---|---|---|
| 9-0-33-7 | Southee T.G. | v England | Wellington | 2014/15 |
| 10-3-34-7 | Boult T.A. | v West Indies | Christchurch | 2017/18 |
| 9-3-19-6 | Bond S.E. | v India | Bulawayo | 2005/06 |
| 10-2-23-6 | Bond S.E. | v Australia | Port Elizabeth | 2002/03 |
| 7-0-25-6 | Styris S.B. | v West Indies | Port of Spain | 2001/02 |

| 10-1-33-6 | Boult T.A. | v Australia | Hamilton | 2016/17 |
| 9.2-1-65-6 | Southee T.G. | v Bangladesh | Dunedin | 2018/19 |
| 6-2-7-5 | Vettori D.L. | v Bangladesh | Queenstown | 2007/08 |
| 7.2-1-17-5 | Boult T.A. | v Pakistan | Dunedin | 2017/18 |
| 10-4-21-5 | Boult T.A. | v India | Hamilton | 2018/19 |
| 10-2-22-5 | Hart M.N. | v West Indies | Goa | 1994/95 |
| 8.4-1-22-5 | Adams A.R. | v India | Queenstown | 2002/03 |
| 7-1-23-5 | Collinge R.O. | v India | Christchurch | 1975/76 |
| 9.3-2-23-5 | Bond S.E. | v Australia | Wellington | 2006/07 |
| 10.1-4-25-5 | Hadlee R.J. | v Sri Lanka | Bristol | 1983 |
| 9.2-2-25-5 | Bond S.E. | v Australia | Adelaide | 2001/02 |
| 10-2-25-5 | Mills K.D. | v South Africa | Durban | 2007/08 |
| 8.3-4-26-5 | Hadlee R.J. | v Australia | Sydney | 1980/81 |
| 10-3-26-5 | Oram J.D.P. | v India | Auckland | 2002/03 |
| 10-3-27-5 | Boult T.A. | v Australia | Auckland | 2014/15 |
| 7.4-1-27-5 | Neesham J.D.S. | v Bangladesh | Wellington | 2020/21 |
| 11-3-28-5 | Cairns B.L. | v England | Scarborough | 1978 |
| 9.2-1-30-5 | Vettori D.L. | v West Indies | Lord's | 2004 |
| 9-1-30-5 | Henry M.J. | v Pakistan | Abu Dhabi | 2014/15 |
| 10-1-31-5 | Neesham J.D.S. | v Afghanistan | Taunton | 2019 |
| 9-1-32-5 | Hadlee R.J. | v India | Perth | 1980/81 |
| 10-2-32-5 | Hadlee R.J. | v England | Christchurch | 1983/84 |
| 10-1-32-5 | Latham R.T. | v Australia | Auckland | 1992/93 |
| 9.3-0-33-5 | Southee T.G. | v Pakistan | Wellington | 2010/11 |
| 10-1-34-5 | Chatfield E.J. | v Australia | Adelaide | 1980/81 |
| 10-0-34-5 | Morrison D.K. | v Sri Lanka | Sharjah | 1996/97 |
| 9.4-1-36-5 | Oram J.D.P. | v USA | The Oval | 2004 |
| 10-0-38-5 | Hadlee R.J. | v Pakistan | Dunedin | 1988/89 |
| 10-0-39-5 | O'Connor S.B. | v Zimbabwe | Wellington | 1997/98 |
| 10-1-40-5 | Henry M.J. | v Sri Lanka | Mt Maunganui | 2015/16 |
| 10-0-42-5 | Harris C.Z. | v Pakistan | Sialkot | 1996/97 |
| 7.4-0-42-5 | Cairns C.L. | v Australia | Napier | 1997/98 |
| 10-1-42-5 | Franklin J.E.C. | v England | Chester-le-Street | 2004 |
| 11-1-45-5 | Pringle C. | v England | Birmingham | 1994 |
| 10-0-45-5 | Ferguson L.H. | v Pakistan | Dubai | 2018/19 |
| 10-0-46-5 | Morrison D.K. | v Pakistan | Christchurch | 1995/96 |
| 9.2-0-46-5 | O'Connor S.B. | v Pakistan | Nairobi | 2000/01 |
| 10-0-50-5 | Santner M.J. | v Ireland | Dublin | 2017 |
| 9.3-0-58-5 | McClenaghan M.J. | v West Indies | Auckland | 2013/14 |
| 10-1-63-5 | Anderson C.J. | v India | Auckland | 2013/14 |

## Most Economical Bowling

| 10-4-8-1 | Chatfield E.J. | v Sri Lanka | Dunedin | 1982/83 |
| 12-6-10-0 | Hadlee R.J. | v East Africa | Birmingham | 1975 |
| 10-6-10-0 | Cairns B.L. | v Sri Lanka | Dunedin | 1982/83 |
| 10-2-11-2 | Tuffey D.R. | v India | Christchurch | 2002/03 |
| 10-5-12-2 | Larsen G.R. | v South Africa | Hobart | 1993/94 |
| 10-2-12-1 | Harris C.Z. | v Pakistan | Napier | 2000/01 |
| 10-5-13-0 | Chatfield E.J. | v India | Adelaide | 1985/86 |
| 10-3-14-2 | Snedden M.C. | v Pakistan | Hamilton | 1988/89 |
| 10-5-14-1 | Larsen G.R. | v Zimbabwe | Wellington | 1995/96 |
| 10-4-14-4 | Vettori D.L. | v Sri Lanka | Dambulla | 2002/03 |
| 10-3-14-3 | Vettori D.L. | v USA | The Oval | 2004 |
| 10-2-15-2 | Chatfield E.J. | v England | Dunedin | 1987/88 |

| | | | | |
|---|---|---|---|---|
| 10-2-15-1 | Watson W. | v England | Christchurch | 1990/91 |
| 10-3-15-3 | Allott G.I. | v Scotland | Edinburgh | 1999 |
| 10-3-15-1 | Harris C.Z. | v West Indies | Wellington | 1999/00 |
| 10-4-15-2 | Bond S.E. | v Bangladesh | Antigua | 2006/07 |

## Most Expensive Bowling

| | | | | |
|---|---|---|---|---|
| 12-1-105-2 | Snedden M.C. | v England | The Oval | 1983 |
| 10-0-105-0 | Southee T.G. | v India | Christchurch | 2008/09 |
| 10-0-96-1 | Anderson C.J. | v Pakistan | Sharjah | 2014/15 |
| 10-0-93-2 | McClenaghan M.J. | v England | Birmingham | 2015 |
| 10-0-91-0 | Henry M.J. | v Australia | Canberra | 2016/17 |
| 10-0-87-1 | Southee T.G. | v England | Dunedin | 2017/18 |
| 10-0-87-1 | Henry M.J. | v Sri Lanka | Mt Maunganui | 2018/19 |
| 9-0-86-3 | McCullum N.L. | v England | The Oval | 2015 |
| 9-0-85-0 | Drum C.J. | v India | Hyderabad | 1999/00 |
| 10-1-85-2 | Southee T.G. | v India | Hamilton | 2019/20 |
| 11-0-84-0 | Cairns B.L. | v England | Manchester | 1978 |
| 10-0-83-2 | Gillespie M.R. | v Australia | Hamilton | 2006/07 |
| 9-0-82-0 | Bond S.E. | v Sri Lanka | Johannesburg | 2009/10 |
| 8-1-82-2 | Southee T.G. | v West Indies | Wellington | 2014/15 |
| 10-0-81-0 | Boult T.A. | v India | Kanpur | 2017/18 |
| 10-0-81-2 | Ferguson L.H. | v India | Mt Maunganui | 2018/19 |
| 10-0-80-1 | Canning T.K. | v Australia | Napier | 2004/05 |
| 10-0-80-0 | Tuffey D.R. | v Australia | Auckland | 2006/07 |
| 10-0-80-1 | Boult T.A. | v Australia | Canberra | 2016/17 |
| 10-0-80-1 | Boult T.A. | v Pakistan | Dubai | 2018/19 |

## Hat-tricks

| | | | | |
|---|---|---|---|---|
| 9-1-35-3 | Morrison D.K. | v India | Napier | 1993/94 |
| 10-0-61-4 | Bond S.E. | v Australia | Hobart | 2006/07 |
| 10-1-54-3 | Boult T.A. | v Pakistan | Abu Dhabi | 2018/19 |
| 10-1-51-4 | Boult T.A. | v Australia | Lord's | 2019 |

## Most Wicketkeeping Dismissals in an Innings

| | | | | |
|---|---|---|---|---|
| *5 | Parore A.C. | v West Indies | Goa | 1994/95 |
| †5 | McCullum B.B. | v India | Napier | 2002/03 |
| 5 | McCullum B.B | v India | Christchurch | 2002/03 |
| 5 | McCullum B.B. | v South Africa | Napier | 2003/04 |
| 5 | Hopkins G.J. | v Ireland | Aberdeen | 2008 |
| 5 | McCullum B.B. | v Bangladesh | Napier | 2009/10 |
| 5 | McCullum B.B. | v Pakistan | Wellington | 2010/11 |
| *5 | Latham T.W.M. | v Australia | Auckland | 2016/17 |
| 5 | Latham T.W.M. | v Afghanistan | Taunton | 2019 |

† *includes one stumping*  * *includes two stumpings*

## Most Catches in an Innings by a Fielder

| | | | | |
|---|---|---|---|---|
| 4 | Bracewell J.G. *(sub)* | v Australia | Adelaide | 1980/81 |
| 4 | Rutherford K.R. | v India | Napier | 1994/95 |
| 4 | Harris C.Z. | v India | Colombo | 2001/02 |
| 4 | Fleming S.P. | v England | Adelaide | 2006/07 |
| 4 | Taylor L.R.P.L. | v India | Dambulla | 2010/11 |
| 4 | How J.M. | v India | Guwahati | 2010/11 |
| 4 | McCullum N.L. | v England | Cardiff | 2013 |
| 4 | Guptill M.J. | v Pakistan | Auckland | 2015/16 |

# WALTER HADLEE TROPHIES

Awarded for the most meritorious batting and bowling performances by a New Zealand player in
one-day internationals under the board's jurisdiction and other one-day matches as designated
from time to time by the Board of Control *(discontinued after 2009/10 season)*.

| BATTING | | BOWLING | |
|---|---|---|---|
| 1988/89 | Jones A.H. | 1988/89 | Snedden M.C. |
| 1989/90 | Crowe M.D. | 1989/90 | Snedden M.C. |
| 1990/91 | Crowe M.D. | 1990/91 | Pringle C. |
| 1991/92 | Crowe M.D. | 1991/92 | Patel D.N. |
| 1992/93 | Crowe M.D. | 1992/93 | Larsen G.R. |
| 1993/94 | Thomson S.A. | 1993/94 | Pringle C. |
| 1994/95 | Parore A.C. | 1994/95 | Pringle C. |
| 1995/96 | Astle N.J. | 1995/96 | Larsen G.R. |
| 1996/97 | Fleming S.P. | 1996/97 | Harris C.Z. |
| 1997/98 | Harris C.Z. | 1997/98 | Cairns C.L. |
| 1998/99 | Astle N.J. | 1998/99 | Allott G.I. |
| 1999/00 | Astle N.J. | 1999/00 | Allott G.I. |
| 2000/01 | Twose R.G. | 2000/01 | Tuffey D.R. |
| 2001/02 | Astle N.J. | 2001/02 | Bond S.E. |
| 2002/03 | Fleming S.P. | 2002/03 | Bond S.E. |
| 2003/04 | Fleming S.P. | 2003/04 | Tuffey D.R. |
| 2004/05 | Marshall H.J.H. | 2004/05 | Vettori D.L. |
| 2005/06 | Astle N.J. | 2005/06 | Bond S.E. |
| 2006/07 | Styris S.B. | 2006/07 | Bond S.E. |
| 2007/08 | McCullum B.B. | 2007/08 | Mills K.D. |
| 2008/09 | Guptill M.J. | 2008/09 | Mills K.D. |
| 2009/10 | McCullum B.B. | 2009/10 | Vettori D.L. |

# RECORD PARTNERSHIPS

## New Zealand v All Countries

**For**

| | | | | |
|---|---|---|---|---|
| 1st | 274 | Marshall J.A.H. & McCullum B.B. v Ireland | Aberdeen | 2008 |
| 2nd | 203 | Guptill M.J. & Young W.A. v Netherlands | Hamilton | 2021/22 |
| 3rd | 206 | Williamson K.S. & Taylor L.R.P.L. v England | Southampton | 2015 |
| 4th | 200 | Taylor L.R.P.L. & Latham T.W.M. v India | Mumbai | 2017/18 |
| 5th | 195 | Taylor L.R.P.L. & Williamson K.S. v Zimbabwe | Bulawayo | 2011/12 |
| 6th | 267* | Elliott G.D. & Ronchi L. v Sri Lanka | Dunedin | 2014/15 |
| 7th | 123 | Broom N.T. & Oram J.D.P. v Bangladesh | Napier | 2009/10 |
| 8th | 94 | Franklin J.E.C. & McCullum N.L. v India | Vadodara | 2010/11 |
| 9th | 84 | Neesham J.D.S. & Henry M.J. v India | Mohali | 2016/17 |
| 10th | 76 | Ronchi L. & McClenaghan M.J. v South Africa | Mt Maunganui | 2014/15 |

**Against**

| | | | | |
|---|---|---|---|---|
| 1st | 201 | Tharanga W.U. & Jayasuriya S.T. for Sri Lanka | Napier | 2006/07 |
| | 201* | Gambhir G. & Sehwag V. for India | Hamilton | 2008/09 |
| 2nd | 331 | Tendulkar S.R. & Dravid R.S. for India | Hyderabad | 1999/00 |
| 3rd | 198 | Root J.E. & Morgan E.J.G. for England | Nottingham | 2015 |
| 4th | 211 | Edwards K.A. & Bravo D.J. for West Indies | Hamilton | 2013/14 |
| 5th | 224 | Shakib Al Hasan & Mahmudullah for Bangladesh | Cardiff | 2017 |
| 6th | 136* | Clarke M.J. & Hussey M.E.K. for Australia | Auckland | 2004/05 |
| 7th | 177 | Buttler J.C. & Rashid A.U. for England | Birmingham | 2015 |
| 8th | 117 | Houghton D.L. & Butchart I.P. for Zimbabwe | Hyderabad | 1987/88 |
| 9th | 118 | Yadav Jai P. & Pathan I.K. for India | Bulawayo | 2005/06 |
| 10th | 103 | Mohammad Aamer & Saeed Ajmal for Pakistan | Abu Dhabi | 2009/10 |

## New Zealand v England

**New Zealand**

| | | | | |
|---|---|---|---|---|
| 1st | 165* | Ryder J.D. & McCullum B.B. | Hamilton | 2007/08 |
| 2nd | 120 | Guptill M.J. & Williamson K.S. | Southampton | 2013 |
| 3rd | 206 | Williamson K.S. & Taylor L.R.P.L. | Southampton | 2015 |
| 4th | 187 | Taylor L.R.P.L. & Latham T.W.M. | Dunedin | 2017/18 |
| 5th | 138* | Styris S.B. & Oram J.D.P. | Gros Islet | 2006/07 |
| 6th | 122 | Rutherford K.R. & Harris C.Z. | Christchurch | 1990/91 |
| 7th | 96 | Williamson K.S. & Santner M.J. | Wellington | 2017/18 |
| 8th | 68 | Congdon B.E. & Cairns B.L. | Scarborough | 1978 |
| 9th | 69 | Santner M.J.& Ferguson L.H. | Mt Maunganui | 2017/18 |
| 10th | 35 | McCullum B.B. & Southee T.G. | Auckland | 2012/13 |

**England**

| | | | | |
|---|---|---|---|---|
| 1st | 193 | Gooch G.A. & Athey C.W.J. | Manchester | 1986 |
| 2nd | 190 | Bairstow J.M. & Root J.E. | Dunedin | 2017/18 |
| 3rd | 198 | Root J.E. & Morgan E.J.G. | Nottingham | 2015 |
| 4th | 136 | Pietersen K.P. & Collingwood P.D. | Chester-le-Street | 2008 |
| 5th | 113 | Gower D.I. & Randall D.W. | Brisbane | 1982/83 |
| 6th | 80 | Bairstow J.M. & Billings S.W. | Chester-le-Street | 2015 |
| 7th | 177 | Buttler J.C. & Rashid A.U. | Birmingham | 2015 |
| 8th | 76 | Nixon P.A. & Plunkett L.E. | Perth | 2006/07 |
| | 76 | Rashid A.U. & Plunkett L.E. | The Oval | 2015 |
| 9th | 47 | Trott I.J.L. & Anderson J.M. | Southampton | 2013 |
| 10th | 29 | Sidebottom R.J. & Anderson J.M. | Johannesburg | 2009/10 |

# New Zealand v Australia

**New Zealand**

| | | | | |
|---|---|---|---|---|
| 1st | 149* | Vincent L. & Fleming S.P. | Wellington | 2006/07 |
| 2nd | 151 | Vincent L. & Fulton P.G. | Melbourne | 2006/07 |
| 3rd | 125 | Williamson K.S. & Neesham J.D.S. | Canberra | 2016/17 |
| 4th | 168 | Germon L.K. & Harris C.Z. | Madras | 1995/96 |
| 5th | 148 | Twose R.G. & Cairns C.L. | Cardiff | 1999 |
| 6th | 165 | McMillan C.D.& McCullum B.B. | Hamilton | 2006/07 |
| 7th | 103 | Oram J.D.P. & Vettori D.L. | Mohali | 2006/07 |
| 8th | 72 | Harris C.Z. & Vettori D.L. | Melbourne | 2001/02 |
| 9th | 74* | McCullum B.B. & Vettori D.L. | Christchurch | 2005/06 |
| 10th | 50 | Mills K.D. & Bond S.E. | Colombo | 2002/03 |

**Australia**

| | | | | |
|---|---|---|---|---|
| 1st | 189 | Waugh M.E. & Gilchrist A.C. | Christchurch | 1999/00 |
| 2nd | 200 | Hayden M.L. & Ponting R.T. | Perth | 2006/07 |
| 3rd | 135 | Ponting R.T. & Clarke M.J. | Adelaide | 2007/08 |
| 4th | 154 | Ponting R.T. & Hodge B.J. | Melbourne | 2006/07 |
| 5th | 220 | Symonds A. & Clarke M.J. | Wellington | 2005/06 |
| 6th | 136* | Clarke M.J. & Hussey M.E.K. | Auckland | 2004/05 |
| 7th | 86* | Marsh M.R. & Hastings J.W. | Wellington | 2015/16 |
| 8th | 97 | Bevan M.G. & Bichel A.J. | Port Elizabeth | 2002/03 |
| 9th | 46 | Marsh R.W. & Lawson G.F. | Adelaide | 1980/81 |
| 10th | 54 | Stoinis M.P. & Hazlewood J.R. | Auckland | 2016/17 |

# New Zealand v India

**New Zealand**

| | | | | |
|---|---|---|---|---|
| 1st | 166 | Ryder J.D. & McCullum B.B. | Christchurch | 2008/09 |
| 2nd | 153 | Guptill M.J. & Williamson K.S. | Auckland | 2013/14 |
| 3rd | 180 | Parore A.C. & Rutherford K.R. | Baroda | 1994/95 |
| 4th | 200 | Taylor L.R.P.L. & Latham T.W.M. | Mumbai | 2017/18 |
| 5th | 147 | Twose R.G. & Cairns C.L. | Pune | 1995/96 |
| 6th | 122 | Cairns C.L. & Harris C.Z. | Nairobi | 2000/01 |
| 7th | 79 | Burgess M.G. & Cairns B.L. | Adelaide | 1980/81 |
| 8th | 94 | Franklin J.E.C. & McCullum N.L. | Vadodara | 2010/11 |
| 9th | 84 | Neesham J.D.S. & Henry M.J. | Mohali | 2016/17 |
| 10th | 52* | Vincent L. & Bond S.E. | Auckland | 2002/03 |

**India**

| | | | | |
|---|---|---|---|---|
| 1st | 201* | Gambhir G. & Sehwag V. | Hamilton | 2008/09 |
| 2nd | 331 | Tendulkar S.R. & Dravid R.S. | Hyderabad | 1999/00 |
| 3rd | 158 | Sidhu N.S. & Amarnath M. | Sharjah | 1987/88 |
| 4th | 136 | Iyer S.S. & Rahul K.L. | Hamilton | 2019/20 |
| 5th | 107 | Sehwag V. & Dhoni M.S. | Dambulla | 2010/11 |
| | 107 | Rahul K.L. & Pandey M.K. | Mt Maunganui | 2019/20 |
| 6th | 133* | Pathan Y.K. & Tiwary S.S. | Bangalore | 2010/11 |
| 7th | 116 | Dhoni M.S. & Jadeja R.A. | Manchester | 2019 |
| 8th | 82* | Kapil Dev & More K.S. | Bangalore | 1987/88 |
| 9th | 118 | Yadav Jai P. & Pathan I.K. | Bulawayo | 2005/06 |
| 10th | 34 | Kulkarni D.S. & Yadav U.T. | Ranchi | 2016/17 |

# New Zealand v Pakistan

**New Zealand**

| | | | | |
|---|---|---|---|---|
| 1st | 193 | Fleming S.P. & Astle N.J. | Dunedin | 2000/01 |
| 2nd | 159 | Guptill M.J. & Williamson K.S. | Auckland | 2015/16 |
| 3rd | 135 | Astle N.J. & Twose R.G. | Nairobi | 2000/01 |
| 4th | 157 | Marshall H.J.H. & McMillan C.D. | Wellington | 2003/04 |
| 5th | 108* | Crowe M.D. & Smith I.D.S. | Wellington | 1988/89 |
| 6th | 132 | Neesham J.D.S. & de Grandhomme C. | Birmingham | 2019 |
| 7th | 115 | Parore A.C. & Germon L.K. | Sharjah | 1996/97 |
| 8th | 57* | McCullum N.L. & Vettori D.L. | Napier | 2010/11 |
| 9th | 73* | Henry M.J. & McClenaghan M.J. | Wellington | 2015/16 |
| 10th | 33 | Germon L.K. & Morrison D.K. | Wellington | 1995/96 |

**Pakistan**

| | | | | |
|---|---|---|---|---|
| 1st | 199 | Yasir Hameed & Imran Farhat | Rawalpindi | 2003/04 |
| 2nd | 263 | Aamer Sohail & Inzamam-ul-Haq | Sharjah | 1993/94 |
| 3rd | 157* | Saeed Anwar & Inzamam-ul-Haq | Sharjah | 2000/01 |
| 4th | 161 | Yousuf Youhana & Younis Khan | Karachi | 2001/02 |
| 5th | 108* | Ijaz Ahmed & Wasim Akram | Karachi | 1996/97 |
| 6th | 105 | Haris Sohail & Shadab Khan | Wellington | 2017/18 |
| 7th | 110 | Haris Sohail & Shahid Afridi | Dubai | 2014/15 |
| 8th | 70 | Shadab Khan & Hasan Ali | Nelson | 2017/18 |
| 9th | 66 | Abdul Razzaq & Umar Gul | Pallakele | 2010/11 |
| 10th | 103 | Mohammad Aamer & Saeed Ajmal | Abu Dhabi | 2009/10 |

# New Zealand v West Indies

**New Zealand**

| | | | | |
|---|---|---|---|---|
| 1st | 136 | How J.M. & Astle N.J. | Wellington | 2005/06 |
| 2nd | 156 | Vincent L. & Astle N.J. | Napier | 2005/06 |
| 3rd | 170 | Astle N.J. & Twose R.G. | Christchurch | 1999/00 |
| 4th | 191 | Ryder J.D. & Anderson C.J. | Queenstown | 2013/14 |
| 5th | 99 | Astle N.J. & Marshall H.J.H. | Christchurch | 2005/06 |
| 6th | 130 | Nicholls H.M. & Astle T.D. | Christchurch | 2017/18 |
| 7th | 111 | Parore A.C. & Patel D.N. | Kingston | 1995/96 |
| 8th | 63* | Vettori D.L. & Franklin J.E.C. | Queenstown | 2005/06 |
| 9th | 44* | Harris C.Z. & Vaughan J.T.C. | Arnos Vale | 1995/96 |
| 10th | 48* | Nash D.J. & Pringle C. | Guwahati | 1994/95 |

**West Indies**

| | | | | |
|---|---|---|---|---|
| 1st | 192* | Greenidge C.G. & Haynes D.L. | Christchurch | 1986/87 |
| 2nd | 184 | Haynes D.L. & Gomes H.A. | Bridgetown | 1984/85 |
| 3rd | 186 | Lara B.C. & Simmons P.V. | Arnos Vale | 1995/96 |
| 4th | 211 | Edwards K.A. & Bravo D.J. | Hamilton | 2013/14 |
| 5th | 91 | Adams J.C. & Holder R.I.C. | Port of Spain | 1995/96 |
| 6th | 85 | Pollard K.A. & Thomas D.C. | Basseterre | 2012 |
| 7th | 98 | Sarwan R.R. & Jacobs R.D. | Port Elizabeth | 2002/03 |
| 8th | 48 | Perry N.O. & Dillon M. | Napier | 1999/00 |
| 9th | 77 | Sarwan R.R. & Bradshaw I.D.R. | Christchurch | 2005/06 |
| 10th | 41 | Brathwaite C.R. & Thomas O.R. | Manchester | 2019 |

# New Zealand v Sri Lanka

**New Zealand**

| | | | | |
|---|---|---|---|---|
| 1st | 137* | Guptill M.J. & Munro C. | Cardiff | 2019 |
| 2nd | 163 | Guptill M.J. & Williamson K.S. | Mt Maunganui | 2018/19 |
| 3rd | 136 | Parore A.C. & Rutherford K.R. | East London | 1994/95 |
| 4th | 154 | Taylor L.R.P.L. & Nicholls H.M. | Nelson | 2018/19 |
| 5th | 93 | Latham T.W.M. & Ronchi L. | Hambantota | 2013/14 |
| 6th | 267* | Elliott G.D. & Ronchi L. | Dunedin | 2014/15 |
| 7th | 85* | Harris C.Z. & Vincent L. | Christchurch | 2000/01 |
| 8th | 64* | Styris S.B. & Franklin J.E.C. | Grenada | 2006/07 |
| 9th | 47* | Cairns B.L. & Boock S.L. | Colombo | 1983/84 |
| 10th | 65 | Snedden M.C. & Chatfield E.J. | Derby | 1983 |

**Sri Lanka**

| | | | | |
|---|---|---|---|---|
| 1st | 201 | Tharanga W.U. & Jayasuriya S.T. | Napier | 2006/07 |
| 2nd | 170 | Jayasuriya S.T. & Tillakaratne H.P. | Bloemfontein | 2002/03 |
| 3rd | 184 | Jayasuriya S.T. & Jayawardene D.P.M.D. | Sharjah | 2000/01 |
| 4th | 127* | Dilshan T.M. & Mathews A.D. | Pallekele | 2012/13 |
| 5th | 110 | Atapattu M.S. & Arnold R.P. | Colombo | 2001/02 |
| 6th | 127 | Samaraweera T.T. & Mathews A.D. | Colombo | 2009/10 |
| 7th | 98 | Siriwardana T.A.M. & Kulasekera K.M.D.N. | Christchurch | 2015/16 |
| 8th | 75 | Perera N.L.T.C. & Malinga S.L. | Mt Maunganui | 2018/19 |
| 9th | 51 | Perera N.L.T.C. & Sandakan P.A.D.L.R | Mt Maunganui | 2018/19 |
| 10th | 44 | Perera N.L.T.C. & Pradeep N. | Mt Maunganui | 2018/19 |

# New Zealand v Zimbabwe

**New Zealand**

| | | | | |
|---|---|---|---|---|
| 1st | 236* | Guptill M.J. & Latham T.W.M. | Harare | 2015/16 |
| 2nd | 157 | Guptill M.J. & McCullum B.B. | Harare | 2011/12 |
| 3rd | 152 | Spearman C.M. & Twose R.G. | Harare | 2000/01 |
| 4th | 130 | Crowe M.D. & Rutherford K.R. | Harare | 1992/93 |
| 5th | 195 | Taylor L.R.P.L. & Williamson K.S. | Bulawayo | 2011/12 |
| 6th | 75 | Cairns C.L. & Harris C.Z. | Hamilton | 1997/98 |
| 7th | 57 | McCullum N.L. & Ellis A.M. | Dunedin | 2011/12 |
| 8th | 79 | Styris S.B. & Vettori D.L. | Harare | 2005/06 |
| 9th | 55 | Harris C.Z. & Larsen G.R. | Bulawayo | 1997/98 |
| 10th | 28 | Franklin J.E.C. & Martin C.S. | Taupo | 2000/01 |

**Zimbabwe**

| | | | | |
|---|---|---|---|---|
| 1st | 124 | Flower A. & Flower G.W. | Harare | 1992/93 |
| 2nd | 120 | Masakadza H. & Ervine C.R. | Harare | 2015/16 |
| 3rd | 154 | Carlisle S.V. & Flower A. | Taupo | 2000/01 |
| 4th | 123 | Rennie G.J. & Campbell A.D.R. | Harare | 1997/98 |
| 5th | 156 | Taylor B.R.M. & Mutizwa F. | Harare | 2011/12 |
| 6th | 112 | Waller M.N. & Chigumbura E. | Bulawayo | 2011/12 |
| 7th | 68 | Taibu T. & Streak H.H. | Bloemfontein | 2002/03 |
| 8th | 117 | Houghton D.L. & Butchart I.P. | Hyderabad | 1987/88 |
| 9th | 89 | Sikandar Raza & Panyangara T. | Harare | 2015/16 |
| 10th | 23 | Strang B.C. & Whittall A.R. | Harare | 1997/98 |

# New Zealand v South Africa

**New Zealand**

| | | | | |
|---|---|---|---|---|
| 1st | 126 | Guptill M.J. & Latham T.W.M. | Potchefstroom | 2015/16 |
| 2nd | 154 | McCullum B.B. & How J.M. | Port Elizabeth | 2007/08 |
| 3rd | 180 | Guptill M.J. & Taylor L.R.P.L. | Hamilton | 2016/17 |
| 4th | 150 | Twose R.G. & Cairns C.L. | Cape Town | 2000/01 |
| 5th | 123* | Taylor L.R.P.L. & Neesham J.D.S. | Christchurch | 2016/17 |
| 6th | 124 | McMillan C.D. & Harris C.Z. | Adelaide | 1997/98 |
| 7th | 84* | Cairns C.L. & Parore A.C. | Brisbane | 2001/02 |
| 8th | 69 | Parore A.C. & Nash D.J. | Brisbane | 1997/98 |
| 9th | 47* | Parore A.C. & Vettori D.L. | Perth | 2001/02 |
| | 47 | Franklin J.E.C. & Mills K.D. | Paarl | 2012/13 |
| 10th | 76 | Ronchi L & McClenaghan M.J. | Mt Maunganui | 2014/15 |

**South Africa**

| | | | | |
|---|---|---|---|---|
| 1st | 176 | Kirsten G. & Gibbs H.H. | Birmingham | 1999 |
| 2nd | 185 | Amla H.M. & Roussow R.R. | Centurion | 2015/16 |
| 3rd | 139* | Kallis J.H. & Dippenaar H.H. | Melbourne | 2001/02 |
| 4th | 145 | Kallis J.H. & Cullinan D.J. | Auckland | 1998/99 |
| 5th | 139* | de Villiers A.B. & Duminy J.P. | Mt Maunganui | 2014/15 |
| 6th | 97* | Rhodes J.N. & Pollock S.M. | Perth | 2001/02 |
| 7th | 84 | de Villiers A.B. & Parnell W.D. | Wellington | 2016/17 |
| 8th | 69* | Klusener L. & Abrahams S. | Cape Town | 2000/01 |
| 9th | 61 | Pretorious D. & Phehlukwayo A.L. | Christchurch | 2016/17 |
| 10th | 67* | Morkel J.A. & Ntini M. | Napier | 2003/04 |

# New Zealand v Bangladesh

**New Zealand**

| | | | | |
|---|---|---|---|---|
| 1st | 158 | Crowe M.D. & Wright J.G. | Sharjah | 1989/90 |
| 2nd | 179 | Williamson K.S. & Broom N.T. | Nelson | 2016/17 |
| 3rd | 131 | Guptill M.J. & Taylor L.R.P.L. | Hamilton | 2014/15 |
| 4th | 130 | Taylor L.R.P.L. & Munro C | Fatullah | 2013/14 |
| 5th | 159 | Conway D.P. & Mitchell D.J. | Wellington | 2020/21 |
| 6th | 86 | Vettori D.L. & Elliott G.D. | Mirpur | 2010/11 |
| 7th | 123 | Broom N.T. & Oram J.D.P. | Napier | 2009/10 |
| 8th | 72 | Taylor L.R.P.L. & Mills K.D. | Mirpur | 2010/11 |
| 9th | 37 | McCullum N.L. & Mills K.D. | Mirpur | 2013/14 |
| 10th | 45* | Oram J.D.P. & Patel J.S. | Mirpur | 2008/09 |

**Bangladesh**

| | | | | |
|---|---|---|---|---|
| 1st | 127 | Imrul Kayes & Shariar Nafees | Mirpur | 2010/11 |
| 2nd | 136 | Tamim Iqbal & Sabbir Rahman | Dublin | 2017 |
| 3rd | 109 | Zunaed Siddique & Mohammad Ashraful | Mirpur | 2008/09 |
| 4th | 154 | Mushfiqur Rahim & Naeem Islam | Mirpur | 2013/14 |
| 5th | 224 | Shakib Al Hasan & Mahmudullah | Cardiff | 2017 |
| 6th | 101 | Sabbir Rahman & Mohammad Saifuddin | Dunedin | 2018/19 |
| 7th | 101 | Mushfiqur Rahim & Naeem Islam | Dunedin | 2009/10 |
| 8th | 84 | Mohammad Mithun & Mohammad Saifuddin | Napier | 2018/19 |
| 9th | 52 | Mahmudullah & Rubel Hossain | Wellington | 2008/09 |
| 10th | 34 | Mohammad Rafique & Syed Rasel | Antigua | 2006/07 |

# CAREER RECORDS

## Averages

| | M | In | NO | HS | Runs | Ave | 100 | 50 | Ct | St | Balls | Runs | Wkts | Ave | 5WI | Best | R/100B | B/W |
|---|---|---|---|---|---|---|---|---|---|---|---|---|---|---|---|---|---|---|
| **Adams** A.R. | 42 | 34 | 10 | 45 | 419 | 17.45 | — | — | 8 | — | 1885 | 1643 | 53 | 31.00 | 1 | 5-22 | 87 | 35 |
| **Aldridge** G.W. | 2 | — | — | — | — | — | — | — | — | — | 114 | 98 | 1 | 98.00 | — | 1-45 | 86 | 114 |
| **Allott** G.I. | 31 | 11 | 6 | 7* | 17 | 3.40 | — | — | 5 | — | 1528 | 1207 | 52 | 23.21 | — | 4-35 | 78 | 29 |
| **Anderson** C.J. | 49 | 44 | 4 | 131* | 1109 | 27.72 | 1 | 4 | 11 | — | 1485 | 1502 | 60 | 25.03 | 1 | 5-63 | 101 | 24 |
| **Anderson** R.W. | 2 | 2 | 1 | 12 | 16 | 16.00 | — | — | 1 | — | — | — | — | — | — | — | — | — |
| **Astle** N.J. | 223 | 217 | 14 | 145* | 7090 | 34.92 | 16 | 41 | 83 | — | 4850 | 3809 | 99 | 38.47 | — | 4-43 | 78 | 48 |
| **Astle** T.D. | 9 | 5 | 2 | 49 | 79 | 26.33 | — | — | 2 | — | 270 | 246 | 10 | 24.60 | — | 3-33 | 91 | 27 |
| **Bailey** M.D. | 1 | — | — | — | — | — | — | — | — | — | — | — | — | — | — | — | — | — |
| **Bates** M.D. | 2 | 1 | 0 | 13 | 13 | 13.00 | — | — | 1 | — | 84 | 52 | 2 | 26.00 | — | 1-24 | 61 | 42 |
| **Bell** M.D. | 7 | 7 | 0 | 66 | 133 | 19.00 | — | 1 | 1 | — | — | — | — | — | — | — | — | — |
| **Bennett** H.K. | 19 | 7 | 5 | 4* | 10 | 5.00 | — | — | 3 | — | 892 | 820 | 33 | 24.84 | — | 4-16 | 91 | 27 |
| **Blain** T.E. | 38 | 38 | 11 | 49* | 442 | 16.37 | — | — | 37 | 1 | — | — | — | — | — | — | — | — |
| **Blair** B.R. | 14 | 14 | 2 | 29* | 174 | 12.50 | — | — | 4 | — | 30 | 34 | 1 | 34.00 | — | 1-7 | 113 | 30 |
| **Blundell** T.A. | 2 | 2 | 0 | 22 | 31 | 15.50 | — | — | 1 | — | — | — | — | — | — | — | — | — |
| **Bond** S.E. | 82 | 40 | 22 | 31* | 292 | 16.22 | — | — | 15 | — | 4295 | 3070 | 147 | 20.88 | 4 | 6-19 | 71 | 29 |
| **Boock** S.L. | 14 | 7 | 4 | 12 | 30 | 10.00 | — | — | 5 | — | 700 | 513 | 15 | 34.20 | — | 3-28 | 73 | 46 |
| **Boult** T.A. | 93 | 40 | 23 | 21* | 159 | 9.35 | — | — | 34 | — | 5157 | 4261 | 169 | 25.21 | 5 | 7-34 | 82 | 30 |
| **Bracewell** B.P. | 1 | 1 | 1 | 0* | 0 | — | — | — | — | — | 66 | 41 | 1 | 41.00 | — | 1-41 | 62 | 66 |
| **Bracewell** D.A.J. | 21 | 14 | 2 | 57 | 221 | 18.41 | — | 1 | 5 | — | 1016 | 845 | 26 | 32.50 | — | 4-55 | 83 | 39 |
| **Bracewell** J.G. | 53 | 43 | 12 | 43 | 512 | 16.51 | — | — | 19 | — | 2447 | 1884 | 33 | 57.09 | — | 2-3 | 76 | 74 |
| **Bracewell** M.G. | 3 | 2 | 0 | 3 | 4 | 2.00 | — | — | 3 | — | 114 | 96 | 5 | 19.20 | — | 3-21 | 83 | 23 |
| **Bradburn** G.E. | 11 | 10 | 3 | 30 | 60 | 8.57 | — | — | 2 | — | 385 | 318 | 6 | 53.00 | — | 2-18 | 82 | 64 |
| **Broom** N.T. | 39 | 39 | 4 | 109* | 943 | 26.94 | 1 | 5 | 9 | — | — | — | — | — | — | — | — | — |
| **Brown** V.R. | 3 | 3 | 0 | 32 | 44 | 14.66 | — | — | 2 | — | 66 | 75 | 1 | 75.00 | — | 1-24 | 113 | 66 |
| **Brownlie** D.G. | 16 | 15 | 1 | 63 | 361 | 25.78 | — | 1 | 6 | — | — | — | — | — | — | — | — | — |
| **Bulfin** C.E. | 4 | 2 | 1 | 7* | 9 | 9.00 | — | — | 1 | — | 102 | 109 | 0 | — | — | — | 106 | — |
| **Burgess** M.G. | 26 | 20 | 0 | 47 | 336 | 16.80 | — | — | 8 | — | 74 | 69 | 1 | 69.00 | — | 1-10 | 93 | 74 |
| **Butler** I.G. | 26 | 13 | 5 | 25 | 84 | 10.50 | — | — | 8 | — | 1109 | 1038 | 28 | 37.07 | — | 4-44 | 93 | 39 |
| **Cairns** B.L. | 78 | 65 | 6 | 60 | 987 | 16.73 | — | 2 | 19 | — | 4015 | 2717 | 89 | 30.47 | 1 | 5-28 | 67 | 45 |
| **Cairns** C.L. | 215 | 193 | 25 | 115 | 4950 | 29.46 | 4 | 26 | 66 | — | 8168 | 6594 | 201 | 32.80 | 1 | 5-42 | 80 | 40 |
| **Canning** T.K. | 4 | 4 | 1 | 23* | 52 | 17.33 | — | — | 1 | — | 204 | 203 | 5 | 40.60 | — | 2-30 | 100 | 41 |
| **Chapman** M.S. | 6 | 6 | 1 | 124* | 161 | 32.30 | 1 | — | 1 | — | — | — | — | — | — | — | — | — |
| **Chatfield** E.J. | 114 | 48 | 37 | 19* | 118 | 10.72 | — | — | 19 | — | 6065 | 3618 | 140 | 25.84 | 1 | 5-34 | 59 | 43 |
| **Collinge** R.O. | 16 | 10 | 4 | 19 | 53 | 8.83 | — | — | 1 | — | 915 | 517 | 19 | 27.21 | 1 | 5-23 | 56 | 48 |
| **Coman** P.G. | 3 | 3 | 0 | 38 | 62 | 20.66 | — | — | 2 | — | — | — | — | — | — | — | — | — |
| **Coney** J.V. | 88 | 80 | 19 | 66* | 1874 | 30.72 | — | 8 | 40 | — | 2931 | 2039 | 54 | 37.75 | — | 4-46 | 69 | 54 |
| **Congdon** B.E. | 12 | 10 | 3 | 101 | 373 | 54.71 | 1 | 2 | 1 | — | 501 | 322 | 8 | 40.25 | — | 2-17 | 64 | 62 |
| **Conway** D.P. | 3 | 3 | 0 | 126 | 225 | 75.00 | 1 | 1 | 2 | — | — | — | — | — | — | — | — | — |
| **Crowe** J.J. | 75 | 71 | 12 | 88* | 1518 | 25.72 | — | 7 | 28 | — | 6 | 1 | 0 | — | — | — | 16 | — |
| **Crowe** M.D. | 143 | 140 | 18 | 107* | 4704 | 38.55 | 4 | 34 | 66 | — | 1296 | 954 | 29 | 32.89 | — | 2-9 | 73 | 44 |
| **Cumming** C.D. | 13 | 13 | 1 | 45* | 161 | 13.41 | — | — | 6 | — | 18 | 17 | 0 | — | — | — | 94 | — |
| **Davis** H.T. | 11 | 6 | 4 | 7* | 13 | 6.50 | — | — | 2 | — | 432 | 436 | 11 | 39.63 | — | 4-35 | 100 | 39 |
| **de Grandhomme** C. | 45 | 35 | 7 | 74* | 742 | 26.50 | — | 4 | 17 | — | 1548 | 1230 | 30 | 41.00 | — | 3-26 | 79 | 51 |
| **de Groen** R.P. | 12 | 8 | 3 | 7* | 12 | 2.40 | — | — | 2 | — | 549 | 478 | 8 | 59.75 | — | 2-34 | 87 | 68 |
| **Devcich** A.P. | 12 | 11 | 0 | 58 | 195 | 17.72 | — | 1 | 3 | — | 324 | 291 | 4 | 72.75 | — | 2-33 | 89 | 81 |
| **Diamanti** B.J. | 1 | 1 | 1 | 26* | 26 | — | — | — | 1 | — | 12 | 25 | 0 | — | — | — | 208 | — |
| **Douglas** M.W. | 6 | 6 | 0 | 30 | 55 | 9.16 | — | — | 2 | — | — | — | — | — | — | — | — | — |
| **Doull** S.B. | 42 | 27 | 13 | 22 | 172 | 12.28 | — | — | 10 | — | 1745 | 1459 | 36 | 40.52 | — | 4-25 | 83 | 48 |
| **Drum** C.J. | 5 | 2 | 2 | 7* | 9 | — | — | — | 1 | — | 216 | 261 | 4 | 65.25 | — | 2-31 | 120 | 54 |
| **Edgar** B.A. | 64 | 64 | 5 | 102* | 1814 | 30.74 | 1 | 10 | 12 | — | 12 | 5 | 0 | — | — | — | 41 | — |
| **Edwards** G.N. | 7 | 7 | 0 | 41 | 164 | 23.42 | — | — | 7 | — | 6 | 5 | 1 | 5.00 | — | 1-5 | 83 | 6 |
| **Elliott** G.D. | 83 | 69 | 11 | 115 | 1976 | 34.06 | 2 | 11 | 17 | — | 1302 | 1179 | 39 | 30.23 | — | 4-31 | 90 | 33 |
| **Ellis** A.M. | 15 | 12 | 1 | 33 | 153 | 13.90 | — | — | 3 | — | 480 | 425 | 12 | 35.41 | — | 2-22 | 88 | 40 |
| **Ferguson** L.H. | 37 | 16 | 7 | 19 | 63 | 7.00 | — | — | 10 | — | 1956 | 1779 | 69 | 25.78 | 1 | 5-45 | 91 | 28 |
| **Fleming** S.P. | 280 | 269 | 21 | 134* | 8037 | 32.40 | 8 | 49 | 133 | — | 29 | 28 | 1 | 28.00 | — | 1-8 | 96 | 29 |
| **Flynn** D.R. | 20 | 17 | 2 | 35 | 228 | 15.20 | — | — | 4 | — | 24 | 25 | 0 | — | — | — | 104 | — |
| **Franklin** J.E.C. | 109 | 79 | 27 | 98* | 1265 | 24.32 | — | 4 | 26 | — | 3836 | 3334 | 81 | 41.16 | 1 | 5-42 | 86 | 47 |
| **Franklin** T.J. | 3 | 3 | 0 | 21 | 27 | 9.00 | — | — | 1 | — | — | — | — | — | — | — | — | — |
| **Fulton** P.G. | 49 | 46 | 5 | 112 | 1334 | 32.53 | 1 | 8 | 17 | — | — | — | — | — | — | — | — | — |
| **Germon** L.K. | 37 | 31 | 5 | 89 | 519 | 19.96 | — | 3 | 21 | 9 | — | — | — | — | — | — | — | — |

| | M | In | NO | HS | Runs | Ave | 100 | 50 | Ct | St | Balls | Runs | Wkts | Ave | 5WI | Best | R/100B | B/W |
|---|---|---|---|---|---|---|---|---|---|---|---|---|---|---|---|---|---|---|
| Gillespie M.R. | 32 | 14 | 8 | 28 | 93 | 15.50 | — | — | 6 | — | 1521 | 1369 | 37 | 37.00 | — | 4-58 | 90 | 41 |
| Gillespie S.R. | 19 | 11 | 5 | 18* | 70 | 11.66 | — | — | 7 | — | 963 | 736 | 23 | 32.00 | — | 4-30 | 76 | 41 |
| Gray E.J. | 10 | 7 | 1 | 38 | 98 | 16.33 | — | — | 3 | — | 386 | 286 | 8 | 35.75 | — | 2-26 | 74 | 48 |
| Greatbatch M.J. | 84 | 83 | 5 | 111 | 2206 | 28.28 | 2 | 13 | 35 | — | 6 | 5 | 0 | — | — | — | 83 | — |
| Guptill M.J. | 189 | 186 | 19 | 237* | 7041 | 42.16 | 17 | 37 | 96 | — | 109 | 98 | 4 | 24.50 | — | 2-6 | 90 | 27 |
| Hadlee B.G. | 2 | 2 | 1 | 19 | 26 | 26.00 | — | — | — | — | — | — | — | — | — | — | — | — |
| Hadlee D.R. | 12 | 8 | 2 | 20 | 56 | 9.33 | — | — | 3 | — | 683 | 410 | 23 | 17.82 | — | 4-34 | 60 | 29 |
| Hadlee R.J. | 115 | 98 | 17 | 79 | 1751 | 21.61 | — | 4 | 27 | — | 6182 | 3407 | 158 | 21.56 | 5 | 5-25 | 55 | 39 |
| Hamilton L.J. | 2 | 2 | 2 | 2* | 3 | — | — | — | — | — | 108 | 143 | 1 | 143.00 | — | 1-76 | 132 | 108 |
| Harris C.Z. | 250 | 213 | 62 | 130 | 4379 | 29.00 | 1 | 16 | 96 | | 10667 | 7613 | 203 | 37.50 | 1 | 5-42 | 71 | 53 |
| Hart M.N. | 13 | 8 | 0 | 16 | 61 | 7.62 | — | — | 7 | — | 572 | 373 | 13 | 28.69 | 1 | 5-22 | 65 | 44 |
| Hart R.G. | 2 | 1 | 0 | 0 | 0 | 0.00 | — | — | 1 | — | — | — | — | — | — | — | — | — |
| Hart R.T. | 1 | 1 | 0 | 3 | 3 | 3.00 | — | — | — | — | — | — | — | — | — | — | — | — |
| Hartland B.R. | 16 | 16 | 1 | 68* | 311 | 20.73 | — | 2 | 5 | — | — | — | — | — | — | — | — | — |
| Haslam M.J. | 1 | 1 | 0 | 9 | 9 | — | — | — | — | — | 30 | 28 | 1 | 28.00 | — | 1-28 | 93 | 30 |
| Hastings B.F. | 12 | 10 | 1 | 37 | 176 | 19.55 | — | — | 4 | — | — | — | — | — | — | — | — | — |
| Hayes R.L. | 1 | 1 | 0 | 13 | 13 | 13.00 | — | — | — | — | 42 | 31 | 0 | — | — | — | 73 | — |
| Henry M.J. | 57 | 21 | 7 | 48* | 211 | 15.07 | — | — | 17 | — | 2970 | 2605 | 103 | 25.29 | 2 | 5-30 | 87 | 28 |
| Hitchcock P.A. | 14 | 7 | 3 | 11* | 41 | 10.25 | — | — | 4 | — | 558 | 468 | 12 | 39.00 | — | 3-30 | 83 | 46 |
| Hopkins G.J. | 25 | 17 | 1 | 45 | 236 | 14.75 | — | — | 27 | 1 | — | — | — | — | — | — | — | — |
| Horne M.J. | 50 | 48 | 0 | 74 | 980 | 20.41 | — | 5 | 12 | — | — | — | — | — | — | — | — | — |
| Horne P.A. | 4 | 4 | 0 | 18 | 50 | 12.50 | — | — | — | — | — | — | — | — | — | — | — | — |
| How J.M. | 41 | 37 | 1 | 139 | 1046 | 29.05 | 1 | 7 | 19 | — | — | — | — | — | — | — | — | — |
| Howarth G.P. | 71 | 66 | 5 | 76 | 1384 | 22.72 | — | 6 | 16 | — | 90 | 68 | 3 | 22.67 | — | 1-4 | 75 | 30 |
| Howarth H.J. | 10 | 6 | 3 | 11 | 21 | 7.00 | — | — | 3 | — | 556 | 304 | 14 | 27.71 | — | 3-24 | 54 | 39 |
| Howell L.G. | 12 | 12 | 0 | 68 | 287 | 23.92 | — | 4 | 2 | — | — | — | — | — | — | — | — | — |
| Ingram P.J. | 8 | 7 | 0 | 69 | 193 | 27.57 | — | 1 | 3 | — | — | — | — | — | — | — | — | — |
| Jamieson K.A. | 8 | 3 | 2 | 25* | 34 | 34.00 | — | — | 2 | — | 412 | 296 | 11 | 26.90 | — | 3-45 | 71 | 37 |
| Jones A.H. | 87 | 87 | 9 | 93 | 2784 | 35.69 | — | 25 | 23 | — | 306 | 216 | 4 | 54.00 | — | 2-42 | 70 | 76 |
| Jones R.A. | 5 | 5 | 0 | 63 | 168 | 33.60 | — | 1 | — | — | — | — | — | — | — | — | — | — |
| Kennedy R.J. | 7 | 4 | 3 | 8* | 17 | 17.00 | — | — | 1 | — | 312 | 283 | 5 | 56.60 | — | 2-36 | 90 | 62 |
| Kuggeleijn C.M. | 16 | 11 | 2 | 40 | 142 | 15.77 | — | — | 9 | — | 817 | 604 | 12 | 50.33 | — | 2-31 | 74 | 68 |
| Kuggeleijn S.C. | 2 | 1 | 1 | 11 | 11 | 11.00 | — | — | — | — | 84 | 58 | 5 | 11.60 | — | 3-41 | 69 | 16 |
| Larsen G.R. | 121 | 70 | 27 | 37 | 629 | 14.62 | — | — | 23 | — | 6368 | 4000 | 113 | 35.39 | — | 4-24 | 62 | 56 |
| Latham R.T. | 33 | 33 | 4 | 60 | 583 | 20.10 | — | 1 | 11 | — | 450 | 386 | 11 | 35.09 | 1 | 5-32 | 85 | 40 |
| Latham T.W.M. | 105 | 97 | 13 | 140* | 2995 | 35.65 | 6 | 16 | 88 | 9 | — | — | — | — | — | — | — | — |
| Lees W.K. | 31 | 24 | 5 | 26 | 215 | 11.31 | — | — | 28 | 2 | — | — | — | — | — | — | — | — |
| McClenaghan M.J. | 48 | 14 | 10 | 34* | 108 | 27.00 | — | — | 4 | — | 2336 | 2313 | 82 | 28.20 | 1 | 5-58 | 99 | 28 |
| McCullum B.B. | 260 | 228 | 28 | 166 | 6083 | 30.41 | 5 | 32 | 262 | 15 | — | — | — | — | — | — | — | — |
| McCullum N.L. | 84 | 62 | 11 | 65 | 1070 | 20.98 | — | 4 | 41 | — | 3536 | 2956 | 63 | 46.92 | — | 3-24 | 83 | 56 |
| McEwan P.E. | 17 | 15 | 0 | 41 | 204 | 13.60 | — | — | 1 | — | 420 | 353 | 6 | 58.83 | — | 2-29 | 84 | 70 |
| McGlashan P.D. | 4 | 2 | 1 | 56* | 63 | 63.00 | — | 1 | 8 | — | — | — | — | — | — | — | — | — |
| McKay J.A. | 19 | 10 | 7 | 4* | 12 | 4.00 | — | — | 3 | — | 926 | 800 | 27 | 29.62 | — | 4-53 | 86 | 34 |
| McKechnie B.J. | 14 | 8 | 4 | 27 | 54 | 13.50 | — | — | 2 | — | 818 | 495 | 19 | 26.05 | — | 3-23 | 60 | 43 |
| McMillan C.D. | 197 | 183 | 16 | 117 | 4707 | 28.18 | 3 | 28 | 44 | — | 1879 | 1717 | 49 | 35.04 | — | 3-20 | 91 | 38 |
| McSweeney E.B. | 16 | 14 | 5 | 18* | 73 | 8.11 | — | — | 14 | 3 | — | — | — | — | — | — | — | — |
| Marshall H.J.H. | 66 | 62 | 9 | 101* | 1454 | 27.43 | 1 | 12 | 18 | — | — | — | — | — | — | — | — | — |
| Marshall J.A.H. | 10 | 10 | 0 | 161 | 250 | 25.00 | 1 | 1 | — | — | — | — | — | — | — | — | — | — |
| Martin C.S. | 20 | 7 | 2 | 3 | 8 | 1.60 | — | — | 7 | — | 948 | 804 | 18 | 44.66 | — | 3-62 | 84 | 52 |
| Mason M.J. | 26 | 7 | 4 | 13* | 24 | 8.00 | — | — | 4 | — | 1179 | 1024 | 31 | 33.03 | — | 4-24 | 86 | 38 |
| Mathieson A.W. | 1 | — | — | — | — | — | — | — | — | — | 24 | 40 | 1 | 40.00 | — | 1-40 | 166 | 24 |
| Millmow J.P. | 5 | 1 | 1 | 0* | 0 | — | — | — | 1 | — | 270 | 232 | 4 | 58.00 | — | 2-22 | 85 | 67 |
| Mills K.D. | 170 | 101 | 34 | 54 | 1047 | 15.62 | — | 2 | 42 | — | 8230 | 6485 | 240 | 27.02 | 1 | 5-25 | 79 | 34 |
| Milne A.F. | 40 | 17 | 7 | 36 | 168 | 16.80 | — | — | 21 | — | 1801 | 1581 | 41 | 38.56 | — | 3-49 | 87 | 43 |
| Mitchell D.J. | 3 | 2 | 2 | 100* | 112 | — | 1 | — | — | — | 30 | 33 | 0 | — | — | — | 110 | - |
| Morrison D.K. | 96 | 43 | 24 | 20* | 171 | 9.00 | — | — | 19 | — | 4586 | 3470 | 126 | 27.53 | 2 | 5-34 | 75 | 36 |
| Morrison J.F.M. | 19 | 16 | 3 | 55 | 301 | 23.15 | — | 1 | 6 | — | 283 | 199 | 8 | 24.87 | — | 3-24 | 70 | 35 |
| Munro C. | 57 | 53 | 2 | 87 | 1271 | 24.92 | — | 8 | 22 | — | 552 | 481 | 7 | 68.71 | — | 2-10 | 87 | 78 |
| Murray D.J. | 1 | 1 | 0 | 3 | 3 | 3.00 | — | — | — | — | — | — | — | — | — | — | — | — |
| Nash D.J. | 81 | 53 | 13 | 42 | 624 | 15.60 | — | — | 25 | — | 3416 | 2622 | 64 | 40.96 | — | 4-38 | 76 | 53 |
| Neesham J.D.S. | 66 | 56 | 10 | 97 | 1320 | 28.69 | — | 6 | 24 | — | 2115 | 2139 | 68 | 31.45 | 2 | 5-27 | 101 | 31 |
| Nethula T.S. | 5 | 3 | 1 | 9* | 12 | 6.00 | — | — | 2 | — | 264 | 249 | 5 | 49.80 | — | 2-41 | 94 | 52 |
| Nevin C.J. | 37 | 36 | 0 | 74 | 732 | 20.33 | — | 4 | 16 | 3 | — | — | — | — | — | — | — | — |
| Nicholls H.M. | 55 | 53 | 11 | 124* | 1487 | 35.40 | 1 | 12 | 22 | — | — | — | — | — | — | — | — | — |
| Nicol R.J. | 22 | 21 | 2 | 146 | 586 | 30.84 | 2 | 2 | 11 | — | 339 | 329 | 10 | 32.90 | — | 4-19 | 97 | 33 |

| | M | In | NO | HS | Runs | Ave | 100 | 50 | Ct | St | Balls | Runs | Wkts | Ave | 5WI | Best | R/100B | B/W |
|---|---|---|---|---|---|---|---|---|---|---|---|---|---|---|---|---|---|---|
| O'Brien I.E. | 10 | 2 | 2 | 3* | 3 | — | — | — | 1 | — | 453 | 488 | 14 | 34.85 | — | 3-68 | 107 | 32 |
| O'Connor S.B. | 38 | 13 | 6 | 8 | 24 | 3.42 | — | — | 11 | — | 1487 | 1397 | 46 | 30.36 | 2 | 5-39 | 93 | 32 |
| O'Sullivan D.R. | 3 | 2 | 1 | 1* | 2 | 2.00 | — | — | — | — | 168 | 123 | 2 | 61.50 | — | 1-38 | 73 | 84 |
| Oram J.D.P. | 160 | 116 | 15 | 101* | 2434 | 24.09 | 1 | 13 | 51 | — | 6911 | 5047 | 173 | 29.17 | 1 | 5-26 | 73 | 39 |
| Owens M.B. | 1 | 1 | 0 | 0 | 0 | 0.00 | — | — | — | — | 48 | 37 | 0 | — | — | — | 77 | — |
| Papps M.H.W. | 6 | 6 | 2 | 92* | 207 | 51.75 | — | 2 | 1 | — | — | — | — | — | — | — | — | — |
| Parker J.M. | 25 | 21 | 0 | 66 | 280 | 13.33 | — | 1 | 11 | 1 | 16 | 10 | 1 | 10.00 | — | 1-10 | 62 | 16 |
| Parker N.M. | 1 | 1 | 0 | 0 | 0 | 0.00 | — | — | — | — | — | — | — | — | — | — | — | — |
| Parore A.C. | 179 | 161 | 32 | 108 | 3314 | 25.68 | 1 | 14 | 116 | 25 | — | — | — | — | — | — | — | — |
| Patel D.N. | 75 | 63 | 10 | 71 | 623 | 11.75 | — | 1 | 23 | — | 3251 | 2260 | 45 | 50.22 | — | 3-22 | 69 | 72 |
| Patel J.S. | 43 | 15 | 8 | 34 | 95 | 13.57 | — | — | 13 | — | 2014 | 1691 | 49 | 34.51 | — | 3-11 | 84 | 41 |
| Penn A.J. | 5 | 3 | 1 | 15 | 23 | 11.50 | — | — | 1 | — | 159 | 201 | 1 | 201.00 | — | 1-50 | 126 | 159 |
| Petrie R.G. | 12 | 8 | 3 | 21 | 65 | 13.00 | — | — | 2 | — | 660 | 449 | 12 | 37.41 | — | 2-25 | 68 | 55 |
| Pollard V. | 3 | 2 | 0 | 55 | 67 | 33.50 | — | 1 | 1 | — | — | — | — | — | — | — | — | — |
| Priest M.W. | 18 | 14 | 4 | 24 | 103 | 10.30 | — | — | 2 | — | 752 | 590 | 8 | 73.75 | — | 2-27 | 78 | 94 |
| Pringle C. | 64 | 41 | 19 | 34* | 193 | 8.77 | — | — | 7 | — | 3314 | 2459 | 103 | 23.87 | 1 | 5-45 | 74 | 32 |
| Rance S.H.A. | 2 | — | — | — | — | — | — | — | 3 | — | 105 | 110 | 1 | 110.00 | — | 1-44 | 105 | 105 |
| Redmond A.J. | 6 | 6 | 0 | 52 | 152 | 25.33 | — | 1 | 3 | — | — | — | — | — | — | — | — | — |
| Redmond R.E. | 2 | 1 | 0 | 3 | 3 | 3.00 | — | — | — | — | — | — | — | — | — | — | — | — |
| Reid J.F. | 25 | 24 | 1 | 88 | 633 | 27.16 | — | 4 | 5 | — | — | — | — | — | — | — | — | — |
| Reid R.B. | 9 | 9 | 0 | 64 | 248 | 27.55 | — | 2 | 3 | — | 7 | 13 | 1 | 13.00 | — | 1-13 | 185 | 7 |
| Richardson M.H. | 4 | 4 | 0 | 26 | 42 | 10.50 | — | — | 1 | — | — | — | — | — | — | — | — | — |
| Roberts A.D.G. | 1 | 1 | 0 | 16 | 16 | 16.00 | — | — | 1 | — | 56 | 30 | 1 | 30.00 | — | 1-30 | 53 | 56 |
| Roberts S.J. | 2 | 1 | 1 | 1* | 1 | — | — | — | — | — | 42 | 47 | 0 | — | — | — | 111 | — |
| Robertson G.K. | 10 | 6 | 0 | 17 | 49 | 8.16 | — | — | 2 | — | 498 | 321 | 6 | 53.50 | — | 2-29 | 64 | 83 |
| Ronchi L. | 85 | 68 | 9 | 170* | 1397 | 23.67 | 1 | 4 | 105 | 12 | — | — | — | — | — | — | — | — |
| Rutherford H.D. | 4 | 4 | 0 | 11 | 15 | 3.75 | — | — | 2 | — | — | — | — | — | — | — | — | — |
| Rutherford K.R. | 121 | 115 | 9 | 108 | 3143 | 29.65 | 2 | 18 | 41 | — | 389 | 323 | 10 | 32.30 | — | 2-39 | 83 | 38 |
| Ryder J.D. | 48 | 42 | 1 | 107 | 1362 | 33.21 | 3 | 6 | 15 | — | 407 | 412 | 12 | 34.33 | — | 3-29 | 101 | 33 |
| Santner M.J. | 75 | 57 | 23 | 67 | 927 | 27.26 | — | 2 | 30 | — | 3385 | 2742 | 75 | 36.56 | 1 | 5-50 | 81 | 45 |
| Seifert T.L. | 3 | 2 | 0 | 22 | 33 | 16.50 | — | — | 7 | 1 | — | — | — | — | — | — | — | — |
| Sinclair M.S. | 54 | 50 | 4 | 118* | 1304 | 28.34 | 2 | 8 | 17 | — | — | — | — | — | — | — | — | — |
| Smith I.D.S. | 98 | 77 | 16 | 62* | 1055 | 17.29 | — | 3 | 81 | 5 | — | — | — | — | — | — | — | — |
| Snedden M.C. | 93 | 54 | 19 | 64 | 535 | 15.28 | — | 1 | 19 | — | 4525 | 3237 | 114 | 28.39 | — | 4-34 | 71 | 39 |
| Sodhi I.S. | 36 | 16 | 4 | 24 | 112 | 9.33 | — | — | 10 | — | 1771 | 1604 | 46 | 34.86 | — | 4-58 | 90 | 38 |
| Southee T.G. | 143 | 86 | 32 | 55 | 679 | 12.57 | — | 1 | 39 | — | 7195 | 6558 | 190 | 34.51 | 3 | 7-33 | 91 | 37 |
| Spearman C.M. | 51 | 50 | 0 | 86 | 936 | 18.72 | — | 5 | 15 | — | 3 | 6 | 0 | — | — | — | — | — |
| Stewart S.L. | 4 | 4 | 0 | 14 | 26 | 6.50 | — | — | — | — | — | — | — | — | — | — | — | — |
| Stirling D.A. | 6 | 5 | 2 | 13* | 21 | 7.00 | — | — | 3 | — | 246 | 207 | 6 | 34.33 | — | 2-29 | 84 | 41 |
| Stott L.W. | 1 | — | — | — | — | — | — | — | 1 | — | 72 | 48 | 3 | 16.00 | — | 3-48 | 66 | 24 |
| Styris S.B. | 188 | 161 | 23 | 141 | 4483 | 32.48 | 4 | 28 | 73 | — | 6114 | 4839 | 137 | 35.32 | 1 | 6-25 | 79 | 44 |
| Su'a M.L. | 12 | 7 | 2 | 12* | 24 | 4.80 | — | — | 1 | — | 463 | 367 | 9 | 40.77 | — | 4-59 | 79 | 51 |
| Sulzberger G.P. | 3 | 2 | 1 | 6* | 9 | 9.00 | — | — | 1 | — | 132 | 102 | 3 | 34.00 | — | 1-28 | 77 | 44 |
| Tait A.R. | 5 | 5 | 2 | 13* | 35 | 11.66 | — | — | — | — | 120 | 88 | 3 | 29.33 | — | 2-37 | 73 | 40 |
| Taylor B.R. | 2 | 1 | 0 | 22 | 22 | 22.00 | — | — | 1 | — | 114 | 62 | 4 | 15.50 | — | 3-25 | 54 | 28 |
| Taylor L.R.P.L. | 236 | 220 | 39 | 181* | 8607 | 47.55 | 21 | 51 | 142 | — | 42 | 35 | 0 | — | — | — | 83 | — |
| Thompson E.P. | 1 | — | — | — | — | — | — | — | — | — | 24 | 42 | 0 | — | — | — | 175 | — |
| Thomson S.A. | 56 | 52 | 10 | 83 | 964 | 22.95 | — | 5 | 18 | — | 2121 | 1602 | 42 | 38.14 | — | 3-14 | 75 | 50 |
| Tickner B.M. | 2 | 1 | 1 | 1* | 1 | — | — | — | — | — | 90 | 88 | 5 | 17.60 | — | 4-50 | 97 | 18 |
| Troup G.B. | 22 | 12 | 8 | 39 | 101 | 25.25 | — | — | 2 | — | 1180 | 791 | 32 | 23.97 | — | 4-19 | 67 | 36 |
| Tuffey D.R. | 94 | 52 | 21 | 36 | 295 | 9.51 | — | — | 20 | — | 4333 | 3534 | 110 | 32.12 | — | 4-24 | 83 | 39 |
| Turner G.M. | 41 | 40 | 6 | 171* | 1598 | 47.00 | 3 | 9 | 13 | — | 6 | 0 | 0 | — | — | — | — | — |
| Twose R.G. | 87 | 81 | 11 | 103 | 2717 | 38.81 | 1 | 20 | 37 | — | 272 | 237 | 4 | 59.25 | — | 2-31 | 87 | 68 |
| Vance R.H. | 8 | 8 | 0 | 96 | 248 | 31.00 | — | 1 | 4 | — | — | — | — | — | — | — | — | — |
| Vaughan J.T.C. | 18 | 16 | 7 | 33 | 162 | 18.00 | — | — | 4 | — | 696 | 524 | 15 | 34.93 | — | 4-33 | 75 | 46 |
| Vettori D.L. | 295 | 187 | 57 | 83 | 2253 | 17.33 | — | 4 | 88 | — | 14060 | 9674 | 305 | 31.71 | 2 | 5-7 | 69 | 46 |
| Vincent L. | 102 | 99 | 10 | 172 | 2414 | 27.12 | 3 | 11 | 41 | — | 20 | 25 | 1 | 25.00 | — | 1-0 | 125 | 20 |
| Vivian G.E. | 1 | 1 | 0 | 14 | 14 | 14.00 | — | — | — | — | — | — | — | — | — | — | — | — |
| Wadsworth K.J. | 14 | 11 | 1 | 104 | 302 | 30.20 | 1 | — | 15 | 3 | — | — | — | — | — | — | — | — |
| Walker B.G.K. | 11 | 7 | 4 | 16* | 47 | 15.66 | — | — | 5 | — | 438 | 417 | 8 | 52.12 | — | 2-43 | 95 | 54 |
| Walker M.D.J. | 3 | 1 | 0 | 10 | 10 | 10.00 | — | — | 2 | — | 132 | 119 | 4 | 29.75 | — | 4-49 | 90 | 33 |
| Walmsley K.P. | 2 | — | — | — | — | — | — | — | — | — | 120 | 117 | 2 | 58.60 | — | 1-53 | 97 | 60 |
| Watling B-J. | 28 | 25 | 2 | 96* | 573 | 24.91 | — | 5 | 20 | — | — | — | — | — | — | — | — | — |
| Watson W. | 61 | 24 | 13 | 21 | 86 | 7.81 | — | — | 9 | — | 3251 | 2247 | 74 | 30.36 | — | 4-27 | 69 | 43 |
| Webb P.N. | 5 | 5 | 1 | 10* | 38 | 9.50 | — | — | 3 | — | — | — | — | — | — | — | — | — |

| | M | In | NO | HS | Runs | Ave | 100 | 50 | Ct | St | Balls | Runs | Wkts | Ave | 5WI | Best | R/100B | B/W |
|---|---|---|---|---|---|---|---|---|---|---|---|---|---|---|---|---|---|---|
| **Webb** R.J. | 3 | 1 | 1 | 6* | 6 | — | — | — | — | — | 161 | 105 | 4 | 26.25 | — | 2-28 | 65 | 40 |
| **Wheeler** B.M. | 6 | 4 | 4 | 39* | 58 | — | — | — | 1 | — | 309 | 315 | 8 | 39.37 | — | 3-63 | 101 | 38 |
| **White** D.J. | 3 | 3 | 0 | 15 | 37 | 12.33 | — | — | 1 | — | — | — | — | — | — | — | — | — |
| **Williamson** K.S. | 151 | 144 | 14 | 148 | 6173 | 47.48 | 13 | 39 | 60 | — | 1467 | 1310 | 37 | 35.40 | — | 4-22 | 89 | 39 |
| **Wilson** J.W. | 6 | 6 | 1 | 44* | 103 | 20.60 | — | — | 4 | — | 242 | 260 | 4 | 65.00 | — | 2-21 | 107 | 61 |
| **Wiseman** P.J. | 15 | 7 | 5 | 16 | 45 | 22.50 | — | — | 2 | — | 450 | 368 | 12 | 30.66 | — | 4-45 | 81 | 37 |
| **Wisneski** W.A. | 3 | 2 | 1 | 10 | 10 | 10.00 | — | — | 1 | — | 114 | 123 | 0 | — | — | — | 107 | — |
| **Woodcock** L.J. | 4 | 2 | 1 | 11 | 14 | 14.00 | — | — | — | — | 164 | 155 | 3 | 51.66 | — | 2-58 | 94 | 54 |
| **Worker** G.H. | 10 | 10 | 2 | 58 | 272 | 34.00 | — | 3 | 5 | — | 6 | 5 | 0 | — | — | — | 83 | — |
| **Wright** J.G. | 149 | 148 | 1 | 101 | 3891 | 26.46 | 1 | 24 | 51 | — | 24 | 8 | 0 | — | — | — | 33 | — |
| **Young** B.A. | 74 | 73 | 5 | 74 | 1668 | 24.52 | — | 9 | 28 | — | — | — | — | — | — | — | — | — |
| **Young** W.A. | 5 | 5 | 2 | 120 | 236 | 78.66 | 2 | — | 2 | — | — | — | — | — | — | — | — | — |

*Cairns' record includes one match for ICC World XI*
*Chapman's record includes two matches for Hong Kong*
*Fleming's record includes one match for ICC World XI*
*Ronchi's record includes four matches for Australia*
*Vettori's record includes four matches for ICC World XI*

# SUMMARY OF ONE-DAY INTERNATIONAL CAREER RECORDS

## Most Matches

| | | | | | | | | |
|---|---|---|---|---|---|
| Vettori D.L. | 295 | Guptill M.J. | 189 | Southee T.G. | 143 |
| Fleming S.P. | 280 | Styris S.B. | 188 | Rutherford K.R. | 121 |
| McCullum B.B. | 260 | Parore A.C. | 179 | Larsen G.R. | 121 |
| Harris C.Z. | 250 | Mills K.D. | 170 | Hadlee R.J. | 115 |
| Taylor L.R.P.L. | 236 | Oram J.D.P. | 160 | Chatfield E.J. | 114 |
| Astle N.J. | 223 | Williamson K.S. | 151 | Franklin J.E.C. | 109 |
| Cairns C.L. | 215 | Wright J.G. | 149 | Latham T.W.M. | 105 |
| McMillan C.D. | 197 | Crowe M.D. | 143 | Vincent L. | 102 |

## Most Runs

| | | *Ave* | | | *Ave* |
|---|---|---|---|---|---|
| Taylor L.R.P.L. | 8607 | 47.55 | Wright J.G. | 3891 | 26.46 |
| Fleming S.P. | 8037 | 32.40 | Parore A.C. | 3314 | 25.68 |
| Astle N.J. | 7090 | 34.92 | Rutherford K.R. | 3143 | 29.65 |
| Guptill M.J. | 7041 | 42.16 | Latham T.W.M. | 2995 | 35.65 |
| Williamson K.S. | 6173 | 47.48 | Jones A.H. | 2784 | 35.69 |
| McCullum B.B. | 6083 | 30.41 | Twose R.G. | 2717 | 38.81 |
| Cairns C.L. | 4950 | 29.46 | Oram J.D.P. | 2434 | 24.09 |
| McMillan C.D. | 4707 | 28.18 | Vincent L. | 2414 | 27.12 |
| Crowe M.D. | 4704 | 38.55 | Vettori D.L. | 2253 | 17.33 |
| Styris S.B. | 4483 | 32.48 | Greatbatch M.J. | 2206 | 28.28 |
| Harris C.Z. | 4379 | 29.00 | | | |

## Most Wickets

| | | *Ave* | | | *Ave* |
|---|---|---|---|---|---|
| Vettori D.L. | 305 | 31.71 | Chatfield E.J. | 140 | 25.84 |
| Mills K.D. | 240 | 27.02 | Styris S.B. | 137 | 35.32 |
| Harris C.Z. | 203 | 37.50 | Morrison D.K. | 126 | 27.53 |
| Cairns C.L. | 201 | 32.80 | Snedden M.C. | 114 | 28.39 |
| Southee T.G. | 190 | 34.51 | Larsen G.R. | 113 | 35.39 |
| Oram J.D.P. | 173 | 29.17 | Tuffey D.R. | 110 | 32.12 |
| Boult T.A. | 169 | 25.21 | Pringle C. | 103 | 23.87 |
| Hadlee R.J. | 158 | 21.56 | Henry M.J. | 103 | 25.29 |
| Bond S.E. | 147 | 20.88 | | | |

## Most Economical Bowling

*(qualification 600 balls)*

| | *Balls bowled* | *Runs conceded* | *Runs conceded per 100 balls* | | *Balls bowled* | *Runs conceded* | *Runs conceded per 100 balls* |
|---|---|---|---|---|---|---|---|
| Hadlee R.J. | 6182 | 3407 | 55.11 | Larsen G.R. | 6368 | 4000 | 62.81 |
| Collinge R.O. | 915 | 517 | 56.50 | Troup G.B. | 1180 | 791 | 67.03 |
| Chatfield E.J. | 6065 | 3618 | 59.65 | Cairns B.L. | 4015 | 2717 | 67.67 |
| Hadlee D.R. | 683 | 410 | 60.02 | Petrie R.G. | 660 | 449 | 68.03 |
| McKechnie B.J. | 818 | 495 | 60.51 | Vettori D.L. | 14,060 | 9674 | 68.80 |

# Best Strike Rates

*(qualification 600 balls)*

| | Balls bowled | Wickets | Balls per wicket | | Balls bowled | Wickets | Balls per wicket |
|---|---|---|---|---|---|---|---|
| Anderson C.J. | 1485 | 60 | 24.75 | Bond S.E. | 4295 | 147 | 29.22 |
| Bennett H.K. | 892 | 33 | 27.03 | Allott G.I. | 1528 | 52 | 29.38 |
| Ferguson L.H. | 1956 | 69 | 28.35 | Hadlee D.R. | 683 | 23 | 29.70 |
| McClenaghan M.J. | 2336 | 82 | 28.49 | Boult T.A. | 5157 | 169 | 30.51 |
| Henry M.J. | 2970 | 103 | 28.83 | Neesham J.D.S. | 2115 | 68 | 31.10 |

# Register of New Zealand One-day Cricketers Who Have Not Played Test Cricket

| | Born | Type | |
|---|---|---|---|
| **Aldridge**<br>Graeme William | 15/11/1977<br>Christchurch | RHB | RFM |
| **Bailey**<br>Mark David | 26/11/1970<br>Hamilton | RHB | RM |
| **Bates**<br>Michael David | 11/10/1983<br>Auckland | RHB | LFM |
| **Blair**<br>Bruce Robert | 27/12/1957<br>Dunedin | LHB | RM |
| **Bulfin**<br>Carl Edwin | 19/8/1973<br>Blenheim | RHB | RFM |
| **Canning**<br>Tamahau Karangatukituki | 7/4/1977<br>Adelaide, Australia | RHB | RFM |
| **Chapman**<br>Mark Sinclair | 27/6/1994<br>Hong Kong | LHB | SLA |
| **Coman**<br>Peter George | 13/4/1943<br>Christchurch | RHB | |
| **Devcich**<br>Anton Paul | 28/9/1985<br>Hamilton | LHB | SLA |
| **Diamanti**<br>Brendon John | 30/4/1981<br>Blenheim | RHB | RM |
| **Douglas**<br>Mark William | 20/10/1968<br>Nelson | LHB | |
| **Ellis**<br>Andrew Malcolm | 24/3/1982<br>Christchurch | RHB | RM |
| **Hadlee**<br>Barry George | 14/12/1941<br>Christchurch | RHB | |
| **Hamilton**<br>Lance John | 5/4/1973<br>Papakura | RHB | LFM |
| **Hart**<br>Ronald Terence | 7/11/1961<br>Lower Hutt | RHB | |
| **Hayes**<br>Roydon Leslie | 9/5/1971<br>Paeroa | RHB | RFM |
| **Hitchcock**<br>Paul Anthony | 23/1/1975<br>Whangarei | RHB | RM |
| **Howell**<br>Llorne Gregory | 8/7/1972<br>Napier | RHB | |
| **Kuggeleijn**<br>Scott Christopher | 3/1/1992<br>Hamilton | RHB | RFM |
| **McClenaghan**<br>Mitchell John | 11/6/1986<br>Hastings | LHB | LFM |
| **McCullum**<br>Nathan Leslie | 1/9/1980<br>Dunedin | RHB | ROB |
| **McGlashan**<br>Peter Donald | 22/6/1979<br>Napier | RHB | WK |

| | | | |
|---|---|---|---|
| **McKechnie** | 6/11/1953 | RHB | RM |
| Brian John | Gore | | |
| **McSweeney** | 8/3/1957 | RHB | WK |
| Ervin Bruce | Wellington | | |
| **Mathieson** | 10/10/1989 | RHB | RFM |
| Andrew William | Hamilton | | |
| **Millmow** | 22/9/1967 | RHB | RFM |
| Jonathan Paul | Wellington | | |
| **Milne** | 13/4/1992 | RHB | RF |
| Adam Fraser | Palmerston North | | |
| **Nethula** | 8/5/1983 | RHB | RLB |
| Tarun Sai | Kurnool, India | | |
| **Nevin** | 3/8/1975 | RHB | WK |
| Christopher John | Dunedin | | |
| **Penn** | 27/7/1974 | RHB | RFM |
| Andrew Jonathan | Wanganui | | |
| **Petrie** | 23/8/1967 | RHB | RFM |
| Richard George | Christchurch | | |
| **Rance** | 23/8/1987 | RHB | RM |
| Seth Hayden Arnold | Wellington | | |
| **Reid** | 3/12/1958 | RHB | |
| Richard Bruce | Lower Hutt | | |
| **Roberts** | 22/3/1965 | RHB | RFM |
| Stuart James | Christchurch | | |
| **Seifert** | 14/12/1994 | RHB | WK |
| Tim Louis | Wanganui | | |
| **Stewart** | 21/6/1982 | RHB | RM |
| Shanan Luke | Christchurch | | |
| **Stott** | 8/12/1946 | RHB | RM |
| Leslie Warren | Rochdale, England | | |
| **Sulzberger** | 14/3/1973 | LHB | ROB |
| Glen Paul | Kaponga | | |
| **Tait** | 13/6/1972 | RHB | RM |
| Alex Ross | Paparoa | | |
| **Thompson** | 17/12/1979 | LHB | LFM |
| Ewen Paul | Warkworth | | |
| **Tickner** | 13/10/1993 | RHB | RFM |
| Blair Marshall | Napier | | |
| **Walker** | 17/1/1977 | RHB | RM |
| Matthew David John | Opunake | | |
| **Webb** | 15/9/1952 | RHB | RFM |
| Richard John | Invercargill | | |
| **Wheeler** | 10/11/1991 | RHB | LM |
| Ben Matthew | Blenheim | | |
| **Wilson** | 24/10/1973 | RHB | RFM |
| Jeffrey William | Invercargill | | |
| **Wisneski** | 19/2/1969 | RHB | RM |
| Warren Anthony | New Plymouth | | |
| **Woodcock** | 19/3/1982 | LHB | SLA |
| Luke James | Wellington | | |
| **Worker** | 23/8/1989 | LHB | SLA |
| George Herrick | Palmerston North | | |

# NEW ZEALAND
# TWENTY20 RECORDS

This section of the *Almanack* is devoted to Twenty20 matches in New Zealand (other than Twenty20 internationals) and has been compiled from the following games:

1. 452 matches in national competitions from 2005/06 to 2021/22.

2. 7 matches involving other teams.

| | |
|---|---|
| 2008/09 | New Zealand A v England Lions |
| 2011/12 | Canterbury v South Africa |
| 2012/13 | New Zealand XI v England *(3 matches)* |
| 2014/15 | Island of Origin |
| 2015/16 | Island of Origin |

## Winners of Twenty20 Competitions

### STATE TWENTY20
| | |
|---|---|
| 2005/06 | Canterbury |
| 2006/07 | Auckland |
| 2007/08 | Central Districts |
| 2008/09 | Otago |

### HRV CUP
| | |
|---|---|
| 2009/10 | Central Districts |
| 2010/11 | Auckland |
| 2011/12 | Auckland |
| 2012/13 | Otago |
| 2013/14 | Northern Districts |

### GEORGIE PIE SUPER SMASH
| | |
|---|---|
| 2014/15 | Wellington |
| 2015/16 | Auckland |

### McDONALD'S SUPER SMASH
| | |
|---|---|
| 2016/17 | Wellington |

### BURGER KING SUPER SMASH
| | |
|---|---|
| 2017/18 | Northern Districts |
| 2018/19 | Central Districts |

### DREAM11 SUPER SMASH
| | |
|---|---|
| 2019/20 | Wellington |
| 2020/21 | Wellington |
| 2021/22 | Northern Districts |

## TEAM RECORDS

### Highest Totals

| | | | |
|---|---|---|---|
| 249-3 | Otago v Central Districts | New Plymouth | 2016/17 |
| 248-4 | Central Districts v Otago | New Plymouth | 2016/17 |
| 230-5 | Northern Districts v Central Districts | Napier | 2018/19 |
| 230-2 | Wellington v Auckland | Auckland | 2020/21 |
| 229-3 | Auckland v Wellington | Auckland | 2009/10 |

### Lowest Totals

| | | | |
|---|---|---|---|
| 72 | Wellington v Northern Districts | Hamilton | 2015/16 |
| 74 | Auckland v Northern Districts | Auckland | 2010/11 |
| 77 | Northern Districts v Otago | Dunedin | 2015/16 |
| 80 | Northern Districts v Central Districts | Hamilton | 2018/19 |
| 80 | Otago v Auckland | Auckland | 2020/21 |

# INDIVIDUAL RECORDS
## Centuries

| | | | | |
|---|---|---|---|---|
| 141* | M.G. Bracewell | Wellington v Central Districts | New Plymouth | 2021/22 |
| 120* | M.J. Guptill | Auckland v Canterbury | Rangiora | 2011/12 |
| 116* | G.D. Phillips | Auckland v Central Districts | Auckland | 2016/17 |
| 116 | D.P.M.D. Jayawardene | | | |
| | | Central Districts v Otago | New Plymouth | 2016/17 |
| 114* | D. Cleaver | Central Districts v Otago | Dunedin | 2021/22 |
| 111* | L.R.P.L. Taylor | Central Districts v Northern Districts | Hamilton | 2007/08 |
| 110 | T.W.M. Latham | Canterbury v Central Districts | Napier | 2018/19 |
| 108* | B.B. McCullum | Otago v Auckland | Dunedin | 2009/10 |
| 107 | T.L. Seifert | Northern Districts v Auckland | Mt Maunganui | 2017/18 |
| 106* | G.D. Phillips | Auckland v Otago | Auckland | 2019/20 |
| 106 | H.D. Rutherford | Otago v Central Districts | New Plymouth | 2016/17 |
| 106 | G.H. Worker | Central Districts v Otago | Dunedin | 2020/21 |
| 105* | L. Vincent | Auckland v Wellington | Auckland | 2009/10 |
| 105* | D.P. Conway | Wellington v Otago | Dunedin | 2018/19 |
| 103* | B.B. McCullum | Otago v Northern Districts | Hamilton | 2011/12 |
| 102 | J.M. How | Central Districts v Wellington | New Plymouth | 2011/12 |
| 102 | L. Ronchi | Wellington v Auckland | Auckland | 2017/18 |
| 102 | A.P. Devcich | Northern Districts v Central Districts | New Plymouth | 2020/21 |
| 101* | B.R.M. Taylor | Wellington v Otago | Queenstown | 2011/12 |
| 101* | R.J. Nicol | Canterbury v Auckland | Auckland | 2011/12 |
| 101* | D.P. Conway | Wellington v Otago | Dunedin | 2019/20 |
| 101 | C.B. Gaffaney | Otago v Central Districts | Dunedin | 2005/06 |
| 101 | M.S. Chapman | Auckland v Canterbury | Christchurch | 2017/18 |
| 101 | W.A. Young | Central Districts v Canterbury | Auckland | 2020/21 |
| 100* | A.J. Redmond | Otago v Central Districts | Dunedin | 2008/09 |
| 100* | Azhar Mahmood | Auckland v Canterbury | Auckland | 2011/12 |
| 100 | C.Z. Harris | Canterbury v Auckland | Christchurch | 2006/07 |
| 100* | H.J.H. Marshall | Wellington v Otago | Alexandra | 2016/17 |

## Fastest Century

| | | | | |
|---|---|---|---|---|
| *Balls* | | | | |
| 40 | T.L. Seifert | Northern Districts v Auckland | Mt Maunganui | 2017/18 |

## Fastest Fifty

| | | | | |
|---|---|---|---|---|
| *Balls* | | | | |
| 14 | K. Noema-Barnett | Central Districts v Otago | Invercargill | 2010/11 |

## Most Wickets in an Innings

| | | | | |
|---|---|---|---|---|
| 4-0-7-6 | K.A. Jamieson | Canterbury v Auckland | Auckland | 2018/19 |
| 3.1-0-23-6 | T.S. Nethula | Northern Districts v Central Districts | Napier | 2018/19 |
| 4-0-28-6 | I.G. Butler | Otago v Auckland | Dunedin | 2009/10 |
| 4-1-28-6 | B. Laughlin | Northern Districts v Wellington | Wellington | 2013/14 |
| 2.2-1-9-5 | A.M. Ellis | Canterbury v Northern Districts | Hamilton | 2015/16 |
| 4-1-10-5 | G.H. Worker | Central Districts v Otago | New Plymouth | 2015/16 |
| 2-0-12-5 | W.S.A. Williams | Canterbury v Wellington | Wellington | 2019/20 |
| 4-0-14-5 | J.D.P. Oram | Central Districts v Otago | New Plymouth | 2009/10 |
| 4-0-14-5 | A.M. Ellis | Canterbury v Wellington | Hamilton | 2014/15 |
| 3.4-0-14-5 | N.G. Smith | Otago v Northern Districts | Hamilton | 2019/20 |
| 4-0-16-5 | A.M. Ellis | Canterbury v Otago | Alexandra | 2017/18 |

| 4-1-18-5 | J.A.Duffy | Otago v Canterbury | Christchurch | 2015/16 |
| 4-1-19-5 | B.M. Tickner | Central Districts v Auckland | New Plymouth | 2016/17 |
| 3.5-0-19-5 | S.H.A. Rance | Central Districts v Otago | Napier | 2021/22 |
| 4-0-20-5 | A.R. Adams | Auckland v Central Districts | Auckland | 2010/11 |
| 4-0-22-5 | R.J. Nicol | Canterbury v Northern Districts | Christchurch | 2009/10 |
| 4-0-23-5 | B.W. Hilfenhaus | Canterbury v Otago | Christchurch | 2016/17 |
| 4-0-32-5 | E.P. Thompson | Central Districts v Otago | Napier | 2006/07 |
| 4-0-39-5 | J.A. Duffy | Otago v Canterbury | Christchurch | 2017/18 |
| 4-0-45-5 | O.R. Newton | Wellington v Central Districts | New Plymouth | 2019/20 |

## Most Economical Bowling

| 4-0-5-2 | I.S. Sodhi | Northern Districts v Auckland | Auckland | 2021/22 |
| 4-0-7-6 | K.A. Jamieson | Canterbury v Auckland | Auckland | 2018/19 |
| 4-0-8-2 | J.M. McMillan | Otago v Auckland | Alexandra | 2013/14 |
| 4-0-8-1 | T.D. Astle | Canterbury v Northern Districts | Mt Maunganui | 2021/22 |
| 4-1-8-1 | M.J. Henry | Canterbury v Northern Districts | Mt Maunganui | 2021/22 |
| 4-1-8-3 | A. Ashok | Auckland v Wellington | Wellington | 2021/22 |
| 4-0-9-2 | M.P.F. Davidson | Canterbury v Northern Districts | Christchurch | 2008/09 |
| 4-0-9-1 | B.J. Arnel | Northern Districts v Canterbury | Christchurch | 2009/10 |
| 4-0-9-0 | B.E. Scott | Northern Districts v Auckland | Mt Maunganui | 2010/11 |
| 4-0-9-0 | M.J. Santner | Northern Districts v Otago | Wellington | 2014/15 |
| 4-0-9-0 | M.J. Santner | Northern Districts v Wellington | Hamilton | 2014/15 |

## Most Expensive Bowling

| 4-0-70-0 | A.W. Mathieson | Central Districts v Auckland | Auckland | 2015/16 |
| 4-0-69-0 | D.S. Hutchinson | Wellington v Otago | Dunedin | 2013/14 |
| 4-0-68-1 | N. Wagner | Otago v Central Districts | Invercargill | 2017/18 |
| 4-0-65-0 | R.J. McCone | Central Districts v Auckland | Auckland | 2016/17 |
| 4-0-63-0 | D.K. Ferns | Auckland v Central Districts | New Plymouth | 2020/21 |
| 4-0-61-3 | M.D. Bates | Auckland v Central Districts | New Plymouth | 2009/10 |
| 4-0-61-0 | A.P. Devcich | Northern Districts v Canterbury | Christchurch | 2019/20 |
| 4-0-60-0 | L.M. Burtt | Canterbury v Otago | Dunedin | 2008/09 |
| 4-0-60-0 | T.G. Southee | Northern Districts v Auckland | Mt Maunganui | 2017/18 |
| 4-0-60-3 | L.V. van Beek | Wellington v Central Districts | New Plymouth | 2017/18 |
| 4-0-60-0 | S.C. Kuggeleijn | Northern Districts v Central Districts | Napier | 2019/20 |

## Hat-tricks

| 4-0-18-4 | T.L. Tsotsobe | South Africa v Canterbury | Christchurch | 2011/12 |
| 4-1-22-3 | S.J.C. Broad | England v New Zealand XI | Whangarei | 2012/13 |
| 2.3-0-10-4 | M.D. Bates | Auckland v Northern Districts | Hamilton | 2014/15 |
| 2-0-12-5 | W.S.A.Williams | Canterbury v Wellington | Wellington | 2019/20 |

## Wicketkeeping

**DISMISSALS**

*(ct/st)*

| 5 | (4/1) | D.C. de Boorder | Otago v Canterbury | Christchurch | 2009/10 |
| 5 | (4/1) | C.D. Fletcher | Canterbury v Northern Districts | Hamilton | 2015/16 |

## Fielding

**CATCHES**
5   P.G. Fulton          Canterbury v Northern Districts                    Hamilton            2015/16

# RECORD PARTNERSHIPS

| | | | | | |
|---|---|---|---|---|---|
| 1st | 201 | P.J. Ingram & J.M. How | CD v Wellington | New Plymouth | 2011/12 |
| 2nd | 188* | N.T. Broom & B.B. McCullum | Otago v ND | Hamilton | 2011/12 |
| 3rd | 143 | D.P. Conway & M.G. Bracewell | Wellington v Canterbury | Dunedin | 2021/22 |
| 4th | 143 | W.A. Young & D. Cleaver | CD v Auckland | Auckland | 2018/19 |
| 5th | 132 | D.J. Mitchell & C.D Fletcher | Canterbury v CD | Auckland | 2020/21 |
| 6th | 112* | A.M. Ellis & B.J. Diamanti | Canterbury v CD | Nelson | 2012/13 |
| 7th | 80 | D.J. Mitchell & I.S. Sodhi | ND v Wellington | Hamilton | 2017/18 |
| 8th | 68* | M.D. Bell & L.J. Woodcock | Wellington v Auckland | Auckland | 2008/09 |
| 9th | 47* | T.G. Southee & B.E. Scott | ND v Otago | Invercargill | 2009/10 |
| 10th | 40 | C.E. McConchie & E.J. Nuttall | Canterbury v Wellington | Wellington | 2018/19 |

# DOMESTIC TWENTY20 CAREER RECORDS

**BATTING**

| | | M | In | NO | HS | Runs | Ave | 100s | 50s |
|---|---|---|---|---|---|---|---|---|---|
| N.T. Broom | O, C | 124 | 121 | 11 | 96* | 3037 | 27.60 | – | 19 |
| G.H. Worker | CD, C, A | 122 | 117 | 9 | 106 | 2970 | 27.50 | 1 | 15 |
| H.D. Rutherford | O | 100 | 97 | 3 | 106 | 2338 | 24.87 | 1 | 11 |
| R.J. Nicol | A, C, O | 98 | 88 | 11 | 101* | 2336 | 30.33 | 1 | 16 |
| A.K. Kitchen | A, O | 127 | 115 | 10 | 66 | 2214 | 21.08 | – | 7 |
| A.P. Devcich | ND | 102 | 93 | 8 | 102 | 2189 | 25.75 | 1 | 14 |
| M.G. Bracewell | O, W | 99 | 89 | 21 | 141* | 2171 | 31.92 | 1 | 12 |
| M.J. Guptill | A | 68 | 64 | 11 | 120* | 2115 | 39.90 | 1 | 14 |
| D.J. Mitchell | ND, C | 91 | 80 | 22 | 88* | 2067 | 35.63 | – | 9 |
| D.G. Brownlie | C, ND | 89 | 85 | 4 | 99 | 1922 | 23.72 | – | 7 |

**BOWLING**

| | | M | O | M | R | W | Ave | R/O | Best |
|---|---|---|---|---|---|---|---|---|---|
| A.M. Ellis | C | 116 | 335.3 | 5 | 2794 | 125 | 22.35 | 8.33 | 5-9 |
| R.M. Hira | A, C, ND | 103 | 338.2 | 1 | 2451 | 109 | 22.48 | 7.24 | 4-13 |
| L.J. Woodcock | W | 107 | 282 | 1 | 2159 | 92 | 23.46 | 7.66 | 3-20 |
| S.C. Kuggeleijn | W, ND | 90 | 295.4 | 3 | 2582 | 91 | 28.37 | 8.73 | 4-18 |
| S.H.A. Rance | CD | 73 | 247.3 | 0 | 1977 | 91 | 21.72 | 7.99 | 5-19 |
| J.A. Duffy | O | 85 | 285.5 | 3 | 2508 | 89 | 28.17 | 8.77 | 5-18 |
| B.M. Tickner | CD | 58 | 211 | 2 | 1825 | 89 | 20.50 | 8.65 | 5-19 |
| B.J. Arnel | ND, W | 92 | 329.2 | 3 | 2649 | 85 | 31.16 | 8.04 | 4-22 |
| L.V. van Beek | C, W | 87 | 266.3 | 2 | 2286 | 84 | 27.21 | 8.58 | 3-15 |
| J.S. Patel | W | 87 | 294.4 | 3 | 2071 | 80 | 25.88 | 7.03 | 4-11 |

# NEW ZEALAND TWENTY20
# INTERNATIONAL RECORDS

## TEAM RECORDS

### Results

| 2004/05 | Australia | Auckland | A 214-5 | NZ 170 | *Australia won by 44 runs* |
|---------|-----------|----------|---------|--------|---------------------------|
| 2005/06 | South Africa | Johannesburg | SA 133 | NZ 134-5 | *NZ won by 5 wickets* |
| 2005/06 | West Indies | Auckland | WI 126-7 | NZ 126-8 | *NZ won bowl-out* |
| 2006/07 | Sri Lanka | Wellington | NZ 162-8 | SL 62-1 | *Sri Lanka won by 18 runs (D/L)* |
| | Sri Lanka | Auckland | SL 115 | NZ 116-5 | *NZ won by 5 wickets* |
| 2007/08 | Kenya | Durban | K 73 | NZ 74-1 | *NZ won by 9 wickets* |
| *World Twenty20* | Sri Lanka | Johannesburg | NZ 164-7 | SL 168-3 | *Sri Lanka won by 7 wickets* |
| | India | Johannesburg | NZ 190 | I 180-9 | *NZ won by 10 runs* |
| | England | Durban | NZ 164-9 | E 159-8 | *NZ won by 5 runs* |
| | South Africa | Durban | NZ 153-8 | SA 158-4 | *South Africa won by 6 wickets* |
| | Pakistan | Cape Town | NZ 143-8 | P 147-4 | *Pakistan won by 6 wickets* |
| | South Africa | Johannesburg | NZ 129-7 | SA 131-7 | *South Africa won by 3 wickets* |
| 2007/08 | Australia | Perth | A 186-6 | NZ 132 | *Australia won by 54 runs* |
| 2007/08 | England | Auckland | E 184-8 | NZ 152 | *England won by 32 runs* |
| | England | Christchurch | E 193-8 | NZ 143-8 | *England won by 50 runs* |
| 2008 | England | Manchester | NZ 123-9 | E 127-1 | *England won by 9 wickets* |
| 2008/09 | West Indies | Auckland | NZ 155-7 | WI 155-8 | *West Indies won eliminator* |
| | West Indies | Hamilton | NZ 191-9 | WI 155-7 | *NZ won by 36 runs* |
| | Australia | Sydney | A 150-7 | NZ 149-5 | *Australia won by 1 run* |
| | India | Christchurch | I 162-8 | NZ 166-3 | *NZ won by 7 wickets* |
| | India | Wellington | I 149-6 | NZ 150-5 | *NZ won by 5 wickets* |
| 2009 | Scotland | The Oval | S 89-4 | NZ 90-3 | *NZ won by 7 wickets* |
| *World Twenty20* | South Africa | Lord's | SA 128-7 | NZ 127-5 | *South Africa won by 1 run* |
| | Ireland | Nottingham | NZ 198-5 | I 115 | *NZ won by 83 runs* |
| | Pakistan | The Oval | NZ 99 | P 100-4 | *Pakistan won by 6 wickets* |
| | Sri Lanka | Nottingham | SL 158-5 | NZ 110 | *Sri Lanka won by 48 runs* |
| 2009/10 | Sri Lanka | Colombo | NZ 141-8 | SL 138-9 | *NZ won by 3 runs* |
| | Sri Lanka | Colombo | NZ 170-4 | SL 148-8 | *NZ won by 22 runs* |
| 2009/10 | Pakistan | Dubai | P 161-8 | NZ 112 | *Pakistan won by 49 runs* |
| | Pakistan | Dubai | P 153-5 | NZ 146-5 | *Pakistan won by 7 runs* |
| 2009/10 | Bangladesh | Hamilton | B 78 | NZ 79-0 | *NZ won by 10 wickets* |
| 2009/10 | Australia | Wellington | NZ 118 | A 119-4 | *Australia won by 6 wickets* |
| | Australia | Christchurch | NZ 214-6 | A 214-4 | *NZ won eliminator* |
| 2009/10 | Sri Lanka | Providence | SL 135-6 | NZ 139-8 | *NZ won by 2 wickets* |
| *World Twenty20* | Zimbabwe | Providence | Z 84 | NZ 36-1 | *NZ won by 7 runs (D/L)* |
| | South Africa | Bridgetown | SA 170-4 | NZ 157-7 | *South Africa won by 13 runs* |
| | Pakistan | Bridgetown | NZ 133-7 | P 132-7 | *NZ won by 1 run* |
| | England | Gros Islet | NZ 149-6 | E 153-7 | *England won by 3 wickets* |
| 2009/10 | Sri Lanka | Lauderhill | NZ 120-7 | SL 92 | *NZ won by 28 runs* |
| | Sri Lanka | Lauderhill | NZ 81 | SL 82-3 | *Sri Lanka won by 7 wickets* |

| 2010/11 | Pakistan | Auckland | P 143-9 | NZ 146-5 | *NZ won by 5 wickets* |
| | Pakistan | Hamilton | NZ 185-7 | P 146-9 | *NZ won by 39 runs* |
| | Pakistan | Christchurch | P 183-6 | NZ 80 | *Pakistan won by 103 runs* |
| 2011/12 | Zimbabwe | Harare | Z 123-8 | NZ 127-0 | *NZ won by 10 wickets* |
| | Zimbabwe | Harare | NZ 187-3 | Z 154 | *NZ won by 33 runs* |
| 2011/12 | Zimbabwe | Auckland | Z 159-8 | NZ 160-3 | *NZ won by 7 wickets* |
| | Zimbabwe | Hamilton | Z 200-2 | NZ 202-5 | *NZ won by 5 wickets* |
| 2011/12 | South Africa | Wellington | SA 147-6 | NZ 148-4 | *NZ won by 6 wickets* |
| | South Africa | Hamilton | NZ 173-4 | SA 174-2 | *South Africa won by 8 wickets* |
| | South Africa | Auckland | SA 165-7 | NZ 162-7 | *South Africa won by 3 runs* |
| 2012 | West Indies | Lauderhill | WI 177-5 | NZ116 | *West Indies won by 61 runs* |
| | West Indies | Lauderhill | WI 209-2 | NZ153 | *West Indies won by 56 runs* |
| 2012/13 | India | Visakhapatnam | *abandoned without a ball being bowled* | | |
| | India | Chennai | NZ 167-5 | I 166-4 | *NZ won by 1 run* |
| 2012/13 | Bangladesh | Pallekele | NZ 191-3 | B 132-8 | *NZ won by 59 runs* |
| *World Twenty20* | Pakistan | Pallekele | P 177-6 | NZ 164-9 | *Pakistan won by 13 runs* |
| | Sri Lanka | Pallekele | NZ 174-7 | SL 174-6 | *Sri Lanka won eliminator* |
| | England | Pallekele | NZ 148-6 | E 149-4 | *England won by 6 wickets* |
| | West Indies | Pallekele | WI 139 | NZ 139-7 | *W.Indies won eliminator* |
| | Sri Lanka | Pallekele | NZ 74-7 | SL 6-0 | *abandoned* |
| 2012/13 | South Africa | Durban | NZ 86 | SA 87-2 | *South Africa won by 8 wickets* |
| | South Africa | East London | SA 165-5 | NZ 169-2 | *NZ won by 8 wickets* |
| | South Africa | Port Elizabeth | SA 179-6 | NZ 146-9 | *South Africa won by 33 runs* |
| 2012/13 | England | Auckland | E 214-7 | NZ 174-9 | *England won by 40 runs* |
| | England | Hamilton | NZ 192-6 | E 137 | *NZ won by 55 runs* |
| | England | Wellington | NZ 139-8 | E 143-0 | *England won by 10 wickets* |
| 2013 | England | The Oval | NZ 201-4 | E 196-5 | *NZ won by 5 runs* |
| | England | The Oval | E 2-1 | NZ | *abandoned* |
| 2013/14 | Bangladesh | Mirpur | NZ 204-5 | B 189-9 | *NZ won by 15 runs* |
| 2013/14 | Sri Lanka | Pallekele | *abandoned without a ball being bowled* | | |
| | Sri Lanka | Pallekele | NZ 142-7 | SL 143-2 | *Sri Lanka won by 8 wickets* |
| 2013/14 | West Indies | Auckland | NZ 189-5 | WI 108-8 | *NZ won by 81 runs* |
| | West Indies | Wellington | WI 159-5 | NZ 163-6 | *NZ won by 4 wickets* |
| 2013/14 | England | Chittagong | E 172-6 | NZ 52-1 | *NZ won by 9 runs (D/L)* |
| *World Twenty20* | South Africa | Chittagong | SA 170-6 | NZ 168-8 | *South Africa won by 2 runs* |
| | Sri Lanka | Chittagong | SL 119 | NZ 60 | *Sri Lanka won by 59 runs* |
| | Netherlands | Chittagong | N 151-4 | NZ 152-4 | *NZ won by 6 wickets* |
| 2014 | West Indies | Rousseau | WI 132-8 | NZ 117-4 | *NZ won by 12 runs (D/L)* |
| | West Indies | Rousseau | WI 165-6 | NZ 126 | *West Indies won by 39 runs* |
| 2014/15 | Pakistan | Dubai | NZ 135-7 | P 140-3 | *Pakistan won by 7 wickets* |
| | Pakistan | Dubai | NZ 144-8 | P 127 | *NZ won by 17 runs* |
| 2015 | England | Manchester | E 191-7 | NZ 135 | *England won by 56 runs* |
| 2015/16 | Zimbabwe | Harare | NZ 198-5 | Z 118-8 | *NZ won by 80 runs* |
| 2015/16 | South Africa | Durban | NZ 151-8 | SA 152-4 | *South Africa won by 6 wickets* |
| | South Africia | Centurion | NZ 177-7 | SA 145-8 | *NZ won by 32 runs* |
| 2015/16 | Sri Lanka | Mt Maunganui | NZ 182-4 | SL 179-9 | *NZ won by 3 runs* |
| | Sri Lanka | Auckland | SL 142-8 | NZ 147-1 | *NZ won by 9 wickets* |

| 2015/16 | Pakistan | Auckland | P 171-8 | NZ 155 | *Pakistan won by 16 runs* |
|---|---|---|---|---|---|
|  | Pakistan | Hamilton | P 168-7 | NZ 171-0 | *NZ won by 10 wickets* |
|  | Pakistan | Wellington | NZ 196-5 | P 101 | *NZ won by 95 runs* |
| **2015/16** | India | Nagpur | NZ 126-7 | I 79 | *NZ won by 47 runs* |
| *World Twenty20* | Australia | Dharamsala | NZ 142-8 | A 134-9 | *NZ won by 8 runs* |
|  | Pakistan | Mohali | NZ 180-5 | P 158-5 | *NZ won by 22 runs* |
|  | Bangladesh | Kolkata | NZ 145-8 | B 70 | *NZ won by 75 runs* |
|  | England | Delhi | NZ 153-8 | E 159-3 | *England won by 7 wickets* |
| **2016/17** | Bangladesh | Napier | B 141-8 | NZ 143-4 | *NZ won by 6 wickets* |
|  | Bangladesh | Mt Maunganui | NZ 195-7 | B 148 | *NZ won by 47 run* |
|  | Bangladesh | Mt Maunganui | NZ 194-4 | B 167-6 | *NZ won by 27 runs* |
| **2016/17** | South Africa | Auckland | SA 185-6 | NZ 107 | *SA won by 78 runs* |
| **2017/18** | India | Delhi | I 202-3 | NZ 149-8 | *India won by 53 runs* |
|  | India | Rajkot | NZ 196-2 | I 156-7 | *NZ won by 40 runs* |
|  | India | Thiruvinanthapuram |  |  |  |
|  |  |  | I 67-5 | NZ 61-6 | *India won by 6 runs* |
| **2017/18** | West Indies | Nelson | NZ 187-7 | WI 140 | *NZ won by 47 runs* |
|  | West Indies | Mt Maunganui | NZ 102-4 | WI | *abandoned* |
|  | West Indies | Mt Maunganui | NZ 243-5 | WI 124 | *NZ won by 119 runs* |
| **2017/18** | Pakistan | Wellington | P 105 | NZ 106-3 | *NZ won by 7 wickets* |
|  | Pakistan | Auckland | P 201-4 | NZ 153 | *Pakistan won by 48 runs* |
|  | Pakistan | Mt Maunganui | P 181-6 | NZ 163-6 | *Pakistan won by 18 runs* |
| **2017/18** | Australia | Sydney | NZ 117-9 | A 96-3 | *Australia won by 7 wickets (D/L)* |
| *Tri-Series* | England | Wellington | NZ 196-5 | E 184-9 | *NZ won by 12 runs* |
|  | Australia | Auckland | NZ 243-6 | A 245-5 | *Australia won by 5 wickets* |
|  | England | Hamilton | E 194-7 | NZ 192-4 | *England won by 2 runs* |
|  | Australia | Auckland | NZ 150-9 | A 121-3 | *Australia won by 19 runs (D/L)* |
| **2018/19** | Pakistan | Abu Dhabi | P 148-6 | NZ 146-6 | *Pakistan won by 2 runs* |
|  | Pakistan | Dubai | NZ 153-7 | P 154-4 | *Pakistan won by 6 wickets* |
|  | Pakistan | Dubai | P 166-3 | NZ 119 | *Pakistan won by 47 runs* |
| **2018/19** | Sri Lanka | Auckland | NZ 179-7 | SL 144 | *NZ won by 35 runs* |
| **2018/19** | India | Wellington | NZ 219-6 | I 139 | *NZ won by 80 runs* |
|  | India | Auckland | NZ 158-8 | I 162-3 | *India won by 7 wickets* |
|  | India | Hamilton | NZ 212-4 | I 208-6 | *NZ won by 4 runs* |
| **2019/20** | Sri Lanka | Pallekele | SL 174-4 | NZ 175-5 | *NZ won by 5 wickets* |
|  | Sri Lanka | Pallekele | SL 161-9 | NZ 165-6 | *NZ won by 4 wickets* |
|  | Sri Lanka | Pallekele | SL 125-8 | NZ 88 | *SL won by 37 runs* |
| **2019/20** | England | Christchurch | NZ 153-5 | E 154-3 | *England won by 7 wickets* |
|  | England | Wellington | NZ 176-8 | E 155 | *NZ won by 21 runs* |
|  | England | Nelson | NZ 180-7 | E 166-7 | *NZ won by 14 runs* |
|  | England | Napier | E 241-3 | NZ 165 | *England won by 76 runs* |
|  | England | Auckland | NZ 146-5 | E 146-7 | *England won eliminator* |
| **2019/20** | India | Auckland | NZ 203-5 | I 204-4 | *India won by 6 wickets* |
|  | India | Auckland | NZ 132-5 | I 135-3 | *India won by 7 wickets* |
|  | India | Hamilton | I 179-5 | NZ 179-6 | *India won eliminator* |
|  | India | Wellington | I 165-8 | NZ 165-7 | *India won eliminator* |
|  | India | Mt Maunganui | I 163-3 | NZ 156-9 | *India won by 7 runs* |
| **2020/21** | West Indies | Auckland | WI 180-7 | NZ 179-5 | *NZ won by 5 wickets (D/L)* |
|  | West Indies | Mt Maunganui | NZ 238-3 | WI 166-9 | *NZ won by 72 runs* |
|  | West Indies | Mt Maunganui | WI 25-1 |  | *abandoned* |

| | | | | | |
|---|---|---|---|---|---|
| **2020/21** | Pakistan | Auckland | P 153-9 | NZ 156-5 | *NZ won by 5 wickets* |
| | Pakistan | Hamilton | P 163-6 | NZ 164-1 | *NZ won by 9 wickets* |
| | Pakistan | Napier | NZ 173-7 | P 177-6 | *Pakistan won by 4 wickets* |
| **2020/21** | Australia | Christchurch | NZ 184-5 | A 131 | *NZ won by 53 runs* |
| | Australia | Dunedin | NZ 219-7 | A 215-8 | *NZ won by 4 runs* |
| | Australia | Wellington | A 208-4 | NZ 144 | *Australia won by 64 runs* |
| | Australia | Wellington | A 156-6 | NZ 106 | *Australia won by 50 runs* |
| | Australia | Wellington | A 142-8 | NZ 143-3 | *NZ won by 7 wickets* |
| **2020/21** | Bangladesh | Hamilton | NZ 210-3 | B 144-8 | *NZ won by 66 runs* |
| | Bangladesh | Napier | NZ 173-5 | B 142-7 | *NZ won by 28 runs (D/L)* |
| | Bangladesh | Auckland | NZ 141-4 | B 76 | *NZ won by 65 runs* |
| **2021/22** | Bangladesh | Mirpur | NZ 60 | B 62-3 | *Bangladesh won by 7 wickets* |
| | Bangladesh | Mirpur | B 141-6 | NZ 137-5 | *Bangladesh won by 4 runs* |
| | Bangladesh | Mirpur | NZ 128-5 | B 76 | *NZ won by 52 runs* |
| | Bangladesh | Mirpur | NZ 93 | B 96-4 | *Bangladesh won by 6 wickets* |
| | Bangladesh | Mirpur | NZ 161-5 | B 134-8 | *NZ won by 27 runs* |
| **2021/22** | Pakistan | Sharjah | NZ 134-8 | P 135-5 | *Pakistan won by 5 wickets* |
| *Twenty20* | India | Dubai | I 110-7 | NZ 111-2 | *NZ won by 8 wickets* |
| *World Cup* | Scotland | Dubai | NZ 172-5 | S 156-5 | *NZ won by 16 runs* |
| | Namibia | Sharjah | NZ 163-4 | N 111-7 | *NZ won by 52 runs* |
| | Afghanistan | Abu Dhabi | A 124-8 | NZ 125-2 | *NZ won by 8 wickets* |
| | England | Abu Dhabi | E 166-4 | NZ 167-5 | *NZ won by 5 wickets* |
| | Australia | Dubai | NZ 172-4 | A 173-2 | *Australia won by 8 wickets* |
| **2021/22** | India | Jaipur | NZ 164-6 | I 166-5 | *India won by 5 wickets* |
| | India | Ranchi | NZ 153-6 | I 155-3 | *India won by 7 wickets* |
| | India | Kolkata | I 184-7 | NZ 111 | *India won by 73 runs* |
| **2021/22** | Netherlands | Napier | | | *abandoned without a ball being bowled* |

# Summary of Results

|  | Played | Won | Lost | NR |
|---|---|---|---|---|
| v Pakistan | 25 | 10 | 15 | – |
| v England | 22 | 8 | 13 | 1 |
| v India | 20 | 9 | 11 | – |
| v Sri Lanka | 19 | 10 | 8 | 1 |
| v West Indies | 16 | 9 | 5 | 2 |
| v South Africa | 15 | 4 | 11 | – |
| v Bangladesh | 15 | 12 | 3 | – |
| v Australia | 15 | 5 | 10 | – |
| v Zimbabwe | 6 | 6 | – | – |
| v Scotland | 2 | 2 | – | – |
| v Kenya | 1 | 1 | – | – |
| v Ireland | 1 | 1 | – | – |
| v Netherlands | 1 | 1 | – | – |
| v Namibia | 1 | 1 | – | – |
| v Afghanistan | 1 | 1 | – | – |
| **Total** | **160** | **80** | **76** | **4** |

# Twenty20 International Captains

|  |  | Results | | | | Toss | |
|---|---|---|---|---|---|---|---|
|  |  | P | W | L | NR | W | L |
| Williamson K.S. | 2012 to 2021/22 | 56 | 28 | 27 | 1 | 23 | 33 |
| Vettori D.L. | 2007/08 to 2009/10 | 28 | 14 | 14 | – | 16 | 12 |
| McCullum B.B. | 2007/08 to 2015 | 28 | 13 | 14 | 1 | 16 | 12 |
| Southee T.G. | 2017/18 to 2021/22 | 20 | 12 | 8 | – | 7 | 13 |
| Taylor L.R.P.L | 2010/11 to 2012/13 | 13 | 6 | 6 | 1 | 6 | 7 |
| Fleming S.P. | 2004/05 to 2006/07 | 5 | 3 | 2 | – | 4 | 1 |
| Latham T.W.M. | 2021/22 | 5 | 2 | 3 | – | 4 | 1 |
| Santner M.J. | 2020/21 to 2021/22 | 3 | 1 | 1 | 1 | 1 | 2 |
| Mills K.D. | 2013/14 | 2 | 1 | 1 | – | 1 | 1 |
| **TOTAL** |  | **160** | **80** | **76** | **4** | **78** | **82** |

# Highest Totals

| | | | |
|---|---|---|---|
| 243-5 | v West Indies | Mt Maunganui | 2017/18 |
| 243-6 | v Australia | Auckland | 2017/18 |
| 238-3 | v West Indies | Mt Maunganui | 2020/21 |
| 219-6 | v India | Auckland | 2018/19 |
| 219-7 | v Australia | Dunedin | 2020/21 |
| 214-6 | v Australia | Christchurch | 2009/10 |
| 212-4 | v India | Hamilton | 2018/19 |
| 210-3 | v Bangladesh | Hamilton | 2020/21 |
| 204-5 | v Bangladesh | Mirpur | 2013/14 |
| 203-5 | v India | Auckland | 2019/20 |
| 202-5 | v Zimbabwe | Hamilton | 2011/12 |
| 201-4 | v England | The Oval | 2013 |

# INDIVIDUAL RECORDS

## Centuries

| 123 | McCullum B.B. | v Bangladesh | Pallekele | 2012/13 |
|---|---|---|---|---|
| 116* | McCullum B.B. | v Australia | Christchurch | 2009/10 |
| 109* | Munro C. | v India | Rajkot | 2017/18 |
| 108 | Phillips G.D. | v West Indies | Mt Maunganui | 2020/21 |
| 105 | Guptill M.J. | v Australia | Auckland | 2017/18 |
| 104 | Munro C. | v West Indies | Mt Maunganui | 2017/18 |
| 101* | Guptill M.J. | v South Africa | East London | 2012/13 |
| 101 | Munro C. | v Bangladesh | Mt Maunganui | 2016/17 |

## Five Wickets in an Innings

| 4-1-18-5 | Southee T.G. | v Pakistan | Auckland | 2010/11 |
|---|---|---|---|---|
| 4-0-21-5 | Ferguson L.H. | v West Indies | Auckland | 2020/21 |

## Hat-tricks

| 4-0-33-3 | Oram J.D.P. | v Sri Lanka | Colombo | 2009/10 |
|---|---|---|---|---|
| 4-1-18-5 | Southee T.G. | v Pakistan | Auckland | 2010/11 |

## Most Economical Bowling

| 4-1-6-3 | Vettori D.L. | v Bangladesh | Hamilton | 2009/10 |
|---|---|---|---|---|
| 4-0-7-1 | Patel A.Y. | v Bangladesh | Mirpur | 2021/22 |
| 4-0-8-2 | Boult T.A. | v South Africa | Auckland | 2016/17 |
| 4-0-8-0 | Ravindra R. | v Bangladesh | Mirpur | 2021/22 |
| 4-0-9-2 | Butler I.G. | v England | Hamilton | 2012/13 |
| 4-0-9-2 | Patel A.Y. | v Bangladesh | Mirpur | 2021/22 |
| 4-0-10-2 | Milne A.F. | v Zimbabwe | Harare | 2015/16 |

## Most Expensive Bowling

| 3.1-0-64-0 | Wheeler B.M. | v Australia | Auckland | 2017/18 |
|---|---|---|---|---|
| 4-0-60-0 | Neesham J.D.S. | v Australia | Wellington | 2020/21 |
| 4-0-58-0 | Rance S.H.A. | v Sri Lanka | Pallekele | 2019/20 |
| 3.5-0-56-1 | de Grandhomme C. | v Australia | Auckland | 2017/18 |
| 4-0-54-3 | Bennett H.K. | v India | Hamilton | 2019/20 |

## Most Wicketkeeping Dismissals in an Innings

| †4 | Phillips G.D. | v West Indies | Nelson | 2017/18 |
|---|---|---|---|---|

† *includes one stumping*

## Most Catches in an Innings by a Fielder

| 4 | Anderson C.J. | v South Africa | Port Elizabeth | 2012/13 |
|---|---|---|---|---|
| 4 | de Grandhomme C. | v England | Wellington | 2019/20 |

# RECORD PARTNERSHIPS

## New Zealand v All Countries

**For**

| | | | | |
|---|---|---|---|---|
| **1st** | 171* | Guptill M.J. & Williamson K.S. v Pakistan | Hamilton | 2015/16 |
| **2nd** | 131 | Guptill M.J. & Williamson K.S. v Australia | Dunedin | 2020/21 |
| **3rd** | 184 | Conway D.P. & Phillips G.D. v West Indies | Mt Maunganui | 2020/21 |
| **4th** | 124 | Williamson K.S.& Anderson C.J. v Bangladesh | Mt Maunganui | 2016/17 |
| **5th** | 81* | Williamson K.S. & de Grandhomme C. v Bangladesh Napier | | 2016/17 |
| **6th** | 85* | McCullum B.B. & Ronchi L. v West Indies | Auckland | 2013/14 |
| **7th** | 54 | Santner M.J. & Wheeler B.M. v Pakistan | Auckland | 2017/18 |
| **8th** | 40 | Styris S.B. & Wilson J.W. v Australia | Auckland | 2004/05 |
| **9th** | 38* | Santner M.J. & Sodhi I.S. v India | Delhi | 2017/18 |
| | 38 | Taylor L.R.P.L. & Sodhi I.S. v Australia | Auckland | 2017/18 |
| **10th** | 36 | Southee T.G. & Rance S.H.A. v Sri Lanka | Pallekele | 2019/20 |

**Against**

| | | | | |
|---|---|---|---|---|
| **1st** | 158 | Sharma R.G. & Dhawan S. for India | Delhi | 2017/18 |
| **2nd** | 99 | Rahul K.L. & Kohli V. for India | Auckland | 2019/20 |
| **3rd** | 182 | Malan D.J. & Morgan E.J.G. for England | Napier | 2019/20 |
| **4th** | 82 | Clarke M.J. & White C.L. for Australia | Christchurch | 2009/10 |
| **5th** | 102 | Collingwood P.D. & Shah O.A. for England | Christchurch | 2007/08 |
| **6th** | 84 | Allen F.A. & Pollard K.A. for West Indies | Auckland | 2020/21 |
| **7th** | 92 | Stoinis M.P.& Sams D.R. for Australia | Dunedin | 2020/21 |
| **8th** | 61 | Harbhajan Singh & Raina S.K. for India | Christchurch | 2008/09 |
| **9th** | 44 | Fernando C.R.D. & Malinga S.L. for Sri Lanka | Auckland | 2006/07 |
| **10th** | 31* | Shoaib Akhtar & Wahab Riaz for Pakistan | Auckland | 2010/11 |

# CAREER RECORDS

| | M | In | NO | HS | Runs | Ave | 100s | 50s | Ct | St | O | M | R | W | Ave | R/O | Best |
|---|---|---|---|---|---|---|---|---|---|---|---|---|---|---|---|---|---|
| A.R.Adams | 4 | 2 | 1 | 7 | 13 | 13.00 | - | - | 1 | - | 12.5 | 0 | 105 | 3 | 35.00 | 8.18 | 2-20 |
| G.W.Aldridge | 1 | - | - | - | - | - | - | - | - | - | 4 | 0 | 45 | 1 | 45.00 | 11.25 | 1-45 |
| F.H.Allen | 6 | 6 | 0 | 71 | 156 | 26.00 | - | 1 | 2 | - | | | | | | | |
| C.J.Anderson | 31 | 24 | 4 | 94* | 485 | 24.25 | - | 2 | 19 | - | 60 | 0 | 495 | 14 | 35.35 | 8.25 | 2-17 |
| N.J.Astle | 4 | 4 | 1 | 40* | 74 | 24.66 | - | - | 3 | - | 6.5 | 0 | 50 | 4 | 12.50 | 7.32 | 3-20 |
| T.D.Astle | 5 | 2 | 0 | 3 | 4 | 2.00 | - | - | 3 | - | 13 | 0 | 116 | 7 | 16.57 | 8.92 | 4-13 |
| M.D.Bates | 3 | - | - | - | - | - | - | - | - | - | 11 | 0 | 107 | 4 | 26.75 | 9.73 | 3-31 |
| H.K.Bennett | 11 | 2 | 2 | 1* | 1 | - | - | - | - | - | 35.5 | 0 | 331 | 10 | 33.10 | 9.24 | 3-54 |
| T.A.Blundell | 7 | 6 | 2 | 30* | 59 | 14.75 | - | - | 3 | - | | | | | | | |
| S.E.Bond | 20 | 8 | 3 | 8* | 21 | 4.20 | - | - | 4 | - | 77.3 | 2 | 543 | 25 | 21.72 | 7.01 | 3-18 |
| T.A.Boult | 44 | 11 | 6 | 8 | 30 | 6.00 | - | - | 16 | - | 165.3 | 1 | 1345 | 62 | 21.69 | 8.11 | 4-34 |
| D.A.J.Bracewell | 20 | 11 | 5 | 44 | 126 | 21.00 | - | - | 7 | - | 51.4 | 0 | 470 | 20 | 23.50 | 9.10 | 3-25 |
| N.T.Broom | 11 | 7 | 1 | 36 | 73 | 12.16 | - | - | 4 | - | | | | | | | |
| D.G.Brownlie | 5 | 5 | 0 | 5 | 6 | 1.20 | - | - | 3 | - | | | | | | | |
| T.C.Bruce | 17 | 17 | 2 | 59* | 279 | 18.60 | - | 2 | 15 | - | | | | | | | |
| I.G.Butler | 19 | 6 | 5 | 2* | 5 | 5.00 | - | - | 3 | - | 59.4 | 1 | 481 | 23 | 20.91 | 8.06 | 3-19 |
| C.L.Cairns | 2 | 2 | 0 | 2 | 3 | 1.50 | - | - | 1 | - | 8 | 0 | 52 | 1 | 52.00 | 6.50 | 1-28 |
| M.S.Chapman * | 33 | 31 | 4 | 63* | 619 | 22.92 | - | 2 | 12 | - | 13 | 0 | 95 | 4 | 23.75 | 7.31 | 1-9 |
| D.P.Conway | 20 | 17 | 5 | 99* | 602 | 50.16 | - | 4 | 11 | 1 | | | | | | | |
| C.de Grandhomme | 41 | 39 | 7 | 59 | 505 | 15.78 | - | 3 | 20 | - | 53.3 | 0 | 461 | 12 | 38.41 | 8.62 | 2-22 |
| A.P.Devcich | 4 | 4 | 0 | 59 | 111 | 27.75 | - | 1 | 2 | - | 12 | 0 | 80 | 2 | 40.00 | 6.67 | 2-16 |
| B.J.Diamanti | 1 | - | - | - | - | - | - | - | - | - | 2 | 0 | 19 | 0 | - | 9.50 | - |
| J.A.Duffy | 4 | 1 | 0 | 3 | 3 | 3.00 | - | - | - | - | 13 | 0 | 76 | 5 | 15.20 | 5.85 | 4-33 |
| G.D.Elliott | 16 | 14 | 4 | 27 | 157 | 15.70 | - | - | 4 | - | 30 | 0 | 218 | 14 | 15.57 | 7.27 | 4-22 |
| A.M.Ellis | 5 | 5 | 2 | 16 | 25 | 8.33 | - | - | - | - | 10 | 0 | 105 | 2 | 52.50 | 10.50 | 2-40 |
| L.H.Ferguson | 15 | 2 | 0 | 14 | 15 | 7.50 | - | - | 4 | - | 54 | 0 | 385 | 25 | 15.40 | 7.13 | 5-21 |
| S.P.Fleming | 5 | 5 | 0 | 38 | 110 | 22.00 | - | - | 2 | - | | | | | | | |
| D.R.Flynn | 5 | 5 | 0 | 23 | 59 | 11.80 | - | - | 2 | - | 1 | 0 | 7 | 0 | - | 7.00 | - |

| | M | In | NO | HS | Runs | Ave | 100s | 50s | Ct | St | | O | M | R | W | Ave | R/O | Best |
|---|---|---|---|---|---|---|---|---|---|---|---|---|---|---|---|---|---|---|
| J.E.C.Franklin | 38 | 31 | 8 | 60 | 463 | 20.13 | - | 2 | 13 | - | | 54.3 | 0 | 417 | 20 | 20.85 | 7.65 | 4-15 |
| P.G.Fulton | 12 | 12 | 1 | 25 | 127 | 11.54 | - | - | 4 | - | | | | | | | | |
| M.R.Gillespie | 11 | 6 | 4 | 7 | 21 | 10.50 | - | - | 1 | - | | 35 | 3 | 255 | 10 | 25.50 | 7.29 | 4-7 |
| M.J.Guptill | 112 | 108 | 7 | 105 | 3299 | 32.66 | 2 | 20 | 64 | - | | 1 | 0 | 11 | 0 | - | 11.00 | - |
| M.J.Henry | 6 | 2 | 1 | 10 | 10 | 10.00 | - | - | 1 | - | | 22 | 1 | 191 | 7 | 27.28 | 8.68 | 3-44 |
| R.M.Hira | 15 | 3 | 1 | 20* | 37 | 18.50 | - | - | 2 | - | | 42.2 | 1 | 337 | 10 | 33.70 | 7.96 | 2-42 |
| P.A.Hitchcock | 1 | 1 | 0 | 13 | 13 | 13.00 | - | - | - | - | | 3 | 0 | 43 | 2 | 21.50 | 14.33 | 2-43 |
| G.J.Hopkins | 10 | 8 | 0 | 36 | 86 | 10.75 | - | - | 4 | 2 | | | | | | | | |
| J.M.How | 5 | 5 | 0 | 31 | 56 | 11.20 | - | - | 1 | - | | | | | | | | |
| P.J.Ingram | 3 | 3 | 1 | 20* | 22 | 11.00 | - | - | 1 | - | | | | | | | | |
| K.A.Jamieson | 8 | 4 | 2 | 30 | 41 | 20.50 | - | - | 3 | - | | 28.4 | 0 | 281 | 4 | 70.25 | 9.80 | 2-15 |
| A.K.Kitchen | 5 | 4 | 1 | 16 | 38 | 12.66 | - | - | 3 | - | | 6 | 0 | 46 | 2 | 23.00 | 7.67 | 1-3 |
| S.C.Kuggeleijn | 18 | 8 | 4 | 35* | 79 | 19.75 | - | - | 6 | - | | 53.5 | 0 | 471 | 16 | 29.43 | 8.75 | 3-27 |
| T.W.M.Latham | 18 | 15 | 2 | 65* | 322 | 24.76 | - | 2 | 8 | 3 | | | | | | | | |
| H.J.H.Marshall | 3 | 3 | 0 | 8 | 12 | 4.00 | - | - | 1 | - | | | | | | | | |
| J.A.H.Marshall | 3 | 2 | 0 | 13 | 14 | 7.00 | - | - | - | - | | | | | | | | |
| C.S.Martin | 6 | 1 | 1 | 5* | 5 | - | - | - | 1 | - | | 23 | 1 | 193 | 7 | 27.57 | 8.39 | 2-14 |
| M.J.Mason | 3 | 1 | 0 | 2 | 2 | 2.00 | - | - | - | - | | 9 | 0 | 65 | 2 | 32.50 | 7.22 | 1-18 |
| M.J.McClenaghan | 28 | 7 | 4 | 6* | 14 | 4.66 | - | - | 7 | - | | 98.2 | 2 | 758 | 30 | 25.26 | 7.71 | 3-17 |
| C.E.McConchie | 5 | 4 | 2 | 17* | 32 | 16.00 | - | - | 1 | - | | 18.1 | 0 | 117 | 7 | 16.71 | 6.44 | 3-15 |
| B.B.McCullum | 71 | 70 | 10 | 123 | 2140 | 35.66 | 2 | 13 | 36 | 8 | | | | | | | | |
| N.L.McCullum | 63 | 41 | 15 | 36* | 299 | 11.50 | - | - | 25 | - | | 187.1 | 0 | 1278 | 58 | 22.03 | 6.83 | 4-16 |
| P.D.McGlashan | 11 | 9 | 1 | 26 | 61 | 7.62 | - | - | 9 | - | | | | | | | | |
| A.J.McKay | 2 | 1 | 0 | 0 | 0 | 0.00 | - | - | - | - | | 5.4 | 0 | 31 | 2 | 15.50 | 5.47 | 2-20 |
| C.D.McMillan | 8 | 7 | 1 | 57 | 187 | 31.16 | - | 1 | 3 | - | | | | | | | | |
| K.D.Mills | 42 | 19 | 7 | 33* | 137 | 11.41 | - | - | 8 | - | | 149.3 | 1 | 1228 | 43 | 28.55 | 8.21 | 3-26 |
| A.F.Milne | 31 | 10 | 9 | 10* | 34 | 34.00 | - | - | 6 | - | | 108.5 | 2 | 854 | 32 | 26.68 | 7.85 | 4-37 |
| D.J.Mitchell | 25 | 23 | 5 | 72* | 392 | 21.77 | - | 1 | 12 | - | | 11.5 | 0 | 121 | 6 | 20.16 | 10.23 | 2-27 |
| C.Munro | 65 | 62 | 7 | 109* | 1724 | 31.34 | 3 | 11 | 17 | - | | 19.4 | 0 | 186 | 4 | 46.50 | 9.46 | 1-12 |
| J.D.S.Neesham | 38 | 29 | 10 | 48* | 416 | 21.89 | - | - | 13 | - | | 63.3 | 0 | 586 | 21 | 27.90 | 9.23 | 3-16 |
| H.M.Nicholls | 10 | 9 | 1 | 36* | 100 | 12.50 | - | - | 3 | - | | | | | | | | |
| R.J.Nicol | 21 | 19 | 0 | 58 | 327 | 17.21 | - | 2 | 5 | - | | 20.3 | 0 | 167 | 5 | 33.40 | 8.15 | 2-20 |
| I.E.O'Brien | 4 | - | - | - | - | - | - | - | - | - | | 13 | 0 | 116 | 6 | 19.33 | 8.92 | 2-30 |
| J.D.P.Oram | 36 | 30 | 7 | 66* | 474 | 20.60 | - | 2 | 12 | - | | 91 | 0 | 793 | 19 | 41.73 | 8.71 | 3-33 |
| A.Y.Patel | 7 | 2 | 0 | 4 | 7 | 3.50 | - | - | - | - | | 26 | 0 | 118 | 11 | 10.72 | 4.54 | 4-16 |
| J.S.Patel | 11 | 4 | 1 | 5 | 9 | 3.00 | - | - | 4 | - | | 33.1 | 1 | 269 | 16 | 16.81 | 8.11 | 3-20 |
| G.D.Phillips | 35 | 30 | 5 | 108 | 645 | 25.80 | 1 | 2 | 19 | 2 | | 8.3 | 0 | 68 | 2 | 34.00 | 8.00 | 1-11 |
| S.H.A.Rance | 8 | 3 | 0 | 8 | 10 | 3.33 | - | - | - | - | | 27 | 0 | 245 | 10 | 24.50 | 9.07 | 3-26 |
| R.Ravindra | 6 | 6 | 0 | 20 | 54 | 9.00 | - | - | 3 | - | | 19 | 0 | 83 | 6 | 13.83 | 4.37 | 3-22 |
| A.J.Redmond | 7 | 6 | 0 | 63 | 126 | 21.00 | - | 1 | 3 | - | | 2.5 | 0 | 24 | 2 | 12.00 | 8.47 | 2-24 |
| L.Ronchi † | 32 | 25 | 6 | 51* | 359 | 18.89 | - | 1 | 24 | 5 | | | | | | | | |
| H.D.Rutherford | 8 | 7 | 0 | 62 | 151 | 21.57 | - | 1 | 1 | - | | | | | | | | |
| J.D.Ryder | 22 | 21 | 1 | 62 | 457 | 22.85 | - | 3 | 7 | - | | 10 | 0 | 68 | 2 | 34.00 | 6.80 | 1-2 |
| M.J.Santner | 62 | 43 | 19 | 37 | 358 | 14.91 | - | - | 26 | - | | 208.2 | 1 | 1515 | 66 | 22.95 | 7.27 | 4-11 |
| B.V.Sears | 2 | - | - | - | - | - | - | - | 1 | - | | 4 | 0 | 32 | 1 | 32.00 | 8.00 | 1-21 |
| T.L.Seifert | 40 | 37 | 5 | 84* | 753 | 23.53 | - | 5 | 21 | 6 | | | | | | | | |
| M.S.Sinclair | 2 | 2 | 0 | 0 | 0 | 0.00 | - | - | - | - | | | | | | | | |
| I.S.Sodhi | 66 | 12 | 5 | 16* | 87 | 12.42 | - | - | 18 | - | | 226.3 | 0 | 1824 | 83 | 21.97 | 8.05 | 4-28 |
| T.G.Southee | 92 | 36 | 14 | 39 | 249 | 11.31 | - | - | 47 | - | | 332.5 | 2 | 2729 | 111 | 24.58 | 8.20 | 5-18 |
| S.B.Styris | 31 | 29 | 2 | 66 | 578 | 21.40 | - | 1 | 8 | - | | 51.3 | 0 | 349 | 18 | 19.38 | 6.78 | 3-5 |
| L.R.P.L.Taylor | 102 | 94 | 21 | 63 | 1909 | 26.15 | - | 7 | 46 | - | | | | | | | | |
| E.P.Thompson | 1 | 1 | 1 | 1* | 1 | - | - | - | - | - | | 3 | 1 | 18 | 1 | 18.00 | 6.00 | 1-18 |
| B.M.Tickner | 8 | 3 | 2 | 5* | 10 | 10.00 | - | - | 1 | - | | 25 | 0 | 234 | 5 | 46.80 | 9.36 | 2-25 |
| D.R.Tuffey | 3 | 2 | 1 | 5* | 5 | 5.00 | - | - | - | - | | 10 | 0 | 93 | 3 | 31.00 | 9.30 | 2-16 |
| D.L.Vettori | 34 | 22 | 6 | 38 | 205 | 12.81 | - | - | 9 | - | | 131.1 | 1 | 748 | 38 | 19.68 | 5.70 | 4-20 |
| L.Vincent | 9 | 9 | 0 | 42 | 174 | 19.33 | - | - | 1 | - | | | | | | | | |
| B-J.Watling | 5 | 4 | 0 | 22 | 38 | 19.00 | - | - | 1 | - | | | | | | | | |
| B.M.Wheeler | 6 | 4 | 2 | 30 | 37 | 18.50 | - | - | 1 | - | | 21.2 | 0 | 216 | 7 | 30.85 | 10.13 | 2-16 |
| K.S.Williamson | 74 | 72 | 10 | 95 | 2021 | 32.59 | - | 14 | 34 | - | | 19.4 | 0 | 164 | 6 | 27.33 | 8.34 | 2-16 |
| J.W.Wilson | 1 | 1 | 0 | 18 | 18 | 18.00 | - | - | - | - | | 4 | 0 | 43 | 0 | - | 10.75 | - |
| L.J.Woodcock | 3 | - | - | - | - | - | - | - | 1 | - | | 10 | 0 | 70 | 1 | 70.00 | 7.00 | 1-30 |
| G.H.Worker | 2 | 2 | 0 | 62 | 90 | 45.00 | - | 1 | 1 | - | | 2 | 0 | 19 | 1 | 19.00 | 9.50 | 1-19 |
| W.A.Young | 8 | 7 | 0 | 53 | 166 | 23.71 | - | 1 | 2 | - | | | | | | | | |

*\* includes 19 games for Hong Kong   † includes three games for Australia*

# SUMMARY OF TWENTY20 INTERNATIONAL CAREER RECORDS

## Most Matches

| | | | | | |
|---|---|---|---|---|---|
| Guptill M.J. | 112 | Williamson K.S. | 74 | Munro C. | 65 |
| Taylor L.R.P.L. | 102 | McCullum B.B. | 71 | McCullum N.L. | 63 |
| Southee T.G. | 92 | Sodhi I.S. | 66 | Santner M.J. | 62 |

## Most Runs

| | |
|---|---|
| Guptill M.J. | 3299 |
| McCullum B.B. | 2140 |
| Williamson K.S. | 2021 |
| Taylor L.R.P.L. | 1909 |
| Munro C. | 1724 |

## Most Wickets

| | |
|---|---|
| Southee T.G. | 111 |
| Sodhi I.S. | 83 |
| Santner M.J. | 66 |
| Boult T.A. | 62 |
| McCullum N.L. | 58 |
| Mills K.D. | 43 |

# Register of New Zealand Twenty20 Cricketers Who Have Not Played Test Cricket or One-day Internationals

| | Born | Type | |
|---|---|---|---|
| **Allen** | 22/4/1999 | RHB | |
| Finnley Hugh | Auckland | | |
| **Bruce** | 2/8/1991 | RHB | ROB |
| Thomas Charles | Te Kuiti | | |
| **Duffy** | 2/8/1994 | RHB | RFM |
| Jacob Andrew | Lumsden | | |
| **Hira** | 23/1/1987 | LHB | SLA |
| Roneel Magan | Auckland | | |
| **McConchie** | 12/1/1992 | RHB | ROB |
| Cole Edward | Christchurch | | |
| **Sears** | 11/2/1998 | RHB | RFM |
| Benjamin Vincent | Lower Hutt | | |

# MINOR CRICKET

## HIGHEST TEAM TOTALS

| | | | |
|---|---|---|---|
| 922-9 | Australians v South Canterbury | Temuka | 1913/14 |
| 741 | Murphy's Pipe Works v North A | Wellington | 1919/20 |
| 709 | Australians v Southland | Invercargill | 1913/14 |
| 701-6 dec | Murphy's Pipe Works v Seatoun | Wellington | 1919/20 |
| † 701 | Bay of Plenty v Hamilton | Hamilton | 2012/13 |
| † 701 | Bay of Plenty v Counties-Manukau | Mt Maunganui | 2016/17 |
| 686 | Nelson City v Buller | Nelson | 1954/55 |
| 683 | Hamilton Old Boys v Eastern Suburbs | Hamilton | 2007/08 |
| 681 | New Zealand v Northern Districts (NSW) | West Maitland | 1925/26 |
| † 678 | Hamilton v Wairarapa | Hamilton | 2011/12 |
| † 659 | Manawatu v Bay of Plenty | Palmerston North | 2009/10 |
| 653-9 dec | Hawke's Bay v Wairarapa | Napier | 1946/47 |
| † 650-9 dec | Manawatu v South Canterbury | Palmerston North | 1993/94 |
| † 649 | Nelson v Wairarapa | Nelson | 1984/85 |
| † 643 | Nelson v North Canterbury | Nelson | 1984/85 |
| † 641-7 | Nelson v Taranaki | Nelson | 1983/84 |
| 633-7 dec | North v Returned Soldiers | Wellington | 1917/18 |
| † 633-9 | Wellington City v Bay of Plenty | Mt Maunganui | 1997/98 |
| † 632 | Nelson v Waikato | Nelson | 1963/64 |
| 629-7 dec | Midland II v Railways | Wellington | 1921/22 |
| 623 | North Canterbury v South Canterbury | Christchurch | 1907/08 |
| 622-4 dec | Canterbury Country v Nelson | Rangiora | 2015/16 |
| 620 | Hawke's Bay v Horowhenua-Kapiti | Paraparaumu | 2009/10 |
| 619-3 | Cornwall Under 19 v Sri Lanka CC Under 19 | Auckland | 1997/98 |
| 612-8 dec | Hawke's Bay v Wanganui | Wanganui | 2015/16 |
| 611 | Australian Academy XI v NZ Academy XI | Lincoln | 1999/00 |
| 609 | Napier United A v Napier United B | Napier | 1898/99 |
| 603-7 dec | Tinwald v Ashburton A | Ashburton | 1927/28 |
| 603-7 dec | Australians v Wairarapa | Masteron | 1949/50 |
| 603-8 dec | New South Wales v South Canterbury | Timaru | 1923/24 |
| 602-9 dec | New Zealand v Melbourne CC | Christchurch | 1926/27 |
| † 602 | Nelson v Hawke's Bay | Nelson | 1959/60 |

† denotes Hawke Cup/U-Bix Cup/Fuji Xerox Cup Challenge match

## HIGHEST INDIVIDUAL SCORES

| | | | | |
|---|---|---|---|---|
| 400 | C.D. Knight | Cornwall Under 19 v Sri Lanka CC Under 19 | Auckland | 1997/98 |
| 381* | C. Egen | Taieri v Kaikorai | Dunedin | 2014/15 |
| 378 | B-J. Watling | Hamilton Old Boys v Eastern Suburbs | Hamilton | 2007/08 |
| 358 | S.F. Golding | St Bede's College 3rd XI v Sydenham | Christchurch | 2006/07 |
| 354 | J.N. Crawford | Australians v South Canterbury | Temuka | 1913/14 |
| 343* | J. Gray | Sydenham v Christ's College | Christchurch | 1917/18 |
| 335 | W.W. Armstrong | Melbourne CC v Southland | Invercargill | 1905/06 |
| 334* | Harold B. Lusk | West Christchurch v St Albans | Christchurch | 1915/16 |
| 324* | D.N. Hakaraia | Waitakere Under 17 v Howick Pakuranga Under 17 | Auckland | 1999/00 |
| 311 | H.M. Butterworth | College B v Wanganui A | Wanganui | 1914/15 |
| 303* | M.D. Bell | Northern Districts Under 20 v Wellington Under 20 | Wanganui | 1994/95 |
| 303* | D. Cleaver | Freyberg v Palmerston | Palmerston North | 2012/13 |
| 300* | W.J. Hendy | Auckland Suburban Association v Christchurch HSOB | Christchurch | 1925/26 |
| 300* | D.T. Meiring | Marist v United | Palmerston North | 2012/13 |
| 300* | S.L. Stewart | Canterbury Country v Nelson | Rangiora | 2015/16 |

**NZC**

## HIGHEST PARTNERSHIPS

*Wkt*

| | | | | | |
|---|---|---|---|---|---|
| 518 | 2nd | A. Young & F.L. McMahon | Wanderers v Taruheru | Gisborne | 1910/11 |
| 455 | 1st | Jasmeet Singh & Parvesh Sethi | Birkenhead 4th Grade v Grafton 4th Grade | Auckland | 2020/21 |
| 449 | 3rd | M.M. Steventon & S.B. Payne | Wairarapa College v Wellington College | Wellington | 2021/22 |
| 441 | 1st | J.E. Mills & H.D. Gillespie | Eden v University | Auckland | 1924/25 |
| 437* | 2nd | R.C. Eden & M.R. Eden | Wanderers v Wakefield | Nelson | 1924/25 |
| 407 | 2nd | D. Crombie & D. Thomson | Naenae College v Marist | Wellington | 1982/83 |
| 394 | 1st | R.S. Scragg & J.V. Hill | Central Districts A v Otago A | P. North | 2001/02 |
| 393 | 1st | M.E.L. Lane & J.S. Lane | Marlborough v Buller | Blenheim | 1992/93 |
| 391 | 4th | T.P.L. Reaney & H.M. Hawthorn | Hawke's Bay v Wairarapa | Napier | 1946/47 |
| 375 | 2nd | A.C. Barnes & S.M. Lynch | Cornwall v Waitakere | Auckland | 1996/97 |
| 374* | 1st | T.D. Astle & K.R. Ambler | Canterbury Under 19 v Auckland Under 19 | Lincoln | 2004/05 |
| 360 | 6th | G. Marshall & H.C. Wilson | United A v United B | Napier | 1898/99 |
| 360 | 1st | B. Sutcliffe & F.J. Craig | Takapuna Grammar School v Mt Albert Grammar School | Auckland | 1942/43 |

## BOWLING

| | | | | |
|---|---|---|---|---|
| 10-4 | A. Rimmer | Linwood 7th Grade v Cathedral Grammar School | Christchurch | 1925/26 |
| 9-0 | W. Blackie | Whareti v Havelock | Auckland | 1909/10 |
| 9-0 | A. Bramwell | Feilding Agricultural College v Public Services | Feilding | 1927/28 |
| 8-0 | S. Fleming | Marlborough College A v Bohally Intermediate | Blenheim | 1967/68 |

## ALL-ROUND CRICKET

| | | | | |
|---|---|---|---|---|
| 107* & 10-39 | D.D. Beard | Palmerston North BHS v Napier BHS | Palmerston North | 1936/37 |
| 157* & 10-29 | A.K. Davidson | Australians v Wairarapa | Masterton | 1949/50 |

## WICKETKEEPING - DISMISSALS IN AN INNINGS

| | | | | |
|---|---|---|---|---|
| 8 (8ct) | A. van der Looy | Lancaster Park Woolston v Riccarton | Christchurch | 2007/08 |
| 8 (8ct) | A.F. Johnstone | St Albans v Burnside West | Christchurch | 2021/22 |

## FIELDING - CATCHES IN AN INNINGS

| | | | | |
|---|---|---|---|---|
| 8 | E. Tait | Buller v West Coast | Westport | 1968/69 |